The
Second World War Diary
of Hugh Dalton
1940–45

The
Second World War Diary
of Hugh Dalton
1940–45

Edited by Ben Pimlott

JONATHAN CAPE
IN ASSOCIATION WITH THE LONDON SCHOOL OF
ECONOMICS AND POLITICAL SCIENCE

First published 1986
Diary copyright © The British Library of Political
and Economic Science 1986
Introduction and editorial matter copyright © Ben Pimlott 1986
Jonathan Cape Ltd, 32 Bedford Square, London WC1B 3EL

British Library Cataloguing in Publication Data

Dalton, Hugh
The Second World War diary of Hugh Dalton 1940–45.
1. Dalton, Hugh 2. States—Great Britain
—Biography
I. Title   II. Pimlott, Ben
941.083′092′4   DA585.D3

ISBN 0–224–02065–X

Typeset by Ace Filmsetting Ltd, Frome
Printed in Great Britain by
Ebenezer Baylis and Son Ltd
The Trinity Press, Worcester and London

Contents

Illustrations

Cartoons

Acknowledgments

This volume and the forthcoming *Political Diary of Hugh Dalton*, covering the years 1918–40 and 1945–60, have been made possible by a generous grant from the Leverhulme Trust Fund to the London School of Economics and Political Science, copyright holders of the Dalton diaries and papers. On behalf of the School, I should like to express gratitude to the Trustees.

I would like to thank the Publications Committee of the School for inviting me to edit the diaries. I am especially grateful to the former Chairman of the Committee, Professor Matthew Anderson, who gave every kind of encouragement and practical help. I wish to thank the International History Department at the School for the warm hospitality shown to our small team during the main period of research; and, in particular, Professor Kenneth Bourne, for his support and friendly interest, and Professor James Joll for kindly making available his room while on sabbatical. I am extremely grateful to Patrick Davis, Publications Officer, for his advice and careful guidance, and to Pat Carman, Alison Forbes and Gus Stewart for help with administration.

My main professional debt is to Dr Dorothy Tarry, research assistant on the project. Her skill, resourcefulness and enthusiasm were an incalculable benefit. I would also like to express my thanks to Greta Edwards, secretary to the project, who carried out the major task of typing the manuscript with great efficiency and accuracy; and to Anne-Marie Rule, Susan Proctor and Audrey Coppard for additional secretarial help. I am particularly grateful to Dr Angela Raspin, Head of Manuscripts and Special Collections at the British Library of Political and Economic Science, for her unfailing assistance, over a long period, with innumerable queries and requests concerning the Dalton diaries and papers and other documents.

Many other people have helped directly or indirectly and I would like to thank once again those already mentioned in the Preface to my recently published biography of Dalton, and especially those who talked to me about Dalton or showed me papers. In addition I wish to thank the many specialists, archivists, librarians and others in cultural institutes, embassies and elsewhere who have interrupted their work to answer telephone requests for information.

A short bibliography is given at the back, listing some of the works of reference and other published sources used. It is appropriate here to express my gratitude to the anonymous compilers of *Who Was Who*, *The Times House of Commons* and *The Times* obituaries. I am also indebted to the authors or editors of the following: W. S. Churchill, *The Second World War* (six volumes), Hugh Dalton, *Memoirs* (three volumes), Brigadier P. Young, *The Almanac of World War II*, Henry Pelling, *Britain and the Second World War*, and D. Dilks (ed.), *The Diary of Sir Alexander Cadogan 1938–1943* – works which became especially valued editorial companions.

I should like to say a very warm word of thanks to my editor at Cape, Jane Hill, whose sharp-eyed thoroughness and fine judgments have greatly reduced the number of errors and infelicities in the academic editing. Those that remain are, of course, my responsibility alone.

Finally, I am grateful to the following for permission to reproduce illustrations: the B.B.C. Hulton Picture Library, for nos 1–6, 8, 13–18, 21, 23, 27 and 28; Wallace Cook, for the cartoon on p. 398; the Imperial War Museum, for nos 7, 9–12, 19, 20, 22, 24–6; and the *Standard*, for cartoons by Low on pp. 28, 44, 49, 232, 434, 523, 761, 815 and 849, and by Vicky on p. 414.

Gower Street,
London WC1
September 1985   B.J.P.

Introduction

Hugh Dalton started writing a diary when he first went off to war as a young officer in 1916. Three years later he published a book,[1] based on his private record. It was a significant beginning: war, and the consequences of war, always aroused his fiercest passions. Though Dalton kept up the diary for the rest of his active life, no section is as full or as rich as the one from which the present selection, providing a companion to that early volume, is drawn. *The Second World War Diary* contains entries for the five years of Churchill's wartime Coalition (May 1940 to May 1945), during which Dalton served first as Minister of Economic Warfare and then as President of the Board of Trade. A selection from earlier and later parts of the diary will appear separately.[2]

Dalton's First World War was a war of mud, mountain snow, movement and percussion, a war (to use his phrase) of 'sights, sounds and smells'. By contrast, his Second World War was a war of minutes and memoranda, of office intrigue and character assassination, of bureaucratic stonewallers, diplomatic fainthearts and political fixers. His record of this Westminster and Whitehall battlefront is undoubtedly one of the most entertaining, and arguably one of the most revealing, accounts of wartime politics and administration to have been written.

Hugh Dalton was the only prominent member of the minority within the Coalition to keep a diary, and his record is the source of most of what is known about the dealings and musings of the Labour leaders who provided the Government's vital underpinning. It also has a much wider interest, partly because of the evocative skills, and partly because of the complex and contradictory character, of the

1 *With British Guns in Italy: A tribute to Italian achievement*, Methuen, London, 1919.
2 *The Political Diary of Hugh Dalton*, covering the periods 1918 to May 1940 (the fall of Chamberlain) and July 1945 to 1960, will be published in 1986.

narrator. Dalton's startling combination of energy, irreverence, imagination and wit, on the one hand, and of cunning, bile and preposterous conceit, on the other, make his diary intensely readable. At the same time, it has a special historical importance because its author was, in ways that need to be understood, subversive.

There have been war diaries by conventional politicians, generals and civil servants, integrally part of the machine; and war diaries by well-connected dilettantes, on the fringes of high politics. Dalton's diary belongs to neither category. It was written by a politician whose ideas and behaviour were profoundly unconventional, yet who exercised great power. Dalton was an intellectual and a fine writer, a vigorous and precise user of words. He was a patriot, bitterly anti-German and impatiently determined to win the war. At the same time, he was a socialist – one of the very few in key positions – and his values and prejudices were quite different from those of most of his colleagues in the Government. As such, and more perhaps than any other Labour minister, he remained an outsider – restless, ambitious and angry, with a fierce belief in the need for great changes both in the running of the war and in the preparations for the peace to follow. Dalton's sense of isolation, and the frustrations that accompanied it, are vital ingredients of the journal.

As well as being an unusual member of the Government, Dalton was a far from typical member of the Labour Party. He was not alone among Labour leaders in his upper-middle- or upper-class background. None, however, had origins so closely bound to the Establishment. Edward Hugh John Neale Dalton was born at Neath, Glamorgan in 1887, the son of Canon John Neale Dalton, a clergyman recently retired from service as tutor to the sons of the Prince of Wales. Hugh's mother was the daughter of a Welsh landowner; her brother was a naval officer who later became an admiral, commanding the Fifth Battle Squadron at Jutland in 1916. Hugh spent his early years in the cloistered community of Windsor Castle and St George's Chapel. He was educated at Eton and at King's College, Cambridge, where he was a member of a circle that included Rupert Brooke and Maynard Keynes. It was at King's, in his first undergraduate year, that he took up Fabian socialism, absorbing the ideas of H. G. Wells and the Webbs.

After Cambridge, Hugh studied economics at the L.S.E., preparing a thesis, later published, on the inequality of incomes. In London he met and married Ruth Fox, a fellow student who shared his Fabian commitment. His studies were interrupted by the First World War. In 1915 he was commissioned, and in 1916 he spent several months with the Army Service Corps in Northern France. Then, at his own request, he transferred to the Royal Artillery, and in 1917 he was sent to Italy. There he remained until the Armistice was signed, gaining an Italian decoration for bravery in the retreat following the battle of Caporetto, and taking part in the final advance.

After the war, Dalton returned to the L.S.E. to teach, and write about, economics. During the next few years he published several books, including a standard textbook on public finance, and took a keen interest in the activities of the expanding Labour Party. In 1924 he was elected to Parliament as Member for Peckham, and began a meteoric rise, rapidly securing election to the Party's National and Parliamentary Executives. Eventually, Dalton was to be Chancellor of the Exchequer, shaping the financial policies of the 1945 Labour administration in its early, radical phase. Between the wars, however, his main political interest was not economics or finance but foreign policy. In 1929 (having abandoned Peckham for the County Durham mining seat of Bishop Auckland) he entered the second Labour Government as Parliamentary Under-Secretary for Foreign Affairs, under Arthur Henderson.

Dalton supported Henderson and the P.L.P. majority against Mac-Donald in the 1931 crisis, and lost his seat in the ensuing election. He spent the next four years travelling (to Russia and Italy in 1932, to Germany in 1933) and rewriting Labour's domestic programme. When he returned to Parliament in 1935, Attlee made him Party spokesman on foreign affairs. This portfolio enabled him to play an important part as an outspoken re-armer and anti-appeaser, skilfully and courageously leading Labour away from its earlier pacifist in-clinations. Indeed, it is arguable that Dalton, more than any other politician, was responsible for the degree of accord between Labour Opposition and Tory dissidents that made it possible to get rid of Chamberlain in May 1940.

During the 'phoney war' period, Dalton shadowed the Air Minister (Kingsley Wood) and the Minister of Economic Warfare (Ronald Cross). He remained adamant that Labour should not join any Coalition of which Neville Chamberlain was head, and he was closely involved in the political machinations, during the Norway debate, which precipitated Chamberlain's departure. By then, Dalton was regarded as one of Labour's three or four most important figures, a likely contender for the leadership should Attlee resign or be forced out, and a necessary element in any truly 'national' Coalition.

Necessary but, to many in the Conservative majority, scarcely welcome. Here was an irony. No Labour leader had been more vociferous on the need to halt Hitler's progress or on the need for adequate defences. Yet none was regarded with deeper suspicion by

Conservative M.P.s. The reason was complex. Partly, it had to do with style. Where others would attack the political enemy, Dalton would deliberately provoke, touching raw nerves. Style was linked to class. Dalton could rile his opponents because he knew the customs of the tribe. His manner – booming voice, rolling eyes, excessive heartiness – together with a taste for jesuitical plotting, aggravated the Tory dislike, behind which lay, of course, a profound distrust of his political beliefs. 'If he was a horse, I wouldn't buy him', was a typical Tory jibe.

To be disliked by Tories was an advantage in times of normal inter-party conflict, as Dalton had been well aware. It ceased to be an advantage when peacetime conflict was replaced by wartime truce. What made it a serious handicap was that one of those who disliked Dalton most was the new Prime Minister himself. Churchill seems to have regarded Dalton's presence in the Government as a penance, one of the tiresome though unavoidable burdens of war. He acknowledged Dalton's ability and political weight, but was irritated by his personality and found his company hard to bear. Dalton, who greatly admired Churchill and was eager to please him, became dimly and anxiously conscious of this disfavour, yet could do nothing to remedy it.

Not every Tory felt as Churchill did, however, and Dalton's origins among the upper class could on occasion be put to positive use. Dalton was certainly not apologetic about his old school, and his conversations were often lubricated with what he called 'Etonian shop'. He was delighted when Gladwyn Jebb, also an Etonian, told him that 'at Eton the Sixth Form are the Labour Party and Pop the Conservatives'.[1] He might have been, in one sense, the bounder of the Remove, but he shared the intimacy of the common culture.[2] The sense of belonging to the same club as many other leading members of the Government and Civil Service comes through strongly in the diary.

Dalton never fully escaped from the implications of this paradox, if indeed he was conscious of it. As an old Etonian in a senior post, mixing with other old Etonians and sharing in their decisions, he had one foot back in the Establishment. As a Labour politician with a principled opposition to great disparities of income and wealth, he had the other firmly outside it. Dalton might have had an easier life if he had moderated his opinions. In fact, he proved the least seducible of politicians, basing himself squarely on Labour Party support and devoting much of his energy to the pursuit of socialist objectives. Especially during his period as President of the Board of Trade, when he succeeded in getting a better deal for the miners and in pushing

1 Diary, 3rd April 1941.
2 See *The Memoirs of Lord Gladwyn*, Weidenfeld & Nicolson, London, 1972, p. 106.

through legislation to encourage investment in the pre-war Distressed Areas, he saw himself as a Trojan horse for the Labour Movement.

Not surprisingly, this brought him difficulties in Whitehall. As a hard-working minister who knew his own mind, he preferred to work with junior, rather than senior, officials, and in each of his departments he surrounded himself with younger men, often drawn from outside the Civil Service, whom he found temperamentally and politically compatible, and from whom he could obtain companionship as well as official advice and assistance. With these his relations were close and informal, and marked by a mutual loyalty. Outside the ranks of his closest aides, however, his dealings with officials were often tense, especially at the Board of Trade. Some felt that he undervalued them, others that he was vain, arrogant or thoughtless. Dalton was conscious of such accusations, but saw no need to change his ways.[1] The more he sought, in the later stages of the war, to use his powers for purposes not directly related to the war or wartime needs, the more he came to regard the Civil Service caste as inherently obstructive. The bad Whitehall reputation he acquired in these years was something he never entirely lived down.

Economic Warfare

This volume of Dalton's diary opens with his first day as Minister of Economic Warfare in the new Government. It was the office he had sought,[2] and it placed him in charge of a department urgently in need of a shake-up. For many months, under Dalton's Tory predecessor Ronald Cross, M.E.W. had been the focus of high hopes, with few results. The spirit of appeasement lingered hopefully; economic weapons were given prominence because of a cautious attitude towards the use of military ones. One consequence was an over-optimistic view of the possibilities of economic pressure on its own – and at the same time a hesitant approach to the implementation of the blockade for fear of antagonising neutrals. An ill-advised claim by Cross early in 1940 that Germany's economic situation was as serious as it had been after two years of the First World War rapidly backfired. Press and parliamentary accusations that M.E.W. could more aptly be described as the 'Ministry of Wishful Thinking' and that the blockade was leaking like a sieve seriously harmed the department's credibility.[3]

1 Diary, 24th February 1942.
2 H. Dalton, *The Fateful Years: Memoirs 1931–1945* (hereafter FY), Frederick Muller, London, 1957, p. 311.
3 W. N. Medlicott, *The Economic Blockade* (History of the Second World War, U.K. Civil Series), H.M.S.O., London, 1952, p. 46.

Dalton, formerly one of M.E.W.'s harshest critics, set about taking blockade policy in hand. The blockade was 'hamstrung by antediluvian British conceptions of prize law', he had declared when still in Opposition. ' ... The time has come to say "Shut up that book and let's get on with the blockade".'[1] Now, in office, his motto became 'belligerency at all times'.[2] Dalton's arrival raised the status of the Ministry. It also made possible a rapid change of direction.

Hitherto, the main work of M.E.W. had fallen into three parts: first, the exercise of contraband control by naval interception; second, the negotiation of War Trade Agreements with neutral countries adjacent to the enemy; and third, intelligence work aimed at preventing contraband evasion and at discovering the economic situation in Germany. The first two of these functions largely disappeared as a result of the changed nature of the war and the extent of territory under German occupation.[3] As a result, emphasis now had to be placed on Britain's own worldwide network of economic interests and facilities, as a means of influencing neutrals and controlling supplies to Germany. M.E.W.'s complex regulatory machinery for 'control at source' involved compulsory 'navicerts' (any ship not issued with a navicert certificate, or with a cargo not navicerted, was liable to seizure); a ship warrant scheme (facilities were refused to ships and shipping lines which failed to obey M.E.W. rules); the refusal of export licences; a black-list (to include so-called 'neutral' firms that traded with the enemy); and financial pressure (to prevent Germans from getting access to funds).

The need to alter the balance of M.E.W. activity in favour of control at source made it possible for Dalton to carry through a thorough reorganisation at the top of the department and to develop a more aggressive approach to blockade policy. At the end of May, he appointed Lord Drogheda and Noel Hall, both 'live wires and warmongers',[4] as Joint Directors under Sir Frederick Leith-Ross, the Director-General. Hugh Gaitskell, a socialist economist already working in M.E.W., became Principal Private Secretary – assuming the role of *chef de cabinet* with instant access to the Minister.

From the start, Dalton made it clear that he was prepared to annoy the Foreign Office – which seemed constantly frightened that a strong blockade policy would upset neutral governments. 'It is not my job,

---

1 *The Times*, 15th April 1940.
2 Douglas Jay in W. T. Rodgers (ed.), *Hugh Gaitskell 1906–1963*, Thames & Hudson, London, 1964, p. 86.
3 Dalton Papers 7/2 (10), Note on the Present Position and Probable Future of Economic Warfare, 27th June 1940.
4 FY, p. 334.

as I see it, to put a brake on the Foreign Office, but rather to act as a spur,' he told Leith-Ross at their first interview. 'Or in other words, it is not my duty to walk about with a watering-can, but rather to light the fires and let the Foreign Office extinguish them if they must.'[1] On 18th May, he sharply rebuked a meeting of M.E.W. and F.O. officials about the conduct of the blockade,[2] and he complained to the Prime Minister that so far the economic war had only been 'half-waged'.[3] It was the beginning of a conflict with the Foreign Office which was to continue throughout his term of office and lead officials to regard him as a disruptive influence, undermining discreet diplomacy.

Dalton's first battle, on a particular issue, concerned oil. Just as Cross had been unrealistically optimistic about the impact of economic warfare in general, so Dalton believed (on the basis of departmental intelligence) that Germany's oil resources were badly stretched. He told Attlee that even on the most unfavourable assumptions, Germany would become 'dangerously short' of oil by the spring of 1941,[4] and he wrote to Lord Hankey, chairman of the interdepartmental committee responsible for preventing oil reaching the enemy, advocating the bombing of oil targets. ' ... [I]t is surely high time to cease being gentlemen,' he declared, 'to become professionals and to do a little "body-line bowling at the Hun".'[5] But Dalton's belief that the enemy 'will not be much above the dying-out figure of 1918 next April'[6] was greeted with understandable scepticism. 'Cabinet discussed eternal question of denying supplies of oil to Germany and got not much further,' Sir Alexander Cadogan, Permanent Under-Secretary at the Foreign Office, noted on 8th June. 'I talked about it to Dalton after. He the "new broom", talking of "vigorous action". Due to ignorance and half to egotism.'[7] It was also due to poor work on the part of the Intelligence Department at M.E.W., though Dalton himself attributed his slow progress over oil targets to the fact that the R.A.F. hierarchy – more inclined to agree with him than the other services – pulled less weight with Tory Cabinet Ministers for social reasons.[8]

It was the blockade that most concerned him, however, and here he

1 Diary, 16th May 1940.
2 PRO, FO 837/500, 18th May 1940.
3 Dalton Papers 8/1 (24), 19th May 1940.
4 Dalton Papers 8/1 (3), 27th May 1940.
5 Dalton Papers 7/2 (2), 3rd June 1940.
6 Diary, 27th May 1940.
7 D. Dilks (ed.), *The Diaries of Sir Alexander Cadogan O.M. 1938–1945*, Cassell, London, 1971, p. 295.
8 FY, p. 345.

faced a series of contradictions. 'Unless we can rigidly blockade Europe, victory will be long delayed if not rendered impossible,' he argued early in July. 'I shall, therefore, do my utmost to resist all proposals to permit the entry of food or other war materials into enemy or enemy-occupied territory.'[1] But it was not so easy. First, there were political problems. The Left in Britain was resolutely hostile to the Vichy regime.[2] Many Conservatives (and some Foreign Office officials), on the other hand, saw no harm in dealing with Vichy if this was possible. Moreover, in order to prevent supplies from reaching Germany, it was necessary to blockade both occupied and unoccupied areas; yet, in practice, it was quite impossible to control merchant shipping passing to and from ports in unoccupied metropolitan France. Finally, the Admiralty was frequently at pains to point out that interruption of ships running the blockade was impossible given the demands on naval resources. Hence it was a long time before the blockade seriously affected any part of the country.[3]

There was also a challenge from another quarter. At a time when the blockade was at its least effective, Dalton had to contend with a campaign against the whole policy on the grounds that it would reduce the civilian populations of Europe to starvation. The campaign was principally American, led by a former President, Herbert Hoover, and although ostensibly humanitarian, it received support from those who backed an isolationist role for the United States. Hence there was the fear that, if the British could be made to seem as heartless as the Germans, the continued supply of American aid to Britain might be placed in jeopardy. The U.S. administration therefore pressed for limited concessions on a 'Milk for Babies' principle (supplies that would be of little use to occupying troops) and the Foreign Office was inclined to comply. It was a classic conflict: M.E.W. wishing to preserve the blockade, against the Foreign Office wishing to protect its diplomacy. Dalton's solution was that Britain should build up large food-stocks to be held 'in trust for the Free Europe of tomorrow'.[4] This was accepted, and Dalton drafted a passage for inclusion in a parliamentary statement by the Prime Minister on 20th August 1940.[5]

How far was the blockade a significant factor in winning the war? The blockade could be justified negatively on the basis of what would have happened without it. Thus, an M.E.W. Press Department mem-

1 PRO, FO 837/1218, 2nd July 1940.
2 See Dalton Papers 7/3 (4), 3rd July 1940.
3 Medlicott, *Economic Blockade*, p. 562.
4 PRO, WP (G) (40) 208.
5 PRO, War Cabinet minutes 225 (40) 5.

orandum argued in November 1942: 'The Axis would be able to trade freely how and where she pleased, import and export goods without restriction, have access to the raw materials of the world, and obtain foreign exchange without interference.'[1] It could be argued positively that fear of the loss of Russian food-supplies and oil encouraged Hitler's attack on the Soviet Union, and that the British blockade was a factor because it removed the possibility of replenishing stocks from other sources.[2] As Professor Medlicott has argued, 'fear of blockade may have been more important than blockade itself in bringing [Germany] to ultimate defeat'.[3] Dalton's claim to be able to 'strangle Hitler' may have been beyond the capacity of his Ministry; but his ability to keep the Führer short of breath, the 'softening up' effect which diverted German resources in order to combat the blockade, cannot be questioned.

How much was due to Dalton personally? He gave his officials 'a definite policy and they know what it is',[4] which had not been true of his predecessor. Moreover, as a new department, M.E.W. needed to be defended by a champion, or risk being cast into the shadows by other, stronger, branches of the war effort. The Minister's tactlessness was unhelpful, and his enthusiasms were sometimes misplaced – due, as Cadogan put it, to ignorance and egotism. But it is hard to argue in retrospect – especially with regard to Vichy France – that Dalton's boldness was wrong and the diplomatic appeasers were right.

In June 1941, the nature of the economic war, and of the blockade, was transformed by the German attack on Russia. Hitherto German-Soviet trade and the 'trans-Siberian leak' had ensured that in the last resort the Germans need not go short of essential supplies. Now this route was sealed. It was calculated that even if the Germans occupied the whole of European Russia, excluding the Caucasus, the economy at their disposal would be badly balanced and short of copper, rubber, tin, wolfram, cobalt, nickel, cotton, wool, leather and oil. The job of sealing off the area under German control could therefore be seen much more clearly. The essential machinery of the blockade, built up since the beginning of the war and especially since the fall of France, was maintained, but now it became easier to operate and increasingly effective. Although the real impact had not begun to be felt until after Dalton left M.E.W., by the autumn of 1941 economic warfare had ceased to be a matter for direction at the top political level. Meanwhile, Dalton's attention had moved elsewhere.

1 PRO, FO 837 1A X/M 03068, p. 13.
2 Medlicott, *Economic Blockade*, pp. 642–3.
3 Ibid., p. 646.
4 Diary, 21st October 1941.

Sabotage

For more than a year, Dalton had been preoccupied by another responsibility; related to, though distinct from, economic warfare – constituting a separate, secret empire. In the summer of 1940, he had begun to take an interest in 'special' operations and 'black' propaganda. There was a pretext. One of the supposed purposes of the blockade and of economic warfare was to undermine the morale of the enemy, and this fitted in with covert propaganda and subversion. It was believed that shortages might eventually drive the people of Europe to resistance and rebellion. Moreover, sabotage in enemy-occupied territory generally involved economically strategic targets, and so tied in with the intelligence side of M.E.W. activities.

From the beginning of June, Dalton had been speculating about the future of two secret organisations, the 'D' Section of the Secret Service, and a body with overlapping functions in the War Office called M.I.(R). 'Everyone wanting everything at once,' Cadogan noted at the end of the month. 'Dalton ringing up hourly to try to get a large finger in the Sabotage pie.'[1] The matter was sorted out at a meeting in the Foreign Secretary's room on 1st July, Dalton arguing that 'there was a clear distinction between "war from without" and "war from within" and that the latter was more likely to be better conducted by civilians than by soldiers'.[2] Ministers and officials present agreed that there should be 'a controller armed with almost dictatorial powers' to take charge. Who should this be? Swinton's name was mentioned – and found favour with the Prime Minister.[3] However, Attlee intervened to ensure that Dalton was chosen – and this decision was ratified by the War Cabinet on 22nd July. 'And now,' the Prime Minister told the Minister of Economic Warfare, 'go and set Europe ablaze.'[4]

Resources were limited, and the administrative problems involved in setting up and operating large new departments were immense. Initially, all subversion was lumped together under the so-called Special Operations Executive (S.O.E.). There were two wings: SO1 (dealing with propaganda) and SO2 (dealing with sabotage). The intention had been that the work of each wing should complement the other. The distribution of functions between the two was unclear, however, and sharp tensions arose between them. Moreover, the problems of M.E.W. in treading on the toes of other departments were magnified a hundredfold with Special Operations. S.O.E. was a source

1 *Cadogan Diaries*, 28th June 1940, p. 308.
2 Dalton Papers 7/3 (2), (FO minute).
3 *Cadogan Diaries*, 11th July 1940, p. 312.
4 Diary, 22nd July 1940.

of irritation to the Foreign Office (where the accusation was made that SO2 ran its own foreign policy), the Chiefs of Staff and the Service ministries (which saw SO2 as a threat to the cover of military intelligence) and the Ministry of Information (which engaged in a battle with SO1 over control of propaganda).

Part of the trouble was the undercover nature of Special Operations. Although the existence of S.O.E. was well known in Whitehall, the Minister of Economic Warfare could not answer questions in the House in connection with any of its duties. S.O.E. was therefore unaccountable – and a failure caused by its activities was likely to redound to the discredit of other departments or services. Moreover, as an organisation with an ambiguous status, and with a high proportion of its senior personnel drafted from outside the permanent Civil Service, it was poorly integrated into Whitehall.

S.O.E. did little for Dalton's reputation. Outside the small group of *cognoscenti*, he could not claim credit for any victories – yet had to suffer the repercussions of tangled official relations with other departments and their ministers. Neither did it help his relationship with the Prime Minister, who was Dalton's only court of appeal in time of trouble, but who took little interest in subversive activities.

Nevertheless, there was an excitement about S.O.E. – and especially SO2 – that captivated him, and soon made Special Operations the centre of his official life. S.O.E. provided a much better opportunity than M.E.W. for 'body-line bowling at the Hun'. Though the idea of setting Europe ablaze through subversion was no more realistic than strangling Hitler through the blockade, S.O.E. did at least provide one of the few aggressive operational units after the fall of France – and this gave it an imaginative appeal even for departments which found its demands tiresome.

SO2 – responsible for subversive warfare of a physical, as opposed to psychological, kind – soon became an entirely separate body (in August 1941, SO1 was absorbed into the Political Warfare Executive, and SO2 took over the title of S.O.E.). Dalton placed SO2 under the direct control of Gladwyn Jebb, S.O.E.'s Chief Executive Officer, who was given the job of providing liaison with Dalton and with the Foreign Office. Jebb, however, was based in Berkeley Square with the Minister, and it was Sir Frank Nelson, executive director of SO2, who was most immediately responsible for running the 'Baker Street Irregulars' at 64 Baker Street, where the SO2 organisation was established. Beneath Nelson was a staff largely recruited through a network of old-boy and City contacts: merchant bankers, City solicitors, Courtaulds' executives and oil men, in particular. Some (like George Taylor, an Australian placed by Dalton in charge of SO2 London

H.Q.) were inherited from the former 'D' Section. Others, including Colin Gubbins, who built up S.O.E.'s overseas networks, were recruited by Dalton himself.

Dalton took a keen interest (some felt too keen an interest) in operations,[1] especially when these seemed to hold out the possibility of spectacular results – though he saw little of any but the most senior staff, and rarely visited the establishment at Baker Street. His main role was to fight for the organisation against its enemies in Whitehall, and here, as with M.E.W., he succeeded in making an impact. Dalton's assertiveness was, indeed, a major factor in turning SO2 into an important instrument of war. 'It was under the regime of Mr Dalton and Frank Nelson that the Services and the government departments first became aware that our existence was sanctioned by the highest authority,' one former official, taken over from 'D' Section, has commented. 'Once they had grasped this they began slowly to give us the facilities without which we could not get anywhere.'[2] The contrast between when Dalton arrived and when he left was striking. In July 1940, there was not a single agent in the whole of Western Europe, and the only work being done was in the Balkans. By February 1942, there were scores of agents and active missions all over the world.

Propaganda

It was the propaganda side of Special Operations that proved to be Dalton's undoing. SO2 rekindled the sense of war as an adventure which Dalton had first acquired as an artillery officer on the Italian Front in 1917–18. It also provided the companionship and cool appraisals of Gladwyn Jebb, the man upon whose judgments he most depended. However, from mid-1941 it was SO1 that took up most of his time. This was because of a growing rivalry with the Ministry of Information over the control of propaganda, which escalated from an administrative dispute between officials into a bitter personal row between ministers. The dispute was the main reason for Dalton's transfer from M.E.W. to the Board of Trade in February 1942.

Since before the war, propaganda had been a Whitehall orphan, moving from one ministerial home to another. In 1938 a secret department was set up and then disbanded – only to be re-established the following spring. Characteristically, the Government looked back to 1918: Sir Campbell Stuart, who had organised a Department of Propaganda in Enemy Countries at the end of the First World War,

1 Jebb wrote later that the Minister, 'though immensely active, did not himself have any great sense of organisation'. (*Memoirs of Lord Gladwyn*, p. 100.)
2 B. Sweet-Escott, *Baker Street Irregular*, Methuen, London, 1965, p. 123.

was drafted to set up a section with the same name for the Second. Established first in Electra House on the Embankment, 'E.H.', as it was called, moved to Woburn Abbey, in Bedfordshire, at the outbreak of war.[1] E.H. was responsible for all propaganda activities and reported at first to the Minister of Information; from October 1939, to the Foreign Secretary; and then, from June 1940, again to M.O.I., now headed by Duff Cooper.[2] Thus, by the time Dalton acquired SO1 as part of the S.O.E. package which was intended to co-ordinate all sabotage and subversion against the enemy, propaganda had been through the hands of two other ministries in the space of a few months.

Dalton was not given all propaganda, but only the 'covert' part. The distinction between what was 'open', and therefore the job of M.O.I., and what was 'black', and therefore belonging to SO1, was the major source of trouble between the two departments. The Prime Minister appointed the Lord President, Sir John Anderson, to arbitrate. The so-called 'Anderson Award', finally agreed on 16th May 1941, gave Dalton secret propaganda, Cooper overt propaganda, and joint responsibility for co-ordination to the Ministers of Economic Warfare and Information and the Foreign Secretary working together – each with a senior official under him – on a triangular Political Warfare Executive. It was a solution that created more problems than it removed: blurring, rather than clarifying, lines of demarcation, and heightening ministerial anxieties and frustrations. Against a background of protests from the Minister of Information that M.O.I. should be given all propaganda or else disbanded, Churchill replaced Cooper with a close friend and personal aide, Brendan Bracken.

Dalton's attitude to Bracken rapidly changed from wariness to hostility and fear, as the diary reveals. Meanwhile, there were other problems in SO1. One was Dalton's uneasy relationship with the organisation's head – Reginald Leeper, 'tall and spare with the thoughtful concentrated face of some old-time papal secretary'.[3] Leeper's suspicions of his Minister may have owed something to Dalton's close attachment to Jebb, twelve years Leeper's junior. At first it seemed that Jebb would be in charge of both SO1 and SO2, but Leeper's appointment, and the move of SO1 headquarters to the main establishment at Woburn in November 1940, made this difficult in practice, and the intention that subversive action and subversive propaganda should be run as a joint enterprise was rapidly abandoned. Jebb, working with the Minister at Berkeley Square House, soon had

1 Sir Campbell Stuart, *Opportunity Knocks Once*, Collins, London, 1952, p. 185.
2 C. Cruickshank, *The Fourth Arm: Psychological Warfare 1938–1945*, Davis-Poynter, London, 1977, p. 17.
3 Sefton Delmar, *Black Boomerang*, Secker & Warburg, London, 1962, p. 64.

little directly to do with SO1 while having a great deal to do with the Minister; and Leeper, aware of Dalton's preference for Jebb over all other aides, kept his distance. As a result, Dalton and Leeper (who became Dalton's representative on the Political Warfare Executive) often felt that they were working at cross purposes. Dalton, for his part, was particularly suspicious of the friendship that existed between Leeper (a Foreign Office official) and Eden, the Foreign Secretary.

Dalton was less interested in the detailed work of SO1 than in that of SO2. According to Lord Gladwyn (Gladwyn Jebb), he 'tended to be bored to distraction by debates on propagandology and political warfare and certainly never appreciated the need for theory as a background for action.'[1] His imagination was initially aroused by the manufacture of sibs (from the Latin *sibilare*: to whisper) – false rumours deliberately spread to confuse or demoralise the enemy. Among those marked 'approved' in October 1941 was the story that 'There have been 200 reported cases during the last week of German soldiers' genitals having to be amputated because of frostbite'.[2] Dalton was also concerned with a proposal to broadcast to Germany on German wavelengths with apparatus which 'would create a raiding Dreadnought of the ether, firing broadsides at unpredictable times at unpredictable objectives of the enemy's radio propaganda'.[3] Early in 1941 Dalton gained the Prime Minister's approval for this project. The transmitter, known as 'Aspidistra', built near Crowborough in Sussex, did not become fully operational until October 1942, though it was extensively used thereafter for broadcasting to Europe.

It was the growing crisis over the administration of propaganda which took up most of Dalton's time, and increasingly sapped his energy. When Cooper was Minister of Information, Dalton made the running, and the situation was containable. The arrival of Bracken, by contrast, rapidly drove Dalton to the edge of despair. Bracken brought to the problem a fresh mind, and a clear aim: to fight for his Ministry's right to exist and to have a major function in the war.

The conflict that followed derived from administrative mistakes for which neither the Minister of Economic Warfare nor the Minister of Information was responsible. Nevertheless, it soon acquired powerful political and psychological dimensions. Dalton saw Bracken as a rootless Tory adventurer; Bracken regarded Dalton as a socialist careerist and intriguer. Soon, Robert Bruce Lockhart, Eden's official representative on the joint committee, was reporting that Bracken

1 *Memoirs of Lord Gladwyn*, p. 102.
2 PRO, FO 898/69/42, 31st October 1941.
3 Cited in Cruickshank, *The Fourth Arm*, p. 106.

was in the ascendant. 'Throughout the negotiations Mr Bracken has been forceful, sometimes pugnacious, sometimes impulsive, yet adroitly skilful in tactics, always good-humoured and always trustable,' Bruce Lockhart minuted his Minister. 'Above all, by quick-fire speech he has proved himself at least the equal of Dr Dalton in argument.'[1]

The dispute was greatly embittered in mid-August 1941 by a paper prepared by the P.W.E. officials which led Dalton to fear that SO1 was to be entirely abolished.[2] This approach had the backing of Bracken, who wanted a separate Department of Political Warfare, run by officials, with ministers effectively excluded. Bracken was prepared to put all M.O.I. and B.B.C. 'war zone' personnel into a common pool, and wanted Dalton to do the same with SO1 staff. Dalton, however, was strongly opposed to such a policy, arguing that the three officials of P.W.E. were insufficiently dynamic, and that ministerial stimuli were needed. Eden replied that if this was so, the best solution was for one minister, namely Bracken, to be solely responsible. Dalton now found himself cornered, with ministers and officials apparently ganging up against him.[3]

Dalton was deeply upset; so perhaps was Bracken. One of the latter's biographers records that, partly because of the 'intransigence' of Dalton, Bracken 'stormed about his office, hinting that he was "thinking of throwing in his hand"'.[4] When Bracken threatened to use his special relationship with Churchill to decide the issue in his favour, Dalton retaliated by appealing to Attlee. 'If it ever came to a showdown, with Labour Party loyalties aroused, I knew that I could beat him,' Dalton later claimed. 'I could raise much greater hell in the Labour Party than he could with the Tories.'[5]

Meanwhile, there was another, private, crisis. Dalton's wife, Ruth, frustrated by inactivity and by the inattention of her husband, had decided to take up war-work of her own – involving a physical separation from Hugh. In the early autumn of 1941 the Daltons gave up their flat in Victoria, Hugh moving into a room in M.E.W., and Ruth temporarily into a hotel. In December, she moved to Manchester. How much this was a result of her desire for useful employment, and how much was due to a personal rift, is not clear. Perhaps both elements were involved. But the effect must certainly have been to

1 PRO, FO 898 9 X/M 05668, 11th August 1941.
2 Dalton to Eden, Dalton Papers 18/2 (3), 20th August 1941.
3 Diary, 10th September 1941.
4 A. Boyle, *Poor Dear Brendan. The Quest for Brendan Bracken*, Hutchinson, London, 1974, p. 281.
5 FY, p. 382.

increase Hugh's feelings of stress, and it can be no accident that in this period his diary provides greatest evidence of anxiety and depression.

By Christmas, Dalton felt that the whole of S.O.E. was slipping from his grasp. His plan now was for a Ministry of Economic and Political Warfare, which he might himself head.[1] But Bracken was putting in a strong bid for all propaganda, with the suggestion that SO2 might be handed over to the Chiefs of Staff. Dalton's response was that if S.O.E. was taken from him, he would resign.[2] But his moods were changeable. A month later he was confessing to his diary that he was 'not quite whole-hearted' in putting up a claim for a Ministry of Economic and Political Warfare, largely because of endless squabbles over propaganda.[3]

Thus, when he was moved to the Board of Trade in the reshuffle of 21st February 1942, his feelings of regret were tinged with a large element of relief. For months he had been preoccupied by propaganda policy, just one aspect of his threefold responsibility – to his own increasing frustration and unhappiness. The relief was undoubtedly shared by the P.W.E. officials, who were now given a new charter by the Prime Minister. The number of responsible ministers was cut to two. Eden was given charge of policy and Bracken of administration, while Bruce Lockhart became Director-General. Woburn propagandists and B.B.C. broadcasters were now brought together at Bush House. Dalton, meanwhile, was confronted by issues of a less arcane nature.

Board of Trade

The move to the Board of Trade was technically a promotion; but the Board provided none of the glamour of S.O.E., and Dalton was now entirely cut off from the operational side of the war. The Board of Trade was a 'residuary ministry' looking after a rag-bag of unconnected problems – including bankruptcy, company law, clothes rationing, films, utility furniture, concentration of industry and much else; in addition, there was a general responsibility for all imports and exports, for trade and industry, and for coal. Three satellite ministers (each with the title of 'Secretary') were gathered under the President's overall suzerainty: D. R. Grenfell was in charge of the Mines Department, Geoffrey Lloyd of the Petroleum Department, and Harcourt Johnstone of the Department of Overseas Trade. Dalton could be held responsible for the mistakes of these men, but, frustratingly, he had no absolute control over their activities.

1 Diary, 20th December 1941.
2 Diary, 5th January 1942.
3 Diary, 11th February 1942.

The new President took part of his M.E.W. team with him. Sir Frederick Leith-Ross, still nominally Government Economic Adviser, joined him at the Board of Trade. So did Hugh Gaitskell, who acted as Personal Assistant before gaining promotion and acquiring an administrative empire of his own. Dalton inherited as Parliamentary Secretary Captain Charles Waterhouse, an old-style Tory who proved extremely useful in putting across potentially embarrassing matters to Tory back-benchers. Dalton was less fortunate in his Permanent Secretary, Sir Arnold Overton, whom he found over-cautious and stuffy, 'a restraining rather than a stimulating influence'.[1]

Coal

The Board of Trade provided a welcome escape from the row with Bracken over propaganda. But if Dalton believed that there would now be a respite from the Whitehall War, he was quickly disabused. Almost at once, he found himself involved in a bitter struggle over coal. A crisis had been brewing for some months. It was a crisis of expectations, not of immediate shortage; no vital war production was ever seriously affected by lack of coal. Nevertheless, the margins were narrow, and the danger of a shortfall seemed great. The problem was how best to guard against this possibility. There were several available approaches: action to increase production with the same manpower; action to increase the size of the work-force, principally by securing the release of face-workers from the Field Army; or action to reduce consumption. Dalton tried all three – and met fierce opposition on each.

The previous summer the Secretary for Mines had produced a rough and ready system of rationing, whereby no domestic coal consumer might receive more than one ton of coal a month, and there had been further restrictions in the autumn. Now, a fairer and more effective approach was considered. Early in March, Dalton, as overlord Minister, asked his old boss at the London School of Economics, Sir William Beveridge, to prepare a scheme for Fuel Rationing. Beveridge accepted, and within five weeks had produced a system which Dalton regarded as 'a very clever and perfect plan', though in need of practical simplifications.[2] Before then, however, the possibility of implementing any scheme had been thrown away by a premature disclosure in the House of Commons. On 17th March, Dalton made the tactical error of announcing the fuel rationing decision and the appointment of Beveridge. Tory back-benchers were outraged – some voicing the opinions of the coal-owners, others opposed to

1 FY, p. 388.
2 Diary, 7th April 1942.

rationing on principle. But there was more to it than the issue itself; Dalton happened, by bad fortune, to have hit a moment in the history of the Government when accord between Labour and Tory benches was at its lowest ebb. 'The rationing plan became a sort of un-acknowledged test of the relative strength of parties and interests within the Coalition Government and in Parliament', as one historian has observed.[1]

At first, Dalton was able to press ahead. Churchill, though sharing Tory misgivings about rationing in general, was even more opposed to the alternative of releasing 7,000 miners from the Field Army. It was opposition from Tory back-benchers (in particular the 1922 Committee), however, that killed the scheme – against a background of serious unrest in the coalfields. Forced to retreat, Dalton suggested that rationing should be postponed until it was possible to present 'a complete programme of action' covering production, consumption and organisation. A White Paper on Coal was published on 3rd June, laying down the principle of 'dual control' – the State directing mining operations wherever necessary while the colliery owners continued to be responsible for the finances of the mines. As a result of pressure from Ernest Bevin, the Minister of Labour, a National Coal Board was proposed – to be presided over by a minister with large powers of direction. A Fuel Rationing Scheme formed an annex to the White Paper, to await a later decision; but rationing was never introduced. Shortly afterwards, a Board of Investigation into Miners' Wages recommended a flat-rate wage increase, a national minimum wage and an output bonus.

It was a defeat: the killing of rationing was the only successful Conservative revolt against Churchill's Government.[2] Yet it was one from which Dalton emerged with some credit. Though his claim to have 'laid the foundation of a New Order in the Coalfields'[3] was exaggerated, the extent of government control of the mines would have been less, and the wages board might not have come about, without him. Will Lawther was not merely indulging in flattery when he told Party Conference a year later that Bevin and Dalton had done more for the mining industry than all their predecessors.[4]

The dispute also had the effect of reminding Dalton that he was a Labour M.P. with socialist objectives. Once the crisis was over, he

1 W. H. B. Court, *Coal*, H.M.S.O., London, 1951, p. 161.
2 See W. P. Crozier (edited by A. J. P. Taylor), *Off the Record: Political Interviews 1933–43*, Hutchinson, London, 1973, p. 323n.
3 Diary, 31st May 1942.
4 Cited in P. Williams, *Hugh Gaitskell: A Political Biography*, Jonathan Cape, London, 1979, p. 114.

turned his attention to post-war plans, which became his main interest for the rest of the war. For this Dalton got little acknowledgment; as with S.O.E., it was an aspect largely hidden from the public gaze.

Post-War Plans

Publicly, Dalton was seen as Minister of Privation – his name associated with all the consumer shortages of the Home Front.[1] He was the man who gave to the ordinary citizen – and the man who took away. The impression that he did the latter with a certain amount of ghoulish enthusiasm was hard to eradicate – especially as the necessity to ration, intensely disagreeable to Tories and Liberals, was seen by Dalton as a perfectly designed instrument of equality. This aspect was much seized upon by Tory editors, eager to find a socialist scapegoat. The *New Statesman* noted 'a vendetta against Hugh Dalton' in the Beaverbrook press at the end of 1943,[2] and the *Daily Herald* accused Conservative newspapers of suggesting that 'while he robs our women of their corsets, he strives without ceasing to imprison the world of commerce in a veritable strait-waistcoat of superfluous Orders and Regulations and Taboos'.[3]

Yet behind this public image as a bureaucratic regulator, Dalton was turning his attention to the task of creating a more prosperous, and peaceful, future. Douglas Jay recalls that Dalton's sympathies at this time were simple. 'He was in favour of miners, the young, white men, socialists, New Zealand, Australia and dwellers in Durham and Northumberland. He was against the Germans, reactionaries, the elderly and the rich.'[4] Of these, his hatred of Germans and reactionaries, and his sympathy for miners and North-Easterners, were most in evidence. In fact, he linked the two. By combining a jingoistic anti-Germanism with the advocacy of industrial intervention in the areas of pre-war unemployment, he was able to make far more progress on post-war plans than if he had pursued domestic reform on its own.

In August 1942 he wrote a long memorandum on Reparations, arguing that after the war the Allies should interfere drastically in the German economy.[5] The circulation of this document led to the setting-up of an interdepartmental committee on Reparations and

1 FY, p. 415.
2 *New Statesman and Nation*, 13th November 1943.
3 *Daily Herald*, 22nd February 1945.
4 Douglas Jay, *Change and Fortune: A Political Record*, Hutchinson, London, 1980, p. 110.
5 Dalton Papers 7/4 (79), 28th August 1942.

Economic Security (the Malkin Committee), whose operations he watched closely. Meanwhile, he let it be known that he was in favour of treating Germany much more harshly than in 1919. He told the Reconstruction Committee in January 1943 that not only should the defeated states be disarmed, but that there should also be a total prohibition of the ownership of civil, as well as of military, aircraft.[1] He tried to convince his old I.L.P. associate, H. N. Brailsford, that in the interests of Anglo-Soviet co-operation, Britain should let the Russians do '*most* of what they like in Eastern Europe and in Germany';[2] and he applauded the Malkin Committee report in the summer of 1943, which prescribed the destruction of the German synthetic oil industry, and a five-year period of 'very substantial deliveries in kind', followed by payment by Germany for international peacekeeping forces. Events overtook such proposals, but Dalton continued to regard the emasculation of Germany as a matter of the utmost importance.

Germany and the problem of the Germans absorbed much of his passion, but not much of his time. He was far more concerned with the constructive opportunities provided by his new job; and, indeed, apart from his first eighteen months as Chancellor, Dalton's period of office at the Board of Trade from the summer of 1942 to May 1945 was the most fulfilling of his life. His absolute powers were limited; very few of his activities were not presided over by a watchful Cabinet Committee dominated by Tory ministers. On the other hand, a finger in many pies and the freedom of *not* being a member of the War Cabinet enabled him to push hard his own plans for the post-war world.

Dalton assumed that a precipitate election would bring a crushing Conservative victory, and he therefore deplored any Labour Party activity that might endanger the electoral truce. He also took for granted that Churchill would win an election held immediately after the war was over. His hope, therefore, was that the Coalition might continue into the peace – as the only way of maintaining a Labour presence in the Government. One scheme was that, when the election came, 'Government' candidates for all three parties would oppose each other in the same constituency, 'varying their emphasis upon one common programme', while ministers should abstain from speaking, and be returned unopposed.[3] When it became clear that Labour rank-and-file pressures for open electoral confrontation could not be resisted, Dalton continued to hold out for a long delay between the ending of the war in Europe and an election – with the

1 PRO, CAB 87/3, 8th January 1943.
2 Dalton to Brailsford, 13th March 1944. Dalton Papers 8/1 (21).
3 Diary, 22nd March 1943.

possibility of Labour rejoining a Coalition once the election was over.[1]

Thus Dalton's concentration on post-war planning – both as a member of the administration and as a policy-maker on the Labour Party N.E.C. was directed at a future government in which Labour seemed likely to be, at best, a junior partner. It was also a product of his immediate experience as a minister working on the Home Front. Pre-war Labour plans had been theoretical constructs, based on limited experience of office. By contrast, Dalton's ideas as they developed during the war took existing government machinery, and its limitations, as a starting-point. There were to be no dramatic panaceas – partly because the pressure of Tory colleagues limited the scope for thinking along ideological lines; and partly because Labour was unlikely to be in a position to introduce revolutionary policies. Instead of suggestions for over-turning the system, these were proposals which the Coalition, in a liberal mood, might be prepared to accept. Labour's 1945 manifesto, *Let Us Face the Future* (much of which Dalton wrote), was not really an alternative to War Coalition policies but a development of them – containing a great deal on which all parties could agree.

But post-war planning by Labour members of the Coalition, and Labour Party policy-making that ran parallel to it, were also part of a complicated political game. Labour ministers who were concerned to advance their political aims were also keen to remain in office – and to do the latter it was necessary to maintain a delicate balance. They needed, therefore, to calculate their value to Churchill (a 'national' rather than a purely Tory leader), against the danger that they might outlive their usefulness; at the same time, and increasingly as the emergency stage of the war passed, they needed to extract as much social reform or promises of future social reform as possible in order to convince supporters that their presence in the Coalition yielded returns. In the second calculation, the future had great advantages over the present – it was far easier to persuade a Conservative-dominated government and a Coalition-minded Prime Minister to grant concessions on tick, than to gain approval for reforms that had an immediate application.

Dalton used a variety of ploys. One was to get colleagues to agree to the setting-up of innocent-sounding ministerial committees – and then to submit well-researched papers advocating reform, in the hope of solidifying Labour ministerial opinion and winning over liberal-minded Tories and civil servants. Another was to galvanise the Labour Party outside the Government on a particular issue. Policies

1 Diary, 26–27th February 1944.

prepared by Dalton and his friends for the Labour N.E.C., and included in the official Party programme, often had as their main purpose a demonstration to the Coalition of the current state of Labour opinion.

Dalton's real opening came after a Cabinet meeting in October 1943, when Churchill issued a short note on the 'Transition Period' – defined as either two years from the defeat of Germany or four years from 1st January 1944, whichever ended first. This was combined with a paper by Churchill listing a large range of topics on which decisions would be necessary. Many fell within Dalton's departmental field, wholly or partly. In his diary, Dalton gives a vivid account of the Prime Minister's address on the subject to the Cabinet:

> ... tonight the P.M., who is in a very good temper and great spirits, says that he has now been led to see this question quite differently. He says that this is because he has been 'jostled and beaten up by the Deputy Prime Minister' [Attlee]. For this, he says, he is very grateful. The Transition has now taken a very firm shape in his mind. We shall not pass direct from war to peace, even apart from the complication of the two-stage ending of the war. Between these two there must be a transition for which it is our duty to make most careful preparations now, and we should rule out nothing important for the simple needs of the Transition, merely because it is controversial. He then elaborated with great dramatic detail, how we should prepare a great book, the Book of the Transition, like the War Book, running to perhaps a thousand closely printed pages, or taking the form of a number of Reports and precise plans contained in drawers, one above another, so that, if any amateurish critic says 'You have no plan for this or that', it would be easy to pull out a drawer, bring out a paper, and say 'Here it all is'. All Parties in Parliament, the country, our returning soldiers, the whole world, would be filled with admiration if we were able to display a series of such plans.[1]

This marked a turning-point in Churchill's attitude to post-war planning. There were to be many checks and disappointments. But the Prime Minister's declaration – conceived as the basis for a possible peace-time Coalition – became a charter to which a hard-pressed minister could appeal. When the going got tough, Dalton was able to draw attention to the priority that had been given to the Transition.

Dalton's main concern was with the problem of providing work in areas of chronic unemployment. A widespread fear remained (as

1 Diary, 21st October 1943.

Dalton was reminded when dealing with the miners in 1942) that peace would bring a return to inter-war 'normalcy'. Dalton therefore decided to use his powers for concentrating and locating industry (shared with Ernest Bevin, the Minister of Labour) in order to guard against this danger. 'Both to secure full employment in the depressed areas, and for other social reasons, I regard some national control of industrial location as essential,' he told Reconstruction Priorities Committee colleagues in May 1943.[1] His proposition was simple: by all means possible, work should be taken to the workers.

In this, Dalton's aim did not depart in principle from that of pre-war official inquiries. Where it differed was in the degree of government intervention that should be involved. In 1934 the Special Areas (Development and Improvement) Act had introduced a measure of 'positive external assistance', but only at a token level. More successful had been the public sponsorship of industrial estates – the first of which was established in 1936. By 1938 government-built factories were employing 12,000 people in the Special Areas, and this approach had become accepted as a regional-policy tool.[2] If development policy in the 1930s had failed, this had not been because of a lack of ideas – but because of a reluctance by government to follow them through.

Dalton's most important inheritance was the Barlow Report on Distribution of the Industrial Population – published in January 1940, and generally ignored. It was the recommendations of this document, in particular the call for 'some form of national planning of industry', which Dalton took as his starting-point. Circulating a paper on the subject to ministerial colleagues, he stressed his concern lest 'a serious outbreak of unemployment' might follow the running-down of war production.[3] He now secured the transfer of Douglas Jay, currently working at the Ministry of Supply, to be his Personal Assistant for post-war problems, and a key member of a band of officials whom he dubbed his 'post-warriors'.

Jay's job was to get Whitehall to prepare for the rejuvenation of pre-war Distressed Areas (renamed Development Areas) as soon as the war ended. There were to be three stages. First came the task of inserting into the projected White Paper on Employment Policy (the famous 'Full Employment' White Paper) a passage authorising an ambitious scheme; the second was to create in the Board of Trade the machinery needed to carry it out; the third was to get through Parlia-

1 PRO, CAB 87/13 X/P 07917, 27th May 1943.
2 D. Maclennan and J. B. Parr (eds), *Regional Policy: Past Experience and New Directions*, Martin Robinson, Oxford, 1979, p. 5.
3 PRO, BT 64/3200 X/P 07825.

ment a Bill which would give the Board the requisite legal powers. The plan was to enlarge the pre-war industrial estates in the Development Areas and add to their number; build what were later called 'advance factories' for sale or let; convert wartime factories to peacetime production and prepare them for sale to private firms; take powers for increased government lending; and control new industrial building in the congested areas of the Midlands and South-East.[1]

By bullying civil servants, fending off Beaverbrook and Bracken, rallying Labour colleagues, and finessing the Reconstruction Committee, Dalton eventually succeeded in inserting a chapter on 'The Balanced Distribution of Industry and Labour' in the Full Employment White Paper. He also won a stiff battle – which lasted until after the Coalition had broken up – to ensure that a Distribution of Industry Bill became law. At a crucial Cabinet meeting on 13th December 1944, Location of Industry was put into the top sixteen Reconstruction Bills for the new legislative programme. Beaverbrook objected, but Bracken was away, and Bevin weighed in on Dalton's side. The Bill received its Second Reading on 21st March. 'It is the first instalment of a debt of honour which we owe to some of the best and bravest of our fighting men,' Dalton told the House.[2] The Bill received the Royal Assent on 15th June – the day Parliament was dissolved. It gave the President of the Board of Trade a wide range of powers to encourage industrial investment in the Development Areas – although a clause proposing the setting-up of Restricted Areas had to be dropped. Despite the need to make this concession, Dalton was well pleased. 'This is the best thing I have done at the Board of Trade,' he recorded. 'If the power, now conferred upon my successors, is strongly and sensibly used there will never be any Depressed Areas again.'[3]

In fact, as Chancellor for the next two years (with Cripps as President of the Board of Trade), Dalton was able to ensure that the powers were given a very strong interpretation. In 1947 the Labour Government made good the concession over Restricted Areas by pushing through the Town and Country Planning Act, which introduced the Industrial Development Certificate (I.D.C.) as a prerequisite for the granting of planning permission. These two pieces of legislation remained the basis of regional policy until 1960, and the reference point for all regional policies to come. Only after 1979 was the structure erected by Dalton in the mid-1940s substantially undermined.

A greater impact was provided in the short run, however, through industrial estates and the provision of factories. The existence of

1 Jay, *Change and Fortune*, p. 112.
2 H.C. Debs [409], col. 837, 21st March 1945.
3 Diary, 29th May 1945.

millions of square feet of ordnance factory in the assisted areas provided the opportunity. In September 1943, Dalton urged the Reconstruction Priorities Committee that post-war arms manufacture should continue in such factories, and that any not so used should be adapted as soon as possible to civilian production.[1] To achieve this Dalton set up a new department headed by Jay and by Sir Philip Warter, Controller of Factories and Storage. Their tool was the wartime building licence system, which channelled to the Board of Trade all applications for post-war industrial building sites.

Building licences and the control of scarce building materials gave the President a power over civilian employment which no minister who was not directly concerned with production for war had exercised in the past. Thus, when Dalton left the Government he was able to boast that he had approved plans for building four million square feet of factory in the North-East alone – creating 26,000 jobs, and indirectly as many more again.[2]

Meanwhile, he had been persuaded of the need to provide a 'macro' approach – to ensure a good climate of international trade and prevent another world slump. In the summer of 1942, the Economic Section of the Cabinet Secretariat was looking for support for the proposals of the economist James Meade for a post-war Commercial Union to implement Keynes's currency plans.[3] Having convinced Keynes, Meade sought the backing of the President of the Board of Trade, hoping to counter Treasury and Board of Trade departmental prejudices in favour of keeping import restrictions. Meade first sought out Gaitskell, and won him over. Gaitskell then redrafted the proposal, and sent a memorandum on the subject to Dalton. Dalton was impressed – and decided that it provided an opportunity for a Board of Trade initiative with 'first-class controversial value'.[4] Meade was thereupon seconded to the Board. Many officials (including Sir Frederick Leith-Ross, who was to be closely involved) remained sceptical.[5] Nevertheless, the idea bore fruit. Long negotiations led eventually to an International Trade Charter in September 1943, the precursor of the General Agreement on Tariffs and Trade (G.A.T.T.). Dalton's contribution had been to persuade colleagues to set up an interdepartmental committee on Commercial Policy, with Meade as a member, and thereafter to give the scheme, through its many

1 Paper on 'Location of Industry and its Control', 2nd September 1943. PRO, CAB 87/13 X/P 07917.
2 *Sunday Times*, 17th June 1945.
3 Williams, *Hugh Gaitskell*, p. 116.
4 PRO, BT 11/2000 X/P 7759, 29th August 1942.
5 Sir Frederick Leith-Ross, *Money Talks*, Hutchinson, London, 1968, p. 293.

vicissitudes, powerful political backing.

On the Home Front, Dalton supported the Keynesian analysis which formed the basis of the May 1944 Employment White Paper. Though his personal relations with Keynes (his former tutor) were cool, Dalton had absorbed some of the influence of his younger economist friends who were enthusiastic about Keynes's ideas. In July 1943, Dalton became Chairman of the Labour Party Policy Committee, and reorganised the sub-committee structure, bringing in new people.[1] In October he asked Gaitskell and Jay to prepare a joint paper on post-war employment and finance, and Evan Durbin to write one on post-war international arrangements.[2] These formed the basis for a paper accepted by the Policy Committee the following April.

'It was largely Keynesian,' Dalton wrote later.[3] In fact, it was an amalgam of White Paper Keynesianism and physical control socialist planning. Wartime controls had increasingly become a party issue within the Coalition, and the more ministers like Beaverbrook and Bracken pressed for decontrol as soon after the war as possible, the more Labour ministers insisted that controls should be maintained. 'I should define Economic Planning, in its widest sense, as the deliberate direction, by persons in control of large resources, of economic activities towards chosen ends,' Dalton had written during the peacetime Depression.[4]

What better description could be given of the activities of wartime economic ministers? Socialism had become what the Coalition had been forced to do because of the exigencies of war.

This volume ends with the reluctant break-up of the administration, and the preparation for an election which Dalton, in common with most colleagues, assumed that Labour would lose. It was also an election in which Labour presented a ministerial team with a greater experience of government and a clearer sense of direction than ever before, as the diary vividly reveals.

1 Labour Party NEC Minutes, 21st July 1943.
2 Diary, 20th October 1943.
3 FY, p. 422.
4 H. Dalton, *Practical Socialism for Britain*, Routledge, London, 1935, p. 243.

Editorial Note

Dalton's diary for the years of the War Coalition is more than three-quarters of a million words in length, with some entries running to several pages. This selection, therefore, includes only a fraction of the available material, and because of the special interest of the period it has been particularly hard to decide what to include and what to leave out. Indeed, the very fullness of the account posed a problem: the author's range of activities at each of his wartime ministries is revealed in the diary in a series of distinct, but closely interwoven, narratives. The alternatives seemed to be to extract occasional passages from each; or to concentrate on some, while neglecting others.

In general, I have followed the second course – even at the cost of cutting out important material. The first alternative would have required a plethora of editorial explanations to fill in the gaps, while sacrificing the natural flow of the original. The second at least has the merit of showing some aspects of the diarist's life in bold relief. Certainly, a simple criterion for selection like 'importance' would have produced a patchwork of passages taken out of context with little continuity. Given the impossibility of publishing the whole diary in full, I have tried to give the selection coherence as an integrated work.

Thus, I have included little in this volume (though there is much in the original) about administering the blockade at M.E.W., or about Dalton's Board of Trade responsibilities for cotton, films, clothes rationing, utility furniture or the supply of tobacco, or about the practical administration of Dalton's attempts to attract industrial investment to the Development Areas. Instead, I have concentrated as much as possible on the war, and on politics. I have included a lot of gossip about operations, and about colleagues; some of Dalton's careful records of talks with leading foreign exiles – especially Poles, with whom he was particularly close – and as much material as possible that relates to the wider background of the war. I have paid special attention to tensions and manoeuvrings within the Coalition, and to the activities of the Labour Party.

Very little material concerns Dalton's private life. Only occasionally did the author use his diary for the purpose of self-examination. Where he did so, I have included what he wrote. Dalton visited his Bishop Auckland, Co. Durham constituency infrequently, preferring to spend spare weekends at West Leaze, his Wiltshire home. Enough references to West Leaze and the Wiltshire countryside have been included to indicate their importance to him.

Dalton himself published three volumes of memoirs during the last years of his life, and in these he quotes and paraphrases material from his diary. Where passages from the diary have already appeared in the memoirs, I have generally not included them here. In this volume, the problem has in fact been slight. Dalton's published account of the war years is compressed into less than a quarter of one of his three volumes, *The Fateful Years: Memoirs 1931–1945*,[1] and very little of this is taken directly from the diary. Nevertheless, *The Fateful Years* is an important source, and I have frequently referred to it, as well as to Dalton's unpublished papers, in linking passages and notes.

For most of his life, Dalton wrote his diary in longhand, using small notebooks or, later on, loose sheets. Between 1937 and 1947, however – including the whole period covered by this book – his habit was to dictate the diary to a secretary. Hence almost all of the original diary for the Second World War is in typescript. There was only one draft. Dalton would read through what had been typed, and make occasional corrections. What makes the diary for the Coalition years different from earlier and later material – and so requiring separate treatment – is partly its sheer bulk (during his years of wartime ministerial office, Dalton produced almost as much diary as for the rest of his life put together); partly the regularity of wartime entries, with a record for almost every day (the main exceptions are holidays and trips); and partly a difference of arrangement that is a product of size, regularity and the pace of the events described. Instead of occasional reflections, and episodes widely dispersed, there is a continuity of plot and sub-plot, with far more detail and, very often, a close examination of policy.

Why did he write so much? Dalton engaged in one form of writing or another throughout his career, and during this period of intense activity, the diary became his main literary outlet. It is likely that his first, war book was somewhere in his mind, and that he saw the diary as the basis for some future publication. A sense of history, and of

1 See pp. 325–466.

history being made, pervades his record of the war years. On one occasion, Dalton discussed diary-keeping with another compulsive diarist, Harold Nicolson, and both agreed that their proudest boast would be that they had served in Mr Churchill's Government.[1]

If, however, the diary was partly a tribute to history, it also served as a tool of the ministerial trade. The use of a secretary helped to blur the distinction between historical record and official *aide-mémoire*. Sometimes Dalton would insert in his diary long private minutes containing detailed accounts of conversations with leading personalities; on other occasions sections from the diary would find their way into his official files. Thus, the diary seems to have been a way of committing details to memory, and ordering thoughts and priorities. Finally (and this point will be further examined in the second volume), the diary was undoubtedly important as a psychological release, even as a way of coping with emotional turmoil. It is noticeable that entries become longer – with, on occasion, a note of desperation – at times of greatest stress.

Although there is an entry for virtually every day for much of the period of the Coalition, Dalton did not compose his diary daily. His usual practice was to dictate a week's material at a single sitting. Hence the date placed at the head of a particular entry (in this volume, as in the original) indicates the date of the events described and not, in general, the day on which the entry was written. Some passages, indeed, written in the present tense, have the strange stylistic feature of referring to events that have not yet taken place. From the reader's point of view, the drawback is that a record made several days in arrears inevitably contains an element of hindsight (though the extent of detail in many entries suggests that Dalton may have used notes when dictating). On the other hand, the author's skills as a narrator are given greater scope: the bunching together of entries often enables him to link the events of several days into a coherent story.

Editorial Style
Apart from leaving passages out, I have interfered with the original text as little as possible. Contractions have been expanded and surnames substituted for initials, occasionally with the first Christian name as well. Where organisations or official bodies are referred to by initials, I have expanded these without square brackets if they are brief, and retained them where they are long (sometimes identifying them in square brackets) or familiar. Dates have been standardised, with the day of the week added. Breaks involving the exclusion of material *in*

1 Diary, 31st January 1941; N. Nicolson (ed.), *Harold Nicolson: Diaries and Letters 1939–1945*, Collins, London, 1967, p. 141.

the middle of entries are indicated by three dots (...). No indication is given if an entry is cut out altogether, or if material has been excluded at the beginning or end of an entry, unless (as happens rarely) the break occurs in the middle of a sentence. Where Dalton himself used multiple dots, these have been distinguished from those indicating missing material by the use of six dots, rather than three. Spelling and other obvious textual errors have been corrected – including (where identification is certain) a large number of typing errors in proper names. Where identification is not absolutely certain, however, I have retained Dalton's original spelling. Many passages in the original contain insertions in the margin, or at the top or bottom of the page, in Dalton's hand. These are often impossible to date: some were apparently written at the time, others when Dalton was preparing his memoirs. To avoid confusion, I have generally relegated these markings to footnotes. Linking passages are intended to provide essential personal and historical background. The division of the material into ten chronological chapters is arbitrary – the text is not so neatly divided.

As many characters in the text as possible have been identified in footnotes. The aim has been to provide basic information – not to give full curricula vitae. The amount of detail provided varies according to the importance of the individual in Dalton's diary, his or her importance in the world, and the information that is available. I have given title or form of address at the time of entry, followed by the last known title, and any earlier name if different from the current one. I have not given details of Privy Councillorships, promotions in the peerage, or honours in general. Birth and death dates have been given where possible. More information is provided about politicians than about officials. Generally each note starts with the position or occupation of the character mentioned at the time of the entry, followed by other information of contemporary relevance (including details of party and constituency, in the case of politicians). After this, earlier or later career details may be given. Senior ministerial posts are automatically listed. Junior posts are given if held at the time of the entry. Otherwise, except for Treasury or Foreign Office posts, junior offices are included under the general rubric of 'junior minister'. With officials, apart from the post or department at the time of entry (where this information is available), usually only the most senior posts are mentioned; ambassadorships, other than those in France, the Soviet Union and the U.S.A., are not normally included, neither are Home Civil Service posts below the rank of Permanent Secretary, unless these are specially relevant. In a few cases, the reader is referred to Appendix A, where fuller biographical details are provided.

Abbreviations

A.C.	Administrative Committee
A.C.O.S.	Assistant Chief of Staff
A.F.H.Q.	Allied Forces Headquarters
A.R.P.	Air Raid Precautions
A.T.S.	Auxiliary Territorial Service
B.E.F.	British Expeditionary Force
B.S.H.	Berkeley Square House
C.C.O.	Chief of Combined Operations
C.D.A.	Chief Diplomatic Adviser
C.E.O.	Chief Executive Officer
C.H.Q.	Country (House) Headquarters
C.I.D.	Committee of Imperial Defence
C.I.G.S.	Chief of Imperial General Staff
C.O.	Combined Operations
C.O.	Commanding Officer
C.O.S.	Chiefs of Staff
C.R.E.S.	Committee on Reparations and Economic Security
C.R.T.	Commercial Relations and Treaties Department (Board of Trade)
C.W.R.	Cabinet War Room
D.A.I.	Director of Air Intelligence
D.C.	Daily Council (of S.O.E.)
D.C.O.	Director of Combined Operations
D.L.P.	Divisional Labour Party
D.M.A.	Durham Miners' Association
D.M.I.	Director of Military Intelligence
D.M.O.	Director of Military Operations
D.N.I.	Director of Naval Intelligence
D.T.	Director of Training

E.A.M.	Ethnikon Apeleftherotikon Metopon (Greek National Liberation Front)
E.E.P.	External Economic Policy
E.H.	Electra House
E.L.A.S.	Ellinikos Laikos Apeleftherotikos Stratos (Greek National Popular Liberation Army)
E.W.O.	Essential Work Order
F.F.I.	Forces Françaises de l'Intérieur
G.O.C.	General Officer Commanding
G.W.R.	Great Western Railway
H.M.G.	His Majesty's Government
I.C.S.	Indian Civil Service
I.D.A.C.	Import Duties Advisory Committee
I.E.P.	Internal Economic Problems (Committee)
I.L.O.	International Labour Office
I.P.W.S.	International Post-War Settlement
J.I.C.	Joint Intelligence Committee (of Chiefs of Staff)
L.P.S.	Lord Privy Seal
L.S.E.	London School of Economics and Political Science
L.S.I.	Labour and Socialist International
M.E.P.W.	Ministry of Economic and Political Warfare (proposed)
M.E.W.	Ministry of Economic Warfare
M.F.A.	Ministry of Foreign Affairs
M.I.(R.)	Military Intelligence (Research)
N.C.L.	National Council of Labour
N.E.C.	National Executive Committee (of the Labour Party)
N.U.D.A.W.	National Union of Distributive and Allied Workers
P.A.S.	Principal Assistant Secretary
P.L.P.	Parliamentary Labour Party
P.O.G.	Prevention of Oil reaching Germany (Lord Hankey's Committee)
P.P.S.	Parliamentary Private Secretary
P.Q.	Parliamentary Question
P.U.S.	Permanent Under-Secretary
P.W.E.	Political Warfare Executive
R.O.F.	Royal Ordnance Factory
S.H.A.E.F.	Supreme Headquarters Allied Expeditionary Force
S.I.S.	Special Intelligence Service
S.O.	Special Operations
S.O.E.	Special Operations Executive
S.W.M.F.	South Wales Miners' Federation
U.D.C.	Urban District Council

U.N.R.R.A. United Nations Relief and Rehabilitation
              Administration
V.A.D.   Voluntary Aid Detachment

In footnotes PRO refers to documents in the Public Record Office, Kew. References to state papers are as follows: CAB, minutes and papers of the Cabinet; FO, the Foreign Office, M.E.W., S.O.E. and P.W.E.; BT, the Board of Trade. FY refers to the second volume of Dalton's memoirs, *The Fateful Years: Memoirs 1931–1945* (1957).

I

Ungentlemanly Warfare

1

Fall of France
May–July 1940

On 10th May Neville Chamberlain resigned as Prime Minister and was replaced by Winston Churchill at the head of a Coalition Government that included both Labour and Liberal representatives – the most truly 'National' administration that there had ever been. Not all ministers were appointed immediately, however, and Dalton – waiting anxiously at Bournemouth where the Labour Party Conference was assembled – was one of the last to be named. Not until 14th May did he receive a message from Churchill asking him to serve as Minister of Economic Warfare. He accepted at once, and returned to London by train. Before he left Bournemouth, he telephoned his wife Ruth, asking her to invite Hugh Gaitskell, a temporary civil servant at M.E.W., to meet him in his London flat at midnight. 'I told him I wanted him to be, in fact, a good deal more than a Private Secretary, more like a *chef de cabinet*,' Dalton later recalled. 'He should be fully in my confidence and feel free to advise me on all questions, both of policy and persons.'[1]

Meanwhile, to meet the emergency, the new Prime Minister had formed a small War Cabinet carefully balancing Conservative and Labour. Chamberlain and Lord Halifax, respectively Lord President of the Council and Foreign Secretary, were included, reflecting the continued influence of the 'Old Gang' among Tory back-benchers; but so too were Clement Attlee and Arthur Greenwood, Leader and Deputy Leader of the Labour Party, who became ministers without portfolio. Outside the War Cabinet, Churchill gave key posts to men he knew and trusted: A. V. Alexander, a prominent figure in the Labour Party and in the co-operative movement, became First Lord of the Admiralty; Anthony Eden, who had resigned from Chamberlain's government in 1938, was made Secretary of State for War; and the Liberal Leader, Sir Archibald Sinclair, became Air Minister. Other new ministers on the Labour side included Ernest Bevin, General Secretary of the Transport and General Workers' Union (Labour), and Herbert Morrison (Supply).

1 FY, p. 318.

Churchill now took over the running of the war, dealing personally with the Chiefs of Staff, and referring major issues to a six-man Defence Committee consisting of himself, Chamberlain, Attlee and the three Service ministers. On the civil side, the most important body became the Lord President's Committee, presided over by Neville Chamberlain.

In the first weeks of the Government, Dalton threw himself into his job with characteristic energy. The new minister's first task was to reorganise his department at the top. M.E.W. could have little immediate impact in the national emergency, however, and Dalton's desire for active involvement in the operational side of the war encouraged his interest in, and ambition to control, the subversive warfare activities which were to be brought together under the Special Operations Executive (S.O.E.).

Wednesday 15th May

I arrive at my office in Berkeley House just after 10 a.m. I attend my first Cabinet, on a small matter relating to the Iberian Peninsula, at 11.30. Duff Cooper,[1] coming out of the Cabinet Room as I come in, shakes my hand and says, 'Congratulations, but you have indeed joined us in a dark hour!' As I come in and sit down, Winston[2] greets me with a cheerful smile, saying, 'Here is the Minister of Economic Warfare. I am very glad to see you.' Halifax[3] smiles and bows in my direction; Attlee[4] and Greenwood[5] grin slightly sheepishly; Chamberlain[6] turns his head the other way; Inskip[7] looks infinitely pompous

1 Alfred Duff Cooper, later 1st Viscount Norwich (1890–1954). Minister of Information 1940–41. See Appendix A.

2 W. S. Churchill, later Sir Winston (1874–1965). Prime Minister 1940–45, 1951–5. See Appendix A.

3 E. F. Wood, 1st Baron Irwin, 3rd Viscount Halifax, later 1st Earl (1881–1959). Foreign Secretary 1939–40; Ambassador to the U.S.A. 1940–46. See Appendix A.

4 C. R. Attlee, later 1st Earl (1883–1967). Lord Privy Seal, and a member of the War Cabinet 1940–42. Leader of the Labour Party 1935–55. See Appendix A.

5 Arthur Greenwood (1880–1954). Minister without Portfolio, and a member of the War Cabinet 1940–42. Deputy Leader of the Labour Party 1935–54. See Appendix A.

6 Neville Chamberlain (1869–1940). Lord President of the Council, and a member of the War Cabinet 1940. Conservative M.P. for Birmingham Edgbaston 1929–40; Ladywood 1918–29. Postmaster-General 1922–3; Paymaster-General 1923; Minister of Health 1923, 1924–9, 1931. Chancellor of the Exchequer 1923–4, 1931–7. Prime Minister 1937–40.

7 Sir Thomas Inskip, later 1st Viscount Caldecote (1876–1947). Lord Chief Justice 1940–46. Conservative M.P. 1918–29, 1931–9. Solicitor-General 1922–4, 1924–8, 1931–2; Attorney-General 1928–9, 1932–6; Minister for Co-ordination of Defence 1936–9; Dominions Secretary 1939, 1940. Lord Chancellor 1939–40.

and puckered; Sinclair[1] squeezes my hand, and Eden[2] smiles very benevolently. King Albert[3] had just left.

The collapse of the French armies on 14th and 15th May in the face of the German advance left the Allies with little means of resistance. By 16th May, when the French 1st Armoured Division, retreating westwards, reached French territory with only seventeen tanks remaining, almost all of the Ninth Army and part of the Second Army had disintegrated, leaving a sixty-mile gap through which the Germans could push their forces without serious opposition. On 15th May, Paul Reynaud, the French Prime Minister, telephoned Churchill to say, 'We have been defeated ... We have lost the battle.' Next day Churchill flew to Paris, accompanied by General Dill, Vice-Chief of the Imperial General Staff, and General Ismay, head of the Military Wing of the War Cabinet Secretariat. Returning next day, Churchill gave the Cabinet an account of his visit – which had brought home the extent of the disaster.

Thursday 16th May
Amusing discussions about Private Secretaries.[4] Offer Hugh Gaitskell[5] the job and he accepts. A conversation, which a less thick-skinned person might have found difficult, with the Director-General[6] who fears that he may be pushed into the background and not consulted about anything. I say, 'If Gaitskell spoke as you said, he was running a bit ahead of the cart. You and I agreed last night that your relations were to be quite frank on both sides, and, if at any time you feel yourself to be improperly short-circuited, you must tell me so.' He then says, 'If you feel that I am not the right person to work with

---

1 Sir Archibald Sinclair, 4th Bart, later 1st Viscount Thurso (1890–1970). Secretary of State for Air 1940–45. See Appendix A.
2 Anthony Eden, later 1st Earl of Avon (1897–1977). Secretary of State for War 1940; Foreign Secretary 1935–8, 1940–45. See Appendix A.
3 A. V. Alexander, later 1st Earl (1885–1965). First Lord of the Admiralty 1940–45. See Appendix A.
4 Handwritten insertion: 'dangerous phrase "Chef de Cabinet" circulating!'
5 Hugh Gaitskell (1906–63). Principal Private Secretary to the Minister of Economic Warfare 1940–42. See Appendix A.
6 Sir Frederick Leith-Ross (1887–1968). Director-General of the Ministry of Economic Warfare 1939–42. Chief Economic Adviser to the Government 1932–46. See Appendix A.

you here, you must tell me and I shall ask the Treasury to give me something else to do.' I say, 'Now *you* are running ahead of the cart. I have never had the pleasure of working closely with you. I have, of course, heard from many others of your great abilities. I did think in 1929 that you were partly responsible for encouraging Snowden[1] to make a fool of himself in the Hague Conference when he nearly prevented Arthur Henderson from pulling off the agreement with the French.[2] But, apart from that, I have nothing critical to say to you at all.' He says, 'Of course, Snowden took his own line on these matters and I had only to give him the facts. I tried to prevent Winston from agreeing at all to the Young Plan[3] in 1938.'[4] I then tell him that my view is that I have come to this Department in order to do everything possible to bring the war to the quickest and cheapest end. If he has the same general approach, there need be no difficulty. 'It is not my job, as I see it, to put a brake on the Foreign Office, but rather to act as a spur. Or, in other words, it is not my duty to walk about with a watering-can, but rather to light the fires and let the Foreign Office extinguish them if they must. The only question I need ask you is "Are you a war-monger or a pacifist?" ' He then gives a long explanation, prefaced by 'Since we are now discussing these very general questions', to the effect that he agrees with me that we should have stopped Hitler long ago; also that we should have introduced conscription much earlier and developed arms production earlier. But, he adds, he still has a respect for law and thinks it most inadvisable that we should push the exercise of our belligerent rights to such a point as will antagonise neutral opinion, especially that of U.S.A. I say I quite

1 Philip Snowden, 1st Viscount (1864–1937). Labour M.P. for Blackburn 1906–18, Colne 1922–31. Chancellor of the Exchequer 1924, 1929–31. Lord Privy Seal 1931–2. Chairman of the I.L.P. 1904–7, 1917–20.
2 The Hague Conference of August 1929, called to settle the question of German reparations. Dalton was Parliamentary Under-Secretary of State for Foreign Affairs at the time. 'The Hague – and what a shameful miasma of a Conference! – has gone on and on,' Dalton wrote in his diary on 27th August 1929. ' ... What a spectacle at Geneva if Snowden has wrecked the Hague! Booed in the streets of Paris!' Later, he wrote that Snowden was the most dangerous obstacle to the early evacuation of the Rhineland. 'He wanted to reopen the Reparations Question, boggle over the Young Plan, abuse the French and Italians and claw back some millions a year from each of them. All this he tried to do at the Hague Conference that summer, in 1929.' (*Call Back Yesterday: Memoirs 1887–1931*, Frederick Muller, London, 1953, pp. 235–6.)
3 The Young Report, product of a committee of financial experts set up by the League of Nations Assembly in September 1928 and chaired by Owen D. Young, appeared in June 1929. The Report reduced and fixed the level of German reparations, and led to the evacuation of Allied troops from the Rhineland in 1930.
4 *sic*. This is presumably a mistake for 1928 or 1929, when Churchill was Chancellor.

appreciate this last point, but in general my view is that when we are at war, there is no law, and I have so spoken to the lawyers, including Lord Finlay[1] yesterday. I told him that, in my view, the British Prize Court would do well to shut up for the duration of the war and let the French take all the ships. They seem to deal with these matters in a more common-sense manner than we do. Finally, I say to Director-General that he will know from what I have said and written that I have held the view that British foreign policy for the last nine years has been in a mess and that in the last stages much of the blame for this was due to politicians having listened to the advice of Sir Horace Wilson[2] and Sir Nevile Henderson.[3] 'I think', I say, 'that you can truthfully say that you are not a Horace Wilsonite?' He says, 'I always thought that Wilson was very good on industrial questions.' 'Yes,' I say, 'that may well be, but he knew less than nothing about international affairs, and no politician should ever have listened to him on such subjects.' He did not disagree.

I ask him to draft the official Treasury letter which I should send to Kingsley Wood[4] regarding the reorganisation of my and his secretariat in the office. I say that it seems to me ignoble that he and I should take part shares in a Private Secretary. This is not what happens in other State Departments. I wanted a Principal Private Secretary (Gaitskell) plus an Assistant, who I thought should be a civil servant and preferably a bright young man from the Foreign Office. I proposed to speak to Jebb,[5] who had been a perfect Private Secretary to me at the Foreign Office and was now with Cadogan[6] and who I knew had worked with the Director-General. This was a good card to play, for the Director-General at once began to praise Jebb and approve my plan. He said that he would like to keep for himself the man whom he had shared with my predecessor. I raised no objection.

We then parted on reasonably, though provisionally, good terms.

---

1 Lord Justice William Finlay, 2nd Viscount (1875–1945). Lord Justice of Appeal 1938–45. Judge of the High Court of Justice (King's Bench Division) 1924–38.
2 Sir Horace Wilson (1882–1972). Permanent Head of the Civil Service 1939–42. Chief Industrial Adviser to the Government 1930–39. Seconded to the Treasury for special duties with the Prime Minister 1935–40.
3 Sir Nevile Henderson (1882–1942). British Ambassador in Berlin 1937–9.
4 Sir Kingsley Wood (1881–1943). Chancellor of the Exchequer 1940–42. Conservative M.P. for Woolwich West 1918–43. Junior minister 1924–31. Postmaster-General 1931–5; Minister of Health 1935–8; Secretary of State for Air 1938–40; Lord Privy Seal April–May 1940.
5 Gladwyn Jebb, later 1st Baron Gladwyn (b. 1900). Chief Executive Officer, Special Operations Executive (S.O.E.) 1940–42. See Appendix A.
6 Sir Alexander Cadogan (1884–1968). Permanent Under-Secretary of State for Foreign Affairs 1938–46. See Appendix A.

Dine, at Spears's[1] invitation, with Blum,[2] Wedgwood Benn[3] (rather sour at not having got anything) and Macmillan.[4] This afternoon news has been very bad, but Blum now, having just come from French Embassy, is more reassured. The drive, he thinks, is being checked. At 3 p.m. today Leith-Ross had come into my room with long face to say that he had drafted a telegram for me to see, to Georges Monnet,[5] urging speed in lifting oil from Constanza, but, he added, 'I don't think it's much use sending it. I doubt if anything will get through to Paris now. They think the Germans will be there by tonight.' Now, at least, it does not look like tonight!

Macmillan very interesting on events leading up to change of Government. I told him of *our* part and reminded him of vain efforts by him and me to begin to do this sort of thing after Munich, now nearly two years ago. He says that Amery[6] was grand. Chamberlain's last effort, at instigation of Sir H. Quisling,[7] who was passionately anxious to prevent. Labour Party coming into Government, was to send for Amery and offer him free choice of *any* office, other than

---

1 Major-General E. L. Spears, later Sir Edward, later 1st Bart (1886–1974). Churchill's Personal Representative with the French Prime Minister and Minister of Defence (Reynaud) May–June 1940. Head of British Mission to General de Gaulle June 1940. Head of Mission to Syria and the Lebanon July 1941. First Minister to Syria and the Lebanon 1942–4.

2 Léon Blum (1872–1950). French Socialist leader. Socialist deputy 1919–40. Prime Minister at the head of the Popular Front Government 1936–7. Tried by Vichy Government in 1942, and interned. Vice-Premier 1948.

3 William Wedgwood Benn, later 1st Viscount Stansgate (1877–1960). Labour M.P. for Manchester Gorton 1937–41; Aberdeen North 1928–31. Liberal M.P. for Tower Hamlets (St George's Division) 1906–18, Leith 1918–27. Secretary of State for India 1929–31, Air 1945–6. Father of Tony Benn.

4 Harold Macmillan, later 1st Earl of Stockton (b. 1894). Parliamentary Secretary at the Ministry of Supply 1940–42. Conservative M.P. for Stockton-on-Tees 1924–9, 1931–45; Bromley 1945–64. Junior minister 1942–3. Minister Resident in North-West Africa 1942–5; Secretary of State for Air 1945. Minister of Housing and Local Government 1951–4; Defence 1954–5. Foreign Secretary 1955; Chancellor of the Exchequer 1955–7; Prime Minister 1957–63.

5 Georges Monnet (1898–1980). Socialist deputy. Minister of Blockades in Reynaud Government March–June 1940. Opposed armistice with Hitler, but abstained in the vote granting Pétain full powers. Minister of Agriculture in the 1936–7 Popular Front Government.

6 Leopold Amery (1873–1955). Secretary of State for India 1940–45. Conservative M.P. for Birmingham Sparkbrook 1918–45; Birmingham South 1911–18. Junior minister 1919–22. First Lord of the Admiralty 1922–4. Secretary of State for Dominions 1925–9.

7 Dalton's name for Sir Horace Wilson. Vidkun Quisling (1887–1945) was Leader of the Norwegian Fascist Party. After the German invasion in April 1940, Quisling became puppet ruler, and his name acquired a generic meaning. Here Dalton is referring to Wilson's advocacy of appeasement before the war.

Premiership itself, if he would bring his rebels in. This was refused. I quote remark of a friend of mine about the Old Man being like a bit of dirty chewing gum sticking to the leg of a chair, and Macmillan said that Bracken[1] had put it another way. He had said, 'It's as hard getting rid of him as getting a leech off a corpse.' Sir H. Quisling used to have a room of his own next to the Cabinet Room in No. 10. The day Winston took over, Sir H. Quisling came to this room as usual, but found that 'the parachute troops were already in possession'. Bracken and Randolph Churchill,[2] the latter in uniform, were sitting on the sofa. No words were exchanged. These two stared fixedly at Sir H. Quisling, who silently withdrew, never to return. Now his room is to be occupied by Morton,[3] the live wire whom P.M. had stolen from my Ministry. But he will be a useful contact, especially through Gaitskell. Macmillan says that the reason why young Tories in uniform voted with us against the Government was because in the Army their loyalty to the King[4] overcame their loyalty to the Old Man[5] and Margesson.[6] When they saw the mess in Norway, some at first hand, they made up their minds. It is, he says, like 1915 when old Asquith[7] told Parliament that there were plenty of shells, and soldier M.P.s came back from the Front and said, 'That's a bloody lie. We only had three shells a day at Festubert.'

Today I have started at least to demonstrate that I want to hot up the economic war by writing a Minute in favour of blockading Hungary, whose Foreign Minister, Csáky,[8] has told O'Malley[9] that Hungary would offer no resistance if Hitler wanted to come through.

1 Brendan Bracken, later 1st Viscount (1901–58). Parliamentary Private Secretary to the Prime Minister 1940–41, although not formally appointed. See Appendix A.
2 Randolph Churchill (1911–68). Conservative M.P. for Preston 1940–45. Journalist. Son of Winston Churchill, q.v.
3 Major D. J. F. Morton, later Sir Desmond (1891–1971). Personal Assistant to the Prime Minister 1940–46. Principal Assistant Secretary at the Ministry of Economic Warfare 1939–40. See Appendix A.
4 King George VI (1895–1952). Ascended the throne 1936, on the abdication of his brother, King Edward VIII.
5 Neville Chamberlain, q.v.
6 David Margesson, later 1st Viscount (1890–1965). Secretary of State for War 1940–42. Government Chief Whip 1931–40. Conservative M.P. for Rugby 1924–42; West Ham Upton 1922–3.
7 H. H. Asquith, 1st Earl of Oxford (1852–1928). Liberal M.P. 1886–1918, 1920–24. Home Secretary 1892–5; Chancellor of the Exchequer 1905–8; Prime Minister 1908–16. Secretary of State for War March–August 1914.
8 Count Istvan Csáky (1894–1941). Hungarian Foreign Minister 1938–41. Immediately after taking office, Csáky confirmed Hungarian adherence to the anti-Comintern Pact.
9 O. S. O'Malley (1887–1974). British Minister to Hungary 1939–41. Ambassador to Polish government-in-exile 1942–5.

In May 1940 it was decided to send Sir Stafford Cripps (now an Independent M.P.) on a special temporary mission to Moscow. Since the Russians refused to accept him except as an accredited Ambassador, he was appointed Ambassador to replace Sir William Seeds. He arrived in Moscow on 12th June.

In the 1930s, Dalton had repeatedly clashed with Cripps, then a leading left-wing Labour M.P., and had helped to bring about Cripps's expulsion from the Labour Party in 1939.

Friday 17th May
Halifax wants to send Cripps[1] to Moscow. I throw some doubts on his suitability. Halifax thinks he might seem new and *persona grata* to them. I say that I have had an uncomfortable experience of him, and that it fell to me, when the Labour Party finally despaired of training him to the House, to put him outside. Halifax asks what my relations are with him now. I say 'rather sketchy'. It is agreed between us that, if he goes, he must have a policeman[2] from my Ministry and must have very close instructions and no power to make a settlement on his own.

Lunch with Gladwyn [Jebb]. He says he feels a little 'groggy at the knees'. He supposes that, if Hitler won the war, he would be crowned Emperor of Europe with the iron crown of Charlemagne, and that no doubt the present Archbishop of Canterbury,[3] always willing to oblige those in authority, would gladly agree to crown him King of England in Westminster Abbey. Sir H. Quisling, he supposes, would come back again in order to negotiate our surrender. He thinks that at our Ministry there has been no policy developed and no unity.

Call from Swinton[4] in the afternoon. His pre-emption plans[5] are still held up by the Treasury.

1 Sir Stafford Cripps (1889–1952). M.P. for Bristol East, Labour 1930–39, 1945–50; Independent 1939–45. See Appendix A.
2 The 'policeman' chosen was M. M. Postan, later Sir Michael (1898–1981). Head of Section, M.E.W. 1939–42. Official Historian of Munitions at the War Cabinet Office 1942. Professor of Economic History, Cambridge 1935–65.
3 Cosmo Gordon Lang (1864–1945). Archbishop of Canterbury 1928–42; York 1908–28.
4 Sir Philip Cunliffe-Lister, 1st Viscount, later 1st Earl of Swinton (1884–1972). Conservative M.P. for Hendon 1918–35. Junior minister 1920–22. President of the Board of Trade 1922–4, 1924–9, 1931. Colonial Secretary 1931–5; Secretary of State for Air 1935–8. Minister Resident, West Africa 1942–4; Minister of Civil Aviation, 1944–5. Chancellor of the Duchy of Lancaster and Minister of Materials 1951–2. Secretary of State for Commonwealth Relations 1952–5.
5 'pre-emption plans': plans for making purchases in neutral countries with the aim of denying to Germany goods needed for the German war effort.

Winston flew to Paris yesterday. He found Daladier[1] and Gamelin[2] in a poor shape, but Reynaud[3] holding up very well. He rallied them, saying, 'Is France defeated because 120 armoured vehicles have broken through your lines? Do you think that these will be able to go on and on for ever? Why, the men inside will have to stop to get a drink or to relieve nature. Pull yourselves together!' (Within two days Reynaud has taken over National Defence; Daladier gone back to the Quai d'Orsay, and Gamelin been sacked.) The P.M. dug them all out for a conference at 1 a.m. in Paris, caught a plane back at 6 o'clock, got to London at 7.30, and was presiding, very fresh, over a meeting of ministers soon after 9. This afternoon he has gone to sleep. A *grand* man!

We have to send the French some more fighter squadrons which, in other circumstances, we should not have been eager to do. Gladwyn told me at lunch that last night the Quai d'Orsay were burning their papers.

After my first visit to the Cabinet, Churchill said, with that half grim, half whimsical smile of his, 'I expect all these buildings will look a bit different in two or three weeks' time.' A good *mot* also by Halifax, the English aristocrat at his very best, 'Invasion? That would be a great bore.'

Saturday 18th May
My secretarial arrangements at the Ministry completed after slight resistance. Gaitskell well in charge. Dingle Foot[4] unexpectedly arrives to be my Parliamentary Secretary. Calls me 'Sir' uninterruptedly all day! I turn him on to focus all the legal stuff.

Jean Monnet[5] comes to see me. He says, 'So long as the French Army exists, France is not defeated.' Even if they have to abandon

1 Edouard Daladier (1884–1970). French Radical politician. Minister of Foreign Affairs 1939–40; Defence 1938–40. Prime Minister 1933, 1934, 1936, 1938–40. Detained during the war. Deputy 1946–58. Daladier remained as Minister of Defence under Reynaud, q.v., until 18th May 1940, and then served as Minister of Foreign Affairs until 16th June.
2 General Maurice Gamelin (1872–1958). French Commander-in-Chief until 20th May 1940.
3 Paul Reynaud (1878–1966). Prime Minister of France 1940. Minister of Finance 1938–40; Foreign Affairs and Defence 1940. Interned 1940–45. Reynaud took over Defence from Daladier on 18th May 1940, leaving Daladier to serve as Foreign Minister.
4 D. M. Foot, later Sir Dingle (1905–78). Parliamentary Secretary at the Ministry of Economic Warfare 1940–45. Liberal M.P. for Dundee 1931–45. Labour M.P. for Ipswich 1957–70. Solicitor-General 1964–7.
5 Jean Monnet (1888–1979). French economist. Chairman of the Franco-British Economic Co-ordination Committee 1939–40. Commissioner for Armaments, Supplies and Reconstruction, British Supply Council, Washington 1940–43. French Council of National Liberation, Algiers 1943–4. Creator of the Monnet Plan 1947. President of the European Coal and Steel Community 1952–5.

Paris. He speaks of need for cutting through interdepartmental red tape and also, more particularly, about coal.

11 a.m. Conference of officials, but this has to be cut short as I have to be in Cabinet at noon. I greet officials, telling them to be mentally prepared for everything short of losing the war, saying that I have been a critic of the half-hearted way, as it seems to me, in which the Economic War has hitherto been waged, but I can well believe that responsibility for this lies not *in* this Ministry, but *outside* it. If we can stabilise the Front in France it will be a great moment for a violent counter-offensive on the economic front against an enemy which will have consumed great quantities of oil, weapons, etc. Then some brief talk on Russian negotiations.

At Cabinet, agreed to send Cripps to Russia, from which, in the end, I did not dissent, having given warnings. I say now, 'We will try and make it go, but if it goes wrong, don't blame me.' P.M. says, with his grin, 'You're on velvet.'

They say that the R.A.F. has done magnificent work over the Bulge[1] and our long-distance raids, on oil stores, etc., are continuing with great effect. Also middle-distance raids on railway and road junctions, lines of communication, etc. Eden says he can't understand why the French don't counter-attack against the Bulge.

Talk at lunch with Attlee, who is in good form. I may be a prejudiced witness, but I think he has made his selections and omissions for Government posts very well. He says that he had absolutely no difficulty about me. Winston was quite keen from the first. This does not, of course, dispose of the rumour that Montagu Norman[2] wanted someone else; it only shows he made no progress with Winston. Attlee says that he left out Pethick [Lawrence][3] because too old, Lees-Smith[4] because too slow, Wedgwood Benn because too recent, and Phil [Noel-Baker][5] because too unbalanced in his judgments, increasingly

1 'the Bulge': the advancing German front line. During his visit to France on 16th May, Churchill learnt from Gamelin that the Bulge was already fifty kilometres wide.
2 Montagu Norman, later 1st Baron (1871–1950). Governor of the Bank of England 1920–44.
3 F. W. Pethick Lawrence, later 1st Baron Pethick-Lawrence (1871–1961). Labour M.P. for Edinburgh East 1935–45; Leicester West 1923–31. Financial Secretary to the Treasury 1929–31. Secretary of State for India and Burma 1945–7. Prominent supporter of women's rights (imprisoned for conspiracy 1912). Old Etonian.
4 H. B. Lees-Smith (1878–1941). Labour M.P. for Keighley 1922–3, 1924–31, 1935–41. Liberal M.P. for Northampton 1910–18. Postmaster-General 1929–31; President of the Board of Education 1931. Leader of H.M. Opposition 1940–41. Lecturer, then Reader, in Public Administration at the L.S.E. 1906–41.
5 Philip Noel-Baker, later Baron (1889–1982). Labour M.P. for Derby 1936–50. See Appendix A.

so these last few months. Also a balance had to be maintained between bourgeois and working-class M.P.s. He has got quite a lot of our people in. Winston was very keen on Ellen [Wilkinson];[1] so was he. Shinwell[2] was offered Under-Secretaryship for Food, with his Chief in the Lords, but turned up his nose and rejected it without even consulting Attlee. Hudson[3] asked for Tom Williams.[4] Winston is fine to work with. Macmillan told me the night before that Winston had been saying, 'My Government is the most broad-based that Britain has ever known. It extends from Lord Lloyd of Dolobran[5] to Miss Ellen Wilkinson.'

Someone said that Chamberlain reminded them of the undertaker who said 'The corpse is upstairs'. This *mot*, when next repeated by me, moved my hearers to great mirth.

On 18th May, Reynaud appointed the ageing Marshal Pétain to his Cabinet as Vice-Premier, moving Daladier to the Foreign Ministry and himself taking the Defence portfolio. Next day General Gamelin, the French commander-in-chief, was relieved of his post. There followed a two-day interregnum, while the French armies waited for the arrival of Gamelin's replacement, General Maxime Weygand, summoned from Syria. Meanwhile the indecisiveness of the French command had led the British commander, General Gort, to conclude that a retreat to the coast and a general evacuation by sea were unavoidable.

---

1 Ellen Wilkinson (1891–1947). Parliamentary Secretary at the Ministry of Pensions 1940; Ministry of Home Security 1940–45. Labour M.P. for Jarrow 1935–47; Middlesbrough East 1924–31. Minister of Education 1945–7. National Organiser of N.U.D.A.W. 1915–47.
2 Emanuel Shinwell, later Baron (b. 1884). Labour M.P. for Seaham 1935–50. See Appendix A.
3 R. S. Hudson, later 1st Viscount (1886–1957). Minister of Shipping 1940. Conservative M.P. for Whitehaven 1924–9; Southport 1931–52. Junior minister 1931–5. Minister of Pensions 1935–6. Junior minister 1936–40. Minister of Agriculture and Fisheries 1940–45.
4 Thomas Williams, later Baron (1888–1967). Labour M.P. for Don Valley 1922–59. Parliamentary Secretary at the Ministry of Agriculture and Fisheries (under Hudson) 1940–45. Minister of Agriculture and Fisheries 1945–51.
5 Sir George Lloyd, 1st Baron (1879–1941). Colonial Secretary and Leader of the House of Lords 1940–41. Conservative M.P. for Staffordshire West 1910–18; Eastbourne 1924–5. Governor, Bombay 1918–23; High Commissioner, Egypt and Sudan 1925–9.

Monday 20th May

Lunch with Mrs Phillimore[1] to meet Norwegians. Meet also, for the first time since we got separated, a number of colleagues. Greenwood and Alexander both very tough and standing up well. Alexander says French are being perfectly useless. Their First Army is no good. General Billotte[2] has been sacked (this turns out not to be true); we had as good as lost the Channel Ports; we don't intend to let our Army in France become a mere bomb trap. They will, if necessary, have to cut their way through whatever lies between them and defensible positions; they are already moving back towards bases further west. Greenwood says that Weygand[3] is 'full of blood'.

Also at the lunch are Lees-Smith and Wedgwood Benn, neither of whom has been asked to join the Government. The former, as it turns out later, is to play a most important role as acting Chairman of the Parliamentary Labour Party. The latter is rejoining the Forces in some appropriate capacity. Lees-Smith says that Gamelin has always been 'cautious', preferring to organise his campaign behind defensive lines. No good at open warfare.

Winston, Greenwood says, has been grand. His visit to Paris pulled the French together. He has also sent a message to F.D.R.[4] saying that his Government will fight to the end: that they will never accept any shameful peace nor any surrender to Germany; if, however, in the stress of war they should later be replaced by another Government which should make such a peace with Hitler, then let the U.S.A. look out for their own skins. And let them therefore now do all they can to help *this* British Government. Greenwood said that he thought he still saw the finger of Sir H. Quisling in some things. I said I hoped that this would soon completely cease. Greenwood said that the Ruhr

1 Lucy ('Lion') Phillimore, née Fitzpatrick (d. 1957). A prominent Fabian and political hostess, whose carefully arranged parties at the Ritz Dalton often attended during the war. Beatrice Webb, who knew her well, gave the following account of a meeting with Lucy Phillimore: 'Lion "beautifully got up" as a voluntary hostess of the diplomatic world, welcomed me warmly. She concentrates on the American and Empire press, and inviting the representatives of the Allied Governments in Great Britain to meet the pressmen, and the Government has encouraged her, though sometimes she gets snubbed by the Foreign Office – she was so when she suggested Halifax as a guest.' (Unpublished diary, 16th July 1941.) Widow of the Hon. R. C. Phillimore (1871–1919).
2 General Gaston Billotte (1875–1940). Commander of the First Group of Armies in France. Killed in a car accident the day after this entry (21st May). Dalton's entry for 20th May appears to have been dictated on 22nd May, or later.
3 General Maxime Weygand (1867–1965). Commander-in-Chief of the French Army, in succession to Gamelin, who had been dismissed on 19th May. Governor-General of Algeria and Delegate-General of the Vichy Government in French Africa 1941–2.
4 F. D. Roosevelt (1882–1945). Democratic President of the U.S.A. 1933–45.

was now a mass of ruins. The Germans were hiding from their public the effects of our air bombing. Only those knew who lived near the targets, though some of these were so spectacular that light and sound travelled great distances around them.

Tuesday 21st May

The news is bad today. Amiens and Arras have been taken and, it is said, Abbeville too. When *will* the French counter-attack? Reynaud has made a panicky speech, speaking of 'incredible mistakes', and hinting at treachery, etc.

John Wilmot[1] settles in at the Ministry. He, Gaitskell and Hancock[2] have my Secretaries' Room to themselves. Reilly[3] and Miss Cracknell,[4] for Leith-Ross, have been put down the passage. I had been told, the first day, that there would be difficulty in finding another room. I had replied that I had been all through this kind of petty obstruction at the Foreign Office ten years ago. I added to Reilly, 'Understand that, if there is one thing I dislike more than another, it is delay in carrying out decisions which have been taken. And what's more, *I won't have it!*' He was rather taken aback and indignant and said something about considering the susceptibilities of the higher staff. He had also been telling me that there would be difficulty in getting a telephone communication between Leith-Ross's room and the room now proposed for him and Miss Cracknell. I said that this was ridiculous nonsense and they had better ring up the Office of Works about it. Next day the thing was all done.

Talk late tonight with Gaitskell and exchange some fundamental thoughts on our present prospects. I say that the great division now is between the stone-colds and the hysterics. I believe that he and I are, and will remain, in the first class. If we lose the war, and have Hitler as Emperor of Europe and King of England, would it be bearable to go on living, especially with Himmler and all that? Anyhow, we have had our lives;[5] much of it has been fun and some has not, and it must end some time and somehow. But we are an immense distance from such large catastrophes as yet.

House of Commons this afternoon presents a funny sight. Herbert

---

1 John Wilmot, later 1st Baron (1893–1964). Parliamentary Private Secretary to Dalton 1940–44. Labour M.P. for Kennington 1939–45. See Appendix A.
2 P. F. Hancock, later Sir Patrick (1914–80). Entered Foreign Office 1937. Assistant Private Secretary to the Minister of Economic Warfare 1940–42.
3 D. P. Reilly, later Sir Patrick (b. 1909). Ministry of Economic Warfare 1939–42. Ambassador to the U.S.S.R. 1957–60; France 1965–8.
4 Miss N. F. E. Cracknell. Private Secretary to Sir Frederick Leith-Ross, q.v.
5 Handwritten marginal insertion: 'I much more than he'.

Morrison[1] is in the corner seat where Ernest Brown[2] used to be. I go and sit next to him. Then on my left, Margesson, then the Old Man of Munich, then Winston, then Attlee and Greenwood, then some more, including David Grenfell,[3] George Hall,[4] and Bob Boothby,[5] who has taken on the job Shinwell refused as 'a bloody insult', namely Under-Secretary to the Ministry of Food, with Woolton[6] in the Lords. (George Hicks[7] speaks of our esteemed colleague as 'Shinbad the Tailor'.)[8] I have to answer Parliamentary Question No. 1 on the Vladivostok leak.[9] I have had to spend some time on getting the answer right, the official who made the first draft here not having the ghost of a notion of how to set about it. He also turned up at 10.40, I having sent for him at 10. I therefore rebuked him and told him that I expected officials to be here not later than 10 a.m. in wartime. This is Baxter[10] of the Foreign Office. I am given quite a friendly greeting from my old friends across the floor, and also from some other parts

1 Herbert Morrison (1888–1965). Minister of Supply 1940. See Appendix A.
2 Ernest Brown (1881–1962). Secretary of State for Scotland 1940–41. Liberal National M.P. for Leith 1927–45. Liberal M.P. for Rugby 1923–4. Junior minister 1931–5. Minister of Labour 1935–9; Labour and National Service 1939–40. Minister of Health 1941–3; Chancellor of the Duchy of Lancaster 1943–5; Aircraft Production 1945.
3 David Grenfell (1881–1968). Parliamentary Secretary at the Department of Mines 1940–42. Labour M.P. for Gower 1922–59.
4 G. H. Hall, later 1st Viscount (1881–1965). Parliamentary Under-Secretary at the Colonial Office 1940–42; Financial Secretary at the Admiralty 1942–3; Parliamentary Under-Secretary at the Foreign Office 1943–5. Colonial Secretary 1945–6; First Lord of the Admiralty 1946–51.
5 R. J. G. Boothby, later Sir Robert, later Baron (b. 1900). Parliamentary Secretary at the Ministry of Food 1940–41. Conservative M.P. for Aberdeenshire East 1924–58.
6 Sir Frederick Woolton, 1st Baron, later 1st Earl (1883–1964). Minister of Food 1940–43; Reconstruction 1943–5. Lord President of the Council 1945, 1951–2; Chancellor of the Duchy of Lancaster 1952–3; Minister of Materials 1953–4. Chairman of the Conservative and Unionist Central Office 1946–55.
7 George Hicks (1879–1954). Parliamentary Secretary at the Ministry of Works 1940–45. Labour M.P. for Woolwich East 1931–50. General Secretary of the Amalgamated Union of Building Trade Workers 1921–40.
8 'Shinbad the Tailor': Shinwell was the son of a Jewish tailor. Dalton, who detested Shinwell, liked the joke so much that he often referred to Shinwell as 'Shinbad' thereafter.
9 Dalton was asked in a Parliamentary Question whether he could report 'any improvement in the matter of the enemy goods being transported through the harbour of Vladivostok' and how far it had been possible to stop this leak in the blockade. He replied that there had been some decline in the import of copper through Vladivostok, and other materials, but that he was 'still not at all satisfied with the position'. (H.C. Debs [361], cols 2–3.)
10 C. W. Baxter (1895–1969). Counsellor, Foreign Office.

of the House. I am said in the press to be confident and audible. ...

At 2 o'clock, before the House meets, Parliamentary Executive. Shinbad, in a state of nervous and egocentric volubility, even worse than usual. We decide, he alone dissenting, to recommend to the Party next day that there should be, in place of the Executive, an Administrative Council consisting of (1) those members of the Executive who are not ministers, and (2) those members of the Front Bench Second Eleven who are not ministers. This will make a convenient number, just over a dozen. In addition, though it is not expected that any of them would be able to attend regularly, members of the Executive who are now ministers should be ex-officio members of the new Administrative Council. Further, we shall suggest to the Party, though it is of course for them to take the decision, that Lees-Smith shall be the Acting Chairman, though Attlee will remain the Leader. This will mean that Lees-Smith will occupy Attlee's old seat and will – a most important point this – put the Business Questions. When this is decided, Shinbad leaps from his seat and rushes from the room in a towering rage. Our remaining business is more speedily concluded without him. He afterwards rushes about among the Party intriguing and making complaint. It seems that he regards himself as the only possible leader in these days.

5 p.m. Meeting in Attlee's room of Labour ministers. First ten minutes taken up with listening to grievances of Paling[1] and Whiteley,[2] who have been appointed to paid offices, the former as one of the Whips, and the latter as Whip and Comptroller of the Royal Household (he is a well-built fellow and will fill the part) without having been invited or consulted. This is obviously a slight slip, but after all, we are at war and the Government had to be formed in a hurry and Attlee had proposed their names to Churchill. Their little dignities, however, are deeply offended and they are doubtful, or say they are, whether they will accept. This momentous problem having been postponed for further consideration, we all briefly report how we are getting on, all briefly except Ernest Bevin,[3] who speaks at immense length and has to be cut short from the Chair. But he is talking good sense.

---

1 Wilfrid Paling (1883–1971). Labour M.P. for Wentworth 1933–50; Doncaster 1922–31; Dearne Valley 1950–59. Junior minister 1941–5. Minister of Pensions 1945–7. Postmaster-General 1947–50.
2 William Whiteley (1882–1955). Government Whip 1929–31, 1940–45. Labour M.P. for Blaydon 1922–31, 1935–55. Government Chief Whip 1945–51.
3 Ernest Bevin (1881–1951). Minister of Labour and National Service 1940–45. See Appendix A.

17

Sir Maurice Peterson[1] comes to see me. He is being dismissed from the Madrid Embassy because stories have reached the Foreign Office, both from British and Spanish sources, that he is not *persona grata* with the present Spanish Government. He was very indignant, and showed me a very cold and critical letter signed by Cadogan. He understood that Sir Samuel Hoare[2] was to replace him and he had been asked to vacate the Embassy at short notice but to leave behind all his personal plate and other belongings for the use of the Embassy. He did not know if there was any other post which at the moment he could hope to fill.

I also received the Yugoslav Minister, and it appears that I am to be, for some British and Foreign diplomats, a sort of unofficial Foreign Office. This is quite amusing, but it will be important not to cause jealousy in the official institution.

Wednesday 22nd May

A busy day. From 10 a.m. to 10 p.m. John [Wilmot] looks over my shoulder while I read the Daily Gloom. Ironside[3] has been over in France and apparently doing well. 'A stupid soldier', some say, but a stone-colder. (Ruth[4] says she heard a cockney say today, 'What we wants is warm feet and cool 'eads.') Ironside found General Billotte 'in a state of indecision'. He reported this to Weygand, who 'sharply reprimanded Billotte upon the telephone'. Weygand is thought to be getting things together, and the German units who have pushed forward into all the towns beginning with A. are very small, the equivalent of old-time cavalry raids, and should be easily nipped off and dealt with.

10.15. Report by my officials on their conference yesterday with Cripps. They seem to have got on quite well when they got down to detail. Gaitskell says that he hopes I shall not say much to Cripps this afternoon. He is afraid that I may make him bristle. The officials have got him into a good mood. I said, 'I expect that yesterday when he was

---

1 Sir Maurice Peterson (1889–1952). Ambassador to Spain 1939–40. Controller of Overseas Publicity at the Ministry of Information 1940–41. Ambassador to the U.S.S.R. 1946–9.
2 Sir Samuel Hoare, later 1st Viscount Templewood (1880–1959). Ambassador to Spain 1940–44 (appointed 1st June 1940). Conservative M.P. for Chelsea 1910–44. See Appendix A.
3 Field Marshal Sir William Ironside, later 1st Baron (1880–1959). Chief of Imperial General Staff 1939–40; Commander-in-Chief, Home Forces 1940.
4 Ruth Dalton, née Hamilton Fox, later Lady Dalton (1890–1966). Hugh Dalton's wife. They married in 1914. See Appendix A.

talking all that rubbish about general principles he was really trying
to show off in front of me and Halifax.'
11.30. Parliamentary Party Meeting. Another monkey-house.

Churchill visited Paris again on 22nd May, and met Weygand at the latter's
headquarters at the Château de Vincennes. The French general outlined a
plan involving a southward advance by the French First Army and the
B.E.F., while other French troops attacked northwards from south of the
Somme. But the plan never materialised and on 26th May Gort decided that
the British retreat to the coast must begin. This decision was approved by
the War Cabinet.

Thursday 23rd May
News a little better this morning but worse again tonight. Abbeville
again occupied. Heavy fighting in and around Boulogne. German
armed forces in rear of allied forces are trying to derange our communications. (Winston announced this in brief statement in House of
Commons.) General Billotte has been hurt in a motor accident and
now replaced. These French generals are doing very badly!
    2 p.m. Shinbad niggling and quibbling about not taking Govern-
ment Whips. In a minority of one on our Administrative Committee.
I leave the room before the end, saying tartly that I have more important work to do than to listen to Shinwell's tripe.
    2.45 p.m. Ramsay's[1] arrest announced by the Speaker. It is ironical
that the first M.P. to be jailed should be a Tory. This follows Van's[2]
line through me to Attlee, and Gaitskell's verbal message from me to
the latter. Anderson[3] has been binged up [*sic*]. Later announced that
Mosley,[4] Beckett[5] and others also in jug. This is some compensation

1 Archibald Ramsay (1894–1955). Conservative M.P. for Peebles and Midlothian
  South 1931–45. Detained in Brixton Prison under Defence Regulation 18B because
  of his outspoken anti-Semitism 1940–44.
2 Sir Robert Vansittart, later 1st Baron (1881–1957). Chief Diplomatic Adviser to the
  Foreign Secretary 1938–41. See Appendix A.
3 Sir John Anderson, later 1st Viscount Waverley (1882–1958). Lord President of the
  Council 1940–43. See Appendix A.
4 Sir Oswald Mosley, 6th Bart (1896–1981). Conservative M.P. for Harrow 1918–22;
  Independent M.P. for Harrow 1922–4; Labour M.P. for Smethwick 1926–31.
  Chancellor of the Duchy of Lancaster 1929–30. Founded New Party 1931; British
  Union of Fascists 1932. Imprisoned under Defence Regulation 18B 1940–45.
5 John Beckett (1894–1964). Labour M.P. for Gateshead 1924–9; Peckham 1929–31.
  Stood as I.L.P. candidate in 1931; later joined British Union of Fascists. Im-
  prisoned under Defence Regulation 18B 1940–45.

for the loss of Boulogne! Ruth says, 'We had to lose Norway to get rid of Chamberlain, and to lose Boulogne to get rid of Mosley.'

Friday 24th May

Yesterday Churchill telegraphed imperatively to Reynaud. There is a Plan, but it is not being fully worked. Strong German elements are through the gap. My personal judgment is that, unless the French attack soon and in force, we shall have to withdraw the B.E.F. [British Expeditionary Force] to this country through such Channel ports as we shall still command. It is obvious, even to laymen, that their supply position, both for food and arms, is becoming seriously difficult.

Churchill was in Paris for the second time on the 22nd; his first flight was on the 16th. We could have no better Premier now.

Noel Hall[1] is a live wire. I take to him. He has been considering certain pessimistic hypotheses. What do then? It has long been foreseen, by those with knowledge, that Germany would reach her maximum strength in May 1940. But even this great strength is brittle. Hall hopes that by April 1941, she should be down to one million tons of oil. This was her dying-out figure in the last war. It is important to observe that there are no really large coal-oil plants anywhere else in Europe outside the present German occupied territory. Romania raises various queries.

If, say I speculatively, Hitler ruled all Europe west of the Soviet frontiers, British sea power would come into its own again. We should operate a continental blockade and stop all cargoes headed for Europe. It is essential, of course, that the U.S. should play on this. It is also to be remembered that the Germans will need *mobile* garrisons in all conquered territories, and that mobility means stores and use of oil.

Later today Admiral Taylor[2] calls. He is our liaison with the Admiralty. A good type of sailor. He says, 'Do you remember Max Pemberton's[3] story of the Iron Pirate? She succeeded in seizing everything

---

1 N. F. Hall, later Sir Noel (1902–83). Head of German Intelligence Section, then Director of Intelligence, at the Ministry of Economic Warfare 1939. Joint Director of the Ministry of Economic Warfare 1940–41. Minister in Charge of War Trades Department at the British Embassy in Washington 1941–3. Professor of Political Economy at University College, London 1935–8. Director of the National Institute of Economic and Social Research 1938–43. Principal of Brasenose College, Oxford 1960–73.

2 Vice-Admiral E. A. Taylor (1876–1971). Conservative M.P. for Paddington South 1931–50; Empire Crusade M.P. 1930–31.

3 Sir Max Pemberton (1863–1950). Editor and novelist. Editor of *Cassell's Magazine* 1896–1906. Author of *The Iron Pirate: A Plain Tale of Strange Happenings in the Sea*, Cassell, London, 1893.

she wanted, but came to a bad end because she ran short of lubricating oil.' He also says, after we have briefly touched on certain pessimistic hypotheses, 'It was much worse in 1780. We had the whole world against us then, including the U.S.' I like sailors in wartime.

Saturday 25th May
Pay an official visit to the French Mission in Lansdowne House. I am shown round, accompanied by Foot and Gaitskell, by Paul Morand,[1] who says that he has spoken this morning to Corbin[2] who reports that Reynaud and Weygand are both calm. Making the round of the Mission and of that section – chiefly Statistics – of my Ministry which is lodged in Lansdowne House is rather like electioneering. Much shaking of hands and the repetition, with only minor variations, of the same sentiments of courtesy, personal interest and good will. Among others presented to me are a large number of French sailors, both officers and ratings. Beneath the surface there is a sense of gravity, and the French know, though no one even hints at it, that we are wondering when their big counter-offensive in France is going to begin.

Call from Dov Hos[3] and Locker.[4] They make certain proposals in the sphere of intelligence with reference to the Balkans and Near East. I hand them over to Hall.

Maisky[5] calls, at his own request, and stays for an hour and forty minutes. Gaitskell says afterwards, 'He stayed so long that we thought you and he had fixed up a complete new Anglo-Soviet agreement.' I give him a good deal of background on recent political events and tell him one or two funny stories with deliberate intention that they shall be reported to the Kremlin. My purpose is to persuade him that this is a really new government and that everything has changed for the better, including the attitude towards his country.

1 Paul Morand (1888–1976). French diplomat and writer. Head of the French Mission of Economic Warfare in London 1939–40; Secretary of the French Embassy and Minister Plenipotentiary 1940. When France fell, Morand left his post and returned to France.
2 (André) Charles Corbin (1881–1970). French Ambassador to Britain 1933–40.
3 Dov Hos (1894–1950). Russian-born Zionist leader and diplomatist. Deputy Mayor of Tel Aviv 1935–50.
4 Berl Locker (1887–1972). Palestinian politician. Political Adviser to the Executive of the Jewish Agency for Palestine 1938–48. Chairman of the Executive, Jerusalem 1948–56. Mapai member of Knesset 1955–61.
5 Ivan Maisky (1884–1975). Soviet Ambassador to Britain 1932–43. Assistant Commissar for Foreign Affairs 1943–5.

Sunday 26th May

All ministers are invited to attend a service at Westminster Abbey with the King and Queen,[1] Queen Wilhelmina,[2] etc., in order to pray for victory. As Foot is pious, though with a Free Church accent, I feel that we are sufficiently represented. I therefore put on a grey suit and a soft collar (since becoming a minister I have generally worn stiff collars!) and spend the day, more usefully, I think, in the office. Master Hancock is alone in charge and I take him to lunch at the Isola Bella, since one may not be able much longer to visit Italian restaurants if Mussolini plays the fool. He is a pleasant and intelligent young man, but very innocent politically.

Albarda[3] to tea with Ruth in my flat, and I leave the office for three-quarters of an hour to see him. The poor man is constantly on the verge of tears. He had to go away in a hurry with other Dutch ministers and left behind his wife in The Hague and his daughter and grandchild in Rotterdam, which was bombed and set on fire over a large area. He says that 10,000 parachute troops came down in a few hours on the morning of Friday, 10th May, around The Hague. They were got up in every kind of way, as Dutch soldiers, priests, nuns, peasants, postmen. The man in charge of the parachute-dropping aeroplane simply turns a handle and they all fall out, twenty at a time. They carry guns, etc., and some of them motor-bikes folded up. The famous bridge into The Hague was occupied by parachutists dressed as Dutch soldiers. They waved their arms in cheerful greeting to genuine Dutch soldiers, who greeted them and then found the bridge occupied and themselves being shot down. He thinks we should realise, more clearly than some do, this new technique. He has told his story to Eden.

There is a blanket over the Front. Fifteen French generals have been sacked. This is in the best French tradition, except that in the great revolutionary wars they shot them as well. I regret to hear that there is some backchat between the principals as to who is and who is not carrying out the Plan.

Spend the evening reading more than usually important papers.

---

1 Queen Elizabeth, née Lady Elizabeth Bowes-Lyon (b. 1900).
2 Queen Wilhelmina of The Netherlands (1880–1962). Queen of The Netherlands 1898–1948, when she abdicated in favour of her daughter, Juliana. She went into exile in England during the Nazi occupation 1940–45.
3 J. W. Albarda (1877–1957). Dutch Labour politician. President of the Dutch Labour Party 1925–39. Minister of Public Works 1939–45. Member of Council of State 1945–57.

Monday 27th May

A vivid day! After having studied the most important and secret papers, I am told at the Ministry that I am not wanted at the Cabinet this morning as only War Cabinet members will be there.[1] Thereupon I write to Attlee and send Gaitskell down to deliver a note direct to No. 12, saying that M.E.W. [Ministry of Economic Warfare] is involved and that I wish to say that, having checked the facts cited in the secret papers, I consider them sound. I enclose certain figures given to me on oil showing that on assumptions very favourable to Germany, she will begin to feel the oil squeeze badly in the autumn, and will not be much above the dying-out figure of 1918 next April. This is a date at the end of a string, which can be drawn nearer by air bombing on synthetic plants and stocks and by other measures, of many kinds, designed to reduce imports. I ask Attlee to put the point to the Cabinet.

Some streaks of defeatism were visible in some of the private papers, not, I thought, due to politicians, and Reynaud, who was here yesterday, will welcome all encouragement.

After a quick lunch I see Attlee at 2.30. He read my note to the Cabinet and gave my figures to the P.M. I therefore give him new copies. He says I need have no fear. There is no shake among the politicians here. Germany's difficulties are very serious. Ministers and high officials will all get a directive from the P.M. not to talk or look defeatist. The short point is that, no matter who comes in or who goes out of the war, we shall fight it out and are confident that, with the resources behind us, we shall win. Attlee is in very good form. Would like some more detail on oil consumption and on the destructions. I tell him of my Balkan pre-emption troubles. He says we shall soon suppress all this Treasury interference with detail. I say that I want to reorganise my Ministry and make an Economic War Council. Need I send it up higher? He says, 'No, do it yourself.'

On my proposal, I see Kingsley Wood *à deux* on Balkan pre-emption, before any officials come in. There has long been a certain roguish intimacy between us two.[2] When Cross went,[3] thinking it was to be *à deux*, to see Simon,[4] he was confronted with six Treasury

---

1 At this time the War Cabinet consisted of five ministers: Churchill (Prime Minister and Minister of Defence), Chamberlain (Lord President), Attlee (Lord Privy Seal), Halifax (Foreign Secretary) and Greenwood (Minister without Portfolio).

2 Dalton had been shadow Air Minister (as well as shadow Minister of Economic Warfare) when Kingsley Wood was Secretary of State for Air in 1938–40.

3 R. H. Cross, later Sir Ronald, 1st Bart (1896–1968). Minister of Shipping 1940–41; Economic Warfare 1939–40. Junior minister 1938–9. Conservative M.P. for Rossendale 1931–45; Ormskirk 1950–51.

4 Sir John Simon, 1st Viscount (1873–1954). Lord Chancellor 1940–45. See Appendix A.

officials. Gaitskell says that he used to call Simon 'Sir'! Wood is where he is in part because we did not black-list him as we did his predecessor. He, therefore, like the P.M., should have, and no doubt has, some feeling of appreciation for the Labour Party. He tells me an amazing Fifth Column tale from Boulogne. Persons purporting to be British Admirals and Generals marched into our Headquarters and demanded in authoritative voices and perfect English accents, 'What is going on here? What are your dispositions? Where are the guards? Where is General X?' When this happened once or twice, we began arresting these people and sent half a dozen of them over to England in a destroyer. When the Guards arrived at Boulogne they had to force their way to defensive positions through seething and utterly disordered crowds of refugees, French soldiers, Belgian soldiers, Dutch soldiers. One of their officers said he had never seen such a sight in his life. Some who have come back say that you get quite used to bombing after a time. At first it is demoralising, partly because it is so noisy, but, as in the old days of two-dimensional war when thousands of shells were fired and most of them did no damage, so it often is with bombs. Somebody else tells me that the worst of being bombed is that you get rather tired.

Just before the officials join Kingsley Wood and me, Sir H. Quisling looks round the door. I stare at him and he withdraws in silence. This is becoming a regular routine.

Kingsley Wood at our Conference is reasonably good. I denounce the Treasury in front of Bewley,[1] his man, and say that in this affair they have expended all their ingenuity in delaying, side-tracking, and, in the last resort, minimising these most essential operations. Swinton, Leith-Ross and Hall weigh in. We shall get something at last out of this.

Kingsley Wood tells me that when the Beaver[2] took over aircraft production, he sent for Nuffield,[3] who, on a Friday, was in the country and said that he would not be back till Tuesday. Whereupon the Beaver sent a message, 'Do you want me to send the Prime Minister's car with a police escort to fetch you?' This brought Nuffield along, but, when he met the Beaver, 'You know, when I got to London I had

---

1 T. K. Bewley (1890–1943). Principal Assistant Secretary at the Treasury 1939–43. Financial Adviser to the Embassy in Washington 1935–9.
2 Sir Max Aitken, 1st Baron Beaverbrook (1879–1964). Minister of Aircraft Production 1940–41. See Appendix A.
3 William R. Morris, 1st Viscount Nuffield (1877–1963). Chairman of Morris Motors Ltd and associated companies; philanthropist. Director-General of Maintenance at the Air Ministry 1939. In May 1940 Nuffield agreed to the suggestion of Lord Beaverbrook, Minister of Aircraft Production, that Vickers should take over the Castle Bromwich aircraft factory.

to ring up from a telephone box to find out who it was I had to see. I had forgotten that it was you.' ...

The Russians have replied to our offer of Cripps that they want a proper Ambassador. They are very touchy and troublesome. This affair runs on for several days and I tell Butler[1] that I am quite prepared for Cripps to be given any title or status that they like and that, now that this experiment is launched, it might well be worth while considering whether we should not leave him in Moscow as a permanent Ambassador. (This would have certain advantages from another angle.)

Dine with Hankey[2] and Geoffrey Lloyd.[3] Hankey gives the impression now of an old man, but he still has ideas and information. Talk on oil, home defence, etc. The Foreign Office is very hesitant towards some kinds of bold action, and our human instruments are not always too good. Two the other day were found drunk in a Danubian brothel. Some of our sailors at the United Services Club where we are dining tell amazing stories of their adventures. A wonderful spirit! Such men cannot be beaten.

Will the Belgians make a separate peace? The Belgian Premier[4] has doubts about the King (soon to be justified).[5] The French are very

1 R. A. Butler, later Baron (1902–82). Parliamentary Secretary at the Foreign Office 1938–41. Conservative M.P. for Saffron Walden 1929–65. Junior minister, India Office 1932–7; Ministry of Labour 1937–8. President of the Board of Education (later Minister of Education) 1941–5. Chancellor of the Exchequer 1951–5; Lord Privy Seal 1955–9; Home Secretary 1957–62; First Secretary of State and Deputy Prime Minister 1962–3; Foreign Secretary 1963–4. Master of Trinity College, Cambridge 1965–78.

2 Sir Maurice Hankey, 1st Baron (1877–1963). Chancellor of the Duchy of Lancaster 1940–41. Secretary to the Committee of Imperial Defence 1912–38; War Cabinet 1916; Imperial War Cabinet 1917–18; Cabinet 1919–38. Clerk of the Privy Council 1923–38. Minister without Portfolio 1939–40. Paymaster-General 1941–2.

3 G. W. Lloyd, later Baron Geoffrey-Lloyd (1902–84). Parliamentary Secretary (Petroleum) at the Board of Trade 1940–42. Conservative M.P. for Birmingham Ladywood 1931–45; King's Norton 1950–55; Sutton Coldfield 1955–74. Junior minister 1935–40, 1942–5. Minister of Information 1945; Fuel and Power 1951–5; Education 1957–9.

4 'the Belgian Premier': Hubert Pierlot (1883–1963). Prime Minister 1939–45. Minister of the Interior 1934–5; Minister of Agriculture 1936–8. Minister of Foreign Affairs 1939. Minister of National Defence 1942–4. Minister of State 1945–54. Leader of the Social Christian Party.

5 King Leopold III (b. 1901). Leopold succeeded his father as King of the Belgians in 1934. When the Germans invaded Belgium, Leopold assumed command of the Belgian army. On 28th May, with the army cornered in the north-east, he decided to surrender. The government declared the capitulation illegal, but could not reverse it. After the war, Leopold was prevented from returning to the throne. In 1951 he abdicated in favour of his son, Baudouin. See Diary entry for 28th May 1940.

bad at destroying their stocks.

Lloyd and I have different estimates from our advisers, his being the more optimistic. But on policy we are all agreed. Oil everywhere should be a primary target. In night raids we lose very few planes and there is reason to think that the effect of our raids on German morale has already been very severe, particularly because they have all been hushed up in the German press and therefore rumour has run ahead of fact and circulated widely.

Tuesday 28th May

8.30 a.m. Hear Reynaud on the air announce that the King of the Belgians has told his troops to surrender. Reynaud phrases it very well.

In the afternoon all ministers are asked to meet the P.M. He is quite magnificent. The man, and the only man we have, for this hour. He gives a full, frank and completely calm account of events in France. When the Germans broke through on the Meuse, French morale for the moment collapsed. Therefore, he flew to France and saw Reynaud and Gamelin. The latter said, 'We have been defeated by German superiority in numbers, in material and in methods.' Churchill said, 'What then are you going to do?' Gamelin merely shrugged his shoulders. Churchill said, 'Will you please leave the room', and then, alone with Reynaud, they went into everything, including the High Command. The French, before this war, had given up all ideas of the offensive. They were hypnotised by the Maginot Line. General Billotte commanding the forces north of the Somme, including our own, had given no important or significant order for four days! Since then he had been killed in a motor accident and succeeded by Blanchard.[1] The French had failed to make a push northwards from the Somme. They had had too few Divisions between the sea and Amiens and their communications had been badly bombed. Therefore, though we had done our best from the north, it had been impossible to close the gap, and we were in grave danger of being surrounded. Now, therefore, it was necessary to fight our way through to the Channel Ports and get away all we could. The act of the King of the Belgians had opened our flank, but this was not so grave as might have been supposed, owing to the inundations on the Ysère, which were perhaps a better defence than the Belgian Army! How many would get away we could not tell. We should certainly be able to get 50,000 away. If we could get 100,000 away, that would be a magnificent performance. Only Dunkirk was

1 General Jean-Georges-Maurice Blanchard (1877–1954). French general. Replaced Billotte on 25th May 1940 as Commander of the First Army. On Weygand's orders, the First Army was dissolved and Blanchard left France in a destroyer on 1st June 1940.

left to us. Calais had been defended by a British force which had refused to surrender, and it was said that there were no survivors. We could only use the beaches east and west of Dunkirk in addition to the port itself. Dunkirk was under a great pall of black smoke, to which our ships were adding artificial smoke so as to screen our embarkations from the air. The Air Force were maintaining the most powerful possible fighter patrols over this scene, and the Germans were suffering immense losses in the air, as on the ground, in their attempts to interfere with the embarkation. The superiority of our fighters was once again being manifested, and on two occasions great flights of German bombers had turned away and declined battle when they saw our fighter patrols. (Sinclair told me, two days later, that it was even more dramatic than this. A large number of German bombers, escorted by German fighters, were approaching from inland. When they saw our fighters, the German fighters turned and fled, leaving the German bombers unprotected. We attacked the German bombers and knocked down twenty-two of them with no loss to ourselves.) The P.M. went on to say that our clawing-down rate was gradually rising, taking an average of one day with another, to 3:1, to 4:1, and lately to 5:1. It was clear that we had killed off most of the best Nazi pilots, unless, which seemed unlikely, they had been holding some of their best in reserve.[1]

He was determined to prepare public opinion for bad tidings, and it would of course be said, and with some truth, that what was now happening in Northern France would be the greatest British military defeat for many centuries. We must now be prepared for the sudden turning of the war against this island, and prepared also for other events of great gravity in Europe. No countenance should be given publicly to the view that France might soon collapse, but we must not allow ourselves to be taken by surprise by any events. It might indeed be said that it would be easier to defend this island alone than to defend this island plus France, and if it was seen throughout the world that it was the former, there would be an immense wave of feeling, not least in the U.S.A. which, having done nothing much to help us so far, might even enter the war. But all this was speculative. Attempts to invade us would no doubt be made, but they would be beset with immense difficulty. We should mine all round our coast; our Navy was immensely strong; our air defences were much more easily organised from this island than across the Channel; our supplies of food, oil, etc., were ample; we had good troops in this island, others were on the way by sea, both British army units coming from remote garrisons and excellent Dominion troops, and, as to aircraft, we were now more than

1 Marginal insertion: '("They're cold meat", our airmen say)'.

ALL BEHIND YOU, WINSTON

making good our current losses, and the Germans were not.

It was idle to think that, if we tried to make peace now, we should get better terms from Germany than if we went on and fought it out. The Germans would demand our fleet – that would be called 'disarmament' – our naval bases, and much else. We should become a slave state, though a British Government which would be Hitler's puppet would be set up – 'under Mosley or some such person'. And where should we be at the end of all that? On the other side, we had immense reserves and advantages. Therefore, he said, 'We shall go on and we shall fight it out, here or elsewhere, and if at last the long story is to end, it were better it should end, not through surrender, but only when we are rolling senseless on the ground.'[1] There was a murmur of approval round the table, in which I think Amery, Lord Lloyd and I were loudest. Not much more was said. No one expressed even the faintest flicker of dissent. Herbert Morrison asked about evacuation of the Government, and hoped that it would not be hurried. The P.M. said Certainly not, he was all against evacuation unless things really became utterly impossible in London, 'but mere bombing will not

1 Marginal insertion: 'If this long island story of ours is to end at last, let it end only when each one of us lies choking in his own blood upon the ground.'

make us go'. It is quite clear that whereas the Old Umbrella[1] – neither he nor other members of the War Cabinet were at this meeting – wanted to run very early, Winston's bias is all the other way. When we separate, several go up and speak to him, and I, patting him on the shoulder, from my physically greater height, say, 'You ought to get that Cartoon of Low showing us all rolling up our sleeves,[2] and frame it and stick it up in front of you here.' He says, with a broad grin, 'Yes, that was a good one, wasn't it.' He is a darling!

Wednesday 29th May

I examine the organisation for the armed defence of my Ministry. We have a number of old soldiers here, and a man named Wingate,[3] ex I.C.S. [Indian Civil Service], is taking charge. They are to have some rifles and a number of others will bring shot guns and ammunition. There will be an armoury in a suitable place and, when the thing gets going, armed guards day and night in all key points.

Mounsey[4] offers me his resignation on the grounds of health and age. He is evidently anxious to get out and, after a friendly conversation, I say I would like to make immediate arrangements to replace him. I carefully do not ask his views on his successor. My first thought is to make [Noel] Hall his successor. Then, talking to Leith-Ross, decide to make Drogheda[5] and Hall Joint Secretaries immediately under Leith-Ross. There may be some Foreign Office chagrin over this.

P.O.G. [Prevention of Oil reaching Germany] Committee[6] meets. Swarms of officials. A lot of fidget about the statistics. Philip Nichols,[7] who has become a first-class middle-aged obstructionist, is there for the Foreign Office. I say that before I came to my Ministry I took the view that oil targets should long ago have been bombarded. I knew that political reasons in the contrary sense were advanced. Those had gone now. I am not much interested in the exact statistics. They do not alter policy. There are also other possibilities of useful action in S.E. Europe. I thus give a lead to any person who may be discontented and

1 Dalton's name for Neville Chamberlain, who was renowned for his rolled umbrella.
2 Marginal insertion: 'and falling in behind you'.
3 R. E. L. Wingate, later Sir Ronald, 2nd Bart (1889–1978). Joint Planning Staff Officer of War Cabinet 1939–45. Indian Civil Service 1912–39.
4 Sir George Mounsey (1876–1966). Secretary at the Ministry of Economic Warfare 1939–40. Assistant Under-Secretary at the Foreign Office 1929–39.
5 H. C. P. Moore, 10th Earl of Drogheda (1884–1957). Joint Director of the Ministry of Economic Warfare 1940–42. Director-General 1942–5.
6 'P.O.G. Committee': this Committee, chaired by Lord Hankey, met between 1939 and 1941. (Hankey was Chancellor of the Duchy of Lancaster 1940–41.)
7 P. B. B. Nichols, later Sir Philip (1894–1962). Foreign Office, London 1937–41. Minister to the Czechoslovakian Government in London 1941; Ambassador to Czechoslovakia 1942–7.

one little man pipes up from the corner and says, 'We have often put up proposals but they have always been turned down.' I say, 'Put them up again to me and if they are turned down I will take them up with the responsible ministers.' Hankey from the Chair says, rather helplessly, 'We have done that before.' I say, rising to leave for another Committee, 'We have now got a largely new Government, and I hope it will have a largely new policy.' We must get a move on here.

Thursday 30th May

Not letting grass grow, I send for Drogheda and Hall and ask them separately whether they will take on joint secretaryship. Both seem pleased and say yes. I send Leith-Ross to the Treasury to fix their salaries. This is arranged. I discuss with Leith-Ross who will be disappointed. He asks whether he may go and speak to Cadogan and Van about some Foreign Office left-outs. I say yes, on the understanding that I have *made my decision*. I am not prepared to discuss this with anyone at the Foreign Office. If Sir Orme Sargent[1] fell down a lift at the Foreign Office and broke his neck, Halifax would not consult me before appointing his successor, and I will have parity. Later, Leith-Ross says that he has seen Cadogan, who is making no difficulties but would like another twenty-four hours to consider whether either Mounsey or Ingram[2] can be employed at the Foreign Office.

Lunch with Foreign Press Association. Duff Cooper the principal speaker, also Van Kleffens,[3] the Dutch Foreign Minister. I have sent a message through Bowes-Lyon,[4] my attractive and intelligent press officer, who is a brother of the Queen, that if I go I shall say a few words. In fact it is thought that I make much the best speech of the occasion and somewhat put Duff Cooper in the shade. I am much congratulated, but perhaps it is not much above the level of loud-voiced and truculent mob oratory. None the less, they like it.

Better news today of numbers being evacuated from Dunkirk.

Friday 31st May

Visit from Van. He still sees no one in the Foreign Office, and no papers, and is consulted about nothing! How much longer will he find

1 Sir Orme Sargent (1884–1962). Deputy Under-Secretary at the Foreign Office 1939–46. Permanent Under-Secretary at the Foreign Office 1946–9.
2 E. M. B. Ingram (1890–1941). Diplomatic Adviser to the Ministry of Economic Warfare 1939–41.
3 E. N. Van Kleffens (1894–1983). Netherlands Foreign Minister 1939–46. Ambassador to the U.S.A. 1947–50; Minister of State 1950.
4 The Hon. David Bowes-Lyon, later Sir David (1902–61). Press Officer, Ministry of Economic Warfare 1940–41. Head of Political Warfare Mission in Washington 1942–4. Sixth son of 14th Earl of Strathmore, and brother of Queen Elizabeth.

this tolerable? All the life, he says, has gone out of the office since he was put on one side. This has shown the rest that vigour and initiative by civil servants is not appreciated. He said this when I complained of Nichols, who, I said, had grown from an attractive and bright young man ten years ago into a solemn middle-aged obstructionist. 'Palsied Pansies of the Foreign Office,' I said to someone. Ruth says I should not repeat this! Anderson, Van says, is a menace, being so slow, timid and unaware of everything. Van tells a terrible tale of high officers at the Home Office, lost files, etc. He has spoken to Attlee and Greenwood, they being in the War Cabinet. I welcome this and urge him to go on. It is a waste of my time always to have to act as go-between. He thinks either George Lloyd or Amery would be much better at Home Office. Van is a little egocentric in these days. There should be a curfew for everyone, and not just enemy aliens, and all roads near the coast should be blocked at night. The French, he fears, are very wobbly. Corbin has been grossly exaggerating the number of French Divisions in the Northern Group. This is a bad sign.

I am summoned to Buckingham Palace and spend thirty minutes with the King. Very easy. No stammering. He asks about M.E.W. and his brother-in-law, David Bowes-Lyon. I say that he is my Press Officer in liaison with the Ministry of Information and is doing very well. He speaks of the really remarkable evacuation of the B.E.F. Hitler, he says, 'wants to come here'. I said that he had fixed the date a little while ago at 20th April. The King says he understands it has now been fixed for 1st August. He wants, the King goes on, to exterminate us and to plant Germans in this island. What will he do next? He will stop at nothing, neither raining gas from the sky nor poisoning our water. That would be the last degradation. But, I say, we have, I hope, effective preventive measures. Scientists, at any rate, have been working on these problems for some time. The King says he has had to remind Winston that he is only P.M. in England and not in France as well!

Talk with Campbell Stuart.[1] As roguish and helpful as ever. He is under Duff Cooper now and finds it works fairly well.

See Leith-Ross. He will announce the changes I am making at the top tomorrow, i.e. Drogheda and Hall as Joint Directors on Mounsey's resignation.

Oil targets and P.O.G. The Air want to go for the oil targets. Nichols obstructs: 'We must help the French.' Alternatively, Italy can make

1 Sir Campbell Stuart (1885–1972). Director of Propaganda in Enemy Countries 1939–40. Deputy Director of Propaganda in Enemy Countries in the First World War. Chairman of the Imperial Communications Advisory Committee and of its successor, the Commonwealth Communications Council 1931–45.

good any deficiencies we create in Germany from her own stocks; thirdly, if we knock German oil targets about badly, Germany will go the quicker into Romania and take their oil. This last snag is really the invention of Geoffrey Lloyd. I say it is a ludicrous deduction from these facts that we should not go for the German oil plants. The right deduction is that we should also do something in and to Romania. This P.O.G. makes me tired! I shall have to do something about it.

The P.M. told us this week that Gamelin had no means of manoeuvre!

The French were as bad as the Poles! The Germans bombed their aerodromes at the beginning of the offensive. … most French fighters were smashed up on the ground. In fact, only eighty fighters survived. This is why we have had to carry the French completely on our backs in the air.

Saturday 1st June

Van has spoken to Greenwood, but not yet to Attlee, who is in France with P.M. Arrange that I will speak today to Amery and he to Lloyd regarding Home Office.

Amery thinks it very unlikely that things are quite as bad as Van says. Van, he observes, is rather French, and inclined to dramatise situations. Amery thinks Anderson is pretty good in a slow, prudent way. Bengal and Ireland have been good training grounds.[1] He was rather concerned to hear Lloyd and Bracken talking the other night as though Anderson must be got rid of. (The appointment of Swinton to deal with Fifth Column is, I suppose, a compromise between all or nothing.)

Much has happened, says Amery, in recent years, and months, which can only be rationally explained as treachery. And yet we know it is really stupidity and muddle. He cites the offer from India of one Division early in September last. This offer was messed about from committee to committee until February, and Belisha[2] could not be got to answer letters about it. Finally, it was accepted in March, Simon, however, making a reservation as to the apportionment between us and India of the cost. Not till late in March was final agreement given.

Likewise the story of the tanks. It was only decided to send an

---

1 Sir John Anderson, q.v. Joint Under-Secretary for Ireland 1918–20. Governor of Bengal 1932–7.

2 I. L. Hore-Belisha, later 1st Baron (1893–1957). Liberal, later National Liberal, M.P. for Plymouth Devonport 1923–45. Junior minister 1931–2. Financial Secretary to the Treasury 1932–4; Minister of Transport 1934–7; Secretary of State for War 1937–40; Minister of National Insurance 1945.

Expeditionary Force to France well after Munich. Before that, the only tanks designed were light tanks to operate on desert sands. Then, the decision on the B.E.F. having been taken, in a very leisurely way a study of heavy and medium tanks began. After a long delay plans and designs were made for a heavy one. Then the Ministry of Supply was set up and two R.A.O.C. [Royal Army Ordnance Corps] officers were moved from the War Office, with whose design they completely lost touch, but gave themselves a step up in military rank. Orders were placed, unawares, with the same firm to manufacture both heavy and medium tanks. Then it was found that the medium tanks were no good anyhow. The first effective flow of supply will begin in April 1941. (Belisha and Burgin [1] should both be hung for this.) I spoke tartly of the obstruction of officials and of inter-departmental delays. Amery said, rather brightly, that an attitude of mind had grown up in the civil service such that, if anyone made a proposal and then two people raised objections, the proposal was held to be defeated by two to one.

I am pressing on with reorganisation in my Ministry. An announcement is to be made in tonight's evening papers, and I agree to putting out within the Ministry a rough sketch of new sections on which Leith-Ross, Mounsey, Drogheda, Hall, Gwatkin [2] and Ingram (whom I shall make Advisers, economic and diplomatic), have agreed. Ingram is not present and is stated to have a slightly sore head, but it has been soothed. The D Plan is being concocted. [3] Campbell Stuart very agreeable (he obviously wants to succeed Ogilvie [4] at the B.B.C.). George Wagner's [5] marriage permit comes through. It has been obstructed by a policeman who has had his head washed by Stuart.

1 E. L. Burgin (1887–1945). Liberal M.P. for Luton 1929–45. Junior minister 1932–7; Minister of Transport 1937–9; Minister of Supply 1939–40.
2 F. T. A. Ashton-Gwatkin (1889–1976). Foreign Office official. Policy Adviser to the Ministry of Economic Warfare 1939. Assistant Under-Secretary and Chief Clerk at the Foreign Office from 1940.
3 'The D Plan': this is the first reference in the Diary to Dalton's attempt to get hold of the subversive operational and propaganda agencies which were to form the Special Operations Executive. One of these, Section D, was currently under the jurisdiction of the War Office.
4 F. W. Ogilvie, later Sir Frederick (1893–1949). Director-General of the B.B.C. 1938–42. Professor of Political Economy at Edinburgh University 1926–34; Vice-Chancellor of Queen's University, Belfast 1934–8.
5 George Wagner (b. 1913). A young socialist refugee from Danzig, who had been staying with the Daltons at Carlisle Mansions. Dalton was trying to hurry through his marriage papers.

Monday 3rd June

Christopher Mayhew,[1] looking very charming and very fit, calls upon me in battledress as a simple gunner. I take him round as my orderly to No. 10, which pleases him. He is now to train for a commission over here and, after that, is probably going into Military Intelligence. I say that, when this stage has been reached, I can, without impropriety, ask for him to be liaison with my Ministry.

The P.M. has a squash of ministers. Things are very much better than last week. We have got out more than 300,000 men. He had thought of nothing but dead, wounded, and long dreary processions making their way to prison camps and starvation in Germany. The French? They will ask us for help, and we must give them more than we can spare, which will still be not all that they ask. We must not denude this island. 'We've got the men away but we've lost the luggage.' This will take some time to make up from our aircraft and munition factories. The French insisted on the post of honour at the end, and so 'after a seemly wrangle we brought the Cameron High-landers away. Otherwise they were to have stayed and died at the end.'

P.M. is much more confident against invasion than he was a week ago. After all, we have the B.E.F. in this country now, hardened veterans. Also, says Geoffrey Lloyd, the Germans are very bad at night flying. In any case, many defence measures are now being taken here.

Eire. Not much to be frightened of. 'They have got something through, but it would be much harder for them to operate against us from there than from France. In any case, let *them* begin it in Eire. Then the Irish will start to fight among themselves, and some at least will be on our side! Indeed, if the Germans begin it, the great majority of Irish will resist, and we can then come in and help them.'

The Beaver gives some very good and encouraging figures on air-craft production. The claw-down rate is steadily at 4:1; initially things stood at, perhaps, $2\frac{1}{2}$:1; we are more than making good our losses, but they are not. Outside of this are the French and the sources of supply from over the ocean.

What will Europe be like after six months? Famine, starvation and

---

1 Christopher Mayhew, later Baron (b. 1915). Dalton had first met Mayhew at dinner with Frank Pakenham in 1935, when Mayhew was an undergraduate, and had followed his career closely ever since. After Mayhew had become an officer in the Intelligence Corps in September 1940 he was attached to Dalton's private office as a personal aide. In 1942 he returned to active service. Labour M.P. for Norfolk South 1945–50. Labour, then Liberal, M.P. for Woolwich East 1951–74. Parliamentary Under-Secretary at the Foreign Office 1946–50. Navy Minister 1964–6.

revolt, most of all in the slave lands which Germany has overrun.

The P.M. wants to be able to say to the House tomorrow, 'If I wavered for a moment, all my colleagues in the Government would turn and rend me.' No one raised any objection to this. Bevin wants to stop 'all this labour floatin' about'. To help this he has pushed agricultural labourers' wages up to forty-eight bob a week. This will revolutionise the countryside. The railwaymen are to get a few bob more, and then all wage rates are to be stabilised for at least four months. As for Fifth Columnism, he says, 'It isn't in the workshop; it's all the upper middle class.' One or two of my colleagues looked down their noses.

Between 26th May and 4th June some 225,000 British, 110,000 French and 2,000 Belgian troops were evacuated from Dunkirk in British vessels, including pleasure-steamers and small boats. Another 50,000 French troops escaped in French ships. On 4th June, Churchill warned the House of Commons that 'Wars are not won by evacuations', adding, 'there was a victory inside this deliverance, which should be noted'. He concluded with a famous peroration: 'We shall fight on the beaches, we shall fight on the landing-grounds, we shall fight in the hills; we shall never surrender ... '[1]

Tuesday 4th June
Winston made a grand speech in the House on the evacuation from Dunkirk, on the victory of our airmen over the Germans, and on our determination to fight to the end and to win. It was very well received, on the whole, by the House. Very grim and determined. 'We shall never surrender.' It was evidently designed, and well designed, to pull ostrich heads out of the sand both here and in U.S.A.

Wednesday 5th June
Have a drink with Campbell Stuart, who is all for Jebb taking over some important work in which we are both interested.[2]

Go on to dine with Jebb, who would like to do it, but must first speak to Cadogan who, I say, I neither like nor dislike, but only non-like. I am still a Vanite. Jebb says that of course Cadogan is very *borné*, but much better than many people think. Jebb thinks that we have been very weak about Italy since the war began, though at an

---

1 H.C. Debs [361], col. 796.
2 Sabotage and subversion, which later became the responsibility of the Special Operations Executive.

earlier stage we should certainly have tried much harder to make a friend of her.[1]

Friday 7th June

To Buckingham Palace to become a Privy Councillor. The ritual is gone through without any crashing errors, though Bracken, who, being first in alphabetical order, has to lead us up in Indian file, tries to shake hands with the wrong people after kissing hands. I drive Charlie Edwards[2] to Paddington in my official car, which much pleases him. He is afraid, today as always in the past, that he may miss his train from Paddington home. I land him there in good time. He is seventy-three but walks very sprightly. He likes being what and where he is and says that only Shinwell is a nuisance.

12.30. To Caxton Hall for ceremony.[3] My presence is really unnecessary since two admirable lady witnesses are already there. I am cutting it rather fine, as I am due at Cabinet at 1 and therefore enter Registrar's Office and apply a slight hustle, telling him who I am and that I must leave there soon for the Cabinet. This perhaps was slightly injudicious, but probably made no difference.

Later in the day the press got wind of my presence and the *Mirror* and the *Mail* in particular seemed to want information as to whether the Minister of Economic Warfare was present today at the wedding of 'a German'. Gaitskell, who knows nothing of my movements, says that he thinks it is almost impossible that the Minister, who has a very crowded timetable, can have found time to attend any wedding. Later I put on Bowes-Lyon to keep the whole thing out of the press, and he does this admirably – he is a very able and agreeable young man, this young brother of the Queen – having rung up a large number of editors and told them that it was a matter of national importance that the name of this German, who was being of great value to this country, should not be mentioned.

Saturday 8th June

Cabinet. Hankey again very long-winded on matters relating to the

---

1 Marginal insertion: 'He says that Van has become hysterical. He should have resigned and gone into politics. He is all sound and fury, and then doesn't follow it up. There can't be two heads in the Office.'
2 Sir Charles Edwards (1867–1954). Labour Chief Whip 1931–42. Joint Government Chief Whip 1940–42. Labour M.P. for Bedwellty 1918–50. Junior government whip 1929–31.
3 The marriage of two refugees, George and Irene Wagner, befriended by the Daltons. The Wagners recall that 'a slight hustle' was actually a characteristic display of rudeness on Dalton's part. See entry for 1st June 1940 and n. 5 (p. 33).

River.[1] He bores the Cabinet. It is 1.15. Winston looks hungrily at the clock. Alexander passes a note to me: '*What* a deployment of detail! Hankey is getting very wordy.' I ask that at long last something may be done to cut the jugular vein of oil. Left to Foreign Secretary, Lord President, Hankey, me and Lloyd to meet and settle. P.M. says all ministers should go away for part of the weekend. They may not have another chance for a long time. Cadogan says to me, going out, that Jebb has spoken to him and he would be willing to release him, good though he is, if H.M. Government should wish it.

Lunch with Attlee. He is a very good G.S.O.I. [General Staff Officer I]. He is doing a lot of push on Home Front, e.g. for communal feeding, rational restriction of imports, etc. He is interested in what I tell him about M.E.W. and possible extensions. He thinks Halifax is going downhill. People are getting rather fed up with him. He is a weak and indecisive nobleman.

Attlee would like to find a job for Shinwell to keep him quiet. Shinwell has been to him and practically admitted that he made a damned fool of himself in refusing the job he was offered when the Government was being formed.

Sunday 9th June
Meet Gladwyn [Jebb] and talk about the lack of coherence in a certain important sphere of war work.[2] Finally left that, as a first step, he should be given an instruction to investigate everything and question everyone in this field, and to report. This should pave the way for his taking charge under whatever political direction shall be decided upon.

On 10th June, Italy declared war, believing that Germany had already won. The same day, the French government left the capital for Tours.

Monday 10th June
Cadogan seems friendly, and I learn indirectly, from Jebb through Stuart, that he is in fact friendly to me. This surprises me a little.[3]

At 6.30 we receive officially in my Ministry the 'Duplicity' message.

---

1 'the River': plan of D Section to block the River Danube to oil barges coming up-river from Romania to Ratisbon or Ulm.
2 A further reference to developing plans for S.O.E.
3 Cadogan had been pressing for Dalton as head of the new secret organisation, against a reluctant Prime Minister. See D. Dilks (ed.), *The Diaries of Sir Alexander Cadogan O.M. 1938–1945*, Cassell, London, 1971, p. 312.

This is the pre-arranged signal that Italy has come in against us. Gaitskell wants me to issue a message to the press on Italy's vulnerability to economic war. This, after a slight hesitation, I do in a few sentences. It gets excellent publicity both in the press and on the air, even up to the morning's B.B.C. news bulletins next day.

Tuesday 11th June

I have a discussion on the phone with Halifax, through the medium of Butler, on the date to be inserted in the proclamation stopping Italian exports. When corresponding action was taken on German exports last November, a week's warning was given! Now it is thought by the Foreign Office that perhaps we can date it from today. I propose instead to date it back a month, so as to catch all Italian exports in neutral ships – Italian ships themselves can be seized anyhow – which are on the seas. It could also be said that this would correspond with the date of Hitler's violation of Holland, Belgium and Luxembourg, which Italy applauded. After some debate I agree to compromise on dating it back one week, and undertaking that consignments to Japan shall, in particular cases, be looked at tenderly.

At 7.30 I am summoned to a Privy Council at Buckingham Palace attended also by Chamberlain, Simon and Halifax (what company I keep these days!). This is to get the King's approval to the Italian export order. We stand and make polite and faintly relevant conversation. Coming out, Halifax says to me, 'Isn't it wonderful how cheerful he is when he must feel that all his Empire may be crashing about his ears'! I say that it is indeed wonderful.

I give a little ministerial dinner party at the House of Commons, admirably organised by John Wilmot, to my principal assistants at the Ministry – Foot, Leith-Ross, Mounsey, Drogheda, Hall, Wilmot, Gaitskell and Hancock. It all goes very well indeed. Wilmot says afterwards, 'They all enjoyed themselves as much as kids at a Sunday School Treat.' We give them little to eat and much to drink.

The P.M. is in France.

Wednesday 12th June

Gaitskell thinks I shall soon have too little to do in the Ministry and wants me to take over part of Greenwood's 'Economic and General Staff' work.

Thursday 13th June

Van and I have a talk. He was hurt by an answer to a Parliamentary Question yesterday saying that he was still Diplomatic Adviser to H.M.G. He says this implies that he is sometimes consulted and may have some responsibility for H.M.G.'s foreign policy. But this is not so. He is consulted no more under this regime than under the previous one. He thinks the Home Office is still most dangerously slow.

Reynaud's two appeals to Roosevelt are published today.

Churchill made two final visits to France. On 11th June, he attended a meeting of the Supreme War Council at the Château du Muguet, near Briaré on the Loire. He returned to England on the 12th, then flew back on the 13th, taking with him Halifax, Ismay and Beaverbrook, and met Reynaud at Tours, where the French government was now based. Next day, 14th June, the Germans entered Paris. Meanwhile, the French government moved on to Bordeaux.

Friday 14th June

5 p.m. Winston has one of his ministers' squashes. Gives an account of his last visit to France and a very vivid appreciation.

French organised resistance is at an end. The Government and the High Command still give orders, but they are not effectively transmitted nor obeyed. You meet men who can talk to you, but have no telephone. General Georges[1] supported Weygand's advice to Reynaud that he should ask for an armistice. Reynaud refused.

Reynaud had asked Churchill 'most solemnly and formally' to relieve France from her promise not to make a separate peace. Churchill had refused. This, he thinks, was the answer Reynaud wanted from him. Reynaud had put this question after a long meeting of the Cabinet.

The French Army has lost the battle. They have no reserves left. Their Divisions have been reduced to the strength of two battalions. In some parts soldiers are wandering in the woods, taking food from passers-by. They state that if they had had twelve more Divisions, they could have won. That may be true, but that sort of thing is true of almost every battle.

Hitler will soon make the French a peace offer. It will be made to

---

1 General Alphonse Georges (1875–1951). General Gamelin's Deputy, and Commander-in-Chief of the Northern and Eastern theatre of operations in France 1939–40. Commander of Anglo-French forces entering Belgium 1940. Went into retirement after the collapse of the French Army, but joined General Giraud in Algiers 1943. *Chef de cabinet* to André Maginot, Minister of War 1925–32. Member of French War Council 1932.

sound very generous. A French government may be found to accept it. The French fleet raises a number of problems and there may be great temptation. There should be a France across the Water. Reynaud and Mandel[1] would be for this. Only too much recrimination is possible on both sides, French and British. But what good would it do? Very few British Divisions have fought in France. At the end, very few indeed. French losses have been out of all proportion to ours, in every sphere.

We here must strike a still more defiant note. We shall defend this island. Weygand said to him, 'You have a very good anti-tank trap in the Channel.' We must intensify the blockade and show great activity in the air. We have more troops here than we have ever had before. All forms of home defence are being vigorously pushed forward. It is a long-standing doctrine that raids may succeed but that large-scale invasion of this island is impossible. Our fighter strength is now greater than before the offensive began. There have been prodigies both of production and repair of aircraft. There will now be very violent attacks made upon this island, but, if they are beaten off at first, they cannot succeed later. Nazidom will lie like a dark pall over all Europe, but, after only a few months, it may dissolve like the snow in spring.

There is no alternative before us except to fight it out; else we shall be first despoiled and then enslaved.

Tonight it is announced that the Germans have been marching into Paris all day! We are back now behind 1870!

Saturday 15th June
Morton says that he is working day and night for Winston. He describes the scene in the garden at Tours. Reynaud was very formal. He said, 'Mr Prime Minister of England: In the name of France I ask you whether you are willing to release France from her promise not to make a separate peace.' Churchill replied, 'Mr President of the Council of France: In the name of England, I say No.' Then, breaking through formalities, he suggested to Reynaud that they two should go and talk together in the garden. Ismay[2] was told to go with them and to take a note. Morton says that the French always have their tails down when Churchill arrives and that, as he energises and encourages

---

1 Georges Mandel (1885–1944). Minister of the Interior in Reynaud's Cabinet. Arrested and interned by the Vichy regime, and murdered in 1944.
2 General Sir Hastings Ismay, later 1st Baron (1887–1965). Chief of Staff to the Minister of Defence (Churchill) and Deputy Secretary (Military) to the War Cabinet 1940–45. Secretary-General of the North Atlantic Treaty Organisation (N.A.T.O.) 1952–7.

them, their tails rise. Mandel is much the strongest. But he is a Jew, whose real name is said to be Rehoboam Rothschild.[1] Reynaud is very susceptible to Winston but he is conscious of having led no large political party and of not being entitled to speak for France. People say to him, 'You can't speak for France. You are only a Boulevardier; you do not know the Provinces.'

On 16th June, Reynaud resigned as Premier. Marshal Pétain succeeded him, and immediately sought an armistice. Britain now faced the combined strength of Germany and Italy alone.

Sunday 16th June

It is put to me that Winston is surrounded by stimulants – his 'Brains Trust', Morton, 'the Prof' (Lindemann),[2] Harrod,[3] Brendan Bracken etc. What he really needs, some think, are sedatives. He is always getting new ideas and collecting what is almost a Cabinet at short notice, and taking sudden decisions of great importance. Most of these are probably very good, but the Chiefs of Staff live in a constant state of terror of what he may do, or decide, without consulting them. The other day, when I came into the Cabinet, he was wigging the Chiefs of Staff like anything, particularly old Pound,[4] who is rather deaf. 'I have been concerned with this problem on and off for the past thirty years and I have never heard it said before that ...... What has become of Sea Power? ...... Who is responsible for this paper ...... ?' Then excuses, and then P.M. again, 'Then it should all be taken back and reconsidered and brought up again in proper form by those responsible. They must be prepared to defend in the Cabinet the statements they put into their papers ...... '

---

1 Mandel was born Louis Rothschild, but took his mother's surname in order to dissociate himself from the banking family, to which he was not related.
2 Frederick Lindemann, later 1st Viscount Cherwell (1886–1957). Personal Assistant to the Prime Minister 1940–42. See Appendix A.
3 R. F. Harrod, later Sir Roy (1900–78). Economist and disciple of Keynes. Served under Lindemann in Churchill's private statistical office at the Admiralty 1940, and in the Prime Minister's office 1940–42. Statistical adviser to the Admiralty 1943–5. Nuffield Reader in International Economics, Oxford 1952–67. International Adviser to the International Monetary Fund, 1952–3; Fellow of Nuffield College, Oxford 1938–47, 1954–8.
4 Admiral of the Fleet Sir Dudley Pound (1887–1943). First Sea Lord and Chief of Naval Staff 1939–43.

Someone said that, when Bastianini[1] was told to return to Italy because she was now at war with us, *'l'Ambasciatore piangeva come un bambino'.*[2]

'I expect the Battle of Britain is about to begin,' Churchill told the House of Commons on 18th June. ' ... Let us therefore brace ourselves to our duty, and so bear ourselves that if the British Empire and the Commonwealth last for a thousand years men will still say, "This was their finest hour".'[3]

Tuesday 18th June
House of Commons. Winston again makes a grand speech – defiant, reasoned, and confident. It is noticeable that he is much more loudly cheered by the Labour Party than by the general body of Tory supporters. The relative silence of these latter is regarded by some as 'sinister'. John Wilmot, whom I ask to feel about and ascertain opinion, tells me that many Tories feel they are quite out of it now. They think the Labour Party has much too large a share, both in offices and the determination of Government policy, and in addition to being a large part of the Government, the Labour Party also continues to be, to a great extent, the Opposition, so far as status is concerned. The Tories, therefore, wonder where they come in. Most of the Tories in the Government are either rebels or near-rebels. So what was the use of having been loyal to the Old Man and Margesson in the now closed chapter of our history? There is some danger in this situation, and it must be watched. One very obvious conclusion is that we must not push the Old Man out of the Government, for he would then become a centre of disaffection and a rallying point for real opposition. Leave him where he is, as a decaying hostage.

With Will Henderson,[4] now attached to Greenwood. The latter seems very slow and unimperative. He is in danger of being run by his

1 Giuseppe Bastianini (1899–1961). Italian Ambassador to Britain 1939–40. Vice-Secretary of the Italian Fascist Party 1921–4.
2 'The Ambassador cried like a baby.'
3 H.C. Debs [362], col. 60.
4 W. W. Henderson, later 1st Baron (1891–1984). Personal Assistant to Greenwood, Minister without Portfolio. Labour M.P. 1923–4, 1929–31. Parliamentary Under-Secretary at the Foreign Office 1948–51. Secretary to the Press and Publicity Department of the Labour Party 1921–45.

officials, notably Hemming.[1] I seek to push Durbin[2] on to Green-wood's immediate staff. Gaitskell is much in this intrigue.

Wednesday 19th June

In the absence of the First Lord and the First Sea Lord, I see Vice-Admiral Phillips.[3] I lapse the protocol and consent to visit him at the Admiralty in his own room. Hitherto I have had a good opinion of him and it was he who passed me a little note in the War Cabinet when I stopped the Italian ships. Today I have come to make sure that the Navy have in the front of their minds the question of the fringe of islands in the Atlantic from which, if Gibraltar went, we could continue to enforce the blockade and control the western gateway of the Mediterranean. His answer on this point is reasonably satisfactory, though he said the islands lack good harbours. Then, however, he begins a political harangue – I feel that I should have had less of this if *he* had been in *my* room, which would have been the proper 'venue'. He does not care anything about the Italians, who are a worthless lot, but the Spaniards are a very different story. To have Spain as an enemy would jeopardise the whole of our control, both of the western Mediterranean and the Atlantic sea routes. It is unthinkable that we should have been brought to such a point. We backed the Bolsheviks in Spain in 1936 and '37 against the only man who, in modern times, has been able to make Spain strong. The horrors committed by the Bolsheviks in Spain were seen by our sailors and are on record. This was the climax of a foreign policy which had first adopted an attitude towards Germany which made war with her inevitable; had then successively alienated Japan, Italy, and now, finally, Spain. The French had not been fighting in these last weeks. This was because they too had become Bolsheviks. Weygand had said that the only tough troops in France were the Poles, and that if he had had ten more Divisions of them, he would have won the battle.

I did not take much part in this talk, but I have been inclined to revise my view that this man should be First Sea Lord. Sailors and soldiers, when they become political, become *very* political. At the same time, one must sympathise with a sailor who sees his problem

---

1 A. F. Hemming (1893–1964). Administrative Head (Economic Section) of the War Cabinet Secretariat 1939–40.
2 E. F. M. Durbin (1906–48). Economic Section of the War Cabinet Secretariat 1940–42. See Appendix A.
3 Rear-Admiral (Acting Admiral) T. S. V. Phillips, later Sir Tom (1888–1941). Vice-Chief of Naval Staff 1939–41. Went down with the *Prince of Wales*, off Singapore, in December 1941.

TOO MUCH DEFENCE IN THE WRONG PLACE

rendered much more difficult by a series of political acts, with an obvious naval bearing.

Friday 21st June

Lunch with Fletcher[1] and Morton. Much of the time engaged in diatribes against Anderson. They are now thinking of trying to frighten Margesson with threats of a revolt in the House unless he is shifted. This is the only thing that moves Margesson. Winston refuses to listen to talk against Anderson, or any other minister. He says, 'I have formed this Government and I don't want to have to change it.' Bracken has, indeed, been forbidden by P.M. to mention Anderson's name again. Attlee has also made a vain endeavour to get a change. P.M., says Morton, is a combination of a genius and a naughty boy. He takes a puckish delight in side-tracking the anti-Anderson campaign. When Morton, the other day, broached the subject, the P.M. turned upon him with a bland smile and, holding out a newspaper, said, 'Have you read this most interesting news about the price of gold in New York?'

1 Lieutenant-Commander R. T. H. ('Rex') Fletcher, later 1st Baron Winster (1885–1961). Parliamentary Private Secretary to A. V. Alexander, First Lord of the Admiralty 1940–41. Labour M.P. for Nuneaton 1935–42; Liberal M.P. for Basingstoke 1923–4. Minister of Civil Aviation 1945–6. Governor of Cyprus 1946–8.

P.M. is naturally greatly focused on home defence, and seems to have ticked off Ironside the other day. He asked the latter how many more guns he wanted, and when a certain figure was mentioned, he leant forward in his chair and said, ' ... (a most expressive monosyllable), General.'

Morton recounts a terrible story, pieced together from versions of Spears and others who have lately been in France, of the complete moral and physical collapse of the Government. This really began, he says, as soon as they left Paris. When they got to Tours there were no telephones and no authority. When they got to Bordeaux the ministers were found eating sardines with their fingers, and Reynaud's mistress[1] is said to have penetrated to a Cabinet meeting and to have been found sitting on his knee, in the presence of the others, tearing up the note which he was trying to draft and saying, 'Ah, but you are still a Frenchman. You are not an Englishman. You can't write like that.' One returned Englishman said, 'This is not France any more; it is Haiti.' All this may well be coloured up, but it is not quite fiction. Lebrun,[2] they say, is 'the best guarded thing in France'. Therefore an attempt to bring him away to safety did not succeed.

Jebb came to see me. He has been offered a job of some importance under Monckton[3] in connection with press censorship. He and Cadogan are trying to think out a plan for better control of problems of common interest to me and others. It is now suggested that Eden and I might have a joint responsibility, with a good soldier jointly responsible to both of us, and, under him, the organisation bifurcating into military and civilian branches. The Foreign Office would fade out of this picture, except that it might be useful to have a relatively junior person from the Foreign Office as liaison with the new organisation. I said that I would be quite willing to work such a scheme, if others agreed.

Saturday 22nd June
For the first time since I became Minister I spent a night out of Lon-

---

1 Reynaud's mistress was Countess Hélène de Portes. She was believed to have a strong, and malign, influence over the French Prime Minister. She was killed in a car accident on 28th June 1940, a week after this entry.
2 Albert Lebrun (1871–1950). President of the Republic 1932–40. Minister in Clemenceau's War Cabinet 1917–18.
3 Sir Walter T. Monckton, later 1st Viscount (1891–1965). Director-General of the Press and Censorship Bureau 1939–40; Ministry of Information 1940–41. British Propaganda and Information Services, Cairo 1941–2. Solicitor-General 1945. Conservative M.P. 1951–7. Minister of Labour and National Insurance 1951–5; Minister of Defence 1955–6; Paymaster-General 1956–7.

don, motoring down to Davenport's[1] house at Hinton Waldrist with the Wilmots.

Sunday 23rd June
It has been a pleasant break, although rain nearly all the time. Motor back after addressing a body of L.D.V. [Local Defence Volunteers][2] in Davenport's back yard. They are amused by my quoting the saying that 'we are now in the Final, and we shall have the advantage of playing on our own ground'. I nearly create a local crisis earlier in the day by inadvertently ringing an outside bell in Davenport's garden. The rule is that no outside bells, and notably Church bells, are to be rung any more, except if German parachutists appear. Fortunately, this bell does not seem to be heard. Halifax told Anderson in my presence yesterday that he thought it would have a most depressing effect throughout the countryside that Church bells should be silenced. Anderson replied, first, that this was done in the last war (which Halifax did not know), and second, that the two Archbishops had given their consent. This rather bowled out Halifax, who could only reply, 'The Archbishops always support the wrong side.'

Terms of the German armistice to Pétain[3] are announced. It is a shocking business. The practical questions now are how far Frenchmen, in addition to the valiant General de Gaulle,[4] will make a France across the Water; how far we can rely upon the French colonies; and what arrangements can be made regarding the French fleet.

Monday 24th June
Still waiting for definite news about the French fleet. Campbell[5] was

1 Nicholas Davenport (1893–1979). City Editor of the *New Statesman* 1930–53; Financial Correspondent of the *Spectator* 1953–79. Davenport lived at Hinton Manor near Oxford. Public Relations Officer for the wartime clothes rationing scheme at the Board of Trade from 1941. Member of the National Investment Council 1946–7. Co-founder of the XYZ Club, a semi-secret study group providing the Labour Party with inside information about the City.
2 'Local Defence Volunteers': precursor to the Home Guard.
3 Marshal Henri Pétain (1856–1951). Pétain had replaced Reynaud as French Prime Minister on 16th June 1940, and signed an armistice with Hitler at 6.50 p.m. on 22nd June 1940. In July, the French Chamber of Deputies assembled at Vichy voted him full powers.
4 General Charles de Gaulle (1890–1970). Under-Secretary for War in the Reynaud Government 1940. De Gaulle broadcast to the French people on 18th June, five days before this entry. Following this appeal, he became the leader of Free French resistance outside France. President of the French Fifth Republic 1959–69. Prime Minister 1944–6; 1958–9.
5 Sir Ronald Hugh Campbell (1883–1953). British Ambassador to France 1939–40; Portugal 1940–45.

very desperate in his last messages from Bordeaux. He was dealing, he said, with 'a crook' (Baudouin)[1] and 'an old dotard' (Pétain). 'French personalities', he says, linger on in Bordeaux, hoping that things will improve. He arranges shipping facilities for them, at their request, and then they do not take it up. Why don't these damned fools come away? Herriot[2] and Jeanneney,[3] whom one had hoped to see away, are now to stay – 'to soften the blow', as they feebly say.

I tell Attlee that, in my view, it is high time that the Cabinet took sharp decisions to disrecognise Bordeaux and to recognise whatever else can be collected. Campbell reports that Weygand has fallen into a 'mysterious disinterested mood'. France, he says, has committed grave sins for which she must now suffer. This old man is a black mystic. Clemenceau[4] once said of him that he was 'knee-deep in priests'.

Stanczyk[5] comes to see me with an attractive young interpreter called Gaszynski. He gives a shocking picture of the scenes in France – French soldiers running away and German soldiers 'controlling the traffic'; French soldiers selling their arms in the streets of Bordeaux; one Polish Division fighting its way south along the coast; two others in the Maginot Line, one fighting its way into Switzerland; Mandel's office at Bordeaux surrounded by armed soldiers, entry refused to all visitors, and telephone communications with the Minister likewise cut off, his secretary saying, 'The Minister is not allowed to speak to anyone.'

Tuesday 25th June
Go to the Cabinet and get authority to blockade France! Both occupied and unoccupied territories are, in effect, to be blockaded and plans to be concerted with the Admiralty for diversion of ships, etc.

---

1 Paul Baudouin (1895–1964). Banker and politician. Foreign Minister in the Pétain Government 1940–41. Minister of State and Member of the Council of Ministers 1940–44. Under-Secretary for Foreign Affairs in the Reynaud Cabinet 1940. Tried and convicted for collaboration 1947. Served five years in prison, and then returned to banking.
2 Edouard Herriot (1872–1957). President of the French Assembly 1936–44. Radical Socialist politician. Prime Minister 1924–5 and for one day in 1926; Prime Minister and Foreign Minister 1932. President of the National Assembly 1947–54.
3 Jules Jeanneney (1864–1957). President of the French Senate 1932–42.
4 Georges Clemenceau (1841–1929). French Socialist leader. Prime Minister 1917–20.
5 Jan Stanczyk (1886–1953). Polish trade unionist, who had escaped to Paris before the German occupation of Warsaw. Minister of Labour and Social Welfare in General Sikorski's government-in-exile.

The French still don't arrive here. Their insularity and non-travelling habit are coming out with a rush.[1] There is no 'French National Committee' around General de Gaulle. It is, as Corbin says to Halifax, 'a construction of the imagination'. French resolution in the colonies seems also to be crumbling. The position regarding the French fleet is still very unsatisfactory and uncertain. We shall 'spare neither patience nor resolution,' says the P.M. today in the House. We are shadowing some of their biggest ships, but we haven't a large enough fleet to do everything we should like to do.

'A very disagreeable message' from the Bordeaux Government is delivered to the Foreign Office by Cambon.[2] Corbin, who won't stay much longer here as Ambassador, would not deliver it himself. It demands the recall of our Consuls, who have been admirably active and tenacious, in North Africa, and the return of de Gaulle to France.

John Wilmot, having read a lump of telegrams from Egypt, the Balkans, Turkey, Iraq, Japan, etc., says, 'When things begin to go wrong, everyone turns against you ...... I suppose they have all had a lot to put up with from the British Empire in their time.'

Wednesday 26th June
Another day of infuriating uncertainty. Still no Frenchman blowing any trumpets anywhere except de Gaulle in London, and his trumpet blasts are becoming a bit monotonous. The 'National Committee' is still only a name. There are rumours of this and that notable Frenchman on his way to England, or in North Africa. Duff Cooper and Gort[3] have gone to North Africa trying to rally something. Still no hard news about the fleet ... These Frenchmen have all become sawdust, or, if you prefer another metaphor, we see before our eyes nothing less than the liquification of France.

National Executive Committee of the Labour Party meets this morning. Long-winded, trivial and rather hysterical, but no damage done.

Thursday 27th June
Bad news from North Africa. Liquification continues. The French

---

1 Marginal note: 'They are too much attached to their mistresses, and their soup [?], and their little properties!'
2 Roger Cambon (1882–1970). Minister at the French Embassy in London 1924–40.
3 General J. S. S. P. V. Gort, 6th Viscount, later Field Marshal (1886–1946). Commander-in-Chief British Field Force 1939–40. Chief of Imperial General Staff 1937–9. Governor and Commander-in-Chief, Gibraltar 1941–2; Malta 1942–4. High Commissioner and Commander-in-Chief, Palestine, and High Commissioner, Transjordan 1944–5.

will to fight is collapsing all round the Mediterranean. How clever of the Germans and Italians to wait a few days and do nothing! Duff Cooper and Gort have not seen Noguès;[1] they have, indeed, been refused an interview. Nor are they allowed to see the bunch of French ex-ministers who have arrived at Rabat, and are being treated practically like prisoners.

There is some move towards my taking over extended responsibilities, but this will need much handling to overcome personal jealousies and bureaucratic obstruction and delays.

"I GAVE YOU A NICE PLACARD IN EXCHANGE, DIDN'T I ?"

Friday 28th June

Lunch with Spears. He says that Van is much past his best. He no longer seems able to take decisions. He has been in the chair of a small committee dealing with Anglo-French things.

Spears said that when, at Bordeaux, Madame Laporte[2] and others jeered at the offer of Franco-British union, he said, 'It is as though England said to France, who had been for many years his beautiful

1 General Charles A. A. P. Noguès (1877–1971). Resident-General and Commander-in-Chief, Morocco 1936–42.
2 The Countess Hélène de Portes, q.v.

mistress, "Now that the Germans have thrown vitriol in your face, I am prepared to marry you".'

Today the Russians take Bessarabia. Our opportunities in Romania continually shrink. The Hankey Committee meets this afternoon and concludes that nothing much new can be done, though some things which have been authorised to be done may yet be done.

Talk to Attlee. French fleet. We must soon pass 'from patience to resolution'.

Dalton made an additional, separate note of his conversation over lunch with Spears on 28th June.

[Spears] says that in France he had less than three hours' sleep on the average for a fortnight. Pétain and Weygand were impregnated with the fear of a Bolshevik revolution. 'If we do not make peace now, the soldiers will shoot their officers.' It was as though one touched France, the façade of which was so familiar, and found that there was nothing solid left at all. It had all been eaten away by white ants. ...

The French political personages, for whom Campbell had secured passages on board ship, were never sure whether they wanted to go or not. He put them on the boat at midday, and at dusk they had run off again back to the British Consulate at Bordeaux to ask the latest news. Spears had even put aboard their mistresses – including Mandel's, 'a fat cow' – to make sure the men would come too.

Reynaud was never a strong man. He was only injected with confidence by Churchill. When Churchill went away he fell down again. His mistress, Madame Laporte, was an Anglophobe. She was always in the next room to the Cabinet at Tours and at Bordeaux. When the great offer of Franco-British Union came through, Reynaud sat at the telephone, with a piece of paper slipping about on a shiny table trying with a blunt pencil to take it down, and Spears held the paper on the table to prevent it from slipping, and then, when Reynaud took it into the next room, Madame Laporte snatched it from the hands of his secretary and said, 'Oh, this is only a trick to make France a British Dominion.' This, too, was the view expressed by many of his ministers.

Saturday 29th June
I receive a document from Cadogan for discussion by a small committee at the Foreign Office. It proposes to give much too much to D.M.I. [Director of Military Intelligence]. I concert counter-measures

and invoke the aid of Attlee. I think it should be under him, with me doing a good deal of it.[1]

Go to the country and only return on 30th June. It has been a rather quiet public weekend. It is clear that German air raids are only practice for the crews. They drop no bombs anywhere that matters. There is a tale at Aldbourne[2] that three bombs dropped 'on the common' some three miles from the village.

The Special Operations Executive (S.O.E.) was set up in July 1940, continuing the functions of several organisations concerned with sabotage and subversive propaganda ('Ungentlemanly Warfare', as Churchill called it) previously under the authority of the Foreign Office and the War Office. In particular, there was the former Section D, hitherto under the control of the Foreign Office, concerned primarily with sabotage; the research section of the general staff at the War Office, originally known as G.S.(R.) and later as M.I.(R.); and the internal department at the Foreign Office, called 'E.H.' or 'C.S.', concerned with 'black' propaganda against the enemy.

After a concerted campaign lasting several weeks to get control of the new, combined organisation, Dalton was asked by Churchill to take charge of S.O.E. on 16th July – with the task of co-ordinating all action by way of subversion and sabotage against the enemy overseas.[3]

S.O.E. was divided into two distinct branches. SO1, concerned with propaganda to enemy and enemy-occupied territories, was placed under a Foreign Office official, Rex Leeper, and operated from Woburn Abbey in Bedfordshire (referred to in the diary as C.H.Q. or, obliquely, as 'the country' or 'a country house'). SO2, which dealt with sabotage and was based on the former Section D, Dalton put under the control of Sir Frank Nelson (referred to by the symbol CD). Gladwyn Jebb, currently private secretary to Sir Alexander Cadogan (Permanent Under-Secretary at the Foreign Office) became Chief Executive Officer (C.E.O.), responsible for liaison with the Foreign Office and the intelligence service. Though nominally associated with SO1 as well, his influence there was slight; in SO2, however, Jebb took the chair at daily policy meetings (the 'Daily Council').

Jebb was based, with a small staff (including Robin Brook as his Personal Assistant), at Berkeley Square House, with the Minister. The other leading official connected with Special Operations was Sir Robert Vansittart, who

---

1 Against this passage Dalton has written: 'I get the assignment from P.M. on 16/7 (just under 3 weeks later) and approved by War Cabinet on 22/7 (3½ weeks)'. The assignment was to take over responsibility for S.O.E.
2 The Daltons owned a house at Aldbourne, near Marlborough, Wiltshire.
3 See pp. xx–xxvi.

became Dalton's Chief Adviser for S.O.E. Vansittart's influence, however, was never great, and soon became minimal.

Monday 1st July

Meeting at Foreign Office: Halifax, Hankey, Lord Lloyd, I, Cadogan, Menzies,[1] Beaumont-Nesbitt,[2] Morton, Jebb. I object to putting everything under the D.M.I. What we have in mind is not a military job at all. It concerns trade unionists, socialists, etc., the making of chaos and revolution – no more suitable for soldiers than fouling at football or throwing when bowling at cricket. Military intelligence, I say, is proliferating everywhere. Surely the War Office have enough on their plate at present. I don't think this quite pleases Menzies and Beaumont-Nesbitt, but they don't put up much fight. Hankey says the Foreign Office have prevented everything so far. Lloyd says to Halifax, 'You should never be consulted because you would never consent to anything; you will never make a gangster.' Morton suggests that we ought to have a single dictator, with a status similar to Swinton, for Home Security. On this broadly we agree. Who should it be? I have in mind Attlee with myself to do a lot of the work. But I do not mention his name in this *galère.* I afterwards speak to him about it and also write to him and to Halifax.

In the evening a meeting of senior Labour ministers – Attlee, Greenwood, Morrison, Bevin, Grenfell and I. Bevin talks nearly all the time. He will have to learn to be snappier. It is thought that the military may be trying to take too much upon themselves just now.

Revez[3] comes to see me. He has escaped from Paris via Bordeaux. More evidence about Madame de Portes. Reynaud was going to marry her when he had succeeded in divorcing his existing wife. She was the friend of Baudouin and Prouvost[4] and pushed them into the Cabinet. Reynaud was completely blind and allowed her to arrange all the appointments except that of de Gaulle. Baudouin had been for many years the agent of Mussolini. The German propagandists said, 'The idea of the Nation is finished; what matters now is Order.' They played on French fears of Communism. Hitler, having had experience

---

1 Major-General Sir Stewart Menzies (1890–1968). Chief of the S.I.S. [Special Intelligence Service] (Code Name 'C').
2 Major-General F. G. Beaumont-Nesbitt (1893–1971). Director of Military Intelligence 1939–40.
3 Revez. Not identified.
4 Jean Prouvost (1895–1978). Millionaire textile magnate, and press tycoon. At the time of this entry he had just joined the Cabinet as Minister of Information.

of Hindenburg, [1] thought Pétain would play a like role. He is an expert in dealing with senile soldiers. Prouvost found that the circulation of his papers had fallen from three millions in Paris to 50,000 in Bordeaux. Therefore, he wanted to go back to Paris! On Sunday, 10th June, Rcvez attended a press conference. He was told, 'There will be another conference here tomorrow afternoon.' But on the Monday everyone had gone. There was no one in the building. Everything was in complete disorder. The whole administration of France went phut in two or three hours. There was no administration and no real Government either in Tours or in Bordeaux. (This shows the weakness of over centralisation. Our diffused regional responsibility, even in moderate measure, is much better.)

On 3rd July the British seized or bombarded the French fleet, at Oran and elsewhere, causing the deaths of more than 1,200 French sailors. The Vichy regime responded by breaking off diplomatic relations. Some on the British side (including the British admiral, Sir James Somerville, in charge of the operation) felt that a grave political blunder had been committed.

Thursday 4th July
In the afternoon Winston makes his historic speech in the House on the necessary action taken at Oran and elsewhere against the French fleet. At the end we give him a much finer ovation than Old Corpse Upstairs ever got.

Friday 5th July
See Kingsley Wood on things generally. I ask him whether it is true that there is a strong movement inside the Conservative Party against Chamberlain's leadership. He says no, 'only a few glamour boys like what's-his-name ...... Cranborne.[2] And he has got a job now, so I daresay we shan't hear much more from him.' On the other hand, he thinks Chamberlain won't last very long. 'I was noticing him in the

---

1 Paul von Hindenburg (1847–1934). 2nd President of the Weimar Republic, in Germany 1925–34. Supreme Commander of the German Army 1916–19.
2 R. A. J. Gascoyne-Cecil, Viscount Cranborne, later 5th Marquess of Salisbury (1893–1972). Paymaster-General May–October 1940. Conservative M.P. for Dorset South 1929–41. Parliamentary Under-Secretary for Foreign Affairs 1935–8. Dominions Secretary 1940–42, 1943–5; Colonial Secretary 1942. Lord Privy Seal 1942–3, 1951–2; Secretary of State for Commonwealth Relations 1952; Lord President of the Council 1952–3; Acting Foreign Secretary June–October 1953.

Chair at a Cabinet Sub-Committee yesterday, and he looked awful.'
He thinks he will soon resign, but he will never go to the Lords. Winston, if he liked, could be leader of the Conservative Party in succession.

We speak of the Governor of the Bank. I say that there will be much
feeling against Catto[1] as successor. He comes from the most reactionary firm in the City, Morgan Grenfell, who, I say, have a notorious
record as partisan Tories and have, I suppose, contributed largely to
the Tory Party funds. Kingsley Wood does not take up this point nor
admit that Catto is intended to succeed Norman. He insists, however,
that he was born at Aberdeen and is of humble origin. Norman feels
the whole world which he built up is collapsing and may not go on
much longer. In three or four months he will be seventy. I ask whether
he would intend to resign in the middle of a year, and Kingsley Wood
says that nothing is actual yet. I say that there is a great deal to be said
for having a Governor from outside the City, which is really a very
narrow circle. We should stop in-breeding. He says he thinks there is
a good deal to be said for this in principle, but who would I suggest?
Old Stamp?[2] 'I can't make out his papers on finance. I like something
on finance that I can understand.' I say that I am not particularly
pressing Stamp, who has become rather old and long-winded. Wood
says, 'He's like me – an old Wesleyan. He always strikes me as being a
talker rather than a doer.' I ask what he thinks about Salter,[3] or Leith-
Ross. I say there would be some advantage in having a man with Civil
Service experience. Personally, I am inclined to think Salter would be
the best. His career has been varied, and a little bit of politics and
Government office lately will have done him no harm. Also he has
written some good books. Kingsley Wood says, 'Yes, I remember one
of them, in which he ticked us all off. He had several pages on me,
neither praising nor downing me too much.' But he thinks that it is important that 'whoever is appointed should have the confidence of the
City'. 'No doubt', he adds, 'I should have a good deal to say about
it.' ...

I also tell him that he ought to have a member of the Labour Party
as Financial Secretary. I think that Crookshank[4] has deserved pro-

1 Sir Thomas Catto, later 1st Baron (1879–1959). Financial Adviser to the Chancellor
  of the Exchequer 1940–44. Governor of the Bank of England 1944–9.
2 Josiah Stamp, 1st Baron (1880–1941). Economist and financial expert.
3 Arthur Salter, later 1st Baron (1881–1975). Parliamentary Secretary at the Ministry
  of Shipping (War Transport) 1939–42. Independent M.P. for Oxford University
  1939–50; Conservative M.P. for Ormskirk 1951–3. Chancellor of the Duchy of
  Lancaster 1945. Minister for Economic Affairs 1951–2; Minister of Materials
  1952–3.
4 H. F. C. Crookshank, later 1st Viscount (1893–1961). Financial Secretary to the
  Treasury 1939–43. Conservative M.P. for Gainsborough 1924–56. Junior minister

motion. He says he thinks so too and supposes he will get it soon. He would be quite glad to have a Labour Financial Secretary. Who? I ask whether he would like Shinwell? He thinks not. (I am thinking of Phil [Noel-] Baker, but do not name him.)

Kingsley Wood is most friendly, and urges me to come back again at any time. He is an engaging little rogue.

Dalton wrote in a separate note: 'I went on 6th July into the country and there met an intelligent group of persons in the Harness Room of an Aristocratic Establishment, now fallen down to the level of practical use as part of our national war effort.

'Before lunch I attended the Planning Committee. It was explained to me that this set-up was prepared soon after Munich. Its task was to disrupt the German Front by broadcasting, by leaflets dropped from the air, and by subversive leaflets, sent through other channels.

' ... I thought it was quite a good show and most of the people much above average.'[1] The Aristocratic Establishment in the country was Woburn Abbey, where the staff of what became SO1 were housed.

Saturday 6th July
With Ingram to a Country House,[2] where I find a good crowd assembled, with whom a useful talk on propaganda in enemy and enemy-occupied territories. I feel that this is all in the air until the Battle of Britain has been fought and won.

In a secret session of the House of Commons on 9th July, Dalton described the present organisation of his Ministry, in five main sections: (1) neutral trade (2) commodity control (3) pre-emption (4) financial pressure, including shipping control (5) economic intelligence and advisory work for the fighting services and other government departments.

1 Dated 14.7.40. Dalton Papers 7/3 (5), (6).
2 'a Country House': Woburn Abbey, requisitioned from the Duke of Bedford at the outbreak of war. In September 1938, Sir Campbell Stuart had been invited to organise a small Propaganda Department, which was moved to Woburn after war had been declared. Later Woburn (always referred to obliquely in this way) became the headquarters of SO1, the propaganda side of Dalton's new organisation.

1934–9. Paymaster-General 1943–5. Minister of Health 1951–2. Leader of the House of Commons 1951–5. Lord Privy Seal 1952–5.

'International Law must keep up with the facts,' he declared, against those who argued that strict legality in the conduct of the economic war should be maintained. 'We must make the law fit the war, rather than the other way round. I am glad to say that these practical requirements are now being realised.'[1]

Tuesday 9th July

Secret session on M.E.W. I speak for one and a half hours at the beginning, and half an hour at the end answering questions. It is said to have been a 'great Parliamentary triumph'. A remarkably friendly and interested reception from all parts of the House. Though I go on so long to a quite full House, I am told that only two members go out during my speech. A Tory said afterwards to Attlee, 'What strikes one about your chaps is that they know their job.' I think I succeeded in conveying a grasp of detail and a sense of vigour as well as telling a story largely unfamiliar to practically all those present. It is also generally appreciated, I think, that much of this could not have been told at all in public session. Foot comes in for half an hour in the middle and does quite well.

Attlee in a sentence as we pass, just before I get up to speak, says that it is settled I am to do something additional. Agreed today. Vansittart, not Gort, to help. Who thought of Gort?

Hancock says late tonight that, lunching with P.M.'s youngest Private Secretary,[2] he heard that I was to be head of No. 6.[3]

Wednesday 10th July

Party Meeting.[4] Hysterics, especially from South Wales, on alleged lack of local defence.

Congratulations from Drogheda, who sat in Peers' Gallery yesterday, thus living a dual life,[5] and from others. ...

7.15. See Attlee. He says it is all right. M.U.W. [Ministry of Ungentlemanly Warfare]. I say I should have same powers as the ex-hyphenate.[6] He agrees. Halifax in favour. I say that it is high time I was told officially, so that things can start.

1 FY, p. 351.
2 J. R. Colville, later Sir John (b. 1915). Assistant Private Secretary to the Prime Minister 1939–41, 1943–5. Principal Private Secretary to the Prime Minister 1951–5.
3 'No. 6': presumably the new secret organisation, though the reference is unclear.
4 'Party Meeting': a meeting of the Parliamentary Labour Party.
5 i.e. as a civil servant and a parliamentarian (in the House of Lords).
6 Viscount Swinton, formerly Sir Philip Cunliffe-Lister, q.v.

Gaitskell very pleased, and he and I have a drink on this.

9 p.m. Fletcher says that there has been a great to-do today. Beaumont-Nesbitt has been pulling every string. Chiefs of Staff Committee – always apt to be girlish – and Ismay threatening to resign. (I don't believe this.) P.M. a little bothered and reluctant. But it is said, I think by Morton, whom Fletcher knows well, that if Attlee digs his feet in he will win.

10 p.m. See Attlee again. He went straight to P.M. at 7.45 from his talk with me and it is true that there has been a strong counter-intrigue. The position of old Hankey is being exploited and it is suggested that Swinton might perhaps do it all. This he regards as fantastic. I tell him something of Fletcher's reports, though not mentioning the source. He says he will stand firm. I press for quick decision. Why should Chiefs of Staff object? I ask. Beaumont-Nesbitt is another story. Attlee says that he insists that much of what we mean must be done from the Left.

Tonight I write to four members of the Cabinet.

Dalton's letters to four Cabinet colleagues urged them to give him support in his bid to take over 'Ungentlemanly Warfare'.

Thursday 11th July
Send Gaitskell with letters to Attlee, Greenwood, Alexander and Sinclair. The two first are together in Attlee's office when my letters are delivered.

To War Cabinet at 12.15. A short item jointly with the Admiralty. All agreed. I was greeted, I thought, with a more than usually friendly smile from the P.M. and, finding myself beside the C.I.G.S. [Chief of Imperial General Staff],[1] noted that he too was most polite.

Arriving at the House, run into Fletcher. He says he thinks it is 'more favourable' today. But Hankey is still in the offing and Swinton is now being presented as 'the man who works 14 to 16 hours a day'. Those who don't want me to have too much ask whether I work as long as that? Or do I 'trust too much to others'?

Attlee rings up just before one and says, 'I am handling it; you can

---

1 General Sir John Greer Dill, later Field Marshal (1881–1944). Chief of Imperial General Staff 1940–41. Head of British Joint Staff Mission, United States 1941–4. Director of Military Operations and Intelligence at the War Office 1934–6. Commander of 1st Army Corps in France 1939–40.

safely leave it to me; you do not need to approach anyone else.' This suggests that he may have been vexed at my writing to Greenwood too, but the latter, seen later in the day, says this is not so.

Greenwood, whom I meet in the afternoon, says that he and Attlee saw the P.M. just before the Cabinet and were very firm. The P.M., just off to inspect some coast defences, told Attlee to 'fix it up with ...... ' I speak of Beaumont-Nesbitt and the rest. Greenwood says, 'Oh the P.M. just brushed all that away at once.'

10.30 p.m. In touch, through Topham,[1] with Attlee, who telephones, 'It is going on all right.'

Friday 12th July

Lunch with Sikorski[2] and Raczynski,[3] Attlee also present. It is clear that Sikorski likes the English better than the French. He is a little haughty about the Czechs – there are 25 million Poles and only, at the very outside, 13 million Czechs and Slovaks; the Poles fought and the Czechs didn't; the Czechs have had a puppet government in Prague all the time; no Pole has accepted such a task for Hitler. ...

I leave with Attlee who says, 'It is all right now. You are to do it, with Van and, if you like, Maurice Peterson and whoever else you like. Swinton will go on doing what he is doing now. I think that he wants watching. I have told them that you will be quite tactful in dealing with the brass hats. The objections raised were not political at all. I think they came from someone in the P.M.'s entourage.' I say, 'Well, it is about time something was settled.'

Saturday 13th July

Speak to Morton after Cabinet. 'Who has tried to upset the Cabinet decision of last Tuesday?' I ask.[4] He says, 'No one. It was the P.M. himself who afterwards had some doubts as to which was the best way to organise it and wondered whether the whole thing shouldn't be under one head, linking up with what Swinton is doing now.' ...

I say I suppose that D.M.I. had really been at the bottom of the trouble. Morton says he does not think so, though no doubt some of the Generals had not liked the idea.

During this conversation he speaks ill of many and well of no one,

1 A. M. R. Topham. Principal Private Secretary to Attlee, as Lord Privy Seal.
2 General W. Sikorski (1881–1943). Commander-in-Chief of the Polish Army 1939–43. Polish Prime Minister 1922–3. Minister of Military Affairs 1923–5. Prime Minister of government-in-exile 1941–3. Killed in an air crash July 1943.
3 Count E. Raczynski (b. 1891). Polish Ambassador in London 1934–45. Acting Foreign Minister 1941–2. Minister of State in charge of Foreign Affairs in the Cabinet of General Sikorski 1942–3.
4 i.e. concerning the setting up of S.O.E.

except the Colonel[1] who, he says, has a mind rather like the P.M.'s.

After lunch I go by car to Richmond Terrace with Attlee. He says, 'It's all settled now; you are to have it.' He thinks Morton worked on the P.M. He says, 'He takes too much upon himself. He wants watching too.' I show impatience at the delay.

I hear later in the evening that Morton rang up Gaitskell and said that everything was now all right and that I should have a letter from the P.M. within forty-eight hours. Either, I think, after my talk with him this morning, he rang up the P.M. in the country, or, Attlee, after my talk with him this afternoon, got on to Morton.

Meet de Gaulle at lunch with Mrs Phillimore. Not an inspiring or romantic figure, rather stiff and a Staff Officer more than a Commander-in-Chief. Reynaud, he says, was *'très mal entouré'*.

He is in favour of setting up a Free French Government in the Cameroons. Here the spirit is very good and both the colonists and the natives remember the Germans and don't want them back. It is also well situated in relation to British West African colonies. De Gaulle quite understands the need to have politicians at the head of the Government. The boat, with 50 deputies on board, including some excellent ministers, is still at Casablanca. The rumour that she had got away from Gibraltar to Marseilles is false. It was on this rumour that P.M. spoke sharply to Alexander and First Sea Lord in Cabinet the other day. Alexander would like to cut her out, but the difficulties are considerable, for she is right inside the harbour, where the French have coast defences and also a number of submarines and small service warships.

Monday 15th July

I hear from Gaitskell that Morton told Hall, who lunched with him, that P.M.'s letter to me should go off today! What circumlocutory gossip! Same channel reports that Attlee 'has been very firm'.

Ingrams hears that Cranborne, as well as Swinton and Lord Lloyd, have been proposed. Elsewhere I hear of Keyes[2] and Admiral Cork and Orrery.[3] (Two days later I hear the latter was proposed by Hankey.)

1 Lt-Colonel L. Grand. Head of D Section, which became part of S.O.E. Dismissed September 1940, when D Section was overhauled.
2 Admiral of the Fleet Sir Roger Keyes, 1st Bart, later 1st Baron (1872–1945). Director of Combined Operations 1940–41. Conservative M.P. for Portsmouth North 1934–43. Commander-in-Chief, Mediterranean 1925–8, 1929–31.
3 W. H. D. Boyle, 12th Earl of Cork and Orrery (1873–1967). Admiral of the Fleet 1938. Served at the Admiralty and in Norway 1939–40. Home Guard 1941–2. President of the Royal Naval College, Greenwich 1929–32. Commander-in-Chief, Home Fleet 1933–5; Portsmouth 1937–9.

Fletcher says that Alexander was rather 'gruff and unfriendly' over my communication. 'The less I know the better.'

Tuesday 16th July

Rung up by Jebb and congratulated. Also by the Colonel [Grand] in a gesture at a P.O.G. Meeting. Draft from Rucker[1] of terms of reference. Jebb to dine at House of Commons. Will he do it? I think yes, and at B.S.H. [Berkeley Square House].[2] He will be an emollient. Vansittart will remain where he is. Jebb quotes Cadogan as having said of de Gaulle, 'It's a pity he has a head like a banana and hips like a woman.' King-Hall[3] also knows too much and speaks to me in House of Commons.

Late that night to Attlee, whom I thank. He says it has been 'a labour of love'. 'They' said that Vansittart wouldn't work with me. This was the last effort. He then rings up No. 10 and P.M. asks me to go round. It is 11.30 p.m.

I find P.M. alone in Cabinet Room, though it appears later that Morton and Lord Salisbury were in Morton's room next door. P.M. says, 'I was just writing to you' (I wonder! I think he had had the letter brought in when he knew I had arrived). The letter to be signed by him was on the table. I ask whether he is really sure that he wants me to do a little more. He says, 'Yes, certainly.' The only doubt raised by some was whether Vansittart and I would co-operate. He has seen him and is quite satisfied. I say, 'Why yes, we are very old friends and all through these years he, you and I have thought the same.' He then commends to me a certain young man who has much impressed him and has not been properly used.[4] Also he says, 'This must come from the Left.'

Lord Salisbury and Morton then join us and much talk about the E.H. [Electra House].[5] I tone down the main attack.

Wednesday 17th July

P.M.'s letter at last arrives. See Lord President on draft. This is

1 A. N. Rucker, later Sir Arthur (b. 1895). Principal Private Secretary to the Prime Minister 1939–40. Seconded for special duties 1941; Deputy Secretary at the Ministry of Health 1943–8.
2 Berkeley Square House was the headquarters of M.E.W.
3 Commander Stephen King-Hall, later Baron (1893–1966). National Labour M.P. for Ormskirk 1939–42; Independent (having resigned the whip) 1942–5. Director of Publicity at the Ministry of Fuel and Power 1942–3.
4 From later entries it appears that 'a certain young man' was probably Gladwyn Jebb.
5 Propaganda department (headed by Sir Campbell Stuart, q.v.), which was shortly to be absorbed into the new Special Operations Executive, as SO1.

substantially agreed. I don't think it necessary to argue too much about words. There is to be no razzle. It would not be worth the candle.

See Sinclair in the afternoon. Very friendly. Likewise, he says, his staff towards me. Later see Vansittart. When asked by P.M. on Monday night (15th) whether he would work with me, he replied saying we had been not only friends, but very close friends, for many years and had thought alike. As to age, there is much less between him and me than between him and Eden. P.M., he says, seemed much relieved at his attitude. I then propose to Vansittart that Jebb should be, under him, my principal officer. He takes this very well indeed and seems quite keen. Later, he develops an attack on Campbell Stuart and proposes in his place Rex Leeper[1] who, he says, has not been at all well treated, has become somewhat discouraged, but has the right point of view in addition to ability and experience, and, if encouraged, would soon revive. I write tonight to Cadogan asking for Jebb.[2] Vansittart had warned me that, if refused, I should go straight to P.M. about this. I am confident that this will not be necessary.

Friday 19th July
First meeting, *à quatre*, with Van, Jebb and Gaitskell; laying plans. Jebb to begin by surveying the existing field. He has already assured Ismay that I shall not tear off his badges of rank when I meet him! ...

Meet Catto at lunch with Leith-Ross. A small, plebeian, undistinguished man. I cannot believe that he would really fill the bill, or, if appointed, be a serious snag, in succession to Norman. (I find that immediately after our lunch I jotted down 'Common little man – not really dangerous!') ...

Gaitskell says that Lady Listowel[3] told him that Virginio Gayda[4] told her that 'Hugh Dalton is the only Englishman who understands Mussolini'.

Saturday 20th July
Enter, for the first time in my life, the Ministry of Information to confer with Duff Cooper on the re-organisation of the Country Establishment.[5] I find him quite reasonable, and it is agreed that

1 R. Leeper, later Sir Reginald (1888–1968). Assistant Under-Secretary at the Foreign Office 1940–43. Head of SO1 1940–43. See Appendix A.
2 Gladwyn Jebb was Sir Alexander Cadogan's Principal Private Secretary.
3 Judith, Lady Listowel, née de Marffy-Mantuano. Married William Hare, 5th Earl of Listowel, junior Labour whip in the Lords, 1933. Hungarian by birth.
4 Virginio Gayda (1885–1944). Italian journalist and editor of *Giornale d'Italia* since 1926.
5 See Diary entry for 6th July 1940, n. 2 (p. 55).

Vansittart and Peterson, whom he is appointing, will have to work out a practical division. This should be based, he thinks, and I agree, on the nature, rather than the manner of delivery, of the material. The Ministry of Information seeks, he says, to give information otherwise not obtainable abroad.

There is too much quack, quack, quack going on. I think it is probably worst of all in the Clubs of the West End, where not only are conversations overheard, but it is noted who goes with whom, and on this basis inferences drawn and gossip continually embellished.

Monday 22nd July
The War Cabinet agreed this morning to my new duties. 'And now', said the P.M., 'go and set Europe ablaze.'

Fletcher to lunch. I tell him that he has hitherto concealed successfully from nearly all the world his Christian name. He says that it is Rex. I ask him to keep things sweet between the First Lord, to whom he continues to be P.P.S., old Keyes and me – a sort of triangular liaison. He says that Keyes has been saying that he has 'sailed into action' against my new appointment, but I understand that, having seen the P.M., he sailed out again!

In the afternoon 'ministers above the line' are invited to Air Ministry to hear Kingsley Wood's Budget proposals for tomorrow. His presentation is very dull. The Budget, reasonable enough in detail, lacks any bigness of conception.

After this performance, Sinclair talks about the Air. Our superiority, man for man and plane for plane, over the Germans is astonishing. They have been sending as many aeroplanes over us, night by night, as we have sent over them, but their results are negligible and ours most formidable. Their pilots, in particular, have very poor maps.

Lindemann dines with me at the St Regis Hotel ... It is conveniently near my Ministry and has the advantage of not being too obvious. I tell Lindemann that I am appalled at the amount of quack quack which goes on in West End Clubs and other public places over matters relating to the war. Some tell me, I say, that the Athenaeum is a little safer than some other Clubs, but I doubt even this. It is always observed, I say, who is with whom, and intelligent guesses are then made as to why they are together. He says there is an old proverb that 'At the Athenaeum you can't hear yourself speak for the noise of the grinding of axes'.

He strikes me as rather old, but very amiable. It is useful, I think, to keep in touch with him since he advises the P.M. on 'everything which has a scientific or technical aspect', including all questions involving statistics. He is, of course, a great Winstonite, and we spend some time recounting and denouncing the errors of the past. Lindemann says that whenever, from 1932 onwards, they had to take a decision in foreign policy, they took it wrong. They would have done much better, he says, if every time they had decided by tossing a coin. Then, at least, they would probably have been right half the time.

Tuesday 23rd July
A bad day, full of delays and irritations! ...

On the other hand, I have a considerable success with Old Keyes, who calls upon me at the House of Commons and with whom I have a hearty and friendly conversation. He no longer fears, I think, at the end that I intend to issue him with daily orders. He grumbles about the Admiralty – as all sailors do – and tells me a long rambling story in favour of the King of the Belgians and against Gort.[1] Gort, he says, 'lost all his records' of events in France leading up to the evacuation at Dunkirk. The Admiral,[2] on the other hand, kept all his and so has, apparently, much the better of the controversy. He has compiled a long report which, he says, the Foreign Office told him was 'unanswerable'. He says that Gort showed no courage at all in reporting home the real situation to the Cabinet. Keyes prepared a full appreciation several days before the collapse of the Belgian Army and showed it to Gort, who said that he entirely agreed with it. Keyes said, 'Then you had better send it home yourself in your own name.' But Gort would not do this, and so Keyes had to send it himself, adding that he had shown it to Gort who agreed with it. In fact, contrary to the allegations of Reynaud and the French and British High Command, the King of the Belgians had given three days' notice, through Keyes, who had conveyed it to Gort, that the Belgian Army could not continue its resistance. It was a cowardly lie to say that the King ordered them to lay down their arms without having told his Allies. Moreover, when Gort consented to a futile southward offensive with troops lacking equipment, munitions and food, in a vain hope of meeting a northward push by the French, which Weygand had promised but which never took place, this had the effect of leaving the Belgians in the air. Keyes made it clear that he regarded Gort as a complete washout and that he had had more than he deserved in being given the appointment of Inspector General of the Forces.

In the afternoon I tell the N.C.L. [National Council of Labour] about the work of my Ministry. They take it very well and are interested and impressed. It is a good story, though most of it cannot be told in public.

1 Gort had commanded the B.E.F., which was evacuated at Dunkirk.
2 i.e. Admiral Keyes, who was Director of Combined Operations, appointed by Churchill on 17th July 1940.

Wednesday 24th July

A rather better day. Spend the morning with the National Executive of the Labour Party. Nothing very important, but it is essential to keep contact and make sure that blunders are not committed.

Thursday 25th July

A swarm of callers in the morning: young Colvin,[1] the P.M.'s protégé – intelligent, critical and indiscreet, it seems; Sir Frank Nelson,[2] who makes rather a good impression; Colonel Harold Gibson,[3] who has been engaged on all sorts of miscellaneous enterprises, recommended by Amery but distrusted by Attlee – he ends by denouncing Sir H. Quisling and saying that neither the Ministers of Supply nor Labour are being well served by their principal permanent officials, Robinson[4] and Phillips,[5] and that there is resentment in high Civil Service circles at the amount of co-ordinating being done by Attlee and Greenwood; Valentine Williams[6] and Brigadier Brooks,[7] who have come up from the country in a great state of concern about the future of their organisation, which they are most anxious should not be split in two.

A final fidget in the middle of the morning about my Navicerts[8] announcement which was to have been made this afternoon in reply to a private notice question. Sir Samuel Hoare[9] is now asking for further delay in order that he may break it gently to the Spanish

1 Ian Colvin. A journalist, who worked first for S.O.E. and later for the Political Warfare Executive and at Combined Operations Headquarters.
2 Sir Frank Nelson (1883–1966). Executive Director of S.O.E. 1940–42. Codename: 'C.D.' See Appendix A.
3 Colonel Harold Gibson (1884–1961). Attached to the Ministry of Information 1940–45.
4 Sir (William) Arthur Robinson (1874–1950). Secretary at the Ministry of Supply 1939–40. Permanent Secretary at the Air Ministry 1917–20. Secretary at the Ministry of Health 1920–35.
5 Sir Thomas Phillips (1883–1966). Permanent Secretary at the Ministry of Labour 1935–44; Ministry of National Insurance 1944–8.
6 Valentine Williams (1883–1946). Journalist, author and playwright. In charge of the SO1 establishment at Woburn.
7 Brigadier R. A. Dallas Brooks, later General Sir Reginald (1896–1966). SO1 Liaison Officer to Chiefs of Staff. Commandant General of the Royal Marines 1946–9. Governor of Victoria, Australia 1949–63.
8 In order to control cargoes from neutral ports at source, all merchant shipping was required to apply for 'navicerts' before embarking, in order to ensure immunity from interception. Much of M.E.W.'s work involved trying to make the navicert system effective. See p. xvi.
9 Sir Samuel Hoare, q.v., at this time Ambassador in Madrid, had been a leading appeaser. This was a typical dispute between M.E.W. and the Foreign Office: the first wanted to make the blockade effective, the second to avoid antagonising neutrals or encouraging the Germans to invade them.

Government. There is also a great dispute about the oil stocks in Spain. My officials take one view and Slimy Sam's advisers in Madrid another. I agree reluctantly to postpone the statement till next Tuesday, since I am anxious just now to be friendly with Halifax and Cadogan, who is being very accommodating in releasing Jebb, but I say to Halifax very firmly that we cannot allow Hoare to begin arguing against Cabinet decisions. I make it pretty clear that, if this is attempted, I shall make serious trouble. It is most important, moreover, not to discourage the U.S.A., who at present are playing up very well about oil (they are inclined, indeed, to play almost too well, since they are now contemplating some plan whereby all exports of oil would be prohibited, though apparently there would be a loophole left through which we would get what we wanted for ourselves). ...

Later see Major Davies,[1] in civil life connected with Courtaulds, who makes a good impression on me (he is No. 2 to Colonel Holland,[2] who is away in Scotland), also Jebb and Cavendish-Bentinck.[3] This latter slightly irritates me, and I tell him that if I come on any obstruction from the Foreign Office or anywhere else I shall report it to the P.M. Major Davies says there has been a lack of drive and decision. He obviously wants me to begin to supply these deficiencies. I find that Quintin Hogg[4] has recommended to Colonel Holland that Crossman[5] and Gordon Walker[6] should be used to inform us about

1 Major F. T. Davies. In charge of training potential agents for S.O.E.
2 Colonel J. C. F. Holland (1897–1956). Head of M.I.(R.) at the beginning of the war. His chief assistant was Lt-Colonel Colin Gubbins, q.v. M.I.(R.) became part of the SO2 organisation.
3 V. F. W. Cavendish-Bentinck, later Baron (b. 1897). Chairman of the Joint Intelligence Committee of Chiefs of Staff 1939–45. Foreign Office adviser to the Director of Plans 1942–5.
4 Quintin Hogg, later 2nd Viscount Hailsham (b. 1907). Conservative M.P. for Oxford 1938–50; St Marylebone 1963–70. Junior minister 1945. First Lord of the Admiralty 1956–7; Minister of Education 1957; Lord President of the Council 1957–9 and 1960–64. Lord Privy Seal 1959–60. Minister for Science and Technology 1959–64; Secretary of State for Education and Science 1964. Lord Chancellor 1970–74 and since 1979. Hogg had been elected at a celebrated by-election in Oxford in 1938; Crossman and Gordon Walker, both socialist dons, had campaigned on the other side.
5 R. H. S. Crossman (1907–74). Briefly head of German Bureau, SO1 at Woburn; then placed in charge of the technical side of broadcasting subversive propaganda to Germany in August 1940. Deputy-Director Psychological Warfare, Allied Forces Headquarters Algiers 1943. Assistant Chief Psychological Warfare Division, S.H.A.E.F. 1944–5. Labour M.P. Coventry East 1945–74. Minister of Housing and Local Government 1964–6; Lord President of the Council and Leader of the House of Commons 1966–8; Secretary of State for Social Services 1968–70. Editor of *New Statesman* 1970–72.
6 P. C. Gordon Walker, later Baron Gordon-Walker (1907–80). Student of Christ Church, Oxford. Labour M.P. for Smethwick 1945–64; Leyton 1966–74. Junior

German conditions. I am surprised and amused at this, but not altogether pleased.

Friday 26th July

Gaitskell says that Lees-Smith said, after my private session speech, that I was the only possible successor to the Prime Minister! This comes from the cold brutality of my speech!

Eccles[1] comes to see me and talks very well about Spain and Portugal. Able and a thruster, but said also to be a social climber and a snob. Spaniards, he thought, were now dropping their isms and gazing with distaste at the Germans just across the Pyrenees. As to oil, there is a difference of view regarding figures of stocks and consumption. Eccles thinks that stocks equal to two months' supply would be reasonable and would be accepted by the Spaniards.

We make a number of jokes about Hoare. 'I was frightened,' he said in Parliament in 1932[2] after his Corridor-for-camels plan had failed. He had stood there, making his apologia, with a bit of plaster stuck on his broken nose – he had fallen down while skating – and as he had proceeded he had begun to cry, and the tears had loosened the plaster so that, when he had left the House of Commons, audibly sobbing, he had had difficulty in finding the door. 'I was frightened'! Lees-Smith, who was sitting next to me on the Front Opposition Bench, had said at this point, 'I never thought I should live to hear a British Foreign Secretary say such a thing in public.'

This incident returns to me when Eccles says that Hoare told him that he was sure that if the Germans entered Spain they would regard him as their most important capture. 'After all, I am a British ex-Foreign Secretary.' He seemed to think that they would take particular delight in putting him into a Concentration Camp. Eccles relates that he replied – though perhaps he did not – 'I think they would attach more value to capturing one or two good British bomber pilots.'

1 D. M. Eccles, later 1st Viscount (b. 1904). Economic Adviser to the Ambassadors in Madrid and Lisbon 1940–42. Recruited to M.E.W. in 1939. Conservative M.P. for Chippenham 1943–62. Minister of Works 1951–4; Education 1954–7, 1959–62. President of the Board of Trade 1957–9. Paymaster-General (with responsibility for the Arts) 1970–73.

2 *sic.* The date should be 1935, however. This reference is to the notorious Hoare-Laval pact, which aimed to extricate Britain from her obligations to Abyssinia. The phrase 'Corridor for Camels' was used as the headline to the First Leader in *The Times* on 6th December 1935.

---

minister 1947–50. Secretary of State for Commonwealth Relations 1950–51. Foreign Secretary 1964–5. Minister without Portfolio 1966–7; Secretary of State for Education and Science 1967–8.

Hoare has already sent several telegrams regarding his mode of escape and, as Jebb said to me this morning, 'When the first German soldier puts his foot on Spanish soil, Hoare will be in Lisbon.' Every night he puts a ladder up against the garden wall before he goes to bed.

In late July, Neville Chamberlain fell ill and had to undergo major surgery. He resigned his office as Lord President of the Council at the end of September, by which time it was clear that he had an incurable cancer. He died on 9th November.

Tuesday 30th July

Chamberlain is to have an operation. It seems most unlikely that he will ever return to active politics. In this fashion, under physical rather than political pressure, will be accomplished the demand that 'Chamberlain must go'.

Another story about Hoare. At Lisbon, dining with Sir Walford and Lady Selby,[1] he was boring on, as usual, about his personal danger if the Germans entered Spain, and of the importance of arranging for his own retreat. Lady Selby, whom I always thought a rather tart and unpleasant woman, said, 'You must remember, Sir Samuel, that you are no longer a politician but have become a diplomat. When a professional diplomat is in a dangerous post, he always acts like the Captain of a sinking ship. He stays to the last.' It is said that Hoare turned very green at this remark. ...

Secret session on foreign affairs. Winston in grand form, both before and during. He now leads the whole House, unquestioned and ascendant. ...

In the evening Wilmot and Jebb and I dine at the House. I am anxious to make them know and like each other. It goes quite well. Jebb says that Ironside, though he can speak eight languages, has a brain the size of a pea. It is a good thing that he is now only a retired Field Marshal. He also says that Van nowadays is very apt to listen to the last word.

Wednesday 31st July

Cripps from Moscow is grumbling that no one will receive him. He

---

1 Sir Walford Selby (1881–1965) and Lady Selby, née Orme Carter. Selby was Ambassador to Portugal 1937–40. Dalton had first encountered him as Principal Private Secretary to the Foreign Secretary 1924–32.

has been kept waiting twelve days for an interview with Molotov, for which he has asked on three occasions. He is refusing to see subordinates. If this goes on, he says, he thinks he should be recalled. This is both amusing and troublesome. ...

Jebb says that I am known in some quarters as 'Dr Dynamo'!

I spend a curious evening at Stornoway House, Beaverbrook's residence. I am invited to dine there at 9 p.m. and find, in addition to Lord Beaverbrook, Lord Horne,[1] who has the delicacy not to mention any of his private interests throughout the evening; Bruce Lockhart,[2] who makes up to me and is most well informed on all sorts of discussions between ministers and their staffs, supposedly secret, which are now proceeding; Clem Davies,[3] who thinks that Lloyd George[4] ought to come back into the Government (a view which I vigorously contest on the ground that we need not older but younger leaders, and that Lloyd George has lost all large following in the country now), and Hugh Seely,[5] P.P.S. to Sinclair at the Air Ministry. Lord Beaverbrook is a most curious character, sitting silent for long periods while others talk and then suddenly bursting forth into violent harangues. No doubt, however, he too is dynamic! Much of the conversation consists in running down various ministers, particularly little Mr Cooper, whose days, Beaverbrook thinks, are numbered. Perhaps Beaverbrook, having immensely lifted the output of aircraft by laying hands, as some allege, on all spare parts, and foreseeing that soon there may be a sharp drop in the output, is anxious to appropriate little Mr Cooper's job and then denounce his own successor. Late in the evening three more curious characters enter, Brendan Bracken, Aneurin Bevan,[6] and Fletcher. The latter, who drives me home, says that Bracken was

1 Sir Robert Horne, 1st Viscount (1871–1940). Conservative M.P. 1918–37. Minister of Labour 1919–20. President of the Board of Trade 1920–21. Chancellor of the Exchequer 1921–2. He died on 3rd September, just over a month after this entry.
2 R. H. Bruce Lockhart, later Sir Robert (1887–1970). Author and journalist. British representative with the provisional Czech government 1940–41. Political Intelligence Department at the Foreign Office 1939–40. Deputy Under-Secretary at the Foreign Office and Director-General of the Political Warfare Executive 1941–5.
3 E. Clement Davies (1884–1962). Liberal M.P. for Montgomeryshire 1929–62; Leader of the Liberal Party 1945–56.
4 David Lloyd George, later 1st Earl Lloyd George of Dwyfor (1863–1945). Liberal M.P. for Carnarvon 1890–1945. President of the Board of Trade 1905–8; Chancellor of the Exchequer 1908–15; Minister of Munitions 1915–16; Secretary of State for War 1916. Prime Minister 1916–22. Leader of the Liberal Party 1926–31.
5 Sir Hugh Seely, 3rd Bart, later 1st Baron Sherwood (1898–1970). Liberal M.P. for Berwick-on-Tweed 1935–41; Norfolk East 1923–4. Junior minister 1941–5.
6 Aneurin Bevan (1897–1960). Labour M.P. for Ebbw Vale 1929–60. Minister of Health 1945–51; Minister of Labour and National Service 1951.

the real cause of the hang-up in recent arrangements regarding myself, having pressed upon the P.M. the view that no minister should be responsible for this particular task.[1] Lockhart had said earlier that Beaverbrook had said to him, 'If it comes to a fight in the Cabinet between Cooper and Dalton, Dalton will win hands down.'

1 i.e. control of S.O.E.

2

Dr Dynamo
August–December 1940

British politics in the last five months of 1940 was dominated by the Battle of Britain, the threat of invasion and the Blitz. For Dalton, now the Minister responsible for S.O.E. as well as for economic warfare, it was a time of intense activity. Blockade policy involved a constant battle (much of it at Cabinet level) between M.E.W. 'warmongers' who wanted to cut off supplies to Occupied Europe as effectively as possible, and Foreign Office 'appeasers' who were concerned not to alienate neutral governments – especially the government of the United States. Meanwhile the Admiralty pointed out the practical difficulty of intercepting ships. At S.O.E., Dalton pushed ahead with staff changes aimed at a more realistic approach to subversion, in place of the cloak-and-dagger romanticism that had pervaded the old Section D.

On the propaganda side, one consequence of the setting up of S.O.E. was a furious interdepartmental row between SO1 and the Ministry of Information. This dispute, which led to the setting up of the Political Warfare Executive (P.W.E.) under joint ministerial control, continued to rage throughout Dalton's period as Minister of Economic Warfare. One of the early problems concerned leaflets. Were leaflets dropped on enemy-occupied territories from aircraft overt or covert propaganda? It was ruled that they were covert, and therefore Dalton's responsibility. Since SO1 was secret, this meant that no Parliamentary Questions regarding such leaflets could be allowed, nor could any be published.

Thursday 1st August
Today we move from discussions to decisions, and I reach a modus vivendi with little Mr Cooper. I begin by proposing to him that I should appropriate an immense kingdom, much more than I expected

70

he would agree to. Against this he argues, not unnaturally, that he could not take responsibility in Parliament for what he did not control. I then ask him to put an alternative plan, adding that it would be a great bore if we had to go to an umpire. We finally agree upon the line of division of Parliamentary discussion, some things, e.g. leaflets and the Country House, continuing to be barred. I hope that this will now hold firm. Jebb very active and useful interviewing First Commissioner of Works and also Generals and Admirals. He thinks the Country House should become a zoo for foreigners. The D.N.I. [Director of Naval Intelligence][1] he says, continues to repeat that he had a most interesting talk with me, and the D.M.I. [Director of Military Intelligence][2] said that he was quite surprised to find me so polite. It is a great thing to have a reputation for brusqueness. ...

Ruth has great doubts about Crossman, but Gaitskell, who was in the same form with him at Winchester and has known him ever since, says that he is brilliantly able, immensely energetic, and overwhelmingly ambitious, and that he will be completely loyal, for the time being, to any Chief who he thinks will aid his ambition.

Saturday 3rd August
Beaverbrook in the War Cabinet. I write and congratulate him. He is a queer chap. Jebb thinks he may be rather a nuisance to us, but I am not very apprehensive about this.

To West Leaze[3] in the evening. In this summer of war there has been more beauty in nature than I ever remember.

Sunday 4th August
I worship Mithra and obstruct the designs of rabbits on my frontier.

Call on Van on way home and find him rather sorry for his tummy. He hopes to be able to come back after a few days' starvation.

Monday 5th August
A bunch of bad reports on a certain officer.[4]

Tuesday 6th August
Fix up Crossman. Say goodbye to Jean Monnet who is off for the

---

1 Vice-Admiral J. H. Godfrey (1888–1971). Director of Naval Intelligence 1939–42. Flag Officer Commanding Royal Indian Navy 1943–6.
2 Major-General Beaumont-Nesbitt, q.v.
3 'West Leaze': the Daltons' house at Aldbourne, near Marlborough, Wiltshire, which they often visited at weekends.
4 Dalton has written in the margin here: '(Grand)'. This entry marks the beginning of a successful campaign, instigated by Jebb, to remove Laurence Grand from the administration of S.O.E.

U.S.A. Warn Attlee against movements further to increase the size of the War Cabinet by addition of Lloyd George. This was told me by Hugh Seely. He said that both P.M. and the Beaver wanted this. I said that Lloyd George was much too old, had lost all grip, had dangerous views about the Peace, and had now no following in the country. Also he talked too much and would waste time in the Cabinet. I hope that this will not succeed.

Thursday 8th August
Greenwood made a long and very dull and unimpressive speech yesterday, after which Shinwell was offensive and later on was squashed quite flat by Bevin. Thinking there might be some fun at the Administrative Committee,[1] I attended today but found Shinwell very subdued. Therefore my carefully marked copy of Hansard and my copy of the Resolution carried at Bournemouth pledging us to 'give full support to the new Government' were not needed.

Saturday 10th August
I go to the Country House, motoring down with Van, who is not at all fit, having duodenitis. He is quite keen about Nelson.

Jebb and Wilmot come down together by another car in the afternoon and we have a conference with Leeper, Williams and Brooks. Great opposition is being raised down here to the idea of some of the staff moving to London to do the broadcasts. I get rather bored with all this, but consent to the matter being re-opened by Leeper with the Ministry of Information.

After the French armistice, British forces in the Mediterranean and North Africa were heavily outnumbered by the Italians, who, however, appeared badly organised and equipped. It was therefore decided, after General Sir Archibald Wavell (Commander-in-Chief in the Middle East) had visited London in August, to send out a contingent of tanks and guns in order to launch an anti-Italian offensive. This was successfully carried out in the Western Desert in December 1940 when Wavell led two divisions to victory against an Italian army of seven divisions, occupying Tobruk early in the New Year.

---

1 The Administrative Committee of the P.L.P. This body took the place of the Parliamentary Executive while Labour was part of the Coalition. See p. 17.

Monday 12th August

Wavell calls.[1] Only one eye and a grim unsmiling expression, but no doubt quite a good General. He complains of things being done in his Command of which he knows nothing. He says we never spend enough on arms in time of peace, and that is why, at the beginning of every war, we have a bad time. It is not only along the coast road that the Italians can attack in Libya, but across a 50 mile strip of sandy country hard enough to carry their mechanised columns. Their great problem will be water. I ask what will happen if Alexandria becomes untenable. He said that he does not think it will, but adds that the only alternative is Haifa, which is not really good enough. ...

Ministers meet at No. 10. P.M. says that he is feeling much more confident than two months ago. Our defences in this island have been immensely improved. The equipment is still short of what we should like, but is rapidly increasing. Our convoys in the Channel which the Nazis have been attacking have been decoys. We have deliberately invited these attacks and had our fighter aircraft suitably disposed to meet them. The convoys have consisted of small vessels only, all manned by naval ratings. We must speak and act on the basis of another year of war anyhow. Meanwhile, discussions of what is to happen afterwards are premature.

Wednesday 14th August

I stay away from the Party Meeting at which Shinbad the Tailor is attacked for too acid and egoistic criticism of his colleagues in the Government. The attack is led, in an amiable fashion, by Walkden,[2] who, however, quotes the Bournemouth Resolution pledging the Labour Party to give 'full support to the new Government'. At a later stage John Wilmot joins in the attack, I am told, in a most mellifluous manner, and after Shinwell has attempted to reply Jimmy Walker[3] brings down an intellectual mallet upon his head. The whole thing is thought by my friends to have passed off well, and it is likely that, for a little while to come, this man will be less of a nuisance.

Citrine[4] to lunch. He thinks that Morrison is the least satisfactory

1 General Sir Archibald Wavell, later Field Marshal and 1st Earl (1883–1950). Commander-in-Chief, Middle East 1939–41; India 1941–3. Supreme Commander, South-West Pacific 1942. Viceroy and Governor-General of India 1943–7.
2 A. G. Walkden, later 1st Baron (1873–1951). Labour M.P. for Bristol South 1929–31, 1935–45. General Secretary of the Railway Clerks' Association 1906–36.
3 James Walker (1883–1945). Labour M.P. for Motherwell 1935–45; Newport 1929–31.
4 Sir Walter Citrine, later 1st Baron (1887–1983). General Secretary of the Trades Union Congress 1926–46. President of the International Federation of Trade Unions 1928–45. Chairman of the Central Electricity Authority 1947–57.

of the Labour ministers, and he hints that I am the best. He says that the statement I made to the N.C.L. [National Council of Labour] the other day on the work of my Department was the best that they had heard. Morrison, he says, is much too much entangled with his officials. He is disinclined to see people without them. (This is a thoroughly bad habit which, from the beginning, I have refused to adopt. I never permit an official to be present when I am speaking to a colleague. If points of detail arise, they can be followed up afterwards, but a minister should know enough about his Department to be able to conduct at least preliminary discussions without officials.)

A major German air offensive, aimed at destroying Fighter Command and so making possible an invasion, began on 12th August. Radar stations, R.A.F. airfields and stations, and aircraft factories were attacked. The heaviest attacks occurred on 15th and 16th August. The assault was met by just over 1,000 R.A.F. pilots in Hurricanes and Spitfires, taking a toll of enemy aircraft in the ratio of roughly 2:1. This was the start of the Battle of Britain.

Friday 16th August
Two air-raid warnings. Take two hours off my working day ...

I preside at a meeting of the Labour Party Policy Committee, when little Laski[1] has a bad time from several of our Trade Union members. He has produced an academic little paper urging that, in order to raise the morale of the people, the Bank of England and the land should be nationalised. It is replied that, whatever the arguments in favour of doing these things may be – and they are well known to all of us – raising morale is not one of them. This is better done by Air Force victories, by full employment, by better dependents' allowances, by improvements in Workmen's Compensation, and by modifications in the Means Test. He goes away with his little tail between his little legs.

Saturday 17th August
Jebb volunteers that he likes Wilmot very much and is amazed when I tell him that he left school at fourteen. As between Wilmot and Gait-

---

1 Harold Laski (1893–1950). Professor of Political Science at the University of London (L.S.E.) 1926–50. Member of the Labour Party N.E.C. 1936–49; Chairman 1945–6. Author and journalist.

skell, he says that the latter is much more intelligent, but the former has a much better judgment.

The move of Halifax, I hear, from the Dorchester to the Foreign Office will be a relief to his officials. At the Dorchester, they say, he leaves important Foreign Office telegrams in the lavatory and the most secret intercepts lying about the floor when he goes out of the room. The officials have always to be dashing round in his immediate wake collecting his 'confidential waste'. Also, they say, he is most unguarded in his conversations with unknown people, some of whom may well be enemy agents. He will let himself be accosted by anyone whose face he has seen before, as he emerges from the lift at the Dorchester, and will converse with them in the most indiscreet fashion. I ask why a man who has been Viceroy of India plus a number of other things should still be so simple. Jebb says that he thinks it is just because he has been Viceroy. In India no one was allowed to come anywhere near him who had not been most carefully seeded, and he therefore got into the habit of thinking that he could speak freely to all within reach.

Monday 19th August
I plan for tomorrow a tremendous barrage against myself in the House of Parliamentary Questions designed to emphasise my case for the blockade.

After much interdepartmental and Cabinet discussion on the question of relief to enemy-occupied territories, the Prime Minister stated the Government's policy in the House of Commons on 20th August. He declared that a strict blockade would be maintained of all countries which had fallen into Germany's power, and that any shortage in Europe was a German responsibility. On the other hand the British government would arrange for the speedy provisioning of any area which threw off the German yoke. This declaration was widely published, and represented the fullest statement of British policy on the general problem of relief. It also led to the setting up of a small section, under Leith-Ross, with Arthur Greenwood and Dalton as the ministers jointly responsible, to collect and organise the surpluses necessary for 'Food and Freedom going into Europe together'. This involved co-ordination with the U.S.A., where most of the surpluses actually were.[1]

---

1 W. N. Medlicott, *The Economic Blockade* (History of the Second World War, U.K. Civil Series), H.M.S.O., London, 1952, vol. I, p. 551; FY, pp. 357–8.

Tuesday 20th August

This afternoon the P.M. makes a great speech in the House in which he has a passage on Blockade and on Food and Freedom going into Europe together which was lifted almost bodily from my brief supplied to him before the weekend. It could not have been better put.

This evening I see Butler and, making no formal complaint, comment upon the slowness of Foreign Office officials. He says that we have the reputation in the Foreign Office of always hustling and browbeating them upon the telephone, so that red-faced and flustered men rush into his room saying that the Minister of Economic Warfare and his minions are on their tails again. He says that it is particularly demoralising to these poor creatures when we ring up the Private Secretaries' Room at the Foreign Office, for there no one ever knows anything about the details of any problem, and they merely start to run around the corridors in high dismay. He thinks the best plan would be to give some one Foreign Office official the job of answering our telephone communications.

Long talk to Wilmot and Gaitskell on personnel. Crossman and Leeper do not like each other. The whole thing is a frightful bore, and meanwhile Gladwyn [Jebb] is away with a chill.

Wednesday 21st August

In the afternoon go with Vansittart to see Halifax, and *his* Man Friday. The purpose of the talk is to discuss how rude we can be to the men of Vichy. The answer is 'as rude as you like'. Halifax says, wonderingly and with a faint far smile, 'I have often wondered whether it would not have been possible to bribe Mussolini, but I do not think we could ever have offered him enough to tempt him, and Loraine[1] always disliked the idea of offering anything to Ciano.[2] He never felt able to hand him £50,000 on the golf links.'

Thursday 22nd August

Gladwyn says that one of the troubles with Van is that his wife is jealous of everyone else and is constantly inciting him to nurse new grievances and jealousies – not least of some younger than himself. This is particularly reprehensible, since he himself got high promotion very young.

1 Sir Percy Loraine, 12th Bart (1880–1961). Ambassador to Italy 1939–40. Dalton had first encountered him as High Commissioner to Egypt and the Sudan 1929–33.
2 Count Galeazzo Ciano (1903–44). Italian Foreign Minister 1936–53.

I lunch at the Drapers'[1] today and am initiated as a member of the Court.

'I am deeply dissatisfied at the way in which the work on surpluses has been handled,' Dalton minuted the Minister without Portfolio, Arthur Greenwood, on 24th August. ' ... We shall, I think, have to re-consider both our methods and our human instruments of doing business.'[2]

Saturday 24th August
I despatch a most violent Minute to Greenwood on surpli. I complain –
(a) that his officers have fallen behind the time-table agreed upon,
(b) that they have only produced, even too late, two 'paltry and jejune' papers,
(c) that they have sent these papers out without my prior approval, and
(d) 'Your staff do not appear to work on Saturday morning. There was no one in the office this morning except the unfortunate Durbin, who has only just arrived.'

Having thus let off some steam, I proceed to Oxford and spend the night at All Souls, whither Hudson[3] and Rowse[4] have invited me. It is quite a pleasant break from the Ministry and they are much interested in political gossip, but, somehow, one feels from their comments that they are far out of touch with any of our real problems. I am favourably impressed by Lathan, who is working temporarily at the Foreign Office as P.S. to Lytton[5] on aliens. He is Left-minded and thinks very well of Gaitskell who, he says, was always intended to make a perfect Private Secretary to a minister. 'There is', he says, 'something velvety about Gaitskell.'

Sunday 25th August
Back from Oxford in the afternoon and complete draft telegram for

1 'the Drapers': Dalton and his ancestors had been associated with the Drapers' Company in the City since the early-nineteenth century, when a member of the family had set up a shop for selling silks imported from the East Indies. Hugh Dalton, like his father, maintained the connection, and both served as Masters of the Company.
2 Dalton Papers 7/2 (11).
3 R. S. Hudson, q.v., was a Fellow of All Souls College, Oxford.
4 A. L. Rowse (b. 1903). Writer and historian. Fellow of All Souls College, Oxford.
5 V. A. G. R. Lytton, 2nd Earl of Lytton (1876–1947). Chairman of the Council of Aliens 1939–41. Junior minister 1916–22. Governor of Bengal 1922–7. Viceroy of India 1925.

Washington with aid of Sporborg,[1] one of my better officials. I have Greenwood's office rung up and find there is nobody there except a night watchman. This is at 7 p.m.

I had said to Gaitskell two days ago, in connection with some Foreign Office arrangement, 'You must give me credit for sometimes being subtle.' He says, 'The trouble is that you are subtle one day and brutal the next.'

Monday 26th August

I am 53 years old today, my first birthday as a Privy Councillor. I celebrate it by much hustling and rowing about surpli. I send a second Minute to Greenwood proposing that Durbin should be hauled across from his office to mine and should work under my close personal supervision along with Rowe[2] to finish the job within a few days.

Thursday 29th August

An excellent day. Lots of hustle! Gaitskell, who had been very doubtful about my proceedings these last few days, is quite won over and enthusiastic. 'You have been in very good form,' he says, and adds that one reason why my Minutes give pain to some is because they are written in such good English! Durbin is also said to be much impressed.

I have now got the appendices to the surpli almost ready and hold a meeting this afternoon with Crookshank and Boothby, Leith-Ross, Catto and Hutton[3] also attending, whereat the rest of us bid down the stupid opposition of the Treasury to sending any telegram to Lothian[4] until after the American elections in November! Catto is very persistent and, I think, very very stupid! (I am told that when this little man is seen trotting round the Treasury with little Kingsley Wood, whom he advises, the world says, 'There go Catto and Doggo.') ...

[Attlee] has told the P.M. that he has had a report from me and considers that I am doing very well in building up a new machine etc. He agrees that he will tell the P.M. that he has had a further talk with me and that I want to see the P.M. within a few days to make a report. I shall then write to the P.M. myself and then, unless summoned,

---

1 Colonel H. N. Sporborg (1905–85). Banker, solicitor and businessman. Joined M.E.W. 1939. Took charge of the Norwegian Bureau of S.O.E. 1940, and then, from 1940–43, headed the Western Directorate of S.O.E., with responsibility for liaison with de Gaulle's secret service. Vice-Chief of S.O.E. 1943–6. Later Managing Director of Hambros Bank.

2 J. W. F. Rowe. Temporary administrative officer at M.E.W.

3 Graham Hutton (b. 1904). Temporary civil servant at the Foreign Office and Ministry of Information 1939–45. Assistant Editor of the *Economist* 1933–8.

4 P. H. Kerr, 11th Marquis of Lothian (1882–1940). Ambassador to the U.S.A. 1939–40. Chancellor of the Duchy of Lancaster 1931. Junior minister 1931–2.

break through to him one day next week.

P.M. says that all the Generals, Admirals and Air Marshals are useless and that he will have his own Planning Committee, containing bright and rather more junior lads drawn from the three Services. Attlee and the Beaver will sit with him, since the burden of Minister of Defence would lie too heavily on one pair of shoulders. The Beaver is constantly engaged in intrigue against all his colleagues in turn. Attlee is dining with him tonight and 'if he puts out a paw I shall hit it hard'. His immediate object of intrigue is Greenwood, but he is reported to have said that he would soon get both Attlee and Greenwood out of the Cabinet. Meanwhile, says Attlee, he is most oleaginously friendly to him. I said that this was the first National Government that we had ever had and he could take it that if any attempt was made to act as suggested, there would be a first-class political row which could not be kept secret and would play into the hands of those elements in our Party who have always been averse from our participation.

Attlee gives a most amusing account of a meeting at which the P.M. roasted Mr Pick,[1] who had adopted a self-righteous and very high moral tone regarding methods of propaganda. 'Nothing tendentious', etc. The P.M. had finally said, 'I am honoured to sit at the same table with a man who so closely resembles Jesus Christ, but I want to win the war.'

Nelson reports this morning that he has now taken charge[2] and finds in his Department good personnel but no organisation whatever.

Saturday 31st August
Hoare is another very weak vessel in Madrid. He asks for ship after ship to be let through. If I left it to him there would soon be no blockade left. I look forward to a time when I may say, if Spain enters the war and he returns and criticises our blockade, 'When you were a minister and I was not, you let everything into Italy, so that she became a store-house of war materials for the enemy. Now, since I have been a minister and you have not, you have wanted the same policy in Spain, but I have succeeded in preventing it.'

I spend an hour on the roof looking out over London. Distant fires and flickers but not very great bombardment.

Sunday 1st September
Lunch at the Mirabelle with Foot to meet Sinclair. It goes very well and

1 Frank Pick (1878–1941). Fourth Director-General of the Ministry of Information 1940–41. Vice-Chairman of the London Passenger Transport Board 1933–40.
2 Of SO2.

we all are very co-operatively conspiratorial. It seems that the idea of bringing Lloyd George into the War Cabinet has faded out a bit. Sinclair says the excuse was that Lloyd George was a man of the Left, so he would do something to balance Beaverbrook. I said that was all rubbish; Lloyd George was much too old, inclined to be a Pétain, pro-German, anti-French, anti-Polish and anti-Beneš.[1] All the wrong things. If the Left needs strengthening in the War Cabinet, I suggested they should bring in Sinclair and another of us. I think he took the hint.

Tuesday 3rd September

At 10.30 this evening I go to see P.M. at No. 10 Downing Street. I wished, before going on leave, to make an oral report to him, following upon a brief written report, of some of my proceedings. But I don't get much chance! He is much more anxious to talk than to listen, and walks up and down the room pouring forth a flow of his usual vigorous rhetorical good sense. 'This is a workmen's war ...... the public will stand everything except optimism ...... the nation is finding the war is not so unpleasant as it expected ...... the air attacks are doing much less damage than was expected before the war began ...... don't be like the knight in the story who was so slow in buckling on his armour that the tourney was over before he rode into the ring.' While I am there he also rings up Lord Portal[2] and asks him to become an additional Under-Secretary at the Ministry of Supply, to help Morrison with control of raw materials. Then he calls for Peck,[3] a young man who is one of his secretaries, and demands that he shall show us air photographs on a screen. These show the guns at Cape Grisnez, the docks at Emden and Wilhelmshaven, etc. The P.M. is childishly pleased with these and also with the mechanism itself. He says, 'Peck you must get some new photographs every day and show them to me every evening.' He is a child of genius. When the Grisnez photograph comes on, he detects a German car travelling along the road, puts his finger upon it and cries, 'Look, there is a horrible hun. Why don't we bomb him?' He is very vexed at the difficulties of communication with France. He says, 'I can't even find an American who would take a

1 Eduard Beneš (1884–1948). President of Czechoslovakia 1935–8; 1945–8. President-in-exile 1938–45. Foreign Minister 1918–35; Prime Minister 1921–2. Co-founder, with Jan Masaryk, of the Czechoslovak Republic 1918.
2 Sir Wyndham Portal, 3rd Bart, 1st Baron, later 1st Viscount (1885–1949). Additional Parliamentary Secretary to the Ministry of Supply 1940–42; Minister of Works and Planning and First Commissioner of Works and Public Buildings 1942–4.
3 J. H. Peck, later Sir John (b. 1913). Assistant Private Secretary to the Prime Minister 1940–46.

letter from me to General Georges. It would be quite a short letter. I should simply say, as Thiers[1] said, *"On pensez toujours! On parlez jamais!"'* The P.M.'s French is incorrect but intelligible and he rushes forward without hesitation or pedantry. 'He would understand that. I should need to say no more. I know that man and a message from me would make a difference to him. I know how he must be feeling.'

Wednesday 4th September
Rather a boring discussion with Van who grumbles about Gladwyn, saying that he always knew from the start that he would not be kept in touch with this side of our work.[2] He is 'not everybody's cup of tea', he says, to which I reply that he is very much mine. Van says that his manner seems to many rather off-hand and his youth is a cause of jealousy. He is, in fact, just forty though he looks less, and I remind Van how glad we all were in 1929 when he himself came along to replace old Lindsay.[3] Van says that someone – I am pretty sure from the tone of the tale that it was Bracken – came into his Miss D.'s[4] room the other day and asked what was all this racket of Gladwyn's. Miss Dougherty, drawing herself up very primly, had replied, 'I am sure that nothing could be called "racket" with which Sir Robert is associated.' To this the visitor had said that Sir Robert knew nothing of what was going on. This is all cheek and nonsense, but it had obviously had some effect upon Van. I tell Gladwyn afterwards that he must work hard to remove this impression (subsequently it seems he does).

Thursday 5th September
To West Leaze for what is supposed to be a fortnight's leave. Take with me the Russian comic novel *Diamonds to Sit On* and some books on Cromwell. Walk to Marlborough, work in the garden and, just occasionally, have telephone conversations with London (the war has destroyed my solitude by compelling me to install a telephone here).

Early in September, the Germans changed tactics, following some R.A.F. raids on Berlin. Hitler, apparently enraged by this effrontery, switched the

1 L. A. Thiers (1797–1877). French statesman and historian.
2 i.e. the SO2 side.
3 Sir Ronald Lindsay (1877–1945). Permanent Under-Secretary at the Foreign Office 1928–30. Ambassador to the United States 1930–39. Vansittart replaced Lindsay as Permanent Under-Secretary in 1930, not in 1929.
4 Miss A. M. Dougherty. Private secretary to the Chief Diplomatic Adviser, Sir Robert Vansittart.

main target of the Luftwaffe to London, rather than the R.A.F. stations which had taken the main brunt of the attack. This was a welcome relief to the greatly stretched resources of the R.A.F., which was now able to recover. But it placed a major strain on the civilian population of the capital. The Blitz began on 7th September, and from then until 2nd November London was bombed every night by an average of 200 planes. In these two months, nearly 12,000 civilians died in air raids, more than 80 per cent of them in London, and damage to property was extensive. Nevertheless, the level of casualties was lower than anticipated before the war.

Tuesday 10th September
Ruth comes down by car in the afternoon and tells me that there has been considerable bombing. I think it is my duty to come up and make arrangements about my staff. I arrive that evening and sleep in the flat, hearing a good deal of distant reverberation.

Wednesday 11th September
Hold a conference at M.E.W. with Foot, Leith-Ross, Drogheda and a few others and tell them to get more beds and bedding and arrange for as many of the staff who wish to do so, with reasonably good grounds, to sleep in. I then return to the country.

Sunday 15th September
Jebb comes to lunch to discuss business. He seems to have re-established quite good relations with Vansittart. I take him for a quick walk through the village and up the Southward, delighting myself with walking briskly up the hill until he asks me not to walk so fast. This is a favourite trick of mine to play on those younger than myself.

Monday 16th September
Wilmot and Gaitskell come by car to spend the night. We go out for a walk along the high road to Woodsend. I make Gaitskell ask me not to walk so fast and then suggest to him that we should run instead but he does not like this idea either. They have both been down to the Country House for the weekend and report that progress is slowly, but only slowly, being made.

Tuesday 17th September
Drive up from West Leaze with Wilmot and Gaitskell. Arrive in Berkeley Square where we find that at 10.15 last night a bomb crashed right in our front entrance, killing two Home Guards on my staff,

flinging a mass of sand and sand-bags over everything, making a crater in the basement, and smashing nearly all glass in front, including my own room, and tearing up quantities of railings and stone work outside. Upstairs everything is a mass of broken glass, burst window frames, tattered curtains and general mess. I take refuge for some days in Lord Finlay's room and start sleeping in the basement in my War Room. This is well ventilated and proof against most hits or sound, though occasionally I am rocked in my sleep by distant bursts.

All this is rather disturbing to the work of the Ministry, but the spirit is generally cheerful. On the other side of the Square two Georgian houses are completely destroyed by a delayed-action bomb which turns them into a mass of brick dust and charred matchwood. There are also other fires and explosions all around the neighbourhood. Hitler seems to have a special spite against drapers' shops in Oxford Street.

Wilmot, with his usual ingenuity, discovers the Lansdowne Club, slightly derelict, across the Square, and he and I tend to have breakfast there and occasionally an evening meal also. The only other denizens appear to be an old colonel who acts as Secretary and a few naval officers.

On 18th September Dalton wrote to Lieutenant-Colonel Grand, former head of the old 'D' Section, sacking him with effect from 20th September.[1]

Wednesday 18th September
Decide to dismiss King Bomba,[2] who has been completely disloyal to his new chief.[3] Two officers in uniform, unwilling to put anything on paper, come and tell me, Van and Gladwyn all about it. Van says that he is sure it is right to get rid of him now, though he advised earlier to give him another chance. I send him a brief and unargumentative letter, since if I see him he will only falsify the interview, as happened before.

---

1 Dalton Papers 7/3 (26).
2 Dalton's private name for Grand. The nickname 'King Bomba' was originally given in Italy to King Ferdinand II, of the Two Sicilies, because of his bombardment of Messina and other cities during the revolutionary troubles of 1849.
3 Sir Frank Nelson, q.v.

It is also decided to move all the staff primarily concerned with propaganda from Lansdowne House to the country. There they will all be together. Van is rather reluctantly converted to this idea, which, however, is urged on him by my other two advisers.

Friday 20th September
To Bishop Auckland,[1] where I stay till the morning of 23rd September. I address five meetings in two days organised by the Ministry of Information, though in fact they are very like the usual Labour meetings so far as the platform and most of the audience is concerned. Very successful. They have suffered little from bombing in S.W. Durham and practically everyone is now at work earning pretty good wages on construction of new aircraft works, military camps, roads, etc. There are also many soldiers in the area and a good deal of money is circulated. Never have I known the place so prosperous. At Shildon less than 100 are now on the live register. It takes a war to do this! They are all in very good heart though wishing to be reassured as to the accuracy of the published statements on German and British air losses.

Monday 23rd September
Ruth returns from West Leaze and I bring her to sleep in my War Room, since there is no other quickly obtainable secure accommodation. This is slightly irregular but may pass for once! I find that King Bomba has written a letter demanding reasons for my decisions and suggesting that his appointment or dismissal is a matter to be decided by the War Cabinet. This is damned cheek and quite baseless!

I have a talk with Attlee who suggests that I should mention this case to the P.M. who, he thinks, will pay great attention to reports of disloyalty and evidence to that effect by officers.

Wednesday 25th September
I have a good report on the parasites (of No. 10). They seem to have been driven back. P.M. is reported to have said that he 'won't have a quarrel with Dalton over this'. I must, however, see him and leave a note on the affair.[2]

Thursday 26th September
I ask Gladwyn to arrange for King Bomba to be sent some distance

1 Dalton's constituency in Co. Durham.
2 'the parasites (of No. 10)': Dalton became increasingly suspicious of Churchill's personal staff at No. 10. The 'affair' was the dismissal of Laurence Grand, who tried to have Dalton's decision reversed – apparently with the support of Lindemann.

off. Of the destinations suggested, I prefer Hong Kong to Ireland. It seems that 'the Prof.' was the biggest nigger in this woodpile. He was very close with King Bomba, hating Government Departments and loving irregular routes, and thinking in terms of personalities. Bracken, whom we suspected earlier, has now been much worked upon by Vansittart and by Gladwyn – more worked upon, perhaps, than he is worth. But it is likely, I think, that he is now neutralised. A rumour circulates that King Bomba, who has now written me a rather crawling and friendly letter, has been announcing that after two months of well-deserved leave, he is to be given a post in the War Cabinet secretariat. This is too much and I ask Gladwyn to work on D.M.I. to get him posted quickly far away. Clearly King Bomba knows he has lost the other game involving an appeal against my right to push him out. 'This shows', I say to Gladwyn, 'that firmness pays.' 'Yes', he replies, 'King Bomba is very like a native. We shall have to send you out to govern Bombay!'

On 14th November 1940, Dalton minuted Jebb: 'I told Sir Alexander Cadogan today that no one could have handled the Grand affair and innumerable other personnel problems with greater skill and persistence than yourself. None the less, it was intolerable that you should have to spend so much time and mind on all this, and that we should be so obstructed by intrigue at home from going full out to fight the Hun and the Wop.

' ... I hope you will see Eden without fail tomorrow, making this the first charge upon your time, intolerable though it is that this should be necessary. I need not rehearse with you what you should say, but rid me, and yourself, of this lousy hair shirt quickly.'[1]

Friday 27th September
Last night the Cabinet War Room was nearly hit by a large shell. There is gloom and despondency over the Dakar fiasco.[2] The Beaver is also said to be very low, suffering from asthma and keeping [to] his room. They have hit two of his important aircraft factories. He has written a memorandum for the War Cabinet like a *Daily Express* article. 'Not another man or another plane should be sent out of this

1 Dalton Papers 7/3 (37).
2 An expedition had been sent to Dakar, in French North Africa, in the hope of assisting General de Gaulle to assume control. The operation failed.

island. We should sit tight and defend ourselves until the U.S.A. comes into the war.' He is inclined, moreover, to be very defeatist – so Gladwyn learns confidentially from Charles Peake.[1] Partly temperament, no doubt, but partly, perhaps, the rich man thinking of his worldly possessions, toying with the notion of a peace which would preserve these.

Saturday 28th September

To Manchester to address the annual meeting of the Lancashire and Cheshire Regional Council of Labour. They are a good sound lot, with only a sprinkling of freaks, and even these not very freakish freaks.

On 16th July, Hitler had issued a directive declaring his intention 'if necessary' (i.e. if Britain refused to accept a negotiated peace) to invade Britain after the middle of August. The failure to gain air supremacy, however, delayed this plan. Early in September a large flotilla of invasion barges had been assembled at the Channel Ports, and for a time invasion seemed imminent. But no order was given, and on 15th September it was decided to postpone an attack indefinitely. This decision only gradually became apparent to the British government, as the weather deteriorated.

Tuesday 1st October

A meeting of ministers to whom P.M. explains present situation. Invasion 'menace' still remains, and will, so long as Germans have in that long row of ports transport enough to put half a million men on board and in the Channel and North Sea on any night they choose. But, as the weather breaks and the season advances, the invasion must surely seem to them more and more difficult. (It seems clear that it was definitely projected for 15th September, but that at the last minute they decided that they had better not.) As my driver says his daughter says, 'Hitler's got the words, but he can't get the music right.' I had a date with the P.M. after this ministers' meeting at which I wished to speak to him on S.O.E., with a passing word on King Bomba, and then leave documents with him. But he asks me to 'let him off' until

1 C. B. P. Peake, later Sir Charles (1897–1958). Head of Foreign Office News Department and Chief Press Officer at the Ministry of Information 1939–41. Personal Assistant to Halifax 1941. Representative to the French National Committee 1942–4.

next week, being pressed and weary, though smiling and friendly. This, however, is a bit of a bore and I decide to send to him, with copy to Attlee, tonight, the document I should have left with him. I blame some of his entourage for failure to interest him, in the right way, in some of the things I wish to tell him.

Wednesday 2nd October
Cabinet in morning. Halifax, without Cadogan who is on leave, is inclined to have wild and woolly ideas. So Gladwyn says. He 'holds colloquies' with Sargent but is not kept straight by him as by Cadogan. This morning he proposed a public statement that, at the end of the war, we should be disposed to discuss Gibraltar with the Spaniards and that this was regarded by us as purely an Anglo-Spanish affair. All present, for a variety of reasons, objected to this. 'Does anyone think that if we win the war, opinion here will consent to hand over Gibraltar to the Dons? and, if we lose, we shall not be consulted' (P.M.). Further, such a publication would lead to embarrassing debate in Parliament, where the strategic Imperialists would combine with the Reds to denounce H.M.G. and Franco. This would completely frustrate Halifax's hopes of good will and furnish magnificent material for the Germans. At the least, it would lead to embarrassing definitions of the meaning of 'discussion'. Attlee thought that, in any case, it was not a purely Anglo-Spanish question, but an international one. P.M. agreed that if, after the war, we could build up some great new Council of the Nations, with a strong secular army, and an appropriate Tribunal, we might then indeed place Gibraltar and other strong points under some international regime. But we were still very far from that point. Further, it was held that such a public statement would seem jittery. Halifax, therefore, was unanimously overruled, a thing I have seen happen before.

At the beginning of October, following the resignation of Neville Chamberlain on health grounds, Churchill carried out a major reconstruction of his Government. Sir John Anderson took Chamberlain's place as Lord President of the Council, in charge of domestic administration. The Chancellor of the Exchequer, Sir Kingsley Wood, and the Minister of Labour and National Security, Ernest Bevin, were taken into the War Cabinet, which now consisted of eight members: Churchill, Attlee, Halifax, Anderson, Greenwood, Bevin, Wood and Beaverbrook, who had been brought in two months earlier. Outside the War Cabinet, there were other changes: Herbert Morrison became Home Secretary and Minister of Home Security; Lord Cranborne became Dominions Secretary; Sir Andrew Duncan became Minister of Supply; Oliver Lyttelton became President of the Board of Trade; and J. Moore-Brabazon became Minister of Transport.

Thursday 3rd October

Bevin has just joined the War Cabinet as part of the recent reconstruction. He says to me, 'Of course I am very new at this game and I didn't know what to say when the P.M. asked me last night. But I thought it would help the prestige of the Trade Union Movement and the Ministry of Labour if I went in. No one has ever put the Ministry of Labour in the forefront like this before.' (I am not sure whether this last was a reference to himself or the P.M.) And now the P.M. will have to teach him to be terse. At present he is terribly long-winded through long habit. I said I had heard that the Beaver was to become Lord President. Bevin was most contemptuous. ''im?' he said. 'Why then 'e'd 'ave to do all the ceremonial. The King would never 'ave that.'

I like this new Cabinet reconstruction very much. Positively, there is nothing wrong with it – except perhaps the increase in the size of the War Cabinet to eight – and negatively, we have escaped several calamities which were much canvassed. Lloyd George has not been brought in. (Only two days ago Lady Astor[1] was saying to me – and therefore, no doubt, had been saying to everybody – that it was indispensable to have Lloyd George or Trenchard,[2] or both, in the War Cabinet in order to 'hold Winston'. I said that I had an open mind about Trenchard, but that I was wholly against Lloyd George who was senile, had no longer any following in the country, was a Welsh Pétain and wrote articles in the Sunday press as though he were a neutral in the war.) We have also avoided having the Beaver without a Department and with a roving commission to intrigue and interfere everywhere. This is particularly important as regards propaganda.

Friday 4th October

Morton to lunch. He is by way of being very co-operative now, and certainly he is keen to get things done. Mr Pick, he says, now asks for one week off in two owing to the strain of his work at the Ministry of Information. Morton adds one more detail of the famous conversa-

---

1 Nancy Astor, Viscountess (1879–1964). Conservative M.P. for Plymouth Sutton 1919–45. Married to Waldorf Astor, 2nd Viscount.
2 Hugh Trenchard, 1st Viscount (1873–1956). Chief of Air Staff 1918, 1919–29. Commissioner of Metropolitan Police 1931–5.

tion with the P.M., who leant across the table extending his hand and said, 'Let me shake your hand Mr Pick. Today I am going down to Dover to watch the air battles. Perhaps tonight I shall be in Hell, and if so I should like to tell the people there that I have shaken hands with the one sinless man since Jesus Christ. Shake my hand Mr Pick.'

Monday 7th October
Early this morning a spot of Spanish drama. Makins[1] was roused from bed at 1.15 and summoned to the Foreign Office. On the way, the windscreen of his car was shattered by a bomb. Arrived, he heard that a telegram had gone from Franco to Roosevelt saying that the latter now had it in his power to take decisive action, which would affect the whole course of the war. Spain would stay neutral if only U.S.A. would send her wheat. It was agreed – Drogheda having given assent on my behalf – that we should agree to this on condition that American agents in Spain distributed the wheat, that none was re-exported, that publicity should be given to the whole affair, and that wheat ships should go over singly and be stopped by us if anything went wrong.

Monday 14th October
In the afternoon, meeting of ministers at Air Ministry, where Sinclair is very frank. Germans are still very inferior to us in night flying, but are working hard at it. There is no sign yet of any deterioration in the morale of their pilots, and all those caught so far were flying at the beginning of the war.

On the other hand, we are making hopeful progress with a number of ingenious devices for night defence. Details, of course, are very secret, but the general principle is, rather obviously, to create artificially at night conditions as favourable for the operation of our fighter aircraft as those which naturally prevail by day. Progress on these lines would make a great difference, but it would be a terrible bore if the Germans made simultaneous and similar inventions.

Germans generally fly at least 15,000 feet over London at night, and by day their tactics now are to come over very high, more than 20,000 feet, with fast fighter patrols, each carrying a few bombs, but with very few bombers. At this altitude some types of British fighters, though superior to the Germans at lower altitudes, are not at their best. Moreover, the quick climb required is a bit of a nuisance. Hence

---

1 R. M. Makins, later Sir Roger, later 1st Baron Sherfield (b. 1904). Acting Counsellor at the Foreign Office 1940. Deputy Under-Secretary of State at the Foreign Office 1948–52. British Ambassador to the U.S. 1953–6. Joint Permanent Secretary of the Treasury 1956–9.

the fact that losses are much more nearly equal in these last days, though they are relatively small on both sides. We have a number of new types, and improvements of present types, coming along satisfactorily.

There was some drop in our production last month, more from interruption of work during warnings than from physical damage by bombs. None the less, our monthly increment was between 1,300 and 1,400, including about 100 imported from U.S.A. This last figure will rise very steeply in the next few months. Last month German production was probably very slightly above this figure, but, over the last four months, we have reason to think that our production, including imports, has been a bit ahead of theirs.

We have also reason to think that if they aim at a continuous and undiminished scale of attack on this country, they cannot send over many more bombers than they are doing now. They could, of course, greatly intensify the attack for a short period, e.g. several days or even a week, but only at the cost of having to reduce it very substantially afterwards and let[ting] it fall well below their recent level. Broadly, and this is also our experience, not much more than one-quarter of the available bomber force can be used each day. The disparity has diminished over the period May to October. ...

Much air activity tonight. Returning about 9 p.m. and on my way to my office on the second floor, a bomb bursts very near the building, in fact in a mews just at the back, blows in all the windows on that side, and puts out all the lights. Miss O.[1] is slightly hysterical and I have to comfort her, but, for my part, I find this bomb burst just near enough to be stimulating, and not too close to be a bother. I therefore don my tin hat, still quite a toy, and call on Gladwyn, who also has a head protection, to come up with me to my Roof of the World. From there we see a most dramatic sight, with fires burning all round the circle. Most of these are soon suppressed by Wilmot's admirable firemen, but one, somewhere in Piccadilly, burns very fiercely. Quite like a *Götterdämmerung* which. must make even German pilots, brought up on all that Wagner stuff, faintly fearful of their future fate. My roof is one of the best lookouts in London. It is also very good for one to have a walk up to the tenth floor, lifts being out of action during the air-raids.

Tuesday 15th October

Joe Kennedy[2] comes to say goodbye. He is most effusive and compli-

1 'Miss O.': a young secretary in Dalton's private office.
2 Joseph Kennedy (1888–1969). U.S. Ambassador in London 1937–41. Father of the Kennedy brothers.

mentary. I don't think he will come back. I shall not be sorry. I always regard him as a defeatist and a crook.

Wednesday 16th October

The rumour grows, through various telegrams and other agencies, that the Germans may attack the Russians in the spring. Certainly the Russians' attitude can best be explained on the assumption that they are very frightened of the Germans but not of anybody else. Kot[1] told Gladwyn the other day that he was in Lwów when the Russians came in last October, and that, behind their 'façade' troops, there were only ragged, ill-trained, ill-armed creatures, mostly suffering from stomach trouble. One must allow a little for high Polish colour, but it is not hard to believe that most of the Red Army is a rabble. ...

Cazalet[2] has got a more or less bogus job as liaison with Sikorski. He is quite innocent about my work. He thinks it a great thing that I have got Gladwyn, of whom he thinks highly, to ease my blockade difficulties with the Foreign Office. (This is the other side of the tale that he has been put here by the Foreign Office to keep a check on this troublesome Minister of Economic Warfare.) Cazalet says that others say that Gladwyn is 'one of the few people who are not frightened of you'. Gladwyn tells me afterwards that he deliberately put this tale around![3]

Thursday 17th October

Clem Davies very haughty to Greenwood and me when offered job of looking after Surpluses. He is, he says, 'a member of the War Cabinet of the greatest concern in this country (Unilevers). There, what I say goes.' He also alleges that before joining them he gave up the biggest practice at the Commercial Bar and that he is now receiving a salary of £15,000 a year. He seems to have no shame about this and is evidently suffering from an extreme form of megalomania. If he were offered a job as Minister for Surpluses, with a seat in the Cabinet, he might look at it! I am sorry I suggested him rather than sticking to some of the other candidates.

1 Stanislaw Kot (1885–1975). Minister of Home Affairs in the Polish government-in-exile 1940–41. Professor of History at Cracow University 1920–34. Deputy-Premier and Minister without Portfolio 1939–40. Ambassador to the U.S.S.R. 1941–2. Minister of Information 1943–5.
2 Lt-Colonel Victor Cazalet (1896–1943). Political liaison officer to General Sikorski 1940–43. Conservative M.P. for Chippenham 1924–43. Killed in an aircrash on 4th July 1943, with General Sikorski.
3 Marginal insertion: 'A sib!'. (A 'sib' was a false rumour, manufactured by SO1 for dissemination abroad in order to confuse the enemy. From the Latin, *sibilare*, to whisper or hiss.)

Friday 18th October

Cabinet. Rather confused and disorderly discussion. The increase in the permanent membership of the War Cabinet leads to the room being fuller and to more people speaking, though not to more knowledge. I urge that we should resume a real blockade of French West Africa and no longer leave alone French merchant ships which are 'escorted', even by such symbolic escorts as sloops, armed trawlers, survey ships, etc. This has become a complete scandal, such third-rate escorts operating a shuttle service in the Straits, passing through one convoy and then returning for the next. There is much support for my view, but the Admiralty say they have no ships. To this plaint, often heard nowadays, I feel inclined to reply, 'If no ships, then why any Admirals?' However, in the end it is decided, as I wished, that the mistaken decision, made without proper consideration more than two months ago, that no escorted French merchant ships should be interfered with, shall be rescinded. Someone says, 'Let us have now a few symbolic seizures!' ...

Christopher Mayhew comes to see me and spends the night in the Ministry. He has now a commission in the Intelligence Corps, which is a new contraption since my time in the Army. He is now between two courses, both of which should be useful to him. I tell him a little about the work here and say that I will ask for him to be seconded when he has completed his second course. I think he will be very useful.

Monday 21st October

Hambro[1] comes to tell me about his experiences on his recent travels and makes, as usual, a very good impression. Go home for an evening meal – quite an amazing and unusual experience – but find the night so dark that I have the greatest difficulty in making my way back to the Ministry. Just now Hitler is being slightly less active in the air.

Thursday 24th October

At lunch with Mrs Phillimore and others, Will Henderson is almost embarrassingly forthcoming. He seems to want me to be in on everybody else's work, on the ground that I alone have real drive and understanding. Both from the national and from the Party point of view, he says, he wants this. He tends to repeat himself and it is all a bit overdone. None the less, I had better see him and let him talk himself out. He says he suggested to Greenwood, when the last ministerial

---

1 C. J. Hambro, later Sir Charles (1897–1963). Banker. Director of the Bank of England. Deputy head of SO2 1940–42. Executive Director of S.O.E. May 1942– September 1943.

shuffle was going on, that I should be 'promoted' to be President of the Board of Trade. I thanked him very much, but said that I would have refused such an offer. I should not regard it as promotion. The Board of Trade was not an ambition of mine. I had a much better staff and was, I hoped, doing much more to win the war at M.E.W. Had it been a question of going to one of the fighting departments, or, needless to add, to the Foreign Office or the Treasury, I would not have said no. Apart from this, I had no wish to shift anyone.

Lothian comes to see me in the afternoon. He is over here for three weeks, goes to Scotland at the end of this week and will then be back in London, when he will have a talk on detail with a number of my officials. I have the impression that he is getting on very well at Washington. He is, I suspect, the sort of man Americans like; very quick to take local colour, as Leith-Ross says, and very fond of 'large ideas', particularly in a vague and unfinished form. The largest one thrown out in our talk today is that of a standing council in Washington representing all the states of pan-America and the British Commonwealth. This, he says, the President threw out the other day.

He thinks Roosevelt will win again, but Willkie[1] has the support of 80 per cent of the Press and is publicised every day in every way. Roosevelt, on the other hand, has been till now keeping out of the limelight and making few speeches. In the long run it won't make any difference to us which wins, but in the short run it would be much better if Roosevelt came back, for then the U.S. administration could go straight ahead, whereas if Willkie won, he would not take over officially until January, and there would be six months of marking time, from November till April, the last three while Willkie's new men were learning their jobs.

But all American opinion, Lothian says, is now solidly convinced that the function of Britain, vital for the U.S.A., is to bottle up the Dictators' exits into the Atlantic. ...

On the blockade, I told Lothian that I was an extremist and was determined to go on saying no, as long as I could, to all proposals to break down the blockade. He argued, not without persuasiveness, that we should soon, on our own initiative, put up a series of conditions and safeguards, subject to which we would let food into all occupied Europe. These conditions should include –

(1) Administration of all supplies coming in by an international commission, largely American.

1 Wendell Willkie (1892–1944). Republican candidate in the U.S. Presidential election of 1940. Lawyer, businessman and writer.

(2) Germans not to take any more food from occupied territories and to replace equivalent of food already taken.

(3) Frontier posts between pre-war Germany and occupied territories to be replaced and manned by Americans and others to prevent violation of above conditions.

(4) Subject to (1), (2) and (3), we should offer to do cat and mouse and let through ships one at a time so long as Germans did not break their word.

He was quite sure that Germans would reject these conditions and that, therefore, we should be able, fairly and squarely, to put blame on them for privation in Europe. He promised to let me have a note of this, and I promised to study it, but told him that my mind was firmly set at present on holding my first line of defence, the straight negative, until I was pushed out of it. So far, no hard push had come. ...

It is reported from another source that the Select Committee of the House of Commons on the Boothby case is packed against him. 'It is', said one, 'a hangman's Committee.' The principal witness against him is to be Simon, who was Chancellor of the Exchequer when Czechs' assets were in debate.[1] Old Chamberlain is dying, but some of his henchmen will enjoy getting their own back, if they can, on one who never loved him.

Sunday 27th October
Sunday. Ruth and I have lunch together – quite an amazing thing! – at the Lansdowne Club. Usually I only see her at breakfast. In the afternoon I walk round Westminster and look at the result of the land-mine which fell in Lupus Street some time ago. Though it did great devastation to bricks and mortar, it killed no one in these houses and only two policemen in all. The inhabitants were all in shelters.

Monday 28th October
Surpluses. Davies will only take the job if made a minister, Salter only if he remains a minister – and this would put too much on him, since he has also North American Purchasing Commission. I have ascertained that Davies has no following, not even in the Liberal Party, and if we turn him down we lose nothing politically. I say this

1 On 17th October, it was agreed that a Select Committee should be set up to examine allegations that Robert Boothby had pressed claims in the House of Commons on behalf of a Czech refugee without declaring an interest. The Committee reported in January 1941 against him, and he was forced to resign from the Government.

to Greenwood and suggest that we should now propose to P.M. either Schuster[1] or Leith-Ross. Lloyd has been most persistent in pressing Schuster's claims on me, and I have suggested to him that he should speak to the P.M. direct.

Greenwood and I then go to see the P.M. in his boudoir in the Cabinet War Room just before the 5 p.m. Cabinet. He comes in looking rather tired and apologises for keeping us waiting, saying, 'I have just had my sleep.' He has not much focused the point at issue but says at once that we cannot make a new ministerial job for Surpluses (Davies should, however, be spoken to nicely and told that perhaps something else may come along for him later on), and 'It looks as though Leith-Ross is the man.' Both Greenwood and I mention that Lloyd has backed Schuster, but P.M. looks very stony and says, 'I know nothing about Schuster.' This means clearly that he knows something he does not like. It also shows that either Lloyd has not pressed Schuster on the P.M. or that he has no great influence with him. I say that Leith-Ross can take on this job quite well in addition to what he is now doing for me, as I have a good deal de-centralised the work of M.E.W. The P.M. says, 'Tell him that he can have some extra staff and an additional Private Secretary.'

Thursday 31st October

See P.M. with Greenwood on Surpluses. I tell the latter beforehand that it will now be quite intolerable if the decision that Leith-Ross should do the job is to be upset. I have seen Leith-Ross after our last meeting with the P.M. and told him to go ahead and make arrangements about staff, etc. Greenwood, as usual, is all flabby and pretends now to agree with me. But earlier in the day he had sent me a copy of a letter, written without consultation with me, to the P.M. saying that he had held up the draft for the letter to sign to Leith-Ross because Davies had rung him up and said that he was now willing to do the job without salary, even though it was not a ministerial post. I bully Greenwood a bit on the telephone and say that this letter should have been shown to me, that it was so worded as to invite the P.M. to reverse his decision (Greenwood denied that this was his intention), and that Davies was no damned use anyhow, and that I regretted having ever put his name forward.

The P.M. takes my point of view and now I hope the damned thing is finally settled.

The P.M., I thought, was looking much better and less weary than two days ago. He is very pleased at reports that German aircraft are turning back and disliking the accuracy of our barrage even when it

1 George Schuster (1881–1972). Liberal National M.P. for Walsall 1938–55.

has to shoot at them through the clouds. We are getting our cat's eyes, it seems.

I said that I was glad that we were turning the main weight of our bomber attacks on to Italy for the next week, and told him that we had produced a very good leaflet, as I thought, to drop with the bombs – 'the curse of Garibaldi'. I said I hoped we should get as far as Rome but succeed in missing the Pope. P.M. said, 'I should like to tell the old man to get down into his shelter and stay there for a week.' ...

A funny story, to be related only to the select. Morrison, when Minister of Supply, sent for, and gave a tremendous wigging to, a North of England firm, Green, Wood and Batley. They had not been doing their share in the arms drive. Having been duly ticked off, their representatives left the room and Macmillan said to Morrison, 'I think you were rather hard on them. After all, they did very good work in peacetime, even though they may not have quite come up to scratch, so far, in time of war.' Morrison said, 'I don't care a damn what they did in time of peace; they're N.B.G. in time of war.' Macmillan said, 'What did you say the name of the firm was? Was it Greenwood and Attlee?'

Durbin dines and spends the evening with me. He is greatly discouraged by the statistics of production, both of aircraft and of various other arms. The effect of air attacks and lost time through warnings has been to push our output sharply down. (This, however, up to a point, was only to be expected, and we must remember that the same thing, probably on a greater scale, will have been happening in Germany whereas beyond the Atlantic these factors do not operate.) He complains also of lack of drive of Attlee and Greenwood and says that Bevin isn't really doing training on any large scale, though he is doing a lot of ballyhoo. Durbin is delighted at being at the centre of things, and says that never before had economists had such a chance of seeing all the essentials laid bare.

He saw Boothby last weekend and heard his story. ... Boothby is a queer chap. Someone said of him the other day that the trouble is that his public life is too private and his private life too public!

Friday 1st November
Lunch with Amery and am shown by Mrs Amery a photograph of their handsome-looking son Julian,[1] who has been getting into some

---

1 Julian Amery (b. 1919). S.O.E. agent in Albania 1940. Liaison Officer to Albanian Resistance Movement 1943–4. Conservative M.P. 1950–66, and since 1969. Junior minister 1957–60; Secretary of State for Air 1960–62; Minister of Aviation 1962–4; Public Building and Works 1970; Housing and Construction 1970–72; Minister of State at the Foreign and Commonwealth Office 1972–4.

trouble for indiscretion in the Balkans and the Middle East and is on his way home to be an airman. I have said that I should like to see him on his return, and I gather that I should win the heart of Mrs Amery for ever if I could make some arrangement to use him.

Friday 8th November

This evening C.D. [Nelson][1] gives a party designed to smooth away many obstacles. I am put between D.M.O. [Director of Military Operations][2] and D.A.I. [Director of Air Intelligence];[3] also present D.M.I., C.D. and Gladwyn. I hear afterwards that D.A.I. thinks I talk too much to D.M.O. and too little to him. It is therefore suggested that I must have D.A.I. alone by himself another time to smooth *him* down. Oh, all these male schoolgirls! D.M.O. is very good and seems prepared to be helpful. They were all horrified when it was said that King Bomba was not going after all,[4] and I think he will take steps to deal with this. I say that if he will release Colonel Gubbins[5] I will not ask him for any more senior officers; also that I have been pressed to appeal to P.M. over case of Gubbins. D.M.O. says that he thinks it would be more difficult to succeed if I did make such an appeal, as the case against releasing Gubbins is very strong. The C.-in-C. Home Forces[6] is most anxious to keep him, but, I gather, the C.I.G.S. [Chief of Imperial General Staff][7] is prepared to let me have him. The issue is not yet quite decided, but D.M.O. is hopeful I shall get him. D.M.O. still thinks it doubtful whether I need a D.T. [Director of Training], but I say that if I get Gubbins, he can do this as well as other duties.

Quite a good evening I thought, not hearing about the D.A.I. till next day.

---

1 Sir Frank Nelson, q.v., Executive Director of S.O.E. 1940–42, was referred to as 'C.D.' within the organisation.
2 Major-General J. N. Kennedy, later Sir John (1893–1970). Director of Military Operations and Plans at the War Office 1940–43. Assistant C.I.G.S. (Operations and Intelligence) 1943–5. Governor of Southern Rhodesia 1946–54. Deputy Director of Military Operations 1938; Director of Plans 1939.
3 Air Vice Marshal C. E. H. Medhurst, later Sir Charles (1896–1954). Director of Air Intelligence.
4 Laurence Grand ('King Bomba'), whom Dalton had wished to have posted abroad, managed for a time to delay his departure.
5 Colonel C. M. Gubbins, later Sir Colin (1896–1976). Director of Operations and Training at S.O.E. 1940–42. See Appendix A.
6 Field Marshal Sir Alan Brooke, later 1st Viscount Alanbrooke (1883–1963). Commander-in-Chief Home Forces 1940–41. Commander Second Army Corps, British Expeditionary Forces 1939–40. Chief of Imperial General Staff 1941–6.
7 General Sir John Dill, q.v.

Saturday 9th November

See Kingsley Wood at No. 11 at his invitation, regarding the application by the Duchess of Windsor to be allowed to send ten thousand francs into France to pay arrears of wages to her servants. I have written Minutes taking strong objection to this. Wood says that the P.M., who always had a soft spot for the Duke,[1] thought of the ingenious device of sending him to the Bahamas, but he is impatient out there and, if thwarted, inclined to throw everything up. He might feel thwarted if we refused this demand of the Duchess. But, to meet my objection, Wood proposes that payment should be made not in dollars but out of the Duchess's sterling assets. He hopes I will agree to this. I say, 'Yes, if you will undertake to answer any question asked in Parliament.'

Dalton first met Colonel Gubbins at the Polish Embassy on 18th November 1939 and was very much impressed by him. 'Next year when I was Minister of Economic Warfare, and looking for a good soldier to help me to plan, and train personnel for, Special Operations in Europe, somebody mentioned Gubbins,' Dalton later recalled. 'At once I remembered this Polish dinner-party and, after much battling with other claimants for his body, I got him, and he rendered splendid service in a field increasingly important to our war effort.'[2]

Monday 11th November

Gubbins to see me this afternoon. I say, 'Do you remember where we met last?' He says no. I say, 'I sat next to you at a dinner at the Polish Embassy immediately after the defeat of Poland. I found then that you shared with me not only an appreciation of the Poles, but what is even more eccentric, an appreciation both of Poles and Czechs.' I say that I hope he will take on a number of functions for me, including liaison with Poles and Czechs, and also be my Director of Training. He says that today battle royal is going on between the C.I.G.S. and the G.O.C. Home Forces for his body, which the former has promised to me.

   Rumour runs riot that Halifax is leaving the Foreign Office and is to be succeeded by Eden. Leeper is said to be bothering about in the hope that if this happens he will supplant Cadogan.

1 Edward, Duke of Windsor (1894–1972). Reigned as King Edward VIII during 1936, before abdicating in order to marry Mrs Wallis Simpson (b. 1896).
2 FY, p. 288.

Tuesday 12th November

Lindemann to lunch with Gladwyn and C.D. [Nelson], and afterwards the Prof. and Gladwyn and I visit Station XIV. A successful trip I think, and the Prof. is quite friendly to me, though still doubtful whether Gladwyn is not too much 'Foreign Office'. I tell the Prof. that he must advise me on the future of this Station and that I shall make no change till he does so. (I write him a letter in this sense next day.)

We deposit Lindemann at Uxbridge and, returning alone with Gladwyn in his car (having used this so that the three of us could talk freely on the way down), we have a good talk on the inner nature of politics and questions of personal publicity. I explain to him that in ordinary days of Party warfare the success of a politician depends on two things only; first, the success of his Party, and second, his own success within his Party. Therefore, for many years I was almost the worst hated by Tories and Liberals of all my Parliamentary Labour colleagues, and this was one reason why I was popular with my colleagues, who enjoyed the way in which I went for our opponents. (I also related to him the story of my election to the Parliamentary Labour E.C. in 1925, the simple-mindedness of Arthur Ponsonby,[1] and the confession afterwards made to me by Scott Lindsay.[2]) Just now, however, when, as the P.M. said the other day of the U.S., 'All our affairs are somewhat mixed up together', everything wore a slightly different aspect. He said that the Tory feelings towards me had only lately, especially since I had become a minister, been changing a great deal. (Wilmot told me earlier this week that he met Tory M.P.s who liked me because I was 'belligerent', now against Hitler as in other days against them. Loftus[3] had said that he would like to see Eden go to the Foreign Office and me to the War Office, because what was wanted there was someone who was prepared to be ruthless with some of the Generals! Wilmot had also explained that I had a very good press with our own Party in the House because, alone among No. 1 ministers, I made a practice of lunching where I had always lunched, among the chaps, and did not even bring Wilmot, though my P.P.S., to lunch at the same table with me.) Gladwyn said that a story was circulating, though as yet not within very wide circles, that

1 'the simple-mindedness of Arthur Ponsonby'. At the end of Dalton's first session in 1925, Arthur Ponsonby proposed Dalton for the Labour Party Parliamentary Executive. In the ballot, Dalton and Ponsonby tied for last place. It was decided that Scott Lindsay, q.v., Secretary of the P.L.P., should draw lots between them. Lindsay did so, and Dalton won – placing him on the Front Bench, where he remained until 1955. Later Ponsonby told Dalton that he had voted for Dalton but not for himself. Dalton replied that he had voted for both of them (FY, p. 160).
2 H. Scott Lindsay (1879–1959). Secretary of the P.L.P. 1918–44.
3 P. C. Loftus (1877–1956). Conservative M.P. for Lowestoft 1934–45.

I was a minister who was not only on top of his job, but was never tired and never ill and generally cheerful, though sometimes righteously and explosively angry. He himself had started the nickname 'Dr Dynamo' which, he said, had gone very well. Meanwhile, many said, looking round at ministers at large, 'Who is there?' Some day P.M. might have a stroke, 'And then?'

Thursday 14th November

After lunching at Drapers' Hall, very near which a land-mine had done great damage last month, I go to the Foreign Office and call on Cadogan on my way to Halifax. ... I speak in particular of the affair of King Bomba and say that he has now pulled some direct wire to Eden, that Gladwyn was going to see Eden today (in fact he couldn't get him, but only J. P. L. Thomas),[1] and that my patience is running very thin indeed. Cadogan says that he thinks we can soon deal with King Bomba if he continues to give trouble. His irregularities and misdemeanours are very numerous. Cadogan says that he would be quite prepared himself to go and speak frankly to Eden about this. ...

I ... go in to Halifax, with whom I have a more intimate conversation than ever before ... he begins to tell me of a great row which he has just been having with the P.M. It is about a private telegram which Lampson[2] sent to Eden protesting against the further transfer of aircraft from Egypt to Greece as being 'quite crazy'. Through some mistake in the Foreign Office – these mistakes seem to me to happen too bloody often! – this communication is treated as 'Departmental secret' and gets a limited circulation, including the King, the P.M., and – as he tells me afterwards – Gladwyn. The P.M. is furious and instructs Halifax to send a message to Lampson rebuking him for his tone and substance. Halifax returns a Minute arguing that this is unreasonable and that the message was not intended for the P.M.'s eyes. The P.M. then minutes back that he is astonished that Halifax is failing to carry out his orders and that the rebuke has not already been sent. Halifax then walks over to No. 10 and tells the P.M. that it is as though he had seen a private letter which was not addressed to him, but that, of course, if he wishes the rebuke sent, it shall be sent. P.M. then says, 'I don't wish to hear anything more about the matter.'

'A most extraordinary man!' says Halifax, and then relates how the first office he ever held was Under-Secretary for the Colonies in

1 J. P. L. Thomas, later 1st Viscount Cilcennin (1903–60). Conservative M.P. for Hereford 1931–55. Junior Lord of the Treasury 1940–43. Financial Secretary to the Admiralty 1943–5. 1st Lord of the Admiralty 1951–6.

2 Sir Miles Lampson, later 1st Baron Killearn (1880–1964). Ambassador to Egypt and High Commissioner to the Sudan 1936–46.

1922. This was under Winston, who was in Egypt when Halifax was appointed, and on returning was furious, having wanted one of the Guests[1] to be his Under-Secretary. Thereafter, for three weeks he would not see Halifax, in spite of many efforts by the latter. When finally he succeeded in breaking in to the presence of his Chief, he said, 'Mr Churchill, I have no desire to be your Under-Secretary, nor to have any other office. I am prepared to resign and leave this office tomorrow, but, so long as I remain here, I expect to be treated like a gentleman.' Then, he said, Winston asked him to sit down and have a drink and became most friendly, and since then their relationship, though having ups and downs, has on the whole been pretty good. Halifax then told me that the P.M. had had a row with Eden because a certain General had written 'so far as I can make out the Prime Minister's scribble ... ' and this – again what shocking staff work! – had been afterwards seen by the P.M. who had thereupon dictated a sharp rebuke to the General and had demanded that the General should be required to initial this rebuke to show that he had seen it.

I said that I was rather relieved to hear that the P.M. just now was pouncing on a number of his colleagues, since I thought that a little half-breeze which I had been having with him might be evidence of concentrated intrigue through him against me. I confessed that I was not always quite sure just how to handle the P.M. Halifax said, 'Always stand up to him. He hates doormats. If you begin to give way he will simply wipe his feet upon you.' He then added with a smile, 'I do not think you will find much difficulty in standing up to him.'

I then asked Halifax whether there was any truth in the rumours that he was going to resign. I said I hoped that they were not true and that, for myself, I would sooner he was Foreign Secretary than anyone else. (In saying this, I had some alternative possibles in mind, including Eden and Lady Astor's nominee, Lothian.) As he knew, there had been many rumours lately and I wondered whether the *démenti*[2] of a few days ago meant what it said. He replied that he had heard nothing either of the rumours or of the *démenti* until the P.M. had told him that he had put out the latter. He had always told the P.M. that he did not wish to stay on one day longer than the P.M. desired, but he did not think that, until we won some victories, anyone else, even an archangel, could do much more than he was doing at the Foreign Office.

I said that when he had been kind enough to propose in these last days, more than once, to come and see me at M.E.W., thus reversing

1 O. M. Guest, F. E. Guest and C. H. C. Guest, three brothers who were Liberal M.P.s, and cousins of Churchill.
2 *'démenti'*: official denial.

the official rule of the road, it had been thought by some of my staff that he was coming *pour prendre congé*.[1] He smiled at this and said that there was no truth in such an idea. ...

Julian Amery calls on me and makes an excellent impression. He is only twenty-one and would, but for the war, still have been at Oxford. He has shown much energy, initiative and resource in these last two years, having been *Daily Express* correspondent in Spain during the Civil War, and thereafter active – some of our diplomats think much too active – in the Balkans. An intelligent young man whom I should like to see effectively used somewhere, and I so minute to Gladwyn later in the evening.

Friday 15th November

I am now told that the Air Ministry will object to Amery Jnr being released. I say, 'Then let them say so, and then, and not before, I will take it up with Sinclair', with whom I lunch today. He is very friendly and easy and I learn from him, for my further reassurance, that he receives at least three violent prods from the P.M. every day, demanding immediate explanations of this and that and a variety of immediate actions. This, he says, is the P.M.'s way and it has much to be said for it, from the point of stimulation. On the other hand, the procedure must take a great deal of the P.M.'s time and somewhat distract him from other matters.

I praise Portal and he says that there was strong pressure for Dowding[2] which he is sure he was right to resist. Dowding has now got stereotyped, keeps things to himself, and has been losing the confidence both of his subordinates and his equals. Within a few days it will be announced that he is being shifted to a job in America, where he can do very good work.

I ask Archie [Sinclair] whether he has any objection to my establishing a relationship with Portal, and he says that he would greatly welcome it. I ask him to drop a word to Portal to this effect. There are, I say, many matters connected with my Other Life[3] about which I should like to talk to Portal, and I have also a relationship from time to time with the Chiefs of Staff. Of these Portal seems to me to be the only one who is alive.

Saturday 16th November

In the afternoon to Denham and spend the night at Van's. Quite

---

1 *'pour prendre congé'*: to take his leave.
2 Air Chief Marshal Hugh Dowding, later 1st Baron (1882–1970). Air Officer Commander-in-Chief Fighter Command 1936–40. Special Duty (with Ministry of Air Production) in U.S.A. 1940–41.
3 S.O.E.

worthwhile. Both he and Sarita[1] are rather ill. She has something wrong with her blood and has to have an injection once a week, otherwise she would quickly collapse. He also says that she has lost a lot of weight. She is, as usual, very charming to me, though her conversation still largely consists of complaints about others, who never see or notice Van. It is all rather one track grievance-pushing, and would become an awful bore if one had much of it. With a little of it now and again one can sympathise, not insincerely. A myth is growing up in her mind and in his that I am the only politician who has ever understood both Van and Hitler!

Sunday 17th November
By car with Van to Country House. He still has some tummy trouble which makes him wake up in the night and want to be sick and not be able. So he loses a good deal of sleep, even though he takes some mild drug each night when he goes to bed. He still has that wonderfully quick mind which has always attracted me, though he has been so long outside the machine that, allowing also for the nervous strain and long frustration through which he has been passing, many of his quick judgments nowadays are quite wrong.

   We talk of persons and types on the journey to Country House. He deplores the pallid trio now running the Foreign Office – Halifax, Butler and Cadogan. And then, below them, I deplore the row of sibilant Assistant Under-Secretaries, throwing in Sargent, with the best brain of them, who is Deputy Under-Secretary, but the man is always half sick. Van says that all these people make the most deplorable impression on the outer world, so dull and slow and never ready to run any risk anywhere. He has heard, he says, from a friend who has recently been doing a motor tour in this country, that in the bar of every public house he visited men were jeering at the Foreign Office over their beer. Moreover, all these poor dull creatures have to compete with another tradition in the public mind, of diplomats who are over-dressed and elegant and amusing and go to bed with Countesses. This legend still lingers, though there is little to support it now, and it makes the public laugh still more at this present lot. I say that I have heard that it needed a special Club to be founded in order to organise the habit in the Foreign Office of calling William Strang[2] by his Christian name. Then, taking this rather obvious opening, I say to

1 Sarita Vansittart, née Ward. Widow of Sir Colville Barclay, a diplomat.
2 William Strang, later 1st Baron (1893–1978). Assistant Under-Secretary at the Foreign Office 1929–43. Acting Counsellor, then Counsellor, to the U.S.S.R. 1930–39. Permanent Under-Secretary at the Foreign Office (German Section) 1947–9; Foreign Office 1949–53.

Van that in this world of dull undaring slow-coaches, he will appreciate why I find Gladwyn so refreshing and have picked him for his present job. He does not argue back on this, but repeats that Gladwyn has got on so fast that he is bound to have created some jealousy against himself and that he would therefore be wise to show a little extra care in his personal relations with those likely to be jealous. His manner, half humorous and half aloof, does not appeal to everyone. It is, Van thinks, like very dry wine, and some people prefer sweet wine. On the other hand, he says, people who drink a lot of dry wine come, after a time, to like it better. I say that the Generals certainly seem to like this particular brand, and this has been very important in recent negotiations which Gladwyn, I repeat, has conducted with very great skill and persistence.

Monday 18th November
Gubbins comes to see me. He is released for the duties I want. He makes a very good first impression. He too is very quick and dynamic.

Gubbins and I lunch with Sikorski at the Hotel Rubens, which is now the Polish military H.Q. Also present Sosnkowski,[1] Kot and Retinger,[2] who seems now most firmly attached to Sikorski. The latter thinks that Gubbins is a colonel and addresses him as *'mon Colonel'*. The Poles are very childish about these matters, and Sosnkowski, who in any case is very friendly to me, saying that no other British name is better known or better loved in Poland, rises to still greater heights of regard when I tell him that I was an artillery officer in the last war. The gathering is, in any case, a *succès fou*. This is not only our impression but is reported by Namier[3] who meets Kot next day. I say to Sikorski, not less than six times during the meal, that I hope when next he sees or writes to the P.M. he will tell him how very excellent our relations are.

Cabinet in the afternoon. Admiralty *contra mundum*. They have no ships to spare, they always say. They are assailed not only by me but by Cross and Lloyd (with special reference to the African trade), backed by Halifax.

Mrs Phillimore has, I learn, a reputation for great indiscretion. I

1 General C. Sosnkowski (1885–1969). Polish infantry general since 1935. Member of the Polish Socialist Party. Minister of War 1920–23, 1924. Inspector of the Polish Army 1927–39. Minister of State 1939–41. Polish Supreme Commander during the Second World War, he was dismissed in 1944 and replaced by General Komorowski.
2 J. H. Retinger (1888–1960). Polish internationalist. Dalton had known him since the 1920s.
3 L. B. Namier, later Sir Lewis (1888–1960). Historian. Political Secretary of the Jewish Agency for Palestine 1929–31. Professor of Modern History at Manchester University 1931–53.

enquire why and it seems that she conducts long conversations on the telephone with Maisky and Quo.[1] These, of course, are listened in to.

Tuesday 19th November
Meet Greenwood at lunch. He says that the P.M. has been prodding Bevin because his training schemes are going too slowly, and that he used to prod Morrison constantly and violently over the output of munitions. It thus seems, as I collect the experiences of colleagues, that they are all much more and worse prodded than I am. There is, therefore, no ground to suspect any special intrigues, or at any rate any special success for intriguers, around the P.M. against me. On the contrary, I seem to be getting off pretty easily.

Greenwood says that he is constantly having trouble with the Beaver, who won't attend, or accept the decisions of, Cabinet Committees, but always says, 'I will bring this matter up myself in the War Cabinet.' P.M. said to Bevin the other day that the Beaver was a magician. Bevin replied, 'Yes, he is an illusionist.'

Greenwood is now starting to have his Economic Policy Committee once a week, which is a long-overdue piece of routine.

The P.M. has finished his controversy with me over Albanians poisoning Italian food. I disclaim all responsibility for these habits, or for encouraging them, but pointed out that 'the weapons used in "total war" vary with tradition. In Albania, with its semi-Oriental background, they appear to include poisoning the enemy's food. In Western Christendom, on the other hand, they include withholding food, unpoisoned, from the enemy, either by blockade or by air and submarine attacks on food ships.'

This, I thought, was rather bright (an even brighter version, drafted for me by Gladwyn, I mark 'Approved, but not sent'). P.M.'s Secretary then wrote to mine that I should be interested to know that P.M. had written in the margin, 'It is the difference between treachery and war.' This is the end of that!

Wednesday 20th November
To the Cabinet. As I enter I hear a voice saying, 'It fairly gives me a pain in the belly.' This is the Beaver commenting on air damage, not severe, to factories in the Midlands. The P.M., as we know, is most mercurial. Today he seemed delighted with the war and is encouraging the Beaver, praising his last week's output.

Discussion on a paper jointly submitted by Duff Cooper and me, with a note of approval by the Chiefs of Staff, on Propaganda. This is

1 Quo Tai-chi (1889–1952). Chinese Ambassador to Britain 1935–41. Chinese Foreign Minister 1941–7.

accepted, in its broad lines, after some rather desultory discussion. P.M. says that he is being pressed to make a statement on war aims. He is told that he will be given material to handle 'in what they call my own inimitable way'. He does not wish, however, merely to pronounce 'unctuous platitudes'. Can we do more just now? He will wait and see what is put up to him. On the paper there is some discussion as to whether we should, in our propaganda, now offer the enemy 'a fair deal' after victory. There is some doubt as to whether public opinion here would not resent such talk now. 'After we have beaten them we may decide to be generous, but people now are saying "skin them alive".' None the less, there must be latitude and suppleness in our propaganda.

Thursday 21st November
It is reported that a party took place at the Romanian Legation in Moscow two nights ago. The German Ambassador arrived late and at once withdrew into a corner to converse with the Italian and the Jap. All three, and particularly the Italian, seemed most delighted. The German showed them a piece of paper. Later in the evening most of the rest of the company, nearly all pro-Axis diplomats, talked in groups with animation and apparent satisfaction. This is interpreted to mean that Stalin has just agreed, and so informed the German Ambassador, to the proposals made to Molotov in Berlin. These, it is surmised, include a free hand for Hitler in the Balkans, including early and strong help for Italy against Greece. The Russians, on the other hand, would continue to pursue benevolent neutrality towards Germany and would receive in return a share in the control of the Straits. They would not at present take any armed action either for or against Turkey.

There are, of course, more grandiose rumours in circulation of promises to Russia, of Iran, Afghanistan, even India. (I would gladly let them have India if they would change over to our side. This has been a favourite idea of mine for years!)

Friday 22nd November
Nelson says that he has evidence that Morton (who, however, seems hardly ever to see the P.M. nowadays) is no friend of his or Gladwyn's or mine, and would much like to discredit our whole show. On the other hand, Nelson says that Hancock told him the other night that Colville, one of the P.M.'s Private Secretaries, not knowing for whom Hancock was working, and gossiping at large about ministers, said that there was 'a prevalent opinion' that the P.M. did not like Dalton, but that this was quite untrue. On the contrary, the P.M. thought that

Dalton was the best of the Labour ministers, having much more drive and energy than the rest, some of whom bored him stiff. Later in the evening when Hancock revealed that he was working for me, Colville had said, 'Ah, then I see why you were so interested in my reference to Dalton earlier this evening.'

'A prevalent opinion' must mean at least two people, and it seems that Gladwyn said something to Colville, who is also very friendly with Hancock, who also knows some of my recent minor discontents. I guess that the P.M. will have liked some of my recent short notes and ripostes.

An impudent attempt by Ministry of Information to steal leaflets from me.[1] Much ado because that fool Stokes[2] put down a question to the Ministry of Information asking that leaflets should be published. On this Nicolson[3] got hold of my simple and liberal-minded Parliamentary Secretary, Foot, and inveigled him into discussions about putting the leaflets in the Library or debating them in secret session. Butler was also drawn into this and, in spite of Gladwyn's earlier reports that he was anxious to play with me, and my offer that if he would, I would let him in to some of my secrets, is now being sticky and obstructive. Nicolson has now written Foot a letter in which he practically suggests that the best solution would be to give leaflets back to Ministry of Information. This is all completely *ultra vires* of Under-Secretaries, and I tell Foot that he has been manoeuvred into an impossible position. I also tell him to leave it to me in the future. I intend to have the whole thing suppressed in Parliament with a high hand (and I so arrange the following week with Halifax and Attlee).

Monday 25th November
Coming out from the Cabinet, I find Bracken and R. A. Butler sitting in the ante-room. Bracken says, 'There is that great brute who, like his friend Mr Bevin, tramples all opposition in the mud. He has no liberal sentiments at all!' And so we drift back to the case of King Bomba. I guess that now I have some reputation for having first got rid of him and then removed him from the country. Bracken says, in friendly fashion, that 'people' came to him and said that my treatment of King Bomba was an outrage and should not something be

---

1 Leaflets for dropping in enemy countries were one of Dalton's SO1 'black' propaganda responsibilities.
2 R. R. Stokes (1897–1957). Labour M.P. for Ipswich 1938–57. Minister of Works 1950–51; Lord Privy Seal 1951; Minister of Materials 1951.
3 H. G. Nicolson, later Sir Harold (1886–1968). Parliamentary Secretary at the Ministry of Information 1940–41. National Labour M.P. for Leicester West 1935–45. Foreign Office and Diplomatic Service 1919–29. Author, journalist and diarist.

said to the P.M. But, says Bracken, he told them that the P.M. was much too busy to be troubled with such matters. Someone had suggested that King Bomba could bring a petition of right against someone, but this also had been discouraged. I said, 'Whatever I have been, I have never been a Liberal.' I fancy that I am now scoring a little in the role of the 'strong man'. Butler, I carry off with me in my car for a drink at my Ministry. He says, 'I never go to the Cabinet and I suppose I never shall. Winston has ruled that Cadogan is the *remplaçant*[1] of the Viscount.[2] He made it quite clear that he regards Cadogan like one of the Chiefs of Staff to a Service minister, and therefore he goes in with the Viscount. Neville never gave such a ruling, and it was left indeterminate in his day, but Winston has made it quite clear.' I said that I did not remember in 1929 any such ruling having been given. Van did not then go to the Cabinet with Arthur Henderson,[3] nor did I remember ever being his *remplaçant* in the Cabinet, though I sometimes was on the C.I.D. [Committee of Imperial Defence]. Butler said that there was also some doubt as to whether he or Cadogan went through a door first; they stood back and waved each other forward. I said, 'I never had any of these difficulties with Van; I always went through the door first.' Butler said, 'I don't mind at all. I see the Envoys a good deal.' ...

I related this conversation afterwards to Gladwyn, who had told me that relations had lately not been very good between Butler and Halifax, who had sometimes ticked off Butler in front of other people. Cadogan, Gladwyn said, regarded Butler as a complete poop, and it was clear from Butler's outpourings to me that he was feeling that his position, *vis-à-vis* Cadogan, was not satisfactory.

In addition to the quarrel between SO1 and the Ministry of Information about leaflets, there was a parallel dispute about broadcasts to enemy-occupied countries. Both battles highlighted the problem created by the lack of a propaganda policy co-ordinated by a single organisation. Dalton's suggestion that he should be responsible for all broadcasts to enemy countries was met with the counter-suggestion that all propaganda should go back to the Ministry of Information. The setting up of the Political Warfare

1 *'remplaçant'*: substitute.
2 i.e. Lord Halifax, q.v., the Foreign Secretary.
3 Arthur Henderson (1863–1935). Labour M.P. 1903–18, 1919–22, 1924–31, 1933–5. Foreign Secretary 1929–31, when Dalton was Under-Secretary at the Foreign Office. President of the Board of Education 1915–16; Paymaster-General 1916; Minister without Portfolio 1916–17. Home Secretary 1924.

Executive, based on an amalgamation of some sections of the Ministry of Information, the B.B.C. and SO1, under joint ministerial control, was an attempt to deal with this.

Tuesday 26th November
Portal to dine with me and Gladwyn at the Lansdowne Club, where we get a private room. This is a great success. Portal is first-class, fresh, thinking for himself, modest and admittedly a bit of an innocent in politics. We all agree that the War will best be won by those who think it's fun! He says he finds the Cabinet most fascinating. He regards the Beaver as a menace, and the combination with Alexander much too obvious. Alexander wants to steal the Coastal Command, and the Beaver is backing him on this. We explain to Portal the layout of S.O. [Special Operations]. Much of this is new to him. He asks if I know anything of a certain Colonel Grand who was recommended to him for employment under the Air Ministry by Professor Lindemann and Lord Swinton. (Thus the plot thickens!) This man was said to be a great authority on industrial questions. Portal asked the D.A.I. [Director of Air Intelligence], who exploded, and Portal therefore declined the offer. I told him of the sequel. On Italy Portal was very sensible and offered many facilities. He thought that we should make it as easy as possible for Italy to leave Germany in the lurch. He would not, for instance, insist on re-establishing the Negus in Abyssinia.

Wednesday 27th November
A Labour Party day. Party Meeting, National Executive, several rounds of drinks at the Marquis of Granby, lunch with Lathan and Garro Jones.

In the afternoon 'Four-Power Conference' in which we mostly discuss attack by Ministry of Information on leaflets and our counter-attack on foreign broadcasts. Gladwyn reads splenetic and almost libellous Minute from Oliver Harvey[1] to Peterson which, through ineptitude of Sammy Hood[2] (Duff Cooper's Private Secretary) has come into his hands. He has taken a copy of it and returned it. It is clear that there is the most frightful rancour against us in the Ministry of Information. Harvey suggests that Leeper and Co. left for the

1 Sir Oliver Harvey, 4th Bart, later 1st Baron (1893–1968). Minister to France 1940. Principal Private Secretary to the Foreign Secretary 1936–9, 1941–3. Ambassador to France 1948–54.
2 Samuel Hood, 6th Viscount (1910–81). Private Secretary to the Minister of Information 1939–41. Deputy Under-Secretary of State at the Foreign Office/Foreign and Commonwealth Office 1962–9.

Country 'after the first bomb had fallen in Berkeley Square'.[1] They have played into our hands and given us another stick to beat them with in the future if we should need it. It is thought that I should go straight to the P.M. next week and ask how he would feel about my taking over the additional broadcasts. If I get him in the right initial mood, I could propose to him that I should then go and talk to Cooper about it. Otherwise Cooper may get in first. The Cabinet Committee on the B.B.C. has not yet met, I learn from Morrison, and I am not in any hurry that it should. Agreed that final tactics should be worked out at the weekend when I shall go to Country House.

Wilmot was disturbed by talk with Gladwyn and me two nights ago regarding co-operation between two wings.[2] Gladwyn and Leeper don't yet pull well together. Wilmot says that they should settle many more questions between themselves and not bring them to Van or me. (I, indeed, deliberately rowed them both at the Four-Power Conference saying that Van and I could not be bothered with all these disputes within the city walls and that it was intolerable that the subordinates of my Under-Secretaries should fiddle about with my instructions, e.g. to P. Willert to go to Gibraltar.)[3] Wilmot thought that Gladwyn should accept, without *arrière pensée*, the fact that Leeper must continue to run SO1. He had been rather taken aback when Gladwyn had said that he thought Gaitskell could run it quite well. This, said Wilmot, would mean under him.

Thursday 28th November
Gladwyn reports that Ministry of Information are buzzing with fury and that all sorts of tales are being put about. Thus Hopkinson[4] asked Gladwyn this morning whether it was true that I had been on the point of being chucked out of my job – I gather he was referring to M.E.W. – the story being that there had been a great row at a meeting of my colleagues (I am not sure whether Labour colleagues or all colleagues) and that I had only been saved because Albert Alexander, who was to have delivered an attack on me, had made a mess of it. I cudgel my brains, without success, to think where this tale could have come from. I have had a brush or two with Alexander over lack of ships to enforce the blockade, but he is not, I think, in any strong position to lead any attack on me either in the Government as a whole or among my Labour colleagues.

1 A reference to the move of the SO1 headquarters to Woburn Abbey.
2 The two wings of S.O.E. – SO1 and SO2.
3 Paul Willert. Executive of S.O.E. Later joined R.A.F.
4 H. L. d'A. Hopkinson, later 1st Baron Colyton (b. 1902). Private Secretary to the Permanent Under-Secretary of State at the Foreign Office 1940. Conservative M.P. 1950–56. Junior minister 1951–5.

Broadcasting to the United States on the night of 30th November, Dalton avoided any hint of a retreat on the vexed question of relief to enemy-occupied countries – drawing attention to Churchill's offer (which he had inspired) of provision for plenty, after the Germans had been defeated, from an accumulated stock.

Friday 29th November
Still on my American broadcast. Take the precaution of showing Halifax the script and asking whether there is anything in it which embarrasses him. He says no and makes only a few very minor suggestions. I have included some departmental suggestions for increased 'aid short of war', including tightening up of export control, black-listing of ships etc. Halifax asks David Scott[1] – hitherto, I have been told, the least feeble of the Sibilants – to come in on this. He reads my page with infinite slowness and solemnity and then says he thinks that it is all right and will put good ideas into the Americans' heads. I then leave Halifax having reinsured myself against any attack by the Ministry of Information or other critics, of whom, no doubt, a good few lie in wait just now! I go on to see Butler who, as usual, gives an impression of having no confidence in himself (Peake says that he is going to suggest to Halifax to make Butler the Governor of an Indian Province. He thinks Halifax would be glad to be rid of him). On emerging from Butler's room I find Scott hanging about in the passage. He says that he thinks perhaps it would be better if, instead of making positive proposals to the Americans, I would just tell them 'where the shoe pinches'. 'So', say I, 'you have changed your mind in the last five minutes since you and I were with the Secretary of State. To turn it round the way you want would be to advertise the weakness of our blockade, and that I do not want to do.' He havers on a little more and then says, 'Well you see what I mean, don't you?' and I reply, 'And *you* see what *I* mean, don't you?' When I report this feebleness to Gladwyn, he says, 'He must have run off to see Jack Balfour.'[2]

Proceed with Gladwyn to record my talk, and find a young man named Ferguson[3] who is very helpful. I rehearse this particular broad-

---

1 Sir David Scott (b. 1887). Assistant Under-Secretary of State at the Foreign Office 1938–44. Deputy Under-Secretary 1944–7.
2 J. Balfour, later Sir John (1894–1983). Counsellor at the Foreign Office 1940–41.
3 Probably J. Fergusson, later Sir James, 8th Bart (1904–73). Talks producer, Overseas Service, B.B.C. London 1940–41. Broadcast nightly on Nazi propaganda, Overseas Service 1941–4.

cast much more carefully, since it is on the whole North American hook-up, than I have done previous ones for this country alone. The chief criticisms are that I go too slow – Americans like their radio talks faster than we do – and the old tale that I drop my voice at the end of sentences. It is agreed that I shall go back next morning to hear the discs played back.

Saturday 30th November

Hear record of my broadcast played back and hate it. We all dislike our voice on records when we hear it. Also this is much too slow and dull. I should have switched it off quite quick had I been an American. Therefore, with hints and stimulus from Ferguson and Gladwyn, I do it all over again, and this time, I believe, damned well. Hearing it played back again *this* time, I am quite moved and should have liked to hear some more! ...

To Country House with Gaitskell. Attend large meeting, the first to be held in the Abbey,[1] where reports are given of various activities. We have taken over the Abbey now and are also extruding Mrs Samuel, the Duke's[2] ex-housekeeper who shares his anti-war views and used to keep, so they say, a nigger night club in Bloomsbury. She is trying to get into the old rectory, now occupied by Leeper and wife and daughter, and has half won over officials of the Office of Works to her side. However, I write a firm letter to Reith[3] which, I think, will finally cook her goose. To make doubly sure, I have asked the appropriate authorities to make a secret report on her, and this, I know, will be adverse.

Take a quick short walk with Crossman.

Sunday 1st December

Gladwyn ... says that [Eccles] would make 'a wonderful Ambassador'. 'He always knows what is in the other chap's mind.' I think very well of his ability, though behind him I always see the finicking, flickering figure of Sir Samuel Hoare. Therefore, my tendency when talking to Eccles is to row and rag him a bit, though I tend to take his advice on detail and have recommended him for an honour. I said to him the

---

1 Woburn Abbey, the new headquarters of SO1.
2 H. W. S. Russell, 12th Duke of Bedford (1883–1953). He was the object of much public criticism because of his pacifism in the Second World War. Before the war, he was Chairman of John Beckett's British People's Party. Beckett was subsequently interned under Defence Regulation 18B.
3 Sir John Reith, later 1st Baron (1889–1972). Minister of Works October 1940–February 1942. Minister of Information January–May 1940. Minister of Transport May–October 1940. Director-General of the B.B.C. 1927–38.

other day, 'This policy of yours and Hoare's goes far beyond appeasement. It is sheer abasement.'

Monday 2nd December
See Halifax over latest threat to our blockade through American pressure to send tinned milk, etc., to Vichy France. I say that I take a most serious view of this, that we cannot hold a line based on a distinction between occupied and unoccupied territory, and that I must take it to the Cabinet and let them decide. I will make a paper which can be discussed at the Cabinet this week. I start making the paper, and this has jumped up to No. 1 on my mental agenda, quite displacing the question about foreign broadcasts about which the people in the Country have, as usual, been instigating me.

No. 2 on my agenda is Italy. Here I feel very explosive, C.D. [Nelson] not yet having got anyone in his Italian section, and nothing serious being done by us to hammer the Italians. I therefore summon Gladwyn, C.D. and A.D. [Taylor][1] to a conference and blow them all up. C.D. is very tired and says he has had no lunch. I say that means he is not running his office right, nor taking time off. His machine is choked. He does not devolve, nor, sufficiently, does Gladwyn. Why don't they ask for more assistants? I have got to take the Italian thing in my own hands. I shall get George Martelli[2] up from the country to hustle about and get things going. I could not answer the P.M. if he asked me, 'What are you doing to Italy?' There is no liaison with D.C.O. [Director of Combined Operations][3] We don't know what he is up to.

I hope this rowing will have done them all good. But I confess that C.D. in particular, and A.D. too to some extent, seems always to make difficulties about everything. I say, 'All these objections of yours would be arguments against doing anything anywhere at any time!' I ask Gladwyn afterwards to make sure that I have not hurt the feelings of the other two too much.

Charles Peake claims the credit for the publicity in the press for my broadcast. He says that if it had been left to Lockhart, practically nothing would have got in at all. I am also vexed at the delay in fixing

---

1 G. F. Taylor (1902–79). Chief of Staff at S.O.E. to Sir Frank Nelson 1940–42, then to Sir Charles Hambro. Special Emissary to S.O.E. Overseas Missions 1943. Australian.
2 George Martelli (b. 1903). Worked for SO2 Italian section; later Head of Italian Region, Political Warfare Executive. Chief Foreign Correspondent of the *Morning Post* 1931–7. Novelist, historian and writer on travel. A cousin of Hugh Gaitskell, q.v.
3 Admiral Keyes, q.v., who was Director of Combined Operations 1940–41.

up Haydn Davies.[1] Peake is to get on with this.

This evening, my staff, mistaking my explosions for tiredness, say that I should have a full weekend in the country. They think that I work too long hours. I say that this is necessary because other people are so slow and must constantly be prodded on.

Retinger to dine alone. He was jealous because I did not ask him to the lunch with the Polish soldiers the other day. But now I think he is quite pleased to have been with me *à deux* and has had his feathers smoothed. It is very odd that he should be so close to Sikorski.

Tuesday 3rd December

After great efforts I break through the barrage of the P.M.'s Private Secretaries, who at first told my own that he was too busy to see me, so that I had myself to speak to them and tell them it was urgent. I go and see [the Prime Minister] at 7.30 p.m. and he sends his armoured car to fetch me. This, I thought, was a kindly act. Before, when I have tried to report to him what is going on, he has talked all the time about something else and I have hardly got a word in edgeways. This time I go determined to talk a lot, even if I have to talk through him and shout him down. But this is not necessary. The poor man is much depressed, particularly because one of our convoys has been badly shot up by eight German submarines, guided by a new technique, in the western approaches. Therefore he sits hunched up in his chair, listening and putting only a few questions as I go on. I begin on block-ade and the Brazilian ship (he asks for a list of the arms on board her), but since now I have agreed with Halifax, there is not much to say on this. I had originally sought the interview in order to put my view against that of Halifax. I therefore pass quickly to Special Operations and tell him how well the machine is running now, Freedom Stations, etc. I give him a few particulars of the French miner, Sicilian sea cap-tain, etc., knowing that he is interested in picturesque detail. I speak of the Italian broadcast[s] and say that ... he could hear them being played. He says rather dolefully, 'I am afraid I couldn't understand them.' So then I tell him there are some nice ones in French. I show him also a telegram about the uniforms and papers of Italians cap-tured in Albania being used to put Anti-Fascist agents in. He likes this very much and I order that a gingering telegram shall be sent off about it. I broach with him the question of foreign broadcasts (enemy and enemy-occupied) and say that I have it in mind to discuss this with Cooper. He says, 'Yes do, but don't commit me.' He is quite vague as to what we do and where.

1 Haydn Davies (1905–76). Journalist, attached to M.E.W. and the Board of Trade 1939–45. Labour M.P. 1945–50.

Wednesday 4th December
It is being whispered by some that I should take Greenwood's job and by others that I ought to go to the War Office where there is needed someone who would be 'ruthless with the Generals'. Very complimentary, no doubt, but I should be a little hesitant about either change.

Thursday 5th December
Conference with Halifax. Also present Drogheda and Foot, the latter having been most eager to be allowed in, and Scott and some other Foreign Office bloke. Halifax is most amiable and conciliatory and it is agreed that we should demand conditions in return for the release of the German arms on the Brazilian ship. Foot makes a few remarks and Halifax leans forward, slightly bored, and says, 'What?'

I hear afterwards that Foot, who leaves before we finish, was immensely uplifted, by the fact that he was in the Foreign Office for the first time in his life (I said to him before, 'When a minister goes to the Foreign Office to see the Secretary of State, he makes for the Private Secretaries' room and walks in as though he half owned it'; I don't know whether he did this well!), by the immense size of the Secretary of State's room, by the most conciliatory and genial tone of the whole conversation, by my skill in handling the discussion, by the forth-comingness of the Foreign Office officials on enemy export control. ...

Gladwyn informs me and Gaitskell that C.D. tells him that there is jealousy and suspicion over the bringing of Martelli to London to binge up Italy. It is being said that Martelli, being Gaitskell's cousin, is in a position to spy and report to me. Gaitskell and I are both most indignant at this, and I say that since there is a shameful vacuum here where Italy should be, and since I have to handle the thing myself, I will not tolerate talk of the jealousy of ineffective underlings. ...

Gladwyn and Gubbins to see me for half an hour before dinner, when I learn that Sikorski is having Gubbins to meet him and also Sosnkowski and Kot together. This looks as though our liaison with the Poles will be simplified and that Gubbins will be able to deal with both their wings, military and civilian. He also gives a good account of preliminary steps taken for training. He is evidently getting a move on and, as I anticipated he would, doing very well.

Bruce Lockhart then joins us for a meal in a quiet place at the Lansdowne Club. It is clear that Lockhart is slightly peeved (Oh, what a crowd of prima donnas I have to command! How much easier if they were a battalion of robots!) because he regards himself as the one and only agent to the Czechs.

Sunday 8th December
Take Hancock for a pretty good walk, via Upham, Liddington Camp, back and through Ogbourne to Barbury Camp, thence down to Marlborough and back over Pulton Downs to West Leaze. As compared with a fortnight ago with Mayhcw, we walk only twenty-two miles instead of twenty-five, and take a quarter of an hour less on the round. Walking less on roads, we make less good pace. But it is a good break.

Tuesday 10th December
Lucas[1] said last night, 'The F.O. is like a chameleon that has grown tired'; it has sat so long on the dull appeasement stone that now it can't brighten, even on red granite or green jade. Poor Old F.O.! It is full of fidgets in these days, suspecting the worst of everyone. But Gladwyn, while admitting the defects of many diplomatic personages, says that the officials will come out with credit when all the archives are opened. For years they urged – all of them, and not only Van – the German danger and the need for rapid rearmament here.

Wednesday 11th December
Yesterday, after our conference at Foreign Office, I stayed behind with Halifax, and told him that Bevin had asked me to help him in preparing his ideas for the reform of the Foreign Office and Diplomatic Service. I added that it was a great mistake to suppose, as some seemed now to do, that Bevin was against Halifax, personally. On the contrary, he spoke to me most warmly of Halifax's helpfulness and receptiveness to his ideas. (More bluntly, I told Cadogan when alone with him afterwards, that he should know that both Bevin and I desired that Halifax should remain at the Foreign Office and that neither of us wishes any change at present in this office. I spoke thus bluntly because there had been a rush of rumour round the office that Bevin was gunning after Halifax, desiring to substitute me for the latter. I said to two of my inner circle two days ago, though I did not repeat this to Cadogan, that I should indeed much like to be Foreign Secretary, but not until, at earliest, we were well on the road to victory in the war and strong enough to make our will and plans prevail in the world. The flutter in these last days has been due, in part, to an article in the *Sunday Despatch*, signed, though obviously not written, by Clynes,[2] attacking the Foreign Office in a most ignorant fashion, attributing all our ills to diplomats, and demanding that there should

1 H. O. Lucas (1905–45). M.E.W. official. Deputy Director of Plans at P.W.E. 1941–4.
2 J. R. Clynes (1869–1949). Labour M.P. for Manchester Platting 1918–31, 1935–45; Manchester North-East 1906–18. Junior minister 1917–19. Lord Privy Seal 1924. Home Secretary 1929–31.

be an 'open competition' for these posts.) ...

Eccles comes to see me before returning to Iberia. He thinks little either of Selby, our retiring Ambassador at Lisbon, or of Campbell who is taking his place. Neither of them has any knowledge of trade and economics, which is the only thing worth discussing with Salazar.[1] Selby, he says, used to crawl into Salazar's presence on all fours, and did not even do this regularly, but only at very rare intervals. ...

A very carefully arranged party at the Lansdowne Club – Bevin, Gladwyn, Wilmot and John Price.[2] It is a very great success. Bevin arrives very tired; he rang up a quarter of an hour before and asked whether he need come, and I said yes. But he gradually revives and gets into exceedingly good form, both amusing and full of sound sense and constructive determination. He gives a remarkable account of the steps he took to restore production after the raid on Coventry. Today, he says, there are 79,000 people working in the factories at Coventry, as compared with 88,000 immediately before the raid.[3] Therefore, allowing for damage to public utilities, etc., the position has practically been restored in full. He himself went up and addressed meetings totalling 30,000 workers. He also made elaborate new emergency arrangements for transport, canteens etc. But he has had to warn off the Beaver, who tried, here as everywhere else, to interfere. He is very anti-Beaver, and we discuss means by which his influence may be diminished. Bevin thinks that a secret session of Parliament, at which aircraft production should be discussed, would be helpful. I say that I will speak a word to Lees-Smith and others about this. Wilmot also tells him of evidence of a huddle, taking place weekly at the Savoy, when the two Cudlipps,[4] with Hore-Belisha, sometimes

1 Antonio de Oliviera Salazar (1889–1970). President of the Council of Ministers, Portugal, 1932–68. Minister of Finance 1928–40. Minister of War 1936–44.

2 John Price (b. 1901). Trade unionist, who worked for eight years in Europe for the International Labour Office before becoming Secretary of the Political Department of the Transport and General Workers' Union, of which Bevin was General Secretary 1922–40. In that year, Price brought out a Penguin Special, *Organised Labour in the War*, with a foreword by Bevin. Price worked for S.O.E., particularly in its relations with European trade unionists.

3 On the night of 14th November, some 450 enemy aircraft raided Coventry, killing 554 people and destroying the city. Aircraft factories on the outskirts of the city however, were not badly damaged.

4 Hugh Cudlipp, later Baron (b. 1913). Editor of *Sunday Pictorial* 1937–40, 1946–9 Military Service 1940–46. Managing Editor of the *Sunday Express* 1950–52. Chairman of Odhams Press Ltd 1961–3. Joint Managing Director of the *Daily Mirror* and *Sunday Pictorial* 1959–63. Chairman of *Daily Mirror* Newspapers Ltd 1963–8 International Publishing Corporation Ltd 1968–73.
Percy Cudlipp (1903–62). Editor of the *Daily Herald* 1940–53; *New Scientis* 1956–62.

Frank Owen[1] and other agents of the Beaver, meet. Bevin thinks that the Beaver might at any time support a patched-up peace, in time to prevent his papers going bust. Just now, of course, they are suffering from loss of advertisement revenue. Southwood,[2] no doubt, shares this view, and so does Harmsworth.[3] Wilmot gives Bevin a piece of paper with a list of those frequenting the huddle. He also observes that all speciality journalists regard the Beaver as an alternative employer, and that he runs this idea very hard. I don't myself take too seriously his menace to the continuance of the war till final victory. More serious at the moment is his constant banditry and intrigues against all colleagues. It should be easy to form a strong anti-Beaver combination. Just now he has, apart from the P.M., who occasionally shows signs of getting tired of him, only one regular supporter in the Cabinet in Alexander, a simple soul whom the Beaver encourages by backing up his claims against the Air Ministry, e.g. for control of Coastal Command.

Wilmot and I both agree that Gladwyn handled Bevin very well tonight. I had warned him beforehand to let Bevin do nearly all the talking and to say whatever he had to say slowly and simply. He plays up very well and we only lightly touch the question of reforms in the Foreign Service, which we shall meet to discuss again *à trois* next week.

Thursday 12th December

Durbin comes to see me to try once more to interest me in Greenwood's job. He says that Greenwood told Hemming, who told him, that there would be a 'comprehensive reconstruction' of the Government over Christmas. Durbin would like this to include my taking Greenwood's job, although he realises that my interests lie elsewhere. But, he says, no job is more important than Greenwood's from the point of view of production, and hence of our war effort. I doubt whether this 'comprehensive reconstruction' is more than one of these constant rumours. More likely, Anderson will take over Greenwood's Production Council. Halifax said to me this week when we were speaking of Bevin and the reform of the Diplomatic Service that, although Bevin had great gifts, he gave the impression of being very conceited, which might upset him in the House of Commons, and I,

1 Frank Owen (1905–79). Editor of the *Evening Standard* 1938–42. Author and journalist. Liberal M.P. 1929–31. Editor of the *Daily Mail* 1947–50.

2 J. S. Elias, 1st Viscount Southwood (1873–1946). Chairman of Odhams Press Ltd.

3 C. B. Harmsworth, 1st Baron (1869–1948). Younger brother of Lord Rothermere. Liberal M.P. 1906–10, 1911–12. Junior minister 1915, 1919–22. Prime Minister's Secretariat 1917–19.

as a friend, might warn him of this. Halifax also found him very long-winded and said that the P.M. in Cabinet, though at the beginning very friendly and polite, now was inclined to cut Bevin short. I said that this was due to the habit of the General Council of meeting for one whole day.

Friday 13th December

Spend the evening with Attlee, who is extremely friendly. He shows me the figures, which I had not seen before, of the voting of the P.L.P. for the Administrative Committee. Pethick Lawrence comes first with 76, I second with 75, and then a group including Alexander, Morrison and Jim Griffiths,[1] with 74. Shinwell, with only 51, fell down to within five of the bottom, and Rhys Davies[2] was pitched off altogether, being the first of the also ran. Chuter Ede[3] and Tom Smith[4] come on, and little Arthur Henderson[5] also slips off, having been for long an absentee. (This is a very good result from several points of view, and I will not deny that I mentioned it to several press-men.) Attlee says, 'The Party generally knows what it is doing on these occasions.'

He is clearly dissatisfied with Greenwood's slowness and inertia, but also very hot against the Beaver. He does not know anything about 'a comprehensive reconstruction' such as was whispered to me yesterday, but Bob Boothby is sunk and his place will have to be filled. This was the job originally offered to Shinwell and refused by him, over the telephone from Bournemouth to the P.M., as 'not interested' and 'a bloody insult'. Attlee now wants Wilfrid Paling to have it and Willy Whiteley to move up in the Whips' Office to No. 2 to Charlie Edwards, with the prospect of succession to Chief Whip

1 James Griffiths (1890–1975). Labour M.P. for Llanelli 1936–70. Minister of National Insurance 1945–50. Secretary of State for Colonies 1950–51; Wales 1964–6.
2 R. J. Davies (1877–1954). Labour M.P. for Westhoughton 1921–51. Junior minister 1924.
3 J. Chuter Ede, later Baron Chuter-Ede (1882–1965). Labour M.P. for South Shields 1929–31, 1935–64; Mitcham 1923. Parliamentary Secretary at the Ministry of Education 1940–45; Home Secretary 1945–51.
4 Tom Smith (1886–1953). Labour M.P. for Normanton 1933–46; Pontefract 1922–4, 1929–31. Junior minister 1942–5.
5 Arthur Henderson, later Baron Rowley (1893–1968). Labour M.P. for Kingswinford Division of Staffordshire 1935–50; South Cardiff 1923–4, 1929–31; Rowley Regis and Tipton 1950–66. Junior minister 1942–7. Minister of State for Commonwealth Relations 1947. Secretary of State for Air 1947–51.

later. I quite approve of this. I also urge that, though we are fairly well represented among No. 1 ministers, we have not enough of No. 2s. Thus there are two Tories at the Foreign Office, two Tories at the Treasury, and four Tories at the War Office. I press the claims of Noel-Baker to *any* No. 2 job other than the Foreign Office. It would do him great good to get his mind, now soddened with lost hopes, frustrations over decades, falsified appreciations of every recent war from Abyssinia through Spain to Finland, and personal relationships gone stale, on to some quite remote Department – either Treasury or, better still perhaps, War Office. I urge also my P.P.S.[1] as No. 2 in the Foreign Office. His temperament, native intelligence and rough outline of knowledge of foreign affairs, would, I think, just fit him in well here. Butler could go to govern an Indian province. Another good claimant from our side is Jim Griffiths, who would do quite well at any Home Front social service ministry.

Attlee says that the new D.M.I., Davidson,[2] is a dour Scot who served in the same regiment as himself in the last war. A great improvement on that salon soldier Beaumont-Nesbitt, whom one always thinks of as on the telephone to Duchesses accepting invitations to cocktail parties.

Saturday 14th December
To C.H.Q.[3] with Gladwyn and Gaitskell for the weekend.

On the way down we discuss the Washington Embassy, vacant through Lothian's sudden death.[4] I relate how Lothian, meeting me twice during his last visit, once near the beginning and once near the end, after an interval of three weeks, made just exactly the same long speech the second time as the first. This was a sign of fatigue. It is ironical that almost his last words to the American Government and people were a stiff defence of our total blockade and a refusal to agree to any plan for letting food through to any part of Hitler-enslaved Europe, including 'unoccupied' France. This declaration he made only on firm instructions from H.M.G. He did his damnedest while over here, and also in his telegrams, to get me and Halifax to agree on concessions. I tried to seem very slow and stupid about it all and kept on obstinately saying no. I had to say no to Leith-Ross as well, and even to Noel Hall, but the Cabinet backed me and so, I am

1 John Wilmot, q.v.
2 Major-General F. H. N. Davidson (1892–1973). Director of Military Intelligence at the War Office 1940–44. Deputy Head of British Army Staff, Washington 1944–6.
3 Country Headquarters, i.e. Woburn.
4 Lord Lothian, q.v., Ambassador in Washington, died on 12th December.

sure, would the House of Commons.

And so travelling down by car, we three discuss names. I don't want Halifax to go, for I doubt whether he would do it well and I don't want him changed at the Foreign Office just now. There are no diplomatic possibles except Van, whose health is bad, and, I think, Clark Kerr,[1] a thruster and a good mixer, but trailing a tiny, oh so tiny, Chilean wife.[2] Gladwyn thought that she would not do at all in Washington. I said that she could symbolise the 'good neighbour' policy to Latin America. Anyhow, he is doing pretty well at Chungking just now. Some awful names of business men and financiers are being mentioned, but I feel that this would be quite the wrong type. Some speak well of Sir Gerald Campbell,[3] now High Commissioner in Canada, previously Consul General in New York. He knows America and, they say, is a very good speaker.

Among politicians there is not much real choice. Greenwood, it is said, has been mentioned, and also Bevin, but only to be quickly dismissed. There are awful rumours about Lloyd George – and he was actually offered it two days later by the P.M., but fortunately refused! I regard him as no better than a neutral in the war, a potential British Pétain, and anyhow, like Pétain, suffering from – in a phrase used to me by de Gaulle – 'senility, pessimism and ambition, a fatal combination'.

Running through this long list we suddenly strike on Cranborne, and the more we discuss him, the better I like him. He has a good political record; he resigned before Munich and was boldly anti-Munichois. Having been at the Dominions Office for a while, he can claim to know the Dominions' point of view. He has charm and distinction and may become at any moment Lord Salisbury, which the Americans would love. Gladwyn says that *his* wife[4] is no good, being very absent-minded and forgetful of people's names and faces, but I refuse to take this very seriously, though I recall that when once I sat at a Nathan lunch, when Bobbity[5] was speaking, between her and Waterson,[6] the High Commissioner for South Africa, she did not

1 Sir Archibald Clark Kerr, later 1st Baron Inverchapel (1882–1951). Ambassador to China 1938–42; the U.S.S.R. 1942–6; the U.S.A. 1946–8.
2 Clark Kerr married Maria Teresa Díaz Salas in 1929, while he was Minister to Chile.
3 Sir Gerald Campbell (1879–1964). High Commissioner in Canada 1938–41. Minister in Washington 1941, 1942–5. Director-General of British Information Service in New York 1941–2.
4 Lord Cranborne married Elizabeth Vere, daughter of Lord Richard Cavendish, in 1915.
5 'Bobbity': familiar name for Cranborne.
6 Sidney Waterson (1896–1976). S. African High Commissioner in London 1939–42.

know who he was, though it was her only official duty to know four people in London, of whom he was one! It is said, however, that Cranborne has very bad health and is ravaged by some bug or other. In that case he ought to go slow, and could go much slower in Washington than Lothian did, reserving himself for the greater persons and occasions, if he were given, what he has not now, an increased and strengthened staff.

I therefore fix on Cranborne and ring up Attlee tonight to suggest his name, and write a note to Halifax next day.

Sunday 15th December

Walk in the pine woods with Con O'Neill,[1] now No. 2 in my German section here. This young man resigned from the Diplomatic Service because he could not bear the late Mr Chamberlain's foreign policy nor its execution by Sir Nevile Henderson, under whom he was serving, unhappily and unwillingly, in Berlin. He is, I hope, now to take charge of one of our Houses. The pine woods are pretty good to walk in.

Butler comes in the afternoon and spends the night. I think he is interested, but he is a curiously indecisive character. I have lately heard that Halifax does not care much for him. He himself is jealous of Eden. I tell him that Cranborne is my candidate for the Washington Embassy. Associating him a bit with Eden, though clearly preferring him, Butler is not over enthusiastic. He says that Eden plays politics too much and does not make a success of his Departments. I tell him the story of Macmillan's effort, just after Munich, to make a three-a-side consultation, and how Eden wouldn't come in.[2] He is, I say, aiming a little obviously at the Leadership of the Conservative Party. Butler, bridling, says, 'He will never get that. The Party will never follow him.' Later he says, 'I have my own shop too, as well as Eden. I know that our Party is not behind him.'

At dawn on 9th December, a British force attacked Italian camps near Sidi Barrani, on the Egyptian coast. In three days, British troops, commanded

1 Hon. C. D. W. O'Neill, later Sir Con (b. 1912). Army (Intelligence) 1940–43. Resigned from Diplomatic Service 1939. Returned permanently to the Foreign Office 1947. Deputy Under-Secretary of State at the Foreign Office/Foreign and Commonwealth Office 1965–72.

2 In the immediate aftermath of Munich, Harold Macmillan had approached Dalton about the possibility of co-operation across party lines against Chamberlain's policy of appeasement. Dalton, and some other Labour leaders, showed interest, as did Churchill. Eden, however, held aloof, demanding 'three-a-side' talks (three Tory dissidents with three Labour leaders), which never took place.

by Major-General O'Connor, took 38,300 prisoners, and large quantities of equipment and stores. Having captured a supply of Italian lorries, O'Connor's army was able to press towards enemy bases at Bardia and Tobruk.

Tuesday 17th December

Lunch, at Garro Jones's invitation, to meet Parkinson,[1] of Crompton and Parkinson, who, Garro Jones says, is friendlily disposed towards us and would be prepared, he thinks, to make a payment to our Party funds if even made a knight! I say that this sort of thing has not been our practice, but in view of future possibilities, nothing should be excluded because it is new. Meanwhile, nothing can be done for some while, as the New Year's Honours are all settled. We can take this up again a little later.

The P.M. holds one of his ministers' meetings in the C.W.R. [Cabinet War Room] and talks to us joyfully of the great victory in Africa. 'In Wavell we have got a winner', and Wilson,[2] his Chief of Staff, has also done wonderfully well. They were most cautious in their forecasts of what they could do; they spoke only, at first, of a 'raid'. They did not know what they might find at Sidi Barrani. They might come up against a hard resistance there. In fact, they didn't, and so they went right on. The Italian Air Force was astonishingly ineffective. Obsolete machines and bad tactics. Many were bombed on the ground, so that we did to them from the air, though of course on a much smaller scale, what the Germans did to the Poles in the first weeks of the war. The battle, said the P.M., is by no means over yet, and it has removed the threat to Egypt and will make repercussions all round the Mediterranean and through the whole Middle East and as far as Moscow. ...

The P.M. says that he is quite sure that Hitler cannot lie down under this. Perhaps within three weeks, and certainly within three months, he must make some violent counter-stroke. What will it be? An attempt, at long last, to invade us? Perhaps a gas attack on us on an immense scale, drenching our cities with mustard? Perhaps a blow through Spain, perhaps through Italy, perhaps to the Mediterranean through France, perhaps through Bulgaria to Salonika? Any of these might be awkward and troublesome, and we must be prepared to face

---

1 Frank Parkinson (1887–1946). Chairman and Joint Managing Director of Crompton Parkinson Ltd.
2 General Sir Henry Wilson, later 1st Baron (1881–1964). General Officer Commander-in-Chief in Egypt 1939–41; Greece 1941; Persia 1942–3; Middle East 1943. Supreme Commander in Mediterranean Theatre 1944. Field Marshal 1944.

difficult hours. There is nothing now to stop him coming through to Salonika. This is the easiest one of all. Why doesn't he do it? The P.M. supposes because he fears that he might get wrong with both the Russians and the Turks.

The P.M. is very optimistic about U.S. aid. They will soon, he thinks, be 'in the war in fact if not in form'. He would say to them, in effect, 'If you want to watch us fighting for your liberties, you must pay for the performance.'

Meanwhile, we shall follow 'that great imposter Triumph' as far as we can and apply all those Biblical injunctions which are also strategical principles: 'Knock and it shall be opened unto you; seek and ye shall find', etc.

He is in a happy, though not incautious, mood.

Wednesday 18th December
At 10 a.m. I visit the Lord President of the Council.[1] He has been appointed by the P.M. as Umpire between Cooper and me on our frontier dispute. He is friendly and intelligent. (I had quite forgotten, till Gaitskell reminded me after our interview, that I had written him, not long ago, a most abusive letter, regarding three of my constituents held too long in internment, telling him that if I had not been his colleague I should long ago have lambasted him publicly in Parliament.) He seems to know a good deal about my organisation and thinks I have some good people running it. He is sure that I am justified in thinking that present arrangements are not satisfactory. The Ministry of Information has not been a success. Perhaps it was wrong ever to create it: perhaps it would be right to abolish it now. But, if we are to keep it at all, we must try to make it self-respecting and effective. Perhaps now that Monckton, who is both 'adroit and agreeable', has succeeded Mr Pick, who was neither, but a complete misfit, things will be easier to arrange. But it would be a humiliation for Cooper and the Ministry of Information if it were announced, as I propose, that the Foreign Office will now take over control of this group of foreign broadcasts. He notes that the present arrangements regarding German broadcasts are reasonably satisfactory, and he would like to try whether this system cannot be extended. I agree to have a plan worked out for this. (I have always thought that this would be the second line where we might find a tolerable compromise.)

Go on to Foreign Office where I see Van. He still has something wrong with his tummy and is going to bed and to starve over Christmas. His judgment is now very uncertain. He wants me, for instance, to write to Anderson arguing back on my first line and proposing

1 Sir John Anderson, q.v.

another conversation, at which Van might perhaps be present. This is not good tactics at all, though I do not bluntly say so. ...

Meeting of Labour ministers in Attlee's room. An hour of slow boredom with Bevin, Greenwood, Alexander rambling on about priorities. I don't believe these silly blighters ever formulate clear decisions or fight them through. This is a frightful tangle into which I am most unwilling to be drawn.

Dine with Cazalet to meet the Foreign Secretary and Lady Halifax. This is the first time – and I suspect that it is a rather carefully arranged first time – that I have met Holy Fox[1] off parade, yet I have felt for some time that I know a good deal about him. I find him charming, amusing and with a pleasantly light touch on personalities. 'He looked at me like a wounded gazelle,' said Peake to me the other night. His eyes do take on that look sometimes, and his face resembles that of some noble animal. Just as men who are much with horses or with dogs come to resemble these, so he is touched with a distant semblance of stags and the like.

We discuss the relation of P.M. and Foreign Secretary. It is, says Halifax, the most delicate of all relationships within the Cabinet. If the P.M. is the sort of man who takes an interest in foreign affairs, the Foreign Secretary must be prepared to defer to him on many points. On very high policy, the Foreign Secretary should, if the P.M. resists him and he cannot persuade him, go to the Cabinet. On very small points the P.M. should not interfere at all. On matters of intermediate importance, the Foreign Secretary should be prepared to make considerable concessions to the P.M.'s point of view. The Foreign Secretary must not get into the mood of thinking that the P.M. has lost confidence in him because he sends across telegrams of his own, or because he knocks about drafts put up to him by the Foreign Secretary. It would be just as wrong for the Head of a Department in the Foreign Office to think that he had lost the confidence of the Foreign Secretary because the latter knocked about his drafts, or for a junior in any Department in the Foreign Office to think, for the same reason, that he had not got the confidence of the Head of the Department.

But P.M.s differ widely in their methods and in the intensity of interest they take in foreign affairs. Thus, Winston himself drafts telegrams to be despatched to ambassadors and to commanders in the field, loving his own power over the English language and his own close grip upon a mobile situation. Halifax does not resent at all such telegrams coming across from No. 10, though sometimes he argues back, and generally gets his way, if he does not agree with their tenor. Chamberlain never drafted such telegrams by himself, although he

1 Dalton's name for Lord Halifax, a devout Anglican and keen huntsman.

intervened much in foreign policy. He would ask Halifax to go over and see him and talk about a situation, but would leave the drafting of the telegram to Halifax and his officials.

Stanley Baldwin[1] desired only not to be troubled with foreign affairs at all. He left his successive Foreign Secretaries completely free. (There was, I recall, though I do not mention it tonight, the famous case of Hoare proceeding to Paris to negotiate the Hoare-Laval Pact, and Baldwin, asked in Cabinet by some of the younger Tories whether all was well, and whether there should not be some discussion now before irrevocable decisions were taken, said, 'I think we all have confidence in Sam; we can safely leave it in his hands.')

Halifax relates that Baldwin, in the year of the Abdication, took three months' holiday (repeat *three* months), at the end of which he asked Eden, then Foreign Secretary, 'Have you had many telegrams about the King?' Eden said no. Then Baldwin said, 'I have had a great many, some from the most extraordinary people. I foresee that I shall have a lot of trouble over this. I hope that you will not bother me with foreign affairs during the next three months.' Yet these were *mois mouvementés* in foreign affairs. Hitler was arming, arming, arming, day by day. But Baldwin was focused on the tactics of the Abdication.

I said that I recalled the MacDonald[2]-Henderson relation in 1929–31, never easy, with no great confidence on either side.[3] (Van[4] was, in fact, the personal cement, for both of them liked and trusted him though they neither liked nor trusted the other.)

Halifax also told this tale of Winston. That in 1929 when the India Bill was up, Halifax one day said to Winston, 'You have the ideas about India of a subaltern a generation ago. There are a number of interesting Indians coming to the Round Table Conference and I really think that it would be very valuable to you to talk to some of them and bring your ideas up to date.' Winston replied, 'I am quite satisfied with my views of India. I don't want them disturbed by any bloody Indian.'

1 S. Baldwin, 1st Earl (1867–1947). Conservative M.P. 1908–37. Joint Financial Secretary at the Treasury 1917–21; President of the Board of Trade 1921–2; Chancellor of the Exchequer 1922–3; Prime Minister 1923–4, 1924–9, 1935–7. Lord President of the Council 1931–5.

2 J. R. MacDonald (1866–1937). Labour M.P. 1906–18, 1922–31; National Labour 1931–7. Prime Minister and Foreign Secretary 1924. Prime Minister 1929–35; Lord President of the Council 1935–7.

3 Dalton had been Parliamentary Under-Secretary at the Foreign Office, and No. 2 to Arthur Henderson, during the 1929–31 Labour Government.

4 Sir Robert Vansittart, q.v., was Permanent Under-Secretary of State at the Foreign Office 1930–38.

Thursday 19th December

See in the afternoon first Haydn Davies and then Maurice Webb.[1] Both say that my stock is very high in Fleet Street and among the Tories. They say that I am the only Labour minister who has been 100 per cent successful, and there are rumbles against others, notably Greenwood. It is being said that I should take his place to run the Production Council and be in the War Cabinet. There are obvious difficulties about this and I am not keen to move, though I can't tell all the reasons for this to either of my visitors. None the less, it does me no harm to be esteemed in wide circles and for such esteem to leak through into the press. Webb tries to defend Cudlipp and the *Daily Herald*. I say that I am not convinced. He asks would I meet Cudlipp. I say the blighter owes me a lunch, since I once took him out, but he has never reciprocated. I am so bored with the journalists' grizzle that they cannot get contact with Labour ministers. He has never tried with me, though the telephone and other means of communication are obvious, and as for Webb, I say, he can always get me whenever he tries. He agrees that this is so.

Friday 20th December

To Foreign Office at 10.30 to discuss with Halifax, Van, Cadogan and Sargent (the last quite calm and friendly after last week's storm)[2] questions regarding Italy. Leeper has put up to Van and me a draft broadcast by the P.M. telling the Italians that we love them, that the Germans don't, and that they should get rid of Mussolini. I thought this draft too long, but not too bad. Halifax accepts, and neither of his officials resists, the idea that the P.M. should be asked to do it. Bardia[3] will soon fall and, after the victory in North Africa, the Greek advance in Albania, the successful bombing attacks on Italian targets,

1 Maurice Webb (1904–56). Journalist, then political correspondent, on the *Daily Herald* 1935–44; *Sunday Express* 1944–5. Labour Party Propaganda Officer 1929–35. Labour M.P. 1945–55. Chairman of the Parliamentary Labour Party 1946–50. Minister of Food 1950–51.

2 'last week's storm': On 10th December, Dalton had recorded a row at a meeting with Halifax and two Foreign Office officials, Cadogan and Sargent, over an allegation that Sargent had sent a telegram to Bucharest calling off an anti-oil action ('the Romanian Bridge') without getting SO2 agreement first. ' ... Sargent is in a terrible temper and, Gladwyn reports, refuses to discuss anything or to maintain any future relations, other than by official correspondence, with SO2,' Dalton noted. 'This is childish nonsense and no doubt will pass away in a day or two ... Probably, on the whole, this row will, however, have done good and will create greater respect by the F.O. for my views and those of my staff.' (Diary.)

3 Bardia, near the Egyptian-Libyan border, fell to the Allies after a naval bombardment, and British tanks entered the port on 4th January 1941. Bardia had been held by four Italian divisions.

on land and in the Gulf of Taranto, we may not get so good a chance again for a long time.

It is then agreed that Halifax and I should go to No. 10 after the memorial service in the Abbey to Lothian, which we shall both attend, and press on the P.M. our view. ...

Therefore, after the service, Halifax and I see the P.M. Halifax begins and I press on the argument, and the P.M. accepts, without resistance. We propose that in his broadcast he should cite his letter to Mussolini when he became P.M. and Mussolini's stuffy reply. 'Only', says the P.M., 'I won't agree to their keeping Abyssinia.' We agree that, at this stage, this need not be mentioned.

I add that I am doing my damnedest to get chaps to make hay in Milan. P.M. says, 'They will be killed.' I say, 'No doubt, but that is all in the war. If they can add only a little to the confusion and loss of morale, they will help us to a quicker victory.' I tell him also of the Slovenes with their leaflets, etc.

We must by all means hit hard at Italy. I stir up much stink in SO2 on this and order a conference for this afternoon. I am tired of excuses and obstruction. I will, if necessary, sack all the subordinates who are failing to do their job. This is a critical moment of the war. Italy is in the market. We must offer, and quickly, a fair price to decent Italians who will get rid of Mussolini and his gang. But there is no place, today, for stupid doctrinaire prejudices against 'Fasc*ism*' as such. If some Fascist toughs will murder Mussolini and a few more and then join with others, representing the Royal Family, the Army, Industry, the Italian workers and peasants, we must not reject them for the sake of some thin theory. What we want is that Italy shall stop fighting against us and, if possible, fight against Germans instead.

As usual, I get Halifax where I want him on this. I tell Attlee and Noel-Baker at lunch with de Gaulle and Mrs Phillimore that this campaign against Halifax is rubbish. I should hate to have, in his place, that wretched Eden, posing before the looking-glass. I have much evidence that Halifax is now nearly as fond of me as I of him, so why change?

De Gaulle at lunch talks Left-wing stuff, whether from conviction or in order to play up, I am not sure. He says that there must be a social revolution at the end of the war. The collectivity must prevail over the individual. He is pleased with the suggestion that to *'Liberté, Egalité, Fraternité'*, he should add *'Sécurité'*. 'Not *Sûreté*' says someone! I say that there is much talk, no doubt quite wrong, about his entourage; that they are reactionary, anti-Labour, and light weight. It would, therefore, I say, do good if he would soon issue such a statement, which would chime in with H.M.G.'s forthcoming declaration on

War Aims. He seemed to me to be pretty sensible and subject to good influences. It is agreed that we should meet again, this same party, in the new year.

Saturday 21st December
Take Gladwyn and Mayhew out to lunch; the latter is still delightfully young and fresh, hardly old enough yet, one feels, to take much responsibility or conduct at all delicate official relationships. But I have confidence that he will soon train on.

To West Leaze in the afternoon, where more bombs have fallen quite near – just up the road opposite Gentry's,[1] blowing in some of his windows and also those of the bungalow on the opposite side of the road. It is now quite clear to all the neighbourhood that Hitler is always coming after me. I am not sure whether this makes me popular or unpopular in the village! On the other hand, Hitler's intelligence seems to be not very good, because I have not been present on either night when he dropped these gifts.

Following the death of Lord Lothian, Churchill appointed Halifax to replace him as Ambassador in Washington. This in turn caused a further Government reshuffle. Eden became Foreign Secretary, entering the War Cabinet, and David Margesson, the Conservative Chief Whip, succeeded Eden at the War Office.

Sunday 22nd December
Leave soon after lunch and visit Attlee at Stanmore on my way home to get the real truth about the Cabinet changes. It is now definite that Halifax is going to Washington. (I hear several days later through Gladwyn that he had to be forced to go, much against his will, by the P.M. This partly because the P.M. thought he would be the best available Ambassador, partly because the P.M. was getting a little tired of him as Foreign Secretary. He has never been in the U.S.A. before and will feel much at sea. He is therefore taking with him Peake for the first month in order to look after all his arrangements. This is tiresome, since Peake is to have the new key post of Foreign Adviser to the B.B.C.) Attlee thinks that it is an advantage to have Halifax

1 The Gentrys were local farmers at Aldbourne.

out, since now the last of the Appeasers will be gone. I say that I regret it because I have worked very hard at my personal relations with the Viscount and now all those hours of studied suavity will have been thrown away. I have now got to make a new start, on somewhat different lines, with Master Anthony. Attlee thinks that I shall find him quite easy to manage. I am much relieved to hear that Lloyd George is not coming in, though there had been a great press campaign in his favour. Attlee takes some credit for preventing this. He says that the P.M. told him when he sounded Lloyd George on the Washington Embassy that he gave the impression of a very old man. Attlee said Yes. 'His nose was as sharp as a pen and he babbled of pigs.' So he looked sitting on the Front Opposition Bench in the House of Commons the other day. I propound that Butler should go to India to govern a Province and that Wilmot might well succeed him. I added that Wilmot, in addition to being young and intelligent, could speak French. Attlee seemed struck with this. I learn afterwards from Ruth and John himself that he can only speak 'waiters' French'! I therefore give him Siegfried's *'Tableau des parties politiques en France'*. Attlee is anxious to get a minor post for George Tomlinson,[1] on whom he seems to have a strong fixation. Quite a good little man, but his promotion would cause much jealousy.

I drop a passing hint that Greenwood is being much criticised for inactivity and that it has been suggested to me by several that I should take over some of his duties, taking with me also, of course, Special Operations. I add that I have of course discouraged all such suggestions.

Dine with Gladwyn at Lansdowne Club and make plans for our next days.

Dalton spent Christmas 1940 in Scotland with the Polish forces, inspecting troops at Forfar and at Arbroath, and making an extensive tour of trenches, gun-pits, pill-boxes and other strong-points. 'From October, 1940, onwards my relations with the Poles, and especially with Sikorski and Retinger, became increasingly close,' Dalton recalled. Sikorski had his own Headquarters at Gask, and his Administrative Headquarters at Perth.[2]

---

1 George Tomlinson (1890–1952). Labour M.P. for Farnworth 1938–52. Junior minister 1941–5. Minister of Works 1945–7; Education 1947–51.
2 FY, p. 372.

Monday 23rd December
Leave the Ministry before dawn and fly in a Flamingo to Perth with Gladwyn, Gubbins and Clifford Norton.[1] There are four or five empty seats which the Poles might have occupied, but they have gone in advance by train. A beautiful flight taking only two and a quarter hours from Hendon. We follow a direct line which passes over Bishop Auckland, then just west of Newcastle and from St Abb's Head strikes out to sea across the Firth of Forth.

Met at Perth by Retinger and drive to Gask, where Sikorski makes his Headquarters. The party here consists of the General, two aides-de-camp, Retinger, another civilian secretary and the General's wife and daughter, who are both fully engaged in looking after the welfare of the Polish troops. The latter are now holding a long line of coast from north of Arbroath to south of St Andrews, including therefore Dundee and the stretch across the Firth of Tay. They have just been asked by the Scottish Command to take over another eleven miles of coast. Sikorski says he will do this if he can get the necessary arms and equipment.

In the afternoon we go for a walk in the woods and the rest of us have a little very mild horse play at Retinger's expense, since he is rather slower than the rest at climbing over walls and fences. He is, as one of my friends said, rather like a sewer rat, but he is clearly completely in the confidence of Sikorski and also easily flattered, so we must make the best of him.

Today is spent in conversation with Sikorski and his staff, and Retinger is much flattered by a talk *à trois* with Gladwyn and Gubbins in the course of which the framework of our organisation is explained to him.

Sikorski is much flattered, I think, by the fact that Gladwyn and I have brought dinner jackets with us and put them on this evening, while Gubbins appears in a kilt. This creates a very happy atmosphere. Sikorski speaks affectionately of Retinger as 'the cousin of the devil'. I prepare and rehearse a short speech in Polish for tomorrow and take my few simple phrases to bed with me.

Tuesday 24th December
A very full day. By car to Forfar where Sikorski and I inspect some 5,000 Polish troops, including 'delegations' from all units in the Polish sector. I am then invited to address them, which I do in a loud clear parade-ground voice, beginning with the greeting, '*Czołem żołnierze!*' ('Greetings, soldiers!') to which they all shout in reply,

1 C. J. Norton, later Sir Clifford (b. 1891). Foreign Office 1939–42. Counsellor to the British Embassy in Warsaw 1937–9.

'*Czołem Panie Ministrze!*' ('Greetings Mr Minister!'). I then proceed for a while in English, and at the end unload my carefully rehearsed Polish –

'*Anglicy i Polacy sąn twardzi. Zwyciężymy. Rozgromimy Niemcōw i ich partnerōw. Niech żyje Polska nieśmiertelna!*'[1]

This is received with immense appreciation and I know that I have done this job very well.

Afterwards I inspect with Sikorski some billets and kitchens and then by his side take the salute as the troops march away. They are a fine lot and I hear from all sides that they are very popular in the district. They are very well behaved and there have been very few cases of crime. On the other hand, a number of marriages have already been arranged between Polish soldiers and Scots girls. All through today, being Christmas Eve, we go through the form of breaking and sharing little wafers of unleavened bread and shaking hands with those with whom we share them.

From Forfar to Arbroath, where there is another small parade in the Market Square and a Polish band which plays the Polish and British national anthems. I inspect these troops also and then we go in to lunch, half-way through which Gladwyn leaves to spend Christmas Day with his family. After lunch we go on a tour of the ditches, gun-pits, pill-boxes and other strong-points. I show great activity and exchange greetings with one detachment after another. We then visit some of the canteens and other arrangements and I say a few words to some hundreds of Polish soldiers who are just about to sit down to a Christmas dinner organised by some Scots Presbyterian ladies.

All these soldiers are far from home; most of them do not know what has happened to their families, but may well expect the very worst. Sikorski said to me driving back, as he heard some locals making jovial sounds, 'I say always to my soldiers that these people have the right to be happy. Their country has not been invaded nor their dear ones massacred, starved and tortured.'

From the sea-shore and the canteens we drive to the Administrative Headquarters at Perth, where Raczkiewicz,[2] the President, is staying. Here we have a meal of fish of various kinds, and Raczkiewicz, Sikorski and I make speeches to an audience of about 200 Polish officers.

---

1 'The English and the Poles are fortresses. We shall be victorious. We shall conquer Germany and her partners. May Poland live for ever!'
2 Wladyslaw Raczkiewicz (1885–1947). President of the Polish Republic in exile 1939–45. President of the Senate 1930–35. Emigré in London from 1945.

Most of them seem to understand English and I am once more in very good form and bring the house down. I tell them that on the day of victory Poland, as the first nation to stand up to Hitler, while others have been grovelling on their bellies, should ride in the van of the victory march. I also recall the old Polish legend of the secret Army under the Hill (somewhere up in the Tatras) waiting for the bugle to blow on the resurrection morning, and how now there is an army, though not secret, along the sea-shore waiting also for the order to go into battle.

Wednesday 25th December
Start with Gubbins and a lady driver at 10.15 and reach Arisaig just before dark at 4.45. We drive right across the Highlands, Perth – Crieff – Glencoe (where we lunch) – Ballachulish – Fort William – Lochailort – Arisaig. I have never seen this country before, and it is, of its sort, very fine. We cross the Moor of Rannoch and run alongside many lochs and see snow on the high levels, Ben Nevis and the rest. I do not think I have ever before seen a 'deer forest', having always regarded Scotland as a rather second-class foreign country which came low down on the order of one's preferences. Gubbins tells me some awful stories. We were sending 120 Hurricanes to Poland, but they arrived too late to be any use. They got to Denmark on 28th August after a six weeks' delay entirely due to a squabble as to whether we or they should pay £4,000 in gold towards the cost of transport. They then had to be sent back from Denmark and right round by the Black Sea, where in turn they arrived too late to be of any use to the Poles, and were then transferred to the Turks. Had they been in Poland when the war began, they might have changed the whole character of the war. The Germans fully expected to find British Hurricanes in Poland, and their planes contained pictures of Hurricanes for the guidance of the pilots.

When the war began, Sikorski was living on his estate. He offered his services but they were rejected. When on the fifth day of the war Smigly-Rydz[1] left Warsaw, Sikorski went to him and said, 'It is your duty to be in Warsaw now directing the defence, but, if you won't go, order me to go and I will stay there till the end.' 'I was offering to sacrifice myself,' said Sikorski, 'but he only told me to go away, as I had no place or responsibility in the Army.'

Kennard,[2] etc., still kept their old acquaintances, said Gubbins,

1 E. Smigly-Rydz (1886–1941). Commander-in-Chief of Polish forces at the time of the German invasion 1939. Following his defeat, he fled to Romania where he was interned, and then escaped to Hungary December 1940.
2 Sir Howard Kennard (1878–1955). Ambassador to Poland 1935–41.

and Mrs Norton,[1] he thought, was 'a menace' and her husband 'a drowned rat'. He told her much too much and she talked most indiscreetly.

The Poles, like the French, had no mass of manoeuvre [*sic*]. They had spread out all their troops along the frontiers. Sikorski said that, if he had been in command, he would have kept a large reserve and held heavily only the south-west corner and the lines in front of Lodz. In these conditions he thought that he could have held out for three months at least.

Thursday 26th December

Spend the day motoring round possible stations and find quite a number in the neighbourhood of Arisaig. Wonderful views over Eigg, Rum and Skye. Gubbins makes a very good impression on me. I am present at his conference with those in charge.

Friday 27th December

Start early from Arisaig, where we have now spent two nights, and drive to Ardkinglas, Cairndow, on Loch Fyne opposite to Inveraray. We arrive soon after two, after another wonderful drive through Highland scenery. This is a large house shared by various members of the Noble family, cousins of Cynthia Jebb.[2] Here we spend three nights, leaving early in the morning of 30th December. And here the war and its cares fall from me like a garment. There are many children here, including Miles, Vanessa and Stella Jebb,[3] all three most attractive and intelligent. Also a Belgian and his wife and two children. Also two lots of Nobles, John[4] who is stationed at Oxford in connection with M.I.5, and Michael[5] who is secretary to Harold Butler,[6] now Regional Commissioner for an area including Oxford, Southampton and Reading. Each of these two has married Jewesses, John the sister of one of my officials at M.E.W., Harry Lucas,[7] and Michael a funny little object said to be only seventeen. In ten years' time she

1 Mrs Clifford Norton, née Noel Hughes.
2 Cynthia Jebb, née Noble, later Lady Jebb. Married to Gladwyn Jebb, q.v.
3 Miles, Vanessa and Stella Jebb: children of Gladwyn and Cynthia Jebb, born 1930, 1931 and 1933 respectively.
4 J. S. B. Noble (b. 1905).
5 Michael Noble (b. 1913). Conservative M.P. 1958–74. Secretary of State for Scotland 1962–4. Minister for Trade 1970–72. Married Anne, née Pearson September 1940.
6 H. B. Butler (1883–1951). Commissioner for Civil Defence, Southern Region 1939–41. Warden of Nuffield College, Oxford 1939–43. Minister, Washington 1942–6.
7 Henry Lucas, q.v., whose sister, Elizabeth (b. 1909), married John Noble in 1934.

will be a frightful dump. I play children's games, interspersed with chess, and climb some hillsides in a mist with Gladwyn and Gubbins who, I think, thoroughly enjoys himself here. Gladwyn shoots two white hares, which lurk only on the higher levels. I am told that eagles also are found near by. On the last day Gladwyn and I go for a rapid walk along the Loch end and over the hillsides to the pass named Rest and Be Thankful. I feel very fit and enjoy making both my companions extend themselves.

Tuesday 31st December
So I am back in London after a week which seems to have been spent infinitely far away, both in time and space. I learn that the functions of members of the War Cabinet have been reshuffled and Greenwood has been relegated merely to the study of post-war reconstruction problems! A new Production Executive and an Import Executive are to be set up, on neither of which is he to serve.

3

Special Operations
January–May 1941

British prospects continued to look bleak during the months that preceded Hitler's invasion of Russia. Lend-Lease, which began in March, provided a vital supply line across the Atlantic, but submarine attacks on British shipping placed this in serious jeopardy. German invasions of Yugoslavia and Greece added to the sense of Britain's isolation, and to a feeling that the enemy was unstoppable.

The Balkans provided S.O.E. with its first major test – and one which it came through with honour, if not with any lasting achievement. Efforts to block the Danube failed almost completely, despite some misleading reports at the time. But S.O.E. agents may have helped to bring about a coup in Belgrade. Elsewhere, S.O.E. was doing less well – and it became clear that the organisation in the Middle East urgently needed investigation. Meanwhile the broad issue of the control of propaganda continued to cause trouble – leading to a fragile truce with the Ministry of Information under the terms of the 'Anderson Award'.

Wednesday 1st January
A bad day! First of all the Honours List. Of all my nominees only Stirling,[1] one of the least meritorious, has got anything, and he a C.M.G. ... I therefore instruct Leith-Ross to write a stiff letter to Sir Horace Wilson, who presides over a committee of officials which winnows the list of recommendations, saying that I am astonished to find that my wishes have been completely disregarded, that I am thinking of taking the matter up in other quarters (i.e. with the P.M.), but that first I should be glad to have Wilson's explanation. Leith-Ross

1 C. N. Stirling, later Sir Charles (b. 1901). Head of Department at M.E.W. 1939–42. Diplomat.

says that he expected to be called in to explain my preferences, but that this was not done. I tell [Noel] Hall that I am fed to the teeth and what I am doing. He thinks, and so does Gaitskell, that the permanent civil servants are simply scratching each other's backs and ignoring the temporaries. As regards Honours in general, I am quite cynical and rather contemptuous, but if the things are to be given at all, they should be given as ministers desire. ...

Other glooms today are a report from Peake that Leeper has been pouring forth 'in the highest quarters' a flood of mischief-making stuff against me. He rang up Gladwyn in a state of great excitement just before lunch to report this, and I ask Gladwyn to check it up. ...

A meeting this afternoon at the Foreign Office to consider Italian propaganda. Eden is in the Chair and, in addition to Duff Cooper and myself, a swarm of officials attend. The meeting runs on easy and amicable lines and the conclusions reached are pretty good. No peace is possible with Mussolini, but if he goes, no other alternative Italian government is ruled out. ...

Stay behind with Eden and bring in Van, Gladwyn and Leeper for a talk on S.O. arrangements. They make quite a good impression. Eden, with whom I have exchanged very friendly letters – I deliberately laid it on fairly thick in order to create good relations from the start – is outwardly very agreeable and not, I think, a very strong character. He thinks well both of Leeper and of Gladwyn, the former of whom ran his Press Department, while the latter was for a short while his Private Secretary and later with him at Geneva during the Disarmament Conference. On the other hand, he does not much like Van, whom he pushed off to be his Chief Diplomatic Adviser when he brought back Cadogan from China to be Permanent Under-Secretary. I spoke well to him both of Gladwyn and Leeper and he said, 'Yes, you have got two of the very best. If I had been here, I would not have let them both go.'

Thursday 2nd January
I have had to beat my first retreat from the front line of the total blockade in response to a special message from Roosevelt to the P.M. urging that a few trial shipments of milk, etc., for children only in unoccupied France, under American Red Cross control, should be let through. It is clear that, not for the first nor the last time, we must give in to Roosevelt's wishes, and I am reasonably assured in this case by his very heavy insistence on the importance of our blockade and on the distinction between occupied and unoccupied territory. I therefore draft with Eden a reply to the P.M. to send to the President, indicating certain conditions and safeguards, and taking it for granted that it

will be announced that this step was taken on the President's initiative. This last point is important in order to meet Parliamentary criticism.

Gladwyn reports that he learns from Peake that it was to Strang that Leeper went and talked rather excitedly. Probably, however, and Wilmot strongly concurs in this, it was not much more than 'a rush of blood to the head' on finding that his old champion had returned as Foreign Secretary. I am not inclined to treat this too seriously, though it will mean that I shall have to keep a watchful eye on Leeper.

Saturday 4th January

Gladwyn reports his conversation with Morton. The latter has pretended to be wholly in my favour, expressing great admiration for my energy and drive. When told that I held him in part responsible for agitation against my decision to get rid of King Bomba, Morton flares up and hotly denies this. It was the Prof., he says, and he himself advised the P.M. that every Minister of the Crown had the right to settle his own staff. Further, he now thinks, in view of what has since come out, that I was completely right to get rid of King Bomba. Gladwyn thought that, in view of this attitude, there was not much more which he could say. I am very angry at this report, which appears to me completely contemptible on the part of Morton, concerning whom I have plenty of evidence that he is consistently unfriendly and tittletattles.

During 1940 Section D and then S.O.E. had been cultivating political leaders in Belgrade and subsidising the Serb Peasant Party, the Independent Democrat Party and the Narodna Odbrana. Through these contacts, it was known that there were elements which were dissatisfied with the pro-Axis leanings of the existing regime and were contemplating a *coup d'état*. At first, the Foreign Office was inclined to keep the possibility of encouraging such a plan in reserve. However, at the end of the year, the Prime Minister had become convinced (partly through intercepts of German communications) that the Germans were about to launch an invasion south into the Balkans; and this belief was reinforced by a Minute from Eden on 6th January 1941 to the effect that German preparations for a southward drive, with the ultimate aim of descending on Greece, were far advanced. In view of these developments, Churchill told Dalton to prepare S.O.E. for action. Dalton responded by sending George Taylor to Belgrade, and S.O.E. began to step up its activities in Yugoslavia, aiming through agitation and propaganda to deter the Regent,

Prince Paul, from yielding to German pressure to sign the Tripartite Pact; and, if this failed, to bring about a coup.[1]

Wednesday 8th January

Conference with Gladwyn and C.D. [Nelson] on Balkans, etc. I decide to send out George Taylor at once to take charge. C.D. has him alone to explain that this is a great mission, ordered from the All Highest, and not a means of shelving him from a key job in the organisation at home. The ground having thus been prepared, Gladwyn and I, after dining with Peake, return and clinch the arrangement. Taylor takes it very well, and now the question is to get him a seat in the next day or two on a bomber. These are scarce and mean that valuable human cargo has to compete with valuable spare parts! ...

I have today sent to the P.M. a letter, a summary memorandum, and a large number of papers relating to progress of S.O. I hope that these will seem quite impressive! I was anxious to see him to report orally, and so minuted to him, but his Secretary tells mine that he would like it in writing and that just now he is asking everybody to do this. In my letter I mention that Morton has more than once told Jebb that the P.M. would like to see me more often on S.O. and would like me to take the initiative in proposing this; also that I would much prefer to tell him myself what is going on rather than that he should get second-hand and possibly inaccurate reports indirectly. The documentation which I now send is formidable. It will probably all be handed over to Morton for comments. (Morton has today rung up and told Jebb that he has minuted to P.M. on Oil papers that he understands that SO2 have been obstructed by Foreign Office.)

Discuss with Peake the handling of Eden. Superficially I have begun well, having up till now written him three letters, one of warm congratulations, the second wholly approving his proposed attitude to trade negotiations with Moscow, and the third inviting him to see H.Q.[2] I have also brought in my principal attendant sprites to tell him about S.O. So far so good, but one never knows who may be pulling him the wrong way behind the scenes.

Leeper, who might, is only in London part of one day each week, and this is probably a good thing. Time was when Leeper breakfasted with Eden every day. Peake is leaving with the Viscount [Halifax] on

---

1 See E. Barker, *British Policy in South-East Europe in the Second World War*, Macmillan, London, 1976, pp. 84–91; D. A. T. Stafford, 'SOE and British Involvement in the Belgrade Coup d'Etat of March 1941', *Slavic Review*, vol. 36, 1977.
2 'see H.Q.': Dalton may have dictated 'C.H.Q.'

the ship next week – his role appears more and more ridiculous, no better than a valet's, ordering Kiwi, etc., for the Washington Embassy! ... Peake will see Eden tomorrow and try to make good blood between him and me. He thinks it is quite good now. (I remark afterwards to Gladwyn that Eden no doubt hopes that he will get the succession to Winston, but that, as things are, this would not be a matter for the Conservative Party alone to decide. We should have to be consulted, and I should not be without influence. Hence, since there is no reason to suppose that Eden and I will differ seriously on policy, it is not against his interest to be friends with me. To Gaitskell afterwards, I permit myself an even further speculation along this line.)[1] Peake says, 'I shall tell him that one day he and you may find yourselves standing side by side facing an angry crowd.' It is thought that Cadogan will be a steadying influence in this next phase.

A story from the Viscount about Munich. When he and Chamberlain and Sir Horace Wilson were returning together from Heston aerodrome, with the cheers of the crowd still in their ears, Halifax said to Chamberlain, 'And now you ought to tell the House of Commons that you have invited the Labour and Liberal leaders to join your Government. Then you will put yourself right with public opinion.' Chamberlain said, 'I'm not sure about that. You had better speak to Horace about it.' And Horace did not approve.

Leith-Ross has put up to me a perfect draft for a letter to the P.M. making complaint about the recent Honours List, the neglect of my clearly expressed preferences, the failure to consult Leith-Ross in spite of the Parliamentary answer to 18th September, the assertion by Horace in reply to Leith-Ross that preferences could not be given to temporaries, and the fact that in other Departments a number of temporaries had been honoured. I must watch for a good moment to pop this in.

On 13th January, a meeting of the Defence Committee considered a report from the Chiefs of Staff which argued that a concerted bombing attack on Germany's seventeen principal synthetic oil plants would bring German production of oil to a standstill by the end of four months. Dalton's request that restrictions on the bombing of Romanian oil supplies should be lifted was opposed by Eden, who was concerned not to sacrifice the British Mission in Bucharest.

---

1 Marginal insertion: 'A.E. P.M. & I F.S.' [Anthony Eden Prime Minister and I Foreign Secretary].

Monday 13th January

Go tonight to Defence Committee, where discussion is supposed to take place on a group of papers concerning attacks on oil. I am accompanied by Gladwyn and Hall. P.M. in the Chair gives the impression of being mentally completely exhausted. Almost alone, he argues against the proposals of the Chiefs of Staff and the Hankey Committee.[1] He goes round and round the same point and is, for him, terribly slow in the uptake and most pigheaded. Portal handles him very well and with extreme good temper and persistence. At the end, the Chiefs of Staff paper is accepted in a grudging provisional fashion subject to reports at short intervals. I can't get my paper discussed at all, the P.M. saying very affably indeed, 'No, no, you needn't go into any detail about that. Provided the Foreign Office and the Treasury and the Service Departments agree you can do what you like.' This really leaves us where we were before. Gladwyn, greatly depressed after the meeting, thinks we have suffered a reverse, or at least failed to make any progress in a most urgent business. I say that, on such form as this, I can't imagine how we can ever win the war.

Tuesday 14th January

Administrative Committee meets in Attlee's room. Shinwell learns nothing from his snubbing at the end of last session. He talks incessantly and makes a great grievance at the proposal that he should not speak for the Party in the debate next week on manpower and machinery of government. I take my share in squashing him and am astonished, not for the first time, at the sheepish submissiveness of some of my colleagues.

Go and see a private view of my film. It is, in its way, not bad, but I am made to speak with a most terrific cold in the nose. [Haydn] Davies tells me that he hears that at three provincial cinemas this film has been cheered. Anyhow, it is seen and heard, he says, by some millions of people.

Attlee tells me that the P.M. has gone away for a week and that everyone agrees that he badly needed a rest.

Wednesday 15th January

Spears to see me, amiable and long-winded, though ostensibly he came to air a grievance of de Gaulle about our leaflets. I ask his view of Eden, with whom, he says, he worked very closely for years on foreign policy. Eden's weakness, he says, is that he is always thinking too much about his career. Therefore, he is not so bold as he should be,

1 i.e. P.O.G. Committee, q.v.

and too much inclined to bide his time and conciliate those in authority. ...

I spend an hour with Eden, first alone, then with Cadogan, Sargent, Gladwyn and, at the end, Taylor who is brought in and introduced to Eden on the eve of his departure for Istanbul. I think that I should have no great difficulty in handling Eden. Alone with him, I speak of the Belgian Government and Pierlot's refusal to broaden it, of the Poles and Sikorski's predominance over all the rest, of Anderson's prejudice against Leeper (he reacts well to this and to my praise of Leeper, saying that this is the old Horace Wilson intrigue), and finally I speak of Lloyd George and of the danger that the P.M. may yet try to bring him into the Government. Eden says that, since Lloyd George was asked some time ago to become Minister of Agriculture and made a number of impossible conditions, and since he declined to consider going to Washington, he does not think that there have been any further approaches. He shares my view that Lloyd George is not only much too old, but is a potential Pétain. Beaverbrook, he thinks, is the only person who would wish to work him in. I say that I could easily get all my colleagues standing on their hind legs and waving their tails in fury at any such suggestion. Eden says he would like to keep in touch with me on this, and if any threat develops, we can concert further. He is evidently pleased with his relations with the P.M., who, he says, tells him everything. I wonder! He also says, concerning my colleagues, that he hopes I will not think it rude if he says how agreeably surprised he has been to find how easy they all are to work with. Attlee, he says, the P.M. likens to a terrier who, when he gets hold of an idea, will not let it go. He also speaks well of Bevin, who, he says, has always a most individual approach. ...

From Eden I descend to see Van, and the talk with him is almost wholly on the further approaches of Morton. This man, says Van, is obviously making a bid for better relations with me. On his own initiative he sought a talk with Van today and said that the P.M. would be writing me 'a nice letter' on my recent report on S.O., but that he would like to advise me to send short and striking reports of incidents from time to time which would interest him more than a long document. I tell Van quite frankly that I suspect Morton of having made mischief with regard to me. Too many rumours reach me from too many quarters for this not to seem credible. I cite Nelson among others. However, I say, I am willing to work with people, even thought I do not like or trust them, if for their own reasons they are willing to work with me. I will therefore wait for the 'nice letter' and thereafter take some further steps about Morton, though, as I tell Van, last time we lunched together I was his host. Van also says that

Morton says that my grasp of M.E.W. matters is most remarkable, that I always have all the details at my fingertips, make a very good impression on these matters in the Cabinet, and nearly always get my way. I reply that I believe this *is* substantially true.

Van says that he would like to see Gladwyn once a week, say for about half an hour, to hear about projects. I say that this would be a very good plan and I will pass it on. I add that I myself am more and more taking personal charge of all the detail on this side,[1] since there are greater difficulties here than on the other. I say this seeking to deflect Van from trying too much to control this detail. His attitude towards Gladwyn is outwardly quite friendly.

Later, when I tell Gladwyn of this, he says that it looks as though Morton realises that now we are doing rather well and are not easily to be shaken, and that therefore he is trying to aid the victors.

Friday 17th January
C.D. gives one of his, as usual, very successful dinner parties this evening, for purposes of co-ordinating the war against the Germans and suppressing the substitute wars in Whitehall. I am put between Sir Orme Sargent (who has been infinitely conciliatory and agreeable since he was almost carried out screaming from Halifax's presence when we had the row about the Bridge) and the D.M.I., a sentimental old fellow who seems to have a great fixation on one of my officers. The D.A.I. is also present and, remembering his grievance last time that I talked too much to someone else, I spread myself to him.

Saturday 18th January
Through the snow by car with Attlee to C.H.Q. As usual, a friendly air and nothing much to say. He says that, following my suggestion, he mentioned Wilmot to Eden 'who was much interested', but clearly this was out of reach as yet, nor would Eden in any case have wished to have one of my inner circle as his No. 2.

I press again that Noel-Baker should go to the War Office as one of the Under-Secretaries. I am sorry to find that he is thinking instead of Milner.[2]

12 noon conference at C.H.Q. attended by Attlee, Vansittart and others. Throughout the day Attlee doesn't react much, but obviously likes it. In the afternoon the usual pilgrimage with recordings etc. In the evening a discussion, not very well staged, on propaganda and invasion. Crossman is a little vexed with me because I don't take more

1 i.e. the SO2 side of S.O.E.
2 Major James Milner, later 1st Baron (1889–1967). Labour M.P. for Leeds South-East, 1929–51. Deputy Speaker of the House of Commons 1943–5, 1945–51.

interest in what Gladwyn calls 'propagandology'. On the other hand, he said to Gaitskell, 'What a good thing it is to be one of the Minister's friends.' Gaitskell said, 'If you weren't, you would never have been here at all.'

Sunday 19th January
This morning Gladwyn explains at length to Attlee what his branch is doing. 'I got quite exhausted', he said afterwards, 'getting no reaction.' None the less, Attlee was obviously impressed.

In January 1941, the Communist *Daily Worker* and Claud Cockburn's satirical newsheet *The Week*, which also took a pro-Soviet and therefore neutralist line, were banned under Defence Regulation 2D, which permitted the Government to suppress any publication that aimed to ferment opposition to the war.

In North Africa, the British forces continued to make progress against the Italians. Following up the victories of December, Wavell advanced rapidly into Libya, and in January 1941 occupied the port of Tobruk.

Wednesday 22nd January
Today's papers are full of news: the fall of Tobruk, of poor Bob Boothby, and of the *Daily Worker*!

As to Boothby, he puts a brave and combative face on it in a statement to the press this morning, but the summary of the report looks pretty damning. Garro Jones,[1] whom I run into, says that he does not believe Boothby can even hold his constituency. But I am inclined to think he may, unless, of course, he goes bankrupt. On personal grounds I am quite sorry about it. But I resist the temptation to write him a personal note of sympathy, realising that this might be given undue circulation.

It now appears that Morrison had already decided the day before yesterday to suppress the *Daily Worker* and the *Week*, but he did not trust some members of the National Executive, and therefore felt he could not say much in front of them, except to try and put them off the scent. He told Wilmot this morning, after defending his action at the Party Meeting against an insignificant minority of objectors, including Rhys Davies and Aneurin Bevan, that he had quite agreed with Wilmot's speech at the National Executive but had not been able to say so.

1 G. M. Garro Jones (1894–1960). Labour M.P. for North Aberdeen 1935–45.

Lunch alone with Hopkins,[1] whom I met in Washington in 1933 when he was in charge of Public Works. Very much a buddy of the President, and very quick on the ball regarding our M.E.W. difficulties with the U.S.A. Very contemptuous both of his State Department and of some of our diplomats. When I told him of a certain recent difficulty, he said, 'Fancy Sumner Welles[2] and Butler[3] sitting up together discussing cotton! Neither of them knows the first thing about it.' His principal remedy was to put a man in the American Embassy in London who was in the President's confidence and would have direct access to me. Then, he said, he could put anything I wanted 'straight on the wires' to the President. He expresses a wish to see me again, and also to see something of our shelters. He was much thrilled by our fine morale, and clearly the P.M. has done good work with him.

Friday 24th January
Lunch alone with [Percy] Cudlipp. He does not make a good impression. He speaks evil, more or less, of all Labour ministers except myself, and says that [Maurice] Webb is all for me. Also, 'I and Webb, we are the *Daily Herald*.' I am left to surmise that almost certainly he speaks evil of me to my colleagues. I do not want to see him often, but probably it will be wise to do so now and then.

A very good day for news. Rubble[4] has come off. A telephone message from Alexander and news brought also from my own staff.

Saturday 25th January
Lunch with Ruth. I tell her that we really are at last spending a weekend together!

Monday 27th January
Gladwyn says that a little bird has told him that Eden is planning to retire a number of diplomats, including Vansittart, and is talking to the Treasury about proportionate pensions.

Tuesday 28th January
House of Commons. Boothby, I think, does very well. 'If only I had realised how this might be misunderstood afterwards ...... all I need

1 Harry L. Hopkins (1890–1946). Special Adviser to the President of the U.S.A. 1940–43. Secretary of Commerce 1938–40.
2 Sumner Welles (1892–1961). U.S. Under-Secretary of State 1937–43.
3 N. M. Butler, later Sir Nevile (1893–1973). Minister in Washington 1940–41. Head of North American Department at the Foreign Office 1941–4.
4 'Rubble' (code name): air support for Norwegian steel-carrying ships running the blockade from Göteborg to the U.K. in 1941.

have done was to add a postscript to a letter or a few sentences to a conversation.' I feel that he is a far better man than most of those who judged him on the Select Committee. Unfortunately, he has broken the Eleventh Commandment, whereas many a financial rascal in Parliament has not.[1]

Ministers' meeting at Foreign Office where Eden gives a good summary. I stay behind and talk to him. I ask whether he would like a copy of my last report to the P.M. He would, and shows much interest. I write, in a covering note sending it, that Gladwyn and Nelson and their team deserve great credit. Eden says that he cannot make out what Hoare is up to in Madrid. He is going to telegraph to him to carry out his instructions. I say that Eccles is able; he replies that he thinks he is also dangerous. I say that I have heard him described as a British Baudouin. Eden is very conscious of many problems whose latest phases are new to him, and of a great mass of detail to be mastered. I think that we shall continue to get on well together.

Wednesday 29th January

Leeper and Wilmot to lunch. Good progress is being made in recasting the hierarchy at C.H.Q. Leeper will now take anything from Wilmot and Gaitskell, both of whom he likes and regards as his friends at court. This suits me very well. He also told Wilmot that, whereas he used to think I was much more difficult to work with than Van, he has now changed his mind. Since I came to a certain agreement with him about our relations, I have strictly kept it, he says, whereas Van is always jumping in excitedly with sudden orders regarding both policy and personnel. ...

Monckton to dinner. He is quite willing to settle the broadcast dispute on the lines that we have a 'common directive' on Italy, as on Germany. He thinks the Foreign Office and B.B.C. should also be in on this. I have no objection. The places of meeting, both for Gladwyn and I, to be left as they are at present. The Ministry of Information to withdraw their claim to leaflets. ...

He goes from me to the Dorchester to find Duff Cooper and report our discussion. 'He doesn't like work', he says of his Chief.

Cripps, he says, writes to him about once a fortnight. He is completely disillusioned with the Russians. He complains that Halifax never gave him any cards to play. I said that, whatever cards he had, he could not play them with effect just now, when the Russians were terrified of Germany. ...

After a little talk with Gaitskell on ministers and their relative

1 Marginal insertion: ' "Thou shalt not be found out." '

capacity for rudeness, I fall asleep and sleep long and placidly. The storm is over.

Thursday 30th January

Will Arnold-Forster[1] to lunch at the House. He still thinks and talks in the terms of long ago. World opinion, he thinks, will be moved in our favour if we make it clear that we intend to reconstitute an independent Abyssinia under Haile Selassie.[2] He had been afraid that delay in recent weeks was due to some desire to appease Mussolini. He is also most anxious that we should continue to repeat (a) that Nazis are not the same thing as Germans, and (b) that we shall do nothing to break up Germany after the war.

On the one point, I ask him where, and consisting of whom, is the 'world opinion' which will be on our side if we say and do these things, and against us or lukewarm if we don't? Let us not, I say, delude ourselves with the belief that virtue, in the condition of today, will bring any quick or large reward. This is an argument not against being virtuous but against being duped.

As to Germany, I tell him that I regret I do not find myself liking these people any better as the war goes on. My mind, in contrast with my view at the end of the last war that it was a good thing that Austria-Hungary should be 'broken up', or rather that its break-up should be legalised, is now moving towards the creation of a Mid-European federal structure, of which the necessary foundation is close Polish-Czechoslovak union, to which should also be added a democratised Hungary, keeping all her gains from Romania and nearly all, but not quite, from Czechoslovakia (e.g. returning Kosice), and also Yugoslavia. These elements being fixed, I should also like to bring in a South German element, Austria plus some or all of Baden and Bavaria. We cannot bear again that all the German tribes should stick together in a solid mass menacing all their neighbours. We should create conditions in which it shall seem to the Austrians and other South Germans preferable to go into the other unit, which should offer them a wider market than that of the old Austria-Hungary, and reasonable self-government, leading them, however, in the last resort, to face a substantial Slav majority. Such a State might, perhaps, even extend, by including Bulgaria and the remnants of Romania, to fill in all the

---

1 Will Arnold-Forster (1886–1952). Writer, and adviser to the Labour Party on international questions. He had worked with Dalton, as Private Secretary to the Labour Government's League of Nations adviser, Lord Cecil, in 1929–31. Married to Ka Cox, who had formerly been a girlfriend of Rupert Brooke.
2 Haile Selassie (1891–1975). Emperor of Abyssinia. Forced into exile in 1936, he rallied Abyssinian patriots in Khartoum in 1940 and crossed the border into Abyssinia the following year. He was reinstated as Emperor in June 1941.

gaps between Central Germany, however organised politically, and the Soviet Union. Essential to any such scheme would be an exchange of populations so as to eliminate the national minorities.

Arnold-Forster is a bit frightened at this, but does not argue frontally against it.

Harold Nicolson wrote in his diary for 31st January 1941: 'Lunch with Sibyl [Colefax]. I discuss with Hugh Dalton whether our children will tell their children that we members of Churchill's Government "were giants in those days". We are not sure that anyone will ever say that Kingsley Wood was a giant. Winston, of course, will emerge as a terrific figure, and perhaps Portal.'[1]

Friday 31st January
Four-Power Conference in my room. Van chatters away about all sorts of unessentials to Leeper and, in the last few minutes, I ask whether Gladwyn has anything new to report. He says no. This is quite a convenient division of the time.

Lunch with Lady Colefax, on whose Lions list I now seem to be inscribed! Nicolson, who is not doing much just now in the public eye, tells me that he does his own diary every night on a typewriter. He appears in this record, he says, as a most blameless character. Reprinting his diary of the last Peace Conference, he added nothing, in spite of overwhelming temptations, and only omitted passages likely to give unnecessary pain to individuals. Are there giants in these days too? The P.M. of course, but anyone else? I say that I think as the war ends, those who took some large apparent share in ending it will look like giants to the next generation, though not perhaps to us who see them close up. Nicolson thinks that his proudest boast will be, to his grandchildren, 'When I was a member of Mr Churchill's administration'.

Maisky comes to protest about our seizure of part of the cargo of a ship and to argue that my references to U.S. exports to the U.S.S.R. are exaggerated. We howl with laughter at each other but get nowhere.

We are invited – Gladwyn and Gubbins and I – to a party with the Poles in Retinger's flat, where Sikorski arrives in due course and there are also gathered Kot and all the aides-de-camp. Retinger produces

1 N. Nicolson (ed.), *Harold Nicolson: Diaries and Letters 1939–1945*, Collins, London, 1967, p. 141.

some bottles of Polish vodka of which, both liking it and desiring to be friendly, I drink a good deal. I should have eaten more of the cold salad, herrings, etc., which are also offered. I leave the Poles with every appearance of dignity and propriety, but my dignity might have suffered a little had they spent the next hour in my company! Next morning, however, I feel completely fit. That vodka, though strong, was a most clean drink.

Saturday 1st February

To Leicester to address a Regional Conference of Divisional Labour Parties. Some 400 delegates, the great majority of whom are very sensible, though a minority are cranks. I tell them that in the next few months each must be prepared to go through greater personal ordeals and personal risks than ever before, and that they should all recover the habit of carrying gas-masks. I have no doubt, I tell them, that we shall frustrate the enemy's efforts, but these will be *immense*. Compared with this, all talk of peace aims, etc., is very secondary. It is strange that even a few can still be such fools as not to sense this priority.

Travel back with Donovan,[1] candidate for East Leicester, a barrister who seems to have more political wits than most of his tribe.

Sunday 2nd February

Read last night Van's *Black Record*.[2] I think it will do good on balance, though many highly educated and traditionally minded people will be shocked. Certainly, however, it may be criticised as being hysterical and venomous in tone, even though it is true in substance.

[Noel] Hall spoke ill on Friday to me of Attlee, obviously echoing Morton. He was said to be sick and small and to bore the P.M., who had rebuked him when he had tried to intervene between the latter and Mr Pick on a famous occasion.

Gladwyn and Nelson to dine with me. ... We discuss little Laski. There is evidence that he not only writes direct to the President but receives answers through the Diplomatic Bag. He gives the President quite a false impression of what is going on here, and his stature in the U.S.A. is far higher than in this country.

1 Terence Donovan, later Baron (1898–1971). Barrister. Labour M.P. 1945–50. High Court Judge 1950–60. Lord Justice of Appeal 1960–63. Chairman, Royal Commission on Trade Unions and Employers' Associations 1965–8.

2 *Black Record: Germans past and present*, published by Hamish Hamilton in 1941, was based on seven radio broadcasts in which Vansittart elaborated his thesis that Germans were aggressive and war-like as a nation. This offended many liberals, who felt that a distinction should be drawn between Nazis and the German people, who had been misled by them.

Following the fall of France, the British government looked increasingly to the United States for military and other supplies. After Roosevelt's re-election as President, it became easier for the Americans to act on Secretary of State Henry Morgenthau's suggestion for financial aid in the form of a gift rather than a loan. After the President had indicated his intentions on 17th December, the Lend-Lease Bill was drafted and sent to both Houses of Congress. The Bill was passed on 11th March and the operation of Lend-Lease started a fortnight later.

Tuesday 4th February

See Hopkins in the morning. We speak again of need for better contacts, and M.E.W., or its equivalent, in Washington; someone at our Embassy there – perhaps Campbell[1] will do, coached by Marris[2] – to handle detail; someone at the American Embassy in London who will specialise on M.E.W. questions, keep in touch with me and, with the approval of the Ambassador, wire direct to Washington, but this person must have the confidence of the President; probably Leith-Ross to go to Washington for a few weeks when the Lease and Lend Bill is through. Hopkins says that there would be a lot to be said for my going, but he quite understands that, if there is an invasion here, I should not want to be out of it. He is a first-class scout for the President.

News from the Foreign Office is that Eden is writing many 'peevish Minutes', but is not really a strong man. He goes about saying, 'There is no control here. I can't imagine what Edward [Halifax] did with himself all day.' It is not thought, however, that he will make any important changes of personnel at present. He is constantly on the telephone to the P.M., who is taking much more charge of the Foreign Office now than he did when the Viscount was there. The latter disliked the telephone, and when the P.M. rang him up and got into full flow, he used to say, 'What's that? I can't hear you.' This used to put the P.M. off his stroke. Also the Viscount had guns in reserve, which Eden had not, and could sometimes give the P.M. the unmistakable impression that he regarded him as a very vulgar and ignorant person. Eden may soon become almost as completely a lay figure as the three Service Ministers. I have been greatly impressed with this lately and am shedding all ambition to become even Air Minister – my first

1 Sir Ronald Ian Campbell (b. 1890). Minister in Washington 1941–5.
2 Adam Marris (b. 1906). M.E.W. 1939–40. First Secretary and then Counsellor (War Trade Department) at the British Embassy in Washington 1940–45.

choice among the three – in time of war. The Chiefs of Staff are much closer to the P.M. as Minister of Defence than to their political Chiefs, and much more influenced. The other day Portal was asked by the P.M. to expound his views, Sinclair sitting silent beside him, and was complimented by the P.M. on his 'diplomatic as well as strategical insight.' ...

I dine tonight with X[1] who gives me an amazing account of his parents and his youth. This, as he tells it, would make a wonderful Chapter I of his Memoirs one day. It also helps to explain his reserve and others of his qualities.

His father wanted to go to the University but was sent instead into the Army and became a gunner officer. He was six foot three, very good-looking, very gay, a very good shot, and 'the life and soul of the mess' in India, where, however, he had sunstroke, the effects of which have never left him. Returning, he married X's mother, then quite a young girl, and by her had three children, X and two daughters, one of whom died, the other being now married to an Italian living near Florence. After the third child, he was advised that his wife must have no more, and, little being known in those days of preventives, he carried on in succession with several other women, including two Gaiety actresses, and is still quite interested in the other sex. He had a large mansion in Yorkshire and stood, in the first years of this century, for Parliament, but always spoke on the platform against his own side and finally, his sunstroke leaping back upon him, became quite speechless at a large public meeting and was howled down by the crowd. He polled fewer votes, X says, than any other candidate who has ever stood anywhere. X thinks he only got 2. The mansion has now been sold and is used as a Club for Sheffield businessmen. It has all been done up with aluminium paint and is incredibly vulgar. There is, for instance, a clock, the hands of which are made to represent a lady's legs. X, the other day, visiting this house with some friends, took them to see the room where he was born, but this was now a ladies' lavatory. X, who was born in 1900, never saw his father from the time he was seven till he was seventeen. He was brought up by his mother, who finally divorced his father. During these ten years his father was wandering about the world with his lady friends, shooting in the Rockies and fishing in New Zealand. In the last war he appeared at a dugout and was given some command at some home station. There he fell foul of the authorities because he carred on a great campaign amongst his men against inoculation, alleging that it poisoned the blood.

1 This is clearly Gladwyn Jebb, whose father, Sydney Jebb, had been the owner of Firbeck Hall in Yorkshire. See *The Memoirs of Lord Gladwyn*, Weidenfeld & Nicolson, London, 1972, pp. 7–10.

Much earlier, having been disappointed of his University education, X's father got a tutor to teach him Greek, was a very quick learner and soon was able to read Homer and Sophocles quite easily.

More recently, he nearly finished himself off by drinking a large tankard, which he thought contained sherry – this is how he likes to drink sherry – but which in fact contained Angostura bitters.

X claims that he is descended also, through his father, from Pitt 'who, after all, was a good Party boss'. His mother, I gather, he finds a bit of a bore and a snob. It is not surprising that he should have been rather a late developer. He blossomed indeed at the University immediately after the war, when it appeared for the first time that he had first-class brains. Between school and University he spent the last six months of the war in an officers' training unit at Bushey, though he never went to the Front. He thinks that this six months was very good for him and that before he was very *maladif.*

In mid-February, the Prime Minister referred in a telegram to Wavell to the 'increasingly menacing attitude of Japan and plain possibility she may attack us in the near future'.[1]

Wednesday 5th February

Leith-Ross thinks that the Japs will make a move southward before the end of March, possibly against North Borneo and the Dutch East Indies. Only two things, he thinks, are likely to stop them, either the U.S. sending their fleet to the Western Pacific (and there are difficulties about this through lack of bases and Jap control of Marshall and neighbouring islands), or by Russians making threatening noises in the north. Of the latter, I say, there is no chance at all at present.

Butler, whom I see later in the day, thinks that the Japs are more likely to attack Burma through Siam. There is nothing to stop them bombing Rangoon from Siamese bases.

See Van for a moment in the afternoon. He is still fidgeting against Crossman and this is beginning to bore me. It is mixed up with the fidget against German Socialist émigrés, who, he thinks, are proposing to issue some joint manifesto against his recent broadcasts, and Noel-Baker who, he says, has been writing letters saying that the Germans are no worse than other people. This is all a bit of a bore,

1 W. S. Churchill, *The Second World War: Volume III The Grand Alliance*, Cassell, London, 1950, p. 56.

and like most other things in which Van now takes an interest, probably much exaggerated. None the less, I must speak to Crossman this weekend.

See Binney[1] this afternoon. A small and unimpressive man for one who has done so well in Operation R [Rubble]. P.M. wants to give some special Honours for this, and I send in a recommendation of Hambro for a K.B.E. (In this queer world of Honours, probably to give Hambro something less than a K.B.E. would be worse than giving him nothing at all!)

Douglas Jay,[2] who is now in the Ministry of Supply and viewed with some suspicion by Andrew Duncan,[3] reports that the latter is a great 'stormer and shouter'. I should never have suspected this. He looks a very reserved and humdrum lower-middle-class Scot. But perhaps *all* ministers really storm and shout, and I am one of the quietest of them all.

Thursday 6th February

I find that Woolton[4] shouts too. He shouted at Leith-Ross yesterday at a conference on the price to be charged to the Dutch for their tea. He asked Leith-Ross why he was bothered to attend at all, and who, other than his experts at the Food Ministry, should know anything about such questions? Leith-Ross apparently told him that his experts were liars! Quite a bright little scene.

Evidence from Woolton's report and also from interrogation of P.W.s [Prisoners of War] that our leaflets have a great effect in precipitating Italian surrender in Africa.

Have Morton along to dinner this evening with Wilmot, Hambro and Hall. He gives an appearance of great affability and makes a great impression on Wilmot, who has never seen him before. I advise Wilmot to remain just a little suspicious.

1 G. Binney, later Sir George (1900–72). Explorer. Seconded from the United Steel Company for service with the Ministry of Supply 1939. Assistant Commercial Attaché Stockholm 1940–42. He was knighted later in the year for 'Special services in the supply of valuable war material'.
2 Douglas Jay (b. 1907). Assistant Secretary to the Ministry of Supply 1941–3. City Editor of the *Daily Herald* 1937–41. Principal Assistant Secretary to the Board of Trade 1943–5. Personal Assistant to the Prime Minister 1945–6. Labour M.P. 1946–83. Economic Secretary to the Treasury 1947–50. Financial Secretary to the Treasury 1950–51. President of the Board of Trade 1964–7.
3 Sir Andrew Duncan (1884–1952). Minister of Supply 1940–41, 1942–5. President of the Board of Trade 1940, 1941–2. Conservative M.P. for the City of London 1940–1950. Chairman of the Iron and Steel Trades Confederation 1935–40, 1945–52.
4 Lord Woolton, q.v.

Friday 7th February

Am summoned to Buckingham Palace by His Majesty this morning and have half an hour with him alone. He shows an interest in M.E.W. but has not, I think, heard very much, if anything, of the rest. I tell him about Rubble and Fischamend.[1] We speak also of gas-masks, and he says he has been thinking that perhaps they ought to have a gas-mask drill in Buckingham Palace and he receive his visitors in his.

Call from the new D.M.I., General Davidson, who makes a very good impression on me. He is an old friend of Attlee, whom he praises for lack of Party spirit or personal animus. Davidson is one of those classless Scots. He is a gunner and has done some Intelligence work before, but not been too long in it to have a fresh mind. He says that the Alpini[2] cracked up in this war because their officers, many of whom were Fascists from low altitudes, neglected their men. In Albania they had hardly any rations and only one thin blanket per man. These blankets, moreover, were in very poor material and tore in pieces. Alpini prisoners captured by the Greeks were in the most miserable physical condition.

He evidently thinks that Gladwyn is a little young for his responsibilities, and is surprised to hear that he is even yet forty. But I sing his praises and so, independently, does Gaitskell, who, taking Davidson along the passage, says what a wonderful combination Gladwyn and I make. Davidson has also heard of 'Dr Dynamo'.

News today is that much evidence, coming through many different channels, accumulates that Jap entry into the war is very imminent. 'Wait for *the* cable next week ... cut off all social contacts and hold yourselves aloof' (I said I thought that this one was all wrong, according to the theory. They should get all they could as late as they could. But I was told that this was the Jap way. Much wooden pride.) They seem also to be settling down in Cam Ranh Bay and other points in Thailand.

Saturday 8th and Sunday 9th February

Gaitskell has a brainwave to secure Walter Adams,[3] a most suitable person now engaged in mere necrophily at Cambridge over the remains of L.S.E.,[4] to come as General Secretary. Acting quickly

1 'Fischamend': another operation.
2 'Alpini': Italian mountain troops. As an artillery officer in the Italian Alps in the first war, Dalton had had experience of the Alpini in action.
3 W. Adams, later Sir Walter (1906–75). Lecturer at the L.S.E. 1938–46. Deputy Head of the British Political Warfare Mission to the U.S.A. 1942–4. Principal of the University College of Rhodesia and Nyasaland 1953–67. Director of the L.S.E. 1967–74.
4 Students and staff of the L.S.E. had been evacuated to Cambridge.

Leeper and Gaitskell go to Cambridge to see him. There is hope that we shall get him.

On the Sunday morning take Ivor Thomas[1] for a walk, broken into sometimes by short runs, round the neighbourhood. He is doing very well and liking it.

Monday 10th February
Lunch with John Carvel[2] of *The Star* along with Gaitskell and Haydn Davies. Carvel says that Butler was offered the Colonial Office in succession to Lord Lloyd on condition that he went to the Lords. He was dissuaded from accepting this by Gretton[3] and Co., who want to keep him in the Commons as they think of him as a future Prime Minister, and by his East Anglian friends.

On 8th February, there was a minor Government reshuffle, mainly involving junior ministers. In fact (despite Dalton's comment) it was a National Liberal, Ernest Brown, who replaced Malcolm MacDonald at the Ministry of Health. Thomas Johnston took Brown's job at the Scottish Office.

Tuesday 11th February
Lunch House of Commons. Short talk with Attlee. Agree with him that last Government changes – Tom Johnston, Tomlinson and Paling – are good from our point of view, Johnston having replaced Malcolm MacDonald[4] and thus it being recognised that a 'National Labour'

1 Ivor (Bulmer) Thomas (b. 1905). Recruited into SO1 Italian section at the end of 1940. Labour M.P. 1942–8. Independent, then Conservative, M.P. 1948–50. Junior minister 1945–7. Writer and historian.
2 John Carvel (1894–1959). Lobby correspondent of *The Star*, which he joined in 1936. In November 1947, Dalton's career as Chancellor of the Exchequer ended after he gave Budget details to Carvel before his speech to the House.
3 John Gretton, later 1st Baron (1867–1947). Conservative M.P. for Burton 1918–43; Derbyshire South 1895–1906; Rutland 1907–18.
4 M. J. MacDonald (1901–81). Son of Ramsay MacDonald. National Labour M.P. for Ross and Cromarty 1936–45; Labour M.P. for Bassetlaw 1929–31; National Labour 1931–5. Junior minister 1931–5. Dominions Secretary 1935–8, 1938–9; Colonial Secretary 1935, 1938–40. Minister of Health 1940–41. High Commissioner for Canada 1941–6. Roving Ambassador in Asia and Africa 1946–69. Dalton is not correct in stating that Johnston replaced MacDonald: Ernest Brown replaced Malcolm MacDonald at the Ministry of Health on 8th February 1941, and Johnston replaced Brown as Secretary of State for Scotland. MacDonald became High Commissioner for Canada, replacing Sir Gerald Campbell, q.v.

place, when vacated, goes Labour again. I speak again of Noel-Baker, who is getting wispier and wilder, though still very good in many ways, the longer he is left outside. Attlee says he is going to push him for the next suitable vacancy – almost anywhere outside the Foreign Office.

He has heard that Van is very nervy and difficult; also that the P.M. is now pretty well satisfied with S.O.

[Maurice] Webb to dine tonight. He is said to be a great fan of mine, but I should not trust him very far. He is not much of a scout, showing no sign of having heard anything of M.U.W. [Ministry of Ungentlemanly Warfare]. He says that Alexander was shown the other night a newspaper article describing how the Germans would use barges etc. for an invasion. Alexander flung the paper down, smote the table, and said, 'These pressmen are a public disgrace, putting such ideas into Hitler's head.'

Webb twitters too much about Party politics after the war. He has some vague fear that something will be 'put across' Labour ministers and that they will be committed to some coupon election or permanent coalition. He says people are talking about this kind of thing on the Stock Exchange and in Tory Clubs. I tell him not to bother.

Thursday 13th February
... I go, attended by Gladwyn and Gaitskell, to pay an official visit to C.D.'s establishment.[1] I spend three hours there and I think the occasion is a success. C.D. writes me a most warm and appreciative letter afterwards, which I feel sure is sincerely meant. I make a short informal speech to the weekly meeting of some two dozen of them, in the course of which I say, 'Happy the Minister who can make his own appointments and start free from all the personal legacies of the past.'

I say that barely six months ago I was given a task by the P.M. and began by appointing Gladwyn and C.D., in both of whom I had and have great confidence, to take charge of this branch of the work. I am satisfied that C.D. has now got together a good team. The building work was delayed, no doubt, by the need to do some slum clearance on the selected site. It is a new departure to have close ministerial control of such operations, and a colleague of mine[2] in H.M.G. recently said to me that in his day it would have been inconceivable that a minister should have directed such things and that he, who had spent more time in certain directions than any other living man, would never dream of telling his Minister what he was doing. I replied,

---

1 'C.D.'s establishment': SO2 headquarters in Baker Street.
2 Clearly Sir John Anderson, Lord President, q.v., a former civil servant.

'Things have changed a great deal, Sir John, since you were nothing more than a civil servant.' This same man had also said that he thought it most remarkable that nothing had come out in public of me or my doings. I hoped that my ministerial control would not be negative, but rather positive. I would undertake to defend them against any charges of impetuosity or undue enterprise or vigour. I would give no such undertaking in the contrary case. The only thing that interested me ... was to win the war. I should perhaps explain that I meant the war against the Germans. The great distinction was between the quick and the dead. I hoped that we could say, as Mazzini[1] said, living an émigré among us and trying to learn our language, when the undertaker called at the wrong house, 'There are no deads here.'

I had only one quarrel with C.D. It was that he never went away for a weekend.

After all this, we had a light buffet lunch and all those present were brought up and introduced to me in turn. I was then taken all round the establishment and shook hands with all, including all the ladies, young and old, many of whom were visibly edified. C.D. kept asking if I was not too tired, but I replied that I never got tired and – afterwards – that it was very like electioneering, of which he and I both had memories.[2] ...

Dine with Spears to meet Pléven,[3] de Gaulle's Breton. Also present Wedgwood Benn and Gladwyn, to whom Wedgwood Benn says, 'I see your name every day on the distribution list.' I think this is all he knows about him!

Pléven does not much impress me. He is not dynamic, and, like all the de Gaulle crowd, can believe no Frenchman outside their little circle is any good or desires our victory. Naturally he denigrates all Vichy and Weygand. This may be true. On the other hand, he says that Pétain is really resisting. But it does not seem to follow from this, in his view, that we should do anything to assist this old man, except intensify the blockade against him. I am astonished to hear that three-quarters of the population of France is in the Occupied zone. The Unoccupied, though it contains Marseilles, Lyons and Toulouse, is for the rest most thinly populated.

1 Giuseppe Mazzini (1805–72). Italian patriot and writer. Member of the Carbonari. Lived in exile in England for a total of twenty years.
2 Sir Frank Nelson, q.v., had once been a Conservative M.P.
3 René Jean Pléven (b. 1901). With Jean Monnet, he was a member of the French Economic Mission in London 1940, and thereafter a member of the French National Committee in London 1941–4. Minister of Colonies in the French Provisional Government 1944; Finance 1944–6; Defence 1949, 1952–4. Prime Minister July 1950, August 1951–January 1952. Minister of Justice 1969–72.

Gladwyn forms a very low opinion of Wedgwood Benn, who, I explain, owed his Secretaryship of State for India in 1929 entirely to his bumsucking of MacDonald. In that office he was a complete failure and had to be put into the background at the Round Table Conference, while he became very unpopular in the Labour Party owing to his weakness and inaction over the Meerut case.[1] He did not like me because he knew that I had several times prevented his getting good by-elections. Since he returned to the House in 1936 he had done his best to ingratiate himself with all elements in the Party, and by not taking sides in any of the more exciting controversies, had built up a certain popularity. He was, however, deeply chagrined at not having any post in the Churchill Government – his exclusion was a tribute to Attlee's judgment. He had since practically boycotted Parliament and had a bogus job in Air Ministry Intelligence. Gladwyn said that he obviously knew nothing about anything and he supposed that he was now too old to have a political future. I said that I thought this was so.

Friday 14th February

[Haydn] Davies brings in a wonderful yarn. He hears from Trevor Evans[2] of the *Express* that three or four people, one of whom was a woman, were offering the paper a most sensational story about M.E.W. The Fascist methods of the Minister; his habit of banishing all those who disagreed with him to a ministerial Siberia, etc. They would furnish a list of names of persons working here before I came, their political records and their present jobs. Tories who expected to be fired by me were now in good jobs, but Reds and Pinks had been pushed out. Even some members of the Labour Party who don't toe exactly the Party line as laid down by me had suffered. But I was very clever and always gave such people an Irishman's rise. They said, 'We will give you the biggest front page scandal about Hugh Dalton, but we want some big money.' Evans had asked whether Wilmot was not my P.P.S. and whether this did not go against the truth of their story. They said, 'Jack is as black as his master.'

Gaitskell and I both think that this is all rather nonsense, probably from someone very far down in the Ministry, probably from some Communist. It seems very unlikely that it will get any further, but Davies is going to try to find out more, and has persuaded Evans, whose identity must on no account be disclosed, to see these people

1 The Meerut Communist Conspiracy took place in April 1929, and the repercussions were still being felt when Wedgwood Benn became Secretary of State for India in June of the same year.
2 T. M. Evans, later Sir Trevor (1902–81). Industrial correspondent of the *Daily Express* 1930–67.

again and get particulars from them early next week.

Vansittart says he attended a meeting of soldiers and officials at No. 10 last night when, at the end, leaflets for de Gaulle were discussed. The P.M. said to Van that he could settle it with me. 'You're his *chef de cabinet*, aren't you?' Vansittart told me that he felt a little old for a Private Secretary's job, but I told him that this was obviously how he was described in War Cabinet circles, as Attlee had used the same expression.

There is some evidence that Alexander and Greenwood are both in Beaverbrook's pocket. Hopkins mentioned the last time I saw him that he had spent a weekend with the Beaver, and that both of these were there. To him, no doubt, this seemed quite a natural weekend party. But to others, less so!

Meet Walt Butterworth,[1] just returned from U.S.A. to their Embassy here. He warns us that the U.S. are very slow to get into war, even with Japan. The quality of the Jap and U.S. Navies are both speculative. Neither has ever taken part in any serious modern warfare. Some good judges think that the Japs will be very weak, but this may be all wrong. Butterworth points out that in a fleet action near Japan, damaged Jap ships may get home, but Americans will be very far from their bases.

Osbert Peake[2] says that Morrison makes no pretence of his dislike of Bevin and says that 'There's too much vitamin I' in the latter's speeches. I ask how Assheton[3] ... gets on with Bevin. Peake says very well. It is amusing to see two Tory Under-Secretaries both being very loyal to their respective Labour Chiefs who are at daggers drawn!

Peake says that he once stayed in the same house as Neville Chamberlain, who, thirty-six hours after his arrival, asked Peake, 'Can you tell me where there is a rear in this place?'

---

1 W. Walton Butterworth (1903–75). American diplomat. Second Secretary at the U.S. Embassy and Special Representative of the Treasury Department in London 1934–41.

2 Osbert Peake, later 1st Viscount Ingleby (1897–1966). Parliamentary Under-Secretary at the Home Office 1939–44. Conservative M.P. for Leeds North 1929–55; Leeds North-East May–December 1955. Financial Secretary to the Treasury 1944–5. Minister of National Insurance 1951–3; Pensions and National Insurance 1953–5.

3 Ralph Assheton, later 1st Baron Clitheroe (b. 1901). Junior minister at the Ministry of Labour and National Service 1939–42. Conservative M.P. for Rushcliffe 1934–45; City of London 1945–50; Blackburn 1950–55. Junior minister 1942–3. Financial Secretary to the Treasury 1943–4. Chairman of the Conservative Party Organisation 1944–6.

On 17th February, *The Times* reported that a group of British parachutists had been captured after landing in a lonely part of southern Italy, on the borders of the provinces of Lucania and Calabria. According to an official Ministry of Information announcement, 'Their instructions were to demolish certain objectives connected with the ports in that area.'

Monday 17th February

Newspapers full of British parachute descent in the heel of Italy. This is the D.C.O.'s[1] operation, in favour of which ours against the toe was postponed. All we did was to lend the D.C.O. one Italian. The thing seems to have been a pretty good failure, and the P.M. didn't know it was to happen and was furious. I hear that Keyes is now refused admission to the P.M. Previously he was always in and out. He writes long, wordy papers and is thought by the Chiefs of Staff to be half-way between a menace and a lunatic.

A great row on the telephone by Morton against Nelson ... This sort of thing is a most frightful bore.

I report Morton to Attlee who dines with me alone this evening after a meeting of Labour ministers. He is duly hotted up.

In addition to the debate about relief to enemy-occupied territories, there was much controversy about trade and aid to neutrals. On 25th June 1940, the Cabinet had authorised Dalton to apply contraband control to all parts of continental France, occupied and unoccupied, and three weeks later it was argued that the same controls should be applied to all vessels bound for French Morocco, Algiers and Tunis. However, the U.S. State Department disagreed with British policy, favouring substantial economic aid to French North Africa.

In October 1940, the Italians attacked Greece, but encountered strong resistance. The Greeks appealed to Britain to honour a pre-war pledge to provide help in the event of foreign aggression. Meanwhile, in North Africa, British forces advanced rapidly into Italian Libya, occupying the port of Tobruk. By early February, all of Cyrenaica was British-controlled. But on 10th February the Defence Committee decided not to order an advance on Tripoli (consolidating the progress that had been made) and instead to concentrate on building up a force to help Greece, which now faced the added threat of German intervention. Eden and the C.I.G.S. (Dill) flew to the Middle East to co-ordinate military and political action. Over the next two

1 Director of Combined Operations: Admiral Sir Roger Keyes, q.v.

months, the Foreign Secretary tried to persuade Yugoslavia and Turkey that if they acted in combination with Britain, the German occupation of the southern Balkans and the Turkish Straits might be prevented.

Wednesday 19th February

Van and Crossman meet today and the latter obviously plays his cards well. Van is now very delighted with him, says that he misread one sentence in one of his memoranda, and asks me to tell Crossman that he likes him very much and would be very glad to see him at any time.

Van says he regards Eden's trip as a great mistake. He is talking of going to Ankara via Cairo. Probably he will get nothing out of the Turks, and in that case his prestige and ours will slump. It looks as though the Turks will do nothing unless attacked, and why should Hitler attack them yet? Van was not consulted about the trip or would have advised strongly against it. He says that his position becomes more and more impossible. He is very full of another series of broadcasts which he is giving in French. I suppose there will be a fuss about this also in due course.

Van is hardly away before Cadogan comes to see me, at my request. So I get the personal contrast at its most vivid. No doubt there is much to be said for Cadogan. Steady, common-sensible, unruffled. I begin on the Americans and the blockade and their attempt to feed Weygand and North Africa with many things, including oil, without reference to us. We discuss tentatively the possibility of sending someone else to Washington. Drogheda is only just back, having been ill with pneumonia. Otherwise, we both agree, he would have been an ideal man could I have spared him. Cadogan, also, I think, is doubtful of the wisdom of Eden's visit. He fears that things will so move that we may have to allow the Greeks, under pressure, to make a separate peace. This might be better than having the country 'devastated to the last acre', and better than putting in some of our own troops and having them not even evacuated, but trapped and destroyed. The Germans, he is sure, have been trying to entice us in force into Greece. This is how they wanted to help Italy. He does not believe that either the Turks or the Yugoslavs will move. Of course, if either or both did, putting our troops in would be a different matter. The Turks, of course, will be able to say that they couldn't do anything because we hadn't supplied them with enough equipment. It will also, of course, be said that we have shamefully abandoned Greece, but what better alternative is there?

He has therefore advised the P.M. to have second thoughts about

Libya and to push on to the boundaries of Tunisia, thus making it as likely as it can be made that Weygand and the French will stand with us. Meanwhile, there are discouraging reports of German infiltration to Casablanca and other parts of North Africa, and these have been communicated to the Americans to try to make them realise the unwisdom of promiscuous supplies.

I mention to him recent troubles with the Camarilla.[1] He says that I shall perform a public service if I can damp them down, but that he is not sure whether it will help me personally to try. He says that he does not himself move much in such circles! I speak to him in praise of Gladwyn and the difficulties made for him by the Camarilla, and broach the question of tail feathers.[2] He says that this shall not be overlooked and we will speak of it again in a few months' time.

Thursday 20th February

Further discussion on the Camarilla. I hear that some 'not flattering' things were said at a recent luncheon party. Someone has complained that I am sometimes too assertive in the Cabinet.

Peake, on the other hand, was surprised and agreeably impressed by the fact that the other night I was so quiet. In fact, I was feeling slightly bored and in very poor form!

Lord Bearsted[3] would like to begin trotting round, but I discourage this.

I see Attlee in the afternoon and he takes, as usual, a very good and loyal line. It is agreed that there shall be a meeting *à trois* early next week, when those concerned have returned to London. I say that I think there should be a meeting with some half a dozen of my H.Q. staff. He thinks this a good plan. He is a good deal vexed by both the communications, copies of which I show him, and says that the other day someone put it into the P.M.'s head that Bevin was doing badly. This is another example of anti-Labour intrigue of which there is too much. He says that he spent an hour with the P.M. yesterday discussing everything most amicably. So much for Morton's yarn.

Fletcher to dine. Appears to be most friendly and claims credit for having encouraged Morton to boost, instead of crabbing, my activities. He was profoundly horrified, he says, at Bracken's behaviour, and I get him to sign, as a substantially accurate record, Tommy

---

1 'the Camarilla': Dalton's name for Churchill's staff at 10 Downing Street.
2 Marginal insertion: 'C.M.G.'
3 W. H. S. Bearsted, 2nd Viscount (1882–1948). Acting Colonel, General List, while specially employed.

Davies's[1] account. The only change he makes is that he warned him, as soon as he started, what Davies was doing. This really makes it worse for Bracken. He suspects Bracken of being violently anti-Labour and thinks that he is carrying on a general campaign. I ask him, without leading him, Morton's views on Nelson and Gladwyn. Morton does not like either of them. He thinks that Nelson is 'out of his depth' and run by other people (he mentioned [George] Taylor and Davies, but this is rather an out-of-date picture in any case). Also he is a legacy from C.[2]

He does not like Gladwyn because he 'punctures' him, i.e. puts some rather simple yet penetrating question after Morton has been building up some great imaginative edifice. Therefore he says that Gladwyn is 'intensely ambitious' and thinks that he can best promote his career by making a success of his present job under me. He regards me, in short, as a horse to be ridden along the road of his own career. All this is rather trivial and unimpressive.[3]

Friday 21st February
Lunch with Bruce[4] to meet Menzies,[5] who has just arrived. Very hearty, amusing and intelligent. He reminds me of 'a classical exchange of compliments' between me and him when I dined with him at the Athenaeum Club at Melbourne in 1938.[6] After a good evening, he said, 'I am delighted and astonished to meet a member of the British Labour Party who has a sense of humour.' I replied, 'I am equally delighted and astonished to meet an Australian Conservative who has some intelligence.'

Gladwyn suggests that I should send [Noel] Hall to Washington.

---

1 Colonel F. T. Davies, q.v., formerly Section D officer, now in charge of training S.O.E. agents.
2 A reference to Sir Stewart Menzies (C), q.v., head of the Secret Service.
3 Marginal insertion: 'Bracken had been abusing me loudly in Carlton Grill at lunch with Rex Fletcher and Tommy Davies. I made Fletcher rather tight and then got him to initial a statement drafted by me with quotes and details. T.D. behaved most correctly.'
4 Stanley Bruce, later 1st Viscount (1883–1967). Australian High Commissioner in London 1933–45. Representative of Commonwealth Governments in the U.K. War Cabinet 1942–5. Prime Minister and Minister of External Affairs in Australia 1923–9.
5 R. G. Menzies, later Sir Robert (1894–1978). Prime Minister of Australia 1939–41, 1949–66.
6 In the winter of 1937–8, Dalton had travelled round the world, spending a month in Australia and two weeks in New Zealand. The purpose was to represent the Labour Party at the hundred and fiftieth anniversary of the first Australian settlement. During the trip, he met many Australian and New Zealand politicians.

He has no sort of opinion of Leith-Ross, even as an envoy for a few weeks. Sir Horace Wilson invented Van's present job. I learn tonight, for the first time, from Gladwyn, that Morton was unfriendly to me as far back as July of last year, i.e. before I took over additional duties. He apparently represented me, most amusingly, as a windbag, a careerist, and a witless fool who shouted contradictory objurgations at my officials! His attempt to get Swinton the other duties and his influence on the P.M. at this time is therefore quite established.

When he heard who my C.E.O. [Chief Executive Officer][1] was to be from this officer himself, he was completely taken aback and had just nothing to say.

Cadogan's reserve. He has three pretty daughters but also a son of whom he never speaks and whose whereabouts is not known. He crawled out of the bushes once as a beater at a shoot attended by Cadogan and some other high society!

Saturday 22nd February
To C.H.Q. Morton is here for the night. Superficially perfect – and writes me afterwards a most oleaginous and excessively effusive roofer. We have a discussion in the afternoon on France, and he does the usual visits. In the evening we see a German film. I mention to him his telephone conversation with Nelson and say I did not like it. He says, 'Oh that was all a complete misunderstanding which has been cleared up now. I thought it was suggested that I was going behind your back.' He then adds that he thinks Nelson is a good chap. ...

Van says he is going to see Bracken again. I tell him that this man has been doing very badly lately, without giving details. Van thinks that Attlee and I ought to see the P.M. and discuss developments, including our need for better transport. 'Give us the tools and we will do the job.' But I do not tell Van about the two incidents which I have reported to Attlee.

I tell Morton that I should like the P.M. to see some of the chaps in my London show. It is this which leads him to say that the P.M. now sees fewer and fewer people and many ministers hardly ever.

He says that the P.M., when he made his fateful decision not to send more fighter planes to France in the summer, said, 'I won't throw any more snowballs into hell.'

Monday 24th February
Further with my C.E.O. [Jebb] on Morton. His conduct last July is

---

1 'C.E.O.': Gladwyn Jebb, Chief Executive Officer of S.O.E. Dalton frequently used these initials when referring to Jebb in his diary.

the more odd because the two chief things I had done up to date should have delighted him – namely, stopping Italian oil and re-organising M.E.W. involving the promotion of Hall. So he has the less excuse for having been unfriendly, but it is a mistake to spend too much time being angry about such things. ...

The War Cabinet is meeting less and less, generally now only twice a week, and nothing of great importance is discussed. One of its members says it is hardly worth belonging to any more.

Morton last weekend said that now the P.M. only saw Beaverbrook, Eden and Alexander; that he never sees Sinclair, nor has he seen Margesson since he sent him to the War Office.

I pass on this last information to Sinclair, whom I see this evening, and to him I also mention Bracken's misconduct. Sinclair says that Bracken was ill and stayed for weeks in Beaverbrook's house. Hence these reflections.

Tuesday 25th February
See Van at the Foreign Office. He is in a great state because the P.M. said that he cannot give his next three broadcasts in French. He has drafted a long letter to the P.M. which he shows me, saying that he is much the best known and loved in France of all Englishmen, that he has been 'their comfort and their pillar' over many years, and that now, when it is known that he is not allowed to speak to them on the air, he will be completely discredited. And much else on the same tune. The practical conclusion, however, only is that he will have to 'decline to take any further responsibility for propaganda'. I ask whether this means that he will disengage from C.H.Q. He says, on the contrary, he will tell the P.M., with whom he is lunching on Sunday, that he will be only too glad to go on helping me, who am an old friend of his. I ask whether he contemplates resigning from Chief Diplomatic Adviser. He says that that may perhaps come next. He does not wish to be drawing a salary and not performing any of the duties which would naturally attach to his post. He has been completely frozen out and is never consulted on anything in the Foreign Office. He is prepared to go on doing all he can 'at half price' (i.e. for a pension on retirement). He says that when Halifax became Foreign Secretary he said to him, 'Of course you are the fifth wheel on the coach, but I didn't make the arrangement. Chamberlain and Eden made it.' This is perfectly true. They did it on the advice of Sir Horace Wilson. At that time Van told Chamberlain that he thought of resigning and going into the House of Commons. This had frightened Chamberlain nearly out of his wits and he said that he would have the very strongest objection to this. Van also felt that he was a little too old a dog to learn new tricks in Parlia-

ment. Chamberlain had then spoken of a peerage, but Van had refused this. He was convinced that at present there was a movement going on among rich people – the same old gang as in past years – to try to get a patched-up peace with Hitler and so save something of their private wealth at least for the remainder of their own lives. I said that I was confident that this sort of thing could easily be smashed.

In the midst of this conversation enter Sarita [Vansittart]. From now on we all weep and wail together in an orgy of self-pity for poor old Van! No one, she says, has borne a more cruel martyrdom for so long and so on! Quite certainly, this beautiful but tiresome woman has been responsible for much misguidance, both of his mind and his emotions.

Gladwyn later comes in to enquire how the talk went, saying that Sir Alec Cadogan is 'all agog' to hear. Van has had almost daily talks with him about the thing for weeks, and he is getting a bit tired of it. Gladwyn thinks that the most difficult situation would arise if Van retired, and was thus no longer entitled to see official papers, and yet continued in any even semi-official relationship with me. He thinks that the two things Van will fight to the end to retain are his room in the Foreign Office and the right to see official papers. I had asked Van earlier today when he would be sixty. He said next June. I said that, in that case, to retire now would make only about three months' difference. I took for granted, though I did not bluntly say so, that anyhow he would be retired at sixty. Gladwyn thinks that he by no means takes this view, and that, although with my full support in earlier days he used to retire all other diplomats rigidly at sixty, thus making a flow of promotion and encouraging the young, he would regard himself now as being in a most exceptional position.

Wednesday 26th February

See Bevin and put him on his guard against an anti-Labour minister campaign in which Bracken is doing his bit. I tell Bevin that the P.M. is being told that he is not doing very well. 'We know', I say, 'where all these tales come from.' Partly from the Beaver and partly from the people round the P.M. I also refer to the American journalist from the Hearst press who has come over in a bomber with a permit from the Beaver and has been defending [Joseph] Kennedy, advocating a compromise peace and getting, according to his own account, some support from a prominent Cabinet Minister. I never know how much registers with Bevin, but I think a good deal more than appears from his manner. ...

Menzies to dinner to meet what he calls my Brains Trust – Director-

General (Leith-Ross), one Joint Director (Drogheda), P.P.S. (Wilmot), C.E.O. (Jebb), Private Secretary No. 1 (Gaitskell). Private Secretary No. 2 (Hancock) was asked but is away with flu. The evening goes pretty well, though it is clear that Menzies knows nothing about M.E.W. When asked by me to say a few words on our work in relation to Australia, he gives a very interesting account of Australian war finance, taxation, rates of interest, Central Bank credit, and all the great expansion of arms manufacture. Bruce, Macdougall[1] (who is clearly breaking up) and Shedden[2] are also there.

Thursday 27th February
My attendant sprites watch most prudently all movements of my lips! My C.E.O. thinks that last night to Menzies I used that significant word Camarilla. Gaitskell, invited to give evidence, says that he is pretty sure I said that the P.M. had a queer entourage. Menzies himself had been abusing Beaverbrook very freely. My C.E.O. also wonders whether it was safe to use to an Australian Conservative the description 'This Churchill-Labour Government'. Repeated to Conservatives here, it might do harm, but Gaitskell thinks that this was perfectly safe. Finally, it is thought that Menzies winced slightly and did not rejoin in like language when I used certain strong words.[3] 'It may have sounded rather too much as though you were showing that you knew the patois.' I welcome all this prudence very much, to overawe my natural rashness of speech, but I discount it a bit too.

Francis Williams[4] has done me proud in the *Strand Magazine*. I write and thank him, saying that I have never been so well done before and that he has beaten Bob Fraser's[5] rendering of me in *Picture Post* and elsewhere, hitherto the best. I hope that Williams may be linked up with Attlee on his personal staff.

1 Probably Frank McDougall (1884–1958). Australian economic adviser and diplomat.
2 Sir Frederick Shedden (1893–1971). Australian Defence Secretary 1937–56; Secretary to the Australian War Cabinet 1939–46.
3 Marginal insertion: 'bloody, bastard, bugger'.
4 Francis Williams, later Baron Francis-Williams (1903–70). Author and journalist. Controller of News and Censorship at the Ministry of Information 1941–5. Editor of the *Daily Herald* 1936–40. Adviser on Public Relations to the Prime Minister 1945–7.
5 R. B. Fraser, later Sir Robert (1904–84). Director of Publications Division at the Ministry of Information 1941–5. Leader writer for the *Daily Herald* 1930–39. Controller of Production 1945–6. Director-General of the Independent Television Authority 1954–70. Chairman of Independent Television News 1971–4. Fraser had been a student of Dalton's at the L.S.E., and had remained friendly with him.

See Attlee in the afternoon. He says that yesterday he spoke to the P.M. about me and my fears and reported two members of the Camarilla, Morton and Bracken. He said that the P.M. was very angry, said that these two had no business to talk like that, in particular that they had no business to use his name, that what they had been saying did not represent his own view, and that he considered that I was doing a good job of work. Attlee said that he had evidently seen, and liked, some of my recent Minutes, e.g. that on the Polish flight. He would probably be sending for me in the course of the next few days, and would begin on my need for more aircraft.

I report this to my inner circle, who are much pleased. Nelson dines with me alone. We make plans for Attlee's visit and tour on Sunday.

Friday 28th February
Our counter-offensive of this week is yielding results! Gaitskell rings up to say that I am invited to lunch with the P.M. at Chequers next Sunday. Van also, as he told me two days ago, will be there. ...

Gladwyn says that he saw Harold Nicolson with Duff Cooper lunching at one of his clubs. (How wise I am to refuse to frequent these places, except the Lansdowne, which is quite different!) Gladwyn said to Nicolson, 'How is the Whitehall War going?' Nicolson was not amused.

Sunday 2nd March
Lunch at Chequers with P.M. ...

I go to Chequers via Denham.[1] Van says that yesterday when he lunched at Chequers 'everything went very well so far as your show was concerned'. P.M. said nothing in criticism, and seemed interested and in agreement when Van said that good work was being done, that it had been built up from nothing, and that, especially in SO2, even better results were to be expected soon. ...

Van said he did not want to go on holding his position of Chief Diplomatic Adviser without feeling that he was performing important duties. The P.M. said, 'I thought when you became Dalton's *chef de cabinet*, though it wouldn't be so glorious as being P.U.S. [Permanent Under-Secretary of State] at the Foreign Office, that it would occupy you. Doesn't it?' Van said that neither he nor I could immerse ourselves too much in detail. He couldn't live in the country and draft documents. He was very glad to work with me, and to go on working, but I had two first-class Under-Secretaries, each with a good team. ...

Arrived at Chequers, I found only Menzies, several women – Mrs

1 Sir Robert Vansittart lived at Denham Place, Denham in Buckinghamshire.

Churchill and, I think two daughters – various underlings, the Prof, Seal[1] and Thompson.[2] P.M. in great form. Complained that his beer was not cold enough. Spoke in praise of onions, of which we had a good supply. *'L'oignon fait la force'*, that, he said, was Baldwin's idea of a joke. It appealed to his mediocre wit. He jeered a little at Halifax, and his draft on Peace Aims.[3] There was 'no precision of mind in it regarding correlation of "rights and duties"'. What duties did a person living on idle investments perform? Yet did Halifax propose to confiscate all such property? Of course not. He then talked of Socialism, the Nationalisation of the railways, and the old Liberal attitude against monopoly. But 'You can never go back and take away from people what they have.' Therefore you could not un-nationalise the Post Office, even if you could prove that it would be more efficiently run by a private company. There must be a profit incentive and there must be a ladder. All this, I thought, was rather superficial. He has not been doing much new thinking on these subjects since the last war.

His mind was much on the sinkings.[4] He told Van yesterday that he was thinking of them all the time. A chart was put out on the floor before lunch. Not so bad as he had thought, in these last weeks, in which, however, most damage is being done from the air. ... The troops were eating too much. They could do with less rations. And they are using too much cotton and wool material.

Through lunch Menzies sat rather silent, a little over-awed, but he will tell the tale all right in Melbourne when he gets back. P.M. said, 'Hitler says that 16 million Jews ought to go and live in Australia. What do you say to that?' He had no good quick answer. P.M. also made the old joke about M.E.W. and M.U.W. of which he is very fond.

After lunch I had three-quarters of an hour with him alone. I offered to send for Gladwyn, whom I was keeping at the end of a telephone an hour away. No, he said, that is too far. I pressed very strongly my need for more aircraft, and read some notes on the present

1 E. Seal, later Sir Eric (1898–1972). Principal Private Secretary to the Prime Minister 1940–41; to the First Lord of the Admiralty 1938–40.
2 Commander C. R. 'Tommy' Thompson (1894–1966). Personal Assistant to the Minister of Defence (Churchill) 1940–45.
3 Halifax had drafted a paper on War Aims. (See D. Dilks, ed., *The Diaries of Sir Alexander Cadogan O.M. 1938–1945*, Cassell, London, 1971, p. 338, 4th December 1940.)
4 Early in February, Hitler had issued a directive stressing the importance of attacking seaborne traffic bound for Britain. The navy and the Luftwaffe were to make a joint effort against shipping. This came to be regarded as the starting point of the Battle of the Atlantic.

position. He asked me to write a short Minute on this and said he would do what he could to help. There is great competition for aircraft. I say that we are now ready for more tools. I say that in particular we are stuck for civil aircraft. He says, rather defensively, 'That is not Beaverbrook's fault.' Vansittart, he says, 'gets things a little out of proportion.' He asks whether we have not many Left-Wing elements at Woburn? (with a slight chuckle). I say that I am accused by others of Fascist methods and getting rid of Reds and even Pinks at M.E.W. I say that our people are being sniped. I want him to be satisfied. He says, 'I am not dissatisfied. I know that you are a very able man.' (This would go all right in a headline, but not much warmth.) He goes on to say that Bracken may have been saying some things which he had no authority to say. Morton has denied saying what he is alleged, and adds, 'He read me a letter saying that he was much impressed with what he had seen.' P.M. adds that Attlee has spoken to him about all this. I press that the P.M. should see some of my chaps. I speak of some of them. I say that Nelson was a friend of [Geoffrey] Lloyd and Alexander. When Tory M.P. for Stroud, he spoke against the Gold Standard. I sometimes wonder whether the P.M. remembers this against him. The P.M. says, 'No, I am not that kind of man.' Brigadier Gubbins seems to register slightly, and of Hambro he says, 'I want to give both him and   a K.'[1] At first he said, 'No, I see no one.' Then when pressed further, 'How many do you want me to see?' Perhaps we shall get something later. He asks, 'What are your relations with Swinton?' I say that I don't find I overlap with him at all. He seems to accept this. ...

I said to the P.M. that anyone who tries to drive a wedge between me and Van will fail. P.M. said no one has tried to do that.

Then, about 3.30 p.m. he said it was time for him to go to bed.

I think that, though there is no great cordiality or intimacy, things have advanced a bit.

Monday 3rd March
Gladwyn and C.D. [Nelson] to dine, and we discuss yesterday's doings. Gladwyn says that the P.M. is a little suspicious of me. It is not clear quite what he suspects me of. Trying to get his job?

Wednesday 5th March
Wilmot and Air Marshal Harris[2] dine with me. This is a good move.

---

1 There is a blank space in this sentence in the text.
2 Marshal of the R.A.F. A. T. 'Bomber' Harris, later Sir Arthur, later 1st Bart (1892–1984). Deputy Chief of Air Staff 1940–41. Head of R.A.F. Delegation to the U.S.A. 1941. Commander-in-Chief, Bomber Command 1942–5.

Wilmot knew him before. A lonely sort of man who would like to have a farm in Kenya or Rhodesia. Said to be very downright and to spit into the fire. There was no fire for him to spit into tonight. Hates the Navy and the Foreign Office, but the Navy a bit more. He is in charge of all the bombers, and the Navy keeps pulling them away. 'Gimme, gimme, gimme.' So, he says, the sailors always cry. And so his lovely bombers go 'grinding up and down in the dark' over the north-western approaches and cannot be turned on to targets in Germany. He found Gladwyn rather difficult, he complains, in today's negotiations. (Gladwyn coming in earlier, asked by me whether he had won, lost or drawn, replied, 'A draw, slightly in our favour.') The principle of the special flight is maintained, we are to have a slight addition to it, and also a chance of part use of machines going on other errands. I said that Gladwyn had been difficult on my instructions. We must keep in touch with this Air Marshal.

Monday 10th March
Gladwyn says that Hambro was much concerned at some remarks of Leeper last weekend, in which the latter spoke of taking up certain matters direct with Morton, who would go to the P.M., who in turn would 'compel the Minister' to do this or that. Not quite clear what! But Leeper, before so speaking to Hambro, had told him that it was all very secret and he must repeat it to no one. Hambro passed a troubled night, then told C.D., who told Gladwyn, who told me. But I must not tell Leeper that I know, or Hambro and C.D. would both feel compelled to resign! I said I thought Hambro was a bloody fool to have promised not to tell me.

I immediately send for Leeper, who comes up rather reluctantly and lunches with me and C.D., whom I invite for the purpose ... Meanwhile, Gladwyn was lunching alone with ———.[1] ——— was the host and got rather drunk. He then proceeded to criticise most people. Gaitskell he appeared to regard as a devil incarnate, always pulling strings. C.D. he thought was not up to his work, and he was not pleased with me, not having forgiven me for having sent for him with others and complained that nothing was being done in his area. He alleged, moreover, that I was filling the place with Labour politicians, citing in particular Crossman and [Ivor] Thomas. Gladwyn told him that I had inherited Crossman from M.I.(R.), into which he had been introduced by a Conservative M.P., one Captain Hogg! Gladwyn notes, however, that much of ———'s criticism was the same as Morton's, and thinks it clear that ——— was passing these criticisms direct to Morton and that this was the reason why Morton flared so furiously when pulled

1 An SO1 official.

up for communicating direct with ——. It looks as though —— should be shifted. It is very extraordinary that he should speak in this way to Gladwyn and not suppose that he would pass it on to me and C.D.

On 6th March, the Prime Minister issued a directive giving the highest priority to defeating the German attack on British shipping routes. Nevertheless, British losses remained serious through most of 1941. The danger that supplies from the United States would be effectively cut off, did not recede until the last three months of the year.

Wednesday 12th March
Gladwyn reports that Laurence Cadbury,[1] with whom we had been dining, says that Alexander is telling journalists that 'in theory' we have already lost the battle of the Atlantic but that, of course, if U.S. will give full aid, we can retrieve it. This makes a bad impression on Cadbury, as upon those with him tonight. Alexander is still in Lord Beaverbrook's pocket, made much of and flattered by being asked to man the piano and sing simple songs during weekend visits to Lord B. I tell them that [Harry] Hopkins, at my third talk, mentioned casually that Alexander and Greenwood (and their wives) were with Lord B. in the country when he went down.

Friday 14th March
Hall and Eccles to see me about American negotiations.[2] I suspect Eccles of trying to get to Washington in front of Hall. He seems to have been busily running round over reservations on the Clipper. Gladwyn tells me that Eccles fluffs up to him and says that it is clear that I am profoundly suspicious of him. He supposes that this is because I do not like his politics, and that I prefer Hall who is a socialist. In fact, Hall is nothing of the kind. I tell Gladwyn that I will try to smooth some of Eccles's feathers down again, though I have doubts at the back of my mind as to whether he would not be prepared

---

1 L. J. Cadbury (1889–1983). Head of Economic Section, Mission to Moscow 1941. Managing Director of Cadbury Bros 1919–59.
2 These concerned supplies to French North Africa, metropolitan France and Spain. Eccles believed that a small relaxation of the blockade as it affected North Africa would have political advantages in terms of swinging the authorities in these areas in a pro-British direction. (See W. N. Medlicott, *The Economic Blockade* (History of the Second World War, U.K. Civil Series), H.M.S.O., London, 1952, p. 570.)

for a compromise peace to save his private wealth. Gladwyn does not think there is any evidence of this.

Thursday 20th March
Winant[1] calls and stays just over an hour. Most of the time he is incredibly tongue-tied and won't look me in the eyes. He brightens up a bit towards the end. He must be brighter than his outward form or how did he ever get anywhere? But he is, I think, a good friend of ours and herein a sharp contrast to his crook predecessor. ... He is an American Man of the Left, with strong sentimental social interests. He speaks of a survey which much impressed him, relating joblessness to age, in our North-Eastern Region. ... I feel he might be soft on Relief questions, and he repeats that we should go slow in pressing U.S.A. along paths of Economic Warfare. He says several times, in different ways, that Leith-Ross should go to U.S.A. 'An older man' – he is comparing him with [Noel] Hall – 'would have more influence' with those at the head of affairs. ... I hope he will talk quicker next time. He has the features and black hair, including thick black brows, of a Western Irishman, but there the likeness stops.

Leith-Ross brings Sir Robert Knox[2] to see me about Honours. A most unsatisfactory man and a most unsatisfactory conversation! He takes the view that Honours are for 'State Servants', i.e. for permanent civil servants. 'The others' should feel it an honour to be allowed to work in the Civil Service during the war. (Yes, he really did say just that!) Gradually, he supposes a few Honours will have to be given to these people, but most of them should wait till the end of the war. If you give them anything now, it will only encourage them to expect something more later. We speak of particular cases, notably Hall and Nicholls,[3] and he is most unsatisfactory on both. I say that it seems odd to me that a man whom His Majesty thinks good enough to make a Minister at Washington may not be thought good enough by Sir Horace Wilson and his Committee for even a knighthood, let alone a C.B. or a C.B.E. Leith-Ross plays no great part in the conversation, though he sticks up for one or two of our cases, and I have the impression that Knox knows that near the top of the Civil Service Leith-Ross counts for little. I tell Knox that if I were a private M.P. and not a minister I should make a row over the quite undue share of the permanent civil servants. I say that, if the public knew on what principles the thing was being run, they would say that the permanents

1 J. G. Winant (1889–1947). U.S. Ambassador in London 1941–6.
2 Sir Robert Knox (1889–1965). Secretary of the Political Honours Scrutiny Committee 1939–65.
3 J. W. Nicholls, later Sir John (1909–70). Diplomat.

173

were scratching each other's backs and keeping the rest out in the cold. I ask whether he realises that when Hall was appointed to Washington, I could find no permanent civil servant in my Ministry who could take over his job, and that I had to bring in a non-permanent from outside.

Friday 21st March

Cynthia Jebb to lunch with me at her own request, she wanting to tell me that Maurice Ingram liked me very much and thought that I disliked him, and would be very pleased if I would take some notice of him. He thinks I think that he was weak over Italy. Philip Nichols dislikes me very much and would be glad if I ceased to be a minister. He also is very defensive about Italy. They only did, he says, what H.M.G. told them to. I reply to her that I should quite like to be nice to Ingram, for whom the plain truth is that I just can't find a use in my Ministry, and am longing for him to get the diplomatic post long promised him. Nichols, on the other hand, I have no use for at all. I regard him as having been a complete disaster. Not only was he quite wrong over Italy, but when I succeeded in reversing the policy, he went about saying that this new minister's line was idiotic and ignorant and quite impossible to carry out. He is also responsible for constant obstruction of all our projects in the Balkans, including the Danube, and I still remember his attempt to appease the Germans at the expense of the Poles in the Foreign Office in 1930. As I say to Gladwyn afterwards, recounting these affairs, 'I never forget. I am like the elephant.'

Sunday 23rd March

A very good walk with Mayhew. We start at 10, lunch at Avebury, where we arrive at 1.30 after a considerable involuntary deviation, tea at Marlborough (Polly's) after a bit more deviation, and then walk straight home, getting in at 7.30. We think we must have walked 30 miles, but, having worked it out most conscientiously upon the map, taking account of all wiggles and woggles, we bring it out at $26\frac{1}{2}$. This is not too bad in itself, particularly as we went at a great pace a large part of the way and frequently broke into a run. As we were coming over the last skyline, Mayhew said to me, 'Now, of course, we ought to run', being quite sure I wouldn't. Whereupon, I said, 'Come on then' and started. We ran down to the postman's gate and then strode up the last hill. He was a little stiff and tired, much more, I think, than I was. I had not taken any kind of vigorous walk since the Christmas break, when I was in Scotland, so I don't think my physical condition is too bad, in spite of my funny life!

Tuesday 25th March
Uproar in Parliament and a great demonstration in favour of the blockade. I have quite a rough passage – a most unaccustomed experience in these days – at Question Time. Outcry from all sections of the House. They are shocked at recent press revelations of trade through Marseilles and at navicerting of American food ships. Really, of course, they should shout at the Admiralty, the Foreign Office and the P.M.! I have it put about that only a very simple-minded person would think that I ask the Admiralty *not* to stop these ships, or that I ask Halifax to persuade Roosevelt to send the food ships! There is some perturbation among my advisers over this demonstration, but on the whole I welcome it and it strengthens my hand for the Cabinet this week.

Wednesday 26th March
Van has been having a bad time with his duodenitis and looks sad and in pain. He has been pestering me with silly little notes on unimportant individual cases. It is rather pathetic.

On 25th March, Yugoslavia signed the Tripartite Pact – following the resignation of Opposition leaders (who were in touch with S.O.E.) from the government. On 27th March, a coup, led by an Air Force General, Bora Mirković, and backed by junior army officers and Opposition politicians, overturned the regime and forced Prince Paul into exile – placing General Simović in command, and putting the young King Peter on the throne. S.O.E. agents had given every encouragement and had done much to prepare Serb opinion for the event. Hence Dalton was delighted by what seemed like a tangible triumph for his organisation. In fact, the Simović government did not denounce the pact, or offer to help Greece, and pursued Prince Paul's foreign policy with little change. In any case, the German invasion of Yugoslavia soon negated most of the supposed beneficial effects. Nevertheless, Dalton later claimed that the coup 'delayed the German attack on Russia by a precious fortnight'.[1] At the time, he made every effort to use the coup as evidence of S.O.E.'s effectiveness – even though S.O.E. direct involvement in the actual conspiracy was slight.

---

1 FY, p. 375.

Thursday 27th March

What a day! Gladwyn comes into my room this morning with a smiling face and says, 'There was a *coup d'état* early this morning at Belgrade.' As the day goes on, we hear more detail, and it is clear that our chaps have done their part well. It was the Air Attaché who went to Simović[1] and finally persuaded him to act. When Simović asked what arms we could supply, the Air Attaché was authorised to say that we would do what we could, but his best chance of getting arms was to attack the Italians in Albania. There was a lot to be collected there. The money we have spent on the Serb Peasant Party and other Opposition Parties has given wonderful value. We knew before that the Air Force would be all right, and, if necessary, would fly away to Greece, but many of those near the top of the General Staff were rotten, and this *coup* was mainly carried out, apart from the Air Force, by Colonels, Majors and junior officers. Prince Paul,[2] 'Our Friend' (Eton and Oxford), has been a complete skunk. He has deceived our diplomats as such gentlemanly skunks always do. Chips Channon[3] told Gladwyn today that he was sure Prince Paul has been behind this *coup*, because he was so fond of King Peter! This is worthy of the Servants' Hall.

Sweet-Escott,[4] who has been in our job for a long while, says that he remembers the black looks he first met at the Foreign Office when it was proposed that we should subsidise the Opposition Parties. 'Prince Paul would be so vexed if he ever found out,' they said.

I had a yap at Gladwyn later in the day because, through some stupid oversight, he had not shown me the telegram he had last night, though he had sent a copy to·Cadogan and shown a copy to Morton at lunch!

Cabinet this afternoon. P.M. says now is the time to go ahead with

---

1 General T. D. Simović (1882–1962). Yugoslav General. In 1941 he led the coup which ousted Prince Paul. Prime Minister and Commander in Chief 1941–2. He had opposed Yugoslav participation in the war on the Axis side.

2 Prince Paul (1893–1976). Regent of Yugoslavia for his cousin's young son, King Peter II (1923–70) 1934–41. Pro-Axis. Forced into exile after the coup.

3 Sir Henry 'Chips' Channon (1897–1958). Conservative M.P. for Southend-on-Sea 1935–50; Southend-on-Sea West 1950–58. P.P.S. to R. A. Butler as Under-Secretary of State for Foreign Affairs 1938–41. 'What a fall,' Channon wrote in his own diary on the same day. 'I dread every wireless bulletin lest it tell us that Paul has been butchered in the traditional Balkan manner; as for myself all my Yugoslav fun is over; no more Bled, Brdo and Belgrade, no more palaces and pomp, no more Regent, I may never see him again.' (R. Rhodes James, ed., *Chips: The Diaries of Sir Henry Channon*, Penguin, Harmondsworth, 1970, p. 363.)

4 Bickham Sweet-Escott (d. 1981). In charge of Western European sections, under George Taylor, at SO2. Previously responsible for the Balkans and Middle East department of Section D.

The Danube.[1] I say that a telegram went this morning. (It did, because the Chief of Staff wanted it, but it was only a repeat of earlier orders.)

...

I win a good victory in the Cabinet, where my five recommendations are all accepted. These are the conclusion of a very good and compact paper, as most think, on blockade of unoccupied France and French North Africa. I am to make a draft, with the Foreign Office, to Halifax, telling him to reason earnestly with Washington against any more blockade concessions, rubbing in that Parliamentary and public opinion is very restive on this subject. As the P.M. says, there will soon be only one country in the world being blockaded, namely our own. Alexander does not put up any serious fight against my proposal that the Admiralty should intercept as much as possible and that no un-navicerted ships and cargoes should be released.

Harriman[2] dines with me alone. He is frank, friendly, intelligent and fairly quick. He does not care much for Laski, who, through Frankfurter,[3] gives the President a queer and misleading picture of our public mind and future probabilities.[4] He does not think much of Cordell Hull[5] and agrees the State Department are remote and difficult. On food, he thinks, the P.M. should make a quite blunt statement to the President of what we feel, not leaving the decision to the latter. I ask may I quote him to the P.M. on this, and he says yes.

The suggestion had been made (apparently by William Stephenson, head of British Security Co-ordination in New York) that Noël Coward should take over S.O. propaganda in the Americas. 'An indiscreet stinker, off his proper beat,' Dalton wrote in the margin of one memorandum on the subject.[6]

Friday 28th March

A stupidity proposed regarding Noël Coward.[7] I react violently

1 The S.O.E. plan to block the Danube. This was carried out, with only limited success, early in April. See entry for 22nd April, and preceding note (pp. 185–6).
2 Averell Harriman (b. 1891). President Roosevelt's Special Representative in Britain March 1941. Ambassador to the U.S.S.R. 1943–6; Britain 1946.
3 Felix Frankfurter (1882–1965). Associate Justice of the U.S. Supreme Court 1932–62. Byrne Professor of Administrative Law, Harvard 1914–39.
4 Harold Laski corresponded regularly with Felix Frankfurter and President Roosevelt.
5 Cordell Hull (1871–1955). U.S. Secretary of State 1933–44.
6 Dalton Papers 7/3 (58).
7 Noël Coward, later Sir Noël (1899–1973). Playwright, actor and song-writer.

against it. Someone over there has gone much beyond his authority. The man is utterly unsuitable and attracts publicity everywhere. I am told that it will upset X[1] if I say no. I say I will risk that. C.E.O. rather weak on this. Thinks the man is very intelligent and amusing. This is a relic of pre-war Mayfair judgments. No use now! I am a little surprised.

Molly Hamilton[2] to see me. We discuss her Memo for Policy Committee, and then go to lunch at Josef's, where Yugo-Slav flag is hung out beside Union Jack and whole place crowded. Many others have thought that this is a good day to eat Serbian.

More congratulations on my Jug achievement. Letter from Ismay on behalf of P.M. and Defence Committee. We are well on top! I make an order of the day and write thanks and appreciation. A wonderful reply comes two days later from my Chief Organiser.[3] It is quite touching.

Saturday 29th March
On top of the world! First news of naval battle in Eastern Mediterranean. In this phase the war goes fast our way. It may reverse a bit later, but never mind that.

On 1st March, Bulgaria signed the Axis Pact, and German troops entered Bulgarian territory. The Bulgarian Army proceeded to mobilise, and to take up positions along the Greek frontier, while the Bulgarians did everything they could to facilitate the southward movement of the German forces. Hitherto, King Boris III of Bulgaria had been under strong pressure from the British to maintain his independence.

Sunday 30th March
Good and occasionally funny conference on Balkans. Lieutenant-Colonel J.[4] – he has jumped up very quick from being a Captain;

1 'X': not identified. Possibly Stephenson.
2 Mary Agnes Hamilton (1884–1966). Journalist and writer. Temporary civil servant 1940–52. Labour M.P. 1929–31. She and Dalton had both been delegates to the League of Nations in Geneva during the 1929–31 Labour Government, and she had known both the Daltons well since that time.
3 Marginal note: 'Taylor'.
4 Probably Lt-Colonel K. R. Johnstone (1902–78). S.O.E., later P.W.E., official. Foreign Office 1926–39, 1945–62. Served in Bulgaria 1931–2.

someone, I think Brig. Brooks, has done a most successful wangle – is rather innocent about the Bulgars. He even wants to 'build up Boris'[1] again. This leads me to make some observations on the way in which British diplomats always seem to be glamoured and bamboozled by local Kings. Why this Servants' Hall mentality? 'I am', I say, 'a Republican for every country but my own.' ... All we ask of the Bulgars now is to be anti-German, that and no more.

Indeed, this lack of objectivity of our diplomats, their tendency to get socially pot-bound and to go native everywhere (except in Czechoslovakia), and to judge people by the kind of dinner parties and weekends they furnish, is a frightful thing. It is a dim consciousness of this which leads to the cry for the 'democratisation' of the Foreign Service. Consider, for example, Prince Paul – 'quite unfit', said the P.M. the other day, 'for public life, fit only for a life of luxurious seclusion.' Yet some propose that this creature should be allowed to come to England, and I have already quoted Channon, who has the Servants' Hall mentality worst of all. He would make a good butler to minor royalty. ...

Later, more talk about Coward. He is a great friend of Brig. Brooks, but I am quite adamant against the suggestion. What if he comes over here and makes a great fuss? I am asked. I reply that I will risk that. My C.E.O. remarked this morning that of course he is a 'roaring pansy'. He is disconcerted – perhaps rightly – when I requote this in front of Brig. Brooks. Later he comes and says that the Brig. thinks I should get the P.M. – also alleged to be a friend of Coward – to agree that he is unsuitable.

Lying awake and reflecting on this and the continuing problem of the River[2] and other things, I decide that I will *not* say anything to the P.M. on this personal case. It would show weakness, I did not go to him when I fired King Bomba, I have a most strong case for refusing this time, and I am inclined to suspect that Brig. Brooks is trying to create a situation in which the P.M. will say I ought to take the chap. I so inform C.E.O. next day.

Dalton was asked in the House of Commons on 1st April about the tonnage of goods imported and exported from the port of Marseilles during the

---

1 King Boris III (1894–1943). King of Bulgaria 1918–43. King Boris signed the Axis Pact in March 1941, and declared war on Britain (but not on the U.S.S.R.) in December 1941.
2 'the River': the plan to block the Danube.

previous December and January, and what proportion of imports he estimated was requisitioned for German or Italian use. He replied that about 450 vessels with a cargo of 500,000 tons had entered, and about 400 vessels with a cargo of about 136,000 tons had left, Marseilles. After adding that a very high proportion of such imports were taken by the Axis, he was pressed to reconsider his decision (made under pressure from the U.S. on humanitarian grounds) to permit two shipments of flour to be landed in unoccupied France.[1]

Tuesday 1st April

Parliamentary Questions on Blockade. I am now pursuing a deliberate policy of maximum publicity for all imperfections in the Blockade. This is chiefly to influence Americans and make American public opinion push old Uncle Cordell [Hull] and his State Department along. Also in a minor degree it is to influence British public opinion and to keep the House of Commons up to the mark. There is a danger that such publicity may react a bit against me personally, but I don't think it will, particularly if a little later I am able to show that there has been an improvement, and attribute this to my policy, including its publicity element. Also I am anxious to make them see that there are naval and diplomatic considerations which hamper the total blockade. The Parliamentary Questions go off pretty well, including my reference to German and Italian pickings of cargoes at Marseilles, over 50 per cent, and some say 80 per cent, of cargoes being taken for the Axis. I am hoping that the U.S., in view of Darlan's latest performances, may say that they won't send the two gift wheat ships after all. I had promised to navicert these but nothing more.

At a battle off Cape Matapán, southern Greece, which began on 28th March, a British fleet commanded by Admiral Sir Andrew Cunningham scattered an Italian force of battleships, cruisers and destroyers. Four Italian cruisers and three destroyers were sunk, and the Italian flagship *Vittorio Veneto* was severely damaged. This victory was important in establishing British naval supremacy in the Eastern Mediterranean.

Thursday 3rd April

As reports come in on naval battle in East Mediterranean, it seems doubtful whether much remains at all of the Italian fleet. Yet it was

1 H. C. Debs [370], cols 830–2, 1st April 1941.

from challenging *this* that first Baldwin and then Chamberlain shrank away in 1935. Chamberlain said that it would be 'Midsummer madness'.

I send a final urgent telegram to A.D. [George Taylor] about the River. It may now be only a matter of hours, and success or failure may be decisive in the outcome of the war. He had done so wonderfully well that I have full confidence in him and know that he will do all possible to crown his work so well begun. ...

Agree with Jebb and Nelson, a letter regarding Coward, with cuttings from Hansard and the press. I ramp a little to C.E.O. on pre-war Mayfair standards. This war is thick with certain undesirable politicians who may not wish me well. Also there was a great stink on 8th August in the House of Commons and in the press. Also a regular dust storm of publicity when he started even to prepare to return to England last week. I would much prefer to turn the whole thing down flat, and am still looking for ways of doing this. ...

In my stimulated and organised publicity for the leaks in the Blockade, high praise should be given to Bowes-Lyon for making much of the fact that, of two French ships lately intercepted, one carried an entire cargo of bananas and the other one million litres of rum and 350 tons of pineapples. It is true that these are almost the only exports of the French West Indies, but it went well to say 'Starving Vichy: See how they live! We have long ago had to give up luxuries like these.'

It occurs to me tonight that if, as up to now is so, this war is much less murderous than the last, there will be afterwards a correspondingly much less vehement anti-war sentiment. This would work both ways as regards prevention of another. It might make us less eager to prevent it, but much more clear-headed as to how. Less pure pacifism and more deliberately devised defences, not merely by arms – though others will have to have enough of these to overawe the Germans in the next, perhaps long, phase – but also by social and political measures.

Gladwyn makes the bright remark tonight that at Eton the Sixth Form are the Labour Party and Pop the Conservatives. The feud, in which I once took my share – the symbol of which was wearing pumps at early school! – has always, he thinks, gone on. It came back to me that, when Captain of my House in my last year, I made sure that there should be no member of Pop in the House by canvassing most vigorously with certain of my friends against the only possible, a certain David Bruce.[1] He was then the son of the Liberal Colonial

1 Colonel the Hon. David Bruce (1883–1964). Fourth son of the 9th Earl of Elgin and 13th Earl of Kincardine, a former Viceroy who was Secretary of State for the

Secretary of that day, and I recall a debate on Free Trade in the House Debating Society when I, from a Chamberlainite angle, ridiculed his argument that 'Imports are balanced by exports'. I went up to Cambridge as a Tory Democrat, my hero being Joseph Chamberlain, whose portrait in my first term at Cambridge adorned my wall, but not in my third.

Saturday 5th April
Coward is coming back to England all the same, but the whole deal is off, to my great relief. ...

C.E.O. says that our best information is that the balloon will go up tomorrow at dawn, when the Germans will attack both Jugs and Greeks and launch the most terrific blitz of which they are capable. Strong German forces, Mounted Divisions, are said to be proceeding down the Adriatic from Ancona to Albania. The Jugs have waited too long. Had they struck earlier, they could have crunched the Italian Army in Albania. Now this may not be possible. The Turks are still mulishly keeping to themselves. We do not ask them to attack, but we would like them to contain substantial German forces.

Early in the morning of 6th April, German armies began a simultaneous invasion of Greece and Yugoslavia, while intensive air attacks were launched on the Piraeus, where British expeditionary convoys were discharging. British attempts to produce a co-ordinated resistance failed. Four Yugoslav Army Corps in the north were rapidly overcome by a combination of advancing Germans, Italians and Hungarians. On 13th April, following a heavy bombardment, German troops entered Belgrade. Meanwhile the Twelfth German Army had moved deep into Serbia and Macedonia, preventing any contact between the Yugoslavs and Greeks, and breaking up the Yugoslav forces in the south. On 17th April Yugoslavia capitulated. 'This sudden collapse destroyed the main hope of the Greeks,' Churchill recorded later. 'It was another example of "One at a time". We had done our utmost to procure concerted action, but through no fault of ours we had failed. A grim prospect now gaped upon us all.'[1]

---

1 W. S. Churchill, *The Second World War: Volume III The Grand Alliance*, Cassell, London, 1950, p. 198.

Colonies during Dalton's final year at Eton. Dalton later recorded that with the help of two friends, 'I organised enough blackballs to keep out, for that year anyhow, one aspirant whom I disliked, and whose election, since he was in my House, would have caused me local inconvenience and rivalry.' (*Call Back Yesterday: Memoirs 1887–1931*, Frederick Muller, London, 1953, p. 34.)

Sunday 6th April
And up she went according to forecast! I hear this at breakfast.

Monday 7th April
Not much Operational news. Still hopes of the River, but not perhaps, according to C.E.O., more than a 30 per cent chance of anything worth while. We have one or two encouraging telegrams from A.D. saying that he has been assured that action will be taken as soon as Yugoslavia is attacked, and that 'the Operation' has been prepared. Meanwhile, the Jugs seem to be in a muddle. Their Government has left Belgrade and is out of touch with their General Staff. Their M.F.A. [Minister of Foreign Affairs] is out of touch with his senior officials who are with Campbell and the other diplomats at Vranjska Banja. It is all too reminiscent of Poland to be pleasant, although one hopes that the terrain favours our side this time.

Wednesday 9th April
Bad news this morning. German mechanised column is threatening Salonika, having broken into the Vardar valley and worked round through Doiran. P.M. will have a job today when he moves a motion, now a bit time-soiled, of congratulations to our Forces for recent victories in North Africa, Mediterranean and Greece. If there were enough good and strong men in Parliament outside H.M.G., there would be danger of an upset. But there aren't, and so there isn't – yet.

Gladwyn asked yesterday what Vansittart was up to just now. I said I thought very little, and he then asked whether I thought, if we were chased out of the Balkans, this would react against Eden. I said I thought not much, for the reason just given and because principle of collective responsibility pretty well accepted at this moment.

P.M. has a difficult job in making his statement this afternoon. It was to have been a triumphal vote of thanks to the Forces and the workers at home for recent victories in Africa, Greece and the Mediterranean. The speech was a strong and sombre performance. Less rhetorical ornament than usual. He announced the fall of Salonika and warned various possible next victims, including Turkey and the U.S.S.R. All turned on the outcome of the Battle of the Atlantic. He got his loudest cheer when he said that the blockade must be maintained. I sent a personal telegram to Halifax afterwards telling him this, in order that he might realise the political atmosphere here.

There is not much sign of boil-over in the House today.

On 11th April, Dalton went on a 'Minister's tour in the North', accompanied by his private secretary, Patrick Hancock. Together they visited a number of S.O.E. and R.A.F. bases. 'It was all rather like electioneering, and therefore not a complete holiday in the ordinary sense,' he recorded. 'But this is not very practicable anyhow in these unordinary days. I still find it fun to fly, and keep up my record of never having been sick in the air.'[1] He returned on 17th April.

Friday 18th April
The meeting at the Foreign Office for which I am fetched back takes place this afternoon. Eden, Alexander, Cross and myself with a few officials. ...

I stay behind and speak to Eden about Vansittart. I say I would like him to go on with me, though I add that he has lately not done a very great deal, particularly since Gladwyn and Leeper have got so well into their respective saddles. Eden says that the P.M. would like to fit him in somewhere and wonders whether he could be an additional Parliamentary Secretary to M.E.W. or to the Ministry of Information. I say that the former would seem very bogus. (It would also, in fact, be a very great practical nuisance for me, but I do not say this.) This idea was put up because Vansittart says that he and I get on well together. As to the Ministry of Information, this might be combined with the British Council and, in any case, a Peerage. I arrange to see Vansittart tomorrow.

Eden tells me that Lampson in Cairo wanted to ask Prince Palsy[2] to lunch, and telegraphed whether he might. Eden replied, 'No, such an act of hospitality would not be understood here.'

I blow off over this incident to Gladwyn, denouncing our diplomats as being men with no sense of national honour. The Snobs' International is a most powerful league of sub-men.

Tonight Gladwyn goes off for a most well deserved week's leave at Ardkinglas. He astonishes me by his industry, both early in the morning and late at night. On Wednesday in the heavy Blitz he could not sleep, since bombs fell both in front and behind the house in Chester Square where he stays, and so he went out to join the fire-watchers instead. He is looking much washed out but has finished several good

1 Diary, 11th–17th April.
2 Prince Paul. ' "Prince Palsy" – this is the P.M.'s name for him – is en route from Athens to Egypt,' Dalton noted on 17th April (Diary).

jobs before going off. I shall try to make sure that he is not disturbed or hauled back before Monday week.

On 17th April, Eden had accepted Vansittart's resignation as Chief Diplomatic Adviser.

Saturday 19th April

See Vansittart at Denham. He has a bad cold but is, I think, happy to have got through his resignation interview with Eden. It is not, however, to take immediate effect, and he has been asked to sketch out over this weekend a picture of what he would like to continue to do. Most of all he wants to be free to write and speak, and notably to broadcast without embarrassing either H.M.G. or his colleagues in the Foreign Office. He would also like to go on with me as at present and to be consulted sometimes too by the P.M. and Eden. He is not attracted by the idea of any political post in the Government, nor by the British Council, which he thinks is a dud show. Nor does he want to engage in details of administration. I say that I should hate any severance of our personal relation.

He says that during the whole of Eden's absence he was never once consulted nor shown any papers. This was the final ground of resignation. He adds to me that he feels that he has warmth of feeling and of temperament which cannot live side by side with the cold fish – Cadogan and Butler who, with Halifax, once made a terrible cold trio.

Monday 21st April

Lunch with Amery. Mrs Amery is still all over me by reason of her son Julian, who I propose should now go to Palestine.

Bring back Morton from this lunch in my car and talk to him cordially, or at any rate apparently cordially, about our progress, throwing in just a word or two of disapprobation of Cooper and the Ministry of Information.

Two early plans by Section D to block the Danube – first by blocking the Greben narrows by destroying the retaining wall, second by mining the over-hanging cliff on the Yugoslav side – failed in the first few months of the war. A third plan, to sink cement-filled barges in the Iron Gates, also failed in April 1940, when German security men, uncovering a somewhat amateurish attempt, informed the Romanian authorities of what was afoot. Despite the embarrassment caused by this incident, a further attempt was made to carry out the third plan – this time working through the Yugoslav authorities in the aftermath of the coup, and on the eve of the German invasion. At the beginning of April 1941 twelve barges were ready for action, and on the 3rd, Nelson, on Dalton's behalf, cabled to Taylor in Belgrade: 'Minister and all high authorities know you realise fully that a successful blocking of Danube before it is too late would be the decisive factor for England in this War ... '[1] On 6th April some half-dozen barges were successfully sunk – but the river was only blocked for a few weeks, and there was no significant drop in Romanian oil supplies to Germany.

News of the operation only filtered through slowly, partly because of the confusion caused by the Balkan invasions. On 17th April, Dalton was informed indirectly that the Danube was blocked, but nothing more. 'There have been a few other references but all quite imprecise, in the telegrams,' he noted. 'It is most tantalising not to know what has happened. The Jugs have been so inefficient that it may well be that plans were made but never executed.'[2]

Tuesday 22nd April

D.M.O.[3] to lunch. I am mobilising him against Reith's officials, who have no sense of security or of the importance of my duties. He plays up very well. He and Davidson are a really good couple. Kennedy says that he thinks Law is the best profession in the world, and Politics the second-best. Both really better than the Army! He says that Smuts[4] always thought we were going to lose Egypt but that this didn't matter so long as we didn't let the Germans go south of the Equator. I say I think this is rather a local South African view. He says that none the less Smuts is a wise old man. Kennedy doubts whether the Turks will now resist. The Germans will get all the Aegean Islands and so Turkey will be encircled. He believes that a number of leading Turks are already in German pay. Marshal Chakmak[5] is in any case too old to count. As to the Russians, he thinks they know that the Red Army

1 Dalton Papers 18/1.
2 Diary, 17th April 1941.
3 Major-General John Kennedy. Director of Military Operations, q.v.
4 Field Marshal J. C. Smuts (1870–1950). Prime Minister and Minister of External Affairs and Defence, South Africa 1939–48. Prime Minister 1919–24.
5 Marshal F. Chakmak (1876–1950). Turkish Chief of Staff 1941–4.

could make no fight against the Germans. Moreover, with mechanised forces, the old argument about Russia being defended by her great distances has gone. The Germans could overrun as much as they liked, though, as I point out, they would meet with new difficult problems of occupation. ...

I see Eden about the River. The P.M. is most anxious to give the public some good news. Can we say the river is blocked? I say not yet, and we go over the skimpy evidence together. He will telegraph to Cairo to ask the Jug Minister there what they know, and also, via Washington, at my suggestion, to the American Minister in Bucharest.

He says the conduct of the Greeks is very moving. They say, 'We are sorry we haven't been able to do more. Thank you very much for all your help. And now please go as soon as you feel you should in order to save as many as you can of your own troops.'

Wednesday 23rd April
Morning at a National Executive. Great waste of time. Afternoon at a Ministerial Committee on Export Surpluses. Equally great waste of time. Menzies, Jordan[1] and Harriman all present. No detail prepared. It is one of the pleasures of my life that I have so seldom to meet my ministerial colleagues on committees. This helps me much to get on with my own work. ...

Leeper tells me that he has seen Eden who has promised to pay a visit to C.H.Q. on 10th May. Leeper also spoke to Eden about Cooper and said that he was 'very idle'; also that we should have charge of all propaganda to enemy and enemy-occupied countries. Eden said he quite agreed, but there were political and personal difficulties. On the other hand, Eden was in favour of our Propaganda Plans for different countries and was also in favour of the proposed French Committee, with the Foreign Office in the Chair. I tell Leeper that Eden had said to me the night before, 'You and Duff are both very combative people and once you start writing rude letters to each other you will go on for ever.' I had replied that he must introduce an element of *soulagement*. Gaitskell says that the game must be to get Cooper to the triangular conference with Eden in the Chair, and for me, though remaining very bland, to make D.C. lose his temper. It is reported that he does this very easily, and that the other night at the Dorchester he literally leapt at the throat of some man who had said something he did not like. He has now left the Dorchester and gone to live at Bognor, whence he arrives very late at his Ministry in the morning.

1 William Jordan (1879–1959). High Commissioner for New Zealand 1936–51.

Thursday 24th April
I am delighted to read in a Colonial Office telegram that Prince Palsy and his wife[1] are to reside in Kenya, with the status of political prisoners, and that a senior administrative official is to live with and watch them; that H.M.G. will pay the rent of their house, seeing that this is in the nature of a prison, but that it will be put to 'our friend' that his large assets in this country should be drawn upon for his keep and other personal expenses. I hope that Lampson in Cairo has read this telegram with profit.

Friday 25th April
C.D. [Nelson] rings up to say that on 6th April six obstacles were sunk in the River. This is not much of a performance.

Saturday 26th April
To C.H.Q. for midday Conference. Oliver Harvey is there in place of Peterson. He is very affable. I tell him that I find it delicate to see much of him, though I should like to, as my relations with his Minister are so bad. And indeed they are! Never a day passes without we exchange brusque correspondence. Soon we must have a show-down at the Foreign Office. The Foreign Office are my natural allies, I think, against the Ministry of Information.

On 17th April, British and Greek leaders agreed that a withdrawal south to the Thermopylae line was unavoidable. A difficult retreat, under heavy aerial attack, followed, but by 20th April the occupation of the Thermopylae positions was complete. Here, for a time, Churchill hoped for a final stand. Lacking Greek support on the British left flank, however, Wavell concluded that any further attempt to hold the Greek mainland must be abandoned. Greece surrendered to the Germans on 24th April. Over the next five days, a seaborne evacuation took place from the small ports and beaches of southern Greece. In all, more than 50,000 out of 62,000 men were withdrawn, many of them to Crete. Meanwhile, a German division commanded by Rommel, which had landed at Tripoli in February, had attacked the British force at Cyrenaica and driven it back to the Egyptian border.

Churchill was heavily criticised for these failures, and early in May the House of Commons debated a motion of no confidence. Lloyd George attacked the Prime Minister fiercely for surrounding himself with 'yesmen'. Churchill replied by comparing Lloyd George to Pétain. In the resulting

1 Princess Olga of Greece (b. 1903).

division the Government won by 447 votes to 3, Lloyd George and Shinwell abstaining.

Monday 28th April
I have issued an order in my Ministry that, from twelve noon to 12.15 every Monday, everyone must wear their gas-masks. We begin this morning and I hold a conference with Drogheda and Stirling in which we agree on action of various kinds and on several draft telegrams to be sent to Washington. It is really much easier than you might suppose. Except, I understand, for those who must wear glasses in order to see. Rather a joke, and also quite a good thing from the point of view of morale. ...

Oliver Stanley[1] dined with me alone in a secluded corner of the Lansdowne Club.[2] ...

He ... asked me what I had thought of the Prime Minister's speech on the air on Sunday. I said that I thought he had done well in a very difficult situation and had heartened his hearers. Stanley said, 'It may have gone down very well with the 99 per cent who know nothing, but the 1 per cent of us who do know, feel rather differently.'

He then began a long tirade against the Prime Minister and the Foreign Secretary, with whom I had said that I found my personal relations developing very satisfactorily, and that this was additionally important for smooth working, since he was so close to the Prime Minister. Stanley said he did not think he was the sort of man who ought to be close to the Prime Minister. He was, he added, vain, weak and unreliable. He had let down Stanley, Malcolm MacDonald and the rest at the time of his resignation. He had promised to consult them, and they had acted together as a group. They were on many points opposed to Chamberlain's Foreign Policy. Eden, however, chose a most frivolous pretext on which to resign, and gave Stanley and others no warning that he was going to do so. So much so that, at the Cabinet, on the proposal that we should begin again negotiations with Italy, Chamberlain had gone round the table, and got the acquiescence of all of them, and it was only then that Eden had quite suddenly said that he could not go on.

1 Oliver Stanley (1896–1950). Conservative M.P. for Westmorland 1924–45; Bristol West 1945–50. Secretary of State for War January–May 1940. Junior minister 1931–3; Minister of Transport 1933–4; Labour 1934–5. President of the Board of Education 1935–7; Trade 1937–January 1940. Colonial Secretary 1942–5.
2 This sentence and the rest of the entry were dictated separately, and appear under the heading, 'Conversation with Oliver Stanley'.

Stanley then proceeded to attack, with such mild vehemence as he could command, the terrible error, as he judged it, of sending anything beyond a small token force to Greece. This, he said, was a crowning blunder. It was the Prime Minister's fault. The decision had been taken against all military and naval advice. It should have been seen from the start that the adventure was quite hopeless. The only real way to help Greece was to win the war. Instead of that we might now lose both Greece and Egypt. We had thrown away a most valuable Air Force in Greece. At least four squadrons of fighters and three squadrons of bombers had been destroyed. It was quite wrong for Eden to have gone to the Middle East and worst of all to go to Athens. There he had been cheered in the streets and smothered in roses. How in such surroundings could he keep his judgment clear. A Foreign Secretary should stay always in the Foreign Office protected by distance and his officials from such local impressions.

I said that I had found it very difficult to form a view, as between Tripoli and Thermopylae. As against what he had said, I saw some force in the argument that Eden might have been able, through the offer of substantial British help, to bring both the Yugoslavs and Turks and a total force of some seventy Divisions into an anti-German bloc in the Balkans. But for Prince Paul, who had had too many friends and dupes in this country, I still thought this would have been a possibility. Stanley replied that it was useless to count Divisions; all that was worth counting was Armoured Divisions, of which neither Turkey nor Yugoslavia had any.

I said I thought we should soon have to have a Parliamentary debate, but that probably it would be best to have this in secret session. Stanley strongly disagreed. It should, he was sure, be a public debate. He added that he would like to speak himself. I asked whether he did not think this difficult, in the light of his present duties. He said not provided he made no use in his speech of any secret information. He would begin by saying that of course they were all behind the Prime Minister, but ...... I gather he would add some critical comments on the ignoring of professional advice and on the weakness of peripatetic diplomacy.

He then added, with a not unhappy smile, that many people were gunning after Eden now. He went on to criticise the Prime Minister, on the ground that he still imposed his strategic conceptions on the Chiefs of Staff, and was most impatient of any criticisms. The three Service Ministers had been reduced to the status of mere cyphers. They were never told, much less consulted, as to what was to be done with the forces for which they were responsible. Everything was settled by the Prime Minister, influenced sporadically by the Chiefs of Staff. He thought the Prime Minister was going to buy in Hore-Belisha, probably in substitution of Duff Cooper – 'So my spies tell me,' he said with a grin – as the only possible leader of an opposition in Parliament. Stanley said that he himself at the War Office under Chamberlain had had a good show. He had had to clean up a much worse mess left by Belisha than the world knew about. Eden he added, when he succeeded him, took no interest whatever in the War Office, and was even worse than Belisha had been. Stanley said that, when the Churchill Government was formed, the present Prime Minister offered him the Dominions Office, but he refused this because he knew that the Prime Minister was impossible to work with. He had seen how he had treated even Eden, his close associate, when he was at the Dominions Office. If any Dominion ever objected to anything, Winston would say to Eden, 'You can't have put it properly to them.' This was when Winston was only First Lord of the Admiralty. Such treatment would be quite unbearable from him as Prime Minister.

We talked a little of the change of Government and of what had preceded it. Desiring to put something into the common pot of gossip, I related to him that of my Labour colleagues, only Alexander at the beginning of the war had been willing to consider, even for a moment, serving under Chamberlain. Nor, I thought, would the Labour Party have been willing, before Norway, to join the Government, even under another Prime Minister. On the other hand, after the Norway Debate, we were practically unanimous in our willingness to join, on reasonable terms, a Government led either by Churchill or Halifax.

I also related to him the story of the efforts of some of us, after Munich, to establish a Parliamentary working arrangement between certain Labour leaders, Churchill, Eden and Duff Cooper, and how Harold Macmillan had acted as a go-between. I told him how, though I had persuaded Attlee and Morrison to join me in a three-sided conference in Macmillan's flat, the plan had fallen through because Eden refused, and Duff Cooper made his attendance conditional on Eden's. So it was left that only Churchill would have met us, and this we judged could be done without so much elaboration.

Stanley said that Churchill was primarily responsible for the fiasco in Norway. He had suddenly refused to allow the Navy to go in to Trondheim. From that time on, an impossible task was thrown on the Army. I told him, wishing to turn the conversation another way, that Hoare at the Air Ministry, with whom I had liaised on behalf of H.M. Opposition, had told me that he thought the heaviest land fighting of 1940 would be in Norway. How laughable and incompetent this judgment had turned out to be! But Stanley turned it back and said, 'Oh, that was what Winston told them all', and yet, he said, this man climbed to power on Norway, who, on his record, least deserved it.

I do not understand why Stanley was so rashly indiscreet to me tonight. I could, if I chose, do him great damage. I conclude that, as I knew before, he is a chronic gossip, and just talks because he cannot keep his mouth shut. The whole conversation left in my mind a disagreeable impression and I shall be most careful what I say to him, or let others say to him, in future.

Wednesday 30th April

The first really good news about the Danube. A telegram from B.[1] reporting that our No. 2 at Belgrade personally supervised an operation in the K. narrows (probably about 8th April) whereby the No. 2, a cautious man and a good judge, estimates that the river will be blocked for at least three months. This particular block is additional to anything due to the destruction of the two railway bridges, and, almost certainly, additional to other barge sinkings at Golubac and Dombrovica. Possible also that there were some further sinkings close to the Iron Gates,[2] though this was not such a good place, as the river here was very deep. No news of any explosion on or near the shore, and this possibility must, I think, almost certainly be washed out. None the less, the result is pretty good, and I send tonight a Minute to P.M. with copies to other eminences.

Thursday 1st May

Agitation about a *Daily Mail* article by Wilson Broadbent[3] referring to sharks in the Channel and hinting, though rather ignorantly, at some of my functions, though not naming me. M.I.5 told Gladwyn that they could prosecute unless particulars of source were given, and could prosecute source if revealed. But this would involve high political decisions, and I should need to go to the Cabinet or at least to approach some leading members of it. The *Daily Mail* have also, by allowing this article, violated a D'Notice against any reference to secret propaganda. Probably the thing has been inspired from Ministry of Information. ...

Give an interview to five selected U.S. correspondents in London and speak from a brief prepared by Bowes-Lyon. This press conference has the most frightful results! On my return from the country on the following Sunday (4th May) I find that Hull has been complaining to Halifax against the references (attributed not to me personally, but

1 'B.': not identified.
2 Near Orşova, close to where the River Timiş joins the Danube.
3 Wilson Broadbent (d. 1962). Journalist on the *Daily Mail*.

to M.E.W.) to the things which the U.S. Government could do to help us, e.g. by bunker control, freezing enemy assets, and co-operation in black-listing. Hull, reported by Halifax to be 'very angry', said that if H.M.G. wanted to make representations on these subjects, they should do so through the proper channels. I have, however, the reply that I personally referred to these three, among other questions, in a broadcast to the U.S. early this year, the terms of which were discussed and agreed with Halifax himself. There were no adverse reactions in Washington then, so why anticipate one now?

A further spot of bother, however, arises from a reference in my talk to the Chase Bank controlling Amexco (American Express Company) who still have a branch in Berlin. This has been cabled out (still under M.E.W.) and has led to furious denials from Aldrich,[1] President of the Chase in New York, and a terrific nerve storm by Wallace,[2] their man in London, who is threatening to make a complaint 'in the highest quarters', i.e. to the P.M. Halifax is so upset that he has sent personal messages to me and to Eden.

For some time there had been complaints about S.O.E. in Cairo – both from Baker Street and from G.H.Q. Middle East. The Cairo organisation was regarded as over-large, expensive, riven with feuds between SO1 and SO2 offices, and unproductive. At last, in the spring of 1941, hints of grave irregularities among S.O.E. staff in Egypt and Palestine persuaded Nelson that an investigation was urgently needed. The question was whom to send. 'Somebody, I never knew who, found us a middle-aged but active merchant banker who was ready to consider taking on the job,' one senior S.O.E. man, Bickham Sweet-Escott, has recalled. ' ... I was detailed to stand by to go with the banker to Cairo as his personal assistant. I spent several agreeable evenings with him at White's. But it seemed to me that in spite of his reputation as a leading banker he had only the faintest idea of what it was likely that he would have to do ... but there was a final hurdle for the banker to take – his interview with Mr Dalton. Mr Dalton was not impressed, and told us to think again.'[3]

Friday 2nd May
As I am leaving London today, it is suggested to me by C.E.O. that I

1 Winthrop Aldrich (1885–1974). Chairman of the Board of the Chase Bank of the City of New York. U.S. Ambassador in London 1953–7.
2 John M. Wallace (1887–1975). Chase Manhattan Bank representative in London.
3 B. Sweet-Escott, *Baker Street Irregular*, Methuen, London, 1965, p. 71.

should see Arthur Guinness,[1] head of the Merchant Banking firm, Guinness, Mahon & Co. (I think this is the title of the gang), who has been pressed upon C.D. as a most suitable 'big man' to send out to Middle East on a quick mission to investigate, report and take necessary action in order to straighten out what is undoubtedly a bad tangle. This man has, as one of his partners, my employee B.C.[2] and is also said to be well spoken of by Hambro. It is these last two, I gather, who have been making the running on his behalf. A little while ago C.E.O. put to me tentatively that this man might be brought into my organisation in London, naming Hambro and B.C. as his backers. I said no, I did not want any more City people. We had enough of these already. C.E.O. said that this man, apart from his standing in the City, was intelligent and amusing and had an Irish wit. But he did not continue to press him against my objections. Now it is suggested that he should go on a brief mission to Middle East. Since time presses, I agree to see him, but I have a dissatisfied feeling that he has been pushed too hard on me. C.D. says, before I see him, that he has only been told that he is one of several candidates whom the Minister is going to see. Guinness, apparently, did not altogether like this.

He is brought in with C.E.O. and C.D. at 12.30. The interview is not a success. He begins by saying that just after the last war he attended some of my lectures at the London School of Economics. I ask him what he has been doing since then. He says, 'I belong to a class for which I am afraid you have not much respect. I am a banker.' This seemed to me a most gauche gambit. I replied, 'Most of you don't deserve much respect. But anyhow the mission we are going to discuss this morning is not a money-lending mission.' From this inauspicious start the conversation made no real recovery. C.D. said afterwards that the man had been very nervous. I said, 'I don't want nervous people in my organisation. I want people of power and self-assurance.' The man produced a piece of paper on which he had written down a number of points. He wanted sufficient status to entitle him to see General Wavell personally, and not merely be fobbed off with some Colonel. C.E.O. said that he thought the rank of local Counsellor would secure this. The man then said that he would prefer to be a Minister. I said, 'I couldn't possibly recommend that. The Foreign Office would certainly turn it down, and apart from that, I don't think it is necessary. The local rank of Counsellor will be quite sufficient.'

He then said – bloody cheek I thought it – that he knew that I had

1 A. R. Guinness, later Sir Arthur (1895–1951). Partner in Guinness, Mahon & Co. (Merchant Bankers) from 1923.
2 Probably B. Clarke, an official at Woburn.

secured the rank of Minister for Noel Hall in Washington. I said, 'That is quite a different case.' He then repeated that he must have direct access to Wavell. I said, 'Of course you must see Wavell at least once, but sometimes he may be too busy with the war to see you and you may have to talk to some members of his staff instead.' The man then began to say that he would be prepared to do the work with a salary, but ...... I cut him short and said, 'That is very public-spirited of you but of course you would be entitled to reasonable expenses.' This was what he was trying to say at some length. He then raised the question of his terms of reference. He was to go out to investigate and report. Personally he would be quite content with this, but was he also to have power to act on the spot? C.E.O. and C.D. had apparently put into his head that he might have some such powers. They should not have done so. I said, 'I think we can find a suitable formula. Telegraphic communication is pretty good and I should certainly expect you, as a general rule, to refer back for authority from me before taking any action.' He then tried to go on discussing this point and bored me terribly. I said, 'I have told you that I will discuss a suitable formula with my officers.' He then said that he was a great friend of Dill and that he would like to take a personal letter from Dill to Wavell. I said, 'I am not sure that that would be wise. I am not sure that Dill and Wavell have seen eye to eye lately.' He amazed me by completely failing to see my point, and twice again raised this suggestion. The third time I said, 'I have told you twice that I don't consider it would be a good move for you to take a letter from Dill to Wavell. Don't you understand?' He then said he knew a lot of other generals, including Adam.[1] I said there would not be the same objection to taking a letter from Adam to Wavell. He then said he could start tomorrow, or the next day. I patiently explained to him that the congestion of communications was such that one could not get passages as quick as that. C.E.O. said that it would probably take about ten days. He did not seem to understand this, imagining that he was so important that he would instantly get a first priority. He had said earlier that he had had no holiday for a long time. I therefore said, 'If you were going ten days hence, you could take ten days' holiday now.' He said that his brother was away for a brief holiday and that it would therefore be difficult for him to go away too without endangering the success of his business. He said, 'Of course I don't know whether you want me to undertake this mission.' I said, 'I am trying to make up my mind as this talk goes along.' I noted with displeasure

---

1 Lt-General Sir Ronald Forbes Adam, later General, 2nd Bart (1885–1983). Adjutant General to the Forces 1941–6. General Officer Commanding-in-Chief Northern Command 1940–41.

that once when I was speaking he turned round and talked through me to C.D. When I said afterwards that the man was not only a fool but had no manners, C.D. said that this again no doubt was due to nervousness. Finally, though unwillingly, I said that I would like him to undertake the mission. The interview then terminated. When he had been got rid of, I saw C.E.O. and C.D. together. I told them that I was most dissatisfied and that the man had made a very poor impression on me. None the less, since it was urgent to send someone, and since they had no one else to suggest, and since they and Hambro thought this man was better than he seemed to me, I agreed that he should go. But his terms of reference must be narrowly drawn, and he must have no power to take any important action on the spot without referring back to me.

Monday 5th May

While waiting to go into the Cabinet, I had a few words with Ernest Brown, who is very hot against Horeb Elisha.[1] Brown said that he himself had been elected Leader of the Simonites[2] at the beginning of this session, by 31 votes to 4 for Horeb, and of these 4, one was Brown's. (Evidently Simonites vote by show of hands, not by ballot!) But after this vote, Sir George Schuster, trying to make a compromise, had proposed, and the rest had weakly agreed, that, though Brown was Leader, Horeb should be Acting Chairman in his absence.

Brown then produced from his pocket a cutting from last week's *Truth* containing a poem derogatory to Horeb. Brown said he thought that the two articles that appeared in *Truth* when Horeb resigned had finally finished him. It might be necessary to remind people of them. Brown said that when Horeb had been invited to lunch at No. 10 (why?) last week, he had tried to collect all the press photographers on the door step, but this move had failed owing to wartime regulations against crowds in Downing Street. Brown said that he thought our great fight which was coming soon would be between those who wanted to make a premature peace and those who, 'like me', intended to fight this thing out to the end. I asked, 'What is Lloyd George doing now?' Brown said, nodding sententiously, 'He is keeping in the background, biding his time.'

The love of Liberals for one another passes the loves of all other political animals. I say this knowing, at first hand, something of the

1 Dalton's name for I. L. Hore-Belisha, q.v.
2 The Simonites were the 'Liberal National' M.P.s who in 1931 had followed Sir John Simon in his support of the National Government. By 1941, the Simonites were almost indistinguishable from the Conservatives, with whom they eventually merged.

mutual loves within the Labour Party and, at second hand, not a little of the Conservatives. ...

Dine with Ingram, a piece of return hospitality. He is rather an old bore, and, falling slightly below the level of diplomatic deportment to which I have been accustomed, commented adversely to me, when the bill was presented to him, on the price charged for the four brandies which we had consumed. (Gladwyn was surprised when I reported this incident.) Ingram spent much of his time denigrating Sir Alexander Hardinge,[1] the King's Private Secretary. He was out of touch, he said, with all political realities. He might dangerously mislead the King in difficult times. He had been offered an Indian Governorship but had refused it. I asked whom Ingram would prefer. He said he thought that Walter Monckton would do it very well. I did not say that just lately I am inclined to blame Monckton for a large part of my trouble with Cooper.

I decided tonight to cancel my invitation to Guinness to go on my Middle East mission. He is, C.E.O. tells me, very sore about his treatment by me last Friday. He says that, after all, he is a Conservative and I am a Socialist and he doubts whether he should work well with me. He supposes that I have heard evil of him from some of my colleagues. I say that none of my colleagues has ever heard of this self-important fool, but that if he is talking like that, I just won't send him. C.E.O., I think, both expected and wanted me to take this line. He adds that Guinness might speak ill of me to Wavell and recommend that all my show should be taken over by the military. C.E.O. says that C.D. was rather upset at the failure of the interview, but that C.E.O. said to C.D., 'If your friend carries on like this, we shall soon be in as bad a way as France was.' I say I am quite clear that this man neither has the other gifts I want nor can be trusted to be loyal to me. The opportunity of getting rid of him comes through news that Taylor is, after all, still safe and sound with Campbell's staff who are being brought by the Italians to Rome and are due to be released, under Anglo-Italian convention for liberation of diplomats. This is very good news, since I had had deep fears either that Taylor was dead or worse, caught by the Gestapo.[2] I shall not be reassured till he has

1 Sir Alexander Hardinge, later 2nd Baron (1894–1960). Private Secretary to the King 1936–43. Equerry and Assistant Private Secretary to George V 1920–36. Private Secretary to Edward VIII 1936.

2 George Taylor, who had been in Belgrade at the time of the coup, had subsequently been captured by the Italians and taken first to Albania and from there flown to Italy, where his captors, unaware of the nature of his responsibilities, treated him with friendliness and liberality. An exchange of prisoners was arranged by the Italian Foreign Ministry, and Taylor was sent in a sealed train to Madrid, returning to England on 17th June. (Interview with George Taylor.)

emerged from enemy-dominated regions, but so far so good. C.E.O. suggests, telling me this news, and I still grumbling on at having been rushed by them over Guinness and have really no confidence in him, and less and less the more I think of that bad interview, that, if I want a get-out, here it is. I eagerly embrace it and ring up C.D. who sadly agrees.

This was done earlier in the evening before I dine with Ingram. I ask C.E.O. to prepare a draft of a letter from me to Guinness. After dinner he produces this, but it is frightfully bad, half jocose and half promising something more in the future, written in a much more familiar tone than I am disposed to adopt towards this bloody fool whom I have only seen once and never want to see again. Therefore, I re-dictate, in his presence, a much terser, though still polite, note expressing regret that, in the changed circumstances, in view of Taylor's early release and unique experience of the Middle East, I no longer feel able to avail myself of Guinness's services, though much appreciating his willingness to undertake, at great inconvenience to himself, a mission which would have had high value for our war effort.

Tuesday 6th May
The first day of the Parliamentary debate. I spend most of the day in the House. Eden makes a poor speech in very difficult conditions, since clearly in public session there are many things, e.g. about the Turks, which he cannot say. Horeb, much applauded by a small claque on rising, makes a speech clever but, having regard to his own past, most impudent. Attlee winds up pretty well.

To see Van and discuss with him the usual themes – our broadcast to Germany, Crossman, Cooper etc.

Then a conference with C.E.O. and C.D. who say that Guinness has received my letter pretty well. Apparently a good deal of social fuss is still being made of him and he is to be had to lunch by various people in the coming week. I say he is not to be told anything more about my organisation. We discuss alternative names. It is thought that Brooks would be best. C.E.O. asks me what I think of the possibility of Wilmot going. I say I don't think this will do. I mention this to John who quite agrees.

Wednesday 7th May
In my bath I change my mind and think Wilmot might do for the Middle East. After my bath, down in the shelter, I put it to him, but he raises four objections –

(1) It would cause the most frightful jealousies in political circles and do me harm. (I say that if this is all, I will face that.)
(2) He does not click with soldiers, finding them stiff and they not quite knowing how to take him.
(3) He only knows the No. 1 and not the No. 2 branch of our work.
(4) There would be much more fuss and trouble with the Camarilla, including Morton who is by nature a jealous *manqué* man and who rang up to ask whether John's speech last weekend, grossly condensed and misrepresented in the press, represented the official view of M.E.W.

He puts this argument quite well next day to C.E.O. who, on the whole, agrees.

Before going to National Executive I have a quick word with Leeper on possibility of Brooks going. He puts on his most obstinate and sheepish look, says Brooks is quite irreplaceable and that he himself could not carry on if he went. Practically a threat of resignation.

Second day's debate in the House. Lloyd George makes a deplorable opening speech, which I don't hear, and P.M., as usual, comes through magnificently at the end. He likens Lloyd George's orations to one of those with which, no doubt, the aged and venerable Marshal Pétain enlivened the last days of M. Reynaud's Cabinet. This will stick now.

Thursday 8th May
Still fidgeting on as to whether Brooks can go. I see him and Leeper together. No progress. At the end I say, 'I am sure you have both tried to be helpful, but I have not been helped by this conversation.' A short point is that no one suitable will go unless I am prepared to make a terrific row by courting resignations and giving orders which will be profoundly unpopular, with terrific reverberations in Whitehall. I am not prepared to do this – at this moment. Brooks says, perhaps truly, that the whole Middle East show is in a pretty good mess – returning troops, prisoners of war far in excess of anything expected, etc. So if our show is in a mess too it will only be like the rest.

Winant has been to see Eden with a protest about my press conference. Bowes-Lyon sees Cohen[1] at the American Embassy this afternoon and is taken in by him to see Winant, who is quite friendly. Eden writes that he would like me to make him a statement which he can send to Winant. Sterling Products Incorporated, an American

---

1 Benjamin Cohen (b. 1894). Adviser to the American Ambassador to Great Britain 1941–2. Office of Economic Stabilisation 1942–5.

concern tied up with the German Bayer Interests, making aspirin, etc., sends solicitor's letters demanding to see me and threatening legal proceedings. I let them be handled by my officials who, supported by lawyers, think they have intimidated them.

The Beaver rings up and asks whether I have seen Wallace. He came to see the Beaver two or three days ago. I say yes. The Beaver sounds friendly, but is such a bloody rascal that I don't trust him not to be adding to the trouble. He says, 'I have been in a lot of press scraps in my life so I don't take them too seriously.' I say, 'You know who my chief Press Officer is, don't you?' He says no. I tell him, just for atmosphere.[1]

Attlee to dine with me alone. Whenever the pressure in the pipe gets too great, I see this little man, who is always most loyal, unruffled and understanding on my affairs. When he arrives, C.E.O. is with me ... It is not understood why neither Eden nor P.M. referred to the River in the Debate. Perhaps because Professor Lindemann has been going round denigrating our claim to have blocked it for three months, as reported by me to the P.M. ... Attlee says he will drop a bomb on this nonsense tonight at Defence Committee, and I will send another chit to P.M. with latest evidence tomorrow, noting that latest story destroys Hitler's yarn that river is open. ...

Attlee says to me, 'No one in the Government except the P.M. and you and I take any interest in Operations.' He suggests that I should sometimes go to the War Room in the evening and cheer up the chaps and see the maps. He says he often goes down. I say, 'Let us go together, you and I and C.E.O. one evening.' He thinks this would be a good plan. I then make C.E.O. who joins us at the end of our meal, motor him to the centre, wishing that they shall become better acquainted. C.E.O. tells me afterwards that the little man was in great form, telling stories all the time.

Saturday 10th May

I go to see H.Q.[2] in time for the 12 o'clock meeting, which is attended by Eden and his most bone-headed and elderly P.P.S., Colonel Ponsonby.[3] The visit, I think, is very successful, and Eden is favourably impressed. My blokes all play up well and he enjoys his afternoon visit. He talks a bit against the Air Force, thus reflecting Dill and War Office, and says that they are most obstinately opposed to dive bom-

1 Dalton's Chief Press Officer was David Bowes-Lyon, q.v., the Queen's brother.
2 'see H.Q.': *sic*. But from the context it is likely that Dalton means, 'I go to C.H.Q.' i.e. Woburn.
3 Colonel C. Ponsonby, later Sir Charles, 1st Bart (1879–1976). P.P.S. to Eden 1940–45. Conservative M.P. for Sevenoaks 1935–50.

bers for army co-operation. He blames, in particular, Harold Balfour for this. (How these Tories love one another!) He also says that if we had had only one armoured division in the Middle East, the Turks would have come in on our side. I wonder!

Duff Cooper has not yet answered his letter of a fortnight ago. Ponsonby tells me, walking round with him alone in the garden, that Cooper is no use and should be fired from his job and sent to the Lords. Peterson, he says, is 'just a block' at the Ministry of Information. Ponsonby asks, on arrival at the Abbey, whether I come down here to sleep every night!

On 10th May the Germans carried out a major raid on London with incendiary bombs. It was the worst night of the Blitz. More than 2,000 fires were started, and nearly 150 water mains were destroyed, preventing effective fire-fighting. Over 3,000 people were killed or injured, and the House of Commons was destroyed by a single bomb.

Sunday 11th May
Drive back in the morning with Gladwyn from C.H.Q. Before starting we had heard something of the damage done in last night's air-raid on London. As we come into London there are some signs of this, much smoke hanging in the air and the streets full of broken glass and charred bits of paper. We drive first to my flat[1] and find that an incendiary bomb has burned out the top flat immediately opposite mine. This will improve my view and it is interesting to see that this old Victorian building, ugly though it is, is yet so solid that this incendiary burnt itself out without spreading either to right or left or downwards through the solid stone walls and floor to adjoining flats. No damage to my own. We then go to Chester Square, where Gladwyn finds that the house some six doors away from No. 20, where he is lodging, is completely gone. It would have made no difference whether last night here one had been under the roof or in the basement. In a public shelter close by, the Mayor of Westminster and twelve other people were killed. As we drive back, we see a working party still digging for human remains in this shelter. Last night also Maurice Ingram was killed while fire-watching on the top of his block of flats above the Mirabelle Restaurant in Curzon Street. They say he was killed quite quickly by some flying projectile.

1 The Daltons had a flat in Carlisle Mansions, Victoria.

De La Warr[1] asks us to lunch and there relates some remarks of Brocket.[2] ... I tell Gladwyn that De La Warr bores me rather because, though he still looks rather young, he bores on like quite an old man. I said to Sargent, whom we meet after lunch, that responsibility for Ingram's death is on the doorstep of the Foreign Office because they delayed so long in sending him out, as promised, to Mexico.

Back at the Ministry in the afternoon. It is a little difficult to work or concentrate one's mind. There have been many tales of where the damage is, so about 5 o'clock I get Gladwyn to drive me down to Westminster and thence to South London. Westminster Hall, which we first visit, has not been badly hit, and the main part of the roof still stands. But then I learn, for the first time, that the House of Commons has ceased to exist. Looking in from the Star Court one sees that the Chamber is completely gutted. Gladwyn and I then work round from the old Members' Smoke Room – where we talk to one of the women staff who was there all last night and says that twelve large bombs fell in the river and two policemen disappeared, leaving no trace – up the staircase, and so under dripping ceilings – the fire brigade often do more damage than the fire – to the entrance to the old Members' Lobby, where, under the sky, lies a great mass of broken bricks, twisted iron and charred bits of wood. The statue of Joseph Chamberlain, however, is still standing, with uplifted hand. His less gifted son has much responsibility for this. We then work round to the entrance to what was once the Chamber itself. Here the destruction by explosions and fire is quite complete: I clamber about among the rubble with my nose full of the smell of burnt wood, and watch firemen still leisurely playing their hoses on some smoking debris. The Members' lavatory in the old Aye Lobby is still intact. Therefore, as a last gesture, I enter and relieve nature. Then we depart. I recall that, apart from little final formalities, the last words spoken in this Chamber were those of the P.M. in his peroration at the end of the Vote of Confidence debate on Wednesday 7th May.

'When I look back on the perils which have been overcome, upon the great mountain waves in which the gallant ship has driven, when I remember all that has gone wrong, and remember also all that has gone right I feel sure we have no need to fear the tempest. Let it roar,

1 H.E.D.B. Sackville, 9th Earl De La Warr (1900–76). Junior minister in the 1929–31 Labour Government. He supported Ramsay MacDonald in 1931 and served in the National Government, again in junior posts, 1931–7. Lord Privy Seal 1937–8. President of the Board of Education 1938–40. First Commissioner at the Office of Works and Public Buildings April–May 1940.
2 A. R. N. Nall-Cain, 2nd Baron Brocket (1904–67). Conservative M.P. for Wavertree 1931–4.

and let it rage. We shall come through.'

And after that we voted by 447 to 3 our confidence in the Government.

Then we drive to South London and make a tour of ruin [*sic*], including John Wilmot's constituency in Kennington. From Newington Butts to the Elephant practically everything is burnt away.

Tonight on the 9 o'clock news it is announced that the House of Commons, Westminster Hall, Westminster Abbey and the British Museum have all been hit, though the damage to the House of Commons is far greater than any of the others.

On 11th May the German Deputy Führer, Rudolf Hess, flew to Scotland intending to contact the Duke of Hamilton and through him persuade the British to accept peace with Hitler in exchange for the restoration of Germany's former colonies. Hitler knew nothing of this scheme, which was a product of Hess's private delusions.

Tuesday 13th May

Gladwyn says that Ismay was able today to give him half an hour. He and the Chiefs of Staff are most delighted over Hess.[1] The P.M. has been thinking and talking of nothing else, and therefore they are free, for once, to carry on the war.

Gladwyn, Wilmot and I dine together. Gladwyn says he has overheard, but must not repeat to me, who was the 'Scottish personality' whom Hess had said he had come to see. I say, 'Was it Lord Brocket or the Duke of Buccleuch?'[2] Gladwyn says he mustn't answer. I say, 'Very well, I shall put it about that it was the Duke of Buccleuch.' Returning to the Ministry I find Bowes-Lyon and McCorquodale[3] outside. The latter says that it was the Duke of Hamilton.[4] He knows this from a man who travelled down by the night train to see Andrew Duncan and who heard it from people who were standing drinks to the ploughman who picked Hess up.

1 Rudolf Hess (b. 1894). Deputy Führer of Germany 1933–41. Tried at Nuremberg and imprisoned at Spandau.
2 W. J. Montagu-Douglas-Scott, 8th Duke of Buccleuch (1894–1973). Conservative M.P. 1923–35.
3 Malcolm McCorquodale, later 1st Baron (1901–71). Conservative M.P. for Sowerby 1931–45; Epsom 1947–55. Junior minister 1942–5.
4 D. Douglas-Hamilton, 14th Duke of Hamilton (1903–73). Served in the R.A.F. 1939–45. Conservative M.P. 1930–40.

After the destruction of the old Chamber, the House of Commons met at
Church House, Westminster. One of the first debates in the new venue was
on the work of Dalton's department.

Wednesday 14th May

My vote is taken in secret session in the miserable 'annexe' at Church
House. The House was in a bad mood, 'an odious mood', as Butler
said to someone. First a long wrangle as to whether the sitting should
be secret or not. This was started by Clement Davies, who is increasingly sour, self-important and intriguing. This grumble was
supported by Winterton,[1] Maxton[2] and a few others. Attlee, who was
leading the House, pointed out that last Thursday, when business for
this week was announced, he had stated that this vote would be taken
in secret session and that no one had raised any objection. This, of
course, was true. Half an hour was wasted with this nonsense before
I was able to get going. This brought us up to 12.25. I did not finish
till 1.55. During this hour and a half I spoke at length and answered,
with great restraint and politeness, a large number of questions, mostly
very stupid. As seen from within a Government Department, especially mine, the House at large appears as a monkey house of utterly
ignorant and ill-conditioned amateurs. I gave them the plain facts
about the Marseilles and Siberian leaks,[3] though most of this was
known before. They fastened on the Marseilles leak and the failure to
enforce our blockade at the Straits. They completely failed to take
my points about Anglo-American co-operation and new methods for

1 E. Turnour, 6th Earl Winterton (Irish peerage) (1883–1962). Conservative M.P. for
   Horsham and Worthing 1918–45; Horsham 1904–18, 1945–51. Junior minister
   1922–4, 1924–9. Chancellor of the Duchy of Lancaster 1937–9. Paymaster-General
   1939.
2 James Maxton (1885–1946). Labour M.P. 1922–32, I.L.P. M.P. 1932–46, for Glasgow Bridgeton. Chairman of the I.L.P. 1926–31, 1934–9.
3 Marseilles and Siberian leaks in the blockade. Since August 1940, the Trans-
   Siberian railway had become virtually the only channel of supplies to Germany
   from the Pacific region – a leak which, however, the British were unable to stop.
   Meanwhile, during the winter of 1940–41, the blockade had almost completely
   broken down in relation to merchant shipping passing to and from ports in unoccupied France, because of the inability of the Admiralty to spare warships to intercept in the Mediterranean, and because of a reluctance to provoke incidents with
   the French navy elsewhere. It was estimated that in the five months ending 1st
   March 1941, ships carrying some 1,750,000 tons of cargo had unloaded at Marseilles.
   A substantial part of this was removed to Germany (see Medlicott, *The Economic
   Blockade*, vol. I, pp. 557 ff.).

relieving the Navy. I demolished the nonsense recently put out in the _Financial News_ and the _Tribune_ about oil stocks in Spain, had a reasonably good run on Relief, and on the German economic situation. I quoted at some length what I had said last year about oil, emphasising my three conditions: (1) large-scale using up of oil by the enemy war machine, (2) continued heavy attacks by the R.A.F. on oil targets, and (3) our continuing to hold the Eastern Mediterranean. It was only on these three conditions, the first two of which have not been fulfilled, that I had said, ten months ago, that the enemy would be in very grave difficulties as to oil in a period to be measured in months, and not in years.

German oil stocks now, none the less, in my considered view, based on the advice of experts, not only of my own but of other Departments, were dangerously low. As Germans improve the Romanian and Yugoslav railways, and still more if they get the sea route round the south of Greece, enemy oil stocks might soon begin to rise again.

Many members received my speech as a cold douche. I am doubtful how my own reputation was affected. At the time, all was so gloomy that I came out pessimistic – as well as a little weary, for I sat through almost the whole thing, only going out for a quarter of an hour for a glass of beer and a sandwich in my room upstairs. But my scouts, Wilmot and others, say that many members thought that I had done well. (This was also the view of my three M.E.W. Peers (Drogheda, Farrer[1] and Hawke[2]) who sat up in the Gallery.) Certainly the chief disapprobation was manifested towards Alexander. At last they had the point that if the blockade was not working, it was primarily because the Navy was not intercepting enemy ships. ...

First K. Lindsay[3] and later the ineffable Cunningham-Reid[4] asked me whether my Department had any responsibility for propaganda to the enemy. I was able to say, 'No, my Department has nothing to do with this.' The second time, I said, 'That is the responsibility of the Minister of Information.' For tomorrow a question has been put asking the P.M. who is responsible. I am inclined to be rather pleased at this, for responsibility for overt broadcasts will now, I hope, be publicly fastened on Duff Cooper. Attempts have been made lately

1 C. C. Farrer, 3rd Baron (1893–1948). Head of Blockade Department at M.E.W.
2 B. W. Hawke, 9th Baron (b. 1901). M.E.W. 1940–43. Government Whip 1943–5.
3 K. Lindsay (b. 1897). Independent National M.P. for Kilmarnock Burghs 1933–45. Independent M.P. for English Universities 1945–50. Junior minister 1935–40.
4 A. S. Cunningham-Reid (1895–1977). Conservative, then Independent Conservative, M.P. for Marylebone 1932–45; Conservative M.P. for Warrington 1922–3, 1924–9.

to try to involve me in this particularly vulnerable activity.

Thence, rather gloomily, to Claridge's where a large reception has been organised by Bowes-Lyon for the British-Dominion Press. They arrive in large numbers and all seem delighted to have been asked. I am conscious of being now in very good form, receiving them all at the entrance, remembering lots of their names and peculiarities, and saying what are called 'a few well chosen words' to most of them.

Thereafter I am carried off by my three Secretaries, Wilmot, Gaitskell and Hancock, to a birthday party arranged by them in my honour at Scotts.[1] This celebrates one year of my administration at the M.E.W. I recall how, on a certain Wednesday at Bournemouth, where I was looking after the last stages of the Labour Party Conference, after a short telephone conversation with the new P.M. in which I was offered, and accepted, M.E.W., I rang up Ruth and asked her to ring up Gaitskell and order him, on my behalf, to wait for me from midnight onwards at my flat, where, half an hour after midnight, I arrived and invited him to become my *chef de cabinet*.

Dalton's SO1 propaganda activities were not officially acknowledged, and his responsibility in this sphere was not generally known to M.P.s or journalists. Hence much embarrassment was caused by the Prime Minister's statement on 15th May.

Thursday 15th May
Great commotion over a supplementary answer given by the P.M. in the House about propaganda in enemy countries. Asked by Neil Maclean[2] what minister was responsible for this, P.M. first replied that several ministers assisted in this important work and H.M.G. took collective responsibility for them. Asked to whom, then, questions should be addressed, P.M. said – most guardedly – either to the Minister of Information or to the Minister of Economic Warfare. Pressed further, he said that if there was any doubt as to who should answer, he would do it himself.

This was really a most frightful gaffe by Churchill. He has never really focused my role in propaganda, nor, apparently, appreciated that for ten months my name has never been mentioned or admitted

1 'Scotts': a restaurant in Coventry Street.
2 Neil Maclean (1875–1953). Labour M.P. for Glasgow Govan 1918–50.

in Parliament or the press as having anything to do with it. I am told that when he made this reply, the House was pretty full, but not a great deal of interest was taken in it. There will, however, certainly be much further bother. He has dropped a bomb through my head cover and we shall now have to put on some new substitute roof.

I went round to see him at the close of the Cabinet this morning with a draft statement which, had he been willing to make it, would have planted responsibility for answering all permissible questions in Parliament on the Ministry of Information, while ruling out many on grounds of public interest. This draft of mine also contained the statement that the Foreign Secretary and I maintain touch with the Ministry of Information in order that all aspects, political and economic, of this work should be properly co-ordinated.

The P.M. did not, however, like this idea at all. He had obviously not focused the problem in any degree, for he said to me in some surprise, 'I had no idea that you had refused to answer questions in Parliament about this.' He said that he would consider issuing any further statement but that, if questions were asked, we must deal with them when they come. He appeared to me to have no sense at all of the secrecy of what I was doing.

I spoke afterwards to Attlee who said that he had been horrified and astonished when the P.M. gave this supplementary answer, but that it was then too late to stop him. He undertook to say something to the P.M. that evening about the difficult situation which had been created. I said, rather angrily, that the P.M. took no interest at all in this particular branch of my work and regarded it as a bloody bone which had been thrown to me in order to appease the Labour Party. Attlee said that he did not think this was so, and added that the P.M. had only last week said that he thought I was doing a very good job of work. I was not much mollified by this.

Hess and Syria[1] have rather overshadowed this nonsense for today, but, following up, Gladwyn invites himself to dine this evening with the P.M.'s secretariat, whom both he and I blame for their failure to keep the P.M. properly informed and on his guard upon this question. The P.M.'s Private Secretaries, Gladwyn and I agree, are a very poor

1 Early in May, Admiral Darlan negotiated an agreement with the Germans to grant the German Air Force landing facilities in Syria. On 14th May, the R.A.F. was authorised to act against German aircraft in Syria and on French airfields. On 15th May, Eden stated in the House of Commons that aircraft sent by the Germans to Iraq had been allowed by the French authorities to use Syrian aerodromes as staging posts. The British government had accordingly taken 'appropriate action'. The same night Marshal Pétain announced in a broadcast that France had been forced to seek an understanding with Germany and to collaborate both in Europe and Africa with Hitler.

lot indeed and it is astonishing that he is content with them. The only one with any personality is Colville, and he is very self-opinionated. Seal, the No. 1, is shortly leaving for the U.S.A. on some naval job. Gladwyn reports later in the evening that he rubbed it in to them as much as he could, but could only do so after dinner, as the P.M.'s brother[1] was present at the meal and this prevented all intimate conversation.

I shall try to get this straightened out, as much as it *can* be straightened out, at the meeting at the Foreign Office tomorrow with Eden and Cooper.

A rumpus with Mr Leathers, who thinks he is going to turn M.E.W. out of the present building without any discussion with me at all. I have arranged for the Office of Works to requisition Lansdowne House just across the Square, and, if necessary, many of us can go in there. But it would be much better for us to remain where we are and for Leathers's additional staff to go to Lansdowne House. Anyhow, the thing must be discussed between us, but he impudently contends that a decision has already been reached at a meeting at which he, Attlee and Anderson were present, though I was not, and though I have received no official notice in writing, nor has Sir Frederick Leith-Ross, of any decision at all on the matter. Hearing of Leathers's refusal to meet me, I ask Attlee whether any decision was taken. He says Certainly not. They only had a preliminary discussion and it was understood that Leathers and I would go into the matter together.

I therefore get Leathers on the telephone and speak to him with some clarity. I ask whether he does not think it an extraordinary thing that any decision on a matter affecting me should have been taken in his presence but in my absence. I also tell him what Attlee said to me and remind him that Attlee is not only a personal friend and colleague of mine but also the Deputy Prime Minister. I say further, 'When you and I have been colleagues a little longer and have got to know each other a little better, you will discover it is no good trying to bluff me in this sort of way. I want this matter discussed on a business basis (I thought this was rather a good line with *him*!) with all the facts and figures in front of us.' Finally, therefore, he agrees to a meeting on Saturday morning at 10 a.m.

The demarcation dispute between M.E.W. and M.O.I. over the handling of propaganda continued to rage. In December 1940 Dalton had asked Cooper

1 Major J. S. S. Churchill (1880–1947). Serving in the Territorial Army Reserve.

to hand over open propaganda broadcasting. Subversion, he claimed, was a single subject. Cooper refused, while agreeing that propaganda policy should be handled as a single entity. He suggested instead that it should all be incorporated into M.O.I. The Prime Minister asked the Lord President, Sir John Anderson, to arbitrate. To Dalton's chagrin, Anderson recommended that the present situation should be maintained, with a continuation of the existing distinction between 'covert' and 'overt' propaganda. But the dispute remained unresolved. On 16th May Eden, Dalton and Duff Cooper met Anderson in order to reach a final agreement. The result was the so-called 'Anderson Award'. The overt/covert distinction would be kept; and, in addition, Eden, Dalton and Cooper would form a Ministerial Committee, each with a senior official in order to provide co-operation. This, however, did not end the quarrel – which continued throughout Dalton's period of responsibility for covert propaganda.

Friday 16th May
Meeting at Foreign Office with Anderson, Eden and Duff Cooper. Before going up, I have a word with Van, who urges me not to lose my temper with Cooper, particularly if he shows signs of losing his with me first and thereby putting himself in the wrong. I square Anderson, I hope, in the Private Secretary's Room before the meeting. I say that I am tired of silly squabbles with Cooper and am quite prepared (1) for the status quo and (2) co-ordination under the Foreign Office.

At the ministerial meeting which follows, Cooper is isolated, 3 to 1, and plays his cards very badly. He says he wants everything now done by my No. 1. Branch. He says that I 'bitterly resent' any criticism and that, in our various scraps, 'the Minister of Economic Warfare always begins it'. This does not make a great impression on the other two. As to co-ordination, Cooper says he thinks the committee now meeting in the Ministry of Information does it. I say no, it is symbolically important to put the committee in the Foreign Office, under a Foreign Office chairman. Both the others agree with this. Anderson is to make a note of our conclusions. When agreed, this is to go to the P.M.

Eden then takes me aside and says that he is afraid this may come upon me as a bombshell, but he is thinking of offering Rio to Leeper. He wants to promote men of ability to Ambassadorial power. He then asks in Cadogan and it is agreed that I should first sound Leeper. Perhaps it may be in the national interest, Eden says, that he should stay where he is. On the other hand, he should not be passed over, and an Ambassador's pension will mean something to him, since he has no private means. Eden adds that, if he goes, I can, of course, have 'anyone you like' from the Foreign Office to take his place. He hints that I might like Stevenson[1] (but of course I shouldn't).

Later talk to Gladwyn about this. I am clear that if Leeper goes, Gladwyn should become responsible for both branches, with a good man at No. 1, the opposite number to Nelson. This might be 'Dixon[2] or Locksley,[3] though both of these are a little young. This, apart from making a better chart, would be a good means of getting rid of 'fissi-parous' tendencies.

Saturday 17th May

Meeting with Leathers on accommodation, three officials aside being also present. He has been trying to dodge a meeting with me and to pretend that a 'decision' has been taken that I should clear out and leave him the whole building. When, having routed him on the tele-phone, I succeed in getting down to a 'business basis' and facts and figures are produced, it is quite clear that Berkeley Square House plus Lansdowne House will more than accommodate our joint staffs, but that Lansdowne House will not accommodate all mine. Therefore, either I remain where I am and he takes Lansdowne House, which I propose, or, in some degree, I, as well as he, am split and give him part of my space, taking part of Lansdowne House in return. It is revealed that the Ministry of Shipping are packed much less tightly than my people, and that the top floor is practically untenanted, for fear of air-raids! It is finally agreed that we should go to a conference with Anderson and Attlee.

I row Gladwyn violently, both before and after lunch, on SO2. I make an *aide-mémoire* afterwards on some of what I said. Too many businessmen; too little political gumption, and biases against the Left; an inefficient machine wherein my Minutes are lost or disregarded; failure to keep me informed of what is going on; a loss of interest by all except me in the Liberator; too many 'smooth-faced explanations'; failure to get the right man to take over my Middle East show. The truth is the war is going rather badly and all these things are shown up sharply as a consequence.

In the afternoon to West Leaze in a most black mood.

1 R. C. S. Stevenson, later Sir Ralph (1895–1977). Diplomat. Minister to Uruguay 1941–3.
2 P. J. Dixon, later Sir Pierson (1904–65). Foreign Office 1940–43. Allied Forces H.Q. Mediterranean 1943. Principal Private Secretary to the Foreign Secretary 1943–8. Permanent Representative at the U.N. 1954–60. Ambassador to France 1960–64.
3 Presumably Peter Loxley (1905–45). Diplomat. First Secretary, seconded to M.E.W. 1939–41. Private Secretary, later Principal Private Secretary, to Sir Alexander Cadogan, June 1941–February 1945, when Loxley was killed in an air crash while travelling to the Potsdam Conference.

Sunday 18th May
Having gone to bed and sleep just after 10 last night, I wake up at 7.30 this morning and then snoozle on again till 11, when breakfast is produced, thus sleeping round the clock. The rest of the day I spend in the garden, getting up three stubs, making a bonfire, and trimming my trees. This makes me feel much better.

Monday 19th May
Conference on Accommodation with Anderson, Attlee and Leathers. Much arguing backwards and forwards. Finally I say I will move 400 of my people from the third floor and let him have that.

Leeper to see me. I tell him that Eden will offer him Rio. His first reaction is quite negative. He is not interested in Ambassadorial gold lace; he feels he is doing a more useful job where he is; his wife's parents are both old, and one of them very infirm, living nearby at Oxford. I tell him to tell no one but his wife, but to discuss with her and then see Eden on Wednesday. Meanwhile I say I do not wish to influence his decision either way, valuing him much where he is now but not wishing to stand in the road of his career, which, moreover, has a more than personal importance. ...

Nelson is back from one week's leave, most unwillingly taken, but looks much the better for it. He, I and C.E.O. dine together and review the week. I say, most sincerely, that I have missed him and that Hambro has not really filled his place, having too many irons in the fire.[1] My fumes are still near the surface and I let fly again about this branch of the show being too much of a businessman's club, and about my Minutes being lost ... and about some of the Country Section Heads being very second-rate.

I hear next morning that C.D. had indigestion and didn't sleep well. I hope it wasn't my fault.

'Rex rang up to say he was ill and could not see Eden tomorrow,' Bruce Lockhart wrote in his diary on 20th May. 'He is worried because Dalton showed no special wish to see him; thinks this is due to intrigue ... '[2]

---

1 'He kept more balls in the air than any man I know,' Dalton wrote later about Hambro. 'In addition to his work for S.O.E., he had his own merchant banking business, was on the Court of the Bank of England and was Chairman of the Great Western Railway.' (FY, p. 369.)
2 Kenneth Young (ed.), *The Diaries of Sir Robert Bruce Lockhart, vol. II 1939–1965*, Macmillan, London, 1980, p. 100.

Wednesday 21st May

Dine at short notice to meet Lord Cecil[1] with Phil and Irene [Noel-Baker]. Cecil is now very deaf and old but still has charm and an affectionate attitude towards me. Last war he was Minister of Blockade, and many of my problems, particularly in Anglo-American relations, are just like his. Thus, before they came in they were furious against our black-list. When they came in, they changed in twenty-four hours and became far more drastic than we had ever been. ...

Leeper cannot come up today. He is in bed with laryngitis, brought on, perhaps, by over-excitement about Rio. So he cannot see Eden for a day or two. I tell Gladwyn to speak to Cadogan and, using judicious language, to hint that Eden might put pressure on Leeper to accept. I have always been in favour of the promotion of younger generations and must not make an exception, even when my own personal interests might be adversely touched.

Thursday 22nd May

Count Karolyi[2] calls, on Kingsley Martin's[3] introduction. Physically a pathetic figure, very lame and hobbling on a stick, and with a split palate, so that, although he clearly knows English very well, he is hardly intelligible. I cannot think that this poor creature could be seriously thought of as a political force in Hungary. His chief reason for coming to see me is to complain that the B.B.C. broadcasts in Hungarian are still pro-Horthy.[4] As if it mattered if they were! Moreover, as I tell him, they are Duff Cooper's responsibility and not mine. He leaves behind, however, a document which, Gaitskell tells me, is pretty spicy and should probably go to M.I.5. I tell Count Karolyi that I will write to Cooper suggesting that he should see him.

I hear that this little pig has now gone to Bognor for three weeks. Meanwhile, I have a most amiable letter from Eden agreeing with my proposed amendments to Anderson's draft note on our meeting *à quatre* last week. ...

Press conference with the Lobby. I tell them of the misdemeanours of Vichy in the economic field, of how the French supply and work for the Germans. This all goes down very well, including the news,

1 Lord E.A.R. Gascoyne-Cecil, 1st Viscount Cecil (1864–1958). President of the League of Nations Union 1923–45. Conservative M.P. 1906–10, 1911–23. Under-Secretary and Assistant Secretary for Foreign Affairs 1915–18. Minister of Blockade 1916–18. Lord Privy Seal 1923–4. Chancellor of the Duchy of Lancaster 1924–7. League of Nations Adviser to the second Labour Government 1929–31.
2 Count M. Karolyi (1875–1955). Leader of the Free Hungarian Movement in London. Prime Minister and then President of the Hungarian Republic 1918–19.
3 B. K. Martin (1897–1969). Editor of the *New Statesman and Nation* 1930–60.
4 N. V. Horthy de Nagbanya (1868–1957). Regent of Hungary 1920–44.

1 Walking to the office, 1st June 1940

2 Diarist. Dictating in the study at Carlisle Mansions, 1940.

3 The Daltons in Battersea Park, 1940. 'What Ruth would really like to do would be to re-plan London.' Ruth was Chairman of the L.C.C. Parks Committee.

above: 4 Lord Halifax at the Foreign Office, 1940
below left: 5 Professor Lindemann in Downing Street, 1940
below right: 6 Herbert Morrison on his way to County Hall, 1940

7 With Czech troops at Leamington, March 1941

which I let out, of the interception of the *Scheherazade*.[1]

We had a great joke in M.E.W. about this ship. I was asked last Saturday by my Lord Drogheda before going off for the weekend, what my view was about stopping her. I said that, since she was carrying American observers as well as oil, I would let her go through, for the Americans, I hoped, would not only 'observe' but also throw their weight about and dish out dollars and make propaganda, and perhaps do other things as well. On my return on Monday morning my Lord Drogheda informed me that over the weekend the Foreign Office had been clamouring for the ship to be stopped, that the Admiralty were panting to send the signal to have her stopped, and that even the poor old State Department had been urging us to stop her. I, therefore, alone stood in the way of this simple act of blockade enforcement. I quickly yielded. I hope the other three partners saw the joke too.

Friday 23rd May

Leeper to see me to say he has refused Rio. I am really a little sorry about this, for it would have simplified many things to put in a younger Foreign Office man to run this side and to give Gladwyn general charge. But that can't be now.

C.D. [Nelson] to see me. I row on about my dissatisfaction with political bias and mishandlings of Danish and French-in-U.S.A. cases. He says that if I feel I have another man who could do better, he will be very glad to resign. He knows that I am worried about the show and does not want me to be worried. I say I have no man in mind who could do better. In C.E.O. and in him I have complete confidence, though further down less confidence in some.

Sunday 25th May

Gaitskell says that Leeper was not at all convinced that I was really sorry he had refused Rio. Gaitskell said that I was always like this and never exercised undue influence on anyone, least of all to keep them if they could do better for themselves elsewhere.

At a meeting of the War Cabinet on 26th May, the Foreign Secretary informed colleagues that the American government wished to continue to

1 'the *Scheherazade*': a French oil tanker en route from the U.S.A. to Vichy-controlled North Africa. After discussion with the Americans, the British eventually agreed to let it through on condition that the oil was to be consumed only on French territory, and that its distribution was to be supervised by American consular officers.

provide economic assistance to the pro-Vichy authorities in North Africa. The Prime Minister felt that the consignments involved were not of great consequence, and was not inclined to take a very stiff line on the matter. Dalton, however, argued that while a number of the commodities it was proposed to send (e.g. sugar and tea) were quite harmless, this did not apply to the cargo of the *Scheherezade*, which was carrying 13,000 tons of oil.[1]

Monday 26th May

Go to Cabinet on question of American supplies for North Africa. We still hear hopeful tales – the Americans always think them more hopeful than we do – of French resistance in this area. Agreed to go on leaving the playing of this hand primarily to the Americans, since North and West Africa is the area in which they will probably begin to make war, but to suggest to them that sugar and tea are more harmless supplies, in case things go wrong, than oil. Bracken, whom I meet just outside the Cabinet door, says that the failure of Roosevelt to speak clearly, or to act, is getting people down. We are always told that he must not get in front of his own public opinion, but the question is will he get in front of Hitler?

Gladwyn tells me that Rex Leeper told him at lunch today that the night when the news came through that the *Hood* was sunk and the *Bismarck* had escaped,[2] Alexander went down to his shelter beneath the Admiralty and played on the harmonium which he keeps there 'Oh God our help in ages past'.

At Cabinet the Beaver makes a row about propaganda to America. We should give the U.S. more news. General sense of gloom. A convoy has been sunk in the Atlantic; we have had heavy naval losses in the Mediterranean (two cruisers and four destroyers sunk and two battleships hit in the 'sea defile' north of Crete); the *Hood* sunk and the *Bismarck* still at large.

Thus, says the P.M., the Germans have established a 'unit superiority' over us. This is the most injurious and distressing naval incident since we missed the *Goeben*.[3]

See Eden over co-ordination of propaganda in Middle East. His letter to me on this subject had painted the picture of a most re-

---

1 PRO, CAB 65/18.
2 H.M.S. *Hood*, Britain's largest and fastest capital ship, was sunk in the Denmark Straits by the German battleship *Bismarck*, the most powerful vessel afloat, in the early hours of 24th May. *Bismarck* did not, however, escape for long. She was sunk on 27th May, after the Fleet Air Arm had destroyed her steering gear with torpedoes.
3 The *Goeben* was a German battle cruiser.

markable man – 'almost ministerial rank', high standing, great experience, first-hand knowledge of the area, etc. I said, 'I suppose you drew this picture with some particular man in mind. Who is he?' He replied, 'How shrewd you are! This draft came up to me from the Department, who went on to suggest Harold Nicolson, but I don't think he would do, do you?' So he had left the description but left out the name! I said I quite agreed, he wouldn't do. He was wetter than the wettest sponge in the fullest bath. I then suggested Burnett-Stuart[1] – whom he didn't like because he had opposed an Expeditionary Force for France, didn't get on with Wavell, and was anyhow too old; Mason Mac[2] – whom he liked but thought was too good for this job; Butler – whom he said he didn't think he could spare, and who might not think the job was good enough for him, counting in due course on having a Department of his own here; and, without much enthusiasm, Pat Hastings,[3] since a lawyer would have some useful qualifications. I said that on the whole I should prefer a soldier, particularly as I thought that there should be high-level co-ordination, not only of propaganda, but of subversion. He said he would think about names and suggested that I should have a word with Dill. He showed me a private wire from Wavell to Dill saying that Special Operations in Middle East was 'a racket'.

This last word excited C.E.O. when I told him and he was all for my seeing Dill at once. Otherwise, he thought, the word would go round and round.

Tuesday 27th May

Mrs Churchill visits M.E.W. to inspect some of our German trophies, e.g. airmen's flying suits and other garments, medicine chests captured from German ships etc. These come to M.E.W. for testing and analysis of materials. She takes away a small tin box of tablets to be taken 'to prevent fear'. The box was about half empty.

Lunch with Drogheda. Van and the Belgian Ambassador also present. Van looks much better and happier already, the beginnings of a new free man. He will definitely retire on 25th June, when he reaches

1 General Sir John Burnett-Stuart (1875–1958). Colonel Commandant 1st Battalion The Rifle Brigade 1936–45. Home Guard 1940–44. Director of Military Operations and Intelligence at the War Office 1922–6.
2 Lt-General Sir (Frank) Noel Mason MacFarlane (1889–1953). Director of Military Intelligence with the British Expeditionary Force 1939–40. Governor of Gibraltar 1940–42. Head of the British Military Mission to Moscow 1942–4. Chief Commissioner of the Allied Control Commission for Italy 1944. Labour M.P. 1945–6.
3 Sir Patrick Hastings (1880–1952). Barrister. Labour M.P. 1922–6. Attorney-General 1924. Playwright.

sixty. He hopes to come to C.H.Q. about every fortnight and to London about once a week. This will suit me very well.

Harriman brings Cohen to see me and C.E.O. The idea is that Cohen should take a verbal message to the President about my show and suggest that I should send someone over (but not Bearsted, Harriman advised me, though I had no thought of this). Alternatively, and as I should prefer, they would send a good American over here. Harriman says that his message has miscarried and got muddled at the other end. ...

Go with Wilmot and Gaitskell to dine with Mackay,[1] Bob Fraser, whom I have not seen for some while, also being there. Mackay is just back from Australia via the U.S. and tells a most awful story of the rottenness of our propaganda to America. I undertake to put him in touch with the Beaver, who is much concerned about all this, and also hates Cooper.

That we have sunk the *Bismarck* is a bright gleam in a dark sky. We have now got a Rook for a Knight and, being ahead before, ought to be winning this naval chess game.

Wednesday 28th May
Dine at home. Tomorrow Ruth goes to the country for a month.

Friday 30th May
... [S]ee L.P.S. [Lord Privy Seal] [Attlee] and draw from him a little more than usual. He admits that Wavell's credit is fast falling and that he has talked too much of not being able to take on any new commitments in the Middle East. He would have let both Syria and Iraq go, and was even prepared to 'ask Raschid Ali[2] for his terms'. He was overruled, and it is to the credit of Auchinleck,[3] C. in C. in India, that he strongly combated Wavell's line. L.P.S. says that Wavell still thinks in terms of 'defending a line' or 'a perimeter'.

There is also a strong rumour that Monckton has resigned and that the Ministry of Information is breaking up.

I hear that the Duke of Buccleuch said the other night at some Club that he thought we ought to make peace, and that Lord Gort, who was present, leaped to his feet and denounced him in unmeasured terms as a 'decadent Duke' and much else! This is Prince Paul's friend.

---

1 Identification uncertain. Possibly Kim Mackay, q.v., later a Labour M.P.
2 Rashid Ali Al-Gailani. Prime Minister of Iraq 1933, 1940–41; sympathetic to the Axis. Ousted in January, he led an unsuccessful *putsch* in April.
3 General Sir Claude Auchinleck, later Field Marshal (1884–1981). Commander-in-Chief, Middle East 1941–2; India 1941, 1943–7.

4

The War of Words
June–September 1941

Britain's chances of winning the war (or at any rate of not losing it) seemed to improve greatly when the Germans invaded the Soviet Union on 22nd June – though optimism was dampened by the Russian reverses which followed. M.E.W. policy was much simplified by the sealing of the 'Siberian leak', and thereafter managing the blockade became largely administrative routine.

More and more, therefore, Dalton concentrated on his 'other life', leaving blockade policy to look after itself. In Cairo, S.O.E. intrigues and inefficiencies caused Dalton to send a team, headed by Sir Frank Nelson, to sort things out. At home, the appointment of Brendan Bracken as Minister of Information escalated the Whitehall propaganda conflict. For Dalton, this now became the source of bitter frustration and anxiety.

The Germans invaded Crete on 20th May, using parachute and airborne troops. The garrison, consisting of two New Zealand brigades and a few British battalions, was insufficient, and after a week of bitter fighting it was decided to evacuate the island. By 1st June, 16,500 men had been taken safely to Egypt, but the Mediterranean Fleet suffered heavy losses in carrying out the evacuation, and 12,000 troops had to be left behind.

Monday 2nd June
C.D. [Nelson], Wilmot and I dine together, and C.D. says that he has heard disquieting stories about the American view of the P.M. and his entourage. Harriman is not impressed, nor, according to C.D., is the Ambassador, who has flown back with Cohen to report frankly. There is much comment on Crete and on our failure to provide air cover for our ships or our men.

It is said that many important decisions are taken over here late at night and in a state of sozzlement. Also that H.M.[1] and P.M. had words about Crete ten days ago. H.M. insisting on putting a number of questions to which no good answer could be made. A search for a scapegoat is going on and already Longmore[2] has been relieved of his command. Wavell may follow.

Tuesday 3rd June

Labour Party Conference. Majority of more than 120 to 1 in favour of a total victory as a necessary prelude to a just peace. Very good spirit throughout the Conference.

Gaitskell says that Cooper has resigned. It is about time it was true. Address Society of Labour Candidates and tell them

(1) that Himmler[3] has got our published list of their names and that they will all have a sticky time unless we win the war;
(2) that when an election becomes possible, we shall resume our normal competitive political activities, but that, in the mean time, they should throw themselves, each in his own constituency, into the war effort in every possible way;
(3) that we should aim at continuing the present Coalition, not only till victory has been won, but till the foundations of peace have been laid;
(4) that, if they want to win when they fight, they had better not have a khaki election.

Dine with C.E.O. [Gladwyn Jebb] with whom I talk very freely on personal matters, and discuss the possibility of the Germans being so discouraged after defeat that they will have no more children. This would make for a much better Europe!

The 1941 Labour Party Conference opened in London on 2nd June. James Walker was in the chair.

---

1 From the context, it seems clear that this refers to the King.
2 Air Chief Marshal Sir Arthur Longmore (1885–1970). Air Officer, Commander-in-Chief Middle East 1940–41. Inspector-General of the R.A.F. 1941. Retired List 1942.
3 Heinrich Himmler (1900–45). Head of the Gestapo and S.S.

Wednesday 4th June
Labour Party Conference. Most of the steam is out of it today and the delegates not much excited about anything. I move the Executive Committee Memorandum on Peace and Blue Prints for the New Britain. Not an exciting speech either.

National Executive elections. The representation of D.L.P.s [Divisional Labour Parties] is smaller than usual and not very representative. None the less, there is a solid block of voting for the seven of us elected, including Jim Griffiths who, to my regret, takes the place of Wilmot. The latter has been blanketed at a series of conferences now for the past four years, never managing to get a proper start, as he has twice come in as odd man out, replacing first Cripps and then Pritt.[1] Also he has been a bit in public obscurity since he has been with me as P.P.S.

The best change is Alice Bacon,[2] young and eager, for silly old Susan Lawrence,[3] who ought years ago to have had the gumption to retire gracefully. Now she has been heaved out, and serve her right! ...

Am summoned to dine tonight with Their Majesties at Buckingham Palace in day clothes. Also present Anderson, Greenwood, Sinclair, Ernest Brown, Van, Dill and Hardinge, and a Lady in Waiting who seems to come from Northamptonshire and Northern Ireland.

I am never wildly keen on meeting my colleagues *en bloc*, either at Buckingham Palace or elsewhere.

The Queen has a very clear memory of her visit to Bishop Auckland and the Trading Estate, including the point that a number of the factories were run by German refugees.[4]

The King has no use for Vichy and is surprised that the Americans have so long had illusions on this. He also has some bad words to say for Kennedy, the ex-American Ambassador, who, he says, was frightened to death of being bombed the day war began. I tell him some of what I hear from Hall in Washington and the difficulty of getting American Economic Warfare policy properly tied up. ...

Gladwyn says that he dined tonight with Hood, Cooper's Private Secretary, and heard that, unless Cooper can get more powers, he will resign and so will his principal officials. This is less precise than the

---

1 D. N. Pritt (1887–1972). Labour M.P. 1935–40, Independent M.P. 1940–50, for Hammersmith North. Pritt had been expelled from the Labour Party in 1940 for writing in support of the Soviet invasion of Finland.
2 Alice Bacon, later Baroness (b. 1911). Labour M.P. 1945–70. Minister of State at the Home Office 1964–7; Department of Education and Science 1967–70.
3 Susan Lawrence (1871–1947). Labour M.P. 1923, 1926–31. Junior minister 1929–31.
4 Dalton had succeeded in helping a number of German refugees to set up factories in his constituency in the late 1930s, thereby providing badly needed jobs.

story that they had all put in their resignations. Hood[1] also says that Cooper is now inclined to go back on the agreement reached with Anderson, Eden and me. Anderson, however, had told me tonight that he had put in a Minute to the P.M. enclosing, at last, a copy of our agreement.

Thursday 5th June

Lunch with Mrs Phillimore to meet officers of the Allied Navies. I sit between the American and the Greek Naval Attachés. These officers are in charge of a certain Admiral Dickens,[2] who was Naval Attaché at The Hague. He knows Hancock of whom he says he is an imperturbable young man. I say that Foreign Office officials are meant to be like that. He says yes, sometimes too much so, as in the case of 'Mr Bland' who always used to say to him, 'Oh, but how sweet of you my dear!' He thought, and so did I, that such language was not suitable addressed to sailors. I told the story to Gladwyn, who has a poor opinion of N.B.[3] who in turn said that Gladwyn was a careerist. I said that one should vary one's vocabulary more to suit one's audience. Hancock says that Admiral Dickens was always demanding at The Hague a much larger room in which to sit, and that he hears that since his return to the Admiralty this is still his chief complaint.

Evening of Thursday 5th June to morning of Monday 9th June

At West Leaze from which the Stamps[4] have now departed, leaving it to us alone.

This is my longest break for some time, and I return full of energy, equanimity and toleration. It rains a good deal and there is not much sun, but it is good warm growing weather. My beeches are doing particularly well and the white-leaved trees are magnificent in the wind, as are the four Aldenham Crabs flowering red against a dark sky.

What should be done about 'black' propaganda? The Ministry of Information still wanted control of it. Dalton, however, countered the demand for unity of propaganda with his own concept of 'unity of subversion': arguing

1 Samuel Hood, q.v., was Private Secretary to Duff Cooper 1939–41.
2 Admiral Sir Gerald Dickens (1879–1962). Naval Attaché, The Hague 1940. Principal Liaison Officer with Allied Navies 1940.
3 G. N. M. Bland, later Sir Nevile (1886–1972). Minister, The Netherlands 1938–42; Ambassador 1942–8. Private Secretary to the Permanent Under-Secretary at the Foreign Office 1928–35.
4 Mr and Mrs Reginald Stamp, friends of Ruth Dalton.

that sabotage, economic warfare and political warfare should be seen as interdependent activities that needed to be organised jointly.

Monday 9th June

From West Leaze in time for conference before lunch on this afternoon's ministerial meeting on 'information'. I ring up Eden and say that I think it a frightful bore that this meeting is summoned. I thought, I say, that we had all agreed on a co-ordination plan as long ago as 19th May before Cooper fell ill. He agrees that it is a great bore but says that he and Anderson will stand by their agreement if I will too. I say certainly.

Having ascertained that Attlee is also to attend the meeting, I see him just beforehand and put him wise. I press, particularly, the view that there must be unification of subversion, and that this matters much more than unification of propaganda.

We meet at No. 12 Downing Street, where the Beaver now operates. He is in the Chair. Also present Attlee, Anderson, Eden, Cooper and I. Also in attendance Bridges,[1] Monckton and Radcliffe.[2] These last two have come to explain, I suppose, why they want to resign, unless the Ministry of Information can get more powers. They take first the matter interesting me; and Anderson, Eden and I all repeat that we are satisfied with what the Beaver calls 'the Anderson Award'.[3] Cooper says that he dares say it will work but that there really ought to be unity of control of propaganda. Attlee repeats several times that there should be unity of control of subversion. Eden says that he has in mind to appoint an Under-Secretary – it is not quite clear whether he means political or official – in the Foreign Office to look after propaganda.

Go with Gladwyn, gate-crashing at my own request, to dine with Nancy Rodd (née Mitford),[4] sister of Unity[5] and wife of Peter,[6]

1 Sir Edward Bridges, later 1st Baron (1892–1969). Secretary to the Cabinet 1938–46. Permanent Secretary at the Treasury and Head of the Civil Service 1945–56.
2 C. J. Radcliffe, later 1st Baron (1899–1977). Deputy Director-General of the Ministry of Information 1941–2; Director-General 1942–5.
3 The 'Anderson Award': the agreement worked out by Sir John Anderson whereby Eden, Dalton and Cooper formed a Ministerial Committee to sort out differences over propaganda and the overt/covert distinction. See above, pp. 208–9.
4 Nancy Mitford (1904–73). Writer.
5 Unity Mitford (1915–48). Younger sister of Nancy. Friend and admirer of Hitler, who arranged for her to be sent back to Britain from Germany after she had attempted to kill herself following the outbreak of war.
6 Peter Rodd (1904–68). Younger brother of Francis Rodd, 2nd Baron Rennell. Married to Nancy Mitford in 1933. (Marriage dissolved 1958.)

younger brother of Francis Rodd.[1] She is writing a novel called 'Wee Free'. The first chapter of this she gave to Gladwyn and Cynthia and it was shown to many in the Foreign Office and M.E.W. and also to me. I thought it great fun and demanded to meet the authoress. Tonight she has the second chapter, which she reads aloud to us two. We cry pitifully at the efforts in the U.S. of the 'League to Help Britain to Help Herself' and at the continuing social frustration of the Nazi conquerors in England.

She has apparently written four or five novels already, and Gladwyn tells me, is much more Left than I am. She and her husband have a small house near the Regent Canal.

Tuesday 10th June
Parliamentary debate on Crete. It is a difficult defence but the P.M. makes the best of it. Someone says that, as between him and his critics, it is more nearly than usual a drawn battle. No other minister speaks and this is a matter of some adverse comment.

I speak to Duff Cooper for a moment after the speech. He is most exceptionally and unnaturally friendly. He complains that the P.M. has mentioned today the names of many British Regiments who have been fighting in Crete, whereas he has been prevented from doing this by the War Office. He says that there is much to be said for me having control of all enemy propaganda. I reply, as so often recently, that I feel it is no use chasing will-o'-the-wisps of administrative perfection. I am quite sure that the 'Anderson Award' will work quite well. When all this is clear, I will deal with the various points raised by Cooper in recent letters.

Wednesday 11th June
Attend weekly Labour Party Meeting at the Annexe. Not very exciting. Attlee passes me this note –

Two women talking: 'There's one thing about this 'ere bombing, it does take your mind off the bloody war.'

[Haydn] Davies calls to tell me of his luncheon last Thursday (5th June) with the Beaver. He went as Industrial Correspondent of the *Star*. A dozen of the other leading Industrial Correspondents were there. The meal came to an end without the host having said anything at all interesting, though he had drunk a lot of whisky. Norman

1 F. J. R. Rodd (1895–1978). Became 2nd Baron Rennell in 1941. M.E.W. Italian Section 1940.

Robson,[1] of the Starmer Press, then asked why they had been invited. The Beaver then began to talk about production. Everything is all right now, he said. The P.M. had put him in charge of priorities, and he was settling all disputes. He then launched forth into a tirade against his colleagues collectively. The P.M., he said, was a grand fellow, but who had he got to help him? Almost nobody at all! He did what he could, but who else was there? There was Alexander and you could search the seven seas and not find a better First Lord. Then there was Herbert Morrison, a clever little chap who was not doing his job too badly. And then there was Eden. But as for all the rest – ! Bevin, for instance, was very little use, though now and again he had flashes of insight and might be worth keeping for that alone.

After this comradely declaration, the Beaver was asked just what the Minister of State did. He answered, 'I am not Deputy Prime Minister. I am not in charge of the Home Front. That is supposed to be Attlee's job. I just help the Prime Minister with anything he wants done.' Then, said Davies, there was a long pause and a silence lasting at least ten seconds. Then they saw that the Beaver was weeping. And then he said, in a broken voice and wiping the tears from his eyes, 'I never wanted to leave the Ministry of Aircraft Production. I loved that job. Don't believe anyone who tells you that I left it of my own free will. I never wanted to be made Minister of State. I wanted to have a Department that would help to win the war.' And then he rose from his seat and rushed from the room, leaving his guests sitting at the table. They waited for a little while to see if he would return, and then themselves rose to go. But as they passed through the adjoining room, there was the Beaver, quite recovered, standing on the hearth-rug. 'Now boys, let's have some more drinks before you go,' he said. And so, soon after, ended what Davies thought a most odd party.

There has been an agitation going on for a little while to build up the Beaver and to make him appear as the P.M.'s No. 2 and successor if any ill should befall him. But, as I pointed out to some who thought his succession was a danger, he would be nothing but for the P.M.'s favour, and nothing if the P.M. disappeared. None the less, he is up to no good and cannot cease from intriguing. 'He is a sick old crook,' said my C.E.O. to me when I told him Davies's account.

I reported this Beaver lunch story to Attlee this evening and hotted him up a bit over it. I said that this sort of thing must be stopped, and he said he would speak to the P.M. about it. I think he will. He said that the Beaver had quite failed to organise M.A.P. [Ministry of

---

1 Norman Robson (1897–1969). Deputy London Editor, and chief of leader-writing staff, Westminster Press 1933–48; Editor 1948–62.

Aircraft Production] and *had* left it at his own desire. Indeed, he had been trying to get out for some time. He was a frightful humbug in personal relations, always flattering his colleagues to their faces. I said that I also heard that Bevan, who frequented the Beaver's parties, got to know much too much about what went on inside. I gave an illustration concerning the proposal to suppress the *Daily Mirror* recently. I said that I thought a united front against the Beaver might soon have to be formed.

...

I also spoke to Attlee about Cooper and suggested, passing on here a bright thought of Gladwyn, that [Thomas] Johnston would make a good successor. Attlee agreed, though he thought Johnston was very wedded to Scotland. He said that Cooper ought to be put into a siding, and the Chancellor[ship] of the Duchy of Lancaster seemed to indicate itself. The present occupant [1] was no use, bored the P.M. to tears, and had been one of the worst influences on his predecessor. Six months before we went to war, Hankey had said that he would sack any member of his staff (then Cabinet Secretariat plus C.I.D. [Committee of Imperial Defence]) who dared to express the view that we should be at war within a year. ...

This morning's *Daily Mail* carries a story that Bowes-Lyon was 'nominated' and 'backed' by the Ministry of Information for a job in the U.S.A. in connection with propaganda. It is also stated that he is at M.E.W. and that 'some Government advisers' had advised against his appointment. I ask Bowes-Lyon about this and he says that a rumour has been going around for some time but that some at the Foreign Office, notably David Scott [2] who, I hear, is soon to be retired, have been much against it. Scott said that the King had formally objected to any member of the Royal Family going abroad in wartime. Bowes-Lyon had rung up H.M. last weekend and had been told that this was the first H.M. had heard of it, so Bowes-Lyon told him that he hoped he would make a row with the Foreign Office about it. I said that it was most odd that I had heard nothing about it. Should I take it up with Cooper and make complaint? Bowes-Lyon said that he thought Cooper was getting so deep in the ...... (he used a most crude expression) that it would really be almost too unkind to tackle him about it. I therefore arranged for Leith-Ross to tackle Monckton. The answer given by the latter is that they had only taken preliminary soundings with the Foreign Office and with Halifax and that I should,

1 Lord Hankey, q.v., Chancellor of the Duchy of Lancaster from 14th May to 20th July 1941, when he was replaced by Duff Cooper.
2 Assistant Under-Secretary of State, q.v.

of course, have been formally approached if these had been favourable. But Halifax, they say, was decisively against it. This is a typical story of Ministry of Information humbug.

Bowes-Lyon says that he hears that both last night and the night before Cooper was 'Oxford drunk'.

I say to Mrs Dean[1] that I am afraid she must get a very lurid view of Government from this diary. I tell her that Gaitskell said to me after a month or two, 'I had no idea that it would be all like this.'

Thursday 12th June

Honours list appears in which, since Hall refused a C.M.G., I have only one O.B.E. (J. W. Nicholls) and one M.B.E. (Thomas Wilson)[2] plus Hambro, described as a Banker, with a K.B.E. But the Foreign Office can think of no worthier recipient of their one C.M.G. for the office, as distinct from the field, than Palsy mi.[3]! This makes me very angry and my first inclination is to write something about it. But I am wisely advised to do no more than speak of it, if opportunity should arise, to Eden, who, after all, resigned on Italy. A civil servant with a worse record, from the point of view of his present Chief's policy, could not be found in all that dreary office. It reflects no credit on Cadogan to have pushed this name.

Bowes-Lyon who also takes this Honour very ill, having once lived for a fortnight in the same flat with this brother-in-law of his[4] and been unable to bear it any more, says that 'there's a lot of dirt in the Foreign Office' and that Palsy mi. and also Makins and 'that second-rater', Cadogan, are still talking appeasement. 'Don't bomb Italy', they say, and 'We must have a strong Germany after the war'. He says that my stock is pretty high in many Conservative circles. This follows my saying that I don't trust the Beaver to fight the war through to the end. He warmly agrees.

The press this morning is full of reflections of an amazing harangue delivered yesterday by Cooper to the Lobby correspondents.

It consisted largely of an attack on Eden and the Foreign Office. Blazing with anger, he declared that the appointment of Sir Malcolm

---

1 Mrs Margaret Dean. Dalton's diary secretary 1937–44.
2 Thomas Wilson (b. 1916). Ministry of Economic Warfare and Ministry of Aircraft Production 1940–42. Prime Minister's Statistical Branch 1942–5. Fellow of University College, Oxford 1946–58.
3 Identified by Dalton in the margin as Philip Nichols, q.v. 'Palsy mi.' is a reference to Prince Paul of Yugoslavia ('Prince Palsy'), to whom Nichols was presumably to be compared. (See entry for 29th May 1940 on p. 29.)
4 Philip Nichols's wife Phyllis, née Spender-Clay, and Bowes-Lyon's wife Rachel, were sisters.

Robertson[1] as Chairman of the British Council had been made and announced by Eden without any consultation with him, but only with the P.M. He declared that 'If there is to be a Minister of Information at all', he must have a seat in the War Cabinet in his own right and control all the news. He said that the Beaver was looking into the whole question and, pending his report next week, those of his leading officials who have offered their resignations would hold their hand. He seems to have said that he had no quarrel with, or complaint against, M.E.W., with whom he had excellent working arrangements.

I thus begin to find myself in a rather amusing and temporarily satisfactory position, though some of my advisers think that Cooper has in no way changed his attitude of hostility towards me and my doings but is only 'containing' me while he fights his main battle with the Foreign Office and Service Departments.

Cripps comes to see me on his first return to England from Moscow. ... He too speaks ill of the Foreign Office and of Halifax, but pays me and M.E.W. a compliment for giving quick decisions and being well organised. I don't know whether this is sincere.

Freeman[2] to dine with C.E.O. [Jebb] and Hambro. He seems well disposed, but I do not trust him very far. He says that Portal[3] has gone sick and thrown all the work on *him*. He says that it is impossible to stand the jamborees with the P.M. lasting up to two or three in the morning. I say that others should imitate the P.M. in going to bed for two hours in the afternoon.

On 16th June, Eden offered Robert Bruce Lockhart, head of the Czech bureau at SO1 and liaison officer to the Czech provisional government, the job of co-ordinating propaganda policy – representing the Foreign Office on the tripartite committee under the terms of the Anderson Award. Lockhart accepted on 19th June, on condition that he be made a Deputy Under-Secretary. This led, a few months later, to his appointment as Director-General of the new Political Warfare Executive.

Monday 16th June
Middle East Committee at Foreign Office. C.E.O. accompanies me.

1 Sir Malcolm Robertson (1877–1951). Conservative M.P. for Mitcham 1940–45.
2 Air Chief Marshal Sir Wilfrid Freeman, later 1st Bart (1888–1953). Vice Chief of Air Staff 1940–42. Chief Executive of the Ministry of Aircraft Production 1942–5.
3 Air Chief Marshal Sir Charles Portal, later 1st Viscount (1893–1971). Chief of Air Staff 1940–45.

Many names are suggested to direct propaganda, etc., in the Middle East. None find much favour. ...

Eden after the meeting tells me that he is thinking of inviting Lockhart to represent him on the Officials Committee under the Anderson Award. I say that I think this would be a very good appointment. He runs out of the room after Cooper, to ask his view and comes back looking a little crest-fallen. Cooper had said that of course Lockhart was a first-class man but that Eden was getting 'too many people in here' to deal with propaganda.

Attlee asks urgently to see me just after lunch. He is a little disconcerted because, having reported the Beaver to the P.M. on the basis of what I had told him for disloyalty to colleagues, the Beaver is now producing signed statements by journalists who were at his lunch that he said nothing against any Labour ministers. I therefore send for Davies whom we cross-examine. He gives, I confess, not quite the same account now as he gave before. He now says that the Beaver said of Attlee, 'He gives wise guidance.' Davies says that he has already been asked to sign, and has signed, the statement to which Attlee refers. I say that the point was, not so much that some Labour ministers were spoken ill of, though there is still some evidence of this, e.g. Bevin, but that, commenting on colleagues, no matter of what Party, to the press, the Beaver, by not mentioning the vast majority, had conveyed the impression that he thought they were very little good. Davies's backslide is slightly embarrassing and illustrates that he is always inclined to exaggerate and get things out of focus. However, when he has left us, Attlee says knowingly, 'They have frightened him', and there, for the moment, we leave it. ...

At 9.45 p.m. to the Defence Committee to present a report of the Hankey Committee on oil for the enemy. The P.M. is most benevolent tonight, smiling upon all. He says that the Air Staff must give old Hankey what he wants, namely at least one very heavy attack on the two principal oil plants in the west. Portal, who looks drawn and ill – Gladwyn says that at his Club he never speaks to anyone and has become neurotic under the strain – says that the Air Staff have changed their view about the vulnerability of oil targets. They now hold that these are not good targets, in the sense of being self-destructive, as at first was hoped. Moreover, most of them have very little 'near miss value', being situated in remote places. The argument is now thought – and here the C.I.G.S. agrees – to be much more in favour of attacking enemy communications. Smiling at me, the P.M. says, in reply to my remark that the Danube is, I am afraid, free again now, 'Never mind, you blocked it for two months. That was good.' ...

Pick up in the Map Room Morton, very pleased with his C.B. on which I have congratulated him and he has replied fulsomely. We go up to his room and he gives me a long account of Hess. He blames Eden for sitting on this news so long. The apple, he thinks, is beginning to go rotten. According to his account, which Gladwyn, to whom I relate it, says is not at all new, since all this came out in the first three days of the questioning of Hess, the latter was completely astonished to find that we were not all starving and cowering in dugouts. He freely admitted to his astonishment and added that, if it had been Goering, [1] he would have committed suicide on discovering the truth. Hess had felt himself rather losing favour with Hitler lately and being left out of important conversations. Therefore he determined to come over here in order to bring back to Hitler what he most wanted, namely, the conditions on which we would make peace. Hess said that the ground plan of *Mein Kampf* remains unchanged. Russia was the enemy, but England, if she wishes, might still be the friend of Germany. Germany would take the Continent of Europe and England might have the rest of the world. Only some evil influences, in both countries, had deflected us from paths of co-operation and had, temporarily, led Hitler to follow other tactics than those which he had laid down in *Mein Kampf*. Hess thought that it would be a terrible mistake if English and Germans went on bombing each other when they might divide the world between them. He had come to the Duke of Hamilton because he was firmly convinced that, behind the façades of Parliament and Free Press, it was really the King and his Dukes who ruled England. Therefore, he must make a contact with one of this inner circle. He had, it seemed, a morbid fear of being poisoned. By whom? By the English? No, of course not, they are an honourable people. By the Jews? No, of course not, not in England. 'You know how to deal with Jews.' Then by whom? It seems by German émigrés, for whom the Nazi leaders have a haunting fear, looking forward to a day of retribution in their own country.

Tuesday 17th June

See Lockhart and urge him to accept Eden's offer to be Under-Secretary at the Foreign Office in charge of propaganda. This, I hope, would mean a perfect tie-up of the officials under the Anderson Award. I find him rather irritatingly reluctant. I say that inside the cage he would have much more influence about everything, including his Czechs, than outside. Also that, if later on the Ministry of Information fades out, at least from foreign propaganda, and the Foreign Office takes formal responsibility, I making my own arrangements with

---

1 Hermann Goering (1893–1946). German Air Minister and Commander-in-Chief of the Luftwaffe 1933–45.

them, he will hold a very key position. I also say that with the Foreign Office my relations now are very good, not only with Eden, but, through Gladwyn and Leeper, with the officials.

On leaving me, in a rather excitable condition, as Gaitskell afterwards reports, he says that I 'put it to me the wrong way' in suggesting that this would be a good job for him; also that I don't realise, he thinks, that Gladwyn and Leeper, far from being, as I seem to imagine, two bright lads loved by all at the Foreign Office, have each many enemies. Thus Cadogan cannot bear Leeper, though [Orme] Sargent is in his favour.

I am, however, the keener to get Lockhart because Gladwyn tells me that Sargent is talking of Sir Malcolm Robertson as an alternative. Gladwyn does not seem to see how great a bore this would be, having to handle this loquacious egoist. (Vansittart told me an amusing tale last weekend of Sir Malcolm Robertson who, it appears, has the habit of sitting under the stairs at the St James's Club and gassing on endlessly. One day some soldier, I forget his name, infuriated by this persistent phenomenon, referred in a loud voice as he passed by, to that 'f. . . .ng old bore'. Having overheard this, Sir Malcolm Robertson demanded that this soldier should resign from the Club, or else he would. Vansittart was asked to intervene, and asked Sir Malcolm Robertson what, in this description, he objected to. Sir Malcolm Robertson said he objected to it altogether; it was most insulting. Vansittart said, 'I can quite understand your feeling insulted if he had merely called you an old bore, but I should have thought that men of our age would think it quite a compliment to be called what he called you.' Sir Malcolm Robertson said that he had not previously thought of it like that, and was mollified.)

Dine in Hampstead with Leith-Ross. Rather dull. I don't much like his wife;[1] his daughter has a spotty face, and why did he ask that dull old stick Sir William Goode[2] to meet me? And Hampstead is far away and takes a long while to get back from there. I come back by tube from Swiss Cottage to Piccadilly Circus and, not having been in the tube at night for a long while, observed with fascinated horror the swarms of night population at each station.[3] Someone says, 'I don't know how we shall be able to get them all out at the end of the war.'

1 Lady Leith-Ross, née Prudence Staples.
2 Sir William Goode (d. 1944). Assistant Secretary at the Ministry of Food; in charge of Communications 1941–4; Head of Cable Branch 1939–44. Former journalist.
3 An estimated 4 per cent of the London population used tube stations as overnight shelters, according to the first shelter census in November 1940. (A. Marwick, *Britain in the Century of Total War*, Penguin, London, 1970, p. 298.)

The coup that ousted King Paul in Belgrade on 27th March (which S.O.E. agents had helped to inspire) had been swiftly nullified by the Axis invasion of Yugoslavia a few days later.

Wednesday 18th June

[George] Taylor arrived back yesterday by air from Lisbon, sent even in advance of the Minister (R.C.).[1] He is brought to see me this morning by Gladwyn. He looks very well and fit. He was captured by the Italians when the Jugs collapsed, near Kator, but he and the rest of the large party, more than a hundred, of captives were treated very well by this comparatively civilised enemy. They passed some weeks at Chianciano and had quite a pleasant time waiting for all the formalities to be completed for their journey on through France and Spain. He is eager to be working again, but I sent him away for several days to see his wife, who thought at the first, as we all did, that he was probably a corpse, and he is to return to London on Sunday night and make me a full report of all his doing. The Jug collapse seems to have been catastrophic, and the Government formed after the coup to have consisted of a number of very elderly politicians who, though their coup was a flagrant defiance of Hitler, believed that if they sat as quiet as mice he would no longer notice them. Therefore, they stated publicly that their foreign policy was unchanged, privately that they were still neutral and could enter into no staff talks with us, and never issued a general mobilisation order. The Croats, moreover, welcomed with open arms both Germans and Italians, and all along the Adriatic coast there was no resistance at all. All things considered, the Slovenes had done better than either the Croats or the Serbs.

I was all for Czechoslovakia and Yugoslavia after the last war, but the failure of the Czechs to blend the Slovaks, and the Serbs the Croats, into reasonably united states, makes me very doubtful whether I was right. These two synthetic countries, with their clumsy long names, are symbols of what Gladwyn often calls 'The Professors' Peace'. He thinks that all the Professors are in hiding awaiting their chance to leap forth from Chatham House and elsewhere to give us just such another! ...

A most amusing development with little Duff Cooper! While Taylor is with me, Cooper rings through direct on the telephone, and addresses me, for the first time ever, by my Christian name. (Indeed, in view

1 Sir Ronald Hugh Campbell, q.v. Ambassador to Portugal 1940–45.

of this approach, I ask again to make sure who it is!) He then says, 'I hear you are going to blitz me again', and goes on to admit that it was most irregular and unfortunate that I was not consulted about Bowes-Lyon. He says that he told Monckton to sound Leith-Ross but, before he could do this, the Foreign Office in Washington had turned down the proposal, so that the whole thing was stone dead. I say that I have indeed been a bit annoyed, since Bowes-Lyon is, after all, *my* press officer and I have not been consulted about the proposed disposal of his body, although London and the press are full of rumours about this. J.T.[1] chiefly – 'A most tiresome young man, I always think,' says Cooper – seems to have been running round asking everybody's opinion and has reported that there might be awkward Parliamentary Questions if Bowes-Lyon went out. I explain further that I have some time ago considered, with Lothian, the question of his going out; I should not be inclined to agree, nor would he wish, that he should be away for more than, say, two months, and he should go under M.E.W. auspices, not least because I could answer awkward Parliamentary Questions, especially from the Labour Party, much more accurately than could Cooper. He says that he agrees with this. 'You and I', he goes on, 'understand each other. You write me a rude letter and I write you a rude letter, or I write you a rude letter and you write me a rude letter back. But what I hate is someone who keeps running to the Headmaster.' This goes, I suppose, both for Eden and the Beaver, and perhaps some Service Ministers too. 'Well,' I say, 'I haven't signed anything yet, though I had rather a good letter in draft for you, but I won't send it now.'

Leeper comes to see me in the afternoon. He thinks that Bowes-Lyon will accept Eden's offer. But Bowes-Lyon wouldn't accept until he had sounded the Beaver, with whom he dined last night, but stayed late as the Beaver was called away for several hours to be with the P.M. Bowes-Lyon, therefore, didn't get to bed till between 3 and 4 a.m. and insists on sleeping this afternoon.

I send for Bowes-Lyon and tell him of my talk with Cooper. He admits that last night he told Sammy Hood that I was getting more and more furious because, though I had received no official information, gossip was constantly reaching me from all quarters of the compass about Bowes-Lyon's proposed appointment, and that I had prepared a most luscious raspberry which I was about to despatch to Cooper. Hood said, 'Oh, that's too dreadful' and ran off to Cooper. Hence the telephone conversation.

1 Not identified.

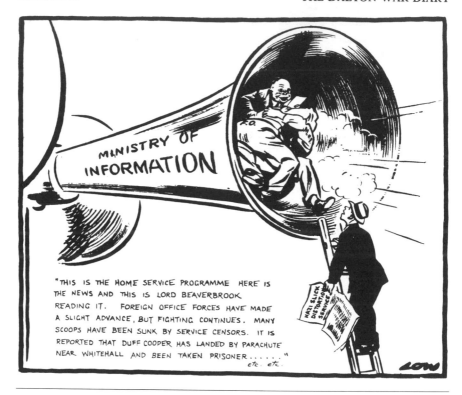

"THIS IS THE HOME SERVICE PROGRAMME HERE IS THE NEWS AND THIS IS LORD BEAVERBROOK READING IT. FOREIGN OFFICE FORCES HAVE MADE A SLIGHT ADVANCE, BUT FIGHTING CONTINUES. MANY SCOOPS HAVE BEEN SUNK BY SERVICE CENSORS. IT IS REPORTED THAT DUFF COOPER HAS LANDED BY PARACHUTE NEAR WHITEHALL AND BEEN TAKEN PRISONER . . . . . . " *etc. etc.*

On 13th June the Soviet news agency Tass denied that any tension existed between Germany and the Soviet Union.

Friday 20th June

A day in the New Forest on a tour of inspection. A very good lot of men have been got together. It reflects great credit on Gubbins. C.E.O. and Gaitskell come with me. The rhododendrons and azaleas are fantastically beautiful, massing everywhere. Going down, we question Can Stalin[1] survive? Certainly, whatever he does now, he has got his country into a jam. It is said that Zhdanov[2] is a possible successor if Russia is going to fight. Zhdanov is very tough and intransigent. He is from Leningrad and pushed the Finnish War.

1 Joseph Stalin (1879–1953). General Secretary of the Central Committee of the Soviet Communist Party 1922–53. Chairman of the Council of People's Commissars 1941–6.

2 A. A. Zhdanov (1896–1948). Member of the Politburo and the Supreme Soviet. Member of the Military Council, Leningrad Front, in the Second World War. Head of Agitprop (Agitation and Propaganda) 1944–8.

Saturday 21st June
Further talk on oil with Mark Turner[1] and others. It is doubtful what the Russians can do in the air, and I am pressed by some to urge that we should send aircraft of our own to bomb Ploesti from Russian acrodromes. I am inclined to think this fantastic – and so does C.E.O. whom I consult. Alternatively, we might let the Russians have a few navigators. C.E.O. has written to Ismay about the problem of the Caucasus oil from our point of view.

Go in the afternoon to West Leaze.

At 4 a.m. on 22nd June, Ribbentrop delivered a formal declaration of war to the Russian Ambassador in Berlin. The Russians were unprepared, and the Germans made rapid advances. Hundreds of Russian planes were destroyed before they could get into the air. Churchill immediately offered to send aid to the Russians in their struggle for survival. 'I have only one purpose, the destruction of Hitler, and my life is much simplified thereby,' he told his private secretary. 'If Hitler invaded Hell I would make at least a favourable reference to the Devil in the House of Commons.'[2]

Sunday 22nd June
I sleep till 9.30 a.m. and then, calling over the stairs for my breakfast, hear from Ruth that the Germans have attacked Russia. This she heard on the 7 o'clock news but did not wake me. I am mentally prepared for headlong collapse of the Red Army and Air Force. On the other hand, it is possible that they may do much better than we think.

A lovely day in the sun. Ruth much better for being here and for sun-bathing. What she would really like to do would be to re-plan London.

Monday 23rd June
Cripps to see me in the evening. He is friendly and business-like. He is going about saying that M.E.W. is the most efficient of the Government Departments and that we always give him quick decisions. He

---

1 R. M. C. Turner, later Sir Mark (1906–80). Ministry of Economic Warfare 1939–44. Banker.
2 Winston S. Churchill, *The Second World War, vol. III The Grand Alliance*, Cassell, London, 1950, p. 331.

has told this to Stokes and Bevan, who have repeated it to [Dingle] Foot.

Tuesday 24th June

Cripps calls again ... Anything may happen in Russia now, and all the Mission may be widely separated. C.E.O. says later today that he hears most secretly from a German source that the Russians have already lost 1,800 planes, half their first-line strength. At this rate, they will be driven out of the air altogether in two or three more days. (Two days later, the Germans are only officially claiming to have destroyed 400.)

Davies arranges for me to meet his friend John Carvel in a remote corner of the Ritz. He won't come to my Ministry. A long story of the influence which he and others – notably, he says, Menzies and Fraser, and also he thinks some people from South Africa – are bringing to bear to get me made Minister of Information. He says he was asked whether he knew me and what he thought of me by Professor Lindemann, that he has had a word with Bracken, and also, so he says, with Mrs Churchill.[1] He seems to have been haunting the Chilterns last weekend. He asks how I would take such a proposal. I begin by saying, quite truly, that it doesn't attract me. I asked for M.E.W. and know that I can do it (no mention throughout our conversation of M.U.W.). I am not sure that I could do Ministry of Information and in any case it is a coffin. Everyone in the country thinks they are experts on propaganda, and any Minister would find himself always ringed round by Aunt Tabithas ('Whatever you do and whatever you say, Aunt Tabitha says "No, *that* isn't the way".')

Moreover, the row now going on shows, if nothing else, that the whole set-up is most unsatisfactory. Nor could I contemplate working with some of the present officials.

Carvel then says, 'How if the job carried a seat in the War Cabinet and it was understood that the Minister was on an equal footing with the Foreign Office and the Service Departments?' I say that that might indeed make a difference, and if the offer were to come with such a condition, I should at least be interested enough to consider it carefully. At present the position of Cooper in the Cabinet is one of complete humiliation. Whereas I never attend except when I have something on the agenda on which I speak and argue, Cooper is always there but never allowed to take part in debate. I say that it would also be necessary, in the hypothesis contemplated, for me to have a completely free hand to deal with the staff. Carvel asks finally, do I object

1 Clementine Churchill, née Hozier, later Baroness Spencer-Churchill (1885–1977). Married to Winston Churchill. Chairman of Red Cross Aid to Russia Fund.

to his plugging my name during the next few days, with the conditions indicated? I say I have no objection, though I think it most unlikely that the thing will go any further, and, as we both agree, it would mean either increasing the War Cabinet by at least two or turning out one of the existing Labour members. He says that this is a difficulty which has been thought of and that it has been suggested that Attlee should go. I say that this is quite impossible. He is the Leader of our Party and any such suggestion would cause a frightful row.

I report this talk afterwards, strictly enjoining complete secrecy, to C.E.O. who thinks that I should also press to sit on the Defence Committee. I say that I should, of course, insist on taking Special Operations with me, and so we should get the much talked of co-ordination by another route. I say that I should want him to come with me and we would define titles and duties when we got there. He says that he would like to do this very much and that such co-ordination would be supported by all the younger people in the Service Departments. I also mention the talk to Gaitskell and say equally that if it came off I should wish him to come with me. This he would like very much. I tell him not to speak of it even to C.E.O. He thinks it is unlikely to happen. So do I.

Dine with Gladwyn at La Coquille, where, among the visitors, are Will Lawther[1] with a lady not his wife, and Mr Pritt with nobody, wondering, I suppose, what to say and do *now*! Gladwyn says that this is a Free French restaurant. '*Ici on parle des opérations prochaines*,' I say.

Wednesday 25th June
To one of Nathan's lunches, where Peter Fraser[2] is the guest. He makes a good speech, but too long and repetitive. He has grown in authority since he became P.M. Maisky is also there, looking very tired, and is called on to say a few words. This sort of audience is not exactly pro-Bolshevik and some of them seem to have difficulty in dragging themselves to their feet when the Chairman proposes the toast of Russia. Great physical contortions are necessary for some these days. ...

I ask Eden to dine, partly in order to keep our relations well manured – I have written congratulating [Oliver] Harvey on his

1 W. Lawther, later Sir William (1889–1976). President of the Miners' Federation of Great Britain, then National Union of Mineworkers 1939–54. Labour M.P. 1929–31.

2 Peter Fraser (1884–1950). New Zealand Labour politician. Prime Minister of New Zealand 1940–49. Minister of External Affairs 1943–9. Attended meetings of the U.K. War Cabinet 1941. Joined the Independent Labour Party in London 1908. Emigrated to New Zealand 1910. Dalton had met Fraser during a visit to Australia and New Zealand in 1938.

appointment as P.P.S. and received an almost too effusive reply, saying how he knows that Eden and I see alike on all foreign questions and that co-operation between our two Departments is most essential – and partly to enable him to meet Taylor and Masterson[1] and hear their Balkan stories. I also ask Gladwyn, C.D. and Wilmot. This makes quite a nice little party on a hot night, though Eden is late arriving, having had to see the P.M., and has to go for a Defence Committee at 9.45. None the less, I think it did good. After he has gone, we all take to abusing the Foreign Office and diplomats, both general and individual. Gladwyn, greatly out-numbered, puts up a very good half-hearted defence!

Thursday 26th June

What is the difference between Hindenburg and a Foreign Office official? Whenever you put a piece of paper in front of them Hindenburg signs it and the Foreign Office circulates it.

Lunch at House of Commons with Wilmot and George Ridley.[2] We are now back again in the Palace of Westminster and using the House of Lords for our proceedings. Ridley is concerned at the intrigues of Laski, who, he thinks, having really nothing else to do, is getting too much influence in the National Executive. ...

Our information is that the Germans counted on the break-up of the Red Army within a month, mass surrenders of troops, the destruction of the Red Air Force and the collapse of the existing Government. They would then organise a series of separate vassal states, exploit their supplies and be able to turn all their forces west in time to invade this country before the autumn. Last year their invasion date was fixed for 16th September, though in the end this was called off. A date later than mid-September would be precarious, owing to uncertainties of weather. If, therefore, the Russians go on fighting for, say, two months, the German High Command will be in a jam. Meanwhile, they are getting no oil from Russia; must transport large quantities eastward over their railway system; and may find their Romanian supplies seriously disturbed. The communiqués are very confused, but there is reason to think that a good deal of damage has already been done by the Red Air Force to oil stocks at Constanza and perhaps also to refineries at Ploesti.

Friday 27th June

Francis Williams to dine with me. He says the chief fault of Cooper is

1 Tom Masterson. Head of the S.O.E. Belgrade office.
2 George Ridley (1886–1944). P.P.S. to Arthur Greenwood (Minister without Portfolio) 1940–42. Labour M.P. for Clay Cross 1936–44.

that he takes no interest in his job, shows up only between 10.30 a.m.
and 6 p.m., takes two hours off for lunch, is generally a little flushed
before lunch and more flushed afterwards, and, when contacts are
arranged for him with the press, spends all his time grumbling against
his colleagues. Thus, at the end of such a lunch the other day, he said,
'I don't know why you think *I* have any information for you. Nobody
ever tells me anything. The P.M. had a press conference this morning;
I wasn't invited, and I don't know what he told them. You had better
go to No. 10 and ask.' Williams further says that decisions are reached
but never acted on, and that Cooper never presses these through. In
short, he keeps no prod sheet. Williams is sure the job could be done
well by any energetic and reasonable minister. He hints that he would
like me to do it. I say that I am not at all attracted. Particularly as the
status of Minister of Information has so declined.

Saturday 28th June
To South Wales by morning train. Address Annual Conference of
S.W. Regional Council of Labour. A good solid body of delegates
and all goes easily. Reasonably good publicity for my speech, both
on the air on Saturday night and in the Sunday papers ... Drive with
George Morris,[1] an excellent fellow, to the top of Caerphilly Mountain, where we have a drink at the Black Cock. It is very full of cheerful
people. Morris says that he thinks the purchasing power of the
population in Wales has increased three-fold since the war. This
allows for invacuees [*sic*], but is chiefly due to the disappearance of
unemployment.

Sunday 29th June
Stay in bed most of the morning. Lunch with Sir Gerald Bruce,[2]
Regional Commissioner for South Wales and a distant relative of
mine, a solicitor who has acted for the S.W.M.F. [South Wales
Miners' Federation] and Mr Caleb Rees,[3] who represents the Ministry
of Information. Then by car to the Rhondda, where I have a good
meeting with a thousand people in Ferndale and make a rather rhetorical speech, which they seem to like. There is a good male-voice choir
and other accompaniments. Back by train and sleep in Ministry.

1 George Morris (1892–1943). Secretary and District Organiser of South Wales
Regional Council of Labour 1937–43. Former steel-worker. Labour Party District
Organiser for Wales 1932–7. Killed in an air-raid.
2 Sir Gerald Bruce (1872–1953). Joint Regional Commissioner for the Welsh Civil
Defence Region 1939–45.
3 Caleb Rees. Regional Information Officer, Welsh Region, for the Ministry of
Information, based at Cardiff. Previously a Board of Education Inspector for
Wales.

On 29th June, the Second Panzer Group under General Guderian and the Third Panzer Group under General Hoth met close to Minsk, cutting off a large Soviet force near Gorodishche. Meanwhile, the Russians came under further pressure from combined German-Finnish attacks in the North. Bobrynsk and Lwów were taken, as the Germans advanced towards Kiev.

Monday 30th June

Attlee to dine with me. He says the Beaver is still asking him what Labour minister complained of his speech to the journalists. But Attlee is refusing to say. He says the Russians had great numbers of their aircraft shot down on the ground because they kept them too far forward and did not camouflage them. We had given them plenty of warnings, but these were disregarded. He is shocked to hear that many people already know of the impending change of Wavell and Auchinleck.

I have been making a great to-do today about the sudden theft of Loxley,[1] of which I only heard late last night. I write to Eden complaining, though not too bitterly, of the procedure, and pressing for Dixon in exchange.

Tuesday 1st July

Pessimistic talk about Russia. Mason Mac [MacFarlane] went out very pessimistic and didn't want to go. He doesn't like the Russians anyhow. One should not believe too much in his reports. He went out thinking that the Russians could not last three weeks. All this from Brigadier Brooks, who says that Lockhart has observed that our staff has always been optimistic about all previous campaigns in this war – Norway, Belgium, France, Libya, Greece, Crete ... This time, says Lockhart, regarding Russia our staff are pessimistic. Perhaps they are always wrong!

I gather, however, from others a general impression that the Russians are doing badly. They are also putting in huge demands for arms and materials from us, and this may be in order to be able to say later on that we let them down because we would not give them what they

1 Peter Loxley, q.v., working as No. 2 to Leeper at SO1 for barely a week, had been ordered by Cadogan to return to the Foreign Office. 'I am most seriously concerned at the effect which this sudden removal of Loxley will have upon the efficiency of my SO1 machine,' Dalton wrote to Eden on 30th June. (Dalton Papers 18/2 (3).) Then followed a row about personnel, which highlighted the friction between the two ministers.

asked for, and that therefore they had no option but to give in. It is also a matter of comment that Stalin has hitherto said nothing. Is he preparing to sell out in a few days? ...

The Free French are also doing badly. They are not being at all loyal to us in Damascus and it is said that their troops are not fighting well. The Syrian campaign is going very much too slowly. ...

Talk on the telephone to Duff Cooper and ask him whether he is satisfied with the way things have gone. He says no, certainly not. I ask if he will open the debate on Thursday; he says no, he is not allowed to do that, it must be opened, he understands, by some member of the War Cabinet, probably Anderson. He says that he has got no Head for his Foreign Publicity Department; can I suggest a name? I ask does he want another diplomat? He says no, he would prefer not. I can't think of anyone who would do. There are strong rumours that nearly all his other leading officials have put their resignations in (Bowes-Lyon hears this from Samuel Hood tonight). It is also said that Cooper, screaming with anger, flings their resignations back in their faces and refuses to accept them. He is said to have told the P.M. that he did not think that ministers should resign in wartime; otherwise he would have gone.

In a Parliamentary Question on 2nd July, G. R. Strauss asked the Minister of Economic Warfare for a statement 'on the release by the British Navy of a French ship carrying valuable supplies, including many thousands of tons of oil, to the Vichy authorities in North Africa'. Dingle Foot, the Parliamentary Secretary, replied that after consultations with the U.S. government, the British government had agreed to permit three ships, one of which was the tanker *Scheherazade*, to sail from the United States to French North Africa, and that the supplies carried were to be consumed solely in French North Africa, their distribution subject to the supervision of American consular officers. When the matter was pressed in supplementary questions by Strauss and Shinwell, the Prime Minister intervened to say that the British government must be guided 'to a very large extent' by American opinion.[1]

On 29th June, Oliver Lyttelton was moved from the Board of Trade to become Minister of State representing the War Cabinet in the Middle East.

---

1 H. C. Debs [372], cols 1358–9.

Wednesday 2nd July

Quite a Parliamentary flutter over the *Scheherazade* and other two ships for French North Africa. The Parliamentary Question to me is No. 71, and, as is our usual practice, I leave it to [Dingle] Foot to take questions on Wednesday. It is just reached on the stroke of twelve, and Foot having given one principal and one supplementary answer, the P.M. bursts in and takes it himself, answering a series of supplementaries by Shinwell and others. This incident, and my absence, is the subject of some comment afterwards among the pressmen. Why didn't I take it? Some suggest that I funked it, others that I had refused because I was in disagreement with the policy and was even on the point of resignation. Gaitskell thinks that there may have been some slight damage to my personal prestige, but I doubt whether there is much in this. Anyhow, it is quite temporary. On the other hand, it is a great advantage that the P.M. should have stated that in this case we are deferring to U.S. opinion. He said many things which certainly not Foot, and doubtfully I, could have stated publicly at this stage. There has been a good deal of press bustle over this for several days, and this has its reflections in Washington, where [Sumner] Welles is being heckled at *his* press conferences. At mine, held this afternoon by Bowes-Lyon, the question was pressed by Americans as to whether the Minister of Economic Warfare was in favour of this policy. Bowes-Lyon said that it was the policy of H.M.G. Another American asked whether M.E.W. would not like to liquidate a number of the personnel of the State Department. Bowes-Lyon said that possibly such feelings might be mutual. ...

Leeper calls in the afternoon to report a long séance at the Foreign Office this morning in which he is trying to get Dixon. He thinks that the chances of this are not too bad. I say that I will lie back until I hear. If I get Dixon, to replace Loxley, well and good; if not, I shall make a row with Eden. I have received a very wooden letter of apology from Cadogan for the way in which the thing was handled. I tell Gladwyn to go tomorrow to the Foreign Office and push further for Dixon. Leeper tells me that both Cadogan and [Oliver] Harvey – who Gladwyn had reported to me had looked very 'po-faced' when the matter had been raised over a cup of tea the other day, and said that Eden would certainly not part with Dixon – had been very helpful.

I hear late this evening some account, following my informant's talk of one and a half hours with Ismay, of recent events. The decision to send Lyttelton[1] to the Middle East was only taken by the P.M. in

---

1 Oliver Lyttelton, later 1st Viscount Chandos (1893–1972). Appointed June 1941 as Minister of State Resident in the Middle East. Conservative M.P. for Aldershot 1940–54. (See Appendix A.)

the train returning from Scotland on Saturday. Lyttelton's instructions were written out by the P.M. in his own hand on a half sheet of note-paper in the train. Everything was settled with a rush and Lyttelton left on the Monday, before I, or a great number of other ministers having some interest in his arrangements, could see him. — One reason for this high speed was so that Lyttelton should see Wavell before the latter left for India. ...

Mr Bentinck[1] has a simple view as to why we are less good (if, indeed, we are) in this war than in the last. It is, of course, always easy to say, looking hopefully from men we know to men we hardly knew, 'They were giants in those days'. None the less, the closer one comes to the top, and the nearer one sees the detail of decisions and the play of motives, the more disillusioned one is apt to become.

Dalton continued to try to prevent his 'secret' responsibilities from becoming known to Parliament, press and public. His cover was particularly hard to maintain, however, when propaganda policy became the subject of debate in the House of Commons.

Thursday 3rd July

I take Parliamentary Question just on the stroke of twelve on the *Scheherazade*, etc. There is still a good deal of concern in the House, which I welcome. I am asked if I was consulted, if it was a Cabinet decision (to both of which I say yes), and whether my Department has not been over-ruled on a question of major policy (to which I say no).

The long-expected debate on Propaganda then begins and I discreetly leave the House, nor do I return at any time during this debate. I sit in my room upstairs, where Foot is instructed to come and tell me if there should develop any clamour for my presence. There is no such clamour not even a word by any speaker, except Anderson in opening, about my Ministry, and he says only that there are other Departments which keep in touch with the Ministry of Information and the Foreign Office, including mine. No one picks up the point. No one, at least of those who speak, but there are great numbers who wish to speak and can't, including Pickthorn[2] and King-Hall, both

1 V. F. W. Cavendish-Bentinck, q.v.
2 K. W. M. Pickthorn, later Sir Kenneth, 1st Bart (1892–1975). Conservative M.P for Cambridge University 1935–50; Carlton 1950–66. Junior minister 1951–4.

of whom I know wanted to refer to me. Indeed, Gladwyn reports to me late tonight that he met King-Hall at dinner at one of those mixed parties of Lady Colefax,[1] and that King-Hall said most indignantly that none of the right people had caught the Speaker's eye and that he in particular had had a long speech prepared, nearly all about the Minister of Economic Warfare. Gladwyn also said that Sir Roderick Jones,[2] who was present, said to him, 'I understand the Minister of Economic Warfare has now taken over the show which Campbell Stuart used to run.' I asked Gladwyn what he replied. He said, 'I changed the subject.'

So we emerge quite scatheless, and now can count on a peaceful run for some while yet. Butler, whom I saw later in the afternoon, said that the debate had been an admirable demonstration of power politics. The Chair had been guided whom to call, and who not. Captain Plugge[3] had made an immensely long and unimportant speech which had occupied much time, and two maiden speakers had been worked in. I myself had squared Phil Noel-Baker, who spoke last before Cooper, and Anderson had made a very long and boring speech to begin with, which had, as nearly as any speech could, taken all life and interest from the proceedings. Butler thought that Anderson had done his reputation some harm by this. He also thought that Cooper was safe now for about two months and that I should not be troubled again this side of Christmas.

Gladwyn heard a rumour that Butler might soon be given a new job, something concerned with finance of devastated districts, so that Eden could bring in one of his little cronies in his place.

The struggle for Dixon still continues. Gladwyn saw Cadogan today and offered, if I could get Dixon, to give back Broad[4] to the Foreign Office. He says that, if it lay with Cadogan, I should get Dixon to-morrow, but it is most difficult to persuade Eden. I said to Gladwyn, 'What is the good of my having here two people, you and Leeper, who are supposed to have such influence in the Foreign Office, and then I can't get a simple thing like this arranged?' He said, 'The Foreign Office is an abstraction. This is simply a question of whether the Secretary of State can be persuaded. I have never pretended that I have any special influence with him. But Rex [Leeper] has great

1 Lady Colefax, née Sibyl Halsey. Well-known political hostess. Widow of Sir Arthur Colefax, a Conservative M.P.
2 Sir Roderick Jones (1877–1962). Member of Advisory Council, Ministry of Information 1939. Principal Proprietor of Reuters 1919–41. Chief Executive and Director of Propaganda 1918.
3 L. F. Plugge (1889–1981). Conservative M.P. for Chatham 1935–45.
4 Philip Broad (1903–66). Diplomat, seconded to M.E.W.

influence with him.' I said that Cadogan's letter to me was a most wooden and stupid communication. I had much rather have had nothing.

Gladwyn also tells me of the fate of [Orme] Sargent's paper, the first attempt to forecast the future and how we are to win the war. There had been discouragement because, although this was the first time that this topic had been put on the agenda of the Defence Committee, the P.M. would not bring it on, saying that it was only a mass of words and that they had more important things to think about. This, although the paper had been passed by the C.O.S. [Chiefs of Staff]. Gladwyn and I consider whether I should not, perhaps, put in a paper direct to the P.M. covering that part of Sargent's paper which is my concern.

Friday 4th July

Cripps (bloody fool!) has leaked Gladwyn's name to David Astor[1] as being engaged in certain activities. Astor therefore comes along with a paper which, happily, does not show much sign of inner knowledge. Gladwyn says there must be some mistake about what Cripps said, though he is, of course, in touch with various people and could pass things on. ...

Policy Sub-Committee[2] meets this afternoon and re-elects me to Chair. Later, and, as I think, unwisely, they decide, by a small majority, to make Shinwell Chairman of the Central Committee on new policy.

This evening I have some of my Daily Councillors[3] to dine: C.E.O. [Jebb], C.D. [Nelson], A.D. [Taylor], A.D.Z. [Davies] and D. Fin. [Venner].[4] Just a little heavy with a little too much sense of frustration in some of their minds. Everyone in this war feels frustrated.

As Chief Executive Officer, Jebb supposedly had responsibility for the whole of S.O.E. The presence of a more senior Foreign Office official as head of SO1, however, restricted his influence, and made it impossible to co-ordinate the two wings. Hence Jebb was keen that Leeper should be moved.

---

1 Hon. F. D. L. Astor (b. 1912). Journalist. Royal Marines 1940–45. Editor of the *Observer* 1948–76.
2 Of the Labour Party.
3 'Daily Councillors': members of the Council of S.O.E.
4 Pilot Officer J. F. Venner, later Group Captain. Director of Finance at S.O.E.

Saturday 5th July

In the small hours of this morning, both of us having returned and done some more work, Gladwyn suggests that I might explore with Eden the possibility of Leeper returning to the Foreign Office and Loxley taking his place at C.H.Q., the whole show being then co-ordinated under one head, as I had so often told him I wanted. I said this would be rather difficult to handle but I would see how things went. It would be an admirable solution, for almost every reason. ...

To C.H.Q. in time for lunch. I make a row about the Italian Prisoners of War in India and how they are to be approached. I say that I will exercise my own judgment on these drafts and clean them up. It is silly to say that there should be 'no propaganda'. The practical question is, is it worth while to try to recruit a Free Italian force? Probably Martelli should be the conducting officer.

Sunday 6th July

Return by way of Chingford, where I speak in P.M.'s constituency. I make a *good* speech and get off most successfully with the lady Mayor of Chingford and, even more important, Sir James Hawkey,[1] Chairman of the P.M.'s constituency organisation, who hated Neville Chamberlain and the old Tory machine and with whom I exchange various political reminiscences, designed to bring out the undoubted fact that it was the Labour Party which determined the change of Government leading to Churchill becoming P.M., and also that I played some personal role in this.

Monday 7th July

My tart exchange with Eden continues. He has today my letter in which I refuse Scrivener,[2] with reasons, and complain again of the way in which Loxley was removed. Lockhart, who, as agreed with me yesterday, was going to suggest to Eden that Loxley should be restored, found him very uppety, refusing to discuss this at all and saying that he had had a letter from me and had already answered it.

Lunch with Tree,[3] who paints a gloomy picture of our propaganda in America. He was out there for some time on behalf of C.D. He saw both Eccles and Hall and thought they were a bit jealous of each other. He also says that Eccles was giving expression to extreme Right-wing opinions.

1 Sir James Hawkey, later 1st Bart (1877–1952). Wanstead and Woodford U.D.C. councillor and former mayor. Chairman of Woodford Conservative Association.
2 P. S. Scrivener (1897–1966). Diplomat.
3 Ronald Tree (1897–1976). Parliamentary Private Secretary to the Minister of Information 1940–45. Conservative M.P. for Harborough 1933–45. Junior minister 1945.

8 The *New Statesman & Nation* observes London. Kingsley Martin on the roof of the paper's Holborn office.

9 King's Cross farewells. Lord Halifax leaves to become Ambassador in Washington, January 1941. *From left:* Walter Monckton (with umbrella), Anthony Eden, Lord Halifax. *Right:* Lord Beaverbrook.

left: 10 General de Gaulle inspects French boys at Brynbach boy scout camp, near Denbigh, August 1940

below: 11 With S.O.E. officers, *c.* 1941. *Left to right:* Gladwyn Jebb, Colin Gubbins, Dalton.

opposite: 12 The Ayes Lobby after the raid of 10th May 1941. Next day Dalton used the Members' lavatory, 'as a last gesture'.

left: 13 Brendan Bracken takes over as Minister of Information, July 1941

below: 14 Member of the War Cabinet. Sir Stafford Cripps at his Gloucestershire home, February 1942.

Cabinet this evening on action to be taken against Jap southward movements. Eden puts up a paper which is criticised as being quite useless and beside the point by [Peter] Fraser, who says that only military force is any good and that economic measures are neither here nor there. Eden is a little testy over all this. P.M. appears very amiable and begs me not to go when this item is over. I find that Sir James Hawkey has been going up to No. 10 and singing my praises. He is most anxious that I should go and speak in the P.M.'s constituency again, next time at Woodford. This liaison can do no harm.

Tuesday 8th July
A tart reply from Eden, with whom I am thus having my first personal breeze. My last letter has caused him surprise, and he resents my observations about 'a member of my staff'.

Colonel Sosthenes Behn[1] calls. This name is almost too good to be true. He is a smooth-mannered rich American whom I would not trust far. He has great financial interests in Germany (telephones, etc.). He is in favour of letting a lot of food through into France. He talks so much that I have little time to reply. I merely say that such ideas are quite counter to the strong feeling of press, Parliament and public here. ...

With Gladwyn to dine with Cazalet, recently back from U.S.A. whither he went with Sikorski. He gives a very depressing picture of our failure to organise propaganda or to make a good impression on the Americans. Halifax is clearly doing very badly,[2] and rumour runs widely that when he comes home next month, he will not return. Cazalet says that he has been trying hard to 'sell him to himself'. He does not seem to realise that he could be the most important Englishman after Churchill and the most important man in the U.S. after Roosevelt. The incident of the hot dog and the Chicago baseball match was frightful. He put it on the ground beside him and left it there instead of eating it. The pressman photographed it and displayed it: 'Lord Halifax's hot dog. He didn't eat it.' So unlike the King and Queen, who munched theirs appreciatively. Then he tried to answer questions the reporters asked him about baseball, which he didn't understand. If only he had talked to them about cricket or football it would have been so much better. He also committed a great gaffe, first in agreeing to go hunting in Virginia, a sport quite unappreciated by the vast American public; and then by going without a pink coat (which, it is understood, his hosts regarded as a great social affront

1 Colonel Sosthenes Behn (1882–1957). American industrialist. President of the International Telephone and Telegraph Corporation.
2 i.e. as Ambassador.

245

to them). Cazalet says that the only way you do business in Washington is by 'having a chat', 'popping in', or 'ringing up'. Halifax can't do any of these things. He always eyes a telephone with deep distrust. He is a little deaf and doesn't hear telephone conversations very clearly. He has no gift for popping in. He only goes to see the President when he has been instructed to argue with him or to make awkward requests. What he ought to do is to ring him up and say, 'Can I look in tonight? I have nothing much to talk about, but it would be just fine to have a chat.'

He also has a very poor staff, though Washington is full now of thousands of British subjects attached to various missions. There is no direct telephone communication between the Embassy and the various Missions downtown. There is no proper accommodation at the Embassy for the staff; some have to sit in passages and others in their bedrooms. Charles Peake, who, according to Cazalet, is a great failure, has to work in his bedroom. Nevile Butler was a most terrible choice for Washington, but is now returning. The temperature in Washington in the summer goes up to nearly 100° and is very humid. It was never meant to be a summer capital, the idea being that Congress and Government both went away.

Wednesday 9th July
See Leeper twice, before and after his visit to Eden. He is most anxious, he says, to remove any personal friction between us. I tell him to press once more for Loxley, carrying this as far as he thinks wise, but that, if I can't get Loxley, I shall have to look outside.

Having had his interview, he comes back and says that he is sure he has removed any personal difficulties. He had said to Eden that he hoped that he and I would not now be antipathetic to each other, since this would make his position very difficult. Eden had said certainly not, and hoped our recent correspondence might now perhaps be forgotten. But, on the question of Loxley there had been no movement. Eden had said that he would still keep the offer of Scrivener if I cared to reconsider it. I told Leeper that of course I should not. It was then agreed that I should make a tentative approach to Bowes-Lyon.

Later Gladwyn tells me that he finds that my relations with Eden are not as good as Leeper thought. He has heard from Leeper that Eden made a great harangue to Cadogan complaining that I interfered too much in foreign policy. 'Am I Foreign Secretary or am I not?' It seems that this had something to do with the Poles, but Gladwyn will try to find out more about this tomorrow. Possibly Cazalet, acting on our talk yesterday, and using my name, has irritated Eden, who is apt to be vain and feminine.

See Attlee this evening ...

I tell Attlee of my breeze with Eden. He says I should see him and have it out with him. He thinks it is very bad to have taken away Loxley, when 'any old Ambassador' could have acted as P.S. to Cadogan! The Foreign Office, he says, have hardly any countries left to look after now and must have an enormous list of unemployed diplomats. He says he has no objection to my telling Eden that I have spoken to him about this.

I also tell Attlee of my paper on the next twelve months' programme. I wish to send this direct to P.M., with copies to him and General Ismay. I think this much better than going round about through Sargent and his crowd. Attlee agrees (he says he does not like the way Sargent is seen lunching with Hore-Belisha). I say I will authorise Gladwyn to tell Ismay that he agrees. Attlee says his relations with Ismay are good and Gladwyn confirms this. I tell Attlee that I consider I should be at the Defence Committee when this paper is discussed. He agrees and asks me to raise this again with him later.

He is very angry with Lord Hyde of Cowes,[1] who has been arguing against any unification of railways beyond the war period. Attlee says that this is a point where we must dig our toes in, and he thinks all Labour ministers will need to stand together. I say that I am sure we will. This arises from my remark that if the Russians do defeat the Germans, Communism will have a great vogue all over Europe.

Gaitskell to whom I repeat this afterwards, says that he thinks in this country it would just bring the Labour Party in while not going so far as to make Mr Pritt Prime Minister.[2] ...

I run into Sir Campbell Stuart, just back from the U.S. He says, 'I do so want to see you. I have got such a lot to tell you. I hear that you are to be the next Ambassador in Washington.' This is a typical gambit.

My relations with Eden being for the moment suspended, I am not sending in various papers I otherwise would.

Thursday 10th July

An enormous assembly at the Savoy at the invitation of the *Sunday Express* in honour of Raymond Gram Swing.[3] It is just a little humiliating, though we shall soon get more and more used to this sort of

1 Dalton's name for F. J. Leathers, 1st Baron (1883–1965). Minister of War Transport 1941–5. Secretary of State for Co-ordination of Transport, Fuel and Power 1951–3.
2 D. N. Pritt, q.v., an Independent M.P. well known for his pro-Communist views.
3 Raymond Gram Swing (1887–1968). Commentator on American affairs for the B.B.C. 1935–45. Journalist, writer and broadcaster.

thing, that the majority of the Ministers of the Crown plus foreign diplomats, British Generals and every kind of notability in the press world have to be collected to help to boost this, I am sure, quite admirable and well-disposed American broadcaster. I saw him for a little while in my Ministry the other day, and he asked whether it was true that there were forces in this country willing to make peace with the Germans. I said that, if there were, they had no real power and were wise enough to keep under cover. I said that, for myself, 'I would sooner be dead than an émigré, even in your most hospitable country.' And this, I was sure, was a most widespread sentiment. ...

Gladwyn has been doing some further ice-breaking at the Foreign Office, first on Oliver Harvey, who, he says, has been constantly telling Eden what a good chap I am and how he and I both think alike on all subjects. Eden, he learns, was really nettled by my last letter about Dixon and Scrivener, and has been in piqued mood ever since. He was also piqued by my attitude lately in the Cabinet, when I gave the impression, he seems to have told Harvey, that I thought he and most of the rest were poor miserable creatures who had no drive and were doing nothing to win the war, and that it was my role to thrust them along. This was over the Far East and the economic measures against the Japs. Eden seems further to have complained that I often give this impression in the Cabinet (probably this refers also to my memo on 'Denial of oil to the enemy: Russia'). His remarks about me and the Poles do not seem to have been very precise. It was part of a general tirade to Harvey, so Gladwyn ascertains, in which he said, 'Am I Foreign Secretary or am I not? All sorts of other people seem to be interfering with foreign affairs ...... for instance, Hugh Dalton seems always to be carrying on negotiations with the Poles ...... ' Gladwyn, however, hotted up Harvey, which was not difficult, against the anti-Sikorski crowd and the undemocratic elements in the Polish emigration, and later saw Makins, who said that he had been very doubtful about letting Savery's[1] recent report go out as print, and that he thought I had been most helpful in my activities designed to build up Sikorski.

Friday 11th July

P.O.G. [Prevention of Oil reaching Germany] Committee. Hankey very anxious for oil offensive on two fronts. We agree to this being recommended to the C.O.S. [Chiefs of Staff]. Some of the accounts of Russian air attacks on Romanian oil targets are discouraging. Many of their bombs don't explode, we are told, and once when they bombed

---

1 F. Savery (1883–1965). Counsellor, H.M. Embassy to Poland 1939–45. British Consul in Warsaw 1919–39.

Ploesti they hit the dummy town instead, which has been constructed near the original. On the other hand, they are attacking these targets night after night and may well do serious damage before long. (I regret to say that when the attack *we* had so long been demanding on a certain oil target was attempted by the R.A.F. some nights ago, they completely missed the town, because they couldn't find it. They don't like to admit this, and therefore merely reported 'No particular results observed'. But a photograph of the place taken two days later showed no visible damage and no craters anywhere in the neighbourhood.)

Take C.E.O. to Middle East Committee at the Foreign Office. Also present Eden, Moyne (not Moyne's a Guinness but Moyne's a Barley Water!),[1] Amery and Duff Cooper, each, except Cooper, accompanied by one official. When I see Moyne, how I miss Lloyd![2] He is frightened out of his wits, such as they are, by every faintest suggestion of action anywhere. He quacks on about 'reactions' everywhere, in Saudi Arabia and Aden and Timbuktu, and he is most anxious to avoid any 'bloodshed', even if this may be necessary in order to eliminate German influence from Iran. He thinks it quite possible that most of the Germans in Iran are there for quite legitimate purposes! ...

I stay behind, as arranged through the Secretaries, to have a word with Eden and to re-establish our personal relations. But the Middle East Committee lasts till after 1 o'clock, Moyne and Amery having yarned on and on about 'reactions' in Palestine, and whether or not one should revive partition. Therefore, I don't have very long, and other people also are hanging about in the room. But we go over to one of the long windows, with a half balcony outside, and have about five minutes. I say, 'Well, we have had one of our pillow fights!' He says, 'Perhaps I wrote you rather a sharp letter.' I say, 'Oh I don't mind that. I daresay mine was rather sharp too. But what I do think was very bad was the way the thing was done. Cadogan made it worse by writing me a most gawky letter.' He says, 'I am very sorry. I really must apologise for the way in which it was done, but we were at our wits' end, owing to [Henry] Hopkinson being suddenly taken away at a few hours' notice.' I say, 'I don't want you to apologise, but I do want to have some assurance for the future. After all, when you thought of making Leeper an Ambassador, you did speak to me about it first and ask me to put it to him.' He says, 'Yes, of course, I should certainly always consult you in any case like that.' I then turn to the

1 Walter Guinness, 1st Baron Moyne (1880–1964). Colonial Secretary and Leader of the House of Lords 1941–2. Deputy Minister of State, Middle East 1942–4.
2 Sir George Lloyd, 1st Baron, q.v. Colonial Secretary 12th May 1940 to 8th February 1941, when Lord Moyne took over.

wider question and ask whether it was true that he thought I interfered in his affairs. He feigns surprise and says, 'No, certainly not. What makes you think that?' I say I had gathered this impression. What about the Poles? At this he seems a little embarrassed and says, 'Oh, did Rex say anything to you about that?' (This was rather a give-away, for Leeper had not in fact told me that Eden had said anything to him about me and the Poles. I had gathered this rather through Gladwyn from Harvey and Loxley.) He then goes on, 'I oughtn't really to have said anything about it. I only got a story from a certain source and I daresay it wasn't true.' I say, 'I have to see Sikorski a good deal because I have to arrange about his money and his parachutists and all that.' Eden says, 'Of course, I quite understand that.' I: 'You don't object to that?' He: 'Certainly not.' I: 'You don't object to my arranging for him to meet other Labour ministers and trade union leaders to talk to them about our ways of doing things?' He: 'Oh, certainly not.' And so this little conversation ends. I say afterwards to Gladwyn, 'We turned a little artificial sunlight on to the surface of the ice. We have melted the surface, but I think there may be still some ice below.' He says, 'It can never be quite easy when a Foreign Secretary has as one of his colleagues someone who knows as much or more than he does about foreign affairs and is also a dynamic personality.'

...

By car this evening to West Leaze with Bob Fraser, who is in quite good form and a very pleasant companion. Though he is now in charge of all publications at the Ministry of Information, he has never seen Duff Cooper and only once has seen a Minute by him. This said that steps should be taken to boost a novel called *Loss of Eden*. This, I understand, painted a scene of Britain invaded by Hitler.

Saturday 12th July
Sun, wind and no shirt on Ogbourne Downs. A very perfect day. I return as red as a beetroot, and shall soon be slightly sore and then peel. In wartime, moreover, there is a shortage of suitable greases, but it was a grand day. Three cheers for Mithra!

Sunday 13th July
Today it rains a lot and there is not much sun. Back in the evening.
Alexander defending Co-op tobacco[1] against critics at the small party of Labour ministers collected by Attlee to meet Peter Fraser the other night, related this story.

1 A. V. Alexander, q.v., was a leading figure in the co-operative movement.

The First Sea Lord came to see him and found he had left his tobacco behind. The First Lord therefore offered him his pouch. The First Sea Lord said that it was very good tobacco. Next morning the First Lord's messenger came to him and said, 'Beg pardon, sir, but the First Sea Lord's messenger has asked me what the tobacco was that you gave the First Sea Lord last night. He says it is the best he has ever smoked and he wants to get in a supply.' This, Alexander seemed to think, finally settled it. My own comment was that it was hardly fair to take the money. No wonder the First Sea Lord holds down his job.

Monday 14th July

See Kingsley Wood about a point concerning Spanish ships ...

Kingsley Wood says that I have a reputation for drive and energy which he thinks is well deserved. (I do not take these compliments too seriously, but I suppose he has heard somebody say something like this.) I ask him whether he thinks that he or Eden has the greater influence in the Tory Party. He says in this Parliament certainly he has, for many of these Tories have memories. But of course he disclaims all possibility of personal rivalries. He says that many of his people dislike Bevin and accuse him of playing politics and attacking the employers. Wood was quite prepared to put over the case for railway nationalisation to the Tory Party. But now that Leathers has gone strongly the other way, he naturally is not very keen to do so, though he still would if the Cabinet so decided.

See Terence Maxwell[1] and like him. I think he would do me quite well in the Middle East, and he seems quite keen to go, even though he has been told all the difficulties. I say that I hear that he is good at Augean stables. He also seems to know Lampson very well.

Middlewood,[2] who is to receive an O.B.E. tomorrow, comes to see me in the Ministry accompanied by his wife, son and daughter-in-law. I take them up to the roof and down to the shelter, and show them some of the neighbouring ruins. They all appear much edified. Mrs Middlewood said that she was quite afraid to come to London lest there should be a raid. ...

Leningrad will be occupied by the end of this week. Moscow will be occupied within ten days. The Germans are now by-passing Smolensk on both sides.

---

1 Captain Terence Maxwell, later Colonel (b. 1905). Staff College, Minley. Leader of M.E.W. Mission to the Middle East (as Counsellor) 1941–2.

2 J. R. S. 'Bob' Middlewood. Five times chairman of Bishop Auckland Urban District Council. Alderman of Durham County Council. A powerful County Durham Labour Party boss.

Tuesday 15th July

[David Bowes-Lyon] ... reports that Bracken is to succeed Duff Cooper in a few weeks' time, when Parliament will have gone into recess. This was told to me by Monckton, who was told by Eden, so it is pretty direct.

Wednesday 16th July

Attend a Parliamentary Party Meeting, now back in the old Committee Room. Not a large attendance. Charlie Edwards has returned, looking very fit, as everyone tells him. He should have resigned long ago. Hear from both Phil [Noel-] Baker and George Lathan, who were present, of the visit of the deputation to the P.M. yesterday on the Ministry of Information. Some dozen went, including three or four from the General Council. The P.M. received them alone, and was most agreeable and expansive. He said he agreed with many of their criticisms and hoped that he would be able to go some way to meet their requests. (One of these had been for a member of the Labour Party to hold political office at the Ministry.) He asked for 'a week or two' to go further into the matter. At the end he talked to them about the war on the various fronts and kept the Cabinet waiting five minutes in order to finish. He said he hoped they would soon come and see him again and that he had enjoyed their company very much. Obviously he was in his best form. ...

See Attlee this evening. He seems in a very happy mood, having had, as he thinks, a most successful meeting with the Tory 1922 Committee, and having arranged, so he says, the party at Buckingham Palace today when all the exiled Monarchs and Heads of State were brought together for a nice little social gathering.

He confirms about Bracken, who, he thinks, has many qualifications for the job, including knowledge of the press and the press lords and of the City. I say that he has a reputation of being reactionary and anti-Labour. Attlee says he does not think this is really so. Anyhow, he will have to be careful, and he is to have a Labour Under-Secretary. I ask is this to be Phil? He says no, he has something better than this in view for Phil, 'with a talking part'. It is Ernest Thurtle.[1] This, I think, is a rather surprising but not at all bad choice. I say that if Bracken tries to use his influence with the P.M. in order to get the better of me, I shall make a row. I recall an incident when he talked long and loudly against me. Attlee says, 'He was ticked off for that;

1 Ernest Thurtle (1884–1954). Parliamentary Secretary at the Ministry of Information 1941–5. Labour M.P. for Shoreditch 1923–31, 1935–50; Shoreditch and Finsbury 1950–54. Junior whip 1930–31.

I don't think he will do it again.' He says that he will arrange a little dinner party at which Bracken and I shall fall on each other's necks.

After one officer, Brigadier Taverner, dispatched to investigate S.O.E. in the Middle East, had been shot down over the Bay of Biscay and captured by the Germans, Dalton noted, 'As Gladwyn says, there is a hoodoo over us in the Middle East.'[1] Now, however, the matter had become more urgent: the arrival of Lyttelton in Cairo on 3rd July brought a powerful witness to S.O.E.'s Middle Eastern misfortunes. 'I was disturbed, in particular, by the lack of security, waste and ineffectiveness of S.O.E.,' the new Minister Resident wrote later.[2] According to Lyttelton's recollection, Dalton replied tartly that he was not accustomed to accept allegations against his staff without evidence – to which Lyttelton responded by threatening to have some officers court-martialled. Clearly the matter needed prompt attention, and a new officer, Terence Maxwell – another peacetime banker – was sent out to take command of S.O.E. in Cairo. He was accompanied on this mission by Sir Frank Nelson and Bickham Sweet-Escott. 'Nobody who did not experience it can possibly imagine the atmosphere of jealousy, suspicion, and intrigue which embittered the relations between the various secret and semi-secret departments in Cairo during that summer of 1941,' Sweet-Escott recalled.[3] Nelson recommended a number of dismissals, which were swiftly carried out. 'O.L. telegraphs that he is "entirely satisfied" with Nelson's recommendations,' Dalton recorded in his diary for 12th August. 'He adds that the latter has performed a difficult task with great tact and firmness.'

Friday 18th July
Gladwyn, C.D. and A.D. [George Taylor] come to see me with Maxwell. The latter now begins to wobble. He thinks that if C.D. goes out, as Oliver Twist[4] is pressing that he should, this will alter the nature of his mission. He will become, he says rather unguardedly, 'small beer' if C.D. is to do the initial reorganising. This phrase makes a bad impression on us all. After he has gone, C.D. says he is afraid he is only thinking of his own career. A.D. says that he thinks I handled Maxwell with great skill and almost got him, at one point, to say yes at once.

1 Diary, 23rd June 1941.
2 *The Memoirs of Lord Chandos*, Bodley Head, London, 1962, p. 239.
3 *Baker Street Irregular*, Methuen, London, 1965, p. 73.
4 'Oliver Twist': Dalton's name for Oliver Lyttelton, q.v.

However, since he won't, I ask him to sleep on it and give his answer next day. He is also a little disconcerted by Oliver Twist's unenthusiastic reception of his name. We had been told by two of our Jewish 'general liaison' men that he was one of Oliver Twist's intimates. Obviously this is not true. He has also told someone that he knows Eden very well, but when I raise this with the latter several days later, Eden says that he hardly knows him at all. None the less, I regard him as a good man and shall be very vexed if he too slips through our fingers. Gladwyn gets him afterwards *tête-à-tête* and tells me that Maxwell thinks I tried to rush him tonight.

Tonight's tale is that the Tory back-benchers are making a great set against Bevin, who has been offered Halifax's job but said, 'If I go out at all, I'll go out through the front door, not the back, and tell the public why.'

Philip Nichols is going as Minister to the Czechs! He wanted ten years ago to give lumps of Poland to Germany and was in favour, on grounds of justice and not of insufficiency of arms, of large concessions of Sudeten-Czecho to Germany in 1938. He has a duodenal ulcer which will keep him out of action for two months, and the only thing which can be said in favour of his appointment is that it is largely a nominal one and will eliminate him from the Foreign Office.

Saturday 19th July

Maxwell has accepted, having been piejawed by C.D. yesterday and asked how he would feel if, having refused, he found that things had gone badly in Middle East, because we had had to send some less good man. What would his conscience tell him? Anyhow, he will go now, so I do not need to see him again for the moment. (Gaitskell says that Gladwyn looked in early this morning, before Maxwell's decision was known, and asked Gaitskell to put to me that if Maxwell turned it down I should not be too rough with him, since this would only make him go about the City saying what a shit I was and what a rotten show the whole thing was. This good and prudent advice turns out now to be unnecessary.) A very good telegram, as I think, is despatched to Oliver Twist offering that C.D. and Maxwell shall both come out together as soon as possible, but the former only to stay a fortnight: as I have deferred to his judgment over C.D. so I hope he will defer to mine over Maxwell.

I regard Hopkinson as a poisonous little blighter who is working against us out there. I tell both C.D. and C.E.O. that they have failed with him. The former is related to him and the latter thinks he is a personal friend.

To C.H.Q. in the afternoon. A rather useful conference on Sibs and

Sibman. A good deal of improvement is possible here, and it would be best to have one man, not specialised on either branch. This is the general view, though Leeper some days later is pushed back on it.

Monday 21st July
Lunch with Nathan,[1] the purpose of his invitation being to suggest that he should either succeed Croft[2] as Under-Secretary of State for War, or be given full command, presumably with the rank of General, of his welfare activities. The first idea he would like suggested to Attlee; the second to Margesson. I say that I will have a word with Attlee and ask Margesson to see him. ...

Cabinet at which a long and not very conclusive discussion on military and economic problems in the Pacific. The Japs will try first to pick up undefended trifles and so build an Empire on the cheap. Indo-China next. ... The U.S. will react a bit to this and we must 'match our action with theirs', even though this might increase the risk of more serious incidents and we have very little force, especially naval, available in the threatened area. ...

[Harry] Hopkins is present for the first six items. Then, before we discuss certain Far Eastern questions, it is desired that he should leave. This is achieved by circulating a bogus agenda, and giving him a copy, in which it is made to appear that the proceedings end with item 6. The P.M. then rises from his chair and says, 'Well, now we will adjourn', and an impression is created of general movement. But in fact only Hopkins really leaves, though P.M. accompanies him into the passage to say *au revoir* and that he is always available, and I see him to the door, fixing a future appointment with him.

When the real adjournment is reached some time later, I say to Cooper on going out, 'I suppose you really *ought* to be congratulated on leaving that place.'[3] He says, 'Yes, certainly. But I don't know what I'm supposed to be going to do in the Far East. I only heard on Thursday that I was to go' (some of us heard on Wednesday). 'Nothing has been arranged and nothing more has been said to me about it.'

On 20th July, Duff Cooper was moved to the Duchy of Lancaster, and Brendan Bracken replaced him as Minister of Information. R. A. Butler became

1 Colonel H. L. Nathan, 1st Baron (1889–1963). Liberal, then Labour, M.P. 1929–40. Junior minister 1945–6. Minister of Civil Aviation 1946–8.
2 Sir Henry Page Croft, 1st Bart, 1st Baron (1881–1947). Parliamentary Under-Secretary of State for War 1940–45. Conservative M.P. 1910–40.
3 i.e. the Ministry of Information. (See following note.)

President of the Board of Education, and was replaced as Under-Secretary for Foreign Affairs by R. K. Law. Ernest Thurtle replaced Harold Nicolson as Parliamentary Secretary at the Ministry of Information. Lord Hankey became Paymaster-General.

Bracken's appointment turned ministerial rivalries over the control of propaganda into a shooting war. The new Minister of Information was in no doubt about his own attitude. When Bruce Lockhart saw him on 23rd July Bracken 'made little attempt to conceal his desire to get rid of Dalton – if Co-ordinative Committee could not co-ordinate, must put up report saying what should be done ... '[1]

Wednesday 23rd July

Meeting of National Executive. Thin attendance but much talk. ...

A good deal of grizzling over appointment of Thurtle as Parliamentary Secretary to Minister of Information rather than Phil [Noel-] Baker. Many who have never loved the latter till now are his admirers today! e.g. Shinwell, who, trying to stir up trouble as usual, says that he thinks this is a 'shocking appointment' and asks whether P.M. makes appointments without consultation with anyone. Someone recalls that Thurtle at the time of Munich called out, 'Well done Chamberlain!' and Barbara Gould,[2] who deteriorates both physically and mentally from week to week, produces a version of a recent conversation with Thurtle in which he said that he entirely agreed with 'the Vansittart letters'. But there is clearly nothing to be done.

I hope, however, that Phil will get something before long; otherwise he will really become discouraged.

After lunching at the House and doing some 'hobbing and nobbing' (a happy and descriptive phrase which I owe to my C.E.O., whom I found so engaged at the Foreign Office some days ago), I settle down in the Ministry to read piles of telegrams and other papers. Hardly started, I am rung up by Bracken, who says that he understands this Committee of Three[3] is very important and he would like to make an

1 Kenneth Young (ed.), *The Diaries of Sir Robert Bruce Lockhart, vol. II 1939–1965*, Macmillan, London, 1980, p. 110.
2 Barbara Ayrton Gould (d. 1950). Labour Party N.E.C. member. Labour M.P. 1945–50.
3 'Committee of Three': set up under the 'Anderson Award' to settle disputes about propaganda, and consisting of the Foreign Secretary, the Minister of Economic Warfare and the Minister of Information. 'Our committee is called "The Committee of Three",' Bruce Lockhart wrote on 10th August, 'and triumvirates generally mean the murder of the odd man by the other two and then a struggle for the crown between the other two.' (*Bruce Lockhart Diaries*, pp. 114–15.)

appointment at once. He suggests that my General (sic) Brooks should represent him on it. I say that he performs indispensable functions for me now and I could not release him. Bracken thinks that 'Joe Hollis[1] could easily find you someone else'. I say that I am sure he couldn't. Anyhow, he asks me to think it over, which I say I will do. I see Brooks later in the afternoon and he expresses deep horror at the idea of joining the Ministry of Information staff. Indeed, he says that nothing will induce him to go. Almost he clings to me weeping! I say that I regard him as one of my linchpins and certainly would not contemplate losing him. If, however, Bracken were willing that my liaison officer with him should represent him on this Committee, I should have no objection. But it would be a very odd and unconstitutional arrangement. ...

Later I hear that Bracken has asked Thurtle to attend the Committee of Three, which is now due to meet on Monday. Bracken has been told that Cooper has left unanswered an invitation from Eden, dated 4th July, to appoint his man, and is terrified of this delay emerging in reply to a Parliamentary Question. It might suit very well if Thurtle were permanently to be a member of this Committee, though he might be encouraged to think it beneath his dignity, as a junior minister, to sit under the Chairmanship of an official. I shall try to see him tomorrow, tell him as much as is necessary and good for him, and smooth the way.

...

C.E.O. has been trying for days to see Ismay, but this is very difficult. Tonight he tried to see Bridges, and took out to dinner Harris,[2] the latter's Secretary, a Fellow of All Souls and said to be quite bright. He brings back an awful picture of how those near the P.M. have to live. Bridges is used as a Principal Private Secretary in addition to being Secretary to the Cabinet. Neither Bridges nor Ismay have had any holiday since the war began and hardly ever have a weekend off. When the P.M. is about, they have to stay up till 2 a.m. and sometimes 4 a.m. and it is said that Ismay, though he has the constitution of an ox and an excellent intelligence, finds that his mind is getting quite numb. The P.M., it is said, regards himself as Commander-in-Chief both of the British Navy in the Atlantic and of the Imperial Forces in the Middle East.

1 Major General Sir Leslie Hollis (1897–1963). Senior Assistant Secretary in Offices of War Cabinet 1939–46.
2 R. M. J. Harris, later Sir Ronald (b. 1913). Private Secretary to the Secretary to the Cabinet 1939–43. H.M. Treasury 1949–52. Cabinet Office 1952–5. Third Secretary at the Treasury 1940–64.

The General de Gaulle is becoming more and more impossible. He is trying to take away, purely for prestige reasons, a number of our trainees to act as 'infantry of the air' in the Middle East, but they will have no aircraft out there! and here there are many tasks awaiting them. C.E.O. is to sit on the doorstep of the C.O.S. [Chiefs of Staff] tomorrow morning to try to get them to oppose this plan.

De Gaulle has been in a terrible state about Syria and there is a dramatic account from Oliver Twist of their talks in Cairo.[1] De Gaulle protests bitterly against the way the campaign was conducted (slow and unenterprising, he thinks) and still more at the Armistice terms and Protocol (signed by General Wavell without proper authority), unduly limiting the contact of Free French or other allied agents with the Vichy elements. De Gaulle came, apparently not having slept and in a terrible state of wounded vanity and unco-operativeness, and tried to leave with Oliver Twist a bombastic written declaration, 'Free France, that is to say France, declines ...... declares ...... repudiates, etc.' He said, in effect, that he would do what he liked in the future with all his own, would not recognise the British in any way in Syria, or as allies in any campaign. Oliver Twist, according to his own account, handled him with skill and firmness and hopes to calm him down soon, but fears that if de Gaulle has another sleepless night we may be confronted with further quite impossible demands.

Thursday 24th July
Spend some time with Hopkins at the American Embassy, most of it alone, and then *à quatre* with Winant and Leith-Ross. Winant is said to get on very well with the P.M., but in my experience of him he is almost speechless, almost inaudible when he does speak, and never looks me straight in the eyes except at the beginning and the end of an interview. They say he has Red Indian blood, which helps to account for his rather curious appearance.

What a contrast is Harry Hopkins! Sharp as a needle, humorous, ready for anything. I say that, since he was last here, when I gave him a memo of M.E.W. questions, there has been a good move forward on all points except one, namely, the creation of an American M.E.W.

---

1 Fearing a German advance into Vichy-controlled Syria, Wavell was ordered to invade the country first. In conjunction with a force provided by the Free French, he attacked on 8th June, and soon met strong resistance. By the end of the first week in July the Vichy French faced defeat, and on 12th July they asked for an armistice. This successful campaign greatly improved the Allied strategic position in the Middle East.

I ask him how this stands now. He says that Wallace,[1] the Vice-President, is to preside over a new set-up which, Hopkins hopes, will be much better than an Inter-Departmental Committee, as some at first suggested. Hopkins, before leaving, saw two letters, one from the President to Wallace offering him this job, and the other from Wallace to the President accepting, but publicity has been delayed pending the collection by Wallace of a good team. Hopkins has urged him not to ask Departments, and especially the State Department, to nominate people, but himself to pick them. Otherwise, the State Department will nominate some old man who will always be obstructing and tiring everybody out. ...

I ask him about Donovan,[2] and say that I would like him to come over here soon to see and discuss our show. Hopkins says he will pass this on and himself thinks it would be a good thing. He would also like to tell the President something about it himself. I hope to arrange a meeting with him and C.E.O. on Monday, by which time we will have a short memo prepared and also let him have a glance at our longer one. ...

Oliver Twist has sent a telegram welcoming the arrival of C.D. [Nelson] and Maxwell, and now we are anxious to get them off as soon as possible. C.E.O. wants me to get C.D. Treasury cover and give Maxwell M.E.W. cover.

I hear that Hoare has written a personal letter to Eden suggesting that Eccles should be sent to America. This is damned cheek anyhow, and no doubt was instigated by Eccles himself. The letter was passed by Eden to Sir David Scott, who showed it to Drogheda, who said he was sure that I should not approve. Nor do I. I am inclined to summon Eccles back to report before long and should like to send him on a mission a great distance away.

Friday 25th July
A regular row in the afternoon between SO1 and SO2 over appointment of Maxwell. Taylor is a good deal to blame for bad staff work and for trying to grab and snatch without consultation. I am asked to see Maxwell this afternoon along with Gladwyn, C.D. and A.D. [George Taylor]. They all march in and proposed Terms of Reference for Maxwell are planted down in front of me. I at once react against

1 Henry Wallace (1888–1965). Vice-President of the U.S.A. 1941–5. Chairman of the Board of Economic Warfare 1942–3. Secretary of Commerce 1945–6. Democrat Presidential candidate 1948.
2 W. J. Donovan (1883–1959). Sent on special missions for Roosevelt in Europe 1940–41. Co-ordinator of Information 1941. Director of Office of Strategic Services 1942–5.

these, since they do not seem either to safeguard my own authority or to have involved any consultation with Leeper and Co. I ask Gladwyn whether he has seen them and he says yes, but it is quite clear that he has not had time to study them. It is A.D. who has drafted them. It is, however, very awkward for me to say in front of Maxwell that they give the latter too much power, and it was very stupid to bring him in before I had had a preliminary look at the Terms of Reference. The only excuse for all this muddling is that everybody is in a rush. None the less, I have first to manoeuvre Maxwell out of the room, then to row the other three, then to suggest that C.D. should see Maxwell alone and get him to agree to *no* Terms of Reference (this is awkward, for it may arouse his suspicions and make him think that I have not complete confidence in him). C.D. goes off and manages this very well, Maxwell having acquired already great confidence in him. Brigadier Brooks, who is hanging about – this again is badly stage managed – is given in the Secretaries' Room a copy of the Terms of Reference with some preliminary amendments of mine. He is, of course, very angry that this is the first he has heard of it, particularly as it is now proposed to give Maxwell complete authority over both SO1 and SO2 in Middle East, i.e. more than was to be given to Taverner.[1] ...

I tell Gaitskell to go down tomorrow with Maxwell and not to allow any dog fights to develop in his presence. A.D. is to be sent away to eat worms with someone else and not to argue in front of Maxwell about anything. Maxwell is just to be shown round and told who does what.

Gaitskell says to me afterwards that Gladwyn and Leeper will never hit it. Leeper is much too suspicious. He think that Gladwyn despises him and realises that Gladwyn always gets the best of any argument, having a much quicker and more incisive mind. Also he is jealous of the fact that Gladwyn sees so much more of me than he does, and he realises that I think much more of Gladwyn than of him. On the other hand, Gaitskell is to make the most of the fact that I shouted at them all this afternoon for not having consulted Leeper and tore up the Terms of Reference and refused even to consider them.

Gaitskell also says that when Gladwyn rang up Leeper on the telephone to try to straighten things out, instead of adopting a deadly serious tone, as Leeper himself did at the other end, Gladwyn treated the whole thing half as a joke and told Leeper he had been getting into terrible trouble and had been ticked off by the Minister.

1 Brigadier R. L. Taverner (1899–1976). He had been shot down while on his way to investigate the S.O.E. machine in Cairo, and taken prisoner. He was released in 1945. (See note on p. 253.)

Gaitskell says that Drogheda told him some time ago that there had been great heart-burning at the Foreign Office when I made Gladwyn an Assistant Under-Secretary of State, and that he does not think Gladwyn realises that he sometimes antagonises people by his rather offhand manner and his apparent lack of interest in what they are saying.

Later this evening I have a triangular talk with Gladwyn and Gaitskell and make them argue between themselves about all this. It is clear that in this case Gladwyn himself had not been properly consulted by his own subordinates over the Terms of Reference etc.

Sunday 27th July
Speak at Woodford in the evening. A very great success! I stand beside the Mayor and take the salute at a march past of representatives of the armed forces, the police and all the A.R.P. [Air Raid Precautions] services of the Borough. Great crowds look on and there are more than two thousand afterwards in the cinema, with a further crowd outside, to whom speeches are relayed from within. I make a very good speech, lasting an hour and a half, during which no one leaves except one woman with a baby. Two patches of generalities and rhetoric, including tributes to the P.M. at each end, and a lump of solid informative stuff about M.E.W. in the middle. Most enthusiastically received, both by the audience and by the small party which comes back to Sir James Hawkey's house afterwards for light refreshments.

Monday 28th July
I lunch with Bracken and have what may prove to be a most useful talk. He gives the appearance of being very friendly and co-operative; says his chief interest is in Home news and in American propaganda; he would like not to have to trouble much about propaganda to enemy and enemy-occupied countries. He does not want to appoint a successor to Peterson; he would like to have 'General Brook' as the man to sit with Lockhart and Leeper on the Committee of Three; he would like this Committee to settle everything without much reference back to ministers except on quite important matters; he says that he and I do not want to be always meeting Eden, whom he finds 'very touchy'. He would like to tell the House of Commons that we three ministers have decided to set up a Department of Political Warfare; that we have put it in charge of people whom we trust, but that neither their names nor any of their activities can be published, since this is a highly secret branch of warfare, as secret as the plans of the Chiefs of Staff. He thinks that this would make a great impression in Parliament and in the press, where 'political warfare' is a much beloved phrase, and

that this would settle for good the question of secrecy. He thinks that the P.M. would back such a plan. ...

After a personal request from President Roosevelt for medical supplies, milk and vitamin concentrates to be allowed through the blockade had been granted in January 1941, an official declaration was issued that no further concessions would be made. U.S. pressure for more relief shipments, however, continued.

Cabinet. Complete defeat of Eden, who wants authority to tell the refugee governments, and particularly the Belgians, that we will be prepared to consider favourably a proposal to let milk through the blockade into their countries on condition that the American Red Cross distributed it. He says that he is sure the Germans would refuse this offer and so we should score. He says that since our blockade in Southern France is not effective, it is difficult to maintain a total blockade against food into other areas. He also says that he has had telegrams from the U.S. proposing that milk should be sent into Occupied France.

I make a speech in reply to this, saying that I am afraid my paper with appendix containing general forecast of food situation in Europe next winter has only come round late this afternoon and that my colleagues will not yet have had time to study it. I strongly urge, however, that there should be no change in policy until my paper has been studied. There will be enough food in Europe this winter to feed all, even though modestly and monotonously, if the Germans will distribute it fairly, and perhaps draw something from their hoarded stocks of over 3,000,000 tons of wheat. The Marseilles leak in the blockade is not as bad as Eden says, and anyhow, even if this leak exists, it is no argument for deliberately making another. I say I have not seen the telegrams he refers to on milk for Occupied France, and any small concession made now must rapidly extend, since we must be prepared to concede to other allies whatever we concede to any one. Nor is this the time to raise the question, since the harvest is just coming in, and for some while there should be no serious shortage anywhere.

The P.M. then weighs in most heavily upon my side. 'Once we leave the high ground of principle and come down into the valley of compromise', we shall face great difficulties. He takes the point about the harvest and declares that we must maintain the principle that the Germans are responsible for feeding those whom they have enslaved. Eden must say this, again and again, to the small neutral allied governments who come to him. The Beaver also backs up this line. Growing weary of the debate, he cries, 'Why should we discuss this any more now? Why can't we wait till after the harvest? I'm told there is going to be a very good harvest in this country.' And no one says a word in support of Eden. It must have seemed very humiliating, but he brought it on himself, particularly by bunging in a paper on Blockade without consulting me first.

Tuesday 29th July
Reflecting on yesterday, I am afraid Eden is rather a light-weight. He reminds me of a little boy trying to clutch all the toys. ...

Wilmot is in great form this evening, very cheerful and amusing. I tell him that his happy gifts of reconciliation will again be wanted between my two Assistant Under-Secretaries. We both agree that it would be much easier if there was only one of them, and if Leeper took a job abroad or in the Foreign Office. One of the grounds of discontent is that both Gladwyn and I work quite late, when most others have gone to bed, and that he often brings me important papers, on which I make important decisions, just before he goes home. Indeed, I often have to tell him to go home and not work any later, since in the morning he has his 9 o'clock meeting with the Daily Council. Those who don't work after dinner cannot expect to be in on all these things, and in any case I won't have the machine slowed up by excessive consultation.

Conversations between the Soviet government and the Polish government-in-exile began in London on 5th July. Poland was represented by General Sikorski, the Prime Minister, and the Soviet Union by the Soviet Ambassador, Maisky. After a long and frigid series of exchanges, agreement was reached on 30th July. Diplomatic relations were restored, and it was agreed that a Polish army would be formed in Russia. The vexed question of frontiers, however, was scarcely settled by a general statement that the German-Soviet treaties of 1939 were no longer valid.

Wednesday 30th July
Say farewell to C.D., who with Maxwell is leaving this evening in a flying boat specially laid on by C.A.S. [Chief of Air Staff], at our

request, for Middle East. I give him a letter to Lyttelton which tries yet once more to make the point that all Subversion is one, and should be under one direction. (There is a confused mass of telegraphing now in process between Middle East and this end, and some of my officials want me to send several more, but I firmly refuse, since these two will soon, bar accidents, arrive in Cairo.) C.D. thinks he will be able to influence little [Henry] Hopkinson, who is his cousin and has, he says a strong family sense! ...

I hear that the Russo-Polish Treaty has been signed at 4 o'clock this afternoon, and as there is a party at the Dorchester from 6 to 7.30, promoted by the Anglo-Polish Parliamentary Committee, I ask for Retinger to come round and see me first. Gladwyn, who has been at the Foreign Office this afternoon, says that, according to Strang, within the Polish Government 'things couldn't be worse'.

Thursday 31st July
Send Eden a letter of congratulation on the Russo-Polish Treaty and his part of it. This is designed to sweeten relations which I apprehend may have become a little sour, though Gladwyn reports that he sounded Cadogan on this today and Cadogan said that he thought our relations were about the same, not much better or much worse, and that Eden was not harbouring any particular grudge against me for bowling him out at the Cabinet on Monday. ...

I give Bracken tonight a copy of my letter to Oliver Twist which Nelson is taking with him. Bracken is still talking very loud about the importance of co-operation, etc., but I am not quite satisfied with a draft he has sent me this evening, to be considered over the weekend, for the new D.P.W. [Department of Political Warfare]. I see an inclination to insert Morton into this machine and perhaps to enable him to take control of it later.

Friday 8th August
Kept waiting for three-quarters of an hour with Eden and Hudson in the anteroom to the Lord President's Committee, while a long jaw proceeds within on coal. Duncan and Grenfell between them have a pretty heavy responsibility for the general muddle over output and failure to keep enough men at work in the pits. It is incredible that, with no export trade, we cannot produce enough coal for our own requirements! Grenfell is now proved to be what I had always thought him, a second-rate, slow-witted, indecisive sheepshead.

Eden is very peevish at being kept waiting and sits down in a corner with a packet of papers. When at last we go in to discuss the Wheat Conference at Washington, it is argued by Hudson, and accepted by

Anderson, that Carlill,[1] our representative at the Conference, has exceeded his instructions by accepting in principle a reduction in our wheat acreage without referring back. ...

I then leave with Eden for a delayed conference *à trois* with Bracken at Foreign Office. Arrived in his room, Eden drinks some milk and admits that he has a tendency to duodenal ulcers. He says that he had a good deal of pain from this about a year ago. I am told that this complaint comes from excessive worry, and no doubt Eden is, more than most men, a nervy fusser.

We three ministers then agree a paper based on a draft of mine which the other two men amend slightly. It is proposed that next our three officials should work out a plan for organisation and operations of Political Warfare.

Get away in the afternoon to West Leaze, taking with me some books and drinks. Just before leaving, I talk to Gaitskell and Brigadier Brooks about sending someone to Moscow, as suggested by Cripps, to discuss subversive propaganda with the Russians. We three all think that Crossman would be the man. Later Gaitskell mentions this to Leeper, who is frightened out of his wits at the very idea. This is becoming a very immobile old sheep, both mentally and in his Old Rectory.[2]

So this evening I make good my escape [to West Leaze] and spend till –

Tuesday 12th August
quite alone, trying to forget the war and all my official duties. I go back to the Romans and read George Gissing's *By the Ionian Sea*, a charming book recommended to me by Gladwyn, Carcopino's *Daily Life in Ancient Rome*, first mentioned to me by the Lord Chancellor (!) and found to be in the possession of Brook,[3] *I, Claudius* in two volumes, and snatches of Gibbon.

It is not hot and rains a good deal, but I perform various mechanical tasks in the garden, notably cutting grass with a pair of shears and making hay on the lower part of my estate with the Gentry family. Gentry has had a hay rick burned down by an evacuee boy and, although they say it was insured, he is therefore glad to get hay from

1 Harold Carlill (1875–1959). Civil servant. Delegate to Washington Wheat Meeting 1941–2.
2 'Old Rectory': at Woburn.
3 R. E. Brook, later Sir Robin (b. 1908). S.O.E. 1941–6, first as Personal Assistant to Jebb, and later in charge of the organisation of resistance in France. A Director of the Bank of England 1946–9. Chairman of the Colonial Development Corporation 1949–53. Merchant banker.

elsewhere. West Leaze, it is estimated, can contribute more than three tons.

Thursday 14th August

Ruth arrives at West Leaze from a visit to evacuees in Cambridge.

Friday 15th August

John Wilmot arrives. Elsa's father died on Monday, so she can't get here till tomorrow. She is very tired after a long and trying time.

Saturday 16th August

Elsa Wilmot arrives in the early afternoon, and Gladwyn in the evening.

Sunday 17th August

We go for a walk on the Downs, but it pours with rain. Wilmot has a tummy ache and turns back early, and the other four of us having got pretty wet, decide not to lunch out of doors on sandwiches as we had intended, particularly as we think John's tummy ache is due to drinking too much cider which has gone a bit sour, and we have only another bottle of the same with us, and therefore we all go back to a late lunch at home. In the afternoon people sleep, and later I win two games of chess, one against Gladwyn and the other against John, and we all go to bed early. I have three rather tired guests this weekend.

Monday 18th August

Return to London, Ruth with a quantity of luggage by train, the rest of us in Gladwyn's car. I pack him off to Scotland this evening by the night train, where he is to have a well deserved leave, and not to return till 1st September. He has worked immensely hard and well for many weeks, starting with the 9 a.m. Daily Council and finishing with me often past midnight in the office. ...

A.D. [Taylor] says that C.D. [Nelson] has left Cairo in a Sunderland and may be home any day now.

Tuesday 19th August

P.O.G. Committee decides to recommend Cabinet to authorise Cripps, at his discretion, to make offer to Russians that, if they destroy Caucasus oil, we will see them through both as regards oil during the war and post-war period and re-equipment of the industry. ...

Receive a draft of a 'plan' for Political Warfare from the three officials. It is awfully bad, both in form and substance, full of confusions and platitudes. The Old Rectory in excelsis! There is to be a ministers' meeting on the 21st at the Foreign Office to consider it. I must send a letter to my two colleagues to reach them before this meeting. It is a most awful bore this continual fidgeting on the Political Warfare front.

Early in August, Churchill and Roosevelt met at Placentia Bay in Newfoundland in order to discuss the situation in Europe and the Far East. The meeting was of great importance in strengthening the Anglo-American accord. Warnings were made to the Japanese, and undertakings were given to the Russians. In addition, the two leaders made an agreement later known as the Atlantic Charter, which expounded a set of principles declaring the right of all countries to democratic elections and protection from foreign domination.

Wednesday 20th August

Van looks in, not having been to see me for some time, and reads some telegrams. He and Sarita were in a car smash the other day and, he says, both narrowly escaped death; she was badly shaken and his car will be out of action for some time. He thinks nothing of the Eight Points agreed by the P.M. and the President. It will be a great mistake, he says, to play this up very much. He also tells me that Montagu Norman was on the *Prince of Wales* and thinks that, if this got out, it would create a very bad impression. What game was *he* up to?

C.D. comes and reports to me at great length on his doings in Cairo. He seems to have done extremely well ... Lyttelton, he says, is anxious to be on friendly terms with me and was a little apprehensive that I should take the line that C.D. need not have come out to Cairo after all. Charges of 'corruption' were quite unproved, though undoubtedly there had been muddle, extravagance, gossip and intrigue in great quantities. ...

Ruth and I lunch with Van Kleffens and a mixed party at Claridge's. Afterwards she comes round to inspect my shelter bedroom, to which we shall move some of our furniture from the flat at Carlisle Mansions. We have decided to give this up in any case and either to take a small service flat somewhere else, or if, as is possible, Ruth goes to do some work in the Midlands, we shall store books and furniture in Swindon, to be near West Leaze, and no longer have a *pied à terre* in London at all, beside my Ministry.

267

The Chinese Ambassador, Wellington Koo,[1] pays a courtesy visit and asks a large number of questions. He is not quite so serene and smiling a character as his predecessor. Some, indeed, regard him as rather sinister.

The arrangements agreed under the 'Anderson Award' on 16th May were not implemented until August, when a charter for a new organisation was approved by the Prime Minister. This was an elaboration of the Committee of Three, a Standing Ministerial Committee to deal with major questions of propaganda policy, supported by an official committee of three, with Robert Bruce Lockhart representing the Foreign Office, Rex Leeper representing the Ministry of Information, and Major General Dallas Brooks (of SO1) representing M.E.W. The charter laid down that this committee would act as a General Staff for the conduct of political warfare. It was proposed that parts of M.O.I., the B.B.C. and SO1 should be amalgamated into an organisation to be known as the Political Warfare Executive (P.W.E.).

Dalton soon became concerned about the scope of this new body. On 20th August he wrote to Eden and to Bracken:

I have been looking through the paper on 'the Executive Committee's proposals for the organisation and conduct of Political Warfare', which we are to consider together tomorrow. This will, in my view, have to be revised considerably, both as to form and substance, before it can be accepted by us as a working basis for our new arrangements.

In the first place the paper reads as though SO1 was to be entirely abolished ... I do not suppose that this can be the intention of the author and, of course, I could not possibly agree to the complete disappearance of one half of the Special Operations Executive created under my charter from the Prime Minister and the War Cabinet, placing upon me the responsibility for 'co-ordinating all action by way of Subversion and Sabotage against the enemy overseas'.

On the other hand, as you know, I am entirely in favour of an effective co-ordination of all forms of political warfare and joint responsibility of the three Ministers concerned in all major questions.

Our three Officials may, perhaps, have misunderstood the meaning of some key words in our agreed paper of August 8th, namely that 'these three Officers should be jointly responsible to the Standing Ministerial

1 V. K. Wellington Koo (Ku Wei-chun). Chinese Ambassador to Great Britain 1941–6. Chinese Prime Minister 1926–7; Foreign Minister 1922–4, 1926–7, 1931. Finance Minister 1926.

Committee which itself will exercise its power of control jointly' ... [1]

Dalton was also worried about proposed relations between the B.B.C. and the P.W.E.; and he argued that the powers proposed for the Executive Committee to deal with staff matters were too wide.

Thursday 21st August

Meeting at Foreign Office with Eden and Bracken to consider the Plan of the three officials. I have sent a long letter, raising various points and objections, which the other two ministers have only got just before the meeting. I have also brought with me an alternative draft. We are due to meet at 4, and Eden has another engagement at 4.30. Bracken cannot arrive till 4.10, so we only have twenty minutes. In this time it is impossible to get down to any detail. Bracken makes a long speech about putting everything into the pool, and says that his decision has been received with horror by all his advisers, that Radcliffe has sent him pages and pages of legal objections, and that the Governors of the B.B.C. have also objected to being robbed of part of their just rights. None the less, he is determined to go ahead. He tries to rush me into saying that I will also put the whole of SO1 personnel into the pot, but this I refuse to do. Eden does not seem to be focusing much and just repeats that everything ought to be joint and the officials ought to get on with their work. Finally, we agree that consideration of the officials' plan shall be indefinitely postponed and that they shall be told to get on with their work on the basis of the ministers' paper of 8th August. It is also agreed that Para. 4 in my alternative draft, about making plans region by region, shall be shown to Lockhart, who is then summoned into the room. He says that it will be very difficult for them to proceed, but he is told to do his best. I foresee that these ministerial meetings are likely to be very brief and sketchy. No doubt this is what the officials are counting on, in being able to run the show largely on their own.

A.D. [Taylor] reports to me that Broad has now twice been drunk, to the point of incapacity, in the afternoon in the office. I agree that in these circumstances he must be at once returned to store at the Foreign Office. A.D. will speak to Mallet[2] about this.

---

1 Dalton Papers 18/2 (21).
2 W. I. Mallet, later Sir Ivo (b. 1900). Assistant Private Secretary to the Foreign Secretary 1938–41.

Friday 22nd August

George Isaacs[1] to see me to get material before going off to U.S.A. He is a good chap. Gaitskell thinks that I should spend more time in the future cultivating Labour M.P.s. ...

Dine with Robin Brook. He also invites Charles MacLaren,[2] Harcourt[3] and Chris Mayhew. I spend a very pleasant evening with these young men, all of whom are intelligent and likeable. Brook is a great find. He has quickness, dry clarity and a sense of humour, like his Master (Gladwyn).

Saturday 23rd August

To C.H.Q. after lunch. After dinner Gaitskell and I discuss with Leeper, Brooks, Bowes-Lyon and Adams. Adams, however, does not say a word the whole evening and Bowes-Lyon only once intervenes, to tell Gaitskell, 'Don't be so cynical.' I cross-examine Leeper as to the meaning of his proposals. Is it intended that SO1 as such should completely disappear? I have the utmost difficulty in getting an answer to this question. It is, as I say to Gaitskell afterwards, like trying to pull teeth out of a sheep. But after much twisting it becomes clear that the answer is yes. At an earlier stage of the conversation we meet an unexpected set-back because, when I tell them what happened at the ministers' meeting on Thursday last (21st), ending with the statement that they should now get on with making their plan region by region, Leeper says that they have had nothing in writing and can't do any more until they have. He thinks that the officials have been badly treated by the ministers. He seems disinclined to discuss anything any further, and it is at this point that Gaitskell says that in this case we had better all go to bed, which leads to Bowes-Lyon's one intervention! Further cross-examination reveals that it is contemplated that I should have no more special relationship to C.H.Q. than either of my two ministerial colleagues (although, of course, on the other hand I should acquire new and joint responsibilities as regards the B.B.C.). For all this, in principle, there is much to be said, but it is clear that in practice the real point which Leeper is after is to evade further ministerial control by me. Indeed I say to him that I have spent a large number of weekends at C.H.Q. by reason of a sense of duty, though I

1 G. A. Isaacs (1883–1979). Labour M.P. for Southwark North 1929–31, 1939–50; Gravesend 1923–4; Southwark 1950–59. Minister of Labour and National Service 1945–51. Minister of Pensions 1951.

2 Possibly Hon. C. M. McLaren, later 3rd Baron Aberconway (b. 1913), who became Brook's brother-in-law in the same year.

3 Possibly W. E. H. Harcourt, 2nd Viscount (1908–79). Serving with the Oxford Yeomanry. A peacetime economist and banker.

should much have preferred to spend them at my country cottage, and that I should welcome having to spend less time here in the future, but that in my view the show will not be efficient without a good deal of ministerial control and stimulus. At a certain stage in the conversation I allow Gaitskell to make the running and myself to remain silent. Every now and then Brooks tried to edge out and to suggest that these are really matters for ministers to decide. To this Gaitskell or I invariably reply that what we desire to ascertain is what the officials themselves have in their minds.

And so to bed, Gaitskell very much excited but I, though a good deal irritated, somewhat less so.

Dalton recorded his discussion on 23rd August more fully in a separate note:

At a certain stage I put to Mr Leeper the question whether his purpose in this new arrangement was not to escape from a measure of ministerial control by me which over a period of months he had found disagreeable. Mr Leeper did not seem disposed to answer this question, and Brigadier Brooks suggested that it was not a fair question to put to him. ...

The various persons present gradually lapsed into more or less embarrassed silence and the conversation petered out. Wishing Mr Leeper Good-night, I said that he was not looking at all well, and I hoped that he would soon be able to take a little leave. [1]

Monday 25th August
See Kingsley Wood on a proposal to forge Reichsmarks. He thinks Montagu Norman will be shocked but will put it to him again! We drift off into a discussion in which Wood says that not everyone accepts the P.M.'s view that the President is a great man. There is another view that he is a yes man to all who speak to him, and Keynes[2] thinks that he is also quite a sick man. The arrangements in the White House are very bad for hot weather – and it is a bad sign that the President has been feeling the hot weather in Washington this summer. He has an old-fashioned air-conditioning mechanism in his bedroom which makes a noise and keeps him awake at night, so he gets up and

1 Dalton Papers 18/2 (24).
2 J. M. Keynes, later 1st Baron (1883–1946). Economic Adviser to the Treasury. Fellow of King's College, Cambridge 1909–46. Treasury 1915–19. Governor of the International Bank for Reconstruction and Development 1946.

turns it off and then is no good for anything in the morning. Also his medical adviser is an old ship's doctor who has been a crony of his for more than twenty years but who has no knowledge at all of modern medicine.

Wood also says that Cripps has been quarrelling with the American Ambassador at Moscow[1] and would like to come home again. I say that he would be a damned nuisance if he did and would probably join up with Shinwell if he came back. Wood says that he has told Eden that he thinks that Cripps should see the job through. ...

Eccles also comes to see me and as usual is plausible and interesting. He says that in U.S. Democratic-Republican enmity is flaming up again. They think that now the Russians will help us to win the war without their bothering much. There is no 'security' in U.S.A. Everything gets into the press. A dozen of the leading American journalists sit all day and all night in a room in the White House drinking highballs with their feet on the table. Nothing can be kept from them. The President is a sick man and more and more with the mentality of an Emperor. He won't do any detailed discussion but always wants to be amused. He still has the gift of 'charming a bird off a twig' and of bright phrase. When Eccles said that he ought to do something or other, the President replied, 'You might as well ask me to piss into the wind.' Halifax is getting on better with him now, but, says Eccles, after he had only been out there a short time he broke down and wept in Eccles's presence because he couldn't get on with these Americans.

Early in the autumn of 1941, the Daltons abandoned their flat at Carlisle Mansions, Victoria – Hugh moving into ministerial quarters in the cellar of his office, Ruth, temporarily, into a hotel. It was the beginning of a separation which lasted until 1945. In December, Ruth moved to Manchester, to take up a post as a liaison officer looking after hostels for women munitions workers. Though they saw each other occasionally, they lived separate lives – and spent the next four Christmases apart.

In 1944 Ruth returned briefly to London, living for a few months in a one-room flat in Hampstead, before going to France to work for the United Nations Relief and Rehabilitation Administration (U.N.R.R.A.). The couple were reunited after Dalton became Chancellor of the Exchequer.

---

1 Admiral William Standley (1872–1963). U.S. Ambassador in Moscow 1941– October 1943, when he was replaced by Averell Harriman.

Tuesday 26th August

Move furniture from 5 Carlisle Mansions to my bedroom at the Ministry, which now will look quite habitable.

Garro Jones asks me to lunch, but simply I think in order to 'maintain contact'. He says that Stuart Campbell,[1] the Editor of the *Daily Mirror*, is interested in running some sort of opposition to H.M.G., but told him that of course Shinwell wouldn't fit the part. He had encouraged Garro, who, however, had not been very responsive. Garro thinks that we should continue a National Government as long as Churchill is Prime Minister, but that, as soon as he pulls out – and he is likely to want to pull out soon after victory so as to have time and opportunity to write the history of these times – we should revert to Party politics. In that situation Garro thinks that we should get a Labour majority, since no effective alternative Conservative leader would be available.

A meeting of ministers at 5 p.m. at No. 10, when P.M. gives us an account of recent events. He seems to me to be in extremely good form, very lucid and rationally optimistic.

He says that he felt that his courtship with the President had been carried as far as it could be by correspondence and that now it was necessary to add a personal contact. The President is a tremendous friend of ours and will do all he can, both to help us to win the war and to consolidate peace afterwards. The most important definite result of the Atlantic Talks was naval. Pound and 'Betty' Stark[2] 'fell in love with each other'. Next month the new convoy system will be operating. ... So long as one American merchantman is being escorted by one American warship, any number of British merchantmen can join in. There will also be other extensions, e.g. around Iceland, of forbidden zones in which loiterers with evil intent may be shot up. And so That Man will have to choose between getting into a shooting match with the U.S.A. or finally admitting that he has lost the Battle of the Atlantic. (The U.S. sailors, I gather, would much prefer the former!) Apart from these preparations, the Battle of the Atlantic has been going very well for us. The last two months of sinkings have been very low. Our decision not to go on publishing them was taken because, at that time, they were so bad that we did not want to encourage the enemy and depress our own people; now we don't want to publish them because they are so good that they might encourage the Isolationists and hamper our friends in America.

1 R. S. Campbell (1908–66). In fact, Editor of the *Sunday Pictorial* 1940–46. Managing Editor of the *People* 1946–57. Editor of the *People* 1958–66.
2 Admiral H. R. Stark (1880–1972). U.S. Chief of Naval Operations 1935–42. Commander of U.S. Naval Forces in Europe 1942–5.

On the other hand, we have been having very great success in *our* attacks, by air and submarine, on enemy shipping. We have never before had such good opportunities for unrestricted submarine warfare and we have some very good new devices for air attack on enemy ships. We have now completely closed the Channel to them and there are no serious signs of invasion preparations in any of the West European ports.

The P.M. still does not think that the Japs will go to war with us. The Americans have been giving them very serious warnings which they may well interpret as meaning that the U.S. will make war on them if they advance any further, e.g. into Thailand. He has said that, if the Americans get involved in war in the Far East, we shall wholeheartedly go in with them. He has been very rude to the Japs in his broadcast on Sunday – 'All this has got to stop' – and he thinks this will have had the effect of checking them. The Russians also have been very firm to them regarding supplies to Vladivostok from the U.S.A.

Meanwhile, the President is gaining time by conducting what is really rather a humbugging negotiation with the Japs on the conditions on which there could be a general guarantee of the neutrality of Indo-China and Thailand. This might be guaranteed, not only by the U.S. and the Japs and the British Commonwealth, but by France and China and everybody else! The President first hoped to keep this negotiation going for thirty days; he now hopes he can spin it out to ninety. Long before then *we* shall be able to put a really strong fleet in the Indian Ocean without denuding the Mediterranean. One of our damaged battleships has nearly completed its repair in the American yards, and a new one is just coming off the stocks.

The P.M. thinks that the Russians are doing very well indeed, and jeers at all the experts who began by saying it would all be over in a few days or weeks. He is confident that Russian resistance will continue through and beyond the winter, though they may lose more ground. He thinks that Leningrad may fall, but not Moscow. He says the German losses have been prodigious. Never in any nine weeks, either of this war or the last, have the Germans lost anything like these casualties. They are behaving with the most complete brutality towards the Russians, murdering them, soldiers and civilians alike, like rats by tens of thousands behind their advancing lines. Our entry into Iran, which can be powerfully defended on other grounds, will also have the effect of establishing a close link, with a route through a warm water port, and so across the Pacific to the U.S.A., between us and them. This will help particularly in the defence of the Caucasus and the whole Volga basin. The Russians have a very good fleet on the Caspian Sea, and of course nobody else has.

Returning to the Atlantic Conference, the P.M. says that there has been a slide back in U.S. opinion since May or June. (Several other people have told me that the President could have brought them right in then, but his health was not good and he could not decide, and so missed that tide, which has not yet returned.) There is a good deal of playing politics and this will only be remedied when they 'unfurl the flag'.

As to Peace Aims, it was the President's suggestion that they should have a statement; the P.M. put up the first draft, which the President amended, and which then was further amended by Cabinet consultations. The P.M. draws attention to two points of sharp difference between this composition and those of 1917. Then we spoke much of a 'war to end war' and of a general organisation afterwards in which all were committed equally to disarm. On the other hand, we were full of ideas of making the Germans pay enormous reparations and of impoverishing them by seizing their trade.

Now we look at things differently. We must disarm the Germans and their accomplices but give no undertaking, which they can afterwards exploit, that we shall give them within any measurable time any sort of equality as regards arms. On the contrary, we must take care to see that we are sufficiently strongly armed to prevent any repetition, in Europe or the world, of these catastrophes. On the other hand, we now take the view that impoverished nations are bound to be bad neighbours, and we wish to see everyone prosperous, including the Germans. In short, our aim is to make Germany 'fat but impotent'.

As I told several people after listening to his broadcast last Sunday, I think that these ideas are both sense in themselves and will go over very well both with the Right and the Left in this country. 'Work and wages but no weapons' is my formula.

Wednesday 27th August

I arrange for Leeper to come and see me, intending to raise a series of small points. Gaitskell then tells me that the three officials ask to come together. Lockhart, who acts as spokesman, says that they have been sent for by Bracken and asked why they are doing nothing. Bracken says that he is prepared to put into the pool all the 'war zone' personnel, both in Ministry of Information and B.B.C. The officials told Bracken that they were not sure that I was equally prepared to put all SO1 personnel into the pool, and they come to ask me if I am. Cross-examined, Lockhart says that what the three of them wish to have is power to 'hire and fire' personnel according to their own ideas and without further reference to ministers. I say that I can't agree to this, nor contemplate that, e.g., Country Section Heads whom I have chosen on the grounds of their competence should come to me and ask for a testimonial for another job because, without further reference to me, three officials have decided to dispense with them.

The right course, I say, is that the officials should prepare a plan and submit it to the ministers for their approval. ...

To lunch with the Dutch P.M.,[1] Anderson, Eden, Morrison and Dill also being invited. I catch Eden for a moment as we are leaving and say that I propose to see Bracken this afternoon and hope to agree with him to give immediate orders to the three officials to put up proposals for dealing with personnel. Eden says that he wishes that they would get on with it, but doesn't dissent from my proposal.

After looking in on Sinclair ... I go on to see Bracken. As usual, he is in a hustle between two meetings. (This is how 'joint' ministerial control is always going to work out in practice.) I produce a draft – a very good precaution on these occasions – and finally he agrees to it in substance. This says that he and I, in agreement with Eden, desire the officials to submit to us as soon as possible their proposed arrangements for complete fusion of Ministry of Information, B.B.C. and SO1 personnel on 'war zone' work. Finally, 'this plan should provide for a single regional Head for each area'. I take this back to the Ministry and send for Stephens,[2] the newly appointed Secretary of the three officials. I tell him that I hand this to him officially and hope that there remain no ambiguities. He reads it through and says he thinks it is quite clear. I then invite Leeper to come back and hand a copy to him. Our relations have become quite cold and distant. I say, 'You have complained that you have had nothing in writing from ministers. Here now is something in writing which I hope is quite clear. Are you going to be in London again before next Wednesday?' (It is Wednesday today and usually this is the only day on which he comes up!) He takes it away, looking more than usually obstinate-sheepish.

Gaitskell and Bowes-Lyon are going down with him in the same car to the country. Gaitskell takes a number of copies of this Ministerial Direction and will use them at his discretion. I speak very frankly to Bowes-Lyon and say that I consider that Leeper, whom I myself had made an Assistant Under-Secretary, has acted most disingenuously towards me. The interview of last Saturday[3] has left a very unpleasant impression in my mind. He has been trying to conceal

---

1 Professor P. S. Gerbrandy (1885–1961). Prime Minister of the Dutch government-in-exile 1940–45. Lawyer.
2 David Stephens (b. 1910). P.W.E. 1941–3. Secretary to the Prime Minister 1955–61.
3 23rd August.

from me his real intentions. Clearly also he is most anxious to escape from any further ministerial control.

Friday 29th August
See Halifax at Privy Council Offices. He says that every night before he goes to sleep he asks himself could he have done any more that day to bring the U.S. into the war. Dealing with their Government Departments, he says, is like a 'disorderly day's rabbit shooting'. Nothing comes out where you expect and you are much discouraged. And then, suddenly, something emerges quite unexpectedly at the far end of the field.

Monday 1st September
Back from West Leaze and have short talk with C.E.O. just returned from leave in Scotland. Tell him of the happenings in the Special Operations world and ask him to do some scouting round. He has a word with Cadogan, who lets drop the remark, though only vaguely, as if repeating something at second or third hand, that he understood the idea was that I should give up propaganda.

Cabinet. Eden has once more put in a paper, without previous consultation with me, on Relief, and once more suggested a voluntary breach in the blockade. This time the pretext is the President's wish to send some more milk, etc., for children in Unoccupied France. This to keep some *raison d'être* there for the American Red Cross. Eden proposes that we should agree to this on condition that we do likewise with the occupied territories. I argue against this and have little difficulty in defeating it. Eden is absent and Cadogan has to state the case, which he does without much fire or conviction. P.M. as usual very good, and this time I am also supported by Woolton, who says that the Americans promised to send us much less milk than asked for, and are sending much less than they promised. This is the second time within a month – the last was on 28th July – that Eden has tried this on in the Cabinet. But I have twice defeated him. If I were he, I should feel a little humiliated.

Leave by night train for Edinburgh.

Tuesday 2nd September
The T.U.C., to keep contact with whom I am here, goes along very smoothly. George Gibson[1] is an admirable Chairman and has done a really good year of office. He is now going to Stockholm on a mission

1 George Gibson (1885–1953). Chairman of the T.U.C. 1940–41. General Secretary of the Mental Hospital and Institutional Workers' Union 1913–45.

which might turn out to be very useful.

Short talk with Attlee on the fuss over propaganda. I say I have the impression that Eden is trying to get too much into his hands. Attlee says that this is probably due to the Foreign Office officials. I say that we must retain, under the new triarchy, effective ministerial control and stimulus. He says that he strongly agrees.

Sunday 7th September

Cleaning up with Ruth at the flat, which we are evacuating this week. I throw away a lot of papers but keep more. I find a letter which I wrote to Ovey[1] from the Foreign Office in 1930 saying that I supposed the difficulties of contact in Moscow were like those of Late Romans trying to get on terms with Early Christians.

C.E.O. tells me that Sargent dropped an incautious remark today when, C.E.O. having said that, quite independently of persons, he thought the right plan was to have one minister responsible for propaganda, Sargent had replied, 'We are moving towards that now.'

There have been no fewer than five Peace feelers in the last few weeks, of which two have come through my channels. No importance should be attached to these as yet.[2]

Tuesday 9th September

Van comes to see me and I give a rough picture of the Peewee discussions.[3] He quite appreciates that difficulty may arise since Eden and Bracken are always in and out with the P.M. whereas I am not.

Wednesday 10th September

Meeting at Foreign Office with Eden and Bracken. I had arranged that Gaitskell should ring up beforehand and say that I wished a meeting with ministers only. The reply came that it was thought that David Stephens should also be there. I said not at the start. I found Stephens hanging about in the Private Secretaries' room. The meeting with my two colleagues was a bit sticky. I said that I did not wish Stephens in at the start because I wished to speak frankly. I then expounded my letter of 6th September, beginning by saying that I had been giving a good deal of thought to this matter and that the three officials were, I was afraid, not very dynamic people, though they had other excellent qualities. Leeper in particular, though I praised his knowledge, ex-

---

1 Sir Esmond Ovey (1879–1963). Ambassador to the Argentine Republic 1937–42. Ambassador to the Soviet Union 1929–33.
2 Marginal insertion: '(P.M. has ruled that no contact of any kind be made.)'
3 'Peewee discussions': discussions about the setting up of the Political Warfare Executive (P.W.E.).

perience, general political outlook and devotion to duty, was, none the less, a student rather than a man of action. This made it all the more important that we should continue to exercise ministerial control and stimulus. I had no doubt that my frequent visits to, and detailed interest in, C.H.Q. had been essential in order to get the thing moving and properly staffed. It had been necessary to take strong action in order to remove certain people, e.g. Valentine Williams.

Eden said that he also had been thinking a good deal about the question and had come to the conclusion that, if we were starting afresh, much the best solution would be to have one minister, rather than three, and one principal official. Therefore, he thought, this minister should be the Minister of Information. He realised, however, that to apply such a plan now would involve going back on our recommendations to the P.M., and therefore he was most anxious to give this novel experiment a good trial. He thought it essential that we should give the three officials as free a hand as possible. This phrase constantly recurred, both from him and from Bracken, who, however, remained silent during this part of the conversation. Nor was I disposed at this point to let myself be drawn. I apprehended, however, that I was faced with a combination of two ministers and three officials who would be glad of an opportunity to say that I had been so difficult and obstructive that the proposals made to the P.M. would not work and we must therefore think again. Since, moreover, there was a Parliamentary Question down to be answered next day, I judged it best not to carry the fight too far this morning but to make sure of having the announcement made tomorrow. It would then become politically more difficult, since I should be publicly representing the Labour Party on the new triumvirate, for the Tory ministers and the officials to disturb the arrangement. We therefore argued on about my detailed proviso, on which I got, though not everything, a good deal. Bracken having said that he thought my character sketch of the three officials was perhaps unduly unfavourable, and that Lockhart in particular had, he thought, dynamic qualities, we had Stephens in to take a note of a rather confused discussion. In the result it was agreed:

(1) that the three officials should always call in representatives of outside bodies when their interests were affected, nor take any such decisions without prior consultation;
(2) that (although I did not succeed in getting the full formula desired by SO2 prohibiting separate P.W.E. representation abroad) P.W.E. should whenever possible, make use of 'existing arrangements' (Bracken said he could not accept a monopoly for S.O.E. abroad, since he also had 'some good people' in some

279

places), and that no independent appointment should be made
by P.W.E. without reference to the Standing Ministerial Committee;

(3) that there was 'no objection in principle' to my detailed proposals on ministerial control and stimulus (provided these
ministerial powers were used reasonably).[1]

Lockhart was called for at the end and it was agreed that we should
have a meeting of the three ministers and the three officials next
Wednesday, when they would report to us what they had done.

An amusing incident followed. Wilmot, lunching at some Conservative Club ... ran straight into the three conspirators, who were
accompanied by Stephens. Evidently they were receiving from him
an account of the proceedings. Wilmot greeted them with his usual
bonhomie, and he thought he had never seen in his life four persons
looking more embarrassed and longing to be left alone. Leeper's
Rolls-Royce was seen sitting outside the conspirators' office at 8
o'clock when I went with John to dine at the Lansdowne Club. Leeper
is working overtime today in London and Primrose[2] has, for once,
been left in the lurch.

Later in the evening I have a good and amusing tactical discussion
with Gladwyn, John and Hugh.[3] What a first-class trio they are! Hugh
had been much depressed by the development of this affair, and felt,
as he has occasionally felt before, that he would now have too little
to do. He is much the most temperamental of my three sprites, but
this is part of his charm. Gladwyn was inclined at first to think that
things had not gone too well for me and SO2 today and to fear that
one thing would lead to another. He is – and this is one of *his* most
satisfactory qualities – very non-political, in the sense of not thinking
very easily in terms of Party sympathies and manoeuvres. John and
Hugh both being first-class at this, saw that I had been right to go
slow today. Gladwyn, however, soon suggested some other next
moves, including the making of a striking memorandum on immediate
problems of Political Warfare – co-operation with Russia, Peace Aims,
etc. – which I should flick soon at my colleagues and the three officials.
This should have a distinct, though rather subtle, Labour Party
flavour. He and Hugh between them are to do this fairly soon. We

1 Marginal insertion, after '(provided these ministerial powers were used reasonably)':
'When Minutes were circulated Eden proposed to leave out words in brackets as
derogatory to ministers! I agreed.'
2 Margaret Primrose Dundas Leeper, née Allen. Married to Reginald Leeper.
3 Jebb, Wilmot and Gaitskell.

drink my last bottle of Wiltshire mead with this discussion, in which there is much fun and forethought. I tell Gladwyn that Hugh finds his 'reserve' rather formidable and, as usual, when I poke him up on any question of habitual behaviour, Gladwyn expresses great surprise and says that he has told Hugh much about his own early life!

I collect Phil [Noel-] Baker earlier in the evening to make sure that the right supplementary question is put to the P.M. tomorrow on King-Hall's Parliamentary Question to bring out the fact that the new body is jointly responsible to the three ministers. ...

I also arrange to have Attlee to dine with me tomorrow. It was at my Council of War tonight decided that I must play up Political Warfare a bit with the Labour Party, who must be made to feel it a great advance that one of their number is now jointly responsible for this branch of the war effort.

Thursday 11th September
The Parliamentary Question on Peewee [P.W.E.] goes off quite well, with a long stream of supplementaries. It is blanketed in the news by P.Q. on the Moore-Brabazon case,[1] leading to a breeze between the P.M. and Gallacher,[2] and, next day, by Roosevelt's speech on Ocean Rattlesnakes.[3] I take occasion, however, to mention to various M.P.s that I am now jointly responsible for all Enemy and Enemy-Occupied propaganda, including B.B.C. broadcasts. ...

At lunch at the House, Chuter Ede relates that when he met, with Butler and various officials, the recent deputation from the Churches on Christian teaching in the schools, Butler asked the Archbishop of Canterbury to conclude the proceedings with prayer. The Archbishop had seemed embarrassed. He had never, he said, been asked to do such a thing outside a Government Department before. After a pause, however, during which all those present knelt, he regurgitated some

---

1 Lt-Colonel J. T. C. Moore-Brabazon, later 1st Baron Brabazon (1884–1964). Minister of Air Production 1941–2. Conservative M.P. for Wallasey 1931–42; Rochester 1918–29. Minister of Transport 1940–41. Following some unguarded remarks by Moore-Brabazon at a luncheon, Jack Tanner, President of the A.E.U., accused the Minister of Air Production of having expressed the hope that the Russian and German armies would exterminate one another, permitting Britain to dominate Europe in the future. Churchill answered a question in the House concerning the speech on 11th September, declaring that the remarks as reported represented neither the views of the Government nor of Moore-Brabazon.
2 William Gallacher (1881–1965). Communist M.P. for Fife West 1935–50.
3 'Ocean Rattlesnakes': on 12th September, President Roosevelt made a radio broadcast in which he pledged protection for merchant navy convoys 'in the defensive waters' of the U.S.A. He also reported an unprovoked attack on an American ship, and the tracking of an American battleship by U-boats.

collect which, Chuter Ede thought, had originally been composed for missions to the heathen. ...

Attlee to dine at my request. I tell him a good deal of the trouble over P.W.E. I say I am not prepared to be a mere lay figure; also that I had had a feeling that a game was being played which I do not care about; also that, since I am now, in view of today's reply by the P.M., openly in joint charge of Political Warfare, I shall be expected by the Party to take a keen interest in these matters. He quite agrees to all this and asks me to let him know if I have any trouble, in which case he will speak to the P.M., who, he says, is the last man in the world to agree that officials should be given a free hand without ministerial control and stimulus. I denounce Leeper as a Foreign Office official who has been disloyal to me, and Attlee passes naturally to a general denunciation of Foreign Office officials and says that he has told Eden that they are no good. As to the Shah,[1] of whom it is now decided we must rid ourselves, the Foreign Office had no alternative candidate ready. Attlee had told Eden that this was very poor. The Germans would certainly have had their puppet ready.

I tell him that M.E.W. is not now a full-time job and that I should not be interested in continuing to do that and nothing else. ...

Gaitskell is still thinking that he might like to go to some post in which he would see more of the inner economics of the war effort. He is, I think, sometimes a little envious of Durbin and Jay. I said that, of course, if he found a good chance of this kind, I should not want to stand in his way, though there would be a good deal to settle, including the difficult question of a successor.

Saturday 13th September

Pleasant lunch with Gladwyn and Hugh in which we discuss 'what is "intrigue"?' How does it differ from diplomacy? Should one not either be quite worldly or quite non-worldly? Is there any stopping place between? Monks, dons, diplomats, politicians ......

West Leaze in the afternoon, where there has been great activity by Ruth in shifting furniture, books, clothes, etc., from our now evacuated flat, partly to West Leaze and partly up the road to the cottage where we store quite a surprising quantity of stuff in one room.

1 Riza Khan Pahlavi (1877–1944). Shah of Iran 1925–41. Following Axis activity in Iran in June and July 1941, the Allies formally asked the Iranian government to expel all Germans from Iranian soil. The Iranians rejected the request, declaring their neutrality. British and Soviet troops intervened on 25th August. On 16th September 1941, the Shah abdicated in favour of his son, Shahpur Mohammed Riza Pahlavi (1919–80).

Monday 15th September
Meet Oliver Stanley at the Lansdowne Club this evening. As usual, he gossips against the Government, including the P.M. Our expedition to Greece was a first-class blunder from every point of view, he thinks, and it is incredible that General Wavell didn't tell the home authorities that he only had one and a quarter Divisions left in Cyrenaica. It is said that this should have been 'inferred' by those at home, but if it had been brought out clearly, it is doubtful whether the Greek expedition could ever have taken place. The C.I.G.S., moreover, was strongly of opinion, before he left England, that it should not be attempted. ...

He likes and thinks well of Shinwell. No accounting for tastes, but I tell him, what he says he did not know before, the story of Shinwell's refusal of a not unimportant post in the Government.

Tuesday 16th September
Retinger to see me, shining-eyed, on his return from Moscow. Like many others, he shines more brightly with high responsibility. He seems to have done good work out there for the Poles. ...

Lockhart calls to take me to visit the B.B.C. underground slum in Bush House. I am insisting on my duty to visit establishments now under P.W.E., whether in London or the country. It is a *frightful* Hole of Calcutta; no ventilation and two dozen people in one not very large room. They have been here since April, having moved from a quite unprotected shedifice in Maida Vale, whither they were pushed after the B.B.C. was bombed. Kirkpatrick[1] and Newsome[2] take me round, but, after a few minutes down below, I begin to feel a headache, though generally pretty insensitive to such things. (I mention this next day at meeting with ministers, and a formal letter is sent to B.B.C. Governors on our behalf.) Kirkpatrick afterwards says that I seem to be the only one of the three ministers who is taking any real interest in this matter.

Wednesday 17th September
... [T]o Foreign Office for first meeting of P.W.E., three ministers plus three officials, plus Stephens. Superficially, the meeting goes off pretty well. On the whole there is an appearance of affability, and most of the

1 I. A. Kirkpatrick, later Sir Ivone (1897–1964). Controller (European Services) in the B.B.C. 1941–4. Director of Foreign Division of the Ministry of Information 1940. Permanent Under-Secretary at the Foreign Office 1953–7.
2 Noel Newsome (d. 1976). Director of the European News Service of the B.B.C. at Bush House 1941–4. Broadcasting Director to the Department of Psychological Warfare of Supreme Headquarters, Allied Expeditionary Force 1944–5.

propositions made are accepted, though here and there I insist on explanations and amendments, in accordance with a talk beforehand with C.E.O. and Gaitskell. Afterwards, Eden says to me, brightly and with a hint of slight relief, 'Well, that all went off very well, I think.' He wears today his agreeable manner, not that of a peevish child snatching all the toys. I recall the story of a funeral, to which, in days of high political tension, Mr Gladstone went. As he advanced towards the graveside, a Conservative old lady was heard to say, 'Oh dear, I hope he has not come here to make a disturbance.'

Crossman to dine. I view this able and energetic man with some detachment. He is loyal to his own career but only incidentally to anything or anyone else. He gives, however, a most amusing picture, supplementing Gaitskell's, of events at C.H.Q. The new Section Heads have a complete contempt for the officials. I urge him, and the other Section Heads, to work in well with Kirkpatrick, whom Crossman likes, though he is so rude to others that some resent it. Crossman says that one of the consequences of the new arrangement is that not only do they lose the 'galvanic stimulus' of ministerial control, but also the steady, sensible and subtle aid of Gaitskell.

Thursday 18th September

Lunch, with Bevin, with Sikorski. Retinger, just returned from Moscow, is there; also Stanczyk[1] and Lieberman,[2] who has just been appointed Polish Minister of Justice in succession to Seyda,[3] the National Democrat who resigned over the Soviet Treaty. Lieberman, who used to frequent the L.S.I. [Labour and Socialist International] is old, sick, garrulous and argumentative and tends to interrupt the conversation when it is getting interesting. But it is cute of Sikorski to appoint him, since this will dig in the Polish Government still better with the British Left.

A gloomy view is taken of Russian prospects in the south, and Bevin says, 'You Poles will soon have to take over Russia.'

This makes them all purr. The Polish Army being reconstituted east of Saratov might obviously, however, move down towards the Caucasus, and Bevin thinks that there might be a Polish General in com-

1 J. Stanczyk, q.v. Minister of Labour and Social Welfare in the Polish government-in-exile.
2 Dr Herman Lieberman (1870–1941). Polish Minister of Justice in the Polish government-in-exile 1941. One of the leaders of the Polish Socialist Party (the P.P.S.). The post of Minister of Justice was left vacant in 1941–2, following the sudden death of Lieberman on 21st October 1941.
3 M. Seyda (1879–1967). Minister of Justice in the Polish government-in-exile 1940–41. Minister of Preparatory Work for the Peace Conference 1942–4. Minister of Foreign Affairs 1923.

mand of the southernmost sector of the Russian front. Budienny,[1] everyone says, is an old bonehead, and has been quite out-witted by the Germans. A Cavalry General! All modern armies have had experience of these.

Fourteen hundred Poles had been condemned to death by the Russians and would have been executed within a few days but for the conclusion of the Polish-Russian Treaty. Therefore, with them this Treaty is most popular. Leading Poles, including several of their Generals, were beaten on the feet by the Russians so that they could hardly hobble, and then, next day, when the news of the Treaty came through, a red carpet was put down for them and a great banquet held in their honour. 'Very oriental!' someone says. ...

C.D. [Nelson] to dine. He and A.D. [Taylor], C.E.O. says, have been excessively disturbed about P.W.E. They see everywhere thin ends of wedges. C.D. is beautifully and simply loyal to me. He has some hates for others. He thinks there will be greed elsewhere to pick from our south wall a now rapidly ripening peach. I think I reassure him. If need be, Party politics can be played on this. Nor would I consent to have only a part-time job. On the other hand, much is going well with us, and the many visits of high-ups, who will talk around Whitehall, to some of our establishments is, so far, very good, though we must not let it go too far. I tell him that no minister has yet been permitted to resign from this Government and there would be obvious great disadvantages if any did.

Tuesday 23rd September

Gladwyn enters and says, 'C.D. has resigned.' When I enquire further, I find that C.D. has worked himself up into a dreadful state, and has not been sleeping, because of all his apprehensions of P.W.E. I send for him in the afternoon and find, as I expected, that he is still, as ever, almost dog-like devoted to me and only thinking that his threatened resignation might help me. I say it wouldn't now and, if ever it would later, I will tell him. It seems that Gladwyn, who joins us in the afternoon after we have been at it for half an hour, has argued back to him on tactics this morning.

I have a long talk with Attlee this evening and parade a series of complaints ... I take the conversation also on to the wider ground regarding our failure to do more to help Russia. He says the Staff have

---

1 Marshal S. M. Budienny (1883–1973). Soviet cavalry officer and politician. Deputy Defence Commissar, Commander-in-Chief Moscow Garrison 1937–40. Appointed Vice-Commissar of Defence in 1940. In June 1941 Budienny was appointed as commander-in-chief of the 'South West Direction', but following the disaster of the Battle of Kiev, he was removed from active command.

been adjured to consider all possibilities. I say I am not satisfied by the familiar argument that we have no shipping. We should seriously consider diverting some shipping, even at cost of letting our food stocks and even rations fall. I hear that some shipping on the North Atlantic is not fully loaded at the other end, or loaded with non-essentials. I seek to give him the impression that I am in a pretty black mood. He says he will 'take it up' and I say probably this is best done in the first instance with Eden. Attlee thinks that Leeper is probably the nigger in the woodpile.

Wednesday 24th September
Long meeting of National Executive Committee, taking all the morning and till 4 p.m., which dislocates my afternoon programme and means that poor little Rennie Smith[1] is once more squashed out from an audience while three Czech ministers are kept waiting twenty minutes. ...

Walter Green[2] is a very slow and indecisive Chairman of the National Executive. Half the morning is spent on complete trivialities. But Attlee comes to ask the National Executive to agree to his signing, with the P.M. and Sinclair, joint letters in by-elections in support of Government candidates, whether Conservative, Labour or Liberal, against opposing candidatures. After a long and rambling discussion, in which some still speak of the 'electoral truce', as though we had not moved beyond that since joining the Government, it is agreed that Attlee may do what he wants, by 13 to 10. Thereupon Shinbad, most excitedly, declares that there will be terrible repercussions outside over this, especially when it is known that it was by such a narrow vote, whereupon I say that when Shinbad has been longer a member of the National Executive, he will no doubt realise that it is a breach of duty for any National Executive member to go outside and say how voting went or who voted which way. Whereupon Shinbad, very indignant, says that some people might lecture him like this, but not I. He knows very well that I have frequently done such things myself. Whereupon the Chairman calls the next item!

Slight fluff in the afternoon over question of publication of long screed of tiresomely written generalities, of which Laski is the author, though many others have lengthened the document by interpolations.

1 Rennie Smith (1888–1962). Joint Editor of *Central European Observer* 1940–46. Labour M.P. 1924–31. P.P.S. to Dalton when he was Under-Secretary of State for Foreign Affairs 1929–31.
2 Walter Green (1878–1958). Chairman of the Labour Party 1941–2. Labour M.P. for Deptford 1935–45. Political Secretary of the Royal Arsenal Co-operative Society.

Finally agreed to wait till November before publishing.

In the luncheon interval, walking in Millbank Gardens, I come upon Sam Watson[1] alone, gazing down into the river. Hitherto I haven't much focused this comparatively young man who, I have been told, is an apt pupil of Will Lawther. He may, however, now that he represents the miners on the National Executive as well as being an increasing influence in Durham County, become important. He used to have the reputation of being near-Communist. This afternoon he seems friendly and begins by denouncing Shinwell. He voted this morning in the majority. He seems entirely bent on winning the war.

Thursday 25th September
Dine with Ruth who is staying at the Royal Court Hotel, Sloane Square, pending some more permanent arrangement about her War Effort. Charles Latham[2] asked this afternoon whether she and others thought he should become a peer. He pretended to regret the prospect very much, but they told him that they thought he should take up this new responsibility. I had heard from Lyttelton this afternoon that Wedgwood Benn is also going to the Lords, and not to Cairo.

Friday 26th September
Gaitskell says that though the three Chief Peewees are no doubt very solid, it should not be impossible to split at least Bracken away from the combination. Hambro, whom I see later in the afternoon, has been most helpful in this direction. He knows Bracken well and is his senior on several Boards in peacetime. He has been to see him and spoken of our serious objections on security grounds to Peewee ambitions – to Brigadier Brooks's secret army, though he does not so describe it to Bracken. The latter says that he is sure nothing of the sort is intended, only a few broadcasters here and there.

1 Samuel Watson (1898–1967). Secretary of the Durham Miners' Association 1936–1963.
2 Charles Latham, created 1st Baron 1942 (1888–1970). Leader of the London County Council 1940–47.

5

Peewee
October 1941–February 1942

During the autumn and winter of 1941–2 the war became a world conflict. The Germans continued to advance on a wide front into Russia, until Moscow seemed within their grasp. The Japanese attack on Pearl Harbor on 7th December followed several months of worsening relations between Washington and Tokyo. With the entry of the United States into the war, the sense of acute danger that had dominated Whitehall and Westminster receded, and domestic rivalries – never far submerged – reasserted themselves. Dalton's uneasy relationship with Eden, and his calamitous dealings with Bracken, made nonsense of 'joint' control of propaganda – until Dalton's move to the Board of Trade in February separated the main antagonists.

Wednesday 1st October
A bit of dust at Party Meeting, Shinbad being more than usually offensive and provoking Attlee to leap to his feet and exclaim, 'That's a damned lie!' I also rise and make an observation about Shinbad's suggestion that our supplies to Russia are 'inadequate' and say that I am looking forward to an opportunity to tell the Party Meeting something about these matters. Shinbad then refers to my 'bravado'. Arthur Jenkins[1] afterwards rebukes him for refusal of share of responsibility [for] the Government and for constant and bitter attacks on Labour ministers.

I tell Arthur Jenkins afterwards that he should have told the Meeting that Shinbad had refused to be interested in, or responsible for, the safeguarding of the people's food.

1 Arthur Jenkins (1892–1946). Labour M.P. for Pontypool 1935–46. P.P.S. to C. R. Attlee 1940–45. Junior minister 1945. Father of Roy Jenkins.

Thursday 2nd October
Kingsley Martin to dine. He seems rather pleased to be taken so much notice of. I ask him to help me over Political Warfare. He already knows the names of the sub-trinity.[1] On the whole, he seems well disposed.

Friday 3rd October
International Sub (Political and Economic Relationships) at Transport House, when we have a general preliminary quack. I emphasise that we must put economic questions well in front this time, speak of the proposals of Professors Hansen[2] and Gulick[3] on Anglo-American co-operation to maintain full employment, to study and finance development schemes, etc. I say that Russia also must be brought in from the start with U.S.A. in any international society worth while; that this must be re-named, since the old name 'League of Nations' stinks to Heaven, perhaps undeservedly, but most potently; that we must be quite flat and clear about arms, none for the Germans and their associates in crime and lots for us, and that, unless we say this flat and clear, we shall get quite wrong both with our own Party and still more with the country. I recall here our past controversy on arms, my attitude, and the moral of all this.

Lunch afterwards with Leonard Woolf,[4] William Gillies[5] and Will Arnold-Forster, but am rather appalled to find the first and third of these much more concerned about some wicked attempt to compel the Emperor of Abyssinia to undertake to accept the views of British advisers rather than to be free to reject them, than with any other aspect of the war! Oh God! Oh Bloomsbury! Oh St Ives!

Saturday 4th October
To Newcastle in time to dine with the Lord Mayor at the Mansion House, where some two dozen guests are assembled, including the Regional Commissioner (Lambert), the Traffic Commissioner (Maxwell), the Chief Constable, the Sheriff, a soldier and an airman from

---

1 i.e. the committee of three P.W.E. officials, Brooks, Bruce Lockhart and Leeper.
2 Professor A. H. Hansen (1887–1975). Special Economic Adviser to the U.S. Federal Reserve Board 1940–45. Chairman U.S./Canadian Joint Economic Committee 1941–3. Professor of Political Economy at Harvard University.
3 Professor L. H. Gulick (b. 1892). Consultative Chief of Staff at the U.S. War Department 1940–42. Eaton Professor of Municipal Science and Administration at Columbia University.
4 Leonard Woolf (1880–1969). Writer and critic. Secretary of the Labour Party Advisory Committee on International Affairs.
5 William Gillies (1885–1958). Secretary of the International Department at Transport House 1920–44.

the local Commands, and a number of Councillors, of whom a good proportion are Labour, as is the Lord Mayor himself. To this little body I make a very successful speech, lasting quite a long time. I tell them that I shall speak frankly and confidentially and, up to a point, do so, though being careful to- say nothing which, if it should get indirectly in the press, would do damage.

Stay with David Adams[1] in his immense Victorian mansion, 'Jesmond Cottage'. His wife is a bit of a bore and he himself is not exactly quick off the mark, but they make me quite comfortable.

Sunday 5th October

Sleep in. 'Demonstration' in the afternoon in Newcastle City Hall with some 700 people present. I make a moderately good speech which is reasonably well received, but it is a bit flat. We are in the dilemma that if we hold meetings on a Sunday afternoon we are told that people are all asleep after their lunch, and if we hold them in the evening we are told people don't like to come out because of the blackout.

Back by night train.

Monday 6th October

I ask Lockhart round for a drink and show sympathy for his toils and trials. He responds a bit to this and says that one of his colleagues is always in the country and the other always running around doing liaising with everyone. I say that I think Lockhart himself should have more authority. He says that this, he thinks, is also the view of the Foreign Office. I quote the recent case of his negotiations with Gladwyn, where, I having agreed to the provisional suggestions brought back by Gladwyn, Lockhart's two colleagues, though only officials, boggled. This, as I said next day to Eden, is not quite *'comme il faut'*.

Tuesday 7th October

Lunch with Mrs Phillimore to meet Attlee, Admiral Muselier[2] and (Naval) Captain Moret[3] (I think). The Admiral is a cross between Nancy and Marseilles, and looks very Midi. Both the Frenchmen speak ill of the General. He has, they say, no political sense, no sense

---

1 David Adams (1871–1943). Labour M.P. for Consett 1935–43; Newcastle West 1922–3. Married to Elizabeth Adams, née Patterson.

2 Vice-Admiral E. Muselier (1882–1965). Commander of Free French Naval Forces 1940–42. He and de Gaulle were on bad terms, and it was only with difficulty that Muselier was persuaded to join the French National Committee in September 1941. Sacked by de Gaulle in March 1942.

3 Captain R. Moret (b. 1901). Chief of Staff to Free French Naval Forces 1940–44.

of humour, and no woman. He is never heard to laugh. ...

Thence to Political Warfare Ministerial Meeting. This is our first for several weeks and there is a lot of detail on the agenda. It does not go badly, the three Peawits suffering a series of rebuffs. They wanted to cease to be anonymous, but ministers unanimously drove them back into their hidden cave; they wanted to begin 'discreet publicity' regarding leaflets, but ministers refused, I quoting from an admirable draft by Leeper prepared for me to send to the late Duff Cooper, arguing that any publicity for leaflets would lead to the most embarrassing Parliamentary situation! Further, the Peawits are sharply called to order by Bracken for issuing, for the education of bomber pilots, a de luxe leaflet. They are told not to do this kind of thing again. I, moreover, insist that they should cease to claim that everything is 'political warfare', including 'the R.A.F. offensive and the Blockade'. I insist solemnly that the P.M., in a public statement, has defined Political Warfare to mean propaganda to enemy and enemy-occupied territories, and nothing more. Brigadier Brooks pompously replies that every word of their paper has been passed by the Chiefs of Staff. I say that is not good enough for me and that the Prime Minister's definition must be followed. Moreover, if I were to admit the terms of this paper, I might find the three chief Peawits sitting one day in M.E.W. and claiming to run the whole show. ...

Thence to House of Commons to hear Ernest Bevin defending his refusal of exemption to the eleven Buchmanites. [1] It is scandalous how much interest is taken in these people, and how little of the right sort, for I am pretty sure that there is a nasty smell at the bottom of the Buchman well and that the thing is really tainted with Hitlerism. Bevin makes free with the scriptures, saying of those who misrepresent him, 'I forgive them for they know not what they do.' (This blasphemy is deeply resented by some Tories near the door, one of whom – Pickthorn – goes out saying, 'Since one can't be sick inside here, one must go out.') There is no challenge to a division. ...

Dine with Cazalet; also present Gladwyn and Fletcher, soon to be ennobled. Rather a dull evening, Cazalet boring on and on about Raids. He has a down on old Keyes, whereas Fletcher thinks that a satisfactory settlement can be got out of his functions and relations to the Chiefs of Staff. Gladwyn says to me afterwards that Cazalet is very stupid but well meaning and is trying in a very vague sort of way to be helpful.

---

1 'Buchmanites': followers of Frank Buchman (1878–1961), founder of the Oxford Group 1921 and of the 'Moral Rearmament' campaign in Great Britain 1938. The issue was whether eleven men of military age who worked full-time for the Group could rightly claim exemption.

Wednesday 8th October
My first official call from the General de Gaulle, with whom it is now permitted for ministers to have official relations. He leaves a memo with me, which can be interpreted as claiming too much, but I give no undertaking except that I will examine it with care.

Thursday 9th October
Dine with Hambro to meet Bracken, Gladwyn and Bowes-Lyon, who, however, leaves early, being also there. Not a success. Bracken was rude, assertive, ignorant, inconsequent, stupid, angular and un-receptive.

Friday 10th October
Attend a Privy Council at Buckingham Palace with Anderson (looking oleaginously happy, for a reason revealed to the world a few days later), Moyne, with a dirty collar and hesitating manner, and Llew-ellin,[1] attending, I think, his first Privy Council. Purely formal.

Saturday 11th and Sunday 12th October
At West Leaze, filling up saucers round trees, lighting bonfires, going for two runs, on Sunday in the dusk and on Saturday in the moon-lit dark (and feeling very fit after them), sleeping, and reading.

Monday 13th October
Back from West Leaze. See my Director General about the next Honours List. I consider that I am entitled this time to two C.s as, owing to Hall's refusal last time, I had none.

Lunch with Gladwyn and Cynthia Jebb. They were not far from me this last weekend, having been staying with Hudson at a house he has just acquired near Pewsey and having found themselves on Sunday shooting at birds on the Downs near Littlecote. Gladwyn tells me that the Littlecote agent related over tea that I had waved an angry spade at the Hunt when they were once passing along the boundaries of my estate. For this reason it had been suspected by many, when the war broke out, that I was a Fifth Columnist!

I told Gladwyn that I only remembered the 'Hunt', a mangy show in any event, having been twice, during the time I was at West Leaze, within sight. It was probably true that, armed with a spade, I had advanced towards my boundary fence to see what was going on, but

---

1 J. J. Llewellin, later 1st Baron (1893–1957). Parliamentary Secretary at the Ministry of Transport (later War Transport) 1941–2. Conservative M.P. for Uxbridge 1929–45. Junior minister 1939–41. President of the Board of Trade 1942; Minister of Supply, resident in Washington 1942–3; Minister of Food 1943–5.

I felt no animosity towards this rustic cavalcade, though equally not much interest in it. Hence there was no basis for this yarn!

They had also spoken, it seems, last weekend, of Bracken, who has a house at Bedwyn, which, however, he is going to sell. They say he has no sense of the country at all, and walks alone through country lanes wearing a dark suit with striped trousers and a black hat. Comment is made on the engagement of the poor old Lord President of the Council, announced this morning, to the widow of Ralph Wigram,[1] commonly known as 'Ava'. She is said to be the most frightful woman and can only have hooked Sir John Anderson in the belief that he would soon be either Prime Minister or Viceroy of India. It is suggested that a telegram should be sent to her: 'You have miscalculated.'

An incredible letter arrives for me today from Bracken – 'Dear Minister of Economic Warfare ...... Yours sincerely' ... What a fool and a nuisance this man is! The result is that I have to spend *hours* – yes, literally many hours – of my own time and that of C.E.O. [Jebb], A.D. [Taylor], and A.D.Z. [Davies] going through old files and making a reply which shall reach this fool, and also Eden, to whom a copy must be sent, tomorrow morning in good time before our meeting.

Tuesday 14th October
Lunch at House of Commons and snaffle Eden in the passage. He is wearing his most affable air today and I play up to his conciliatory gifts and diplomatic skill, with a view to this afternoon's meeting. ...

Lord Hyndley[2] gives a dinner party in honour of Attlee, about to leave for the U.S. to represent H.M.G. at the I.L.O. [International Labour Office]. Most of those present are Labour members of the Government, including Under-Secretaries. But the P.M. graces the occasion by his presence and Kingsley Wood, Moore-Brabazon, James Stuart[3] and Harvie Watt[4] are also there. The P.M. is in very

1 Ava Wigram, née Bodley, widow of Ralph Wigram (1890–1936). Wigram was a diplomat at the British Embassy in Paris 1924–33, where he met Dalton and Henderson in 1931. Ava married Anderson, the Lord President of the Council, in 1941.
2 J. S. Hindley, 1st Baron Hyndley (1883–1963). Commercial Adviser to the Mines Department 1918–38, 1939–42. Controller-General at the Ministry of Fuel and Power 1942–3. Chairman of the National Coal Board 1946–51.
3 J. G. Stuart, later 1st Viscount (1897–1971). Joint Parliamentary Secretary to the Treasury and Government Chief Whip 1941–5. Conservative M.P. for Moray and Nairn 1923–59. Junior whip 1935–41. Secretary of State for Scotland 1951–7.
4 G. H. S. Watt, later Sir George Harvie-Watt, 1st Bart (b. 1903). Parliamentary Private Secretary to the Prime Minister 1941–5. Conservative M.P. for Richmond, Surrey 1937–59; Keighley 1931–5. Junior whip 1938–40.

good form and, in addition to making a short and cordially phrased speech about Attlee and H.M.G. generally, holds forth at great length on the war and kindred topics. During a large part of this he makes me his principal audience and also calls across the table to me about the latest news from Montenegro. I tell him that I have sent him in tonight a note on the latest developments there. Following this up, as the party is dispersing I catch him by the door and urge him to pay a visit to my Stations. He says, 'Yes, I must' and seems most friendly. Therefore, next day I send for M. [Gubbins] and have made out an attractive afternoon's programme which I bung in with a pressing invitation. If I could get him on this trip, I am pretty sure that he would be interested and would focus my doings better thereafter.

Wednesday 15th October

Some fun at, and after, Party Meeting. Yesterday Shinbad had pursued a long dialogue with the P.M. at Question Time over the Russian campaign and the 'disquiet' felt in the country owing to our inadequate assistance. He had seemed to be playing up for an early debate on this subject.

I therefore came to the Party Meeting, by arrangement, with Lees-Smith and Scott Lindsay, armed with particulars of economic aid to Russia. I had originally hoped to be able to make a fuller statement on recent work of M.E.W., including P.W.E., in which I am anxious to inspire a reasonable interest in my Labour colleagues. Clearly, however, it is better tactics – this thought flashed on me, as many tactical revelations do, in my bath this morning – to concentrate on Russia.

There is some delay in my getting on, as many small points are first discussed at tedious length by small people (it is astonishing how the smallest people in the Party talk largest, longest and oftenest at Party Meetings). Several people, including Ellis Smith,[1] call from time to time for me to speak and ask when I am to come on. About 10.30, therefore, I am called and speak for about a quarter of an hour, giving a good deal of detail, but not much statistics, on non-military supplies to Russia, emphasising that on most commodities the Russians have had, and are to have, all they ask for, that shipping is a considerable difficulty, and ending up by a reference to P.W.E. and co-operation with the Russians as to propaganda.

This statement is very well received and a series of questions is put to me, practically all of which are genuine and friendly enquiries. Shinbad, however, who always sits with his back averted from the

1 Ellis Smith (1896–1969). Labour M.P. for Stoke-on-Trent 1935–66. Junior minister 1945–6.

platform during the whole of our proceedings, rose from his place and ostentatiously left the meeting in the course of my statement. He was observed striding down the passage alone with a black face. This, therefore, all goes very well and no one presses for an early debate on Russia. There has been a considerable interest in the press on this subject, and pressmen hung about members afterwards. A considerable leakage, with substantial elements of accuracy, afterwards appears. On the whole, it does *me* good and Shinbad harm, and is also helpful to the Government. How it all happened I do not enquire.

Attend a Nathan lunch, where Attlee is the principal speaker. He does quite well in his funny little unimpressive way.

Despite predictions that Stalin would be forced to capitulate within a matter of weeks, the Russians fought on against the advancing Germans. By October Moscow was in immediate danger. On 12th October the Soviet authorities began to prepare for a siege. Meanwhile arrangements were made for the evacuation of many government departments and the whole of the diplomatic corps to Kuibyshev, on the Middle Volga. By now, the enemy was only fifty or sixty miles from the capital, having broken through the defences near the Velikie-Luki-Moscow road at Volokolamsk.

Thursday 16th October
Lunch at House of Commons. Shinwell has called Carvel a 'bloody swine' for the two paragraphs in the *Star Man's Diary* on our Party Meeting and has threatened a libel action. Silly ass! I am well pleased with the leaks in the press on yesterday's meeting and my statement. ...

Tonight I see a telegram from Moscow. All diplomats and foreign journalists, except Cripps and one or two others, were to leave by 9 p.m. on the 15th. Cripps has burnt nearly all his files. This recalls a moment last year when Gladwyn told me that at the Quai d'Orsay they were burning all their papers. It gave him, he said, a queer feeling in the tummy. Molotov, Cripps and a few others are leaving by air for the new capital on the Volga.

Friday 17th October
John Carvel to see me. He is quite pleased, as am I, over the *Star Man's Diary* and other disclosures. The provincial press have done it well. Now we must try to get Shinwell off the Administrative Committee [of the P.L.P.].

Cadogan wrote in his diary for 21st October: '3.45 meeting of P.W.E. Dog-fight between Dalton and Bracken. Inconclusive ... '[1] Bracken had a number of complaints, including the accusation that an SO1 propaganda agency had approached a news agency in South America offering to pay for the inclusion of articles – and the news agency turned out to be owned by the Ministry of Information. Dalton became 'white to the top of his bald head with rage', according to Bruce Lockhart.[2]

Such battles soon became routine. Bracken pressed constantly for the reorganisation of all propaganda, making clear his desire to get rid of Dalton in the process, and hinting at the allegedly left-wing nature of the propaganda that emanated from Woburn Abbey.

Tuesday 21st October

Weekly meeting of P.W.E. with seance following at which Cazalet, Cadogan, Gladwyn, A.D.Z. [Davies] and Radcliffe are also present. A most infuriating afternoon! Bracken is worse than ever. He brings no papers, has studied nothing, is arrogant, rude, inconsequent, critical, purely destructive. I am told that he makes a bad impression on several of those there. I show great restraint, but shall not in-definitely continue to do so. ... Whatever I or Gladwyn say during this talk is at once seized upon, twisted and made into some fresh ground of complaint.

The L.P.S. [Lord Privy Seal] [Attlee] is on his way to U.S.A., and, if we are to have a flaming row, it will be best to play for time till the little man returns. Meanwhile, this other man is always hanging about No. 10. On the other hand, it is not clear that much heed is paid there to what he says, though my last invitation for a visit to No. 17 has not been picked up. ...

Dudley Ward[3] dines with me and dwells affectionately on past memories. He also says that it is extraordinary how M.E.W. goes on so well – he admits it *does* go on well – when the Minister is largely concerned with other and engrossing duties, likewise the Director General with Surpluses, and of the two Directors, one is a sick man and the other deeply fascinated by problems of military intelligence.

1 D. Dilks (ed.), *The Diaries of Sir Alexander Cadogan O.M. 1938–1945*, Cassell, London, 1971, p. 409.
2 Kenneth Young (ed.), *The Diaries of Sir Robert Bruce Lockhart, vol. II 1939–1965*, Macmillan, London, 1980, p. 125.
3 Dudley Ward (1885–1957). M.E.W. 1940–44. Former Treasury official and banker. A Cambridge contemporary of Dalton and Rupert Brooke.

I say that it goes well because I have a very good band of officials, because I have a definite policy and they know what it is, and because there are no bottle-necks, but direct access to me from below the level of Directors. Also, I might add, a most efficient private office.

Wednesday 22nd October
Speak at National Trade Union Club. My speech seems to have been a fair success and odds and ends are reported in different papers. I am following Gaitskell's advice and spending a good deal of time just now in Labour Party circles.

Francis Williams to dine, also Wilmot and Gaitskell. I am most tactful in not making any personal reference to Williams's Minister,[1] who has promoted him and with whom he appears to be getting on quite well.

Pursue a line started at breakfast this morning. The Beaver is playing up to the Communists on Aid to Russia. Some shop stewards are trying to by-pass trade union officials and go straight to ministers, especially the Beaver. Moore-Brabazon a few days ago went to an aircraft factory and tried to address the men. They greeted him with boos and cries of 'We want Beaverbrook'. If Russia were to collapse, there might be a very sinister and formidable combination in favour of a negotiated peace. 'Let us all make peace together'; 'How can we ever expect to win the war now?'; 'If Germany will evacuate West Europe, why should she not have more space in the East?', etc. In this combination you might find the Beaver and his papers, Southwood ('Always an appeaser to the finger tips', says Williams, with deaf old Dunbar[2] always against war, and Percy Cudlipp, who is said, only a fortnight ago, to have been talking most defeatist stuff and declaring that we could never win), Kemsley[3] and his papers, the *Daily Mail*, the Communists, Montagu Norman and a bunch of money-lenders in the City, etc.

A slight variant on this theme is that the Beaver is trying to build himself up as the only man in the Government with any push and go. Michael Foot[4] has been saying that if only the Beaver had gone to

1 The Minister of Information, Brendan Bracken, q.v.
2 J. W. Dunbar (1888–1955). Editorial Director of Odhams Press Ltd.
3 Sir James Berry, 1st Baron, later 1st Viscount Kemsley (1883–1968). Chairman of Kemsley Newspapers 1937–59. Editor-in-Chief of the *Sunday Times* 1937–59. Chairman of Reuters Trust 1942–59.
4 Michael Foot (b. 1913). Journalist with the *Evening Standard* 1938–42 (Acting Editor 1942). Labour M.P. 1945–55, and since 1960. Secretary of State for Employment 1974–6. Lord President of the Council and Leader of the House of Commons 1976–9. Editor of *Tribune* 1948–52, 1955–60. Leader of the Labour Party 1981–3.

Moscow in September 1939, he would have fixed everything up with Stalin and there would have been no war. (Michael Foot and Frank Owen are constantly speaking now on the same platform as Harry Pollitt[1] and other Communists.) John Gordon[2] of the *Sunday Express* is going round, says Williams, telling everyone that the war has been hopelessly mismanaged by the Government, that at this rate we can never win, that the only man who can put things right is the Beaver, that Parliament is a bit out of date, and that a number of 'the younger Generals in the Army' would back a Beaver Government. It might be that a Beaver Government, taking office to wage the war more ardently, might soon become a Peace-by-negotiation Government.

I do not think, nor do any of my three companions, that a Beaver Government could come into office except as a result of a serious Parliamentary set-back to the present Government. Of this there is no sign. The P.M. could carry a vote of confidence any day in the House by a majority of several hundreds. The Opposition Lobby would not muster more than two dozen at the most. If anything were to happen to the P.M. now, it would not be the Beaver who would succeed him. The men of Fleet Street tend always to over-estimate their political influence and importance. The tale about the younger Generals is, I believe, sheer rubbish. The House of Commons has a very firm foundation of the national will to wage war till we win. None the less, the Beaver, I am sure, is up to no good (it is reported that Eden said this to a friend only a few days ago) and we should all be on our guard and keep our ears open. Certainly at some moment we may need a sudden showdown between warmongers and peace-mongers.

Thursday 23rd October
Sit beside Eden while Phil [Noel-Baker] opens general debate in House. He does extraordinarily well and could not, except for a few occasional critical passages, have made a better defence of the Government, even if speaking from our box. Also, as usual, his speech is admirably phrased and the balance is better than usual. ...

Ruth to dine with Phil and Irene.[3] She is now to have an interview on Monday morning which she hopes may lead somewhere.

---

1 Harry Pollitt (1890–1960). Secretary of the Communist Party of Great Britain 1929–56.
2 J. R. Gordon (1890–1974). Editor of the *Sunday Express* 1928–54. Director of Beaverbrook Newspapers 1931–69.
3 Irene Noel-Baker, née Noel (d. 1956). Married to Philip Noel-Baker.

In late September Beaverbrook and Harriman had been sent to Moscow by their respective governments to arrange the long-term supply of the Russian armies. An agreement was reached, and a protocol signed setting out the supplies which Britain and the United States could make available to Russia within the period October 1941 to June 1942. On 4th October Beaverbrook telegraphed to Churchill: 'The effect of this agreement has been an immense strengthening of the morale of Moscow. The maintenance of this morale will depend on delivery … ' The Mission was given no formal entertainment almost until the last night, when they were invited to dinner at the Kremlin.[1]

Friday 24th October
Dine with C.E.O. who cheers me up a bit out of a fit of rather deep depression by telling me a story, which he swears comes from a first-class source, of the banquet given at the Kremlin, when Stalin sat at the head of the table, Beaverbrook and Harriman on each side of him. There was no common language and no interpreter within reach. Therefore, there was no conversation at all at the top of the table. Stalin was served by an attendant with special food and drink, no doubt a habitual precaution against food poisoning. A bottle of red wine was first planted in front of him. Beaverbrook, wanting to warm up the atmosphere, stretched across for this bottle and poured himself out a glass with a friendly grin, but this was not returned. Stalin scowled and without a word recovered the bottle. Next his attendant brought a bottle of Caucasian champagne, and champagne glasses were set before the guests. But this time Stalin was running no risks. Still scowling ferociously, he stretched out his hand and appropriated the still empty champagne glass of the Beaver and placed it, inverted, over his own bottle, where, except when he refilled his own glass from this bottle, it remained.

Wednesday 29th October
The press today is full of rumours that the Beaver will resign – at least for a time – owing to asthma and the strain of his recent trips abroad. A parallel rumour circulates, though not in the press, that he wants

---

1 Winston S. Churchill, *The Second World War, vol. III The Grand Alliance*, Cassell, London, 1950, pp. 416–18.

to be the Production Dictator and let Layton,[1] between whom and the Beaver there is a queer and long-standing affinity, go to the Lords and take over the Ministry of Supply. ...

Another Beaver-Stalin story:

Stalin. 'What do you think of Maisky?'
Beaver. 'He or she?'
Stalin. 'Maisky.'
Beaver. 'Rather a bore, don't you think?'
Half an hour later.
Beaver. 'What do you think of Cripps?'
Stalin. 'Rather a bore, don't you think?'

Another story, this time of the Beaver accompanying the P.M. in June 1940 to France just before she fell. Weygand, even then, was expatiating on the theme that France had sinned and must be redeemed through suffering. Whereupon Beaverbrook said, 'I am a Calvinist. I know that no one is redeemed through suffering. Many are destined to suffer – and suffer and suffer for ever, but they are never redeemed.' Weygand said to another Frenchman afterwards, 'What a curious view of religion that man has.'

On 29th October, an internal row in SO2 about personnel flared when Dalton accused Sir Frank Nelson of 'concerting' behind his back. Nelson immediately announced his intention to resign, and wrote to the Minister giving his reasons. 'I have been increasingly aware of late that you may perhaps be better served by someone who is not so adamant in his views as I am, as to the necessity of the "man in charge" of the Office being allowed to deal himself with the Staff, except in very senior and special instances,' Nelson wrote.[2]

'I suspect A.D. [Taylor] of being the nigger in this woodpile,' Dalton noted. 'He hinted to C.E.O. of "other resignations".'[3]

---

1 Sir Walter Layton, later 1st Baron (1884–1966). Director-General of Programmes at the Ministry of Supply 1940–42; Chairman of the Executive Committee at the Ministry of Supply 1941–2. Chief Adviser on Programmes and Planning at the Ministry of Production 1942–3. Head of Joint War Production Staff 1942–3. Chairman of News Chronicle Ltd 1930–50; Star Newspaper Co. Ltd 1936–50. Editor of *The Economist* 1922–38.
2 Dalton Papers 18/2 (40).
3 Diary, 29th October 1941.

Thursday 30th October

Today I have an orgy of sweetness and light, first with C.D. [Nelson] and then with the Peawits. ...

I have told Gaitskell that if C.D. rings up to arrange to see me, it should not be till the afternoon, so that I can first get C.E.O.'s report on this morning. On my return from P.O.G. [Hankey Committee], Gaitskell says that C.D. rang up and wanted to come this morning, but he put him off till 3 o'clock this afternoon. C.D. had said, in a heavy voice, 'I am afraid it may be rather a long interview.' The time had then been fixed. A little later C.D. rang up Gaitskell again and said that of course he wanted to see me alone. Gaitskell replied that this of course was what was intended.[1] ...

I tell C.E.O. that I shall try honey-pot tactics this afternoon and aim first at getting the resignation withdrawn. We will see where we get to and then think again. He says I ought to think what I would do if I can't get the resignation withdrawn, or if others resign as well. On the first point he and I and Gaitskell were inclined to think yesterday that M. [Gubbins] would be the best successor.

C.D. stays with me for three-quarters of an hour. He combines what I think is quite genuinely a strong personal regard for me with an obstinate adherence to certain so-called 'principles' (I am sure A.D. [Taylor] has put all this into his head) which should be adopted in running the show, now that it has grown to its present size. I read him the Charter, which is quite in conflict with much that he suggests. Following a line concerted with C.E.O. at lunch, I suggest at a certain point that I should talk separately to each member of the Daily Council and get their views. I would then have a general talk with the whole lot of them. The resignation is duly withdrawn 'at any rate for the present'. ...

And so to P.W.E. The Brigadier [Brooks] is absent on leave. Everything goes swimmingly. No continuance of my row with Bracken. On the contrary, he is most amiable to all, though very much on the lookout against unnecessary expenditures, even on the secret vote.

Dalton recorded in a separate note:

C.D. came to see me on the 30.10.41. I began by asking him to wash out from his memory our telephone conversation of yesterday. I was sorry that I had spoken to him so abruptly, and no doubt I had not well chosen

1 Marginal insertion: '(A.D. [Taylor] had probably put this second call into his head.)'

my words ... He said he fully accepted this and asked me to think no more about it.

After some further general conversation, he said that he considered S.O.E. could not go on as it was. His position was being undermined because he could never say yes or no, but must refer everything up.

Nelson proceeded to elaborate three principles designed to limit Dalton's and Jebb's interference in staff and administrative matters:

> He drew an analogy between himself and 'C.', who, he said, never reported any of his detailed proceedings to the Foreign Office. I said that I did not think this was at all an exact analogy. He said that I could always deny knowledge of anything that was done. [1]

It was then agreed that Dalton should interview separately senior officials who were members of his 'Daily Council', chaired by Jebb. Most of these argued in favour of a reduction in red tape, and the need to refer matters up for higher authority. It was suggested, in particular, that the Minister should lay down general policy, and not interfere with – or even necessarily seek to know about – operational details. There was some resentment of the role of Jebb and of the Foreign Office.

There was also a general feeling that the Foreign Office interfered too much in the detailed working of the S.O.E. machine; and a demand for closer contact with the Chiefs of Staff and its planning machinery. Underlying all these complaints was a recognition that changes were needed to take account of the fact that S.O.E. was becoming operational, with more and more agents in the field. [2]

Following these consultations, Dalton decided on a clearer division of responsibility between Jebb, who was to deal with 'political' questions only, and have nothing to do with operations; and Nelson who was to be solely responsible for operations, except where these involved the Foreign Office or any other non-Service Department, in which case Jebb might be involved. Nelson was also given the absolute right to hire and fire within S.O.E. [3]

Monday 3rd November

On this and two succeeding days I interview separately six members of the Daily Council and make records of what they say. ... Much nonsense is talked, alongside of some sense, but what a cabal! It

1 Dalton Papers 18/2 (41).
2 Dalton Papers 18/2 (42–53).
3 Dalton Papers 18/2 (54).

becomes more and more clear that it is largely directed at C.E.O. A.D. [Taylor] has clearly been at the bottom of this. ...

Dine with Durbin and Norman Chester,[1] a Manchester economist, now in one of the circuses, at Martinez. Gaitskell tells me later that they both thought I was not much interested in my Department. I don't know how they got this impression, for I told them, I thought, several amusing stories of how it all began. Perhaps they expected a solemn lecture on my problems of today. But it would have been altogether too much of a bore to do this kind of thing.

The scale and effectiveness of partisan resistance in Yugoslavia, under the leadership of General Draja Mihailovitch, had increased sharply since August. So too had German and Italian efforts to stamp it out. On 29th August, a puppet government was formed in Serbia under General Neditch, formerly War Minister. One of the first acts of this regime was to announce the imposition of the death penalty, summarily and without right of appeal, for 'Communist and anarchist activities'. On 1st October, the Yugoslav Vice-Premier in exile, Dr Krek, declared that the Germans were pursuing a policy of deliberate extermination of the Slovenes as a nation. On 3rd November, following a month of intensive activity by the Germans against the partisans, Neditch appealed to Serb patriots to end their armed resistance, maintaining that a hundred Serbs were shot for every German killed.

Meanwhile, in September, there had been heavy fighting between partisans and German troops south-west of Belgrade, with heavy casualties on both sides; and a partisan raid on Kragujevac had led to the capture of a large quantity of arms and ammunition. By the end of the year, despite repressive counter-measures, there was talk of a 'Third Front' in the Balkans, while Mihailović was estimated to have an organised force of 80,000 troops, including many officers and men of the Yugoslav army, under his command. On 28th November, Churchill minuted to Ismay that 'everything in human power should be done' to help the guerrilla fighters in Yugoslavia.[2]

Tuesday 4th November
Today A.D. [Taylor] and A.D.P. [Boyle[3]]. The former is as clever as a

---

1 D. N. Chester, later Sir Norman (b. 1907). Member of Economic Section, War Cabinet Secretariat 1940–45. Warden of Nuffield College, Oxford 1954–78.

2 Churchill, *The Second World War, vol. III*, p. 752.

3 Air Commodore A. R. Boyle (1887–1949). Director of Air Intelligence 1940–41. Appointed Director of Intelligence and Security at S.O.E. 1941.

monkey, but the latter is much the most sensible witness so far, putting down most of our troubles to the fact that people are over-working and not taking enough time off. ...

Weekly P.W.E. goes quietly until Other Business, when Bracken explodes with a complaint about some leaflets pushed under the doorways of the Thais! It is not known who did it but it has greatly embarrassed our Minister,[1] who has sent home a screaming telegram about it. It is suggested that I may have had something to do with it. I say I think this most unlikely but have had no notice of this question, which therefore had better be examined by the officials between now and next time. Bracken then raises a more general question of competing organisations doing 'porpaganda'. He says that either this matter must be settled by the ministers or referred to the P.M. I say I think we had better look at all this next time, and that, to my mind, there is no difficulty of principle. But this is a vexatious little blighter and I am irritated by his constant attempt to play the P.M. card. He is too much inclined to say, 'I was talking to the P.M. yesterday'; 'At lunch today the P.M. leaned across the table and said ... ' (even, it seems, if there were some thirty people present). When L.P.S. [Attlee] comes back from U.S.A. I must have another word to him about all this. Eden on the other hand, is, I think, generally bored with Bracken's methods.

Summons for Juggery,[2] first for 10 p.m., afterwards put to 10.45. I arrive at C.W.R. [Cabinet War Room], taking Glenconner[3] with me, though it is most unlikely that he will either be wanted, or allowed, in the inner room. We find Cranborne also waiting in the Mess-Anteroom. I do not get in till 11.45. P.M. in a good mood. We have a useful discussion. All possible is to be done to help the guerrillas. A further conference on lower level with the Admiralty tomorrow.

Wednesday 5th November

Invite myself to tea with Mrs Amery,[4] who has signed a letter in *The Times* on a Relief Fund for Juggery.[5] She is very fond of me but comes in with a catch in her breath, saying that she hopes I have not brought her any bad news. She feared that I had come to tell her that something

---

1 Sir Josiah Crosby (1880–1958). Envoy Extraordinary and Minister Plenipotentiary, Bangkok 1934–41.
2 'Juggery': discussions relating to Yugoslavia.
3 C. G. Tennant, 2nd Baron Glenconner (1899–1983). Director of Hambros Bank and I.C.I.
4 Mrs Florence Amery, née Greenwood. Married to L. S. Amery, q.v.
5 The Yugoslav Relief Society, formed under the patronage of King Peter and Queen Marie of Yugoslavia, was appealing for funds and equipment.

had happened to her younger son.[1] Her elder son[2] has just been interned in France. He was apparently in a Sanatorium for T.B. I am at once able to reassure her. She is prepared to write a letter holding up ill-advised appeals and broadcasts and arranging for [Dingle] Foot – who is very much excited about this letter in *The Times*, and has spoken on the telephone to old Lord Crewe,[3] another of the Secretaries, who has expressed great contrition – to go with her to the next, and indeed to any future, meetings of the Committee. ...

Maurice Webb gives me, over the telephone, a story of impending ministerial changes, including the following: Kingsley Wood to go to the Lords, Eden to the Treasury, Cranborne (though he is said to be hesitating about the offer) to the Foreign Office, George Hicks[4] into the War Cabinet to replace Greenwood, who would busy himself with supplies for Russia. Jim Griffiths also to enter the Government. I say that this all sounds rather unlikely, but Webb has sometimes been right before. Eden would go to the Treasury (1) because there isn't much to do there, and (2) in order to give him a wider Departmental experience, since he is regarded as a possible successor to the P.M. I tell Webb that I think it most unlikely that this would be consummated with Attlee away. Webb supposes that such very rapid promotion for Hicks would create great feeling in the Labour Party. I think it might.

Hancock, to whom I talk later this evening on his own future – he is shortly to be medically examined and, if in a high grade, would then be de-reserved as from a date next month – says that the gossip is, both in the Foreign Office and among intelligent Conservatives outside, that Eden has not been doing so well lately, but that it would be read by many as rather a disgrace if he were shifted to the Treasury. Personally, I would rather have Lord Cranborne to deal with.

1 Julian Amery, q.v.
2 John Amery (1912–45). Amery was among a group of twelve detained by the Vichy Government on 4th November, and interned at the Grand Hotel, Vals-les-Bains, as a reprisal for the arrest of seven French nationals in Syria. In 1945 he was executed by the British after pleading guilty to several charges of collaboration with the Germans, Italians and Vichy French.
3 R. O. A. Crewe-Milnes, 2nd Baron Houghton, 1st Marquis of Crewe (1858–1945). Joint Secretary of the Yugoslav Relief Society. Lord President of the Council 1905–8, 1915–16. Colonial Secretary 1908–10. Lord Privy Seal 1908–11, 1912–15. President of the Board of Education 1916. Ambassador to France 1922–8. Secretary of State for War 1931.
4 E. G. Hicks, Parliamentary Secretary at the Ministry of Works, q.v.

Thursday 6th November

C.E.O. has had a further talk with C.D. after this morning's Council and reports that the latter is looking very ill and feeling very low and conscious of strain. He is now saying that in any case he would like to resign and make way for a younger man. He does not suggest who this should be. Not, apparently, M. [Gubbins] for whom he speaks of a larger responsibility in his own section and who, he says, is unpopular with some; nor, apparently, A.D. [Taylor] who, he says, is a very good Chief of Staff. C.E.O. urged on him that his resignation now would do much damage in Whitehall and encourage the snipers who, the more we succeed, the more are they jealous. ...

I lunch today with Sir Percy Loraine. There was no reason why he should have asked me unless he wanted something from me, for his social circles and mine would not normally intersect. And so, quite early, it appears.

He is, he says, a war casualty, for, if Italy had not gone wrong, he would have continued as Ambassador at Rome for three years longer. So here he is, at the height of his powers, and with an unrivalled experience of the Middle East, where he has spent twenty-five years of his life and served in Persia, Turkey (twice), Egypt, Greece and Italy. I say that people seem to be falling over one another in the Middle East just now and that Sir Walter Monckton is the latest addition to the swarm. Sir P. Loraine sniffs contemptuously at the name of the late King's legal adviser and goes on to say that what he would really like would be 'the job Oliver Lyttelton has got'. I say that I understand Oliver Lyttelton doesn't like it much, feeling that he has been pushed out on a limb, doesn't know what is going on at the centre, and is not helped by the Departments at home.

Sir P. Loraine then talks in praise of the Turks. ...

We then, inevitably, spoke of Italy, and he related various conversations with Ciano who, however, was always very much *petit garçon* when the Duce was about. Italian policy was always based on an estimate of military events outside Italy. She had come in on our side in 1915 because she thought we were winning; and on Germany's side in 1940 because she thought we were losing and that it would soon be too late to share the spoils. Hitler had not welcomed Mussolini's entry into the war in June 1940. Ciano had asked Loraine, when France was toppling, what we should do when she fell. Loraine had said we should go on with the war. Ciano had asked, 'What with?' Loraine had said he declined to answer the question in that form but that the war could only end when Britain either won or surrendered, and that Britain would never surrender. Ciano had shrugged his shoulders incredulously. ...

He told me a story of anti-British placards put up in Rome which said, among other things, 'England has missed the bus.' But some Italian wrote underneath, 'But she is rich enough to take a taxi.'

Towards the end of our lunch he asked whether I thought that we were making progress with 'welding the whole nation into one class', which he seemed to think was most desirable. I said that taxation, rationing, etc., had moved us a fair distance already towards greater equality. He said, 'Don't you think that what are called the Upper Classes have been behaving very well?' I said that I thought the majority of people in all classes had been behaving well, though there were some bad patches, no doubt, in all. He asked whether I thought that it might not be a useful service for him, seeing that he was a large landowner (I did not quite apprehend the significance of this reason for his proposal), to go round making speeches for ten minutes or a quarter of an hour at factories on 'the anatomy of the war', particularly in those areas where he owned land and was therefore well known. I said I thought this was a most excellent idea but that of course it would fall under the Ministry of Information. I asked in what areas he owned land, and he replied in Northumberland and in Suffolk, and then a long rigmarole about how his ancestor in Northumberland bankrupted himself by guaranteeing a loan for the relief of the local poor during the Napoleonic Wars. This had meant that the estate had had to be broken up. I asked whether he had since got the lost land back again. He said that his present Northumberland estate had 'come through the female line'. I said that if he was inclined to do some speaking, I was sure he would be most acceptable at Warship Week demonstrations, etc. all over the country.

I never see this diplomat without recalling that it was he who once apostrophised me as 'Mr Parliamentary Under-Secretary of State'.

Friday 7th November

[Haydn] Davies reports that there will now be no Cabinet changes nor any important rearrangements of functions, though minor rearrangements touching Ministry of Works and Ministry of Labour, and also perhaps touching Supply and Admiralty.

The statement widely published (except in the *Daily Express*) some ten days ago that the Beaver was ill with asthma, very much overtired and nearly at the end of the six months for which he had undertaken to run Supply, was given out on the Beaver's own instructions through J. B. Wilson[1] to Stacpoole[2] of the Press Association. Wilson

---

1 J. B. Wilson (1878–1968). Chief Publicity Officer at the Ministry of Supply under Beaverbrook 1940–41. *Daily Express* News Editor 1912–40.
2 E. P. Stacpoole (1902–80). Lobby correspondent of the Press Association 1936–66.

added, 'Now you can all start to speculate on the Beaver's future.'
Hence began all the guesses at Cabinet changes.

The P.M., however, was much displeased when he heard of this,
feeling that the Beaver was trying to force his hand, and objecting
also to attacks being made, e.g. by Clem Davies on Kingsley Wood,
on individual ministers. Some changes had been under consideration
before, notably the disappearance of Moore-Brabazon from the
Government and his replacement by Gwilym Lloyd George,[1] but
even this is off now.

It is also known that the Beaver had drawn up a short list for
assassination: Kingsley Wood, Anderson and Greenwood. This
came to the ears of Anderson, who went straight to the P.M. and
received, not only an assurance on his own position, but an assurance
that the Beaver would not be allowed to become Deputy P.M. for
the Home Front, which is said to be his ambition. ...

This afternoon I see C.D. alone. This too goes easily. I begin by
getting rid of his offer to resign, repeated today though in a very
different manner from last week. I say that, with these new changes,
he must go on at least for several months, and then, if his health is
really not good enough, we can think again. But I hope it will be. I
then read over to him, having given him a copy, my scheme of new
arrangements. He obviously likes them, but asks whether he could
not take them away and discuss them with his people. I say no, he
must not do this, he and I must take our responsibilities. If he agrees
to this scheme, I will have the Council in tomorrow morning and tell
them that these are my decisions. So he agrees. And then I send for
C.E.O. and tell him that we two have agreed on a certain paper which
I have shown C.D. And C.E.O., playing up very well, says, 'I haven't
seen it yet.' And so I give him a copy and he reads it through and then
says he agrees too. (Of course he drafted it for me and I haven't altered
his draft much.) And so all has gone on swimmingly, but I felt with
C.D. that it was a little bit like doing a major negotiation with a
backward child!

Saturday 8th November

Receive the Council, minus C.E.O. and C.D., this morning. I give
them rather a formal address, with some history of what has gone
before, and end by reading to them my 'decisions' on future organisation. I then invite observations, but there are none.

---

1 Gwilym Lloyd George, later 1st Viscount Tenby (1894–1967). Parliamentary
Secretary at the Ministry of Fuel and Power 1942–5. Liberal M.P. for Pembroke-
shire 1922–4, 1929–50. Conservative M.P. for Newcastle-upon-Tyne North
1951–7. Junior minister 1931, 1939–42. Minister of Food 1951–4; Home Secretary
1954–7.

Tuesday 11th November

House of Commons reassembles. Ruth has started today her new duties and thinks she will like them, but she wants some more of my margarine coupons!

At the Administrative Committee Shinwell demands that he shall be allowed to make the principal speech on the address. He goes on and on, awkwardly insistent, and declares that, if not chosen by the Party, he will go to the Speaker and put in his claim. It is clear that other members of the Committee do not wish Shinwell to speak, but, over-delicate, they hesitate to say so bluntly. One by one being asked to speak instead, they make excuses, but finally it is decided that Griffiths shall kick off, though he protests that he knows nothing about strategy and will find it difficult to follow the P.M. This decision having been taken, Shinwell rises abruptly and leaves the room.

P.W.E. meeting, followed by a meeting of Eden, Bracken and myself alone. Bracken, as usual, has a long string of grievances, which he puts with his customary rudeness. I say that I am getting rather tired of all this and, in particular, very tired of the suggestion that things have been concealed from him by my people. I say, 'I am rather tired of being told that I evade issues or am a liar. I may have other qualities which are displeasing to the Minister of Information but I am not that sort.' Eden, slightly embarrassed, says he thinks that there are several alternatives; we might extend the P.W.E. area, or let the Minister of Information take all propaganda. I say there is a third alternative, namely to keep the present system, which is not working at all badly. But I am willing to consider the possibility of extending the P.W.E. area. It is agreed that we shall think over the matter and meet again for further discussion. These talks create in me a sense of deep depression. This continual fratch is a vile waste of time, not only mine but my staff's as well. I am not sure which is worse, Eden's green eyes or Bracken's brainless bad manners. Gladwyn tells me that Eden has told Cadogan that of course certain arrangements were made before he came back to the Foreign Office and he is not sure that this is the right set-up. Meanwhile, Attlee is still dangling about in the U.S.A., and, on these inner questions, there is no one else whom I can mobilise. Therefore I am playing a bit for time till his return. ...

[Noel] Hall to dine. Very full of himself, his achievements in Washington and the way in which all the diplomats and consuls tried to keep him down. He is a frightfully patent intriguer. I had forgotten how patent. Last night he was at a *partie carrée* with Bracken, Radcliffe and Tree. I am most careful not to ask what was said. He would go back and tell them that I had shown interest.

Wednesday 12th November

At Party Meeting results of elections for Administrative Committee are announced. The only changes are that Barnes[1] and Ellis Smith come on in place of Clynes, who did not stand again, and Kennedy,[2] who would have been well advised to do the same. He is now only a walking corpse, with a faint residue of mental trouble. I learn from Ritson[3] at lunch that a few of our colleagues had been organising a vote against all ministers. They had been going round with ballot papers in which the names of all ministers were struck off, because 'they have got a job already'. This movement showed itself in the order of voting, though it did not, judging from the figures, affect more than about a dozen of the voters. The list, in order, ran: Griffiths, Pethick [Lawrence], Noel-Baker, Wedgwood Benn, Lawson,[4] and then Alexander, the top minister, and then some other non-minister, and then myself, and then, two places down, Herbert Morrison, and two places below that, Grenfell.

But the great joke and semi-sensation was over Shinwell! As the names and votes were read out and his did not appear, his face became more and more grave. When the name of Ellis Smith was reached, Will Thorne,[5] who was announcing the results, said, 'And those are all elected', and then went on to read a list of 'non-elected' with *their* votes. And so we went down to the thirties and twenties, and still no Shinwell, and still the wonder grew! His name was not read out at all, but old Pethick in the Chair, Lees-Smith being ill in bed, said in his fussy old way, 'I think there is the name of one candidate which has been left out.' Then someone came up from the back of the hall with a slip of paper, from which it appeared that Shinwell had come in last but one among the elected, and his name was missed out from the enumeration – by mistake? I wonder. This is probably the best solution. If he had been pushed off altogether, he would have made even more trouble. He left the meeting, as usual, before the end, and was afterwards seen gesticulating with Thomas Balogh[6] in the sandwich bar. ...

1 Alfred Barnes (1887–1975). Labour and Co-operative M.P. for East Ham South 1922–31, 1935–55. Minister of Transport 1945–51.
2 Thomas Kennedy (1876–1954). Labour M.P. for Kirkcaldy 1921–2, 1923–31, 1935–44. Government whip 1924, 1929–31.
3 Joshua Ritson (1874–1955). Labour M.P. for Durham 1922–31, 1935–45.
4 J. J. Lawson, later 1st Baron (1881–1965). Labour M.P. for Chester-le-Street 1919–49. Junior minister 1924, 1929–31. Secretary of State for War 1945–6.
5 W. J. Thorne (1857–1946). Labour M.P. for West Ham 1906–45.
6 T. Balogh, later Baron (1905–84). Hungarian-born economist. Oxford University Institute of Statistics 1940–55. National Institute of Economic Research 1938–42. Fellow of Balliol College, Oxford 1945–73. Reader in Economics, Oxford Univer-

Dine as the guest of Sir Alexander Mackenzie Livingstone,[1] a social engagement fixed once before but then put off, as I had that night to be at the dinner given to Attlee on his intending departure for the U.S., the P.M. and others being there. Sir Alexander Mackenzie Livingstone was in Parliament with me as a Liberal from 1924–9 – and then no more – in which years, he says, he joined the Labour Party.[2] He would like, he says, to return to Parliament as a Labour member. He now walks with a stick, and hobbles mentally as well. Gaitskell says that he has been very odd on the telephone, having rung up several times about this party tonight, asking whom I would like to sit next, etc. But it is quite a pleasant party, George Hicks entertaining us all with a series of moderately lewd stories admirably told. Alexander is also there and holding forth most proud-smilingly about the exploits of his Navy. ...

C.E.O. says that everything is swimming along very well for the moment at Baker Street, that he is being consulted more than ever before by C.D. and A.D. [Taylor]. He brings me four drafts – one to the P.M. complaining of recent indiscretion by the *Daily Mirror* and *Daily Sketch*, a second to Eden on our work in the Americas, a third to Bracken, dealing at great length with the latter's latest series of complaints and putting forth some constructive suggestions for extending the P.W.E. area, etc., and a fourth to Buckingham Palace explaining to Hardinge, following up Gladwyn's own talk with him, that there are three ministers in charge, and not one only, and that perhaps Their Majesties would prefer to lunch with Bowes-Lyon and then be taken round sub-ministerially. He is *damned* good, this principal officer of mine. He creates in me not only confidence in him but renewed confidence in myself. I let him have the first and fourth draft back straight away, but the second and third, being more complicated, I shall sleep on and play about with.

And so, having read a few pages of *Scum of the Earth*,[3] which is now my bed book, I sleep very well, much better than for some nights past, till I am awakened –

---

1 Sir Alexander Mackenzie Livingstone (1880–1950). Liberal M.P. for the Western Isles 1923–9. Joined Labour Party 1930. Supported MacDonald in 1931 and became Vice-Chairman of the National Labour Committee.
2 Marginal insertion: '(But in 1931 he went *Nat* Lab! I checked this up afterwards.)'
3 By Arthur Koestler, published by Jonathan Cape in 1941, an account of the author's experiences in France between August 1939 and June 1940.

---

sity 1960–73. Economic Adviser to the Cabinet 1964–7. Consultant to the Prime Minister 1968. Junior minister 1974–5.

Thursday 13th November

– in time for one of my breakfast parties with Wilmot and Gaitskell in my bedroom.

Lunch at Yugoslav Legation where, out of a party of nearly twenty, the only non-Yugoslavs are Bruce Lockhart, Ambassador Biddle[1] and I. ...

Biddle, who, as usual, oozes sentiment and compliments, says that as I entered the room he thought how very fit I looked, in spite of all official cares. It was 'wonderful' (his most hard used word) how at my age I had retained a respectable figure in the region of the stomach (I forget just how he put this). I said that sometimes now, when I was in the country, I went out for a run in the dusk. He said that in London he sometimes went for a jogtrot round the Park. I said that we might perhaps go out together one morning. This would make a good press paragraph for both of us. What time did he start? He said about seven. I asked whether he wore shorts. He said no, only a pair of grey flannel trousers. I think I must follow this up.

I bring back Lockhart for a few words on P.W.E., etc. It is clear that Gladwyn is holding Lockhart very well, it being an advantage that he knows M. [Gubbins]. If these two could handle all my relations with P.W.E. I should be quite happy to leave it without any ministerial interference at all. Lockhart is still evidently harassed by the weight of his duties. Now, he says, the three Peawits spend much time in considering how they can keep questions off our ministerial agenda which otherwise may lead to 'another explosion' by Bracken. He says that Eden is awfully bored with Bracken's way of carrying on. I propose to him an extension of the P.W.E. area, especially in the Far East which might anyhow soon be thrown into their laps if war broke out there. He is a little shy of this, but I more and more lean towards this sort of plan. ...

Address five or six hundred members of my staff in the canteen this afternoon on the work of the Ministry. Gaitskell has prepared me a very good basis for this, and I gather that the talk goes quite well. 'He has forgotten nobody,' said one of the young ladies coming out afterwards. I had indeed recited in due order nearly all the different sections of the Ministry, explaining how each played their indispensable part. I got the best laugh when I said that the Chilean Ambassa-

1 A. J. D. Biddle (1896–1961). U.S. Ambassador Extraordinary and Plenipotentiary to the governments of Poland, Belgium, Norway, The Netherlands, Greece, Yugoslavia and Czechoslovakia and Minister to Luxembourg 1941–4. Ambassador to Poland 1937–40. He accompanied the Polish government in forced moves from Warsaw to other cities, and eventually to Angers in France. Interim Ambassador to France 1940.

dor, when I sent one of my senior officers to apologise to him personally for great and unjustifiable delay in dealing with a case regarding Chilean wine, soon afterwards died. The shock and surprise at receiving an apology from a British Minister of the Crown had been too much for him. ...

Tonight I entertain Carvel with Wilmot, Gaitskell and [Haydn] Davies. He is, I think, a good friend of mine. He says that Attlee was told that he could have the Washington Embassy if he wanted it. I think this is a bit unlikely. Carvel is close friends with Harvie Watt, whom he will arrange for me to meet, probably next week, with one or two notable people, two of whom are wives of the War Cabinet. It will be interesting to see whether he can hook these. He says that Lord Beaverbrook, and to a lesser extent Bracken, are not in favour now with the P.M., but that Anderson is. The P.M. said to Anderson, 'Max has moved from A to B, but you are still A, and I take you in alphabetical order.' He thinks the P.M. will always stick to Anderson, whom he first met and appreciated when they were both young men at the Home Office.

Friday 14th November
After dinner I put the finishing touches, with the aid of Gladwyn and Gaitskell, to my long reply to Bracken's latest impudences. I have deliberately delayed a day or two so as to give time for the L.P.S. [Attlee] to return. I am very conscious of the attempt being made to force me into a corner while he is away.

A night or two ago I walked round late in the evening to C.E.O.'s room and spoke to him of these 'embarrassed, transient, jealous, embittered phantoms' of politicians who drift across the civil servant's sky line. We win our battles today and lose them tomorrow; we come in and go out, generally at quite short intervals. To me, sometimes, the idea of going out has great attractions. I should regain my freedom of expression; I should regain full freedom of speech. I should declare in a loud voice that the P.M. was *très mal entouré* ('But what good would that do?' Gladwyn asked). Anyhow, whatever happened, I had a tender feeling for his future career and hoped that hunting with him during this period would not have damaged it. Indeed, I liked hunting with him and would not care for it, in these conditions, with many others. As usual, he was astringently calm and sensible. 'We shall come through all right, I expect,' he said. This depression lifts considerably in the next few days.

Saturday 15th November
I get [Robin] Brook to bring me some papers, Gladwyn having gone

off, as his habit is, by a very early train this Saturday morning and returning on Sunday afternoon. I draw Brook on recent events and he says at once that clearly A.D. [Taylor] has been at the bottom of the intrigue, for it was no less, against C.E.O.'s position. Though he has not been long enough with the latter to be 'conscious of an acute loyalty' to him, yet he thinks it most disgraceful that there should be so little recognition of how much he has done for the others. Brook gathers that C.D. is not much liked by those some distance below him, who find him very rude in personal dealings and contemptuous of many of their suggestions. He thinks, I gather, that if I had got rid of C.D. this time, it might have been better. But I explain to him that this is impossible.

Ruth lunches with me. She is off next week to South Wales on the first of her visitations. She is most delighted to have got a definite full-time occupation at last so close to the war effort. She is the first of a new class of 'liaison officers' between the Ministry and the new Ordnance factories which are putting up hostels for their workers, a great majority of whom will be women. She may, later on, be stationed in one of the regions, coming occasionally to London, or may be stationed in London, going out from time to time to visit the regions. I am most delighted that she feels at last well fitted in.

Monday 17th November
Back from West Leaze. Lunch with Phil [Noel-Baker] and Leonard Woolf, who, now that Virginia has been dead some months,[1] looks better than he has for years. She must have been a frightful strain. He thinks that we should only recognise the exiled governments as definitely 'provisional', since we don't know what will emerge in these various countries later on. I am inclined to agree with him in substance, though not exactly in form. I think that those who stay behind and face the Nazi death, torture and starvation music will have great pride in themselves and some contempt for those who hopped it early on and only sent exhortations from a safe distance.

Gladwyn hears from Cadogan that Eden was much offended by my letter.[2] He thought I was trying to interfere with 'foreign policy', telling him what he ought to do. He was never consulted about this set-up. He is not at all sure it is the right one. He thinks that Gladwyn is 'keeping his end up' pretty well but that I am a most dangerous

1 Virginia Woolf, née Stephen (1882–1941). Writer. Virginia Woolf drowned herself on 28th March 1941.
2 'my letter': the content of this letter is not known, but it may have been related to Dalton's 'long reply to Bracken's impudences' referred to in the entry for 14th November.

person. He is going to write me a most furious letter. Cadogan had asked him why he did not have a frank talk with me on the subject.

Gladwyn comments on this story that Eden doesn't really like 'frank talks'. He prefers brooding and exploding to his own officials about the wickedness of outside intermeddlers. Gladwyn says that Cadogan is going to draft a 'mild reply' to my letter for Eden to sign. (As appears later, I forced a frank talk, the 'furious letter' was never written, and Cadogan's 'mild draft' took its place.)

On 18th November, British forces began to advance into Cyrenaica. By evening they had penetrated fifty miles into enemy territory.

Tuesday 18th November

Lunch with Maisky alone. We are waited on by a Russian maid who has only the dimmest idea of what to do with the food. The service is so slow that after an hour the coffee has only just been produced and Maisky has let it stand for five minutes without pouring it out. I have to say that in ten minutes I must be away for a meeting of the P.W.E. He says Oh dear, he hoped to have a much longer talk. Not yet socially very clever!

I am very cautious with him, having had previous experience of his leaky habits. This time I try to get *him* to talk. He says he does not think we have any clear idea as to *how* we are going to win the war. The P.M. is very brilliant and very determined, but, Maisky thinks, he is trusting a good deal to our national luck, which has never forsaken us yet but which, Maisky suggests, should not be too much counted on. Our Navy and Air Force both think that they will contribute very much to the final victory. But the Army seems to have no such pride in itself. He then relates how, when his Military Mission arrived, he took them round to Eden, Sinclair and Alexander, and in each case they were received in a most friendly atmosphere, asked to sit down and offered cigarettes. When, however, he took them to the War Office, Margesson, accompanied by two not very senior officers, received them most stiffly. All remained standing and the interview lasted only some five minutes. ...

P.W.E. meeting this afternoon goes fairly smoothly till the end, when, as usual, Bracken explodes. This time over alleged complete lack of preparation of propaganda in Middle East, with the Offensive already started this morning. Nothing has been done, the whole machinery has been broken up (this is obviously the tale he has heard from Brooks) and there should be an enquiry into the whole business. All this in front of the three P.W.E. officials. I merely say that he is wrong, not for the first time, in his facts. ...

I stay behind and talk to Eden. I summon up all my reserves of charm for this vain, feminine creature. He has been in a great stew over the very tart letter, as he thinks it, which he had from me last weekend, on Gladwyn's excellent draft. Gladwyn hears that he minuted to Cadogan, 'This looks like a lecture by the Doctor on how to run my job.' On this side, however, our conversation is friendly. He says he understands that Gladwyn and Cadogan have had a good talk. He thinks it is remarkable how, for an improvised organisation, we have got on so well. He has never been opposed to recruiting agents in South Africa, but on other matters thinks that our Ministers should always be consulted. I say I quite agree, but surely they should have discretion without referring everything home. He thinks they will exercise discretion in what they refer home or not. I say I don't think there is much between us on this and shall be very glad to talk to him further in detail at any time. I say that only to the P.M., to him and to the Lord Privy Seal am I prepared to speak quite freely on these secret questions. I ask whether Gladwyn has not confidence here of the Foreign Office and that he was my first appointment, specifically to keep relations good. Eden says yes, he has their confidence.

Then, turning to Bracken, I say that I shall pour out to Attlee the story of what I have had to put up with during his absence. It is quite intolerable that Bracken should always be running round to the P.M. Eden says he doesn't think the P.M. pays much heed to what Bracken says. He doesn't register.

Wednesday 19th November
At Party Meeting this morning, Morrison makes an effective statement on 14B.[1] This is well received and accepted with all but unanimity. Shinwell jumped up after Morrison and, at tedious length, repeated his arguments, though putting them less well and maundering off into reflections on the possibility that he himself might one day be imprisoned, as he had often been in the past, etc. The Party gets very impatient with this, and finally old Pethick [Lawrence] rises

---

1 *sic.* But probably a typing error for Defence Regulation 18B, under which the Home Secretary was empowered to detain any person believed to be of 'hostile origin or associations' or to have taken part in activities prejudicial to public safety. The Regulation had been introduced under the Emergency Powers (Defence) Act of August 1939. Its provisions were attacked by some on the Left as a threat to individual liberty.

in the Chair and asks him to bring his conclusions to an end as there is other business to get through before eleven, and only ten minutes left for it. Shinwell's stock is pretty low in the Party just now, and I hear from Ede that there is a good deal of discontent with him among miners in Seaham. Last weekend he made a speech, in which he said, 'I beg the Government not to be more afraid of me than of Hitler.'

Lunch at House of Commons and hear some amusing gossip from Rex Fletcher. He is not now in touch with A.C.O.,[1] who, he says, is humourless, industrious, and most ambitious to become First Sea Lord and so retrieve the naval reputation of his father, who had to give it up, on the ground of his German connections, in 1914. This man, being the cousin of the King, has a snob value in the Services and, having married one of Ashley's daughters, is rolling in Cassel money.[2] He was most unwilling to give up the command of the *Illustrious* and had to be specially summoned back by the P.M. himself.[3] (I hear later today from C.E.O. that he is having to start right at the beginning, as we had to more than a year ago, and fire practically all the existing top lot.)

Fletcher says that Keyes's dismissal was his wife's fault.[4] A satisfactory agreement had been reached with the Chiefs of Staff and Keyes had accepted it, but his wife persuaded him to write a five-page letter to the P.M., going back over all the old ground of Zeebrugge and Gallipoli and saying that 'I cannot accept this diminution in my status'. This was the only sentence which caught the P.M.'s eye, and he thereupon told the C.O.S. [Chiefs of Staff] to leave the matter in his hands. He then told Keyes to go. The press leak, about his Commandos being his 'babies', etc., also came from Lady Keyes. (Fletcher says she has an enormous moustache and he calls her 'The Marchioness Budienny'.[5]) Keyes said, 'I only spoke to one press man and I thought he was the man from the *Sunday Graphic*, whom I have always found to be a gentleman and who never repeated anything

1 A.C.O.: L. F. A. V. N. Mountbatten, later 1st Earl (1900–79). Commodore Combined Operations 1941–2. Chief of Combined Operations 1942–3. Supreme Allied Commander S.E. Asia 1943–6. Viceroy of India 1947. Governor-General of India 1947–8. First Sea Lord 1955–9. His father, Prince Louis of Battenberg (1854–1921), a grandson of Queen Victoria, was First Sea Lord 1912–14, when he resigned. In 1917 Battenberg gave up his German titles, assumed the name of Mountbatten, and was created 1st Marquess of Milford Haven, Earl of Medina and Viscount Alderney.

2 Louis Mountbatten married in 1922 the Hon. Edwina Ashley (1901–60), granddaughter of Sir Ernest Cassel.

3 Mountbatten had commanded H.M.S. *Illustrious* in 1941.

4 Sir Roger Keyes, q.v., was married to Eva, née Bowlby.

5 A reference to Marshal Budienny, q.v., Soviet Vice-Commissioner of Defence, who was renowned for his luxuriant moustache.

that I told him in confidence.' This conversation, however, was on the telephone and was not to the *Sunday Graphic* man at all.

In order to placate the deaf old Admiral, he had then been offered a peerage and the Governorship of Northern Ireland, in place of Abercorn,[1] but he didn't want the peerage – 'He said he didn't think he'd earned it'.[2] (I asked Fletcher, 'How does one earn a peerage?' He said, 'I am quite the wrong person to answer that question!') – and then Abercorn refused to quit Northern Ireland.

I say that I hear – I had heard it from [Maurice] Webb only an hour before – that Alexander is doing too many luncheons and speeches, and that people are asking whether he has not got enough work to do at the Admiralty. Fletcher said that Alexander was certainly very much taken up with social events. 'You and I', he said, 'got through all this when we were young, but Alexander finds it a thrilling new experience. And so he goes to all these luncheons and dinners, and off in the afternoon to have his portrait painted at the expense of the Co-operators and the weekend before last he went to Knowsley[3] and took me with him.' He was made a tremendous fuss of by Lord Derby[4] and a host of other people, and purred with pleasure all the time. 'When I have been away for a weekend, I write my hostess a Jemima,' said Fletcher, 'but on Monday morning when Alexander got back to the Admiralty, he found a Jemima from Derby, thanking him for having found the time to go, and saying that Derby had taken a vote of all the members of his family and that they had all voted that Alexander was quite the most delightful and interesting man they had met for years and that they all had the most complete confidence in the Navy so long as he remained First Lord.'

I ask whether Alexander was still so thick with the Beaver. Fletcher said no, this had cooled off a good deal but the Beaver was clever enough to warm it up whenever he wanted to.

Fletcher thought that the Beaver's relations with the P.M. were now very bad. I asked him, quite casually and not seeming to attach much importance to it, about Bracken's relations to the P.M. Fletcher said he thought that these were cooling off a good deal. He thought the P.M. had become rather bored with Bracken as P.P.S., always running in and talking about everything, and had therefore decided to give him the Ministry of Information partly in order to see less of

1 J. Albert, 3rd Duke of Abercorn (1869–1953). Governor of Northern Ireland 1922–1945. Conservative M.P. 1900–13.
2 Keyes accepted a peerage in 1943.
3 Knowsley, at Prescot, Lancashire, was one of Lord Derby's three country homes.
4 Edward Stanley, 17th Earl of Derby (1865–1948). Conservative M.P. 1892–1906. Junior minister 1900–3, 1916. Postmaster-General 1903–5. Secretary of State for War 1916–18, 1922–4. Ambassador to France 1918–20.

him. Bracken, Fletcher thought, was not quite so well or readily received at No. 10 nowadays and was rather regretting the old husks.

Fletcher had met Rose Rosenberg[1] the other day. She had had her face lifted, so that now she looked like a wax doll. He asked her, 'How is the old man?' She said, 'Do you mean my husband?' He said, 'No, I mean old Ramsay.' She said, 'But he is dead.' He said, 'Oh is he? Old Ramsay MacDonald and old Stanley Baldwin, I know one of them is dead and the other isn't but I always forget which is which.' ...

Attlee comes to dine with me. He only got back yesterday from the U.S.A. At dinner I encourage him to talk. He is very pleased with his trip and with the President, whom he saw twice, and with the other ministers, who he thinks are a very good lot. Ickes[2] is very much our way politically. John L. Lewis[3] is a crook suffering from acute inflammation of the ego. The I.L.O. [International Labour Office] Conference itself went very well. They passed unanimously a resolution declaring that the complete defeat of Hitlerism was essential for their future work. ...

After dinner I brought him back and told him what had been going on, particularly with Bracken, during his absence. I reminded him of Bracken's conversation in the Carlton Grill last February, vouched for by two witnesses.[4] He said that he had taken this up with the P.M. at the time and that Bracken had been ticked off. I said there had been an improvement for a while, but that since we had been together on P.W.E. he had been completely impossible and bloody-minded. I then showed Attlee all the correspondence between myself and Bracken. He read it all through – though there is now a damned lot of it – snorting with indignation. He said, 'This man is not fit to be a minister in the middle of a war.' I said that he had clearly wanted to bring on a crisis, while Attlee was away, and to tell some cock and bull story to the P.M. and get him on his side. I had played for time and prevented this. I objected very strongly to Bracken continually running round to the P.M. and giving him an account of our affairs. It placed me in an intolerable position. Attlee said that he quite agreed, and that Bracken must be either a P.P.S. or a minister conducting his business properly with his colleagues. I said that Bracken was always saying, when we were together, 'As the P.M.

1 Rose Rosenberg (d. 1966). MacDonald's Personal Private Secretary 1924, 1929–35. Private Secretary to MacDonald as Lord President of the Council 1935–7. She married Laszlo Hoenig in 1939. The marriage was dissolved in 1954.
2 Harold Ickes (1874–1952). U.S. Secretary of the Interior 1933–46.
3 J. L. Lewis (1880–1969). President of the United Mine Workers of America 1920–60. Vice-President of the American Federation of Labor.
4 See entry for 20th February 1941, and n. Bracken had (allegedly) abused Dalton over lunch at the Carlton Grill with Rex Fletcher and Tommy Davis.

said to me last night ... ', or 'I was lunching with the P.M. yesterday and he said ... ', or 'I have to be round at No. 10 in ten minutes'. I said that I couldn't possibly agree to Bracken having to do with anything secret, except within the P.W.E. area. Attlee quite agreed. He said the Ministry of Information was the worst Ministry in Whitehall. (Ministers apart, he has a great down on the staff both at the Foreign Office and the Ministry of Information.) I said that I had heard indirectly from General Ismay that Bracken and [Desmond] Morton, not being friends of mine, put ideas into the P.M.'s head about my other wing and lessened his interest in it. I showed Attlee the report prepared by C.E.O. for Cadogan, and his covering letter, on the other wing; also recent letters from the Polish Deputy Prime Minister and the D.N.I. [Director of Naval Intelligence]. He thought all this seemed quite good. I said I had some minor difficulties with the Foreign Office but wouldn't bother him with these now. My immediate preoccupation was Bracken. I said, however, that Eden had hinted at one of our ministers' meetings that all P.W.E. might be turned over to the Ministry of Information. I said that I couldn't agree to this for a moment. I judged that it was important, other considerations apart, that one of the Labour ministers should be in on propaganda. If the Party thought that an attempt was being made to edge us out of this, there would be a row. Attlee warmly agreed. He said that he was seeing Bracken tomorrow, the latter having asked to see him in order to get information on the U.S. He would take occasion to speak to him on what I had told him. I think he will play up quite well.

The L.P.S. [Attlee] told me this evening that he had had trouble with Makins in the U.S.A. 'He was supposed to be my Secretary, but he tried to run me on a Foreign Office string. I wasn't having it.' The I.L.O. Conference had passed a resolution in favour of setting up a special Commission to study post-war problems. A few days later Makins brought the L.P.S. a draft for a communication from him to the Foreign Secretary, proposing that this Commission should be presided over by Van Zeeland[1] and that H.M.G. should be represented by Leith-Ross, who would have been the only British representative on the Commission. L.P.S. asked why he had produced this document without first discussing with him the general line. Makins said, 'It is only a draft' and added that he had been discussing it with the Embassy and the State Department while L.P.S. had been away for a few days. L.P.S. said that he had no authority to enter into

1 Paul Van Zeeland (1893–1973). Belgian politician and economist. Prime Minister 1935–7. Left Belgium for London and then for the United States after the German invasion in 1940. Returned to Belgium in 1944. Minister of State 1948. Foreign Minister 1949–54.

such discussions. Nor did he understand why any communication should be sent at this stage to the Foreign Secretary. The proper minister to communicate with was the Minister without Portfolio, who had charge of post-war planning. The L.P.S. told Makins that he had no use for Van Zeeland, who had been a member of a most reactionary government in Belgium, and that the whole make-up of the Commission was wrong, since the I.L.O. was tripartite and there should therefore be three British representatives, one of whom must be a good trade unionist. The L.P.S. therefore tore up Makins's draft and summoned a meeting of the British delegation, including my brother-in-law[1] and George Gibson. He then made his own draft and sent it off to Greenwood. Makins had said to him that we should not allow the I.L.O. to usurp the functions of the League of Nations. The L.P.S. replied, 'The League of Nations is dead and the Foreign Office helped to kill it. The I.L.O. is still very much alive.' Makins replied that the Economic Section of the League was still alive in some place, the L.P.S. forgot where, on the American Continent. The L.P.S. told Makins that this meant nothing at all. It is quite clear that Makins showed great ineptitude in his handling of the L.P.S.

I said that I knew Makins only very slightly. He was reputed to be one of the abler Foreign Office officials. I had only once had any direct dealings with him since I had been at M.E.W. and this had not been satisfactory. While Halifax was still at the Foreign Office and Labour ministers in the Government were trying to get the Belgian Government widened so as to include Socialist and Liberal elements – a line in which we were getting some support from Halifax and even from the P.M. – it had been suggested to me that I should ask Makins to lunch, since Belgium was one of his responsibilities. I had done so, but had discovered that he thought very much better than I did of the present Belgian Government, and much preferred Gutt,[2] the little agent of the Société Générale, to our friend Camille Huysmans,[3] whom he obviously regarded as a dangerous and undesirable character. It had then become clear to me that, so far as Makins exercised any influence on this subject, it would be directed to frustrate the wishes of the Labour ministers.

1 Sir John Forbes Watson (1879–1952). Director of the British Employers' Confederation 1921–52. Employers' Member of the Governing Body of the International Labour Office 1928–52. Married to Dalton's sister, Alexandra Mary (Georgie), q.v., since 1918.

2 C. A. Gutt (1884–1971). Belgian politician. Belgian Minister of Finance 1934–5, 1939–45; Managing Director of I.M.F. [International Monetary Fund] 1946–51.

3 Camille Huysmans (1871–1968). Belgian Socialist politician. Minister of Sciences and Arts 1925–7. Speaker of the Chamber of Representatives 1936–9. Prime Minister 1946–7. Minister of Education 1947.

As for Van Zeeland, I reminded the L.P.S. that his famous 'Plan' for European settlement had principally consisted in procuring very large loans from Britain, the U.S.A., and the small moneyed States in Europe, to Hitler and Mussolini. He was the chief apostle of money-lenders' appeasement.

Thursday 20th November

In my talk with Attlee last night he said that he had got on quite well with my brother-in-law [Sir John Forbes Watson]. I showed discretion here and did not say what a dull dog I always found him. But one day, said Attlee, Sir John suddenly exploded with indignation and said, 'I have been representing the British employers at international conferences for years, in half a dozen capitals, and I have never yet been asked inside a British Embassy or Legation.' Attlee then spoke to Halifax, who invited both Sir John and the trade union representatives to luncheon. If he had not been spoken to, there is no evidence that he would have done it. Attlee said to me, 'I said to your brother-in-law, "I suppose the Foreign Office think you haven't got a dinner jacket."'

I get this morning a most reasonable and friendly letter from Eden in reply to mine about the wilful child and the dangerous toy. I send a note to Gladwyn saying, 'You were quite right. Firmness pays, and I think that Cadogan has done some good work over this.' Gladwyn says later that this looks very much like Cadogan's draft. Gaitskell thinks that my talk with Eden the other day has also helped it through.

Friday 21st November

Have a few moments with Attlee just before lunch at No. 11. He did not speak to Bracken yesterday but thinks it will be better to speak to the P.M. when he can catch him at the right moment.

Saturday 22nd November

To West Leaze by the six o'clock train with Christopher Mayhew, who is now a Captain and wears uniform.

Before going to bed we go for a quick run in the dark up the road to Dudmore.

Sunday 23rd November

A wonderful day of sun and breezes. We walk and run most vigorously from 9.45 to 2.15, stopping only for a quarter of an hour, sitting first for a few minutes on the Sarsen Stone, looking down at Ashdown House along an axial line from above, and then having a drink at the

Queen Victoria in Aldbourne. We begin by running over a piece of plough just across the road and down the hill to Lower Barn, then strike past the Giant's Grave, over the Swindon road, and up to Peaks, from which we do a two hours' swerve first to the left and then round to Ashdown, and then swiftly up the rising ground beyond it and so back, beelining to Peaks again, from which we go down to the village, running a good part of the way. I am delighted at my endurance and find Mayhew, aged twenty-six, a perfect partner on such an enterprise. After this energy, and lunch, we go to sleep in front of the fire, and after tea play chess. He has gained much self-confidence, he says, during the past year. He is still in some ways surprisingly young and immature and has not yet grown a very firm or worldly judgment, but he is extremely nice.

Monday 24th November
Gladwyn and I dine together and discuss tomorrow's P.W.E. meeting. He thinks that I should now take quite a stiff line with Bracken and refuse to go on arguing any longer. It is clear that writing letters is no good and that none of the arguments or explanations put forward are seriously considered. He reports to me that Ronald Tree told de la Warr, who told it back to him, that I was a most sinister figure and was organising a Gestapo of my own staffed with members of the Labour Party. Also that Hood gave Gladwyn the impression that the talk in the Ministry of Information was that they should take it all[1] over and that what was left of S.O.E. could be done by 'the military' or C.![2] ...

Later this evening, having further conferred with Gladwyn, who says, 'We want allies very badly', I decide to try to catch Eden before tomorrow's meeting.

What is all this worth? Sometimes I feel that I should be much happier outside it all. I recall how, after my third Parliamentary defeat, returning to the School of Economics and entering the crowded lecture hall, where my appearance, after a much publicised fight, was much applauded, I said, 'What shadows we are and what shadows we pursue!' Whereat Gladwyn replies, quoting from neither he nor I remember which Greek author, 'All is laughter; all is dust; all is nothing.'

All that is left of his Greek or mine is a bagful of tags, but he has more in his bag than I. 'Those who believe themselves worthy of great things become worthy.'

1 Handwritten insertion: 'all propaganda'.
2 'C.': Sir Stewart Menzies, q.v., head of the Secret Service.

Tuesday 25th November

Attend Administrative Committee, where Shinwell, for the first time in his life, sits silent, though with his habitual pitying, contemptuous look.

I am anxious to see Eden before the P.W.E. meeting at 3, but this can't be managed, so I have a few cryptic words with him on the telephone and arrange to speak to him after the meeting.

The meeting itself goes better than usual. Several points on which I expected a row – Middle East reinforcements and Aspidistra[1] – go past easily.

The only slight flutter is over a Parliamentary Question on which I ask for information as to the reply proposed to be given by Bracken. It is a silly thing about the Horst Wessel song having been played, etc. etc. Bracken says he does not think an important executive like ours should spend time on such trifles. I say, 'That is a matter of opinion. Each of us must have his own view as to what is important.'

I then have a short time with Eden alone and speak with him frankly on the lines agreed last night. I say that I could not for a moment agree, nor would my political friends, to any proposal to edge me out, and that, though Eden and I have put our Party politics aside for the duration of the war (I think he rather likes this), Bracken has not. I say that I have shown great patience with him in correspondence but that it is clear that many things are being said which should not be. I cite Tree, who obviously only echoed his master's voice, but it is intolerable that such things should be said, particularly by a fellow who puts up the P.M. for weekends. I then recite my Council – a Foreign Office official, a Conservative M.P., a member of the Bank of England Board who is also Chairman of the G.W.R. [Great Western Railway], a regular soldier, an ex-Director of Air Intelligence, a Director of Courtaulds ...... ! I ask him! Eden seems to take all this very well. He says, 'Perhaps I have sometimes been rather inept in the Chair.' He is sure the P.M. is not at all interested. He has never spoken one word to Eden about this subject. He thinks that I have been 'very wise' in my correspondence with Bracken. Might it not be a good thing for me to mention this to Attlee? I say that I have already done so and he has read the correspondence. ...

1 'Aspidistra': Code name for a powerful transmitter to be built at Crowborough for P.W.E. in 1942. Aspidistra could be used for breaking into enemy transmissions, or for jamming them. It was used with some success to mislead enemy forces, creating the impression that its broadcasts emanated from an official German source.

It seems that Cripps is not doing very well just now. He makes a great fuss over small things and won't give straight answers to important questions. He is in a nervy state. I say I have had long experience of him, and now he only eats raw carrots! Eden says that the Beaver treated him very roughly when in Moscow, which he had much resented.

Eden was pleased, I gather, with my last letter – and indeed it was intended to please him – but I fear that our plan of fortnightly meetings with Cadogan and C.E.O. will now have to stand over till his return.

I then go straight to No. 11 and tell Attlee what has passed. I repeat that it will mean a first-class political row if any attempt is made to monopolise P.W.E. When the battle in Libya has died down, he will speak to the P.M. I dwell on the insecurity of Bracken and quote the Gestapo story.

Tonight, after these two talks, I feel much brighter! The Celt in me[1] jumps up and down these days, contrasting, as I tell C.E.O., with his most level English imperturbability.

Dine with Ruth, who has had some days in South Wales and is now going off to the North-West. She is very much interested in her new duties. She may be stationed later on in Manchester.

Wednesday 26th November
Wilmot and Brook lunch together today. The former likes the latter very much and finds him very quick, loyal and lucid; not much interested yet in politics, thinking politicians are 'just a bag of monkeys', as indeed most of them are. John, not having been in on the detail of the last few weeks, reports that Brook says that there is a certain 'insularity' at Baker Street and an inclination to press the distinction between policy and operations too hard. In this Gladwyn and I are in the same boat. Some of those at Baker Street felt 'a little bruised' and 'anti-Minister' and Brook thinks that it would have been a good thing for me to have accepted C.D.'s resignation, doubting whether he is quite a big enough man for the job. I encourage John to maintain this contact. He wanted to tell me this in the absence of Gaitskell, not because anything was said against the latter, but because he might have taken the line that John shouldn't 'bother the Minister' with all this. John says that he wanted to tell me so that we shouldn't repeat our experience with C.H.Q. ...

---

1 Dalton's maternal grandfather, Charles Evan-Thomas, came from a long line of Welsh landowners.

Early in November the Japanese government made a final attempt to get a permanent settlement which would safeguard the Japanese position in China and provide access to urgently needed raw materials, and in particular, oil. It was decided in Tokyo to go to war if agreement was not reached by the last week in November. The negotiations took place in Washington. On 22nd November Japanese proposals and the draft of an American reply were shown to Australian, British, Chinese and Dutch representatives. The British, though concerned not to appease Japan, were nevertheless anxious to avoid war and were prepared to give the Americans a free hand. In spite of this, Hull told the President on 26th November that all governments concerned were either hostile to the American proposals or hesitant about them. The outcome was a virtual ultimatum, demanding the withdrawal of all Japanese forces from China and Indo-China. Faced with these terms, the Japanese government decided to go to war.

A Munich in the Far East? Troutbeck[1] comes down to the House with latest telegrams and information. Bennett[2] was with the P.M. till 3 a.m. this morning and the question is being dealt with strato-spherically, not even a Cabinet. They want to buy three months. Stimson[3] – how I keep on remembering 1931 and his book and Simon, but he is now seventy-two years old! – Knox,[4] after all these terrific bellifist speeches! – pressing Hull. ...

Leith-Ross, who always hates the Japs, says that trying to appease them now will merely make them think that we are too weak to fight, and this is quite likely to make them go full steam ahead. Thailand in the role of Czechoslovakia?

Thursday 27th November
Cynthia Jebb to lunch. She wants Gladwyn to have ten days in Scotland over Christmas and the New Year. I say he may. Butler, she says, will never get far because he worries so frightfully over everything. The other day he couldn't sleep because he wasn't sure whether he shouldn't write a letter to a Bishop who had made a

---

1 J. M. Troutbeck, later Sir John (1894–1971). Foreign Office. Seconded to M.E.W.
2 J. C. S. Bennett, later Sir Sterndale (1895–1969). Head of Far Eastern Department of the Foreign Office 1940–42, 1944–6.
3 H. L. Stimson (1867–1950). U.S. Secretary of War 1940–45. Formerly Secretary of State 1929–33. Aged seventy-four, not seventy-two. Dalton may have been referring to his book *Democracy and Nationalism in Europe* (1934).
4 W. F. Knox (1874–1944). U.S. Secretary for the Navy 1940–44. Republican candidate for Vice-President 1936.

speech partly going back on what he had said to Butler at a conference at the Bank of England on religious instruction in our schools! And he worries too, she says, before every party, large or small, that he organises, whether it will be a success or not. And he is most old-fashioned in his views and wants to return to the age of Pitt and the great country houses, and thinks that Socialists are quite frightful. And, living in his constituency, he worries even more because he never dares dismiss anyone in his employment. His wife,[1] Cynthia thinks, is perhaps a little too bracing with him, and this only makes him worse. I tell her that Butler had had ambitions to be made Deputy Leader of the Tory Party when the present P.M. took it over, and that there had been evidence of a press campaign aiming at this. She says that de la Warr would, she thinks, rather like to come back now to the Labour Party. No doubt he made a mistake in 1931, but he is full of energy and good will and feels now rather under-used. I say that if he really wants to come back, I think that probably it could be arranged. Jowitt was not only back now but in the Government. On the other hand, de la Warr had had a long innings as a minister, simply because he was about the only remnant of the Ramsay MacDonald crowd who could be plausibly given anything. He had not done too badly out of his connection with MacDonald. She then returns to her familiar charge about Philip Nichols, who, she says, is really longing to be spoken to nicely by me. I say I think that this would be a waste of my time. Francis Noel-Baker[2] was sitting at the next table, and, after he had gone, she said, 'I hope he didn't think that "Phil" meant his father.' I said I would take steps to remove any such idea.

Friday 28th November
Eccles to see me. He has blotted his copy book with Eden, who, he says, has also been indescribably rude to 'Francis Rennell' – thus we must learn to describe Mr F. Rodd. I say that this is most justifiable. Rodd is almost an 18B case. He has been going about London saying that 'there is no Government' in this country.

Saturday 29th November
Robin Brook to lunch. He is anti-King's and Sheppard[3] and Rylands.[4]

1   Mrs Sydney Butler, née Courtauld (d. 1954).
2   F. E. Noel-Baker (b. 1920). Captain in the Intelligence Corps during the Second World War. Labour M.P. for Brentford and Chiswick 1945–50; Swindon 1955–68. Son of Philip Noel-Baker, q.v.
3   J. T. Sheppard, later Sir John (1881–1968). Provost of King's College, Cambridge 1933–54.
4   George Rylands (b. 1902). Fellow of King's College, Cambridge and University Lecturer in English Literature. Like Dalton and Brook, an Etonian and Kingsman.

He recalls the latter's liaison with Topsy,[1] a most unusual adventure for him – and how? – and then talks of Gerald Shove,[2] who never asked him to his house, although he taught him for two years. He had evidently a great contempt for this pedagogue, who, I say, I had known very well when I was up. But he had married a twittering little wife, a very bad poetess, with a ridiculous Christian name – Fredegond[3] – given her by her cruel scholar of a father, F. W. Maitland.[4] I tell Brook that I had once eagerly asked Shove whether he thought I should ever make any success of a political career, and that he had made an encouraging reply.

Sunday 30th November
Gardening, filling saucers and getting out one rather easy stub.

And then I go back to Catullus. I rediscover, after many years, poems III and V in Macnaghten and Ramsay's edition.[5]

III is about the sparrow

Qui nunc it per iter tenebricosum
Illuc unde negant redire quemquam

and V, let us give and take thousands of kisses, now while we may, for –

Soles occidere et redire possunt.
Nobis cum semel occidit brevis lux
Nox est perpetua una dormienda.

After listening to the nine o'clock news I walk, and partly run, to Woodsend and back. The moon is nearly full. I have put my Whitehall-war-worries well away today but now give a few thoughts to future tactics. I shall, most certainly, threaten to resign and blow a lot of gaffes unless I can secure some real improvements.

---

1 'Topsy': not identified.
2 G. F. Shove (1887–1947). Fellow of King's College, Cambridge and University Reader in Economics. An undergraduate Fabian contemporary of Dalton's.
·3 Fredegond Shove, née Maitland. Poetess and cat-lover.
4 F. W. Maitland (1850–1906). Professor of English Law at Cambridge 1888–1906.
5 *The Poems of Catullus*, edited and selected by H. Macnaghten and A. B. Ramsay, Duckworth, London, 1899. Hugh Macnaghten had taught Dalton Classics at Eton. Macnaghten translates the lines quoted by Dalton thus: III 'And now he journeys whence they say/ No steps retrace the darkling way'. V ' ... suns can set and rise:/ For us the brief light dawns and dies/ Once only, and the rest is night.' (*The Poems of Catullus*, Cambridge, 1925, pp. 5 and 9.)

On 1st December, the Japanese emperor ratified the decision of his government to fight against the Americans and British in the Far East.

Monday 1st December
Gladwyn's hunch is that the Japs won't fight (so is that of various other people).

I go over the ground with Gladwyn and am not very pleased at the present state of things. Apart from trouble with Bracken, there seems a constant Foreign Office block against our projects. ... Our Operations now are few and far between. Our last reports have been most bare, long tales of what has not been done, with most of the blame put upon the weather. We are living on the past. I tell Gladwyn that just now I am particularly anxious for a successful operation or two.

The telegrams over the weekend show that Hull is still peeved. He seems to keep no Private Secretaries at the State Department. When Halifax asked for a copy of a certain paper – Hull's most important declaration to the Japs, as amended after pressure from the Chinks – Hull fumbled about on his desk amid a pile of other papers and couldn't find it.

Tuesday 2nd December
On returning from the P.W.E. meeting, I find Bracken's latest letter. This is so offensive that I decide not to answer it. In the next few days, however, I give Attlee a copy of this letter and notes on the reply which I might have made.

Wednesday 3rd December
I have been trying several times to catch Attlee, to whom I hand over further papers relating to Bracken and speak with emphasis and indignation. I just cannot go on like this and my patience is exhausted. He says he will make a memo for the P.M. on the matter. This last conversation takes place on the following day (4th). Today Attlee has two Cabinets, one Defence Committee, and an L.P. Administrative Committee, where there is visible great restiveness, partly owing to Anderson's incompetent handling of the Government case in the House, and much rebel activity in the wings. ...

Gladwyn says that if the Russians march on, we may yet have a Communist Europe – 'And then we shall be boiled, unless we have made something here that will appeal to our own people. If we have just gone back to millions of unemployed and individualist capitalism, we shall deserve our fate.'

Thursday 4th December
George Rendel[1] to dine. He clearly liked the Bulgars much better than the Serbs, who are now his charge. He thinks that a very grave mistake was made in not giving Boris the Garter. We had given it both to Carol and to Paul. 'The King never mentioned it to me, but I am sure that he felt it very deeply.'

We spoke of King Peter. Rendel said that he was mentally not more than sixteen and a half. I had already heard that he was spending five days a week at Cambridge (Clare). Rendel had visited, last week-end, the Queen Mother at her 'cottage' in Bedfordshire. After a talk with her alone, he had gone out and found King Peter playing darts all by himself in a shed at the back of the house. This had so profoundly shocked Rendel that, as soon as he returned to London, he began to make arrangements for King Peter to be attached to the Brigade of Guards.

Friday 5th December
Lunch with Mrs Phillimore. Attlee is there and Moret and Labarthe,[2] both of whom denounce de Gaulle. Go back with Attlee to No. 11 and speak to him further on Bracken. I dine with him tonight at his Club. He has seen Bracken and told him that his P.P.S. should talk less. Gladwyn says that this, no doubt, is why Tree cut him yesterday evening when they met at Lady Colefax's weekly Pay for Yourself dinner party. Attlee also says that Bracken denies being motivated by animosity against me and my affairs. I tell Attlee that I just refuse to believe this and give him some further letters. He says that this thing must now go to the P.M. and I say that I will agree to this only if (1) Bracken's letters are put before the P.M., and (2) if Attlee himself is present. Further, if the thing, being complicated, is referred to someone else for consideration, this must, I say, be a minister and not an official, especially Morton.

Saturday 6th December
To West Leaze with Patrick Hancock.

1 G. W. Rendel, later Sir George (1889–1979). Minister, then Ambassador, to the Yugoslav Government in London 1941–3.
2 A. Labarthe (1902–67). Editor of *La France Libre* and *Tricolor* in New York. Scientist.

At 6 a.m. Hawaiian time (afternoon in England) on Sunday, 7th December, forty Japanese torpedo-bombers, fifty high-level bombers and roughly the same number of dive-bombers, with an escort of some fifty fighters, attacked the American naval base at Pearl Harbor. In an hour and a half, the Japanese destroyed four battleships, crippled two, sank half a dozen cruisers and destroyers, and damaged or destroyed more than 200 aircraft, killing or wounding 3,581 servicemen and civilians.

Sunday 7th December

A very good day, and I take Hancock for a three and a half hours' walk on the Downs, with rather little running but a good deal of fast walking uphill. We come back via Baydon and call in at the pub, where one has a sense, in the slow Wiltshire bucolic talk, of the complete remoteness from all that absorbs my nights and days.

Nine o'clock news says the Japs are in. They have begun by attacking the Americans. This, from our point of view, is much the best way for them to begin. It will unite all the Americans in one great warlike fury. But this, I say to Hancock, will lengthen the war by two years. We must now begin to make plans for 1946.

Monday 8th December

Meeting of Labour ministers decides that we should insist at Party Meeting on seriousness of violation of Standing Orders by Shinwell, etc. All this row, however, is now blown away by the war news.

This does not prevent great waste of time by Shinwell, both at the Administrative Committee and the National Executive Committee this afternoon. At both of these I take him up and he becomes infuriated. At the second gathering he says that I am 'exceedingly objectionable' and that I am trying to prevent him from speaking. I say that I am not doing this but only observing that however long he speaks he will say nothing new, and the longer he speaks the fewer people will remain to listen and to vote at the end, and that this no doubt is part of his calculation. At the end we carry some almost meaningless motion saying that the National Executive 'views with concern' recent disunity in the Party but will take no action until the matter has been dealt with by the Parliamentary Party – which, of course, it isn't!

331

On 11th December, Germany and Italy declared war on the U.S.A.

Friday 12th December
Sir James Hawkey to lunch with me. Most affable, and soon the talk leads on to Bracken, Sir James leading it, and I tell him that this is by far the worst of all my colleagues. I hot him up a good deal about this and he is almost on the point of rushing off to the P.M. at once. But I discourage this, though leaving it that he may mention it to the P.M. when next he sees him. Of course this is all on the basis of P.W.E. Hawkey says that at the time of Dunkirk, Bracken, then just made P.P.S., was talking most defeatist stuff, saying he did not see how we should ever win. A parson told Hawkey that, having heard Bracken on this line, it had quite spoilt his sermon. He had not known what to say to the people. Gladwyn and Cynthia also lunching at the Lansdowne Club, I bring Hawkey across and join them, and Gladwyn plays up well. Hawkey says the only way to deal with Bracken is to 'treat him rough'. He also says that he was at one time a master at Bishop's Stortford.[1] I had not heard this before.

Gladwyn says that one of my staff is going to present me with a book entitled 'How to Get Rid of Bracken' but the trouble is that it takes seven years, and then the bloody stuff may grow again. I shall keep in touch with Sir James Hawkey! He says that when he praised me to the P.M. after my visits to the constituency, the P.M. lowered his eyebrows, as his way is, and said, 'Yes, he is a very able man.' (This same epithet was used on a certain occasion at Chequers.) ...

On 10th December Dalton minuted to Jebb: 'Captain Mayhew will shortly be taking up his duties in my Private Office ... It will be a great convenience to me to have Captain Mayhew as my Assistant Private Secretary in view of his knowledge of Baker Street and S.O.E. work generally, and in view also of his great discretion.'[2]

---

1 In the 1920s Brendan Bracken had taught at Grimwade House, a preparatory school attached to Bishop's Stortford College, a minor public school in Hertfordshire.
2 Dalton Papers 18/1.

Saturday 13th December
I collect Mayhew for lunch and tell him that I wish him to accompany me on my tour from 22nd December over Christmas. He would like this. He now is quite attracted by the prospect of coming here.

I get a very satisfactory short note from Attlee on his approach to the P.M. He put the case 'strongly', and the P.M. was much 'impressed with the impropriety' of the behaviour of 'the offender'. From now on, Attlee writes, he thinks that 'this warfare will cease'.

Sunday 14th December
Wet all day, so I read and sleep. Ruth is clearing things up and packing for her move to the North.

Jebb was awarded the C.M.G. in the January 1942 New Year's Honours. In his citation, Dalton wrote that, in creating a completely new organisation of a highly secret character, Jebb had shown 'varied ability of the first order, wide knowledge, quick intelligence, constant initiative and resourcefulness, marked organising power, great discretion and tireless energy'.[1]

Monday 15th December
Back with Ruth from West Leaze. She goes to Manchester tomorrow and has lots of travelling at the start, but will be based at the Grand Hotel. ...

Gladwyn has received this morning a 'letter of offer'. He says that he supposes he has me to thank, or is it the Foreign Office? I say it is I, and there was some resistance from the Foreign Office. Later I show him the correspondence and also his 'citation'. I ask him, 'Can you deny any of this?' and he says, 'I should think I could.' He has always been very detached about these things, and refused, when at the Foreign Office, to serve on the Honours Committee. But he thinks the Foreign Office should be grateful to me for having taken him off their list.

Tuesday 16th December
John Wilmot and I are to dine together, but join up at the Lansdowne Club with Gladwyn, Cynthia and the wife of Butler, whom I have never met before, though I have heard much about her. She is neither

1 Diary, no date.

good looking nor well dressed nor elegant but I can see what is meant when it is said that 'she is very good for Butler'; a manageress with ambition. Gladwyn says she was meant to be a boy. ...

Wilmot relates that a number of spinsters were sitting at long tables in a room in the Censorship Department going through intercepted correspondence. An old Blimp was in charge, on whom one spinster eagerly advanced and, holding up a letter, said, 'I am quite sure, sir, that this letter is by a Lesbian.' Whereupon Blimp, raising his eyebrows and his voice, cried, 'Gad, madam, I wonder if any of you girls can speak Lesbian.' Wilmot says that this story was told to Miss Cracknell, who didn't see the point, and then to Miss Wood who did, and explained it to Miss Cracknell afterwards.

Gladwyn produces this one –

The Commissars' Club at Kalinin
Is the best Club that I've ever been in
Said a chap from Odessa
'You watch me undress her'
As he brought a young girl of thirteen in.

Wednesday 17th December
Nathan lunch for Peter, King of the Jugs. Among those invited to meet him in the ante-room and be presented are Beneš, Raczynski (in the absence of Sikorski), Amery, I, Law, Addison, Rendel and – Nichols. The latter is now Minister to the Czechs. He has been suffering from a duodenal ulcer. He stands looking rather awkwardly away from me, and I, therefore, partly for my own amusement and partly to oblige Cynthia Jebb, advance upon him and ask after his health. He says that he is now quite well again. I say that I was sorry to hear that he had been ill. And that is all.

At the lunch I sit between Beneš and the Egyptian Ambassador who bores me. ...

[Beneš] has been speaking in these last days with 'Minister Nichols'. I say that of course he knows that this man has a bad record, having been Munichois and also an appeaser, right up to her entry into the war, of Italy. His political errors, I add, date back and are continuous. 1930 he wrote a Minute proposing that large chunks of Western Poland should be given to the Germans, on the ground that Germans were better people than Poles. I had had to put my thumb on this.

Beneš said that he thought Nichols now realised his errors. He had frankly admitted some of them. I asked, 'Did he give you the impression of a Guilty Man?' Beneš said, 'Yes.' I said, 'Perhaps this will make him all the more eager to do the right thing now. I hope so.' ...

A most interesting talk with C.E.O. and Gaitskell on future possibilities, and especially the creation of a Ministry of Economic and
Political Warfare. This is very difficult, but not too difficult, I think,
to try. It would be linked up with the necessary decline in work at
M.E.W. I shall speak to Attlee about it.

I saw the latter for a minute or two this morning, just before he
went in to take Parliamentary Questions. I asked, 'Did you show the
P.M. any of the letters?' He said, 'Yes, I did, and he was very much
shocked.' I said, 'I understand that Bracken is now preparing some
paper for the Cabinet, but I think this most unsuitable to be discussed
in the Cabinet. It should be considered by some one minister, acting
as arbitrator.' Attlee said, 'I am handling this at present and any papers
will come to me. If you have any more trouble with him, let me know.'

I tell this both to C.E.O. and to C.D. on the telephone. To the latter
I say, 'We have some down days and some up days. Yesterday was a
down day; today is an up day.' We are agreed that my words to
Sinclair on the telephone yesterday had probably led to his ticking
off, even though very mildly, Freeman,[1] and to today's new offer.

Thursday 18th December

See John Carvel at House of Commons. He gives me more particulars
of Macmillan's most clumsy intrigue against the P.M. He wrote a
letter to poor old Harry Fildes![2] The latter was showing it to Carvel
when he had to go off to the telephone, taking the precious letter with
him. He didn't take any action on it, not even replying. The movement
against the P.M. among the Tories is confined at present, I think, to
disgruntled and not at all important back-benchers. ...

Eccles is trying to be sent on another mission to Washington, and
has so tried to persuade Drogheda and Stirling, to deal with proposed
negotiations with French North Africa on the lines of my Minute to
the P.M., which the Foreign Office swallowed whole, proposing
direct trade between French North Africa and the U.S. and ourselves, thus deflecting supplies from French North Africa away from
Metropolitan France. I don't accept the view that none of our people
in Washington is capable of conducting these negotiations, and,
moreover, as Drogheda admits, there would be a scream from the
Foreign Office, and shrillest from Eden on his return, if Eccles was
again to be used on an important and semi-political mission, so soon
after having blotted his copy book with the Foreign Office over his,
as Eden thought, too political telegrams from French North Africa.
Later in the evening, I encounter Eccles with his wife and father-in-

1 Sir Wilfred Freeman, Vice-Chief of Air Staff, q.v.
2 Sir Henry Fildes (1870–1948). Liberal National M.P. for Dumfries 1935–45.

law. I ask her whether she wants him to stay at home or go away again. She says she prefers the former. This will give me an extra argument.

This was after I had been persuaded to go with Gladwyn and Cynthia to one of Lady Colefax's parties. I can bear these once in a while, but would be terribly bored to go too often.

Hear late tonight that Bertie Lees-Smith[1] is dead. He has been suffering badly from asthma for some weeks, and away a good deal. His will-power and firmness in the Chair have been, I thought, weakening for some time. I last saw him two days ago climbing into Phil [Noel-] Baker's car in Palace Yard to go to an N.C.L. [National Council of Labour] meeting. I last spoke to him the day before, when I asked after his health. He seemed a bit low and said that he had had this trouble all his life, and that it always came on in the winter. He could not sleep at night and always had to sit up in bed. The last words he said to me were 'Very few people have got a physique like yours. You don't realise, I expect, what it means to you.'

He was a first-class colleague, sensible, balanced, kindly, quite without any sign of bitterness, envy or egoism. He had a rather gentle sense of humour and I always found him most easy, agreeable and helpful to work with. He had not a first-class brain, nor was he a great orator. But he was, perhaps, a better politician, in the best sense, by reason of these two defects. He filled, since this Government was formed, a special niche in the House. His place will not be very easily filled. I suppose, in the first instance, old Pethick [Lawrence] will take it on. But he is getting *very* old and has not Bertie's width or poise. The only other possible candidate is Phil.[2]

Bertie was Ismay's cousin and always took an interest, at one time rare in the Labour Party, in the Army, and, to a lesser extent, in the other fighting services. Questions of strategy, and also of military organisation, interested him a good deal, and he used to go off quietly and spend time with Army and Air Force Units. On these matters he was a good deal more than an amateur, though a little less than an expert.

On 7th December (London time) the Japanese began an invasion of Malaya. On 16th December there was a second wave of landings, and British forces were compelled to withdraw from Penang on the west coast and from their

1 H. B. Lees-Smith, q.v.
2 Marginal insertion: 'or Jim Griffiths'.

defensive position at Gurun. Meanwhile, the Italians had inflicted heavy losses in the Mediterranean, including (during the night of 18th–19th December) the sinking of two battleships in harbour off Alexandria.

Friday 19th December

The House of Commons in one of its bad, ragged moods. A very bad spirit, pessimism and discontent with the conduct of the war; but no leadership of any opposition. There is evidence that the old gang of Chamberlainites are fanning up each other's animosities against the Churchill Government. If only they had a leader, they would put the Government in danger. Malaya now is a little like Norway in May 1940. The P.M. being away, Attlee and Alexander spoke for the Government, but neither made much headway. Reference to the P.M. received hardly a cheer. The Far East has got people down. It was a secret session. ...

Colonel Nicholls[1] to dine. I have not seen him for twenty-five years, when we were subalterns in the 35th Divisional Train,[2] first at Perham Down and then in France. I remember him as being good on a horse and at the piano and rather an agreeable companion. He was then – and therefore still is – six years younger than I am.[3] He says that I made a great impression upon him in 1916 and that he remembers my saying that I was going into Parliament after the war. He asked me whether I was going to be Prime Minister and I said, 'Yes, probably.' He also says that I put 'ideas about the under-dog' into his head 'over our rum'. We both thought little of our C.O. or of the way in which the 35th Divisional Train was run. And therefore he went into the Air Force just before I went into the Artillery. Since then he has been in India and elsewhere, pursuing his career as a regular soldier. Now he is Chief Signals officer at the headquarters of the Third Corps. We get on very well together and he is full of recollections of me in the last war. I think he remembers rather more than there really was. He talks, quite sincerely I think, about politics in a rather uninstructed, well-meaning, Left-minded way, saying how 'grand the men' are and

1 Lt-Colonel L. B. Nicholls, later Major-General Sir Leslie (1895–1975). Served with Dalton in the Army Service Corps 1915–16.
2 '35th Divisional Train': During the First World War, goods were sent by train from base supply depots at Channel ports in Northern France to railheads. Here a complete 'section pack grocery train', made up of trucks packed with one day's groceries for one division, were handed over to the supply officer of the divisional column and thence transferred to the horse-drawn vehicles of the 'divisional train' for conveyance to each brigade.
3 Actually eight.

how some officers don't realise this, and how right it is that everyone should go through the ranks and how difficult it is for men promoted from the ranks to get their bearings, and how he has tried to help in such cases and in various ways, and how, after this war, we must not repeat the mistakes we made after the last war. He asks me whether I am ever free for a weekend, and I say yes, for the next one. So we fix that.

Saturday 20th December
Gladwyn to lunch and concert plans for pushing M.E.P.W. [Ministry of Economic and Political Warfare]. I will begin with Attlee. Bracken is said to be ill and out of action.

See Attlee at three, while Gladwyn goes over to the Foreign Office. I give Attlee a copy of the note about Macmillan's intrigue against the P.M.; push the claims of Ivor Thomas for a by-election; and expound in broad outlines the scheme for M.E.P.W. He takes the latter pretty well and I say that I will make a note of it for him over Christmas.

To West Leaze by the usual train.

Monday 22nd December
Christopher Mayhew to lunch, and then we start on our Christmas tour of my Stations. ... Today, however, our car breaks down within half an hour of our destination – Sir Thomas Bazley's[1] country house. The next day, 23rd, we have a car smash, overturning a grocer's van at the side of the road and ourselves skidding round and shooting on to the grass verge, no one, however, being hurt though Mayhew has a black eye and a scratch near by.

Saturday 27th to Monday 29th December
Weekend with [Leslie] Nicholls at The Bridge House, Mordiford, Hereford. Very pleasant and easy. They encourage me to sleep late in the morning and I am taken out on Saturday evening, the 27th, to an evening party of rather uninteresting people. (Gaitskell says, when I relate this on Monday, 'It is just as well to remind oneself occasionally how dull most of those people whom one meets in the country really are.') On the Sunday we go to lunch with an enormous number of members of the Bulmer family, into which Ivor Thomas, who meets me at the station the night before, has now married. A faint flavour of rural radicalism in the cider.

Nicholls wants to go into politics after the war and thinks the Labour Party the only possible. I will arrange for him to meet Attlee.

---

1 Sir Thomas Bazley, 3rd Bart (b. 1907). Of Hatherop Castle, Fairford, Gloucester-shire, where a training school for Danish irregulars was housed.

I also drop a hint to him, without saying what it is, that he might find a change over in the near future to a show run by me, interesting. He is inclined to like this idea.

Monday 29th December
Back from Hereford. C.D. comes and reports on a number of matters, including that he hears that Lt-Colonel L. B. Nicholls has the reputation of being 'a first-class officer'. I say that he would be completely loyal to me and there would be something to be said for putting him in charge of our Signals.

Dine with Gaitskell and Thomas. See Brigadier Brooks in the distance and think to myself how very annoyed he would be if I succeeded in pushing Thomas into Parliament now!

Thursday 1st January [?]
Write a long letter, mostly news, to Ruth, now based in Manchester. I miss her a lot.[1]

Friday 2nd January
C.D. to see me (C.E.O. still being on leave) for our weekly talk. He is very anti-Foreign Office and says that they are involving us in great risks of losing the war. This repercusses a little against C.E.O. I suspect A.D. [Taylor] of working steadily in this sense. I have got the C.I.G.S. [Brooke] to dine with me next week and ask C.D. whether he would like to come. I say that I propose to have C.E.O. and M. [Gubbins]. He is not keen to come himself and hints that it would be better if C.E.O. did not either, though he does not wish to hurt his feelings. It would be much better if M. were to talk direct to C.I.G.S. Soldiers understand one another but do not like talking shop either to politicians or civilians. C.I.G.S. would not want to 'hear about politics'. ...

[A] report brought by Gaitskell, through P.,[2] who had seen a telegram at the War Office, to the effect that Eden had been very sticky with the Russians over (1) Baltic States, and (2) Persia.[3]

I discuss this with Gaitskell later this evening. It has been said that Cripps has long wanted to resign from the Moscow Embassy and would like either to come back into politics here or be Viceroy of India. It would be a frightful bore, in nearly every way, if he came back and constituted himself Leader of the Opposition here. If, how-

---

1 This entry is inserted in handwriting.
2 'P.': not identified.
3 Marginal insertion: '(some truth in (1), though not without some justification but none in (2).)'.

ever, he blows the gaffe and attacks Eden for being difficult with the Russians, there might easily be a first-class crisis and Eden might have to be sacrificed. I shall sound Attlee on this when next I see him. Meanwhile, I tell Gaitskell that I feel that I am being furnished with more pretexts, if I should need them, for a strong line.

Sunday 4th January
Attlee to dine. I speak to him very frankly about Eden, Bracken, etc., and expound my ideas in favour of M.E.P.W. [Ministry of Economic and Political Warfare].[1] He says that he quite agrees and will discuss the matter with Eden tomorrow.[2]

The War Cabinet on 5th January discussed a Memorandum by the Foreign Secretary proposing that, in view of famine conditions following the German invasion, the Foreign Office and M.E.W. should consider ways of promoting shipments of wheat from Turkey to Greece – on the understanding that Britain would not be involved to the extent of a private undertaking to the Turkish government to replace grain so shipped. Discussions turned mainly on whether such a concession would create a breach in the whole blockade policy. No conclusion was reached, but Dalton and Eden agreed to discuss the matter further.[3]

Monday 5th January
Cabinet. Greek Relief again, this time on a paper by Eden. It is not a good paper and contains a number of mistakes. After he has expounded it, Kingsley Wood at once leaps in and says this is impossible and has already been decided. Attlee then cross-examines him. I later make a statement, substantially repeating what I said before, and the only new support which he gets is from Amery. I offer to consider the matter further with Eden and through our officials, but without commitment. This is agreed to.

See Attlee after the Cabinet and ask him how discussions are going. He has seen Eden and put up to him my proposal, supporting it, according to his own statement. Eden had said that Bracken had proposed that he should take all propaganda and that my other responsi-

---

1 i.e. a possible new ministry with this title.
2 Marginal insertion: 'He says B.B. "had his head bruised by the P.M." '
3 PRO, CAB 65/25.

bilities should be transferred to the C.O.S. [Chief of Staff]. Eden had not said that he was in favour of this and Attlee had said that it was quite impossible, and that the Labour ministers must have a proper share of the conduct of the war. I said to Attlee that of course if anything of this kind happened, I should not regard M.E.W. as a full-time job and should not go on. Attlee said that he had told this to Eden. The talk had ended with a suggestion by Attlee that the two of them, with Anderson, should consider it further in the hope of settling something before the P.M.'s return. The P.M. was very bored with questions of organisation and would not wish to be troubled with this.

Perceiving a 'gap of understanding between our two countries', Churchill had sought to smooth relations by sending Eden on a mission to Russia. Eden set sail from Scapa Flow on the night of 7th–8th December, just as the news of Pearl Harbor broke. In conversations with Stalin and Molotov on 16th–18th December, Eden discussed the frontiers of post-war Europe. In particular, Stalin demanded the restoration of the position in 1941, before the German attack, in respect of the Baltic States, Finland, and Bessarabia, the incorporation within the U.S.S.R. of the Baltic States, and the restoration of the 1941 Finnish-Soviet frontier.[1]

Tuesday 6th January
It is reported, from more than one quarter, that at one of the banquets given when Eden was in Moscow, Voroshilov[2] got so drunk that he fell across Stalin's knees, but that Timoshenko,[3] on the other hand, arrived at the banquet very drunk but got more and more sober as the proceedings went on. Stalin asked Eden, 'What does your Winston Churchill do when his Field Marshals get as drunk as this?' ...

P.W.E. meeting, the first for a month. No butter melts in anyone's mouth. We all approve the reports put up by the officials and Bracken is quite oleaginously polite to me. But we have not time to consider my paper, and this, therefore, is postponed. To make sure that I should have no trouble with Bracken, I went in before the meeting to see Eden alone, leaving Bracken and the officials in the outer room. I said that I hoped he would rule out of order any attempt by Bracken

1 Churchill, *The Second World War, vol. III*, pp. 471–3, 538–9.
2 Marshal K. Y. Voroshilov (1881–1969). Commander of Soviet North-Western armies defending Leningrad. Chairman of Presidium of Supreme Soviet 1953–60.
3 Marshal S. K. Timoshenko (1895–1970). Commander of South-West Soviet armies. Led Soviet invasion of Poland 1939.

to raise contentious points, or any matter touching my other activities. He said he hoped that this would not be necessary. While we were thus speaking, Lawford[1] came in rather hurriedly to say 'Mr Bracken is here', but he had been there before me, so evidently impatience was growing outside. I remained after the meeting alone with Eden and laid myself out, with a sustained effort, to be nice to him. Gladwyn had this morning, on my suggestion, gone round to see Oliver Harvey and to explain how much I admired Eden, how baseless, in the present political situation, would be any suspicion on his part that I was after his job, how like-minded we were on all large issues, and how eager I was to work with him. Gladwyn said that Harvey had taken all this very well, and it seems that he had passed some of it on before this afternoon's meeting. Eden spoke fairly freely to me about his visit to Moscow and said that he would let me see the record of the talks, though he begged me to keep this very much to myself as he had refused it to several members of the War Cabinet.

Wednesday 7th January

First Lord Drogheda and then [Dingle] Foot on Greek Relief. Both opposed to any concession. I am a little fluctuant, being anxious not to have a further row with Eden.

Lunch with de Gaulle. Not a very well assorted party and the whole thing a bit sticky. Lord Cherwell,[2] Sir Edward Bridges and Radcliffe (Ministry of Information) are the other British visitors. No delicate questions are raised, but the thing does not go very well. We lunch in a private room of the Connaught Hotel, where the cooking is generally good, but de Gaulle, wishing, I suppose, to seem very English, has ordered some very desiccated boiled beef cooked altogether in the English manner.

Administrative Committee in Attlee's room. After dealing with small business, they skirt round and round the question of 'discipline' and Shinwell, who leaves, as usual, before the end. As usual, we end nowhere.

Bruce Lockhart to dine with me and I encourage him to talk. He says that the influence of Harvey on Eden is very great. They go for a walk together every morning. Leeper lives almost wholly in the country.[3] He generally only comes up on a Tuesday and they spend the whole of that day in their Executive and Ministerial Committee Meetings. Therefore Leeper maintains practically no contacts in

1 V. G. Lawford (b. 1911). Assistant Private Secretary to the Foreign Secretary 1939–46.
2 1st Viscount Cherwell, formerly Frederick Lindemann, q.v.
3 i.e. at Woburn.

London. Eden often asks, 'Where is Rex? Why is he never here?' Lockhart understands that Leeper may be offered Chungking, and that Clark Kerr is likely to succeed Cripps at Moscow. I say that Leeper is fifty-four this year and should surely by now be an Ambassador. The pension will be very important for him.

As for Brigadier Brooks, Lockhart says that he is 'entirely built up on Hollis'. This in reply to my ingenuous suggestion that he has many contacts in all the Service Departments. Lockhart says no. But he sees Laski from time to time, who, says Lockhart, 'is a great enemy of yours'.

Lockhart says that Eden said, after our last ministerial meeting, that it was 'the best we have had yet' and that he hoped that I and Bracken were now prepared to settle down together. Lockhart said that he thought this was hoping too much. He added that Eden had been very much displeased with Bracken's methods and that his last letter to me had been 'the letter of a lunatic'. I said that I had not replied to it but had passed it on to the Lord Privy Seal [Attlee], together with other correspondence. Lockhart said that there was obviously much to be said for 'putting under one hat' all P.W.E. and S.O.E. I said that either I should wear this hat or no one would. I said that I had drafted the resolution on which the Labour Party had entered the Churchill Government: 'Full share of responsibility as an equal partner', etc.

He said several times that Bowes-Lyon was an ambitious intriguer and was spending much time with Bracken. This is a new suggestion. I said that I was sure that Lockhart himself and Jebb would always settle matters satisfactorily if not interfered with by others, either vertically or horizontally.

Lockhart says that Eden has referred my propaganda paper to him for a Minute. He will express agreement with it, except that each of the Allied Governments should be treated on their merits. He says that Eden lives a very busy day. He spends much time seeing the Ministers of Allied Governments and unimportant States. He also makes his own records of these conversations. Lockhart says that Sir Edward Grey[1] would never have seen anybody less than an Ambassador. (I tell this to Gladwyn, who says that he understands that Eden lives in a constant whirl, people rushing in with papers and doors opening and shutting in all directions, like the best French farce. There is no time, I say, for deep reflection. Gladwyn says that it is because Eden is constitutionally incapable of deep reflection that

1 Sir Edward Grey, 3rd Bart, 1st Viscount (1862–1933). Liberal M.P. 1885–1916. Parliamentary Under-Secretary of State for Foreign Affairs 1892–5. Foreign Secretary 1905–16. Ambassador to the U.S.A. 1919–20.

he prefers this ineffective way of life.)

It was tonight that Clement Davies was to have given his great dinner party, on the eve of the re-assembly of Parliament, at the Reform Club. This was to gather together all the important opposition elements and make a plan to hot up the Government. I have Haydn Davies in the lounge keeping his eyes open, and he reports next day that only Clement Davies and Horabin[1] were there. All the others had fallen out and Clement Davies said loudly that he was going off to dine with his wife. Shinwell had said in a public speech last weekend that he had heard that there had been stories about a dinner party on the eve of the meeting of Parliament but that he would not be there. There is a story that they all met and dined and plotted somewhere else on some other night this week, and this may well be true.

At talks in Washington between 22nd December and 7th January, Churchill, Roosevelt and other political and military leaders confirmed the policy of seeking to defeat Germany before Japan. They also established the Combined Chiefs of Staff to direct the Allied war effort. On 3rd January, General Wavell was made Allied Supreme Commander of the joint American–British–Dutch–Australian Command, with the task of holding the 'Malay Barrier'.

Thursday 8th January

House of Commons sits for one day and Attlee and Eden make speeches. Things go pretty easily and the stock of H.M.G. has gone up again, largely owing to the P.M.'s activities and publicities in the U.S. and Canada and to the fact that people are getting more used to an unsatisfactory situation in the Pacific. ...

Dine with Spears, who has got a K.B.E. in the Honours List. He is to be British Minister in Damascus and Beirut. He is accepting this, but not with great enthusiasm. He has now very little use for de Gaulle, whom he describes as 'the warrior monk', and absolutely none for de Larminat,[2] 'that blue-faced Jesuit'. Catroux[3] is a bit better, but no

---

1 J. L. Horabin (1896–1956). Liberal M.P. for North Cornwall 1939–47. Labour M.P. 1947–50.
2 E. de Larminat (1895–1962). Deputy Commander of the Free French Forces in Syria and Lebanon 1941. G.O.C. Free French Forces in Libya 1942–3. Chief of Staff to de Gaulle 1943. Commander of the 2nd French Army Corps in Italy and Provence campaigns 1943–4.
3 Georges Catroux (1877–1969). Commander-in-Chief of the Free French Forces in Levant 1941–3. French Ambassador to the U.S.S.R. 1945–8.

enthusiasm even for him. Charles Peake is taking over Spears's liaison job, and of him he is contemptuous. 'The diplomats always stick together and find each other jobs.' He is also impatient with Morton, whom he says is 'the fifth wheel on any coach'. Also present at the conversation is Spears, Junior, very Jewish-looking and, apparently, not physically fit to join the Army. He was at Eton and Magdalen and has now, apparently, been taken on as a temporary in the Foreign Office. He was a Chess Half Blue at Oxford. During my conversation with his father, I also played chess with him, making my moves very quickly without reflection. None the less, I hold out against defeat for a considerable time.

Earlier in the day I had been inclined to give way to Eden over Greek Relief to the extent of one shipment of wheat from Egypt. This was to be hedged about by various conditions, including prior agreement with Russia as well as with America. Gaitskell, however, comes in and persuades me to change my mind and to maintain my reputation in the Ministry and elsewhere. This will please Lord Drogheda, who is therefore to see the Foreign Office tomorrow and tell them that we cannot budge.

Friday 9th January
C.C.O. [Mountbatten] calls and stays for an hour. ... He asks many questions about the origin of my show and its relations with others. He is anti-de Gaulle and anti-Foreign Office. I arrange for exchange between his man Haydon[1] and M. [Gubbins] of major directives. Our talk reaches a tremendous finale of enthusiastic agreement on the subject of the French industrial workers – and the Comte de Paris,[2] Comité des Forges,[3] etc. I ring the bell for my P.W.E. paper and show him the relevant passages. He says he is astonished and delighted that any member of the Cabinet should hold such opinions. He supposes that he and I would be the only two out of any dinner

---

1 Brigadier J. C. Haydon, later Major-General (1899–1970). Vice-Chief of Combined Operations Staff 1942–4.
2 The Comte de Paris (b. 1908). Son of the Duke de Guise and Princess Isabelle de France.
3 'Comité des Forges': a group of right-wing French industrialists. In a separate note, Dalton recorded: 'There has been much talk of the Comte de Paris, as a rallying point for wider popular support, and of Vichy Generals who were on the point of coming over to our side, and, from the same source, persistent tales that the traditional ideas and forces of the French Left – Republican, Democratic, Radical and Socialist – now counted for nothing, and that every personality ever connected with the *Front Populaire* was irredeemably discredited. I have never believed this story, and the evidence of the B.B.C.'s most interesting monthly surveys is all the other way ... ' (Dalton Papers 18/2 (55).)

party of thirty people drawn from those who were running the war who would hold such opinions.

All this is good as far as it goes and quite amusing, but he may become, or be presented by others as, an uncomfortable acquisitive force. ...

Visit Lansdowne House and go round the top floor where my Censorship Department is housed. Accompanied by Sir Frederick Leith-Ross and Mayhew I show interest in all the details and shake hands with all the staff, some of whom, I think, are very pleased to be visited. I make a row in a room used as a typing pool, which appears to be much too dark, overcrowded and noisy. I say very audibly that I have seen plenty of unoccupied space and that the number in this particular room should be much reduced. Someone says something about the difficulty of getting Treasury to agree to more supervisors, and I say that, if this difficulty is raised, they should refer it up to me.

Return from this tour in time for my usual weekly meeting with C.E.O. and C.D. This goes on for more than three and a half hours, i.e. till about 8.45, and both C.E.O. and Gaitskell think that I have been tiring C.D. out. He does not look very well and is having further trouble with his tummy. C.E.O. and I are not sure whether, on physical grounds, he will be able to go on very much longer. In that case, we both agree that M. should succeed him. He would be difficult in some ways, but a great improvement in others, and he has a good deal more political sense.

I go to dine with Gladwyn at the Travellers' Club, waiving, for this once, my objection to the standard West End Clubs. He says, 'Surely no one who may see us together there will accuse you of conspiring with me!' The dining room is nearly empty, but Sir Horace Wilson is intriguing with someone, and offers a congratulation to Gladwyn on his recent tail-piece. I say to Wilson, 'I am glad that you approve of my nomination.'

Dalton made an additional, separate record of his conversation with Mountbatten.

The C.C.O. [Mountbatten] came to see me today and stayed for an hour. I said I was glad to hear that there were good contacts between his Show and S.O.E.; I wished for full co-operation with him. He said that he had already had valuable help from us in his Norwegian raids.

He asked me various questions about the origin of S.O.E. and its relation to other bodies, particularly S.I.S. He said that he had the impression there was rivalry, and some difficulty as regards signals. ... I said that my chief preoccupation was to make sure that we had a system of communications which would not only work well now, but could be relied upon to work when the balloon went up in Western Europe.

The C.C.O. then spoke about the directive which had been given to him, to be ready for an invasion of Europe in the spring of 1943. There had been some reference in this to patriot forces, and these, he understood, were my concern. He asked what we were doing in this connection. I then told him of our directive from the Chiefs of Staff and of our paper dealing with secret armies, etc.[1] He said he would very much like to see this, and I said I should be glad for him to do so, on condition of our seeing his directive. We agreed that such papers as we interchanged should be seen by very few people. He asked whether I would agree that his Brigadier Haydon should get into direct touch with M. I said that I should be very glad.

Reverting to Intelligence, he said that he was puzzled by the many bodies at work, S.I.S., S.O.E. and J.I.C. [Joint Intelligence Committee]. I explained to him that S.O.E. was not supposed to collect intelligence. He said that we must get a good deal anyhow, and what did we do with it? Could he have it? I thought we were here getting on to rather dangerous ground and said that I was sure arrangements could be made for us to keep him in touch. I then expatiated on the relation of M.E.W. to the J.I.C., and on the growing importance of economic intelligence and the valuable work done by Colonel Vickers.[2] ...

He then spoke ill of the Foreign Office, not, he explained, the present Foreign Secretary, whom he knew very well, but 'the machine'. They

1 'our paper dealing with secret armies, etc.': In the early summer of 1941, Dalton and his senior officers in SO2 had put forward proposals involving the notion of a huge reallocation of resources in order to arm secret forces in Europe for eventual use against Hitler. These ideas were fully expounded in a report prepared by the Future Operations Planning Section of the Joint Planning Staff. According to this document, the blockade and strategic bombing should be supplemented by subversion, including the organisation and arming of patriotic forces on a massive scale. Behind this idea lay Dalton's ambitions to place S.O.E. at the very centre of strategic planning. (See 'The Distant Future', extract from the Joint Planning Staff's Review of Future Strategy, 14th June 1941, JP (41) 444 in PRO, CAB 79/12, reprinted in D. Stafford, _Britain and European Resistance, 1940–1945_, Macmillan, London, 1980, pp. 234–8.)

2 C. G. Vickers, later Sir Geoffrey (1894–1982). Deputy Director-General, M.E.W., in charge of economic intelligence, and member of Joint Intelligence Committee of Chiefs of Staff 1941–5.

were adepts at passing the buck and hindering action. I said that under my Charter I was required to get the consent of the Foreign Secretary to any operation affecting Foreign Office interests and that, although we often had differences of opinion with the Foreign Office, and sometimes suffered great delays, I owed a very great deal to the activities of the C.E.O. in breaking through or finding ways round Foreign Office objections. But in many cases I would often have liked to go much faster than the Foreign Office agreed to. The C.C.O. said he thought we should have given Pétain an over-dose of sleeping draught six months ago. It would have been easy to put this old 'ga-ga' out of the way and the results would have been splendid. He was not sure that it would make much difference now.

He then spoke ill of de Gaulle, saying that there was very little difference between him and the Vichy Generals. What we had to tell the French, he said, was that they had to get rid of their French Fascists, who were in league with the Germans. He hoped that we were in touch with the French workers, from the 'pink trade unionists' to the Communists. I said that I had insisted, in recent discussions with General de Gaulle, that we must have the right to co-operate with any group of Frenchmen in France or outside, who were prepared to work for the common cause. He said that this was quite right, and that he hoped that General de Gaulle was not told too much about what we were doing. I said we had various agents in France, who were in touch with the French workers, and that I myself strongly held the view that it was the French industrial working class on whom we must count. This pleased the C.C.O. very much. ... Our conversation ... ended in an atmosphere of enthusiastic political agreement.

Tuesday 13th January

Go again, with other ministers, to the Foreign Office later in the afternoon to hear Eden give an account of his visit to Russia and talks with Stalin. I think he tells them rather dangerously much, including the substance of all the conversations on which I had seen the fuller record, even to the particulars proposed to be put into the secret Protocol on new European frontiers. Voroshilov, he says, 'had to be helped from the room' at 4 a.m. Timoshenko was most impressive to look at; he looked like a huge Mongolian peasant. Stalin is quite a small man, no taller than Beaverbrook; his physical movements are rather like those of a cat. Eden tried hard to think of him as dripping with the blood of his opponents and rivals, but somehow the picture wouldn't fit. Eden couldn't quite make out why Stalin was so insistent on getting a Treaty reference to the Baltic States, for, when we had won the war, the Russians would be in possession of them, he said, and we shouldn't be in a position to put them out.

I think, on the other hand, that it is natural, particularly in view of the long haggle over debts, gold, ships, etc., connected with these three potty little places, that Stalin should want it cut and dried at last. Eden was most impressed with the good clothing and equipment of the Russians, and its great superiority over that of the Germans. Stalin said, 'The Germans don't surrender much to us.' Eden went out to Klin to the scene of recent fighting. The road, one of the big broad highways of Russia (Moscow–Leningrad) was littered with broken tanks. The scorched earth policy had been applied, in some places quite completely, in others not. Klin was about two-thirds destroyed, but they had lunch at a large house which did not seem to have been damaged at all. They asked him if he would like to see some German prisoners. When he said yes, there was a great scurrying about, and it was some time before they could be produced. They then said, 'We were keeping these for identification purposes.' He saw no cages, such as we keep for prisoners, near the front. They insisted on his being photographed beside some frozen German corpses. Everybody crowded round and took great interest in this photograph. It made him wonder whether there were quite as many German corpses as they all alleged, e.g. 12,000 German dead in Klin alone.

Stalin did not seem to think much of the British Army, though he had a great respect for our Navy, Air Force and equipment.

It was very difficult to remove the suspicions. Stalin could not be got to see why he and Eden could not just sit down and sign a Treaty. On the second morning Eden found him sitting with a newspaper cutting in front of him; this reported the Anglo-Turkish Treaty. Stalin said, 'If you can sign a Treaty with Turkey, why can't you sign one with me?' Eden explained that this had taken months to negotiate and had required the concurrence of the Dominion Governments. Next day, Stalin having thought more about the matter, said, 'If you don't think I am the sort of person with whom you want to sign a Treaty, why don't you say so?' Eden found him very straight, direct and reasonable. He never raised his voice or harangued, as Hitler and Mussolini used to do. Altogether, if I may summarise the general impression, quite a nice gentlemanly fellow!

Friday 16th January
Two inebriated newspaper men[1] seek an interview with me to tell me that the most tremendous changes are about to be made in the Government. M.E.W. is to be abolished and a War Cabinet to be

1 A marginal note indicates that one of them was John Carvel.

constituted from which all ministers with departments are to be excluded. Thus, e.g., Eden and Bevin are to be pushed out. Tom Johnston and Duncan are to enter the War Cabinet without portfolios and, of various alternatives, rather cloudily exposed, the most likely seems to be that I may succeed Lord Halifax in Washington! This conversation lasts too long and was not, says Gaitskell, who finally is most helpful in breaking it up, at all a good show. These journalists seem not to have any sense of the political limitations on ministerial reshuffles.

Saturday 17th January
I was hoping to get away to West Leaze by a morning train, thus making a rather longer weekend of it and getting rid of the remains of a cold. But I am rung up on the scrambler by Bridges, who says that the P.M. is expected back at 3 o'clock this afternoon at Paddington and the Lord Privy Seal [Attlee] thought that as many ministers as conveniently could would like to meet him. So I postpone my going till the 4.45 and take Mayhew (rather thrilled) round with me to the station after lunch. A considerable crowd, including most members of the Cabinet. As the train draws in, Bracken is seen rushing about, part lunatic, part showman and part bell-hop. A policeman, who seems to know no one by sight, advances upon us and says, 'Only Cabinet Ministers allowed on the platform!' He then descends upon the Lord President, of whom he demands, 'Are *you* a Cabinet Minister?' Anderson says that he is the Lord President. The policeman then hustles Lord Simon, not even asking whether he is anybody, but repeating raucously, 'Only Cabinet Ministers allowed here!' Lord Simon replies very deprecatingly, 'I am the Lord Chancellor.' The policeman then withdraws. The P.M. emerges from the train looking a little pale and very cheerful. With a number of others I shake him by the hand, and also his wife, who is looking very radiant.

Then, having had tea with Mayhew, in Paddington Hotel, I escape.

Monday 19th January
Back from West Leaze by a later train which gets me in in time for lunch with Mrs Phillimore alone with three Frenchmen, Comert,[1] Hauck[2] and Labarthe. They all say de Gaulle and all his principal associates are deplorable. Listening to Frenchmen in London, it is hard to foresee any future for France in our lifetime.

---

1 P. Comert (1880–1964). London Editor of *France* 1940–48. Chief of Press and Information Service of the French Ministry of Foreign Affairs 1933–8.

2 H. P. L. L. Hauck (1902–67). Director of Labour, Free France 1941–4. Director of Industrial Relations of the French Ministry of Labour and Social Security 1944.

Sir Campbell Stuart to see me this afternoon. He has nothing much to say, and does not ask for a job. I repeat to him that I handed over Bracken's correspondence to Attlee and that since then there has been an improvement. He speaks ill of Leeper and asks whether, if he could be got rid of, Jebb would not better represent my interests on the triumvirate of officials. But, he adds, this should not be mixed up with Baker Street, which, he hcars, is going very well. This non-mix-up idea has, no doubt, been put into his head by Bracken. ...

Crossman comes to see me about German Workers' talks. He has seen Bracken today, who had pretended to be very friendly and has said that he is not going to let him down, in reply to a Parliamentary Question by some Tory which picks a phrase out of its context and suggests that our broadcasts are pro-German. Crossman is not, at this moment, a great favourite of mine, and he talks nonsense, as I find out when checking up afterwards, about the German Workers' talks. He says that they are entirely addressed to the old membership of the S.D.P. [Social Democratic Party]. But this is quite untrue.

Tuesday 20th January
P.W.E. meeting this afternoon is again uneventful. We are still in the era of Precarious Peace. Eden is delayed and does not get back to the Foreign Office till 3.20. It is hinted several times by Harvey and others that we might like to begin, but Bracken and I both say that it would be much better to wait for the Foreign Secretary. The point, of course, is that neither of us is willing to let the other take the Chair.

Wednesday 21st January
Party Meeting unanimously elects old Pethick [Lawrence] to succeed Lees-Smith. Ellen Wilkinson says to me that strong pressure was exercised by 'the machine' to prevent any other nominations. I say that, if this was so, I took no part in it, either way. She says that she nominated Jim Griffiths, and was rung up by Scott Lindsay and tremendously bullied. In fact, he seems only to have asked her whether she had Griffiths's consent, and the answer was no. I am glad that Pethick has been given the job, for it is mostly honorific and ceremonial and is best held, at this stage, by an old man who will not make a personal challenge to members of the Party who are ministers. Griffiths might have been quite awkward, being ambitious, effectively rhetorical, and with streaks both of slyness and of innocence. Nor would it have been very convenient to bring him up too fast on the National Executive.

Old Pethick, having been elected to the Chair, makes a frightful mess of it when we come to discuss whether the P.M.'s speech in the

House next week should be recorded and broadcast the same night. This proposal had been turned down by the Cabinet while the P.M. was in the U.S., but has been resuscitated, largely, I hear, as a result of Bracken's officious activities, and the P.M. has been persuaded to put down a motion permitting this to happen. It has aroused a lot of criticism, some stupid but on balance sound. It would create a precedent which might be dangerous; it would either eliminate all interruptions or reproduce them; in the former case it would not be a Parliamentary record, in the latter case it might create an impression of factiousness, opposition and discord quite out of scale with reality. Moreover, the sort of speech that goes well in the House is quite a different thing from that which goes well on the air. I gingered up the Administrative Committee yesterday to take a strong line against. They were inclined to be hivvery-havery, but Lindsay mentioned that the Cabinet were against it and Bracken had dug it all up again, and, being the only minister present, I told him that this was true. This morning the *Daily Herald* says that the Administrative Committee will advise the Party to vote against, and *The Times* and *News Chronicle* are also hostile. On the other hand, the *Telegraph* and *Express* are in favour.

At our Party Meeting the debate becomes quite disordered and Pethick does not seem to understand the elements of Chairmanship, namely the need to *put* the question straight away: 'Those in favour ...... Those against'. Instead, he asks plaintively, 'Would you now like to vote on ...... ?' The result, of course, is a mixed yell and a general atmosphere of excited disorder. He surpasses himself, before putting the final vote, asking, 'Does anyone else want to raise any point of order?' But no doubt he will improve with practice.

The P.M., having sensed that there is a lot of opposition, merely rises to say that he does not propose to move the motion.

I sit myself near the steps of the throne but out of sight from the Chamber, though well within hearing – this hidden nook is rather a discovery! – in order to hear, without being seen, Bracken's replies to questions. But he is not reached, standing at No. 91 on the order paper. ...

Thence to lunch with the Turk, 'Aras[1] in Wonderland', as Gladwyn calls him. A swarm of guests, including the Chinese Ambassador, the Lord President and his new wife, and Mr and Mrs Richard Law.[2]

1 Dr T. R. Aras (1883–1972). Turkish Ambassador in London 1939–42. Former Turkish Foreign Minister.

2 R. K. Law, later 1st Baron Coleraine (1901–80). Parliamentary Under-Secretary at the Foreign Office 1941–3; Minister of State at the Foreign Office 1943–5; Minister of Education 1945. Conservative M.P. for Hull South-West 1931–45; Kensington

The last named female is planted opposite to Aras between Anderson and myself. She is quite quite frightful, an account which I had had of her from Gladwyn being much below the truth. She is, I understand, an American, but I hear her getting completely bogged regarding her legal status and nationality in a conversation with the Lord President, who finally asks her, 'But surely you have not got a Nansen Passport?' My conversation with this woman begins very inauspiciously. I said across the table to her husband, 'In a moment I must introduce myself.' He replied, 'She is an extreme Socialist.' I, therefore, taking this gambit, said, 'Your husband has just told me that you are an extreme Socialist.' She said, 'How can he possibly have told you that? You could not have heard anything he said across the table.' I said, 'Well, *are* you an extreme Socialist?' She said, 'Oh, no, I am only in favour of a slight change.' Her idea of conversation seemed to be to contradict anything I said while it was generally clear that she was completely ignorant of the subject. Thus, when I remarked that it was extraordinary that the Russian Army seemed to be so much better equipped than the Germans, she replied that it was not at all extraordinary because they had been preparing for war for such a long time. I said that I thought the Germans had been preparing for longer. She told me this was not so. I also suggested that the Germans had a higher level of industrial efficiency and organising power. She replied that this was not so. When I said something about the Poles in Russia, she said that it would never be possible to get them to fight on the same side as the Russians against the Germans. The Russians, she said, had driven them from their homes and this the Poles would resent much more than being murdered by the Germans. I asked her whether her husband liked being at the Foreign Office. She said that it was better than the War Office, where, though she had supposed that he would get to know something about the war, he had been told nothing. But she did not think she really liked him being in the Government at all. 'The Foreign Office must be very stuffy,' she said. 'Do you mean the atmosphere or the people?' I asked. To this she replied, 'I suppose they must all be great experts in their own subjects.' A quite deplorable female.

Of the Lord President, as we left the dining room, I asked that he should present me to his wife. He did so and we sat in a corner for a quarter of an hour. We both praised the Prime Minister and Lady Anderson's first husband.[1] She said – really much too obvious – that

1 Ralph Wigram, q.v.

South 1945–50; Haltemprice 1950–54. Married to Mary Virginia, née Nellis, from Rochester, New York.

he had had a very high regard for me and he so well remembered a visit which Arthur Henderson and I paid to Paris in 1931. His death had been hastened because he felt that he had failed to make successive Governments realise the coming German peril. The difference between him and the P.M. was that Churchill felt that it was *they* who had failed, and not he. She then said that she remembered so well going to tea with my mother, and overdid this theme a good deal. She thought that as a small girl she had seen me as a large schoolboy. She asked whether I saw much of Sir Frederick Leith-Ross. I said, 'Why, but of course, he is my principal adviser.' She said, 'He thinks that I have made a *mariage de raison*.' I said, 'Would you like me to speak to him about it?' She said, 'Oh no.' I said perhaps, none the less, I could rebuild a bridge between them. A very false and unattractive woman!

Thursday 22nd January

C.E.O. has seen Cadogan who reports that Eden is being very silly and difficult again. Everything seems to be going on well and then suddenly he pours out deep suspicion of me, my functions and intentions. 'Who is Foreign Secretary, I or ...... ?' He is constantly afraid that I want to 'control foreign policy'. He seems to fear that at some moment some great movement will start in some foreign country, Italy or Germany, and that I shall say it is all mine and that therefore I must run the Peace Conference and he be elbowed out. Which is really all too childish and silly, as Cadogan agrees. Moreover, the little man will never face up to it with me. Last time I saw him I asked him whether he was quite happy with the way in which our affairs were working. He said yes, quite. These outbursts only occur when I am not there. Cadogan thinks that Harvey may have been hotting him up, which, if true, is disappointing after the trouble taken by C.E.O. – and me – with him. ...

Dine with Ruth at Royal Court Hotel. She seems to be thoroughly enjoying her work in the North-West, though it means a lot of travelling and awkward hours. She hates Manchester, particularly the centre of the city. It is frightfully black and sordid, and the Lancashire people are all undersized and wizened, the offspring of our Industrial Revolution. She likes Nottingham best of all the towns which she has been to, though Leeds is Paradise compared with Manchester. In the North one has much more the sensation that everyone is engaged on war work. In London this is not so.

Complete final draft of letter to P.M. reporting on Postmaster.[1]

1 'Postmaster': interception of Axis vessels off Fernando Po in January 1942.

C.E.O. is particularly good at drafting this kind of document, and he is the only person who can do it. The rest are *incredibly* bad at drafting, even for lesser people than the P.M.

Saturday 24th January
To lunch with Nathan. He asks Mayhew on the telephone whether I prefer lunching in a Club or a hotel. Mayhew says that I am not very keen on Clubs and therefore Nathan has chosen the Carlton Grill. But the reason why I am not very keen on Clubs is because I don't like it being observed who I am with, nor my conversation overheard. These objections apply even more to the Carlton Grill than to most Clubs! Nathan, of course, wants to put in again his claim to a post in the Government. Now that we have more Labour peers, he thinks that we should have more Labour ministers as well. He merely wishes me to know that he is willing and available to serve. He suggests to me that I should move to the Dominions Office. ...

Mayhew dines with me. He says that people in general think C.E.O. 'very iceberg'. He himself, he thinks, gets on much better with him now, especially since the evening when Hancock came to dine with us.

I discuss with Gladwyn the question of making a dossier against the Foreign Office. I say, not for the first time, that I am anxious to do nothing that will spoil his own prospects. He says that fighting the Foreign Office on some of these issues now won't do this. It might antagonise the present Foreign Secretary, but Foreign Secretaries don't last very long. The officials, on the other hand, will respect him all the more for having taken a strong line, and will say that if he fought well against the Foreign Office when he was outside it, he will fight very well for it when he is inside it again.

Monday 26th January
Ivor Thomas has got Keighley! I wire him my heartiest congratulations. This is my first real success in getting into the House of Commons one of my protégés of the next generation. It will be a nasty jolt for Leeper, Brigadier Brooks, etc.

Lunch with John Carvel at the Charing Cross Hotel to meet Harvie Watt. This has taken the hell of a long time to arrange, but now, at last, it goes very well. Also present Captain Ian Harvey,[1] a friend of Mayhew at Oxford, and a rising young Conservative politician. I tell Harvie Watt that P.M.'s solidest support is in the Parliamentary Labour Party. We first shed Harvey immediately after lunch, then

1 I. D. Harvey (b. 1914). Served Royal Artillery 1940–3. Conservative M.P. 1950–8. Junior minister 1956–7. Joint Parliamentary Under-Secretary at the Foreign Office 1957–8.

proceed to a wine shop in Villiers Street, where we drink some port and discuss the problems of Party machines, and I then take Harvie Watt back to No. 10. While we are still with Carvel, Harvie Watt says that Duncan is being talked of more and more as a possible Conservative Prime Minister. To follow the P.M., he says, it is no good having a 'cheap imitation Winston'. On the contrary, you want something quite different, very solid, competent, experienced and unexciting. This sounded to me anti-Eden and not without interest, since Harvie Watt is tied up with the Party machine.

Going back in the car, he says that people are saying of course we have confidence in the P.M., but not in all his ministers. 'We may not have much confidence, for instance, in Grenfell, or Attlee, or Kingsley Wood.' I don't rise to any of these names, though I am interested that these are the ones he mentions to me. If there is no reconstruction of the Government, there may be serious grumbling soon. He thinks Bevin is doing much better now in the House.

In announcing the shipment of wheat to help meet the Greek emergency, Dalton told the House of Commons that the British and American governments continued to regard it as incumbent on the Germans to feed the countries occupied by them.

Tuesday 27th January

Make my announcement in the House in answer to a Question on Relief Shipment of wheat to the Greeks. All sections of my answer are applauded, first the reassertion of our general attitude on Blockade, and second the announcement of the exceptional concession to the Greeks. The latter applause is the louder. The Supplementaries come out well, especially the question by Jack Lawson as to 'what guarantee' there is that the Germans will not take the food. I reply, 'None.'

P.M. speaks for an hour and a half. It is not one of his best speeches, but it is, on the whole, a pretty convincing statement. He is insisting on a vote of confidence. He says at the end that he feels the weight of the war more heavily now than in the summer of 1940. There is a great deal of criticism about, partly directed at him for doing too much and, so it is said, interfering with decisions of Chiefs of Staff, etc., and partly at his colleagues, or some of them, not generally very specifically named.

Wednesday 28th January
Dine with Pooley[1] at the Savile Club. We hear the Beaver on the 9 o'clock news. Laudation of P.M. and announcement of many figures of production. Alan Barlow,[2] of the Treasury, asks, 'Why must we listen to that bastard?'

During his visit to Moscow, Beaverbrook had clashed violently with the British Ambassador, Sir Stafford Cripps. On his return, Beaverbrook sent Churchill a list of 'Eight important points of difference between Sir Stafford Cripps and me' that had become apparent during the Moscow Conference.[3]

Thursday 29th January
Incredible stories of the behaviour of the Beaver in Moscow. He took possession of Cripps's office in the Embassy and turned him out of the room. When he wanted him, he opened the door and bellowed, 'Cripps!' When dining out, he demanded that an orchestra should be produced, and two rather decayed musicians were discovered. He demanded that they should play the Volga Boat Song but was told they couldn't; they were 'only a Caucasian band'. He then ordered that they should go away and learn it and come back again and play later in the evening. Once he tried to take them with him in another car behind his own, but when they reached their destination they had disappeared. They had been arrested by the police.

Friday 30th January
Leslie Nicholls to dine with me. I also ask the L.P.S. [Attlee], who likes men in khaki. We get on very well and the latter reminisces about his old batman.

Saturday 31st January
To West Leaze by the 12.30. Still some snow. Run round a bit and find myself locked out, my key of the front door breaking in the lock. I therefore have to walk up to Irene's cottage to get a duplicate. She has suddenly ceased to be shy, which much eases things. Her key works, so I don't have to break the glass as I feared might be necessary.

1 Sir Ernest Pooley (1876–1966). Clerk to the Drapers' Company 1908–44.
2 Sir Alan Barlow, 2nd Bart (1881–1968). Joint Second Secretary to the Treasury 1938–48. Principal Private Secretary to the Prime Minister 1933–4.
3 A. J. P. Taylor, *Beaverbrook*, Hamish Hamilton, London, 1972, p. 491.

Sunday 1st February
Snoozle till lunch and after lunch take a short run round in the snow. It is very cold and some of our pipes have burst. Sit up late tonight reading stuff on South America. It is all very dramatic – perhaps unreasonably so, but can one be sure and is one not running great risks in doing so little?

I must counter-attack the Foreign Office with a well prepared dossier if they try more interference (but a few days later, when I demand such a dossier, very little is forthcoming).

Monday 2nd February
Lunch with Phil and Irene [Noel-Baker] to meet the King of Greece.[1] As Kings go, he is fairly intelligent. Gilbert Murray,[2] looking very ancient, and a Greek A.D.C. make up the party. Irene says in Greek, when the King arrives, that we will not talk about food till after lunch. He and I then sit in a corner, and I speak particularly about parcels for Greek prisoners of war and the evacuation of Greek children to Egypt, etc. On the question of direct wheat shipments to Greece, I tell him that H.M.G. has decided [on] only one shipment. The King said that he heard that the German Governor of Athens, when called upon by a Greek lady responsible for organising Relief, who asked for food to be supplied, treated her with great rudeness, did not ask her to sit down, and said, 'We want you Greeks to die. At present we have to keep a large garrison here. When there are fewer of you, we shall not need so large a garrison, and there is the door.' He spoke also of the shocking and quite needless cruelty of the Bulgarians and of the massacres perpetrated by them against the Greeks.

Tuesday 3rd February
P.W.E. meeting. Bracken back towards his old form – reckless rudeness. He is, as Gladwyn says, simply a guttersnipe.

In December 1941, the *Prince of Wales* and *Repulse* were sunk by Japanese aircraft with the loss of 1,000 men. By the end of January, the Japanese had overrun the whole of Malaya, leaving Singapore isolated and ill-defended. Against this background, a three-day debate was held in the Commons on a

1 George II, King of the Hellenes (1890–1947). King 1923–4. Returned to the throne 1935 following a plebiscite. Set up a government-in-exile in Cairo after the German invasion of Crete 1940.
2 Gilbert Murray (1866–1957). Co-President of the League of Nations Union 1938–1957. Regius Professor of Greek at Oxford University 1908–36.

Vote of Confidence. On the vote, the Prime Minister won by 464 to 1, with only a handful of deliberate abstentions. 'P.M. makes a most masterly speech ... ' Dalton wrote in his diary on 29th January. Churchill hinted that he was about to appoint a Minister of Production, a concession to his critics, who had been demanding a more effective co-ordination of the existing supply ministries. On 4th February, it was announced that Beaverbrook had been given the job of Minister of War Production. Sir Andrew Duncan replaced Beaverbrook at Supply, and Colonel J. J. Llewellin took Duncan's place at the Board of Trade.

Wednesday 4th February
Long Meeting of National Executive Committee lasting into the afternoon. Chiefly on much too long document, 'the old world and the new society', which is written in Laski English and very remote and unprofitable. ...

Lunch at House of Commons with Attlee, to whom I say that the effect of the washing of Bracken's head is now fast wearing off and that it will have to be done again. I ask how he is getting on with M.P.E.W. [Ministry of Political and Economic Warfare] project and he says he will try and get a meeting this week. I repeat that I think it would be best for them to see me and Bracken separately.

Call on Secretary of State for Air, infinitely charming as usual, and leave with him an *aide-mémoire* provided by my E.R.D. [Economic Research Department]. The point is that, if we strike out [*sic*] a new invention, making it easier to bomb a target, say of ten square miles, even without moon, it would be a disastrous mistake to repeat what we did last war with tanks at Cambrai. We should save up the use of the new weapon – which, after an interval, the enemy will discover and counter – until we can use it as a massive surprise. My advisers strongly hold that economic targets, notably in the Ruhr, could be suddenly devastated by a series of really massive attacks under these new conditions, but that to let the thing go off at half cock would simply fritter it away. In the former case we might decisively affect the issues of the war; in the latter case, nothing important would happen.

I put all this to Sir Archibald Sinclair, who is most sympathetic, and says that this point of view is well understood at the Air Ministry. They attach great importance to this argument. They have Cambrai always in mind. On the other hand, from the military and political, as distinct from the economic, point of view, there is very much to be said for acting as quickly as we can, while the Russians are still pushing the Germans back, and while Germany is still in the grip of winter, so that the effects of air bombardment on morale are correspondingly large, and while the war moves so ill for us on all fronts other than the Russian. These considerations have to be weighed against each other. He adds that training has been lengthened, in order to give more weight to new methods of navigation. We have now to make dog legs round the most formidable flak which defends most interesting targets. The development of German defensive power in this way has been very great, though they have not, happily, countered, as we thought they might have done, directionally, etc. There is no shortage, as I had heard, of trained crews for Halifaxes, but only of crews trained with the very latest [*sic*]. There has been great disappointment both over the weather, which, according to their records, has been the worst for fifteen years – the whole period during which accurate records have been kept – and over the delay in big output of heavy bombers. These last had severe teething troubles, but these are now over and the Air Staff are very pleased with the results. The Lancasters, the latest, are the best of all. Soon, aided by the latest developments, we should see some really formidable results. K.G.100 practised fire raising by a few well directed leaders, and then the rest just came in and bombed the blaze. We should be able to imitate these tactics. Our latest incendiaries should make a greater blaze than ever, and the fear of being misled by a decoy fire is thought to be small. On leaving, I say that Medhurst is being very helpful, but I do not take it any further than this, since we still have great difficulties.

Phil [Noel-Baker] is to come to this building and live upstairs on the fourth floor as Parliamentary Secretary to the Ministry of War Transport. I hear a rumour of this from Gaitskell this evening, and ring up Phil to ask whether it is true that the Beaver has been fired and he is taking his place. Phil says, 'Not exactly.' I ask what then, and he says that he is succeeding Llewellin. I say that I am very glad and that he is clearly right to take it. He says he has had great doubts. I am sure he has, but it is a first-class thing that he has now been put into a Governmental job far removed from the Foreign Office. It will do him a lot of good.

The gossip is that Cripps originally as good as accepted the Ministry of Supply but that Bevin then worked upon him and told him what a dreadful man the Beaver was, so that Cripps then said that he would only take it on if he was a member of the War Cabinet. This was refused and the P.M. is said now to be very angry with Cripps. It is said that Bevin saw the latter three times; also that Cripps made a great row with Maurice Webb and the *Herald* and demanded that they should publish a denial of the statement that he had been offered a job. He said he had an angry telephone conversation with Webb and said,

'The press are trying to hound me out of public life again.' Webb said, 'If you will authorise me to publish a statement by yourself, in inverted commas, "I have not been offered the Ministry of Supply", I will do so.' Cripps then climbed down. Gaitskell says it looks as though he is just as big a fool as ever in domestic politics.

Bowes-Lyon to dine. For more than a month he had not heard of any suggestion, till yesterday, that he should go to the U.S. He talks a great deal, without any incitement from me, against Bracken. He is particularly vexed about the outburst over Aspidistra. He says it is just B.B.C. jealousy. He has taken a great interest in this particular project. Bracken, he says, is just a very small man who hates me personally and is therefore prepared to sacrifice everything to scoring off me. He has heard from Hood today that Bracken has just received a very severe snub from the P.M. and has been told to mind his own business and not interfere in other people's. Bowes-Lyon says that he has only seen Bracken once since last November (this is quite contrary to what Lockhart told me; he said he was always in and out with him). The only time he saw him then was when he went over to see Tree, who he says is a very stupid man. Bowes-Lyon further adds that Bracken has been a Minister for Political Warfare for six months and has never been down to C.H.Q. nor got to know any members of his staff. He has seen Dick Crossman once for five minutes in connection with the P.Q. Stephens, he says, is perfectly useless. Brigadier Brooks is realising that he is more and more out of his depth. To Leeper, Bowes-Lyon remains curiously loyal. He says he is much the toughest and best of the three. Bowes-Lyon now says that they all feel the lack of ministerial control at C.H.Q. I say that it was to get rid of this that the whole intrigue was worked, but that I remembered he had been very vexed with Gaitskell when the latter had brought out this point. He does not deny this. He says that he has got into trouble for suggesting the name of Grand to do something for us in Persia. ... I tell him that Grand was a friend of Bracken. I also tell him that I handed Bracken's letters to Attlee, who showed them to the P.M. I am inclined to think that Bowes-Lyon is, on the whole, honest and that the charges against him, of intriguing with Bracken, are not true. He asks whether I will go down and stay a weekend with *him* at Paris House. I say that, in principle, I should be quite glad, but that I have no free weekend for a long while.

Thursday 5th February
To lunch at House of Commons. Webb very busy and full of himself. He says he has seen the three letters which Cripps wrote to the P.M., the first accepting Ministry of Supply, the second and third raising

difficulties. The second only reached No. 10 Downing Street after the P.M. had made his final speech in the Vote of Confidence debate, having thought that everything was settled. It was written with the advice of Aneurin Bevan who, with Strauss,[1] is Cripps's chief adviser. Bevan had thought it very clever to send the letter so that it reached No. 10 only after the P.M. had spoken. Now the P.M. is ramping round denouncing Cripps with every kind of imprecation. Bracken had fixed things up, he thought, with Cripps so that they should show a united front, and was quite surprised when the latter cried off. On the whole, Webb says, the press today is critical of Cripps, except *The Times*.

News from U.S.A. through our channels is disconcerting. It is said that they are more anti-English in many significant ways than before they came into the war. Strong pressure, e.g., against our publicity. C.E.O. writes a Minute urging again, 'at the risk of boring you', that unless this country can take the leadership of a Western European bloc after the war, we shall degenerate into a rather miserable outpost, whose chief aim in life will be to keep Europe divided. The alternatives are to be dominated by the U.S.A. or Russia. U.S.A. after the war will take charge of South America, Far East and perhaps Australia and New Zealand as well. A West European Federation, on the other hand, might exercise dominant control over most of Africa, the Middle East and perhaps India. All this, he thinks, will become very clear in a few years' time, and those who can foresee it now should be thinking ahead. I reply that there is much force in this argument, but that Western Europe just now is an unappetising plateful. By all means, however, let us think ahead.

Friday 6th February
Lunch with Attlee at his Club and then take him on to see our Ops Room. M. [Gubbins] is most adequate and produces, as advised by C.E.O., a number of young officers in khaki to explain. Attlee stays for an hour and says practically nothing, as is his way, but I think is pleased and interested.

It is said that a frightful telegram has come in from the Auk explaining Libya and attributing the enemy's success to better generals, better tanks, more of them, and no spare parts on our side. He hopes to hold a line a good deal further back.

After the regular weekly meeting with C.E.O. and C.D. [Nelson], the latter and I dine together. I think I leave him purrier than I found

1 G. R. Strauss, later Baron (b. 1901). Labour M.P. for Lambeth North 1929–31; 1934–50; Lambeth Vauxhall 1950–79. Junior minister 1945–7; Minister of Supply 1947–51.

him. He gathers from Conservative country circles, Carlton Club, etc., that the P.M. is riding for a fall. C.D. wants me and Attlee to assert ourselves, though it is not clear quite how. He has also got quite keen on uniting us, although operational, with the Intelligence side. He speaks again of the possibility of his own resignation, not through discontent but because he thinks a younger man should soon take it on. I say that I suppose M. would be the natural successor. C.D. says that M. would be on his merits the best choice, but not a fortunate one, for he is difficult personally and likes only to work with people whom he himself has picked. Also he had no No. 2 who could take over. C.D. thinks that it would be best to seek some young man, preferably from the North of England, a civilian with great energy and no politics. He thinks there must be many such. ...

Later this evening Gladwyn reports that he has had Retinger to dine and the latter has been much concerned at hostility to me in the P.M.'s entourage. What we are doing is either suppressed or misrepresented and described as 'inefficient, amateurish, etc.' Gladwyn is inclined to think that Retinger gets some of this wrong, and has told him that my position is politically so strong that there is no chance of my being shifted. None the less, there is, of course, much truth in what Retinger has heard.

Gladwyn also tells me that there has been a further fuss in the Foreign Office over his seeing Departmental Secrets. Eden said they should not go outside the office and finally Cadogan only got the present arrangement continued on the basis that Gladwyn showed them to *no one* else at all, unless permission had been got on each one separately.

Going to bed, I think that we just don't deserve to win the war. We are all fighting each other instead of the enemy, and with such zest. P.M.'s entourage ...... Mr Bracken ...... Eden and his telegrams ...... !

Saturday 7th February
To West Leaze, but before leaving I ask Retinger to come and see me. He gives a very Polish and political interpretation of affairs. His account is that I have many enemies, partly because I am a Socialist and partly because I am known to have courage and energy and am thought to be personally dangerous. Therefore, he says, there is sabotage of my work in the Air Ministry and War Office by all the Blimps, and the P.M. is just not told of what I do and no reports are passed on. I have, he says, many enemies in the P.M.'s entourage. I ask him who, and he says the Beaver and Bracken, both of whom are always speaking ill of me, and General Ismay. (This last one is a bit

surprising, but he says it comes through Zamoyski.[1] I connect it a bit with C.D.'s rather unfortunate appearance before the C.O.S. [Chiefs of Staff] some time ago. He has never been a second time, leaving it now to M. This, however, I don't tell Retinger.) On the other hand, he says that the Prof. [Cherwell] is friendly to me. Morton he doesn't know anything about. Eden, Monckton and Lockhart, he says, are friends of mine (he doesn't know quite all about that!).

Monday 9th February
Harvie Watt to lunch. We talk very freely and I like him. He doesn't know much of what I do, and I just mention it in passing. He describes how packed the P.M.'s days and nights are, and I say that I think ministers ought not to bother him except on big questions. Harvie Watt says that most are very good that way, but a few aren't. We speak of possible Cabinet shuffles and he says that there are some who want to see Attlee, Greenwood, Eden and Kingsley Wood all out of the War Cabinet and replaced by Cripps and Duncan. I say that, as regards Attlee and Greenwood, this would lead to a riot in the Labour Party, and they would no longer support the Government. Attlee and Greenwood, whatever others may think of them, happen to be the Leader and Deputy Leader of the Labour Party, from which Cripps was expelled four years ago.[2] There is particular feeling, I say, against him still, in many trade union circles. Harvie Watt says that the argument for getting him into the Government is that otherwise he may become a focus of opposition. What kind of office do I think he might be offered? I say that he made quite a good Law Officer in 1931 but I doubt whether he would be willing to be Solicitor-General again. Harvie Watt says perhaps a sinecure office, such as Postmaster-General. I say that Cripps told me, four days before the German attack, that Russia would only last four weeks and that it was a great misfortune for us that they were being dragged into the war in 1941 rather than waiting till 1942.

Harvie Watt likes Greenwood, chiefly, I gather, because they often have drinks together. He doesn't think much of Attlee, who, he says, cannot effectively lead the House in the P.M.'s absence. But who could? Herbert Morrison, he gathers, is very unpopular with his own Party. In the various changes which have been discussed, no one, he says, has suggested that I should lead the Government! If anything happened to the P.M., he thinks there would be a strong feeling that Anderson should succeed, at any rate for a time. I say that this does

1 Tadeuz Zamoyski. Chief of Economic Section of the Ministry of Finance, Polish government-in-exile.
2 Cripps had actually been expelled three years previously, in 1939.

not inspire me at all, and that the Labour Party would expect to be consulted, not as to who should be Leader of the Conservative Party, but as to who should be P.M. He says that for the succession to the Leadership of their Party, there are groups supporting Eden, Stanley and Margesson. Kingsley Wood has completely passed out and has few friends and little influence.

Harvie Watt says that he had a great admiration for Neville Chamberlain, who, though he had a bad exterior, was a most honest and decent man and really keen on pushing young men on. Baldwin, on the other hand, though he talked much about this, did nothing for any young man, except Geoffrey Lloyd! Baldwin only once spoke to Harvie Watt, and that was when he came and stood next door to him in the lavatory and, laying his hand on his shoulder, said, 'Young man, adjust your dress before leaving.' But Baldwin was wonderfully shrewd. I said that I knew he had made a parting speech to Under-Secretaries, etc., in which he said, 'Never be rude or sarcastic to the Socialists; never score points, however inviting, at their expense; one day we shall need them.' I contradicted this with Chamberlain's reception of me and others on Air Force deficiencies, when he had opened by saying, 'I suppose I can take it for granted that you come here not for Party but for patriotic reasons.' I also gave Harvie Watt an account of the proceedings immediately before and at our Bournemouth Conference in May 1940, which led to the change of Government.

We discuss possible new recruits to the Government. He doubted whether Phil [Noel-Baker] was very well placed at War Transport, though I thought he was. As I knew, he said – though I didn't, but only pretended to – it had been proposed that he should go as No. 2 at the Board of Education, but Chuter Ede had not been willing to shift. Colonies had also been spoken of, but, I suppose, Phil was a bit too viewy for that, as for the Foreign Office. Harvie Watt said that Grenfell and Montague were talked of as two Labour ministers who were not worth their places. I praised Griffiths, who, I said, had come on very fast and had, I thought, considerable further powers of growth. Also Wilmot, whose praises I sang and whom Harvie Watt seemed already to think well of and to have in mind. I also said a little on behalf of Garro Jones, but to this he didn't respond much. Turning to his side, I praised Harold Mitchell (bearing in mind the off-chance that he might fit in with me in a new situation). This went very well indeed. Harvie Watt said he knew him very well, thought very highly of him and sat with him on the Boards of several Companies. But he was terribly shy. I said that I thought this would soon pass. Harvie Watt spoke well of Jack Lawson and I agreed, but hinted that he was already fully occupied.[1]

Just as we were leaving the Connaught Hotel, where we had lunched, I said that Harvie Watt's duties, which he had defined as being to keep the P.M. in touch with feeling in the House, were very different from his predecessor's. He said that this was so, and that Bracken hardly ever used to go near the House. He said that he was not at all happy at the Ministry of Information and had been talking of giving it up. I made no comment on this, and Harvie Watt said that this was a ministry which had become a graveyard of reputations. It was left that Harvie Watt and I should meet each other every few weeks. This may be a very useful contact, particularly if I appear primarily as an authority on Labour Party affairs and personalities.

A long string of interviews in the afternoon, ending up with a visit from Lockhart. I show him my draft letter to Eden on Aspidistra, which Gaitskell and Mayhew think I ought not to send, because too polemical and unnecessary. Lockhart thinks it would be very useful, since it includes much which the officials cannot put into their paper. He says, without any pumping from me, that Bracken has been in a very curious mood for some weeks. Neither Radcliffe nor his other officials can do anything with him at the Ministry of Information, either on P.W.E. or anything else. It is said that yesterday he put in his resignation to the P.M. (We often used to hear this about Duff Cooper, but in the end it happened!) Lockhart thinks that Bracken is very disappointed. He always used to be seeing the P.M. but doesn't do so now. When he writes the P.M. a letter, it goes down to the bottom of the tin. The P.M., he says, gave him general assurances of backing, but has not carried them out.

In order to counter pressure from both sides of the Atlantic on the question of relief shipments to Greece, Dalton arranged that he should be asked in the House about 'the manner in which Germans and Italians have carried out their legal and moral responsibility to feed the Greeks'. Dingle Foot replied on his behalf that, so far from feeding the Greeks, the Germans had been organising on a large scale the export of foodstuffs from Greece to Germany.[2]

---

1 Marginal note: 'Regional Commissioner in North-East.'
2 H. C. Debs, 10th February 1942 [377], col. 1,368.

Tuesday 10th February

P.Q.s. I give two, for which I particularly wanted publicity, to Moelwyn Hughes,[1] but the silly blighter wasn't in his place. He is a worthless Welsh waffler! One on German starvation of Greece – famine as an instrument of German policy – was just caught on the second round and put by Evelyn Walkden.[2] It was answered by Foot and made, I am told, a considerable impression on the House. ...

I get away, after much confabulation with C.E.O. and Gaitskell, my reply to Eden – (1) a most honeyed personal letter, and (2) an argumentative, though not unconciliatory, enclosure on modes of co-operation and demarcation of functions. I am to have a discussion with him on Thursday (the day after tomorrow).

I also take some pleasure in writing to Sinclair explaining that Hood, who Sinclair complains has been guilty of leakage of projected operations, and attributes to me, is not either an official of mine or of P.W.E., but of the Ministry of Information, where, I am afraid, this leakage must have taken place.

Dine with C.I.G.S. [Brooke] in his ground-floor flat in Marsham Street. Also present Findlater Stewart,[3] thought by many to be one of our very best civil servants, Weekes,[4] a General on the Q. side, and two junior officers. Findlater Stewart speaks slowly with a Scots accent, but has, I should think, a good clear judgment and co-operative capacity but not, perhaps, much energy. C.I.G.S. is, I still think, pretty quick and good. A good deal of talk is about tanks and the difficulties of design and output. The Beaver vehemently denies that there are no spares. He says that, if there are none in Libya, that is not his fault. C.I.G.S. says that he has been having a bad time in the Cabinet lately, and adds, 'I don't get too much support from my secretary.' I think he means his Secretary of State! He says that the P.M. carries an amazing mass of detail in his head. He knows where every battleship and every cruiser is, and their capacity and endurance, and where most of our destroyers are. He knows a great deal about aircraft and often puts the C.I.G.S. to shame by knowing, quicker than he, where particular brigades and other units are. But it is a little disconcerting when he telegraphs direct to Commanders in the field without consulting C.I.G.S. – and, of course, I suppose,

1 Moelwyn Hughes (1897–1955). Labour M.P. for Carmarthen 1941–5; Islington North 1950–51.
2 Evelyn Walkden (1893–1970). Labour, then Independent, M.P. for Doncaster 1941–50.
3 Sir Samuel Findlater Stewart (1879–1960). Permanent Under-Secretary for India 1930–42.
4 Probably Colonel (acting Major-General) R. M. Weeks (1890–1960). Director-General of Army Equipment at the War Office 1941–2.

without consulting his Secretary of State for War. Sometimes, C.I.G.S. says, the P.M. is just like a child who has lost its temper. It is very painful and no progress can be made with the business. One feels that a nurse should come and fetch him away. But this is when he is very tired. He has tremendous powers of resilience and recovery, particularly if he gets his sleep in the afternoon.

Wednesday 11th February

Lunch at House of Commons and tick off Moelwyn Hughes for not being in his place yesterday to put my two important questions. I add that I shall not give him any more. He takes great umbrage at being spoken to bluntly in front of a number of others and threatens afterwards to raise the matter at a Party Meeting! He then goes to the Library and writes me a letter, which he shows to Haydn Davies, demanding that I should 'withdraw' something or other. Davies tells him not to be such a silly ass and he afterwards comes into the bar and consents to have a drink at my expense. I see no reason, in this incident, to vary my judgment on him noted a day or two ago.

At lunch reference is made to Ivor Thomas.[1] Arthur Jenkins knows and likes him very well and describes his early days. Milner claims credit for having got him the seat, through having told him to go and talk to Tom Snowden.[2] I say it is a great thing that he is under seventy, and, indeed, under forty. George Woods,[3] who is sitting opposite, says sourly, 'Then he has still got a great deal to learn.' This comment is, I am afraid, very typical of the outlook of too many Labour, and indeed other, M.P.s. ...

See Attlee at No. 11 and show him the correspondence between Eden and myself on co-operation and demarcation of functions between him and me. The essential point is that I must have a right of appeal, in the case of disagreement with Eden, either to the Defence Committee, or, in very important matters, to the P.M. direct, or to some other minister conversant with the issues, and I have added in my letter that the only one such is Attlee. The latter says he is sure the

---

1 Ivor (Bulmer) Thomas, q.v., gained the seat at Keighley in February 1942, following the death of H. B. Lees-Smith in December 1941.

2 Thomas Snowden (1875–1949). Worsted manufacturer in Bingley, Yorkshire, and a member of West Riding County Council. Labour M.P. for Accrington 1929–31. Thomas had told Dalton a fortnight earlier that he had been informed 'that Tom Snowden was the real king of Keighley. He therefore went to see him and, he thinks, made a good impression. Snowden, without giving any promises, worked on many key people and withdrew his support from Titterington, a well-known local man who had been expected to win.' (Diary, 28th January 1942.)

3 Rev. G. S. Woods (1886–1951). Labour M.P. for Finsbury 1935–45; Mossley 1945–50; Droylsden 1950–51.

principle I am putting up is right. Clearly he has not been getting on very well with Eden lately, for he says that 'He's a funny little bird. He's got no status of his own. He's only a Private Secretary to the P.M.'; and again, when I tell him that Eden objected to my taking to the Defence Committee a difference of opinion between him and me on Turkey, because this was 'foreign policy', although my proposition for dealing with certain Turks was supported by the Commanders in Chief Middle East, 'Questions of foreign policy often come up on the Defence Committee, particularly as regards Turkey; that's the only reason why he is allowed to attend the Committee.'

My reply to Eden, to which I put the finishing touch last night, has gone off this morning, which will give him twenty-four hours to think it over before seeing me tomorrow afternoon. Gladwyn is to come over with me and 'hang about' until such time as Eden and I want him and Cadogan to come in and join us.

I tell Attlee some of what Harvie Watt had told me, including the notion that Attlee, Greenwood and Wood should be pushed out of the War Cabinet, and replaced by Duncan and Cripps. I said that I had told Harvie Watt that this would lead to withdrawal of Labour Party support from the Government. Attlee sniffed and said, 'No doubt that is the sort of thing that *some* people are saying.' I asked whether personal relations in the War Cabinet were good just now, and he as much as said they weren't. But I didn't press him any further.

Thursday 12th February
In the afternoon see Eden on the relations between him and me. He is anxious not to commit himself in detail. Cadogan and C.E.O. are called in at the end of our talk and it is agreed that they shall make a draft. ... He then goes on to say that of course he has no secrets from me, and that, if he had been Foreign Secretary at the beginning of the war, he would have objected to M.E.W. being an independent department. He would have kept it under the Foreign Office. Likewise my other activities. But 'Edward [Halifax] always wanted to get things away from the Foreign Office.' This perfectly illustrates again how Eden is like the little boy trying to clutch all the toys. Edward used to give his toys away to other children. When I tell this to Gladwyn afterwards, he says, 'And he doesn't even play with his toys, he only fiddles with them.'

Monday 16th February
Gladwyn to dine. He started off very early this morning and is sleepy. He heard from Butler over the weekend that the Beaver, Bracken,

Horeb,[1] and his immediate followers, Lord Winster[2] and one or two more are going to form a Centre Party. Butler disapproved of this very much. I told Gladwyn that Harcourt[3] had said the last word in this sort of thing. 'I know the Centre Parties only too well. All centre and no circumference.'

Tuesday 17th February
Several P.Q.s, including one much too-long-for-the-House answer on Anglo-American co-operation in Economic Warfare. Not a happy atmosphere at the end of questions when P.M. adopts a rather too firm tone. There will be a debate next week. There is a general sense of irritation and unease. All governments are judged by success, and we aren't having much at present. Many accusations are being made, behind the scenes, of undue interference by P.M. in naval, military and air movements. W. G. Hall,[4] beside whom I sit at lunch, says, 'The P.M. was quite rattled this morning.' In fact his epithet perfectly fits Hall and some others. He says he hears that the P.M. goes late at night, having drunk a lot of whisky, into conference with the Chiefs of Staff and that anyone who reads the Admiralty signals from about midnight will realise that it is the P.M., and not the First Lord or the Admirals, who is directing the fleet. Next morning many of these signals are reversed. I say that I think this is quite a fantastic story. Hall then goes off on to dive-bombers, but I can't pin him down. George Hicks says that the P.M. will have to get rid of some of the burden he is now carrying or 'he will get into bad odour'. I try to encourage people to attack the Beaver, but not with much success, though I hear that Bevin was 'most indiscreet' at the Administrative Committee this afternoon – I couldn't go – and denounced the Beaver vehemently.

An inconclusive, rambling debate on B.B.C. Overseas Services, which goes near to touching P.W.E. Most of the critics cancel each other out. Bracken replies in a scrappy but fairly conclusive fashion. Now Parliament will, I expect, be content to leave P.W.E. matters alone for a bit. ...

Mayhew to dine with me at the Viking. He is rather engaging and I talk to him very freely. He says it is a great experience to work with me, but that I suffer fools most impatiently. He thinks that if I had suffered

1 Hore-Belisha, q.v.
2 R. T. H. Fletcher, q.v., had been created 1st Baron Winster.
3 Sir William Harcourt (1827–1904). Liberal M.P. 1868–1904. Solicitor-General 1874. Home Secretary 1880–85. Chancellor of the Exchequer 1886, 1892–5.
4 W. G. Glenvil Hall (1887–1962). Labour M.P. for Colne Valley 1939–62; Plymouth Central 1929–31. Financial Secretary to the Treasury 1945–50.

them more patiently, I might now be Prime Minister. I say it is much simpler than this. Everything would have been the same, except that if I had not lost my seat in 1931, I should now be Leader of the Labour Party with whatever that implies.[1] For many years, I tell him, I exercised the most tremendous control, even in the presence of the greatest fools. Only recently have I allowed myself the luxury of showing some of them – and by no means all of them even yet – what I think of them. I say that in my Utopia we should wash out old age. Everybody would die young, perhaps never later than thirty-five. I praised energy and enterprise. He is inclined to favour a sort of stationary state, with a Chinese streak – tolerance, contemplation, etc. But he realises that this does not appeal much to me. I say that, on the other hand, I can, when required, and out of wartime, sit and relax quite completely in the sun. Phil [Noel-] Baker, who Mayhew thinks has a Chinese streak, can never do this.

We work out that Ivor Thomas, who took his seat in the House today, has by his arrival reduced the average age of the Parliamentary Labour Party by two months. He is thirty-six and Lees-Smith was sixty-two. A few more such by-elections will get us down quite a lot.

Wednesday 18th February

For a few moments at Party Meeting. A good deal of excitement, but Attlee, who speaks at the end, does not do at all badly. I see him later alone and tell him that Swinton is trying to stage a come-back and is talking about 'co-ordinating' everything and everybody. Attlee takes very ill to this idea and says that he would never be acceptable, having been one of Neville Chamberlain's men. (I had heard this morning that Swinton had come across to C.D. at the Club and said that he was just the sort of man to co-ordinate my show and C. [Menzies]'s and M.I.5 and everything else. He knew it all, he said, and knew all the people, and got on with everybody – 'I get on very well with Dalton,' he had said – and did not trouble himself with detail but only exercised high executive power. This, of course, is a throw-back to the attempts made long ago to give him all the works.[2])

1 In 1931, Dalton lost Bishop Auckland by 755 votes. Attlee, on the other hand, held Limehouse by 451. 'If, instead of just losing my seat in the general election of 1931, I had just held it, I should almost certainly have become Deputy Leader of the Parliamentary Labour Party that year in place of Attlee, and succeeded Lansbury as Leader in 1935, or earlier,' Dalton wrote later. 'In that case I might well have continued as Leader from 1935 onwards – there has been much continuity of Leadership in the Labour Party – and become Deputy Prime Minister to Winston Churchill in the War-time Coalition and Labour Prime Minister, leading a great Parliamentary majority, immediately after the war.' (FY, p. 19.)

2 In the summer of 1940, Churchill had considered placing Lord Swinton, rather than Dalton, in charge of the secret organisations which became S.O.E. (see pp. 57–9).

The Japanese assault on Singapore began on 8th February. A week later, the British garrison surrendered and some 80,000 survivors went into captivity. Meanwhile on 12th February, three German warships, the *Scharnhorst*, the *Gneisenau* and the *Prinz Eugen* had evaded both the Royal Navy and the R.A.F. and slipped through the English Channel en route from Brest to Germany. It was a humiliating week, and Churchill decided that more changes in government were necessary to meet his critics and revive the image of his administration. Despite Attlee's objections, Cripps – who had gained a high reputation in Moscow – became Leader of the House. Beaverbrook found that the Ministry of Production, to which he had only been appointed on 4th February, was not what he expected, and resigned on 19th February; he was replaced by Oliver Lyttelton, brought back from Cairo. Greenwood, a failure as a minister, was sacked, and his place in the War Cabinet taken by Cripps. Kingsley Wood also left the War Cabinet, while retaining his post as Chancellor of the Exchequer. Margesson was replaced at the War Office by his Permanent Secretary, Sir James Grigg. Moore-Brabazon was replaced as Minister of Aircraft Production by Colonel J. Llewellin, who relinquished the Board of Trade after only eighteen days in this office. Dalton was moved – theoretically promoted – to the Board of Trade, leaving S.O.E. in the hands of the new Minister of Economic Warfare, Lord Wolmer (later the Earl of Selborne). Other changes included the appointment of Cranborne as Colonial Secretary, Portal as Minister of Works and Planning, and to complete the reshuffle, on 4th March, Jowitt as Paymaster-General (with responsibility for post-war reconstruction problems) and Sir David Maxwell Fyfe as Solicitor-General.

Thursday 19th February

A bad Parliamentary Party Meeting. Attlee is there, but rather smaller than usual. Great desire everywhere for a small War Cabinet of members without departmental responsibilities. This has become a mere tin can formula. Someone even tried to move that the Labour members of the War Cabinet should be 'instructed' to present this view to the P.M. This was, of course, ruled out. But it showed the tone. Shinwell said that the trouble was that Attlee, Greenwood and Bevin were all playing for position and could not agree who should go out.

Lunch with Winster. Very anti-Alexander, who, he says, is a mere office boy and laughed at by all the Navy. Thus he went out of his way to praise Pound at a luncheon, which was very irregular and undesirable, and Pound felt that he had to praise him back. And so he said at some public function that 'We have got a very good First Lord. He always takes the bump for the Navy.' Winster said that the true story of the *Prince of Wales* and *Repulse* was the following. The proposal to send them out without an aircraft carrier was minuted against right up through the Admiralty, including the First Sea Lord and the First Lord. The P.M. then summoned the First Sea Lord down to Chequers and poured forth upon him a great flood of political arguments, as a result of which the lame, deaf, sleepy old gentleman returned to London prepared to say that the ships should go. This was what was called 'getting the approval of the Admiralty'.

Later in the day there is much gossip about imminent changes. It does not occur to me that I am likely to be involved, but there is a grand rumour going round that the Beaver is out (this turns out to be true and is by *far* the best of all the changes. That he should be a good deal in America would be better still, and that ...... [1] would be best of all). I saw Attlee twice and Morrison once during today, 'to maintain contact'. On the former I pressed once more the desirability of M.E.P.W. [Ministry of Political and Economic Warfare] and the value of linking this with S.O.E. Morrison seemed to have no scouts out at all. He just didn't know a thing about what was going on. And I am pretty sure that this was genuine and not put on.

Late tonight the new War Cabinet is known. The entry of Cripps as L.P.S. is very interesting. If he has grown out of being a bloody fool, he will be first-class, and, in any case, if things go badly for a few months, his stock, now artificially inflated, will fall heavily and he will have to bear a large part of the responsibility.

Friday 20th February
Catch Attlee after a lunch with Mrs Phillimore. I say that I suppose there are going to be a few more changes. He says, 'Oh yes, we are going to get rid of some more of these bloody Tories.' I ask him whether I am likely to be affected. He says, 'Certainly not,' and I therefore go, as arranged, to the North for Shildon Warship Week.

Saturday 21st February
A very good show in Shildon.[2] It is snowing, but I spend two hours going round the shops this morning. They are doing a great deal of important war production work. In the afternoon we have a procession headed by myself and a police sergeant, followed immediately by a very good band from the Loyal North Lancs; and large detachments of Army, Air Force and various Civil Defence Services. This is perfect

1 *sic*. No name is given.
2 In Dalton's constituency.

electioneering, for all come to their doors and windows as they hear stirring music and the first things they see is their own Member heading the procession. In addition, considerable crowds line the route. When I first asked the sergeant at the starting point who would give them the step and show them the way, he said he would. I said, 'I will march with you.' He was rather taken aback and thought that perhaps he had better ask the Inspector. I said, 'You need not ask the Inspector. He will not stop a Minister of the Crown, who is also the Member for this constituency, from marching at your side.' He then said he hoped that I should keep step. I said that I was well used to marching in all situations and at all paces, and that in the last war I had marched some of my troops right off their feet.[1] So all went well.

I then took the salute alongside of Captain de Burgh and afterwards proceeded to the Hippodrome, where I made a short urgent speech. I had just sat down when I received a message saying, 'Don't interrupt your speech, but as soon as you can, ring up Whitehall 4464 Chequers.' I rose and left the meeting, saying, with a wave of the hand, 'I have got to go and telephone to London about the war.' I went to a telephone in an A.R.P. shelter close to the U.D.C. [Urban District Council] offices. After some considerable delay, I got on to Martin,[2] the P.M.'s Private Secretary. After a moment, the P.M. himself came on.

P.M. 'Are you alone in the room?'

H.D. 'No, but I soon can be.' I signal everybody out.

P.M. 'I am making, as you know, some changes in the Government, and I want to change your office.'

H.D. 'Where do you want me to go?'

P.M. 'I want you to take the Board of Trade.'

H.D. 'This is a bit of a surprise. Do you want an answer now? I am coming back tonight and shall be in London early tomorrow morning.'

P.M. 'I should like an answer soon, because I am making a number of changes which all go together and one depends on another. Can you give me an answer in an hour?'

H.D. 'I suppose the Board of Trade is a very full time job.'

---

1 Dalton had been in command of the last three British guns in the retreat to the Tagliamento, following the Italian defeat at Caporetto in 1917. He reached the river only a few hours ahead of the advancing enemy; and was awarded an Italian bronze medal for his courage and resourcefulness.

2 J. M. Martin, later Sir John (b. 1904). Principal Private Secretary to the Prime Minister 1941–6; Private Secretary 1940–41.

P.M. 'Yes, quite full time. You will have many important duties and you will have to do what you can with what remains of the trading community.'

H.D. 'So that would mean that I should give up all the other duties which I am now doing.'

P.M. 'Yes, you would.'

H.D. 'Very well, I will take it, but on one condition. Can you tell me that you have confidence in my capacity to do it well?'

P.M. 'Yes, I have complete confidence in you, and after all, much of the work will not be very different from what you have been doing at M.E.W.'

H.D. 'Very well. Thank you very much. I accept.'

I could not, of course, tell either Frank Addison, nor the Myers, nor any other of my good friends at Shildon what had happened. But many knew that I had been having a conversation with the Prime Minister, and some guessed that it had something to do with the Government reshuffle.

II
Whitehall Ablaze

6

Coal Scuttle
February–August 1942

Military and naval reverses – especially in the Far East – encouraged criticism of the Government during the first half of 1942. Some of this discontent rubbed off on ministers and departments with no responsibility for operations, and it was Dalton's misfortune, as new President of the Board of Trade, to find himself at the centre of the worst domestic political row of the war so far. The production of fuel, the organisation of the coal industry and the vexed question of whether or not coal should be rationed provided a symbolic battleground for groups and individuals who wished, for a variety of reasons, to disagree among themselves, and with the Government.

The dispute was, however, more than an excuse for a battle amongst hostile factions. At stake was the future organisation of coal-mining in Britain, and the future relationship between central government and the miners. These were matters which deeply concerned Dalton as an M.P. for a mining area which had experienced high levels of unemployment before the war. The eventual outcome – abandonment of the proposed fuel rationing scheme, but a measure of requisitioning short of full state control – greatly facilitated the process of nationalisation a few years later.[1]

Sunday 22nd February
Having travelled through the night, I arrived at King's Cross at 3.30 a.m. and slept a bit in my shelter at M.E.W. But not much, because I was revolving many problems. Handing over S.O.E. twangs my heart strings and I shall feel very desolate and unfriended if I lose the daily presence of those who have been for twenty-one months my trusted inner circle. Gladwyn and I lunch at the Gourmet and that

1 See Introduction, pp. xxvii–xxviii.

evening he and I dine with C.D. [Nelson] and discuss future possibilities and arrangements. I am to be succeeded at M.E.W. by Wolmer,[1] who has been out of politics for many years and has never held any office higher than Assistant Postmaster-General, from which he had to resign because he made a public speech saying that postmen were thieves, slackers and liars and that the Post Office should be run as a private company to earn a large dividend, presumably by charging a lot more for the stamps and having much fewer deliveries. He is also said to be very religious, High Anglican, and was associated with the P.M. in the latter's die-hard opposition to the India Bill. He is thought not to be very clever.

I propose to Gaitskell that he should come with me as Principal Private Secretary to the Board of Trade, and I also arrange (next day) with Wilmot that he should come on as my Parliamentary Private Secretary. I hope his long period of sickness is nearly over and that he will once more be available next week. Gaitskell wants to think it over, particularly as Leith-Ross had talked to him about promotion to the rank of P.A.S. [Principal Assistant Secretary] in connection with Surpluses and post-war food relief. It has long been understood between Gaitskell and me that, having done twenty-one months in my Private Office, he shall have whatever good chance of promotion comes along.

Monday 23rd February
A day of good-byes. Leith-Ross wants to come on with me, bringing his Surpluses with him and resuming his old role, though he has never lost the title of Economic Adviser to H.M.G. This could most easily be held at the Board of Trade. He tells me that I shall find the machine there good but slow. This is rather flattering to me, since, at the beginning of my time at M.E.W., he and I had quite a sharp exchange which resulted in his offering me his resignation. But he is not too bad at certain jobs and I should be quite glad to have him at the Board.

At noon Wolmer comes to see me. He seems a little deaf, but shows great keenness and interest in the work. He begins by saying that he understands a great part of it is very secret. I say yes, our economic intelligence *is* very secret, and I talk a bit about Vickers and his chaps. Wolmer says, 'I suppose you get a lot of it from spies.' I say, 'Yes, some.' Then, after I have given a long lecture on food relief, and control of imports into European neutrals, and Navicerts, and Anglo-American co-operation, he says, 'But there are some other things you

---

1 R. C. Palmer, Viscount Wolmer, later 3rd Earl of Selborne (1887–1971). Minister of Economic Warfare 1942–5. Conservative M.P. 1910–40. Junior minister 1922–9.

do, aren't there, which are very secret?' I ask, 'What did the Prime Minister say to you?' He says, 'Oh, he told me that you had lots of agents in Europe, and that you blew things up, and dropped people from parachutes, and he asked me, before he gave me the job, "Would you be prepared to assassinate Hitler?"' I ask, 'Did the Prime Minister tell you that you were to take over all that side of my work?' He says, 'Yes, the Prime Minister said I was to take over *all* your work.' I say, 'In that case I can tell you a good deal, but it will take some time and we had better have another talk tomorrow.'

Afterwards I break this news to Gladwyn who is quite dumbfounded and thinks there must be some mistake. He just cannot conceive of Wolmer running S.O.E. I say that, at any rate, if Wolmer has it that will eliminate a number of the worst solutions which we have feared, including (1) Morton getting hold of it, (2) the Foreign Office running it, and (3) the Chiefs of Staff running it. At any rate now it will continue to be in [the] charge of a Minister of the Crown.

Later in the day I speak to Attlee about this, and he says of Wolmer, 'He is not such a fool as he looks; he is very tenacious, and he is quite close to the P.M.' I repeat this to Gladwyn and to C.D., whom I see together, and they both think that this is a pretty shrewd comment. Eden had put in a hurried Minute to the P.M. asking that no decision should be taken about S.O.E. until he had been consulted. He had not been consulted. The P.M. had just acted on his own and plunged. Never having focused very clearly what I did, he just thought of it altogether as 'M.E.W.', and so, as Gladwyn said, 'He had poured out the baby with the bath.' But having done it, he won't budge. He will say, 'I have said it and I stick to it.' He won't let Wolmer down. There will be frightful consternation in many quarters which were intriguing against me. They won't be sure at all that they have gained by my translation. And if Wolmer gets keen on it, he may do it rather well. I arrange with Gladwyn that he should seek out Morton and congratulate him on having advised the P.M. to make such a good new Head of the show, assuming that Morton had been consulted. (It is really a great joke when people who are always boasting of their influence with the P.M., and using it for wrong purposes, find that at critical moments things are done without any word with them and in a way that they dislike.) When this conversation took place a day or two later, Gladwyn found it impossible to sustain, as Morton from the start made a wry face and made it pretty clear that he thought the P.M. had made a gaffe.

At Board of Trade.[1] Talk with my predecessor. I say I will take P.Q.s tomorrow. There are three, and simple. Sir Arnold Overton[2] is then brought in and introduced. He makes a bad start by suggesting that it may not be in order for me to answer the P.Q.s since the Order in Council confirming my appointment may not have gone through. 'In any case, I shall answer the P.Q.s,' I say, 'and you must look after the Order in Council.' ... I am to occupy the suite designed for himself by Sir Henry, now Lord McGowan.[3] It is on the sixth floor. The panelling in the principal office is such that Oliver Lyttelton, when installed here, said, 'I feel like a lonely cigar in a cigar box.' There is also some funny business about the lighting. But the whole thing is, as Lord Curzon said about his wife's bedroom, 'of unexampled magnificence'. There is a large room opening out of the office which was previously used as a sitting-room, which I shall make a bedroom. There is a bathroom just down the passage and the most superb lavatory, although one of the windows is broken and therefore it is very cold, in black and gold.

Gaitskell comes with me, having signed with me a Treaty. I am not to keep him needlessly too late at night and he is, after a month, to be considered for promotion. This completely suits me and I now contemplate that he will be of very great use to me at the Board of Trade in a high post with a roving commission on policy.

In the afternoon I take the oath. This is a quick and simple business. *I* say nothing but merely hold aloft a red testament.

I have my first talk with Overton alone this afternoon. But I tell him that I have the impression that there are too many permanents and too few good temporaries here, in contrast with M.E.W. I say that we must push on with various policies.

See Attlee late this evening. He has had great difficulties about Greenwood, who is now to be out altogether. But there was nothing else for it and Attlee says that Greenwood has no great support in the Party.

Tuesday 24th February

Today I formally hand over M.E.W. I say many farewells to officials, who, nearly all of them, are rather sorry that I am going. I have chased

---

1 The headquarters of the Board of Trade were housed in the I.C.I. building, overlooking the Millbank.
2 Sir Arnold Overton (1893–1975). Permanent Secretary at the Board of Trade 1941–5; Ministry of Civil Aviation 1947–53.
3 Sir Harry McGowan, 1st Baron (1874–1961). Chairman of I.C.I. 1930–50.

and hunted them about and shouted at many of them, and written splenetic Minutes, but, faced with the possibility of a Minister who may be more inert, I think they are inclined to regret the change.

I appear in the House at eleven to answer my questions, but all three are missed on the first round. Dingle Foot arranges for two to be asked on the second round, and I get a reasonably friendly cheer on making my bow. I am making great efforts to get Harold Mitchell[1] to come to the Board of Trade as my Parliamentary Secretary.

Wolmer comes at six and stays for over an hour. I expound S.O.E. on the basis of my latest report to the P.M. Towards the end I call in my C.E.O. [Jebb] so that Wolmer may get used to his face. He asks me afterwards whether I think he made a good impression, and I say, 'Yes, not bad, but you mustn't mumble or talk too fast.' Wolmer's tempo isn't quite mine. Gladwyn dines with me later at the Viking and we talk of many things. At the end of these nineteen months, when he has been the strongest and firmest of all my personal supports, I have never felt uneasy when he was handling any negotiation, however tricky. Sure-footed, quick as a needle, industrious almost to a fault, sitting up much too often much too late, always able, as when we were together twelve years ago, to put me out of a bad into a good humour, a wonderful scout, a most pleasant companion, a joy to have about the place, whom I shall miss sorely, for there is no pretext under which I can take him with me to the Board of Trade. I gave Wolmer a copy of my 'citation' of him for his C.M.G.

Wednesday 25th February
All the morning at a National Executive.

Mitchell to see me at my request in the afternoon. I tell him that I want him to come as my Parliamentary Secretary. He likes it and is flattered but doesn't jump at it as quick as a young politician should. He has just been made Vice-Chairman of the Tory Party organisation. I say that so far as I am concerned, he can go on holding that as well, and that I don't think it means much work. He says he will consult the Whips and tell me again. ...

C.D. to see me in my cigar box. He says again that he thinks he will soon give up and that a younger man should take over. I say that he should keep on for a bit with Wolmer. He said of course he will do this if required to do so. I give him the hint that it would make things

---

1 Colonel H. P. Mitchell, later Sir Harold, 1st Bart (1900–83). Conservative M.P. for Brentford and Chiswick 1931–45. Vice-Chairman of the Conservative Party 1942–5.

go better if he moved out A.D. [Taylor] and put Glenconner in his place.

To Liverpool Street Hotel to meet Wilmot, who, though still hobbling a bit, seems to be nearly able to return to duty. He quite realises the much greater scope he will have as my P.P.S. at the Board of Trade and has arranged to spend more time in London and would like to sleep at the premises. I shall arrange this.

I sleep tonight for the first time at the Board of Trade.

On 12th March, Dalton asked his old boss at the L.S.E., Sir William Beveridge, to prepare a scheme for fuel rationing. 'This inquiry was not one that I would have chosen, nor did it improve my reputation,' Lord Beveridge later recalled. 'I was not asked to say whether fuel should be rationed. That was settled before I began.'[1] By mid-April, Beveridge's plan was ready – consisting of a points system, with interchangeable coupons. However, Dalton met some powerful resistance to this scheme, from miners as well as coal-owners. By the time of the debate on the rationing plan on 7th May, resistance from Conservative back-benchers had become so strong that Cripps, Leader of the House, promised a further Government White Paper on rationing proposals as material for yet another debate.

Thursday 26th February

This afternoon my first experience of the Lord President's Committee.[2] It is awfully slow, and ministers talk much too long and say the same thing one after another. A discussion on future quotas of trade, labour for the malting industry, our future import programme, and – and this is the only point that closely touches me – oil imports. I say that I am in favour of stopping the basic ration for motorists. A great quantity of cars now on the road should be laid up and stripped of their tyres for other and better uses. Several ministers at once assert that they have long been in favour of abolishing the basic ration and that

1 Lord Beveridge, *Power and Influence*, Hodder & Stoughton, London, 1953, pp. 287–8.
2 During the war successive Lord Presidents – Neville Chamberlain, Sir John Anderson, Clement Attlee – had overall responsibility for economic planning, through the powerful Lord President's Committee. The great prestige of this Committee was built up while Sir John Anderson was Lord President from October 1940 to September 1943. The Committee dealt with matters affecting the whole of domestic administration.

these ideas are not new. [Geoffrey] Lloyd puts up a most feeble paper by one of his officials, long, inconclusive and unclear, and attaches to it a note of his own. Very feeble. I am keeping fairly clear both of Lloyd and Grenfell, until the weekend, when we know who is to be where.

Gladwyn calls on me at my cigar box at 5.15. I tell him that I have spoken to Eden in the House today and said that I had hesitated much to go to the Board of Trade because it would mean that I should be so cut off now from Eden. The latter had said something about Bracken taking P.W.E., but I had reacted most adversely to this, saying that one could not confide such tasks to a street urchin, and recalling Jos Wedgwood's[1] famous saying, 'If a man must be a Tory, at least let him be a gentleman.' Eden had said, 'Just like old Jos!'

To Baker Street for a farewell, first to the Council and then to some two dozen others down below. It goes off pretty well, and I think most, here too, are sorry to lose me and much more uncertain than M.E.W. of what the future may hold for them.

Dine in my cigar box with Gaitskell, food being brought up from the canteen. I think it will be convenient often to dine in here, for there is nowhere very close ...

Dalton inherited from his predecessor three satellite ministries, the Mines Department, the Petroleum Department and the Department of Overseas Trade; and three ministers ('Secretaries') in charge of them: D. R. Grenfell (Labour), Geoffrey Lloyd (Conservative) and Harcourt Johnstone (Liberal).

Friday 27th February
Geoffrey Lloyd is sure that he is going out, but asks me to lunch and shows me round his Chart Room at the Petroleum Department. This is pretty good. He says this Government is a racket and that Bracken decides everything. I say not quite everything.

Monday 2nd March
Dine with Hyndley. Gaitskell has arranged this. We must move fast over this coal business. I find Hyndley most satisfactory, but he takes a most grave view of the prospects and insists that we must get men back from the Army in substantial numbers. Compared with this,

---

1 Josiah Wedgwood, later 1st Baron (1872–1943). Liberal M.P. 1906–19, Labour M.P. 1919–42, for Newcastle under Lyme. Chancellor of the Duchy of Lancaster 1924.

nothing else matters much. Grenfell, he says, is frightfully conceited and really does not understand what it is all about. He has been very difficult to handle by my predecessors and there have been scenes in public. Hyndley hopes he is going. Sir Alfred Hurst,[1] he says, is not at all a good Head of the Office. He is an individualist, both in outlook and in methods of work. I hear from other sources that he is openly disloyal to his Minister. Hyndley shows me a copy of a letter which he has written, but not sent, to Grenfell, with copies to P.M. and myself, saying that he must resign unless something is done about manpower. He agrees now not to send this.

Tuesday 3rd March

Ask Attlee at the House when the changes are coming out. This constant delay, so that I don't know who is to be either my Parliamentary Secretary here or the three Heads of my satellite Ministries, makes it impossible really to get down to work. Attlee says plaintively that the P.M. and the rest of them have had so much to do, especially on India, that it has not been possible to finish the list. He hopes it will be out tomorrow. He says that he has put his foot down against the P.M.'s wish to shunt Grenfell. Attlee told the P.M. that he just couldn't stand a second row about firing a Labour minister just now, after Greenwood. I said that I thought this was deplorable, and that Grenfell was no use. If he stayed, it would mean that I should have to spend infinite time humouring him, and then do most of the job myself. I would much have preferred, if it had to be a miner, Jim Griffiths. Attlee said that he did not think any other miner would be willing to take Grenfell's place. They would all stick together and say he had been victimised. He begged me to do my best to work with him, and, if I found it was impossible, we could consider it again after an interval.

Cripps said to me that he understood it had been decided to pass the buck to 'the dynamic Doctor' and that it would be up to me to say, a little later, that Grenfell must go. I said to both of them that I thought the solution was that Grenfell should be made Postmaster-General, which would look like promotion. To this Attlee replied that Grenfell was too proud and suspicious to be taken in by this and would refuse. Cripps said that he thought all such transactions were quite wrong in principle and should not be encouraged.

Lunch with Duncan, with whom I think that, over most of our common field, I can do business. He too thinks Grenfell quite hopeless, and is horrified when I tell him that he is to stay after all. He said he had to take the whole thing out of Grenfell's hands. His advice

1 Sir Alfred Hurst (1884–1975). Under-Secretary at the Mines Department 1940–42. Cabinet Secretariat 1942–4.

on personnel is that I should fire both Hurst and Nott-Bower[1] and ask Horace Wilson[2] for some bright new No. 1 from outside. For No. 2 he would move up Fulton.[3] He would also promote Harold Wilson[4] to be Director of Programmes, and bring in Young,[5] of Bolsover, as Adviser on Production. I said that there should, I thought, also be a trade union adviser high up on the chart, and he thought Lawther might come in on a level with Young. I draw him on Hyndley and he is very favourable, but he did not suggest him as No. 1.

In the evening I have a preliminary coal talk with Attlee, Bevin and Grenfell. Two frightful long-winds out of three. Largely it is atmosphere making. I say that we must have more men, and have to keep dragging the subject back to this, Bevin and Grenfell wandering over the whole thing. I get Bevin to say that he would be willing to release e.g. 50,000 men from the Army for the pits on a period of leave, and bring out 20,000 from the pits to the Army to be trained. This won't quite do, but it is progress. Much talk on the psychological value of a National Board, and Bevin offers Emerson[6] to discuss this with our officials. I raise the point of firing Hurst and he has no friends here. Grenfell says that he thinks he has brought him to heel lately! Attlee long ago advised that he should be got rid of. Grenfell says that he thinks Nott-Bower would make a good No. 1.

Wilmot reappears after his much too long absence through illness and seems reasonably fit. He dines with me in my office.

Wednesday 4th March

Wilmot goes to Party Meeting, while I do some work. He says later that there was a long discussion, adjourned till next time, on a motion

1 W. G. Nott-Bower, later Sir Guy (1890–1977). Under-Secretary at the Mines Department 1942. Deputy Secretary at the Ministry of Fuel and Power 1942–8.
2 Sir Horace Wilson, q.v., was Head of the Civil Service 1939–42.
3 J. S. Fulton, later Baron (b. 1902). Principal, then Assistant Secretary, at the Mines Department 1940–42. Principal Assistant Secretary at the Ministry of Fuel and Power 1942–4. Vice-Chancellor of the University of Wales 1952–4, 1958–9; University of Sussex 1959–67. Chairman of the Departmental Committee on the Civil Service 1966–8.
4 J. H. Wilson, later Baron (b. 1916). Economic Assistant at the Mines Department 1942. Director of Economics and Statistics at the Ministry of Fuel and Power 1943–4. Labour M.P. 1945–83. Junior minister 1945–7. President of the Board of Trade 1947–51. Prime Minister 1964–70, 1974–6.
5 T. E. B. Young, later Sir Eric (1891–1973). Production Director at the Ministry of Fuel and Power 1942–3. Formerly Managing Director of Bolsover Colliery.
6 *sic*. Probably H. C. Emmerson, later Sir Harold (b. 1896). Under-Secretary at the Ministry of Home Security 1940–42; Chief Industrial Commissioner at the Ministry of Labour 1942–4. Deputy Secretary and Director-General of Manpower 1944–6. Permanent Secretary at the Ministry of Works 1946–56; Labour 1956–9.

to exclude ministers from the Administrative Committee. The silly chumps were not compelled to vote for ministers last time, but did so, and that was only a few months ago. They also insisted on taking nominations and a ballot for the post of Chief Whip in succession to Charlie Edwards, who has at last been pushed out at the age of seventy-five! This makes Attlee look a fool, as he had as good as promised the job to Whiteley, who will no doubt be elected after all this paraphernalia. A large number of private members of our Party have nothing to do except to belly-ache, and they are not being at all well handled by anyone.

Pay my first official visit to His Majesty as President of the Board. He does not seem to focus my new problems particularly, though he takes an interest in overalls. He asks me some questions about S.O.E. and what sort of people they are whom we use, and about Fernando Po, and the bomb at Tangier. He says that David Bowes-Lyon is going to America and told him that I was the first person to give him the news. 'What was Leeper doing?' asked H.M.

I summon Sir Horace Wilson to my room this afternoon. We do not discuss Munich, but I tell him that I have decided to get rid of Hurst and that I am minded to put Hyndley in his place unless Wilson can produce for me at once a first-class man from outside. He says there would be difficulty in this, as anyone who would be good enough for the Mines Department will already be holding down a good job somewhere else. I tell Wilson that both Attlee and Duncan have advised me to get rid of Hurst, and that no one has spoken to me in his favour. Nor does Wilson, though he says that he had hoped that he would gradually improve, but evidently this has not happened. I leave it that I will get Grenfell's formal approval and Hyndley's, and then, this done, will let Wilson know so that he can put up a Minute to the P.M. on the change. He also offers to save me and Grenfell the awkwardness of seeing Hurst and breaking it to him. This I agree to. ...

Have Grenfell round and spend more than an hour with him. Most of the first part I have to let him talk. The real purpose of the interview is to get him to agree to Hyndley in place of Hurst. This is quite easy. It is also convenient that he regards Gaitskell as an old friend and comrade.

I send for Hyndley, who is not finally tracked down and collected till 11.30 p.m. I then press him – this has been Gaitskell's idea, which I accept, as the best available – to take Hurst's place. He is a little reluctant, saying that it is not his job to be a regular civil servant. I say I think this can be managed by letting Nott-Bower do a lot of the routine. I press Hyndley hard, in the national interest, to accept. He would like to sleep on it and tell me tomorrow.

Thursday 5th March

I tell Gaitskell when I go out this morning, to get on to Hyndley and get his reply to my proposal of last night. The answer is that he will take it provided certain not difficult conditions are made.

I then send Gaitskell round to see Sir Horace Wilson, and he afterwards reports to me a most amusing conversation. I told him to tell Wilson that I wanted Hurst out of the office tomorrow. This message profoundly upset Wilson, who said that Hurst was a distinguished and honourable man who could not be treated just like that. Gaitskell said that he only just refrained from reminding Wilson that there was a war on and that unsuccessful generals were fired even quicker than this. A question was raised by Wilson about Sir Ernest Gowers[1] coming in, and though I was a little irritated at this possibility of new delay, all agree that Gowers is a first-class man, though unlikely to be available. Wilson asked Gaitskell, rather indignantly, 'Are you a civil servant?' Gaitskell then gave an account of himself and Wilson a little cooled down. But he had been very hoity-toity. He knows what I think of him, for some of it I have publicly spoken and written. Gaitskell says that he has two enormous photographs in his room, one of Baldwin and the other of Chamberlain!

Later in the day Gaitskell went round to the Mines Department and ran into a room in which Hyndley, Hurst and Nott-Bower were confabulating. Hurst was in a great state of indignation. Gaitskell quickly withdrew. Hyndley later told him that Hurst had taken it very badly.

See Mrs Churchill to try to dissuade her from asking for more wool for clothes for Russia. She says that Madame Maisky[2] is very acquisitive. But clothes are needed, not so much for the general population in Russia, but for the re-occupied territories, where the Germans have stripped them almost naked.

Meeting of ministers in P.M.'s room to discuss draft declaration on India. A good deal of Conservative opposition to going as far as is proposed. ...

Dine with Campbell Stuart. The old rascal is anxious to gather up some gossip, and I give him a good deal. He wants me, as President of the Board of Trade, to travel round the Empire with him in attendance, but I do not feel that the moment is quite ripe for this!

He thinks, as Levy[3] thought at luncheon, that Cripps is playing to

1 Sir Ernest Gowers (1880–1966). Chairman of the Coal Commission 1938–46. Permanent Under-Secretary for Mines 1920–27. Chairman of the Coal Mines Reorganisation Commission 1930–35. Chairman of the Royal Commission on Capital Punishment 1949–53. Author of *Plain Words: A Guide to the Use of English* (1948), etc.
2 Madame Maisky. Married to Ivan Maisky, q.v., Soviet Ambassador.
3 Thomas Levy (1874–1953). Conservative M.P. for Elland 1931–45.

be, and might succeed in being, the next P.M. (I shall need a good deal of convincing on this, though Bevin said the other night that he felt the present set-up could not last very long and that the P.M. in Cabinet now seemed to alternate between being 'a beaten man', sitting collapsed in his chair and plaintively saying, 'I suppose this is another of the concessions that I must make for the sake of national unity', and a violently aggressive, resentful, man. There was no doubt, he thought, that the P.M. felt the loss of Beaverbrook very badly. Attlee, on the other hand, thought that things were not as bad or insecure as they seemed, and that the P.M.'s attitude was due to the fact that we had taken a bad knock, worse in some respects than many people guess, at Singapore.) Stuart said that the Beaver was not going to America and that he thought he was genuinely ill. He said, what I well knew, that Bracken hated *me* quite exceptionally and he was sure that the manoeuvre by which he had first worked in Brooks was suggested by the Beaver. Stuart said that Brooks frequently stayed weekends with the Beaver, and the story was the more likely because, when Bracken first made the proposal to me, he could not even get the chap's name and title right but spoke of him as 'General Brook'.

Early in March, Rangoon came under increasing pressure, falling to the Japanese on the 8th. Meanwhile the German submarine war was taking a serious toll on British shipping. These strains came on top of earlier disasters in the Far East, and Rommel's successes in North Africa. At home, Churchill's leadership continued to be the subject of criticism. 'Poor old P.M. in a sour mood and a bad way,' Cadogan wrote on 4th March. 'I don't think he's well and I fear he's played out.'[1]

Friday 6th March
Lobby lunch with P.M. as guest and Maurice Webb in the Chair. The latter makes a pretty good and most self-confident speech, well-turned but asserting the right and duty of the press to criticise helpfully. P.M., who has sat looking depressed – and Harvie Watt, who sits next to me, says that he has been in a state of frightful gloom and has unloaded on to him half an hour of 'most awful stuff' – is clearly feeling the burden of our misfortune. But, towards the end, he lifts the audience and sends them away feeling at least braver, if not happier, men.

1 D. Dilks (ed.), *The Diary of Sir Alexander Cadogan 1938–1943*, Cassell, London, 1971, 4th March 1942, p. 440.

Monday 9th March
Wilmot tells me that he met a Tory businessman who said, 'You Socialists are getting in everywhere, I must say I do admire you. One of you is Deputy Prime Minister, and you have got control of the Navy and the Police and Scotland and all our Trade, and now you have worked in one of your members as Archbishop of Canterbury.'[1]

At the beginning of March, the Prime Minister decided to send Cripps, the Leader of the House of Commons, to India, with a specific radical offer: dominion status for the subcontinent as soon as possible after the war, and in the meantime a series of steps towards that end. The offer concluded with a call for co-operation by the popular parties in a national wartime administration. Details of the proposed mission were given to Parliament on 11th March.

Tuesday 10th March
Meeting of ministers on India in P.M.'s room at the House. The proposed declaration has been modified a little and Cripps is to take it out with him to India and try to get all to agree. Meanwhile, it will not be published. P.M. says that Cripps has volunteered to go on this most thankless task and that this has deeply moved him. A threat of resignation from a high quarter out there will just not be accepted.

Wednesday 11th March
Party Meeting is a frightful exhibition. Attempt by Alfred Edwards,[2] supported by the usual crowd – Shinwell, Bevan, etc. – to remove ministers from Administrative Committee, which has been subject of debate for two meetings, is finally terminated by the previous question being moved and carried by 50 to 3. Pethick [Lawrence] has ruled that no change can be made during the currency of the present session.
    Lunch with Maisky, who complains about delay in our agreeing with them about their future frontiers. They want their 1941 frontiers, subject to a Curzon Line frontier with Poland, whom they would be glad to see take East Prussia and up to the Oder. He says there are still

---

1 William Temple (1881–1944). Archbishop of Canterbury 1942–4. Archbishop of York 1929–42. President of the Workers' Educational Association 1908–24.
2 Alfred Edwards (1888–1958). Labour M.P. for Middlesbrough East 1935–48; Independent M.P. 1948–9; Conservative M.P. 1949–50.

doubts in Russia about our sincerity and determination to fight the war to a finish. I say that he himself must know better. He says he does, but that some, like Stalin, have never been out of Russia and find us more difficult to understand. There is still great suspicion, he says. Meanwhile, we are too subservient, he thinks, to the Americans. We should, no doubt, consult them, but 'consult' is not the same as 'obey'. I say that Litvinov in Washington should be able to do some good. Maisky says he is sure he will.

We then speak of military events. He thinks that the Japanese are not good, but that we are 'much worse than I expected'. He cannot think that an Empire such as has been seen in Malaya can ever be reconstructed in the same way. I cannot honestly dissent from all this. He does not touch any of the matters covered by my new Department

2.30 to 5.30 p.m. in the Chair at the Coal Production Council. This is a most impossible instrument. But Gaitskell, who comes with me, is quite thrilled by the proceedings, and Fulton afterwards said that he found the meeting 'quite inspiring'. What earlier ones must have been I can't think. The miners' leaders unload great quantities of complaints and Horner[1] makes by far the most effective speech, summing up a series of practical proposals to increase output. For the owners there are only Evan Williams[2] and Lee,[3] as for the past twenty years. Williams, Gaitskell thinks, is a pure Galsworthy type. Lee is clever, sly, and obstructive. The miners like having me in the Chair, and we wink a bit at one another. Lawther, not generally very complimentary, tells me afterwards that I have done very well. In particular, they were delighted because at one stage I said, 'There is no difference of status here', i.e. between owners and miners, and 'Everyone is equal on this Council.' I have to carry Grenfell with me all the way with compliments and encouragements. He is my Calvary! No decisions emerge from these three hours. I arrange for the miners' leaders to come and see me tonight at 9 p.m. I then go across and have a word with Lee, so that he shall not think I am too one-sided, and say that I look forward to a talk with him soon.

Feed in with Wilmot and Gaitskell. Later, Ebby Edwards,[4]

---

1 Arthur Horner (1894–1968). President of the South Wales Miners' Federation 1936–46; General Secretary of the National Union of Mineworkers 1946–59.
2 Sir Evan Williams, 1st Bart (1871–1959). Colliery owner. President of the Mining Association of Great Britain 1919–44.
3 William Lee (1886–1971). Colliery owner. A director of the Mining Association of Great Britain.
4 E. Edwards (1884–1961). Secretary of the Miners' Federation of Great Britain, then of National Union of Mineworkers 1932–46. Labour M.P. 1929–31.

Lawther, Ernest Jones[1] of Yorkshire, and Arthur Horner turn up. Jim Bowman[2] is the only absentee. These five carry the Federation. They encourage Wilmot to stay and we have a two hours' seance, from which Wilmot goes early, wanting to get to bed, and Horner passes out in charge of Grenfell, who takes him downstairs and puts him in a taxi and then returns. Horner is apparently quite incapable of carrying even a small quantity of whisky. But at an earlier stage, he is most lucid and most determined to do all possible to win the war.

The points discussed are

(a) supplementary clothes rations for the miners, which they wish to be equally distributed between underground and surface workers, even though this should mean a considerable cut in the total allocation to the industry, and

(b) the future handling of the National Authority Plan passed by the N.C.L. [National Council of Labour]. As to this, Ebby urges very strongly that the next step is for me and Grenfell to meet the owners and see how far they can be moved in our direction. Meanwhile, no further talk on our side alone will advance matters.

I get the others to agree to this and, next day, I write a letter to Lee inviting the Mining Association Executive to meet us next week.

So today I have spent five hours on coal and am pretty tired. Much the most tiring experience, as I used to find when Chairman of the National Executive of the Labour Party, is to have to sit in the Chair for long periods patiently listening to rotund rubbish and knowing that from all this will emerge no decisions. But at least I have created a good atmosphere today and tonight with miners' leaders.

Thursday 12th March
Beveridge[3] to see me. I have decided this morning, on a suggestion made to me yesterday by Gaitskell, through Fulton, to offer him the job of making my fuel rationing scheme. He is, I think, inclined to accept. He will tell me definitely tomorrow. He wants to bring with

---

1 W. E. Jones (1895–1973). General Secretary of the Yorkshire Miners' Federation 1939. Seconded to act as Regional Labour Director at the Ministry of Fuel and Power 1942–4. President of the National Union of Mineworkers 1954–60.

2 J. Bowman, later Sir James, 1st Bart (1898–1978). Vice-President of the National Union of Mineworkers 1938–49. Chairman of the National Coal Board 1956–61.

3 Sir William Beveridge, later 1st Baron (1879–1963). Director of L.S.E. 1919–37. Writer on social questions, and a member of many government and statutory bodies. Responsible for the 1942 Report on Social Insurance and Allied Services. Liberal M.P. for Berwick 1944–5.

him Stephen Tallents,[1] with whom he worked on all this in the last war. I say I will agree to this, though I make no commitment as to keeping Tallents when Beveridge moves on after having launched the scheme. ...

A good talk with Bevin, who is disposed to be quite friendly. I think we can co-operate well now. He thinks it would be wiser for him not to be in with me and Grenfell in our talks with the coal owners. He thinks the miners would dislike it. He suggests the title of 'National Joint Council' for the national body. He will direct youths into the pit, as my agent, if ever I request it, but he thinks we should first have a further go with both sides over the Youth Charter for the Mines which he prepared, but to which both sides returned 'most fatuous replies'. He had told Evan Williams the other day that he would no longer allow the mine owners to call themselves 'employers'. 'In this war', he had said, 'you are not employers any more; you are only agents of the State.' Williams, he said, had taken this quite well.

Next to see Anderson, on his invitation, to discuss a prodding letter. Norman Brook[2] sits in with us and is quite useful. We go over a good deal of ground and I think that relations with Anderson should also be quite easy. At one stage he suggests that, on advertisements, the Ministry of Information should be consulted. I say that I hope not until Kingsley Wood and I are agreed. Then perhaps Anderson would summon the Minister of Information to attend his Committee. I add that one of the great pleasures of my new job is that I no longer have to see the Minister of Information. Anderson says, with a smile, 'My Committee is intended to be a forum, not an arena!'

Friday 13th March
Beveridge agrees to make a report to me on 'the most effective and equitable methods of restricting and rationing fuel and power'. ...

Dine with Hyndley. He is still most concerned about the manpower problem, including, as a particular case, Grenfell!

Saturday 14th March
Conference with Bevin on cotton labour. He is disinclined to use his powers to direct married women in Lancashire, who are no longer working, to the mills. It would cause, he says, 'a great upset'. 'After

1 Sir Stephen Tallents (1884–1958). Controller (Overseas Services) at the B.B.C. 1940–41. Principal Assistant Secretary at the Ministry of Town and Country Planning 1943–6.
2 N. C. Brook, later 1st Baron Normanbrook (1902–67). Deputy Secretary (Civil) to the War Cabinet 1942. Permanent Secretary at the Ministry of Reconstruction 1943–5. Additional Secretary 1945–6, Secretary 1947–62, to the Cabinet. Joint Secretary to the Treasury and Head of Home Civil Service 1956–62.

two years as Minister of Labour, I am still 'uman.' I say I will think over his proposal to re-open *four* mills recently closed, but that it would be much more efficient to direct the necessary labour to the nucleus firm. The policy proposed is a reversal of concentration. ...

Leave with Gladwyn for West Leaze by the six o'clock train. We have a good exchange of gossip this evening. My successor is frightfully slow but well-meaning and keen. He has been edged out of P.W.E. and, since I am no longer on the scene, Bracken has collared it, subject to control of 'policy' by Eden and occasional meetings between the two little people, Law and Thurtle, to discuss secondary matters. I confess I have lost all interest in this particular branch of the war effort, though Gladwyn puts some malicious thoughts into my head, such as running a whisper that brass hats are in charge of P.W.E.

Gladwyn had told Selborne[1] that he was spending the weekend with me, and the latter had expressed apprehension lest I should try to take him away to the Board of Trade. He had told Gladwyn, though in a manner quite friendly towards me, that it was not good for a civil servant to be taken round too much from department to department by one particular minister. Gladwyn had said that he did not think I *had* any intention of using him at the Board of Trade. I said that, as I had told him before, this was so. It would not be good for him and it was not clear that there was any particular job in which he could particularly fit at the Board.

He said that many Conservatives thought that immediately after the war, when we returned to Party politics, there would be a big Labour majority and a Labour government for about two years, but that they would make such an unholy mess of everything that the Conservatives would then return with a large majority. I said that whether a post-war Labour government made a mess of things or not depended largely on the general situation. We might have luck or not. Meanwhile, an increasing number of our people were getting practice and experience in government departments and I thought that we could probably furnish a government containing four or five good people in key jobs which was as good as almost any government could ever show. I said that I did not want to lead the Labour Party, this possibility having passed in 1931, but that on the hypothesis we were discussing I should demand the Foreign Office. I thought that a Labour government with Bevin as P.M., me at the Foreign Office and Herbert Morrison at the Treasury would have the makings of something pretty good. He agreed, and I said that, if I found myself at the Foreign Office, I should want to use him in some very key position. He said he

1 Viscount Wolmer, q.v., had become the 3rd Earl of Selborne on the death of his father on 26th February 1942.

thought that he could ginger up the Foreign Office and be of service to me, but we both agreed that everything might come out differently. I might get so angry with my colleagues that I might at any time pass out in a flaming apoplexy, and either he or I might, even in this war, be blitzed. So it is all, perhaps, not much more than a rather amusing gossipy pipe-dream.

Gladwyn said that he had specifically asked Lord Selborne whether he wanted him to go on, and Lord Selborne had said, 'Oh yes, certainly, I like you.' He had also sought from Cadogan an assurance in writing that the Foreign Office wanted him to go on. Cadogan had given this assurance, though C.D. and others were constantly telling him that Cadogan had turned against him. He had heard that Eden had said of him, 'He is a very able man.' I said that this was very funny, because months ago Gaitskell had asked me what I thought Eden thought of Jebb, and I had said, 'The same as the P.M. thinks of me. You will remember that he said to me at Chequers, "I know that you are a very able man".' This, I had told Gaitskell, meant just what it said but not a little bit more! Gladwyn said that Bracken was a Firbolg or bog squatter, one of those aboriginal inhabitants of Ireland before the conqueror came. This was clear, both from his physical features and from his conduct.

C.D. and Co. were raging ever more hysterical against the Foreign Office, with whom they wanted Lord Selborne to have a show-down, but Gladwyn thought Lord Selborne was much too sensible to try these tactics, which could only end in his defeat. The 'Treaty' which I had negotiated, on the level Cadogan–Jebb, with the Foreign Office was much amended by Eden, who tried to put a quick one past Lord Selborne. The new draft would have made it impossible for S.O.E. to do *anything*, e.g. even to train an agent, in Europe. Lord Selborne, coached by Gladwyn, wrote back to Eden that he 'preferred the original draft', which he understood had been approved by his predecessor. But Gladwyn was amused when he said, 'After all, the Foreign Secretary is a gentleman.' Little, Gladwyn said, did he yet know his Whitehall. He had seen my correspondence with Bracken and had given it back to Gladwyn, saying, 'Most deplorable', referring, I understand, to Bracken's part rather than my own. He was being taken round various Stations and had spent two days in the Operations Room. He had said that he was most impressed by the quality of the members of the Council. He, however, went home fairly early and never did any work after dinner, or at least took no secret papers home. This led to a considerable block and many papers were lying for more than a week waiting for him. He had not yet had time to read a single secret telegram.

Sunday 15th March
Take Gladwyn for a quick walk from ten to two, via Snap, Upham, Sugar Hill, Peaks and the Village, where we stop for two pints of Four X. I make Gladwyn walk briskly up steeply inclined Down slope and fairly fast most of the way, but when I suggest that we should jog downhill, as a 'substitute for equitation', he shows unwillingness, which I shall bring up in future when I want to rag him.

After lunch we sleep and after tea play chess, I winning two games, and then we inspect the damage by frost. The electric pump is split right across, a number of pipes burst, and a large lump of the upstairs lavatory just fell out. They have not had such frost for a generation.

Dalton's announcement in the House on 17th March of his intention to introduce fuel rationing initially provoked little reaction. However, it gave opponents vital time to organise.

Tuesday 17th March
12 noon till 8.30 p.m. Coal debate. I sit in the Chamber all the time except for half an hour, 2 to 2.30, when I get some lunch. Grenfell is not so bad as might have been feared, and sticks closely to his typewritten brief. I come in about 5 p.m. and speak for half an hour, painting a black picture of the situation, stating that I and Grenfell are in touch with both sides of the industry 'to see whether some common ground cannot be found for a programme of action, *and change* to meet the special emergency of the war.' The words 'and change' I add, when on my feet, to the carefully prepared official statement, but I am sure it is right to add them. I then announce the decision to impose fuel rationing and my appointment of Beveridge. This is not received with any marked enthusiasm by the House, but quite well, I think, by the public outside.

Thursday 19th March
Lunch in and get Hyndley across for a few words before I meet the Mining Association.

This is an impressive performance in my large Conference Room, from 3 to 5.15 p.m. A whole roomful of coal owners! Gaitskell says afterwards he has never seen such a collection of hard-faced twisters. I have Grenfell on my right (fortunately he keeps silent throughout

398

the proceedings, having been heavily warned by Hyndley beforehand that he should leave this meeting to me). Hyndley is on my left and Nott-Bower, Fulton and Gaitskell are also in attendance.

I begin with a speech of welcome, in the course of which I say that I look forward to discussing with them the way in which the coal industry can make its full contribution to the war effort. I add that I am sure they will not deny that their relations with their men have been worse, over a period of years, than in any other important industry, and that this suspicion and ill feeling must now be removed in order that all shall do their best. I add that it is for consideration whether there should not now be set up some national authority for the industry, on which owners and men will both be represented. I say that, as they will have seen, I told the House of Commons that production was insufficient, and I am most anxious to get back men from the Army, though they know that there are great difficulties in this. On the other hand, it is deplorable that the industry has become so unattractive that youths are not going into it. My speech takes about a quarter of an hour, and I then invite Evan Williams to respond.

He takes an hour and a quarter and goes over all the old ground from before the last war onwards, of their troubles of 1920, 1921, 1925, 1926, 1930, 1931, up to 1936, from which date, according to him, everything has gone along very nicely. All the troubles in the industry, he says, have been due to 'political interference' by successive governments. If they had only been left alone, all would have been well. They would, of course, have liked to pay better wages, but the money wasn't there. He regards the proposal for a national authority as being politically motiv[at]ed and thinks that it would do no good at all, but only harm, to the industry. He, as hotly as his advanced age and sly temperament allow, denies that the relations of owners and men are bad. On the contrary, they are very good, whenever there is no political interference. The owners will be prepared to consider, on its merits, any proposal put forward for improving the efficiency of the industry. (This seems like a get-out phrase put in to please a minority of his colleagues who do not want to be too negative.) He agrees with me about the men from the Army and the importance of making the industry more attractive to youths.

At the end of all this, I thank him for his most interesting historical survey and ask any others to speak. There is not much response, though one or two say shortly that they agree with Sir Evan Williams. I am succeeding in keeping Grenfell quiet through occasional references to him in my speech, and occasional whispers with him on the procedure, e.g. suggesting that I should let the coal owners all have their go before either of us speaks again.

It is now twenty to five, and Sir Evan Williams says that there is another question which they would like to discuss with me, namely, coal prices. He wonders whether we have time for this today. I look at my watch and say that I must be away in about twenty minutes, but I shall be delighted if we can open the discussion on coal prices today. Thereupon, all the coal owners brighten up and in quick succession say that this is a most urgent matter on which there has been great delay. More than a quarter of the companies are making a loss and have to be subsidised from a levy ... which, I ascertain, is collected and distributed by themselves without the Mines Department having any detailed knowledge of it. We pay them enough 'to keep them just breathing', says Sir Evan Williams of the poorer pits. I say that I am afraid the Chancellor of the Exchequer may not look very kindly on a proposal to increase the price of coal, since he is very keen to keep down the cost of living, but I will report to the Lord President's Committee all that has been said today, both on organisation and prices, and suggest that we should have another meeting soon with only two items on the agenda, namely, the question of a National Authority and the question of prices. ... At this point there are signs of deep concern among the owners. Sir Walter Benton Jones[1] hastens to say that these two questions are quite separate and should not be linked up together. He would be very glad to come with Mr Lee and tell me all about prices. It is most urgent that this should be settled. I feel that I have now got them in a thoroughly uncomfortable position, and say that I cannot say more until I have reported to my colleagues. I then shake hands warmly with Sir Evan Williams, who says, 'We have only had our first round with you.' ...

Sir James Hawkey rings up to tell me of a lunch *à quatre* at No. 10, with the P.M. and their two wives. He says that in the course of conversation he praised me to the P.M. as 'a man of quite outstanding ability and exceedingly loyal to you'. Thereupon, the P.M. broke into the conversation of the two women – he and Hawkey had been talking alone in one corner of the room – and said, 'Clemmie, I think you will be very interested in something Hawkey has just said to me.' Hawkey then repeated his tribute and Mrs Churchill said, 'Oh I'm so glad to hear that.' Hawkey thought that this meant that someone had been speaking ill of me to her. I said, 'Almost certainly Bracken.'

Friday 20th March
A very interesting meeting of the Lord President's Committee. I report the proceedings with the coal owners arising out of a discussion on

1 Sir Walter Benton Jones, 2nd Bart (1880–1967). Chairman of the United Steel Companies Ltd 1928–62.

getting miners out of the Army. The War Office having got all the figures wrong, I am returning to the charge and demanding all ex-miners from Units in this country, whether Field Force or not. The line is taken by my colleagues that they must be assured, before recommending this to the Cabinet, which most of them seem inclined to do, that vigorous action is being taken to make the coal industry stand up to its duty, and I am asked to investigate a number of questions and to report back to the Lord President's Committee with a scheme for reorganising the industry. This is a perfect remit, given to me and not to Grenfell, who makes a very poor impression, bumbling on about how difficult everything is. Bevin says to him at one point, 'Of course, I know you will always defend everything in the industry. You are the biggest conservative I have ever met.' Bevin nudges me at another point in the discussion and whispers, 'Would it 'elp you if I asked for you to put up a scheme?' I whisper that it would. This Committee, then, is better than usual, but I am told that Oliver Lyttelton said, when he became President of the Board of Trade, and became a member of a series of ministerial committees, that he felt that he had joined a lot of second-rate debating societies, and this is just what I have been telling Gaitskell and others when they have been eager for me to sit in on other ministers' business as well as my own.

Pass an Honours List put up by Overton. I am horrified to find that Grenfell has recommended Lee for a knighthood!!! This is how the Workers stand up to the Capitalists! A most incredible performance! I strike it out, having the last word on these recommendations of the satellite ministries.

Then to lunch with Electrical Development Association. I am in exceptionally good form and make a very good speech, full of impromptu jokes and with much praise of electricity. I always know when I have done *very* well, but not always when I have done either rather well or rather badly. ...

Dine with Hyndley. Gaitskell and Fulton also there. The latter disappoints me a little. He is not a real economist and he gives the impression of being rather frightened of everything. But in the kingdom of the blind, the one-eyed man is king, and so it is in the Mines Department. I am very pleased with the proceedings of the Lord President's Committee, about which I tell them, and I think *they* are reasonably hopeful too.

Saturday 21st March
A muddle has been made over a special issue of coupons for bank messengers. It seems that a special issue has been made to the English

Clearing Banks but nothing to the Scots. Hence a row in Scotland. Political ineptitude by officials.

In the afternoon to Watford for a private conference of delegates from the five Parliamentary Divisions in the County. George Brown, [1] one of Bevin's young men, who helped me to hoof Cripps out of the Labour Party four years ago, is in charge. He is an excellent chap and I should like to see him in Parliament. I talk to them quite frankly about current matters.

Wednesday 25th March

National Executive is an even worse waste of time than usual. We have a wonderful gift of concentrating at great length on the trivial.

Lunch with Johnston at House of Commons and fix up with him about coupons for Scots bank messengers' uniforms. This had led to needless fuss, and almost to a debate in the House of Lords, because some official of mine wrote a tactless letter! ...

A long meeting, accompanied by Grenfell, with miners' leaders; Edwards, Lawther, Bowman and Horner. Jones cannot be there. I have made a separate note of this. I have to head them off the idea that they will be shown the draft of my paper for the Lord President's Committee next week! Or that we shall see them again before 3rd April, when the next discussion on Lord President's Committee takes place. Bowman thought that it might be useful if 'the movement' were to send a deputation to the Lord President's Committee before we do any more. But I get this out of their heads. I tell them that I will do my best to get colleagues to agree to a National Authority. I say that we must handle colleagues a bit beforehand and so they must leave the details to us, but I tell Bowman, who makes a complimentary speech to me afterwards, that my views on coal have not varied for many years, and I will do my best to get them accepted. Edwards is pessimistic on the whole thing. When I say that on Lord President's Committee the coal owners have not got a friend, he says that they have so often heard this before that they do not believe it. Such friends always turn up at the last moment. ...

Gaitskell, who has been dining with Spearman, [2] reports that there is a good deal of anti-P.M. feeling in the Tory Party, but, as usual, they

1 George Brown, later Baron George-Brown (1914–85). Labour M.P. 1945–70. Junior
minister 1947–51. Minister of Works 1951. First Secretary of State and Secretary
of State for Economic Affairs 1964–6; Foreign Secretary 1966–8. Deputy Leader of
the Labour Party 1960–70. Brown had made a celebrated anti-Cripps speech at the
1939 Labour Party Conference. He was a member of Bevin's union, the T.G.W.U.
2 A. C. M. Spearman, later Sir Alexander (1901–82). Conservative M.P. for Scar-
borough and Whitby 1941–66.

have no answer when asked who they would like as his successor. Spearman tonight, when pressed, said he supposed it would lie between Anderson, Lyttelton and Butler!!! He said that after Singapore it was reported that Churchill had quite lost his head and almost thrown his hand in. I do not believe this.

Thursday 26th March

Lunch with *The Times* on the invitation of Sir Campbell Stuart. Sit between the latter and Sir Harold Hartley,[1] a keen little scientist who has been working for M.E.W. as well as for Board of Trade on fuel problems. He is now on the Board of *The Times*. He says that one reason why the Germans don't use gas is because they are very short of clothing, and, if we retaliated with mustard, we should rot so much of their clothing that they could not replace it. I have a word with Barrington-Ward,[2] the new Editor. He is the brother of F. T. Barrington-Ward,[3] which gives me a gambit. I don't like him much, but it is useful to have met him.

Receive a deputation of colliery managers, headed by Mr Charlton, rather a surly brute. I begin by ragging him a bit for having written to *The Times* and not to me.[4] We then listen to their story, which is not very new, except that several of them put great emphasis on short-shift working by the men, i.e. though the shift below ground is seven and a half hours, many men, so they say, come up after five and a half, or little more, having hewed their bit and earned the wages they are accustomed to. Very often this leads to coal being left on the conveyor face and to delay in later operations, as well as to the loss of additional coal which these men might have hewed.

This last meeting started at 4 and I close it down at 5, having the three Panjandrums of the Mining Association coming to see me at 5.15. (I did not want Grenfell to know that they were coming, but Hyndley afterwards tells me that just as they were all emerging, I having left some moments before, from the meeting with the colliery

---

1 Brigadier-General Sir Harold Hartley (1878–1972). Scientist. Vice-President of, and Director of Research for, London Midland Scottish Railway 1930–45. Honorary Adviser on development of Home Produced Fuels at the Ministry of Fuel and Power 1939–47. Chairman of the Fuel Research Board 1932–47.
2 R. M. Barrington-Ward (1891–1948). Editor of *The Times* 1941–8.
3 F. T. Barrington-Ward (1880–1938). Barrister. Dalton had been his pupil when studying for the Bar before the First World War.
4 T. S. Charlton. Manager at the Cortonwood Colliery Co. Ltd near Barnsley and President of the National Association of Colliery Managers. On 17th March *The Times* published a letter from Charlton complaining about the failure of the Board of Trade and the Mines Department to consult his Association about the danger of a coal shortage.

managers, Grenfell saw the three P.s coming along the passage. He asked Hyndley, 'What do you think they are doing here?' very suspiciously. Hyndley said, 'I really don't know. I expect they have asked to see the President.' But Hyndley says that next day Grenfell's suspicions, he thought, had disappeared.

I have one and three-quarter hours with the three P.s, alone except that Gaitskell is here as a witness and to take a note. They are most shifty, especially Sir Walter Benton Jones. They are most anxious to interest me in their case for a price rise, and, on my request, Lee undertakes to send me particulars of the output produced at various rates of profit and loss and of the distribution of the levy between firms. They say that they would like to discuss with the men the scheme which has been put through the N.C.L. [National Council of Labour]. Could I not help to arrange this? I say that this is not a simple matter. The men, it seems, have said that they are bound by this scheme and can't discuss it. I propose to them an extension of the Kent scheme, whereby boys are credited with £10 a year to accumulate till they reach the age of, say, twenty-three. This would be a solid inducement to go down the pit. Williams chuckles and says that he doesn't think this would be much good, because, if the boys had the prospect of more money, they would do less work. After they have left, Gaitskell says that he thinks they will be saying amongst themselves, 'Well he's not such a bad chap after all. Of course he has to put up a show for the sake of the Labour Party, but I don't think he will push it to extremes. I think we made quite an impression on him.' But Lee will say, 'Don't be too sure. We didn't really get anything out of him, did we?' ...

Hear from Gaitskell that Robbins[1] said of my paper on tobacco, 'It is so well written that the President must have done it himself.'

Friday 27th March
Lord President's Committee. There must be a further bias against exports. Turning to tobacco, the general line in my paper is that, unless I can be assured of large and regular imports, so as to keep stocks at or above six months, there must be restriction of supply, and this should, in my view, mean higher tax plus rationing. But to ration tobacco alone would at once make an immense and active black market. Therefore, it should go in with other things, either a few, or a much larger number. I would hand it over to the Ministry of Food.

General apprehension at idea of rationing. Bevin says we mustn't

1 Lionel Robbins, later Baron (1898–1984). Director of the Economic Section of Offices of the War Cabinet 1941–5. Professor of Economics at the L.S.E. 1929–61. Chairman of the Committee on Higher Education 1961–4. Dalton taught Robbins at the L.S.E. just after the First War. Later they were academic colleagues.

push things too far. He thought Cripps in his speech on 'austerity' struck the wrong note. We may easily upset people. Others object to rationing because they think the supplies would be too small, e.g. sixty cigarettes, or two ounces of pipe tobacco, or eight average-size cigars a week. Woolton doesn't like it at all, and complains that he has not been consulted, though there have been discussions on the official plane. Nicotine, he says, is not an alternative to proteins. Why didn't I tie up tobacco with cosmetics! This indeed is passing back the buck! Finally it is agreed that for the time being I must have my imports, and that officials shall consider what would be the best rationing scheme if we had to come to that. ...

Conference on coal with Gowers, Hyndley, Wilmot and Gaitskell. The two first are of the opinion that the coal industry should be run on Public Corporation lines. But they are both very doubtful whether this change can be brought about during the war without interrupting the flow of output. Even if one put in very strong district bosses, they might encounter a good deal of obstruction and ca-canny in a number of pits. It is clear to me, however, though I don't say so at this conference, that my next move must be to put up a scheme on these lines to the Lord President's Committee. Gowers is getting a little old, but he is a most able man, with a clear brain, a sense of irony, and has a very low opinion, based on long experience, of most coal owners. In an admirable paper, of which I now have a copy, he says that the men, though they made every sort of tactical mistake, were absolutely right in 1925–6 in resisting wage cuts and longer hours.

Sunday 29th March

Gladwyn to breakfast at 9.45 bringing with him a great quantity of papers relating to my work with him. We go through them and I keep some and let him keep others. He puts the case, quite truly, that, if the Camarilla got to know that I had taken away official papers, they would raise a frightful stink at No. 10. This is quite wise. We go to lunch at the Lansdowne and afterwards walk quickly in the Park – it is a day which whispers of spring. Lord and Lady Leathers[1] are reclining in chairs beside the lake and he urges me to do something about coal. I say I have a paper coming this next week.

Monday 30th March

Grenfell this afternoon for an hour. I say that I propose that he should take the Chair at this week's Coal Production Council. He seems pleased at this but finds it necessary to make the same long speech about his not being nobody, which I have heard so often before. I then

1 Lady Leathers, née Emily Baxter.

try out on him the general line of my paper. I say that he and I must put in a paper on which, if necessary, we could stand, and even resign. He agrees, though very flatly, as his way is.

Tuesday 31st March
Reconstruction Committee with Jowitt[1] in the Chair. A rather servile Jewish-looking man is waiting in the passage to usher Jowitt and me into the Conference Room – I had had a few words with Jowitt first – and says, rather obsequiously, 'This is your seat, President.' It soon appears that this man is Sir Alfred Hurst! The Treasury and other Departments have circulated an immense printed paper of more than 120 pages on currency policy, etc. Bevin comes in late, gives the appearance of being slightly flushed, and proceeds to denounce the whole paper, saying it is an Anglo-American bankers' conspiracy against the working class: it would doom us to two million unemployed; if it were thought that this was what we were fighting the war for, our people would refuse to go on one day longer: if people outside knew that Labour ministers were being asked to agree to this sort of thing, it would break up the Government. And so on! ...... In fact, the proposals were most enlightened and reasonable – or so Gaitskell had explained to me at lunch, I not having had time to read them. Why, though, was Russia left out? I said I thought this was injudicious. I then proposed that Keynes and Hopkins[2] should be sent for to explain their paper. This was done. They appeared and sat at the end of the table. The room was full of other ministers, including Kingsley Wood, Hudson, Ernest Brown, Butler, Law, etc. Bevin was now much milder, and both expert witnesses dealt cleverly with him. It was finally agreed that this paper, with a mass of other stuff, might be put before the Americans who were coming over to discuss economic questions.

Dine at Paddington Railway Hotel with Sir James Milne.[3] Also present George Hicks, who kept us all in a state of great mirth by an unending fund of funny stories, two blokes from the G.W.R. [Great Western Railway] and Carvel. Hicks afterwards told me that he was

---

1 Sir William Jowitt, later 1st Earl (1885–1957). Solicitor-General 1940–42; Paymaster-General 4th March–30th December 1942; Minister without Portfolio December 1942–October 1944. Labour M.P. for Ashton-under-Lyme 1939–45. Liberal M.P. for Hartlepool 1922–4; Preston 1929. Labour M.P. 1929–31. Supported MacDonald and National Labour in 1931, but later rejoined the Labour Party. Attorney-General 1929–32. Minister of Social Insurance 1944; National Insurance 1944–5. Lord Chancellor 1945–51.

2 Sir Richard Hopkins (1880–1955). Permanent Secretary at the Treasury 1942–5. Second Secretary 1932–42.

3 Sir James Milne (1883–1958). Director and General Manager of the Great Western Railway 1929–47.

very concerned that I looked so tired. He even rang me up the next day to say the same thing and to explain that this was why he had told so many stories in order to keep me in a good mood. I said I was indeed a bit weary, but was going away for the weekend. Very friendly and solicitous!

I hear tonight that it is being said in the Mines Department, at least by [Harold] Wilson and his friends, that my paper on coal is 'the best ever'. It also has a good reception at the War Cabinet Secretariat, and the economists there are going to press it upon the Lord President.

Wednesday 1st April
Jowitt comes to see me. He says that Ernest Brown and his Ministry of Health, both Minister and officials, are the most inefficient thing in the Government just now. He also senses that there is a feud between Foreign Office and Treasury, and thinks that he will do best for a while to back Foreign Office. He finds Makins and other officials quite helpful. He says the P.M. has taken no notice of him at all since he has had this job. I say he must not be surprised at this. It is the lot of many ministers not engaged very directly on operations. He asks whether I have any doubts about the outcome of the war, and about next autumn. I say none, though we shall no doubt pass through some tight places. ...

Lunch with Sir James Hawkey, as devoted as ever to the P.M. and to me. He repeats himself a bit, including the conversation at No. 10 the other day when he and his wife were lunching alone with the P.M. and Mrs Churchill. He says that when he praised me to the P.M., the latter said, 'Well, I have promoted him', and Hawkey said, 'Not nearly enough' and made rude remarks about Kingsley Wood, who, he said, was no better than a country barber's assistant. Sir James Hawkey had a black outlook on the war. He could never get out of his head, he said, the fear that the Russians might make a separate peace in the East.

Harriman to see me and to ask me to agree to prohibit export of all woollen cloth to U.S.A. other than the specifications imposed by U.S. Government regulations. I said I agreed to this in principle. He then asked whether they could import, say, two million tons of coal a year to enable them to free some coastwise shipping. I said that this was much more difficult.

Tuesday 7th April
Beveridge, with whom Tallents, comes to talk about his fuel rationing. He has made a very clever and perfect plan, though it is administratively complicated and I feel that we should seek some practical simplifications. Overton and Gaitskell also present. The latter makes

some good suggestions. Beveridge says that he has squared nearly all the interests. He will let me have a summary by the weekend.

To see Attlee about coal. I tell him about Beveridge's rationing scheme, and then try to binge him up both on release of soldiers and my plan for reorganisation. I point out the political troubles of delay.

Wednesday 8th April

Lunch at Spanish Embassy, but the Ambassador is ill in bed and the party a bit flat. Kirkpatrick is there and I take him to Bush House by car to ask how P.W.E. is getting on. He says that things are going pretty well, and I gather that Brigadier Brooks is a bit demoted, direct contact now being established with the War Office. How far away it all seems!

Thursday 9th April

Cabinet on coal is put off owing to India. Cripps has now failed to get agreement with Congress, but these latter are starkly exhibited, especially for American eyes, as mere ridiculous word-mongers.

Special meeting of N.E.C. at Transport House which decides to approve Attlee's 'decision', in which I and other ministers consulted concurred, to send some junior Labour members of the Government to speak for Grigg[1] against Brockway[2] in Cardiff East.[3] I say that it is all just too simple. Are we in favour of the Government or not? Are we in favour of the war or not? If the answer to both questions is yes, as it is, how can we refuse to support a member of the Government, who happens not to be either a Tory or a Liberal, against an opponent of the war? I had to leave early, but this view finally carries, though some of my prize colleagues say that they are sure that we shall do Grigg harm and turn votes to Brockway by openly supporting the former![4]

Dine at Isola Bella with Wilmot, Carvel and Haydn Davies. This is

1 Sir James Grigg (1890–1964). Permanent Under-Secretary at the War Office 1939–42. Secretary of State for War 1942–5. National M.P. for Cardiff East 1942–5. Principal Private Secretary to successive Chancellors of the Exchequer 1921–30.
2 Fenner Brockway, later Baron (b. 1888). Author and journalist. Labour M.P. for East Leyton 1929–31; Eton and Slough 1950–64. General Secretary of the I.L.P. 1928, 1933–9; Chairman 1931–3. Editor of *Labour Leader* 1912–17; *New Leader* 1926–9, 1931–46.
3 The I.L.P. (which was opposed to the war) contested the by-election at which Grigg, new Secretary of State for War, sought to enter the House of Commons. This was an embarrassment to the Labour Party, which was concerned to maintain the electoral truce.
4 Marginal insertion: 'Go down and ask not, how would Christ vote, but how would Stalin vote?'

really a party for Carvel, but he is *most frightfully dull*! Later Gaitskell and a lady friend of his join us. Davies has now started at Board of Trade.

Friday 10th April
War Cabinet on coal. P.M. *contra mundum* for one and three-quarter hours; a very remarkable performance. The trouble is the proposed release of 7,000 miners from the Field Force.[1] Grenfell says, when asked, that they will produce 300 tons each, i.e. just over two million tons a year extra. (Of course this is wrong, though I don't find it out till afterwards. Three hundred is the average figure for *all* workers in and about the mines. For coal-face workers the figure is 800. Therefore, the increment of output in question is over five and a half million tons a year. I send, two days later, a correcting Minute to Anderson on this.) The P.M., however, won't give in and says he will put up a series of alternative ways of saving two million tons of coal, e.g. by harder rationing, lower stocks, less munition production, etc. Anderson and Lyttelton are particularly vexed at his obstinate resistance. The former gets red in the face and constantly shrugs his shoulders, protesting, 'All this has been taken into consideration. We have thought of all that.' It is agreed that a small committee of ministers, including myself, shall make a plan for reorganising the mining industry.

Dalton spent the weekend of 10th to 12th April staying with Mayhew's family in Norfolk. 'Go for a run with C.M. from 7.30 to 8.30 – thus repeating our habits of last Christmas except that this time the sun has risen,' he recorded. 'The yokels are amazed to see us running across ploughed fields and along roads. Go in feeling very fit.'[2]

Tuesday 14th April
Budget in the afternoon. Kingsley Wood waffles on for two and a half hours. What a fall from the old days! This country barber's assistant, however, gives me two friendly references, on un-taxing utility cloth, clothes and underwear, and on talks on post-war with businessmen.

1 'I am not at all convinced we should be wise to pull the Army to pieces at the present time,' Churchill had minuted to the Lord President on 30th March (PRO, PREM 4/9/8).
2 Diary, 11th April 1942.

The speech was subjected to a run of utterly inane interjections by Gallacher, MacLaren and Stokes – three of our worst fools. My political friends give me great credit for the repeals on 'utility', but the Co-operators, as usual, say that it is not enough.

Beveridge's proposals for fuel rationing were submitted by Dalton to the Lord President's Committee on 14th April. The intention was now to start the scheme in June, to help build up the summer coal stocks.

Friday 17th April
Lord President's Committee this morning approves the adoption of a fuel rationing scheme on the general lines of Beveridge's report. He himself is allowed in, though not without some grumble by Kingsley Wood and others. He does not, in fact, play a very prominent part in the discussion, as I expound the scheme and all he does is to answer a few questions. ...

All ministers are in favour of the scheme except Duncan, who makes a furious attack upon it. His arguments vary from a complaint that Scotland will get too small a ration, to objection to 'placing us all in chains', and to the statement that any rationing scheme will check production, and that our stocks at $15\frac{1}{2}$ million tons are grossly excessive, and that 5 million tons, properly distributed, would be quite enough. He gets no support from other colleagues, though Grenfell says that it will be a serious thing if people find next winter that they cannot get more coal when the weather is very cold if they have exhausted their ration. ...

Daily dose of Beveridge. He is very troublesome.

Gladwyn comes to pick me up here for dinner at the Isola Bella. He says that, while waiting in the Private Office, he thought that 'the atmosphere was quite good' and noticed that both Overton and Sir Thomas Barlow,[1] on emerging from my room, seemed quite cheerful! I tell him that, apart from not having him working with me, I find my present job much more interesting and exciting than my last. He says that the Earl [Selborne] has been instructed, in a Minute by the P.M., in response to a complaint by Eden about activities in Portugal, to

---

1 Sir Thomas Barlow (1883–1964). Director-General of Civilian Clothing 1941–5. Chairman of the District Bank Ltd and Barlow and Jones Ltd. Younger brother of Sir Alan Barlow, q.v.

act always in neutral countries in Europe under the direction of the Foreign Office. I say that Eden never tried that on with me, and that my half-bluff, of the danger of a row with the Labour Party, and my playing up of Attlee for a bit more than he was worth, did, after all, succeed. He says that the Earl was simply knocked backwards by the members of the Council and kept on saying that he had never met a finer lot of chaps in his life. C.D. is going on sick leave, having had a pretty poor doctor's report, and will be resigning soon on the quite genuine ground of ill health. The question is who shall succeed him? Gladwyn wonders whether he ought not to move across and take it over himself, but the Foreign Office don't like this, and Cadogan said, 'That would mean that you would become a regular thug yourself.' Other alternatives, from within the present lot, would be either Glenconner or M. [Gubbins]. I said that I thought either of these would do, and I should be inclined to prefer M. Gladwyn said that this would mean that the whole thing would be militarised. I said I could not believe that we could sit inactive through another summer and, therefore, the moment for more active and widespread operations than ever before would be near. Gladwyn said that C.D. favoured Hanbury-Williams.[1] I said that I had only seen him once, when he called on me with Sam Courtauld.[2] I thought he was a mere stuffed shirt. Gladwyn was inclined to agree.

Saturday 18th April
Get up early and catch 8.35 train for West Leaze. Ruth has been here since Thursday (16th) on a short leave, and to exchange winter for summer clothes. She has had a laudatory notice in the *Starman's Diary* yesterday evening. She is said to be 'a great factor in maintaining output' in the North, and to be arranging for dance-floors and other comforts in hostels. She says that in fact the hostel building programme has been grossly overdone and that a number of hostels have been built which will never be occupied at all!

Sunday 19th April
Make bonfires and mow the lawn.

Following the decision taken by the War Cabinet on 10th April, a Cabinet Committee on the Reorganisation of the Coal Industry was set up. The Lord

1 J. Hanbury-Williams, later Sir John (1892–1965). M.E.W. 1942. Managing Director of Courtaulds Ltd 1935–42; Deputy Chairman 1943–6; Chairman 1946–62.
2 Sam Courtauld (1876–1947). Chairman of Courtaulds Ltd 1921–46.

President (Sir John Anderson) was Chairman. Other members included the Minister of Production (Lyttelton), the Chancellor of the Exchequer (Wood), the President of the Board of Trade (Dalton), the Minister of Labour (Bevin), the Minister of Supply (Duncan) and the Secretary for Mines (Grenfell). The Deputy Prime Minister (Attlee), Lord Privy Seal (Cripps) and Minister of War Transport (Leathers) attended the last two meetings, when the final proposals were being prepared.

Monday 20th April

Back from West Leaze just in time to change from country clothes and attend the first meeting of the Coal Committee, with Anderson in the Chair. Others are Bevin, Lyttelton, myself, Duncan and Grenfell. We begin with a fuss about a leakage in this morning's *Daily Express* which states that our Committee has been appointed, names Anderson, Bevin, Duncan and me as members, though adding a total membership of seven, states that the miners' plan is being considered by us and that it is likely to be adopted. All this over the signature of Trevor Evans, tacked on to a tale of how Jimmy Bowman is looking after the underground training of lads in Northumberland and how the Government is appointing soon a Committee with Sir John Forster[1] in the Chair to consider recruitment of juveniles for the pit. This is a most blatant and vexatious leak and I have little doubt that it came from the Mines Department and probably from Grenfell himself. It is agreed that the rigours of the Law can properly be applied to the persons concerned and Anderson will raise it in the Cabinet, proposing that the Attorney-General should interrogate Trevor Evans as to his source, and also George Crist, the *Daily Telegraph* man who got advance notice of fuel rationing.

As Dalton put it to a fellow M.P. a few days later, in advocating the rationing of fuel he was implementing Labour's policy of rationing necessities.[2] Opposition, however, did not just come from the Tory benches. Some mining M.P.s were also suspicious, and pressed for more direct methods of controlling the coal industry.

---

1 Sir John Forster, later 1st Baron (1888–1972). Barrister. Served on the Railway Staff National Tribunal 1940–60. President of the Industrial Court 1946–60. Chairman of the National Arbitration Tribunal 1944–72.

2 Chuter Ede, unpublished diaries, 25th April 1942 (British Library).

Tuesday 21st April

Make my announcement in the House on fuel rationing. Quite short, stating only that I received Beveridge's report last week, that H.M.G. have decided to introduce a comprehensive fuel rationing scheme on the Points system, that this will begin on 1st June for coal, coke and paraffin, and as from about the same time – by last meter reading before 15th August – for gas and electricity. I add that each house will be rationed by present needs and not by past consumption, and that each person will have a personal ration in addition. This is hoped to save ten million tons of coal a year and I have already set up a department at the Board of Trade to administer it.

There is a most surprising uproar of interrogative disapproval from all parts of the House. Some say we should dig more coal, others that the scheme will cost too many officials, others that it is unworkable anyhow, others that the poor will be penalised, others that the Beveridge report should be published, others that a debate should first take place in the House before a decision is reached. I go on to a meeting of the Lobby Correspondents, many of whom think that the scheme is already dead, or stillborn. I do not accept this view and am most urbane, says Wilmot, for three-quarters of an hour. I expect that my ministerial colleagues will be in a flutter, but they are much firmer than I thought.

I see Anderson in the afternoon and tell him – following a talk I have had with Beveridge and the others immediately after lunch – that I think I should agree to publish Beveridge's report. He agrees to this, provided I can square Kingsley Wood and Cripps, who is returning tonight. I ring up Wood and fix him.

Laski dines with me alone at the Board of Trade. He says that, during the time that he was with the late L.P.S.,[1] he was never given any real work to do. Most of this evening he spends in denigrating poor little Attlee. But, when I ask him for his alternative for the leadership, he can only suggest – I fancy quite insincerely – myself. Whereupon I tell him that my ambitions lie not along that road but along certain other alternatives. He thinks that our next Annual Conference will be a scene of wild and indignant disorder against the failure of Labour in the Government to get any socialism at all. This little fool lives in an unreal world of his own making.

Wednesday 22nd April

All morning at Labour Party National Executive. Middleton[2] is sixty-

---

1 i.e. Attlee, the former Lord Privy Seal.
2 J. S. Middleton (1878–1962). Secretary of the Labour Party 1935–44; Assistant Secretary 1903–35.

HOT BRICKS

five on 12th March next and it is decided to recommend to the Whitsun Conference to keep him on from year to year until we see our way clear to appoint a successor, having regard to the fact that there would now be an unduly narrow field of applicants. This is rather deplorable, though the arguments for it are strong. ...

Further session with Beveridge – also Wilmot, Overton, Watkinson,[1] Gaitskell and Reddaway.[2] I have this morning squared Cripps on the telephone to publishing the Beveridge Report, provided, as I would in any case have done, that I make it clear that we are not committed to the details. This will best be done, I think, by a letter from me to him. We go through a simplified application form for a Fuel Ration Book and then consider how far, without exposing ourselves to criticism, we can make minor amendments in the draft of his report.

1 G. L. Watkinson, later Sir Laurence (1896–1974). Principal Assistant Secretary (Industries and Manufacturers) at the Board of Trade; Under-Secretary 1942–6; Deputy Secretary at the Ministry of Fuel and Power 1947–55. Watkinson had helped Dalton on coal; later, he took a leading part in Dalton's plans for the location of industry.
2 W. B. Reddaway (b. 1913). Statistics Division, Board of Trade, with final rank of Chief Statistician 1940–47. Lecturer in Economics at Cambridge University 1939–55; Professor of Political Economy 1969–80.

He is, as usual, inclined to be a little sticky on some points, but gives in on others. ...

The press reception of my fuel rationing announcement yesterday is very critical and, in spots, most hostile. It is difficult to explain just why they, and the House, reacted so violently. Wilmot, who went back there last night, says that some were already having second thoughts. It is, he thinks, because the war is not going visibly very badly at this moment that they have reacted a little against 'austerity'. If we had lost a battleship, or a colony, yesterday, they would have been quite different. I have not much doubt that we shall get them round. Wilmot proposes that, if we get the Beveridge report out next week, we might have a debate the week after, in which I would begin by explaining the scheme in detail, then there would be scope for criticism all round, and then – I add – Cripps can wind up.

By early April 1942, the Japanese had sunk 112,000 tons of merchant shipping in the Indian Ocean alone, together with one British aircraft carrier, two cruisers and four smaller naval vessels. Meanwhile, Japanese forces continued to advance in the Philippines against the Americans, and in Burma against the British.

Thursday 23rd April
Secret Session. P.M. speaks at great length and very well, and carries the House. First a very sombre picture, naming places which may well be lost to the Japs in the near future, and various misfortunes (principally naval, and what a hell of a run of bad luck we have had!) in the near past and present. Enough, but not too much, on Singapore. Events there quite out of harmony with our traditions and our previous experience. Many different persons and sections have been blamed. Meanwhile, it would do no good and would only divert active men from the immediate business of the war to hold an inquiry. Great praise for New Zealand. Their one Division is still in the Middle East with no request for its recall. Japs have choice of many moves by land and sea. Perhaps next into China?

Then to the future, and the grounds for undiminished confidence. American production. Recent consultations; Hopkins and Marshall[1]

---

1 General G. C. Marshall (1880–1959). Chief of Staff, United States Army 1939–45. Special representative of President Truman in China 1945–7. Secretary of State 1947–9. Instigator of the Marshall Plan for European economic recovery.

in London; the matters discussed; their return to U.S.A.; exchange of messages between P.M. and President. This most dramatically ends the speech. 'Who wants a public session after that?' one Tory asks me.

Lunch at House of Commons and encourage M.P.s to talk fuel rationing. Chuter Ede says that he has larger rooms than most. Do I take into account the size of rooms? Westwood[1] says that he is in favour of fuel rationing but there will be a tremendous row if we are proceeding in ignorance of the fact that miners get free coal. It seems as though all assume that we know nothing.

Friday 24th April

The proof of the Fuel Rationing White Paper is finally carried away to the printer by Preston,[2] after Beveridge has had a final poke at it this morning. But he has raised no difficulties at this stage, not even, as I feared he might, on the terms of my letter to him, in which I merely say that H.M.G. have decided that there must be a comprehensive scheme of fuel rationing, deliberately omitting to commit myself even to the broad outlines of his plan. I am more and more sure that the right procedure is to get agreement to the proposition that fuel must be rationed, and then to say that [as] for the details his plan is a basis of discussion, though a very good one, on which we may, but are not likely to, improve much.

I.L.O. [International Labour Office] lunch with Bevin in the Chair. Jowitt and I and Law are the only other ministers, the rest of the company consisting of officials and delegates of workers, employers and governments, including my brother-in-law,[3] whom I have not seen for a number of years. He is as stupid as ever, and bores on at length about his political views, undefined, not being the same as mine. I am inclined not to want to see him again for many years. Burge[4] said, when I came in, 'I hope there won't be a scene; your brother-in-law's here.' I said, 'Oh dear no; I will go across and introduce myself to him.'

Talk to Cripps about coal. I tell him what has been happening as regards (1) manpower from the Army, (2) reorganisation, (3) fuel rationing. He reacts very well. On (1) he thinks we should go on pressing for more men from the Army, on (2) he hopes that I will stick

---

1 Joseph Westwood (1884–1948). Parliamentary Under-Secretary for Scotland 1931, 1940–45. Labour M.P. for Stirling and Falkirk Burghs 1935–48; Midlothian and Peebleshire 1922–31. Secretary of State for Scotland 1945–7.

2 G. E. Preston (1910–59). Principal Private Secretary to Dalton at the Board of Trade 1942–5. Personal Assistant and Private Secretary to Dalton at the Duchy of Lancaster 1948–9.

3 Sir John Forbes Watson, q.v.

4 M. R. K. Burge (1894–1968). Director of the London Office of the I.L.O. 1924–45.

to the proposals in my paper, since this, he thinks, would make a first-class occasion for a show-down with the P.M. on wartime Socialism, and on (3) he thinks that we should put down a motion in the House simply approving fuel rationing without reference to details or the Beveridge plan. He would like himself to wind up the debate which I, of course, would open.

I spoke to Waterhouse before lunch and said I would be glad, if they desired, to speak to the 1922 Committee on fuel rationing next week, as I was speaking to the Labour Party Meeting. Promptly after lunch an invitation came for next Thursday afternoon. Waterhouse thinks that the fuel rationing scheme is just in the balance. Beveridge, he thinks, is not very popular with my Party, and many in his think that he is 'a funny old fellow with his head in the clouds and his feet in the pond'. Waterhouse says the real question is what shall we do with the munition worker who has used up all his ration before the end of the period and will therefore have to go to bed in the dark and eat uncooked food and have no heat in his house, and who therefore stays in bed next morning and won't go to work? He also says that this scheme is thought to be 'a benefit for Grenfell', since he has failed to increase production.

Despite a widespread view that the rationing plan would have to be dropped, Dalton refused to give way under pressure. He determined to publish the scheme and fight for its implementation. It soon became clear, however, that Tory backbench protests could not be stilled, and that some form of compromise was unavoidable.

Monday 27th April
Gaitskell says that through the press the vested interests are working like tigers against fuel rationing. He has done his best with several of them.

This too raised at the War Cabinet. The P.M. says, 'Don't let them all form up on you.' He is very friendly. I say I will fight as much as need be for the war effort, but I don't want to fight needlessly or fruitlessly. He says that this is not a central issue in the war effort at present and we should try to avoid any unnecessary vexation. 'But', he adds afterwards, 'we must all stand together.' He wonders whether a broadcast by him appealing for economy would not be worth while. He is inclined towards appeals, with a rationing scheme prepared in the background, to be introduced if appeals fail. I thank him, but say that I fear there are great difficulties, particularly in knowing whether the appeals have been successful or not, and also in losing valuable time. Lyttelton is working against the scheme. It is he, he himself admits, who put this last suggestion into the P.M.'s head. He says to me that, though I may get away with it for the moment, I shall soon be facing fifteen P.Q.s a day.

Tuesday 28th April

The White Paper is out today. At Question Time I get a heavy barrage, particularly on the silly point about the number of officials required to run the scheme. It is thought that I face it with good temper. Sir Douglas Thomson[1] has a question down about the number of officials who were on the staff of M.E.W. when I left and on the staff of Board of Trade now, and how many of these were established civil servants. I sense that he is trying to get at Gaitskell or Haydn Davies. The answer is 'Twenty-nine, of whom five, including Sir Frederick Leith-Ross, are established civil servants.' This was carefully drafted by me. The trick works. The introduction of Sir Frederick Leith-Ross's name leads my questioner in his supplementary to ask whether most of these are with Sir Frederick Leith-Ross. My answer is 'Practically all', and I then add something about the nature of his work and the fact that many have not yet, physically, been able to move from M.E.W. to Board of Trade owing to lack of accommodation. This lengthy and conciliatory supplementary answer makes it impossible for him to pursue the subject. I heard afterwards that some time ago the Tory Head Office were told that at M.E.W. I relied on six men who were all temporary and all Labour candidates, and that all of these I had taken on to Board of Trade. Therefore, Sir Douglas Thomson held in his hand a supplementary question, assuming that my answer would be 'Six, none of whom are established civil servants', 'How many of these are Labour candidates for Parliament?'!

Thursday 30th April

Shaving in bathroom with Wilmot I say that there are only three alternatives – victory, resignation, or some kind of huggery-muggery, which does not attract me at all. There is, I say, much to be said for resignation and regaining freedom. Wilmot does not think I should really enjoy this very much!

This is a busy day. First, at ten o'clock, I meet the Labour Party Meeting and expound the case for rationing. I say that it is in line with

1 Sir (James) Douglas W. Thomson, 2nd Bart (1905–72). Conservative M.P. for Aberdeen South 1935–46.

our policy. Increasing production is important, but not less [are] cutting consumption and providing that there is equitable distribution of an assured ration to all. If we don't do this now, next winter will be worse than last. Wilmot says afterwards that he thinks I made a very good speech. I was not so sure. Next we get a string of questions on pretty obvious detail. I hold my reply to all of these and do not finally deliver it, for then follow a series of speeches and just after eleven o'clock there is an upsurge of loyal, sensible miners – Tinker,[1] MacDonald[2] and Jim Griffiths – as well as Bevan, who has made a very good speech – all ready to move that equitable fuel rationing be accepted in principle. Others had proposed that the matter should be adjourned, or that we should make our acceptance of rationing dependent on Government's acceptance of N.C.L. [National Council of Labour] plan. I sit next Greenwood and keep on repeating to him that we cannot have any such tie-up. He flabbily agrees and, on the whole, gets us through the meeting pretty well. Finally, the acceptance in principle is unanimous.

Return to the office and excogitate my speech for the 1922 Committee this afternoon. I lunch in and Gaitskell rings up, just as I am starting for the House, to say that he has been lunching with Braithwaite[3] who is very pro-me and wants to come with me to the meeting and make suggestions on the way. We go together in the car and Braithwaite says that I shall 'get them' if I insist that my policy is to keep the home fires burning next winter and to get fair play for all.[4]

There are some 150 present, and I cannot complain of my reception. I speak, then answer a number of questions, and then depart, leaving them to debate. I don't propound the Beveridge Scheme but only the broad necessity for cutting consumption, and hence for rationing, with special demolition of the demand to withdraw two Divisions from the Army. Maybe we made a mistake in letting so many miners join the Army, but that was long ago and now they are trained soldiers, and some of the very best we have.

Levy immediately before the meeting urges me to 'withdraw' the

1 J. J. Tinker (1875–1957). Labour M.P. for Leigh 1923–45.
2 G. MacDonald, later Sir Gordon, 1st Bart (1888–1966). Labour M.P. for Ince 1929–42. Paymaster-General 1949–51.
3 Probably A. N. Braithwaite, later Sir Albert (1893–1959). Conservative M.P. for Buckrose 1926–45; Harrow West 1951–9. Braithwaite was a Director of Huddersfield Collieries Ltd, among other companies, so would have had an interest in the fuel situation.
Possibly, however, J. Gurney Braithwaite, later 1st Bart (1895–1958). Conservative M.P. for Holderness 1939–50; Sheffield Hillsborough 1931–5; Bristol North-West 1950–55. Junior minister 1951–3.
4 Marginal insertion: 'He wants me to put him on a committee to advise on it.'

scheme; otherwise, he says, I am committing political suicide. Waterhouse, who before was very pessimistic as to the Tory attitude, tells me afterwards that he thinks I have done very well but that the prejudice is still almost too strong for me. Gridley[1] gets up during the meeting and asks whether I will consider substituting 'restrictions' for rationing for coal for gas and electricity. I say that I will consider anything which gives me both economy and equity. He then asks whether I would agree to the postponement of the debate. I say no.

Later I hear that they were considerably impressed by my statement and answers and have unanimously agreed that there must be a reduction in consumption, but that they want a simpler scheme without coupons, and therefore suggest a postponement of the debate. This is not too bad.

Thence to Lord President's Committee, where the Lord President, smiling, says that his scouts tell him that I have made a considerable impression on the 1922 Committee. Kingsley Wood also says the same. ...

Dine with Maurice Webb, Gaitskell and Haydn Davies. There is a general sense of victory. Webb says that I have won a most remarkable triumph today. My stock, he says, is very high. Then follows the usual denigration of Attlee.

Friday 1st May
It is clear that the coal owners are spending a lot of money trying to get rid of me.[2]

Robin Brook to dine. Gladwyn is on leave and returns in a few days. He is going back to F.O. It is not yet settled what post he will fill there. Brook himself will return to the pool and no one will remain at Berkeley Square House except perhaps a quite junior secretary. The F.O. will have a man who will attend the meetings of the Council, but not otherwise be in the machine. It is not yet settled who this will be. He is referred to by Sir Alexander Cadogan as 'the Foreign Office spy'! Hanbury-Williams will succeed Nelson, who, as I knew already, is retiring on quite genuine grounds of ill health. He does not know anything about the show, nor about Whitehall.

Brook said that it had been clear for some time that Gladwyn and the Earl [Selborne] were not meant for one another. The latter, he says, though he supposes him to be about my age, is old enough in all other respects to be my father. He starts work soon after 10 a.m. and

---

1 Sir Arnold Gridley, later 1st Baron (1878–1965). Conservative M.P. for Stockport 1935–50; Stockport South 1950–55.
2 Marginal insertion: 'E.W. [Evan Williams] is giving lunches at the Savoy and talking against me when drunk.'

is quite tired by 6 p.m. He takes a little work home, but never deals with more than a small fraction of it. He takes long weekends and takes no work away with him, and in addition he attends many ecclesiastical functions in working hours. Thus, the other day he was reported at 11.30 a.m. to be attending the enthronement of the new Bishop of Portsmouth.[1] He does not know his way about Whitehall and Government circles, never having been a No. 1 minister before, and is not willing to be advised. He can neither make a good draft himself nor accept a good draft when presented by another. Access to him is now only got by application in the Private Office. He is also almost unbelievably slow in understanding the simplest things. Thus the pace of everything has been almost inconceivably, as compared with my days, retarded. Moreover, he takes decisions, including decisions to evacuate strong points, quite unexpectedly, and quite without any appearance of principle or of any plan of campaign. He has thrown away, notably to the Foreign Office, several such strong points and has been given a few very small sops in exchange. It is always being said that he is very close to the P.M., but so far no advantage seems to have flowed from this.[2]

Brook astonished me by saying that the Earl's relations with Bracken were now even worse than mine had ever been! I did not press him for the reasons, but he said that the Earl had completely misplayed his cards and acted in a most irregular and indefensible manner towards this most unlovely colleague.

It would, in any case, Brook thinks, have been impossible for Gladwyn to continue to work with such a Chief, whom it is inevitable that he must deeply despise. For some time there had been mutterings of a coming storm, but the critical point was only reached last week just before Gladwyn went on leave. The Earl then said that he did not want him to go on. Gladwyn had for some time found that his access to the Earl was more and more difficult, and his advice less and less heeded. It was clear to Brook that several people had been at work on the Earl undermining Gladwyn. He thought that Charles Hambro had been prominent in this. I said that this accorded with the notes of my conversations with all the Councillors[3] when they threatened rebellion. Hambro, I said, could never forget that Gladwyn had been his fag.[4] Moreover, said Brook, the Earl, as a Director of the National Provincial Bank, would look up to Hambro as a Director of the Bank of

1 Rt Rev. William Anderson (1892–1972). Bishop of Portsmouth 1942–9.
2 Marginal insertion: '([Dingle] Foot is *persona gratissima* and always in and out and Drogheda has easy access.)'
3 i.e. members of the S.O.E. Daily Council.
4 At Eton.

England. I said that I supposed George Taylor, on previous form, had also been in on this. Brook said he thought Taylor had changed sides recently. He thought Tommy Davies had been with Hambro. I said that, after I had gone, it was inevitable that Gladwyn should be subject to heavy attacks, mostly under water, from three separate sections: (1) those who hated me, and therefore hated Gladwyn because he was so conspicuously and so intimately my man; (2) those who disliked Gladwyn for his own sake, either because they did not like his manner, or because they were discomforted in debate by his quicker wits, or because they were jealous of his quick promotion, and his place in the last New Year's Honours List; and (3) by those who hated the show as a whole and were anxious to discredit all who held key positions in it. This was a formidable combination,[1] and of course the three classes overlapped a lot.

Brook said that Gladwyn had been a good deal upset when the crisis came but would no doubt have recovered his equanimity on his return from leave. He had been on the point of writing to me but had not done so before going away.

I said that I heard that the Earl had sent in a most glowing paper on the show as a whole, though I had not yet seen it. Brook said that he supposed that, although the Earl had been so short a time in office, he would already be claiming much of the credit.

Monday 4th May
Just before I go to dinner, Maurice Webb rings up and says that Lawther had made an amazing outburst to a pressman at Newcastle, saying that the miners are all against coal rationing, that there must be no interference with miners' coal, that the Executive of the D.M.A. [Durham Miners' Association] is so disturbed at his report that they have decided to send a deputation to London to see the miners' M.P.s, and the Durham County's M.P.s and the President of the Board of Trade, to protest. All this is wonderfully helpful! If it appears in the press tomorrow it will create a furore. Webb says that he is trying to get on to Lawther and to try and restrict him on to miners' coal and not to coal rationing in general.

Tuesday 5th May
Attlee urgently wishes to see me and I look in on him at 9.40 at the Dominions Office. I had thought – he had been most anxious to see me last night – that it was something to do with Will Lawther's outburst. But not so. It is that Grenfell has sent in a letter of resignation, addressed to the P.M., asking Attlee to forward it. In this letter he

1 Marginal insertion: 'H.G. thinks Drogheda did his best to down Gladwyn.'

makes complaint that he has never been treated like a proper minister, and that he has never been properly taken into consultation, that he has always been opposed to miners leaving the pits for the Army, that he had tried in vain to get them back, that he had had one interview with the P.M. in which he had explained his 'personal grievances', and that now he wished to resign. Attlee says that this is quite the wrong moment for this to happen. I note that Grenfell in his letter makes no complaint against me, nor against anyone else personally. I tell Attlee that he has never made any complaint to me about his position. On the other hand, I have let him take the Chair at the Coal Production Council partly because it is a mere talking shop and a waste of my time, and partly to appease Grenfell. I have had him in with me whenever I have had large meetings with miners or mine owners. Also on many other occasions. He has wasted my time abominably.

Attlee says that he saw Grenfell last night and that he was very difficult and complained that he was 'led about like a dog on a string'. I suppose by me?

Wednesday 6th May
A word with Butler who says that the Tories are against fuel rationing because they are afraid that it will mean that they won't get enough for their country houses. If I could offer them not only the proposed household ration but also something based on a datum period, they would all agree. I repeat this to Gaitskell, who thinks it is absolutely true, and most disgraceful. If I were to quote it outside, he says, it would do great damage.

Early this morning I tabulate a list of reasons for the resistance, among the Tories, to the Beveridge Plan.

(1) An instinctive feeling against the rationing of coal.
(2) A dislike of miners; why can't they work harder?
(3) A dislike of coupons and 'officials'.
(4) A dislike of Labour ministers in general (the *Daily Telegraph* is now daily gunning against one or other of us, Morrison, or me, or in this same group, Cripps; one of the methods is a selective printing of hostile letters).
(5) Some dislike of me in particular, though with many Tory M.P.s I am the most popular of the Labour ministers, but a recognition that I am rather 'clever' and a fear that I am trying to put through nationalisation of the mines by a side wind. (The Labour Party, on the other hand, think that rationing may be a device for evading nationalisation by a side wind.)
(6) A feeling that this plan is 'a benefit for Grenfell' and only necessary because he has made a mess of his job.

Returning to Butler, he also spoke of Jebb and said that he thought he had been treated very badly. He understood that 'the military' had been making a set at him, thinking that he occupied a position of too much influence. Butler said that Jebb might, he heard, be put in charge at the Foreign Office of a new Economic Section such as Gwatkin once had. He also remarked that Gladwyn's manner made him many enemies, but we both praised in unison his good qualities.

Meeting of Emergency Executive Council of Labour Party. Discussion on Conference arrangements. They want me to move the International resolution. It is not drafted yet, and is left for me to draft. I raise the question whether it is convenient for a minister to do this. I say it depends a good deal on what sort of resolution it is. Some are too stupid to see the point. We postpone decision until we have settled the resolution. ...

Lunch at the House. Erskine-Hill[1] is just going off to lunch with the P.M. He is anxious that I should not have misunderstood the attitude of the 1922 Committee. They are still most opposed to coupons. I say that I understood this from their announcement in the press. I suggest that he should tell the P.M. that Erskine-Hill and I will be able to arrange it between ourselves.

Further fuss about future procedure. Waterhouse rings up to the Board that the Chief Whip is very much concerned because Cripps was heckled at the end of questions and, in my absence, could not give a clear answer as to what would happen next.[2] He had said that I would explain in my speech tomorrow. They all clamoured for an undertaking that there would be a second debate on the Government's proposals. I agree with the Chief Whip that it may be said to the 1922 Committee, who are meeting again this afternoon, and also to the House tomorrow, that, having listened to all suggestions which may be put up tomorrow, the Government will publish a White Paper on their proposals, and, if there is any strong desire in the House for a further debate on this White Paper, it shall happen.

This afternoon at 3.30, as requested, I attend a meeting of Durham Labour M.P.s to meet Lawther and a 'deputation' from the D.M.A. on Durham miners' coal. On this Lawther has sent me a most hysterical letter, as well as having given a most ridiculous interview last

1 Sir Alexander Erskine-Hill, 1st Bart (1894–1947). Conservative M.P. for Edinburgh North 1935–45. Chairman of the 1922 Committee 1940–44.

2 In Question Time on 7th May, Cripps (as Leader of the House) had been asked by Arthur Greenwood to say something 'as to the conduct of the Debate on fuel rationing'. Cripps replied that Dalton would be giving an answer; that there would be a new White Paper; and that, if there was a demand for one, a further debate as well. (H.C. Debs [379], col. 1411.)

week to the press. Hardly anyone turns up to this meeting, only Whiteley, Ritson and David Adams in addition to myself. After an interval, during which people go out hunting for the missing, Lawther appears, but his 'deputation' has got lost! Lawther is very friendly and puts across the story that, when he reported to his Executive his talk with Beveridge, they all went in off the deep end and, although he told them that nothing was finally settled, there was a danger of all the pits in Durham being stopped, as a protest against any attempt to interfere in the slightest way with present arrangements for miners' coal. (Gordon MacDonald told me earlier today that the miners' M.P.s had given Lawther what for at a meeting yesterday. 'It is deplorable', said MacDonald, 'that Lawther should be our President at present. He always leads from behind; you never know where he is. But you have got thirty good friends in the miners' M.P.s in this House.') ...

It is therefore left that there shall be further discussion later, and that I shall see, if desired, a deputation from the miners' M.P.s on this subject. Meanwhile, Lawther can go back to Durham and assure his Executive that no sudden decision will be taken without full consultation with them.

Nearly at the end of this meeting, the 'deputation' from the D.M.A. appears, in the form of two large, friendly, stupid miners, both of whom know and like me quite well. They seem quite reassured by my statement. How everyone helps me!

On 7th May, Dalton addressed the House for more than an hour on the subject of fuel rationing, commending the Beveridge scheme in principle, without committing himself to all its details, and inviting suggestions from the House. He argued, in particular, that the only alternative to rationing was to take 30,000 miners out of the Army – the equivalent of two divisions. To do so would be 'to pick the eyes out of large sections of our striking force'. A comprehensive fuel rationing scheme was therefore urgently necessary, not only to reduce total domestic consumption, but also 'to make an equitable and orderly distribution of the diminished quantity'.[1]

Thursday 7th May
Fuel rationing debate in the House. ... I begin to speak at 1.15 and don't finish till 2.40. Out of this hour and 25 minutes a good deal is occupied by answering a series of questions and interjections. It is

1 H.C. Debs, 7th May 1942 [379], cols 1461, 1478.

generally thought that I make out a formidable case, very difficult to answer. ...

I spend a good deal of time expounding the main features of the Beveridge report. I make it clear that we are not committed to this particular plan but are inviting suggestions from the House. The only suggestion comes from Gridley. All the rest merely talk about more production, or propaganda to economise fuel. Gridley's scheme is pulled to bits by Cripps at the end, in a rather injudicious, unkind speech, which much worries the Chief Whip who is sitting beside him, as well as Gerald Palmer,[1] Cripps's Tory P.P.S., who sits behind him biting his lips. But by this time the House is rather thin.

Wilmot makes excellent arrangements for speakers on our side, but George Isaacs, whom he had briefed, rushed away in a fit of temper because Ivor Thomas was called before him, and he suspected that this was through the machinations with the Chair of me or Wilmot. Jealousy is the foundation of public life. Green eyes glare from every thicket at every passer-by in the political jungle. Thomas doesn't do well, I am told – while he spoke I was having a late lunch at 3.45 p.m., having taken the precaution to have a relatively large breakfast at 8 consisting of two sausages and a rasher of bacon. He seems to be unpopular, partly because thought to be supercilious and partly because known to be intelligent and young. He will get over it in time. He is young enough for it not to matter that he is unpopular now.

Dine with Wilmot and Gaitskell at the Coquille. General feeling is that we have had a very good day indeed. It has gone very much better than I expected. I thought that there would be much more declamation against coupons. Erskine-Hill was going to speak towards the end of the debate, but, thinking the life was all out of it, lurched off, having first spoken to Kingsley Wood, and asked whether his act would be regarded as an act of 'desertion'. Wood had said no.

Always when I have a momentary success in this infinitely protracted business, my close adherents think we have won a final victory. I am always more doubtful. We are not yet out of the wood. We have today undertaken to make a White Paper to be issued next week, and then, if desired, for another debate to take place. I am not at all sure how this will go. ...

Friday 8th May
Press Gallery buffet lunch at House of Commons. Cripps is the guest. He is most frightfully dull. Never a flicker of humour. Winterton,[2] on

---

1 G. E. H. Palmer (b. 1904). Conservative M.P. for Winchester 1935–45. P.P.S. to Sir Stafford Cripps.
2 Lord Winterton, q.v.

the other hand, is very funny, relating how thirty-five years ago he went with other young Tories to Dundee to try to defeat the present Prime Minister, then a Liberal candidate, at a by-election caused by his promotion. The P.M.'s supporters used to empty buckets of ...... on to the speakers at the open-air meetings. These Tories, therefore, went round in a gang and always had one man on guard to warn the others of what was coming. But one of their party, now a Duke and even then very deaf, did not hear the warning and got a bucketful right on his head. Whereupon, said Winterton, he left the meeting looking and smelling like an amateur sewage farm, while the successful marksman cried from aloft, 'Thus perish all bloody Tories.'

The press generally think I did very well yesterday and that the battle is as good as won. ...

At six o'clock I have a conference, which Cripps attends, and also Beveridge, Overton, Watkinson and Gaitskell. Not very satisfactory. Beveridge full of egoism and petulance. He thinks the new White Paper should say that the Government had adopted the Beveridge plan, just like that, subject to a few very minor alterations. (He afterwards tells Watkinson, whom I have asked to make a draft for the White Paper, that he does not consent to any change at all in the wording of his first report.) He is a most tiresome man! He also wanted to be allowed to begin to broadcast in favour of his scheme forthwith, i.e. before the House of Commons had even seen my White Paper, let alone considered it. I say bluntly that this is hopelessly bad policy and would set everyone against it, him and me. He seems not to understand. I wish these people would realise that I am a professional politician and they are not.

Following this confabulation I am in deep gloom.

Saturday 9th May

Visit Kingsley Wood at the Treasury and discuss the prospects. He says he is afraid that Wardlaw-Milne[1] and Herbert Williams[2] may divide against our proposals. This might mean forty or fifty Tories in the Division Lobby against the Government. Wood by himself would do us more good than harm, but with Wardlaw-Milne as well it might be awkward. Wardlaw-Milne, he thinks, made a very bitter and unhelpful speech on Thursday. I say that I am seeing Gridley, and indi-

---

1 Sir John S. Wardlaw-Milne (1878–1967). Conservative M.P. for Kidderminster 1922–45.
2 Sir Herbert Williams, later 1st Bart (1884–1954). Conservative M.P. for Croydon South 1932–45; Reading 1924–9; Croydon East 1950–54. Junior minister 1928–9.

cate the concessions which I think we might make to him. Wood says that the Chief Whip has rung him up in some concern, and he is seeing him this afternoon. Wood says, 'You and I had better do a bit of whispering next week.' He seems quite sound on the general question. I ask about Erskine-Hill. He says that he carries some weight, but not as much as is supposed. His chief use is to go about whispering, if he can be got to whisper the right thing. He went to lunch last week with the P.M. and they got talking about this matter. P.M. wanted to know all about it. Wood thinks this is a great mistake. P.M. ought to stick to the war. He doesn't understand these domestic questions. Wood quite agrees that the matter should come before the War Cabinet so as to get a final decision.

Gridley calls at 11.20 and I take him on for a meeting at 11.30 at Gwydyr House where I take the Chair, with Cripps, Beveridge, Watkinson, Gerald Palmer and Gaitskell. A long and most unsatisfactory meeting. Gridley is very self-important, very slow and stupid, very anti-Beveridge, and quite fanatically anti-coupon. He argues back against Cripps's points in Thursday's debate, but very inconclusively. He and Beveridge wrangle together on everything including what the Coal Merchants think. Cripps suggests that I should get hold of the Coal Merchants on Monday morning and confront them with Beveridge and Gridley and see whether they prefer, if there must be rationing, coupons or marking off. I agree to this. This is as far as we can get. ...

I send away all my officials and dictate a draft White Paper on fuel rationing for the War Cabinet. This is very nearly Beveridge, but put freshly and more simply, and with a few new details (e.g. actual rations) and a few faint concessions to Gridley. It is a good paper, very clear and simple.

Sunday 10th May

Gladwyn to breakfast. He brings with him a quantity of papers, which we work through. A lump of these is to be destroyed; a lump to be kept by him; and a lump by me. A particularly key paper, for which I had asked, is to be retyped in riddles with a key to these in a separate envelope.

Gladwyn has just returned from leave, immediately before which he was 'sacked by the Earl'. For some fortnight beforehand he had felt that things were not very good. It is clear that an intrigue has been conducted against him by a number of people. He and I agree that Charles Hambro was prominent in this. Hambro 'lives by bluff and charm'. Gladwyn says that the Earl, being a Director of the National and Provincial Bank, looks up to a Director of the Bank of England! The Earl is stupid, slow and – worst of all – quite unpredictable. He keeps no records of any of his conversations, and this lands him in much trouble. He met Bracken at some Club for luncheon and some days afterwards said that they had reached a quite definite agreement on the division between their two shows in Mid-East and elsewhere. When Gladwyn raised this question with the Earl, he said, 'Oh I settled all that with the Minister of Information.' He then wrote off a letter, based on his recollection, which was vehemently repudiated by Bracken. Gladwyn had sensed a gradual cooling off in his own relations with the Earl – I said that I thought the other Earl [Drogheda] had also played his part in bringing this about – and things had come to a head when Gladwyn had put in a Minute proposing that, in view of C.D.'s retirement, he should himself move to Baker Street and should, with M. [Gubbins] take charge; he of politics and M. of the operations. The Earl had asked him to come and speak to him and had then said that he had come to the conclusion that Gladwyn's position was too difficult, since it gave rise to divided loyalties. The Earl was in favour of a policy of 'complete honesty with the Foreign Office'. This was going to operate through a Foreign Office nominee, or spy, sitting in on the Council. I press Gladwyn as to who was intended for this role, and he said O'Malley. He and I both agreed that this appointment would be ridiculous. This man was no better than a neutral in the war. Gladwyn thought that the Earl had got a child's conditioned reflex: G.J. – trouble with F.O. There had been a violent incident, resulting from Campbell[1] 'making a clean breast' to Salazar over S.O.E. The Foreign Office thought this was right. Jebb thought it was quite wrong, and said so in no equivocal terms. This was what finished things off.

There had been much talk about an 'enquiry' and vague hints of 'corruption'. The only sphere where any sort of case could possibly be made was North America. Here Beaumont-Nesbitt had perhaps employed some unsuitable agents ... The Earl had made his own 'enquiry' and had sent in a glowing report to the P.M. of substantially the same material that I had sent in in my final report, dwelling particularly on the high quality of staff over which 'Mr Jebb and Sir Frank Nelson preside'. Even after this there had been pressure for an enquiry, and the name of Mr Justice Singleton[2] had been suggested by the P.M. But this had been resisted for some time, and it had then been found that Singleton was not available in any case.

1 Sir Ronald Hugh Campbell, q.v., Ambassador to Portugal 1940–45.
2 Sir John Singleton, Lord Justice Singleton (1885–1957). Judge of the King's Bench Division 1934–48. Conservative M.P. 1922–3.

Hanbury-Williams had now been brought in as No. 2 to Hambro. He was a complete innocent, both as regards operations and as regards Whitehall. Gladwyn had been telling him various things which had profoundly disturbed him. I said that I thought he was no use. It was thought that pressure for the 'enquiry' had come from Eden. Now in F.O., Gladwyn thinks, there is some regret at what had happened. They say now that they have lost the only two people whom they trusted, namely Gladwyn himself and C.D. George Taylor has changed sides at the last moment, Hambro has told Hanbury-Williams, and is now devoted to Gladwyn! In the Foreign Office it is thought, Gladwyn says, that he has been badly treated, and it is not yet decided what he is to do. He himself would like to be the Foreign Office official in charge of relations with P.W.E. and S.O.E. Lockhart would then live in Bush House. Gladwyn would then have, as his No. 2, Ward,[1] whom I don't know but of whom he speaks highly. This would indeed put him back into a position of great influence, but it seems to me unlikely that this could be arranged. Cadogan does not wish him to go abroad, but wants to keep him in some job close to the war effort. He is proposing to Cadogan that he should have the substantive rank of Counsellor as from the time when I appointed him Acting Assistant Under-Secretary of State.

Gladwyn asks me, and so does his wife, with whom and him I lunch, whether I think he would do well in politics. I say I think not. He is good at handling small groups of intelligent people, but I doubt whether he could handle large groups of unintelligent people and anyhow politics is a chancy business and he should not forget the failure of that bright boy Harold Nicolson. He says finally that he thinks it might be useful for him to let it be known that he was thinking of taking up politics in the event of the Foreign Office failing to find him something reasonably good.

Watkinson to see me. He is working out details very well.

Dine with Leslie Nicholls, who is soon going to Middle East and is friendly and sentimental. Conference after dinner with Gaitskell.

In June 1942, a separate Ministry of Fuel and Power was created, no longer under Dalton's jurisdiction. Dalton had been keen on this separation from the start, partly because of difficulties in managing Grenfell, but mainly for organisational reasons. 'I told both Churchill and Attlee that I was equally

1 Possibly J. G. Ward, later Sir John (b. 1909). First Secretary at the Foreign Office 1941–6.

willing to be Minister of Fuel and Power, or President of the Board of Trade, without Fuel and Power,' he recalled; 'but that it was impossible for any man, however fit and however hard a worker, to do justice to both these jobs in the conditions of this war.'[1]

Monday 11th May

Beveridge breaks to me the not unwelcome news that he thinks the time has now come when we should divide our forces, at least temporarily, so that he can regain his freedom to speak and write. With an appearance of reluctance and broken-heartedness, I acquiesce. ...

Dine in and go later to Attlee, with whom I discuss coal rows, including Grenfell, rationing, and reorganisation. He has had a long talk with Hyndley, who is most anxious for Grenfell to be shifted but not sacked. I say that I am more and more keen on the creation of a separate Ministry of Fuel and Power. At present I can't get anywhere near my many other problems at the Board of Trade. Attlee wonders whether Hyndley could not become Minister in the Lords, with Grenfell as his second-in-command in the Commons. I say I don't think this would do, both because Grenfell would be terribly offended and because he would be quite unable to handle the business in the Commons. I press that he should be made P.M.G. [Postmaster-General], in which case Morrison[2] could become M.F.P. [Minister of Fuel and Power] with a Labour Under-Secretary. Alternatively, Attlee suggests Grenfell might become Secretary to the D.O.T. [Department of Overseas Trade]. But I don't think this would do; it would be clearly demotion. I suggest again making him Joint Under-Secretary at the Foreign Office, but Attlee does not think that Eden would jump at this. Attlee says that Grenfell says that, 'up to a certain moment' in Duncan's time, Grenfell was Minister of Mines. From that time on he has been treated as an office boy. Grenfell thinks this is so under me. I say that he has never frankly complained to me about anything. Attlee says, 'The trouble is he never does speak frankly; he only broods. And', he added, 'you have got a very quick mind and he has got a very slow one.'

1 FY, p. 388.
2 W. S. Morrison, later 1st Viscount Dunrossil (1893–1961). Postmaster-General 1940–43; Minister of Town and Country Planning 1943–5. Conservative M.P. for Cirencester and Tewkesbury 1929–59. Financial Secretary to the Treasury 1935–6; Minister of Agriculture and Fisheries 1936–9; Chancellor of the Duchy of Lancaster 1939–40; Minister of Food 1939–40. Speaker of the House of Commons 1951–9. Governor General of Australia 1959–61.

Tuesday 12th May

A bathroom brain-wave! I am in danger of being isolated and shot up on fuel rationing. This, in itself, is not a sufficient issue on which either to resign or to have a tremendous battle. Hardly anyone, *pace* Beveridge and Gaitskell, both of whom are 'too intelligent', as Wilmot says, is eagerly behind me, though I am supported pretty well by *The Times, Yorkshire Post, Manchester Guardian, Daily Herald* and *Economist*. Therefore, think I, let me rejoin the main body of my natural allies. If we are to have a row on coal, let us have a big row on the thing as a whole, including organisation. Therefore, let me propose to the Cabinet that we postpone further consideration of fuel rationing until we can place before the House a complete programme of action, covering production, consumption and organisation. This will not be till after Whitsun, but that will have the further advantage of allowing passions to cool. Meanwhile, it can be truly said that we are acceding to the wishes expressed in various parts of the House, both among those Tories who clamoured for more production rather than – or as well as – rationing, and those Labour Members who feared that the rationing proposals were a dodge to shelve reorganisation.

Wilmot, to whom I confide this thought, is enthusiastically in favour. Gaitskell also thinks it quite bright. I, therefore, proceed to the House to answer my questions at eleven, the Cabinet being at noon. I canvass both Attlee and Cripps on the Bench, and get their agreement. Likewise Kingsley Wood, emerging from the lavatory, in a walk down the passage. Likewise Anderson, with whom I have a longer talk in his room. He has a new coal fear. There may soon be large numbers of American soldiers in this country desirous of heating themselves up to the temperature they are accustomed to in the U.S.A. He says that it is being said by Tories that I only got the support of the Labour Party to rationing by telling them that the alternative was a lengthening of miners' hours, which otherwise the Tories would propose. I tell him that this is quite untrue. (Another rumour running about these days is that I got the Labour Party to support rationing because I told them that nationalisation would soon follow!) I also tell Anderson that it really is essential to create a separate Ministry of Fuel. The present task of the President of the Board of Trade is quite intolerable. I propound to him also the idea of moving Grenfell to the Post Office. He says that W. S. Morrison has been rather a failure, both at the Ministry of Agriculture (over milk) and at the Ministry of Food. But it is important, he agrees, 'to provide for Grenfell'. This seems now a major problem of the war. He thinks that Gwilym Lloyd George might make a good Minister of Fuel and Power. His appointment would also appease his old father, which would have political advantages. I also think well of it, since he is neither Conservative nor Labour. He could have another miner as his Under-Secretary, plus Geoffrey Lloyd. But this does not yet 'provide' for Grenfell, who certainly would not be willing to take over No. 2 to Woolton. Anderson thinks that the question of Minister of Fuel and Power might be raised in Cabinet this morning, since Grenfell will not be there.

At the Cabinet we spend an hour and twenty minutes on this one subject. I have never thought so ill of the P.M., nor been so vexed by him before. He talks more than half the time, and has clearly not concentrated his mind on the details of the subject at all. This is another and a worse repetition of our seance the other day on men from the Army. He argues at immense length, almost alone, against a substantial majority of his colleagues. He is quite unconvinced of the need of any rationing. He thinks that a broadcast appeal by himself would do the trick, followed up by a press campaign. We explain at tedious length that at this season of the year it is important to stock up and that it is impossible to be sure whether coal goes into the cellars, as it should, or the grate, as it should not. Therefore it would not be possible for months to determine whether his appeal had succeeded or not. And then it would be too late. To this he can only reply that the Air Raid Wardens could carry out inspections of people's cellars to see whether they were storing or burning their coal! He has received a letter from Dugdale,[1] Chairman of the Tory Party organisation, saying that the feelings of the Party are very strong against the Beveridge scheme. They think they would lose a lot of votes at by-elections. The Chief Whip, a poor, wispy creature, I begin to think, says that opinion in the Tory Party in the House is very much against the scheme and that at least sixty or seventy, and perhaps a hundred, Tories would vote against the Government on it, and many more would abstain. The P.M. says that last year they were told things would be very awkward in the winter, and yet they weren't. Why should it be any worse this time?

Eden is very wobbly, and Lyttelton significantly silent during this discussion. Anderson, Bevin, Cripps and I, with faint support from Attlee, put the other view. Sinclair, called in to represent the Liberal Party, is also more or less on our side. I, however, present the view, at an early stage of the meeting, that we should postpone the decision till after Whitsun and then do the whole thing in one. This is rather gratefully accepted by most, though the P.M. maunders on much too long trying to get us to agree that we should put all rationing schemes

1 Major Sir Thomas Dugdale, later 1st Baron Crathorne (1897–1977). Government Whip 1937–42. Conservative M.P. for Richmond, Yorks 1929–59. Minister of Agriculture and Fisheries 1951–4.

aside and let him go on the air instead. This is finally discouraged on the grounds that it would be unfair to him to risk a failure. I come out from this meeting very vexed. The P.M.'s mind is nowhere near the merits of this problem, and he has been wholly swayed by Cherwell, who will have told him that on the figures rationing is not necessary, and by the Tory Party representations. He does not react at all to my observation that Erskine-Hill did wrong to write to the Sunday papers. Attlee and Cripps are also, momentarily at least, very furious at the

THE NEW METER, MUM

manner of the meeting. I don't think many people realise how well I have now reinsured my political future. Now, a number of us will sink or swim together. Had I not performed this tactical manoeuvre, there might have been some danger that I might sink alone.

The P.M. had been very struck by Low's cartoon of the meter. As for Beveridge, he said, 'He's getting very long in the tooth.' Cripps thinks that Lyttelton is the sinister influence behind the scenes in this and other matters. ...

Coal Committee. Gowers and Major Egbert Cadbury[1] give evidence. The former is in favour of nationalisation after the war and

1 Major E. Cadbury, later Sir Egbert (1893–1967). Regional Controller at the Ministry of Fuel and Power, S.W. Region 1941–50. Managing Director of J. S. Fry and Sons Ltd 1920–63; Cadbury Bros Ltd 1943–63.

against it while the war is on, on the ground that it would create too much commotion. He would like Regional Commissioners with drastic powers to give orders for reorganisation, closing collieries, moving men, etc. Any Company which failed to comply should be taken over. He does not think that his Coal Commission would be of any value for any such purposes as this.

Dine with Attlee to meet Evatt.[1] Also present Bevin, Alexander and Greenwood. The latter is quite deplorable. He arrives half squiffed and constantly interrupts, with a stream of fatuous nothings, the conversation of everybody else. But Evatt seems to think it is not a bad evening!

Thursday 14th May

On Tuesday, the day before yesterday, it was just three weeks since I gave the Parliamentary answer, on 21st April, on fuel rationing which, much to the surprise of most of us, started the storm which has now taken all my time to navigate for these twenty-one days. And we are not yet in harbour. It has been a most crashing bore, though it may be that we shall get more of our own way on organisation, now that everything is to be taken together, than we would have done otherwise.

This is what is in Pethick's mind, I find, when I raise the matter at the Administrative Committee today. The miners' M.P.s, who are a majority of this Committee, see at once the advantage of tying everything up together. I do not disguise from them that it was the 1922 Committee which obstructed, if not upset, my applecart, and I say nothing to discourage verbal reprisals, some of which are promised this weekend. There is increasing evidence of a seething discontent in the mines. Now it focuses on wages. The elderly miner finds he is getting less money than his son and daughter working at munitions, and that they say and think that 'the old man's no good'. Horner last week, for the first time, failed to get a good hearing in South Wales. At the end of his speech someone said, 'Why do you talk of everything under the sun, except our wages?'

Sunday 17th May

Some Thoughts (better written than dictated)[2]

West Leaze

I feel almost out of office. It's a mixed sensation. I should be free of routine and responsibility for all things large and small in a Depart-

---

1 H. V. Evatt (1894–1965). Australian Labour politician. Australian representative in U.K. Cabinet 1942–5. Australian War Cabinet 1941–6. Member of Commonwealth Advisory Council 1941–5. Attorney-General and Minister of Foreign Affairs 1941–9.

2 This entry is handwritten on a loose sheet of lined notepaper.

ment, and of those boring long-drawn-out Committee meetings with colleagues, and even of the War Cabinet – how dreams fade when one wakes – with desultory, uninstructed monologue, and suggestions that A.R.P. wardens should look in people's cellars to see whether they're burning or storing coal! I should be able to spend a week, or even weeks, on end down here in the summer. (But without Ruth or other visitors for short spells, it would be very lonely. And arrangements about services and rations would be tiresome.)

I should be free to speak and write again, as I felt and not as I was constrained by ministerial prudence, and the perpetual pending of undecided, and therefore unmentionable, questions. If I went out the right way, I might greatly strengthen my position in the Labour Party.

On the other hand, I should miss, after a week or two, a great many things. The power to take decisions, a lot of which may make a bit of difference – some inside knowledge of what is going on; the prestige, and the conveniences, including the salary, etc., of being a minister. I should have to try to find, I suppose, a small service flat somewhere, preferably in Westminster, or a temporary provisional abode with someone, and there would be a bother about my furniture, and my letters, and Mrs Dean, whom I have now got firmly employed at the Board of Trade.

And, on a longer view, I should miss the chance of having anything serious to do with the settlement at the end of the war – or should I? For how would I go out of office, and who else would go? Certainly we are approaching a Coal Crisis. If the Tories come to party-life again over rationing, what will they say to taking over the mines in some form? And other necessary changes? And, if these aren't done, how can some of us, or any of us of the Labour Party, stay in the Government? But the more *they* play the party [game] the closer I must keep to my political friends. Beyond all this, coal is a very great danger to our war effort.

Monday 18th May

Lunch with Mrs Phillimore. Also present Attlee and two Jugs, Jovanović[1] and Ninčić.[2] Nothing of any note said at lunch. Afterwards I tell Attlee that we may be nearing a crash, and that I anticipate some liveliness at the Labour Party Conference next week. I said I was quite disgusted at the last proceedings at the War Cabinet. We seemed to

---

1 Slobadan Jovanović (1869–1958). Prime Minister and Minister of the Interior in the Yugoslav government-in-exile 1942–3.

2 Momčilo Ninčić (1876–1949). Yugoslav economist and politician. Minister of Foreign Affairs in the Yugoslav government-in-exile 1941–3. Vice-President of the Radical Party.

get nowhere and there had been no thought by those not on the Lord President's Committee. He said, with some irritation, that it was always like this. I said that something must soon change or we should not avoid a break.

Coal Committee. I had come back from West Leaze in a state of great gloom, and disposed to think that we were on the edge of a major political crisis. Maybe I am still right, but this afternoon's proceedings were strangely easy and optimistic.

Both Dalton and Bevin regarded the Committee set up by the War Cabinet in April to consider reorganisation of the coal industry as an opportunity to do something for the miners. Bevin advocated a separate, independently chaired, National Wages Body and this was broadly accepted on 19th May.

A White Paper on Coal was agreed by ministers on 1st June. This laid down the principle of 'dual control' – the State directing mining operations wherever necessary while the colliery owners continued to be responsible for the finances of the mines. Much of Bevin's formula, including a National Coal Board, was adopted. A Fuel Rationing Scheme formed an annexe to the White Paper, to await a later decision; but rationing was never introduced.

Dalton was much relieved at the outcome. What had looked like becoming a humiliating personal defeat became, in the end, a compromise. Yet, if not a humiliation for Dalton, it was certainly a victory for the 1922 Committee – the only successful Conservative revolt against the Churchill administration; and there was some justification in Aneurin Bevan's jibe: 'The State steps in, not in substitution of private interests, but as their guardian.'[1]

Tuesday 19th May
Cripps mentions to me on the Bench that he had a very unsatisfactory talk with the P.M. last night. The latter, he says, is back where he was weeks ago and against all real action; against any form of rationing 'until December', and against anything that would upset the mine owners or the Tory Party. Cripps says he is prepared to go out on this. I say that we must have a word about it before nightfall.

Communications come pouring in from Durham, by letter and telegram, about unrest in the coalfields, largely due, it seems, to the high wages being earned by workers in munition factories. They are sending a deputation jointly from the owners and the men on Friday afternoon. I am trying to arrange to see Lawther on Thursday morn-

1 Cited in M. Foot, *Aneurin Bevan: A Biography*, vol. 1, MacGibbon & Kee, London, 1962, pp. 358–9.

ing, i.e. after the miners' leaders have seen our Coal Committee. ...

Anderson, I and Grenfell with Lord Hyndley now always trailing along like another little dog – he looks just like one – go over a draft War Cabinet paper on manpower in the pits. Not bad at all. A demand is maintained for men from the Fighting Front, though in moderate numbers. Rationing is kept in as an essential means of economy, and there is a veiled reference to the coming hosts from the West. Also to other possible 'operations' which would absorb shipping and railway transport otherwise available for moving coal.

I play for presenting to the War Cabinet our proposals as a whole, and therefore delay my new ration paper over the weekend. It should come to a head about the same time as organisation. These two, with manpower, will make three papers to be bound into one.

After a short interval we meet again in Anderson's room at the House for Cabinet Coal Committee. Very discursive. Bevin talks nearly all the time. I say at one point, 'I want to support you, but you won't let me get a word in edgeways.' It is really a disease: perpetual verbal diarrhoea. He has, however, produced quite a good paper on the functions of a National Board, proposing that this should be under the Chairmanship of 'The Minister' and that there should be a separate National Wages Body, from which the Minister should keep free. This, therefore, should have an independent Chairman. Kingsley Wood is very much on his guard against the National Board being anything more than 'advisory', a word he frequently repeats. Lyttelton is very disappointing in all these coal discussions. He has never intervened at all except to protect the financial interests of colliery companies against losses due to working for maximum output in the short run. Judged on this form – I am sure he is often quite good and much broader-minded on other problems – he has only the narrowest financier's outlook.

...

Dine with Victor Cazalet, who thinks we cannot possibly win the war with the present P.M. He has, however, no good alternative. He has heard that the P.M., acting, as always, on impulse, is always on the point of firing high commanders in Whitehall or in the field. Thus, he hears, he almost fired Portal the other day, and Auchinleck – and everyone but Pound! Cazalet is also much disturbed at the prospect of our letting the Russians have the small Baltic States. He hears that Molotov[1] may be arriving here any day now to sign a Treaty. He thinks that Eden has under-estimated the opposition to this in Parliament, and that some members of the Government, including Duff

1 V. Molotov (b. 1890). Soviet Foreign Minister 1939–49, 1953–6. Deputy Chairman of the Council of Ministers 1953–7.

Cooper, might resign over it. He says that Cripps has been pushing for this and asked him to come and see him about it the other night. He says the Poles are very much disturbed at this. I say they need not be. They are quite in a different class from Lits and Lats. He gives me a copy of his 'Private Diary' of his trip with Sikorski to Russia, with an inscription 'To a lover of the Poles ...... hoping this will blow away some of the coal dust.' I had said that I came to him trailing clouds, not of glory but of coal dust. On coal itself he has not much to say, nor, deliberately, have I. This nice little man has no judgment and carries no guns. But he is a reed through which other people's talk blows.

Thence, at 10.30 p.m., to see Cripps in his flat at Whitehall Court. The inevitable Lady Eno[1] sits in. He says that the P.M. on coal has swung back and is now 'most reactionary'. He would like just to make a broadcast appeal, and have a press campaign, and let things go, without rationing, till December. Then, if we were really short of coal, we could close down several large munition works, since we shall then have produced more shells than we can ever hope to fire. Also we must do nothing that would antagonise the owners or the Tory Party. The 1922 Committee have now reported to the P.M. that there should be no rationing but only appeals, and this has influenced him a good deal. Cripps says that this is an issue on which he is prepared to resign. It is essential to requisition the pits. Otherwise our Regional Directors will be thwarted. The question is, who runs the Government? Is it the 1922 Committee? I refer again to my paper of 31st March, by which, on merits, I stand. I say that I should be prepared for a deal, having a second-rate rationing plan for the time being, provided we got effective reorganisation of the industry. But I shall not at present agree to any concession. I say that we must keep in touch and not act independently. I also say that it is essential quickly to create a Ministry of Fuel and Power. The present position at the Board of Trade is quite impossible. I have no time for anything but coal and, even when dealing with this, there is the continual ambiguity and heavy burden of Grenfell. Cripps says that the P.M. is now at last quite decided to make this new Ministry. Gwilym [Lloyd George] is definitely designated for it, with Gordon MacDonald as Parliamentary Secretary. Cripps would have preferred Griffiths; he is inclined to think that MacDonald has 'a slack manner' as an administrator. I, on the other hand, defend MacDonald. Cripps says that the P.M. would like to get rid of all our other 'proposals' and simply to announce the creation of the new Ministry and some propaganda for economy. I say this is quite impossible. Cripps says that the P.M. is

1 Dalton's name for Lady Cripps, née Swithenbank, later Dame Isobel (1891–1979).

going to tell Attlee that he is determined to get rid of Grenfell. Cripps also adds that it is 'settled' that the latter is to be Chairman of the Development Commission. This is said just as we are parting, and I think he probably means Forestry Commission. But I am not at all sure that Grenfell would accept this. Perhaps at this stage it wouldn't matter much if he didn't.

Thence to call at 11.15 p.m. on Attlee at No. 11. I have the impression that he is seeing less of the P.M., while Cripps is seeing more. He gives me the impression tonight of being rolled up very tight in a frightened little ball. He was rather afraid of his followers over coal. At next week's Conference, he thinks, 'They might help us a lot, but I am afraid they won't.' I say that he must be prepared to spend a lot of time, both in the Conference and in National Executives; also that we ought to have a meeting of Labour No. 1. ministers during the weekend.

Wednesday 20th May
Coal Committee from 3 to 5 p.m. ... After the meeting, I have a few words with Bevin and Grenfell. Bevin says that he is afraid the miners' leaders may miss the chance of a lifetime in rejecting our proposals for a National Board. If this Government broke up, if anything happened to Winston, we might get a most reactionary Prime Minister. In that case, the men would get nothing. I tell him that Cripps is threatening to resign unless we requisition the pits. He is very impatient at this and says he has no tolerance for anyone who talks like that. Cripps has found, coming into the Government at a late stage of the war, that much more has been done than he supposed and that there is much less scope for large changes now. Just before we left the meeting Bevin had been momentarily indignant with me because I said that nobody knew what 'requisition' meant, and that I would be quite prepared, if we requisitioned the industry, to give up coupons and have a second-rate rationing scheme instead. Bevin said, 'You mustn't let down your colleagues like this.' It was he, he reminds us, who used the word 'requisition' in the House. As to rationing, he hopes that I shall stick to it. He will make a statement tomorrow in Parliament, in the course of which he will 'let out a few figures' which will astonish the world. These will, I gather, hint at the coming of the Americans in great swarms. The result will be to widen the coal gap to be filled by increased production on the one hand and rationing on the other. He is very keen that I should stick to a drastic rationing scheme.

The developing crisis in the coalfields had produced eighty-six short strikes in the first three weeks of May, involving 58,000 men. 12,000 men came out on strike at Bolsover on 21st May.

Thursday 21st May

Haydn Davies to see me. I say that, on the whole, I think he had better go back full time to the *Star* as their second Parliamentary representative. He will continue to see me at the House and have favoured access to the Press Department here, and we shall thus remove one vulnerable point. He agrees to this quite happily, particularly as I lead in, by a reference to forthcoming by-elections in London, [to the subject of] Labour seats and undertake to say a word to Shepherd.[1]

Douglas Jay comes with Gaitskell to discuss the terms of his transfer. We agree to leave it for the moment, until things become clearer as regards the new Ministry of Fuel and Power, etc.

Lunch with Sikorski and Retinger only. Sikorski is sixty-one today and I score by knowing this. It was in the *Daily Telegraph* List of Birthdays, which I always read, since I find that people are most delighted when one knows this detail on the right day. Molotov arrived last night. Sikorski is very much concerned lest the Anglo-Soviet Treaty should adversely affect Polish interests. He might even feel moved to make a public protest about this. I say I hope this will not be necessary. What interest, I ask, has he in the Baltic States, apart from Lithuania? He admits none in Ests and Lats. Even as to Lits, he admitted that he didn't want Memel, particularly as I impressed on him that he should get the whole East Prussian coast and Danzig. 'Yes, and Königsberg,' he said, with an eager look in his eye. I said that, as he knew, Stalin had offered him the line of the Oder. He said that that was 'only a provocation'. He could not take over an area containing so many Germans. I said that he can drive them out, but he still seemed to think that this was too large an operation. In East Prussia there were all the Kashubians. He was also quite prepared to take the whole Silesian coalfields, but not, certainly not, the Oder. Nor could he agree, he said, to surrender any of East Poland. The Russians, he added, were claiming both Vilna and Lwów. I said that I should be against his giving up either of these historic cities, but thought that, in return for satisfactory Western frontiers, he could agree to some rectification in the East. But the picture must, of course,

1 G. R. Shepherd, later Lord Shepherd (1881–1954). Labour Party National Agent 1929–46.

be seen as a whole. He said the Americans would be very much against our signing away the Baltic States. He recognised, on the other hand, that the Russians must have warm water ports in the Baltic. I said that, perhaps, we could make some arrangement for 'cultural autonomy'. In fact, I think it is too silly for words to boggle over the Baltic States. The Russians will get them when they drive the Germans back and we shall never take any steps to dispossess them.

Sikorski said at the Kremlin Stalin said to him that he himself would sign the Soviet-Polish Treaty. 'This is the first time I ever signed a Treaty,' Stalin said. He then pointed to Molotov and said, 'I keep him to sign Treaties which will never be observed.'

From the Poles to the Coal Committee. Oh God! Oh Montreal! This afternoon we have the owners. They are not *quite* so frightful as last time and put in a paper in which they support the proposal for a Regional Officer with large powers. They make a great song about men leaving the pits with bogus medical certificates.

When they have withdrawn, Anderson says that he thinks now our line is pretty clear. We are agreed (1) on the need for a Regional Officer with powers, (2) for some kind of National Body, (3) for some better arrangements for dealing with absenteeism. Bevin then says, 'Have we made up our minds to reject requisitioning?' Anderson says he thinks we are all impressed with the difficulties of this and adds, looking towards Grenfell, 'I think the Secretary for Mines is against it?' Grenfell says, 'Yes.' I then say that I incline to the other view. I put in a paper on 31st March from which, though I hope my mind is not unduly fixed, I have as yet seen no reason to withdraw on any substantial point. Our purpose is more coal. This can only be got if we have the good will of the men. We have been told that they attach great importance to requisitioning. We must take this most seriously into account. Moreover, we are still waiting for the answers of the men to the questions put to them by Anderson. We cannot reach a decision till we have these answers. In further discussion Duncan says that requisitioning was tried in the last war and failed, and Lyttelton raises some point about financial arrangements. (I am coming to take rather a black view of both these colleagues. Often they seem only to be capitalist stooges in our midst.) I say that I think all these objections can be met, and Anderson asks me to make a paper on the subject. This I agree to do. This is to be taken on Tuesday next, the same day as my paper on fuel rationing.

Later in the evening I go to No. 11 for a confab with Attlee, Cripps and Bevin. I give the first two, before Bevin arrives, some account of what has been going on. Cripps is most insistent that we stick to requisitioning. He repeats that this is an issue on which we really ought to fight. Attlee, still rather frightened of the situation, agrees. Bevin is not quite so sure, but attaches great importance to his own declaration on behalf of H.M.G., in which the blessed word 'requisition' first appeared. He hopes that I will quote this in my paper. Bevin did not like the conference with the miners. He wonders whether Grenfell is in league with some of them. He noted that Grenfell is against requisitioning. 'And he is a miner.' He linked this up with Bevin's remark that the miners were not all agreed with the N.C.L. [National Council of Labour] scheme. Bevin has bad memories of the miners in 1926. 'They are very queer people.'

Friday 22nd May
10 a.m. Lord President's Committee. We start on Anderson's paper for the War Cabinet on manpower. I had hoped that this would go quickly through, but Bevin is frightfully long-winded, as usual, and just when I am trying to get away at the end of an hour – the National Executive of the Labour Party having been in session since 10.30 a.m. – Duncan bursts in with a query, 'When can we have this subject discussed without impatience?' I was inclined to reply, 'We have been discussing it with great patience many hours a day for many weeks now, and reaching no hard decisions.' He declared that our stocks are much too high and could be cut by a further five millions. In that case, says Anderson, we should not need to ask for any men from the Army. Duncan then says that he is very keen on getting men from the Army, but he is against rationing. Our rationing scheme, he says, went through in one hour in one meeting. It was much too rushed. I say that all this has been gone into time and time again and our advisers are satisfied that stocks cannot safely be cut any lower. None the less, it is agreed that decision on this point should be postponed and a further meeting held – also next Tuesday – for further discussion between ministers and officials.

This palsied delay and single minister's liberum veto is quite appalling. Duncan as Minister of Supply has no locus in this. It is because he was once P.B.T. [President of the Board of Trade] that he is intervening.

At 11.45 a.m. I reach the National Executive. They have not done much harm so far in my absence. ...

After lunch I receive, with Grenfell and the officials, a deputation from Durham, owners and men. Both want a higher price for coal, and the men want higher wages, both relatively to munition workers and to miners in other coalfields.

The Labour Party Conference opened at Central Hall, Westminster on 25th
May. On the first afternoon, there was a unanimous vote in favour of the
National Council of Labour's Coal Plan – strengthening Dalton's hand. 'It
is not, I think, in anyone's mind that any break-up of the Govt, or even
resignations from it, are impending,' wrote Dalton.

On 26th May, Dalton attended three ministerial meetings on Coal. At the
first, Duncan argued that coal stocks were too high. 'Duncan is excitable and
very persistent,' Dalton noted. ' ... [he] is really working to demolish the
case for rationing.'[1] At the second, the War Cabinet Sub-Committee, requisitioning was discussed inconclusively. The third was the Lord President's
Committee.

Tuesday 26th May
Lunch with Gaitskell, who produces material for this afternoon's
meeting. This is at three, the full Lord President's Committee. We
begin by looking at Lord Hyndley's note on stocks, etc. Duncan is
still very much excitable and seems to think, more and more, that he is
still President of the Board of Trade. We do a little marking up of
outcrops and fuel economy, and a little marking down of stocks, thus
turning the deficit in Anderson's manpower paper into a small
surplus. But there are still the 'contingencies'. I am then invited to
expound my fuel rationing paper. This I do very well, so much so that,
when Anderson then asks for views as to what rationing scheme is
best, on the assumption that we are to have one, they all, without
exception, support my scheme in Appendix A. Leathers says that,
'speaking with a good deal of knowledge of the coal trade', the non-
coupon scheme is quite unworkable. Lyttelton says that my scheme
is most simple and ingenious and 'makes much the best of a bad job'.
Even Duncan and Kingsley Wood, both of whom stress the assumption, say that mine is the best way. So far so good! This is the nearest
approach to a 'decision' which we have taken since we started.
  Then follows a yambling discussion as to whether, after all, we need
a rationing scheme at all. On this we are about equally divided. Anderson says that, if we are to ration at all – and he thinks it would be most
imprudent not to – it would be well to begin at once, before the situation becomes too critical. Attlee, Cripps and Bevin are also all for
rationing now, though Attlee with the proviso that our reorganisation
plans will not make a sufficiently large difference in a short period.

1 Diary, 25th, 26th May 1942.

Leathers says the same. Wood, Lyttelton and Duncan are against, and Grenfell says, 'I would prefer to get through without rationing.' So this Welsh goat has now gone against Party policy both on requisitioning and rationing! This should be let out. Lyttelton says that he is anxious to save the President of the Board of Trade from the embarrassments of having to administer a rationing scheme. Wood says that he thinks an appeal by the P.M., backed up by suitable publicity, would do the whole thing. I say that I don't want to put the P.M. in a bad personal position, if, as seems likely, we get into a jam in mid-winter. I also draw attention, somewhere in the middle of the yamble, to the fact that, given the readjustment of the statistics, there is now no case for asking for more men from the Field Force. This is the general view and, when put to those present, all except Duncan and Grenfell agree. What a bore!

The 'whole picture' is to be looked at again tomorrow afternoon by the full Lord President's Committee.

Later I go and see Cripps. He is still inclined to think that this is an issue on which we should be prepared to break. He had a word, he says, with Bevin, who says that he is embarrassed by the fact that Grenfell won't go with me. And he is a miner! Cripps says that the argumentation is very strong on 'requisitioning' – or, if you would prefer a new word, 'leasing' the mines from the owners for the period of the war. Otherwise, the Regional Controllers' orders will encounter great delays. He says that he has arranged that there shall be a good leader in *The Times* tomorrow or the day after; also that last week the *Statesman*, *Economist* and *Spectator* were all good. He says that the P.M. is quite firm on making a Minister of Fuel and Power but that he heard that now the Minister might be Harry Crookshank (whose doctor has forbidden him to go to West Africa) in place of Gwilym [Lloyd George], who was now likely to be made a Minister of State in that unhealthy part of the world. There would be a miner as Under-Secretary, either MacDonald or Griffiths. Cripps says that Attlee says that he too would face a row on this coal business, but Cripps is not sure whether, if the P.M. talked to him earnestly about keeping up the unity of the family, he would persevere. (Gaitskell says that Durbin says that Morton says that the P.M. cannot 'face a row with the 1922 Committee'.) ...

I remark to Wilmot this morning that it would just be perfect if tomorrow I lost my seat on the Labour Party National Executive. This would give me my final touch of strength, prestige and influence in the coal talks! He says he does not think this is very likely, and reminds me that this was also my own view a few days ago when I was relatively undepressed.

Wednesday 27th May

I heard late last night from Gaitskell, who had heard it in the Strand Palace Hotel from George Dallas,[1] that there was no change in our section of the National Executive. This is not surprising. The figures were announced this morning, and I was No. 5, comfortably ahead of Herbert Morrison and George Dallas. The odd man out this year is John Parker,[2] some considerable distance behind, who polled a fairly large vote by reason of (a) a pre-canvass stand-in on a ticket, Dallas tells me, with Laski, Shinwell, Phil [Noel-Baker], Jim Griffiths, Sorenson[3] and Strauss, and (b) a speech on the first day of the Conference saying that, unless we soon began to get more of our own way, we should go out of the Government.

Ebby Edwards gets me in a corner and speaks ill of his colleagues. He says that he has never known wage discussions conducted so badly as this time through the press by Lawther. As for the 'Miners' Plan', this was originally a plan for joint control by owners and men during the war. But, when it was before the N.C.L. [National Council of Labour] Coal Sub, Shinwell got them to put in the blessed word 'requisition', but this word does not make sense with the rest of the document, as was brought out when the miners' leaders appeared before the Cabinet Sub the other day. Edwards says that he never believed in the joint control scheme and thinks you should have either nationalisation or nothing. He says that the miners' organisation is in a very bad state. There is certainly a great lack of mental grip as well as of good comradeship among the miners' leaders.

3 p.m. Another meeting of the Lord President's Committee to consider his draft of a report to the War Cabinet. Rationing is not covered, but everything else tries to be. After slowly ploughing through the earlier pages, and making a few amendments and projects of re-drafts, we come to the passage about requisitioning. Here Bevin says that he has been thinking about it all night and been much troubled, particularly by the differences of opinion between me and Grenfell. He had drafted, he says, yesterday evening, a statement which then seemed a reasonable compromise, but 'looking at it again late at night', he didn't like it and tore it up. He now proposes that we say that we will take 'full control over the industry'. He realises that it is very

1 George Dallas (1878–1961). Chief Organiser of the Agricultural Workers' Union. Labour M.P. 1929–31. Member of the Labour Party N.E.C.
2 John Parker (b. 1906). Labour M.P. for Romford 1935–45; Dagenham 1945–83. Junior minister 1945–6. General Secretary of the New Fabian Research Bureau 1933–9; Fabian Society 1939–45.
3 Rev. R. W. Sorenson, later Baron (1891–1971). Labour M.P. for West Leyton 1929–31, 1935–50; Leyton 1950–64.

important to give something to the men on psychological grounds. After some desultory discussion Lyttelton says that he thinks it would be financially silly to 'lease' all the mines, since you might often be paying much too much on the basis of pre-war profits, and some much too little if you were working out their coal uneconomically quick. Therefore, he suggests, you should eliminate the Boards of Directors entirely from the running of the mines and lay it down that the word of the Regional Controller always goes, subject only to the right of the Directors not to delay obedience to the Regional Controller's orders, but only to put in a claim, consequent on the carrying out of the order, for financial compensation. Some special tribunal would have to be set up to deal with this. ... Lyttelton, who is sitting beside me, looks hopefully at me more than once during this discussion and says that he doesn't think there is now anything much between us. He and I and Cripps remain afterwards and talk further about it, and I try to get Lyttelton to be quite explicit in the sense summarised above and Cripps to agree. I think I have very nearly succeeded, but we are to meet again at 10.15 tomorrow, by which time Anderson and his scribes will have tried to put into writing Lyttelton's proposition. Kingsley Wood seems a bit frightened of it, but all the others are reasonably unperturbed (Duncan is missing, thank God!). Lyttelton also said, when questioned, that of course the Regional Controller would have the right to fire the manager or the nominee of the Board, and of course, in suitable cases, to 'take over' the mine. Bevin said afterwards that Lyttelton's great idea was to avoid a political row and that Cripps was very anxious to get an excuse to resign, because he was already fed up with being Leader of the House. (This was said in one corner of the room after the meeting had broken up, while Lyttelton and Cripps were arguing in another corner.)

On leaving, I had a further word with Cripps and said I thought we were fairly near agreement on Lyttelton's formula. He rather grudgingly said he thought this might be so. We then had a word on rationing. I tried to stiffen him and he was not unwilling.

Thursday 28th May
Coal Committee at 10.15 till lunch, and again after lunch from 3.15 to 5.30. ... In the end we get substantially what I want on Regional Controllers. Cripps also is content with the final forms of words, and any idea of his, or any group of us, 'having a showdown', with the P.M. over this evaporates! Kingsley Wood treats poor old Grenfell just like his little 'dog on a string'. He drags Grenfell in to support opposition to requisitioning, opposition to rationing, and a statement that in 90 per cent of the mines there would be no need for any inter-

ference. He constantly says, 'I agree with the Secretary for Mines on this', or 'After all, the Secretary for Mines has much more knowledge of this than any of us'! I say at one point, 'Since we are all making the most of our allies, I think the Minister of Production and I are in agreement about this.'

Reorganisation having been disposed of, we then turn to rationing, and Cripps takes the initiative in proposing that the introduction of this should be delayed in order to see the effects of the proposed changes on production, and that meanwhile we should appeal for voluntary economy while getting ready the rationing scheme, issuing the form and making the assessment.

I had intended, and so informed Gaitskell, that I would stand out today on rationing and only give way tomorrow at the Cabinet. But, Cripps having jumped in like this – and he was before one of the stoutest supporters of immediate rationing – I don't feel it is worth carrying the fight further today. Only Attlee, and he rather faintly, is now in favour of immediate rationing anyhow. The ground has been largely cut from under our feet by the changes we have now agreed to in the figures of outcrops, industrial fuel economy and de-stocking. So we are all in accord on this as well!

At the end Attlee with a frightened look says that perhaps we ought to consult some more people before finally reaching our conclusions. He even hints at the possibility of calling in all other No. 1 ministers. This horrifies me, since our reorganisation proposals would be likely to be furiously opposed by a number of Tory ministers, whereas it should be pretty easy quietly to square our Labour colleagues.

In the luncheon interval I have a word with Wood, telling him that, if they will all accept reorganisation and my rationing scheme, I might be willing to postpone the operation of the latter. I think this works a bit.

Despite a numerical inferiority in tanks and infantry, Rommel launched a new North African offensive on 26th May. After initial advances, the relative inability of the Afrika Korps to absorb losses began to show, and on 30th May Rommel ordered a tactical withdrawal. Axis reverses proved only temporary, however, and by early June the tank battle had turned decisively against the Allies.

Friday 29th May

War Cabinet, nominally all on coal, from 11 a.m. to 12.30. P.M. in a very expansive and agreeable mood. The Libyan battle is said to be going well (we have heard this before; I hope this time it is true). ...

The P.M. makes quite a speech at me, expressing great appreciation of my accommodating spirit in regard to this scheme on which, as he knows, I have spent so much labour. He goes on to praise the miners.[1] He is sure something must be done to improve their wages. Perhaps some special war allowance could be given. The Treasury must not be difficult about this. It is agreed that we should have a draft White Paper ready for the Cabinet on Monday evening. This should be in the Vote Office on Wednesday. The 'two sides' should be met and told immediately beforehand what we propose. The following week there should be a two-days' debate, with the Government putting down a resolution.

And so we all separate purring!

Saturday 30th May

Working on the draft White Paper. Cripps comes to see me, being most anxious to see the draft. He makes some useful suggestions. He is anti-American. He says they have just stopped all supplies, a quick and sudden decision, which destroys our plans for fifty new squadrons of the R.A.F. Everything is now being kept for the American Army and Air Force which is coming over. When they arrive in great numbers, there will be ill feeling because they will have so many dollars to spend. They will demoralise everything and everyone. They are always telling us now just where we get off. They are treating us like a poor dependency. Lyttelton has gone to Washington because Roosevelt summoned him. He now is sending for Leathers and Bevin. It is as though we were all his servants. The P.M. has always gone in for appeasing the Americans, letting them have whatever they like. Cripps thinks that he ought to go over again to Washington and say, 'This must stop.'

I finally finish my redraft, and so to West Leaze.

Sunday 31st May[2]

A fortnight ago I thought I was as good as out, and was thinking of details such as where to find a service flat, what to do with my furniture now in Board of Trade, how long a break I could take at West Leaze, what book I should next write – with how much scandalous and inner disclosures.

1 Handwritten insertion: 'who work out of sight of the sun.'
2 All of this entry except the final paragraph (see overleaf) is handwritten.

And now I feel almost triumphant – though we're not right through yet. In a short time I shall get rid of my responsibility for coal, but, before I let it go, after three and a half months, I shall I hope have laid the foundation of a New Order in the coalfields, and a more sensible wage system, and made a good push to increase production. On rationing I make the 1922 acccpt points and coupons, but not for immediate application – a respite first. On release of more men from the Forces, we stand pat.

All this, assuming that my White Paper goes through the Cabinet tomorrow, and the scheme through Party entanglements and Parliament.

Cripps has been a good ally, and Bevin pretty useful. Grenfell is a dunderhead and a disgrace. Lyttelton at the end played up very well.

And now for a further spell at Board of Trade minus Coal.

What new twists and turns of political fortune?

It's ups and downs, sure enough!

I garden and play patience. I mow till midnight by moonlight. There is a bright orange full moon.

Monday 1st June

After lunch, Lord President's Committee considers Home Front problems. R. A. Butler wants to set up a Committee on how the Public Schools can be brought into proper relation with the rest of our educational system, or, in other words, how a number of boys from Secondary Schools, or below eleven plus, shall be woven into the boarding school system, and how State grants shall be made for this. Much to Butler's surprise, as he told me afterwards, there is no opposition in principle to this. He had expected Duff Cooper and others to explode at the mere idea. He thinks that it would be best to have as Chairman someone who was not educated in England and therefore will have no biased experience. Various names are suggested, and Bevin asks, 'What about Beaverbrook?' The talk then drifting on to the old subject of religious education in the schools, and Butler having said that he hoped to get a final answer from the Church of England within a few months, Bevin makes a great oration in which he declares that ever since he can remember, we have been 'baffled by the Bishops' whenever we have tried to open the gates of education to the children of the poor. 'All these Bishops', he says, 'have had all the education there was, and now they are denying it to the children of the masses.' I suggest that a time limit might be imposed on the Bishops, and Butler tells me afterwards that he will find it very helpful to tell them that his colleagues expressed impatience at their delay.

Cabinet at 7.45 considers the 'final' redraft of the White Paper. It goes through pretty easily, though a few further bright ideas are thrown up by my colleagues which Bridges and [Norman] Brook undertake to put into shape for next day. It is left in the end to Anderson and me to settle 'without further reference to anyone' the 'final' version. The P.M. only asks on what page it is stated that rationing will not be introduced at once. When satisfied that this is in, he takes no more interest. They all swallow Reorganisation without any effort at all. ...

Gladwyn to dine at the Coquille. He says there is nothing for him yet at the Foreign Office. He wonders whether they are really trying. He was very indignant at Sargent having said the other night, 'Oh, I thought we had disposed of you now and that you had joined the Treasury.' Gladwyn says that when Sir Horace Wilson heard that he was available, he asked for him to replace Playfair[1] 'for a few weeks' while the latter was advising Hanbury-Williams!

Tuesday 2nd June
A bunch of P.Q.s go easily. Maurice Webb, to whom I give a faint adumbration of the coming White Paper,[2] says that Strauss has been giving a series of lunches at which he has been puffing Cripps and saying that he is the only person of any decision on the Left in the Government and that all our scores are due to him alone. Webb was asked to such a lunch the other day.

Norman Brook, who has a very good mind, brings me the veritable 'final' revise of the White Paper. It reads pretty well. Anderson is on the telephone endlessly to Ava.[3] She just won't stop talking. He is much embarrassed when Brook and I are in the room and says, 'No, I am not alone.' He sounds very cooing and endearing. ...

At Lord President's Committee. I raise the question of the miners' wages. What are we to do next? It is agreed that Anderson and I (with Grenfell) should see both sides the day after tomorrow and promise them an immediate enquiry into the wage claims and a less hurried enquiry into the wage structure generally.

1 E. Playfair, later Sir Edward (b. 1909). Treasury 1934–56. Permanent Under-Secretary of State for War 1956–9; Permanent Secretary at the Ministry of Defence 1960–61. He had recently been working on an enquiry into S.O.E. (See p. 456.)
2 This announced that ' ... the Government have decided to assume full control over the operation of the mines, and to organise the industry on the basis of national service, with the intention that the organisation now to be established will continue, pending a final decision by Parliament on the future of the industry.' (Cmd 6364.) The White Paper was published on 3rd June.
3 Lady Anderson, q.v.

Wednesday 3rd June

Wakened by an Alert just before 3 a.m. It is long since the last. I half-expect the Huns to come in great and desperate force. But the All Clear goes after twenty minutes, and I to sleep again.

Get up rather late and attend a Reconstruction Committee, with Jowitt in the Chair, where the first item is a paper for which I take responsibility, on Post-War Relief. But I frankly tell them that I have been so thick in coal that I have had little thought to give to this, and ask Leithers [Leith-Ross], who is with me, to expound. I find myself in a coalition with the Foreign Office and the Ministries of Food and Agriculture against the Treasury. Wood wants to make no commitments on anything till the war ends. It is finally agreed that we should have a small committee of officials to try to reach agreement.

Maisky comes to see me, ostensibly to ask me to reopen my decision not to permit more clothing, in excess of a final £10,000 worth, to go to Russia. But we only reach this after half an hour of gossip, in which he says he is now very hopeful about the War. He likes very much our latest air-raids, is fairly satisfied with Libya, and very pleased with the Russian success in checking the German offensive. I don't ask about Molotov, who, I heard from Gladwyn Jebb two nights ago, had been 'hiding in a suburb' but had now gone home.[1]

Lunch with Iranian Minister,[2] where I am the principal guest, sitting on the Minister's right with Sir Alexander Cadogan on his left and opposite Richard Law and Dingle Foot! Some thirty other persons, mostly from the Near East, are also present. The Iranian Minister was teaching Persian at Cambridge until very recently, when he was made an Envoy. He knew Donald[3] and Petica Robertson[4] well and was in Cambridge when the latter was killed in an air-raid. He does not like the Russians much and says that in Persia no one speaks Russian, although they are next door. French, and then English, are, he says, the most favoured foreign tongues.

Cadogan says, when I tell him that I hope soon to be rid of coal, 'You are very good at knowing when to give things up.' I give him and Law a lift in my car and, as they get out, ask him when he is going to make some provision for Gladwyn. He says it is rather difficult. He

1 Marginal insertion: 'The suburb was Chequers! He had really gone to U.S.A.' A Russian delegation, led by Molotov, had arrived in London on 20th May to discuss questions relating to a post-war settlement, especially as this might affect East Europe; and the vexed issue of the Second Front.
2 Seyed Hassan Taquizadeh. Iranian Minister to Great Britain 1941–4; Ambassador 1944–7.
3 Donald Robertson (1885–1961). Emeritus Professor of Greek at Cambridge University 1928–50. Fellow of Trinity College, Cambridge from 1909.
4 Petica Robertson, née Jones (d. 1941). Married to Donald Robertson, q.v.

could easily make him a Counsellor in Latin America, but this was not welcome. He was minded now to make him the head of a new or refurbished Economic Section at the Foreign Office. Gladwyn thought he would not like this, but Cadogan thought, after he had been doing it for a short while, he would get quite interested in it, as people always did in a new job. Cadogan was quite surprised to find how unpopular Gladwyn had made himself with so many people. The Service Departments were very much opposed to him and therefore it had not been possible to put him on Joint Planners or anything else very close to the war effort. Gladwyn, he said, was always writing him letters about himself and this was becoming rather a bore. His unpopularity had taken Cadogan quite by surprise. I said that he and I, who both knew Gladwyn so well, did not notice the 'off-hand manner' complained of. But in any case, it was a great pity that he should be wasted. ...

When all the rest have gone away except Bevin and I, Attlee says that it is now all fixed that Gwilym [Lloyd George] is to be the new Minister of Fuel and Power with Tom Smith as Under-Secretary. (I had met the latter coming out and he seemed very pleased. I had asked him whether he was taking it and he said yes. I congratulated him. He despises Grenfell and is also a good sound fellow in himself.) Grenfell, said Attlee, is going right out. He has been offered several jobs but has refused them all. He is in a very black mood and says he is 'being sacked' because he is thought to be inefficient. This is just about it, but of course everybody is having to deny it. Attlee asked Hyndley to try and get him in a better mood, and the latter reports he has made some improvement. Grenfell was also to see the P.M. this evening, and perhaps *he* will be able to charm him. He is threatening, I hear, to 'defend himself if attacked'. I said I couldn't imagine why anybody should bother to attack him; we should all be much more eager to forget him.

Thursday 4th June
10 a.m. Special Meeting of P.L.P. to consider the White Paper. Not at all a good atmosphere. No one says this is a good scheme. Only the critics are vocal. I begin with an exposition of the scheme. Then Gordon MacDonald, obviously speaking from a prepared statement, says that the miners have not yet taken any decision on the scheme. The present position is that they do not support it and accept no responsibility for it. The miners' M.P.s are meeting the Miners' Executive officials later on. Then comes a stream of critical questions. ...

At the end of the meeting Attlee gets up and says that he wishes it to be clearly understood that the replacement of Grenfell implies no reflection whatever upon him. Thereupon, Grenfell gets up and makes a very painful speech, complaining that he has not been consulted before being removed, that he is confident he has always been right in everything he has done at the Mines Department, and that one day he will speak out and tell the full story. With this the meeting somewhat unhappily adjourns.

The impression created is very bad. I say to several of the miners that really they should not once more miss, as so often in past years, the opportunity of making a solid advance, even if they do not get all they want at once. If they were to swing the Party against the White Paper it is difficult to see how I could continue in office. Nor, for that matter, would it be at all easy for other Labour ministers to go on. And if I went out on this, I should go out in the worst way possible, having failed to carry the Labour Party with me in this particular compromise. It would be a much worse personal position than if I had resigned a little earlier because I could not get as much as I wanted from my colleagues. ...

2.15. MacDonald comes to my room for a few minutes before the Administrative Committee. He thinks that 'it will be all right', but this morning the atmosphere was disturbed because they had all read in their newspapers, without expecting it, that Grenfell was out and Tom Smith was to be the new Under-Secretary at the Fuel Ministry. This upsets both Grenfell's friends and MacDonald's, because he had been told only yesterday that *he* was to be the new Under-Secretary. Indeed, Lloyd George had asked him yesterday afternoon, 'Have you heard anything yet?' and when he had said no, had expressed surprise and said that he himself had been asked what he would think of Mac-Donald as his Under-Secretary and had replied that there was no one in the world whom he would prefer. MacDonald hints that Tom Smith is not the kind of man who will 'stand up'. MacDonald says further that there is a terrible lack among the miners of willingness to take responsibility, both on the industrial and the political side. Each is trying to pass the buck to the other. ...

Much desiring a break, I go with Wilmot and Gaitskell to the London Fire Brigade H.Q. whence we proceed to the Caledonian Market to see some boxing between a Polish team and a team from the London Fire Service. The Poles do very well and win by four matches to three. We then return with Major Jackson to dine at the Fire Station, where I press the bell and give an alarm which results in the very rapid manning and going into action of a number of fire engines. After dinner we look in at the tail end of a Discussion Circle, attended by some sixty firemen, in a school in St Pancras. They are discussing Parliament, and I have the impression that they are a very bright and thoughtful lot. I make a short speech, which is well received, and then go home to bed having forgotten, for a brief two hours, about coal dust.

On 22nd May 1941, the Minister of Health had announced the formation of an interdepartmental committee of officials to undertake a survey of existing national schemes of social insurance and allied services, including workmen's compensation. Sir William Beveridge was made chairman. In December, Beveridge circulated the outline of what became the welfare state. Social insurance would be based on a national minimum, and it would involve three assumptions: a National Health Service, family allowances, and the maintenance of full employment. Long before the Beveridge Report appeared, the press was full of optimistic rumours, and as early as April 1942 a Home Intelligence report observed: 'Sir William Beveridge's proposals for an "all-in" social security scheme are said to be popular.'[1] But it was not until May 1942 that Beveridge turned his undivided attention to the problems of social insurance or, more generally, of post-war social reform.

Friday 5th June
Get hold of Beveridge, in order to make sure that he is not writing embarrassing letters to *The Times*. But he shows no sign of any intention to do this. He has now almost forgotten, I think, about fuel rationing, and got quite absorbed in his report on Social Services, which he says will be 'quite revolutionary'. He is a little vexed that in our latest White Paper we make no reference to him, or explicitly, to his previous plan. I promise to say a nice word about him and it in the debate next week. ...

Lunch with Mrs Phillimore. Also present Attlee, Beneš and Raczynski. I have to leave early for an N.C.L. [National Council of Labour] Sub-Committee on Coal, but not before Beneš has expressed the view, which he says he has steadily held and expressed for a long time, that the Germans cannot stand more than one further war winter. He does not think they will last beyond May 1943.

---

1 Cited in P. Addison, *The Road to 1945*, Jonathan Cape, London, 1975, p. 215.

In response to disquiet in Whitehall about the effectiveness of S.O.E., a special enquiry into the workings of the whole machine had been ordered by Lord Selborne, at the request of the Treasury. The investigation was conducted by John Hanbury-Williams, assisted by Edward Playfair. Though the resulting report was broadly favourable, stress was placed on the need for improvements in organisation and administration.

Tuesday 9th June

Dine with Robin Brook at 10 Devonshire Place. Gaitskell accompanies me and we find Hancock also there. We discuss problems of quite another world, that of military and diplomatic operations. I tell them that I haven't read a Foreign Office telegram for weeks, if not months. Brook is now 'Policy Adviser' to M. [Gubbins]. The latter is to be promoted. ... The 'investigation' is still going on, not leading anywhere much. The worst they can say is that there have been rather a lot of cars and secretaries and that, perhaps, in the U.S.A. everything is not quite as clean as it should be. I ask who has been pressing for the 'investigation'. Brook thinks it was Eden. The latter has several times squashed the Earl [Selborne]. (On the other hand, when he and the Earl put up to the Cabinet a proposal to let milk through the blockade for Belgium, there was an explosion from the Chair and it was said that the Earl's predecessor used not to take such a line! The line was rejected.) Brook thinks it clear that Hambro has been getting hold of everything. It was certainly he who manoeuvred Gladwyn out, though it was quite clear, after only three days, that Gladwyn and the Earl were not made for one another. Miss O. reports that, when the Earl was dictating something to her in Gladwyn's presence, the latter, after one or two vain attempts at intervention, flung himself back in his chair and threw his handkerchief over his face.

Wednesday 10th June

10 a.m. Party Meeting to decide 'finally' their attitude towards the White Paper. Jimmy Walker makes a very good speech and, in the end, the decision to support the Government in the Division Lobby is taken by an overwhelming majority, only four or five voting against. This morning there is no need for me to speak.

Anderson opens the debate pretty well. Slow but sure. ...

Twenty-eight speeches are made today and we let all the would-be orators exhaust themselves. Cripps and I, with Lloyd George and

Tom Smith and two Whips, sit on the Bench till 9.20 p.m., listening, for the most part, to sheer rubbish.

Thursday 11th June
Gaitskell says that what strikes him about the coal debate is that all the Government spokesmen's persuasions are addressed to the Labour Party. The Tories, he thinks, are at a very low ebb and almost apologetic for their existence.

Dine, with a great sense of weary freedom, with Wilmot at Josef's.

On 11th June, Gwilym Lloyd George was sworn in as Minister of Fuel and Power. For Dalton, it was an important turning-point. First at M.E.W., and then at the Board of Trade, there had been little time to look beyond the short-term crises that dominated his ministerial life. The hiving-off of fuel changed the pace, providing new opportunities to think and plan for the post-war world.

Friday 12th June
I wake today with no responsibility for coal. A most happy sensation! The press is pretty good, except the *Daily Telegraph*, which has a most malicious write-up of the Parliamentary proceedings, designed to discredit the President of the Board of Trade. This coal owners' paper has been consistently the worst since we had our first brush on rationing.

Looking back, there were two crisis peaks; the first when it seemed that I, and some others, might have to resign because we could not push our colleagues far enough on reorganisation, and, second, for a brief period when it looked as though I might have to resign because I could not carry the Labour Party, and in particular the miners, in support of the reorganisation section of the White Paper. This last crisis was resolved last Friday, a week ago today, when the Miners' Federation Executive came down in favour of the scheme. The miners' leadership this time has been good. They have learnt the lesson that their traditional policy of 'all or nowt' always ends in nowt. This time they have gone to the other extreme and followed the advice once given by the Rev. William Hodgson:[1] 'Keep on nibbling at the cheese, boys.'

1 Rev. William Hodgson. Vicar of Escomb and Secretary of the Bishop Auckland Labour Party when Dalton was adopted as candidate.

Now, after I have had three nights away, I must look again at the Board of Trade, both persons and problems. ...

Hugh Gaitskell went off last night for five days' leave, which he has well earned. He has been most valuable to me throughout my coal phase and will, I know, be not less valuable in the next phase, however that may shape itself.

Tuesday 16th June

I go to bed early with a cold, having begun to pick up various non-coal problems, including Leith-Ross's visit to U.S. and his instructions, on which Kingsley Wood is apt to be very sticky, but Eden, Jowitt and I are united against him, thinking it not enough that Leith-Ross should sit and listen in silence to what the Americans say and then leave the room, but rather that he should be forthcoming up to the point of undertaking that we will maintain the rationing of food, clothing, etc., after the war until the most urgent needs of distressed allies have been met; furniture, hollow-ware and rubber footwear, etc.

In mid-June, Gladwyn Jebb was given responsibility for a new department in the Foreign Office, to deal with a number of long-term problems, including relief after the war, refugees, civil government in liberated countries, and armistices. Under Jebb, this department became a machine for thinking out Britain's long-term foreign policy.

Friday 19th June

Stay in bed to get rid of my cold.

Long talk with Gaitskell on our future activities, particularly external economic relations. I have a locus here which I have not yet exploited through lack of time and also because it is a little bit Economic text-book, and this still repels me.

Meanwhile, I have a note from Gladwyn saying that he has been offered by Cadogan, and has accepted, the headship of a new Economic and Reconstruction Section at the Foreign Office. This will be good in many ways, but may be tiresome in others, if Eden has it in mind to try and snatch more influence over external economics. And I hear from other sources that there is talk to this effect.

Sunday 21st June

Get up late just in time to receive Gladwyn at 12.30 for lunch. We find several of my haunts closed and end by going to what is now called the Cigale in Romilly Street. Under the new 5/- regulation the food tends to be everywhere the same and less in quantity. This is, no doubt, wholly right. ...

I warn Gladwyn that there must be reciprocity between the Foreign Office and me over Economic and Reconstruction questions on the one hand and political questions on the other. The purpose of his new Department can, no doubt, be very innocently and plausibly stated but, in the light of my previous difficulties with Eden and the latter's tendency to an unpleasant-childish acquisitiveness, I shall be rather suspicious.

I ask Gladwyn how my coal adventures had looked to him. He says that he has the impression that I have had to retreat a bit, and that I have been left to do most of the fighting on my own. He says that Winster, who always professes a great admiration for me, says that I was left in the lurch by my colleagues, Bevin ostentatiously walking out of the room in the middle of a difficult Parliamentary Labour Party Meeting. (This last is not quite just.) Winster says that he thinks my short-term credit with the Labour Party has been lowered, but not my long-term. Peake and others say that all the Committees in the Reorganisation scheme are mere eye-wash and will make no difference. Gladwyn senses that I am 'not popular' with Keynes. I say, 'I know that. It is because I have always refused to sit at his feet.'[1] In fact Keynes was much against the Beveridge rationing scheme. ...

I spend the evening finishing Rowse's *Cornish Childhood*, a charming book of which he has sent me a copy. With this his publishers enclosed a letter to H. G. Wells,[2] and a few days later I received from the secretary to Noël Coward an apology and a letter addressed to me, with the further statement that Coward had now received a letter addressed to him by Rowse which had been enclosed in a copy of the book sent to Bernard Shaw![3] The publishers must have had tremendous fun mixing up all the letters.

---

1 Dalton had been taught by Keynes at Cambridge in 1909–10, and both had been part of the same circle. They had seen little of each other since, even though Dalton had become, like Keynes, a professional economist.
2 H. G. Wells (1866–1946). Author, historian and writer on scientific and social topics. Fabian pioneer.
3 George Bernard Shaw (1856–1950). Playwright, social critic and Fabian pioneer.

Monday 22nd June

Jowitt to lunch with me. He is very vague and lacking in exact conviction. He seems to have practically no staff and has, as yet, no official car. He asks me how one gets one. I suggest that he should get his Private Secretary to enquire. Though vague, he seems very co-operative.

On 20th June, Rommel's forces penetrated the defences of Tobruk. Next day Tobruk fell to the enemy. By the 24th, Rommel had reached a point south-east of Sidi Barrani, and British troops were forced to withdraw from positions at Sollum and Sidi Omar.

Tuesday 23rd June

In P.M.'s absence, Attlee makes statement on Tobruk. The House is uneasy but less difficult and excited than I had expected. Wardlaw-Milne gives notice that he and some of those with whom he has been consulting will put down a motion of No Confidence in the central direction of the war.

Dine with Lord Hyndley, Wilmot and Gaitskell. I rag Lord Hyndley about the press attacks on him. 'Banker-Peer to control your coal', and 'The Miners' friend' followed by a long list of his directorships. I say it is high time that Gwilym Lloyd George announced his other appointments.

Thursday 25th June

A confused Party Meeting which ends in the defeat, though only by 33 to 30, some 6 or 7 ministers voting in the majority, of a proposal to put down *at once* a motion demanding an enquiry into Libya. The matter is now adjourned till next Tuesday. I was myself not clear whether such a motion would be either good or bad. H.M.G. could hardly have treated it as a vote of no confidence if it came with the support of the Labour Party, but it would have done something to undermine Attlee's position, since it would be known that he had tried to dissuade the Party from such action. Now pride of place will remain with Wardlaw-Milne's censure motion, which is subscribed to, up to date, by some 20 Members, of whom 7 or 8 belong to our Party.

Friday 26th to Monday 29th June
Weekend of sun and solitude at West Leaze, except that Evan Durbin comes over to lunch on the Saturday and talks rather intelligently. He thinks the Germans, having lost two big wars, won't be able to try again. The Russians have done so marvellously in building up their industry in a short time that they will soon, after this war, tower over Europe. I ask him whether he still thinks the Russians are as bad as the Germans. He says yes. I argue against this. I say the Russians are indifferent to the individual, whereas the Germans like concentrating, with sadistic glee, upon him. I think the Russians are callous rather than gleeful over human suffering, and anyhow they are further away from us.

I was in a depressed mood about the war, which, when I had heard on Monday morning last about the fall of Tobruk, seemed to extend itself immeasurably. I had not liked the large surrender at Tobruk. Durbin said that the attraction was all into the Air Force and the Navy, and the Army got what was left, on all levels. He thought the war couldn't last beyond next year. He said 'victories' were no use to Hitler. The only thing that is any use to him is 'Victory'.

Mrs Emily Lowther has her husband home on leave, but she leaves plenty of food in the larder. I mow the lawn a lot and trim my trees and make a bonfire and play my hundredth game of Triangle Bridge. (I have got it out 26 times in this 100.)

Sir Frederick Leith-Ross had arrived in Washington on 28th June to discuss a draft plan for a Relief Organisation. On 29th June, he was instructed by the War Cabinet to say in the discussions that 'as part of the common plan, His Majesty's Government will be prepared to continue in this country, after the end of hostilities, a system of rationing of food and clothing, and other suitable measures of control over essential commodities, so long as the available supplies are not sufficient to meet the urgent needs of Allied countries which have regained their freedom.'[1] The talks that ensued led eventually to the setting up of the United Nations Relief and Rehabilitation Administration (U.N.R.R.A.).

Monday 29th June
War Cabinet. Discussion on joint paper of Eden, me and Jowitt on instructions for Sir Frederick Leith-Ross in Washington. Everyone

1 PRO, CAB 65/27.

is tired, garrulous and inconsequent. A most deplorable discussion which goes on for an hour and a quarter. But in the end we get the instructions through substantially unchanged. Attlee in the Chair, in the absence of the P.M., is *frightfully* slow and obstructive.

Wednesday 1st July

Vote of Censure debate begins.[1] Wardlaw-Milne proposes that the Duke of Gloucester should be made Commander-in-Chief. This is very ill received, particularly on the Labour benches, and quite upsets the speech. The general view is that this Duke is the least mental member of the Royal Family.

As I am still tiresomely deaf, my Private Office gets in touch with Duncan's and are recommended Dr Trapnell, who arrives with an immense apparatus, inspects and syringes my left ear – rather an unpleasant though not exactly painful process – whereupon my hearing is completely restored. He seems quite a good physician.

Thursday 2nd July

Answer an arranged Private Notice Question on the Wheat Agreement.[2] This goes over all right. Vote of Censure debate is continued, the House having sat up till 2.30 a.m. this morning when it was counted out by McGovern,[3] who had spoken for three-quarters of an hour himself!

I distinguish myself by missing the Division! The House being very crowded and it being impossible to get a seat, I went away to my room and there did some work by myself and succeeded in misjudging the time, arriving just after the doors had been closed and in time to hear the result – 475 to 25 – announced by the Tellers. I was exceedingly angry and learned afterwards that the Division had been called at four minutes to five. The bells are not audible in the far distance, and the absurdity of the thing is that I hardly ever use this damned room at all. It is much too far away for general convenience. I think that I shall never use it again!

I go round to see the Deputy Prime Minister and pour forth my

1 The censure motion was proposed by Sir John Wardlaw-Milne and seconded by Aneurin Bevan.
2 Following discussions in Washington, the British, Canadian, Australian, American and Argentinian governments had agreed on the outline of a wheat convention which would later be submitted to a larger conference of the countries concerned. It was also agreed to set up a Wheat Council to administer a wheat pool to make supplies available to territories liberated from the enemy. The Council was intended to fix wheat prices and maintain a scheme of export quotas.
3 John McGovern (1887–1968). I.L.P., then Labour, M.P. for Glasgow Shettleston 1930–59.

indignant regrets. But he doesn't take it very seriously and invites me to dine with him.

Friday 3rd July
Re-elected Chairman of the Labour Party Policy Sub-Committee. ...
Christopher Mayhew to dine with me. He has been having a very good time in Wales with his Phantom troop. He is still very eager to get a by-election and has seen Attlee about this – half showing his old school tie[1] – and Shepherd. It is difficult to arrange, but we will go on trying.

Sunday 5th July
This Sunday morning I am driven over by the Ministry of Information to Hemsworth. Bacon,[2] the Ministry of Information officer for the area, plays up during our journey and we have an interesting talk about the problems which will arise when one or two million American soldiers are stationed in this country. They will buy all the stuff they can, and they may not altogether like our ways, or we theirs. They will seem much richer than we, especially their soldiers than ours, and they will buy all the girls and all the drinks. They may boast that they are winning the war for us, as well as keeping us going in other ways. There is a danger that they may go back to the U.S.A. with anti-British feelings, just as many British and American troops came back anti-French from France at the end of the last war, and the antipathy may be mutual. These are dangers to be watched for and guarded against, but they will need a good deal of watching. Another trouble is that many of the American soldiers will be Negroes, and the white Americans will tend to set about the coloured Americans even in our streets or our pubs, and then the British may sometimes take the part of the coloured Americans. Some of the difficulties may be diminished by giving the Americans, so far as possible, special towns and zones. But this cannot be done completely. With food rationing, to give them hospitality will be difficult, but a scheme may be able to be developed in which they will bring to our houses packets of their own food to be eaten in common. They will, however, annoy some of us a good deal because they have no sense of their host's private property and will carry off souvenirs from our houses, even sometimes breaking up our household goods for this purpose. So it all sounds a bit difficult!

Good meeting at Hemsworth Hippodrome with little George Griffiths, M.P.[3] About a thousand miners react very well to my exposition of the Coal White Paper and the need for more output.

1 Attlee and Mayhew had both been at Haileybury.
2 R. K. Bacon. North-East Regional Information Officer at the Ministry of Information.
3 G. A. Griffiths (1880–1945). Labour M.P. for Hemsworth 1934–45.

Monday 6th July

Harcourt Johnstone[1] to lunch with me. Rather a ridiculous person with not quite enough brains or energy. He wants to form a combine with the Foreign Office against the Treasury. He says that 'the dark forces' have lately again been in the ascendant. I ask who these are and he says Phillips[2] and Hubert Henderson.[3]

Conference of Home Front ministers. 'Quack, quack!' A frightful waste of time. Jowitt is supposed to be expounding his reconstruction plan, but everybody wanders all over the field. ...

Summoned to a Cabinet for seven-thirty to discuss a Minute by the P.M., obviously instigated by a cock-eyed version by Cherwell of the discussion last week, at which neither the P.M. nor Lord Cherwell was present, on Leith-Ross's instructions, and especially on the rationing undertaking.[4] Jowitt and I wait till after eight, the Cabinet getting hopelessly behind their timetable, and then finally it is decided that this point will not be taken at all. Meanwhile the instructions have been telegraphed to Leith-Ross, who has acted on them, and the matter has now got as far as the President. So Lord Cherwell is too late. But he is a damned nuisance all the same – and all the time.

Emerging with Jowitt, I meet Gladwyn in Downing Street. I go with him and have a drink and a snack at the Queen's Restaurant, Sloane Square, where Cynthia is also meeting him. He says he has now become simply a Foreign Office official again. He rather likes Hubert Henderson and wants me to come and re-make my acquaintance with him. I tell him that his immediate chief, Nigel Ronald,[5] has written a most indiscreet letter to one of my officials proposing that we should discuss with the exiled governments how we should all get on if the Americans completely washed their hands of Europe after the war. I say that I think this is a most undiplomatic suggestion and that it would do very great harm if it got out.

Wednesday 8th July

Party Meeting. Alfred Edwards, of Middlesbrough, is put on the car-

---

1 Harcourt Johnstone (1895–1945). Parliamentary Secretary at the Department of Overseas Trade 1940–45. Liberal M.P. for Middlesbrough West 1940–45; Willesden East 1923–4; South Shields 1931–5.
2 Sir Frederick Phillips (1884–1943). Treasury Representative in the United States 1940–43.
3 Sir Hubert Henderson (1890–1952). Economic Adviser at the Treasury 1939–44. Drummond Professor of Political Economy, and Fellow of All Souls College, Oxford 1944–51.
4 See linking passage before 29th June 1942, above, p. 461.
5 N. B. Ronald, later Sir Nigel (1894–1973). Assistant Under-Secretary at the Foreign Office 1942.

pet, quite properly, for making a most stupid speech to the effect that attacks on the Government by Labour M.P.s are always rehearsed beforehand – when pressed, he can only give as example Gordon MacDonald and myself at the Party Meeting on the Coal White Paper – that 'nepotism and hypocrisy' are rife, that the Labour Party should leave the Government, and that the P.M. would do much better 'with men of his own choosing'. Disloyal and dyspeptic.

Sir Arthur Salter is back from the U.S. No one in Parliament knows who he is when he rises to answer a question from the Front Bench! He tells me that the Americans have helped us wonderfully, and promptly, over ships and supplies. They have imposed a very stiff gasolene ration on themselves, which will cut very deeply into all their motoring habits.

I say that I sense in certain circles, both at the Foreign Office and the Treasury, an anti-American prejudice. He says that this is very real. It is the jealousy of the old British governing class at 'the passing of power'. He remembers how, at the end of the last war, over shipping, when we had the power, we made all our allies, and even the Americans, feel their inferiority. But at Washington the Americans have never made us, in this war, feel like suppliants, not even during the period of their neutrality.

Thursday 9th July
At the Cabinet, in the P.M.'s room at the House of Commons, an hour is spent wrangling round the rationing formula in Leith-Ross's instructions. The P.M., egged on by little Kingsley Wood, is much against any immediate 'commitment'. He has written a most eloquent and cogent Minute based on someone's misrepresentation to him of the meaning of our formula. He says he thinks it means that we undertake now, even though the Americans go on eating enormous and unrationed meals, to come down, after the war, to the level of Romania. The truth is that he dislikes rationing as such and does not readily accept the view that it will be necessary to continue it, in any case, for some considerable time after the war. He and Bevin have quite an argument, the latter saying that our people are better fed now than they have ever been, and that we cannot 'go back to chaos' after the war. To which the P.M. replies, 'You are trying once more to pre-judge the settlement of our post-war problems. What you call chaos others might call freedom.' The P.M. has also got it into his head that some of us still want 'rationing for rationing's sake', 'hordes of officials', 'the people clamped down in a bureaucratic grip', etc. He is really very tiresome this morning, but in the end it is agreed that a telegram shall be sent to Leith-Ross which, in effect, varies his

instructions very little. He has already acted on them and communicated, in confidence, our formula to Acheson.[1] Probably it has got by now to the President, so Wood has been a little too late! ...

Wilmot and I dine with Sir Jocelyn Lucas, M.P.,[2] who gives Wilmot two of his books on Dogs. He is, I think, a little barmy. He has with him a wife who gushes without much comprehension and a young Wavy-Navy officer who escaped from Hong Kong the night it fell. He takes a most objective view of the Japs. He says they are fanatically brave; if they die in battle, they go straight to Heaven; if they die otherwise they go first to Purgatory. They behaved badly at Hong Kong, but then they always do, and did much worse things to the Chinese at Nanking. They feed our prisoners on rice, chucking sacks of it through the barbed wire and leaving them to cook it as best they can. On the other hand, they only have rice themselves and there is no obvious reason why they should feed us better. The guards are said to be quite prepared to instruct the British prisoners how to cook the rice. The worst thing in the camps is the lack of medical necessities.

Wednesday 15th July

Luckhurst Scott[3] comes to ask my view on Joad[4] as a Parliamentary Labour candidate. This view is adverse. He is against the war, or was, and has not recanted. Also his past life might lead to most embarrassing questions, as with the Blanco-Whites.[5] I say there are many far better men whom we should push in front of him. ...

Lunch at the House and run into Maurice Webb, who says that his information is that the P.M. is most anxious to have the Beaver back in the War Cabinet. He feels a longing for his companionship, feeling

---

1 Dean Acheson (1893–1971). U.S. Assistant Secretary of State 1941–5. Secretary of State 1949–53.
2 Sir Jocelyn Lucas, 4th Bart (1889–1980). Conservative M.P. for Portsmouth South 1939–66. Lucas wrote several books on dogs: *Hunting and Working Terriers*, *Simple Doggie Remedies*, *Pedigree Dog Breeding*, etc. Married to Edith Kekewich, née Cameron.
3 A. Luckhurst Scott (1886–1952). Chief Assistant to James Middleton as Secretary of the Labour Party.
4 Cyril Joad (1891–1953). Philosopher, author and broadcaster. Professor of Philosophy at Birkbeck College, University of London 1930–53.
5 G. R. Blanco-White (1883–1966), Barrister, and Recorder of Croydon 1940–56; and Amber Blanco-White, née Reeves (1887–1981), who had known Dalton at Cambridge, when she was an undergraduate at Newnham and Treasurer of the University Fabians. Writer on finance, literature and ethics. She stood as a Labour candidate in 1931 and 1935. Before her marriage, Amber Reeves had a celebrated affair with H. G. Wells, which resulted in the birth of a child. Joad was well-known in Fabian and left-wing circles as a philanderer. Hence Dalton's comment.

acutely at this time the burden of the war. From none of his other colleagues does he get so much stimulus. But there is much opposition. Both Cripps and Bevin talk of going out if the Beaver comes in again. The P.M. is said to be quite prepared to lose Cripps now, his stock having fallen. As for Bevin, it is more doubtful if he would stand firm on going out. But a number of Tories are against the Beaver coming back, and Webb thinks that it is impossible for the P.M. to have his way. It is also rumoured that Garro [Jones] may soon be appointed Under-Secretary to Lyttelton. This would not be at all a bad appointment.

Thursday 16th July
Gaitskell has discovered that Sir Horace Wilson does not go until his sixtieth birthday, 21st August. This is later than I had hoped. I conclude that I must broach some of the questions of personnel with Sir Arnold Overton before that.

Friday 17th July
To my constituency in the afternoon. This is my first visit since I became President of the Board of Trade, but there is no suggestion that I have left them too long.

In the light of the Coal White Paper, Bevin and Dalton had appointed a Board of Investigation into Miners' Wages, presided over by the Master of the Rolls, Lord Greene, with Harold Wilson as secretary. On 18th June the Board reported in favour of an unconditional flat-rate wage increase for all mine-workers, plus an output bonus, and a national minimum weekly wage – initially set at £4.3s for underground workers and £3.18s for surface workers. These recommendations were accepted.

Saturday 18th July
At Bishop Auckland. Sleep late and then see a lot of people. Private Delegate Meeting in the afternoon and Public Meeting at night. I make a long speech, mostly on coal, expounding the White Paper. (I had told the delegates a bit more about this and the difficulties over rationing. I had told them bluntly that the Labour Party was not at all keen, least of all the miners, and that this had been one of the reasons why, though I had got the Party's support 'for the principle', I had

decided to make concessions on this provided we got something good on reorganisation.) I say at the Public Meeting that we had got more in the White Paper than either the first or the second Labour Government was able to achieve for the miners, and I gave a long list of the new gains, including prominently the increase in wages. The reception is very good, and a vote of thanks is moved and seconded by Bland and Jack Bell,[1] it being thought fit that two miners' representatives should do this. One of them says that Lawther said the other day that I had been largely responsible for laying the foundations for a New Order in the coalfields. From this source, this is quite unusual praise!

Sunday 19th July
Play two sets of tennis in the morning and catch an afternoon train back to London. I am extremely fortunate in my constituents.

Monday 27th July
I have been having several consultations with Sir Arnold Overton lately on rearrangements near the top. I want two live wires immediately under him, to take charge of home and external problems respectively. For the former I want Watkinson, and for the latter some outsider. Twentyman[2] has been spoken of by Gaitskell and is in fact now in London. ... Sir Arnold Overton said that he had been the Treasury official in touch with the Board of Trade before the War, and that he was certainly an able man, though he understood that he had quarrelled with Woolton and French[3] at the Food Ministry, and he was now out of touch with Board of Trade war developments. I said that I still held the view, which I had expressed to him early in my time here, that the Board of Trade were a very slow and uninspiring lot. 'There is no zzzip here,' I said. He replied that much of the work here was necessarily dull and never reached me. There was a great mass of routine. Therefore, it was not to be expected that I should find quite the same interest here as either at the Foreign Office or M.E.W. I persisted, however, that I was dissatisfied and that we must have some new blood high up.

As to Watkinson, he was very anxious that Owen,[4] who was his senior, should not be passed over. I said I thought that he might be sent to America or to represent us in Lyttelton's Department. I also

1 Local activists.
2 Edward Twentyman (d. 1945). Second Secretary at the Ministry of Food 1941. Former Treasury official. Killed in an air crash March 1945.
3 Sir Henry French (1883–1966). Secretary at the Ministry of Food 1939–45.
4 G. S. Owen (1892–1976). Principal Assistant Secretary (Industrial Supplies) at the Board of Trade 1940–42. Ministry of Production 1942–5. Under-Secretary at the Board of Trade 1945–52.

said that I wished to get rid of Somervell,[1] whom I found frightfully slow and lifeless. He said that Somervell's health was not very good. I said that I would like to find something for him which would look like promotion but which would clear him out from the Board of Trade. My picture was that under Sir Arnold Overton there should be two live wires, and that Hodgson[2] should be left where he was for the time being, dealing, no doubt, quite competently with his relatively small technical field. Sir Arnold Overton said that he would make enquiries about Twentyman, including his rank. He said that the Treasury did not much like the rank of Under-Secretary. I said that this was great nonsense, seeing how many Under-Secretaries they had, both at the Foreign Office and the Treasury. He replied that several of the so-called 'Under-Secretaries' at the Foreign Office had not really got that rank. (I ascertained later from Gladwyn that this was quite untrue.)

While Sir Arnold Overton was talking with me about these matters, Gladwyn rang through on the telephone in reply to an earlier enquiry by me, to say that he was free to dine with me alone tonight. I told him later that this incident must have aroused Sir Arnold Overton's suspicions. On the whole, however, it is best, if he should have any suspicions, that he should think I was being incited by permanent civil servants outside the Board of Trade.

Gladwyn and I dine at the Coquille, where everybody is looking very ingratiating-shame-faced, after a recent conviction – a breach of food regulations. I tell him that I find many of the Board of Trade officials frightfully slow and boring and that I am on the look-out for new blood. He does not know Twentyman but suggests that I might like to consider either Lee[3] of the Treasury, who, he says, is a tremendous worker, very energetic, pretty intelligent, and with a reputation for being generally offensive – I say I don't mind this at all – or bringing back Noel Hall from Washington. I am inclined to like this less, since Hall is one who specialises in disloyalty and is absurdly egoistic. He has, I think, on the whole done pretty well in Washington, and I recall that it was on Gladwyn's suggestion that I sent him out there. He says that Fraser[4] makes a deplorable impression when repre-

1 R. C. G. Somervell (1892–1969). Under-Secretary at the Board of Trade 1941–52.
2 Sir Edward Hodgson (1886–1955). Second Secretary at the Board of Trade 1941–6. Principal Finance Officer 1946–9.
3 F. G. Lee, later Sir Frank (1903–71). Assistant Secretary at the Treasury. Permanent Secretary at the Board of Trade 1951–9; Ministry of Food 1959–61. Joint Permanent Secretary at the Treasury 1960–62. Master of Corpus Christi College, Cambridge 1962–71.
4 A. R. Fraser, later Sir Ronald (1888–1974). Assistant Secretary at the Board of Trade. Minister (Commercial) at the British Embassy in Paris, September 1944–9.

senting the Board of Trade at interdepartmental meetings. Keynes and others simply make rings round him. He is not only stupid, failing to see any of the points, but, conscious no doubt of being no match for the representatives of other departments, ineffectually rude as well.

We have a few words on the Rationing Declaration incident, and he says that to mention 'reconstruction' to the P.M. is like suggesting to an elderly uncle that he ought to be thinking about his will.

Returning after dinner, I am quite vexed at the very miscellaneous mass of business which I have to deal with, and the general failure to bring any of the matters now hanging about to a proper conclusion, as well as by the failure of most of the high officials to provide me with any stimulus at all. This business of stimulus, between a minister and his officials, should not always be a one-way prod.

Gladwyn had talked at dinner about the series of important speeches recently made by leading Americans on post-war affairs. No one at the Board of Trade had directed my attention to them. And why the hell hadn't they?

Wednesday 29th July
Disgraceful scene in the House over old age pensions. Shinwell makes a demagogic appeal which results in forty-nine Labour Members repudiating poor old Greenwood, who had accepted an assurance by Bevin, on behalf of the Government, that further steps would be taken next session for improvement of old age pensions. The House, including a section of the Labour Party, has got into a shocking state of mind. The sooner they are dispersed, the better for all concerned.[1]

Thursday 30th July
Lunch with Gaitskell to meet Twentyman. I like the latter, though he has a bit of a beard. But at any rate he shaves his cheeks! I broach with him, at the end of lunch, the question of coming to the Board of Trade, of which he has a very poor opinion. But I get the impression that he might be interested to come in to help to stir it up.

Friday 31st July
Sir Horace (Munich) Wilson calls at my invitation to discuss reinforcement of Board of Trade. I say that I must have more life and energy near the top. I speak of Twentyman, and Sir Horace Wilson, though warning me that Twentyman did not get on with French, nor later with Woolton, speaks well of his abilities. It is agreed that he shall speak to him. I say that I want a bifurcation under Overton into Home and External, and want the new man to take the latter.

1 Marginal note: 'Generally like this at end of July'.

Tuesday 4th August

We are now in the last week of Parliament and I have quite a lot of P.Q.s, which go off more than usually well. I then seek out Woolton and ask him for the release of Twentyman. He says that he would be quite willing. He adds that Twentyman, though very intelligent and just what I want as an energiser, has a difficult temperament. He has had a lot of grief in his private life and his nerves are not good. He used to sit up working too late at night, and this reduced his efficiency. He stimulated those below him but quarrelled a lot with those above him. When the Blitz was on, he did not like it at all, and this was rather too obvious. Woolton will, however, write to Sir Horace Wilson to-night and say that he is quite willing for me to have Twentyman. He then proceeds to speak ill of French. He says that, soon after he came to the Ministry of Food, he told French that he wanted it reorganised on certain lines. Three months passed and nothing happened. Woolton then said to French that he was getting tired of waiting for his instructions to be carried out. French said he must go and consult Sir Horace Wilson. Woolton said that indeed *he* must insist on his going to Sir Horace Wilson and telling him that Woolton was getting very tired of waiting for the reorganisation. When French saw Sir Horace Wilson, he asked, 'Did Lord Woolton shout at you and tell you he was the Minister and must be obeyed?' French said, 'No, he was very quiet.' Sir Horace Wilson replied, 'Then you are in mortal danger. You had better do it quick.' And then, it seems, it was done!

Woolton also said that, after a few weeks, French said to him, 'The right arrangement is that ideas should come up through the machine to you, but you are always sending ideas down through the machine. I am afraid this will lead to great confusion.' Woolton said that, when he took on Twentyman, 'I wanted to be stimulated.' 'That', I said, 'is exactly my position. Stimulus between a minister and his department ought not to be all one way.' Woolton said he had also said to French: 'I know that you are trying to delay because you think I may not last very long as a minister, then you may get somebody who will let you go on doing what you like.' ...

Later I go to the tail end of a most deplorable Party Meeting. The Administrative Committee have recommended a resolution re-affirming confidence in Greenwood's leadership and laying it down that in future decisions must be taken on the floor of the House by the Leader. An attempt is made by the malcontents to have this motion put in two parts, they alleging that they are all in favour of the first part but that the second involves a criticism of those who voted against the Government last week. [1] The proposal to divide, after much wrang-

1 i.e. on old age pensions.

ling and shouting, is declared to be defeated by 45 to 32. Shinwell then challenges the vote, which was counted by S.L.[1] and Hockley, and tellers are appointed to recount. But the second time the majority is rather larger, 50 to 31. The resolution as a whole is then carried by 66 to 4, a good few abstaining. This will look very satisfactory to the outer world. But I fear there will be a repetition soon. There are a lot of good demagogic wickets available, e.g. servicemen's pay and allowances.

Twentyman turned down the offer of a job at the Board of Trade, and on 5th August Dalton resumed his search. One suggestion was H. Wilson Smith, an Under-Secretary in charge of Establishments at the Treasury and until recently Principal Private Secretary to the Chancellor of the Exchequer, Sir Kingsley Wood. Dalton consulted Jebb, who described Wilson Smith as 'quite first class', and Sir Horace Wilson, who felt that the Chancellor would be unwilling to let him go. Dalton therefore button-holed Wood after lunch, and went back with him to No. 11 Downing St.

Wednesday 5th August

I tell [Kingsley Wood] that I am very much dissatisfied with the top lot at the Board of Trade and must have some new blood and live wires. He says that he greatly blames my predecessors for not having taken this up before. It is well known that the top of the Board of Trade is very second-class. He will do his best to help me. I say that I would like Wilson Smith.[2] He says that *he* is very good indeed and he will see what can be done, though he can make no promises. I say that this must be regarded, not simply from the point of view of the interest of him as Chancellor for the time being, or me as President for the time being, but of improving the efficiency of the public service. He says he agrees.

...

Dinner to Nash[3] – second meal with him today – at St Ermin's.

1 Probably H. Scott Lindsay, q.v., Secretary of the P.L.P.
2 H. Wilson Smith, later Sir Henry (1904–78). Under-Secretary in charge of Establishments at the Treasury 1942–6. Permanent Secretary at the Ministry of Defence 1947–8. Additional Second Secretary at the Treasury 1948–51.
3 W. Nash, later Sir Walter (1882–1968). New Zealand Labour Party politician. Minister of Finance in New Zealand 1935–49. Deputy Prime Minister 1940–49. Leader of the Opposition 1950–57. Prime Minister and Minister for External Affairs 1957–60.

Selection of members of National Executive and Administrative Committee of Parliamentary Party. Nash is in wonderful form. To illustrate his thesis that there are no inherently inferior races, he cites the Maoris, and the great progress they have made in recent generations. He tells a story of a Maori and a Scotsman disputing at Gisborne, on the east coast of the North Island, where the Maoris are very strong and a Maori was once elected to Parliament by white votes. The Maori said to the Scotsman, 'I am a better Scotsman than you are.' 'How is that?' asked the Scotsman. 'My grandfather ate a Scotsman,' said the Maori. And it was true!

Thursday 6th August
Kingsley Wood telephones that, immediately after I saw him yesterday, he sent for Wilson Smith, who felt that he had so recently taken on his present job, and that the work here would be so responsible and such new ground for him, that he preferred to continue where he was. Wood added that he would do his best to find someone suitable for me. This is most unsatisfactory. The Board of Trade has such a bad name, it seems, and is regarded as such a poor show at the top, that bright people are disinclined to come here! ...

Dine at the Soviet Embassy, other guests being Morrison, Dobbs,[1] Laski, Dallas, and Burrows,[2] who, I think, will turn out to be more use than most of our recent recruits in the Trade Union section. After some general jaw, Morrison propounds to Maisky the idea of a Labour Party delegation to Moscow. He does it very well. Others follow up and Maisky replies that he will consult his Government, that his personal view is that such a visit would be valuable, but that, as we all agree, the time is not at present opportune.

We then drift off on to a discussion of the future of Germany, and the opinion is expressed that the Germans should be compelled to repair damage, particularly in Eastern Europe. Reparations should be not in money but in kind and in labour. In particular, they should hand over machine tools to those whose industry they have destroyed, and should send labour gangs, e.g. to repair the Dnieprostroy Dam. The view was also expressed that it was an unhealthy condition in Europe where Germany was very highly industrialised while the countries to the east of her were largely restricted to agriculture and extractive industries. All these countries should have their share of

1 A. J. Dobbs (1882–1945). Chairman of the Labour Party 1942–3. Executive of the Boot and Shoe Operatives Union. Killed in a motor accident the day after he had been elected M.P. for Smethwick in 1945.
2 F. Burrows, later Sir Frederick (1887–1973). President of the National Union of Railwaymen 1942–4. Governor of Bengal 1946–7.

European industry. Also that the Ruhr should, in some form, be internationally controlled. Maisky said that he did not accept the view that Germany could not with advantage be broken up. When it was said that the result would be a long period of disordered struggle in order to reunite the German tribes, he was not so sure. What would Europe look like twenty-five years hence? Possibly national rivalries would by then have been removed in some wide federation. There must be, if we were to avoid economic disaster, economic planning on a European scale. He then led the conversation in an anti-American direction. He criticised the proposal that the Relief Commission should be centred in Washington. America might be the Germany of tomorrow. It would have immense need to penetrate world markets with its exports. It was the kind of country which might easily go Fascist. The influence of Wall Street was likely to reassert itself before long. All this was eagerly applauded by little Laski. I had to leave before the rest, and Maisky seeing me out said that he was afraid the P.M. had got 'an inferiority complex' about the British Army and this was why he was so reluctant to invade Europe. On the other hand, feeling in Russia regarding this country would be most adversely affected if we did not open a Second Front to help them very soon.

Friday 7th August
Lord President's Committee. I put in a paper on Advertisements, proposing to cut the percentages allowed in the newspapers. It is concluded, however, that the best course would be to approach the papers and to say that, for shipping reasons, we must cut newsprint by about 23,000 tons a year. The best way to do this would be by printing fewer copies. Kingsley Wood and Bracken are to handle this. The War Cabinet have agreed to a cut of some 200,000 tons a year of civilian raw materials and, as I point out, the choice may be between newsprint and wool, between fewer newspapers or a smaller clothing ration.

Dudley Ward comes round with a telegram for Leithers [Leith-Ross]. He says that both the Foreign Office and the Treasury are now very concerned about the stage which the talks in the U.S. have reached. It is proposed that Leith-Ross should come back 'for a few days' for consultation and then return to Washington. I don't object to this. The American Departments are squabbling among themselves, and their draft scheme is a mass of unsatisfactory verbiage. Keynes is said to be interfering a great deal in trying to reverse previous decisions of ministers. Ward finds Gladwyn very good in the Economic Section at the Foreign Office. He has become 'much more human' since leaving M.E.W. When Ward first heard that Gladwyn was to be his opposite number at the Foreign Office, he was rather concerned, but he has now been quite reassured.

Monday 17th August
George Tomlinson told me, soon after he went to the Ministry of Labour, that he used to go into the office early in the morning and write half a dozen of his most important letters in his own hand, and get them off before the Private Secretary arrived, so that the latter 'didn't get to know too much'.

I am told that Sir Andrew Duncan, when President, used to shout quite a lot at Sir Arnold Overton (I have never done this yet). Sir Andrew Duncan is said to have taken no interest in the work of the Board and to have been very chagrined during his second period here, having been pushed back by the Beaver from the Ministry of Supply. He is said to have stopped all initiative by the officials and to have given way to all claims by every vested interest. 'That man is a bloody coward, and probably a bloody crook as well,' someone said of him, rather unkindly.

One of the boldest initiatives to emerge from the Board of Trade during Dalton's presidency derived from a paper prepared by James Meade, a young economist (and associate of Keynes) in the Economic Section of the Cabinet Secretariat. The paper concerned the possibility of an international commercial union after the war, Meade arguing in favour of a world system in which there would be a general expansion of purchasing power, with discriminations and restrictions on foreign trade reduced or removed. The idea was for a Commercial Union to complement Keynes's proposed Clearing Union.

Tuesday 18th August
Take Wilson Smith out to lunch and pump him on possible reinforcements at the top of the Board of Trade. He is very good and very quick, but says that, from the selfish point of view, he would not care to come himself as it was much paraded that he had been promoted very young to take charge of all Establishments, and it would be said that something had gone wrong, if he moved too soon. When I say that I have heard well of Woods,[1] Lee and Playfair, he says that these

1 J. H. E. Woods, later Sir John (1895–1962). Principal Assistant Secretary at the Treasury 1940–43. Permanent Secretary at the Ministry of Production 1943–5. Member of the Economic Planning Board 1947–51.

are the three on whom people are always fixing their eyes. He argues that the Treasury have exported lately to the limit, and that they are very thin underneath. Most of their Heads will be retiring in a year or two. The outcome of our talk is that Liesching[1] of the Dominions Office is the best man available. Middle forties, energetic, intelligent, knowing something of external economics, and having set up three offices of British High Commissioners in Dominions, which was quite a new show. On the other hand, he may be very difficult to get, as he is spoken of as the one rising light of the Dominions Office. I tell Wilson Smith that I am speaking tomorrow to the Chancellor and will follow this up. ...

Gaitskell to dine, and tell him about Liesching, who, he agrees, sounds promising. I ask him to do some scouting about this new discovery before tomorrow evening.

Read, before going to bed, a paper by Meade[2] and Gaitskell on Commercial Union. This is quite bright, though with some little defects, and ties up pretty well with the paper on the Clearing Union. I discuss this with Gaitskell next morning and agree that I will put it round to the officials, with a laudatory Minute, so that it shall emerge as a Board of Trade official paper. This will be better than a ministerial paper, since it is rather free trade and might, therefore, provoke outbursts from more than one quarter.

Wednesday 19th August

See Kingsley Wood about personnel here. He thinks Liesching is the best man available. I will tackle Attlee about him tonight, and Wood says that he will do his best to help me to get him. We are at No. 11 Downing Street and it is a sunny morning. We look out through the open window into the garden at the back. There is no one there. Wood says, 'Ah, I have seen a lot of Prime Ministers walking about there among the flowers, and there were flowers for them in the end.' He has served in each of the Baldwin Governments, and also under MacDonald, Chamberlain and the present P.M. He says that Keynes and [Hubert] Henderson and others are always 'running in' to him and saying, 'Why don't you do so and so?' I say that not enough do this

---

1 P. Liesching, later Sir Percivale (1895–1973). Assistant Under-Secretary of State at the Dominions Office 1939–42. Second Secretary at the Board of Trade 1942–6. Permanent Secretary at the Ministry of Food 1946–8. Permanent Under-Secretary at the Commonwealth Relations Office 1949–55.

2 J. E. Meade (b. 1907). Economic Assistant 1940–45, and Director 1946–7, of the Economic Section, Cabinet Office. Professor of Commerce, with special reference to International Trade, at the L.S.E. 1947–57. Professor of Political Economy and Fellow of Christ's College, Cambridge 1957–68.

at the Board of Trade. I hear that they say at the Treasury, 'You will never do much with that little fool.'

Take Gladwyn out to lunch and ask him about Liesching. Very favourable. He is able and much respected, though not 'superlatively amusing' and inclined to retire in the evening to the company of his wife in Hampstead. I ask if he can hold his own in a battle of wits with the Treasury and the Foreign Office. Gladwyn says yes. He is inclined to be earnest and speak with passion about the Commonwealth. He thinks that I should like him.

He says that Maisky came in the other day and declared at great length to Eden against Wall Street and the Americans generally. I said this was the same as I had had at the Soviet Embassy the other night. Gladwyn thinks that there may be a repetition at the end of this war of the situation at the end of the last, with the United States taking the same attitude towards Germany that we took then, and we taking the same attitude as the French took then, both as to security and reparations. He thinks it quite possible that the Germans will fly into pieces, and that the westerners in particular will rush into our arms asking to be saved from both Prussians and Russians. The argument might be used that, in order to get reparations out of Germany, we must hold her together. This, he thinks, would be a great mistake.

Today there is news of our big raid on Dieppe.[1] This enables me to write a short note to Lucas, saying, in monosyllables, how responsive is H.M.G. to suggestions!

Discuss appointments with Overton and tell him that I am trying to winkle Liesching out of the Dominions Secretary this evening. He likes this idea. I leave over till tomorrow other consequential questions.

Attlee to dine at the Lansdowne. He gives me an impression of greater strength and on-the-spotness than recently. Perhaps acting as P.M., with the Labour Party scattered and Parliament up, makes him feel better. He says the raid went very well and we certainly destroyed many more of their aircraft than we lost of our own. But enemy losses are difficult to check exactly, since the Air Force always 'count every feather', whereas the Admiralty count nothing unless it is quite visibly 'in the bag'.

He talks a bit about the changes in the military command in the

---

1 On 19th August, more than 6,000 troops (including nearly 5,000 Canadians) went ashore on the French coast near Dieppe, midst heavy fire. Casualties were severe and, despite Dalton's record a few days later (Diary, 24th August), the air battle which was precipitated by the attack went in favour of the enemy. However, the raid was useful in providing evidence of the problems involved in attempting a seaborne invasion of France. There was also a limited success on the western flank, where a coast defence battery was captured and destroyed.

Middle East. The Auk [Auchinleck] has been a great disappointment lately. We have been urging him to attack, but it is impossible to give too many orders from Whitehall to the Commander in the field. He certainly missed a great opportunity of counter-attacking Rommel[1] when he was first halted, when his troops were at their weariest, before his lines of communication had been put in order or reinforcements had reached him from across the sea. But that chance was missed. Our Staff are always wanting to wait another week until they have completed their own preparations, forgetting that the enemy is doing the same.

Garro [Jones][2] was personally picked by Lyttelton, who thought him the best of the available House of Commons bunch, better than any Tory. Attlee could not have pressed for this post to be given to us, as he has already increased our quota much above what arithmetic entitles us to. The Tories, no doubt, will be very sick, but Garro is likely, we both agree, to do well.

Passing to my own affairs, I lead up, without much circumlocution, to a request for the transfer of Liesching. He says that he has already heard that this was coming. He adopts, on the whole, quite a forthcoming attitude, and says that, though Liesching is his best man, he does not think that any minister should stand in the way of the promotion of a good civil servant, even if it means moving to another department. He asks for an assurance that if Liesching comes to me, he will be No. 2 to Overton. I say that this is my intention. He asks me to put my request on paper, which, later that evening, I do.

Thursday 20th August
Poor old Craig Henderson[3] toddles in to see me about his Retail Trade Committee. He has no grip at all. He says that he once had a talk with 'Mr Duncan' ...... then he hesitates, and is not sure whether he has got the name right. I say, 'Sir Andrew Duncan?' He says, 'Oh yes, yes, Sir Alexander ... no, I mean Sir Andrew.'

Monday 24th August
Christopher Mayhew comes to take me out to dinner and tells me about Dieppe. A lot of his Company were in it, and he just missed being detailed for it on the ground that his training had not been quite long

---

1 General Erwin Rommel (1891–1944). Commander of German forces in North Africa 1941–3, Northern France 1944.
2 Garro Jones became Parliamentary Secretary at the Ministry of War Production on 10th September.
3 W. Craig Henderson (1873–1959). Leader of the Parliamentary Bar 1938–49. Chairman of the Committee on Problems in Retail Trades.

enough. He takes a rather gloomy view of the operation. In the centre, he says, it was just a massacre, and there was a muddle at one of the other landing places. The only place where they did well was where, under Lovat,[1] they put out of action the German battery and radio location station. This was well done. And so, of course, was the air. The Germans here were taken quite by surprise, and it was three hours before any of their fighters, and six hours before any of their bombers, appeared on the scene. Our ground troops, however, came up against great obstacles. Our tanks got stuck against a sea wall. Our objectives had included the whole town of Dieppe itself and something considerably further inland. These, of course, were not reached at all. On the other hand, the Canadians in particular were delighted, having for several years had no one to fight except the guards and the local inhabitants of places where they were billeted. The morale of all those returning from the other side, some of whom he met on arrival, was magnificent. No doubt important lessons have been learned for another time.

He then gave me an account of an evening with Cripps and his family. He ran into John Cripps,[2] whom he had known at Oxford, and was asked to go along. He was the only outsider present. The rest were Cripps, his wife, son, Personal Assistant (David Owen)[3] and some other hanger-on. The whole conversation was whether Cripps should resign or not and if, as Cripps appeared to take for granted, the P.M. fell, who should succeed him and what Cripps should do in that event. Should he or should he not serve under Eden? This was discussed at great length. I said to Mayhew that it all sounded a most nauseating, egoising performance, and quite remote, in nearly all its calculations, from probabilities. He agreed. He said that, when asked what *he* thought, he said, flat-footedly, 'When you came back from Moscow, you had quite a mystique, but of course you have lost most of that now and I suppose, if you stay on in the Government, you will soon lose the rest.' Cripps seemed to agree, and this, Mayhew thinks, is really the reason why he is always fidgeting about wondering whether he ought not to try to improve his personal position by resigning. He told them that the chief reason why he didn't resign was because he

1 Lt-Col. Lord Lovat, 17th Baron (b. 1911). Served with Lovat Scouts 1939–42. Brigadier, Commandos 1943. Under-Secretary for Foreign Affairs, 1945.
2 J. S. Cripps, later Sir John (b. 1912). Son of Sir Stafford. Editor of the *Countryman* 1947–71.
3 A. D. K. Owen (1904–70). Personal Assistant to Sir Stafford Cripps as Lord Privy Seal 1942, and a member of Cripps's Mission to India. General Secretary of Political and Economic Planning (P.E.P.) 1940–41. Assistant Secretary-General at the U.N. (Economic Affairs) 1946–51.

didn't want to let the Beaver in, and that the Beaver was working away to form a Peace Party which would come into action 'when Russia collapsed'. I told Mayhew that I thought this was all a farrago of nonsense. There was no reason at all why the P.M. should fall; there was nobody to take his place; even if he met with an accident, I did not for a moment believe that either Eden or Cripps would be asked to replace him, but much more probably Anderson. Nor did I see where the Beaver and his Peace Party were going to gain much strength. Nor did I think that Russia would collapse. So there was really no point of contact anywhere between Cripps's reflections and reality. Cripps also said that he thought that Shinwell should be in the War Cabinet! Also that he was afraid that, after the war, our politics would revert to pre-war Party lines. He would much prefer the formation of a new Progressive Party, which, those present understood, he would lead. Mayhew asked how this Party was to be composed, and who would now follow Cripps. He said, 'Chiefly some of the more progressive Conservatives in the House.' I told Mayhew that I had heard a little while ago, from Maurice Webb, that Cripps had been had along to an evening gathering of a group of about thirty Conservatives, who led him on and persuaded him that they all thought the same as he did and would like him to be their leader. He sucked all this up and, at the end of the meeting, said that they must all meet again soon. When he had left, there was much laughter at his expense. Bevin told me a few days later that this same lot had asked him along and tried to tell him the same tale. But he had said, 'You can't catch an old dog like me as easily as that. I am not Stafford Cripps!'

Following the fall of Singapore in February, Churchill had set up a sub-committee of the War Cabinet to look at the problem of India, where opposition to British rule threatened the war effort. One member was Sir Stafford Cripps, known for his sympathy for, and personal friendship with, leaders of Indian opinion. In March, Cripps was sent to New Delhi with a 'Draft Declaration' containing proposals for post-war elections and the extension of political rights, with the eventual aim of establishing a Union of India with Dominion status. This historic document conceded India's right to self-determination for the first time. It was not, however, enough for Congress leaders, who objected to a proviso that Provinces wishing to retain their present constitutional position should be allowed to do so. While the Japanese made rapid advances in the East, the Cripps Mission foundered on the 'separatist' implications of the terms, and on the refusal of the British to allow any immediate constitutional change. Cripps blamed Gandhi, who was widely quoted as saying that the Cripps offer was a post-dated cheque on a crashing bank.

With the departure of Cripps, Gandhi took the position that India could only be given a stake in its own defence against the Japanese if it was immediately granted independence – an attitude interpreted in London as 'defeatism'. On 14th July, the Congress Working Committee declared that British rule must end at once. To make India 'a willing partner in a joint enterprise' it was necessary that Indians should feel 'a glow of freedom'. This 'Quit India' proposal was endorsed by the All-India Congress Committee in Bombay on 8th August. Next day Gandhi, Jawaharlal Nehru and other Congress leaders were arrested. Although Gandhi had stressed non-violence as a basic principle of his campaign, a wave of rioting followed. On 12th August, the British Labour Party and the T.U.C. issued an 'earnest appeal to the Indian people', declaring that the civil disobedience movement would seriously injure the hope of Indian freedom and give encouragement to the enemy.

In July, Gandhi had described his attitude towards the Allied war effort in characteristically ambiguous terms. 'We do not want allied troops for our defence or protection,' he wrote in the Indian press. 'If they left these shores we expect to manage somehow. We may put up a non-violent defence. If luck favours us the Japanese may see no reason to hold the country after the allies have withdrawn if they discover they are not wanted.' But he also condemned the behaviour of the militant Congress leader Subhas Chandra Bose, at that time in Berlin, who favoured supporting the Axis against the British. 'Subhas Bose's performance can only fling India from the frying pan into the fire,' he declared.[1]

Tuesday 25th August
Call from Sir Theodore Gregory,[2] as he is now known. I had not seen him for quite a long time, and he is much more cheerful than of old and in quite good form. Whereas he always used to seem to feel himself very inferior to most of his surroundings, he has been feeling so bloody superior to the Indians out in India that he wears now quite a happy aspect. He says that all Englishmen in India now agree that the

1 See *The Times*, 20th July, 20th, 21st August 1942; B. R. Nanda, *Mahatma Gandhi – A Biography*, Oxford University Press, 1981 (first published 1958), pp. 447–70.
2 Sir Theodore Gregory (1890–1970). Economic Adviser to the Government of India 1938–46. Dalton and Gregory had been colleagues at the L.S.E. in the 1920s when Gregory had been Cassel Reader in International Trade 1920–27 and Cassel Professor of Economics 1927–37.

only thing to do with these hopeless people is to come out and let them go to hell their own way. This cannot be done during the war, but should be done as soon as possible afterwards. The Moslems have a perfect case for Pakistan, since the Hindus simply do them down by mental agility as well as by superior numbers. His only doubt about Pakistan is whether there are enough really intelligent Moslems to make it work at all. He says that the Indian capitalists are the worst of their kind anywhere in the world. They have no interest in their country, nor in any abstract aims, but only in making money. Gandhi's[1] latest move, including his statement that he would be willing to negotiate with the Japs, is due to the attitude of Indian capitalists controlling Congress, which has become a mere job-trust. The Indian capitalists are most emphatically opposed to any scorched earth policy which would reduce their profits. Subhas Bose,[2] now ostentatiously with the Nazis, has been known by every well-informed person in India for some time to be a Quisling. But, in spite of this, when there was a rumour a few months ago that he had been killed in an air crash, Gandhi sent a much publicised message of sympathy to his wife. There is no doubt that Congress leaders are quite prepared to appease the Axis. All their support in America is gone. ...

Sturrock,[3] a not very bright South African Minister, comes to see me and brings with him, amongst others, Liesching. I arrange for the latter to stay behind, and broach with him the possibility of his coming here. He is correct and guarded, but I think would be attracted. I say I hope he will come. (I learn that that day he lunches with Overton, and several days later seeks out Gladwyn and asks *him* about me. 'Of course I cracked you up,' said he, 'and told him he mustn't be frightened of you. He seemed quite surprised to hear that you were really quite human.' Who, I wonder, has been expatiating to him upon my inhumanity?)

I put to Gaitskell tonight the possibility, suggested by Overton, that he might be P.A.S. [Principal Assistant Secretary] in succession

---

1 Mohandas Karamchand, known as Mahatma, Gandhi (1869–1948). Leader of the Indian revolutionary national movement. President of the National Congress 1924–34, 1940–41. Leader of a Satyagraha (non-violent) campaign for freedom of speech and writing and action regarding war.

2 Subhas Chandra Bose (1897–1945). Indian Nationalist leader. Co-founder (with Nehru) of the Independence League in 1928 to promote the idea of complete Indian independence. President of Indian National Congress 1938–9.

3 F. Claud Sturrock (1882–1958). South African United Party politician. Minister for Railways and Harbours 1939–43; Minister of Transport 1943–8; Finance Minister 1948.

to Nowell[1] and under Watkinson. This would be subject to my still having a call on him, within reasonable bounds, for special jobs. The alternative would be to remain an Assistant Secretary and my Personal Assistant and to take over all Reconstruction. (Next morning, having thought it over, he says he thinks he would be a fool to refuse once more the possibility of P.A.S. I tell him I think he is right, and that it would be quite easy to make all sorts of adjustments to suit both him and me and the work.)

Wednesday 26th August
Attain the Elder Statesman-like age of fifty-five. I feel, however, fitter than I should, when younger, have thought possible in such old age. ...

Go in the evening to the Fabian Summer School at Frensham and am duly lionised. I give them a long talk in the form of reflections of a Labour minister after two and a half years in office in this Government. After that I sit up with them answering a lot of questions. Not too bad a bunch.

In late July, the Americans reluctantly agreed to a joint Anglo-American invasion of North Africa (Operation Torch) under General Dwight D. Eisenhower's command. The invasion was to be preceded by an attack by the British Eighth Army on Rommel's force at El Alamein. Early in August, Churchill and General Brooke visited Cairo, and decided to replace Auchinleck with Alexander, who had carried out the retreat in Burma before the advancing Japanese. Meanwhile, Churchill decided to visit Stalin in order to explain personally why it was impossible to open a Second Front in 1942. Accompanied by General Brooke, General Wavell, Air Marshal Tedder and Sir Alexander Cadogan, and by Averell Harriman on behalf of the Americans, Churchill left Cairo on 10th August, arriving in Moscow two days later. The party went back to Cairo on the 17th, and returned to England on 24th August.

Thursday 27th August
Press Conference on Clothes Rationing, in which I explain that, for shipping and supply reasons, clothing coupons must be spun out, so that the second lot must last for $5\frac{1}{2}$ months instead of $4\frac{1}{2}$, and it may

1 R. M. Nowell (1903–73). Principal Assistant Secretary (Commercial Relations and Treaties) at the Board of Trade. Nowell had moved over from Industries and Manufacturers (Division I).

be necessary to extend the 14-month period during which existing rations were to run. I emphasise, however, the special advantages to be bestowed on children and industrial workers, and the press takes it all very well. I say that we shall soon have no more hats and that everyone with natural hair should go about without one. This also is well received. (Cunliffe[1] sends me a short Minute asking whether I also think that those with beards should go about without collar and tie. I say that this is a bright thought which I will propound later.)

Lunch alone with McGowan in his private room at his office. He is very hardboiled but we both feel, I think, that each might be useful to the other. He evidently likes to keep in close touch with ministers and, in the course of our talk, asks me to get a knighthood for one of his directors. In return I ask him to turn his experts on to making me a report as to how the German war potential can be bust up after the war.

Keynes (Jeremiah Malthus, as we used to call him) – now a Baron on the Board of the Bank – comes to talk to me about cotton. Very bright and stimulating, as always. But he and I both know that neither of us much cares for the other. ...

Dine with Lady Colefax and am somewhat run after by persons interested in the films. Knickerbocker,[2] the American journalist, just arrived from some war front, wants coupons for a new suit. [Desmond] Morton, whom I have not seen for some time, talks most unguardedly to me about the P.M.'s visit to Moscow and Middle East. He always dramatises and exaggerates, but his tale is as follows:

In the Middle East the morale of all our people was most deplorable. The Auk had completely lost confidence in himself. Everybody was always looking over their shoulders towards prepared positions to which to retreat. The units at the Front were hopelessly mixed up, and there was no evidence of good staff work. The Auk had 180 Generals on his staff. This number has now been reduced to 30 by his successor. We should, of course, have hit Rommel hard when he reached his furthest point of advance. The P.M. and C.I.G.S. [Sir Alan Brooke] both went up to the line and followed different routes, and met that evening to compare notes. 'Both', said Morton, 'came back with faces like boots.' They were both convinced that drastic and speedy action must be taken. Already there had been a very great improvement. But

1 Hon. Geoffrey Cunliffe (1903–78). Director of Office Machinery at the Board of Trade 1941–2. Business Member of the Industrial and Export Council at the Board of Trade 1941.
2 H. R. Knickerbocker (1898–1949). American newspaperman who covered the Battle of Britain and the North African campaigns.

it was only just in time. Alexander,[1] the Auk's successor, has hitherto been in charge of brilliant retreats. He was the last man off the beaches at Dunkirk and since then he has done Burma. Williams Thompson,[2] who sat next to me at dinner, and is on the staff of Mountbatten, said that he thought the appointment of a man with this record, good though it was of its kind, would have a very bad effect, since it would be generally assumed that we were going to repeat Dunkirk and Burma in Egypt,[3] (Gladwyn, whom I brought back afterwards to talk alone, said that he heard that Alexander was a typical brave, brainless Guardsman, with beautifully burnished boots. When some junior officer rushed up to him at Dunkirk and said, 'Sir, the situation has become quite catastrophic,' Alexander said, 'I don't understand these long words.' Gladwyn also said that Casey[4] had blotted his copy book badly in Cairo by completely getting the wind up when Rommel was advancing, and issuing all sorts of notices advising flight. Indeed, Mrs Casey[5] had flown away in an aeroplane, but Lady Lampson[6] had angrily refused to go with her.)

Morton then talked about the visit to Moscow. He said that on the first day the Russians could not have been nicer and everything seemed [to be] going very well. On the second, everything changed and they were violently offensive, declared that we were doing nothing to help them, that we always betrayed all our allies, that we had never done any good in land fighting, and that it was a bloody disgrace that we hadn't opened a Second Front in Western Europe long ago. Whereupon, said Morton, reporting the version of Rowan,[7] the P.M.'s Private Secretary who was with him, the P.M. launched into a superb philippic and denounced the Russians with even greater ardour than Stalin had denounced us. What had they been doing, he demanded, when we were

1 General Sir Harold Alexander, later 1st Earl (1891–1969). Commander-in-Chief Middle East, in succession to Auchinleck. Supreme Allied Commander, Mediterranean Theatre 1944–5.
2 Major R. B. ('Mike') Williams Thompson (1915–67). Served in S.E. Asia Command. Chief Information Officer at the Ministry of Supply 1946–9. Later worked in public relations. He became a close friend of Dalton, who made several unsuccessful attempts to find him a parliamentary seat.
3 Marginal note: 'First mention of Mike'.
4 R. G. Casey, later Baron (1890–1976). Australian politician. Minister of State Resident in the Middle East and member of the U.K. War Cabinet 1942–3. Australian Minister of External Affairs 1951–60.
5 Mrs Casey, née Ethel Marian Sumner, married to R. G. Casey, q.v.
6 Lady Lampson, née Jacqueline Castellani. Married to Sir Miles Lampson, q.v., at this time Ambassador in Cairo.
7 Sir Leslie Rowan (1908–72). Assistant, then Principal, Private Secretary to the Prime Minister 1941–7. Second Secretary at the Treasury 1947–9, 1951–8.

fighting alone to save the liberties of the world? They had been supplying warlike goods in great quantities to the enemy and half hoping for our defeat. Why were they in the war at all? Only because they had been pushed into it and couldn't help themselves. Would they even have held out as long as this if we had not supplied them with large quantities of tanks and other arms? The result was a complete and immediate reconciliation. Stalin rose and said, 'I know now that I have been speaking to a real man. Let us go away together and have some drinks.' So off they went, alone with interpreters, to Stalin's private house, and talked from midnight till 5 in the morning. The P.M. had been able to tell Stalin a good deal which much interested him about things that might happen in the not far distant future. Morton said that the P.M. and the others thought very highly of Timoshenko and several other Russian Commanders. But there was a queer phoney political feeling always in the background. They did not see the Politburo, but they had the impression that Stalin went to and fro between it and them, and that his power was by no means so great as some supposed. On their first arrival in the Kremlin, one of his staff said to the P.M., while they were waiting for the Russians to come in, that almost certainly there was a listening apparatus in the wall, so he must be careful. The P.M. said, 'We will soon deal with that. The Russians, I have been told, are not human beings at all. They are lower in the scale of nature than the orang-outang. Now let them take that down and translate it into Russian.'

7

Minister of Privation
September 1942–April 1943

The war began to move decisively in favour of the Allies during the autumn of 1942. Victory at El Alamein in early November was followed by a success-ful Anglo-American invasion of Morocco and Algeria. The same winter, huge German losses at Stalingrad marked the limit of Hitler's eastern advance. The Allied attack on Tunis in May, crushing Axis resistance in North Africa, paved the way for a re-invasion of Europe.

Dalton took a keen interest in these developments, while himself exercising an increasing influence on the Home Front. His wide-ranging responsibilities – from films to cloth for trouser turn-ups – brought him into contact with Labour and Tory ministers with whom he had had few dealings in the past. He also seized every opportunity to develop important new ideas about post-war commercial policy. Meanwhile, the Beveridge Report became the central issue in domestic politics.

Monday 31st August to Friday 4th September
Visit to Manchester, accompanied by Preston. ... The visit was, I think, well worth while. I learned a good deal, chiefly by absorbing as I went along, and listening to a series of people talking, each in a slightly different way, about the same problems. Also many of the leading cotton people, who had never seen me before, and had only heard evil rumours concerning me, were, I think, faintly reassured to find me, after all, relatively human.

Saturday 5th September
Take Watkinson out to lunch and find him very keen and good at his new job. I am quite sure that I have done the right thing in promoting him, in spite of doubts and opposition.

I dine with Robin Brook, who says that 'they' are now doing very well in Poland, fulfilling their complete programme and dropping both persons and things according to plan. He sees a good deal of Morton, but always feels slightly embarrassed because the latter was clearly very antagonistic to Gladwyn Jebb, for whom he himself worked, I know, with great loyalty and appreciation for a number of months, even though working in a subordinate capacity to Gladwyn was not easy, for lack of cut-and-dried instructions. He says that at the Foreign Office they all say of Jebb, 'Very able ...... yes, but ...... ' I ask what he thinks 'Yes, but ...... ' means. He says he thinks it means that Gladwyn always laughs at the wrong place, and laughs alone, and the others don't like it. He gathers that this often happened in the Council at Baker Street. And behind it, one must admit, he says, that there is 'a certain arrogance'. He thinks that this will mean that at a certain point Gladwyn's career will be side-tracked. I say that I had jeered at Gladwyn sometimes for what I called his gullibility, and his mistaken belief that he was generally popular. Brook said that this 'gullibility' was really because Gladwyn was so keen on his job that he didn't realise that other people don't base their judgments solely on the merits of work-issues, but introduce many more personal considerations.

Churchill had visited Moscow in mid-August, mainly to explain to Stalin why no Second Front in the West was planned during 1942.

Sunday 6th September

Take Retinger to lunch and arrange with him that I can accept the invitation of the Polish Squadron to go to Exeter next Thursday, since air transport both ways will be provided. We then talk of other things, and he gives an account of a talk Sikorski and he had alone at Chequers with the P.M. last weekend. The P.M. said quite frankly that, in his recent talks with Stalin, he did not mention Poland. He did not feel that he could do anything for them on this occasion, since he had so much to answer regarding our own reverses and our slowness over the Second Front. But he had assured Sikorski that, 'At the Peace Conference I shall be able to help you a great deal.' Retinger said that both the P.M. and Eden, and Roosevelt and Stalin, had now given the Poles private assurances that they should have East Prussia and Danzig, and they counted also on themselves and the Czechs getting Silesia.

Monday 7th September

All ministers of Cabinet rank are invited to lunch at the Admiralty, and the P.M. makes one of his very attractive, intimate and amusing speeches to his 'pals and comrades'. He recalls our first gathering just before Dunkirk, and how then all seemed very black and we were all prepared to give up everything, including life itself as one of the least things to give up, rather than give in, and how we, by our united determination to go on to the end, sustained him in those days. And now, in spite of all, the prospect is immeasurably brighter. He gave an account, much on the lines that I had heard before, of his visit to the Middle East and Moscow. He said very frankly that Auchinleck had become a very dangerous failure and that the spirit of the troops was not at all good, though he hoped that now it had been improved.

Of Stalin he said many complimentary things. Also 'He is very genial out of business hours' and this he had appreciated. He thought that they had got on very well together. The last night, he being due to catch a plane away at 5 next morning, Stalin asked him, when they had finished their formal business about 7 p.m., whether he had any preoccupation that evening. When he said no, Stalin said, 'Then let us go and have some drinks together.' (In Russia, the P.M. explained, they never say 'Come and have a drink', but 'Come and have some drinks.') They then repaired to the Kremlin, to Stalin's private apartments, which were conveniently, but by no means luxuriously, furnished. Stalin then proceeded himself to draw the corks from a large number of bottles, in the midst of which process a pretty red-haired girl entered. She kissed Stalin, who looked to see how Churchill reacted to this. 'And I confess', said the P.M., 'that I acquired a quite definite physical impression.' It was Stalin's daughter.[1] Stalin then asked, 'Do you mind if we have Molotov as well?', and added, 'There is one thing you can say in defence of Molotov: he can drink.' So Molotov was allowed in too. Then they had drinks and food and drinks and talk till 3 a.m., and then the P.M. said that he must go to pack up, as his plane left at 5. The P.M. is quite convinced that the Russians will fight on and on until victory. 'Even if we and the Americans were to throw in our hands tomorrow, I am sure that they would go on.'

This afternoon Leith-Ross comes to report on his return from the U.S.A. The Americans will do nothing till after the elections in November, for fear of something getting out. Reverting to other arrangements, Leith-Ross says that, just after I left M.E.W., Eden was 'quite savage' against Gladwyn because the latter put up such

1 Svetlana Iosifovna Alliluyeva (b. 1926). At the time of this entry Svetlana was sixteen. She was Stalin's daughter by his second wife, who had killed herself in 1932. Svetlana defected to the U.S.A. in 1967 and returned to the Soviet Union in 1984.

resistance to the suggestion of a Treasury enquiry into our Organisation. This reminded me of the attribution to Selborne of the conditioned reflex: 'G.J. – rows with the F.O.'

Tuesday 8th September

11 a.m. Question Time in the Monkey House ... I stay on after questions to hear the P.M.'s speech. It is pretty good, on anticipated lines. Even while he is speaking, the House begins to empty, and when he has finished, practically everybody goes out to lunch. The whole debate, indeed, collapsed shortly after, and Cripps – silly ass – instead of saying that this shows that the House is completely satisfied and that the Government has received the equivalent of an almost unanimous vote of confidence, preaches a priggish sermon on the duty of M.P.s to stay and talk. He is rapidly losing all that is left of his 'mystique'.

On 29th August, Dalton sent Eden a memorandum urging that attention be given to the problem of reparations when Germany was defeated. 'Certainly the European victims of Germans, especially all those tough Slavs lying to the east of her – Russians, Poles, Czechs and Yugoslavs – will expect very solid compensation indeed for all the unspeakable maltreatment they have suffered,' Dalton wrote. 'Nor in this country will it be easy to put across the argument that we should be content to accept nothing.'[1]

Wednesday 9th September

Attend Memorial Service in the Abbey to the Duke of Kent.[2] The damn thing has no character at all. Smooth unctuosities by actor-priests, and beautiful music; but it might just as well have been for any notability. I recall having made the same comment on a similar service I attended when some Australian ministers crashed in an aeroplane at Canberra. I said then, 'No smell of the Bush in the Abbey this morning.'

...

1 Dalton Papers 7/4 (80).
2 Prince George Edward Alexander Edmund, Duke of Kent (1902–42). Youngest surviving son of George V, and younger brother of George VI. Married to Princess Marina of Greece. Chief Welfare Officer, R.A.F. Home Command, with rank of Air Commodore. He was killed in an air crash in the north of Scotland on 25th August 1942.

I get Gladwyn to come round for a moment before dinner to find out where my Reparations paper has got to in the Foreign Office. It appears to have got nowhere, though I sent it off with a suitable letter to Eden on the 29th August. Gladwyn has not yet seen it, though it should, as a matter of routine, have been at once referred to him. He will find out what has gone wrong. I tell him that Kingsley Wood had said to me, with a slight chuckle, 'My instincts are all with you, but I will have to discuss it with my officials. Anthony won't like it a bit.' Gladwyn added that he had congratulated Liesching the other day, and the latter, rather horrified, had asked, 'How do you know?' Leith-Ross, just returned from the U.S.A., was not so complimentary about Liesching as everybody else had been. He thought that I might find him rather 'pettifogging' and added that he was rather like, both in appearance and manner, what Overton had been at his age.

On 10th September Dalton flew to Exeter from Hendon aerodrome, accompanied by Victor Cazalet and others, in order to visit a detachment of the Polish Air Force.

Thursday 10th September

On the way to Hendon this morning Cazalet poured forth again his old tale of woe about the higher direction of the war, very anti-P.M. and anti-Pound. The higher direction, he says, is 'very messy', the same subjects being successively discussed by the Chiefs of Staff Committee, the Defence Committee, and the War Cabinet. He thinks the War Cabinet should take complete charge of the war. I am not much impressed by this, and say so, but there is more weight, I think, in his criticisms of the Admiralty. Pound has certainly gone on too long, but the P.M. likes him and A. V. Alexander now makes no attempt to 'interfere' in appointments, leaving all these to be settled by Pound, who has recently been putting a number of his personal friends into key posts – Portsmouth Command, Orkneys and Shetlands, etc. Alexander, Cazalet says, is quite content to be a cipher and to leave the running of the Navy to the P.M. and Pound, retaining his honourable status and exercising no real influence. I say that I am sure that Pound should be replaced by someone younger; that it is a good rule to change men in high command every few years, in view of the immense strain upon them. I daresay all he says about Alexander is quite true. He also hears that the feeling among high-ups at the

Admiralty is not at all good, that Pound is very unapproachable and has, too obviously, his own pets. We both agree that Sir James Grigg is a great failure at the War Office, not having, as Cazalet says, any idea of how to deal with human beings. He is a most unimpressive minister in the House, and much less good with the Generals than Margesson was. Cazalet also relates that Mountbatten, though a great pet of the P.M., is still being completely held up by the three Services, the Heads of all of which are very jealous of him. In the Dieppe raid there was only a handful of the personnel of Combined Operations, and the War Office in particular are very vexed at the continuation of the Commandos under a separate head. Cazalet goes on to say that, bad as we are, the Americans are, in every respect, much worse. ... Cazalet should always be taken with very large doses of salt, and he has nothing really 'constructive' to propose, least of all an alternative P.M. He tells me that in 1923–4, on his first election to Parliament, he became P.P.S. to Swinton, who was then President of the Board of Trade. He had also been invited by Austen Chamberlain to be *his* P.P.S. at the Foreign Office, but Swinton had 'fixed it with Austen on the telephone' – much to Cazalet's dismay, and Austen, therefore, had to fall back on Eden as second choice. It was clear – this conversation taking place in front of little Roberts,[1] who no doubt reported it at the Foreign Office – that Cazalet thought that if he had only gone to Austen in 1924, he might have been Foreign Secretary now, instead of Eden. He said, 'My Party has never done anything for me.' I said, 'Perhaps you joined the wrong Party.'

Sir Richard Hopkins, Permanent Secretary to the Treasury, visited Dalton on 28th August to tell him that the Treasury would allow him to have Percivale Liesching, a civil servant at the Dominions Office, transferred to the Board of Trade to work as No. 2 to Overton.[2] Dalton was delighted by this significant victory in his campaign to make the Board more dynamic. There was some difficulty about grading – the Treasury wanted Liesching to be a third Second Secretary, rather than an Under-Secretary. Dalton happily consented.

---

1 Identity uncertain. Possibly F. K. Roberts, later Sir Frank (b. 1907). Foreign Office. Ambassador to the U.S.S.R. 1960–62,
2 See entries for 18th and 19th August, pp. 475–8.

Tuesday 15th September
Liesching to lunch. He is a good buy. A bit of a Tory no doubt, and a little solemn, solid and conventional. But good brains and a good Whitehall reputation and very pleased at the substantial promotion in the Whitehall hierarchy which I have got for him. (I hear from Noel Hall some days later that he was getting rather 'waspish' because he felt that he was being kept down and not given enough opportunity.) He will start in with me as soon as Attlee gets back from Newfoundland with Clutterbuck,[1] who will succeed him at the Dominions Office. I tell him that I don't want long Minutes written, and he says that this is not his way.

Friday 18th to Monday 21st September
At West Leaze alone this weekend. The weather is pretty bad and I spend most of the time reading Carr's two books *Twenty Years of Crisis* and *Conditions of Peace.*[2] He is an able fellow and has read a lot. He has been much influenced by Marx and has some quite advanced and satisfying views on domestic policy. But he is pretty perverse in International Affairs. He was a failure as a Foreign Office clerk and had to take up the profession of Professor instead, at Aberystwyth. He hates 'Utopians', the League of Nations and Poland. On the other hand, he condones the Germans. He is said to be a great influence on *The Times*, and I must see him soon. He will like me to make conversation about his books. All authors do!

Monday 21st September
Back from West Leaze. Noel Hall to see me and to tell the tale of his successes in Washington, both with Americans and with Halifax. He says that immediately after Pearl Harbor, Kingsley Wood sent a telegram suggesting that we could now get better terms out of the Americans. Hall says that he told Lord Halifax that, if this were attempted, he would resign, and that Lord Halifax authorised him to draft 'a strong reply', after which no more was heard of this proposal.

---

1 P. A. Clutterbuck, later Sir Peter (1897–1975). Assistant Under-Secretary at the Dominions Office 1942–6. Permanent Under-Secretary at the Commonwealth Relations Office 1959–61.
2 *The Twenty Years' Crisis 1919–1939. An Introduction to the Study of International Relations* and *Conditions of Peace* (Macmillan, London, 1939 and 1942 respectively) by E. H. Carr (1892–1982). Professor of International Politics at the University of Wales 1936–47. Assistant Editor of *The Times* 1941–6. Foreign Office 1916–36. Assistant Adviser on League of Nations Affairs 1930–33. Director of Foreign Publicity at the Ministry of Information 1939–40.

Wednesday 23rd September

N.E.C. all the morning. Organisation Sub recommends that Laski – 'little liar Laski', as someone called him the other day – should be severely censured for writing an article in *Reynolds'* referring to the 'paralysis' of the Labour members of the War Cabinet etc. [Sam] Watson, using this as a means of attacking Shinbad, who, he says, is even worse, moves that we should have special N.E.C. in a fortnight's or three weeks' time devoted solely to the question of Party discipline. He would like to expel both Laski and Shinbad. After some exchanges of amenities, it is agreed to hold this meeting, and that Attlee and Bevin should be asked to attend.

Dine with Sir Alexander Mackenzie Livingstone, who is entertaining a party of American soldiers and airmen, including General Doolittle,[1] who bombed Tokyo – a squirrel-faced, humorous-looking little man. Our host announces that he gave me the choice of meeting King Haakon[2] next week or the American Army this week, and that I plumped for the latter. General Pile[3] is also of the party. He is certainly, as I used to think years ago before I had met many Generals, quite one of the most intelligent of his kind. He says that the defence is once more rapidly overhauling the attack in air warfare. The curve of our losses in night raids over Germany is mounting sharply. This is due, not so much to their flak, as to improved methods of using night fighters, which just fly up a searchlight beam which has already fastened on an attacking bomber. Therefore, he says, we may either win the war before Christmas by increasingly heavy air attacks, before their defence has been still further perfected, or experience such heavy air losses next year that it will be necessary to seek some quite new line of attack, the perfecting of which may take anything up to two years. He says that, on the one hand, our recent air attacks have been exceedingly effective, but that, on the other, 'Harris may be too late,' since our night bombers, including the newest and most perfect, are not sufficiently heavily armed to be able to fight off enemy fighters. On the other hand, the American Fortresses, flying by day, will be able to go on through the next phase, when we may be fading out, for these are most heavily armoured and armed and can most effec-

1 Major-General J. H. Doolittle (b. 1896). U.S. aviator. He led the first air attack on Tokyo in April 1942. Commander of U.S. Air Force in North Africa 1942. Commander of Mediterranean Strategic Air Force 1943–4. Commander of Eighth U.S.A.F. in Great Britain 1944–5.
2 King Haakon VII (1872–1957). King of Norway 1905–57. Forced into exile when the Germans invaded.
3 General Sir Frederick Pile, 2nd Bart (1884–1976). General Officer Commanding in Chief, Anti-Aircraft Command 1939–45. Director General of Ministry of Works 1945.

tively defend themselves by day. General Crain, an American who is sitting between us, tells of the great success of the Fortresses against Jap Zero fighters in the Pacific. One Fortress was recently assailed by six Zeros, of which it shot down five and frightened away the sixth. Our heavy bombers are made for speed and load, not for defence. The Fortresses carry a much lighter load but are armed with twelve guns which between them can fire in any direction. Pile thinks that, if German morale cracks in the next few months, as it may, the Russians will simply advance against no resistance from the East, and we shall be able to make a landing, without much resistance, in the West. But he wonders where we shall meet. He would like it to be in Berlin, but he thinks that it may be on the Rhine. All this may be a bit fanciful, but I set it down now to check up on later.

Following a letter from the Durham Miners' Association about a retiring age for M.P.s, Dalton wrote to the Secretary of his own constituency party, Councillor W. N. Davis: 'I daresay I am about the youngest of the present group of Labour M.P.s in the County, and therefore I am not immediately affected ... '[1]

Thursday 24th September
Shinbad rang me up, in a most amiable tone of voice, to enquire whether I had had a letter from Swan[2] about Durham Miners' M.P.s retiring at sixty-five. I said I had. He asked whether I had yet replied. I said I had. This disappointed him, as he was clearly anxious to concert a reply. I said that I was wholly in favour of the principle, and that I had proposed this very scheme in a book published in 1934 (on p. 41).[3] I said that I had added, in my reply to Swan, that I had only

---

1 Dalton Papers 8/1 (46).
2 J. E. Swan (1877–1956). Labour M.P. for Barnard Castle 1918–22. General Secretary of the Durham Miners' Association 1935–45. Member of Labour Party N.E.C. 1932–41.
3 *Practical Socialism for Britain*, Routledge, London, 1935, p. 41. 'Even a retiring age of seventy would have some effect in reducing the present average age of the Chamber, and one of sixty-five would be still more effective. A convenient compromise, which would avoid any additional cause for by-elections, might be found in fixing sixty-five as the maximum age for any candidate at a Parliamentary election.' Dalton was to make the 'age question' a major campaign in the 1950s – when his own resignation from the Shadow Cabinet on grounds of age helped to clear the Front Bench of ancients. Shinwell was one of the loudest protesters then, as in 1942.

just turned fifty-five and that the answer to the question, whether I intended to contest the Bishop Auckland Division at the next election, was yes. I asked him how old he was. He said fifty-seven.[1] Then, said I, *you* will have eight years to run before you reach the age in question. He admitted that this was so, but added that the whole thing was a manocuvrc 'to get us all out', and that he had sent a letter to his D.L.P. [Divisional Labour Party] and would insist on it being discussed. He said that the claim of the D.M.A. [Durham Miners' Association] that they made a financial contribution to each of our constituencies was all nonsense. The contribution which they made was very small, and they received a much larger contribution to *their* funds from the miners' lodges in his, and no doubt in other, constituencies. He did not think that age was the principal question in determining whether an M.P. should retire, though he appreciated that I might feel somewhat bound by having expressed an opinion on the subject some years ago. I said that I did not think that either he or I need fear any immediate consequences from this move of the D.M.A., but that I was firmly in favour of a fixed retiring age for M.P.s and a younger Parliamentary Labour Party. ...

To one of Lady Colefax's parties, where Gladwyn tells me that Eden says that he found my paper on Reparations, etc., 'very interesting and stimulating' and sat on it for several days. A number of officials have now written Minutes on it, and Gladwyn understands that Eden is likely to write to me shortly, accepting my proposal for a committee of officials to examine this and kindred questions.

Friday 25th September

... [T]o Lord President's Committee, where a long morning is spent on Fuel and Power. My locus this morning is confined to the sale of electrical and gas appliances, but I listen with some amusement to a long discussion. Gwilym [Lloyd George] appears, attended by Tom Smith, Hyndley and Innes[2] (this is most irregular and unself-reliant). He is evidently anxious to edge away from rationing, though the output has fallen further than the most pessimistic of the alternative hypotheses of three months ago. The miners and the owners were right when they told me that a flat increase in wage rates, unrelated to individual output, would mean less coal, and not more. Bevin produces figures to show, in accordance with his talk with me already noted, that the mines are no worse off, as regards age composition, than

---

1 Marginal note: 'This was a lie. He was born in 1884.' The first sentence is then crossed out. In fact, Shinwell was just over fifty-seven years and eleven months.
2 John Innes (1881–1961). Director of Services at the Ministry of Fuel and Power 1942–5. Deputy Secretary at the Ministry of Fuel and Power 1945.

munitions, building and other industries. Gwilym is hounded back to the White Paper Annexe,[1] from which he does his utmost to extricate himself. But he is reminded by quotations from speeches of Anderson, Cripps and myself in the House that, if rationing is to be adopted, it will be according to the White Paper. He is asked whether he has yet got the coupons printed. He says no, and adds that he is advised that it will take twelve weeks. Anderson raises his eyebrows at this, and it is hinted, pretty broadly, that he should have put this printing job in hand long ago; he must now do it at once. He is reminded that Parliament has been told that it will be the duty of the Minister of Fuel and Power to tell the War Cabinet when the coal situation is so serious that rationing is inevitable. He is asked whether this moment has yet come. He says no, and adds that the figures for gas and electricity consumption show some evidence of the success of the appeal for voluntary economy; at this time of year these figures are generally mounting sharply, but this year they have been mounting much more slowly, and in the last fortnight they have even shown a decrease. On sale of appliances, I say that I am against prohibition, since this would be administratively vexatious, and because, properly used, these appliances make for fuel economy. It is left that Gwilym and I shall discuss the matter without any need to refer back to the Lord President's Committee. I have said that we could arrange to reduce manufacture a bit later, and to discourage ostentatious display in the shops.

Lunch alone with Dunbar of the *Herald*. Deaf old fool! He says, quite truly, that Middleton is no use as Secretary of the Labour Party, and that we should not have kept him on. He thinks that we should offer £5,000 a year for the job, when all sorts of people would be attracted by it who would not look at it now. He doesn't see the point that no one could be appointed to, and succeed in, this job who was not already well-known and respected in the Labour Movement. He complains of Citrine's preoccupation with international affairs and of Bevin's megalomania. He also talks platitudes about the importance of international economic arrangements after this war. At the end he comes to the real point, and says that the newspapers really cannot cut down their advertisements any more.[2] To ask them to do so would be an infringement of the freedom of the press! It seems that Kingsley Wood and Bracken, meeting the Newspaper Proprietors the other day, mentioned me as particularly interested in such reductions.

---

1 The Annexe to the Coal White Paper. This recommended fuel rationing.
2 Dalton had been proposing a reduction in the advertising space permitted in newspapers in order to save paper.

Wednesday 30th September

Labour Party Meeting. A most chaotic discussion, with an even more chaotic close, on the composition of the Administrative Committee, now due to be elected for next session. There has been a lot of talk in what are called 'rebel circles' – this term is used in self-praise by the occupants of these circles – about the undesirability of ministers being members of the Administrative Committee. On the other hand, there is a very strong and simple argument against laying down any rule on the matter put at this morning's meeting by George Muff,[1] namely that all members of the Party should be equally free to be nominated or not and to vote for which nominees they choose. No minister, after all, is on the Administrative Committee except by the votes of his colleagues. If it were decided to exclude all ministers – and P.P.S.s would find it practically impossible to combine a seat on the Front Opposition Bench and frequent speeches of criticism of the Government, with their role in the Department – there would be a very poor rabble to choose from. This morning George Daggar[2] makes a long, rambling, rancorous speech, from which we infer that, when one has subtracted from the Administrative Committee all those who are now members of the Government, all those who have been chucked out of the Government, and all those who are ambitious to enter the Government, there is no one left except George Daggar. He points out that there is now a majority of one on the Administrative Committee for the members of the Government. (This is because there has been much recruitment from the Administrative Committee to the Government, including recently Tom Smith, Phil [Noel-] Baker and Garro Jones.) Daggar ends up his speech by suggesting that the members of the Government should meet among themselves and select three of their number to sit on the Administrative Committee. Right at the end of the meeting, an alternative proposal is suddenly put up by John Parker that not more than one-third of the Administrative Committee should be ministers. A vote being taken on this, it is declared carried by 38 to 37, but then Scott Lindsay says that he didn't notice whether anybody on the platform voted. I did, quite visibly, against the proposal, though all others on the platform abstained. So this makes 38 to 38, and Greenwood declares that the motion is not carried. Commotion, protests, etc. A very stupid end to a very stupid discussion. But I feel very doubtful whether it is really worth while for me, or, for that matter, for a number of my other colleagues, to stand again for the Administrative Committee. One cannot go very often. When one

1 George Muff, later 1st Baron Calverley (1877–1955). Labour M.P. for Kingston-upon-Hull 1929–31, 1935–45.
2 George Daggar (1880–1950). Labour M.P. for Abertillery 1929–50.

does go, most of the talk is rubbish and has nothing much to do with one's Departmental affairs. One could always go specially if these affairs were in question.

Conference with officials on clothing for Russia. They think we could and should give them a good deal.

Lunch with Eden to meet little Peter, King of the Jugs.[1] Also present Butler, Sargent, and the King's Equerry, who speaks little English but gives the impression of listening in very intently. Perhaps in order to report the talk elsewhere. The King is a funny little creature, who doesn't want to go back to Cambridge. His stay there has not, it seems, been a success. Nor was his period with the Guards' Armoured Brigade a success. Eden says, beforehand, that we should try 'to interest him in something' and to do our best for him, since he is the only possible link after the war between the disparate elements in his Triune Kingdom. The poor little chap gives me the impression of having adenoids, and, though faintly shrewd at times, is rather unimpressive. It seems that we might manoeuvre him into some other armoured formation, since he is clever at taking machines to pieces and putting them together again.

Return with Eden to Foreign Office to discuss clothing for Russia, relief, etc. Very friendly. I congratulate him on his Coventry speech. It seems that Maisky is in a mood to make trouble about many things, and has not only been complaining about our failure to give more clothes, but also about the plans for relief, which he says have not been properly revealed to him, and also Eden tells me, about our recent convoy to Russia. Although we had 75 warships protecting it, and got through 27 merchant ships, we lost 8 of the latter out of 35. These were all lost on the first day, in the course of the most concentrated torpedo bombing air attack of the war. When Maisky heard the news, instead of saying how good it was that we had got in 27, he complained about the loss of the 8. 'Your sailors could not have been paying proper attention,' he said. He seems to have imagined them all playing Crown and Anchor below decks.

I asked Eden what he thought of my paper on Reparations, etc. He said he liked it very much. I asked whether he agreed with my proposed procedure for a committee of officials. He said yes, provided Kingsley Wood agreed. I said he did. Eden thought that he had already sent me a letter about it.

1 King Peter II of Yugoslavia (1923–1970). Son of King Alexander. He succeeded to the throne in 1934 with Prince Paul as Regent. King Peter was granted full power after the coup in 1941, but fled to Cairo following the German invasion. He was dethroned in November 1945 by Resolution of the Yugoslav Assembly.

Friday 2nd October

My officials, who think I have been much too resistant to letting the Russians have clothes, have now concocted a list of available supplies worth £3,000,000, of which 5 per cent only represents the value of second-hand clothes. Eden thinks this is very handsome. But we must insist on controlling all supplies through Board of Trade.

Monday 5th October

E. H. Carr to dine with me. An angular, personally unattractive, but quite intelligent person. On home affairs he is very progressive; on foreign affairs very clear-headed on the whole, but with patches of obsession. 'Utopians', League of Nations, Poles, Germans. ... He says tonight that his great aim is to prevent Germany and Russia combining after this war. He will be a useful ally, on home affairs certainly, in *The Times* office. He agrees that the present P.M. is indispensable, but also that he is *très mal entouré*, and thinks it absurd that he should not sometimes say something striking on post-war affairs, even, e.g., that we shall not tolerate unemployment any more.

Tuesday 6th October

I agree to let my name go forward for the Administrative Committee, estimating that, though there is a small 'map room gang' which is campaigning against ministers generally, they will not get very far, though they may push off one or two. Walker has withdrawn his name, after consenting to nomination by Wilmot, and Ridley, whom I press to stand, says that he wants to reserve all his energies for next year, when he will be Chairman of the National Executive. He finds our new recruits deplorable and says that, if we could only get into the House Durbin, Gaitskell and Molly Hamilton, with a few more like them, we should soon revolutionise the Parliamentary atmosphere and the reputation of the Party in the country. Leslie[1] tells me that he is over sixty-five, but that he has replied to the D.M.A. that age is no criterion of fitness, that he is much fitter than many younger men, and that the question of next time must be decided between his Union and his D.L.P. [Divisional Labour Party]. Willie Stewart[2] says that *he* is sixty-five – though he doesn't look it ... There will clearly be a good clearance in County Durham next time.

Monday 12th October

Labour Party National Executive holds a 2½-hour inquest into the

---

1 J. R. Leslie (1873–1955). Labour M.P. for Durham Sedgefield 1935–50.
2 W. J. Stewart (1878–1960). Labour M.P. for Durham Houghton-le-Spring 1935–45.

misdemeanours of Laski. Unsuccessful efforts are made to introduce those also of Shinwell. Walker says that he knows that Laski approached Bevin a little while ago and asked him whether he would run for the leadership against Attlee. Laski is very nettled at this, but admits that it is true, adding that Bevin at once turned it down. (Attlee is present through all this.) Laski says, looking across at me and Bevin, who are sitting side by side, that he has completely lost confidence in Attlee's leadership and thinks there are only two possible alternatives, one of which is Bevin. He does not name the other, but no doubt he remembers that he made a similar proposal to me, which I received without warmth. (Shinwell next day said that Laski ought to be expelled from the Party for intriguing, though not a Labour M.P., about the Party leadership, a matter lying within the jurisdiction of the Parliamentary Labour Party!)

Wednesday 14th October
Mrs Phillimore asks some of us to lunch to meet Winant, of whom I have so far seen surprisingly little. He has great charm of manner, a great underlying earnestness, great good will, I am sure, and a certain amount of superficial twinkle. In addition to Attlee and myself, there are present Wilmot, Arthur Jenkins and Ivor Thomas. Mrs Phillimore now wants to ask 'some of the younger people in the Labour Party' to meet persons of eminence, and she leaves the choosing largely to me.

Thursday 15th October
Meeting with Harcourt Johnstone and principal officials on commercial policy. I tell them frankly that, until now, the Board of Trade has played a dreary and inert part, in comparison with the Treasury and other Departments, but that, now that changes have been made in the personnel, etc., I hope and expect that we shall be much better. We have before us Gaitskell's relatively short and audacious paper on Commercial Union,[1] and a much longer document by Leith-Ross and Clay[2] giving both a long historical survey – 'background' they call it – and a rather unemphatic and lengthy series of suggestions on future policy. Clearly some present want to give the latter precedence, in time and status, over the former. But this I won't have.

Friday 16th October
Lord President's Committee, as a result of which I am now to take

---

1 Based on the earlier paper by Meade.
2 Sir Henry Clay (1883–1954). Economic Adviser to the Bank of England 1930–44. Professor of Economics at Manchester University 1922–30. Warden of Nuffield College, Oxford 1944–9.

over the control of books as well! That *I* should do this had been recommended by a committee of officials chaired by Osbert Peake. Bracken and Butler both dislike this, and the latter, beside whom I sit, judiciously leaves lying under my eye the draft of a letter from himself to Bracken in which he says that he does not like at all this proposal, and that either he or Bracken should take on the job. I say, quite early, that I am personally quite indifferent as to whether I or someone else takes charge, but that I am sure that there should be a single minister in charge and not a Ministerial Committee. At this point I look fixedly at Bracken – he and I recalling, I am sure each equally vividly, our past clashes – and he at once assents. Several other members of the Committee, including the Chairman and Bevin, are strongly for my taking it. If it should be thought, says the Chairman with a smile, that spiritual and cultural values would be ignored by the materialist President of the Board of Trade, he felt sure that I should be most willing to consult my colleagues, and that a standing committee of officials to advise me would be most useful, and, he was sure, quite acceptable to me. I thereupon observe that the Archbishop of Canterbury is a member of my Board of Trade, though I have not lately summoned him to any of my meetings, and that only yesterday I was accosted by the Chaplain to the House of Commons[1] on a most spiritual problem, namely, the supply of clothing coupons for the choir and vergers of Westminster Abbey. Bevin adds that, after all, I was pretty spiritual myself in the last generation,[2] and, further, that he has a very good working arrangement with the Board of Trade regarding labour and doesn't want to have to start all over again with the Ministry of Information or any other Department. And so, with thanks to Peake for his valuable labours, the thing goes through, after a snub has been administered to the British Council, whose paper allocation, we decide, is to be made not direct, but through the Foreign Office.

Monday 19th October

Afternoon at Foreign Office, (1) with Eden and Maisky, and (2) with Eden, Attlee, Leith-Ross and Ronald. ...

Maisky ... seems to like my clothing offer. I shall be taking out £3,000,000 worth of stuff for him. When I name this figure, he sits up straight, with a surprised grin, and says, 'Oh, thank you!' Eden said afterwards, 'I have never known the little blighter say thank you for

---

· 1 Rev. Canon A. C. Don (1885–1966). Chaplain to the Speaker of the House of Commons 1936–46. Chaplain to the King 1934–46. Dean of Westminster 1946–59.

2 Dalton's father, John Neale Dalton, q.v., had been a Canon of St George's Chapel, Windsor.

anything before.' The stuff is to be distributed by a joint committee of British Red Cross (Mrs Churchill's Fund), the Soviet Red Cross (Mrs Maisky) and the T.U.C., with Board of Trade officials in attendance. …

Subversive operations in Czechoslovakia suffered a severe setback after the killing in May 1942 of Reinhard Heydrich, the German military leader, by two S.O.E.-trained Czech agents. In the bloody repression that followed, the Czech underground was virtually wiped out and the network set up by S.O.E. agents in the months before the assassination collapsed.

Dine with Robin Brook. He says that the whole Czech network is now destroyed. The Germans have simply gone on killing, torturing and imprisoning key people until there is nothing left. Not quite in accord with the easy-oozy theories sometimes current among soft-minded civilised people that you cannot, if you are brutal enough, destroy what you dislike. Brook thinks it will be almost impossible to recreate this network, though others take a different view. Likewise the Polish network in France has been destroyed, and will be almost impossible to recreate. Here there had been much indiscretion and some mismanagement, and Mikolajczyk[1] nearly came unstuck over it. Librach, 'his stooge', was even more seriously discredited. One consequence is that the Polish military have taken over even more of what were previously civilian activities. Meanwhile, on the other hand, in Poland itself the network remains, with an almost fantastic multiplicity of links. Great success has been achieved both in reinforcing from the air and maintaining wireless contacts.

I tell Brook what Pile said the other night. He thinks this much exaggerated, and our heavy bombers much less vulnerable than Pile had argued. He says that the curve of our losses is not rising, as Pile said. At present it simply has no trend, but jumps up and down from raid to raid. The success of the American day bombing is due to their amazing bomb-sight. It is, he thinks, out of the question that the Germans should be able, within a reasonable time, to reproduce this incredibly complicated mechanism, even if they captured one intact.

1 Stanislav Mikolajczyk (1901–66). Deputy Prime Minister and Minister of Home Affairs in the Polish government-in-exile 1941–3. Prime Minister (following death of Sikorski) July 1943–November 1944 when he resigned.

And this it is designed that they should not be able to do, since pieces of the mechanism blow off, according to plan, if there is a danger of capture, or if the plane hits the ground hard. So far, the American fighter has been a great disappointment, and our superiority here is quite unchallenged. General Marshall-Cornwall[1] has just come in as No. 2 to M. [Gubbins]. The reason for this odd arrangement is not clear. Perhaps the General is going to take over from M., or perhaps from Hambro, for whom Brook has an increasingly low opinion. He says he blunders over everything, and his bluff will not always carry him through.

Tuesday 20th October
P.Q.s include one on supplies to Russia, and I take the opportunity of unloading news of our impending large additional consignments, ending up by saying that I am sure the House will agree that we should do all we can to aid our Russian allies, but that all we send must be a subtraction from the ever-diminishing supplies available to our own civilian population. This is said in order to create a good atmosphere for resisting further claims for industrial supplements etc. To my horror, Maurice Webb in the *Daily Herald* next day says that this means an early cut in our own clothing ration, and I have a vision of an ugly rush to all the shops to clean up supplies, and an early exhaustion of the present bunch of coupons. With some little difficulty, Wilmot and Simmonds[2] get Webb to put in a para next day saying that it is not intended to alter the ration during the present rationing period. ...

Patrick Hancock to dine with me. I have not seen him for some time. He is very cheerful and pleased to see me and other old friends again. He looks back, I think, to the time when he was with me at M.E.W. as much more fun than his life at the Foreign Office now.

Wednesday 21st October
The voting for the Administrative Committee has come out very well. Wilmot comes in just before lunch to tell me that he has won his bet with me that I should get more votes than any other minister. I am, indeed, second on the list of 39 candidates for 19 places. I get exactly 100 votes, Jim Griffiths getting 104. If I had not snubbed 5 chaps some time or other, I should have been on top! All retiring members who

1 General Sir James Marshall-Cornwall (b. 1887). G.O. Commander-in-Chief Western Command 1941–2.
2 C. C. J. Simmonds. Director of Public Relations at the Board of Trade 1943–6.

sit again were re-elected, and, in addition, Montague,[1] Milner[2] and Creech Jones.[3] Shinwell only just saved his bacon, getting 53 votes as against 47 for Dobbie,[4] the highest unsuccessful candidate. Morrison was 4th, but Alexander dropped to 10th place with only 79 votes. His remark, 'when I brought the Army away from Dunkirk', has been quoted a good deal lately. Wilmot says that my vote was distinctly noticed, when announced at the Party Meeting, and he himself took steps to inform the press, and told John Carvel to tell Harvie Watt, who, later in the day, when Wilmot was trying to get out from the Second Bench, said, 'Don't give yourself such airs, just because your Chief has got a lot of votes' – this in a most friendly fashion. These relative votes have great importance for a very short time, but after a while all that is remembered is whether one is actually on or off the Administrative Committee or other body. Meanwhile, for the next week, say, I could safely force a major issue almost with anyone, from the P.M. downwards. But, in fact, there is no major issue which I wish to force!

Smuts speaks this afternoon in the Royal Gallery, specially arranged for the occasion, to an audience of M.P.s, Peers, and other notabilities from within the British Commonwealth. It is a remarkable performance, lasting nearly an hour, admirably phrased, and delivered, although read word for word from manuscript, so well as to sustain interest throughout. He has a weather-beaten, outdoor face, which contrasts magnificently with the pale faces of Lloyd George in the Chair, the P.M. and the Speaker. Simon, the only other occupant of the platform, has a flushed, but not a really healthy, red face. Smuts makes, it seems to some of us, two gaffes. First, he says that we should all be 'most grateful for Pearl Harbor', since it brought America 100 per cent into the war. Second, he speaks of the Russians 'bleeding Germany white, as only Russia can'. On the other hand, he makes one first-class crack in declaring that one of our peace aims must be 'Japan for the Japanese'.

The P.M., again some of us thought, looked tired, too pale and not very well. He said only a few rotund and complimentary words at the end. [David] Lloyd George on the other hand, made a quite shocking

1 F. Montague, later 1st Baron Amwell (1876–1966). Labour M.P. for Islington West 1923–31, 1935–47. Junior minister 1929–31, 1940–42.
2 Major James Milner, Labour M.P. for Leeds South-East, q.v.
3 A. Creech Jones (1891–1964). Labour M.P. for Shipley 1935–50; Wakefield 1954–1964. Junior minister 1945–6. Colonial Secretary 1946–50.
4 W. Dobbie (1878–1950). Labour M.P. for Rotherham 1933–50. President of the National Union of Railwaymen 1925–8, 1930–33.

performance, Pétain to the life. 'This terrible and perplexing war.' He said nothing to show which side he was on. He has been neutral and defeatist from the start. But today he looked very, very old. I think he will fade out soon.

'I am in a good patch now,' Dalton scribbled on the typescript of his diary entry for 22nd October, which dealt with the Retail Trade Committee. ' ... Both the Labour Party and the Tóries like me a lot! This compares well with four months ago, when I had just emerged from the Coal Scuttle. I have now had just eight months at B of T, and have come to like, rather than resent, its infinite variety.'

Friday 23rd October

Having a quiet morning, I reconstruct my Prod Sheet, and find quite a number of items to enter from scattered slips. This device is the key to efficiency, and I think that probably ministers can be grouped in two classes, the efficient ministers who keep a Prod Sheet, and the duds who don't.[1]

The Mexican Minister[2] comes, asking for wool! As Belloc[3] once said in another connection, 'He might as well have asked for the stars or fairy gold'. I undertake to send him a long-winded story of why he can't have any. Like many diplomats, he has a frightened look, and is no doubt being bullied by his government at home. ...

To West Leaze this evening, taking with me the paper on Commercial Union, which I must put into their final shape myself, having taken account, but not too much account, of all the frightened and too prudent shrieks of my higher officials.

1 'All ministers should keep a "Prod Sheet" ... ' Dalton wrote later. 'On this should be entered a note of pending questions which the Minister thinks important and does not wish to be postponed or forgotten, as may easily happen in the rush of a busy office, even without deliberate delays by some of those concerned. Every few days the Minister should go through the Prod Sheet with his Private Secretary and prod the laggards.' (*High Tide and After: Memoirs 1945–60*, Frederick Muller, London, 1962, p. 23.)

2 Señor Dr Don Alfonso de Rosenzweig Diaz. Envoy Extraordinary and Minister Plenipotentiary for Mexico.

3 Hilaire Belloc (1870–1953). Poet, satirist and critic. Brooke had introduced Dalton to Belloc's work at Cambridge, and Dalton became a keen admirer. After leaving Cambridge, Dalton and a friend founded a 'Belloc Club' in London.

Monday 26th October

Gladwyn Jebb for a drink before dinner. Still no letter from Eden convening Reparations Committee, and Gladwyn will 'chase this up'. It is said to have been with the Private Secretaries four days ago. The Foreign Office is very inefficient at the Private Secretary level. I sound Gladwyn as to the atmosphere with Russia, and he thinks that it is full of danger. This makes it all the more important that we should give them no excuse to increase their suspicion that we don't really want to co-operate with them, e.g., consultations on Relief Organisation. (Eden's letter comes in, quite satisfactory and evidently based on a draft by Gladwyn, two days later. I nominate Liesching and Clay to represent me.)

Tuesday 27th October

Winster gives a frightful picture of the Admiralty and the way in which A. V. Alexander is completely in the hands of the Admirals and, in particular, of old Pound. Moore,[1] the Deputy First Sea Lord, is, he says, a complete yes man, and was chosen for this reason. Alexander, like most other First Lords, is so glamoured by the operational side of the Navy, and by the cocked hats, etc., that he spends all his time ineffectively playing about with this side of the show and leaves untouched the incredible inefficiency of the civilian administration, headed by Markham.[2] Here he could really do good work, but he doesn't think of it at all. It is a constant complaint that 'you can never get a decision at the Admiralty', and this is largely the fault of the civil side. Also Admirals returning from the sea to Whitehall, to the ways of which they are quite unused, quickly become more bureaucratic and circumlocutory than even the worst civilian bureaucrats. I notice a tendency, however, on the part of Winster and Bowles[3] to think that I ought to be taking more interest, if not more share, in the operational side of the war. So long as I am President of the Board of Trade, this would mean that, with even less excuse than Alexander, I was neglecting my primary job for others.

Winster is very anti-Commando, both on principle and because he thinks Mountbatten is not big enough to do it. In principle, he thinks, it discourages the general body of the troops. They are told that, when some very daring and important operation is on, it is handed over to these picked forces, because the poor old P.B.I.[4] isn't up to it. In the

1 Admiral Sir Henry Moore (1886–1978). Vice Chief of Naval Staff 1942–3; Commander-in-Chief, Home Fleet 1944–5.
2 Admiral Sir Henry Markham (1897–1946). Permanent Secretary at the Admiralty 1940–46.
3 F. G. Bowles, later Baron (1902–70). Labour M.P. for Nuneaton 1942–64.
4 'P.B.I.': Poor Bloody Infantry.

Navy they have always set their faces against any idea of a 'crack ship'. Destroyers, submarines, etc., come up for duty according to a roster. They are all on the same footing. I say that I recall that in the last war, the Germans first, with their Storm troops, and then the Italians with their 'Arditi' – also known as 'Black Flames', whence the Fascist badge – went in for picking the eyes out of ordinary units in order to create such special units. Neither we nor the French did this. Winster also complained that the Commandos were not numerous enough for large operations. Of Mountbatten, he said that he was much too meticulous. It has been represented that the success of the Dieppe raid was illustrated by the fact that the troops had all re-embarked within twenty minutes of the time scheduled for re-embarkation. But how fantastic to *schedule* a time for re-embarkation, before one knew whether the raid had fully succeeded or not. He said that Mountbatten always worked things out on a minute and complicated timetable beforehand, and that this was about the limit of his mental powers. Also that he had now collected around him an enormous staff of hundreds of officers, and that his Intelligence work was done by Casa Maury,[1] who, I understood, though I did not wish to show too much ignorance, was some kind of celebrity in the world of art. No wonder, said Winster, that the three Services looked with the greatest disfavour upon so-called 'Combined Operations'. He told a tale of how Mountbatten at his country house, entertaining a large party, asked them all the night before what time they wished to leave in the morning. Nearly all of them said 11 o'clock. He then drew out a list whereby Lord A's car would call at 10.55, Mr B's at 11 o'clock, the Dowager C's at 11.05, etc. All this was announced to the guests. But, through some gap in staff work, it never got into the operational sphere, and next morning the butler asked Mountbatten at breakfast what time the various guests were going, and no arrangement had been made about any of the cars.

We spoke also of the Labour peers. Winster said that Addison was very old indeed and could not go on much longer. He had wondered whether Latham would make a good successor. He seemed to him to be well-informed and a practised speaker. Wilmot very loudly, and I less loudly but with emphasis, declared against this. Little Lord Latham of London, as we always call him, is in every respect, except in his ambitions, a small man. It seemed to us that Winster himself would be much better, and that things should so be worked, if possible, that Winster should become new deputy to Addison, so that the suc-

1 Wing Commander the Marquis of Casa Maury (1895–1968). Invited in 1941 by Mountbatten to set up and run the Intelligence Staff of Combined Operations H.Q. Former racing-driver.

cession should come easily. He seemed pleased at this and won't, we think, forget it. How to do it is more difficult. All the rest of the Labour peers are quite impossible: Nathan, with his creaking Sam Browne belt, Southwood – Camrose[1] had asked Winster why Southwood sat on the Front Bench and Winster had replied, 'The *Daily Herald* is always found in the front rank' – Listowel,[2] always white with stage fright and rather reassured to find that Labour peers were tolerated after all, Snell,[3] very old indeed and deafer still, and anyhow the Master of the Horse or some such something in the Government, Faringdon,[4] a pansy pacifist of whose private tendencies it might be slander to speak freely, Marley,[5] a complete nitwit who had remained in China until it seemed that England was less dangerous – and what else? We remembered nothing else.

Wednesday 28th October

Labour Party National Executive all the morning. Further desultory discussion on the misdeeds of Laski. Morrison urges him to 'undertake not to write again criticising leaders personally, though reserving the right to discuss tendencies, etc.', and little Laski, with not a very good grace, accepts and the thing is left there.

Postscript from last night. Winster told two stories of how the Admirals play up to King Albert.[6] They are awfully good at this sort of thing, and he most easily caught.

1 Returning up the Thames from a Fleet inspection, in some sort of well-appointed craft (I forget its description), accompanied by nine Admirals all in their cocked hats, there was a slight, but only a very slight, disturbing movement on the water. King Albert, towards the end, turned silent and a little green. For the Admirals, of course, used to tempests in the open sea, the movement was imperceptible, but, as they stepped ashore, one Admiral said,

---

1 W. E. Berry, 1st Viscount Camrose (1879–1954). Editor-in-Chief of the *Daily Telegraph* 1928–54; *Sunday Times* 1915–36.

2 W. F. Hare, 5th Earl of Listowel (b. 1906). Junior minister 1944–5. Postmaster-General 1945–7. Secretary of State for India and Burma 1947–8. Junior minister 1948–51.

3 H. Snell, 1st Baron (1865–1944). Labour M.P. for Woolwich East 1922–31. Junior minister 1931. Leader of the Labour Party in the House of Lords 1935–40.

4 A. G. H. Faringdon, 2nd Baron (1902–77). Fabian. Treasurer of the National Council for Civil Liberties 1940–45.

5 D. L. Aman, 1st Baron Marley (1884–1952). Junior minister 1930–31. Six times an unsuccessful Labour candidate 1919–29. Chief Government Whip in the House of Lords 1930–31; Chief Opposition Whip 1931–7.

6 Dalton's name for A. V. Alexander, q.v.

'You stood that splendidly, First Lord. I confess I was feeling a bit queer myself towards the end.'

2 They were receiving, in the Admiralty War Room, wireless reports of some hot naval engagement. King Albert showed keen, and even slightly emotional, interest in the news as it came through. An Admiral said, 'I know just how you feel, First Lord. You are saying to yourself, "I wish to God I was in command myself, out in the middle of it all." ' ...

Ellen Wilkinson to dine with me. This has been on the cards for some time, but always put off. She is still a most devoted worshipper of Herbert Morrison, and puts me second. What she would like would be Morrison to lead the Party and me to be his deputy. She would like us two to go into the War Cabinet, putting out Attlee and Cripps. The difficulty about all such plans is that the right moment never arrives to put them into execution! She says that Morrison, having been deeply absorbed with his job until recently, is now feeling that he has got it into running order, and is taking much more interest in wider questions, including post-war problems and the future of the Labour Party. Bevin, she says – though I think she puts him third in order of merit among Labour leaders – is quite grotesque in his garrulity. She says that he accompanied Gwilym Lloyd George to a press conference the other day – nominally called by the Ministry of Fuel and Power – and that he literally talked for fifty minutes, leaving Lloyd George five, and then went on to answer all the pressmen's questions. His is an extreme case of what I am beginning to call the General Council disease. They meet in London for a clear day, and there is never any need to be terse. Ellen Wilkinson had a bad knock the other day when her car was run into from behind and she had a fracture of the skull. She tends now to get most excruciating headaches, and she drinks more than one small glass of sherry. Whenever we meet and talk, at rare intervals, she is always planning to bring me and Morrison together. I say that I am always very willing for this to happen. My feelings towards him are entirely benevolent, though I tell her that I know – from Wilmot, of whom she speaks most highly – that Morrison was much chagrined when he found that I was trying to supplant Attlee by Greenwood in the early days of the war. But this, as she well knows, because I told her at the time, was because I judged that Morrison had retired so completely to his tent in the County Hall that he would just not have polled the votes required. Greenwood, on the other hand, had done extremely well at the outbreak of the war, never before or since had he reached the same high standard, and it seemed to me that *any* substitution was better than none. But that was a phase which has passed.

Thursday 29th October
John Wilmot tells me a queer yarn of a man called Macdonald[1] who came to see him, and has since written to him, about the formation of a new Centre Party. ... John says that this man Macdonald alleged that he had Sam Courtauld behind him, and that other businessmen were interested. He had sent John a long farrago of a programme, amateurish but not ill designed to attract support from many quarters. It advocates religion, patriotism, and, in broad terms, private enterprise, but it adds the expansion of public corporations and public utilities, family allowances, the immediate raising of the school-leaving age to sixteen, etc. It wants an improved higher direction of the war, with the P.M. no longer Defence Minister, and with members of the Cabinet chosen not for their Party influence, but for their ability. It is suggested that this might lead to many changes. The leader of the new Centre Party would be chosen later, but meanwhile, provisionally, by those M.P.s from the Conservative, Labour and Liberal Parties who would be willing to join at once. Macdonald has been very pressing for some reply, but John and I agree that, even at the cost of seeming to be rude, it would be most unwise for him to put anything on paper, or even to initiate a telephone conversation. On the other hand, we think that Ivor Thomas might be used as a willing stooge and encouraged independently to get in touch with this man and find out what he can. I am not inclined to take the thing seriously, but it is mildly amusing. ...

Return to welcome Sir Walter Citrine, whom I have not seen for a long time. He comes at 4 and leaves at 6.10, two hours and ten minutes, and yet I am always given to understand that he is too busy, on the rare occasions when he is in England, to see anybody! Very friendly, and anxious to get my support for Trade Union representation on this and that. This now is his great prestige preoccupation. I hook him for forthcoming afternoon party with the two 'high-powered ladies' – Sir Thomas Barlow says he does not care for H.P.L. – Mrs Churchill and Mrs Maisky, next week, to discuss the future arrangements regarding clothes for Russia.

On 3rd November, the War Cabinet accepted a Joint Memorandum by

1 Not identified.

Attlee, Dalton and Eden concerning the draft agreement for the creation of a United Nations Relief and Rehabilitation Administration. In the discussion, there was some objection to a statement in the Memorandum that before a reply could be sent to the Americans, consultation was necessary with the Soviet Government 'in virtue of the terms of the Anglo-Soviet Treaty of Alliance'. As a result, the last phrase was deleted.[1]

Tuesday 3rd November

A heavy day. Morning Cabinet, when the joint paper by Attlee, Eden and myself on post-war Relief and Rehabilitation at last goes through. Poor old Leithers [Leith-Ross] is quite pleased and surprised! My two colleagues ask me to explain the paper to the Cabinet, which I briefly do. The American scheme for setting up the Relief and Rehabilitation organisation, resulting from Leith-Ross's talks in Washington, is approved, subject to our reserving the right to move small amendments on detail later, and to the increase of the Policy Committee from four to seven members, so as to include Canada. Discussion hinges mostly on the question whether we should consult the Russians before replying to the Americans. On this the P.M. says that the Foreign Office are 'now putting it about' that we can never speak to the Americans without having first got the permission of the Russians. He appears to be reading from some note. Eden says that the Foreign Office have never said this, and that he doesn't know where the P.M. got this idea from. The P.M. says, 'I know what is going on' and passes across the table the Minutes of the meeting at which Leith-Ross had a row with the Foreign Office, with observations by Ronald marked in red ink. Eden says, 'Well, perhaps he was a little pedantic.' It seems that Cherwell has been putting the P.M. up to this. At any rate, this is better than his poisoning the P.M.'s mind against the Relief and Rehabilitation scheme, as some of us feared might happen. The P.M. makes a jesting allusion to 'these barbarous Asiatics'. There is less danger that this may get outside the Cabinet room, since Bracken is not present. Finally, the only amendment made in our paper is to strike out the phrase 'in virtue of the Anglo-Soviet Treaty'. But the procedure remains that, before replying to the Americans, we inform the Russians that this is how we are minded to reply and invite their observations, but within a time limit of a fortnight.

...

Tea Party of what Sir Thomas Barlow calls 'high-powered ladies'.

1 PRO, CAB 65/28.

Mrs Churchill and Madame Maisky both come, trailing attendants, and so does Citrine, with Tewson,[1] to inspect a quantity of garments made of rabbit skins, etc., which I am now prepared to liberate for export to Russia. It goes pretty well until Mrs Churchill's Jewish attendant, Sir Arthur Abrahams,[2] tactlessly raises the question of money. Who will pay for this nearly £3,000,000 worth of supplies? Thereupon, the Maiskaya starts to be very awkward. She says her government wants drugs more than clothes, and all the money available should be spent on drugs. She almost gets as far as saying they don't want any clothes at all, even though it is explained to her that all the drugs available for Russia from now to next June have already been ordered, and that there are surpluses in all the three Funds after these have been paid for. I didn't want to be too much of a Chairman, but should have liked to put my thumb on Sir Arthur Abrahams. However, it is finally left, after a good deal of confusion and not entirely good-tempered talk, that Sir Thomas Barlow should take the Chair next week at a meeting attended by the substitutes of the Big Three, and go into all these questions of detail. Mrs Churchill, descending in the lift, said of the Maiskaya, 'Poor thing, I often think she doesn't understand English very well.' (Next day Maisky rings me up and I say, 'I had a very pleasant tea party here yesterday.' He asks, rather ironically, 'Was it a very *pleasant* party?' Evidently his wife had given him an exaggeratedly qualifying description of the scene. I insisted that it *was* very pleasant, though I added that some rather irrelevant discussion had taken place about money. He said he thought it was a great mistake that money was mentioned. I said I agreed, and in any case it did not concern me, whose only duty was to provide supplies. Money must be discussed between the Foreign Office, the Treasury and himself. He quite agreed. I said that I had told Sir Thomas Barlow to rule out of order next week any further discussions about payment.)

Thursday 5th November
To Denham Studios with Wilmot, Preston (representing the official side of the Board of Trade, both Overton and Liesching having fallen out, pleading urgent Committees) and Willy Hall, who is now paid by the film producers to be their Vice-Chairman and look after their interests in Parliament and with the Departments – much more fun

1 H. V. Tewson, later Sir Vincent (1898–1981). Assistant General Secretary of the T.U.C. 1931–46; General Secretary 1946–60.
2 Major Sir Arthur Abrahams (1878–1944). Stockbroker. Chairman, Stores Department, and Vice-Chairman, Finance Committee, of Red Cross and St John's War Organisation.

than being the Finance Officer of the Labour Party![1] We are shown a number of interesting things and then lunch with Arthur Rank,[2] the big financial noise in British film production, who strikes me as a first-class Methodist humbug. He says that his real interest is in religious films, but he has gradually been led to take an interest in films as a whole. I should not trust him far.

On 23rd October the Eighth Army, commanded by General B. L. Montgomery, opened its preliminary bombardment on enemy positions at El Alamein. A force of 200,000 British troops and 1,100 tanks faced 100,000 Germans and Italians and over 500 tanks in the Western Desert. After twelve days, Montgomery succeeded by force of numbers in breaking through, and Rommel (who had taken command of the Axis armies on the first day of the fighting) was compelled to order a full retreat. More than 30,000 prisoners were taken and five-sixths of the German tanks were destroyed. With a large haul of captured tanks and transport, the British counted this as a total victory; but Rommel managed to extricate an army which the advancing Eighth Army was unable to pin down.

On 8th November, the Anglo-American invasion of Morocco and Algeria (Operation Torch) began – against Vichy French opposition. The landings were successful and on 10th November Admiral Darlan, for the French, ordered a cease-fire throughout North Africa. By the middle of November all of North Africa apart from Tunisia (which the Germans and Italians were in the process of occupying) was in Allied hands. The British and Americans, joined by some badly-equipped French troops, pushed eastwards and by 28th November they were within fifteen miles of Tunis.

Sunday 8th November
It was this morning, going round Pattisons Mills at Whitehaven, that a police inspector first told us the news of the American landings in French North Africa.[3] And so, through this amazing weekend and the next days, the news poured in. 'This is not the end; it is not even the beginning of the end, but it is perhaps the end of the beginning.' In this admirable and characteristic phrase, the P.M. two days later sum-

1 Hall was a contender for the Party treasurership, made vacant by the recent death of George Lathan, q.v.
2 J. Arthur Rank, later 1st Baron (1888–1972). Film promoter.
3 Marginal note: 'TORCH'.

med up the situation. I said, 'We can see the great tide turning today on the North African beaches.' This, following so fast on the great victory of the Eighth Army, changes both the immediate, and the ultimate, prospects of the war, and still more changes all our feelings. The critics of the 'higher direction of the war' – the Shinwells and the Belishas and the rest – will all have sunk well out of sight and mind today. And Crazy Cripps will have to think again about the prospect of the P.M. falling from power and find some new excuse for his own resignation from the Government, in time, as he sees it, to save part of what Mayhew so happily called his 'mystique'.

Monday 9th November
Drive along the Front at Morecambe and form the view that it would be an excellent place for a Labour Party Conference,[1] provided only we could get enough accommodation – and I think, adding in Lancaster, we probably could – and I inspect, in particular, the Midland Railway Hotel, very functional, with plenty of dining accommodation but only forty bedrooms, right on the sea. Speak at the Mayoral lunch, and, having enjoyed a good deal this very varied jaunt, catch a train from Lancaster, reaching Euston at 9.15 p.m.

At Dalton's suggestion, two interdepartmental committees were set up to deal with aspects of post-war financial policy. One concerned the problem of Reparations from Germany, and was based on Dalton's memorandum on this subject written in August.

The other committee was established after the circulation of Meade's paper on the possibility of an international commercial union after the war. 'By far the best course now is to seek big cuts in tariffs everywhere, and in other trade impediments, within a new international association, world-wide if we can make it so; if not, as wide as possible,' a Board of Trade memorandum declared on 5th November. 'We can lose nothing by putting up this project tactfully. We should gain immensely by its acceptance.' Dalton sent this paper to Anderson, Attlee, Eden and Kingsley Wood, suggesting that a small committee of officials from the Foreign Office, the Treasury, the Dominions Office and the Board of Trade, 'together with an economist from the War Cabinet Economic Secretariat' (namely Meade), should be convened to discuss the idea. All ministers approached responded positively. 'I entirely agree

1 Dalton underlined the last seven words and wrote in the margin: 'We did in 1952, and I was beaten for N.E.!' At the 1952 Labour Party Conference in Morecambe, Dalton and Herbert Morrison were ousted from the N.E.C. by Richard Crossman and Harold Wilson, after a successful campaign by the Left.

with you that it is no good our trying to patch up old machinery in a case where entirely new plant may be necessary,' Eden replied. 'What we must do is to think up constructive and practical ideas of large scope calculated to catch the imagination and fire enthusiasm both here and in America.'[1]

Tuesday 10th November

Parliament is prorogued. The new session begins tomorrow. Kingsley Wood wishes to see me on the Reparations etc. Committee. He says he is sure that I want it to succeed. I say of course. He thinks then that it should be well manned. He would like to put on Keynes, but thinks that to balance him I should put on Leithers [Leith-Ross]. I say that I am putting on Liesching and Clay, or, if as now seems likely, the latter is soon leaving me, some other good economist. I say that I will not in any case put on Leithers, who reacted, as was his right, to my paper by putting in a statement of his own which showed that his views were far removed from mine and that he could not possibly act as my representative. Liesching, on the other hand, is now, in effect, No. 2 to Overton and has quite enough official standing to face any other member of the Committee. I add that I am not at all keen on Keynes coming on, in view of his attitude in *Economic Consequences*,[2] in which, I point out, he not only showed much disloyalty to his political chiefs of that day, but grossly exaggerated the German case, showed much political prejudice against other states, now again our allies, particularly France and Poland, and is therefore likely to take a wrong and tiresome view today. Wood says that he will speak to Keynes about this and warn him that he must not run any such line, but he is sure that Keynes would be deeply affronted and hurt if he were left off a Committee dealing with this subject, and he has, says Wood, been most helpful to him in many ways. I say that it is, of course, for him to choose his own chaps and that I only hope he will rub into Keynes the need to weaken Germany so much that she will be industrially unable to repeat her crimes in future.

Dine tonight at No. 10, where the P.M. revives the ancient custom of reading aloud to his ministers behind closed doors the King's Speech. What a lot of ministers! I am told it is the largest dinner party that has been given for very many years at No. 10. All ministers who

1 Dalton Papers 7/4 (74)–(78), (91), (93), (103).
2 *The Economic Consequences of the Peace,* Macmillan, London, 1919. This was Keynes's celebrated attack on the Treaty of Versailles, and especially its economic clauses. It gave encouragement to those who felt that Germany had been unfairly treated.

sit in the Commons, plus the Mover and Seconder of the Address, plus the Speaker, plus Smuts, Bruce, Harvie Watt, Bridges and Martin. Smuts makes a most brilliant and unprepared little speech in perfect English after dinner. Attlee proposes the health of the P.M., who makes a short reply. We are all very, very happy.

Wednesday 11th November

See Meade, who is coming here to replace old Feet of Clay,[1] who is going, most inappropriately, as I think, to snatch and grab for ships in Washington. Meade will be a great improvement, from every point of view. He seemed less gawky than of old, and less ill than I had been led to expect. He will be an acquisition. At present he is to be part-time with me and part-time still with the War Cabinet Economic Secretariat, commonly called Anderson's Circus. He will represent me, along with Liesching, on the two important Committees which I have instigated by my memoranda on Reparations, etc., and on Commercial Union. He says that he is really much more keen about the latter, but he appears to be quite sensible about the former also. He confesses that he is also in the habit of influencing Lord Cherwell, who, he says, is very keen on Commercial Union. I say I am delighted to think that one who is apt, sometimes most unhelpfully, to influence the P.M., should, in turn, be influenced by Meade. I was very right to prefer this economist to Harrod.

Lunch at House of Commons and, just before two, we all crowd into the Chamber. The Address is moved this session by Walkden and seconded by young Thorneycroft.[2] Both do well, especially the former, and I doubt whether any private Member from our Party could have excelled in eloquence, humour and straightforward horse sense, my Honourable and genial, though aged, Friend, the Member for South Bristol. (There is what Wilmot calls a vomit-making row within the Labour Party because Walkden moved the Address rather than John Parker, whose name had been suggested by the Administrative Committee. There had, I understand, been some murmurs against this choice through the 'usual channels', the chief point being that Parker is a young man who is neither a minister nor doing any war service, and it is felt that he would be less useless in the Armed Forces. ...)

The P.M. is batting today on a very easy wicket, but he runs up a

1 'Feet of Clay': Dalton's private name for Sir Henry Clay, q.v.
2 G. E. P. Thorneycroft, later Baron (b. 1909). Conservative M.P. for Salford 1938–45; Monmouth 1945–66. Junior minister 1945. President of the Board of Trade 1951–7; Chancellor of the Exchequer 1957–8. Minister of Aviation 1960–62; Defence 1962–4. Chairman of the Conservative Party Organisation 1975–81.

very good score. Never before has he been able to count so many lately hatched chickens of victory. It is observed that all the Higher Critics are either absent, e.g. Wardlaw-Milne, or looking sick as mud to think that, without much aid from them, we are winning, e.g., Horeb-Elisha, Shinwell, Stokes, etc. ...

I am due to dine this evening with Sir Cecil Weir[1] at 55 Park Lane, which, I learn later, adjoins the Dorchester. Parly Charlie[2] asks whether I will give him a lift, and we attempt to start in the car just before 7.45. There is, however, the densest fog tonight that I remember, at least since the last war, and we bump violently first on one curb and then on another. Thereafter Parly Charlie walks in front of the car holding a white handkerchief behind his tail, while I perform a flanking movement near the curb with an electric torch. (Why we ever tried to take the car along like this, I really don't know, except to prove it could be done.) We arrived, after an hour and a quarter's steady marching, at the Dorchester, having passed quantities of cars and buses marooned and motionless among the mists. We park the car in the Dorchester garage, whence Sullivan[3] goes home, and Parly Charlie back into the mist to try to find his daughter. I spend the night in Weir's pyjamas, rather small for me, in Warter's[4] unoccupied flat, since it seemed that return to Millbank would be a quite hopeless adventure.

Thursday 12th November

Major Williams Thompson, known to his friends as Mike, spends the evening with me. He is very bright and intelligent and would like to be a Labour candidate. I arrange for him to send me some notes about himself which I will pass on to Shepherd. He is only twenty-seven. He says that Mountbatten has surrounded himself with a group of his personal friends, most of whom are not very good at their jobs. Though his relations with the Air Force and the Navy are reasonably good, those with the Army are quite frightful. His principal lieutenant here is Brigadier Haydon, who is thought nothing of in any Army circles, except the Irish Guards.

1 Sir Cecil Weir (1890–1960). Controller-General of Factory and Storage Premises at the Board of Trade 1941–2. Director-General of Equipment and Stores at the Ministry of Supply 1942–6.
2 Captain Charles Waterhouse (1893–1975). Parliamentary Secretary at the Board of Trade 1941–5. Conservative M.P. for Leicester South 1924–45; Leicester South-East 1950–57. Junior government whip 1936–9. Junior minister 1939–41.
3 Not identified. Probably the chauffeur.
4 P. Warter, later Sir Philip (1903–71). Controller-General of Factory and Storage Premises at the Board of Trade 1942–5. Chairman of the Associated British Pictures Corporation Ltd 1947–71.

Sunday 15th November
Lie in bed and hear the joy bells[1] on the wireless from 10.15 to 10.30 – Westminster Abbey, Saint Cuthbert's, Edinburgh, Armagh, Llandaff (blitzed), some small village church in Lancashire and Coventry (blitzed). Later in the day I hear the sounds also going over the air to French and Italian listeners. It means a lot. The self-respect of the British Army is on the way to being re-established. Last week, when the news was known, a British General was seen to rush in front of the waiting queue at a bus stop and to leap upon the moving vehicle. One onlooker said that he would not have dared to do this a week before.

Tuesday 17th November
Look in on Attlee and tell him that I am very dissatisfied at the slow progress we are making with post-war decisions. He says he agrees and shows some signs of irritation with the P.M., who, he says, 'always closes everything down'. I speak to Attlee about Eden's War Cabinet paper on the Four-Power Plan[2] (on which Gladwyn had asked me to excite the interest of Attlee) and he says he is sure that the lines suggested are right and that we ought to be talking much more in detail both to the Americans and the Russians. I say I hope he will say this in the War Cabinet. I add that the present procedure, whereby a large committee of officials, presided over by Hurst, sits on all projects, is not at all satisfactory, and I have been trying to break through this in the case of both Reparations, etc., and of Commercial Union. Attlee is in on the latter, but I am interested to notice that, on the former, he says that he would take away all machine tools from Germany and distribute them among her victims, Poles, Czechs, Russians, etc. He asks me to put down on paper any ideas which I may have for improving the efficiency of our post-war planning. But the real trouble is not so much with machinery as with persons.

Wednesday 18th November
Liesching to see me on Reparations etc. in preparation for the first meeting of the Committee, to be held this afternoon. I have agreed to this body being called the Committee of Reparations and Economic Security, henceforth to be called C.R.E.S. Meade cannot be there today, since he is meeting his wife and family returning after two years in Canada. I tell Liesching that I feel so strongly on the matters to be discussed at C.R.E.S. that, in certain circumstances, though I am not

1 Marginal insertion: 'for ALAMEIN'.
2 'The Four-Power Plan' was a proposal for an international organisation based on co-operation between the Allied Great Powers. The paper put to Cabinet was a summary (written by Jebb) of a much longer document prepared in the summer.

by nature a Resigning Robert, I might feel moved to take a very strong line. My mind, I say, is quite clear that the power of Germany to prepare and make war must be greatly weakened, and that this is both a British interest, a European interest, and, indeed, an interest of all humanity. Neither Italy nor Japan would have given any serious trouble had Germany not been there to lead. Liesching says that he is in complete agreement with my view, but doubts whether monetary reparations would be a policy politically able to be maintained over any long period, and also whether it would not do us damage through reaction on our exports. I say that I regard all these details as quite debatable and hope the C.R.E.S. will go into them fully. ...

This afternoon the first meeting of C.R.E.S. is held. I tell Liesching to come and report to me immediately it is over, and Gladwyn dines with me later. So I get two versions, which happen quite to agree. I want these two to get together, and I think they will.

Liesching says that the discussion today was nearly all on procedure, and that he and others urged that they should begin by considering broad questions of 'Economic Security' before 'Reparations'. This seems to have been more or less agreed. Keynes, towards the end, 'showed signs of putting on his old racing colours', declaring that we should consider nothing except British interests, and that any payment of reparations by or to anyone could not fail to damage us. He had also suggested that we should consider whether payments for 'relief' should be made by the Germans. Liesching, Gladwyn and others had thought that this was not the sort of question that should be given a high priority in their discussions. Liesching said that he thought Keynes had raised this in the hope of getting Leith-Ross on to the Committee. Probably true. I can see that we are going to have the sort of trouble I anticipated, but I think there are enough good men on the Committee to get through it. Robbins, apparently, said that he intended to put in a paper on his own. I think that this should be the right sort of stuff. (Gladwyn tells me that Robbins, while speaking very highly of me – as he damned well ought to, seeing that it is only through my efforts that he became a Professor[1] – thinks that I regard things too much from a political point of view.) C.R.E.S. is to meet at least once a week, and oftener if required.

Gladwyn doesn't add much to this account, and we go on to discuss other things. Eden's War Cabinet paper on the Four-Power Plan, on which I have not yet written to him, was to have been taken, at Eden's request, today, and Eden had been down to Chequers to discuss this

1 In 1926, Dalton had used his influence to secure for Robbins, his own former pupil, the post of professor and head of the economics department at the L.S.E. Since then, Robbins's ideas on economics and those of Dalton had sharply diverged.

and other things with the P.M. But now the P.M. is very much occupied and wants it postponed, suggesting that Eden should talk to Smuts about it. The P.M.'s general line has lately been that we must, of course, disarm the Germans completely, and then we shall be all right. He doesn't like the idea of entering into commitments in Europe, even though the Norwegians and others are asking us to *take* air bases on their territory. He is also reported to have said, in reply to a question as to the role of Russia, that Russia should be counted as Asia, a non-European world. It is thought that Kingsley Wood and Cherwell are egging him on against closer relations with the Russians and that recent victories have made him less, rather than more, disposed to think in concrete terms of post-war plans. Eden is said to be getting rather desperate about all this and, it is thought, would welcome some sympathy and support from me.

Thursday 19th November
Mayhew looks in to see me for a short while, having just missed North Africa as he just missed Dieppe. He looks very fit and happy and distinguished himself by swimming across a pond in Richmond Park with his braves last week under the eyes of General Paget,[1] who, being distantly related, thereupon asked him to lunch.

Friday 20th November
At Lord President's Committee there is argument as to whether Jehovah's Witnesses should be denied their paper supply. The Home Office are against such action, but little Mr Cooper, whom one seldom sees these days, thinks Morrison's arguments all bosh, and I am inclined to agree with him. It is sheer pitiful impudence to say that there is no effective means of preventing the waste and misuse in such cases of this scarce material. Finally it is agreed that Osbert Peake[2] should collect once more the committee of officials who made the plan for books, and see whether something cannot be done for other forms of printed matter, so as, at the very least, faintly to discourage Jehovah's Witnesses.

Mrs Phillimore gives a lunch for Poles plus younger Labour M.P.s. It is a great success, most of the younger M.P.s present never having seen a Pole before. Many of the latter acquit themselves quite well, and Sikorski holds court at one end of the table and has brought to

1 General Sir Bernard Paget (1887–1961). Commander-in-Chief Home Forces 1941–5. Commander 21st Army Group June–December 1943. Commander-in-Chief Middle East 1944–5.
2 Osbert Peake, q.v., was Parliamentary Under-Secretary at the Home Office 1939–44.

him, one by one, the various younger members of our Party, most of whom are noticeably elevated.

On 3rd October, Sir Stafford Cripps wrote to the Prime Minister declaring that he was in fundamental disagreement over defence. For the moment, Churchill did not react. After the victory at Alamein, however, he felt strong enough to demand Cripps's resignation. Cripps now became Minister of Aircraft Production, outside the War Cabinet. His place in the War Cabinet was taken by the Home Secretary and Minister of Home Security, Herbert Morrison. Cranborne replaced Cripps as Lord Privy Seal (outside the War Cabinet), and Eden replaced him as Leader of the House of Commons. Stanley became Colonial Secretary, and Colonel Llewellin became Minister Resident for Supply in Washington.

Saturday 21st to Sunday 22nd November
Two full moons and very still.[1]

On Sunday night (22nd) Cabinet changes are announced on the air. Morrison succeeds Cripps in the War Cabinet and the latter drops down to Minister of Aircraft Production, thus becoming a lodger downstairs in my own building. This hole is made by the appointment of Llewellin to Washington. Cranborne is to be Lord Privy Seal, and Oliver Stanley returns to the Government as Colonial Secretary. Eden is to lead the House of Commons.

I write at once to Morrison, 'Congratulations! The War Cabinet is strengthened.' Next morning the *Daily Herald* begins its leader with these same last five words. It is, indeed, a great improvement. Nearly all Cripps's 'mystique' is now gone, and he has missed all his chances – never really good – of resigning with credit. He has, I think, been very skilfully played by the P.M. He may, of course, be quite good at the Ministry of Aircraft Production, but seldom has anyone's political stock, having been so outrageously and unjustifiably overvalued, fallen so fast and so far. I add in my letter to Morrison that I would like soon to have a meeting and a talk, and I write also to Ellen [Wilkinson] summarising my letter to Morrison.

Tuesday 24th November
Liesching and Meade for a preliminary talk on C.R.E.S. They show me a paper by Robbins, which, on the whole, I like. It contains positive proposals for the repair of damage by the Germans after the war,

1 Marginal insertion: '(I think of air operations)'.

while recognising that most of the benefit of this will go to others and not to us. Much is made in this paper of the argument that, if we assume large monetary reparation payments by Germany, of which only a very small fraction comes to us, the effect on our terms of trade will be bad, for German exports being very like ours, the tendency will be to push down our export prices. I ask Meade what would happen if Germany, instead of increasing exports, reduced imports. He was not

ready with an answer. I decide to see Robbins, after a long and deliberate interval, and seek to line him up with other members of the Committee, who are, on the whole, of my mind.

Today I say farewell to Clay, who is going to Washington quite soon. The story that he had a great deal of important unfinished work here turns out to be untrue. Seeing him this afternoon, immediately after Meade, I rejoice at the exchange.

Labour ministers jointly give a reception at Admiralty House to members of the three Executives[1] and principal officials. A very jovial party, which I think does good. Lawther today is holding forth, almost in unctuous tones, about the splendid work which Bevin and I did on

1 'the three Executives': the Administrative Committee of the P.L.P., the General Council of the T.U.C. and the Labour Party N.E.C.

behalf of the miners when we set up the new White Paper organisation. I say that I would like him to repeat all this publicly!

Frank Nelson dines with me at the Lansdowne. He looks reasonably fit and has a very interesting and not very responsible job sitting near the centre of things in the Air Ministry and seeing all the most exciting telegrams, but not having to take any real decisions. He says that Hambro has been a failure as his successor; also that Gladwyn was much hurt because I did not take him with me – I am pretty sure that this is not true, since I discussed all this quite frankly with Gladwyn at the time and neither he nor I contemplated that he would fall out so quick with my successor. As to this, Nelson says that they never got on from the first moment, but were like two cats arching their backs against one another. He repeats that Jebb makes himself most unpopular by his manner, and doesn't know it. He thinks that the only person who could really explain this to him would be his wife. He says that, when I left, Jebb was like 'a sheep without a shepherd'. He thinks that Operations in North Africa have been going even better than is commonly realised.

Wednesday 25th November
Labour Party National Executive in the morning. Long and yambling discussion of a silly little motion by Laski that the National Executive should seek an interview with the P.M. on the 'higher direction of policy'. This meets with little favour. It is pointed out that there is to be a meeting with Jowitt on 9th December, and it is thought by some that there might thereafter be a meeting with Labour War Cabinet Ministers. All this, apparently, in order to ascertain what 'decisions' have been taken by the Government. It is feared by Laski and others that decisions favourable to the point of view of the 1922 Committee have already been taken. At a certain point I intervene to say that, though I don't intend to make any sensational revelations this morning, they may take it that the real danger is not that decisions favourable to the 1922 Committee will be taken, but that no decisions will ever be taken at all. Ministers, I tell them, constantly obstruct one another from taking decisions, and that I am only really happy when I am free to act in a Departmental field not subject to interference by my colleagues. But, passing to the counter-attack, I tell them that equally dangerous is the prolonged indecision of the Labour Party itself. The Beveridge Report to be published in a day or two is, I understand, to be referred, in the first instance, to four sub-committees, representing T.U.C., the Co-op, our own National Executive, and the Parliamentary Party. Each of these sub-committees, I gather the N.C.L. [National Council of Labour] have decided, is to meet sep-

arately and to report separately to its parent body. These parent bodies having separately considered the sub-committees' reports, a meeting of the N.C.L. is then to be called to see whether any decisions can be agreed. This, I bluntly say, is fantastic. When I look around at our litter of committees, I say to myself, 'Never was so little decided by so many.' The 'Central Reconstruction Committee', presided over by Shinbad, has produced no decisions for months. Do we yet know whether they are in favour of the Uthwatt Report?[1] No. We must buck up our own processes if Labour ministers within the Government are really to be helped along. All this is taken pretty well, and Morgan Phillips,[2] in particular, nods much approval from a corner. He has been suffering under the indecisive verbosity of Shinbad.

Robbins to see me, slightly uncertain at the beginning of our relationships, but after a while we settle down to discuss C.R.E.S., I having told him that the issues raised here are, in my view, so important that I would be prepared to go great distances and run great risks to get my way. I add, knowing that he has been saying to Gladwyn and probably to others that I am inclined to be 'too political', that there are just a few questions on which I am prepared to take this line, though I regard a great many others as suitable for merely tactical treatment. I tell him that, on the whole, I agree with the line of his paper.

Leith-Ross gives me an account of Relief as it now stands.[3] The Americans have moved quickly forward by the President's appointment of Lehman,[4] who is obviously designed to be the future Director-General of the Organisation, to organise American participation in the arrangements. Leith-Ross had a talk last week with Maisky, following Eden telling the latter what we intended – this in pursuance of the War Cabinet decision. Maisky was full of the most ridiculous suspicions, e.g. that the Relief Organisation might be intended to be supra-Governmental and might, e.g., distribute food in Russia, as Hoover did last time, without any reference to the local authorities, and that there was some sinister intention in a harmless phrase about the Organisation providing for the resettlement of 'exiles and prisoners of war'. He wished to be assured that it was not intended to send back

1 Departmental Committee on Compensation and Betterment, chaired by Sir A. Uthwatt; appointed January 1941; reported September 1942. (Cmnd No. 6291.)
2 Morgan Phillips (1902–63). Secretary of the Labour Research Department 1941–4. General Secretary of the Labour Party 1944–62.
3 On 9th October, Leith-Ross had complained to Dalton that the Foreign Office had 'gone all Russian' on the question of consultation over relief. (Diary.)
4 H. H. Lehman (1878–1963). Governor of New York State 1933–46. Director of the U.S. Office of Foreign Relief 1942–3. Director-General of United Nations Relief and Reh bilitation Administration (U.N.R.R.A.) 1943–6.

White Russians into Soviet territory against the will of the Soviet Government. There is much advance in getting down to details with the Russians, partly because it will give them confidence in our good faith, and partly because it will keep us mindful of their state of mind.

I take Leith-Ross on to dine with Wilmot and Gaitskell – a M.E.W. reunion. Leith-Ross tells amusing stories of his early days as junior Private Secretary at No. 10 when Asquith was P.M. in 1910. There were no Cabinet Minutes and no officials ever attended. The only records were the letters written after each Cabinet by the P.M. to the King in his own hand, giving an account of what had passed. And these letters were taken away by each P.M. when he resigned. If a minister wanted to raise any question in the Cabinet, he just rang up the P.M. beforehand. He then said his little piece in Cabinet, no notice having been given to his colleagues and no papers having been circulated, and generally was told that he could do what he wanted. Then it never came back to the Cabinet again. Evidently this method, though hopelessly 'unbusinesslike' and casual, led to much less interference by ministers in each other's work, and far less impediment to quick decisions. Lloyd George had gone to the other extreme when he organised the Cabinet Secretariat under Hankey, and there had been, since then, a vast increase in all the apparatus. Leith-Ross said that Lloyd George had frequently had a number of officials in Cabinet when matters which they were dealing with in their Departments were being discussed, and it was quite usual for officials, rather than ministers in the first instance, to be called upon to give explanation. In this respect we had now swung back to a far more ministerial arrangement, since neither in the War Cabinet – except for Chiefs of Staff and Secretaries – nor in the Lord President's Committee – again except for Secretaries – were the officials admitted. In the latter part of Leith-Ross's service at No. 10, there was one lady typist. The proposal to extend this practice throughout Whitehall had met with great opposition. The Treasury had been inclined to favour it, as a means of economy, and replacement of male by female labour. The Admiralty had thus addressed the Treasury –

> Their Lordships cannot conceal their preference for boys, although they are prepared, in this case and with great reluctance, to experiment with girls.

I cannot date this exactly, but it must have been when Leith-Ross was a junior at the Treasury, before he went to No. 10.

Today in the House 95 members voted against the Government on the issue of equal compensation for war injuries for men and women, and this after a Select Committee had been offered and most conciliatory speeches made by Attlee and Womersley.[1] For the Government there voted 229. The minority included 39 Tories and 35 Labour, the rest being oddments. It would have been a bore if there had been more Labour than Tory in this lobby. As it is, I get the impression that there has been a good deal of stickiness in the Government handling of this matter, and too great fear of 'repercussions'.

Thursday 26th November

I say a few words – a very rare proceeding on my part – at the Party Meeting. This was supposed to be about Reconstruction, with special reference to next week's debate. Jowitt sat silent through the Meeting, but I made a few points at the end on matters relating to the Board of Trade – notably post-war relief for Europe, based on collaboration between ourselves, the U.S. and Russia; the future of distressed areas, and the control of the location of industry. I ask members to assist in the debate by making positive and practical suggestions. I am afraid the great majority of my hearers are mentally and emotionally incapable of such a feat.

Saturday 28th to Monday 30th November

At West Leaze. It now gets dark very early, and there is a dankness in the air and in the garden. I take a moderate amount of exercise, but return to London on the 30th still with a tummy chill.

See Willie Whiteley, who is doing his job[2] pretty well, and infinitely better than that old fool Charles Edwards, who never went to the office at No. 11 Downing Street at all! Whiteley says that conversations have been going on about the Speakership. It had been thought, till Gwilym Lloyd George went to M.F.P. [Ministry of Fuel and Power], that he would be the best successor. Mrs [*sic*] Carey Evans,[3] old Lloyd George's daughter, has been saying that Gwilym is very 'uneasy' at M.F.P., and that the old man has been bleating that he would like to see his son in the Speaker's Chair before he dies, and adding that Shinwell (!) would make an admirable M.F.P. [Minister of Fuel and Power]. Whiteley has warned Attlee to watch out on this, and has told him that such an appointment would meet the most furious opposition on the part of many people, including, in particular, the miners' M.P.s. I say I don't think it is conceivable that such

---

1 W. Womersley, later Sir Walter, 1st Bart (1878–1961). Minister of Pensions 1939–45. Conservative M.P. for Grimsby 1924–45. Junior minister 1935–9.

2 Labour Chief Whip.

3 Lady Carey Evans, née Olwen Lloyd George (b. 1892). Elder daughter of David Lloyd George.

an appointment could be seriously considered. Of other candidates, W. S. Morrison and Crookshank, he says, have been spoken of, 'but the P.M. won't look at either of them'. Whiteley thinks that Crookshank has had rather a raw deal. I don't know why he or we should be solicitous about this, though, in fact, he would not make at all a bad M.F.P. Whiteley says that they were at one time pressing the claims of Jim Milner for Deputy Speaker, but it has now come to light that he is mixed up, as a solicitor, with some very unsavoury clients. He was involved in a minor degree, it seems, in the Czech scandal which brought down Boothby. Whiteley, therefore, thinks that George Oliver[1] should have one or other of the two junior Chairs. I say that he would do quite well, provided he is not too long-winded. Whiteley adds, the talk turning to Lawther, that the latter paid a tribute, which was very well received, to Bevin and myself by name at the mass meeting of miners addressed by the P.M., for the work we have done over the Mines Reorganisation scheme.

After this interview I lie low, and stay in, washing out all other engagements.

Tuesday 1st December
Chill on the tummy having developed violent and disagreeable features during the night, I stay in bed and – an even rarer proceeding than speaking at a Party Meeting – am visited by a doctor. ... He pulls rather a long face at me in the morning, but comes again in the evening very much brighter, having played about with my blood in the interval. He agrees that tomorrow I may resume normal activities. An occasional day in bed is probably a good move.

Wednesday 2nd December
I have an audience of His Majesty, at the start of which, I having said that I am having a bit of fuss over Luton hats,[2] he says, 'I gather you are moving them to Newcastle.' This shows how false ideas spread everywhere! He is interested in various aspects of the work of the Board of Trade, though he doesn't think that utility suits really save any material. I am to send him a copy of the booklet on Utility Furniture. He finds it more and more difficult to purchase suitable presents for people, e.g., silver boxes, or even silver cigarette cases, and he thinks that the prices of these have gone up very high, by more than

---

1 G. H. Oliver (1888–1976). Labour M.P. for Ilkeston 1922–31, 1935–64. Junior minister 1945–7.
2 Dalton had been dealing with a false rumour, fired by misleading press stories, that the Luton hat-making industry was to be uprooted and transferred to the north-east coast.

300 per cent since before the war, partly, he supposes, due to Purchase Tax – I must put him in touch with Mr Prater – but partly because the shopkeepers add up their accounts wrong, so as to give themselves, until detected, a considerable advantage! He thinks Americans are inclined to be troublesome and to take things too much into their own hands, e.g. in North Africa. ...

Dine with Hyndley and Gaitskell. Quite like old days when I was Minister for Coal. I think I am really being canvassed to agree to the recommendations of the Interdepartmental Committee proposing the increase of 1/- a ton, as against the 1/9 originally put up by M.F.P. [Ministry of Fuel and Power]. Gaitskell, who represented me on the Committee, has done quite well in getting off 9*d.* out of 1/9. Hyndley says that the output went down sharply the week after the Prime Minister addressed the miners! Since then, it has come up again, and is now running between 4.1 and 4.2 (million) per week. In the summer, even without holidays, it was often down to 3.8 or 3.9. The mild winter so far has been a great piece of luck, and so has the absence of air attacks, so that transport has not been interfered with at all. We are hoping to get through the winter without rationing, though what may come next spring remains to be seen. The argument that the introduction of rationing would mean the use of considerable manpower is of increasing importance, as manpower gets shorter and shorter.

Hyndley says that the P.M. was very nervous when he arrived at the Central Hall to address the miners. He apparently expected some hostile interjections about the Second Front. He took a little while to get into his stride, but he had a tremendously good reception all through, being enthusiastically applauded both at the beginning, at the end, and at intervals all through. He began: 'War is fought with steel, and steel is made from coal.' Half-way through he spoke of our bombing attacks on Germany and Italy, and said we were repaying what the enemy had done to us 'with interest, with compound interest, and soon they will get a bonus'. This was received with a roar of delighted approval. He ended with a long passage on what men and women would be able to say they had done for victory when all was over. 'Some will say, "I was a pilot in the Battle of Britain"; others will say, "I bombed the enemy's submarines"; others will say, "I was with the Army at El Alamein"; others will say, "I was in the Merchant Navy and brought the ships safely home"; others will say, "I made the shells"; and you will say, "I cut the coal".' Hyndley's only criticism was that he should have said 'won' and not 'cut', for the latter might seem, to a pedantic critic, to limit the appeal to workers at the coal face. But it was very well taken, and Lawther made an excellent speech proposing a vote of thanks. Evan Williams, on the other hand, who seconded him, was too long and very nearly got the bird from the audience. Hyndley thinks that his present minister listens to too many people before making up his mind, particularly on appointments. [T.E.B.] Young is not very easy in harness with civil servants. The National Board is not yet set up – after six months! – but the rest of the machinery is working pretty well.

On 4th December, the Foreign Secretary wound up a two-day House of Commons debate on Reconstruction with an appeal that the United Nations should develop in peace the co-operation built up in war. He referred to the future functions of the 'Anglo-American-Soviet Coalition', and declared that on the four Great Powers – Great Britain, the United States, Soviet Russia and China – must rest the main responsibility for extending the system of common security after the war, and for re-establishing the economic life of the devastated regions.

Friday 4th December

Group Captain Grant to see me, at Frank Nelson's instigation, to express great gratification that I should wish to spend Christmas with the R.A.F. He will make all arrangements and accompany me, probably to the east coast, spending two nights at one Station and a third at another. This will be a good change from Whitehall. ...

Cherwell, who came to see me yesterday, said that he was very glad that I was 'standing up for the civilians'. He was quite sure that 25 per cent could be cut, both from stocks and from the current supplies of the Services, both as regards clothing and equipment, and also as regards most sorts of armaments – excluding special cases such as aircraft and tanks – without any damage to the war effort. He did not think that Portal was going quite far enough on this. I said I greatly welcomed his support, and I also gave him copies of my two papers on Reparations and Commercial Union. He seemed to be in favour of my general thesis on both. He is full of suspicion of 'the Foreign Office' and of Leith-Ross; the former because 'they say we mustn't speak to the Americans unless we have the permission of the Russians', and the latter because he wants to expand 'relief' into 'reconstruction' and run the whole of post-war Europe.[1] He likes Meade.

---

1 In the Washington talks, the Americans had been concentrating on pure relief to the starving and destitute, and were reluctant to extend the functions of the proposed

Gladwyn to dine. He has been in the House these last two days on the Reconstruction debate. He thinks Eden did very well, both in manner and matter. Much of his speech, he thinks, was quite bold. He himself, of course, made the draft, and got in a good deal more than he expected, though some of his more striking passages were cut out. Eden was warmly congratulated both by Maisky and Raczynski, both by Erskine-Hill and Gallacher! Who says there is no wide agreement on post-war policy? Eden did not consult the P.M. beforehand, but there has been no adverse reaction.

Sunday 6th December

Walk through the Parks with Will Henderson, and lunch with him and little Arthur.[1] W.H. is very bitter at not having got one of the recent by-elections. He attributes it wholly to the fact that he offered less money than Bowles at Nuneaton, or Ivor Thomas at Keighley. He feels that his reputation has been damaged by association with Greenwood. He is, as usual, very complimentary to me, and I think is quite sincere, but I doubt whether he carries much weight anywhere just now.

Will Henderson thinks that any minister should have the right to appoint his own principal civil servant, without reference to anyone outside the Department. I said I thought the right way to put it was that the minister should get the P.M.'s approval. It should be kept on a ministerial plane. The P.M., no doubt, would consult someone and would also himself have some knowledge of the persons of Whitehall. The minister, quite unaided, might be an easy dupe for some designing bureaucrat, or might often so lately have reached his office that he did not know anything about the various candidates. I related certain experiences of my own, and said that here, as elsewhere, a determined minister with knowledge – I hope I didn't pat myself too hard on the back here – could get his own way. I cited the case of Lees-Smith and Pelham.[2] Lees-Smith got his way, on approaching Attlee, against Warren Fisher.[3]

1 Arthur Henderson, q.v., son of 'Big' Arthur Henderson, the former Foreign Secretary.
2 Sir (Edward) Henry Pelham (1876–1949). Permanent Secretary at the Board of Education 1931–7. Lees-Smith was President of the Board of Education in 1931.
3 Sir Warren Fisher (1879–1948). Permanent Secretary at the Treasury and Head of the Civil Service 1919–39.

relief organisation further. Leith-Ross, however, insisted that transport, fuel and raw materials were no less significant. Leith-Ross succeeded in getting 'Rehabilitation' added to the title of the new body – but this was not allowed, as he would have wished, to cover reconstruction.

Little Arthur is much concerned about his powers and status at the War Office. He thinks that duties should be definitely 'delegated'. I point out that the Secretary of State is responsible to Parliament, and must know what is going on, and relate my own experiences (1) as No. 2 to his father, whom I saw every day but who delegated nothing to me except the Boxer Indemnity Bill, I having dodged an attempt by the officials to delegate the negotiations on Russian debts and claims which had been landed on Ponsonby[1] in 1924, (2) with Dingle Foot at M.E.W., to whom, contrary to the advice of the officials, I delegated nothing, though I let him chase practically every rabbit he put up to me, and hear that he thought himself admirably treated, and (3) with Waterhouse at the Board of Trade, whom I frequently make Chairman of Committees, and who sees my engagements and has the right to break in when he chooses. I said it all really depended, not on 'constitutional positions', nor paper schemes, but on personal relations between the No. 1 minister and his No. 2. I rather took little Arthur aback by saying that the chief purpose of Under-Secretaryships was to provide training facilities, within Government Departments, for future No. 1 ministers, and that no man, therefore, should be made an Under-Secretary unless he had reasonable prospects of being promoted later. Little Arthur said, 'Then you do not think we have any real constitutional importance?' I said, 'No, not much.' He is a wooden little chap, but does his best. ...

Will Henderson in the Park had said how important it was, both to learn to run a government department, and in fact to run it, and I had said that my happiest days were those when I saw neither Parliament nor my colleagues, but simply sat in my chair and ran the Board of Trade, or bits of it. I quoted the criticism made of some Frenchman that 'he was a great orator, but always apt to mistake a great speech for a great deed'. And this, I said, was true of many little orators also.

What at the Foreign Office they call 'The Four-Power Plan', in support of which Gladwyn said he had been working very hard since he went back, is faced by no defensible alternative. Amery, however, put up a paper supposing that both we and the Americans and the Russians should 'keep out of Europe', each of us having large enough extra-European estates to administer, and it being desirable that the Germans should have some 'outlet' in a sphere natural and appropriate to them. This frightful plan, which found no support in the Cabinet, Gladwyn calls 'The No-Power Plan', but it is much worse

1 Arthur Ponsonby, 1st Baron (1871–1946). Liberal M.P. 1908–18. Labour M.P. 1922–30. Parliamentary Under-Secretary of State at the Foreign Office 1924. Junior minister 1929–31. Chancellor of the Duchy of Lancaster 1931.

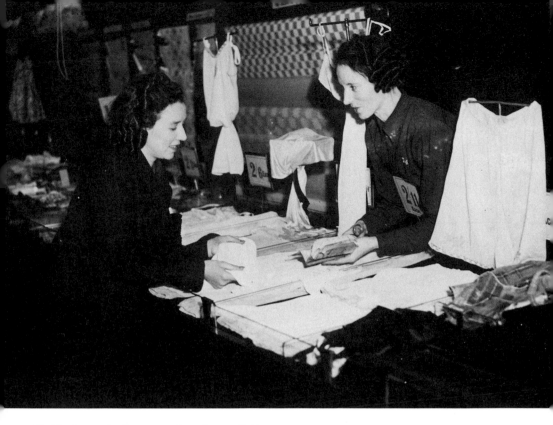

15 Clothes rationing comes into force, 1941

16 Concert in Aldwych tube station, January 1942

17 Ruth and Hugh in St James's Park, June 1942. Ruth had been working in the North of England since the previous December.

18 Dalton and Attlee at the Labour Party Conference in the Central Hall, Westminster, May 1942

19 Molotov meets British war leaders at No.10 to press for a Second Front, May 1942. *Going down the garden steps:* Molotov and Churchill, followed by Maisky, Attlee and Eden. *On the top step, left:* Ismay; *right:* Lyttelton.

20 Sir William Beveridge (*second from right*) entertains American officers to tea in Oxford, *c.* 1943

21 A toolmakers' works meeting discusses the Beveridge Report, March 1943

22 Quebec, August 1943. *Front row:* Eden, Roosevelt, Countess of Athlone, Churchill. *Back row:* Earl of Athlone (Governor-General of Canada), Mackenzie King, Cadogan, Bracken.

than this. It is the German Victory-through-Defeat Plan.[1]

Monday 7th December
Dine this evening with Morrison and Ellen Wilkinson, the latter having arranged the party, at the Howard Hotel, where Morrison now
seems to stay. We talk pretty frankly about persons in the Party, and
I repeat, deliberately, though quite casually in the course of the
conversation, that it is not part of my ambition to be the Leader of
the Party. I had thought that the conversation might have gone a little
further than it did, but it was quite useful that it went even thus far.
I suggest to Ellen Wilkinson that we might repeat a party, I taking
the initiative and adding Wilmot. She would like this.

Tuesday 8th December
Dine with Evan Durbin, who has now been working for some weeks
with Attlee. The latter, he says, told him at the start that he had no
experience in 'using assistants'. It was therefore left to Durbin to
invent his own methods. He looks after all Lord President's Committee papers, as well as War Cabinet papers which are economic, and
hopes later on to deal also with Labour Party papers, though he is
doing nothing in this line as yet. He says that Attlee is very variable,
and often very irritable. Did he show this latter side to his colleagues?
I said no, I thought he didn't dare. Durbin says that Attlee has many
too many Committees to attend, and is, he thinks, very much over-
worked. He also thinks that he is very conscious of difficulties in the
Labour Party.

Wednesday 9th December
T.U.C. Deputation to Labour ministers at No. 11 Downing Street on
Trade Disputes Act.[2] The atmosphere is not very good. It appears,
though none of us had realised this before, that the General Council's
'consultations with the Conservative Party' were not, as we had
supposed, with influential members of the 1922 Committee, or with
such Tory ministers as R. A. Butler, but with a small number of
persons, quite of the second class, representing the Conservative
Associations in the country. Only two of these were M.P.s, namely

1 'Amery was an isolationist – a sort of English Luce,' Lord Gladwyn wrote later.
  'Under his plan Germany would shortly be in a position to dominate Europe'.
  (*The Memoirs of Lord Gladwyn*, Weidenfeld & Nicolson, London, 1972, p. 119.)
2 The Trades Disputes and Trade Unions Act (1927) limited the political activities
  of unions. The labour movement had long campaigned for its amendment or re-
  peal.

Headlam[1] and Gwilym Rowlands![2] Naturally they go nowhere. They then met the 'Liberals', including again only one M.P. and five outsiders, led by Comyns Carr.[3] They are only asking now for two changes in the Law, the right of the Civil Servants' Association to affiliate to the T.U.C., and the removal of the prohibition on a local authority to make trade unionism compulsory on its staff. On this second point there has been some legalism lately which has been helpful from the T.U.C. point of view. It is left that Labour ministers in the War Cabinet shall take up this question again with the P.M., who, it seems, would be quite prepared to agree to the T.U.C. request if there were not serious Conservative opposition, and try to get things moving. ... Attlee does not make a very good impression, and one of the General Council leaders says, 'If you don't know what is going on, that only shows how little you are consulted, even though you are Deputy Prime Minister.'

A Russian winter offensive had started along the river Don in mid-November. On 23rd November, the Russians crossed the Don at Kalach, and began the encirclement of Stalingrad.

Thursday 10th December

Maisky comes to see me, bringing me samples of cloth offered by the T.U.C. which he says are not good enough for the Russians. I gather that the Clothing Committee is going pretty well. He comes, I think, to tell me another thing, namely that he has now got a favourable reply from his Government to the proposal put to him when some of us dined at the Soviet Embassy some while ago, of a British Labour Party delegation to visit Russia. He thinks the visit should be made before the end of the winter, and that the delegation should consist of leading people in the Party who will be able, on their return, to get the National Executive to agree to whatever they themselves have agreed to in Moscow. He has already told this to Morrison. I asked whether he contemplated that Labour ministers should go. He said that this

1 Sir Cuthbert Morley Headlam, 1st Bart (1876–1964). Conservative M.P. for Newcastle upon Tyne North 1940–52; Barnard Castle 1924–9, 1931–5. Junior minister 1926–9, 1931–4.
2 G. Rowlands, later Sir Gwilym (1878–1949). Conservative M.P. for Flint 1935–45.
3 A. S. Comyns Carr, later Sir Arthur (1882–1965). Barrister. Liberal M.P. for East Islington 1923–4.

was a matter for us, but that he very much hoped that some would. I said that I could see a good deal of difficulty here, but that we would have to go into it. I think that in Moscow they have the intention to try to get us to agree to something rather difficult, e.g., either as to peace terms in some detail (as when Eden met Stalin), or as to the formation of some new International, possibly merging Second and Third, and thus involving our own relations with the British Communists. This will want careful watching. And, in fact, I don't see how Labour ministers could expect to get the consent of their colleagues to go on such a trip.

I talk to Maisky a bit about the war, and he says that we have a long way to go before we meet in Berlin, though, he adds, 'You have further to go than we have.' I say that I myself would much like, for several reasons, to go on the proposed mission, though I think it very unlikely that I shall be able to, but I remind him that I have a very consistent record in regard to Russia, never having said anything rude about them in public – British Communists are quite another story – having, on the contrary, said nice things about them in my book in 1928,[1] having had some share in the resumption of diplomatic relations with them in 1929,[2] having visited their country and praised their planned economy in 1932,[3] having taken the leading part in poking up the Old Umbrella[4] by weekly Questions in Parliament when we were trying to secure the Anglo-Franco-Soviet Pact in 1939, and having refused to visit Finland, and having maintained a firm silence on the subject of the Russo-Finnish war in 1940. I had always wanted, I said, to confront Germany with the choice of peace, or war on two Fronts. He says, 'Yes, you have a very good record.'

Saturday 12th December
Before leaving for Birmingham to address meeting of West Midland Regional Council of Labour ... speak to Preston about toys. I read in bed this morning in the *Daily Express* a loud grizzle about our quota restrictions hindering the supply of toys for Christmas. I said I saw no point at all in inviting another fuss, in Parliament and in the press, about this silly little matter. What *was* there to be said for my officials

1 *Towards the Peace of Nations. A Study in International Politics*, Routledge, London, 1928.
2 When Dalton was Parliamentary Under-Secretary for Foreign Affairs in the second Labour Government.
3 Dalton visited the Soviet Union as a member of a New Fabian party in 1932, and wrote an essay about Soviet planning in a book edited by Margaret Cole shortly after his return. ('A general view of the Soviet Economy, with special reference to planning', in *Twelve Studies in Soviet Russia*, Gollancz, London, 1933.)
4 'the Old Umbrella': Neville Chamberlain, q.v.

sitting tight, at Christmastime, on stocks of toys already manufactured? One toy before Christmas was judged, by our poor sentimental compatriots, to be worth more than ten in the New Year. I,
therefore, judged that *all* stocks in wholesalers' hands should now be
let out, below a certain price. I told Preston that I would like an Order
signed today. He should go into it at once and – on my return today
at 9 p.m. – either leave me a note saying that the Order had been made,
or parade all principal officials who had been making difficulties
about such an Order, along with himself, in order that we might have
a pleasant Saturday-night conference about it.

Tuesday 15th December
Beveridge is being married today,[1] and I send a personal note to the
Dorchester, where, this afternoon, he is holding a reception, making
excuse for my absence that I have been engaged – and I have – in a
discussion of his Report by the National Executive of the Labour
Party.

Social Insurance and Allied Services – Report by Sir William Beveridge was
published on 1st December 1942. This long-heralded document set out
Beveridge's proposals for a national health service, family allowances, full
employment and a comprehensive system of social insurance. The report was
intended (according to its author) not only to bring about the abolition of
physical want, but to give a new sense of purpose to democracy, and hence to
promote the war effort. It was an immediate best-seller. 635,000 copies were
quickly sold, and a public opinion survey showed that 86 per cent of the
population believed that the proposals should be adopted, against only 6 per
cent who thought they should be dropped.[2]

Wednesday 16th December
A very full day, beginning with a seance on surgical corsets and how
to prevent unworthy people claiming these. I am not very happy
about the proposals of the officials, requiring two medical certificates
for each afflicted person, one before and one after the fitting of these
supports, a plan which seems to me to be vexatious and ineffective.

    Casey to see me. An industrious and stupid man, with, so I am
told, a rich and ambitious wife. It is said that it was she, rather than

1 To Janet Mair, his close friend and colleague at the L.S.E.
2 P. Addison, *The Road to 1945*, Jonathan Cape, London, 1975, p. 218.

he, who fascinated our P.M. on a railway trip in the U.S.A. and persuaded the latter to offer her husband the post of Minister of State in Cairo. He admits to me today that, at one moment, he thought it was all up in Egypt, and had all prepared for taking flight. But he says that the transformation of the Army, when the High Command was changed, was quite amazing, within a period of three weeks. Till then our troops, as any troops after so long a retreat would have been, were quite demoralised. But when Alexander and Montgomery[1] had taken over, everything changed. He thinks it very awkward that Rommel has retired from El Agheila, since our lines of communication will be greatly lengthened and there is no water in the Desert of Sirte. I speak to him with caution on our post-war commercial policy, since Liesching has warned me that he is returning via Washington – he did not admit this to me – and may speak unguardedly to Hull and others. To me he says that he does not think the Dominions much care where they sell their produce, so long as they sell it, and that the U.K. does not much care where we buy our food and our materials, so long as we can buy them. Therefore, he would be quite prepared to wash out Imperial Preference in return for a general expansion of trade, and a lowering of U.S.A. and other tariffs. He says that, unless Australia can build up sufficient external markets to allow of a large increase in population, 'the Japs will get us in thirty years' time'. They have nearly done it this time.

Lunch with the Belgian Ambassador.[2] Devonshire – diminutive Duke of,[3] who, it is said, wants to be the next Viceroy, but the P.M. doesn't think he is up to it – says that there are only 462 British civil servants in the whole of India. This shows how far Indianisation has gone. I say that this figure ought to be used as propaganda in the U.S. and elsewhere. He also says that, out of many thousands of letters, censored at the source, to Indian soldiers from their relatives, only ten make any reference to Congress. Of these ten, nine are frankly hostile to Congress, and the tenth is quite objective. I say that the Government of India ought to be able, on this basis, to organise,

---

1 General B. L. Montgomery, later Field Marshal, 1st Viscount (1887–1976). Commander of Eighth Army during campaigns in North Africa, Sicily and Italy 1942–4. Commander-in-Chief, British Group Armies and Allied Armies, in northern France 1944. Commander of 21st Army Group 1944–5. Commander, British Army of the Rhine 1945–6. Chief of Imperial General Staff 1946–8. Chairman of Western European Commanders-in-Chief Committee 1948–51.

2 Baron de Cartier de Marchienne (1871–1946). Belgian Ambassador in London 1927–46.

3 Edward Cavendish, 10th Duke of Devonshire (1895–1950). Parliamentary Under-Secretary for India and Burma 1940–42. Junior minister 1936–40, 1943–5. Conservative M.P. 1923–38.

indirectly and discreetly, some alternative political party to the Congress, and prevent the latter from winning so many elections. He does not seem to think this feasible.

Robbins to dine with me. It is a long time since we have had a meal together and he is slightly self-conscious. But he talks sense on the whole, and is quite amusing. He is strongly on my side on both my Committees (and it was to make sure of this that I invited him to dine with me). He says that Cherwell, once Lindemann, is obsessed with the collapse of the German Home Front in 1918, and the need to prevent any such risk in this country. Hence his opposition to fuel rationing, and his solicitude for the civilians as against the Services in disputes about clothing, etc. Robbins relates that, in June 1940, when things looked blackest, the Beaver, at his most impish, said to Lindemann, after dwelling on the enormity of German armed might and the few miles separating us from them, and the fact that Lindemann's mother had been a Frankfurt Jewess, 'When they come here, they will murder me, but they will torture you, Prof!' And Lindemann wriggled on his seat and looked most uncomfortable.

Robbins says that Beveridge, whose Plan he supports, has still unlimited personal ambitions. He sees himself as a possible future Prime Minister, and certainly as a member of the War Cabinet in the near future. He thinks that he can hear, already, a cry going up next year, after confused political debates and convulsive popular movements in his support, of 'Send for Beveridge!' He has been keeping very dingy company, with Clem Davies, Horabin, and, in the background, Balogh. All these are embittered by our victories. Robbins says that Bridges and Norman Brook – he agrees with me that this is one of the best civil servants – both sleep, with him and others, in Cabinet Offices. Bridges never finishes till very late. Now that we two have renewed relations, we shall, no doubt, meet from time to time, and work, on the whole, in harmony, at least during the war.

Saturday 19th December

Attend two sessions of Labour Party Central Reconstruction Committee, with Shinbad in the Chair. Too many people, too much talk, too little outcome. Lunch with Laski, who tells me that he lunched alone with the Prime Minister last week! P.M., he says, spoke warmly of Bevin, Morrison and myself, saying of me that, though he and I approached politics from quite different angles, he had a great respect for me, and that I always expressed my views most clearly. But Attlee was never mentioned throughout the conversation. What a little liar! He also spoke ill of Leith-Ross, thinking him to be a man of no intellectual gifts at all, but this, of course, is quite the wrong ground on which to criticise Leith-Ross. It was surely in a moment of weakness that Laski admitted that he had never met him before.

Monday 21st December
A sense of less to do just before Christmas. ...

Morgan Phillips to dine, and talk about Policy Committees, Transport House, etc. He is a little disappointing and stays too long. I have to hint broadly at 10.20 that I have still a good deal to do. He is very cagey, when I try to draw him on his own ambitions for the future. But I am sure that they are large.

Tuesday 22nd December
First meeting of Cabinet Committee on the 'Reform of the Foreign Service'. It goes pretty easily, and pretty well for Eden, whose draft White Paper got stuck the other day in a lump of more or less critical rejoinders by his colleagues. This afternoon we meet at No. 11, with Attlee in the Chair. Simon, absurdly rubicund and healthy-looking – does he, I wonder, ever remember that others remember *his* record at the Foreign Office! – Kingsley Wood, myself, Hudson and Duff Cooper, are the other members, 'appointed by the P.M., after consultation with the Foreign Secretary'. Stanley also appears, because Cooper's paper refers to the Colonial Office. Not a bad discussion, as a result of which Cooper's project for dividing the external service into two world-branches, East and West, wherein the Eastern should include, not only diplomats and consuls in China and Japan, but colonial administrators in Malaya, and perhaps the I.C.S. [Indian Civil Service] as well, and also the High Commissioners in Australia and New Zealand, life for a British Eastern-world official being passed entirely within this field, and similarly for the Western rest-of-the-world, was turned down. Simon pointed out that it would logically involve the creation of two Secretaries of State, one for the East and one for the West, an impossible arrangement. The point was also made that administering Malayans had little in common with being a diplomat in Chungking. Cooper thought that after the war China would 'have to be dealt with' and would be much more difficult, and perhaps more dangerous, than Japan. There were many more Chinese, he said, and they were much cleverer. Clark Kerr, whom all present unitedly praised, had, he said, been necessarily a child in the hands of the Chinese for the first twelve months of his mission, though for the last two years he had been completely on top of it, and was now doing very well in Moscow.

There was some talk on 'transferability' between the Foreign and the Home Services, and Eden got away pretty well in resisting this, though I suggested that he might admit in his White Paper that in very exceptional cases transfers might take place.

Wednesday 23rd December

Lunch with deaf Dunbar, alone at the Howard Hotel. Wilmot had accepted, but never wanted to go, and has a good excuse today in that he has lost his voice. Dunbar says that he is very much happier than when we last met, because he understands that Labour ministers are meeting each other more frequently, because several good speeches on Reconstruction have been made, e.g. by me and Morrison, and because he has now got Citrine interested in Reconstruction. He is awfully stupid, and a crashing bore, as well as being so deaf that one has to shout and repeat simple sentences.

I look forward to leaving London tomorrow and forgetting all my shop for several days.

Dalton spent Christmas Day and Boxing Day visiting R.A.F. Squadrons stationed at Bircham Newton and West Raynham, staying the night of 27th December at the Wilmots' house at Diss.

On Christmas Day, Dalton was told by his R.A.F. hosts that Admiral Darlan was dead (he had been killed in Algiers by a pro-Gaullist assassin on 24th December). 'They ask me what I think,' Dalton recorded in his diary. 'I say that I am most delighted, and that it might now be possible for the French factions to unite.'

Tuesday 29th December

With Attlee to lunch with Mrs Phillimore to meet Roger Cambon, Dejean[1] and Comert. They all think that Darlan's[2] death has been a bad blow for de Gaulle. The latter is still ludicrously above himself. He said of Giraud,[3] when he was appointed to succeed Darlan, 'Yes.

1 Maurice Dejean (b. 1899). Diplomatic Adviser to the French Committee of National Liberation 1942–3. National Commissioner for Foreign Affairs with the Free French 1941–2. Previously *chef de cabinet* (for Foreign Affairs) to Daladier and Reynaud at the Quai d'Orsay 1939–40. Ambassador to U.S.S.R. 1955–64.
2 Admiral François Darlan (1881–1942). Commander-in-Chief of the French Forces 1941–2. Assumed authority in the name of the Vichy regime in French North Africa October 1942.
3 General Henri Giraud (1879–1949). Commander-in-Chief of the French Forces in North Africa and High Commissioner 1942–3. Giraud, defeated during the Fall of

He is a good soldier. I think that I could use him and give him some military command.' The lack of any political, non-military, figure-head for a United France is pitiable.

Friday 1st January
The arrival of the New Year makes everyone feel, perhaps, unduly optimistic. Everything seems so much better than twelve months ago, when the Japanese had only been in the war a few weeks and we felt quite over-mastered for the time being.

Monday 4th January
Home Front Ministers' Meeting, at which Woolton makes a rather glum speech about our food prospects. Taking everything into consideration, the months from April to August are likely to be difficult, and it may be necessary, he says, both to ration bread and to stop the production of beer. Supplies of bacon are now down to only $3\frac{1}{2}$ weeks' supply, and of edible fats 12 weeks'. Submarine sinkings are still very high, and may go higher, and much shipping may be required for other purposes, some of which, as Anderson says, 'kindle the imagination of the fighting men'. Portal, who gives the impression of having had an extra good lunch, says, 'Don't take all this too seriously. Woolton is only trying to blackmail the supply departments. We have heard all this sort of thing before.' He also keeps on saying, in a loudish voice, that these meetings are a great waste of time and he has a lot of work to do. With this I sympathise.

It now appears that some arms factories may be suddenly closed down in the near future, on the ground that we have now got sufficiently large stocks of certain kinds of munitions to meet all possible contingencies, particularly of munitions which are now no longer any use! This will be liable seriously to dislocate our labour arrangements, especially in Scarlet areas. Thus, it is rumoured that some arms factories in Luton may soon be closing down.[1]

Try to square Anderson – I think I have – on the desirability of bringing the Commercial Union Report before his Committee rather

1 Marginal insertion: '220,000 workers to be switched, chiefly to aircraft and tanks. We have 14 years' supply now of *some* arms.'

France in 1940 and interned by the Germans, had escaped to Vichy France and from there to North Africa, before the Torch landings. Here the Americans backed him against de Gaulle. Following a stage-managed reconciliation between the two generals at Casablanca in January 1943, Giraud became joint President, with de Gaulle, of the French Committee of National Liberation. He resigned from the Committee in October of the same year, however, and within a few months had been entirely eclipsed by his rival.

than Jowitt's, so as to cut out I.E.P. [Committee on Internal Economic Problems]. Anderson agrees that, when the Report is ready – I hope within a week – it shall go, in the first instance, to the small group of ministers immediately concerned, and that we shall then decide the next steps.

Later I see my three representatives on the Committee, Overton, Liesching and Meade, and hear from them the atmosphere at the last meeting, when Hubert Henderson produced a minority report, basing himself entirely on the balance of payments, and seeking to prove that the proposals of the majority would inconveniently stimulate our imports, strike out of our hands all financial measures for restricting them, and do little to expand our exports. His minority report, which I found awaiting me last night on my return, is, as usual with him, dangerously plausible and completely negative. But he was quite isolated at the last meeting. Waley[1] went with the majority, and so did all the others, including Ronald, about whom we had had some doubts. Keynes, moreover, in a note, declares his approval of the 'general layout', though raising various points, some of them important, on details; and fearing lest our report, if it 'saw the light', might not do damage to the administration in the U.S.A. Many of his points can easily be met and, on procedure, there is no reason why our proposals should 'see the light' until a much later stage, since they could be communicated, as a confidential *aide-mémoire*, to the State Department, with no reference either to Congress, or the press, or the House of Commons.

At a War Cabinet meeting on 5th January, Lord Woolton (Minister of Food) argued that Britain should give the Americans an undertaking that this country would make food stocks available for purposes of relief to liberated territories, and that food or clothing rationing would continue until severe shortages in Allied countries had been overcome. Sir Kingsley Wood (the Chancellor) felt that such an undertaking was unnecessary, and that the views of the American President should be ascertained first. This was agreed.[2]

Tuesday 5th January
War Cabinet on Relief Stocks. One hour and forty minutes on this

1 S. D. Waley, later Sir David (1887–1962). Principal Assistant Secretary at the Treasury 1931–46. Third Secretary 1946–7.
2 PRO, CAB 65/33.

item alone! A most futile and irritating discussion in which all ministers, except the P.M. and Kingsley Wood, are in favour of proceeding on the broad lines suggested by Woolton and supported by me. At a certain stage I become too bored to go on, since no arguments make any impression. But Attlee, Eden and Woolton are all very angry, especially with Wood, who, along with Cherwell – now promoted, as Paymaster-General, to sit at the Cabinet table – have been putting 'a lot of crude rubbish', as Attlee said afterwards to me, at the P.M., who naturally has not had time to study the thing properly. ... Eden says to me afterwards, outside, that he is going to write to Wood and tell him that if we are all starving at the end of the war, it will be Wood's fault.

I get Attlee to dine with me tonight, in order to work off our indignation at this morning's meeting and because I have not had much talk with him for some time. He says that the P.M. has struck a very bad patch lately. He has again become very conscious of the burden of the war, of the slow progress in North Africa, and of the shipping losses. Also he still lets Cherwell run to him at any time. Attlee says that, now that Cherwell is a minister, he should take his place with other ministers and not be allowed always to get in first. There must be, if necessary, a show-down over the Beveridge Report, but he thinks that the P.M. will be in favour of this. Attlee tried to get Listowel into the Government as Under-Secretary either for Colonies or India in the last reshuffle, but could not manage it. The P.M. said, quite truly, that the Labour Party had done very well in recent appointments. (I am quite glad that he didn't get in this poor little wisp of a peer, for he would have been very little use and it would have roused great jealousies elsewhere.) I say that I should like Wilmot to get an Under-Secretaryship soon, and Attlee, most amiable, says that he quite agrees, and if Lyttelton had consulted *him*, he would have recommended Wilmot as his Under-Secretary instead of Garro Jones, whom Lyttelton took without consulting anyone. Attlee thinks that we have now reached a stage when some of the P.P.S. should get promotion. He says that Devonshire, who has now been made Under-Secretary to Stanley,[1] has a great contempt for the latter. When Derby[2] once said that 'the Stanleys never run away',

---

1 The Duke of Devonshire, q.v., was Parliamentary Under-Secretary of State to the Colonies while Oliver Stanley, q.v., was Secretary of State.
2 E. G. V. Stanley, 17th Earl of Derby (1865–1948). Conservative M.P. for Westhoughton 1892–1906. Junior minister 1900–3, 1916. Postmaster-General 1903–5; Secretary of State for War 1916–18, 1922–4. Ambassador to France 1918–20. Oliver Stanley's father.

Devonshire was heard to remark, 'They have been running ever since Bosworth.' And some historian added, 'No, ever since Bloors Hill' (which, I understand, was an engagement a few years earlier!). (I hear from Gladwyn a few days later that Stanley strikes him as being very wet in discussions on the future of Europe. He doubts whether 'it would be wise, and would not be too great a strain on our resources, to attempt any occupation of Germany'.)

Attlee says that he doesn't know what the Russians will want in Europe after the war. Possibly they will wish to absorb all the Slav States. I said that this might well be, though hitherto Stalin had expressly disclaimed such intentions. I should not like, however, them to try to absorb Germany as well, as a Soviet Socialist Republic, or we might find the Germans running Russia as well as Germany. This is the greatest of all dangers in the background. Attlee said that this time we must make no mistake in rendering Germany unable to repeat her aggressions. We had, he said, been too tender to her last time, though he admitted that he did not think so then, but we could not afford to do this twice.

Thursday 7th January
Spend the morning at St Ermin's talking with representatives of the Allied Socialists and a few of our National Executive members about Relief. They are much concerned because 'nothing has been done'. I have explained that there are large stocks, of wheat, coffee, wool, cotton, etc., but these are overseas and the problem will be to find the shipping to fetch them. Several Allies attach importance to actual purchase of overseas stocks by the United Nations, though admitting the strong case for pooling, as against stocks in the separate owner-ship of separate nations. Laski asks to what sort of Governments we propose to entrust the administration of liberated countries, and what guarantee we have that the weapon of Relief will not be used against the parties of the Left, or against revolutions from the Left against Fascist Governments. I find this a bit much, and tick him off in front of the foreigners, which, I think, will have been no bad thing. I say that, so long as Labour ministers are in the Government, by the will of the Labour Party Conference, that should be sufficient guarantee that the democratic process shall operate in all liberated territories. On the other hand, I tell him frankly that ministers have not been sitting round discussing hypothetical political situations in liberated countries. But we are fighting this war, I remind him, against Nazism and Fascism, and I, as President of the Board of Trade and the minis-ter principally responsible for Relief, or any of my colleagues, should not be likely to use Relief as a means of bolstering up Fascism in any

part of Europe. He says that it is most unfair to suggest that this is what he meant. I said, 'Then why try to be clever?' And we pass on.

At lunch afterward André Philip[1] sat himself down beside me – he is, anyhow, a very pushing fellow – and explained in a self-confident manner how, when he was in Washington, he had put President Roosevelt in his place. He had told him that he knew nothing of Europe, and less than nothing of France, and that his action in recognising Darlan had ruined all prospects of French resistance. He had also stated, earlier in the morning, that there would be no food problem in France, since their production, and also their herds, were well maintained. I said I doubted this very much. I was not impressed at all by this Socialist Protestant Professor.

Friday 8th January
Julian Amery comes to see me, to ask me whom he should approach to get in touch with Englishmen who fought in Spain with the International Brigade. Some of these, he says, would be most useful in impending (S) Operations in Juggery. I turn him on to Ellen Wilkinson, failing whom, Phil [Noel-]Baker, but advise him not to say where they will be acting. Bailey,[2] he tells me, is now with General M.[3] who, however, is now in loose association with the Italians and meanwhile fighting against the Partisans. But he is said also to be suborning and penetrating the Jug Quisling organisations, including Nedić's[4] staff, and he is still, after the last shift in the Jug Government in London, their Minister of War! This last shift has, at any rate, got rid of Ninčić. This is all to the good, though old Papa Slobodan[5] is becoming more and more of an absurdity, and now purporting to be Minister of Foreign Affairs as well as Prime Minister and Minister of the Interior.

1 André Philip (1902–70). French Socialist politician. Economist. Commissioner for the Interior in the French government-in-exile 1942–3. Finance Minister 1946. Minister of National Economy 1947. Professor of Economics at Lyon University 1926–42.
2 Col. S. W. Bailey. S.O.E. 1939–41 (Belgrade, Cairo and U.S.A.). Senior Liaison Officer with Mihailović 1942–4. Bailey had been dropped by parachute at Mihailović's headquarters on Christmas Day 1942.
3 General Dragoljub-Draza Mihailović (1893–1946). Leader of the Yugoslav resistance in 1941. Came to co-operate more closely with the quisling Prime Minister, Nedić, and thus lost the confidence of the Allies, who finally gave their support to Tito and the Partisans. Mihailović was executed in July 1946.
4 General Milan Nedić (1882–1946). Prime Minister of Serbia 1941–4. Deputy Commander-in-Chief, General Staff 1936–41. Minister of War 1938. Died in prison, while awaiting trial for treason.
5 Slobodan Jovanović, q.v.

Lunch with Mrs Phillimore and a number of the staff of the American Embassy. Sit next to Freeman Matthews,[1] now Chargé d'Affaires, who was till recently in Vichy. Pleasant, but not very intelligent, I thought. We spoke of André Philip, who, I said, had made a bad impression on me. Freeman Matthews said that while in Washington Philip had shown no sign whatever of any gratitude for the American action in North Africa. He was, body and soul and cheque-book, in the pocket of de Gaulle.

Jowitt to see me, at my request, when I succeed in getting his agreement to the Commercial Union paper going to the Lord President's Committee. I suggest to him that, as regards Reconstruction, ministers should take more on themselves and leave less to officials, and I tell him how sorry I am that he was ever saddled with Hurst. He says, 'He has been doing a little better lately.' But he agrees to my proposal on Commercial Union, since, as I point out, it relates to 'current policy'.

On 10th January a major new Soviet offensive began round Stalingrad.

Sunday 10th January

Gladwyn Jebb to lunch, after which I inspect his suite on the top floor at the Foreign Office. Much better quarters than many senior officials have, and he has got an Under-Secretarial carpet which looks very handsome! He shows me some Minutes which he and others have been writing about Anglo-American relations, but I tell him that much of this minuteering in the Foreign Office seems to me to be only beating the air. He does not disagree. We go over the Minutes, made by him with some care, of the last meeting of the C.R.E.S. [Committee on Reparations and Security]. That Woman Keynes has now veered round to favouring, on grounds of Economic Security, the division of Germany into a number of small and semi-independent States, in preference to the cutting off from a Unitary Germany of such extremities as East Prussia, Upper Silesia, and the Saar, particularly on the ground that the latter arrangement would leave disgruntled German minorities just outside the German frontiers. I say

1 H. Freeman Matthews (b. 1899). U.S. diplomat. First Secretary at Vichy 1940–41. Counsellor at London Embassy 1941. Minister with the Department of State, Chief of Division of European Affairs 1943. Director 1944.

that this must be looked at very carefully, or we shall be landed with a Germany still unitary and still possessed of these debatable extremities. My own view has been that the German population in the areas to be transferred should retire within the new German frontiers. In the case of *industrial* Upper Silesia, i.e. the old Plebiscite area, the Germans were, even in 1919, admittedly in a minority. (I have already noted that, but for Lloyd George and Keynes, the Poles would have got the whole thing then, which would have been much better both for Poland and for the prospects of peace.) Gladwyn says that the P.M. recently sent Eden a Minute asking for his observations on the proposal to detach East Prussia from Germany, and suggesting that this would be in breach of the Atlantic Charter. Gladwyn had put up a Minute to the Secretary of State giving reasons to the contrary, both under Article 2 and Article 6 of the Atlantic Charter. In Article 2, 'the peoples concerned' must surely include the Poles as well as the Germans, and under Article 6, the Poles could surely strongly argue that they could never hope to 'live in peace within their boundaries', or whatever the exact phrase is, if they were still encircled by the Germans and practically cut off from the sea, as in the inter-war period. But this is a sign that someone has been inciting the P.M. against the transfer. ...

Gladwyn says that he gets on well with [David] Owen, who is much more sensible than his master, Cripps. They have been trying to fuse a rather 'waffly' paper by the Secretary of State with a series of dogmatic points made in a paper by Cripps, while he was still a member of the War Cabinet. The silliest of these, postulating in unreal detail the future Government of the world in five major groupings, at least two of which are quite absurd, are likely to be withdrawn. Meanwhile, Gladwyn hopes that Clark Kerr, who is returning to Moscow at the end of this month, will be authorised to talk detail with the Russians on the future of Europe. It is high time this began. So long as we refuse, their suspicions of our intentions are most natural. Clark Kerr has been meeting Crossman and Ritchie-Calder[1] and others, so as to acquaint himself with the views of some of the Young Left.

Wednesday 13th January

Ruth dines with me and Wilmot at the Acropolis and likes her pilaf! They had been rung up from my office to ask them to keep a table for three, and, as we were leaving, the little Cypriot waiter asked Wilmot, 'In what Government is the gentleman a minister?' Wilmot replied,

1 P. R. Ritchie-Calder, later Baron (1906–82). Journalist, author and broadcaster. Foreign Office 1941–5.

'In the British Government, in Mr Churchill's Government.' 'Oh, my!' said the astonished waiter.

Thursday 14th January
Preside at a Labour Post-War Finance Committee, which is attended by all our tribe of experts, including, for the first time, Mrs Joan Robinson,[1] the best living, or dead, woman economist, but not, I am amused to find, by either Shinwell or Laski or any other of the outside elements. I have been a good deal bothered by the lack of progress in the work of this committee, and, with the aid of Wilmot, have been stimulating the production of papers. We have today quite a bunch, one by Chris Mayhew, written some time ago, on Foreign Exchange Control, another by Durbin on Post-War Monetary Policy, and a third by Jay on Post-War Financial Problems. After quite a useful discussion, we ask some of those present to go further into all this and prepare a single draft.

Friday 22nd January
I ask Tewson and Woodcock[2] to come and see me on post-war talks and how to relate the T.U.C. with them. As usual, very sensible and co-operative. I say that I am quite prepared to see either the full General Council or any sub-committee they may appoint. I also agree with Tewson and Woodcock the insertion of a sentence in our stock letter to Trade Associations saying that 'no important decisions will be taken without consultation with the trade unions concerned', and that it may, therefore, be convenient if the questions we ask are first considered through the medium of any joint machinery existing in the industry.

Wednesday 27th January
Morning at L.P.N.E. [Labour Party National Executive]. A slight wobble over the attitude to be adopted towards the Communist request for affiliation, but finally the recommendations of our Joint Committee for (1) a flat refusal, (2) the issue of a reasoned statement why, to be prepared by a small drafting committee, (3) the office to be given full powers to influence votes on this subject at the next Annual Conference, are carried by 15 to 4 – Laski, Shinwell, Barbara

1 Joan Robinson, née Maurice (1903–83). Lecturer in Economics at Cambridge University 1937–49; Reader 1949–65; Professor 1965–71. Married to Austin Robinson, q.v.
2 George Woodcock (1904–79). Secretary to the T.U.C. Research and Economic Department 1936–47. General Secretary of the T.U.C. 1960–69.

Gould and Sam Watson, who was very pro-Communist in his earlier days.

Laski is in a minority of one in objecting to the postponement, for the time being, of our proposed delegation to the U.S.S.R. Morrison makes a very good statement on this, and adds that Maisky told him yesterday in confidence that, the state of the war being what it was and our Second Front not yet having been opened, he thought it would cause embarrassment, and perhaps unpleasantness, if a 'goodwill mission' from this country came just at present. Ellen [Wilkinson] chides Laski with not seeing the point when the man he wants to visit very politely informs him that he is not wanted. Will Arnold-Forster is unanimously appointed Temporary Assistant to Morgan Phillips. He has been through a very tragic time, and I hope he will like this and fit in.

Thursday 28th January
Receive four dreary blokes from the F.B.I. [Federation of British Industries] this morning to talk about post-war. 'British industry' at the top is profoundly unimpressive.

Tuesday 2nd February
First of two days' Parliamentary debate on Post-War Financial and Economic Policy. A placid House, and Kingsley Wood, who speaks fairly early, full of most advanced ideas! Controls of all sorts must be continued after the war, and, in particular, control of new capital issues and of raw materials. It may well be that there will be a number of public enterprises, 'as recently suggested by the Home Secretary'. I tell Maurice Webb afterwards to put in the *Daily Herald* that Wood's advanced views are the result of successful pressure by Labour ministers, and that I shall dot his i's and cross his t's next day.

Wednesday 3rd February
And so I do when winding up the debate. I also give an account of what I am doing, for post-war studies, at the Board of Trade. My speech is well received by the House generally. The contributions of private Members have, however, been quite deplorable. Hardly a fact is cited, or a single fresh thought thrown up. Even Schuster, who begs me to remain into the luncheon interval to hear him, and tells me in advance that he thinks he has something important to say, is really rather feeble.

The final German surrender at Stalingrad took place on 2nd February.

Monday 8th February

Clark Kerr to see me. I begin, desiring to avoid all excuse for Foreign Office jealousy at my having summoned their Ambassador, by raising with him (1) post-war commercial policy, and (2) Relief, with both of which I am primarily concerned, on the first of which we may at any time wish to sound the Russians, and on the second of which there have already been discussions, both with Litvinov in Washington and Maisky here, and communications to both from Moscow. I find that Clark Kerr knows nothing whatever about either, has received no telegrams on either subject, and has heard nothing about either at the Foreign Office! I, therefore, write down for him one or two principal papers which he should take back with him to Moscow.

Having thus played my departmental gambit, we speak more generally. He says that, on his return, he will demand as much liberty to see people in Moscow as Maisky enjoys here. Personal contacts are still practically nil in Moscow. He has seen Stalin a few times, and Molotov more often. Stalin doesn't argue, he thinks aloud, without any reserves, and he laughs from his stomach. Thus he will say, 'Don't you think that chap over there is bloody ugly?' Molotov they call 'Stone-bottom'. In fact, he is made of stone from top to toe. He never laughs at all, and the utmost response Clark Kerr has ever got from him to his best cracks is that Molotov takes off his exceedingly thick glasses, wipes them and puts them on again. He is a frightful niggler in negotiation.

Our official relations are not really good. The P.M.'s visit was well worth while, and he and Stalin – particularly after the 'man to man' talk, which Clark Kerr says he insisted was essential – have feelings of mutual respect, though not of personal liking for each other. But the Russians want from us one thing and one thing only now, namely, large-scale military operations on the Continent of Europe. They want us and the Americans to die too. There is just no substitute for this. If and when such operations succeed, there is no real reason why our relationships should not become first-class. He often feels that it requires only a little turn of the wrist to make a wonderful Anglo-Soviet honeymoon. He is convinced that, if once they trust us, they will be tremendously keen to play with us on everything. But at present they don't trust us, and still think we are playing politics. The delay in starting our European offensive feeds this powerfully. Further, they attach quite undue importance to small things said and published here. Stalin, for instance, referred to the publications of de Courcy,[1] Lord Phillimore,[2] etc. When told by Clark Kerr that they were of no importance whatever, he did not believe it. When assured that H.M.G. had no responsibility for them, and did not agree with them, he still thought that some Department of H.M.G. must be behind them. 'Which of your Departments', he asked, 'is encouraging them?' Clark Kerr thinks that the Russians trust him, and Eden, but not 'the Foreign Office', the officials of which they think are still living in the 1880s. Maisky and his wife still don't understand much of English ways and of who counts how much. But they have their own developed, and effective, technique for poking people up, by constantly shooting in complaints about everything.

I ask whether he thinks there is any danger of Stalin making a separate peace. He says he would not rule this out, if we continue to seem to them to be doing nothing to help them. The Russians, for more than a year now, have been stretched to the utmost, like a piece of elastic on the point of breaking. They might well say, when they have cleared the Soviet territories, 'Now we will pause, and build up reserves, and re-equip, and let the British and Americans begin to do their share of the fighting.' Hitler, moreover, must always have the faint chance of a negotiation, so long as he can say that he realises he did wrong to attack Russia but he is willing to make ample amends, and that the real enemies to both of them are the Anglo-Saxons.

Even if none of this happens, it will still be pretty disastrous to our prestige in Europe if the Russians arrive in Berlin in their tanks and we travel peacefully to meet them by train. In the same way, our prestige in the East will be ruined if we let it seem that the United States, without much help from us, has defeated Japan.

The Poles in Moscow have been very foolish, and Ambassador Kot was a disaster. There is no doubt that many who were distributing parcels among their compatriots were simply spying. And they were all talking much too much. When Kot came away, a fat and cheerful Pole who acted as Chargé d'Affaires said to Clark Kerr, 'You can never stop a Pole talking, any more than you can stop a woman talking.'

Clark Kerr found the officials at the Foreign Office completely out of touch, and out of understanding, with realities in Russia. He has now arranged for a regular exchange between young men from the

1 K. H. de Courcy (b. 1909). Co-founder of the right-wing Imperial Policy Group in 1934 and its Secretary 1934–9. Publisher of *Review of World Affairs.*
2 Lord Phillimore, 2nd Baron (1879–1947). Co-founder of the Imperial Policy Group.

Northern Department of the Foreign Office and the Embassy at Moscow.

I am quite sure that, when I spotted this particular diplomat long ago, as one of the very best of the bunch, I was right. He could not be improved upon for this particular job, which I told him was by far the most potentially important in the world today. ...

Dine in with Morrison and Wilmot. Very successful. Morrison thinks the post-war Board of Trade should be on parity with the Treasury. We should have an industrial, as well as a financial, budget, and all ministers in charge of other industries should be subordinate to the Board of Trade. I say that I will let him have some notes on these possibilities. We must also run him for Treasurer of the Labour Party.[1] He liked this evening very much and told Wilmot that he would take steps to be able to repeat it at the Home Office.

Tuesday 9th February
I expound to the four senior officials principally concerned the ideas of the Home Secretary on the post-war Board of Trade. Ministers, I say, are only passengers through their departments, but 'the gang goes on'. Overton asks, 'The gang?' I say, 'Yes, the gang.' But ministers, in their brief passage, can do either much good or much evil, and here is a chance for the officials to help ministers to do great good to the Board of Trade. So I hope for their ideas on this. They should be, and I think are, departmentally delighted.

Friday 12th February
A deplorable Party Meeting, not very well attended, to discuss the Beveridge Report. It was to run for three hours, from 10 to 1, but the first two were taken up with yowling because Greenwood had put his name to an all-party resolution on which the debate was to be hitched, he opening it, whereas a number of other resolutions had been put upon the paper, including one by some Liberals, in stronger terms demanding early legislation. In fact, I guess that none of these others will be called, but I don't think the Administrative Committee have handled the business very well. As usual, many of the speakers show a complete lack of any sense either of proportion or trust in elected leaders. ...

... [P]roceed to my dentist and have a tooth out. Though it is not exactly the sort of amusement one chooses, it is not really so bad in fact as in anticipation. I should like injections, producing numbness of the nerves, on many other occasions than in the dental chair!

1 Marginal insertion: 'He ran, and was beaten by Greenwood, through Bevin's influence. Vacancy through Lathan's death.'

Saturday 13th February

Leith-Ross says that Noel Hall is to come back, and that Selborne will probably offer him to me. He has fallen out with many in Washington.

Leith-Ross also wonders whether we should not take over Relief through the blockade. Lehman is doing this for the Americans. Leith-Ross says that, as no doubt I know, Eden and Selborne are now in favour of sending relief, e.g. to Belgium, but that the P.M. is still against it. I say, 'And so am I.' I add that I hear that the P.M., when Eden and Selborne said that they agreed with one another, looked sternly at Selborne and said, 'The Cabinet are not accustomed to hear such arguments from the Minister of Economic Warfare. Your predecessor would never have taken such a line.' In any case, I don't think this would fit in well with the rest of Leith-Ross's work, and I much discourage such an idea. Possibly Drogheda, who no doubt is anxious also to get rid of Hall, put this into Leith-Ross's head.

Tuesday 16th February

Beveridge debate begins, and Anderson speaks for the Government in the afternoon. He pulls out no loud stops and emphasises nothing. A most miserable and inept presentation. I don't think he did it on purpose, but, as someone said, if Lloyd George at his best had had to speak on that brief, he would have made everyone believe that we were arriving in Paradise tomorrow. Morrison says that the P.M. was very obstinate in the Cabinet yesterday on the question of timing. He said that we could not introduce the Beveridge scheme until after an election. Morrison said, 'Does that mean a khaki election? This is the first we have heard of it. If so, we had better begin to prepare for it now.'

Wednesday 17th February

Party Meeting, at which the amendment expressing dissatisfaction with the Government's declared policy, put down late last night after a scratch meeting of the Administrative Committee, is discussed. Final decision is left till tomorrow's meeting. Attlee and Morrison both speak, but without much success. Here once again, we have a nauseating example of collective ministerial incapacity to decide anything. Morrison tells me that he saw the P.M. late last night. He was 'not too bad' but has been much influenced by Kingsley Wood, in particular, against any financial commitments now. ...

Wilmot told me that Maurice Webb tells him that Bracken at a press conference this afternoon said, 'The Government is going to get tough with its critics', and added, 'We don't care if Mr Maurice

Webb writes five columns every day in the *Daily Herald* instead of two.' It is also reported that Wood has had a spectacular success in the Cabinet, and that Morrison was beaten. Whiteley tells me next day that Attlee 'fought like a tiger' against the P.M. in the Cabinet, but without success.

Wood spoke in the House today and only made things worse than yesterday.

After listening to Anderson and Wood, the main Government spokesmen in the Beveridge debate, the Parliamentary Labour Party put down an official amendment to the Government motion. This amendment, which called for legislation along Beveridge lines as a matter of urgency, secured 121 votes – including the overwhelming majority of Labour Party back-benchers. The vote threatened the foundations of the Coalition, and Bevin, who was un-enthusiastic about the Report, believing it to cut across trade union interests, came close to resigning from the P.L.P. The importance of the clash, how-ever, was that it firmly identified the Labour Party in the public mind with the highly popular Beveridge proposals.

Thursday 18th February
Third day of Beveridge debate. Meeting of Administrative Com-mittee at 9.30 and of Parliamentary Party at 10. The Administrative Committee proposes that the Party shall support its own amendment, if called, but not everybody else's amendment. Bevin speaks at the Party Meeting and makes a mess of it. He begins quite well by pointing out that there are many things in Beveridge which are not acceptable to the trade unions, or on which consultation with trade unions will be necessary. Therefore, they should not swallow Beveridge whole. So far so good, but he then begins to shout, protest and threaten, which he is always too much apt to do, and which undoes it all. He says the Party amendment is a vote of censure on him, that they never gave him an opportunity of speaking before it was put down, that this is not the kind of treatment he has been accustomed to, that this is not the way they do things in the unions, and that, if this is the way things are to be done, he will refuse to go on. (It is not clear what this means. It was thought at first that he meant that he would resign from the Government. Later, it was thought that he meant that he would resign from the Labour Party. In any case, he was going about late

that evening saying that he was 'through with it all'.) Barnes makes a good speech immediately afterwards and turns them all against Bevin, saying that if anyone threatens to resign because they are unwilling to accept the view of the majority, that resignation should be accepted. This is loudly cheered by an excited Meeting. He then goes on to make a most sensible suggestion, namely, that the Party should only press its amendment to a division if Morrison, who is to wind up today, does not put a different aspect on the case from the two earlier Government spokesmen. But Greenwood, in the Chair, whether through general weakness or design, does not take this point, and the Party finally votes, practically unanimously, to divide on its own amendment. This is illogical, since the amendment expresses dissatisfaction at the policy of the Government, and this policy may or may not be modified in Morrison's final speech. There is a vague reference this morning to 'consultations on the Front Bench' after Morrison's speech, but in practice this is quite an unworkable procedure. ...

Morrison, winding up for the Government, makes a grand speech. I am quite sure that if this had been made on the first day, there would have been no crisis at all. But it is by now much too late to retrieve the ground lost by Anderson and Kingsley Wood, or to stop most of the Party voting for their amendment against the Government. Wilmot and certain others have been lobbying to secure abstentions, and have a certain measure of success. At least twenty-four of our members, who remain in the House till the end, don't vote. I advise Wilmot to abstain rather than to vote with the Government, since abstention is permissible under the Standing Orders, and I don't wish him to make himself unduly vulnerable. The minority vote, 119, is nearly the same as that in the Tory revolt against the Catering Bill,[1] 116. Of the 119, 98 are Labour members, the rest being Liberals and other oddments. But no Tories.

I return a little weary to the Board of Trade. We cannot have many more such incidents. This one has been incredibly mishandled by all concerned from start to finish, except by Morrison. But what a lot of our Members don't see is that they run a risk of the P.M. appealing to the country, on the ground that he must know where he stands, with the result that the Labour Party would be scrubbed out as completely as in 1931. As Wilmot and I agree, many of our colleagues are complete innocents, while a small minority is fixedly set on breaking up the Government. Master Shinwell today has been rushing about with

1 Bevin had managed to get Cabinet approval for his Catering Wages Bill, designed to improve working conditions in the trade. However, 116 Conservatives showed their displeasure by voting against the Second Reading.

a maniacal glint in his eye. He reminds me of the chap who was determined to set fire to the house and burn it down for his own delight. Greenwood cuts a very sorry figure, rising just before the division to say that he intended now to vote for the amendment.

I put the scrub-out point to Maurice Webb, who rang me up on the telephone later. It would not, I said, be very clever, from any point of view, to install in 1943 an overwhelmingly Conservative majority which need not again go to the country till 1948.

Friday 19th February

Mayhew to dine with me. He has just had his one-week-in-three-months leave. He comes back afterwards and helps me to concoct my advance for my speech in Birmingham tomorrow. He is going to help to run his father's East Anglian papers after the war. I quite approve of this.

Sunday 21st February

Stay in all day, don't shave – since I have sent away all my staff for the day – and read funny old Pethick [Lawrence]'s autobiography.[1] He has no sense of humour, as we knew, and succeeds in making everything seem very flat. But he has had quite an interesting life, of a sort, and is clearly very fond of his wife.[2] At points quite blush-making, including the Song of Spring at the beginning, wherein he and the flowers in his garden burble to each other and send messages to her in South Africa.

Hear Eden at the Albert Hall on the wireless. Not bad, but not quite so good as it might have been. Too much, in a not very long speech, about Hitler and the 'Bolshevik bogy' and how it won't work now. This theme has been overdone a good deal lately. I am sure it cannot please the Russians.

Monday 22nd February

I ask Retinger to call, to feel my way for my talk with Sikorski on Wednesday – day after tomorrow. I say that this is the worst possible moment for Poles to quarrel, either publicly or privately, with Russians, since there is a great wave of pro-Russian feeling here, in view of their victories, while we seem to be doing so little. I say that I hear that Polish claims to a frontier on the Black Sea and the Dnieper, and to include Kiev, after the war, are floating about. This is disastrous folly. He says that Sikorski wholly agrees with me and that no official or

---

1 *Fate Has Been Kind*, Hutchinson, London, 1943.
2 Emmeline Pethick Lawrence, née Pethick (d. 1956). Her husband incorporated her name into his own at the time of their marriage in 1901.

authorised person had ever made such suggestions for post-war frontiers. He adds that the Russians are treating the Poles in Russia very badly and have decreed that all Polish citizens picked up east of the line to which the Russians advanced in 1939 are to be treated as Soviet citizens, even if they came from West Poland, in retreat before the German advance.

Take Attlee out to lunch in view of tonight's Labour ministers meeting. He does not seem very worried about it, and most of our talk is on other things. He says that he is satisfied that the estimate of 5,000,000 Germans out of the war – killed, prisoner or severely wounded – is not too high! Also that Alexander in Tunisia is writing a book 'How Green is My Ally'. The Americans seem to have lost a large number of their Sherman tanks, quite intact.

Labour ministers meet later in the afternoon. Many of them seem very thin-skinned, and to feel that their position has been rendered very difficult by last week's vote. Bevin – about whose intentions many press rumours are circulating, it being said that his intention is to resign, not from the Government, but from the Labour Party – is very indignant with the Parliamentary Labour Party, but not so violent as the press suggests. Attlee, he and Morrison have to go to a War Cabinet, and I take the Chair. I had previously said that, in my view, most of those who voted against the Government did not realise what they were doing, but that it was clear that this sort of incident could not often be repeated. We were, however, in the Government, not by any decision of the P.L.P., but by the will of the Annual Conference, which alone had the right to bring us out. Between Conferences the National Executive exercised the powers of the Conferences, but not the power to reverse a Conference decision. I said bluntly that, if this sort of thing went on, and if, for example, the electoral truce was broken up, there would be a General Election in which the Labour Party would be 'scrubbed out', worse than in 1931. When I was in the Chair, a number seized upon the point about the Annual Conference, and some wanted to pass a resolution to be conveyed to the National Executive. I discouraged this, since the meeting had no constitutional status, but undertook to report to the National Executive on Wednesday that some had expressed the view that there should be a special Conference summoned forthwith, and others that the National Executive should 'protect' ministers. Some of these little fish suffer from haemophilia.

Tuesday 23rd February
Administrative Committee in the morning. Desultory talk, mostly by Shinwell. ...

Gladwyn Jebb to dine. He says that Eden is going quite soon to the U.S., accompanied by Cadogan, Strang and himself. It has been put off, for the moment, owing to the P.M.'s illness. The principal discussion will be political, and Eden will press that we should now talk detail on the Peace Settlement, both with the Americans and the Russians. He does not think Eden will be led into any detailed talk on economics, either on the Treasury or Board of Trade side. We agree that Phillips[1] of the Treasury is a frightful old woman. Gladwyn says that his telegrams read like cautionary letters from a very third-rate solicitor. He agrees that it would be very useful if Liesching were there at the same time, to counter-balance the Treasury if necessary, but thinks it would be difficult to include him in Eden's personal party, since there would be jealous outcry from a number of other Departments. He suggests that I might arrange for Liesching to be in Washington, independently, at the same time. He says that they two like each other and are in close touch. He insists, in reply to my usual scepticism, that he is quite popular and well dug in at the Foreign Office. He is not one of Eden's intimates, and he thinks he never will be, but he is allowed to see all papers and his own suggestions are generally well received. He thinks that his relations with Cadogan are also still quite good, and that the latter was misled by Ismay and Morton into believing, when the change came at M.E.W., that Gladwyn was much more unpopular with the Services than he ever really was.

He thought Anderson's speech on Beveridge was ludicrously inept, and that, whereas the Government were expected by all to say, and were really trying to say, that they thought the Beveridge Report was a jolly good thing and that they were going to act on most of it, they succeeded in creating the impression that they were both shifty and hostile. He has met, by request, Morrison's Mr Leslie,[2] and thinks him very intelligent. Morrison has submitted a draft on his next speech, which is largely on foreign affairs, and, Gladwyn thinks, very good. So good, indeed, that it has not aroused much enthusiasm in Eden. The latter, he says, 'does not reason out a problem, as you or I do', but gets there by a queer process of his own. He is very sensitive to atmosphere, and, if you choose to use the word in this sense, very feminine.

Wednesday 24th February

Another Administrative Committee this morning, at 9.30. A speech by Shinwell, but no decision. Then a Party Meeting. Desultory talk,

1 Sir Frederick Phillips, q.v. Treasury Representative in the U.S. 1940–43.
2 C. S. (Clem) Leslie. Morrison's publicity adviser from 1937. In the 1942–3 period, Leslie helped to write Morrison's speeches on post-war reconstruction policy.

much by Shinwell. There is no longer a Chairman in the Chair. Greenwood gives no guidance, controls nothing, and seems mostly paralysed, though I suspect an occasional touch of malice against ministers. Morrison at the Party Meeting gives them a very good pie-jaw, telling them that the Labour Party seems often to want to be a Suicide Club, and that there is much too much talk about 'safe seats', no matter how grave the blunders committed. On this the point is that we can never get power unless we win, and hold, a very large number of the weaker seats. Aneurin Bevan makes a long, rambling address, obviously in a state of great pique because, in spite of the Beveridge Report fuss, which was perfectly timed to help her, Jennie Lee[1] lost the North Bristol election, though her successful opponent absolutely refused to commit herself for or against the Beveridge Report. This result casts some doubt on the readily accepted allegation that the whole country is hungering and thirsting after Beveridge.

At 11 go from Party Meeting to National Executive and find them quacking away about the Communist affiliation.[2] Several, including Jim Griffiths, who, as Wilmot and I agree, has got a very spongy under-belly, are wobbling towards measures of compromise, e.g. entering into discussions with the Communists, believing that the vote may go against us at the Conference. Fred Burrows says that the N.U.R. is quite firm and that there is no reason to suppose that we cannot defeat the Communists, provided that the necessary preparatory work is done and people don't get cold feet. ...

T.U.C. this afternoon pass unanimously a vote of confidence in Labour ministers, and were restrained only with difficulty from adding a vote of condemnation on the Parliamentary Labour Party. Speeches in this sense were also made at the N.C.L. [National Council of Labour] yesterday. ...

Gaitskell to dine, and we discuss the incredible crudeness and stupidity of the Labour Party, which now tends to overshadow the indecisive ineptitude of the Government. I try to poke up the work on post-war financial policy which Gaitskell and others have been doing, but it seems very difficult to get any sense out of a 'drafting committee', even of bright people. Better soon to give out tasks one to each, and for me to go through them when they come in.

---

1 Jennie Lee, later Baroness (b. 1904). Labour M.P. for Lanark North 1929–31; Cannock 1945–70. Junior minister 1964–7; Minister for the Arts 1967–70. Married Aneurin Bevan, q.v., in 1934.
2 'the Communist affiliation': the desire of the Communist Party to affiliate to the Labour Party. See entry for 27th January, pp. 548–9.

I thought this morning 'the crisis' was petering out. Tonight I am not so sure.

Thursday 25th February

Another meeting of Labour ministers at No. 11 Downing Street tonight. There has been a fantastic number of meetings this week on the Beveridge fuss. This evening it emerges that, at the tail end of the National Executive yesterday, after 2 p.m., it was proposed by Walker, and seconded by Ridley, that a vote of confidence in the Labour ministers should be passed, as at the T.U.C. Against this, it seems, from a letter from Middleton to Attlee ... that this would be equivalent to censuring the Parliamentary Labour Party. Since, however, the mover and seconder would not withdraw, this (as an amendment to a resolution merely reaffirming the earlier resolution of the N.C.L., in favour of the principles, though not necessarily of all the details, of the Beveridge Report) was defeated by 13 votes to 4. Most clumsy! Bevin and others make a great to-do over this and declare that it is equivalent to a vote of no confidence in the Labour ministers. But it is really not quite this. They suggest a further meeting of the National Executive to be called, from which such a vote of confidence should be demanded, failing which a special conference to be called, at which a vote of no confidence in the Executive should be proposed, etc, etc. Bevin, very full of peasant suspicions, especially against Maurice Webb and other persons unnamed – possibly Morrison – declares that there is a double conspiracy going on, partly to break up the Government and partly to change the leadership of the Labour Party. As usual, much abuse of 'the political side', which is taken to include the National Executive. But I have to point out that this last body abounds in trade union representatives. None the less, I am more than half inclined to support the proposal for a special National Executive, but it is finally left, Morrison weighing in against stirring the whole thing up any further, that, unless reports appear in the press suggesting that the National Executive has expressed lack of confidence in ministers, we should do no more for the present. If, however, such rumours circulate, then Attlee should have a free hand to demand a special meeting. All this has become the most *frightful bore*. As Simmonds[1] says to me later this evening, when I ask him for his frank opinion, at the beginning the Government came out of it much worse than the Labour Party, but, with the passage of days and the constant stirring up of crisis mud, the Labour Party has now come out of it much worse than the Government. Ground which had

1 O. E. Simmonds, later Sir Oliver (b. 1897). Conservative M.P. for Birmingham Duddeston 1931–45.

lately been gained has been lost again, and many intelligent people are now saying that the Labour Party is N.B.G.[1] I fear this is quite true, though it may soon pass.

Bevin says that he went straight to the T.U.C. tonight, since it was at their request that he first entered the Government. They are a strong and sensible, though slightly wooden, element in all this flotsam and jetsam.

I say tonight to the two Cazalets, whom I meet dining with Lady Colefax, referring to Scott's *Behind the Urals*, that the Russians are completely indifferent to human suffering, whereas the Germans cultivate it like a fine flower. It is thought that this is a very bright remark, as indeed it is!

Saturday 27th to Sunday 28th February
At West Leaze for the first time for a month. Work in the garden till 7.30 p.m. I notice the lengthening evenings more because my mind has been on the cycle battery shortage.

Monday 1st March
Home Front Ministers' Meeting. ... A general jaw on next steps regarding the Beveridge Report. Jowitt is to 'co-ordinate' the various inquiries of different Departments, and to have, for this purpose, a small high-powered staff of officials. [Ernest] Brown and Thomas Johnston are to discuss the 'unified medical service' with the doctors, etc. – Brown said to me that he thought it would take fifteen months, in which case there will be another row before long – Bevin is to examine necessary changes in unemployment benefit and assistance, and so forth. Someone has said, 'Never has any Government got so little credit for doing so much so quickly.' But neither Anderson nor Kingsley Wood, both of whom are at today's meeting, seem to be oppressed by any sense of guilt or wasted opportunities. ...

A 'directive' was recently issued, relating primarily to research work closely connected with the war effort. It indicated that we should proceed on the assumption that the war in Europe would be finished before the end of 1944, and the war against Japan before the end of 1946, the latter being likely to require from us 'quite a considerable effort'.

Tuesday 2nd March
Dine at the Great Western Hotel, the party being organised by Carvel and Haydn Davies, and including Wilmot, Harvie Watt – whom I don't see much of, but with whom I judge that my relations are very

1 'N.B.G.': No Bloody Good.

good – Cranfield,[1] the Editor of the *Star*, who does not impress me at all – I hear that he has been demoted in Fleet Street, having once edited the *Daily Mail*; he has an old-fashioned Liberal outlook, desiring to abolish the House of Lords but, on the other hand, to do nothing to enforce any orders or regulations, any efforts to do this being described as 'snooping' – Desmond Morton, whom I seldom see now but still regard as one of the slimiest snakes and a close friend of some of my worst enemies, and other less obtrusive persons.

Wednesday 3rd March

The Speaker[2] died today. He had only been ill, with bronchitis, for a week, but he was seventy-three and had been giving an impression, for some time, of losing his grip. He succeeded Whitley[3] in 1928, in my first Parliament, and it is interesting to recall that it was the Labour Party who made him Speaker. He had been Chairman of Ways and Means for several years and had given an impression of slow-witted impartiality. Hope, now Lord Rankeillour,[4] the Deputy Speaker, was completely unacceptable to the Labour Party. He was a complete contrast to Fitzroy and oozed quick-witted bias. We had gone to the length of putting down a motion on the paper condemning his partiality in the Chair. Baldwin, then P.M., and other leading lights in the Tory Party, realising that Hope was impossible, wanted Inskip. But the Labour Party were against this candidature, since he too seemed to us a partisan and had often made pompous and not very benevolent debating points against us. We therefore encouraged MacDonald to tell Baldwin that we would support Fitzroy, but would vote against Inskip. It being much desired to avoid a vote, Fitzroy got it, and Inskip became less friendly than ever towards the Labour Party.

I myself should like to see Clifton Brown,[5] the Deputy Speaker,

1 A. L. Cranfield (1892–1957). Editor of the *Star* 1941–57. Editor of the *Daily Mail* 1935–9. In November 1947, Cranfield (as Editor of the *Star*) was responsible for publishing the Budget disclosures, telephoned in by Carvel, which resulted in Dalton's resignation as Chancellor of the Exchequer.
2 Hon. E. A. Fitzroy (1869–1943). Speaker of the House of Commons 1928–43. Conservative M.P. for Northamptonshire South 1900–6, 1910–18; Daventry 1918–43. Deputy Chairman (not Chairman) of Ways and Means 1924–8.
3 J. H. Whitley (1866–1935). Speaker of the House of Commons 1921–8. Liberal M.P. for Halifax 1900–28. Junior minister 1907–10. Chairman of the Committee on the Relations of Employers and Employed (Whitley Committee) 1917–18.
4 J. F. Hope, 1st Baron Rankeillour (1879–1949). Conservative M.P. 1900–6, 1908–29. Junior whip 1915–16. Junior minister 1916–21.
5 Douglas Clifton Brown, later Viscount Ruffside (1879–1958). Conservative M.P. for Hexham 1918–23, 1924–51. Speaker of the House of Commons 9th March 1943 until 1951.

succeed to the Chair.[1] But there will be a great intrigue to get it for Gwilym Lloyd George.

Tewson to see me. I say that I should like to put in George Woodcock for an Honour, but Tewson thinks that this might cause ill-feeling among his seniors, and I agree to defer it. He speaks ill, as usual, of Madame Maisky and all the trouble over clothes to Russia. He expresses great sympathy for [Sir Thomas] Barlow. The Russians, he says, are very arrogant, as well as being difficult on details ...

Dine with Sir Alexander Livingstone and sit beside Averell Harriman, who, as usual, gives an impression of being very pro-British. He says that most Americans believe that we are so damned clever that we have already got all our post-war plans worked out to the last dot, and intend to inveigle the Americans into accepting them to their own great disadvantage. In view of our chronic indecisions, this is really frightfully funny, but I tell Harriman that decisions come even more slowly in a Coalition than in a one-Party Government. Harriman says that he is afraid that the U.S. are falling down on their promises of food and other supplies for us. Their price control and rationing have begun with tremendous muddles, and so have their manpower arrangements. We have the great advantage in food rationing in so far as we import the bulk of our supplies, but it is administratively impossible to control everything that happens on the farm. The Republicans in Congress are feeling the ground for a fight with the President, but they have not found solid enough ground yet. In particular, they will be very chary of doing anything which can be construed as an attack on the war effort. Harriman does not think much of Sumner Welles, or his last speech in which he said that discussions on post-war problems with the Allies were overdue. Harriman thinks that the President may now be feeling that the war may end sooner than he expected a little while ago, that he cannot run again on the New Deal, the domestic electoral trend being conservative, and that, therefore, he must be prepared to run, partially at least, on pleasing post-war plans.

Thursday 4th March
Lunch over Simpson's in Piccadilly and propose the health of Poland. Barnby,[2] in the Chair, says he is very glad that the Board of Trade is in the hands of an Old Etonian. This gives him great confidence for the future! ...

Thence to Bishop Auckland for three and a half days.

1 Marginal note: 'He did.'
2 Hon. Francis Vernon Willey, 2nd Baron Barnby (1884–1982). Conservative M.P. for Bradford South 1918–22.

Saturday 6th March

Sleep in, visit the Trading Estate across the road, and hear plans of Ernest and Henry[1] for turning over from making aeroplane parts to making button-making machinery after the war. They have much enterprise.

Afternoon, receive constituents at Lightfoot Institute for three hours, then for tea with Ernest Proud, and return to two and a half hours' private meeting of delegates.[2]

I find the latter discussing, rather vaguely, the reform of local government, but after three-quarters of an hour of this, I am invited to speak and do so at some length. I begin with the war, the coming climax, the U-boats, the Russians, etc., and then go on to post-war problems, saying a good deal about Beveridge, but sandwiching it in among my visit to state factories, Bevin and Hicks's Charter for the post-war building trade, and my own contribution to the Miners' Charter last June. I tell them frankly that I have never known any case so mishandled, both pro and con the Government, as this Beveridge scheme. I say that I was not in on this, and that, perhaps, if I had been, the mess might have been less. I say that I know Beveridge better than most people, having served both under and over him; that he is not 'one of us' and has no first-hand knowledge of industrial conditions; that there are a number of things in his Report to which we could not subscribe, e.g. the penalising of miners and railway workers because their jobs are inherently more risky than a carpenter's, and the proposal to take twenty years to reach the appropriate rate of old age pension. Both of these criticisms are well received, as I knew they would be, by my audience. I then add that, none the less, the Beveridge Report is a fine and stimulating document and that, out of 23 suggested changes, the Government has set only one aside, has referred 6 to further consideration, and accepted the remaining 16, together with the three 'assumptions', child allowances, comprehensive health services, and full employment. I then blow my own trumpet over child allowances, and recall that I only just succeeded last year in persuading the Labour Party to get in front of the Government. I praise Morrison saying that he is about the only person who came with any credit out of the three days' debate in the House of Commons. I remind them that Beveridge did not himself propose that his scheme of benefits should begin to operate till 1945, so we have plenty of time, even on that basis, to work out plans and take account of finance. I tell them, more than once in different connections, that

1 'Ernest and Henry': Bishop Auckland factory.
2 Of the Bishop Auckland Labour Party.

23 Ernest Bevin walks to the Ministry of Labour, July 1944

Warsaw, August–October 1944:

24 When the battle ended. General Bór-Komorowski, leader of the partisans, and S.S. General Bach-Zelewski, commander of the German units. 200,000 Poles died in the Rising.

25 Polish resistance fighters

26 London suburbia, October 1944

27 A rocket bomb hits Farringdon Market, March 1945

28 Planning for peace. Dalton and Harold Laski at the Labour Party Conference in Blackpool, June 1945

they may take it from me that Labour ministers in the Government are exercising no small influence, and that, were we not there, the result would be much less satisfactory. All this goes over very well, and, when questions are invited, very few are asked, and none of them hostile. One man gets up and says that he was present this afternoon in Durham at a conference on the Beveridge Report, and that he is sorry to say that several of the speakers had shown lack of confidence in the Labour members of the War Cabinet. This news is greeted with evident disapproval by the delegates. Blenkinsop[1] then gets up and says he does not know whether 'our' Member would like a vote of confidence. I say, 'Yes, please', and he then moves it, and it is seconded and carried unanimously. They are a grand lot! But, as I often tell my weaker brethren, every M.P. gets out of his constituency what he puts into it.

Dalton's decision to impose a ban on trouser turn-ups in order to save cloth caused public irritation, and much ribaldry in the press. 'If Dr Dalton will come to the House of Commons with a large red patch in the seat of his black pants I will endeavour to have his picture published free in this newspaper,' wrote one columnist, ' – rear view only.'[2]

Tuesday 9th March
Elect the new Speaker, Clifton Brown. It takes a damned long time, but I think he will do all right.

Lunch with the Belgian Ambassador and go on to open a Make Do and Mend Exhibition at Charing Cross. There I make an impromptu vow not to buy a new suit till the end of the war!

The evening papers report remarks by Mr Langley, Stipendiary Magistrate at Old Street, in a prosecution for evasion of regulations against turn-ups. He seems to have let off four defendants, who pleaded guilty, very lightly, and then said that he had purposely imposed only nominal penalties, in order to encourage representations to secure a change in the law. We have had trouble with this Magistrate before, and I write to Morrison enclosing a cutting from the *Star*.

1 A local party member.
2 *Daily Express*, 6th April 1943.

Friday 12th March

Maillaud[1] to lunch with me. I have not seen him for a long while, but I have recently written to him praising his little book on France.[2] I find him, as I used to do, very clear-headed and sensible. He was in North Africa for a month, including the time when Darlan was shot. He had a long talk with Giraud, and would much prefer to live under his *'liberté humaine'* than under de Gaulle's *'liberté démocratique'*. Giraud, he says, is a typical old General, with conservative tendencies but no clear political ideas or ambitions. He would never wish, differing here from de Gaulle, to be the head of a French government. He wants only to fight and beat the Germans. He said to Maillaud, 'Yes, I too would have gone to England had I been able, in the summer of 1940. But I would not then have indulged either in politics or in slanders.' He also said that undoubtedly some of the Jews had behaved very badly, but so had 'many of my own middle class', both having enriched themselves at the expense of France. Maillaud said that the de Gaullistes in France were now being urged, from their Headquarters in London, to show the maximum of activity. But this, he said, only means that a number of brave men died, and suffered, to no good purpose. It would be much better to hold themselves in until sabotage and other acts could really help our invasion of the Continent. But in this tactic, he said, de Gaulle was both playing up to the Russians, who also always favoured it, and staking out further claims for himself. Maillaud thought that there was a real risk of civil war in France between the de Gaullistes, who were everywhere being organised, even though in small numbers, and various other factions, some of whom would follow Giraud, some the Communists, some the leaders who had remained in France. He also feared that, in order to emphasise themselves on the morrow of liberation, de Gaulle and his adherents would adopt an anti-British line. Nor, he thought, should we lose sight of the possibility that, particularly if Anglo-Russian relations were not very close, the Russians would have an interest in making France both Communist and, in some measure, anti-British. On the other hand, he himself believed that Britain, France and Russia could be good friends and, between them, provide sufficient power to keep Europe at peace for a long while. Maillaud said that he

1 Pierre Maillaud (1908–48). French journalist. B.B.C. French political commentator 1940–44. Havas Foreign Services 1931–40. Founded *Agence française indépendente* 1940. He became Secretary of the Radical Socialist Party in 1947 under the name of Pierre Bourdan, and served in the Ramadier Government as Minister for Youth, Arts and Information.

2 Pierre Maillaud, *France* (with a foreword by D. W. Brogan), Oxford University Press, London, 1942.

had seen too much of Generals – his father having been one – to be much impressed by them. Returning to France, he said, he would 'feel very humble' in the presence of those who had stuck it out. He is still running his post-Havas agency and is quite independent of de Gaulle or any other French faction. He spoke highly of Massigli, who, he said, stood for the best, though not the universal, tradition of the French civil service, good brains and honesty of purpose. Leger,[1] he said, was in the U.S.A., likewise independent of all factions.

Saturday 13th to Sunday 14th March
At West Leaze. Sit in a deck-chair on the terrace after lunch on Sunday and go to sleep in the sun for one and a half hours! I am feeling rather fretful about P.Q.s, which, it is clear, are being organised by that little bounder Herbert Williams[2] in order to snipe and embarrass me. There is also a P.Q. for next Tuesday to the P.M. by another Tory prize twerp, Simmonds, trying to make trouble about the reference at Bishop Auckland to retaining State factories after the war. I had sent a note, on Private Secretary level, to the P.M. before leaving London, but he has only just got back and will have been out of touch with everything, and I am afraid they may trip him up on Supplementaries. But I forget all this for a while in fixing wires from the balcony to sustain the new growth of the ceanothus. None the less, I write to Ruth that down here I feel more inclined to resign and write some scabrous memoirs than to return to boredom at the Board of Trade! I suppose 'they' will try to use the Official Secrets Act to prevent the publication of all the most interesting things which one day I shall want to say.

Monday 15th March
Cynthia Jebb to dine with me. She thought that I rang up the other day to make sure whether or not Gladwyn had actually left with Eden for Washington. She amuses me by much feline gossip against Clark Kerr, I having told her that he is undoubtedly much the best of our diplomats, and that I had so informed all members of the Labour Party, and that Phil [Noel-]Baker said that he agreed with me. She thought this last point alone was fatal, since Phil had notoriously the worst of judgments regarding people. She added that Clark Kerr dyed his hair, mis-stated his age in *Who's Who* – representing himself to have been two years younger than he was, and, when this

---

1 Possibly Alexis Léger (1887–1976). French Secretary-General for Foreign Affairs 1933–40. He came to London in June 1940, and later went to New York.
2 Sir Herbert Williams, Conservative M.P. for Croydon South, q.v.

was discovered, having removed the date of his birth entirely from this work of reference – that although he wore a kilt and talked about his 'place' in Scotland, he was really an Australian and his 'place' only a bungalow by the roadside. She also made malicious allegations about his intimate life and the unfortunate little Chilean whom he married when in South America but had been separated from for a number of years.[1] But I told her at the end that even though all this and more were true, I stood by my opinion that he was the best of our diplomats. So much the worse for all the rest! Anyhow, he is sixty-one now, though he doesn't look it, and he will, no doubt, retire after another year or so. I hope he will be able to pull off some big success, with the aid of some external factors, at Moscow before he goes.

Tuesday 16th March

Start an official visit to the West Riding, accompanied by Barlow, Weir, Warter and Preston. I spend the first two nights in Bradford and the next two in Leeds. ... It was a bit exhausting, rather like electioneering, rushing from place to place and group to group, showing all the time affability and interest, making too many speeches, public and private, being friendly to the press but not telling them much, and being a little too much entertained.

At Bradford I stay with Bailey,[2] my Wool Adviser. He has a Swedish wife, who had spent much of her time in Finland, and a very Swedish-looking daughter. She is not very interesting, but is a very good hostess. On Tuesday (16th) the Baileys ask about twelve people to dine, and on Wednesday (17th) I dine with Behrens[3] and some thirty people at the Union Club. Here I make a rather successful impromptu, seated, reminiscent speech, about Queen Victoria, and my father[4] (they lap this up), and King George V, and how odd, yet potent, the British Crown is, like the British people – illustrated by some old chestnuts about the General Strike and the football behind the German lines on 1st April 1915 – and then, in effect, a summary of

1 Sir Archibald Clark Kerr's marriage to Maria Teresa, née Diaz Salas, was dissolved in 1945.
2 R. Bailey, later Sir Reginald (1894–1953). Adviser to the Board of Trade on Wool Exports 1939–53. Married Hjördis Marie Frederikson in 1919.
3 E. C. Behrens (1885–1975). Chairman of Sir Jacob Behrens & Sons Ltd. Chairman of the National Wool Export Group 1942–58.
4 Canon J. N. Dalton (1839–1931). Tutor to Prince Albert Victor (Eddy) and Prince George (later King George V), sons of the Prince of Wales 1871–84. Chaplain-in-Ordinary and Deputy Clerk of the Closet to Queen Victoria and King Edward VII. Canon of St George's Chapel, Windsor 1884–1931. Father of Hugh Dalton.

Chapter I of *Practical Socialism for Britain*,[1] and the old pussycat's remark to my mother[2] about my 'having gone the same way as poor Arthur Ponsonby'.[3] And so I end by saying that we find in many of our national habits and attitudes 'the rational root of our patriotic self-esteem'. Is it really very shocking to humbug all these poor people like this? Several come and thank me warmly afterwards. Behrens said that I had done more to bring them together by this speech than he could have thought possible.

Monday 22nd March
See Morrison, at his request, this afternoon, when we discuss the P.M.'s broadcast, and procedure for the Whitsun Conference. Morrison is now inclined to treat me very much as a close ally, which is all to the good. He says that he succeeded in improving some passages in the P.M.'s speech, and in particular in getting him to say that there was an increasing field for State ownership, particularly as regards monopolies. For the post-war election, I suggested, not for the first time, that we might have Government candidates, Conservative, Labour and Liberal, fighting each other in the same constituency, varying their emphasis upon one common programme. Ministers should have unopposed returns and abstain from speaking! I said that in the final jam something like this might be the only way out. He thought perhaps it might. I said it was essential we should have no redistribution of seats this side of the next election. He said that this was his own view and he was so advising the War Cabinet.

Wednesday 24th March
All morning at Labour Party National Executive. As might have been expected, they soon drift on to the P.M.'s broadcast and, in particular, the post-war election passages. But, quite amazingly, nearly everyone agrees that it is undesirable to make any public pronouncement or pass any public resolution at this stage. Shinwell says little; it appears later that he has been sickening for flu, and Morrison makes a quite sensible speech which carries a good deal of support.

At [C.C.J.] Simmonds's suggestion, I take him and Stuart Camp-

1 Dalton's book, written before the 1935 General Election, outlined the programme of a future Labour government. Chapter I begins with a warning about the danger of foreign aggression.
2 Catherine Dalton, née Evan-Thomas (1863–1944). Married Canon Dalton in 1885.
3 Arthur Ponsonby, q.v., who served as a minister in the first two Labour governments, was the son of a private secretary to Queen Victoria. Like Hugh Dalton, he had grown up in the community of royal retainers and courtiers at Windsor.

bell,[1] Editor of the *Sunday Pictorial,* out to lunch. The latter is a frightful man, gibbering political rubbish which I find most irritating. He thinks the two most striking public men today are Acland and Shinwell; also that it is a great pity Franco has not declared war on us, so that we could upset him in Spain; also that the trade union racket is responsible for most of our political ills. After a very bad first half, we gradually pull out and do better, and towards the end he is inclined to be helpful and, after I have worked fairly hard with indiscretions of various kinds about my Labour colleagues, to be quite impressed with my knowledge and judgment. I find it rather impudent that he did not start at this point, for after all he is a sheer political ignoramus. Possibly this meal was just, but only just, worth while.

Wilmot, who, with Gaitskell, dines with me tonight, says that at the Party Meeting this morning Attlee gave quite a good reply to some critics of the P.M.'s broadcast, and that there was very little violent feeling or speaking against it in the Party. My own view is that it may have done good in bringing some of these purveyors of 'nagging negatives' up against realities. What they find hard to see is how completely, now and till after victory, the P.M. personally dominates the scene, so that any attempt to fight him at elections, or any conduct likely to provoke him to fight them, would mean that they would be blown away like feathers in a tempest.

Thursday 25th March
Fulton takes me to dine at the Reform Club, where there is hardly any food and the service very slow. How different – dingy, socially uninteresting and replete with mediocrities – these London Clubs look to a Minister of the Crown at fifty-five as compared with an eager, young, unknown idealist of twenty-five! This Club seemed like a great lions' den in those days. Great authors, great editors, great Parliamentarians, swarming everywhere. And tonight not even Sir William Beveridge is here, but only Clem Davies and Sir John Monck,[2] who tells the foreign diplomats where to put their feet – I am surprised that he comes to this relatively plebeian social centre – and little Gilbert Ponsonby,[3] still looking very childlike, though he is now the father of three children, the eldest of whom is ten. Fulton is treating his war experiences at Fuel and Power as raw material for post-war uni-

---

1 R. S. Campbell, q.v.
2 Sir John Monck (1883–1964). H.M. Vice-Marshal of the Diplomatic Corps 1936–45. Acted as Marshal 1939–45. Marshal 1945–50. Extra Gentleman Usher 1950–64.
3 G. J. Ponsonby (d. 1981). Lecturer in Commerce at the L.S.E. Sir Ernest Cassel Reader in Commerce 1950–64. Nephew of Arthur Ponsonby, q.v.

versity lectures on 'political science'. He is a nice character, but is not really very clever.

Friday 26th March
Lobby lunch, with Herbert Morrison as the guest. He went on rather too long and was not quite at his best. He gave special character sketches of the P.M., Anderson and Beaverbrook, praising all three. It will have been noted that he omitted all his Labour colleagues from this list. He will have seemed, I think, to the audience, to have taken a certain pleasure in being the minister responsible for hangings, though I am sure it was not his intention to convey this. He said that the P.M.'s reference in his recent broadcast to post-war affairs would have set 'all the politicians chattering' and so it had. It was difficult to foresee the political set-up immediately after the war, but he would do his best to 'prevent the Labour Party from committing suicide', which it had sometimes tried to do before, 'not quite unsuccessfully'. But if he failed, and it insisted on committing suicide, he would commit suicide with it, for his whole political life was bound up with it, and he owed it everything.

Wednesday 31st March
Address the weekly Parliamentary Party Meeting on post-war plans at the Board of Trade. My voice is very unpleasant, owing to a cold, but I seem to succeed in pleasing the Party, while not telling them anything very new, beyond what I said in the House on 3rd February. But I stress the extent to which I am consulting trade unions, both nationally and for each industry, and my contacts with the Co-ops. Also plans for pre-war Distressed Areas. Wilmot tells me that he heard a number of favourable comments afterwards, and there were no criticisms at the Meeting. On the other hand, some of the worst bellyachers were absent. They take no interest in hearing what Labour ministers are doing.

Go, very unwillingly, to an afternoon party at Buckingham Palace. It is, I suppose, as near an approach as we have in wartime to a 'royal command'. Hundreds of male eminences, in the Government, the higher reaches of the Civil Service and of the fighting services, and in the world of foreign diplomats in London ... together with their mostly-not-very-eminent-looking wives. Tramp in Indian file past the King, Queen and the two Princesses,[1] and then stand tightly jammed in the Gallery for longer than I like. I look at Princess Eliza-

1 Princess Elizabeth (b. 1926). Acceded to the throne as Queen Elizabeth II in 1952. Princess Margaret (b. 1930).

beth and wonder what sort of trouble she would give, as Queen Elizabeth II, to the President of the Board of Trade of that future day. But they both look quite nice little girls, and seem to enjoy being shaken hands with by everybody. I think these functions are a frightful bore, in this respect also holding unwaveringly to an opinion first fixed many decades ago.[1]

Friday 2nd April

Attlee to see me, since I am not 'going out' today, to discuss Commercial Policy and the War Cabinet. He is sure that the very long draft telegram, prepared by his blokes and mine, would not be read by the P.M., who would seize upon one small point and monologue on about it, so that we should get nowhere. Or else he would have some silly note prepared by the Prof, who is nearly always wrongheaded. (I said I thought in this case he might be better than usual, having been briefed by Meade.) Liesching was with me just before Attlee arrived, and I told him to go out and deliberately cross his track. I suggest to Attlee, after a little, that he should return. We then talk *à trois*, and it is agreed that Liesching's amendment to our Joint Memorandum should be adopted, making us propose that the Dominions should be asked to send chaps here, 'within, say, four weeks', to discuss the whole thing; also that I shall make a note summarising the three Views and the three Main Issues, the long telegram going into an appendix.

Attlee then goes away, but apparently says nothing to his officials, who are thrown into a state of extreme excitement, confusion and jealousy, feeling that Liesching is having it both ways, and, in their absence, is advising both Attlee and me. He has to do his best to make it all clear on the telephone, but they will all be running round in rings when they get the revised papers, and still more when Attlee returns from the country on Monday morning.

Saturday 3rd April

Work on note for War Cabinet, summarising Views A, B and C on Commercial Policy.[2] Meade, who had tried his hand, was much too wordy and indefinite.

Gaitskell says that, when he gets into the House, he will propose that only junior ministers should answer letters from M.P.s. He thinks, and I quite agree, that it is a shocking waste of my time that I

---

1 Dalton later recalled that when his father had offered him the chance, as a young man, of being presented at Court to King George V, he had declined. (*High Tide and After*, p. 10.)
2 See entry for 8th April and preceding linking passage, pp. 576–9.

should have to spend so long on this. But, especially in a Coalition Government, it is not so easy, because (a) one has to be so damned nice to everyone, and (b) Labour M.P.s writing to me would not be content with a refusal from Waterhouse, and similarly in other cases.

Sunday 4th April
Walk to Battersea Park and see Ruth's shapely tea-house[1] sitting, a little grimier than it was and rather disconsolate, between the boating pond and the deer pen. Still too many evergreens and not enough flowering trees in this park.

Read chunks of the *Iliad* and keep clear of shop.

Double Summer Time begins this morning. A very clever invention!

In January, Churchill made another journey to North Africa, this time to meet President Roosevelt for an (initially secret) conference at Casablanca. The conduct of the war was discussed against a background of mounting optimism because of Alamein and Stalingrad. Eventually it was agreed that Sicily must be captured, that there should be a joint Anglo-American bombing offensive against Germany, and that plans for a cross-Channel invasion should be put off until 1944. At a press conference on 24th January, Roosevelt declared that the Allies would enforce 'unconditional surrender' upon all their enemies. In addition, Generals de Gaulle and Giraud were brought together, and made to shake hands in front of the press.

Meanwhile the Eighth Army had resumed its attack on Rommel, whose army had abandoned Tripoli and withdrawn into Tunisia. Here, the Germans launched an attack on the American and French troops holding the southern sections of the Front. At Casablanca it was decided to concentrate everything on taking Tunis, with Alexander as Eisenhower's deputy, virtually in charge of all the operations. Early in March, Rommel left for Germany and did not come back. The Germans continued to reinforce their armies by air throughout April, but the Allies retained a massive naval and air superiority, and Axis losses were heavy. The Allied attack on Tunis came on 6th May, and quickly succeeded. The first assault, mainly by the First Army, came on 12th May. The enemy now capitulated, and a quarter of a million prisoners passed into Allied hands. For Britain, and the United States, it was the greatest victory of the war so far.

---

1 As Chairman of the L.C.C. Parks Committee, Ruth Dalton had been responsible for adding to the amenities of London parks.

Tuesday 6th April

P.M. talks to No. 1 ministers. He has not held one of these general talks for some time. He says that the great battle in North Africa will begin this week. We have a superiority in men of more than two to one, in guns and aircraft of a good deal more. He thinks it will be a Stalingrad. Hitler has been constantly pouring in reinforcements and supplies by sea and air. We have sunk and destroyed much, but much has kept on coming in. This is Hitler's usual obstinacy. But we need not regret it. Hitler is, moreover, playing for time, and we have reason to know that he hopes we shall not start any new large land operations till 1st July. This probably means that he will by then have trained and ready the last 2,000,000 men whom he has scraped and squeezed out of German reserves of manpower. He is still immensely powerful; particularly if the Russians slow down, he could easily detach some thirty Divisions from the Eastern Front for other duties. He may still either push down through Spain or attack Turkey. If we must choose, we should prefer the former. Much thought has been given to our next move after clearing North Africa. There are practically no German troops in Italy or in the islands. The P.M. has been carrying on a double flirtation with Roosevelt and Stalin. The former has gone pretty easily. His relations with the President are most intimate and friendly. He does not want to use the direct approach on routine questions, but on questions of outstanding importance he is always pretty confident that it will work. Stalin is more difficult. But he has received two telegrams from him lately. One is thanking Churchill for the film *Desert Victory*. This has clearly been much appreciated. It is being shown in many parts of Russia. It demonstrates, says Stalin, how bravely and how skilfully the British are fighting. It disposes of the stories put about by those miscreants who allege that the British are not seriously in the war. The second telegram is in reply to a discouraging message about convoys.[1] He takes the news very well, though not, of course, with pleasure. Further, Stalin always telegraphs congratulations whenever we raid Berlin. He evidently takes very great satisfaction in this. And no wonder!

The P.M. says that we often look back to May 1940, but we may also look back with great satisfaction now to twelve months ago. Then he was frightened, yes, very frightened, that the great pincer movement would come off, and that the Japanese would march through India and the Germans across the Caucasus and both meet in Persia. But neither happened. It was at this moment that Gandhi told us to quit and leave her, in his own words, 'to God, that is to say,

---

1 Marginal insertion: 'No more for six months by northern route.'

to Anarchy'. Then followed a superb philippic against Gandhi, and the utter humbug of his so-called fast. First we were told that the fourth day would be a critical day; then it was to be the seventh, then the eleventh. All the time, quite clearly, he was really taking nourishment. He had no doubt counted, a year ago, on two Japanese army corps being made available to him to enable Congress to rule over the rest of India.

Giraud and de Gaulle. The latter, though he has undeniable qualities, is a great fool and very anti-British. At Casablanca the P.M. could have got him 50:50; *'les deux grands chefs militaires'*. But, though Giraud came at once when invited, de Gaulle stood on his dignity and argued and delayed four days. Meanwhile, Giraud, with all his decorations and wound stripes, and his story of how, at the age of sixty-two, he had slid down a wire rope, smuggled into the prison by his wife, and so escaped, had become the hero of all the Americans, civilian and military. So, when de Gaulle at last arrived, Giraud was quite on top, and had been promised by the Americans equipment for seven French Divisions in North Africa, which will be incomparably the strongest French armed force anywhere. And so it was no longer possible to get for de Gaulle even 25:75! If ever the latter comes to power in France, he will try to build up his popularity by being anti-British. If he were to come out now to Algiers, he might fly off to Brazzaville or Syria and do much harm in either.

The P.M. says that the U-boats cannot win the war for Germany, nor starve us out. But what they can do is to spin out the war, to delay the movements of troops and supplies, to wear out our civilian reserves and wear down our standards of living. The Americans had planned to have thirty Divisions in England by now. But in fact they only have one, and in North Africa seven or eight. This is due to the U-boats.

In domestic politics, says the P.M., 'Everything I say and everything I do has only one object, to keep the forces together.' He thinks this can be done. No one can see far ahead, but he sees no reason why for the next year or eighteen months at least, we should not all go on together. He makes a specially friendly reference here to 'our colleagues of the Labour Party' (in fact, only I, Jowitt and Whiteley are present).

Wednesday 7th April
At Party Meeting Attlee does much better than usual and reads out a prepared statement, which he is giving to the press, to the effect that we entered the Government in order to win the war, that this is still our first objective, that, however, the situation is so far improved

575

that we can now begin to think about post-war plans, that Labour ministers are taking their share in making these, that no one can tell when or in what circumstances the war will end, or a general election take place, that, as the P.M. himself has said, the question of what Government shall be in office will depend upon the decisions taken by the various Parties, including the Labour Party, that we shall take our own decision at the appropriate time, that, meanwhile, the Party is not committed, nor are the Labour ministers, to any particular line, and that the Labour ministers all remain, as hitherto, faithful to the policy and decisions of the Party.

This goes down very well, and the storms that have been brewing for some time are wholly stilled. ...

This morning the P.M. announced that the Eighth Army had broken through again, and that our men are now out in the open country pursuing the enemy.[1]

This lunch and speeches last so long that I miss a meeting of the Election Sub, called in order to discuss the electoral truce. All ministers on the National Executive, plus Bevin, are invited. Dobbs and Middleton had both been very wobbly about the truce, but all the rest had come out strongly in support of it, and a para is now to be included in this sense in the Executive Report. ...

Gaitskell to dine. We are both rather tired, but he promises over Easter to think out a scheme whereby I may stimulate selected sectors of the Home Front, as I did with Commercial Union.

On 8th April, the War Cabinet considered a Memorandum by the President of the Board of Trade on post-war commercial policy, which summarised the three views (labelled A, B and C) held among the ministers chiefly concerned. View A was that a general clearance of barriers towards world trade was particularly in the interest of Britain, in order to make possible full employment in the export trade. Such a clearance could best be secured by a multilateral commercial convention open to adherence by all States. Under the convention tariffs should be restricted, preferences reduced, export subsidies banned, State trading regulated to avoid discrimination or excessive protection, and quantitative import restrictions only permitted within strictly defined limits. However, there should be an interim post-war period during which these restrictions might continue on a diminishing scale, and

1 Marginal insertion: '(Wadi Akarit)'. On 6th April, the Eighth Army attacked enemy positions at Wadi Akarit in North Africa, taking 5,000 prisoners. Next day, enemy troops abandoned defences in the area and retreated.

thereafter they should be used only in certain circumstances, disputes being settled by an international authority. It was proposed that Britain should take the initiative in proposing such a plan to the American government and to the United Nations.

The War Cabinet decided to take the initiative in putting forward proposals on the lines of View A, though amended to preserve the freedom of a country to maintain quantitative import restrictions without obtaining the permission of an international monetary authority if it could be shown that the country had an adverse balance of payments.[1]

Thursday 8th April

War Cabinet.[2] Two and a half hours on post-war commercial policy. I open the discussion, which at some stages seems to be going very badly. But, after much meandering and trite talk, the P.M. puts to the vote the question who is in favour of 'View A as amended by Lord Cherwell'. (The latter merely suggested that we should reserve the right to use quantitative import restrictions when our balance of payments was in danger, and not when some international authority declared that it was in danger.) Both Kingsley Wood and I said that this quite met our view. The vote was 15 or so to 2 (it was a largely attended Cabinet). The 2 were Duncan and Amery. The former, however, who had hitherto remained quite silent, but who tends, when not coached beforehand, to take the opposite line from me, had very little to say when asked by the P.M. to explain himself. And Amery was quite satisfied when I told him that I was as much opposed to M.F.N. [Most Favoured Nation] as he was. 'Nothing for nothing' was my motto, I told him. He said that in that case he had no further objection to View A. Then, after further rambling, it was decided that a Committee should prepare a more precise version of View A as amended, with suggestions for procedure (the P.M. thought that we should not bring in the Dominions; it was a bad plan that 'no one may talk, unless all talk at once'; he would prefer 'bilateral conversations with the U.S.A. for the conclusion of a multilateral convention'). Further, the Committee should work out the relation of all this to the 'bancor' and should have thrown in as well the plan for Buffer Stocks ('I thought you said Butter Scotch,' said the P.M. to Jowitt after a technical discussion on this matter had been proceeding for some minutes, 'I am getting very hard of hearing').

The Cabinet Committee – 'We must put all the cleverest people on

1 PRO, CAB 65/34.
2 Marginal insertion: 'Frightfully good.'

it,' said the P.M. – is to be, going round the table, Lyttelton, Cherwell, Cripps, myself, Stanley, Johnston and Wood. Jowitt is to be summoned when Butter Scotch is in question.

All this looks like a remarkable success. But I don't quite understand where a lot of the opposition went to in the last round. For Lyttelton and Hudson had both grumbled heavily against View A, yet finally voted for it as amended. The *deus ex machina* was Lord Cherwell. He had clearly briefed the P.M. right, having himself been briefed by Meade, Johnston afterwards said that he was sure the P.M. had made up his mind from the start what was to happen, and had deliberately given the impression of rambling about in order to mislead and entrap those who took the opposite view. He had said, e.g. to Wood, that these quantitative restrictions would mean the riveting on our economy of state trading as absolute and as arbitrary as that of Russia. 'They have one multi-millionaire, controlling in one hand the movements of 180,000,000 human microbes.' The P.M. constantly apologised for being rusty about these trade matters, but revived his memories of years ago and the 'beautiful precision' with which Free Trade and the Gold Standard had worked 'not in this disastrous century but in the last'. He still thought that we should correct our balance of payments by raising the bank rate. But no one supported him on this. He asked me a number of questions on quotas, and who imposed them, and when they began, and whether they were really much worse than tariffs. He was most anxious that, whatever we said, we should 'use the right language'. We should make our approach in terms of the freest possible exchange of goods and services, freedom rather than restriction, abundance and not scarcity. This would be in line with the declarations of President Roosevelt that 'All the men in all the lands shall live out their lives in freedom from want.' He said that he had spent forty years of his life opposing Imperial Preference. He believed that it had done nothing but harm. He was very furious with Lyttelton, who said that we were no longer a creditor, but a debtor, nation. The P.M. vehemently denied that we should owe anybody anything at the end of the war. On the contrary, we should send in a bill to the whole world for having defended them. We should begin with India. He would be for whole-hearted repudiation of any debts alleged to be owed by us when we were seated on the pinnacle of victory. But he had rebuked Sumner Welles, in the presence of the President, for having said that he was out 'to break Ottawa' and that the U.S. had favoured freedom of trade for many generations. The P.M., though he admitted that he had forgotten the dates and the names of the authors of the latest and most monstrous American tariffs, had told Sumner Welles that it was all the fault of the United States that trade had been restricted and that the 'Joe Chamberlain movement' had sprung up in the early years of this century. 'This man was certainly abashed by what I said,' said the P.M.

After the Cabinet, both Anderson and Jowitt say that they think that I have every reason to be pleased with today's doings.

Friday 9th April
Ellen Wilkinson to lunch. She would like more show at the next Labour Party Conference, and would also like, in which I encourage her, to be the next Vice-Chairman. On seniority she is entitled to this. The alternative is little Laski, which might be deplorably ill-timed.

Labour Party Policy Committee in the afternoon, when we provisionally allot a number of the speakers for the Conference. I can't work Ellen in anywhere, but there are some gaps left open. Shinwell, Laski and Gould are early in attendance, trying to corner good places for themselves.

Monday 12th April
Dine with Victor Cazalet, the others being Peter, King of the Jugs (who seems to me less and less interesting every time I meet him), and a Frenchman just returned from 'underground' activities in France. He says that what should be done is to bring out Lebrun from France, and that this could easily be arranged, who would then take precedence of both the Generals. But de Gaulle will fight to the end against this. The mentality of the exiled French, he says, is deplorable. They are most averse to any reinforcement from France, fearing that each newcomer will do one of them out of his job.

Tuesday 13th April
Woolton is being a bit of a nuisance, egged on by his don, John Maud.[1] He has suddenly discovered that telegrams have been passing with Washington regarding the constitution of the U.N.R.R.A., and thinks that the whole matter should again be reviewed by ministers. I take some rather active counter-measures, including the incitement to jealousy of Eden and Attlee, to neither of whom has Woolton sent a copy of his foolish letter, arguing as above to Anderson. We have now reached a point when the Canadians will accept the proposal

---

1 John Maud, later Baron Redcliffe-Maud (1906–82). Deputy Secretary, then Second Secretary, at the Ministry of Food 1941–4. Master of Birkbeck College, London University 1939–43. Ministry of Reconstruction, then Lord President's Office 1944–5. Permanent Secretary at the Ministry of Education 1945–52; Ministry of Fuel and Power 1952–9. Master of University College, Oxford 1963–76. Chairman of the Royal Commission on Local Government in England 1966–9.

that they should have the Chair at the Supplies Committee, in return for agreeing to four, as against seven, members of the Policy Committee. Also it is to be recorded that the limitation to four is not to be regarded as a precedent in other post-war consultations. I write vigorously to Anderson – and canvass on the Bench in support of my thesis Eden, Attlee and Kingsley Wood, all of whom agree with me – that it is unthinkable that after all this persistent toil we should now do other than wire *at once* to Halifax saying we accept this latest American-Canadian accord. 'It is not the work, it's the bumble bees that tire one out.' I recall this saying of Sir Ronald Lindsay at the Foreign Office in 1929.

Wednesday 14th April
Dine with Ambassador Biddle, who has invited some forty people, mostly representatives of exiled governments, to meet Lehman. The latter sits between Varvaressos[1] and Gutt,[2] but has no opportunity of talking to any of the others. Nor does Biddle arrange for him to make even an informal speech, nor does he shuffle people round. And so, after several hours, the Party breaks up, some thirty-five out of the forty having had no opportunity to exchange a word with the guest of the evening, from whom, no doubt, they are expecting vast American largesse. I am reminded of the Diary of Ambassador Dodd,[3] and his comments on the inanity of diplomatic dinners. I am the only British minister present.

Lehman is learning as he goes along, and is already inclined to tell the foreigners that they will get much less than they expect. There will be a shortage, from now on, not only of ships, which we always knew, but also of food, clothing, etc.

Friday 16th April
To Newcastle.

Saturday 17th April
Talk, without the press, to our Northern Regional Conference and tell them that Labour ministers are doing a lot of good work and that it is not possible to go on in the Government and scrap the electoral

---

1 Kyriakos Varvaressos (1884–1957). Greek economist, politician and diplomat. Minister of Finance in Tsouderos Cabinet 1941–3. Ambassador at large 1943. Vice-Premier in Vulgaris Cabinet 1945. Economic Adviser to the International Bank for Reconstruction and Development 1948–56.
2 C. A. Gutt (1884–1971). Belgian politician. Minister of Finance 1934–5, 1939–45. Managing Director of the I.M.F. 1946–51.
3 W. E. Dodd (1869–1940). U.S. Ambassador to Germany 1933–7. Diplomat and historian.

truce. A very sensible response from the delegates, though one or two are, naturally, rather wistful about by-elections.

Monday 19th April

Take Gladwyn Jebb to dine ... and hear of his recent visit with Eden to U.S.A. It seems to have been a great success, many useful personal relations having been established. ... Halifax, he says, has no mass appeal, but is quite good at handling a party of sixteen or so. Several of these were arranged for Eden while he was there, and Halifax guided the talk quite skilfully, bringing in all the Senators and other Americans by their Christian names. Gladwyn related that one night at the Embassy Sol Bloom,[1] the 78-year-old Chairman of the House of Representatives Foreign Affairs Committee, who dyes his hair black and is, of course, a Jew, held forth as follows: 'When your Ambassador first came over here, we didn't care for him one little bit. We felt he was aristocratic and quite high-hat. But now, after he has been with us a little while, he has become quite democratic, quite one of the common men.' And then, calling across the room to Halifax, he cried out, 'Hi, Mr Ambassador! I was telling our young friend here that when you first came over you were quite aristocratic, but now you aren't aristocratic any more, are you? You have become quite democratic, haven't you? Now you are quite a common man, aren't you?' Whereat Halifax smiled wanly. Gladwyn says that the new Government buildings in Washington are very good indeed, both as architecture and for practical uses. But the British Embassy is quite frightful, most inconvenient in every way. Sir Arthur Salter lives in a comparatively small house. I explain that this was his wife's, and that she had fallen in love with him when acting as an American Geneva hostess when he was one of the League lions. Gladwyn said that he was asked to go and see Salter, and arrived at this house and was shown into a room where Lady Salter was also sitting. I asked, 'Was she knitting all the time?' And he said yes, and that it was most embarrassing, because Sir Arthur Salter began to ask questions on most secret official matters, and he did not know how much he could say in front of this lady. I said that the only time I had lunched with him at the Connaught Hotel, Lady Salter had likewise been knitting and immovable. I told him that it was just the same as going to see Sir Stafford Cripps, except that Lady Cripps didn't knit.[2]

1 Sol Bloom (1870–1949). Congressman for New York. Chairman of Foreign Affairs Committee 1939–49. Bloom was seventy-three, not seventy-eight.
2 Yet Dalton later wrote, describing one particularly tense interview with Cripps in 1939, 'I should have preferred a *tête-à-tête*, but Lady Cripps remained knitting throughout our conversation ... ' (FY, p. 212.)

There was an earlier precedent, I recall, in the case of Stephen Walsh,[1] when Secretary of State for War in the first Labour Government. He used to drink a good deal, and Mrs Walsh, in order to help keep him away from the bottle, used to sit with him all day in his room in the War Office. Cavan,[2] then C.I.G.S., was much embarrassed by her presence when he brought in important papers for the Secretary of State. But the latter used to say, 'Never mind mother. She's always here.' It is also related that Mrs Walsh was heard to say, when leaving the Royal Garden Party, 'My shoes are tight, and my stays are tight, and Stephen's tight, and I want to get home.'

Wednesday 21st April

Meeting at the House on Beveridge, attended by members of the Administrative Committee, some members of the Executive Committee, and various 'ministers concerned'. Bevin makes a very good statement, explaining how defective Beveridge is in many points, and saying that he has got some very much better plans, especially as regards unemployment insurance, which he is putting up to his colleagues in the Cabinet. There is not room for 'crisis' here, and I think that a speech by Bevin at the Conference will settle the whole matter. ...

... [T]o No. 11, where Attlee and Noel-Baker have a little Frenchman, who has just come over from France and is returning soon. He is in charge of one of what used to be *my* organisations. He is very pro-de Gaulle and, when questioned by me as to what he means by saying that 'All France is Gaulliste', he replied that they are in favour of de Gaulle because they believe he is a symbol both of resistance and democracy! He also brings various stories designed to show that most Germans are not Nazis and are now 'looking to Britain and America to free them from Hitler'. I must say I thought that this fairly took the bun! But dear old Phil [Noel-Baker], who is also very pro-de Gaulle, thought that it was grand. I asked the little Frenchman what was thought of Giraud, and he replied that 'all France' thought he was a Fascist and still in touch with Pétain. I wonder how long this crew around de Gaulle will go on calling themselves 'the Fighting French', when all the real fighting is being done by Giraud's troops, equipped by the Americans, in North Africa. The little man also said that Blum had only *not* escaped to England because he was not sure, as a result of a direct correspondence which he had had with our P.M., whether he would really be welcome. Both Attlee and I repudiate this. We knew that efforts had been made to get him out, but that this

1 Stephen Walsh (1859–1929). Labour M.P. 1906–29. Secretary of State for War 1924.
2 F. Lambert, 10th Earl of Cavan (1865–1946). Chief of Imperial General Staff 1922–6.

had become impossible, partly because he had hesitated, but also because he had been in prison. I say the same had been true of Jouhaux,[1] and the little man did not deny this. Rather discouraging.

The Inter-Allied Food Conference at Hot Springs, Virginia opened on 18th May. Richard Law, Minister of State at the Foreign Office, led the British delegation. The Conference recommended the setting up of a permanent organisation for food and agriculture. The eventual result was the establishment of the Food and Agricultural Organisation of the United Nations.

Thursday 22nd April

War Cabinet ... [A] tiresome wrangle, with one of those monologues by the P.M., to which we are becoming very accustomed, about instructions to our delegates at the Food Conference. Should they be allowed to say that we were prepared to continue rationing after the war? The old, old story. The P.M. says only if the Americans undertake that *they* will continue rationing, and then we can say that we will do not less than they. Otherwise, we may 'find ourselves all melted up with the Chinese and the Indians'. He says that Woolton wants to keep on his 40,000 bureaucrats after the war, restricting people's freedom, and that is why he presses this. Woolton becoming quite vehement, urges the P.M. to 'face realities'. Then a long yarn on what happened at the end of the last war. The P.M. says that he, at that time, was not a member of the War Cabinet but 'only a functionary', 'only looking after the Army, and dealing with mutinies'. But he gives great praise to Lloyd George and says that his insight and judgment at that time were quite wonderful. He was in his prime, only in his fifties, and it is quite wrong to say that in 1918–19 great errors were committed. On the contrary, the Government of those days did very well. But everybody 'misbehaved' and within a week of the Armistice the political parties were at one another's throats. There were also many riots, and armed troops marching on Whitehall, demanding to be demobilised. He hopes that those of us who will be in charge this time will do as well as Lloyd George's Government did. Kingsley Wood then adds that the only bright feature of this period was a most

---

1 Léon Jouhaux (1879–1954). Secretary of the Confédération Générale du Travail. Dalton had wanted him to be extricated from Vichy France in the autumn of 1941, but before this could be achieved, Jouhaux was arrested by the Vichy administration. He spent most of the rest of the war in prison.

satisfactory General Election! Morrison, sitting beside me, takes all this very ill, and says afterwards, when we go off to lunch with Sikorski and Retinger, that it is 'very wearing' to have to listen so often to all this stuff. He adds that it is all very well for us in the Labour Party to be talking as though we might perhaps graciously consent to remain in an all-Party Government after the war, when it is quite on the cards that the Conservatives will pass a resolution, at their Annual Conference or elsewhere, demanding that this all-Party Government should be ended.

Sikorski had specially asked me to arrange for him to meet Morrison again. But he wanted only to talk about the difficulty of Polish-Russian relations. He was very full, quite naturally, of the massacre of 10,000 Polish officers, and is quite convinced, despite the Russian denial, that it was the Russians and not the Germans who murdered them.[1] He says the Germans have only now proclaimed this fact, because they are beating up the anti-Red bogy and are trying to win over the Poles to this thesis. He hears from Poland that the German repression has sensibly abated in the last few weeks. Also a rumour that Maisky may soon succeed Molotov. He is not sure that the former would not prefer to stay in London, where life is better and safer. He related that when he dined at the Kremlin, the menu covered both sides of the card, and at a certain point, when they had only got about half-way down the first page, he told Stalin that he could not eat any more. Whereat, Stalin stopped the meal, and all went into another room and drank instead. Many of the Russians present were much disappointed to miss so much food. Sikorski is leaving in a few days' time for the Middle East. He will not go on to Moscow, but counts on the impending Anglo-American approach to secure the release from Russia of all the Polish citizens who are still alive, including 65,000 orphaned children. This, he says, is what he now asks, in view of the massacre of the 10,000 officers. Morrison said to me afterwards, 'That was very noble. I thought he was going to demand some monetary compensation.' ...

I am to dine tonight with Mrs Phillimore to meet some Frenchmen. I hear today that Pierre Viénot[2] is to be among them. This is a great and delightful surprise.

---

1 On 13th April German radio publicly charged the Soviet Government with the murder of 14,500 Polish officers and other prisoners at Katyn. On 17th April, the Polish Cabinet in London issued a communiqué declaring that an approach had been made to the International Red Cross in Switzerland to send a delegation to Katyn to conduct an inquiry. The Soviet authorities responded to this move by breaking off diplomatic relations with the Polish government-in-exile.

2 Pierre Viénot (1897–1944). French Socialist politician. Under-Secretary of State for Foreign Affairs 1936–7. Interned in 'protective custody' in 1940, and deprived of

And there sure enough, was Viénot! He was looking rather ill and tired and, when asked whether he could now speak English – he used hardly to have a word, though he knew German well – he said that he had tried to learn English in prison with the aid of a Linguaphone, but his English was painfully laboured and spoken with a most unreal accent, and we soon went back into French. He arrived only yesterday, by plane. I shall hear much more of his adventures when I get him alone. But it seems that he did not have a very bad time, having been let out of prison after four months, though sentenced by the Tribunal to eight years for 'desertion' from Vichy, and had since been living under police surveillance, though not, apparently, very strict. His wife is still in France. He says that Herriot[1] is physically in a bad way, in a clinic, and 'weeping all the time'. Jouhaux also is taking captivity very ill. On the other hand, he had seen, he said (though I don't quite understand how), both Blum and Reynaud fairly recently. The former, he said, was evidently suffering from the effects of a long period of solitude, but the latter was comparatively lively and writing a good deal. Viénot was inclined to defend de Gaulle, though he had not yet had an interview with him. I said, however, that his régime here was a purely personal dictatorship. Viénot may be a very useful influence, if he is physically fit enough to have any influence at all. I would have carried him off to West Leaze, in spite of all obvious difficulties of food, etc., but he said he had a number of engagements in London in the next few days.

With him were poor old Queuille,[2] a Radical Socialist Senator, who was a minister for ten years, first for agriculture, and then for food, from 1930 to 1940, and was thought of as a possible President of the Republic in 1938. A possible civilian figurehead, I suppose, but very faint and ancient. Much brighter and younger was General Cochet,[3] of the French Air Force, who had escaped from a German prison. Attlee said to me that this was much the best bunch of Frenchmen who had yet been got out from France.

---

1 Edouard Herriot, q.v., President of the French Assembly.
2 Henri Queuille (1884–1970). French Radical Socialist leader. Commissioner in the French Committee of National Liberation. Three times Prime Minister, and member of twenty-three different Cabinets in the Third and Fourth Republics.
3 General G. R. Cochet (1888–1973). After his escape he at first headed de Gaulle's Secret Service in Algiers, but was replaced in September 1943 by Jacques Soustelle.

---

citizenship in 1941. Escaped from France to join the Fighting French in 1943, and came to England as de Gaulle's Ambassador. A close friend of the Daltons, and especially Ruth.

Friday 23rd April

By early-morning train to West Leaze, where I stay until the 29th. The south-west wind blows hard nearly all the time, but lots of lovely things are hastening out in the garden, and, while I am here, I see the whitebeams actually breaking, and many of the service trees and the beginning of the white lilacs.

Read Herodotus, the Father of History, as recommended by Peter Lucas, and refresh my memories of Croesus, Cyrus, etc., and also Van's *Lessons of My Life*,[1] all, of course, on the one theme – the wickedness of Germans – but, though tending to tediousness through repetition, very full of bright phrases. The style of Oscar Wilde, and other bright young writers of the 1890s, has much influenced Van.

Evan Durbin stays two nights (27th and 28th), and we go for a walk on the 28th, to Marlborough, round a circle in Savernake Forest, happily losing our way, and back again through Marlborough. Eighteen or nineteen miles, I suppose, and a healthy good blister on my left heel!

He has written a memorandum on foreign policy, much of which is very good sense, but he fears the Russians in the future and thinks the Germans should be kept just strong enough to help us to resist them. I say that this is much too delicate an operation for this world and looks needlessly far into the future. He also thinks that we should get an agreement on foreign policy between all parties in this country, our weakness in the inter-war years being largely due to party divisions on this. He, therefore, proposed that there should be early inter-party discussions. But I think I persuade him that this would not work. That we should be more united after the war than before on foreign policy is most desirable, and we may be able to achieve this, but talks now, at any rate outside the Government, would be no good. He is feeling, he says, the effects of his 'too long apprenticeship', and I greatly sympathise. But it is largely this damned war, though the difficulty of getting young and able Labour candidates adopted and elected to Parliament is a very serious one. We agree that it is amazing how few people, outside their own circle, are known to leading people in D.L.P.s. Durbin says that Transport House have worked very hard for him, even, clearly, to the extent of canvassing Chairmen of D.L.P.s beforehand. He thinks that the best way to help some of the younger people would be for the *Herald* to run a series of personal puffs of them.

1 Sir Robert Vansittart, *Lessons of My Life*, Hutchinson, London, 1943.

8

Post-warriors
May–December 1943

The invasion of Sicily, the fall of Mussolini and the Italian capitulation during the summer and autumn of 1943 made the end of the war seem much closer. One effect was to focus attention on post-war plans.

As a former Foreign Office minister with ambitions to become Foreign Secretary, and as a leading member of the Labour Party N.E.C., Dalton played an important part in shaping Labour's views on a possible post-war international settlement. But his first concern – from this time until the end of the Coalition – was with measures for ensuring that mass unemployment should not return after the war to the regions which had been hardest hit by the Depression.

The death of George Lathan, the Labour Party Treasurer, created a vacancy that provided the most hotly contested internal election of the war. There were three candidates: Greenwood, Morrison and W. G. Hall. Though Hall had the backing of the miners (who nominated him), the real contest was between Greenwood and Morrison. Dalton was strongly behind Morrison, regarding Greenwood (no longer in the Government) as a spent force.

Wednesday 5th May
Labour Party National Executive from 10 to 1.15 and from 2 to 4.30. A pretty good day. Shinwell is out-manoeuvred and defeated on almost all points, and, on several, receives surprisingly little support. We decide that the National Executive shall flat-footedly recommend the continuance of the Electoral Truce. The voting on this is 17 to 7. The

587

minority are Shinwell, Laski, Griffiths, Openshaw,[1] the only trade union representative in the minority, two women – Gould and Bacon – and the old fool of a Chairman, Dobbs. ... On the treasurership I hear that Morrison will have the votes of the General Workers and the cotton unions. I hope that Ellen [Wilkinson] will be able to get him the vote of the N.U.D.A.W., and that Burrows will get him the N.U.R., some leading members of which are said, however, to be for Greenwood. The miners' vote will be left on a sandbank, in support of Willie Hall, who told Wilmot that he would be willing to retire if he thought that this would help Morrison. But the latter is not sure that it would, since the miners are awkward people to handle. Best, therefore, leave them as they are. I suspect that the Transport Workers may support Greenwood, partly because of Bevin's hatred of Morrison, and partly because some of their underlings are in the Greenwood orbit. But, on the whole, I think that Morrison's chances are pretty good.

Thursday 6th May

Viénot to dine. He gives a long and interesting account of his doings in France; he went, on Reynaud's instructions, to North Africa immediately before the Armistice and remained for three weeks in Morocco, when he was arrested by orders of Vichy as a 'deserter' and brought back to France and imprisoned for four months under very bad conditions. He was then tried and sentenced to eight years' imprisonment on this most fantastic political charge, but was immediately released. He then lived for some time near Grasse in comparative freedom, but was then arrested again, and imprisoned, with other politicians and Generals, first at Vals and then at Evaux. He was then released on grounds of health and went to a sanatorium in Savoy, near Chamonix. Here he assumed the leadership of the secret society 'Liberation', and was then brought over, through the agency of S.O.E., to England by an aeroplane from somewhere in Angoulême. From Savoy to Angoulême he made his way by train, being passed on from point to point by trusted men. The aeroplane, piloted by a most cheerful young Englishman, arrived with the greatest precision at the appointed hour and place. We have a long talk about de Gaulle and Giraud. He is most definitely in favour of the former, of whose deficiencies I, however, speak very frankly. I hope that Viénot and others may do something to civilise and moderate de Gaulle. He speaks very highly of the spirit of resistance in France as a whole.

[1] R. Openshaw (1891–1962). Official of the Amalgamated Engineering Union. President 1954–6. Member of the Labour Party N.E.C. 1941–8.

Early in May, Allied armies in North Africa began to make decisive gains. On the afternoon of 7th May, Tunis and Bizerte were captured by British and American forces.

Saturday 8th to Sunday 9th May
What a weekend! 'Tunis and Bizerte have been occupied' and everything has gone with a wonderfully perfect rush. It is the 'Blitzkrieg' over again, and exactly as in France in May 1940, with the roles reversed. We have crushing superiority in the air, in tanks, and in numbers, and race through to Tunis, as the Huns raced through to Paris, leaving large sections of their army cut off and hopelessly disrupted and demoralised behind our forward rush. So this method is no German patent. It only requires intelligent use of emphatically superior means of modern war.

High winds blow all the weekend, blowing away, symbolically, the dreams and the defences of the enemy. ...

Our military, when asked how large they estimated would be the civilian populations in Europe requiring 'relief', (a) by the end of this year, (b) by next spring, and (c) by the end of next year, have replied (a) 25 per cent of the population of occupied Europe, (b) 50 per cent, and (c) 100 per cent. They may, of course, have been giving large margins of safety in each case. But evidence seems to be accumulating that we are further, and more firmly, on towards victory than I had recently supposed.

The Pensions and Determination of Needs Bill, brought forward by the Government, aimed to give supplementary pensions to widows with dependent children, and to make various adjustments in the financial conditions to be taken into account in the consideration and granting of applications. Labour critics attacked the 'needs test' which accompanied the application for supplementary pensions. They also demanded an increase in the basic pension. The row was partly an expression of anger at the delays attending Government action on the Beveridge Report.

Tuesday 11th May

Another fuss brewing over Old Age Pensions. The Government have been rash enough to propose to introduce another Bill, giving more money to some. This has produced the usual complaint that still more money is not being given to many others. I don't know the details, but I smell the prospect of another row, which will be exploited by the disruptionists and bellyachers.

Wednesday 12th May

I go down to the House determined to do my duty and sit in and listen to Wood expounding the Clearing Union. But he is so frightfully dull that I come out after ten minutes.

Thursday 13th May

Sir Thomas Barlow tells me that some in the clothing industry are complaining that too much favour is being given to the West Auckland Clothing Company.[1] Sir Thomas Barlow has been telling them that I have had nothing to do with this, but I give him some background of the history and useful doings of this firm, and thank him for warning me of these rumours and grumbles. It is not unnatural, I daresay, having regard to all the facts, including *their* nationality[2] and *my* politics, and their location and the cuts imposed on output and labour force in other parts of the country, that these growls should be heard.

Friday 14th May

Paul Winterton,[3] on leave from Moscow, and his wife to dine. He has developed very well and his present experience in Russia results from my having urged him to go out there with his Acland Scholarship, and to learn Russian, a number of years ago. He looks very fit and is very interesting, 'objective', as he himself claims, and intelligent. He says that the Russians are struggling along on a very low standard of life indeed. The civilian rations are extremely poor. So is their clothing, etc. They are simple-minded people and they are just hanging on and will go on doing so. But the idea of a Second Front in Europe is now an obsession with them. He does not think they will want to do much outside their frontiers when the war is over, but he thinks that they will insist on exterminating all the top layers of the German army,

---

1 In Dalton's constituency.
2 The West Auckland Clothing Company was owned and run by a family of German Jewish refugees.
3 Paul Winterton. Correspondent for the *News Chronicle* in Moscow, and the author of several books on Russia, including *A Student in Russia* (Co-operative Union, Manchester, 1931), based on his experiences as an Acland Scholar in 1931.

S.S., etc. He says that their atrocities on the Russians are quite beyond belief, and that they often give him nightmares. (He appeared to be very steady and well-balanced, and to retain a considerable cheerfulness and sense of humour, so that this last remark means more than if he were in a nervy condition.) He saw one letter to a German soldier from his wife asking the former to send her some children's underclothes and bedding. 'It doesn't matter if they are blood-stained, for I can wash them.' He saw at Rzhev women and children lying about dead and mutilated, and houses where the Germans had carried out a senseless destruction, not only of human beings but of all the poor little articles of household furniture and equipment. And he has related already in the *News Chronicle* a story of the Russian woman in the streets of Khar'kov who told him that when she was passing down the street, she was seized by a German officer who told her that she had now got to witness a hanging, and held her by the arm, compelling her to watch while some Russians were flung out over the balcony across the street with ropes tied round their necks. He also had much first-hand evidence at Khar'kov of the total massacre of all the Jews in that city, who were driven out to a barbed-wire encampment outside the city, kept there without food or shelter for several days, and then simply mown down by machine guns to the number of many thousands. He says, without waiting for me to say it, that there is no other nation in Europe who would behave in this continuously and unfailingly atrocious fashion to foreigners whose lands they had invaded. He says that the Russians have quite made up their minds what they will do about this, and that it is therefore most likely that the Germans will try, at a certain point, while holding the Eastern Front, to let the Western Front give way, thinking themselves likely to be better off with us and the Americans than with the Russians.

He shares my high opinion of Clark Kerr and says that he is very accessible, unconventional and intelligent, and is just beginning to get on very well with Stalin. It is most important, in his view, that we and the Russians should maintain a close co-operation for many years after the war. This, he thinks, will be pretty difficult and will need great patience and forbearance on both sides. They are fantastically ignorant of us, and of everything outside their own country. Also it is most important that we should be 'objective' and frank about their points of weakness, as well as their points of strength. We should never talk as though Russia was, or was likely soon to become, any sort of earthly Paradise, where living standards must, particularly after the interruption and devastation of war, remain very low for a long time to come. He was very sympathetic towards the Poles, and was sure that the Russians had destroyed great numbers of them in captivity. On the other hand, it was only realistic to admit that Poland had no chance whatever of independent survival, unless she got on good terms with Russia. Otherwise, there would soon be merely a Polish Soviet Socialist Republic. He asked me a good deal about Poles and others and evidently enjoyed meeting me again. He is an almost, though not quite, first-class young man, and I am very glad that I started him on his Russian road. He may well have some political role to play after the war.

Tuesday 18th May
Meeting of Labour ministers in Attlee's room to discuss fuss over Pensions Bill. My own view is that the Government should say they will withdraw the Bill if the Party does not accept it, without a fuss and a vote.

Wednesday 19th May
Party Meeting. Long wrangle over Pensions Bill. Finally decided by 48 votes to 43 that we will accept the recommendation of the Administrative Committee to support the second reading against any reasoned amendment. Greenwood in the Chair is a little less flabby than usual. After the vote there is a scene with Shinbad shouting that he will not honour the decision, and Fred Montague[1] and others shouting back. 'Quite a bear garden,' says Greenwood from the Chair. It really is hardly worth while to bring in these piecemeal Bills, which always lead to these fusses. But no one seems to feel much political crisis in the air just now. ...

   Wilmot and I to dine with Douglas and Peggy Jay[2] in Hampstead. They are both in very good form and seem to be getting on better than they used to. They have two children, no help and a tall, thin house, five storeys high. Jay tells some good stories about the impression made on our seamen at Archangel by the Russians. Some who were Communists thought they had been hoaxed, and that this could not be Russia at all, because the conditions were so primitive and uncomfortable. They thought that an imperialist government had landed them in backward Finland instead. Others were shocked because the Soviet police used to hit people, including women, over the head with clubs and leave them lying in the road, if they crossed the streets at points other than those indicated for pedestrians. A tale was also told of a Russian naval officer who came on board a British

1 Frederick Montague, later 1st Baron Amwell (1876–1966). Labour M.P. for Islington West 1923–31, 1935–47. Junior minister 1929–31, 1940–2.
2 Margaret (Peggy) Jay, née Garnett. L.C.C. Councillor. Married Douglas Jay in 1933; divorced 1972.

ship and got very drunk. Next day some other Russian officers came, in reply to an invitation, accompanied by a political commissar. The latter began by apologising for the misconduct of the officer yesterday, and said, 'He has been shot.' The Englishman said, 'Oh, I hope he is not seriously injured.' Whereat the commissar replied, 'Yes, he is dead. Our officers are not allowed to get drunk on Allied ships.' Another Russian was reported to have been shot for adding up some figures wrong, when making some nautical calculations, and so 'attempting to commit sabotage by giving false information'.

Thursday 20th May

See Lyttelton, who has been trying to put across a fast one, or rather has been put up to it by some of his officials – some think by David Eccles – in the form of a paper for Lord President's Committee tomorrow, suggesting the formation of an interdepartmental committee under Portal, drawn from Foreign Office, Ministry of War Transport, Ministry of Supply, Department of Trade, and God knows who, as well as the Board of Trade, to 'advise' on practically every matter relating to supplies for the civilian population. I say that this is the most frightful poaching, and I cannot agree. Lyttelton says that his intention was to help the civilians to get a proper allocation at an early stage. I say that, there having been no consultation either between him or me, or between officials, before he bunged this in, it should not be pressed tomorrow, but discussed by his officials and mine, with no others. He agrees. ...

Second reading of Pensions Bill carried by 236 to 61. Of Labour Members, 68 vote for, and 54 against. Many Members of all parties seem to have abstained.

Friday 21st May

Lunch with Norwegian Chamber of Commerce and am told that I lectured to them exactly twenty years ago on 'Labour and Capital' and that a most animated discussion ensued. I say that I then was an innocent university teacher.[1]

Monday 24th May

Jules Moch[2] calls, attired in French naval officer's uniform. He was 'Minister for Co-ordination' in Blum's first Government. He is an intelligent, and not at all unpleasant, French Socialist Jew. For Blum

---

1 At the L.S.E. In 1923, Dalton published a short polemical book, *The Capital Levy Explained*, which advocated a once-and-for-all tax on private fortunes.
2 Jules Moch (b. 1893). French Socialist politician, who had served in the Popular Front Government of Léon Blum. Served in successive governments 1946–58.

he fears the worst already. The Germans, carrying him off along with Gamelin and others into Germany, refused his request that he should be accompanied by any woman relative. This, admittedly, because he was a Jew! Gamelin was allowed to take his wife.

Moch is very anti-Giraud, who, he says, is a Fascist, and so are practically all his entourage, both military and civilian. Sensing, perhaps, that I am not enamoured of de Gaulle, Moch admits his weaknesses, but says that, all through France, he is a symbol of resistance. Moch fears that, if the agreement now being negotiated between the two Generals (Eden tells me two days later that 'everything is now settled', on the day when de Gaulle leaves for Algiers) comes off, de Gaulle may easily be trapped. He will take two men with him, one of whom is Massigli, who might easily desert to Giraud; Giraud will have with him two men, both of whom will stick to him. Therefore, at the critical moment, de Gaulle may be in a minority of 4 to 2. I dwell, as always, discreetly with the French, on de Gaulle's defects, his tendency to personal dictatorship, his poor civilian entourage – so far, his vanity, his ignorance of politics. I tell Moch how he missed his chance at Casablanca.

Although he hoped that Labour might increase its representation, Dalton took for granted that Churchill would win any general election held immediately after the war. He therefore took an increasing interest, shared by politicians on both sides of the House, in possible ways of reconstituting the Coalition after an election had been held.

Harvie Watt to dine. A most interesting evening. He is not keen on Eden. His is, he says, 'purely a press-made reputation'. If he had been at a 'business Department', e.g. the Treasury, or the Board of Trade, he would have made a mess of it. At the Foreign Office it is quite easy. Mere platitudes and amiable generalities. But, Harvie Watt thinks, Eden has been improving his position and is probably now the only possible successor to the P.M. as Tory leader. Harvie Watt's own favourite is Oliver Stanley. Kingsley Wood, he says, is working his way back, and is well liked by the P.M., who thinks he has his ear to the ground. But Wood 'has no prospects'. In the House of Commons, both Lyttelton and Cripps are complete failures. Lyttelton was thought of, at one time, as a possible Tory leader. But not now, by anyone.

Therefore, he might well like the idea of going to India as Viceroy. This job has been hawked round a lot, and at least eight ministers have now refused it. Cripps is a complete prig. (Who told me that, when, in the presence of the P.M., Cripps asked to be excused to answer the telephone, the P.M. said, when he was gone, 'There, but for the grace of God, goes God himself!'?) Harvie Watt says that Sinclair cuts no ice now either with his party or with mine. We speak of younger people, and he thinks that, on our side, only Wilmot and Arthur Woodburn[1] are first-class. I tell him that I hear the P.M. thinks Wilmot a pacifist who, by his victory at Fulham, postponed our own rearmament.[2] I say this is quite false, or I, who led, often by the scruff of the neck, the Labour Party to support rearmament, would have no truck with him. Harvie Watt says that there is nothing in this. If true, this is most satisfactory. Harvie Watt says that, of Labour ministers, only Morrison, Bevin and I have been increasing our reputations. None of the others count. He adds, for me especially, that the P.M. likes ministers whom he can leave alone to do their jobs, without interference. Thence we turn to the post-war election. I ask him what he thinks the P.M. has in mind. I say that it would be most hard, if not impossible, to persuade our party to accept an election in which the strength of parties, as in 1935, was stabilised. He at once agrees that this would be quite wrong, and a demand which nobody would make of us. He is sure the P.M. had not this in mind. The P.M. used to say there should be no general election for two or three years after the war. But Beaverbrook has worked assiduously on him, and has made him feel that it would be wrong to continue this effete Parliament any longer than was necessary. On the other hand, the P.M. has said that he wishes the National Government to go on, not only till the war is won, but also to make the Peace and shape the first post-war years. But at other times he has heard him say, 'If the Socialists won't co-operate, then I should like to lead the Conservative Party to victory in an election.' He thinks the P.M. has not really thought the thing out.

I hint, going into no detail, at the possibility that we might have an election, on a common programme, with more than one Government candidate in a constituency. He thinks that this might have the effect

---

1 Arthur Woodburn (1890–1978). Labour M.P. for Clackmannan and East Stirlingshire 1939–70. Junior minister 1945–7. Secretary of State for Scotland 1947–50.
2 After winning an unexpected by-election victory at East Fulham in 1933, Wilmot had described the result as a symptom of a public desire for peace. This interpretation was widely believed, and gave rise to Baldwin's 'appalling frankness' speech three years later, in which the Prime Minister said that the loss of the Fulham seat 'on no issue but the pacifist' had helped to convince him of the political impossibility of rearmament. Churchill had been particularly contemptuous of this remark.

of letting a number of Independents in. But I am sure he has not really thought it out. Nor, I daresay, has the P.M.

He says that Tories don't much take to Morrison. He sends the P.M. accounts of Parliamentary proceedings every few days. He regrets that Attlee has made difficulties about political Honours in wartime. It would be much easier to bring young men on, if we could make old men Baronets or Peers, especially those who, as Under-Secretaries, could not 'make the grade' of No. 1 ministers. I said that I had no objection, in principle, to such arrangements. He asked me to use my influence with Attlee to get him to modify some Minute he had written on this subject.

Tuesday 25th May
Labour Party Administrative Committee. A long wrangle on last week's vote on Old Age Pensions. Greenwood, as Chairman, is most indignant at the lack of discipline among the members of the Administrative Committee itself. The Administrative Committee recommended to the Party Meeting, and it was carried by a small majority, that there should be no vote against the second reading of the Bill. Two members of the Administrative Committee – Shinwell and Daggar – spoke, without authority, from the Front Bench in the opposite sense, and, of those members of the Administrative Committee who were not ministers, 4 voted with him for the Government, and 5 against. Members of the Party, other than members of the Government, voted 51 with him and 49 against. This is sheer anarchy, and will utterly discredit the Party, and its leadership. ...

My economists and other officials confer with me on full employment, in the light of a paper on this subject for the Reconstruction Priorities Committee. I shall make a paper emphasising the Distressed Areas, and the need to push new industries into them.

Churchill and Roosevelt met for the 'Trident' Conference in Washington from 12th to 25th May. They decided to aim for an Allied invasion across the Channel at the beginning of May 1944. The British undertook to prepare plans.

Wednesday 26th May
Party Meeting, at which Shinwell, Bevan and other miscreants are noticeably absent. Pi-jaws from Greenwood in the Chair, and from

Attlee, on last week's indiscipline. It all leads nowhere! Too large a section of the Party has been allowed to get both sour and out of hand. But, just now, no one senses a Governmental crisis. The war is going too well, and most men's minds are elsewhere.

[Lord] Winterton and I lunch at the House. This is a long-standing engagement, made at his suggestion. He starts off at once, discussing post-war politics. He is much against an early return to Party politics. No doubt, he says, if the P.M. led the Tories into battle, he would sweep the country. But this would not last long. There would be a reaction, and we should come in. And then, in view of the great difficulties confronting any party, another reaction, out of which Mosley or [Sir Richard] Acland,[1] or some other ... might emerge triumphant. No matter who won the first, or the second, post-war election, national interests would suffer. Therefore, he favours a post-war agreement between the parties. He does not think this should be impossible. He, with Hogg and Hinchingbrooke,[2] has formed a Conservative Reform Committee. They organised motions and speeches and claques and counter-claques at the Conservative Party Conference last week. They were very successful. They are determined to hold in check the reactionary elements in their party. They would be quite prepared for a continuance of controls, for much state action and some state ownership, if we would agree to a strong defence and Empire development policy. I said I thought there would be little difficulty on these last. We, particularly the trade union leaders, were most firm now upon defence. We were, I thought, more sympathetic, and more closely in touch, with the Dominions, two of which have Labour Governments, than were the Tories. (Winterton said that he was afraid that this was so.) As for the Colonies – Winterton had praised Creech Jones for his persistent advocacy of Colonial development – I said we were less keen, but not at all antagonistic. I then say that the difficulty of a post-war election would be, if it was demanded of us, to accept the stabilisation of party strengths in 1935. Winterton said that he agreed that this was quite out of the question. At the same time, he was most eager for an early election. Many M.P.s, both in his party and ours, were too old and no use. 'This is a most discreditable House of Commons,' he said. Not showing my hand, I asked him

1 Sir Richard Acland, 15th Bart (b. 1906). Liberal, then Common Wealth, M.P. for Barnstaple 1935–45. Labour M.P. for Gravesend 1947–55. Co-founder of Common Wealth, a left-wing populist party which won a series of by-elections, uncontested by Labour because of the electoral truce, in the final years of the war.
2 Victor Montagu, Viscount Hinchingbrooke, later 10th Earl of Sandwich (b. 1906). Conservative M.P. for Dorset South 1941–57, 1958–62. Independent Conservative 1957–8. Chairman of Tory Reform Committee 1943–4. (Renounced peerage 1964.)

how he thought an election could be worked. He said he saw no reason why, the leaders having put out a common programme – he supposed we must still admit the right of these wretched Liberals to a place, though they now represented nothing, and would be ground out of existence in any genuine election – and the P.M. having drafted some appealing statement, in favour of great social advance, but no return, as yet, to party warfare, and suggesting to the electors that they should support a Government candidate, several Government candidates should not run in any one constituency. Tory and Socialist candidates would all support the Government, but the Tories would chide the Socialists with having voted against arms before the war, and Socialists would chide Tories as having been Men of Munich. But what would all this matter, this probing of the ghosts of long ago? I said that this was a most interesting idea, and that I should like to think further about it. Winterton said that he still saw the P.M. sometimes, and he would suggest it to him. I said I hoped he would.

This, surely, was a most interesting conversation. If he carries as much weight as he thinks, it may also have been most important.

Nearly all Labour ministers and a few others are invited to a sherry party at the Great Western Hotel. Harvie Watt again tackles Wilmot on political Honours, and Attlee, joining in the conversation, says he never objected to these for M.P.s, but only for outsiders who 'came crowding in'. Harvie Watt asks Wilmot to ask me to try to do something further to clear up this point with Attlee. I should be quite willing to do so.

On 22nd May, the Soviet Union announced the winding up of the Communist International, ostensibly to demonstrate that the U.S.S.R. had no expansionist aims. This decision raised, once again, the question of relations between British Communists and the Labour Party.

Friday 28th May
Special Labour Party Executive to consider latest situation resulting from Stalin's dissolution of the Comintern. All but unanimously, we are for no change. Shinwell and Laski, alone, are for refusing affiliation at the Annual Conference but offering to enter into conversations with the Communist Party. Watson, loyal to the M.F.G.B. [Miners' Federation of Great Britain] decision, puts up his hand, all alone, in

favour of accepting Communist Party affiliation on condition that they agree to our constitution. Jim Griffiths for once is in the majority on both issues. Afterwards he tells me that the Communists are losing much ground in South Wales by abusing absentee miners and denouncing them as 'criminals', for not doing their utmost for the Soviet Union. He says Lawther is only backing Communist Party affiliation because he fears that otherwise Horner will beat him for the Presidency of the M.F.G.B.

Tuesday 1st June

Administrative Committee at which Shinbad is trying to argue that, because they all recognise that, whatever the Parliamentary Party decision, Labour ministers must vote with the Government, so long as we are in it, it follows that ministers should not have the right to vote, either at the Administrative Committee or at the Party Meeting, when it is being decided how the Party shall vote in the House. This impudent attempt gets no support, but, as usual, wastes time. ...

Dine with Evan Durbin at the White Tower. The Greek food is good, but I prefer the Acropolis. We discuss – many intelligent people are discussing this now – how we all felt in the summer of 1940. The sense is very deep now that the tide has turned right round, so that 1940 is now quite distant and detached history.

Thursday 3rd June

Peggy Jay to dine with me. She thinks Douglas would like to go into politics after the war. I say that he should be better at telling people what he wants. She says that at Winchester they never learnt to do that. He was pressed very hard at the Ministry of Supply not to come to me, when I was angling for him, but, since, for reasons which she quite understands, I am no longer angling for him, his superiors at the Ministry of Supply have lost much interest in him! I think that she and he would like to come for a weekend to West Leaze.

Dalton had been reminded while dealing with the miners in 1942 of a widespread fear that peace would bring a return to mass unemployment on the same scale, and in the same places, as in the past. He therefore decided to use his powers as one of the ministers (with Ernest Bevin at Labour) responsible for concentrating and locating industry to provide some security against the danger of a future Depression. His ideas were drawn from several sources: from his own investigations into the Distressed Areas as Labour Party Chairman in 1936–7; from observations of socialist planning and the location of industry in the Soviet Union; and from the Report of the Royal Commission on Distribution of the Industrial Population (the Barlow Report) published in January 1940.

Dalton set out to do two things – to use the selective allocation of building licences (over which he had the power of veto) to ensure that industry went to areas where it would be needed after the war; and to stimulate the Cabinet into providing legislation in order to establish permanent post-war control of the location of industry by central government. Serious policy discussions began in May 1943, after the Reconstruction Committee had considered a paper by Dalton on Distressed Areas.[1] Preparations for another, more comprehensive, paper were quickly undertaken.

Friday 4th June
Afternoon meeting with my post-warriors to discuss Location of Industry. I am anxious quickly to put in a wide-reaching paper, but we seem to be entangled in a mass of commitments to interdepartmental consultations. I make a Minute of one of their papers, 'But this Heath Robinson (interdepartmental) construction must quicken up. Or we shall miss a number of important buses.'

To West Leaze.

Saturday 5th to Sunday 6th June
Mostly sunshine; much digging, carting and embanking; a goat gets loose in the gloaming and has to be reshackled before it can devour the young leaves on my trees.

The draft agreement for the setting up of the United Nations Relief and Rehabilitation Administration was published on 11th June. According to the preamble, the purpose was to ensure that the populations of liberated countries should receive food, clothing, shelter and health aid, and that arrangements should be made for the return of exiles to their homes, for the resumption of production and for the restoration of essential services. U.N.R.R.A. was to be run by a central committee consisting of representatives of China, Russia, the U.S.A. and Britain, with a director-general. President Roosevelt proposed to convene an international conference to approve the scheme.

---

1 27th May 1943; PRO, CAB 87/13 X/P 07917.

Thursday 10th June
The announcement about the U.N.R.R.A. has been made by the President in Washington. The press references here this morning are, however, very meagre. Leith-Ross is now to take a Press Conference of diplomatic correspondents this afternoon, and I shall have something to talk about at our Conference next week. Meanwhile, I tell Maurice Webb to crack the thing up in the *Herald* tomorrow, and to mention my name in connection with it. ...

Attend the première of Rank's new film, *The Life and Death of Colonel Blimp*. The P.M. turns up, and there are quite a number of ministers and other notorious people in the Dress Circle. I take George Preston. The film is much too long, more than two and a half hours, and I don't like at all the pro-German sentimentality of Blimp. It does not have a very enthusiastic reception, and many will dislike it for other reasons, e.g. the *Daily Mail* next morning, because foreigners will not understand our self-caricature. Another criticism is that *this* Blimp is not Low's immortal creation, but a much inferior, flabby creature, with no sharp outline.

In the contest for the Labour treasurership, there was some uncertainty about the voting system to be adopted at Party Conference. Was it first past the post, or exhaustive ballot? If there were to be two votes, there was some chance of swinging first-ballot trade union support for Hall, the likely also-ran, behind Morrison.

Friday 11th June
National Executive all morning, preparing for Annual Conference. George Oliver[1] attends for the Conference Arrangements Committee and, as usual, does very well; practical, experienced, good-tempered and witty. As the programme now stands, the votes for Executive, etc., will be taken – as I suggested they should be – on Monday between 12 noon and 5 p.m. After the usual preliminaries, the first real business is the pronouncement of *The Labour Party and the Future*.[2] Attlee will

1 George Oliver, q.v., was Chairman of the Conference Arrangements Committee.
2 The statement of the N.E.C. to the 1943 Conference, outlining post-war aims. 'In this document', Attlee told delegates on the first day, 'we envisage a planned economy in which the resources of the nation are used in peace as they have been in war, to serve the needs of the community.' (Labour Party Annual Conference Report, p. 121.)

move this, and Morrison wind up, just before lunch. This will give him a pull with whatever votes are still free for the treasurership. No other Executive candidate will have as much chance of getting in. Shinwell starts an attempt to work himself in with a 'Progress Report' for the Reconstruction Committee, and I pass a note to Morrison saying that so long as we hold the Monday morning programme and the Monday vote, it does not matter if Shinwell gets a bit more of a show than had been intended some other day.

Go to lunch at the Cock with George Ridley, Sam Watson and Morgan Phillips. The rumours are that the Transport Workers and the N.U.D.A.W. are both voting for Greenwood, the former because he is nominally one of their members, the latter through the machinations of Luke Hogan[1] and Billy Robinson. There are also fears that the General Workers may go the same way. On the other hand, the N.U.R. and the cotton unions are thought to be probably for Morrison, who should also pick up a large quantity of small pieces. Will Hall has not only the Miners, but the Iron and Steel Workers and a few more. Although we could have got his withdrawal a month ago, when Wilmot canvassed him (but it seemed both to Morrison and me that he had better stay put, since the Miners' vote, we then thought, could not be relied on), it is said that now his ambition has been fired and he quite believes he may win. Morgan Phillips says that he will get the support of practically all the constituency party agents, who think he has done very well for them over their superannuation scheme. Watson says that he thinks if Hall were to withdraw before the Miners' delegate meeting on Sunday morning, it would be possible for Will Lawther, just as the meeting was breaking up, to say, quite casually, that since their first choice had withdrawn, he took it that their vote would now go to Morrison – who had, in fact, received a good deal of support when the original nomination was being discussed, Greenwood not having been in the running at all. On the other hand, there is a danger that this manoeuvre might miscarry, through the intervention of Ebby Edwards, who tends to oppose everything proposed from Durham, and Ridley thinks that, if it were announced at the last moment in the Conference that Hall had withdrawn, there would be a suspicion among the delegates that there had been a wangle. On the whole, therefore, we decide that it is not wise or worth while to make any further approach to Hall. I suggest, however, that we might leave open the possibility, when we know more about where the big votes are going, of getting someone to raise in the Conference, before

---

1 Luke Hogan (1886–1954). Divisional Organiser for N.U.D.A.W., and a delegate to the 1943 Labour Party Conference. A member of Liverpool City Council from 1921, and its leader for fifteen years.

the vote is taken, the question of a second vote between the first and second candidates if the first has not a clear majority. This would do Morrison no good if he was only third, and, until we know more, it is not clear that it would help anyhow.

Ridley is very conscious of the responsibilities and possibilities of next year, and we discuss the possibility of a meeting of 'the hard core' of the Executive at regular intervals, especially before monthly meetings.

Sunday 13th June

National Executive in afternoon to take account of Group meetings and resulting composites. On 'Post-war treatment of enemy peoples' Stokes and others have a composite attacking [the] Fight for Freedom Group and declaring generally that Germans are good chaps and that no one should hate them, to which the Iron and Steel Trades have an amendment declaring that they don't want to exterminate anybody, but that most Germans are to blame for what is going on, and that Germany must be completely disarmed, as laid down in Atlantic Charter, and 're-educated' so as to give her a chance of becoming a decent member of future international society. ...

After the National Executive, I bring back George Ridley, Sam Watson and Morgan Phillips to my room, and we check up the prospective votes for the treasurership. All the big unions have now taken their decisions, several of them this morning.

Of the Big Six, Greenwood has got the Transport Workers, the N.U.R., and the N.U.D.A.W.; Morrison the General Workers and the Cotton Textiles; Hall the Miners. There have been some close shaves, Burrows being broken-hearted because he only just failed to pull the N.U.R. for Morrison because a number of his delegates 'were grumbling about fire-watching', and Morrison having got Cotton only by the casting vote of the Chairman of the delegation.

Of the middle-sized unions, Greenwood has the A.E.U. and the E.T.U.; Morrison the R.C.A. and the N.A.T.S.O.P.A.; Hall has Iron and Steel.

These votes add up as follows:

Greenwood	974 [,000]
Morrison	491
Hall	470

Therefore, so far, Greenwood has a clear majority over both the others. There remain the smaller unions, the constituency parties and other oddments. Of constituency parties, we anticipate a total vote of

400,000 of which Morrison should certainly get a very substantial majority. Provisionally, we give him 300,000, Greenwood 100,000 and Hall nothing. This brings the vote to:

Greenwood	1,074 [,000]
Morrison	791
Hall	470

It is, therefore, clear (1) that if the first vote settles it, Greenwood is in and the Miners have thrown away their vote of 413,000, and (2) that if there is a second vote between Greenwood and Morrison, and the Miners swing over to the latter, he is in.

Watson is pretty sure he can get the Miners' vote for Morrison, Lawther and Bowman being also very keen to do it. On the other hand, there is a certain amount of anti-Morrison feeling among the Miners, including some in South Wales, and also Yorkshire, who are very pro-Greenwood. It is agreed that some delegate should ask, at the opening of the Conference on Monday morning, before the votes are taken, that, if the first candidate has no clear majority, there should be a second vote. Ridley gets on the telephone to Watkins and, I thought, fixed this definitely. Watson will do his best to make sure that the Miners' second vote goes as desired.

The Labour Party Conference was held at the Central Hall, Westminster from 14th to 18th June. Alfred Dobbs was in the Chair.

Monday 14th June

Old Dobbs makes a much better Chairman's speech – and throughout the week a much better Chairman – than I had expected. Just after he had finished his oration this morning, I am told that Fred Watkins[1] won't raise the point as arranged yesterday, since the R.C.A. have had a delegate meeting this morning and have felt that it would be invidious for them to raise it, since they have nominated Morrison. I, therefore, incite various people to run about the hall and try to get someone else to raise it. Wilmot succeeds in doing this, getting hold of Mrs Bamford,[2] who in fact is voting for Greenwood, and asking her to raise the question, and not to argue or to ask him why. She does

1 F. C. Watkins (1883–1954). Labour M.P. for Hackney Central 1929–31, 1935–45.
2 Mildred Bamford. Labour Party Conference delegate from Hammersmith South in 1943 and 1944.

so, but rather ineffectually, and George Oliver, as Chairman of the Conference Arrangements Committee, merely says that this is not a matter for him. But Greenwood's supporters will have been put on their guard. Most inept!

Returning to the Conference after luncheon, I am mounting the stairs with Phillips when Lawther meets us. I take him aside and ask whether he does not think there should be a second vote. He says yes certainly, and he thinks he can put the Miners' vote on to Morrison. I ask whether he will authorise me to tell the Chairman that Lawther has approached me and say that, as a matter of principle, he thinks there should be a second vote. He agrees. I, therefore, write notes both to the Chairman and to Middleton, proposing that a special Executive Committee should be held to decide this question, in view of Lawther's approach to me. This is done at the close of the day's sitting. The Greenwoodites, however, are in full force and full cry. Robinson, Walker and Dallas sit together in the front row and try to shout everyone else down. They say that there is no precedent for a second vote, and that, if we agree to this, we shall have to recast our whole method of election, including that in each of the panels of the National Executive. Shinwell also swells the hubbub, characteristically, by insinuating that persons and organisations unnamed are trying to do a wangle on behalf of some candidate unnamed. None the less, it is moved and seconded that we should recommend the Conference tomorrow, before the vote is announced, that there should be a second vote if no clear majority. This is supported by Ridley, Watson, Laski, Phil [Noel-] Baker, Burrows (though rather hesitatingly), and myself. It gets 11 votes to 10, Middleton being in a state of great dither and trying to make sure that he counts every adverse vote. Then someone says to the Chairman, 'But you have got a vote too.' The Chairman says he gives his vote against the recommendation, so that it is not carried. Another close thing, just the wrong way!

I talk further with Watson, who will tell Lawther what has happened and consider with him whether, as a last resort, the Miners should not raise this question themselves tomorrow at the opening of business, before the votes are announced. He is inclined to think that this is all too late. Afterwards I do some telephoning to Morrison, Ellen Wilkinson, and then to Lawther at the Strand Palace. Since he is likely to be sitting in a crowd having drinks, I arrange that Miss Lowndes[1] should try to get through first without mentioning my name, and if pressed should give her own. (He has a number of lady friends.) This works, and he comes on to the 'phone not knowing who wishes to

1 S. A. Lowndes. Private secretary to Dalton at the Board of Trade 1943–5.

speak to him. He says there has been a buzz since this afternoon among the Greenwoodites, who know, of course, of our manoeuvres and of the special Executive Committee. He thinks that if the Miners did raise it tomorrow, it would only create a strong pro-Greenwood reaction and he is not dead sure of his delegation. It might be that they would insist that the Miners' vote should be broken up into coalfields, in which case Yorkshire and probably South Wales would go for Greenwood, though Durham and some others would go for Morrison, but not enough to change the first vote. We leave it that he will think it over and talk to some of his friends before tomorrow morning.

Morrison, on the telephone, is, very naturally, very indignant. 'This is the third time,' he says, that they have turned him down, for the leadership in 1935, for the secretaryship, through imposing the ban on its being held by an M.P.,[1] and now this. 'They know quite well what they are doing,' he says. He would rather like a row tomorrow, if it can still be arranged, and would be prepared to say that he would ask for a second vote if he were on top without a clear majority.

I am afraid it is now too late.

As expected, Arthur Greenwood won the contest for the Party treasurership – obtaining 1,253,000 votes against 926,000 for Morrison and 519,000 for Hall.

Tuesday 15th June
The voting is announced. No one raises the question of a second vote. ... Morrison does better than I expected on his vote, and evidently swept nearly all the board of constituency parties. There were 450,000 of these. The total vote of the Conference is unusually high, being over 2,600,000. The only other changes on the Executive Committee are that Collick[2] comes on in the trade union section in place of Bolton[3] who doesn't run again, and that John Parker takes the place vacated by Morrison. I get a very solid vote of 300,000 and Phil [Noel-Baker] falls down below me, as I forecast would be the case

1 See entry for 25th October 1943 and n., p. 657.
2 P. H. Collick (b. 1897). Assistant General Secretary of the Associated Society of Locomotive Engineers and Firemen (A.S.L.E.F.) 1940–57. Labour M.P. for Birkenhead West 1945–50; Birkenhead 1950–64. Junior minister 1945–7.
3 H. P. Bolton. E.T.U. delegate on the N.E.C. 1942 and 1944.

when he became a minister. But the top five, down to and including Phil, all have a clear majority of the total constituency party vote. Dallas and Parker, who bring up the rear, are a long way behind, but both comfortably in front of the runner-up. Ridley will be Chairman and Ellen Vice-Chairman next year.[1]

The public will not take well the election of Greenwood and the defeat of Morrison. It will strengthen the view that we are bad judges of ability in the Labour Party, or that our judgments are clouded by jealousy. Of Greenwood it used to be said in Whitehall, when he was a minister, that 'the poor old chap couldn't even sign his name after midday'. In fact, out of ministerial office, he is not quite so bad as they think. None the less, the thing is most unfortunate. Morrison is saying that he won't run again for the Executive Committee for several years, but I expect he will change his mind twelve months hence. Some of the press say that he has now got the asset of personal sympathy for the first time in his career. I am now the only minister of Cabinet rank left on the Executive, apart from Attlee. I can foresee that I shall have to spend even more time on Party business next year, and to take a larger share in next year's Conference. Speaking in public at Party gatherings while a minister in this mixed Government is, I find, a very tiresome and unsatisfactory business. But much may change, and things seem very different, twelve months hence. The vote for Greenwood was largely a 'testimonial vote'. People thought he had had a raw deal; he was a decent chap, a good old crony, he had done a lot of work for the Party, etc. Rather pathetic!

The Conference, apart from this incident, went very well and reached a series of very good decisions. It flatly reaffirmed the electoral truce by 6 to 1; it flatly turned down Communist affiliation by 3 to 1 (the Miners voted in the minority and it is clear that the great majority of the constituency parties voted in the majority); it beat off an attack on Labour ministers for their votes and speeches on the Beveridge Report by nearly 2 to 1; it carried, without a vote, the Previous Question on a resolution which tried to commit us to leave the Government as soon as hostilities with Germany were ended, following an undertaking by Attlee that the Party Conference should decide the matter when the time came (which anyone would have assumed would be the case in any event); it carried by nearly 2 to 1 the Iron and Steel amendment to the Stokes resolution referred to above.

This last event occurred on the morning of Thursday, 17th. Till then I had been most assiduously in attendance, but then I returned to the Board of Trade.

1 Marginal insertion: 'I could have lost half my votes and still got on.'

Monday 21st June

Talk with pram-makers, who ask for more metal. The supply of babies, and even of first births, is running ahead of the supply of prams. I say that I will do my best, and I hear later that pressure on the Ministry of Supply has been effective.

It is most remarkable, most time-absorbing, and sometimes most irritating, that I should be regarded as a sort of universal provider for the civilian population. And so, apart from being expected to produce more prams, more razor-blades, more alarm clocks, more tea-cloths for pubs, more children's shoes (and to prevent the prices of any of these things being excessive, and, on the other hand, not to issue too many Orders, and not to have too many officials to enforce them, or to inspect anything or anybody, lest this should appear to be 'Gestapo'), I receive also letters from M.P.s, replies to which I must, if the writers are not to be grossly offended, sign and vet myself, reporting that, e.g., some lady has tried in eight different shops to get an outsize corset and will I please do something about it, or again that a lady has lost her clothing coupons in a tram, and will I please replace them, or again that someone wants to publish a most important book and the publishers can't get the paper, and will I please provide it. It is a little difficult to prevent this mass of urgent, short-term detail from blocking the vistas towards the brave new post-war world.

Wednesday 23rd June

My talk with Eden is very friendly. ... He says he isn't at all anxious now to have a second Parliamentary Under-Secretary, though he was thinking of it some months ago. If he did, he thinks the new minister should be from the Labour Party, and probably a trade unionist. He would wish to consult Attlee and me on who would do. He does not think Phil [Noel-Baker] would fit in, and that he is doing very good work where he is now. I say that I agree that it is much better for him to be off foreign affairs for the moment. I suggest no name, but think a bit. Creech Jones, we mention, made a very good and sensible speech on the Foreign Service Bill. He would evidently be a possible. Could he learn, however, to be less long-winded?

I tell Eden that I like the various post-war Foreign Office papers he has been putting out. He says it is most difficult to get the Cabinet ever to consider these. He is getting very tired of the P.M.'s regular joke, when these come up, 'I suppose it is thought that the war is now going so well that we needn't trouble about it any more, and can amuse ourselves this afternoon.'

Friday 25th June
Gladwyn Jebb to dine. He has been very busy with post-war plans and many of these have found shape in the various Foreign Office papers. But these are never properly discussed in the Cabinet, but either accepted perfunctorily, as with 'Armistice and related problems', or postponed indefinitely. He is most anxious to get joint political planning, probably in London, with Americans and Russians of sufficient authority, both military and civilian, sitting in with us. The Americans, he thinks, still regard Europe as a lump of undifferentiated putty, which can be 'moulded' this way or that, without much reference either to history or nationality. The P.M. came back from Washington somewhat imbued with these same ideas, and influenced also by Cripps's crackpot notion of dividing Europe arbitrarily into some six or seven synthetic 'States'.

We speak of the future of Relief, and he strongly urges that Leith-Ross should agree to become one of Lehman's Deputy Director-Generals. This would mean that he would be, not a Board of Trade, nor a Treasury, nor a Foreign Office, official, but an international official of great standing and influence.

I spoke bluntly to Gladwyn about the intrigues of certain officials. ... I also said that Bridges should stick to taking an accurate note of what the P.M. said in Cabinet. This was his proper function, and he might be wise to remember that some day someone else will be P.M. Anyhow, I was quite content with my arrangement with Eden that there should be a transfer of ministerial responsibility after, but not until, the U.N.R.R.A. was a going concern with Lehman in the saddle.

Monday 28th June
Douglas Jay to dine. He has been asked whether he will become prospective Labour candidate for Oxford University. He says he met the most frightful lot of people, dim and wildly eccentric and totally out of touch with all reality, at Oxford last week, when the matter was broached. Some were for approaching A. D. Lindsay.[1] We agreed that Jay might say that, if they couldn't get Lindsay, he would accept, provided he could square this with his Ministry. I told him that it would give him an important increment of status in the Labour Party if he were a candidate, and make it easier to shift him to a better seat.

He thinks that we are producing far too many heavy bombers. A grotesquely high proportion of our total labour force and material is going into this. Therefore, he says, we are short of landing craft for

1 A. D. Lindsay, later 1st Baron (1879–1952). Master of Balliol College, Oxford 1924–49. Independent Progressive candidate in the Oxford by-election of 1938, with local Labour Party and Popular Front support.

the invasions and of much else, which could otherwise have been provided. He does not think we are getting any *decisive* results from our air bombing. The R.A.F. have had their way, and have been given their head, and the result is, he fears, that we shall neither bomb the enemy out of the war, nor have enough forces to invade Europe effectively this year, nor even perhaps next. He says that the Air Force have not yet sunk a single enemy battleship or aircraft-carrier in any sea. The American, Japanese and German bombers have all done better, because, he thinks, none has a separate Air Force. Our Air Force also failed, fantastically, to hit the *Gneisenau* and *Scharnhorst*. The *Bismarck*, on the other hand, was destroyed by naval action, including the Fleet Air Arm. It may, he thinks, be argued that it *was* we who began the bombing of cities and civilian populations. Hitler did not start on us until we had attacked the Ruhr. It may also, Jay thinks, be argued that we *did* hold back strong air forces from the Battle of France, and that, if we had thrown them all in, the result might have been different. We are now losing hundreds of heavy bombers a month, whereas our big battleships last for years, and in spite of our vast bomber production, the wastage is so great that, at any given moment, we have only a few months' supply of these monsters. In none of our battles, before El Alamein, did the Air Force play any real part at all.

I set all this down, omitting some striking figures, as a record of what he said. I think it wildly out of focus. The real effectiveness of our air bombing remains to be checked up later on. My own view is that it *is* becoming one of several decisive factors. But, like the blockade last time, the results won't show clearly till the end is reached. Everyone's view must be discounted by their natural bias, and the Ministry of Supply are furiously opposed to Ministry of Aircraft Production, [which] has put all its factories in the wrong places and is voraciously snatching both labour and material from the Ministry of Supply.[1]

Tuesday 29th June
Ruth to dine with me and John Wilmot at the Board of Trade. She has seen Viénot and would very much like, later on, to go across to France and help to get things going again. Also she wants all possible done to put him in touch with useful people here. I tell her that Jebb, who has recently met him, has told me of Eden's reactions.

Wednesday 30th June
Dine, after a longish interval from these occasions, with Lady Colefax

1 Marginal insertion: 'And D.J.'s brother is in the Navy.'

and find myself between her and Lady Phipps.[1] The latter was always said, when her husband was Minister at Vienna, to be a Socialist. She says that the American Ambassador Dodd at Berlin was a complete idiot, never knowing anything that was going on, and never understanding anything that was said to him. The only subject on which he was interesting was on the Old South. He was writing a history of this in six volumes. At the end of the Civil War the South was in a state of complete devastation. Martha Dodd,[2] she says, had a series of love affairs with young Germans. The first few were Nazis, but later she fell in love with a young Jew, and it was only from this moment she turned anti-Hitler.

Lady Phipps then began to talk the most frightful drivel, which nearly launched me into a most ferocious argument. But I refrained, feeling a little weary. She thought it was a terrible sort of war in which the soldiers stayed fretting at home, and had no chance to fight or die for their country, while women and children were bombed from the air. I said the worst thing about the last war was that so many young men were killed and so few old people, or women of any age. In this respect I thought this war was much less evil. She did not seem to see the point at all, and said that there was something beautiful in a young soldier dying for his country, but nothing beautiful in civilians being killed. I said that if the bombing of German civilians – and, after all, it was quite false to draw a line between a soldier in uniform and a civilian making arms for the soldier or otherwise assisting the 'war effort' – resulted in shortening the war and saving lives of large numbers of British soldiers, who would otherwise be slaughtered as on the Somme and at Passchendaele in the last war, I was all for it. She said she was sure that the soldiers hated it. I said I would rather that they hated it and survived than died loving old-fashioned war – and they didn't love that anyhow. A silly woman! But I connect her reaction with Jay's and wonder whether Goebbels[3] isn't having another mild success. Lady Phipps also said that this extermination of whole classes, e.g. the Jews, by the Germans, 'was started by the Russians'. Until they set an example, no one ever did such things. The Germans, she said, never did it in the last war.

Thursday 1st July

Lunch with Viénot, who is looking very much better and has put on 8 lb. since he arrived in England. He has been appointed representative of the French National Committee in London. If they were offi-

1 Lady Phipps, née Frances Ward. Second wife (m. 1911) of Sir Eric Phipps, q.v.
2 Martha Dodd, née Johns. Married to Ambassador Dodd.
3 Joseph Goebbels (1897–1945). German Minister of Propaganda 1933–45.

cially recognised, he would, I suppose, be the Ambassador of France. He thinks it very mistaken, from every point of view, that recognition is still withheld. It has a bad effect in France, and this is exploited by the Germans. He is very apprehensive of American economic imperialism in Europe. He thinks they will press for the setting up of conservative and right-wing governments everywhere. He says their preference for Giraud over de Gaulle is most mistaken. The American intervention through Eisenhower[1] was 'most brutal'. The two French Generals were sent for and bluntly told that no change could be made in the present attributes of General Giraud. He must remain both Commander-in-Chief and Minister of War. Viénot says that he has confidence in the stability of the National Committee, because, subjected to this most severe crisis, it survived. De Gaulle did not, on this occasion, 'go through the roof', but merely retired to his own room, and remained there for twenty-four hours, with great dignity! I said that he must really try to understand Anglo-American impatience at the perpetual quarrelling of the Generals, and their backers. We were about to embark on important military operations, based on North Africa, and could not be expected to tolerate the possibility of riots, civil war between French factions, and the compromising of our lines of communications. He said he did not think that these were real dangers, and added that the promise to furnish arms for the French in North Africa had not yet really begun to be kept. Hardly any equipment had yet arrived.

We talked on, discursively, for some while, and I urged him not to seem a partisan of de Gaulle. He said that now he was a supporter of the National Committee, though he had his own preference for the one General over the other. Giraud, he said, was the most completely reactionary type of old regular soldier. 'Order', he had said, 'must, of course, be maintained when we liberate France; if necessary, with machine guns.' De Gaulle, he said, was, no doubt, a 'difficult' man, but part of his rigidity had been due to the persistent German and Vichy propaganda that he was nothing but an English agent, paid by the English. He had felt that he must prove this false. Further, if French trust in de Gaulle, still passionate, was dissipated, the Communists would come into their own, and the prestige of Russia be enormously enhanced relative to that of Britain and America.

We spoke also a little on Relief, and I arranged for him to see Leith-Ross.

He has great qualities, including as Ruth says, a most surprisingly

1 General Dwight D. Eisenhower (1890–1969). Commander-in-Chief, Allied Forces in North Africa 1942–4. Supreme Commander, Allied Expeditionary Force 1944–5. President of the United States 1953–61.

unFrench sense of what is 'practical'. Already, I think, he is sensing London a little better. He has, he says, practically no staff and a very great deal to do. I shall keep in touch with him.

An hour's talk with Sir John Anderson. I begin the conversation by asking him to explain to me the 'background' of recent moves concerning Relief. He is moderately apologetic, explaining that it was, of course, wrong for officials to circulate recommendations touching the functions of ministers, without ministers first having been consulted and their agreement secured. He can only excuse this on the ground that everything has been in such a rush. He is still apprehensive that U.N.R.R.A., when set up, with 'forceful' Americans in charge and a quantity of 'greedy and destitute' small European allies clamouring for supplies, may put us in the U.K. in a frightful hole. Hence the need to insist on the powers of the Combined Boards.[1] This is all very well, but I am horrified by his further suggestion that we should now ask the smaller allies to accept our own view of the relative functions of U.N.R.R.A. and the Combined Boards. He is a little apprehensive of Leith-Ross's attitude, and of his view of U.N.R.R.A. I say that both Leith-Ross and I have the sensation that manoeuvres have been going on and that there has been a lack of frankness among officials. Why have they not approached Leith-Ross direct? Anderson says that he thinks some of them find Leith-Ross very difficult to approach. 'He sits and mumbles', and they can't hear what he says, but generally get the impression that he is very sensitive. Anderson asked what role I think Leith-Ross should play, and I suggest Chairman of the European Committee. Anderson says he thinks this would be a good plan. Would there not also be a Deputy Director to Lehman? I say yes; would he think this a suitable post for Leith-Ross? He says he thinks so, if the latter would like it? I say I think perhaps he would. I have mentioned it to him. But it would mean his becoming an international and no longer a British government official. Anderson did not seem to have thought of this, but I said that this might have several advantages.

He branched off into saying that the Foreign Office was very ill-equipped for taking the place it should take in economic discussions. He spoke unfavourably of the capacities of Ronald. I praised Gladwyn, of whom he said that he had also 'heard good accounts'.

Friday 2nd July
With Wilmot to Snitterton, near Matlock, for weekend with Broad

1 The Anglo-American Combined Boards were responsible for the allocation of all supplies. There were British fears that U.N.R.R.A. might prove a rival to them – to the detriment of this country's national requirements, especially of food.

and his wife. An attractive old house in a rather good neighbourhood. Atmosphere of hero-worship, and I talk to them about trees and hedges. They have a good yew hedge. Walk up to plateau of Stanton Moor, owned by National Trust, from which grand views all round. Memorial Tower to Reform Bill of 1832. More trees cut down than planted. Descend to pub at Birchover, where we sit, unrevealed, while yokels behind their tankards declare that (1) P.M. is a grand man, and (2) that rationing of everything must go on after the war — 'all fair and square'. I assent and reveal my identity, and the publican, an ex-miner who was taken prisoner in the last war and made by the Huns to work in a Polish mine ... invites me to have one with him and gives me a free cigar. I have no doubt that consumers are all for controls and rationing. This desire must be mobilised at the right time.

On 4th July General Wladyslaw Sikorski, head of the Polish government-in-exile, was killed in a plane crash just after leaving Gibraltar, possibly as a result of sabotage.

Monday 5th July
Today we have heard of the death of Sikorski. This is deeply moving and very disturbing. I had a warm affection and high regard for this man. He combined, as few others, the best qualities of statesman, soldier and patriot. There is no other Pole to take his place. Clearly his functions of P.M. and Commander-in-Chief must be split. Retinger comes to see me, red-eyed and worn out. Sikorski had specially asked for a Czech pilot, who had flown him in U.S.A. This pilot is the sole survivor, though badly injured. Victor Cazalet also was on this plane. He was friendly, humane, *manqué* and generally ineffective. But up in the Elysian Fields he will be able to say that he died with Sikorski, and on active service. I recall that, in the General Strike of 1926, I met him on Paddington Station, strike-breaking. I said, 'What are you up to?' He said, 'I am prepared to die, if necessary, for my country.' I said, 'Don't be so bloody melodramatic.' After that, he learned much, and I often enjoyed his company.

Thursday 8th July
With John Wilmot to Royal Court Hotel, [1] where he and Molly Hamil-

1 Ruth had moved into the Royal Court Hotel after the Daltons gave up their flat in Carlisle Mansions. She was presumably staying there now, on a brief visit from the North.

ton are dining with Ruth. They are going on afterwards to see Viénot.
...

Irene [Noel-Baker] dines with me alone and pours forth about Phil
and his future. She says that some say that I am determined to be
Foreign Secretary in any Labour government, and should simply kick
Phil downstairs if he got in my way. On the other hand, she recalls
that I once said to some Conference, 'I don't care much for some of
my colleagues, but I love Phil.' I quote to her the wise saying of Arthur
Henderson, 'Never fix your mind too much on any one office, or the
result will be disappointment and bitterness.' I tell her that, if we win
the next election, Phil will be in the Cabinet[1] – she did not seem to have
realised this – and that, whatever office he held, he would have a general voice in all policy. I said that the only people who really influenced
events were politicians in office. Next to them in influence came their
departmental advisers. No one else normally counted for much. She
had thought that Phil might do better if he retired and became a
publicist. I said this was a lousy life and counted for nothing. Phil and
I were at an age when, if we won the next election, we should have great
power to influence events, but, if we lost it, we should be too old, by
the time the next one came, to do much. She did the usual gloom about
Attlee, and said she heard it was not he but the P.M. who insisted on
Phil being brought into the Government. I said that the P.M. wanted
him, but that Attlee had pressed him on his shortlist, and that I had
pressed Attlee much on his behalf.

Later I took her home and had a talk with Phil. I said that we must
meet and talk and that I would try to make a realistic paper on foreign
policy. (I noted that he had not yet reacted to my knockout blow in
reply to his tripe for the French, but he explained that this was only
because he had been too busy.) I must keep a little closer to him this
year than last. Left alone, he has queer streaks of unreliability. Properly guided, he has great value. And, in any case, a most attractive
personality.

The invasion of Sicily ('Operation Husky') began with airborne landings during the night of 9th July. General Eisenhower was Supreme Commander, with
General Alexander as his deputy, in charge of the 15th Army Group, com-
prising General Patton's Seventh Army and General Montgomery's Eighth
Army. On 10th July, the U.S. Seventh Army landed in the Gulf of Gela,

1 In fact, Noel-Baker did not become a Cabinet Minister until October 1947.

while British forces invaded south of Syracuse. The British met little initial opposition, but the Americans soon encountered heavy resistance from the Hermann Goering Panzer Division. By 14th July, Axis forces were being pushed back all along the front and both Allies had consolidated their positions. Nearly half a million Allied troops were landed in Sicily before the invasion was complete.

Saturday 10th to Sunday 11th July

At West Leaze. Continuous rain and I can cut no grass! At 12 noon on Saturday, 10th July, Ruth comes and wakes me up to tell me that the invasion of Sicily has begun. Last time we spent a weekend together here, Bizerte and Tunis unexpectedly fell! These rare occasions have a good influence on the course of the war.

Monday 12th July

Waterhouse says that he has authorised the prosecution of Lady Astor[1] for trying to obtain a fur coat from the U.S.A. without an import licence. I am rather pleased at this. He says that, if I like, I can put all the responsibility on him. I say that I shall say that it was, quite rightly, not referred to me for my decision, since there should be no discrimination in favour of the wealthy and influential, but that when I was told that it was intended to prosecute, I expressed approval. It would be fun to put her in jail! Waterhouse says that she is 'appealing to the Attorney-General'.

Tuesday 13th July

[Leo] Amery gives a lunch to ministers and others to meet Wavell. The latter makes a most remarkable and attractive speech. The Wyke-hamist scholar soldier! A number of Latin quotations, a number of stories of sport, some straightforward and rather fresh comments on India, and an impressive and direct manner. Amery relates that when Wavell was in command in Egypt just before France fell, he had a very small and poorly equipped force, on paper far inferior to the Italians just across his Western frontier. But he had been well buttressed by two powerful French armies, the one in Syria and the other in Tunisia, so that in North Africa and the Near East as a whole, the Anglo-French position was very strong. Then Italy came into the

---

1 Viscountess Nancy Astor, Conservative M.P. for Plymouth Sutton, q.v.

war, and two days later France fell, and, a few days afterwards, the two French armies were in clear dissolution. This news was brought to Wavell while on the golf-course by some excited subordinate who expected him to rush back at once to his office. But Wavell merely said, 'I don't see there is anything that I can do about it' and went on with the game. This story strikes a responsive chord in me. There is enough for busy people to bother about without bothering over troubles one has no power to cure.

...

Reconstruction Priorities Committee, with Anderson in the Chair. Two hours of it, but the results are not too bad, if only the Minutes come out clean. I pursue, obstinately and repetitively, my line that ministers must do more and officials less. ... On Location, I begin by saying that I would like to do a paper, in consultation with Jowitt and W. S. Morrison, but I finally get away with the initiative entirely in my own hands. Someone, I say, must kick off the ball or the game cannot start, and I am prepared to 'make a map' of the problem, by way of beginning. Bevin, rather disgruntled and jealous, keeps boring on about transport being fundamental, and, therefore, there should be a representative of Ministry of War Transport on the Steering Committee[1] (a new proposal of Anderson's to consist of five officials only, from Treasury, Ministry of Labour, Board of Trade, Economic Section, and Reconstruction Secretariat – a vast improvement on the wretched old Internal Economic Problems [Committee], which I think we are slowly stifling). I say that we know, broadly, *where* the new industries are required, and that we must see that there are suitable transport facilities for these regions. Anderson agrees with me. Finally, I say that, granted transport is most important, what is required is not an official from Ministry of War Transport on the Steering Committee, but the Minister himself to attend this Committee. This is plain sense, and taken by Anderson. But I don't believe that Bevin really sees the point at all.

Wednesday 14th July
Party Meeting, at which much incredibly loose talk and rubbishy rhetoric is released on the need for planning – i.e., the setting up of one minister to deal with everything. These fools have just no sense at all of what government means, or what are either the inter-relations of ministers or the proper limits of what any one minister can do. Almost they make me a defender of our drab delays!

1 The 'Steering Committee': the Official Committee on Post-War Employment, set up by the Reconstruction Priorities Committee on 13th July.

Thursday 15th July

Dick Law to see me. He thinks that he should probably go as leader of the delegation to the U.S. to discuss Relief – when probably, as it now seems, there will be almost simultaneous discussions of monetary, commercial, buffer stock and investment problems. He agrees, and thinks Eden agrees, that Leith-Ross should be internationalised, once U.N.R.R.A. can be born. I stress that there is danger of national and self-regarding forces winning too much ground here; the Food Ministry, for instance, wishing to dole out peas, and the Treasury pennies, to those whom Anderson describes as 'greedy and destitute European nations'. I say I often feel ashamed at how little we have suffered in the war, and that it would be both morally wrong and politically short-sighted, to follow this line too far. As to our own people, they will take an 'internationalist' policy in these matters, if it is properly put to them. We agree that he should have a talk with Leith-Ross and then convene an interdepartmental meeting, himself in the Chair, to discuss 'instructions' for the declaration. He asks why I have feelings about Maud and Robbins, both of whom I had mentioned at the Foreign Office the other day. He had found them both very good at the Food Conference. I said that Maud had, I gathered, intrigued violently on the Combined Board side against U.N.R.R.A. and that Robbins was fantastically anti-planning. There had, I thought, been a good deal of unfrankness towards poor old Leith-Ross. Anyhow, committees, if not presided over by a minister, must still be presided over by Leith-Ross, who was much more distinguished and senior than any of the other officials concerned. I think he took this point. I said that, the period of gestation of U.N.R.R.A. being so prolonged, I was now inclined to hand it over to Eden before long, provided we could find a suitable pretext, e.g. the completion of the instructions for the delegation. We agreed to keep in touch over these matters.

Monday 19th July

Lord President's Committee. I have a fight against Bevin, Duncan and Ben Smith,[1] representing Cripps, all of whom want to put various people into uniform for the first time. Bevin's is the most dangerous and the least defensible. He wants a walking-out uniform for members of his new Corps of Domestic Helps in hospitals, etc. I get strong support in resisting this from Anderson, Wood and Morrison. Bevin

---

1 B. Smith, later Sir Ben (1879–1964). Parliamentary Secretary at the Ministry of Aircraft Production 1942–3. Minister Resident (for Supply) in Washington 1943. Labour M.P. for Rotherhithe 1923–31, 1935–46. Minister of Food 1945–6.

takes it very badly. The other two claims, being smaller, are referred to officials, and it is agreed that Anderson shall umpire if we cannot settle them. ... Then follows a discussion on withdrawing coupons from various part-time uniformed people, and Morrison claims that, if he is to agree to this, for his part-time Fire Service, the Home Guards must also make a surrender. I don't press for this, or even speak in favour of it, but Anderson thinks it should be done and the Committee so 'decides'. This leads to some fuss and trouble, for the War Office strongly opposes and [Sir James] Grigg sneaks to the P.M. Bits appear in the press, where I, not unnaturally, am blamed for having made this proposal. The P.M. and I send each other Minutes on the subject which cross, he being much concerned that nothing shall be done to upset the Home Guards, and I explaining that this was not my proposal and that I do not press for it. A P.Q. is asked and Waterhouse is able to say that 'no decision has been taken' to withdraw these coupons. The thing is then referred back to the Lord President's Committee for reconsideration.

Tuesday 20th July
Have a word with Anderson at the House over Relief. He is now most punctilious in consulting me on these matters, and I suggest to him that once we set up U.N.R.R.A., Leith-Ross should become an international figure, working under Lehman and presiding over the European Committee. He thinks this a good plan and says he will back it.

Wednesday 21st July
Labour Party Policy Sub-Committee. I am unanimously invited to take the Chair. We then unanimously decide to liquidate the Reconstruction Committee. Before the decision is taken, I ask Shinwell's opinion. He replies, very angrily, 'I have no objection to the Committee being wound up.' Then, after the decision, he stamps out of the room. This man has shot his bolt and lost all support on the National Executive.

Meeting of ministers under Lord President on Relief. Leith-Ross comes with me, but he is not at all fit. The usual long yarn about Combined Boards, etc. I am fed up with the whole thing. And, in fact, when the time arrives, we shall just have to chuck into liberated territories whatever we can quickly lay hands on. And this will be so, whatever has been decided, or still left undecided, about U.N.R.R.A. or any other paper constitution, or any report by nutritional or any other inter-Allied experts.

On 22nd July, American troops entered Palermo, the Sicilian capital. Late in the afternoon of 24th July the Fascist Grand Council met in Rome, and in the early hours of the following morning passed a resolution moved by Count Grandi inviting the King to assume command of land, sea and air forces. On the afternoon of 25th July, Mussolini was dismissed and arrested and Marshal Pietro Badoglio became Prime Minister. On 28th July the Fascist Party was formally dissolved, and on the 29th the Italian government announced the arrest of prominent Fascists and the release of political prisoners.

Saturday 24th July

Work on my Location paper. This is gradually improving in shape, but I find it very hard to finish it off.

Gladwyn dines with me. He was to have gone to Washington to try to tie up our plans for post-war settlement with the Americans, but his trip has been postponed. The U.S. government and we have hitherto been working quite separately, e.g. on Armistice terms. There is now a possibility of the Italians surrendering soon, and what then? The U.S. think that we ought to have a military government, and are prepared to install earnest American officers with suitable staffs in every Italian town and village. We think that this would be vastly wasteful and most irritating to all. We should like an Italian anti-Fascist government which would help us to beat the Germans and save us from the administrative bother and waste of manpower of an Occupation. He thought there was much to be said for having the Princess of Piedmont,[1] the Crown Prince's wife, as Regent for her little flaxen-haired boy aged six.[2] She is a Belgian, and he thought this combination might be not unpopular outside as well as inside Italy. I said I thought a Republic would be better, but I recognise that this might mean bringing back some frightful old greybeard such as Sforza[3] as first President. I hoped that there was no prospect of our

1 Princess Marie José, daughter of King Albert I of the Belgians, married the Prince of Piedmont (who reigned from May to June 1946 as King Umberto II of Italy) in 1930. The Prince of Piedmont was the son of King Victor Emmanuel II of Italy and Helena of Montenegro.
2 Victor Emmanuel (b. 1937). Only son and second child of the Prince and Princess of Piedmont.
3 Count Carlo Sforza (1873–1952). Sent to Paris as Ambassador in 1922, and remained abroad thereafter, as an anti-Fascist, following Mussolini's rise to power. Returned to Italy after the fall of Mussolini in 1943. Minister Without Portfolio 1944–5. President of the Council 1945–6. Minister of Foreign Affairs 1947–51.

recognising, after the surrender, Grandi[1] or any of the prominent Fascists. He said there was no fear of this, but that practically everyone in the country had had, in order to keep their jobs, to pretend to be a Fascist. But they were all taking their tesseras off now. I said that I had no desire at all to treat the Italians badly, but I was a little afraid, if we treated them too nicely, of this being used as a precedent for Germany later. It is the latter who have always been the only really dangerous people. Gladwyn and I agreed that, whatever came later, it was obvious sense to discuss with Badoglio,[2] if he showed willingness to give us the unconditional surrender of Italy, and particularly of airfields, ports and rail and road communications, for the continuance of the war against Germany. Further, Gladwyn said, and I agreed, that we ought by now to have had quite a lot of Anglo-American-Russian talks on questions of detail. But the P.M. had been much against bringing in the Russians – 'those Mongols' – to interfere in the affairs of civilised Europe. The Foreign Office had got off, with great difficulty, a telegram to Moscow on our plans. Russian recognition of 'Free Germans' was a hint to us that, if *we* didn't take them into our confidence, they would start doing things on their own. Gladwyn thinks that it is much easier to foretell Russian than American policy over a period. The Russians are very realistic, but may well become 'black reactionaries' after the war. Anyhow, they will consistently pursue what they conceive to be their own interests, and it should not be difficult to agree with them what these interests are, and what ours are, nor need these clash. The Americans, on the other hand, are much subject to tidal waves of sentiment, prejudice and hysteria, and these may go in any direction. F. Rodd[3] in Sicily was Eisenhower's appointment, in order to avoid the possibility of having La Guardia[4] forced upon him. Gladwyn agrees that Rodd has very bad judgment, and that there is a danger, if he has any real influence, of all sorts of undesirable Italians, e.g., Volpi,[5] having a voice in the future. I remind

1 Count Dino Grandi (b. 1895). Italian Minister of Justice 1939–43. Foreign Minister 1929–32. Ambassador in London 1932–9.

2 Marshal Pietro Badoglio (1871–1956). Italian Prime Minister and Minister for Foreign Affairs (after the arrest of Mussolini) July 1943–June 1944. As Badoglio was not appointed to head the government until 25th July, this diary entry must have been misdated (or Dalton placed this part of the conversation on the wrong day). The entry appears to have been dictated on the 27th.

3 F. J. Rennell Rodd, 2nd Baron Rennell of Rodd, q.v., was a Major-General in the Civil Affairs Administration in Italy at this time.

4 Fiorello La Guardia (1882–1947). American lawyer, politician and Mayor of New York 1934–45. Head of the U.S. Office of Civilian Defence 1941–2. Director-General of U.N.R.R.A. March–December 1946. Served in Italy in the First World War, having been U.S. Consul at Fiume in 1902.

5 Count Giuseppe Volpi di Misurata (1877–1947). Fascist Minister of Finance 1925–9.

Gladwyn of how I had had to get rid of Rodd from M.E.W. and of his incredible account, in conjunction with Lord Greene,[1] whose fatuous 'mission' to Rome had been decided on just before I took over, of official Italian inclinations and purposes. I recalled how he had asserted that Mussolini would have sold us large quantities of arms for use against Germany, and might even have come in on our side, had the British War Office not foolishly insisted on including in the list of items to be sold, some particular gun in which the Duce took a special interest. Gladwyn said that he would look up some of the papers of that time and make use of them to try to diminish any possible influence which Rodd might acquire.

He related that when Macmillan[2] brought Makins[3] to see Eisenhower, he said, 'You see, General, this man has come to help me in the same way as Murphy[4] helps you. He represents our Foreign Office in the same way as Murphy represents your State Department.' Whereupon, Ike replied, 'If that's all he represents, you had better tie a stone round his neck and chuck him into the Mediterranean.'

Gladwyn asked me whether I thought there was any chance that the Labour Party would break up. I said, 'No. It may break down, but it will never break up.'

Tuesday 27th July

... [T]o War Cabinet, where for $2\frac{1}{2}$ hours we discuss mainly the financial relations of this country and India, on which the P.M. is most persistent and eloquent. Our debt to them is piling up at the rate of £250 million a year and is already over £800 million. Parliament does not know this, nor does the country and it would be quite intolerable that, when the war ended, we had really to pay all this. The P.M. says that we should (a) tell Parliament the truth and (b) be prepared to put in a counter-claim at the right moment for the cost of defending India from the Japs. Kingsley Wood and I are asked to make papers on the financial and trade aspects of the matter. I say, when asked my opinion by the P.M., first that the size of this debt is quite new to me,

1 Sir Wilfred Greene, 1st Baron (1883–1952). Master of the Rolls 1937–49. Accompanied Lord Rennell on a mission to Italy in 1940, to seek to persuade the Italians to break the Axis Pact. Lord Appeal in Ordinary 1949–50.
2 Harold Macmillan, q.v., was British Minister (and Chairman) of the Advisory Council for Italy 1943–5. Minister Resident at Allied H.Q. in North-West Africa, then in Mediterranean 1942–5.
3 R. M. Makins, q.v., served on the staff of the Minister Resident in North-West Africa, and then in the Mediterranean (with Macmillan) 1942–5.
4 R. D. Murphy (1891–1978). United States Representative in Algiers 1943–4, with rank of Minister. U.S. member of the Advisory Council for Italy under Macmillan 1943–4. Political Adviser (with rank of Ambassador) to Eisenhower 1944–5.

second, that I am sure there would be great indignation in the country at the suggestion that we should have to pay it, and third, that, if we tried, it would make even more difficult the question of our balance of payments.

Friday 30th July

I find the officials, Watkinson, and still more Welch,[1] terrified of the policy of putting London out of bounds for new industries. They think that this would kill all sorts of promising new enterprises as well as being politically impossible. I must rely on my intrepid Temporaries to binge up these palsied Permanents![2]

Lunch with Southwood, whom I have never really met before, but who makes upon me an impression of honesty, common sense and broad humanity, without egoism. Southwood[3] says that Beaverbrook said to him, 'You take all your ideas from your own newspaper; I put my own ideas into mine.' Southwood added, rather pleasantly and simply, that he thought it was quite a good thing to take his own ideas from the *Herald*, since he had confidence in his staff and they were experts to an extent that he would not pretend to be. He said that I was not liked by the *Express* or the *Mail*. I said I knew this.

Tuesday 3rd August

Answer P.Q. on clothes rationing and announce that the basic ration will remain the same for at least five months and children's and industrial supplements go on as before. This is received with less interest than the press and my post bag would have led one to expect. There is more interest in my reply to the Astor woman who, having been convicted last week of illegally soliciting clothes – to wit a fur coat and other articles – from the U.S., and fined £50 and £10 costs, jumps up and asks as an irrelevant Supplementary, whether I think that everyone knows that if they bring clothes into this country from abroad, they must surrender coupons. This, of course, is not the point at all, but I don't want to be led aside, and merely answer, 'I should be very much surprised to hear that any responsible citizen was ignorant of the regulations.' This was much cheered. ...

Dine with Horabin. Half crook and half cracked, I think. He shows

---

1 A. E. Welch (b. 1906). Principal Assistant Secretary, Commercial Relations and Treaties Department at the Board of Trade.
2 Marginal insertion: 'Only test of where to put an industry, Welch thinks, is cost of production even if this brings much more to London!'
3 J. S. Elias, 1st Baron, later 1st Viscount, Southwood (d. 1946). Newspaper proprietor. Chairman and Managing Director of Odhams Ltd, publishers of the *Daily Herald*.

an inclination to join the Labour Party and says that Megan Lloyd George,[1] Clem Davies, and Professor Gruffyd[2] would come with him. Also, he thinks, though I don't – Gwilym [Lloyd George]. He is in touch with 'the old man' but admits that he is getting rather feeble. He talks the usual bunk about trade union domination of the Labour Party and is also furiously anti-Eden. He says that the members of the Labour Party whom he knows and likes best are Shinwell, Aneurin Bevan, Silverman[3] and Bowles! I don't think he would be much catch. Meanwhile, I have procured him an exit permit to go to America on business.

Wednesday 4th August
W. S. Morrison to see me, at my request, to discuss Location of Industry. I don't know how much I can count on him, but he talked very good and encouraging sense today, both on the impossibility of moving large numbers from the Distressed Areas, the need for getting new industries in, and the desirability of stopping the further industrial growth of London, Birmingham, etc.

Thursday 5th August
Labour Party Policy Sub-Committee, with me in the Chair, and Shinwell's resignation accepted without regret, get through a good deal of work in re-arranging all our Committees for the coming year. This is not a bad bunch of chaps now.

Friday 6th August
McGowan to see me in my series of Talks with Big Industrialists on Location. He pretends to be very sympathetic and says that he regards it as a national duty for I.C.I. to help in starting up new enterprises in what would otherwise be post-war depressed areas. We are to discuss particulars further.

The House of Commons went yesterday into recess. What a good thing! I confess to feeling rather sleepy, and look with drowsy distaste towards the *New Statesman*, which would be better named the *Bellyachers' Bulletin*, lying on my desk.

---

1 Megan Lloyd George, later Lady Megan (1902–66). Liberal M.P. for Anglesey 1929–51; Labour M.P. for Carmarthen 1957–66.
2 Professor W. J. Gruffyd (1881–1954). Professor of Celtic at the University College of South Wales and Monmouthshire (Cardiff). Chairman of the National Confederation for the Preservation of Welsh culture.
3 S. S. Silverman (1895–1968). Labour M.P. for Nelson and Colne 1935–68. Pacifist.

Wednesday 11th August
Spend most of the day at Datchet.[1] The two Old Ladies seem quite changeless, and both in better health and mood than when I last saw them.

Thursday 12th August
11 o'clock. Ellen Wilkinson on uniforms for part-time Fire Guards. I tell her that most of my colleagues seem to be suffering from nervous uniformitis, a fantastic disease after four years of war. I say that it is understood that *some* of this crowd have their uniforms already, and I won't inquire just how many. But I won't agree, in principle, to any new class being put in uniform for the first time. We then speak of other things. She says all General Secretaries of trade unions, including her own Hallsworth,[2] would love to be M.P.s. That is why they talk of the House of Commons and of 'politicians' with such studied contempt. She finds much spitefulness against her in her own union because she is a minister.

Tuesday 17th August
Leave for West Leaze – I hope for a week.

Evan Durbin, q.v., and Douglas Jay, q.v., had been closely associated with Dalton's pre-war efforts to rewrite Labour's domestic policy. Both men had written influential books about socialism and socialist economics. Durbin was the author of *The Politics of Democratic Socialism* (1940) and *What Have We to Defend?* (1942), Jay of *The Socialist Case* (1937).

Tuesday 24th August
And so it was, with pretty good weather, except on the one day when I went on a full-sized walk, with Evan Durbin, carrying three bottles of beer, to Uffington, where we picked up his wife[3] carrying luncheon for three persons. It was very windy, even in the ditch running round the earthwork, and, soon after we started off home, it began to rain

1 Dalton's mother, and her companion Mrs Battye, had been living in Datchet, Berkshire, since the death of Canon Dalton in 1931.
2 J. Hallsworth, later Sir Joseph (1884–1974). Secretary-General of the National Union of Distributive and Allied Workers. Ellen Wilkinson, q.v., had been National Organiser of N.U.D.A.W. since 1915. Hallsworth had been a parliamentary candidate in 1918.
3 Marjorie Durbin, née Green (b. 1910). M. 1932.

heavily. We sheltered for a while in a Dutch barn, but were all three quite drenched when we got back. He spent two nights with me, and she one, and, after they had gone, Douglas Jay came for three nights and Peggy for the last one. He was really looking very ill and couldn't walk at all, or do more than sit in the sun. But we played some games of chess and he was much better when he left. I broached with him the possibility of his coming, at last, to the Board of Trade to take part in post-war plans. He would be very good at this, quite apart from my present team of post-warriors being over-driven, reduced by sickness and preoccupied with immediate jobs as well, for he has a quite exceptional knowledge of government factories, what they make, the character of the labour force, the local transport arrangements and the local employment situation. But it is no good my asking for him if he is going to go on being ill. So I left it rather vaguely, while he goes off for three weeks more sick leave.

I kept off shop pretty successfully during the week and cut a lot of grass. But I encouraged these two intelligent visitors to talk, and here are some of the things they said.

Durbin thinks that our post-war troubles will be with the Russians. They will want, soon if not at once, to expand, like every other Great and Growing Power. And then they will begin to threaten our interests. He doubts whether talking to them will be any easier than talking to other lunatics, such as Hitler (I think, and tell him, that all this seems to me too gloomy). ...

He said that none of the Treasury officials knew any economics and this might have disastrous consequences. They only knew about a few strictly limited topics – Public Finance in the narrower sense, Foreign Exchange and the technique of Public Borrowing. If left to themselves, half a dozen high officials at the Treasury would land us with two million unemployed at the end of the war.

He was most optimistic about U-boats, having recently been reading some secret papers. We had, he said, been carefully preparing for some time new weapons and tactics, and we suddenly loosed all these in a blitz against U-boats just over three months ago. The results were terrific, and at least ninety, as had been announced, were destroyed in three months. It was difficult, he thought, to see how they could ever come back again in real force. Meanwhile, imports were pouring in, and the Battle of the Atlantic, he thought, was quite definitely won.

Jay, as I have already said, seemed to me quite ill and in a fuss about his health, food, family, etc.[1] But he said some very intelligent things. He asserts that there are not any fewer passenger trains now running than before the war. Ministry of War Transport pretends to have taken

1 Marginal insertion: 'And morbid about money.'

off some trains and issues bogus time-tables. But, in fact, for every train taken off another runs in duplicate, or makes an engine pull many more coaches. Therefore, many more people than before the war are now trying to travel, and this, not fewer trains, is why there is all this crush and inconvenience. And this, he says, is merely an inflationary symptom, like the unprecedented queues at cinemas, or that quite new phenomenon at London stations, a queue for taxis, including many people who have never driven in a taxi before. People have been given a lot of money and this is headed off, by rationing, etc., from many normal vents, and thus flows in increased volume towards the unblocked vents, including travel.

He says that Sir Andrew Duncan is often very rude to the officials. Once Jay, with a number of others, attended a conference with the Minister, when Sir William Brown,[1] then Permanent Secretary, ventured to say, 'I think it would be best' to do so and so. Whereat the Minister shouted, 'What business have you to think? I don't ask you to think. I am the only person here who need think ......' Sir William Brown, on leaving the room, said to Jay and the rest, 'What can one do, when a lunatic is appointed Minister? He thinks he is Churchill, Beaverbrook and Napoleon rolled into one.' (I think Sir Arnold Overton has relatively a very easy time!) Jay thinks that Duncan is now 'subsiding' and contenting himself with saying to the officials, 'Well, it's an order by the Prime Minister and it must be carried out.' Jay says that officials are always filled with consternation when they hear that 'ministers are intervening' in any matter. For this will surely mean that either a lunatic, or at any rate an unworkable, 'decision' is about to be handed down.

In sharp distinction with Durbin, he believes that it is with the Americans, and not with the Russians, that we shall have our worst post-war troubles. We shall be very much in their power, since they will have a Navy three or four times larger than ours, and a Merchant Navy double or treble ours. They will, therefore, in the last resort, be in a position completely to dictate to us, and to cut off our food supplies if we show independence. This is a state of affairs which has never existed in our history before. When we realise it, we shall not like it at all, and there will be a tendency for us to line up, he thinks, with Western Europe in a combination against American Imperialism. (I think that this, too, like the other prospect, is much too gloomy, and that, given reasonable sense on both sides, though there may be diffi-

1 Sir William B. Brown (1893–1947). Permanent Secretary at the Board of Trade 1937–40. Acting Secretary at the Ministry of Supply 1940–42. Secretary, Petroleum Division, Ministry of Fuel and Power 1942–3; Home Security 1943–5. Permanent Under-Secretary at the Air Ministry 1945–7.

cult moments, there will be no 'last resort'. None the less, as Jay points out, we may have some very troublesome successors to Roosevelt and Hull, who may want to use their undoubted powers harshly.) ...

As to post-war arrangements, Jay is convinced that we cannot just close down R.O.F.s [Royal Ordnance Factories] in places where there would be consequential unemployment running into thousands. It will be necessary either that these R.O.F.s shall go on making arms, even after peace, or that they shall switch over to some other suitable production. For this he thinks there may be additional legal powers required. If so, we should seek them now.

Friday 27th August

Watkinson is still rather frightened of the Barlow Report,[1] and my inclinations in regard to it. He says once more that I, as President of the Board of Trade, should emphasise to my colleagues the economic dangers of too rigid a closing of any area to new industrial development. He is afraid, I think, that I am too conscious of the *social* objections to big cities and the needs of the Distressed Areas to do justice to the other side of the argument. But (a) I refuse to be unduly departmental, particularly when this particular Department on this particular issue has, as I have often told them, such a lousy record, as shown by their evidence to the Barlow Commission, and (b) I am deeply concerned with *economic* considerations when I seek to prevent heavy unemployment in the difficult areas and all the wastes, of fixed capital, etc., involved in labour drift from these areas to the Great Wens. Later this evening I return to redrafting my long-delayed paper on Control of Location, which has been held up, partly because I have had so many other things to do and it has gone a bit stale in my mind, and partly because I have been waiting for the Local Surveys we have been organising, in order to be sure which look like being, in default of remedial action, the blackest post-war areas.[2]

[1] The Royal Commission on the Distribution of the Industrial Population, chaired by Sir Anderson Montague-Barlow, had published its Report in January 1940. The Report urged that Greater London (including the Home Counties) should be put out of bounds for new industrial development, as part of an attack on the concentration of population in urban areas, which it deplored. It also recommended the 'decentralisation or dispersal both of industries and industrial population', and the encouragement of industrial diversification in each region by means of the national planning of industry. Dalton seized on this Report eagerly as ammunition in his fight for the industrial development of areas of high unemployment.

2 In a paper entitled 'Location of Industry and its Control', Dalton urged the Cabinet Reconstruction Committee that arms production should be kept in the old 'Distressed Areas' after the war, and, where this was not possible, ordnance factories should be adapted to civilian production (2nd September 1943; PRO, CAB 87/13 X/P 07917).

Tuesday 31st August
P.M.'s broadcast tonight is as good as ever – I am an addict of his oratory – and there is much emphasis on friendship with Russia and appreciation of their contribution to victory.

Wednesday 1st September
Attlee summons a meeting of myself, Bevin and Morrison, with Piercy[1] and Meade, whom I take with me as an expert, to consider the proposed instructions for our Washington delegates on monetary questions. Bevin is very much afraid we are drifting back to the gold standard, and that we shall be at the mercy of 'an America with a nineteenth-century outlook'. I think the question of the rate of exchange is more important than either (a) the amount of gold, if any, to be subscribed by States joining the Clearing Union, or (b) the currencies in which the Fund can deal, though here it would be much better to restrict dealings to an international currency – Unitas or Bancor – falling back, however, if pressed, on an ingenious suggestion of Meade's that the Fund should only sell sterling to any central bank, on demand of the latter, and should only buy sterling from the Bank of England. But this last is a little too subtle for my colleagues. It is finally agreed that I shall write a letter to Kingsley Wood today and raise the point in Cabinet tomorrow, when the others will back me up if necessary. (I do this, but not much backing up is required next day.)

A 'Meeting Between British and American Experts with Reference to Article VII of the Mutual Aid Agreements' took place in Washington in September 1943. These exploratory talks covered a wide range of post-war economic problems, including commercial policy, and were intended to provide an agenda for further study by the respective governments. The British mission was led by Richard Law, Minister of State. The talks resulted in a broad agreement on the need for a multilateral convention on commercial policy, supplemented by an international trades organisation to interpret it.[2]

---

1 W. Piercy, later 1st Baron (1876–1966). Principal Assistant Secretary at the Ministry of Supply and Ministry of Production, and Personal Assistant to the Deputy Prime Minister, during the Second World War. Formerly L.S.E. lecturer. A Director of the Bank of England 1945–56. A friend of Hugh and Ruth Dalton since L.S.E. student days.
2 See R. N. Gardner, *Sterling-Dollar Diplomacy*, Clarendon Press, Oxford, 1956, pp. 101–9.

Thursday 2nd September

Economist luncheon to celebrate their centenary. A roomful of eminent persons. Keynes, sitting next but one to me, says that he saw my letter to Kingsley Wood on gold, rates of exchange, etc., and quite agreed with it. Speeches by Wood, Montagu Norman and Herbert Morrison, all read from carefully typed scripts. Private secretaries and others had laboured mightily. Wood's was a very good speech, but I am sure he had not looked at it before he rose to deliver it. Montagu Norman said that the Bank 'welcomed instructed criticism', regretted that *The Economist* did not confine itself wholly to finance and the City, and praised the Bank of England for being a private institution animated by public spirit. Morrison made some rather wicked quotations from articles ardently defending the gold standard the week before we came off it, and demanding, on the morrow of the last war, the swift suppression of all controls.

Dine alone with Gladwyn at his flat ...

We discuss the present top lot at the Foreign Office. He says that Cadogan stands out a mile. He is a good influence on the P.M. when left alone with him. He will be sixty this year. He will stick it, out of a sense of duty, till the end of the war, and will then insist on retiring. He wants to be out of it all.

Sargent is even older, very clever, but very sick, nervy and malicious.

Peterson and Newton[1] are grotesque as leading figures.

Then comes Strang. Gladwyn thinks that he will probably succeed Cadogan. He has his points. Gladwyn says there are very few people who could really tackle the job of Permanent Under-Secretary. He thinks Makins could, and he himself could. But both of them would be thought to be too young. We agree that the Civil Service everywhere is very old and tired at the top. It was much better in the last war. Warren Fisher,[2] he says, became Permanent Secretary to the Treasury at the age of forty-three. Of Eden, he says, 'He has antennae in all directions, but no brain. He doesn't read papers, he only sniffs them.' ...

Tomorrow the party leaves by ship for Washington, to engage in 'preliminary, informal, non-committal, purely official, discussions' with the Americans on Article VII ('Monetary, Commercial, Commodity and International Investment Policy'). Law will lead them. A final flutter and telephone call from him tonight, asking whether I don't think we could accommodate old man Hull by agreeing to his bilateral negotiations, even though we still propose a multilateral

1 Sir Basil Newton (1889–1965). Foreign Office 1942–6.
2 In fact, Sir Warren Fisher, q.v., became Permanent Secretary at the Treasury when the First World War was over, at the age of forty.

approach. I am horrified at this and tell him that he can go into all these matters on the boat, but that there are most definite Cabinet decisions on them which Liesching in particular is most competent to explain to him. Someone has been getting at him at the last moment. I suspect Ronald. (But next week it turns out to have been Penrose.) Keynes and Waley will be there for the Treasury; Ronald for the Foreign Office; Liesching, Meade and Shackle[1] for me; Robbins for the Economic Secretariat, and a few secretaries as well. There are very great possibilities in these talks, but we are getting very close to that 'night wherein no man can work' in American politics, i.e., the month before the Presidential campaign. Anyhow, the delegates are well instructed and a pretty able lot. (I ring up Liesching, who has left the office to pack his bags, and tell him of Law's conversation with me. I rely on him to coach Law on the boat.)

The instructions are finally passed at a War Cabinet today. The points put by me in my letter to Wood were well received and generally supported, particularly the need to avoid having the value of sterling tied too tightly either to gold or to any other currency. I argue, moreover, against allowing the right to depreciate our exchange being decided by a vote in an International Governing Body. We should, I said, and this was generally supported, aim at some objective statistical test, as in our proposals on quantitative import restrictions in the Commercial Union scheme. Wood undertook to instruct the delegates in this sense before they left.

Monday 6th September

Kingsley Martin to dine with me at Josef's. As usual, he seems to get everything wrong way up. He began with a great denunciation of 'your friends the Poles'. He said they were all bent on fighting the Russians. I asked him what Poles he knew. The answer seemed to be none at all except Szapiro.[2] I took him through all their leading personalities and he had to admit he had met none of them. He asked what I would do with Poland, and I said move her physically to the west and politically to the Left. I asked whether he would resist Poland getting East Prussia. He said he didn't like it at all, but didn't think he would resist it. I said another alternative was that Poland might become a Soviet Socialist Republic. He said this would mean the most horrible resistance and massacre, and agreed with me that the fact that the Poles were Roman Catholics made this solution particularly difficult.

1 G. L. S. Shackle (b. 1903). Statistical Branch, Prime Minister's Office 1939–45. Professor of Economics at Liverpool University 1951–69.
2 Jerzy Szapiro (1893–1962). Principal Secretary at the Polish Ministry of Reconstruction. Journalist. Warsaw correspondent on the *Daily Herald* 1926–39.

He seemed quite incredulous that anyone, anywhere in the Government, was taking an interest whatever in any post-war problems. I naturally could not tell him much, except that he was wrong. He was afraid – he is always physically afraid of someone – of the Eighth Army on their return to England. Attempts were being made, he said, already to organise them as a political force. He had heard of some man who had been going about the City, with the approval of some Generals, trying to raise a large sum of money to use this military force as a 'Fascist' instrument. How bored I am with this dreary old bogy, appearing always in new hysterical disguises! And they will have to invent some new epithet in place of 'Fascist' now. Also he was afraid, as always, in the years before the war, of Mosley and of the 18B *détenus.*[1] They might have great influence when they got out. They were, he had heard, all keeping careful notes of everything that was said or printed against them. And they would start a tremendous lot of libel actions when they came out and might arouse great public sympathy. He thought it was a great mistake that Morrison had not published something to show that he had some real case against Mosley. I said I didn't believe any of this at all. It would be enough to discredit them to ask on whose side they had been before and at the beginning of the war. Also to ask Mosley where he had married and who his witnesses were. Martin was quite astonished when I said the answers were: in Berlin, Hitler and Goering.

I said that all this would much better be published later on. Timing was essential. If published now it would be forgotten. It had been published years ago and forgotten already. In reply to his bleating questions about the political near-future, I said that here again much turned on timing. We had in the Labour Party, I said, too many experts in the art of losing elections, and too many people who specialised in total ignorance of the views and sentiments of the great mass of their neighbours.[2] It would, I said, be total lunacy to fight an election, if it could be avoided, against the present Prime Minister while the laurels of victory were still bright upon his brows. Martin agreed that we must lose in such a case, but was inclined to think that it might be the best thing to do, in the circumstances. This led to my last remark. I said I had now reached an age in political life when I wanted either to have power or to retire and plant trees. I was not interested

---

1 '18B *détenus*': those detained under the extended powers given by Defence Regulation 18B (1A), in May 1940. The Regulation was used against fascists, anti-Semitic propagandists and others, mainly on the extreme right, whose views or conduct were believed to be prejudicial to national security.
2 Marginal insertion: 'I once told Cole, "We must win power by the votes of the football crowds." He was terribly shocked!'

any more in impotent gyrations in Opposition. Therefore, my simple plan was, though it might be quite impossible to execute it, to continue an all-party government, and to screw as much good policy as we could out of our colleagues while it lasted, until such time as we could fight an election and *win it* with a Labour majority. Also I judged it most important that we should have many younger and more interesting candidates. He seemed to think it quite impossible that any of this could happen. He also said that I was still, it seemed, conceiving politics in terms of the old parties. I said I was. You could change the contents of a political bottle more easily than the label, and these old bottles were very hard to break. He was inclined to agree, but wondered whether there might not be some 'regrouping'. I asked what sort. He said, 'A Centre Party, for instance.' On this I quoted my favourite dictum of Harcourt's. 'I have heard much talk in my time of Centre Parties. I know them all. All centre and no circumference.' He said he agreed. The trouble is he always does say he agrees with whoever is speaking to him at the moment. Then he meets someone else and agrees with *him*. I quote the saying, though not the author, that Eden had 'no brain, but antennae in all directions'. Martin said that this was the exact opposite of Cripps. I told him I thought campaigning against Attlee as Leader of the Labour Party, as Laski did in his articles in the *New Statesman* and elsewhere, did no good at all, but rather harm since it generally sapped confidence and could have no effect, except perhaps in the opposite direction to that intended, on the leadership.

This, I reminded him, was determined, not by any general sentiments of public opinion, nor by the Annual Conference of the Labour Party, nor even by the T.U.C. and the 'trade union bosses', but by the members of the Parliamentary Labour Party. And these, quite certainly, had no intention at all of making a change. These tired old men were enthusiastic for social security, and applied this to the Party leadership as well. 'Too much Beveridge!' he said. I added that, after an election, with much new blood, it might be very different. My own attitude was well known. I had always preferred Morrison and had done my best, first to get him the leadership and later the treasurership of the Party. Both efforts had failed. Martin invited me to one of his *New Statesman* lunches. He said I should meet Laski, Brailsford[1] and Vallance.[2] I said I should enjoy this very much. A queer creature. ...

Wilmot has just returned from ten days in West Cumberland. He is very pleased at the progress he seems to have made towards the suc-

1 H. N. Brailsford (1873–1958). Socialist journalist and propagandist. Editor of the *New Leader* 1922–6. Leader-writer successively on the *Manchester Guardian, Daily News* and *Nation*.

2 A. Vallance (1892–1955). Journalist. Editor of the *News Chronicle* 1933–6.

cession to Tom Cape.[1] ... Archie Rowe[2] is ... very keen that Wilmot should have it. And so, oddly enough, is Cape himself who has a special link with the Wilmot family. In 1934 he told Wilmot he was tired of living in a hotel and would like a suitable lodging in London. He lodged for six months with Wilmot's mother, and hence has a warm personal feeling towards the family. I have told Wilmot how great a blessing it is to move from a London constituency, which makes a stale slave of one, to a northern constituency, where greater native loyalty blends with much greater distance to make one's rarer visits much more highly appreciated.[3] Rowe told Wilmot to tell me to beware lest in the redistribution in Durham Lawther might contrive something to my disadvantage. I spoke the other day to Shepherd, and went into the figures. It is clear that County Durham must lose at least one member, and much the smallest electorate is Barnard Castle, only 46 per cent of the quota. Next smallest are Spennymoor and Bishop Auckland, each between 70 and 75 per cent of the quota. All these three lie together and compose South-West Durham. Therefore, much the easiest and most obvious adjustment would be to split Barnard Castle into two roughly equal halves, as regards electors, and to join one to Spennymoor and one to me. This would bring both of us close on 100 per cent of the quota. I should think that I could comfortably carry my half of Barnard Castle, even though it would contain the town of Barnard Castle itself and a substantial rural area. But some mining communities would be bound to come in too. My constituency, in that case, would be increased by about one-third in electorate, but doubled, or perhaps trebled, in area. In much of this area, however, particularly if it included the higher reaches of Teasdale and Weardale, there are very few inhabitants, though much natural beauty. I am not, therefore, much bothered by this prospect. An alternative and less convenient procedure would, of course, be to keep Barnard Castle in existence and bring it up to quota by adding bits from each of the other two, the residues of these two being merged into a second constituency. This would mean splitting the Bishop Auckland Division, which would be a bore. But it would also mean making the area of the Barnard Castle Division uncomfortably large. I don't think this plan would have much support. But I must discuss this when I am in the North next month.

1 Thomas Cape (1868–1947). Labour M.P. for Workington 1918–45.
2 Councillor Archie Rowe. Full-time party agent for Workington.
3 Dalton was elected as Labour M.P. for Peckham in 1924. Following a row with his local party, however, he decided not to stand again for the same seat, and in 1928 he was selected for Bishop Auckland.

Tuesday 7th September

Watkinson reports progress. He is still perturbed about my Location policy. I tell him that I have told Overton that it is 'against the constitution' for any of my officials now to say anything outside the Department in conflict with my own views. I find this long semi-resistance getting rather irritating. ...

Ruth comes to dine with me in the office, after which we two and Simmonds go to the B.B.C. where I broadcast after the 9 o'clock News. ... I am told that it went well. Indeed, all the early opinions were quite favourable. John Wilmot, whom I find waiting for me later, said that he had been afraid it might go badly, but that it was most strikingly good, and very much better than I did at M.E.W. (Pulham, bringing me my tea and papers next morning, said that he had enjoyed it very much. It was 'all plump and plain'.) Wilmot said that I managed my voice much better than usual, and avoided a 'schoolmasterly tone', which sometimes crept in, as with his brother Horace! Wilmot had originally thought my script looked rather too much like baby talk, talking down to the audience, but, he said, it did not come over at all like that, and a number of his constituents assembled round his radio at his Committee Rooms enjoyed it very much.

On 15th August, Badoglio, head of the new Italian government, secretly sued for peace. Organised resistance to the Allies in Sicily ceased on 17th August but the Germans by this time had begun to make preparations for massive troop reinforcements in Italy. An armistice agreement was reached with Badoglio on 3rd September, and made public five days later. Meanwhile on 2nd September an Allied division landed without opposition at Taranto, and was quickly joined by two more divisions. Further landings followed at Reggio di Calabria on 3rd September and Salerno on 8th–9th September. At Salerno, there was strong resistance: but after a few days' heavy fighting the Allied armies found it possible to link up and capture airfields at Foggia. Naples was taken on 1st October.

The public announcement of Italy's capitulation on 8th September, as well as the landings, had an important psychological effect. The loss of a major, though weakened, ally also had an immediate impact on German strategy, compelling Hitler to take divisions from the Russian Front to reinforce Italy and to replace Italian garrisons in the Balkans. It also eliminated the Italian fleet, and by making available the equipment of several Italian divisions, turned Tito's guerrillas in Yugoslavia into a powerful army.

Wednesday 8th September

12.20. Meeting of ministers of Cabinet rank specially summoned at Foreign Office. Eden informs us that at 5.30 p.m. this afternoon Eisenhower will announce Italian unconditional surrender and the granting of an Armistice, the terms of which cannot, for obvious reasons, yet be published. They would tell the Germans too much and give them a chance to try counter-measures. Political, economic and financial terms to be imposed will be announced later. Negotiations were opened some weeks ago by the Italian General C, who came to Lisbon and said Badoglio would like to change sides and fight with us against the Germans, Italy thus becoming a United Nation. (This was the first really serious approach, though there had been other unimportant ones before.) It had to be explained that things could not be done so simply. So he returned, though he took an unexplained long time getting from Lisbon to Rome. Then there came another Italian General, Z, who discussed upon a basis of reality, and the arrangements for the surrender were made. The Armistice was, in fact, signed in Sicily last Friday, i.e. five days ago. But it could not be announced till now. The Russians, as well as the Americans and ourselves, are associated, and in agreement, with the action taken. There will be other striking developments within the next week.

Bevin, just returned from the Southport T.U.C., is, as usual, very full of himself. He says he was particularly pleased because he got a much greater ovation from the delegates than did the Russian visitors. This was when he was first introduced by the Chairman. After he had finished his speech, the applause first died down and then rose up again. He received a series of deputations in his hotel while he was there. There was, he thought, growing resentment among the delegates at the domineering attitude of the General Council towards the floor and at the nagging attitude of Citrine in particular against Labour ministers. ...

I incite Ellen Wilkinson to be on my side over Location. She says she doesn't want again to have to lead a march from Jarrow. She thinks that Sir Kingsley Wood and Sir Richard Hopkins paralyse leading permanent officials everywhere. All know that their future careers depend on Treasury approval. I think this old tale is a bit over-told. But she is quite right to say that Hurst is a most evil influence and that Jowitt is as weak as a rabbit in dealing with him, though he detests him personally. ...

We all sit round in the Private Office and listen to the 6 o'clock, and also to the 9 o'clock, News. It isn't easy to assess how large or how swift the consequences are likely to be. There are said to be nearly twenty German divisions in Italy, and these brutes will, I suppose, make a good deal of resistance. The Italians are now being encouraged, by Eisenhower and by Badoglio himself, to turn against the Germans. Eden said today that Eisenhower was most anxious to make the fullest possible use of Italian assistance. On the other hand, most of them are utterly sick of the war and will be little use. But we shall gain soon many valuable vantage points and the German forces will soon be seen to be spread too thinly to hold all their outposts. Meanwhile also the Russians are advancing at great speed over a wide front.

Thursday 9th September
See three of my colleagues on my Location of Industry paper:

(1) Morrison, accompanied by Ellen Wilkinson. He begins quite well by saying that he agrees with a large number of my propositions. But goes on less well, thinking that we should have more details, and that trying to redistribute unemployment between different areas is dodging the larger question of how to maintain full employment everywhere. Not very good.

(2) Kingsley Wood. He, of course, wants to hang things up until we have a lot more reports from the Steering Committee, and produces a note from Hopkins, who is away on leave, promising that the Steering Committee will have a report on other aspects of all this by the end of this month. Wood says that Portal[1] came to see him and said that we couldn't possibly tell now which areas would be most distressed at the end of the war, and that I was 'in too much of a hurry'. I said that Portal had told me quite the opposite, namely that my proposals were very good, that he supported them and would like to be on the proposed committee.

(3) Bevin. Much the best of the three on my paper. He has a real understanding of the problem, and says that his man Phillips has submitted a paper very much on the same lines as my own, to be sent to Overton. It has not yet come, but he will have it sent off at once. He suggests that we should co-operate.

...

All are still agog over events in Italy. There are rumours of landings everywhere and of far-reaching repercussions all through Occupied and satellite Europe. And Persia tonight has declared war on Germany!

It was very lucky I got in my broadcast on Tuesday, the night before

---

1 Sir Wyndham Portal, q.v.

the Italian news broke. Otherwise, I should have been quite blanketed. Meanwhile, Beaverbrook is blanketed, in his attacks on me. I always speak of him now as 'That asthmatic ape'. Meanwhile, I have, as yet, received *no* abusive letters regarding my broadcast, but quite a number of complimentary ones and many of the usual type, beginning with general approval and going on to some particular grievance.

Saturday 11th to Sunday 12th September
At West Leaze. Dine on arrival with the Browns. Mrs Brown much thrilled by my broadcast. She thought the ladies particularly liked being directly addressed about their stockings.

Tuesday 14th September
Cripps to see me on Location. He cannot say yet what will be done with all his factories after the war. Unless they keep them going in Bristol, there will be heavy unemployment there![1] He thinks it is all part of a much larger question. So they all say. About the most sensible letter from any of my colleagues on my Location paper is from Gwilym Lloyd George, who really deals with practical points as they arise. I have hopes of him as a good ally. ...

Dine with Attlee, just back from a week's holiday in Cardiganshire. He says the position at Salerno is not so bad as alarmists have been saying. (Bevin and Portal this afternoon have been glooming frightfully. 'Another Dunkirk.' 'The Americans have given way in the south.' 'You can't direct a war by political instructions from Washington,' etc.) I press Attlee to press the P.M., at a suitable moment after his return, to think of post-war tactics. The easiest way would be not to hurry a post-war election, provided we could hold our own people from reckless disengagement. They are great experts, we agree, at suicide. I also suggest that we might try to get the P.M. to address, on some suitable occasion, our own Party Meeting. Attlee is much fitter and fresher and in pretty good form and sensible. But he really doesn't, one feels, have an effective pull on the Party.

Thursday 16th September
An hour with Halifax. As full of charm as ever, but very airy and unattached to earthly detail on monetary and commercial policy. He thinks, on my exposition of the Commercial Union, that this should appeal to Hull. He is, Halifax thinks, a very fine old man, very Nineteenth Century and 'quite pathological about North Africa' and France generally. [Sumner] Welles is resigning, not through any diff-

---

1 Sir Stafford Cripps was M.P. for Bristol South-East.

erence of view on policy, but because Bill Bullitt's[1] 'smearing campaign' against his private life has attracted much attention. The President has had to pay some heed to it, and, Halifax says, it seems that the allegations made are not wholly untrue.[2] This is a great pity, for Welles is a fine man and has greatly improved in the last few years. In particular, he is now much more of our way of thinking on Russia. He is now always on the look-out to prevent the appearance of snubs or neglect and is much more accommodating over their western frontier. He says now, e.g., that he thinks the U.S. has been too rigid about the Baltic States. It is being suggested that he should go to Moscow for the Foreign Secretaries' talk. Eden, Halifax thinks, is quite justified in being a bit annoyed because it is always thought that 'London is untouchable' as a place for talks between the Big Three. Halifax says that he would not say this 'outside the walls of this room', but that he thinks the P.M. somewhat idolises the President. The latter is most uncomfortably susceptible to political breezes. Once recently he made a certain statement about Russia 'at the Pacific Council, where, as you know, we discuss everything except the Pacific, with the Chinese, the Dutch, the Australians, the New Zealanders, etc.' When Halifax reported this home ('You know how we have to fill up our telegrams with little bits of gossip'), interest was taken and he was asked to find out more exactly what the President meant. But, when he asked Welles to pursue it, the latter replied, by telephone, that he had spoken to the President, who had flatly denied ever saying any such thing. This had made Halifax feel that 'The President is, perhaps, a little like Lloyd George. You never quite know when you have got him, or whether he will not slip through your fingers.' Hull, he thought, was apt to feel a little hurt and indignant at the 'rough treatment' he sometimes received from the P.M., and by his 'cyclonic manner'.

The President was now quite keen to meet Stalin. He had at first thought it would be better for them to meet *à deux*, since the P.M. had already met them both separately, and Stalin might think that, at a meeting *à trois*, he would be out-numbered by 2 to 1. The President, therefore, had played with the idea of meeting Stalin in Alaska. But he had now given this up, since Stalin seemed to like the notion of a

---

1 W. Bullitt (1891–1967). Special Assistant Secretary to the U.S. Navy 1942–3. U.S. Ambassador to Russia 1933–6; France 1936–41. President Roosevelt's special representative in the Near East 1941.

2 Marginal note: 'That he was homosexual.' Rumours that Welles was to resign began in August. His resignation – apparently on the grounds of disagreements with Hull – was not confirmed until September. At the time, it was thought that Welles would be offered a roving Ambassadorship, or some other compensation for the loss of his post, but he never held high office again.

talk *à trois*, and it was now likely that, after the ground had been prepared by the Foreign Secretaries, the three Big Men would meet at Teheran. It was essential, Halifax thought, that they should settle here the question of Russia's post-war western frontiers. Otherwise, the Russians would soon be arriving in debatable districts, and there might well be risings and bloodshed, e.g. as between Russians and Poles. This would produce the most shocking impression. We and the U.S. should try to make a reasonable bargain on behalf of the Poles and push them hard towards accepting it. Sikorski had said to him that no government-in-exile could, of its own free will, agree to the cession of any part of the national territory. But such a solution might be imposed by stronger allies. (It was typical, Halifax said, of the President's approach to such matters, that he had once said that there were more Lithuanians in the U.S. than in Lithuania, and that he must take account of this in deciding his attitude towards the Russian claim.)

We then spoke of post-war politics. Halifax thought it would be very bad if the Coalition broke up soon after victory in Europe. He had spoken both to Bevin and Morrison on this, and both agreed with him. He asked my view. I said that it was most desirable to re-juvenate this Parliament, and I had toyed with the view that we might have an agreed programme, backed by the three party leaders, but that in each constituency each party should be free to run its own candidates. ... Halifax said he liked this idea very much, and that Morrison had propounded something of the same kind. I said that I had first propounded it to Morrison, who then had thought it pro-bably impracticable. Halifax said he thought the P.M. would prefer to go on into the Peace with a National Government, if we would play. But, if he were suddenly to be irritated by some intransigence or awkwardness by the Labour Party or the T.U.C., he might lose his temper and plunge for an election. There were, Halifax said, various people, including Kingsley Wood, of whom he evidently has a low opinion, who had rejected any such idea as that put up by me. And they had, unfortunately, more influence than they deserved with the P.M. Halifax thought it was a pity the P.M. had become Conservative Party Leader. It would have been better to let old Salisbury have this. He hoped that I, and my Labour Party colleagues, would do our best to win over the more long-headed [*sic*] of our Party to our view. I said that, of course, if we plunged back to a party fight, there was no doubt that the P.M. and the Tories would sweep the board. I did not think, however, that this would be good for the country. In particular, it would not be good that we should be officially absent from the Peace Conference. Last time great evil followed from the fact that the Labour

Party were not in at the peace-making, and therefore went much too far, in after years, in criticising the Treaty, and hence, almost necessarily, in supporting our ex-enemies against ex-allies. Halifax quite agreed with this, and added that such a Tory sweep would be very bad, after a short interval, for the Tory Party itself. Any government holding office immediately after the war would soon become most unpopular. Even the P.M.'s popularity would soon fade if we got into economic and financial difficulties at home. After a very short time, there would be a tremendous sweep against a purely Tory government in the post-war years, and the Tories would be violently swept out again.

Monday 20th September
Lunch with Němec[1] ... [who] says that he knows nothing of the whereabouts of his wife and family. Nečas[2] is ill, he says, largely because he thinks *his* wife and daughter have been executed by the Germans. Beneš has just heard that a brother of *his* has just been executed. Kosina[3] has heard that his wife and children have been made 'hostages' by the Germans.

Meeting of Reconstruction Priorities Committee, to which I go to present the argument that not all building labour and materials must go to dwelling houses, but some to industrial buildings, including repair of these. Portal, who presents 'the main paper, in which the Board of Trade is not mentioned at all, gives me the impression, even at 4.30 p.m., of having drunk a great deal at luncheon. He looks blearily around and successively agrees with all his critics. 'I quite agree with you my dear chap ...... That is exactly what I meant ...... We should always be hand in glove ...... ' The paper is referred back, for the second or third time running, for further consideration. The status of the Board of Trade is recognised.

Late tonight Watkinson brings me the latest draft of his Location paper. It is really quite good, though I suggest various amendments. There are many ingenious suggestions in it, and it is not any longer out of line with my own thought and written statements of policy.

---

1 František Němec (1902–63). Social Democrat Minister for Social Welfare in the Czech government-in-exile.
2 Jaromír Nečas (1885–1945). Czech Socialist Minister for Social Welfare 1935–8. Member of the governing body of the International Labour Office. Fled to Britain in 1940, and served in the Czech government-in-exile.
3 J. K. Kosina. Czech Military Intelligence officer before the war.

Tuesday 21st September

Kingsley Wood died this morning, quite suddenly. Only yesterday he had been very alert, cheerful and sensibly talkative at the Reconstruction Priorities Committee. It was his heart. He had been in office twelve years running and was sixty-two. I found him, as a colleague, personally agreeable, always shrewd, often helpful, though sometimes deliberately deceptive and one of the principal obstructionists to the taking of decisions. He was a bad influence, in the last respect, on the P.M. He was more of a professional machine politician than any other Conservative member of the Cabinet. From this point of view his disappearance is likely to be a good thing.

Parliament reassembles after six weeks' recess, and, though this is my day, none of my Questions are reached. [Sir James] Grigg makes a worse fool of himself than usual and is howled at from all quarters of the House. The P.M. makes a very long speech, with an hour's adjournment in the middle. It is, almost wholly, powerful and persuasive.

Churchill, Roosevelt and other Allied war leaders met in Quebec in mid-August to discuss future strategy.

Wednesday 22nd September

Dine alone with Bruce Lockhart, whom I have not seen for some time. He is very full of himself, and how hard he works. He is now labelled, he says, at the Foreign Office as a Russian, and no longer as a Czechoslovak, expert. He is bothered about the prospects of the two Anglo-American-Soviet conferences. The Russians will definitely want to talk details, about frontiers, etc. There is still great reluctance to do this, on the part of the P.M. and, he thinks, the Americans. Eden, on the other hand, would like to do it, and went out to Quebec boasting that he would 'bell the cat'. But he didn't. Lockhart says that Eden's relations with the P.M. are good, but 'because he pays the price' of always giving in. Lockhart thinks that there is a distinct danger of the Russians being alienated by our reluctance to talk. Stalin, he says, won't come further out than to Teheran, though he has been urged to do so, in semi-humorous telegrams, pointing out that the other two are 'old men', more easily fatigued than he by long journeys. But Stalin's life would be in danger in, e.g., Cairo. The Russians, Lockhart thinks, are sitting holding two scales, in the one our twenty years'

Treaty and collaboration, in the other a policy of deliberately foment-
ing, as of old, disturbance and chaos everywhere, save in German–
Russian relations, which would again become ordered and intimate.
He is pretty sure they would prefer the former, but, if they grow too
vexed with us, may turn to the latter. They are brimful of suspicions
of all kinds, which will need much exorcising.

As to Italy, Eisenhower wants Badoglio to be fully recognised at
once, as an ally. The P.M. had stood up to this a bit, and Eden stood
up to the P.M. till 3 a.m. on his return, insisting that recognition should
be conditioned by a broadening of the base of Badoglio's Government
to include men from all the parties of the Left, including the Communists. He thinks the P.M. finally stuck to this in the telegram to
Washington drafted in the small hours. There was, Lockhart says,
great confusion, even among the Chiefs of Staff, as to the date and
hour of the Armistice. It might easily have come out twenty-four hours
wrong either way!

I said that I was much perturbed lest an easy settlement with the
Italians, which, on isolated merits, I would favour, should be treated
as a precedent for the Germans. I was delighted that the P.M. had
said so vehemently in the House yesterday that the German case was
quite different. Lockhart said that he was afraid the Americans were
weakening on this too, and Warburg,[1] of the American P.W.E., was
arriving today to reconsider policy towards Germany.

Lockhart spoke also of the latest developments in the dim under-
world of S.O.E., P.W.E., etc. (I said that I had grown used now to the
sunlit spaces and clearly marked frontiers of the upper earth.) He
said that Charles Hambro had certainly been responsible for poisoning Selborne's mind against Gladwyn Jebb, who had been 'for a while
quite down and out', but had been taken up again by Cadogan and
now was, he heard, again doing very well. Looking back, the trouble
from the start had been the jealousy between Leeper, conscious of his
seniority and at the same time of his physical remoteness from me,
and Jebb. Hambro had been dismissed partly because he didn't concentrate sufficiently on his work, and partly as a scapegoat for a first-
class row in the Middle East. It seems that S.O.E. had been extracting
the wrong kind of Greeks from Greece, contrary to the desires of our
High Command. Glenconner – I said that I thought well of him – had
also been blamed for this, and Leeper, who, of course, had been on
the other side, had gone to bed in high fever. Many of the Greeks in
question were strongly anti-King, and it was still the policy of H.M.G.

---

1 J. P. Warburg (1896–1969). American author. Deputy Director (U.S. Propaganda
  Policy) of the Office of War Information, Europe 1942–4.

to back the King – up to a point. The military in the Middle East had now demanded that S.O.E. there should come under them (this was a claim made in my time). Selborne had been summoned to a Defence Committee and had 'read a paper for an hour and a quarter'. At the end everyone had been bored and sleepy, and it had been decided that Lyttelton should act as umpire. The scale of S.O.E. and P.W.E. had both expanded enormously, and so had the 'integrated Anglo-American organisation'. Listening to all this, I felt rather glad it was no longer my province.

Following Sir Kingsley Wood's death, Sir John Anderson became Chancellor of the Exchequer with a seat in the War Cabinet, the appointment taking effect on 28th September. Attlee replaced Anderson as Lord President of the Council, and Cranborne took over Attlee's responsibility for Dominion Affairs. R. K. Law became Minister of State, and Lord Beaverbrook returned to the Government as Lord Privy Seal.

Monday 27th September

... [L]unch with the *New Statesman*. They give one a damned good lunch, and I was interested to see the gang who run this often most irritating and unreal paper – Kingsley Martin himself, Cole,[1] Brailsford (whom I had not seen for years), Driberg[2] (who is now their Parliamentary Correspondent), Aylmer Vallance, Joad (only a recent addition to these lunches, I gather), Roberts[3] and an eager, bright-eyed young man whose name I didn't catch. They are terribly concerned with things which matter, relatively, very little, e.g. whether Polish and Czechoslovak citizens who, generally, no doubt, being Jews, don't want to join the Polish or Czechoslovak armed forces, are *really* being given an effective option to join the British instead; further, whether such persons, joining the British forces, ought to be

---

1 G. D. H. Cole (1889–1959). Socialist writer, publicist and organiser; author of detective novels. Fellow of University College, Oxford 1925–44; Chichele Professor of Social and Political Theory, Oxford 1944–7. Earlier he had been associated with the Guild Socialist movement. In 1931, he and his wife Margaret had founded the New Fabian Research Bureau.
2 T. E. N. Driberg, later Baron Bradwell (1905–76). Independent M.P. for Maldon 1942–5; Labour 1945–55. Labour M.P. for Barking 1959–74.
3 R. E. Roberts (1879–1955). Literary Editor of the *New Statesman and Nation* 1930–32. Journalist.

terrorised by threats from their co-nationals that they will be given hell after the peace, having so opted, and whether, having effectively opted, they ought to be compelled to serve in the British Pioneer Corps rather than any other units, and whether they can be protected from ill treatment from the British, as well as from their own co-nationals. I said, rather bluntly, on all this, that a definite statement had been made that the option was genuine, but that, having opted, they couldn't really be so bloody choosy, and that some of them seemed to think they were entitled, as refugees, to contract right out of the war. These remarks of mine at any rate had the effect of shutting the subject up. I then talked to them pretty freely and off the record on personalities and tendencies within the Government; on the incredible indecisions, some calculated and some not, which beset our post-war plans; on the evil influence of the late Sir Kingsley Wood in this regard, and on the utter futility of the still faintly breathing Sir William Jowitt. I urge them to urge the Government to make its mind up some time on Barlow, Uthwatt, Scott,[1] etc.

Asked what my views were about a Coalition after the war and an election, I said my view was most profoundly simple. Next time we had a general election, I wanted to win it. And this could not be done if the Labour Party merely arranged for a duel between itself and the present Prime Minister, while he stood at or near the highest pinnacle of his fame. This remark also seemed to have a damping effect upon further discussion of this topic.

My God! At what astronomical distances this mob live from the Great Simplicities! Their cleverness is all. But it was quite a pleasant occasion, and I think they liked me being there. The article in the next Number, on Home Front, was pretty good, and reflected, without divulging anything awkward, a number of my suggestions.

Call on Attlee for the first time since the Government changes. I asked whether he personally wished to be congratulated or not, on translation from Dominions Secretary to Lord President. He wasn't sure, and, throughout the talk, seemed rather glum. He said he had protested violently against the reintroduction of the Beaver. I said I hoped the latter wouldn't intermeddle with any of *my* affairs. Attlee said that every minister was saying this. All the Home Front ministers wanted him to go abroad, but the Foreign Office were eager he should stay at home. Anyhow, I said, if he went on attacking me personally in the *Express*, I should now be able to take it up with him officially. Anderson will keep on Reconstruction Priorities Committee, which Attlee will now join for the first time. He will himself take on the Lord

1 Report of the committee set up in 1941 under Lord Justice Scott to consider the future of the countryside.

President's Committee. I said that Jowitt was no damned good at all, and that his staff was lousy; it would be much better to wash out his job completely, push Simon off the woolsack, and sit Jowitt in his place. It could then be said that Attlee, as Lord President, was generally responsible for 'co-ordinating' post-war stuff. He admitted that Jowitt's position was 'being considered'. I said he was quite useless as a politician, though no doubt a good lawyer. Attlee didn't disagree. As regards the Foreign Office, he said the P.M. was very insistent that there should be a trade unionist there as Parliamentary Under-Secretary, and that the P.M. himself picked George Hall. Attlee, as I knew, had Hall next on the list for a No. 1 office. He repeated again tonight that he had done very well at the Colonial Office under Lloyd, and had frequently stood up for his own ideas. I said I was sure he would do all right at the Foreign Office, but that it was a pity he was sixty-two, and so had little power of growth. Why not, I asked, Creech Jones? Attlee thought that answering Foreign Office questions in the House was a skilled business, which Hall might be trusted to do well, but that perhaps Creech Jones would make some blunders. He was, I repeat, rather glum throughout our talk. The only time he really smiled was when I asked, 'In view of all this shove-halfpenny business, am I to understand that I am to go on being President of the Board of Trade?' Whereat he smiled most affably and said, 'Of course.'

Wednesday 29th September

Ministers' meeting at Foreign Office on Malkin Report.[1] I thought it not a bad meeting, since all were agreed that we should go at least as far as the main propositions of the Report. Even Attlee, always apt to be shaky on such points, said that he was in favour of lopping off some extremities of Germany. But Selborne and Cherwell, both probably feeling a bit 'left out', thought that we should dismember Germany, and that therefore this plan was based on a wrong assumption. Anderson pompously took the same view. Eden said that he was still a bit inclined to favour dismemberment, though difficulties had been pointed out. He thought we should at least encourage any separatist tendencies. I said that, even if we adopted dismemberment, there were still many points in the Report which held good, e.g. destruction of synthetic oil plants, loaning of labour service and contribution to cost of occupation and peace-keeping, also removal of machine tools, etc. The two main dissentients argued, however, that the levy for peace-keeping was in any case quite inadequate and should be in-

1 Marginal note: 'On "Reparations and Security".' Sir William Malkin (1883–1945). Legal Adviser to the Foreign Office 1929–45.

creased. It was finally agreed that we should leave it over, until a decision had been taken as to whether we favoured dismemberment or not.

Gladwyn Jebb, whom I saw later, was horrified at the report he had had from Coulson[1] of the meeting. He said that Selborne and the Prof were both very stupid about this. The former thought of Germany in purely anthropomorphic terms. You kill your enemy and then cut him up into little bits. But this had no real meaning. As to the Prof, he would tell him that he understood that he wanted to be much more kind to Germany and to set up a lot of little Badoglios whom we would have to pet and encourage.

Friday 1st October
Take out to lunch my Australian 'second-cousin-once-removed' (?) Douglas, whom I met in Sydney in 1938 at the house of his father, who is my reprobate and near-convict uncle's son, 'Cousin George'. Quite a pleasant lad, now a Pilot Officer in the R.A.A.F.,[2] but not violently exciting. (How seldom one's relations are!) I put him in the train to Datchet where he will pay a dutiful visit to my mother.

Saturday 2nd to Sunday 3rd October
At West Leaze. More than 800 American soldiers are now billeted in the villages round here, and –

Monday 4th October
– as I am getting up, half a dozen of them perform manoeuvres, doing no damage I think, in front of the house, only frightening Mrs Shepherd's two goats, which leap about excitedly. These American troops are very well spoken of and look very fit and decent. Mr Dew says that since they have been here, not one 'rough word' has been spoken in his pub.

Returned to London, the chief interest is post-war rates of exchange. As I think I recorded last week, all those who know the subject and are keen on pulling something off with the Americans, are now in Washington – notably, on the monetary side of things, Keynes, Waley and Meade. (Liesching also reports that on Commercial Policy we have also had an unexpectedly good opening, and that the Americans are by no means against the multilateral approach, nor pressing to complete bilateral treaties.) Meanwhile, at this end, while the cats

---

1 J. E. Coulson, later Sir John (b. 1909). Diplomat. Seconded to Ministry of Economic Warfare 1939–41. Seconded to War Cabinet Offices 1941–2. Returned to Foreign Office as Acting First Secretary 1942.
2 Marginal note: 'The Germans shot him down.'

are away, the mice, led by the rump of the Treasury and the bloody Bank of England, who have been always wrong on policy, for an even longer period than Montagu Norman has been Governor, are trying to play. In particular they are trying to play the new and untried Chancellor [Anderson]. Overton went to two meetings last week, at the first of which, according to private information which reaches me, he made an excellent statement of the Board of Trade case, carefully agreed with me, and put in writing by him to Eady[1] afterwards, emphasising our interest in preventing exchange depreciation by foreigners, and urging that the Keynes–Waley proposal – which allows everyone to depreciate 10 per cent 'unilaterally' within ten years, and the second 10 per cent, provided the Board are informed, with the penalty that if the Board don't approve, either the second 10 per cent must be reversed, or the country in question leave the Board – is quite reasonable and should be supported. But now the rump of the Treasury, plus the Bank, want a policy of no commitments. They want, in short, to sabotage the Clearing Union plan altogether. At a second meeting held last week, the Treasury produced a draft telegram urging that for a 'transitional period' of five years (!) everyone should be free to do anything they liked. This is said to have 'received the approval of the Chancellor'. Hearing of this beforehand, I tell Overton to dig his feet in and to say that, if it is desired to turn down the Keynes–Waley proposal, the matter must go to the Cabinet. He tells me today that he attended the meeting, was rather impressed by Eady's arguments, is inclined to recommend me to accept the Treasury telegram, but had no difficulty in getting it agreed that the matter should be considered by ministers.

Hence a War Cabinet at 6 p.m. tonight. Meanwhile, much activity. Harrod comes to see me this afternoon, an emissary from Cherwell, who 'is going to take a very strong line' at tonight's meeting against the Treasury telegram. While I am discussing the matter with Overton, Gladwyn rings up to ask what my reactions are, as he is just going to speak to Eden. He says that not only the Prof, but also Cranborne and, he thinks, with very little pressure, Eden, are against the Treasury. The Prof, no doubt, will have briefed the P.M. I tell him that I think five years is too long.

At the War Cabinet Anderson is decisively defeated. He gets no solid support, and there is a strong combination against him on the 'transitional period', which I point out is a quite new feature, not included in the previous Cabinet Directive. Those who speak in the same sense include the Prof, Cranborne, Eden and Beaverbrook! The P.M. half apologises for bringing him into the Cabinet at all, but says,

1 Sir Wilfrid Eady (1890–1962). Second Joint Secretary at the Treasury 1942–52.

'I have asked Lord Cherwell and Lord Beaverbrook, as I myself am a complete child in this matter, and they both have great experience of bucket shops.' The P.M. protests, almost too much, that he has given no thought to the matter, and doesn't understand it. But, as I have noticed before in previous cases, comes out with a very clear and sensible suggestion, i.e., that we should telegraph to our delegation, saying (1) that we like their plan very much, and (2), that we should like them to discuss further with the Americans and suggest to us any ideas on the 'transitional period', not giving them any views of our own on this latter topic or leading them at all. 'Quite a short and simple telegram,' says the P.M., but to make doubly sure it doesn't go wrong, he confides the making of it to Anderson, assisted by Attlee, who had spoken briefly and sensibly on the subject, Cherwell, Beaverbrook and myself. Anderson had tried, as a last-minute get-out, to get us to agree to a long-winded additional paragraph which he had brought along, 'in case the general feeling of the Cabinet should be the other way', but this was so full of calculated ambiguities that it was thrust aside contemptuously. Not a very good début for the Chancellor!

The P.M. tells us that he, Roosevelt *and Stalin* have signed a joint declaration recognising King Victor and Badoglio as the Government of Italy, as soon as they have declared war on Germany. All the evidence is that the Russians are now most anxious to get down to detail with us on all points. Meanwhile, Eden is getting very frightened of the Mediterranean Commission,[1] fearing they will try to do too much off their own bats.

Wednesday 6th October

Put on a boiled shirt and a dinner jacket for the first time for a long while, in order to attend a large party at Claridge's, with the P.M. in the Chair, to wish a final goodbye to Wavell, who really *is* going to India this week.

Thursday 7th October

Cherwell rang me up yesterday to say that Anderson had refused suggestions made by him, and also by Overton on my behalf, regarding the telegram to our delegates in Washington on exchange rates. He has already protested to Anderson and had in reply 'a pompous letter'. I send, at Cherwell's suggestion, a letter of my own to Anderson, to which, two days later, he replies. ...

---

1 The Mediterranean Commission had been set up by the Allies after the surrender of Italy in order to deal with Italian affairs.

This incident illustrates several things:

(1) Our delegation at Washington is too strong. It includes, both in the Treasury, the Board of Trade and the Economic Secretariat representatives, the most intelligent people who have, moreover, the most knowledge of the subject, since they have been shaping policy over here. We have left behind, at the Treasury, Eady plus Sir Hubert Henderson, who is still trying to wriggle back to his doctrines which were so emphatically rejected first by the Overton Committee and later by the Cabinet; at the Board of Trade, Overton has to do it all (and is not by nature a highly pugnacious animal), since none of the underlings in C.R.T. [Commercial Relations and Treaties] know anything about it; in the Economic Secretariat, Robbins and Meade are both away, and we are left with Dennison,[1] a second-rater, in charge. Therefore, one must be constantly on the watch to see that our delegation out in Washington is not being thwarted and mal-instructed by people at this end who combine, in varying proportions, ignorance, jealousy and other preoccupations.

(2) The Treasury are very resentful at 'interference' by others, whether ministers or officials. They try to brush all other arguments aside and to dictate policy even to the War Cabinet. They have a new Chancellor, who, as an old civil servant, is rather amenable to their pressures. They are, finally, very short-handed. Hopkins is ill, Phillips is dead, and a number of their younger people are lent this way and that in the public service.

(3) I am horrified to find that the Bank of England are allowed in on these discussions. They really can't have it both ways. Either they are civil servants or they are rank outsiders. But here we find them trying to edge round to sheer defiance of Cabinet decisions. What a speech I could make on all this, if my lips were unsealed! Having mal-advised every government for more than twenty years, they are still at it. Now their line is that we must accept 'no commitments' of any kind regarding our exchange rates. Let foreigners depreciate as much as they like, so long as we are free to do the same. Overton tells me that

---

1 S. R. Dennison (b. 1912). Chief Economic Assistant, War Cabinet Secretariat 1940–46. Fellow of Gonville and Caius College, Cambridge 1945–58. Professor of Economics at Queen's University, Belfast 1958–61; Durham and Newcastle Universities 1962–72. Vice-Chancellor of the University of Hull 1972–9.

Cobbold, whom he thinks is very clever, came to the last meeting but one, and Clay, whom I was delighted to get rid of to Washington, whence he has now drifted back to London, to the second. But *he* seems to have said nothing at this last meeting.

Dalton had been concerned to get Douglas Jay, currently at the Ministry of Supply, to transfer to the Board of Trade in order to work on post-war problems. On 13th October he obtained the formal consent of Sir Andrew Duncan, Minister of Supply, to the change. Dalton explained to Jay that the latter 'would be entirely concerned with post-war questions and would work direct to me, though you would, of course, be in constant touch with others working in this field and would co-operate, I am sure, most harmoniously with other members of my post-warrior team. You would come across with your present rank and emoluments.'[1]

Tuesday 12th October
Write to Duncan confirming his agreement, made orally after a ministers' meeting, to give me Douglas Jay.[2]

Then discuss with Watkinson how the latter would work. There has been a good deal of obstruction and reluctance at my high-official levels, with a fear that Jay and I know each other too well, and that, if he becomes my Personal Assistant, the others would be by-passed and squeezed out. Therefore, Watkinson having a bad cold, I give him tea with a lot of rum in it, and then another cup, and assure him that all will be well – and, indeed, much better than well – and that, as I told Overton, 'I am always right about personnel.' I tell him that I said to Overton, when he was being a bit difficult about Jay, 'Do you remember how you obstructed me when I wanted to promote Watkinson to be an Under-Secretary?' Watkinson then says that of course I have put it all so clearly that he no longer has any apprehensions. Gaitskell had also told me earlier in the day that he had already mentioned the matter to Alix Kilroy,[3] who said she was most de-

1 Dalton Papers 7/5 (16).
2 Marginal insertion: 'In exchange for Weir and Lee.'
3 Alix Kilroy, later Dame Alix, Lady Meynell (b. 1903). Principal Assistant Secretary Division IV, Industries and Manufactures Department of the Board of Trade. Under-Secretary 1946–55. Married Sir Francis Meynell, q.v., in 1946.

lighted, and so they all ought to be, for the reinforcement of a first-class brain can do their team nothing but good.

I then write to Jay ... and send a copy of this to Overton, asking him to push it through with Ministry of Supply. In this letter I have told Jay that he would (1) be only on post-war, (2) work to me, (3) co-operate harmoniously with the rest of the team. I also told him that I have now discussed and settled all this with Overton and Watkinson.

Thursday 14th October
Dine with Hugh Gaitskell at Hampstead. An extremely nice party is collected, including Bob Fraser, whom I had not seen since his silly little Betty came back from her travels, Douglas and Peggy Jay, Jenifer Hart[1] (now at Home Security and very intelligent as well as attractive, with whom I swap stories of the relations of civil servants tò each other and to ministers), and Raymond,[2] Gaitskell's step-son, a nice young man now in the Air Force and obviously liking it very much.

'As you know, I have a mandate from the National Executive to make a draft on the International Post-War Settlement,' Dalton wrote to Will Arnold-Forster on 17th October. ' ... Among the documents I have been reading is your Atlantic Charter Commentary. We all owe much to you for having done it. It has, like all else you write, great clarity and a background of great knowledge.

'But it is much more than its title suggests. It is really a very far reaching, and at some points very detailed, statement on the Post-War Settlement ... ' Hence, Dalton tactfully suggested, it should be published under its author's name, and not as official Party policy.[3]

Tuesday 19th October
Labour Party International Sub-Committee. I succeeded in killing the project of Will Arnold-Forster's Commentary on the Atlantic

---

1 Jenifer Hart, née Williams. Principal at the Ministry of Home Security. Later Fellow of St Anne's College, Oxford.
2 Raymond Frost (b. 1925). Dora Gaitskell's son by her first husband, Dr David Frost.
3 Dalton Papers 7/10 (32).

Charter being published officially by the Party. I had already written him a letter ... which I thought was very friendly, followed by eight sides of detailed comment in my own scrawl, composed last weekend at West Leaze. The other members of the Committee agreed, I having expounded briefly my reasons, as in the letter, except Phil [Noel-] Baker, who squeaked that we ought soon to publish something on the Atlantic Charter. Arnold-Forster, however, took it very ill, and even suggested that he should resign his post and repay the salary he had drawn from the Labour Party during the past few months, while he had been working at this document. He is rather a silly little man. His Commentary was full of the most egregious impossibilities for a Party document, though legitimate enough for an individual contribution. He wanted, e.g., to commit us to giving Massawa to the Ethiopians; Gibraltar to some undefined international body; Formosa to China; while denying in advance Greek claims to Northern Epirus, Polish claims to East Prussia, and Russian claims to the Baltic States. ...

Bob Fraser sends to see me Major Kenneth Younger,[1] grandson of a famous Tory Chief Whip and Beer Baron, who was at Winchester and Oxford, but who has joined the Labour Party and been most assiduous in attendance at the meetings of the South Kensington D.L.P. He speaks Russian and has been in M.I.5. He would like to run for a hopeless constituency. This can always, be easily arranged.[2] I liked him.

War Cabinet on U.N.R.R.A. Lyttelton, I and Law submit a joint paper, which comes through quite happily. Law, who dines with me afterwards, and is rather new to Cabinet discussions, was very shocked because clearly hardly any of our colleagues had read the paper, and there was no real discussion on it. I told him that what mattered in Cabinets was not the discussion but the conclusions. If these were right, the discussion didn't matter at all. ...

Today at Questions I was heckled, both by Hammersley[3] and Hogg, and by Shinbad, on the Commercial Talks in Washington. I spoke afterwards with Hogg and learn that he had heard from 'someone on the fringe of official knowledge' that Keynes had been bargaining away both Imperial Preference and our right to do bulk purchases. I assured him that this was all nonsense, and spoke of Liesching and other personal factors, including my own prejudice in favour both of the Dominions and of Socialism, and I think reassured him. But it is

1 Hon. K. G. Younger, later Sir Kenneth (1908–76). Labour M.P. for Grimsby 1945–1959. Junior minister 1947–50. Minister of State at the Foreign Office 1950–51.
2 Marginal insertion: 'He ran for Grimsby and won.'
3 S. S. Hammersley (1892–1965). Conservative M.P. for Willesden East 1938–45; Stockport 1925–35.

clear that someone has been leaking, and I divide my suspicions between Sir Hubert Henderson, who, like Hogg, is a Fellow of All Souls, and Balogh who also hangs about the fringes of Oxford and is one of Shinbad's drainpipes. This is rather irritating.

Wednesday 20th October

Leith-Ross to see me and to say goodbye. He is leaving for the U.S. tomorrow and, unless he becomes an international official, comes now under the Foreign Office and no longer under me. He has taken it all very well and I hope will fix something up with Lehman, though Law says that he bearded Lehman in his office and asked him whether his intentions towards Leith-Ross were honourable, to which Lehman replied that he did not think Leith-Ross at all a good administrator, rather a muddler indeed, but that he would like him as his financial adviser, to live in Washington. Law hoped that Leith-Ross would not be dashed at this, and thought that I might break it to him. But I thought it unwise to go so far as this, and only told him how important I thought – and he agreed – the finance of U.N.R.R.A. would be, and how it would need most skilled handling.

Labour Party Finance Sub-Committee meets in my room and I get it just where I wanted it. That is to say, I arrange that Gaitskell and Jay shall between them make a paper on post-war employment and finance, and Durbin one on post-war international economic arrangements. They will make use of any or all of the material already collected and we will have a meeting on their draft in due course. This was the whole purpose of the meeting. The rest of the time was filled up with discursive observations by all on a large variety of papers. This did no harm and kept them happy.

Jay remains to tell me that he is to change over at the end of next week. I have been stirring up the Ministry of Supply, partly by poking up Overton to follow up his first formal letter to Sir William Douglas,[1] following my confirmation to Duncan of his agreement now to let me have Jay; partly by inciting Preston to warn Tippetts[2] that, if something wasn't settled soon, I would raise hell. Jay reports that a few days ago he was summoned by Sir William Douglas, who said that he had told his Minister that he considered it most wrong for ministers to make arrangements between themselves for swapping staff, without consulting the officials. To this Duncan had replied, 'Well, we agreed to it, didn't we, when the President of the Board of Trade gave us

1 Sir William Douglas (1890–1953). Permanent Secretary at the Ministry of Supply 1942–5; Ministry of Health 1945–51.
2 R. B. Tippetts (b. 1913). Principal Private Secretary to Sir Andrew Duncan, the Minister of Supply.

Weir and Lee?' On which Sir William Douglas had said to his Minister, 'You may have agreed; I never did.' Jay then said that anyhow it seemed all settled now. 'Not necessarily,' said Sir William Douglas. 'If you were to tell me that you were unwilling to go to the Board of Trade, I could reopen it.' But Jay said that he did not feel able to say that he was unwilling. 'And then', he said, 'Douglas became much more formal.' This, Preston says, when I relate it to him, is the old-fashioned Treasury approach to Establishment questions. Jay anxiously asks me whether, having been imprisoned for some time in a cell looking out upon a well, he could have here a room, no matter how small, which faces the sun. He also hopes that any lady attached to him will be able to type. He does not even mind if she can't do shorthand, being quite willing to dictate straight on to a typewriter. At the Ministry of Supply they gave him a lady attendant who was very agreeable but could neither type nor do shorthand. Therefore, he always depended on the pool.

Thursday 21st October

A most remarkably and surprisingly good and important Cabinet. The P.M. has issued a short Note on War – Transition – Peace. In this he argues that we should fail completely in our duty if we had not got ready, before the German war ends, complete schemes for the Transition Period, during which we should ensure for all our people Food and Employment. The Transition Period he proposes to define as either two years from the defeat of Germany or four years from 1st January 1944, whichever ends first. He is anxious to speed up all preparations now being made. There is also circulated a paper by the Prof, listing a large range of topics on which decisions will be necessary. Quite a surprising number of them fall within my Departmental field, either wholly or partly.[1]

Very great credit is due to Attlee and, in a lesser degree, to Morrison, for having brought about this remarkable change in the P.M.'s attitude. They have both been having a great go on him, and tonight the P.M., who is in a very good temper and great spirits, says that he has now been led to see this question quite differently. He says that this is because he has been 'jostled and beaten up by the Deputy Prime Minister'. For this, he says, he is very grateful. The Transition has now taken a very firm shape in his mind. We shall not pass direct from war to peace, even apart from the complication of the two-stage ending

---

1 Dalton wrote to Churchill in reply: 'So many of the questions listed by you belong, in whole or part, to the Board of Trade that I feel I should be on any Ministerial Committee which is to hasten the making of the Transition Plan.' (Dalton Papers 7/5 (68).)

of the war. Between these two there must be a transition for which it is our duty to make most careful preparation now, and we should rule out nothing important for the simple needs of the Transition, merely because it is controversial. He then elaborates, with great dramatic detail, how we should prepare a great book, the Book of the Transition, like the War Book, running to perhaps a thousand closely printed pages or taking the form of a number of Reports and precise plans contained in drawers, one above another, so that, if any amateurish critic says, 'You have no plan for this or that', it would be easy to pull out a drawer, bring out a paper, and say, 'Here it all is.' All parties in Parliament, the country, our returning soldiers, the whole world, would be filled with admiration if we were able to display a series of such plans. And so, he thinks, there might be a whole week's debate, or longer, in Parliament, and one day it would be the Chancellor of the Exchequer, followed by the Minister of Labour, who would expound in detail their part of the Plan, and next day, it might be the President of the Board of Trade, followed by the Minister of Agriculture. And so it would go on ...... They would be spellbound! ...... And even if we made a few mistakes, as we should, for after all, we are all only simple people and not archangels, we should at least have got great credit for our Plan.

So now he will spend the weekend reading Reports of all that is in hand, and considering how our machinery should be improved. There follows a good deal of chitchat on detail, e.g. as to the future of agriculture, the relation of efficiency to exports and to the needs of the Transition, etc., and there are a few casual references to the next general election, whereon the P.M. is a bit cautious, saying it all depends on whether the parties break up or hold together; that if we hold together, we shall be more masters of our fate, but that if we break up, he, assuming he continued P.M., would not feel able to delay more than a month or two an appeal to the country, particularly as we should then all be getting into training for a good old dog-fight and he would, no doubt, be accused, if he postponed the election, of clinging to office rather than testing the opinion of the electors.

It also emerged very clearly that another factor which had made him change his attitude was a considerable optimism regarding the duration of the war. 'I don't think it will happen,' he said, 'but what would be said to us if Germany were suddenly to collapse now, and we had nothing prepared?' He thought the odds were about 6:4 against a total German collapse within the next six months. He was sure that when they went, they would go completely. As to how long the Japs would go on afterwards, he was not at all sure. The psychological effect on Japan of the fall of Germany would be tremendous, and already there was much evidence that the Jap will to war had greatly weakened. Moreover, with Germany out of the war, the Russians would want, he thought, to join in the war against Japan. Stalin had never concealed his hatred, and distrust, of the Japs. The Russians, moreover, had various ambitions in the Far East and there was no reason why we should thwart them. As to our own contribution, time and distance were limiting factors, and the U.S.A. would naturally take the principal part in the war against the Japs. Both we and the U.S. had an enormous preponderance now in battleships and aircraft carriers. Admiral King,[1] when the P.M. had told him that, now that the Mediterranean was clear, we could send him some heavy ships to help him in the Pacific, had received this offer coldly. He had gone on to tell the P.M. that already the U.S. had two battleships to one against the Japs in the Pacific.

This Cabinet, in short, went very well. I spoke afterwards with Attlee and congratulated him on the success of his efforts. He said there had been a frightful row last week, and loud explosions from the P.M. But now that the smoke had cleared away, the P.M., having invited various Tory ministers, including Butler and Crookshank, to this meeting – they had both been dumb throughout – had now led the Tory troops through the breach which we had made in their defences. I told Attlee that it was nonsense for ministers without departments or staffs – notably Jowitt, but others also might be named – to try to deputise for or try to compete with people like myself who had large staffs working on these post-war problems. I therefore counted on being effectively in the picture when the new drive began. He expressed strong agreement with this view and asked me to send him a note on the whole matter.

Monday 25th October

Lunch with Dunbar, who thinks that H.M.G. has heard of something really serious in the way of German secret weapons and, for this reason, is pushing on with preparations to invade Europe across the Channel.

Meeting of National Executive Sub-Committee on Party secretary-ship. We recognise we are divided on the Parliamentary bar.[2] Middleton is then asked to leave the room, which he does with a very bad

---

1 Admiral E. J. King (1878–1956). Commander-in-Chief of the U.S. Atlantic Fleet 1941–5. Chief of Naval Operations 1942–5.
2 The 'Parliamentary bar': at the 1934 Labour Party Conference it had been decided that the Secretary of the Party should not be an M.P. Dalton pressed for this decision – much to the annoyance of Morrison, who wanted the job, but only if he could also serve in Parliament at the same time.

grace, and one or two of us then have to push hard to make sure that on Wednesday, two days hence, the National Executive takes a definite decision on his resignation. Ridley had proposed a slow procedure which would have put this off for another month. But we all agree that we should back each other up on the Executive Committee in support of the proposal that he should go at the end of March and his successor be in office for a month before this. Ridley is to see Middleton and put this bluntly to him and offer him £500, in addition to his pension, to write the History of the Labour Party.

Wednesday 27th October
National Executive from 10 to 12, when I have to leave, before the end, for the Cabinet. A most blush-making business over Middleton. First, quite a good discussion on whether we should seek to lift the Parliamentary bar on his successor. All the argument is against, by me, Walker, Laski, Shinwell and Barbara Gould – a most powerful and unwonted coalition. But we only get our way by one vote, 11 to 10. Still, that suffices. Then Ridley from the Chair asks the staff to withdraw, so that he can report what happened at our Sub-Committee, after Middleton had withdrawn. All the staff troop out, except Middleton, who sits, flushed and immobile, in his chair. There is an awkward silence. Then Ridley says, 'I think, Jim, the Executive would wish you to withdraw.' Middleton sits tight and then snaps, 'Have you tested the Executive?' Ridley says, 'I think it would be kinder to you, Jim, if we were to discuss this when you have withdrawn.' Middleton, getting more worked up, yaps, 'I want no kindness.' Then Laski says that in University circles, anyone whose position is affected by proposals regarding appointment or reappointment always withdraws. 'They find this much the wisest way.' No response. Then Walker says, 'Well, if he wants to stay, I'd let him stay. We can all say what we think quite frankly in front of him, though he may not like it.' And Shinwell adds to the sweetness of life by remarking, 'I am supposed to say offensive things sometimes, and I may say something offensive in the course of this discussion, and if Jim cares to stay and hear it, he can please himself.' After this, it is generally agreed to let him stay. He then asks, 'May I make a statement?' Ridley says, 'Certainly.'

Middleton then rises from his seat – normally we remain sitting – and gulping at first with emotion, though gradually recovering himself, and flushing ever redder and redder, says that he has been more than forty years in the service of the Labour Party; that he began at 9*d.* an hour, part-time, the same as he was earning at his trade; that he has been conscious ever since he succeeded Arthur Henderson that the Executive has never given him the confidence which they gave to his predecessor; that he could tell them how Henderson managed to do the two jobs, but that he himself has never had, as Henderson had, an Assistant Secretary; that he has never claimed to be 'a big man', nor a Knight, nor a K.B.E., nor thought of a salary for himself of £1,500 or £2,000 a year (this in response to remarks made in the discussion on the Parliamentary bar that we wanted to have 'a bigger man next time' who could deal with Sir Walter Citrine on an equal footing, and who ought probably to be paid this higher salary); that he had done his best, etc., etc.; that he thought he was at least entitled to fair play, and courtesy, etc., etc.; that it was only two days ago that he was faced by Ridley with the prospect of retiring next March; that this had come to him as a great shock; that anyhow he should go on till the Annual Conference, since no one else would be able at short notice to make all the necessary preliminary arrangements; that he was not going himself to resign, but that, if the National Executive desired him to go, it was for them to take the decision; that he had already had three offers to write his autobiography and therefore he did not propose to accept the suggestion, made by Ridley, that he should receive £500 after his retirement for the writing of the History of the Labour Party. All very small, and pitiful, and typical! However, we moved on, through a rambling and not unkind discussion, to the unanimous view that he should go next Whitsun, and, as I understood it, that a successor should be appointed, Secretary Elect, subject to confirmation by the Conference, a month or two before this. No one said that he should stay on beyond Whitsun. ...

I should, with Gaitskell, have dined tonight with Rank, but the fog is so thick that we dine in instead.

There had been a row earlier this evening in the House of Commons over Morrison's wretched Workmen's Compensation Bill. Bevan had been more than usually hysterical and abusive, and forty Members, mostly ours, had gone into the Lobby in favour of an amendment to improve the position of the single man. Meanwhile, the whole Bill had been agreed with the T.U.C., the M.F.G.B., and, within Parliament, with the Administrative Committee and the Party Meeting. But this did not prevent several members of the Administrative Committee from breaking loose tonight! We are an undisciplined rabble!

Thursday 28th October
I receive Vincent Auriol,[1] Blum's ex-Minister of Finance. He was not

1 Vincent Auriol (1884–1966). General Secretary of the French Socialist Party (S.F.I.O.) in the Chamber of Deputies 1919–36. Minister of Finance 1937. Voted against the Armistice in 1940; interned, but escaped to London in 1943. Prime Minister 1946. President of the Fourth French Republic 1947–53.

good at this, but is a decent little man. He has just escaped from France, by aircraft, and is going on to Algiers. Gradually, he thinks, enough experienced men are gathering round de Gaulle to make the latter incapable [of] doing harm. He knows we here have found him difficult, but repeats the story, which I had heard from Viénot, that Vichy and the Germans represent de Gaulle always as the hireling of the English and, therefore, he had to give some proof that this was a lie. Auriol gives nauseating details, not to be set down here, nor easily to be forgotten, of how the Germans torture Frenchmen to obtain confessions and information. All this, when told in detail, strengthens my view that a very large number of Germans, for very many co-operate in these practices, are just not tolerable except as corpses. Auriol escaped with nothing on save what he stood up in, and with no overcoat, with a false passport, having grown a beard, which he only shaved off on arrival in England. His wife is still in France, liable to the worst horrors if caught by the Huns. I had already sent, at Viénot's request, 150 extra clothing coupons for each of a list of Frenchmen recently escaped. Auriol asked whether he might have an extra 50. I let him have them gladly.

Friday 29th October
Go to see Anderson and talk to him on Films. ... I mention Beaverbrook's interest in Black Spots.[1] He says that we must not make things too hard for the P.M., who is conducting the war with great skill. The P.M. was very unhappy during the period when Beaverbrook was not one of his colleagues. He is a sensitive artist, attaching great value to 'presentation' and the quality of the spoken word. He likes to have around him certain people, whose responses will not be jarring or unwelcome. He has valued Beaverbrook for this for many years. We must not, therefore, be too particular, even if things are sometimes not done in quite the most regular or orderly way. On the other hand, he adds, 'I should take the very strongest objection' to any interference by Beaverbrook in the work of Departments or of Ministerial Committees of which he was not a member.

By lunchtime, on my return to the Board, Preston had sent to Peck my two personal papers on Location, with a hint that Beaverbrook might find 'useful background' in the Barlow Report.[2] If he now

1 'Black Spots': Dalton seems to have been alarmed by signs that Beaverbrook might take an interest (and by implication a hostile interest) in post-war Location Plans. 'Black Spots' may, therefore, mean unemployment black spots.
2 Marginal insertion: 'Peck had rung up Preston and said that Beaverbrook had been talking to the P.M. about Black Spots, and the P.M. would like Beaverbrook to have something to read on this.'

comes back with some tale about everything being stuck, nothing being done, we can rebut him, with the strong aid of Anderson, by telling him that a policy is being recommended to ministers next month.

Waterhouse feels very strongly against Beaverbrook's interference. He hopes I will speak also to Attlee and Bevin about it. He has himself been speaking to James Stuart and Harvie Watt. None of them has any evidence yet of any other raids by Beaverbrook. It is hoped by all – except the Foreign Office – that he is soon leaving for Washington, for a long stay, and thence to Moscow.[1]

See Attlee this afternoon and speak of Beaverbrook. He says it is very difficult to know what *is* going on, with Beaverbrook and Cherwell always hanging round the P.M. I said that Anderson said, when I asked him whether the present untidy arrangement of Ministerial Committees was now to be modified, that 'this depends on personal matters, on which the P.M.'s mind is in a state of flux'. Attlee said this was certainly so. Evidently Jowitt is part of the problem. Attlee said that the latter had been a damned fool to accept such a rotten staff, all other people's rejects. Attlee is seeing the P.M. on Monday, and will repeat that we must pull things out of the hands of officials and hurry to ministerial decisions. On the other hand, he was against making too much difficulty with the P.M. over Beaverbrook, just at a time when the P.M. was beginning to take a really live interest in post-war.

Monday 1st November

Lunch with Southwood, who makes himself very affable. We speak of the succession to Middleton, and he more or less offers Maurice Webb, though adding a warning that we should have to chain him down to his office chair, prevent him from appearing frequently on the public platform, and make sure that he did not try to run the show too much as a personal venture. I told him of the rumours about Beaverbrook and post-war, and he said that he was quite sure public opinion would not for a moment tolerate this. I said that he might have to come out with a strong blast in the *Herald*. He said he would certainly be prepared to do this if anything came of it, but he could not believe that it would.

Make my first call on the new Soviet Ambassador, Gusev.[2] I liked him. He is much younger and more typically Russian-looking than Maisky. To be exact, he is, and looks like, a native of Leningrad. These North Russians have a special look which is not easily defined,

---

1 Marginal insertion: 'Waterhouse says no one gets to the P.M. except Beaverbrook and Bracken.'

2 F. T. Gusev (1904–73). Soviet Ambassador to Britain October 1943–6. Deputy Foreign Minister 1946–55.

but I think I recognise it. His English is fair and his general attitude most friendly. He obviously feels very new to it all, and we don't get into any deep waters. He says that Maisky told him that I was one of those whom he saw most, and I expatiate on ordinary lines – my long desire for Anglo-Soviet co-operation, the apparent great success of the Moscow Conference, the need for them and us to be the two great pillars of post-war security in Europe, etc. I must see more of him and find out how far he is more than a pleasant diplomatic robot.

War Cabinet. Mention of Indian sterling balances. I tell the P.M. he understated the gravity of it and that these are now increasing not by £1,000,000 but by £2,000,000 a day.[1]

Leaving the Cabinet, I have a word with Bevin and ask him whether he knows that Beaverbrook is taking an interest in post-war matters. He says, 'I know things have been going on, and I told the Old Man I wouldn't stand it, but the Old Man said, "He won't interfere with *you*." ' I said that this was all very well, but that if he began interfering with anybody, you would never know where it would stop, particularly as a number of these problems were of joint concern to several of us, e.g. Location to Bevin and me. But we had now reached the door and he went grunting off into the dark.

Tuesday 2nd November

Tell Attlee that I have been thinking over the threat that Beaverbrook might be put in charge of post-war plans, and that I have quite definitely come to the conclusion that, if this is done so far as the Board of Trade plans are concerned, I shall ask the Prime Minister to relieve me of my office. I will not work to Beaverbrook, though of course I could not object if the P.M. put him on some committee merely as a member. But I will only work either to the P.M. himself, or to such trusted and experienced chairmen of committees as Attlee and Anderson. I add that Waterhouse is also much upset at these rumours, and that, though he has not said quite so much to me, I should not be at all surprised if he was prepared, as I was, to resign rather than be put under the Beaver. Conservatives in general feel even more strongly against the Beaver than our own Party. Attlee knows, I say, that if decisions have been slow, as they have, this is not my fault, and I have constantly pressed and badgered my colleagues and my officials to get on with it. The fault lies with the procedure whereby everything is considered by inter-departmental official committees, instead of being handled by ministers themselves. I add that an additional reason why I won't serve under the Beaver is because I know, from three sources, that he has

1 Marginal insertion: '(But this was wrong. It is £1m+)'.

been doing his best to damage me personally and that he used to incite his staff, day by day, to 'down that bugger Dalton again tomorrow'. Attlee says that he entirely understands and shares my point of view and that when he sees the P.M. on all this – he is seeing him tonight, instead of last night – he will put the case very strongly. I say that, if he cares to do so, he can tell the P.M. what I have said about myself and Waterhouse.

I go on to Morrison and tell him the same. He said he hadn't heard that the Beaver was being run for post-war Controller. On the other hand, he thinks that Bevin's remark to me is the best evidence he has had so far of this. Morrison himself is having rows all round just now; with a section of our own Party over Workmen's Compensation, and now, he tells me, with the P.M., incited by Bracken, over his recent speeches. Hitherto the P.M. has not minded his speeches on post-war control at all, but now he is angered by them. Morrison wonders whether the Beaver's interest in 'Black Spots' may not be because the P.M. wants something on this for an election programme. Morrison is a little suspicious of the P.M.'s intentions over the next election. He thinks we should have this out with him, and that Attlee ought to insist on knowing more.

Wednesday 3rd November
Attlee whispers to me at the Party Meeting that he saw the P.M. last night and they had 'quite a row, as we usually do', but that the result was that Beaverbrook is not to have anything to do with post-war. I thank him for his intervention but get no chance to pursue it today. I tell this to Waterhouse, who says that Stuart has heard no more, but that there is a rumour that the Beaver was trying to 'supervise' W. S. Morrison at Town and Country Planning!

Thursday 4th November
Jay to see me. He will start here next week. He says that, taking his leave of various people at the Ministry of Supply, he sensed a good deal of hostility to the Board of Trade. He thinks Lord Portal is behind a lot of it; also the I.C.I. men, who swarm at Ministry of Supply (he mentioned one Bain,[1] in particular, of the Chemical Control). But much worse seems to have been Turner,[2] the Second Secretary under whom he has been working. This man spoke most indiscreetly, as it seems to me, and said that, of course, the Board of Trade was trying

1 F. Bain, later Sir Frederick (1889–1950). Deputy Chairman of the I.C.I. Chemical Control Board at the Ministry of Supply 1941–4.
2 G. W. Turner, later Sir George (1896–1974). Second Secretary at the Ministry of Supply 1942–8. Permanent Under-Secretary of State for War 1949–56.

to get hold of all post-war policy, but that the Treasury would certainly not permit this. He said the Treasury took a most unfavourable view of the Board of Trade activities. He hinted that the President of the Board of Trade was thought to be personally responsible for the quite unnecessary hustle which was now going on, and that 'the other Departments wouldn't stand for it'. ... Jay deduced that there was strong hostility (a) to me, (b) to temporary civil servants as such, and (c) to the waxing of the Board of Trade and the waning of the Ministry of Supply. Also they are still very sore at my having done a direct deal with Duncan over Jay. ...

Wilmot and Durbin to dine, chiefly in order that we may see whether the latter would like to be a candidate for the Labour Party secretaryship. In view of the Parliamentary bar, he is pretty definite that he doesn't want it.

Friday 5th November
Receive a report from Liesching, Meade and Shackle, on their Washington discussions. They have done well and were a good combination; Liesching very clear-headed, incisive, firm but friendly; Meade very expert on all points of theory, able to hold his own, and a bit more, with the American theorists, and most ingenious in devising new formulae; Shackle an immense repository of dry knowledge of all detail, past and present, relating to Commercial Policy, our own and everybody else's. The next thing is to try to get something soon to ministers. Meade says that the Prof says that it is important to get this in while the P.M. is in the country.

Monday 8th November
Douglas Jay to see me on arrival. I hope and think that he will fit in well. I give him, to begin with, a few odd jobs and urge him to make the acquaintance of the various people concerned. He is still inclined to niggle a little on his personal position, and I tell him that I will look after this so long as I am President, and he adds that, when I cease being President, he will probably want to leave anyway!

Immense Reception at the Soviet Embassy. The invitation is from 4 to 6. I arrive soon after 5 and find the place quite packed, and hundreds of people pouring in and out. I am seized upon by Kuimov, a little man in the Trade Delegation, whom I met with Holmes[1] and Dobbie months ago. He says, 'Vodka at 6 o'clock. You must wait.' But, in fact, bottles of vodka appear about 5.45, and we all begin to

1 Probably H. E. Holmes, later Sir Horace (1888–1971). Yorkshire N.U.M. official. Labour M.P. for Harmsworth 1946–59.

drink, including a rather reluctant Sir George Nelson,[1] whom, however, I overbear, urging him only to eat between his drinks. I ask, as usual here, for Major Lebedev,[2] who appears magnificently arrayed in uniform, with heavy red epaulettes, looking very pleased with himself. Many representatives of the Red Army and Red Air Force are here today, and all most impressively dressed. But the Red Air Force, to my surprise, has blue and white round its collar. Soon after this, I am taken down to a lower room, where the only other Englishman is a British Officer, a Major very full of vodka already, rather excited and loudly shouting sentiments of undying friendship. The rest are Russians, about two dozen, including Gusev and his wife. She speaks now just a little English. It is all most friendly, and I feel, and shall, I think, still feel the same tomorrow, even when the vodka has worn off, that the Moscow Conference[3] has made a real difference, and that the feeling is now soaking through to these Russians that we are prepared to play in the same team with them, and that there is no reason why we should have serious quarrels now or in the future.

Proto-types of *Vergeltungswaffen* (reprisal weapon) rocket-powered bombs had been developed at the German research plant in Peenemünde on the Baltic. First tests took place as early as 1942.

Tuesday 9th November
Lunch at Mansion House – annual event with pikemen (they look much more impressive at a distance!), etc. The P.M. makes a speech in which, for the first time in public, he elaborates his theme of Food, Work and Homes in the Transition. He says that all ministers are now giving close attention to these preparations. This switch-over has not yet been fully appreciated or seized upon by the press. It is much more remarkable than they yet apprehend. He hinted also that the enemy might have new and powerful weapons, but that we should be ready for them and they could not affect the outcome of the war. (There is a lot of talk just now about a new German Rocket Bomb. Various

1 Sir George Nelson, later 1st Baron (1887–1962). President of the Federation of British Industries 1943–5.
2 Major Anatoli Lebedev. Assistant Military Attaché at the Russian Embassy in London.
3 The Moscow Conference of 12th to 16th August 1942, at which Churchill explained to Stalin his reasons for not opening a Second Front in Europe that year.

committees are sitting to consider it, and what it might do, and what we should do if it did. A speech by Ley[1] the other day was noted in which he said that Hitler had a tremendous Secret Weapon, but that the wretched English, by their 'terror bombing', had interfered with its production and postponed the day when it would come into use. It is said that a certain raid on a relatively small target on the Baltic lately had this in mind, and that it succeeded. Others are sceptical about the whole thing. They ask why, if the thing is any good, it hasn't been used long ago, in the hope of doing at least something to counter the ever-increasing Anglo-American air attacks on Germany, and old Dunbar, it will be remembered, said that he understood that plans for the Second Front across the Channel were being speeded up, in order to forestall the Rocket Bomb, capable of being fired from a range of 150 miles, and liable to do great damage on impact. So they all say! And others add that at the rosiest, such a projectile at such a range could not be aimed with any great exactitude, and that, e.g., a strong wind might blow it far from any intended target. New weapons often go awry. Roy Robinson[2] told me that, when at the beginning of the war some – including myself and Amery – wanted to set the Black Forest alight, he always said that this was practically impossible. And then some clever chap in some hush-hush back room invented a balloon which was supposed to blow from here over Germany and then descend and burn their forests. But some of these wretched things, he said, got into the wrong air currents, and blew back and dropped in some of Robinson's nice new conifer forests and did a little, but not excessive, damage, so that he had to ring up the hush-hush man and say, 'Hi, you damned fool, your bloody balloons are blowing the wrong way today.') ...

Look in at meeting of Polish Socialists in London at Stratton House. They are celebrating their Independence Day. Rather a moving sight, some one hundred of them in a long, low, half-lit room, most with sad, worn faces. No one here but has relatives and friends already massacred, or in course of being tortured, or missing and undiscovered, in their native Poland. Stanczyk in the Chair. When I arrive Ciolkosz[3] is making a long speech. Thereafter I speak shortly. Words are worth so little at such times.

1 Robert Ley (1890–1945). Leader of the German Labour Front. Reich Organisation Leader of the Nazi Party 1932–45. Committed suicide while awaiting trial at Nuremberg.
2 Sir Roy Robinson, later 1st Baron (1883–1952). Chairman of the Forestry Commission 1932–52.
3 Adam Ciolkosz (1901–78). Polish Socialist politician. Member of the Polish government-in-exile.

Wednesday 10th November

The election of our new Administrative Committee has gone astonishingly well. Morrison has a very good vote and is top of the ministerial list – now stupidly separated from the non-ministerial. Phil [Noel-Baker] and Tom Williams are the other two. Westwood and Garro [Jones] are defeated. I didn't stand, nor did Alexander. There had to be at least two new non-ministers. In fact, there are three; Wilmot, who gets a very good vote of 69, Woodburn with 61 and Parker with 55. Then followed Daggar with 54, the last elected. Shinwell had 53 and so was off, by one vote! This is a great rebuff, much better than I had hoped. He takes it very badly, left the Party Meeting in the middle after the figures were read out, and told the press that 'This is the worst day's work the Labour Party has done for a long time. I don't intend to take it lying down.' This will now be an altogether different Administrative Committee, with quite a different balance of opinion and temperament inside it. Wilmot will have a great opportunity of improving his Parliamentary reputation. There are now three P.P.S.s on the Administrative Committee, Creech Jones, Wilmot and Woodburn.

I saw Attlee for a moment later in the morning. I had not had time for a word with him since this day last week, when he whispered to me at the Party Meeting that he had seen the P.M. and that the Beaver menace to Reconstruction was off. Today we discuss this a little further. He says that it was clear that protests came in to the P.M. from many quarters at the bare idea of letting the Beaver loose in this field. It was hoped, by all except the Foreign Office, that he was really going off soon to Washington. Attlee said that he had told the P.M. very frankly that he received much false information from the two B.s.[1] Attlee had been much annoyed because the P.M. had told him that he had heard that Attlee was very unpopular with the Tories in the House. Attlee said he knew that this was not true.[2] On the other hand, the plans now made for Reconstruction, etc., were, he thought, quite satisfactory.

Elections in July and August 1943 in Syria and Lebanon, where the Free French controlled the administration, resulted in overwhelming Nationalist

1 Beaverbrook and Bracken.
2 Marginal insertion: 'The P.M. had also said that he heard that I was very unpopular in my Department. Attlee said this was all rot, though no good Minister was ever popular with *all* his staff.'

victories. On 7th October, the Lebanese government, distrusting promises of post-war independence, proposed to abolish the French position in the republic. A month later, the French authorities arrested the Lebanese President and most of his ministers. The British government was outraged by this high-handed action, and threatened to withdraw recognition from the French National Committee. As a result, on 22nd November the arrested politicians were released, and negotiations began for the eventual independence of Syria and the Lebanon.

On 12th November, Lord Woolton became Minister of Reconstruction, and was replaced as Minister of Food by Colonel Llewellin, who, in turn, was replaced as Minister Resident for Supply in Washington by Ben Smith. On 17th November, Ernest Brown replaced Duff Cooper as Chancellor of the Duchy of Lancaster, and H. U. Willink became Minister of Health.

Thursday 11th November

In the House today Eden's statement on the Moscow Conference and Anderson's on Mutual Lease-Lend both went very well. Anderson is gradually acquiring a Parliamentary manner, a gift which Eden has had for many years. The Moscow proceedings are all made to sound most friendly and important, and I have no doubt that so they were.

Lunch at No. 10 in small downstairs dining room looking out on the garden. P.M. says he has a bad headache and is rather glum and relatively silent. Mrs Churchill, however, fully makes up for this. She is a first-class hostess. To me she talks a lot about Russia, and I to her about Sir James Hawkey, whom she is seeing tomorrow. Other visitors are old Garvin[1] and his much younger wife,[2] Mr and Mrs[3] Harvie Watt and Sir Edward Bridges. The P.M. is obsessed by the tendency of Indians to breed right down to the margin of subsistence, and often below it, as now in Bengal. He does not see what we can do to stop it. He is also, very naturally, furious with de Gaulle – 'that is a bad man, most unfriendly to this country' – for his coup in the Lebanon, to which the French had promised independence but where they have just kidnapped all the members of the new Government!

I went off with Harvie Watt, with whom I had a very frank talk. The new Cabinet shuffle will be announced tonight. Woolton, as expected, will be Minister of Reconstruction. Jowitt, who has an unfailing capacity to accept impossible jobs under undignified con-

1 J. L. Garvin (1868–1947). Editor of the *Observer* 1908–42.
2 Mrs Viola Garvin, née Taylor.
3 Bettie Watt, later Lady Harvie-Watt, née Taylor.

ditions, is to stay on, in effect as his Under-Secretary. Ernest Brown is to be dumped down to be Chancellor of the Duchy. This, with the withdrawal of his 'speaking part' from Mabane,[1] now that Llewellin is to come back to be Minister of Food in Woolton's place, is a nasty blow for the Simonites. Duff Cooper is to be an Ambassador somewhere to the French, and Ben Smith is to go to America in Llewellin's place. He did very well there lately. The P.M., Harvie Watt says, would also have liked to get rid of Simon, Amery and Grigg. But, since it is now desired to send back as many war criminals as possible to the scenes of their crimes, there is no longer much of a job, as was at one time expected, for Simon as President of some great International War Criminal Tribunal, and so, for the moment, he sticks on. The P.M. is fed up with the other two, but won't get rid of either of them while so many people are gunning after them.

I speak very bluntly about the influence of Beaverbrook and Bracken, and tell Harvie Watt my own reaction and Waterhouse's – which he had had direct already – to the suggestion of any interference with us. Waterhouse says that the P.M. knows that practically everyone hates the Beaver. He said the other day, 'I know that if I put it to a vote of the Cabinet, at least three-quarters of them would vote against my taking Max back. But that is not the way things are done in this country. The Prime Minister still has the right to choose a few of his own colleagues.' I said that I was much irritated by the dropping in the P.M.'s ear of tales, nearly all lies (about, e.g., internal relationships in the Board of Trade). I said that Attlee had told me that, when the P.M. had referred to one of these tales the other night, Attlee had told him that it was quite untrue, and that he supposed the P.M. had got it from Beaverbrook, who had long been running a personal campaign against me in his papers. Whereat, Attlee had reported, the P.M. had made a loud snort and said that everybody was always against the Beaver, and changed the subject. Harvie Watt said that he frequently told the P.M., both orally and in written Minutes, that I was one of the most successful ministers in the House and that only a few very reactionary Tories objected to my being where I was. A much larger number objected to certain other Labour ministers. Harvie Watt also said that Waterhouse was always exceedingly loyal to me in conversation in Tory circles.

Dine with Garro [Jones], who got into very hot water with the P.M. the other day, because he had made what I frankly thought was a most stupid speech about the future of our relationships with the

1 Sir William Mabane, later 1st Baron (1895–1969). Liberal National M.P. for Huddersfield 1931–45. Junior minister 1939–42. Minister of State at the Foreign Office 1945.

U.S.A. The P.M. had said, 'Under-Secretaries, when making speeches, should confine themselves to platitudes.' Garro likes Lyttelton very much and is clearly rather fascinated by his job. We gossip a bit about the old topics of Party leadership, etc., but I formed the view that, though he is a nice chap, and a good friend of mine, his judgment isn't really very good.

Friday 12th November
Dine with Bob and Betty [Fraser], who now have a top flat with a very fine view in East Heath Road, Hampstead. Bob says that Dick Crossman is very ill indeed, having neglected phlebitis, which is now showing signs of spreading up his legs. He had been a crashing success – with occasional crashing indiscretions – in North Africa. Eisenhower thought the world of him. But he was so ill out there that he was flown home with a doctor in a bomber, and then, instead of going into hospital here, worked for two days in the office and then collapsed. He will be a great loss if he dies. A most powerful, though not a very lovable, character.

Bob now wants to be a politician again, after a long fallow period. But when he talked to Hindley Atkinson[1] the other night, the best offer the latter could make him was to fight Pritt at Hammersmith. I had not seen these two together since 1940, nor their 6½-year-old daughter, Rosalind,[2] since she was a baby.

Saturday 13th November
Liesching reports that the Treasury are at it again. Eady and Co. are trying to hold up the report to ministers on the Washington talks, and Eady even suggested to Overton that there should first be a meeting of officials 'to brief ministers'. Overton replied, Liesching being in the room, that 'this would lead us into rather deep water'. Liesching thinks that such a meeting was designed to give Hubert Henderson an opportunity to wave his arms about and reopen many old closed questions. Liesching hears that Keynes has not seen either Anderson or Hopkins since his return. This suggests a high-powered intrigue to lessen his influence. On the other hand, he has been very slow in preparing his own part of the report to ministers. We have done ours. I shall write to buck up Law, who led the Delegation and is putting in a covering note to the Cabinet on the Report. I also incite Meade to speak to Cherwell.

Robin Brook to lunch. Very quick and keen and amusing as usual.

1 London Labour Party Organiser.
2 Rosalind Fraser, later Gilmore (b. 1937).

He says Gubbins is a very bad judge of character and has been making frightful trouble by appointing and dismissing large numbers of people in Cairo. He has been stupid enough to appoint Sporborg as his No. 2. The latter is, of course, the stooge of Hambro, whom Gubbins only recently succeeded. He will certainly be disloyal.

Monday 15th November

Hopkins, it is understood 'under ministerial direction', has written to all Permanent Secretaries a quite Henry James letter, the point of which is that 'private conferences' with Sir William Beveridge on his plans for full employment should not be attended by officials, temporary or permanent, lest they might say or imply by what they did not say, something which would give Sir William Beveridge an inkling as to the Government's own proposals. This is rather a blow for Watkinson, who enjoys sitting round with Sir William Beveridge and his economists, and has done so with my full authority and approval. But I am rather glad the thing has been brought to a head, for I have been getting uneasy, particularly since Beveridge has been publicly attacking Morrison, who, he ought to know, is the best friend of his old plan in the War Cabinet. Douglas Jay tells me that Kahn,[1] now at the Ministry of Supply, met him at the Reform Club the other night and, pointing to Beveridge sitting alone at a table in the corner, said, 'Look at that old chap. Everybody has been forbidden by the Treasury to speak to him. If we were seen sitting at the same table, we would be dismissed from the Civil Service, I suppose.' I wouldn't wonder if we hear more about this. But, in that case, I think Anderson will have to answer any public queries.

Dine with Tom Marshall,[2] whom I had not seen for a long while, and Evan Durbin, who now live together at 20, Princess Road. Marshall is now working in the new Historical Research Section of the Foreign Office under Gladwyn Jebb. He is still both intelligent and charming. We have a sweepstake on the likeliest month for the Germans to fold up. I say July 1944, but most of the others put it a month or two earlier.

1 R. F. Kahn, later Baron (b. 1905). Temporary civil servant in various government departments 1939–46. Professor of Economics at Cambridge University 1951–72. Fellow of King's College, Cambridge. Architect of the Keynesian 'multiplier', and close friend and colleague of Keynes.
2 T. H. Marshall (1892–1982). Head of the German Section and Deputy Director of the Research Department at the Foreign Office 1939–44. Head of Social Science Department at L.S.E. 1944–50. Professor of Sociology at L.S.E. 1954–6. Director of Social Sciences Department at U.N.E.S.C.O. 1956–60.

Since L.S.E. days, when Dalton had had politically-minded Jews among his students, he had taken a keen interest in the Palestine problem. Now the provision of a Jewish national home became one of his personal causes. At a meeting of the International Sub-Committee of the Labour Party N.E.C. on 16th November, Dalton presented his first plans for a post-war International Settlement. His views were strongly pro-Zionist. 'The Arabs have not done very well since the last war, either for themselves or for us,' he wrote. 'We should not give in to their policy of Dog in the Holy Manger. They have many wide territories of their own, compared with poor little Palestine. Indeed I would like to extend the Palestinian boundaries either into Egypt or Transjordan. There is also something to be said for throwing open Libya or Eritrea to Jewish settlement, as satellites or colonies to Palestine.'[1] After five months of haggling, the demands were less naked, but still (as Oliver Stanley put it) 'Zionism plus plus'.[2] In April 1944 the N.E.C. International Committee finally passed Dalton's draft on the International Post-War Settlement. This called for Anglo-American-Russian co-operation as the cornerstone of a new World Organisation, and laid emphasis on the menace of Germany and on the need for resettlement of German minorities. It also included a key paragraph in which 'the Arabs' were presented as a single people, whose territory could readily absorb their Palestinian compatriots: 'Let the Arabs be encouraged to move out as the Jews move in. Let them be compensated handsomely for their land and let their settlement elsewhere be carefully organised and generously financed.' The statement suggested that the present boundaries of Palestine might be extended by agreement with Egypt, Syria and Transjordan and that Russian and American support should be sought for the execution of this policy.[3] This commitment aroused keen interest among Jews; though (as the following entry shows) Dalton was originally more interested in the passages which referred to Germany.

Tuesday 16th November
International Sub [-Committee of the Labour Party]. I put over my first sketch of the Post-War International Settlement. It is extremely well received, much better in some quarters than I had expected. Poor little Gillies is terrified of my Palestine paragraph, and thinks this should be referred to a separate committee. I say this is all nonsense.

1 Dalton Papers 7/10 (43).
2 Diary, 28th April 1944.
3 Labour Party Annual Conference Report 1944, pp. 4–9.

He likes all the rest. Dallas, Walker and Burrows are all very complimentary, but the most surprising case is little Laski, who, looking rather ill and telling us that he has had a heart attack, takes half an hour to go through my draft point by point and express complete approval, except, perhaps, on Basic English, which he thinks we should get someone else to propose. He is deeply touched by my Palestine paragraph and also by my earlier reference to the German atrocities. He, like most of the others, is quite prepared for the transfer of population. The more I think, and speak, on this point, the more firmly am I persuaded that, amid the immense inevitable movements for repatriation and resettlement of prisoners-of-war, slave labourers and exiles, the deliberate transfer of some few millions of German minorities back behind the new German frontiers would be a relatively small addition to our problem. This, moreover, would be the unique moment for carrying out this movement, and, once it was done, it would take the sting out of Labour agitations for frontier revision.

The most critical of all my colleagues, and the only one who really argues back against some points in my paper, is Phil [Noel-Baker]. He is a terrible old Genevan Tory. He bothers on for a reference to Mandates, but gets no support on this. ...

Have a word with Overton on the Steering Committee. He is finding it a frightful drain on his time, since they are meeting practically every day. I gather also that he is frequently practically alone against a combination of three Treasury officials – Hopkins, Barlow and Eady, but why all three? – and Robbins. He says, however, that Hurst has given him fair support on Location. Old Phillips[1] seems a bit of an old buffer, and not much use for this purpose.

Wednesday 17th November
Meeting of Sub-Committee on Labour Party secretaryship. Middleton is much calmer now that his date of retirement is decided. We plan to get all nominations in by the end of January and then, through this Sub-Committee, to make a long Short List and finally to bring, say, the six strongest candidates before the full National Executive for interview. The salary must be increased, but the general feeling is that we should not offer more than £1,000 rising to £1,250, or resentment will be caused. Most trade union General Secretaries, I gather, get £1,000, but not a predetermined incremental scale. ...

Douglas Jay to see me, having read through Minutes and papers of

---

1 Marginal insertion: 'of Ministry of Labour'. Sir Thomas Phillips, q.v., was Permanent Secretary at the Ministry of Labour 1935–44.

the Steering Committee. It seems that on Location there is much opposition on the Committee to our proposals and a good deal of concern
among my post-warriors. I must have a conference on this next week.
Jay says that Robbins is talking too much at the Steering Committee
and put in a most preposterous paper – a copy of which I saw – on
Location.

Thursday 18th November
With Hugh Gaitskell, his wife Dora,[1] and George Preston to a Rank
film, *The Demi-Paradise*. This shows a Russian arriving in England,
being received at first in our characteristically ungracious way, but
later being caught up in our middle-class social life. At first he hates
us, particularly our lack of seriousness and sense of humour, but
gradually, particularly after we become allies, he comes to understand
and like us very much. A good film, though it could stand a bit of
cutting.

Herbert Morrison aroused serious hostility when he released Sir Oswald
Mosley, the fascist leader, from detention on grounds of ill-health. As a
result Morrison faced deputations, a back-bench P.L.P. revolt, and a threat
of resignation from Ernest Bevin. The Prime Minister, however, gave Morrison his full support. 'I am convinced 18B should be completely abolished, as
the national emergency no longer justifies abrogation of individual rights of
habeas corpus and trial by jury on definite charges,' Churchill telegrammed
from Cairo to the Home Secretary on 25th November. ' ... Any unpopularity
you have incurred through correct and humane exercise of your functions
will be repaid in a few months by public respect.'[2]

Wednesday 24th November
A bloody awful day! First, from 10 to 1, a National Executive, most
of which is taken up discussing the Mosley case. Little Ellen [Wilkin-
son] who is apt to be much too publicly emotional about her Chief,[3]
makes an impassioned defence, with sobs in her throat, but it really
isn't very convincing, except to the purists for civil liberty, who like to

1 Dora Gaitskell (formerly Frost, née Creditor), later Baroness. Married Hugh
   Gaitskell in 1937.
2 W. S. Churchill, *The Second World War, Vol. V, Closing the Ring*, Cassell, London,
   1952, pp. 635–6.
3 Marginal insertion: 'Morrison'.

think that 18B is being administered leniently. Sam Watson wants us to pass a resolution 'strongly protesting' against Morrison's action. We get this toned down to 'regretting', and this is the best that could be hoped to do.

Thursday 25th November

Morrison today gets a vote of 51 to 43 in the Parliamentary Party Meeting, as a result of which the Party will not put down anything approximating to a Vote of No Confidence. I don't go to the Meeting, partly because I am fed up with the whole thing, partly because I should be much embarrassed in having to defend the way the thing was done, partly because I have lots else to do. Wilmot appears to have been helpful, particularly in drafting the recommendation of the Administrative Committee. So now, rather to my surprise, Morrison will get away with it after all.[1] With every day that passes, interest will decline.

None the less, I consider that he has made a thorough mess of it. I suspect that he has been badly advised by pedantic officials. Also he is much too inclined to get 'upstage' about his 'judicial functions' and not to show much resourcefulness in procedure. I am quite sure that it was quite wrong to speak of the 'release' of Mosley, and also a pretty bad mistake to do the thing three days before Parliament reassembled – instead of waiting and making the first statement in the House – and then putting out such a jejune press notice. Leslie, I hear, knew nothing about it till it had happened. Yet Morrison keeps this clever Australian Jew to advise him on publicity! It would surely have been possible, when these doctors made their representations, to have them up and cross-examine them – and this should have been a good bit of fun in itself – and I would have been inclined to ask them now to go on with the good work and examine the health of all the poorer and obscurer *détenus* as well – and to make them say just what additional steps and facilities were required. And then it would surely have been possible to say that somewhere, in some prison or other institution controlled by the Home Office, such facilities could be provided. And, therefore, all that need have been done, to meet the doctors' case, would have been to transfer this *détenu* from one place of confinement to another; but, neither in fact nor in name, to 'release' him.

I would also have wanted to know, had I been Morrison, why these highly paid, fancy physicians, and notably Dawson of Penn,[2] were

---

1 Marginal insertion: 'letting out Mosley'.
2 Bertrand Dawson, 1st Viscount Dawson of Penn (1867–1945). Physician in Ordinary to the King and Queen. President of the Royal College of Physicians 1931–8.

brought in for this one particular case. Nor can I conceal from myself that, having always hated Mosley worse than any other man in public life – and I don't really *hate* many of them – and remembering vividly many of his misdeeds, including the fact that he was married at Berlin, about 1936 or '37, with Hitler and Goering as witnesses of the ceremony, I would not have been at all sorry to let him die, provided there was not too sharp a comeback from anywhere that mattered. When so many millions are dying, including so many who are so worth while, it is revolting to me that any step, however small, should have been taken to prolong the life of this filthy blackguard, who was clearly marked out to be Gauleiter of this country had the Huns got ashore. I do not think much care would have been taken, even on the recommendation of Lord Dawson of Penn, of the health of most of us under *his* regime.

And therefore, quite frankly, I am almost wholly in sympathy with all the row. But, on the other hand, it would have been a monstrous thing if Morrison had gone down because of this one blunder. None the less, we ministers must remember that our political lives hang always by a thin thread.

Monday 29th November
Go to see Bevin and raise with him, first the P.M.'s latest Minute on Woolton's functions, which seems to suggest that they are practically nil, the duty both of 'formulating' and 'executing' policy remaining 'with the Department concerned', and, second, the hold-up on the Steering Committee. On the first, Bevin says that he went and made a row with the P.M., in the latter's bedroom, when the news of Woolton's appointment was first announced. He wanted to know whether Woolton was going to take over all his work at the Ministry of Labour, because if so, he would go back to his union next day. He also wanted to know whether the P.M. had put Woolton in at Beaverbrook's suggestion. The P.M., he said, 'took this very badly' and said that he was just off to meet Stalin and that his mind was full of other things, and that it was really too much to ask him to go into detailed questions at this moment. But he assured Bevin that there was no intention that Woolton should interfere in the work of the Department, except when it was necessary to bring several of them together, and that he would leave a note behind him which could be circulated as a Minute, making this clear to all ministers. It seems that the P.M. did leave a very rough note, and that this, in his absence, has been cleaned up a bit and circulated over his initials. It was designed to be 'a reassurance' to ministers generally that Woolton would not butt in on them. I then told Bevin that I had told Attlee that he could tell the P.M. that, if

Beaverbrook were given any supervisory powers over me, I should resign, and that almost certainly Waterhouse would do the same. Bevin said, 'We would all have done the same here, me and George Tomlinson and McCorquodale,' and he had also let this be known to the P.M. We then passed to the Steering Committee. He said, 'Poor Phillips is quite broken-'earted about it. He says they are not getting on at all. He says that your man Overton puts up your point of view, but not with much conviction.'

For many purposes Bevin is by far the best of all my colleagues, in spite of his mountainous defects, of egoism, garrulity and peasant-minded suspicion. Wilmot said to me the other day, 'I think Bevin likes you.' I said, 'Why?' He said, 'Because he is always abusing all the others, but he never says anything about you.'

Tuesday 30th November

John Wilmot, with whom I discuss the prospects tonight, is rather gloomy about the atmosphere over Mosley. He thinks that if the Party breaks loose, as it may, and votes solidly against the Government on the Mosley amendment to the Address, the Government may break up and we may all have to go out. I am inclined to think that this is a little over-drawn, but it looks to me quite on the cards that Morrison may feel he ought to resign, if more of our Party vote against him than for him in the Division.

Crowds of people are leaving their work in order to form delegations and deputations to M.P.s and ministers, and I saw with amusement a large crowd with banners gathered outside the building which I share with Sir Stafford Cripps – but they were aircraft workers, after him, not me!

Wednesday 1st December

Party Meeting. On and on about Mosley. 55 to 38 against allowing a free vote to members on the motion put down, in effect a vote of no confidence in the Government, by certain of our Members ... This indiscipline and anarchy is preposterous.

Morrison makes a not very convincing speech, as it seems to me, in the House, but we finally, I hope, are finished with this thing now. A majority of Labour M.P.s votes with the Government, and the total Government majority was very ample. But Morrison has made a sad mess of this case.

An amendment had been moved on the Address regretting the lack of mention of any national policy for a better location of industry, designed to prevent a recurrence of unemployment in areas hardest hit before the war. On 8th December, Dalton announced his intention to use the granting of building permits for industrial development as a lever for influencing the location of industry in the transitional period from war to peace. He also suggested that arms factories could be switched to civilian production, or adapted as trading estates.[1]

Friday 3rd December
Confer with Woolton and Lyttelton on next week's Location debate. They came up to me at the end of the Lord President's Committee this morning and said they were afraid that I should have a rather difficult job in dealing with this Amendment since so little had been decided, and they would like to do their best to help! Sir Alan Barlow is produced this afternoon as Acting Chairman of the Steering Committee. I am a little cold to him and ask whether there is anything on which the officials have agreed that they shall recommend to ministers. To my surprise, he says they are agreed on the use of building permits for the Transition. This is a bull point which I must make the most of. Woolton seems, quite naturally, not to realise much about the detail of any of this, but I think he genuinely does want to help to produce decisions.

Tuesday 7th December
Dine with Douglas and Peggy Jay. Peggy says that he is now really much better, the transfer plus a fairly easy opening period having done him good. His naval brother comes in and tell us of his experiences with the Russians. Archangel sounds a bit dreary and slushy, but he says that the Russians, once they start on a job, go full split until they finish it, and their naval people seem to get on very well with ours. They are good at their work and also at drinking.

Wednesday 8th December
Three amendments are taken in the House today on the Address, and on the second of these, on Location of Industry, I make a rather successful speech ... I go a bit beyond anything that my colleagues have agreed to, but not much beyond the rough note which I cleared with

1 H. C. Debs [395], cols 1064–74.

Woolton. The speech gives a good deal of satisfaction in the House and also to some of my officials. We can now go forward a bit faster, I hope, with the industrialists.

Thursday 9th December
1.15 to 3.0. Act as host, in the absence of Mrs Phillimore, to six American journalists. I notice, as on previous occasions, that they are tremendous experts at suspicion of seemingly harmless persons and transactions. I talk to them fairly frankly about the Labour Party, and impress on them that it is the Annual Conference of the Party, and not the Parliamentarians, who will decide whether we stay in or go out of the Government later on. I also make the point that it takes two to stay together, and that perhaps the Tories may think, at a given moment, that they would do better if we broke up.

Friday 10th December
Spend morning, and lunch, with Allied Socialists at St Ermin's, seeking their views on the International Post-War Settlement ... They don't add much, but they oppose nothing of importance in my plan, which I don't positively disclose to them, only asking them questions. The most intelligent is Brodson (?),[1] the Luxembourg Minister of something or other. He says that an army can only, in the next stage, become international at the staff level, though, in the light of our war experience, an air force can become international lower down. Most are for 'decentralisation' in Germany, and it may be that this will prove the magic formula. If you 'decentralise' enough, the result will not be practically different from 'dismemberment', e.g. if you 'decentralise' the right to make war. They all undertake to send particulars of German conduct in their own countries. I am inclined to think that we should make a separate publication of this, collecting also something from the Soviet Embassy. None wants German labour gangs in their territory; they think the Russians should have the monopoly of this form of reparation. Most are scared of any European organisation, political or economic, which would exclude Britain and Russia. This, one of them says, would be nothing less than a Great Germany. But, if you include Britain and Russia, you have already gone as far east as the Pacific and included the whole of the British Empire. In that case, you are already world-wide, and why, then, have any special European organisation? There is some sense in this.

1 Probably V. J. H. Bodson (1902–84). Vice-President of the Luxembourg Labour Party. Minister of Justice 1940–47.

Saturday 11th December
To Hampstead in the evening to dine and sleep with Bob and Betty [Fraser].

Sunday 12th December
Sleep in most of the morning and, after an admirable lunch, go for a quick walk, with occasional jogs, on Hampstead Heath with Bob and Betty. We overtake Douglas and Peggy Jay, but rapidly out-distance them. A most dingy man, alleged by Bob to be his immediate superior[1] and ranking as the equivalent of a P.A.S. [Principal Assistant Secretary], makes a very poor impression on me. He was, I hear, an advertising agent before the Ministry of Information took him on. His worst break, speaking to a Minister of the Crown, was to refer to 'some chap at the Ministry of Supply' when it appeared that he was intending to indicate Sir Andrew Duncan. This was apropros of the allegation of Driberg that Sir Andrew Duncan was going to leave the Government in order to take up a post at £20,000 a year with the British Employers. Following a formal denial of this, Driberg was fired from the *Daily Express*, so that, though 'William Hickey' still writes, it is no longer Driberg.

Rosalind, now aged six and a half, has a penetrating voice, great self-confidence and strong character. She was, for a short while, at school with some nuns. Towards these she is quite vindictive. We discuss together how to make life unpleasant for 'the silly old nuns'. She would like me, first of all, to take all their coupons away, and then take away all their blackouts, so that they must either sit in the dark or turn on the light, and, if they turned on the light, we would take them all away and put them in gaol.

Wednesday 15th December
Very interesting Cabinet on 'Demobilisation'. Bevin now proposes a quite fresh approach. Is this, he asks, one war or two? If one war – and unless we insist on this, the whole machine will break in our hands and no one will be willing either to go and fight the Japs or to do anything except what he likes at home – we should consider 'demobilisation' as coming only when Japan is defeated. Till then, men should only be 'released'. On release from the Forces – with liability to recall – they should be subject to direction. They should go, not where they like, but where their labour will be most useful, whether for export, or for re-equipping the home market. Similarly, workers

---

1 Possibly G. S. Royds (1897–1964). Controller of five divisions of the Ministry of Information 1942–5. Founder in 1927 of the advertising agency G. S. Royds Ltd.

in war industries should continue, during the second stage of this 'one war', to be subject to direction. No one should be able to leave an arms factory or any other Works covered by E.W.O. [Essential Work Order], without Bevin's permission, and then only on condition of going where he or she is directed.

I am wholly in favour of this revolutionary proposal, provided it can be put across politically. Age + Length of Service would continue to be the criterion for 'release', as it has hitherto been suggested for 'demobilisation'. 'Block releases' would be ruled out for men leaving the Services, though 'a limited number of specialists' ... would be 'released' out of their turn. On the other hand, civilian labour would be dealt with on the basis of 'block releases'. Thus we would pull out from an arms factory first of all those who were miners or builders or textile operatives or furniture makers, and so build up our 'labour allocations' in industries important to be expanded quickly.

There is general support, among others too, though less cautiously than by me, for this idea of 'the one war'. Evidently also the idea has distinct political attractions for Bevin and me. Some, however, have grave doubts whether this *can* be put over politically. But the alternative is very bad. Cripps thinks that after a few months, if everyone is free to leave his aircraft factories, he will have great difficulty in maintaining anything like the output required. And I can see large numbers of people, both from the Services and other industries, going into the wrong occupations, and embarking on all the 'inessential productions' which we have banned, while production which is really essential is left most ill provided for. It is finally agreed that Bevin shall discuss the matter further with Service ministers and also with the Supply ministers and with me. 'What would you do about the furlough and the gratuity?' somebody asked. 'Oh, that is only a detail,' replied Bevin. He was a really great man tonight.

At the end of November, Churchill, Roosevelt and Stalin met in Teheran to discuss grand strategy, Stalin giving his support for Overlord and the invasion of southern France as soon as possible. It was decided to back Tito's partisans in Yugoslavia; to change boundaries in eastern Europe in order to take part of Poland into the Soviet Union, and to give Poland part of Germany; and to press Turkey to enter the war.

On 2nd December, Churchill and Roosevelt flew from Teheran to Cairo to continue the Anglo-American discussions. On 12th December, Churchill flew on to Tunis, to spend one night with General Eisenhower before visiting the Italian Front. Next day the Prime Minister fell ill, and pneumonia was diagnosed. His doctor, Lord Moran, feared a total collapse. On 27th December Churchill went to Marrakesh to convalesce. This was his second attack in 1943: in February he had suffered a milder bout of pneumonia, his first serious illness since 1922.

Thursday 16th December

I.L.O. [International Labour Office] lunch with Bevin in the Chair. This thing has kept alive in the most surprising way – in spite of the continual presence of my brother-in-law, who is at the lunch today, looking drearier than ever.

Llewellin to see me, our first contact since he has returned as Minister of Food. He gives the impression of having handled the U.N.R.R.A. Conference pretty well. But he gives a most awful account of Sir George Rendel, 'the one diplomat who was there', as he contemptuously observed. It was an Anglo-Russian dinner party, and all was going very well. Successive toasts were being proposed, in the Russian fashion, and they began with such simple ones as 'To Victory', 'To our Common Cause', 'To the Red Army', 'To the R.A.F.', etc. And then Sir George, rising in his turn, said, 'Now *I* will propose a toast. I give you the toast "To Hitler's attack upon Russia".' Thereupon a great commotion, and to make it worse, he began to make a speech. 'Let me explain. What I mean is that from the moment we were in the war together, all the old misunderstandings began to disappear. Before Hitler attacked you, neither of us realised the great qualities of the other ...... ' The translator tried to be diplomatic, but one of the Russians who understood English shouted out, 'No, he did not say that at all.' Whereupon Llewellin rose and said, 'I give you the toast of "The Future",' and the incident passed over.

Later that evening in the hotel bar, Llewellin said to Dean Acheson, 'It was as though I had proposed to Americans the toast "To the Japanese attack on Pearl Harbor".' Whereupon Jan Masaryk, who was there, said, 'I give you the toast of Munich.'

Dine with Winster and a chap in Air Force uniform whose name I don't catch when he is introduced to me, but who emerges, in the course of the talk, as a peer and the Lord Lieutenant of some county. It turns out to be Brownlow,[1] who was one of Edward VIII's entourage.

---

1 P. F. A. C. Brownlow, 6th Baron (1899–1978). Staff Officer to Deputy Chief of Staff 8th U.S. Air Force 1943–4. Personal Lord in Waiting to King Edward VIII 1936.

Tonight the news of the P.M.'s illness appears for the first time in the evening papers. I said that there had been much running about during last night's Cabinet and Winster said that he was at Beaverbrook's house – wherever this is now – and that the latter came in very late and looking very white and drawn. Clearly it is serious. (During the next two days the bulletins are much better, and there seems ground for hope that, reasonably soon, he will be back again. But this second dose of pneumonia in less than a year raises some very grim thoughts and very deep queries. We owe this man, as our War Leader, an immeasurable debt. But how much longer, at this pressure, can he go on?)

On 29th November, Churchill had presented to Stalin the Sword of Honour, which the King had had specially designed and wrought to commemorate the defence of Stalingrad. 'When, after a few sentences of explanation, I handed the splendid weapon to Marshal Stalin he raised it in a most impressive gesture to his lips and kissed the scabbard,' Churchill recalled. 'He then passed it to Voroshilov, who dropped it.'[1]

Friday 17th December
Lunch with the Jebbs, including Miles and Vanessa. Both distinctly handsome, but I hear that Stella is going to be the beauty of the family!

Gladwyn tells me, while we are alone, some of the smaller incidents at Teheran. The presentation of the Sword of Stalingrad was – up to a point – very impressive. The P.M. made an appropriate allocution, and it was a moving moment when Stalin took and kissed the sword. But then, not being used to handling this kind of weapon, he passed it to Voroshilov at such an angle that the sword fell out of the scabbard and struck the ground. Whereupon Voroshilov performed various drill movements to replace it, and got it in the right ceremonial position again.

Gladwyn said that Stalin is very small in stature, smells very strongly of scent – he thinks that this is a Russian rather than a personal characteristic – and has a most curious complexion, a sort of greenish-blue hue.

On the occasion when he said, 'Until now I have always called him

1 Churchill, *Closing the Ring*, p. 321.

"Prime Minister Churchill", but henceforth I shall call him "My fighting friend",' the P.M. replied, 'Tell him that I have always called him "Uncle Joe" behind his back.' But the translator, translating this last sally into Russian, treated 'Uncle Joe' as untranslatable, and repeated it in English. Stalin's face remained completely blank. This was a missed opportunity, for the translator might well have said in Russian 'Little Uncle Joseph'. This would have sounded both affectionate and amusing.

Many of the projects in which Gladwyn was personally interested could not be raised, since the P.M. was already sickening at Teheran and wasn't up to discussing them.

He formed a very poor impression of Casey at Cairo, saying that he had 'a mind like a snipe'. There was a great fuss about his being appointed Governor of Bengal. The India Office said that it was quite impossible for a plain Mr to be Governor of a Province. He must be either a peer or a knight. But Casey said that he couldn't become either, or his return to Australian politics would be rendered impossible. (We agreed that it would almost certainly be impossible anyhow, particularly after a term of office in Calcutta.) So a new precedent is to be established. He will govern Bengal as plain Mr Casey.

Monday 20th December
First meeting of Reconstruction Committee with Woolton in the Chair. I am there for a discussion on clothing for demobilised soldiers. Woolton begins by beaming round the room, which contains sixteen ministers and about half a dozen officials, and starts off. 'Gentlemen' – we are quite unaccustomed to being addressed in this fashion – 'I hope that we shall now soon be able to reach a series of important decisions. All the material has now been collected by our advisers. I do not think, gentlemen, that there is anything more which we can ask them to do. It might even be that a wrong decision would be better than no decision at all.' He couldn't have got it better, if I had written his notes. But Portal, with his usual post-lunch manner – it is now 3.30 p.m. – whispers in my ear, 'The silly b...... thinks he is still trying to sell something across the counter. He has got nothing to sell really at all.'

I hear that Norman Brook is determined to make this thing succeed if he can. He is a very able and clear-headed man and his rise has been rapid. If he falls down on this, many will rejoice and he may find it hard to rise again; if he succeeds, he will be one of the outstanding war figures in the Civil Service, of whom in this war, as contrasted with the last, there are damned few.

Before the Teheran Conference, Churchill and Roosevelt met in Cairo to discuss joint operations and to consult General Chiang Kai-shek about policy in the Far East. Churchill was impressed by the Chinese leader and his wife. However, he found the presence of the Chinese a distraction from the main business – especially as far as the Americans were concerned. 'All hopes of persuading Chiang and his wife to go and see the Pyramids and enjoy themselves till we returned from Teheran fell to the ground,' he recalled, 'with the result that Chinese business occupied first instead of last place at Cairo.'[1] In spite of Churchill's arguments, Roosevelt promised the Chinese a major amphibious operation across the Bay of Bengal within the next few months – diverting vital resources from Overlord.

The major purpose of the further Cairo meeting after the Teheran Conference was to resume talks with the Turkish leaders in the hope of bringing Turkey into the war. Churchill and Roosevelt met President Inönü on 4th December, but without result.

Tuesday 21st December

Ministers' meeting at Foreign Office, where Eden gives some account of the recent Conferences.

At Cairo the difficulty was to prevent the Americans from promising the Chinese everything, including several large-scale amphibious operations, so that there would not have been enough left for the Russians! It was rather invidious to have to keep on intervening to counsel caution and calculation. But the P.M. fell for Madame Chiang,[2] and feels now that he likes both her and her husband much better than he did before, never having met either of them. She was a most accomplished interpreter. Eden also thinks that *they* both felt better for having been brought into the Club.

There was also some difficulty over a declaration about post-war territorial arrangements in the Pacific. The first draft had been made by the Americans and shown to the Chinese before they showed it to us. It gave the Chinese everything, including Formosa and the Pescadores, but it was very doubtful whether, on a strict reading, either we or the Dutch would have got back anything of what the Japs have seized. We succeeded in getting a better draft agreed with

1 Churchill, *Closing the Ring*, pp. 289–90.
2 Madame Chiang Kai-shek, née Mayling Soong, married Chiang Kai-shek in 1927.

the Americans, and the final result was not bad. But Dr Wang[1] kept on saying monotonously throughout the discussion, 'I prefer first draft.'

The President also said some most unfortunate things to the King of Greece when the latter came to see him. We had been working very hard, in order to get the Greeks to fight the Germans rather than each other, to persuade the King to declare that he would not go back to Greece, after her liberation, unless and until he was invited by a properly elected national assembly. It was very difficult to get him to say this, but in the end he did. The Americans had been just as keen on his saying it as we had, and both the State Department and the U.S. diplomats concerned had been helping things along, and the President had been carefully briefed on all this, finally by Harry Hopkins. But, says Eden, whenever he meets anyone, he likes to create a friendly and favourable impression, and, therefore, when the poor little King was shown in, the President began by saying, with a broad smile, 'Don't let anybody bully you into giving an undertaking not to go back to your country. I am sure they will all be only too delighted to see you again.' ......

Teheran. Here again the Americans were promising the Russians everything, including all that they had previously promised to the Chinese, and we again had the ungrateful task of expressing doubts. One day in particular was very sticky, and we had to point out that our resources really were getting very strained and that we could not do all that was being talked about.

Stalin was very jovial off parade. He is very able. He took charge himself of all the military discussions. He brought with him no prominent soldier except Voroshilov, and everything, in the military talks, was referred back to him for his approval. He said that he would keep on with partial offensives all through the winter, leading up to a big push in the spring – timed to come just in front of ours – which in turn has a fairly wide date range. He realises that the great problem is ships. He will be very tough with the Germans. The President wants to break Germany up into three or four separate States and to join Bavaria to Austria. Stalin is against this. He wants no Germans in any federal groupings of States which may be formed in Central or South-East Europe. The hatred of Germans has gone very deep in Russia. A separate peace by the Russians is quite out of the question. Stalin also spoke very ill of the French. He said that they haven't really fought; their whole society is rotten; they cannot be trusted in any strong points and therefore the Americans should take Dakar

1 Wang Ch'ung-hui. Secretary-General of the Chinese Supreme Defence Council. Minister of Foreign Affairs 1937–41.

and the British Bizerte. (The President lapped this up, but we were rather disconcerted. It would shock de Gaulle, who thinks he has been having quite a good flirtation with Stalin, to hear all this.) As to the Poles, Stalin wants the Curzon Line, but is quite prepared for Poland to go as far west as the Oder, with transfer of German populations westward. Eden said they had some discussion on the eastern frontier, and Stalin said, 'We regard that as all settled. Here is our line on the map.' Eden said, 'Do you mean the Ribbentrop-Molotov Line?' Molotov looked rather disconcerted at this, but Stalin said, 'We generally call it the Curzon Line. It is the same thing, isn't it?' Then there was some discussion about Bialystok, where Eden said the people were mainly Poles and Stalin agreed and redrew the line on the map to exclude them. We tried very hard to get Lwow for the Poles, but Stalin insisted that, although there were a lot of Poles in the city, the countryside was entirely Ukrainian. Stalin also thought that the Russians ought to have Königsberg, as a 'warm water port', but Eden thought this was going a bit far. Stalin did not speak very ill of the present Polish Government in London, but complained that the Poles were killing Partisans on their territory, and that a situation was developing very much like that in Yugoslavia.

The President, with his mind full of the elections, did not want to get involved in a discussion on Poland, and this, therefore, was entirely an Anglo-Russian affair, the President sitting in a corner and feigning sleep.

Eden said he had seen the Poles since he returned, but they were all waffling. They have no successor to Sikorski. But they intend at a certain moment to order a general rising in Poland, and this is a card which may be worth something to them when the time comes.

Stalin was also very hot against the Bulgars.

Finally, the Cairo Conference with the Turks was very heavy weather. We got nowhere at all until the last day, and not very far even then. The Turkish Foreign Minister talked incessantly and was most obstructive. The Turkish President was better, and it is he in the last resort who will take decisions. But whenever anything is suggested to the Turks, they always ask for more arms and equipment first.

Dalton had been invited to stay over Christmas with Morgan Philips Price, Labour M.P. for the Forest of Dean, and his family, in their house at Taynton, near Gloucester. He arrived on Christmas Eve.

Friday 24th December

... [H]ere [at Taynton] I spend four very pleasant nights and days; sleeping a lot, eating a lot, and spending nearly all of every day plugging about through muddy woods and fields in my very superior leather + rubber boots. Mrs Price,[1] it will be recalled, is a German, who, as a young Communist, Philips Price[2] met when he was in Germany as Correspondent of the *Manchester Guardian* at the end of the last war. She is very definitely a good Hausfrau, but rather a tiresome woman. She still speaks with a strong German accent and never lets one long forget her origin. I don't encourage much political conversation, but, given half a chance, she advocates the total extermination of all 'Nazis', both old and young. He, on the other hand, is much more interested in Russia and is very Russophil. He has just published a short book, a potted history, which has gone very well, called *Russia through the Centuries*. He argues that this great people did not suffer any fundamental change in 1917, but that everything has been a natural succession for centuries. He still speaks Russian and maintained, he says, an hour's conversation of a sort with Gusev in London the other day. He thinks Tchaikovsky the greatest of all composers, and we listen to a good deal of him on the gramophone.

His other great interest is agriculture and forestry and, in particular, his own estate. I am shown and told a lot about all this and am taken on some very interesting tours of his woodlands, many of which were planted by his grandfather, who sat as Liberal M.P. for Gloucester for twenty years. ...

The house is very full of visitors, refugees and retainers of all sorts and nationalities. They have a very good Austrian (Aryan) cook, who is accompanied by her Austrian (Jewish) husband, who helps about the place. There are also three or four English retainers, whose roles are a little obscure. They all come in and sit round on Christmas Eve, when a Christmas Tree is lighted and presents distributed to all. The rest of the party consists of Peter, their rather good-looking son, who is physically unfit for the Army and doing Films instead, a young Polish soldier, who has come all the way from Scotland to spend Christmas with them, they having offered to take 'one Pole' over this season, and a very wispy and inarticulate little German Jewish refugee boy from Breslau. Their daughter Tatiana was married only a few weeks ago to a young man in the Canadian Black Watch, who has now gone back to Canada to train for a commission.

1 Elisa Philips Price, née Balster. From Halberstadt, Germany. M. 1919.
2 Morgan Philips Price (1885–1973). Labour M.P. for the Forest of Dean 1935–50; Whitehaven 1929–31; Gloucestershire West 1950–59.

I find that we last stayed here from 29th June to 1st July 1928, when I wrote in the Visitors' Book, 'We have seen the snows of Central Asia, and heard the songs of Kurds and Armenians, and eaten the most divine raspberries and strawberries of Gloucestershire – and all in one weekend!' He put on again, at my request, the records of the Kurdish and Armenian songs. This time I wrote in the Visitors' Book, 'Since July 1928, the whole world has rolled away, but the charm, the friendship and the hospitality of this house remain unchanged.'

I meet during these days various other local notabilities, from the bailiff to neighbouring farmers and the Deputy Director of Forestry for the Forest of Dean. It is all very healthy and cheerful and non-Board-of-Trade. ...

I wish we had more men like Philips Price, who, in addition to taking an intelligent interest in other matters, can beat the Tories at their own local country game. His wife tells me that what he would really like most of all now would be to be sent on a mission to Russia. But this is not really very practical, for he is getting rather deaf and goes off to sleep at the least excuse, particularly after lunch.

Wednesday 29th December
No one much about.

Garro Jones to dine. He has got a queer, half-baked, political judgment. He says that we should not rush, just after victory over Germany, into an election against the P.M., but thinks that 'as a condition of maintaining the Coalition', the Labour Party should then claim an *equal* share with the Tories of seats in the Government. In particular, he thinks we should have either the Foreign Office or the Treasury or both. This is really very raw.

He is also apt to have strong, but not very firmly based, opinions on matters lying outside his own field, e.g. on price control and location of industry. He is also still very anti-Attlee. On the other hand, he is very pro-me!

Thursday 30th December
The gossip is that, at the last ministerial reshuffle, when Woolton was moved up, Gwilym Lloyd George was offered the Ministry of Food and, after two hours' meditation, accepted. Shinwell was then invited by the P.M. to become Minister of Fuel and Power, and also accepted. That evening, however, Lloyd George changed his mind and told the P.M. so about 11 o'clock. He felt, on second thoughts, that a move now would look as though he had been a failure at Fuel and Power, and he wanted to have one more shot. So he stayed where he was, and Shinwell had to be told that the offer was off, and Llewellin was

fetched back from Washington, and Ben Smith sent out in his place. This is both interesting and amusing. On the one hand, it would have finally blown up any reputation Shinwell has if he were to fail to get the coal;[1] on the other hand, many of the miners hate him, including the Durham leaders, and his appointment would have had a bad reception from them. Equally it would have had a very bad reception in the Parliamentary Labour Party, where he has recently been pushed off our Administrative Committee. But the old device of putting awkward people in tight spots hasn't yet quite gone out of fashion.

Friday 31st December
Lunch with Mrs Phillimore – and Attlee. Coming away, I take occasion to throw a fly over him to check up the truth of the reported offer to Shinwell. I say that Shinwell and his mentor, Balogh, are telling everyone that he was offered Fuel and Power and was willing to accept it. This, I said, was very stupid. Attlee, looking slightly defensive, quite agreed that it was very stupid, but didn't deny that it was true. I then said that, if he had taken office, it would have made a very bad impression in the Parliamentary Party and would have upset a number of miners' leaders. Attlee again assented and then relapsed into a rather uncomfortable reserve. He did not even say, this time, as he told me at the time of Beaverbrook's re-entry to the Government, that he had fought very hard against it.

Gladwyn Jebb to dine. I had not talked to him of the Teheran and Cairo Conferences since Eden's official exposition. He agreed with me that the Cairo Conference with the Turks had been a flop. Both the Turks – the President and the Foreign Minister – were deaf and neither spoke English, only a very Turkish kind of French. Our own Prime Minister, as we know, talks very fluent French but with a distinctly English accent and often translating faithfully the most idiomatic English. It was, Gladwyn said, the thing that finally knocked up the P.M., having to shout at these two Turks for hours on end in his French. Whatever was proposed, they always said they would like, before considering this, to have some more arms, some more from us and some more from the Germans.

Dixon, he says, is doing quite well as the new Principal Private Secretary. He will make a good Private Secretary of 'the nursemaid type', and this, at present, is what is required, as so often with politicians. When Horace Seymour[2] succeeded Selby as Principal Private Secretary to Simon, he came into the Private Office and asked what

---

1 After Shinwell became Minister of Fuel and Power in the Attlee administration, this comment turned out to be oddly prophetic.
2 H. J. Seymour, later Sir Horace (1885–1978). Ambassador to China 1942–6.

sort of a man this present Foreign Secretary was. When it was explained to him that he was not quite so bad as some people painted him, but that he was sometimes very difficult, argumentative, inclined to tantrums and full of easily injured vanity, Seymour replied, 'Oh, I quite understand. I think I shall be able to manage him. I have children of my own.'

9

Background to Overlord
January–August 1944

During the spring and summer of 1944 the War Cabinet was concerned with preparations for, and then the consolidation of, the Normandy landings. Meanwhile the Red Army advanced rapidly in the East, and the Allies moved slowly up the Italian peninsula, encountering fierce German resistance.

At home, Labour's document on 'The International Post-War Settlement', drafted by Dalton, and including among its most important recommendations a proposal for a Palestinian settlement favourable to the Jews, was passed by the National Executive. The Government's celebrated Full Employment White Paper was published in May.

Articles of Agreement for an International Monetary Fund were finally settled at Bretton Woods, New Hampshire, in July.

Saturday 1st to Sunday 2nd January
In London. On the Sunday afternoon visit Dick Crossman in the Nursing Home at 18 Bentinck Street. He had nearly died of thrombophlebitis and has had to lie quite motionless for weeks. He is still not allowed to use his left hand. But what a dynamic, even if, as I have said before, not very lovable character. I stayed for two hours, during nearly the whole of which he harangued me with great vigour both of voice and mind. He had a wonderful time in Africa.[1] He says it is so

1 Crossman had been Deputy Director of Psychological Warfare, A.F.H.Q. [Allied Forces Headquarters], Algiers for several months in 1943. During this time he had been with Eisenhower and Harold Macmillan in Algiers and Italy, working on the propaganda possibilities created by Mussolini's fall from power. In 1944–5 he was Assistant Chief of the Psychological Warfare Division of S.H.A.E.F. [Supreme Headquarters, Allied Expeditionary Force].

wonderful to be out of reach of control and interference by various offices in London and to be in direct touch with soldiers, who see much more clearly than civilians the importance of political warfare, just because it will save casualties and hasten victory. He is very pro-Ike, and says that he has done a simply grand job as the leader of the Anglo-American team. He always gives the benefit of the doubt to an Englishman and, at the higher levels, there is just no duality at all. Crossman's own American associates were also first-class. He had a great thrill in actually negotiating the timing of the Italian Armistice and the publicity connected with it. He flew across from North Africa to Sicily with Jackson,[1] his American opposite number, and, on arrival, at the rendezvous with the Italians, they found a number of Italian Generals but no British or American. The latter, it seems, had just flown off somewhere else, and Crossman and Jackson with one comparatively junior British officer had instructions to get on with the job. It was rather complicated trying to make sure that nothing came out too soon to compromise operations, or too late to have the hoped-for propaganda effects. Crossman quite agrees that the Italians, including their Generals, are the best diplomats alive. With such small means they achieve remarkably good results. One Italian, whose eyes were like deep brown pools of understanding, said, 'We are not really interested in unconditional surrender; what we want is to become one of the United Nations. We will give you all the help we can against the Germans.' Harold Macmillan, Crossman thought, was doing very well. He is also a good diplomat. At their first meeting, he said, 'We are like the Greeks in the later Roman Empire. They ran it, because they were so much cleverer than the Romans, but they never told the Romans this. That must be our relation to the Americans.' Montgomery was, for many reasons, most unpopular at the War Office. He had sent back to London under arrest one of his Major Generals of the Eighth Army who had ventured to argue with him. This had caused great trouble at the War Office, because they had had to find three Lieutenant Generals to sit as a Court Martial on this man. (Sir Basil Brooke[2] next week in Northern Ireland told me this story. When his uncle, Sir Alan Brooke, the C.I.G.S. [Chief of Imperial General Staff], was asked by the King what sort of a man Montgomery was, the C.I.G.S. said, 'He is a very good soldier, but I think he is after my job.' The King said, 'What a relief! I thought he was after mine!' In

---

1 C. D. Jackson (1902–65). Deputy Chief of the Office of War Information Overseas, North Africa and the Middle East 1943–4. Deputy Chief of the Psychological Warfare Division of S.H.A.E.F. 1944–5.

2 Captain Sir Basil Brooke, later 1st Viscount Brookeborough (1888–1973). Prime Minister of Northern Ireland 1943–63.

Northern Ireland the Montgomeries are a cult. The old mother is always turning up and telling people who she is, and a younger brother of the General said, 'I hardly know him. I have only seen him twice since he was seven. But he sounds a clever bloke. If ever I want a room in a hotel, I find it very convenient to be able to say that I am his brother.')

Crossman also related, to my horror, that he had heard our General Alexander make an after-dinner speech to an Anglo-American party in which he said, 'There are only two first-class races in the world, we, the Anglo-Saxons' – and here he fixed his eye upon a rather Latin-American looking U.S. General – 'and the Germans. It is one of the tragedies of history that twice in our lifetime we should be fighting each other instead of fighting on the same side. If we were allies, we could beat the whole world.' (Some may think this story incredible, but I recall the case of Wully Robertson[1] in the last war, who went round with Lloyd George as his C.I.G.S. to many inter-allied conferences and always showed the utmost hostility to all our allies, particularly to those who, like the French and the Italians, didn't speak English. When any one of these was speaking Wully assumed an air of deep suspicion and hardly veiled hostility and used to whisper in a loud voice to his next-door neighbour, 'What is the fellow saying?' And once, at the end of one of these seances, he said, 'If only we and the Boche were allies, how easily we could beat all this crowd!') Crossman explained that between the German Panzer Divisions and the Eighth Army in Africa there had grown up a great mutual respect for each other's efficiency, combined with great contempt on both sides for Italians and French. He told me of a German officer, a prisoner-of-war, with whom he himself had spoken and who had said 'our war' in the desert had been 'a gentlemanly war', fought with great skill and courage by good sportsmen on both sides, and that lives had only been sacrificed, on both sides, for good military reasons. This German officer, before being captured, had been fighting on the Russian Front. 'That', he said, 'is quite a different war. It is not a civilised war. It is a barbaric war. The Russians drive us back, not through their military skill nor their soldierly qualities, but only by their mass of numbers. They send in great masses of infantry, sometimes of cavalry, and [we] shoot them down, and still they send more and more, and in the end they get there. Their gunners put down a terrific barrage, not scientifically on a selected target, but anyhow all over the place, and then they shift their barrage about until it falls

1 Field Marshal Sir William Robertson, 1st Bart (1860–1933). Chief of Imperial General Staff 1915–18.

on us and not on their own men, and they have so many guns and so much ammunition that, in the end, they shell us out. But that is only barbarism and mass murder.'

Tuesday 4th to Thursday 6th January
With George Preston to Northern Ireland. Quite an interesting trip, the best part of which was the flight there and back. We took 2½ hours with a head wind going out; only 1¾ hours with a following wind coming back.

...

In between these flights we saw something of Ulster. I was put up by Basil Brooke, the 'Prime Minister' of this petty provincial government, in a small official residence just opposite the vast Parliament House. Not a bad chap, an ex-regular soldier, with more idea of how to organise and get things done than most of the Northern Irish notabilities. He is, in fact, quite good at pressing the claims, and contributions to the war effort, of the Six Counties. The first night there was a dinner party, the real purpose of which was to get me in a corner, surrounded by the linen manufacturers, who were to explain to me how important their industry was, both now and post-war. These included an old frog called McCready,[1] a very hard-boiled and self-opinionated capitalist employer; Mulholland,[2] brother-in-law of Sir Basil Brooke, also Speaker of the Ulster House of Commons, a more agreeable and better-educated man, with film star features; and Dermot Campbell,[3] recently elected M.P. at Westminster. The real trouble these people are going to have is to get their raw material. There will be no difficulty in selling their products, particularly abroad.

For the next day and a half I have a series of interviews with representatives of various industries – linen, clothing, etc. – and visit a large number of factories of interest to the Board of Trade – one linen, two clothing, prams, nursery furniture, etc. At the first clothing factory I stand upon a table and make a speech to several hundred girls. A very jolly and enthusiastic scene, including singing, in which they all join, of 'There'll always be an England ...... There'll always be a Britain ...... Red, White and Blue, what does it mean to you?

1 H. L. McCready (1876–1950). Chairman of the Linen Industry Post-War Planning Committee 1943–4. Chairman of the Central Council of the Linen Industry 1946–50.
2 H. G. H. Mulholland, later Sir Henry, 1st Bart (1888–1970). Speaker of the House of Commons of Northern Ireland 1929–45. Chairman and Managing Director of York Street Flax Spinning Co. Ltd, Belfast. Married to Sheelah, daughter of Sir Douglas Brooke, 4th Bart, brother of Sir Basil Brooke.
3 J. D. Campbell (1898–1945). Unionist M.P. for Antrim 1943–5.

...... ' The factory is stiff with Union Jacks of every size, including a lot of small ones strung along above the sewing machines. This is 'loyal' Ulster, and I don't doubt that it is all most sincere, even, as by tradition, most fanatical. I was to have gone to a factory in Falls Road, but this was changed at the last minute. They feared some clash of Orange and Green. As one of the officials said to me, 'If they had shot you, it would have helped to advertise the I.R.A.'

Friday 7th January
In Lord President's Committee for an hour, during the last minutes of which I said twelve words, agreeing with a paper by Stanley that control of cotton export prices to the Crown Colonies was neither practicable nor necessary. Not an economical, or even amusing, use of time! A concourse of twenty ministers, who should have been doing useful work in their departments, sitting round the table and palavering disjointedly, with poor little Attlee hardly visible or audible in the Chair.

...

With Wilmot to Golders Green for George Ridley's funeral. It was, no doubt, as his widow said afterwards, just as he would have liked with no Christianity and three quite good addresses – by Sorensen, who also read passages from William Morris, Fred Watkins and Attlee. The Red Flag was played on the organ, but there was no other music.

For my part, I still think that if you are going to have such a gathering at all, it should all be a bit more dashing and dramatic – even if only, as Ponsonby once said he would like, to have one of the House of Commons policemen to stand beside the grave, or before the door through which the remains go to be burnt, and cry, in a loud clear voice, as late at night when 'the House gets up', 'Who goes home?' This is a good Parliamentarian's alternative to the bugler playing the Last Post, though I like that too.

Dine with John Wilmot, who is much shocked at the offer of office to Shinwell. Had this come off, he says, it would have had the most disintegrating effects in the Labour Party, and he wonders whether this was perhaps part of the intention. Everyone would have said that the path to office was through disloyalty, and many imitators would have been encouraged. Decent loyal people, on the other hand, would have been greatly discouraged and there would have been a serious row among the miners who, particularly in Durham, hated Shinwell. Wilmot also thinks that the incident reflects little credit on Attlee, who must either have freely agreed to the idea or been over-ruled and bullied into accepting. Wilmot has lately read again the terms of the

P.M.'s Four Year Plan Broadcast and noted the possibility of a government of men from all parties 'who would be willing to serve'. Wilmot says, 'mentioning a few names at random', how would it seem if, at a given moment, say, Bevin, Alexander and Shinwell were to be 'willing'. All this is speculation and it is easy to make too much of it. Between Now and Then lies a steep bloody mountain to be climbed. But maybe some are thinking more than I am of how to get down the further side most comfortably.

Monday 10th January
Dine alone with Ellen [Wilkinson] at Dolphin Square. She lives in a flat on the twelfth floor and, the lift being automatic and probably unreliable, as I had heard, I walk up, which she thinks rather a feat. The only other person, she said, who had walked up twelve flights to see her was Harry Pollitt. I said this would make a good press par. She is very anxious not to lose her full Chairman's year after next Conference, and hears that there are some intrigues to put her in only for the four remaining months this year. I say this would be wrong. We discuss the prospects of the next Annual Conference and I remind her that it will take place when the fighting may be at its bloodiest height, and this, I am sure, will influence, for the Executive favourably, the atmosphere.

In 1944, Dalton spent much time pushing in a broad, popularised fashion the Keynesian analysis which formed the basis of the Full Employment White Paper published in May. The Labour Party Policy Committee accepted what were, essentially, the ideas of his young 'post-warriors' – Durbin, Gaitskell and Jay – on 17th April. The Labour Party paper on Full Employment and Financial Policy committed a Labour government to keeping full employment by maintaining purchasing power and by opposing the need to balance the Budget year by year, while calling for international agreements to stabilise rates of exchange. There was also a strong commitment to national control of the location of industry and the redirection of industry to the Development Areas. The document anticipated the Full Employment White Paper by just over a month – though the ideas embodied in the latter had, of course, been widely discussed by relevant Cabinet Committees long before this. It is possible to see in these plans an outline sketch of the main direction of Labour's economic strategy on the Home Front in the first two and a half years of the post-war government.

Tuesday 11th January

Dine, rather weary and with a cold, in a private room at the Reform Club with Piercy, Wilmot, Durbin, Gaitskell, Jay and Berry,[1] where we discuss a draft for the Labour Party's Financial Committee on Post-War Employment. Quite a good meal, with plenty of drink, which causes me rapidly to revive. A good paper and a good evening, but it is left to me, as usual, to knock it about a bit before putting it up to its next hurdle.

Friday 14th January

Lord President's Committee. I put in a paper proposing to take the restrictions off men's suits, in view of decision to make non-austerity suits for demobilised soldiers. I put it up to my colleagues, I explain, only because it might be thought that the removal of these restrictions might encourage the view that there is no longer the same need for economy and concentration on the war effort. I propose, further, to down-point austerity and up-point new non-austerity. The silly colleagues all squeak with delight at the proposed 'derestriction', and none take the point of a possible blow to morale. On the contrary, they all begin to clamour against any up-pointing of the new non-austerity – hoping, no doubt, each of them, to be able to replenish their wardrobes. This clamour is so loud – and I am so disinclined to let them have any further opportunities of discussing my administrative details – that I merely, for the sake of form, 'reserve my position', undertaking that, if I remain convinced that non-austerity should be up-pointed, I will bring this back to the Committee. But, after this, I shan't up-point, and shall give them no more opportunity to discuss it.

This Lord President's Committee is rapidly losing business to Woolton's Reconstruction Committee, and is becoming a place where odds and ends are considered in an atmosphere of jovial irresponsibility!

Tuesday 18th January

Parliament, called by some 'the monkey house', reassembles. I have a bunch of P.Q.s, which go off quite well. Jests about Hogg's Oxford Laundry. Another lost cause: lost drawers ...... [2] (Sir Philip Warter is

1 H. V. Berry, later Sir Vaughan (1891–1979). Chairman of the Southern Region Manpower Board 1941–4. Member of the Union Discount Company of London Ltd 1925–45. With Nicholas Davenport, Berry had been a founder of the XYZ Club, a City-based group of socialists that fed ideas on financial policy to the Labour Party.
2 Quintin Hogg, M.P. for Oxford, complained about Board of Trade 'zoning' regulations that had allegedly compelled some of his constituents to use a particular laundry which regularly lost 'between 7 and 8 per cent' of its total weekly wash. 'Is

rather shocked; he thinks M.P.s should treat these grave questions more seriously).

Friday 21st January
Lunch alone with Melchett[1] – McGowan being in bed with lumbago. Melchett, of course, is a very intelligent fellow, and our conversation is on a higher mental plane through the absence of McGowan. He says that the evolution of arms has alternatively favoured the regular armed forces and the mob. Up to the outbreak of this war, it was going all against the mob, and it seemed that a small highly armed force could dominate vast multitudes. But lately it has gone the other way. Small and relatively cheap firearms and other weapons have been invented, largely for sabotage and irregular and underground warfare. And thus, at close quarters, the sticky bomb can do in the tank; and small bombs and hand-grenades, not to speak of small weapons such as tommy guns, have reversed the situation. There is now being invented a silent pistol, so that one person can shoot another and just walk out of the room, without a sound. And so, he says, one person could shoot another at a cinema and, barring a cry from the victim, no one else guess what was on. The post-war world will be dangerously full of highly trained and easily equipped gangsters. All the underground movements are being trained in this sort of thing.

He says that he is spending a great part of his time – and, it is horrible to have to confess it – in conducting experiments as to how things can be made to burn. In the later developments of air attack, high explosive has become completely secondary to fire, and even the largest block-busters are now mere secondary 'morale effect'.[2]

Saturday 22nd January
A good barrage starts up about 4 a.m. and I hear later that a quantity of incendiaries were dropped on the Houses of Parliament but that most of them failed to go off and that no serious damage was done, though a new hole seems to have been burnt in the roof of Westminster Hall. I suppose they were really aiming at the Board of Trade!

---

1 H. Mond, 2nd Baron Melchett (1898–1949). Deputy Chairman of I.C.I. Liberal M.P. 1923–4; Conservative M.P. 1929–30.
2 The text reads, 'moral effect', but it is hard to make sense of this. A typing error has therefore been assumed.

---

this another lost cause for Oxford?' cried another M.P. 'Lost drawers,' replied Hogg. Dalton answered the question by saying that he very much regretted the lost drawers, but could not hold himself personally responsible. (HC Debs [396], cols 6–7.)

699

Friday 28th January

Two hours at Reconstruction Committee, considering with a large swarm of colleagues Chapter V of the Steering Committee's Report on Location of Industry. On the whole, a very satisfactory afternoon. I had been prepared to make a row and to tell them, at the end, that the delay and indecision over this had become so intolerable that I had now no recourse left except to send a Minute direct to the Prime Minister. But nothing like this turned out to be necessary. The desiccated and sinister Sir Alan Barlow – I much prefer my own Sir Thomas – squatted beside Anderson and whispered in his ear from time to time. Woolton invited me to begin. I said that, broadly, I favoured the proposals of the Steering Committee as a minimum, though I had some reservations on points of detail, and thought that in some respects the proposals were timid and inadequate. None the less, they would give us a start. After some further obvious explanations of the elements of the problem, I said that, following the long delay on the Steering Committee, we had been caught short in the debate on the Address, when amendments had been moved on Location, and that I had been asked by the War Cabinet to speak, but had been commiserated with because there was practically nothing that I could say. However, Woolton and Lyttelton had made helpful suggestions and, in the result, I had got away with it pretty well, and Parliament and the press had been favourable. But we could not go on any longer, without grave embarrassment, without a policy. In particular, before my speech on 8th December, and still more since, hundreds of industrialists had approached me and my officials asking for guidance, and it was impossible to give them any reply. I therefore pressed that I should have, that very afternoon, the agreement of my colleagues to telling industrialists and others that the Government would like them, in the national interest, to consider the possibility of putting factories into any of the following four areas:

(1) South Wales – as a whole, that is to say, including Cardiff, Swansea and Newport, and not merely within the bounds of the old Special Area,
(2) Industrial Scotland, including Dundee, and also Glasgow, thus again going beyond the bounds of the old Special Area,
(3) The North-East coast, i.e. Tyneside and the County of Durham, and
(4) West Cumberland.

At the end of the meeting, when we were just breaking up, I pressed again for this authority and got it. I shall now also be able to say something about industrial building facilities in these areas. This, I am convinced, is the most potent of all the available inducements now and in the Transition. None of the colleagues argued against this today. By getting this authority [to] write letters, I have made sure that these four areas will soon have to be publicly announced, for some of the letters will certainly be shown or reported to the press. Some of my colleagues, frightened of public announcements, seem not to foresee this obvious next move on the chess board. But that's their funeral. I shall be very glad for the areas to be announced, and not at all sorry to be pressed to make certain additions to them.

I get good support from Portal, who has a practical knowledge of this question, and has come much nearer to my way of thinking in the last few months. Also from W. S. Morrison. The chief difficulties are made by Lyttelton who talked a lot of capitalistic hot air about the need to approach the question 'from the point of view of industry and not from the point of view of areas'. In fact, however, I squared him by relating how Sam Courtauld and I talked to each other, he saying he would like to have a few more plants in new places, and that he wants lots of water, and I giving him a list of half a dozen places, with plenty of water, in these difficult areas which he can inspect. Lyttelton said, 'Oh, that *is* the industrial approach', and he made no difficulty about my naming the four areas to the industrialists. Attlee, well briefed, I should think, by Durbin, asks some helpful questions about the quantity of industrial building available in the various areas. He enables me to emphasise that, in the North-East, particularly, there is a great shortage, since for a long while a strategic bar was put up on all arms production there. Clearly, therefore, in the North-East we must build more factories, in addition to making full use of what are there now, if we are to employ the population. Otherwise we shall only be providing good houses for some of the unemployed. The shortage of factories, I explain, is less severe in South Wales and Scotland, but, even there, some new industrial building is needed.

Cherwell backs me up pretty well and is specially strong on having all our permanent arms production in these areas. He also thinks that we ought to be able to vary the volume of arms production, like Social Security contributions, according to the general state of trade. This is a bright idea. Bevin spends most of his speech in an ideological pillow fight with Lyttelton. These are Defence Areas, he says, and we must look after them in peace as in war. They were neglected by private enterprise before the war. Everything was closed down following some talk in the back parlour of some Bank. He glared at Lyttelton as much as to say, 'And no doubt you were there.' He thinks that the local authorities could have done much better in attracting, and even financing, industries to these areas if they had been allowed to do so. But the law prevented them. 'You call this private enterprise; I call it slavery.' If private enterprise continued to fail, the State and the local authorities would have to deal with this direct. I was interested to notice (1) that he made no difficulty at all about my four areas, and (2) that he showed no desire to play a prominent part in the administration of the new scheme. On (1) we have been intolerably obstructed by his officials, but it is clear that these have not put the matter up to him. On (2) some people here have been longing to pass this baby to the Minister of Labour, but he seems not, for the moment at least, to want it. He is deeply involved in his latest manpower squeeze and in his Disabled Persons Bill in Parliament.

There is some discussion on the proposed Barlow Ban,[1] with suitable provision in exceptional cases, on Greater London. This is strongly supported by W. S. Morrison and me and Herbert Morrison. Some other ministers hedge, but a majority are frightened of it for the moment. Cranborne makes the bright suggestion that we might say that London is not to be spread any further but we shall build it all up higher. He has noticed several two-storeyed houses and wonders why they could not be built up higher.

At the end of the meeting I get my authority to tell industrialists about my four areas, and it is agreed that Woolton, Lyttelton, Portal and I – to whom Cherwell is afterwards added – shall produce a statement of policy in the light of discussion. Quite a good afternoon, and *most* of my officials, to whom[2] I relate this afterwards, are rather pleased.

Wednesday 2nd February
Quite successful *partie carrée* at the Acropolis, where Ruth and I entertain Phil and Irene [Noel-Baker]. The latter, whom I had not really intended to ask but who, as we know from experience, always pushes herself in when she can, was much better than usual, and Phil was very quick and bright. Later Ruth and I ran into A. P. Herbert[3] with wife and Philip Nichols.

Thursday 3rd February
Tom Fraser, M.P.,[4] to dine. He is a pleasant, though curiously un-

---

1 The 'Barlow Ban': the Barlow Report had recommended a ban on new industrial development in Greater London.
2 Marginal insertion: 'and E.B.'
3 A. P. Herbert, later Sir Alan (1890–1971). Independent M.P. for Oxford University. Barrister, playwright, author and journalist.
4 T. Fraser (b. 1911). Labour M.P. for Hamilton 1943–67. Junior minister 1945–7. Minister of Transport 1964–5.

assertive, young man. He succeeded old Duncan Graham[1] a year ago, but has been seen very little in the House, and has only spoken twice. He is feeling his way and says that he was very unwilling to accept the candidature, not feeling himself sufficiently qualified. He seems to have been taking some interest, not only in the inevitable mining questions of his constituency – he himself worked in the pits until a candidate, though he was also Secretary of the next door D.L.P. – but [also] in Colonial questions, and has joined the Fabian Committee on these. He has a sense of humour, doesn't drink, and is, I think, less than thirty. He might go quite some way. He says that he is shocked at the amount of jealousy everywhere. He was most delighted to have been asked tonight. He has, I think, been left very much to his own resources.

Thursday 10th February
Meade to coach me just before lunch on tomorrow's War Cabinet. There have been great comings and goings by the officials trying to get all the ministers primed right. Great efforts have been made with Bevin's advisers, it is thought with some success. Cherwell has written a wonderful Minute for the P.M. which Meade has seen and approves. (It was, apparently, a very personal and rather abusive Minute, and Cherwell told me that the P.M. said, 'You had better circulate it', but Cherwell had to explain this wouldn't do at all.) ...

Hazel Crompton,[2] at her own request, comes to tea. I had not seen her for, perhaps, twenty years. Her parents both died last year well in their nineties.[3] She discovered various old Carbonari relics[4] with all our signatures. I said that she must show them to me. She still keeps up with Beryl Power.[5]

Dine, though rather weary, with Leslie and Doris Nicholls. He is very cheerful and I am arranging for him to join the Fabian Society. He still thinks he would like to do politics after the war. If he gets half a chance, he would be quite a good candidate. He has been getting on very well with the Americans and is a great admirer of Patton,[6] and

1 D. M. Graham (1867–1942). Labour M.P. for Hamilton 1918–42.
2 Hazel Crompton. Sister of Dalton's Cambridge friend, Nigel Crompton, killed in the First World War.
3 Colonel R. E. B. Crompton (1845–1943). Elizabeth Crompton, née Clarke (d. 1943).
4 The Carbonari was a literary and dining club founded by Dalton, Rupert Brooke and other friends at Cambridge in 1906.
5 Beryl Power (1891–1974). Assistant Secretary, Housing and Welfare, at the Ministry of Supply 1941–5. Organiser and speaker for the National Union of Women's Suffrage Societies 1912–14. Sister of Eileen Power, the medieval historian.
6 Lt-General G. S. Patton (1885–1945). Commanding General, U.S. Seventh Army in Sicily 1943–4. Commander of Third Army in France, Belgium, Luxembourg and Germany 1944–5. Commander of Fifteenth Army in France 1945.

sure that, if he had been in command at Anzio, they would have broken right through and got to Rome.

Following the Washington talks on Article VII in autumn 1943, Richard Law, Minister of State, had become a vigorous advocate of the compromise plan for the setting up of an International Monetary Fund. This steered a course between American proposals for a new currency of international account and Keynes's idea for a clearing union. The new plan was attacked on the Left by such economists as Thomas Balogh, who opposed an international scheme that might subject the British economy to external influences, particularly to the economic fluctuations of a free-enterprise country like the United States. It was also attacked by the Bank of England and by the Conservative Right on the (essentially similar) grounds that financial control would leave London, and sterling exchange would be replaced by dollar exchange.

'Imperial' critics were concerned, in particular, that the plan would tie sterling too closely to gold and that it ruled out such devices as Imperial Preference. The War Cabinet considered Britain's attitude to the plan on 11th February.

Friday 11th February

... [T]o War Cabinet at No. 10. A large gathering to consider Law's paper on the Article VII talks. This is a good statement, and quite brightly written, though rather long. Officials from the Dominions and India are due in ten days' time. What line shall we take? The Beaver has put in a ludicrous paper, making a direct frontal attack, on the ground (a) that this is the Gold Standard all over again, and (b) that we are abolishing Imperial Preference. As to (a), this is the sheerest piffle, the latest arrangements at Washington being about as different from the Gold Standard as can be conceived. Bevin, who is always a little difficult on this point, has been warned that if he makes a row today he will be isolated along with Beaverbrook and the Bank of England, who are now at the bottom of a lot of Treasury resistance to the new monetary plan. This warning has had its effect. As to (b), the plain truth is that the Dominions now no longer care much about Imperial Preference, and that here is a wonderful opportunity to sell it in return for a good multilateral arrangement. The alternative is gradually to have it whittled away with no quid pro quo.

There is a substantial majority in the War Cabinet for going ahead along the lines suggested. Law opens very well and briefly. Attlee, who has to leave early, tells the P.M. he is in favour of this whole line and that he and I are in agreement and that I know his views. Anderson is pontifical and emphatic and, though half persuaded, I think, to the 'long-term objectives', is very anxious that we should not be committed in a transitional period of uncertain length. Lyttelton is very good and lucid on the exchange arrangements and wholly demolishes the Beaver's assertion that we shall be chained to gold. He is, as previously, sceptical of getting anyone to agree to the multilateral convention, but is not unwilling that we should have a try. Moreover, he is always departmentally eager to appease the Americans and cannot, therefore, go back on this negotiation. I say that my chief aim is to clear as many roads as possible for our exports, not in some distant period, but from the end of the German war. I add that I have always been strongly opposed to the Gold Standard, and support this monetary plan precisely because it steers clear of the gold trap. Cherwell is very hot in support of the Law paper, and then the Beaver waves his arms and talks more arrant rubbish, thinking that Canada might easily be persuaded to enter into bilateral barter arrangements with us and join the sterling block. When told by me and Law that the Canadians are very strongly in support of these proposals, he says that, just as in 1912 they drove out Laurier[1] over reciprocity, so now they would drive out Mackenzie King.[2] All this is utterly remote and silly old man's fever fancy. Cranborne confirms that the Dominions have become very uninterested in Preference, and Hudson adds his usual stuff, boring us all and making no converts. It is incredible how these rambling discussions succeed one another, every few months, with no new arguments and no one changing sides and never any really firm decisions. Brief support for the right line is also given by Woolton, Herbert Morrison and, most surprisingly, Bracken, who sees the point that quota restrictions on our exports of manufactures hit hardest those lines which give us most employment. The P.M., a little torn between Cherwell and the Beaver, says that he knows nothing about these things and has not had time to pass this paper through his mind, but that it is clear that the majority of the Cabinet are in favour of going forward with the negotiations on the lines suggested, and

1 Sir Wilfrid Laurier (1841–1919). Liberal Prime Minister of Canada 1896–1911. 'Reciprocity' was a movement calling for the abolition or reduction of customs duties between Canada and the United States. In late 1911 (not 1912), Laurier was defeated in the so-called 'reciprocity' election, and the matter was dropped.
2 W. L. Mackenzie King (1874–1950). Prime Minister of Canada 1921–6, 1926–30, 1935–48. Secretary of State for External Affairs 1935–46.

that a small committee of ministers should look at it and report again to the Cabinet. He names as the Committee Anderson, to be Chairman, Lyttelton, myself, Law, Cherwell and the Beaver. Not a bad Committee.

Sunday 13th February

Address a public meeting at Battersea. This has been well advertised and is reasonably well attended. But I dislike very much addressing public meetings now. One feels held upon a chain with a row of reporters sitting waiting to pounce upon unguarded phrases. Hinley Atkinson is there and we walk back together, after tea with Douglas[1] and his wife.[2] Atkinson quite understands my feelings. The audience, he says, are always waiting for 'those few reckless words' which would warm them up but would make most disastrous headlines. He is a very strong supporter of Maurice Webb for the secretaryship of the Party. I still feel, however, that he can't get it.

Monday 14th to Thursday 17th February

These four days are dominated by perpetual meetings of the Cabinet Committee on External Economic Policy.[3] We meet twice a day on each of three days and finish with a majority report by the five of us and a minority report by the Beaver. A most infuriating performance. The Beaver talks at least half the time or, I should say, shouts headlines at the rest of us – these are the same as he shouts at the War Cabinet next week, as to which see later note.[4] He also shows great skill in obstruction. He several times proposes that the Committee should adjourn, sometimes on the pretext that we should give the Bank of England a chance of preparing an alternative plan, sometimes in order that we may have time to prepare an alternative plan ourselves, sometimes in order that Hudson and Tom Johnston shall be summoned to the Committee and heard. On the 16th (Wednesday) the Beaver and I shout at each other a good deal in the morning. We are now discussing, no longer Currency, but Commercial Policy, and I take a larger share in expounding the plan. When I have spoken a few sentences, he shouts, 'Have you finished?' I shout, 'No.' He shouts, 'Tell me when you have finished.' I shout, 'You will know soon enough when I have finished, just as I know when you have

1 F. C. R. Douglas, later 1st Baron (1889–1980). Labour M.P. for Battersea North 1940–46. Parliamentary Private Secretary to the Board of Trade 1940–45. Chairman of the L.C.C. Finance Committee 1940–46. Governor of Malta 1946–9.
2 Minnie Douglas, née Smith.
3 The small Cabinet Committee set up on 11th February to consider the War Cabinet's attitude to the Monetary Plan.
4 See entry for 23rd February.

finished. You have talked a great deal more than I have for the last few days and now you had better listen to me for a change.' Through this Anderson sits immobile and expressionless in the Chair. But at the end of this seance the Beaver invites me to lunch alone with him in his flat in Arlington House. It is a very good lunch, with some very good Rhine wine of which he makes me drink the larger part, a wing of chicken, some dates from Marrakesh, some rather good Canadian cheese, and a large brandy. He says, 'I think you are doing very well in this Committee. You are putting your case very clearly and with great good temper.' He also says, 'I think you are doing your job very well at the Board of Trade.' I say, 'You used not to think that when you were attacking me every day in your paper. Apart from the *Express*, I used to have quite a good press. Since you have joined the Government, even the *Express* has stopped attacking me.' He says, 'Oh, there was nothing personal about that. And now, of course, we can't criticise anything that the Government does.' He then went on to denigrate Law and Eden. 'You want someone really tough at the Foreign Office,' he said. 'I would let Eden have anything else he likes. He can lead the House of Commons and succeed the Prime Minister as Leader of the Tory Party.' He also said it was shocking how the Government was being run by 'the three Profs' – Cherwell, Keynes and Robbins. He wanted me to draft, in time for our meeting this afternoon, something on Imperial Préférence and Agriculture. This was, perhaps, why he asked me to lunch. I did so, and brought the draft with the paper to the meeting in the afternoon. They were accepted by the others, but the Beaver didn't like them. They went into our majority report. The Bank of England, who were hauled before us on the Beaver's suggestion, Law having injudiciously suggested that Keynes should give evidence, which gave the Beaver his opportunity to spin out the proceedings, made, I thought, a quite deplorable impression. Catterns,[1] the Deputy Governor, and Cobbold[2] came. They obviously hated the very idea of any kind of international bank. Its assets, they held, 'must inevitably deteriorate', until it was 'all filled up with levas and dinars – and perhaps that would be the intention'. The proposed fund could not possibly be 'passive' because no active-minded banker could disinterest himself in the fate of his assets. Therefore, it was inevitable that people would ring up on the telephone and advise sales or purchases of sterling. It would all, they thought, be under the influence of foreigners. They assumed that it

1 B. G. Catterns (1886–1969). Deputy Governor of the Bank of England 1936–45.
2 C. F. Cobbold, later 1st Baron (b. 1904). Executive Director of the Bank of England 1938–45; Deputy Governor 1945–9; Governor 1949–61.

would be located in Washington. This would mean the break-up of the sterling block and that everyone would soon 'look askance at sterling'. When someone asked whether they would like it to be in London and not in Washington, Catterns exclaimed, Oh, good gracious no! We don't want the thing here.' Anderson thought, and Lyttelton and I agreed, that the Bank were totally unconscious of post-war realities, and in particular of our need to get very substantial assistance from the U.S. during the transitional period. This wretched Beaver is tolerated by all because he has this queer influence over the P.M. This has been a most intolerable week.[1]

Friday 18th to Monday 21st February
Visit my constituency for the first time for nearly six months. Very busy but very easy and successful, even more so than usual. Meet B.A.U.D.C. [Bishop Auckland Urban District Council] for talk on future of the area. Take them over my speech of 8th December. Sit for three hours in a room at the Town Hall receiving constituents, who are being schooled by Will Davis[2] to bring pieces of paper with them on which particulars of their 'cases' are written out. This is now enjoined in premonitory advertisements in the local press. Very good delegate meeting with Middlewood – a very tiresome fellow, said by Davis to be very disloyal both to me and him behind our backs to *non-Labour people*, but always very fulsome to my own supporters to my face, and a most admirable chairman, from my point of view, of such meetings as this – presiding. After he had buttered me up, I made a long and rather good speech about the war and the coming events, and our post-war plans, and the difficulty of getting decisions, and how far, broadly, we had got. All this went very well.

Tuesday 22nd February
P.M. today makes a speech of an hour and a quarter on the war and the international situation. He had said last week that it would be 'the most sombre speech' he had made for a long time. But it wasn't, and it even ended with the hint that perhaps victory might be near. He had some interesting passages on Poland, Yugoslavia and Greece. On Poland he said, in effect, that we were against the Poles ever having had Vilna and that we thought the Curzon Line was just, but added that he and Stalin had agreed that the Poles should be 'compensated at the expense of the enemy both in the North and in the West'. It is

1 Marginal insertion: 'Churchill said to me, after the Bank had given evidence, "Does that make you feel our money is safe with these people?" We both thought not.'
2 W. N. Davis. Secretary of the Bishop Auckland Labour Party from the 1930s to the 1950s. A teacher. Dalton's closest friend and ally in the constituency.

the first time this has been so clearly stated. He also made some reference to transfer of population and declared that the Germans had 'no rights' under the Atlantic Charter. This is all new – for the public – and in much firmer outline. On Yugoslavia he went all out for Tito[1] with exuberant eulogy, brushed aside Mihailović and made only faint praise of King Peter, adding that we should not seek to force Monarchy on any country that didn't want it. On Greece he never even mentioned the King. There was more interest, for those who know anything about such things, in his reference to foreign affairs than in his references to the war.

The War Cabinet on 23rd February had a preliminary discussion on a proposal to hold an oil conference in Washington, and then considered a paper presented by the External Economic Policy Committee set up on 11th February, which recommended that discussion with the Dominion representatives on the monetary plan should proceed 'on the basis that, while no commitment will be entered into, our expectation is that at the appropriate time we shall find it to our advantage to participate in these schemes, with or without modification'. The paper stressed the importance of arrangements to govern the transitional period after the ending of Lend-Lease, and expressed doubts about the possibility of Britain committing itself to the scheme for an International Monetary Fund unless latitude in regard to contracting out of convertibility continued 'until such a time as we can be really satisfied that we can maintain convertibility indefinitely'. It also stressed the need for discussion about reductions in Imperial Preference.

In a dissenting Minority Report, Beaverbrook attacked these recommendations, and in particular those concerning Imperial Preference. It was not for Britain, he declared, 'to take even the shortest step either towards promoting an attack on Imperial Preference or towards a weakening of the Dominions' adherence to that principle of Empire'. He went on: 'The Financial Plan restores the Gold Standard in the form of a "Gold Fund" ... If we accept the "Gold Fund" we lay ourselves down to die.' A note submitted by Bank of England representatives agreed on this last point, declaring that implicit in the plan was the idea that gold-convertible currencies were better than other currencies, and that acceptance of the mechanism envisaged in the plan meant that 'we say publicly that we are working towards a system where sterling will be less useful'.[2]

---

1 Josip Brož, known as Marshal Tito (1892–1980). Yugoslav communist leader. After the German invasion, he led and organised the Partisan forces. President of the National Liberation Committee from 1943. Prime Minister and Minister of National Defence 1945–53. President of the Republic 1953–80.
2 PRO, CAB 66/47 W.P.(44) 121, 18th February 1944.

709

Wednesday 23rd February

War Cabinet from 6 to 9 p.m. First hour on Oil. The Americans are riding a very high horse. They have decided, in spite of our very definite suggestions to the contrary, to hold (1) an early conference at Washington (we had suggested a later conference in London), (2) with the President presiding 'in the Cabinet Room at the White House', attended by a powerful team of ministers (we had suggested preparatory discussions at official level), and (3) to discuss Middle East oil only (we had suggested a wider discussion on all oilfields, including Mexico, Colombia and Venezuela, in the last two of which the U.S. had large reserves). Their latest telegram is equivalent, it is said tonight, to demanding that we should send out a team of ministers with a halter round their necks, like the burghers of Calais. All this is thought by some to be high-handed brigandage, and short-sighted politics, and most ill-timed, coming so soon before the Great Operation. The P.M. will send a suitable reply, suave but resistant and repetitively argumentative. The Americans are being difficult all round, apart from operations – persistently difficult, over Lend-Lease. ...

'Iraq, isn't that just a silly name for Persia?' asked the P.M. this evening, and pretended not to know where any of the oil places were upon the map, which had to be brought and explained to him. 'We may be only poor, God fearing men, serving the Lord Jesus Christ in humbleness of heart, but that's no reason why we should allow ourselves to be knocked about.'

This first hour is not an auspicious opening for the main business, which is to consider the report by Anderson and the rest of us suggesting instructions to our officials in the talks with the Dominion officials, who were here on Monday (today is Wednesday). There is some anti-American feeling in the air which the Beaver, supported this time most vociferously by Bracken, who last time was on my side, and, in his dull, deaf, boring way, by Hudson, makes the most of. Clearly many ministers, including the P.M., have not even read our short report. Anderson expounds it with heavy over-emphasised lucidity. And then the Beaver begins to shout headlines, 'It is a gold fund', 'The Bank says it is the gold standard', 'We are giving up our economic empire', 'The Americans will never agree', 'Let us have another committee with some new ministers on it who know something about agriculture', and so on, again and again and again, ringing the changes, meaninglessly. Others try to speak, Lyttelton in support of Anderson, I in explanation of the Imperial Preference clause and of Australian attempts to make a bilateral treaty with the U.S., Cherwell in explanation of the gold standard. But the Beaver claims to answer each one in turn, and goes on shouting through our speeches, and Bracken joins in: 'We can't give up Imperial Preference', 'What could the Australians expect to sell in the U.S.?', 'Let us hear the Minister of Agriculture'. Then Hudson speaks at great length, and several of us interrupt him, both the P.M. and I, saying he wants to raise the price of food rather than rely on subsidies. He protests loudly that this is 'most unfair'. 'I have not been allowed to state my case.' And the Beaver shouts, 'The Committee refuses to hear the Minister of Agriculture. He was not allowed access to us.' The whole thing develops into the worst pandemonium I have ever seen in the Cabinet. Towards the end, four or five ministers are often shouting at once and the P.M., I think, deliberately allows the thing to get out of hand, explaining that he hasn't had time to read the papers, and doesn't pretend to understand it, but thinks it should be thoroughly discussed, and why anyhow should we be hustled, 'just because a few officials from the Dominions are here; they can be entertained for a few days, and given drinks, and taken round to see the bomb craters'. He joins with some delight in baiting Hudson, and says, 'Aha, so you say subsidies are no use to you? You don't want them any more.' Both Attlee and Morrison try, in a minor sort of way, to help the thing along, and poor Cranborne, who, though Secretary of State for the Dominions, and, therefore, perhaps entitled to speak on this, has the weakest voice in the Cabinet, quite fails to make himself heard above the din. He was understood to be trying to say that the Dominions were not really much interested now in Imperial Preference. He managed to get this out after Bracken, who had been shouting very loudly at this end of the table, some of his shouts interchanged with mine, suddenly shouted, louder than ever, 'Let us hear the Dominions Secretary.' But the latter came out on the wrong side for him.

Then, at 9 o'clock, the P.M. said that it was clear we could reach no decision that night, but he saw no harm in this Cabinet paper being given to our officials on the clear understanding that the Cabinet had reached no decision upon it. I said, 'And they can have the minority report as well.' And the Beaver shouted from the other end of the table, 'So it's clear these are only bits of paper – only bits of paper – they don't mean a thing. We must have another committee, with other ministers.' But by this time the P.M. had risen from his seat, and this amazing seance was at an end. Cherwell, whose remarks had been very sensible, but who had exercised much less than his usual influence – in the last resort I think the two Bs beat him down – said, 'I don't believe anyone outside our committee had really read the papers at all.' And that, I am sure, was true. I said to Eden going out, 'If you took as long to settle foreign policy as we take to settle this sort of thing, we should be in a fine mess.' It is, indeed, quite intolerable that when a committee so obviously strong and competent, judged by any standard, either departmentally or personally, as ours – Anderson, Lyttelton, myself, Law and Cherwell – with the Beaver thrown in – has made a careful report on a subject which has been before the Cabinet, on and off, in much the same form, since April 1943, the whole thing should be thrown back in confusion, even though the great majority of our colleagues would be quite prepared to accept our views, simply because three men make trouble, of whom two belong to 'the entourage'. Unless we change these methods, we shall go very wrong very soon.

Thursday 24th February
Lunch with Mrs Phillimore and two Frenchmen. One, recently arrived from France, says that 'the resistance' is not divided into political parties but is more prepared, probably, than we in England for large changes after the war, both in the direction of European 'federation' – in loose form, e.g. unification of currency, transport services, etc. – and internally in Socialist direction, especially through public ownership of heavy industry. He thinks Germany should be admitted from the start to any new international organisation, but with very low status, this only being raised to that of other members gradually and in accord with German good behaviour. He thinks countries on the Atlantic seaboard will be much more stable and closely bound to England than anything to the east. He is not hopeful about south-east Europe.

Afterwards I go back with Attlee, who says that he and others today protested to the P.M. about last night's pandemonium in Cabinet and the impossible position in which our officials were now placed. P.M. said he thought we were really all agreed on three things: (1) no return to the gold standard, (2) no abolition, or even reduction, of Imperial Preference, except in return for sufficient tariff concessions by Americans, and (3) no increase in the price of food by taxation. He inveighed again, with great emphasis, on this third point. Anderson said that these three points would suit him and the P.M. said he would issue a short Minute.

Friday 25th February
Labour Party National Executive meets today for ordinary business and –

Saturday 26th to Sunday 27th February
– continues over the weekend. The discussion is surprisingly good and

sensible. Bevin was invited but refused, obviously because he cannot trust some of those present not to leak. Attlee and Morrison are both there.

A good deal of talk on the Electoral Truce, for the termination of which there is still no pressure from any of the important trade unions, though one or two of the trade union members of the National Executive speak in favour. The feeling of D.L.P.s is very human and natural, but in my view it is really impossible to get out of it so long as we are in a National Government. Morrison, however, suggests that it might be possible for two or three candidates, all 'supporting the Government', to be put up by the principal parties to run against each other at by-elections, from which all ministers would abstain either from speaking or from sending messages. I am myself very sceptical about this, but it is left that one or two Labour ministers might have a word with the P.M. and his colleagues about it.

Much more important is the question of what we shall do after the defeat of Germany. There is no dissent from the view that *at the first election after* the defeat of Germany, we should fight as an independent Party and seek a clear majority. At an early stage in the discussion I myself support this view, but give three reasons why we should seek to interpose an interval of months. Morrison thinks an interval of a year – between the German surrender and our own election. For this there are three separate reasons: (1) because the P.M.'s prestige, though it will fluctuate up and down between now and then, will certainly be at its peak when Germany surrenders and for a short while afterwards; it would be suicide for the Labour Party to get into an election just then – but, for this same reason, the Tories may think this much the best time; (2) because we are bound by our Conference resolution of May 1940 to join the Government in order to secure 'a swift victory and a just peace'; it isn't our fault that things since then have not been 'swift', but it is clearly part of our duty to take our full share in drawing the first broad outlines of the Peace; it is only ministers who can do this, and the T.U.C., for example, are deluding themselves if they think that any delegation of theirs, hanging about the Peace Conference in a 'consultative capacity', will count for anything; it is important for the future that we, as well as the Tories, shall have broad responsibilities for the Peace Settlement, so as to increase the chance of a 'national' foreign policy hereafter; and (3) because it would be very wrong to hold a general election before a substantial number of men from the Armed Forces had been demobilised and absorbed again as civilians into the life of the community; they must be able to express their views to their friends and relatives and, e.g., to speak at public meetings; no arrangements for 'absent voters' or 'proxy votes' are any substitute for this; it was Lloyd George's greatest crime in 1918 that he rushed the election in such a way as, in effect, to disfranchise millions of men in the Services. Broadly, the National Executive accepts my view on all this, though the phrase 'Leave the Government as soon as Germany is defeated' dies hard. Nor can any thoughtful person rule out from his mind the possibility that the P.M. may not be able, or inclined, to go on much beyond the German defeat. If he were out of action, our course would be much easier and our chances much brighter.

There is also some talk of the possibility of (1) a new coalition after the next election, and (2) some 'coalition of the Left' in the form of an electoral compact. As to the former, obviously nothing can be settled yet. It must depend on the results of the election itself. On the latter, there is, I think, a tendency to over-estimate both Common Wealth and the Communists. But it would be out of the question to make any formal arrangement with either of them before the eve of the election. Possibly some arrangement with Common Wealth might then be worth while, e.g., leaving them undisturbed in a certain number of rural Divisions which we could not hope to win.

There is also some discussion on the connected question of the Alternative Vote. We are all against [Proportional Representation], but on Alternative Vote we are uncertain and divided. I am inclined myself to be against it, but it is worth looking at again.

On Sunday evening (27th) I go down to stay the night with Beaverbrook in his house near Leatherhead! Following our row on the E.E.P. [External Economic Policy] Committee and in the Cabinet, he had sent a message conveying this invitation. It would have been quite wrong to refuse.

I arrive at 6.30 p.m. and find only Bruce Lockhart, who has been having a very bad time in hospital with some kind of skin disease. He is still pretty run down. 'It is not the hard work, it's the hard worry' which makes many people ill in this fifth year. Beaverbrook, I am told, 'is resting' on my arrival. He appears soon afterwards and is almost excessively affable. He raises, throughout my stay, no awkward questions at all. I had thought that he might launch forth on the gold standard or Imperial Preference, but neither of these is even mentioned; or try to pump me on the proceedings of our Executive during this weekend, but not a word on that either; or try to involve me in some intrigue against some other Labour minister, or someone else, but not a hint of this either. On the contrary, a lot of talk about oil, and American intentions in the Persian Gulf and in Saudi Arabia, and a lot of desultory talk on other topics, and some appearance of interest in some of the things I am doing, and the promise of support on any proposals I may make for dealing with cartels.[1] No other guests except Sholto Douglas[2] and his wife,[3] who arrive just in time for dinner, stay the night and leave very early. He is now commanding Coastal Command. From Fighter Command he had gone to America, but had apparently not got on very well there. Fighter Command exists no more. It has been cut in two, in preparation for coming events. We are given some very good champagne for dinner, but a ham which is served has not been properly cured. This leads to a great outburst by Beaverbrook next morning to one of his attendants. After dinner we all go and look at a film, a rather crude old-fashioned story of Jack the Ripper, dating back to London in the Eighties. Beaverbrook's private cinema is filled with 'staff' and, I suppose, a certain number of locals. After this, various things are discussed, including even Emerson's one good poem, which, someone not having got his glasses, I am encouraged to read aloud. After this faint literary whiff, we go to bed, not much past midnight. Quite different from the stories I had heard of people sitting up drinking and intriguing till 4 a.m.!

Monday 28th February

I come down to breakfast at 9.30 and find Bruce Lockhart hanging about. His attitude to Lord Beaverbrook is always rather that of servant to master, though, of course, he isn't working for him now. He says he does not know whether he will be 'sent for' before Beaverbrook leaves for London. Beaverbrook has been down early for breakfast, unexpectedly, and suggests that he and I should drive up to London together. On the way he enquires about films, and Rank, and my arrangement with him, and then goes on to speak ill of the Liberals and their failure to observe the Truce. All, I repeat, most excessively affable and ending with a threat to invite me again in a week or two's time. No doubt there is some game on.

The communiqué issued after our National Executive was most austere. 'Discussion concentrated round the winning of the war and various questions which would subsequently arise.' There had been

---

1 'I listened to [Dalton] and Max discussing "cartels" for an hour and agreeing to line up together in the effort to have them suppressed', Bruce Lockhart recorded in his own diary on the same day. 'I.C.I. was regarded as the chief offender.' (Kenneth Young, ed., *The Diaries of Sir Robert Bruce Lockhart, vol. II 1939–1965*, Macmillan, London, 1980, p. 282.)

2 Sir William Sholto Douglas, later Marshal of the Royal Air Force, 1st Baron (1893–1969). Air Officer Commander-in-Chief, Coastal Command 1944–5; Fighter Command 1940–42; Middle East Command 1943–4. Air Commander-in-Chief, British Air Forces of Occupation, Germany 1945–6. Commander-in-Chief and Military Governor, British Zone of Germany 1946–7.

3 Lady Douglas, née Joan Denny.

no troublesome leakage, though, naturally enough, some intelligent guesses. It was generally stated that we were all in favour of going on with the coalition till the war in Europe was won, and of maintaining the truce meanwhile, and that we were looking for younger candidates for the next election, including a fair proportion from the Services. All this was true enough. Some think there was no leak because W. A. Robinson was absent. Some even think that he not only talks loudly and unguardedly in pubs, but literally *sells* leaks to the press. Someone at lunch recalled a speech of his in his own constituency in which he said, 'And today there is such poverty that many mothers have not a drop of milk to give their babies ...... and, if anyone says to me, "What about foreign policy?" I shall reply, "I plead, 'Not Guilty'." ' Another tale related of him is that a colleague at a conference invited him to share a taxi from the Conference Hall to their hotel. He accepted the offer and went off to fetch his coat. He did not come back, and after waiting ten minutes, his colleague took the taxi on himself. Later, after lunch at the hotel, Robinson came up to him and said, 'Thanks so much for giving me a lift in your taxi.' His colleague said, 'But I waited for you for ten minutes and you didn't come back, so I had to go on without you.' Robinson said, 'You must have been bloody drunk not to remember that I did come with you in the same taxi.'

Robinson was absent this time because he is very disgruntled. His union[1] have decided that they will not nominate him again for the National Executive, and that, having reached the age limit, they will not run him again for Parliament. I recall other occasions when he has been a great nuisance at evening, or sometimes even at afternoon, meetings of the National Executive. It has always been a bad sign when he rises to his feet in order to address us. Once or twice evening meetings have had to be adjourned, and I recall one famous occasion when Arthur Henderson was still struggling on as Chairman of the Disarmament Conference, and Robinson rose and said, 'There is one question I particularly want to put to Mr Henderson. Is it true or is it not that they are all burrowing away like rabbits?' No one understood this, so he went on to explain, 'People tell me they are all burrowing away like rabbits, like bloody rabbits, burrowing away under the Maginot Line. I mean the French.'

At the end of February 1944, it was decided to build a number of new 'Standard Factories' in the Development Areas, ready for immediate occupation

1 National Union of Distributive and Allied Workers (N.U.D.A.W.). W. A. Robinson, q.v., ceased to be on the N.E.C. after 1943–4, and left Parliament in 1945.

and intended as bait for industrialists.

Meanwhile, Dalton succeeded in getting a statement of government intent on location included in the Employment White Paper which was being drafted by government economists. Having obtained the support of the Reconstruction Committee at the end of January, Dalton managed to get the following paragraph inserted:

> It will be an object of Government policy to secure a balanced industrial development in areas which have in the past been unduly dependent on industries specially vulnerable to unemployment. The Government will encourage the establishment of the new enterprises in these 'Development Areas' by the following means ... [1]

This, and other passages in the White Paper, became Dalton's official Charter, 'on which I relied in much subsequent argument'.[2]

Wednesday 1st March

A distinctly good meeting, beginning at 9.45 a.m. and lasting till nearly 12, on Location of Industry. Woolton, Lyttelton, Bevin, Portal, Cherwell, W. S. Morrison and myself. Our final agreement, to be put into the draft of the White Paper on Full Employment, is very satisfactory. All our inducements for Development Areas are kept intact and it is emphasised that the Government will itself build factories in these areas. The Board of Trade are to have powers to *require* all industrialists to come and talk to them about their plans, and to *prohibit* developments in 'congested areas'. This seems almost too good to be true, being the Barlow Ban in small and undefined instalments. It may get back at the next stage, but it is remarkable to have got the rest so far. Responsibility for administering policy on Location generally is to be vested in three ministers jointly, President of the Board of Trade, Minister of Labour and Minister of Town and Country Planning. They are to have a joint office for this purpose and a joint staff, and Regional Boards. Special Areas legislation is to be repealed. Bevin wastes a good deal of time pressing for a State Corporation to *operate*, as well as build, factories if private enterprise won't play. It is finally agreed that there shall be some 'last resort' phrase in the draft, but we don't want to suggest that all our powers and inducements will be ineffective, nor to give private enterprise an excuse for not trying to play.

1 *Employment Policy*, Cmd 6527.
2 FY, p. 443.

Thursday 2nd March

Visit two Utility furniture factories in the afternoon, and dine with Meynell,[1] who provides us with a very good dinner for a rather amusing company – Miss Kilroy, Evelyn Sharp,[2] John Maud (whom it was part of the plan to get me to meet), Joad and myself. All gossip rather freely. I think it does no harm to tell Maud how well, in my view, Woolton is doing.

Friday 3rd March

To West Leaze, for the first time, Mrs Shepherd says, for seven weeks.

Saturday 4th to Sunday 5th March

I sleep a lot and finish my redraft of 'International Post-War Settlement'. But, as regards 'Full Employment', my other job for the Labour Party, I find the draft by Jay and Gaitskell so frightful that I just can't do anything with it.

Therefore, I ask Durbin next week to try his hand, which he does, with some success, though briefly. We all know pretty well what we want to say on Full Employment; the trick is to say it well.

The American Army have poisoned Mrs Shepherd's goats. The two big ones died in great pain. Their tongues were swollen and discoloured. It seems that the Americans fed them on bits of my yews, not knowing that this was poisonous to all stock. So Mrs Shepherd has carried off the two little goats out of harm's way!

The place is getting fuller and fuller of Americans. At night their aircraft are a beautiful sight, flying round in formation with red and green lights. 'Quite like fairyland,' the children say. But the troops are apt to knock up people's houses at 4 a.m. and ask for water, which some people find a bore, and they drive their Jeeps everywhere and are said to be getting very bored with their long training.

I get, for once, a little exercise and do some digging and wheeling, which leaves me feeling a little less paunchy than before.

Monday 6th March

I am now taking quite a few new factories into the three main Development Areas. But the difficulty, and the slowness, is illustrated by the case of Treorchy. Three new radio valve factories are to be built, and I have got it agreed that one is to go to Scotland, one to the North-

---

1 F. Meynell, later Sir Francis (1891–1975). Temporary official at the Board of Trade (Adviser on Consumer Needs) 1940–45. Book designer, publisher and poet. Typographical adviser to H.M.S.O. 1945–66. Later married to Alix Kilroy, q.v.
2 Miss E. A. Sharp, later Baroness (1903–85). Civil servant in the Ministry of Housing. Permanent Secretary at the Ministry of Housing and Local Government 1955–66.

East, and one to South Wales. Within these areas the firms concerned may, within reason, choose their sites. In South Wales, Cos-
sors, rather to my surprise but quite to my delight, chose a flat piece
of ground more than half-way up the Rhondda Valley at Treorchy.
Bulldozers arrived and excavations began. It is to be a rush job, since
more valves are badly needed for the Forces, and it will be a good
post-war proposition. The local people are all delighted. William
Mainwaring, M.P.,[1] is friendlier than ever. Then, suddenly, Mainwaring writes to say that there is great local indignation because it is
learnt that the local colliery company – the Ocean – are pulling strings
with the Ministry of Aircraft Production and the Ministry of Fuel and
Power to stop it, on the pretext that they plan to use this ground – the
only ground available – as a recreational centre and a playground for
the children of the Rhondda. This drives me nearly mad. It is a bare-
faced effort by these unspeakable coal-owners, who have reduced this
whole area to misery and dereliction, in addition to spoiling its natural
beauties, to stop the creation of *any* alternative employment being
found for the men, youth – and even women – of this valley. They
know that, if such alternative arrived, no one will go down their
damned pits any more, unless the whole miner's life is changed for the
better.[2] We shall have this sort of impudence in every mining district
where we introduce – as I plan to do in a great number of cases – new
light industries. The coal-owners have, let the long years pass, including the years when all the men were out of work, without using
this piece of ground for any purpose, though they refused some years
ago to sell it, because, they said, they might want it for 'industrial
development'. I find that the Ministry of Aircraft Production officials,
locally and at the centre, are quite sound on this, and that Cripps has
sent to that old humbug Lord Davies,[3] who has written to him, a firm
reply. I then write to Mainwaring, and have sent to his Town Clerk,
who has also written to me, a letter of reassurance. All the local people,
except the owners' agent, are mad keen for this new factory and think
they see at last a hopeful change in the industrial prospects of the
Valley. And then, late one night this week, Cripps sends me *another*
letter from Lord Davies, mixing a lot of sanctimonious humbug about
recreation and planning with a hardly concealed protest against anything being done to make it more difficult to get labour, particularly

1 W. H. Mainwaring (1884–1971). Miners' leader. Labour M.P. for Rhondda East
   1933–59.
2 Marginal insertion: 'and that the women will earn better wages in the new factory
   than the men in the pits'.
3 David Davies, 1st Baron Davies (1880–1944). Liberal M.P. for Montgomeryshire
   1906–29.

young labour, for the pits. I ring up Cripps and am pleased to find that he is standing quite firm. Some day I shall let loose this story. (I heard no word from the Ministry of Fuel and Power; I would have kicked them hard if I had.) ...

Dine with Gladwyn Jebb, whom I had not seen for some weeks, in their flat. Also present Cynthia Jebb and Oliver Harvey, who is, I think, finding his job rather heavy for him. He is not only King of Poland but King of Algiers. He was very much impressed on his last visit to Moscow by the tremendous developments of every kind. He and I have always both been, with obstinate persistency, very eager for close understanding with Russia. He fears that, if we make a mess of this, we shall find, not so much a hostile power in the East as an enormous Sphynx. We shall never know what they are thinking nor hence what it would be prudent or practicable for us to do.

Wednesday 8th March
Dine with Phil [Noel-Baker] at R.A.C. [Royal Automobile Club] to meet Weizmann[1] and Bakstansky.[2] I all but tell them that I have drafted a very hot paragraph for the Labour Party on post-war Palestine. I hint as much on leaving. Weizmann is very conscious of the influence of the Arabs in the Middle East itself, and of the hostility of British officials, and especially of Moyne,[3] who is still in Cairo. Over here the P.M. is very friendly, and so, he knows, is the Labour Party. He met the P.M. the other night, who said to him, 'We agree so completely that there is nothing for us to discuss. I am on your side; the Labour Party is on your side; Amery is on your side. What more do you want?' Weizmann is sure he is sincere, and, of course, pre-occupied. I said that we were all preoccupied. Weizmann understood that there had been 'some discussion' in the Cabinet the other day on Palestine. I said he must not take too seriously rumours of 'some discussion'. Much of this was only a desultory five or ten minutes' exchange of banalities, resulting in nothing even faintly approaching a 'decision'.

He is also very full, tonight, as I have known him on previous occasions, of his chemist's plan[4] to turn sugar and sunlight into any-

1 Chaim Weizmann (1874–1952). Honorary Adviser to the British Ministry of Supply 1939–45. President of the World Zionist Organisation and Jewish Agency for Palestine 1921–31, 1935–46. President of Israel 1948–52.
2 L. Bakstansky (1904–71). General Secretary of the Zionist Federation of Great Britain and Ireland. Well known to Dalton as a student at the L.S.E., when Dalton was a lecturer.
3 Lord Moyne, q.v., had been Deputy Minister of State in the Middle East since 1942, and became Minister Resident in the Middle East shortly before his death in 1944.
4 Weizmann was a research chemist by training, and had taught chemistry and bio-chemistry at the universities of Geneva and Manchester.

thing you want, e.g., especially oil or rubber. But the oil companies, he says, are sabotaging all this. There is no reason why the whole of Africa, where sugar cane would grow like a weed, and where there is always sun, should not become a great factory of synthetic products. He would like to start a 'pilot plant' somewhere in this country to show what can be done by his methods. I ask him to let me have a note on this. He says he also talked to Bevin about it, and Bevin gave him his private address to send his memorandum to, not wishing it to go to the Ministry of Labour.

Thursday 9th March
Kulski[1] brings to see me Nowak,[2] of the Polish Underground Army and before the war a teacher of Economics at Poznań University. These are very brave people. They are sabotaging much German transport by rail and road, especially aircraft parts. They are also distributing – and this may be a good deal less useful, though they love doing it – quantities of Underground newspapers, including some in German. In the East, he complains, the Red Partisans are not co-operating with their bands at all. They are dropped by parachute and, he says, loot and burn mercilessly. I suspect there is much exaggeration in all this. But clearly there is, in present conditions, no real co-operation. This is terribly sad.

Friday 10th March
Crossman to see me. He limps a bit and must not stand long, nor work more than half time. Otherwise he has made an amazing recovery. He wonders whether it is worth his while to be Principal of Ruskin, if offered it. I say I think not. He thinks he could win Coventry next time, redistribution or not. But he would like to be something else than an M.P. I say that the House of Commons is such a blind world that he would clearly come to the front. He has been asked to join the staff of the *Observer*. This is now run by David Astor. He would prefer it to the *New Statesman*. But this would be after victory in Europe. Now he is working with the Americans on P.W.B.[3] He will cross when Ike crosses. The latter wants, Crossman thinks, to cross as soon as possible so as to be free from undue interference by our own

---

1 Wladyslaw Kulski (b. 1903). Polish diplomat. Counsellor to the Polish Embassy in London 1940; Minister 1942–4. After the war, he became Professor of International Law and European Government at the University of Alabama.
2 Jerzy Nowak (1898–1949). Chief of the Economic Department of the Prime Minister's Office in Poland before the war. Managing Director of the Bank of Poland 1936–45. Member of the Financial Committee of the League of Nations 1940–45. After the war he taught Economics at the Polish University College, London.
3 'P.W.B.': Psychological Warfare Bureau.

P.M. and others. Crossman thinks that getting on with Americans is frightfully easy, if only one will talk quite frankly and not give the appearance of being too clever, but very few English seem to have achieved it. Ike has set a wonderful standard at the top, but as soon as anyone gets mixed up with 'government', good relations seem almost impossible. I tell him a bit of our conclusions at our 'private' National Executive weekend. He doesn't agree. He is, as I expected, rather concerned lest there should be too large a Poland and, in consequence, too revengeful a Germany. I say that, as he knows, Stalin wants Königsberg and that I would give the Poles all the rest of East Prussia with Danzig and all Upper Silesia, but, in their own interests, not much beyond. He thinks this would not be too bad.

Tuesday 14th March
On the Bench today Eden says to me, 'A fine thing! The same day we read in the press that Stalin is exchanging Ambassadors with Badoglio, we get a telegram from Roosevelt saying he has finally made up his mind that Italy must at once become a Republic, and both without any previous discussion with us!' ...

Ruth is in London today and we speak of her post-war plans and the various ways of going to France. I say I think she should not have anything to do with U.N.R.R.A., but that she should let me and others pull strings to get her some special position. She doesn't really much like this way of doing things. But I think it would be best. She is going on to dine with Viénot.

I have Durbin to dine with me, and we go over the line that he should take at Clay Cross. We think he has a fair chance, though the odds will be against him. (This turned out to be a complete fiasco. Most of the delegates were only interested in how much money the candidates could put up, and lapsed into apathy both before and after statements on this subject. Durbin, following my advice, named no figure, but was vaguely encouraging. They didn't think this nearly good enough, in view of firm offers both from the miners and the R.C.A. [Railway Clerks Association]. These two were left in to the last, when the former got it. This is very disappointing, and, indeed, infuriating. But it is very difficult to see what to do.)

Earlier today I talked to Waterhouse, who said that he thought that, if anything happened to the P.M., a great many Tories would much prefer Anderson as his successor to Eden. They think Eden much too specialised on foreign affairs, and much too young, and much too 'spoilt darling of fortune'. I think that, in a Party election, we should do much better against Anderson than Eden. He is such a dull dog, and dullest of all on the air.

Jowitt says that he thinks our draft paper on Restrictive Practices is quite the worst paper he has ever read. I said I quite agreed and had myself blown off about it. It is largely concocted by ——, who can no more draft a document suitable for ministers than I can sing a solo. I have said this to several people. When I was young they tried my voice, some man striking the piano first here and then there, and after a few shots, he stopped and said, 'You have a very strong voice but absolutely no ear.' Since then I have only joined in choruses. I am not at all ashamed of this particular disability, nor have I been seriously handicapped by it in life. I tell several people this in relation to ——, and hope it may be passed on. I have given instructions that Jay is to redraft the whole thing in a cleaner, crisper and more challenging way.

Wednesday 15th March
Attend an afternoon party at Buckingham Palace. Frightfully boring!

Thursday 16th March
Lunch with Bruce Lockhart to meet Beneš, who talks of his plans for post-war politics in Czechoslovakia. Proportional Representation is to be abolished and there are only to be three parties, the Right, the Centre and the Left. The Left is to include, for a start, the two Socialist Parties and the Communists. The latter, therefore, cease to exist as an independent party. If they misbehave, the more moderate Socialists will join the Centre and the Left will be sunk. On the other hand, if they behave, the Left will probably govern the country. He explained all this to the Kremlin and it was well received. When they invited him to a State Banquet, the Russians asked whom he would like to have invited too. He suggested various names and then they said, 'What about the Czech Communists here?' He said he would be very glad if their leaders were invited too. So three of them came, and afterwards they called personally to thank him, because, they said, they had been in Moscow many years but had never before seen Stalin or been allowed inside the Kremlin.

Saturday 18th to Sunday 19th March
At West Leaze. Write the first half of the Labour Party declaration on Full Employment and Financial Policy. It is extraordinary how little use most of the drafts made by other people are. I must try to complete this *next* weekend.

Wednesday 22nd March
I get a letter by the first post this morning from Mrs Battye saying that my mother is very ill indeed and is not expected to live long, and that last night she was rambling about me and others of the family. This

is a very bad day for such a crisis, since it is a National Executive, morning and afternoon, including the election of the new Secretary of the Party. But I motor down in the afternoon (I should have had to do this anyhow, since the line from Waterloo to Windsor is blocked following last night's air-raid). Mrs Battye is getting very blind and very deaf, but has two other people helping her, a nice young V.A.D.,[1] Miss Dickie, and, for part of the day, the District Nurse. My mother has only been in bed for a few days and, indeed, wrote me a quite coherent letter, with no mention of illness, on the 14th, i.e. only eight days ago. She had had a bad bronchial cough which had somewhat tired her, and, as Mrs Battye explained, Attlee[2] (the doctor, a cousin of C.R.A.) had found, when he examined her a few weeks ago, a lump in her left breast. But it was giving her no pain and was not growing, so, having regard to her age, after an examination at the hospital they decided to do nothing about it. She is now suffering, as Dr Attlee told me when I went to see him this afternoon, from 'senile heart' and there is just nothing to do except to wait, and to keep her out of pain. I went up several times to see her today, but there was no sign of recognition, either by sight or hearing. She was quite unconscious, breathing very heavily, coughing a little, looking quite waxen. (Looking at this pallor, I remembered a passage I wrote in *With British Guns in Italy* on the colour of those very near to death.)[3] I can't believe that she can live much longer. But she is making a peaceful and painless end and she has had twelve and a half years of quite happy widowhood – a good deal happier, indeed, than the later years of her married life. It has helped happiness that she has been well looked after by Mrs Battye and various servants and that she has combined great physical toughness with low mentality and very little imagination. She has not been really 'worried' by the war and she has had enough small things to interest her locally – the Parish Church, the local Savings Group, the trees in her little garden at the back, etc. She has out-lived her sisters and all but one of my considerable army of uncles. Only my uncle Llewelyn[4] will survive her. Last December she was eighty years

1 'V.A.D.': Voluntary Aid Detachment.

2 Dr W. H. W. Attlee (1876–1962). Consulting Physician at King Edward VII Hospital, Windsor, and Staines Cottage Hospital.

3 Dalton wrote in *With British Guns in Italy* (Routledge, London, 1919, p. 248): 'The more I look at dead bodies, the more childish and improbable does the old idea of personal immortality appear to me! ... in a ditch, two wounded lay on stretchers, covered with blankets. One, only lightly wounded, gave us directions. The other was very near to death. His face was growing pale already, as only the faces of the dead are pale ... '

4 Llewelyn Evan-Thomas (1859–1947). Surviving brother of Catherine Dalton, née Evan-Thomas. Catherine Dalton was one of eight children.

old. The longer my sister Georgie[1] can be kept out of all this, the better. She would only make a fuss and be stupid and pompous and jealous. Mrs Battye wrote to her a week ago that my mother was ill (Mrs Battye says she also wrote to me, but I never got the letter). Dr Attlee also wrote to Georgie before he took my mother to the hospital to be examined. Mrs Battye has had no word from Georgie, nor has she communicated with me. But, since we had a certain difference of opinion early in 1932, we have had no direct communication. At some moment I shall have to tell her what I am arranging, but not till death has come.

At today's National Executive, we have the usual fidget on the Electoral Truce. After some discussion it is decided that Shepherd shall approach his opposite numbers 'to consider the operation of the Electoral Truce'. This is quite harmless and will take more time. We are playing our time on this, before the Second Front starts. Then all this triviality will be forgotten. My document on International Post-War Settlement should have been distributed today in galley proofs. But these have not arrived, and it appears that the printers were blitzed last night. So we shall have to have a special National Executive a fortnight hence to consider this one item. This is rather a pity, for it is likely to be more closely examined then than it might have been today, run through with other items.

This afternoon we chose the new Secretary. Right up to the last moment there were faint intrigues going on, with which Tom Williamson[2] and Harold Clay were associated, to try to put the whole thing off and carry on with Middleton, at least till the end of the war!! But no one, when it came to the point, dared propose this, though Clay said, before we began the interviews, that he supposed this 'didn't rule out second thoughts'.

...

I vote throughout for [Maurice] Webb, though without tremendous conviction, and conscious that he would have been a great speculation. He had his solid cohort of supporters, but the majority were clearly determined not to risk him. He has succeeded in making himself very unpopular.

Morgan Phillips is forty-one, so that, barring accidents, he can, if he chooses, go on for twenty-four years! Solemn thought! Within his limits, he is supremely competent. He has been a first-class Secre-

---

1 Lady Forbes-Watson, née Alexandra Mary ('Georgie') Dalton (1891–1974). Hugh Dalton's sister. Hugh and Georgie had disliked each other since childhood.
2 T. Williamson, later Baron Williamson (1897–1983). Labour M.P. for Brigg 1945–8. General Secretary of the General and Municipal Workers' Union 1946–61. Chairman of the Finance and General Purposes Committee of the Labour Party 1940–47.

tary of our Policy Committee. He understands how to make a memorandum and to guide discussion and to state a case. But he is not a commanding personality. He is not outstandingly intelligent. And he is very Welsh, in the derogatory sense. He is, I understand, a terrific intriguer and without deep personal loyalties. But he may grow, and he has a wonderful chance. Anyhow, the thing is done and we must make the best of it.

Thursday 23rd March

Underhill,[1] whom I ask to call, says that the Public Trustee, when acting as Executor, 'generally leaves it to the relatives'. I said that this was not what I wanted. I wanted him to do the whole thing and that was why he had been appointed. I said that I would like to see his representative as soon as would be appropriate.

I ring up Datchet twice today, but she is still living, contrary to all expectations. They give her drugs to make sure she has no pain and prevent her from becoming restless. There is nothing else to be done, and, for the moment, I make no plans and write no more letters, having written last night to Ruth.

War Cabinet before lunch. Attlee in the Chair, the P.M. being absent. Several say afterwards how much quicker things go when he *is* absent. Law, in particular, who complains that the P.M. 'doesn't know how to be Prime Minister. He wants to be Sole Minister.' 'That Bedlam,' he said over the telephone to me, speaking of the Cabinet. ...

Robin Brook to dine. He is carrying greater responsibilities than ever and has been down with jaundice. He is evidently being a great success at his job. I shall take him down to West Leaze the weekend after this. He would like his wife[2] and two babies to live in it, if I agree, for a month or so. He is one of the most appreciative of all my visitors to West Leaze. He says that Gubbins tremendously enjoys travelling about the world and being close behind all the Fronts in turn. This also they like best at home, for Brook says that Gubbins is a very bad administrator and a very bad judge of men. I think he overdoes this criticism.

Friday 24th March

Jay and later Warter discuss with me the 'score sheet' of new factories built or building in Development Areas. This is beginning to look quite important, but I impress on both of them the importance of doing something for South-West Durham, which is, after all, one of

1 Dalton's solicitor.
2 Helen Brook, née Knewstub, later Lady Brook (b. 1907). Founder of the Brook Advisory Centre for Young People 1963; Chairman 1964–74; President since 1974.

our most serious 'survey areas' and where, even apart from my own constituency, there are many possibilities of new building.

Overton to see me, bearing in his hand a copy of Woolton's covering note to our joint recommendations on Location. In this Woolton says that, having thought it over, he thinks that full responsibility for Location policy should be placed in a single minister, and not on a group, and that this single minister should be the President of the Board of Trade. Overton grins rather sheepishly and asks whether I have seen this. I say, 'Yes and oddly enough I did not myself suggest it to Woolton. I know you won't like it at all.' He doesn't reply to this. ...

I ring up Datchet three times today. Still no real change, though she is getting gradually weaker and has not recovered consciousness. Last night she was rather restless. Her physical tenacity is amazing.

Saturday 25th March

She died just after 11 o'clock this morning. I heard when I telephoned at 2 p.m. She had never recovered consciousness nor heard the guns firing near by last night. So I went down this afternoon, reaching Datchet just before 3. A second doctor had just come to view the body, as a condition for cremation. The dead shrink very quickly. (I remember, too, writing in my *British Guns* that 'The more I see of dead bodies, the less I believe in immortality'. I still feel like that. This belief is, except for a few philosophical experts, mere wishful and unplausible sentimentalising.)

And then I have to see Mr Hunt, the undertaker, a smooth-mannered, red-faced, clean-shaven, subservient, rather sly-looking person, who, however, turns out to be quite efficient. He will bring the coffin round on Sunday night and we shall go on Tuesday to Woking for the cremation, in good time for which he will procure a small, simple, chaste bronze urn.

Sunday 26th March

I sleep a bit; send a Death message round to *The Times*; and then finish off my joint paper with Jowitt on Restrictive Practices. I like turning aside to this. I have to do a lot of cleaning up. I am very vexed that not only ——, but others who *can* do better if they tried, serve up such shambling stuff to ministers. They have no pride in form or style.

Tuesday 28th March

Arrive at Datchet just after noon. Thence to Woking. It is a great thing that I go alone. The process takes two hours. Now they use gas burners, two rows of them, one on each side of the coffin containing the body. Before the war they used solid fuel. From the burned remains pieces of wood forming part of the coffin are first picked out and then the pieces of bone are passed through a special machine which grinds them to powder. The resulting ash is quite heavy. Today, when the small casket was brought out, quite full and still warm, it weighed, we estimated, 7 or 8 lb. Oh, how quick and clean and final!

The garden round the Woking Crematorium is really rather lovely. Today was a warm spring afternoon. The buds of flowering trees and others were just breaking and, except that not far off the railway ran, with trains rattling along it and in sight – though this will be cured when some of the trees grow up – one could have imagined oneself deep in the country.

Then we drove back, Mr Hunt with me in the car, his myrmidons and the hearse having been sent away before the two-hour wait, through that most familiar but rather attractive countryside, past Virginia Water, with new coniferous plantations, and along the river by Egham, back to Datchet, where I drop Mr Hunt, and then on up to the Deanery, where I leave the ashes.

Back at the office I hear that the Whips have sent an S.O.S., and going down to the House join in a Division in which the Government is defeated by one vote – 117 to 116 – on an amendment to give women teachers equal pay with men (Clause 82 of Butler's Bill).[1] This is the first time this Government has been beaten. Most other governments I remember suffered this fate fairly often.

In January 1944, General Eisenhower was appointed to command the impending invasion of northern France. By delaying the proposed invasion in the south, more landing craft were made available for a five-division attack on the Normandy coast: three divisions of the British Second Army (in-

1 'Butler's Bill': the 1944 Education Bill, introduced by R. A. Butler, President of the Board of Education. Major provisions included compulsory daily religious services in all state-aided schools; the raising of the school-leaving age to fifteen (not in force until 1947); and free, universal secondary schooling in three categories: grammar, technical and modern. The Tory Reform Committee felt that the Bill did not go far enough, and moved two amendments, one calling for the raising of the school-leaving age to sixteen by 1951, and the other demanding equal pay for women teachers. On equal pay, 37 Tories rebelled and, in combination with Labour back-benchers, defeated the Government by one vote – as described here. Next day, the Prime Minister called for a reversal of this vote, and the amendment was overturned. The Bill became law in August. (See P. Addison, *The Road to 1945*, Quartet, London, 1977, pp. 238–9.)

cluding a Canadian division) on the left flank, and two American divisions on the right flank close to Cherbourg. The date of the first landings – 'D-Day' – was provisionally fixed for 5th June.

Meanwhile, in Italy, the Fifth Army had opened a heavy attack on enemy positions south of Monte Cassino. On 22nd and 23rd January a major landing was successfully carried out at Anzio, more than sixty miles behind the German front line. However, by the end of January the Allied army found itself hemmed in, and repeated attempts by the Fifth Army to break through failed, despite a heavy bombardment of Monte Cassino.

The Russians moved forward rapidly against the Germans at the beginning of 1944. They relieved Leningrad in January, driving the enemy back to the Estonian frontier. In February they encircled some 50,000 German troops at Korsun. In March and April, they moved past Odessa, crossing the Dniester on a 300-mile front.

Wednesday 29th March
This afternoon a ministerial meeting, Woolton, Anderson, Bevin, Lyttelton, the Prof and myself, with a number of officials. I sense that Woolton and a number of the rest are almost completely exhausted. I sense, on the other hand, that Bevin, who arrives late, has had much to drink. He is almost incoherent and continually returns, long-windedly, to points that have been settled. The officials look demure while this goes on and on and Woolton leans towards me and whispers, 'He is very tight.' We all, both drunk and sober, agree that the draft presented to us this afternoon on post-war employment is completely lousy. It is, I think, by Dennis Robertson,[1] and is a sort of extract from an economic text book, full of long words, long sentences and all quite abstract. Not a fact or a figure anywhere! We all agree this must be scrapped, and something intelligible to the ordinary Member of Parliament substituted; and that we must begin with the Transition, which will interest people most.

Woolton gives me the impression of being completely bogged just now in his job and has suffered some shock from being knocked about in the House of Lords debate last week. He has had no political training to harden his skin and his sensibilities. He particularly resented little Lord Latham's reference to a 'Government in Slumberland' and the same little peer's interruption, when Woolton said 'Our under-

---

1 D. H. Robertson, later Sir Dennis (1890–1963). Sir Ernest Cassel Professor of Economics at the University of London 1939–44; an adviser to the Treasury 1939–44. President of the Royal Economic Society 1948–50.

takings still stand', 'Stand still.' 'I call that very cheap,' Woolton had replied. And at the end of the debate, Lord Beaverbrook had waved his arms and shouted at the Lords. So many had been brought up from their backwoods and country kennels that a Government majority was assured. So there had been no vote; only great discomforture. Going out, Lyttelton complained to me of Woolton's Chairmanship, that he had to 'sit twice a week through several hours of this'. There was no direction, he complained. The whole discussion was just like a heap of sand. 'And', he added, 'it is pretty stiff that we should be expected to do all this, when we have to be thinking most of the day and night about the war.'

Wanting a change of companionship, I collect Bob Fraser to dine with me. I am a little late because Attlee suddenly summons a meeting of Labour ministers at No. 11, where we discuss tomorrow's proceedings on the Education Bill. The War Cabinet have decided to make the House vote against the Clause as amended by yesterday's vote, and to make this a vote of confidence. It is quite clear that, once more, a large number of our silly Members fell into a Tory trap and voted without any consideration of the real point at issue. Attlee says that he will tell the Party Meeting tomorrow that, unless not only the Government gets a good total majority, but [also] a substantial majority of our own Party vote for the Government, he will resign and hopes we will all back him up. No one challenges this view.

The truth is that we are all showing various signs of disorder and strain, while waiting for the invasion. And the Russians are rushing on so fast that there is an uncomfortable feeling that, even if we do the invasion very well, we may seem rather small beer and late in the day, and may only meet the Red Army somewhere west of the Rhine. There is, further, the daily humiliation of the news from Cassino, where, in spite of 'the war's greatest air bombardment' and every other kind of effort by all arms, we are still baffled by a bunch of bloody Germans in the rubble of a wretched little Italian town on a hillside. Something has been going very wrong here, and it, together with the lack of exploitation of the Anzio bridgehead, raises gloomy thoughts for the future.

On my return tonight I write a careful letter to my brother-in-law, replying to lucubrations from him and Georgie. The latter is still living on old grievances of having been 'completely ignored' some twelve years ago when Ruth and I had to tidy up, quite unaided by her, my father's affairs and my mother's future arrangements.[1] It would

---

1 After Canon Dalton died in July 1931, it had been necessary for his widow to vacate the house that went with the canonry at Windsor.

be sad, were it less silly. My first inclination is to write a rather sharp letter, but I finally tone this down into a more 'dignified' allocution.

Thursday 30th March

A very useful meeting with Warter and my four Regional Controllers from the Development Areas. I give them a clear and strong lead on policy and say that this is a subject on which I both feel very strongly and know a good deal. There are many subjects on which, until duly briefed, I know much less than the officials. But this is the other way round. It is a very simple problem. These areas had too few factories in them and too little variety of industry. The remedy is to put more factories in them with a greater variety of industries. If this is persistently followed for several years, the problem will be solved – for *these* areas. And no others, if the same policy is steadily followed, can ever become nearly half as bad again. ...

Ruth arrived last night from Manchester and comes this morning to an early lunch. We then go down by car together to Windsor, where the funeral in St George's passes off very easily. A few old ladies attend and the service is quite short and simple, without music, except for a little on the organ as we come in. Evans,[1] aged eighty-nine, still walks in front of the Dean bearing his silver poker, much as he used to do forty or fifty years ago. My father's protégés last well.

Ruth and I call at the Deanery about a quarter of an hour before the service and walk in immediately behind the Dean, who carries the casket. We find Georgie and John [Forbes-Watson] already established in their stalls next to ours. I suppose it will be a new grievance that they were not also invited to the Deanery and to join in the procession. When it is finished, we are just going off when Georgie comes rushing after me, having shown no particular warmth, or, indeed, emotion, at any stage in the proceedings, to ask whether it is clear that she will be able, whenever she likes, to go down to Datchet and stick a label on anything she wants, and buy it at the probate value. I say, 'Oh yes, of course.' She then begins to complain that she has not yet received a copy of the Will. I say I am sure the Public Trustee will send her one before long. She then goes on to complain several times over that she has been left completely in the dark about everything for many years. John, hovering in the background, says, 'We haven't even ever seen the Marriage Contract.' This is really too fantastic for words, for she has been a Trustee of our parents' marriage

---

1 Canon Dalton's sailor servant, acquired on the *Bacchante* voyage in 1883, when the Canon accompanied Prince George and Prince Eddy on a world trip. Evans was a verger of St George's Chapel.

settlement for about twenty years! I really don't feel I want to see her again.

Back in London, I leave Ruth at Euston, going back to Manchester tonight, and then get to the House in time to take part in the vote of confidence in the Government, deleting Clause 82, by 425 to 23.

The International Sub-Committee of the N.E.C. did not finally pass for publication the statement on 'The International Post-War Settlement', drafted by Dalton, until 18th April. 'It has been a long struggle of successive reviews, compromises, and conciliations,' recorded its author in his diary. James Walker, a trade union member of the N.E.C. and one of Dalton's allies, put it more strongly. In a letter to Dalton on 17th April, he described the critics of Dalton's draft in the following terms:

> So far as Baker is concerned, he is simply a credulous fool who always believes the last man he met, Laski is more dangerous because he suffers from an over-weening vanity in his belief of his own knowledge of men and affairs ... [Y]ou will have learned by this time that conciliation with these people does not pay. They are very much like the Germans, when you conciliate they regard it as a weakness and try to get more than you are offering. [1]

Wednesday 5th April

A most remarkable meeting of the National Executive this afternoon. It was a special meeting to consider my draft on the International Post-War Settlement, which, after prolonged consideration by the International Sub-Committee at, I think, five meetings, beginning with a preliminary study of my Conversational Memorandum, had now been sent up, after much amendment, and some improvement, to the National Executive. It was a rather thin National Executive. But most of the pro-Germans were there, including three – Laski, Phil [Noel-Baker] and Clay – who had taken a good deal of part in the discussions on the International Sub and had never made any direct challenge there to my layout. Indeed, Laski had embarrassed and surprised me at the first meeting by saying how wonderful he thought it all was, and nearly weeping over my Palestine paragraph, on which he afterwards wrote me a most emotional and effusive letter.

1 Dalton Papers 7/10 (80).

But afterwards, sinister omen, he wrote and said he hoped I would read Brailsford's Penguin.[1] (I did and wrote to Brailsford ...) No doubt Laski has since been confabulating with the *New Statesman* crowd, and especially Brailsford and Kingsley Martin, and they have told him that my draft is quite frightful. Anyhow, this afternoon they have obviously prearranged an attempt at sabotage. Jim Griffiths, who as I have remarked before is very wet and has a spongy under-belly, not having read the thing before, moves that the whole draft be referred back. ...

John Parker, also a member of the International Sub, who has taken no effective part there in making alternative proposals, is noticed to be sitting with Laski and Clay, and gives a silent vote in favour of the reference back. Several of my most stalwart supporters are absent, including Jimmie Walker, who is having an operation on his eyes, and Billy Robinson, who is fed up with the whole thing, and Jennie Adamson,[2] who always backs me through thick and thin. None the less, the motion for reference back is defeated by 9 to 7, after some vigorous interventions on my side by Burrows and Tom Williamson, during whose speeches the atmosphere tends to rise. I, on the other hand, am very suave and patient, saying only that I think it rather an odd procedure that this motion should be supported by a number of those who are supposed to have co-operated with me in producing the document in the Sub-Committee and never challenged it there, and that, of course, it would be quite easy to meet a number of points raised, e.g., altering the order of paragraphs and changing their relative length. Laski then unctuously says that my reply has done much to make their task easier. I deliberately reserve my fire on the main issues to a later occasion. We then have a lengthy discussion, paragraph by paragraph, and I undertake now to prepare a revised draft in the light of this. I also seek to implicate Phil and Laski by specifically inviting them to redraft certain of the paragraphs to which I attach the least importance.

They are rather a cowardly lot, this minority, and I am not going to hunt them out into the open prematurely. But we may have to have a showdown before we are through. One result of this further delay is that it will not now be possible to get this document out much more than a month before the Conference. This, I think, will suit me all right. Earlier on there was a great effort to get it out early, so as to allow conferences expounding it [to be] held all over the country. I never liked this, because all the silly pro-German factions in the

1 H. N. Brailsford, *Our Settlement with Germany*, Penguin, London, 1944.
2 Janet (Jennie) Adamson, née Johnston (1882–1962). Labour M.P. for Dartford 1938–45; Bexley 1945–6. Junior minister 1945–6. Member of the N.E.C. 1927–46.

D.L.P.s would then have had plenty of time to get their counter-campaign going. And so would some of the German émigrés so active in our midst. But now there will be very little time for this. The only trouble on the other side is that some of the big unions may say they have not had time to consider it.

I proceed straight from this lengthy meeting to take the Chair at the Finance Sub-Committee of the Policy Committee. Here we guide through another of my own precious drafts – no one at present in the Labour Party Executive seems capable of drafting anything except me – on Full Employment. Old Pethick [Lawrence] appears and is very sensible, as usual. But George Benson[1] is ... notoriously in the pockets of the Treasury officials and possibly one of the leaks to them regarding our affairs. He is opposed to all modern thought on matters of finance and puts his case so slowly and long-windedly that I make another heavy draft on my stock of patience. In the end the document emerges not much changed.

Beaverbrook gives a large ministerial dinner tonight to Berle[2] and Warner,[3] who are over here to discuss Civil Aviation. I tell Berle how impressed I was by Berle and Means's classic *American Corporations*,[4] also by his speech about German responsibility for the massacre of Jews. He makes a most eloquent and well-arranged after dinner speech. I think that probably it is a very good thing we have him here, to exorcise his suspicions and anti-British inclinations and to flatter his vanity, which is considerable.

Thursday 6th April
To West Leaze in the evening for five nights.

Friday 7th to Tuesday 11th April
The spring is beginning. ... I begin to think that, when I leave office, I must start at once to write, though not necessarily to publish, my autobiography.

Tuesday 11th April
Return this afternoon to London, rather grudgingly. It does not seem

---

1 G. Benson, later Sir George (1889–1973). Labour M.P. for Chesterfield 1929–31, 1935–64.
2 Adolph A. Berle (1895–1971). U.S. Assistant Secretary of State 1938–44. Ambassador to Brazil 1945–6.
3 L. W. Warner (1885–1959). Deputy Director-General of Aeroplane Production at the Ministry of Aircraft Production 1943–4; Director-General 1945.
4 Adolph A. Berle, Jnr, and Gardiner Coit Means, *The Modern Corporation and Private Property*, Macmillan, New York, 1933.

that people have been bestirring themselves unduly over the Easter weekend.

Thursday 13th April
War Cabinet on manpower for Jap war. The Chiefs of Staff pitch their claims very high, and Lyttelton wants to have an alternative study made on lower figures. This is accepted, the C.I.G.S., who is a very able man, being very adaptable, but explaining that it is very difficult for the Chiefs of Staff to make any estimate until they know more about what is to happen in Europe, e.g., how large the Armies of Occupation will have to be and what areas we shall have to occupy, either alone or jointly with others. Lyttelton and I both stress the need to lift civilian standards and push export trade as soon as Germany is beaten. The P.M. is always very responsive to this, though also very insistent that we must 'do our utmost', whatever that may turn out to mean, to help the Americans to beat the Japs. He says that, at Teheran, Stalin said that it would happen on the very next day. 'And so, with everybody gathering in, they might not really fight it out, but might offer terms, short of unconditional surrender, which it might be well worth our while to examine.'

The P.M. seemed to me to be in very good shape tonight; confident, equable, not tired, and with his sense of humour always quite near the surface.

The outcome of the Washington talks on post-war economic problems was the *Joint Statement by Experts on the Establishment of an International Monetary Fund*, made public in a White Paper in April 1944. The main proposals of this document were incorporated into the Articles of Agreement of the I.M.F. in July 1944 at Bretton Woods, New Hampshire.

Friday 14th April
War Cabinet on Monetary and Commercial Policy. It is agreed, after long wrangle on usual lines, that Anderson may publish the latest version of the Monetary Plan, though making it plain that we are not committed to it and that we expect it to be discussed by the House of Commons and the public before we take our decision. On the other hand, Anderson had wanted to say that we were in favour of the 'broad objective'. There was a long wrangle as to what this might mean or

imply. Finally the P.M. said that he could easily draft some 'broad objectives' which we could support, and begin with 'maximum exchange of goods', reasonable stability of prices, etc., most of which, however, belongs to the Commercial and not to the Monetary compartment. Not much time is left to discuss Commercial Policy and the Beaver keeps on shouting that he wants the Commercial Plan published as well. I keep on repeating that there is no Commercial Plan yet, which is quite true in the sense of a detailed technical scheme agreed with the Americans, though the officials have published a long story of their recent talks with the Dominion and Indian officials. The Beaver keeps on shouting, 'I only came to the Cabinet this morning in order to support the Doctor. I thought he wanted to publish his plan.' It is, on the whole, a very genial Cabinet. Bevin says to the Beaver, 'You want to strangle the one plan at birth and do an abortion on the other.' This was thought by all to be very funny. The P.M., as yesterday, was in an exceedingly good mood and full of benevolence towards all. But he said, 'I really cannot be expected at my age to start to get up all these currency questions which I have thought nothing about for nearly twenty years.' And it is true that, in this field, he is willing to be led. But he is embarrassed when people try to pull him violently in different directions.

To see Bevin at his request. He wants to do a wangle with me to help work on post-war models. ...

He then passes to his favourite topic of abusing colleagues. This afternoon it was Lyttelton and Cripps. He had, he said, told Cripps at the Cabinet the other day that he didn't know why he didn't mind his own bloody business. 'Some of them looked rather surprised when I said that,' he said. 'But I stuck to it.' Cripps, it seems, had hurried down to Bristol, when the miners' strikes were on, and seen the Central Electricity Board and told them that, owing to lack of coal, electricity supply ought to be cut down by 20 per cent. The truth was, said Bevin, that Cripps and his Ministry of Aircraft Production had wasted electricity and manpower in the most disgraceful way and they were using the excuse of the strike in order to retrench. Cripps had put in a fantastic demand for 212,000 more workers. He had never expected to get them, but Bevin had produced them for him. And then he had been in a complete mess and had no work for most of them to do.

He then said that he had been asked 'last Monday' (10th April) to go and see Attlee. He had found him and Herbert Morrison 'with their heads close together', though 'they looked up rather hurriedly' when Bevin came in. He had obviously interrupted them in the middle of a very confidential conversation. Then Attlee asked whether he had heard about the proposed Cabinet reconstruction. Bevin said no, what was it? Attlee said it was proposed to move Gwilym Lloyd George from Fuel and Power to Information, give Bracken the Dominions, and Cranborne the Foreign Office, with Eden continuing as Leader of the House. Bevin asked, 'Have you agreed to all this?' Attlee said it had been talked about between him and the P.M. Bevin then asked, 'Did you raise no objection?' Attlee said, 'No.' Bevin then said, 'You ought to be ashamed of yourself, letting all these jobs go to Tories. Why shouldn't one of our people have the Dominions? After all, there are Labour Governments in Australia and New Zealand, and a great left-wing movement growing in Canada, and an important Labour Party in South Africa. There are plenty of our men in the House who could do that job very well.' Then he asked, 'Who is to go to Fuel and Power?' Attlee said that the P.M. wanted Shinwell. 'Then', said Bevin to me, 'I really lost my temper, and I said, "Bloody hell! If that bugger is brought in, I shall go out, and you can tell that to the P.M. I won't stand for it. He is just another nominee of Beaverbrook." ' Bevin then continued with the obvious point that to reward Shinwell would be to put a premium on disloyalty and discourage all the decent people in the Party who had played the game and supported the Government in moments of difficulty. He also said that that very morning he had got the miners to support the new Four Year Plan for wages by telling them that Shinwell had said in the House of Commons that they were going to turn it down. This, he said, had irritated them very much, and many who before had been in doubt, now voted for the plan. Bevin thought – he *would* – that it was solely his intervention that had stopped any Cabinet reconstruction taking place at all.

Thursday 20th April
Attlee to dine with me. He says he has told the P.M. that he really mustn't put Shinwell in the Government. He thinks the Beaver is running Shinwell. We discuss certain possibilities and agree that the best line to take at the Annual Conference will be that there can be no change in the Election Truce, but that at the first election after the defeat of Germany, we shall fight as an independent party, adding, if this could be squared with the P.M. beforehand, that it would be a great mistake for this election to come too quick.

Saturday 22nd April
Warter drives me down in the afternoon to his house at Cobham. A very pleasant break. He has a good North Country cook, who, however, is quite deaf.

Sunday 23rd April
Get up late. Go for a short walk before lunch with my host, and sleep in the sun in the afternoon. It is a very good sun!

Drive over to Beaverbrook's in the evening, where we find Fulbright,[1] a Rhodes Scholar and rising Democratic politician from Arkansas, who is now running for the Senate. Fairly young and quite well disposed, but, like most of them, rather slow. Warter remains to dinner and is amused. The Old Man has some wonderful trees, including some very old yews, below his terrace, over which we look forth. The talk is chiefly about the need to keep up good future relations between U.S., Soviet Union and ourselves. The Beaver, to his credit, has, in recent years at any rate, been very good on Russia.

Monday 24th April
John Wilmot back from his tour in the West Indies. This seems to have been a very great success and he has a wonderful story about flying up the great river in British Guiana with three other M.P.s, the Governor of the Colony and the pilot, in a very old plane, and flying first up, and then over the edge and down, the highest Falls in the world, said to be some 850 feet, with a river the size of the Thames above and below. Also very much impressed with the efficiency and smoothness of Pan Air. He doesn't think much of the white population in the West Indies, nor of the Indians in British Guiana, but finds the negroes very engaging and very keen to remain in the British Empire!

'The Commercial Plan in its present form is intended to destroy Imperial Preference and re-ruin the agricultural industry,' Beaverbrook had reported to the War Cabinet on 18th February.[2]

Wednesday 26th April
Early meeting with Anderson and Law to consider whether we should jointly meet Stettinius[3] and talk to him on Commercial Policy. There has been evidence that the State Department is very vexed at our

1 J. W. Fulbright (b. 1905). U.S. Congressman for Arkansas 1943–5; Senator for Arkansas 1945–74.
2 PRO, CAB 66/47. W.P. (44) 121.
3 E. R. Stettinius, Jnr (1900–49). U.S. Secretary of State, August 1944–June 1945. Industrialist. Chairman of the Dumbarton Oaks Conference, and leader of the American delegation.

delays on this, and papers have come in, both from Washington and Ottawa, saying that it is generally realised at Washington, and that the Canadians understand in much more detail, naming Beaverbrook, Amery and Hudson as the obstructionists, that we are stuck, split and in recession on Commercial Policy. The State Department is also pressing, in rather heated and indignant telegrams to the Foreign Office, and in high-level telegrams from President to P.M., for an answer to their proposal to set up a Steering Committee on international economic problems. We three finally decide that it would be embarrassing to meet Stettinius formally. Anderson is entertaining him to dinner and this, we think, should be enough. Anderson should say some soothing but delaying words to him. ...

Oliver Stanley comes to see me to say how very disturbing is our Palestine paragraph in I.P.W.S. [International Post-War Settlement]. It is, he says, 'Zionism plus plus'. It is tacked on, he feels, rather unnaturally, to a long and helpful statement on Europe. It will not, he hopes, be much played up in our propaganda. I say that I don't think it will. But I remind him that the Labour Party has always taken a pro-Jewish line in Parliamentary debates for many years. He is afraid that it may do harm in Palestine, both by encouraging the Jews to believe that the next British Government, which they think may well be a Labour Government, will do everything for them, and equally by unsettling the Arabs.

Thursday 27th April
John Wilmot tells me privately that the Duke of Windsor seems to be working very hard in the Bahamas. He has practically given up drink, taking only one glass of wine with his dinner, and nothing between meals. Mrs Simpson said to them, 'The Dook's working very hard.' Wilmot had the impression that the 'Dook', who now speaks with a strong American accent, would like 'a spot of promotion soon'. But it is difficult to see where to send him. ...

War Cabinet on Commercial Policy. New subject! Finally agreed that I should prepare a fresh paper – this will be about No. 100! – to be put in for the Dominions P.M.s next week, making it as non-controversial as possible, and explaining that ministers here are not united and that an all-party government finds it much more difficult than a party government would, to reach agreement. Amery presses to be allowed to put in to the Dominion P.M.s an alternative programme, but the P.M., very bored with him, shakes his head violently and says, 'No, no, no.' The P.M. is on my side – he says to me tonight, 'I agree very much with many of the things you say' – but is troubled by the split, and the active pro-Preference agitation, in the Tory Party.

But he warns Hudson, who is as difficult as usual, pressing his demand for the right to impose quota restrictions on food imports into this country, 'You are preparing for yourself a terrible electoral disaster. I remember 1906, when less than 100 Conservative Members were returned.'[1]

Very weary after all this, I go to bed early. This National Government will never reach decisions on many of these questions. I feel tonight that it is imperative, soon, but not too soon, after the defeat of Germany, to burst open this ragbag of all the political parties and try for a majority of our own. The P.M. said tonight, 'I am always doing my best to hold you all together until we have won the war.' It is amusing to observe that Beaverbrook is not on the list of those attending the Dominion P.M.s talks. Clearly this is because Mackenzie King would hate it so. The latter, I am told a few days later by Sir Frederick Whyte,[2] keeps at the end of his study in Ottawa a little shrine, with a curtain drawn in front of a photograph of his mother. Mackenzie King has never married. He has no personal friends. He is incredibly 'astute'. With a few short breaks he has been P.M. of Canada for twenty years. His moral strength comes from his belief that he is constantly in communion with his mother.

Thursday 4th May
Attend Administrative Committee for first time this session. Pethick [Lawrence] talks good sense about the Monetary Plan. He has seen Keynes and proposes to give cautious support to the Plan in the debate next week. This is agreed to.

Friday 5th May
Lunch with Percy Cudlipp at Boulestin's. He is clever and quick, but not really very attractive. He says, as often before, that Labour ministers don't keep him informed so that he can be helpful in the *Herald*. Attlee tells him nothing. Bevin is friendly when they meet, but everything may change within twenty-four hours. We speak of the Party secretaryship. He says Maurice Webb was much hurt by not getting it. We wonder whether he should not now try to enter the House. I think he should, since there will be great openings for able young men in the next Parliament. He says Webb's health is now pretty good, though he tells me, what I did not know before, that Webb as a boy had very poor health and spent some years in a sanatorium. We speak also of the I.P.W.S. [International Post-War Settlement] and

1 *sic.* In fact, 157 Conservatives were returned in 1906.
2 Sir Frederick Whyte (1883–1970). Liberal M.P. 1910–18. Head of the American Division of the Ministry of Information 1939–40.

I tell him the story of the composition of this. He is frankly frightened of my Palestine paragraph. He has more sympathy with Arabs than Jews. He asks, rather absurdly, why the Jews shouldn't all go to the British Empire and the U.S.A. Why need they go to Palestine? He thinks that many people will dislike the sentence saying that the good Germans cannot restrain the bad Germans. I said I thought this was very friendly towards the Germans, and I cannot understand why so many people are so much more anxious to be nice to Germans than to Russians and all the other European peoples whom Germans have overrun, oppressed and tortured. We agree to meet again soon.

To West Leaze this evening.

The draft White Paper on Employment Policy was considered by the War Cabinet on 19th May 1944, and published the following month. This looked at the short- and long-term prospects for employment, and outlined a programme for the encouragement of exports, action to maintain both public and private investment and the regulation of consumption. The last would be achieved by adjusting the level of social insurance contributions and local authority public expenditure – a scheme put forward by James Meade. Though only mildly Keynesian, the document was revolutionary in a political sense. It committed the Government to preserving 'a high and stable level of employment'. It also contained a separate chapter on 'The Balanced Distribution of Industry and Labour'.[1]

Meanwhile, Beveridge had been conducting a private inquiry into the full employment aspects of his Plan, and had been persuaded to adopt a Keynesian approach. This inquiry came to be regarded in official quarters with suspicion, and in the autumn of 1943 civil servants employed as advisers by Beveridge were required by the Treasury to withdraw. There followed what Beveridge later described as the 'White Paper Chase' – the attempt by the Government to publish its full employment plans before the appearance of Beveridge's private report. Though Beveridge's more radical private document, *Full Employment in a Free Society*, was not published until November, by then it had already had a major impact in speeding up the official commitment to full employment.[2]

Monday 8th May
This afternoon we have another go at the Draft White Paper on Full

1 Cmd 6527.
2 See J. Harris, *William Beveridge: A Biography*, Oxford University Press, Oxford, 1977, pp. 434–41.

Employment in Woolton's Reconstruction Committee. The bit on Location of Industry comes through pretty well unscathed. The bit about stabilising purchasing power and not bothering too much about balancing the Budget has been toned down a good deal under the pressure of the Treasury. This passage 'now reads like an antiphon by Keynes and Eady', as Cherwell says. I ask Hopkins whether he does not think this is a step back from the Steering Committee's Report. He says he thinks not, but this is for the general public, whereas the Steering Committee's Report was for a narrow circle of ministers and officials. Some of us think it most desirable to get this White Paper out before Beveridge. If so, we must hustle. It is left that Woolton will now revise it and circulate it once more, and, if no strong objections develop, it will then go to the War Cabinet. I wonder whether some tiresome person, the P.M. or another, will sprag it there. Certainly this is not government in too great a hurry!

Tonight I attend the War Cabinet meeting with the Dominion P.M.s to discuss 'economic policy'. There were two items on the agenda, (a) Monetary Policy, and (b) Commercial Policy. Anderson was to expound the former and I the latter. Anderson begins, and then the Dominion P.M.s speak in turn. Mackenzie King sticks to the point and hands in a neat little typewritten statement. But then Curtin[1] brings everything in, protection for Australian secondary industries, Imperial Preference, state trading, migration, etc. He is very insistent on Imperial Preference. They are now producing, he says, for a population of seven millions, with a large part mobilised for war, an output enough for twelve millions. (The Australian Labour Party has always been extreme high-protectionist.) Then Fraser, following this cue, says very little about money, but much in favour of Imperial Preference and protection of New Zealand industries. He adds, what Curtin didn't, that quantitative restriction of imports is vital to New Zealand. And then Smuts says that he doesn't believe the Americans will ever agree to reduce their tariff. I felt I couldn't get in before this, since the rota of Dominion P.M.s must be observed. (The Indians, and Huggins[2] from Southern Rhodesia, are rather obviously treated as being 'below the line'.) Also I feel, particularly after Curtin's and Fraser's speeches, that there is just no hope of getting on, and that it would be a great tactical mistake even to suggest further official discussions with the U.S. on this. I, therefore, merely

1 John Curtin (1885–1945). Australian Prime Minister and Minister of Defence 1941–5. Chairman of the Advisory War Council 1941–5.
2 Sir Godfrey Huggins, later 1st Viscount Malvern (1883–1971). Prime Minister of Southern Rhodesia 1933–53. Prime Minister of the Central African Federation 1953–6.

explain briefly the need for the U.K. to expand its exports by at least 50 per cent, i.e. from about £500[m.] to about £750 million pounds a year, and add that we must therefore look to increased exports, both inside and outside the Empire. I add that, although there are differences of view on this within our three-party Government, all parties are anxious to develop Empire trade by all practicable means. There is no proposal here that Imperial Preference should be abolished, except by unanimous agreement of those concerned, or even reduced, except in return for a substantial quid pro quo. This must include better terms of entry for British goods, not only into the U.S. market, which took only about 6 per cent of our total exports before the war, but into other non-Empire markets, including many in Europe where we were blocked out before the war by quota restriction. In this rough sketch we have safeguarded, I suggest, the right to subsidise home production without limit, and likewise, subject to reasonable conditions, infant industries and state trading. But frankly I feel I am making a rather perfunctory statement, merely in order to get it on the record. There is just no hope of moving on along this line at all for the present.

Tuesday 9th May

Gladwyn Jebb to dine with me. I have not seen him for some time. He says, as previously, of Eden that 'he has no mind, only a mass of antennae'. Further, it is very difficult to discuss foreign policy nowadays with him, because, as soon as one begins, the Chief Whip is announced. He is fascinated by leading the House of Commons. He risked his arm, however, the other day, by saying that we would recognise the French C.N.L. [Committee of National Liberation] when we landed in France. Jebb thinks the Prime Minister's influence on foreign affairs is not at all good. He is incurably romantic. He had Fitzroy Maclean[1] down to Chequers the other day with one or two others recently returned from the Balkans, and harangued them for four hours about the merits of the Yugoslav and Greek bandits. None of them could get a word in edgeways to report to him what had actually been happening. Also he has now an intense personal feeling against de Gaulle, which colours his whole outlook on France. This may result in de Gaulle becoming thoroughly unco-operative with us. And yet it is imperative that we and the French should work closely together after the war. De Gaulle will be tempted to try and play us off against the Russians, and even perhaps against the Ger-

---

1 Brigadier F. H. Maclean, later Sir Fitzroy, 1st Bart (b. 1911). Conservative M.P. for Lancaster 1941–59; Bute and Ayrshire North 1959–74. Led the British Military Mission to the Yugoslav Partisans 1943–5. Junior minister 1954–7.

mans. The Russians, meanwhile, are still very suspicious that we want, after the war, to make friends with the Germans again and use them against the Russians. ...

Gladwyn thinks that it is inevitable, as the Russian armies move forward in the East, and as Poland and Czechoslovakia are liberated, that, whatever happens in the West, there will be the most unimaginable chaos in Germany, where all the prisoners-of-war and slave labourers will, no doubt, rise against the Germans. He does not see how food supplies, communications, etc., can possibly be maintained. He thinks we have not yet fully envisaged the extremities to which a great part of Europe will be reduced in the last phases of the war.

Aneurin Bevan and fifteen other Labour M.P.s incurred the wrath of the Labour whips by voting against Regulation 1AA, a measure introduced by Ernest Bevin imposing penalties against any person instigating an unofficial strike. The Administrative Committee of the P.L.P. proposed that the whip should be withdrawn from Bevan, with the likelihood that expulsion from the Party would follow; but the P.L.P. decided only to report him to the N.E.C., and Bevan was merely required to sign an undertaking to obey Standing Orders in future.

In July 1943, Churchill appointed Fitzroy Maclean, an M.P. and former diplomat, to lead a mission to the Yugoslav Partisans in the field, with authority to make direct recommendations back to the Prime Minister about future actions towards them. 'What we want is a daring Ambassador-leader with these hardy and hunted guerrillas,' Churchill told the Foreign Secretary.[1] The mission was parachuted into Yugoslavia in September. It found that, following the Italian surrender, six Italian divisions had been disarmed and two had changed sides to fight alongside the Partisans against the Germans. The Yugoslav Partisan Army, now 200,000 strong, was able to occupy most of the Adriatic coastline and keep up a widespread resistance against the Germans. Faced with this massive evidence of Partisan strength *vis-à-vis* the rival followers of Mihailović, the British government withdrew official support from Mihailović in December. At the end of May 1944, under heavy pressure from the British, King Peter (in exile in London) dismissed Mihailović from his government, and asked Dr Subašić to form a new Administration.

---

1 W. S. Churchill, *The Second World War*, Vol. V, *Closing the Ring*, Cassell, London, 1952, p. 412.

Wednesday 10th May
Party Meeting. By 71 to 60 my colleagues, as I thought they would, dodge the issue on the proposed expulsion of Aneurin Bevan and refer the matter to a joint meeting of the National Executive and the Administrative Committee, with a view to the prevention of future occurrences of this kind! It will now evidently be wise to let the whole thing go to sleep and give Bevan no further opportunity for self-advertisement. ...

In the afternoon hear in a Committee Room at the House a statement by Brigadier Fitzroy Maclean on Tito. He looks much improved since he shaved off his long, drooping moustache. But he speaks very, very slowly and is very guarded in all references to matters outside his immediate mission. He says Tito has 300,000 men, organised in ten Corps which intercommunicate by wireless and by couriers. Tito, he thinks, is the greatest master in Europe of guerrilla tactics. His following is 50 per cent Serb, 30 per cent Croat, and the rest Slovene and Moslem. The original driving force behind his organisation was Communist, but all parties are now in it. The German reprisals are exceedingly brutal. When they come to a village from which all the men have gone up into the hills with Tito, they massacre indiscriminately all the women, old and young, and all the children. The Partisans count it a defeat unless they kill at least five Germans for every man they lose. Mihailović is unquestionably co-operating with the Germans. This has been so since the end of 1941.

Thursday 11th May
Reception by Cranborne to a multitude of people vaguely associated with the Dominion Prime Ministers Conference, including swarms of officials from all Departments. I have a word with Norman Robertson,[1] who is very sad at what he calls the 'confused and ignoble end of the Commercial Policy proposals'. He asks why I didn't intervene earlier and with more emphasis. I say that I couldn't break into the series of Dominion P.M.s and that, in fact, the policy was now quite impossible for political reasons in this country. There had been strong representations against it by the Conservative Party to the P.M. who himself was in favour of it, so far as he had had time to study it, and there had even been a threat of resignation by at least one Conservative minister (Amery, though I did not name him). Liesching afterwards said to me that he quite realised the thing was now politically impossible here, and that he supposed what was most likely was a series

1 N. A. Robertson (1904–68). Under-Secretary of State for External Affairs, Canada 1941–6. Clerk to the Privy Council and Secretary to the Cabinet 1949–52. High Commissioner for Canada in U.K. 1946–9, 1952–7.

of bilateral arrangements between the U.S. and the various Dominions, in which each of the latter would make concessions which would be helpful to them but not to us. None the less, by this most unsatisfactory means, the British Empire would be able to escape any American charge of bilking on Article VII. After an interval it may be possible, I think, to resuscitate our general plan. But not yet.

Friday 12th May

Warter and Jay to see me with very good news. I.C.I. want to build a large new works, to employ 5,000 people, south of the Tees and a few miles east of Middlesbrough. This would be a perfect location from the point of view of Cleveland, where the ironstone mines seem bound to go completely dead within a few years after the war. It would also draw both labour and supplies – especially coal and salt – from Durham County on the north bank. Sir John Nicholson[1] asks whether, if they decide to go ahead, they will have as good industrial building priority as the Development Areas. I tell Warter to say yes, and it is now clear that the balance of advantage is definitely in favour of bringing in the industrial strip on the south bank of the Tees into the N.E.D.A. [North-East Development Area].

Tuesday 16th May

Joint meeting in the afternoon between Administrative Committee and National Executive on the eternal, and now incredibly boring, Bevan case, and 'discipline' generally. After two hours of talk it is decided, on the motion of Sam Watson, by 21 to 9, to call on Bevan to state in writing, within seven days, that he is prepared to obey the Standing Orders of the Parliamentary Party, failing which the National Executive be recommended to expel him. Also decide that a Sub-Committee of eight, four from each body, should consider future arrangements designed to prevent a repetition of these incidents.

Thursday 18th May

5.15. Visit Norgeby House and other neighbouring establishments in Baker Street, at invitation of Selborne, to see how things have got on. And indeed, they have got on famously. Operations all over Europe have grown immensely. Last month all records were broken both for dropping and picking up personnel, dropping stores and dropping containers. Great quantities, in particular, have been dropped in Belgium and in Savoy, to help the Maquis, and elsewhere in southern France. They have 120 planes for this last month. The training establishments in the country have not been much expanded, but there is

1 Sir John Nicholson (1879–1959). Deputy Chairman of I.C.I.

very good interworking with the Americans, and I met one bright young American officer in charge of the Operations Room. The other principal characters were familiar – Sporborg, Colonel Barry,[1] Tommy Davies, Archie Boyle, Robin Brook and Venner. ... In addition to all that is being done from here, there are large operations from Italy, from which stuff is being poured into Yugoslavia on a great scale, and also into Poland, Czechoslovakia and Greece. The news about Poland is that the Germans are as brutal as ever but also all very venal. The Polish Underground Movement is said to be establishing pretty good relations with the Red Army but to be fighting furiously with the Polish (Communist) partisans. Some of the Poles who have recently come out from Poland have been speaking very bluntly to the Poles over here and are much more favourable to a real understanding with the Russians. In Czechoslovakia almost everything had been smashed up by the Germans until recently. But now there are some small beginnings of revival. There is not much good to report from north Italy. Italians do not, it seems, take easily to guerrilla activities. I ask about Germany. They say that there is still absolutely nothing there. Some people talk vaguely about 'having lines into Germany', but I have been totally right in telling people that there is no effective underground movement in that country.

Friday 19th May
War Cabinet at noon. The Full Employment White Paper, called 'Employment Policy', is *finally* – repeat *finally* – approved, subject to Woolton and Anderson putting in some extra sentence to meet the Beaver's view that not quite enough is said about the need to stimulate private investment if trade looks like drooping. The P.M. admits that [he] has not read the paper and that he asked the Prof for a short note on it, but that the Prof has produced a very long note, and that he has not had time to read this either. But he has read the first sentence, in which the Prof says that he regards this as a very bold and ably conceived plan worthy of full support. The P.M. adds that he notices that the Committee which prepared this plan 'contained all the best brain power of the Cabinet', but, before finally committing himself, he would like to hear the view of the Lord Privy Seal, who was not on the Committee. The latter says that he regards this as 'a magnificent scheme, a first-class scheme', and we should all certainly support it. Woolton then begins to give some general explanations, dwelling in particular on the proposed variation in the social service contributions

---

1 Colonel R. H. Barry, later Major-General (b. 1908). In charge of the operations section of S.O.E. 1940–42. Chief of staff and director of plans at S.O.E. 1943–5.

according to the state of trade. The P.M. says he understands that what is proposed for public authorities is the exact opposite of what would be generally done by private persons, that when things look bad, they should not draw in their horns but push them out and launch forth into all sorts of new expenditures. Woolton replies that this is exactly so, and that it will be necessary to do a good deal of education of the public mind upon it. The P.M. says, 'I suppose that at such times it would be helpful to have a series of Cabinet banquets – a sort of Salute the Stomach Week?' Amid the laughter following this happy quip, the White Paper is approved for publication.

David[1] and Freda Hardman[2] to lunch at the Acropolis. They are both very nice and friendly. His name is one of several now being considered for Darlington, and I strongly urge him, she supporting me, not to enter into any entanglement at Dudley or elsewhere in the Midlands, until Darlington is definitely settled. He says that Windle[3] is pressing him to consider one of the Midland seats, as we are very anxious to get a new and better lot of candidates there. I say that this is quite all right from the point of view of the Head Office, but that Darlington would be, for Hardman, very much better, in addition to the fact that I should like to have him next door to me.

Wednesday 24th May

P.M. opens two-day debate on Foreign Affairs. It was by no means one of his best speeches; particularly at the end, he gave the impression of being very tired. There was little fire in this speech, and he stumbled over his words; 'Communism' or 'Christendom', he wasn't quite sure which he meant to say at one point! There was, however, a very frank passage about the Turks, saying that we had been disappointed by their excessive caution and that, since they showed no inclination to come into the war on our side, we had ceased to send them arms, which were badly needed by those who were fighting. He was rather grudging about the French, and the objection to giving full recognition to the F.C.N.L. until we knew who really represented the mind of France.

Bevin, meeting me just afterwards, shook his head over the P.M.'s speech and hinted that his health and stamina were again rather poor.

1 D. R. Hardman (b. 1901). Labour M.P. for Darlington 1945–51. Junior minister 1945–51. Former Cambridge don, and Borough and County Councillor. Dalton had known him since the 1922 Cambridge by-election when Dalton had stood as Labour candidate.
2 Freda Hardman, née Riley.
3 R. T. Windle (1888–1951). Assistant National Agent of the Labour Party 1929–46; National Agent 1946–51.

But Bevin is apt to be alarmist on this matter. Attlee told me later that the P.M. had been sitting up till 3 a.m. preparing this speech. In any case, on the eve of great events, it must be a great effort to concoct this sort of oration, and I really don't know why he thought it necessary, just at this moment, to do it at all.

Meet at lunch, along with Durbin, Cobb,[1] Managing Director of Mullard's Valves. This man makes a good impression on me and is very anxious to become a Labour candidate. He is to be put into touch with Elland and, like others, is being pressed by Transport House to take an interest in Birmingham. He thinks he could go on in his present business even if elected, and has many right ideas on trade and, in particular, on distribution. He would be a very welcome addition to our Party. He has had a mixed life, having started as a small boy doing a milk round, and having been a sailor and a number of other things and travelled in most parts of Europe and Asia. He is now forty-three and full of energy.

Thursday 25th May
Berl Locker to see me. He is, naturally, very pleased with our Palestine paragraph, particularly as we have put it in, as he says, without any pressure from the Jewish Agency. (He is, of course, their liaison man with the British Labour Movement.) He argues against our giving way – which we have no intention of doing – to the suggestion that we should amend the reference to 'encouraging' Arabs to move out as Jews move in. He agrees that it is quite clear that 'encouragement' in this context does not mean 'compulsion'. I ask him to send me any further points on this.

...

Am invited to dine by Sir Frederick Shedden, and supposed that we should be alone together. I had yesterday received a note from Curtin, in which he said he was very sorry that the pressure of official engagements was so heavy that he could not find time for the talk with me to which he had been looking forward. Tonight, however, on arrival at Shedden's room at the Savoy, I find Curtin is there, and we dine *à trois*. After some general talk, Curtin begins to criticise the P.M. and, still more, his entourage. 'That old boy's no friend of yours,' he says (he means of the Labour Party generally), 'and the people round him are even worse. That old Professor, for instance. He said to me, "Of course everybody knows New Zealand would have gone bankrupt if the war hadn't come at the right moment." I said, "Your crowd, including the bankers in the City of London, tried to

1 F. A. Cobb (1901–50). Radio engineer, and General Manager of Mullard's. Labour M.P. for Elland 1945–50; Brighouse and Spenborough 1950.

keep New Zealand's temperature down to about 95. She got it up to about 99 and could have kept it there, if you hadn't tried to force her down again to sub-normal. But the war just stopped that game." '

As to the Beaver, Curtin related that he said to him one day, 'You must come down and stay with me. I want to talk to you.' Curtin asked, 'What about?' The Beaver replied, 'Oh, anything', and Curtin said, 'Well you can talk about anything here if you want to', i.e. in the Cabinet Room at No. 10. Nor had he been at all taken by Bracken. Then he said, 'I have been looking about and listening a good deal while I have been here and I am not at all happy about the state of the British Labour Party. I hear that Bevin does not intend to go on after the next election. Herbert Morrison ought to go and get his hair cut. He looks too eccentric and lots of people don't take to him. They think he is conceited and too much identified with London. I don't think he goes down well in the country as a whole. As for Clem [Attlee], of course no one can say anything against his sincerity or his loyalty, but he doesn't look to me much like a Prime Minister. I don't think the country thinks he does.' I then related the story of 1935 and the contest for the leadership of the Party, and the part which I had played on behalf of Morrison. Curtin then looked at me rather hard and asked, 'Does that mean you feel bound to him for next time?' I said, 'Not necessarily.' I had referred, in connection with this story, to Greenwood. Curtin said, 'Well, of course I hadn't been thinking of him at all – for obvious reasons.' I said, 'Yes, everybody knows he is the victim of his habits.' (I noticed that neither Curtin nor Shedden were drinking anything but water at this meal, though they had insisted that I should have a double whisky. Curtin was supposed, at one time, to be drinking too much, like most Australian politicians, but I gather that he has firmly checked this habit lately.) He then went on to say, in the most direct language, that he considered that I would be by far the best Leader of the Labour Party, and that I had gifts which none of the others possessed. He understood, in particular, that my relations with the trade unions were good. He said he supposed, looking at me, that I was about fifty. I said I should soon be fifty-seven. He said, 'Well anyhow you look quite healthy. You ought to have another ten years of public life in front of you.' I said that it had never been one of my ambitions, at any rate since 1931, ever to be the Leader of the Labour Party, though I should like, if the chance came, to be either Foreign Secretary or Chancellor of the Exchequer in a Labour government with a strong Parliamentary majority. He persisted, however, in his view, and added, 'If I were you, I should seriously consider the question of coming out of the Government if some good reason presents itself. Of course you can't and shouldn't do it until the big operation has been launched and is well under way. But there would be a lot to be said for your crossing over to the other side of the House before the Government breaks up and before there is a general election. It is not good that it should all be left to Shinwell, and it would help your personal position a good deal if you came out by yourself for some good solid reason. And I think you might easily find one.'

I have put down what he said for purposes of record. I thanked him very much for speaking so frankly and said I appreciated the personal friendship which had made this conversation between us possible. I would certainly think over all he had said. We must see how things develop. It was not easy to look very far ahead, and I agreed that it would be quite out of the question for any of us to pull out of the Government – except on some most vital pretext – until the war had moved well into its next stage.

Friday 26th May
Mild row with Anderson at meeting of Lord President's Committee. Anderson is suggesting that arrangements for transfer of staff from one Department to another should be looked after by an official committee with a Treasury Chairman. This, he says, is 'not to interfere' with existing interdepartmental arrangements, unless these result in deadlock. I say that I should like this to be more clearly put into the paper, since it would be quite wrong for ministers, or their Permanent Secretaries, to be prevented from discussing staff transfers with one another and making arrangements. I then say, addressing Attlee in the Chair, that I remember how helpful he was when I invited him to dine with me in order to arrange for the transfer of Liesching from the Dominions Office. Anderson rather raised his eyebrows at this, and I went on to say that I did not want to be told in future that arrangements I made with my colleagues had to be held up pending consideration by 'some committee of officials sitting at the Treasury'. Whereupon the Chancellor, getting, to my surprise, very red in the face and raising his voice, exclaimed, 'If ministers are not prepared to co-operate, I shall withdraw the scheme. I have tried to make it quite clear that the ordinary interdepartmental arrangements will go on.' He is very official-minded still.

On 25th May, Dalton had raised with Overton the possibility of promoting Douglas Jay to the rank of Principal Assistant Secretary, and putting him in charge of a new Section in the Board of Trade responsible for Location policy.

Wednesday 31st May

Further talk with Overton about new Location Section, at the end of which I bring him to acquiesce in my own view. There is no other candidate now in the Board of Trade, apart from Douglas Jay, for the new P.A.S. [Principal Assistant Secretary] post, and Overton has no other name to propose except Beer,[1] to be brought back from Ministry of Supply. I repeat that I can't agree to anyone acting, particularly in a Section in which I take so active an interest, as P.A.S. unless I know him and have seen him in action. I repeat, for the third or fourth time, the virtues of Jay. Overton thinks that both Jay and Warter are 'positive' and that perhaps someone who is more of an 'administrator' to work with Warter would give better results. I don't agree with this, but again repeat that I want Palmer[2] to keep a general eye on the whole thing and that I think that he would supply whatever qualities of caution and Whitehall knowledge are needed to restrain these other two wild horses! ...

Dine with Crossman, not quite physically recovered from his illness, though, as usual, full of mental energy. He is very anxious now to get to Germany with P.W.E., and is full of ideas as to our buying up or otherwise taking over German radio stations and film industry. This, he thinks, will be the only way to 're-educate' the Germans. I ask him to discuss this with Gaitskell. He says a good deal about the nonsense of the American official attitude towards France and their refusal to recognise or deal with the F.C.N.L. [French Committee of National Liberation]. Roosevelt and Hull are most to blame, no doubt, but our own P.M. is not quite blameless. So it looks as though, when the first landings take place, no authoritative French voice will speak to the French people. There is trouble now about de Gaulle's proposed visit to this country, owing to American refusal to participate officially in the talks, and it therefore seems that de Gaulle will, in any case, arrive too late to be of any use for *this* purpose.

No one, therefore, will be in a position to give orders to the Resistance Movement in France to help us. (I am not sure that this matters as much as Crossman says, since I cannot imagine the French Resistance Movement doing anything else.) Crossman says he quite understands why so many civil servants, permanent and temporary, despise ministers and are always trying to do things which they think ought to be done, without letting ministers know, for fear that they might try to

---

1 H. Beer (1896–1970). Principal Assistant Secretary at the Ministry of Supply 1941–6. Permanent Under-Secretary at the Board of Trade 1946–56.

2 Sir William Palmer (1883–1964). Principal Industrial Adviser to the Board of Trade 1944–6.

stop them. He says that, as regards his two present ministers, Eden 'has no moral courage' and always tries to dodge difficult questions, and that Bracken is an utterly contemptible character, who takes no real interest in his job and whose answers to Departmental questions in the House bear no sort of resemblance to the truth. He is always looking, likewise, for ways to keep out of trouble and is trying to acquire cheap popularity by repeating that he is the first minister who, when the German war is over, will close down his Department.

Thursday 1st June
See Warter and tell him that Jay is to be P.A.S. and work with him, both to keep in touch with Palmer. He is quite agreeable to this, though apparently the idea had been put into his head that there was some distinction between 'executive' and 'administrative' functions, and that some permanent civil servant would be required for the latter. When I said that the other man who had been suggested was one of those who had given official Board of Trade evidence to Barlow that nothing could or should be done about Location, he made a wry and surprised face.

Friday 2nd June
Assemble my new Location Squad – Palmer, Warter and Jay, and, with Overton, discuss broadly the new arrangements. I think they make a good trio – this wily and experienced permanent, who has so surprisingly high a reputation in Whitehall and with ministers generally; this distinguished young businessman, and this brilliantly able and dynamic temporary – Socialist, Economist, and Fellow of All Souls!

I take away a mass of notes and documents on Location to West Leaze.

Saturday 3rd to Sunday 4th June
At West Leaze working mainly on Location. Ruth, during her recent visit, has performed, as she warned me, some 'drastic operations' in the garden. She has cut down the beeches outside the kitchen to half their height. But this both gives more light and will make them grow up much bushier at the bottom. She has also decapitated two birches near the gate, but this again will be for their good! She says she had some very good sun-bathing and has certainly come back very brown and fit-looking after this long-delayed break in the country. She has also done a great tidying up of the books, including Hansards, which I recently moved down from the cottage up the road.

On 5th June, General Eisenhower issued the order which put 156,000 Allied troops into France by the following evening. After a heavy bombardment of coastal defence batteries, and a variety of calculated diversions to confuse the enemy, the first seaborne troops landed on Normandy beaches shortly before dawn on the 6th. The Germans were taken by surprise, and Hitler's 'Atlantic Wall' was quickly penetrated.

Tuesday 6th June
The Invasion of France began today at first light. It is very hard to think or speak of anything else. But I have, very unwillingly, to give my mind to preparing my speech for the House of Commons tomorrow on Location of Industry, which is being raised on the Board of Trade vote. I spend all day on this. As usual, the trouble is that one has, not too little material, but much too much.

Wednesday 7th June
Bracken says that the P.M. is very tired – and who can wonder? De Gaulle was got here just in time to be told about the Operation before it began, and to speak on the air to France. The Americans have been quite intolerable over this. Recently we have indications that Hull does not share the President's unyielding distaste for de Gaulle and the F.C.N.L. But there is also evidence now that the President himself is preparing a move in de Gaulle's direction. And, therefore, it is very important that we should not sit at the end of a bough which we might suddenly find the President was sawing!

Discussion on Location in rather a typically Parliamentary day. I make a long and, I fear, rather uninteresting and unincisive speech. It is largely in the form of quoting, summarising and commenting on successive paragraphs of Chapter III of the Employment White Paper.[1] I am more than usually conscious of the difficulty of coalition government and of using language which will not lead to an uproar on either side of the House. There must be compulsion on employers regarding Location – at least negatively, through refusal of building permits if necessary – but there must not be too much compulsion, and there must be inducement and discussion as well. All this is difficult to put over. Waterhouse, winding up, makes a pretty poor speech, giving the impression of not really knowing his stuff – though he had worked hard at it and thought he did – and at one place quite losing his way. But no great harm is done.

1 The chapter dealing with 'The Balanced Distribution of Industry and Labour'.

Thursday 8th June

Waterhouse very much upset at having made such a bad speech yesterday, and says that he thinks he ought to resign. I tell him not to think any such thing. He had been inclined both to offer me his resignation and to write to the P.M. doing the same. I said he should on no account write to the P.M., and I would not dream, for a moment, of considering his going. We all had our good and bad days. He had had a rather bad day yesterday, but no real or lasting harm had been done. It had come out all right in the press. He mentioned that his son was likely to be leaving for France in a few days. This sort of explanation affects many people's actions just now.

...

Ruth comes to dine and tell me of her start with U.N.R.R.A. She enjoys it very much and is obviously much happier and better placed there than she was in Manchester. Their office now is in Portland Place, just opposite the B.B.C. She is in the 'Areas and Services' Department – they have a curious nomenclature – but this is what she likes, because it is from here that arrangements will be made for sending out 'Field Missions' and she is in the section dealing with France, Belgium and Holland. As she said before, her great desire would be to go to France as soon as this is possible. And this may now be much sooner than we thought before the Invasion started, provided this goes well. Her further picture is that she might go on from France to Berlin in order to arrange for the repatriation of all the French now in Germany. These are immense undertakings. ... She will go on staying, for the time being, with Miss Jephcock in Hampstead, which is very convenient. We speak also a good deal of political prospects and of how things might develop here.

In a speech in the House of Commons on 24th May, Churchill defended negotiations that had taken place with Spain, indicated his gratitude to the Spanish government for keeping out of the war, and declared that 'Internal political problems in Spain are a matter for the Spaniards themselves'.[1]

Friday 9th June

Gladwyn Jebb to dine. He is rather tired and discouraged by the failure to get rational consideration of post-war foreign affairs. He

1 H. C. Debs [400], col. 771.

blames the P.M. for this. He won't leave things alone and his interventions, in this particular field, are romantic and ill-judged. An old autocrat surrounded by bad advisers! Instead of getting down to sensible detailed discussions – if he *must* meddle with detail – he spends literally hours monologuing about Tito and various partisans and bandits of all sorts all over Europe. He has all this quite out of proportion. On Spain it is quite natural that a commotion has arisen as a result of his praise of Franco and the Spanish government. It was all totally unnecessary, but he made it up at 2.30 a.m. on the morning of his speech and the Foreign Office didn't see the draft until about an hour before it was to be delivered. They did their best to tone it down, but with hardly any success. Then again his speech was much warmer towards the Italians than towards the French, and this again was very ill-judged. As to the French, there is really no sensible alternative to recognising de Gaulle and his Committee. Eisenhower, to whom has been given the ungrateful duty of deciding which Frenchmen to co-operate with in France, is himself strongly in favour of recognising de Gaulle. This is a most ironical and stupid situation, which may be cleared up as we move forward in France, but which should never have been allowed to arise in this form. It is primarily due to the strong feelings of the President, and to a lesser extent of the P.M. Gladwyn hears that Bracken, for once, is taking the right line on something in his private advices to the P.M. and is urging that de Gaulle should be recognised. It has, in particular, been quite fantastic to print these new French currency notes without even the superscription 'République Française'.

The American reporters have been very indignant because they have not been allowed to cross to France in larger numbers to witness what one of them described as 'the greatest event in human history since the Crucifixion'. To which someone made reply that that particular incident was very well and fully covered by only four reporters.

Saturday 10th to Sunday 11th June
Stay in London, feeling that it is wrong to travel just now, and polish off miscellaneous arrears of private correspondence, of varying degrees of importance, and start reading up papers and books on iron and steel. My strong impression is that this last industry is both inefficient and sinister, and that it is my duty to do something about it. But I am not quite sure what!

Monday 12th June
Meet at lunch with Mrs Phillimore, Schoenfeld,[1] American chargé

1 H. F. A. Schoenfeld (1884–1952). U.S. chargé d'affaires to exiled governments in London 1943–5.

d'affaires to the Allied governments in London. He is a State Department man and has a smooth manner, but is really, I think, very stupid. He has some queer preconceived view of the British being less 'democratic' than the Americans, because, he thinks, our people are prepared to leave everything in the hands of 'a small group'. In other words, we don't stand up for ourselves and think for ourselves to the same extent as Americans. He is very confused as to what the 'small group' is composed of, but I think he really means a few hereditary peers. (All the old standard arguments against hereditary titles are reinforced by the fact, which is constantly being impressed on me when I talk to Americans, that much more significance is attached to this rubbish in the U.S. than here, and that we are all thought to be still dominated by Dukes [and] Earls and bossed by Barons!) Then he seems to shift to some conception of a group as 'possessing advantages' and charges both me and Attlee with being part of the 'group' in this sense. But when we point to Herbert Morrison, the third member of the party, and tell Schoenfeld that he is the son of a policeman and never went to a secondary school, the argument seems to break down. I then explain that in the County of Durham all the public affairs are indeed in the hands of 'a group', but that this principally consists of Durham miners, and that highly educated and wealthy Conservatives greatly resent this state of affairs. But at this point Schoenfeld says that I am misrepresenting his argument. He also seems very surprised that we are not more sensitive to his charge, which he seemed to think was a rather crude and indelicate one for a diplomat to make. Mrs Phillimore says that he must come and meet the members of the T.U.C. I urge him to do this, saying that in America there is no equivalent of our trade union leadership.

Wednesday 14th June
We decide, after long hesitations, to institute another prosecution in London of Civil Defence workers who have refused to give in coupons for their uniforms. Wilmot is much troubled by the local position in Lambeth, where an earlier prosecution, incompetently presented, failed, and where, as a result, all the Civil Defence workers are being incited to refuse to surrender coupons and to cock snooks, when they pass him in the street, at the unfortunate and, as it would appear, somewhat pompous and self-opinionated Town Clerk. I myself had been reluctant to prosecute, because I feared that prosecution might coincide with heavy air attack, in which some Civil Defence workers would be, and all would be liable to be represented as, heroes. I did not think it would look good for a man to appear in the Police Court in the morning and be fined for violating one of my regulations and

then to go in the afternoon to Buckingham Palace to receive a George Cross! Now, however, the argument for having another prosecution is overwhelming, and the Home Office are very insistent that we should.

The Government presented a Town and Country Planning Bill on 20th June, to make provision for the acquisition and development of land for planning purposes.

Thursday 15th June
War Cabinet to consider Town and Country Planning Bill and White Paper. Finally it is agreed that both shall go forward, but not till after further wails by Selborne, very loudly and persistently, and by Cranborne, less plangently, on behalf of the poor landowner, who is having his property compulsorily taken from him at the values of four years ago, without any adjustment to correspond to the fall, since then, in the value of money. Attlee also reports from the Legislation Committee that the Lord Chancellor and the Attorney-General think the provisions regarding landowners will be thought most inequitable and will not be capable of effective defence. The rest of us, however, all stand firm and, to my surprise, the Beaver, when invited to express an opinion, warmly supports both the Bill and the White Paper and says that he would have no difficulty in defending either of them in the House of Lords, and this, of course, finally settles it and satisfies the P.M., who before had had doubts. It is becoming more and more visible, with each succeeding week, that the P.M. will swallow anything which both the Beaver and Cherwell support. He becomes visibly more and more dependent on these two and less and less interested in the opinions of others. Even Lyttelton, who was at one time always treated as the expert on business questions, seems much less in favour now.

Talk later in the evening with Salter and his wife,[1] with whom I go back to the Connaught Hotel, where they are still living. They speak very ill of Ben Smith, who, they say, has not got a real job to do at all, made himself ill by eating and drinking too much, and used to try to entertain Americans by telling them a lot of very dirty stories. This,

1 Lady Salter, née Ethel Mather Bagg. Widow of Arthur Bullard, writer, of Washington, D.C. Married Sir Arthur Salter, q.v., in 1940.

Sir Arthur and Lady Salter say, is not the thing to do in Washington. Salter adds that there never was a job for Ben Smith's predecessor, and that, if I will cast my mind back, I shall remember that it was only invented when it was desired to get him fixed up somewhere else because he was making such a mess of the Ministry of Aircraft Production and because something had to be done for Cripps. Salter says that across the water, the P.M. stands out much more clearly in his essential character than he does here, and it is widely known and said in the U.S. that he is *très mal entouré*. Salter will not long go on, he thinks, with U.N.R.R.A., but for the moment he is looking into its organisation, which needs much improvement.[1]

The first V-1 flying bomb exploded in England, near Gravesend, on 13th June. Soon a hundred bombs a day were crossing the Channel from launching-sites in northern France. By early September, when the German launching-regiment withdrew to escape capture, some 20,000 people had been killed or seriously injured by this assault. There had also been a great deal of damage to property, as well as dislocation caused by the evacuation of about a million schoolchildren.

Tonight we have a lot of pilotless aircraft flying round. We had a few a week ago, but this was treated as a dead secret. This time the public are to be told the truth, and Morrison makes a statement next day in the House. Our *first* impression is that they are not really very serious and certainly they cannot be aimed with any great precision. But they may well be something of a nuisance in the next few weeks (until we have occupied the Pas de Calais, as Little Arthur says to me).

Friday 16th June
I was told the other night, the story coming from Waldorf Astor,[2] the tale that de Gaulle had a torture chamber in Duke Street, supervised by Passy,[3] where the victims were those Frenchmen who had been too

1 As Parliamentary Secretary at the Ministry of War Transport, Sir Arthur Salter, q.v., shared responsibility for the organisation of U.N.R.R.A.
2 W. W. Astor, later 3rd Viscount (1907–66). Conservative M.P. for Fulham East 1935–44; High Wycombe 1951–2.
3 'Passy': code name for Colonel André Dewravin, head of de Gaulle's intelligence branch, the Bureau Central de Renseignements et d'Action Militaire, whose office was at 10 Duke Street.

intimate with the British. I must say that this seems to be a very tall story. But he made the very sensible suggestion that we should have taken the opportunity, if we did not like de Gaulle well enough to recognise him, to recognise the group of French Parliamentarians, drawn from all parties, who were over here about a year ago and then went on to Algiers. In fact, however, the de Gaulle problem is likely to solve itself gradually, untheoretically, and in a very English fashion, by no definite act of 'recognition', but by the acceptance by the British and American military of de Gaulle's nominees as administrators in the French areas successfully liberated. This is already beginning in Normandy.

Saturday 17th to Sunday 18th June
In London, paying visits to several of the scenes of the flying bomb incidents. Their blast is, quite clearly, nearly all horizontal. It is still surprising how few people, as a rule, are killed.

Friday 23rd June
Awakened at 2 a.m. by flying bombs and one comes fairly close when I am in my bath at 9 a.m.!

Lunch at Soviet Embassy, with Sir Thomas Barlow, in celebration of his services in providing clothing for the Soviet civilians. Gusev still very slow and tongue-tied, but it is not true to say that he won't speak English.

Leave for West Leaze with Bob Fraser. Train is very crowded and the morale of some of the passengers is not high. It is sensible that any one not now working in London should, if they conveniently can, get out and stay out.

Saturday 24th June
Bob shows great assiduity in mowing my lawn, or part of it. The first time this has happened for years.

Monday 26th June
Dine with Frank Nelson, looking very fit, due no doubt to freedom from worry. Party mostly Air Force, plus Gubbins. Nelson still shows signs of having liked working with me very much.

Tuesday 27th June
Only thirty-four P.Q.s in all. I think the buzz bombs are encouraging Members, outside London, to keep in touch with their constituents.

Wednesday 28th June

National Executive all the morning and Joint Meeting of National Executive with General Council and Administrative Committee in the early part of afternoon. Flying bombs near overhead in the morning make us move down from the pleasant top floor Board Room, nearly all glass, to a stuffy room on the third floor. But I think the flying bombs also help to shorten the speeches, except, of course, Shinwell's. We are to consider, month by month, whether it is possible to hold the Annual Conference. The National Executive accept, with approval

"DAMMIT, YOUNG MAN, WE MUSTN'T PUT THE CART BEFORE THE HORSE!"

and without amendment, my draft message of salutation to the Armed Forces and to the Resistance Movements in Europe.

This afternoon's Joint Meeting is opened by harangue, wholly justified, I think, by Citrine on the lack of discipline in the Parliamentary Party. He complains that Bevan, when he made violent attacks on the trade union leaders, was not only not dealt with afterwards but was not even subjected to any criticism or interruptions at the time. Several others of the General Council spoke in the same sense and some threatened to come down into the constituencies of offending M.P.s and denounce them. This, of course, is exactly what they ought to do, or better still, work on their local branches in these constituencies. If, as Wilmot put it to me, all the trade union branches

761

in North Lambeth began to pass votes of censure on Strauss and threaten to procure another candidate next time, he would soon [revert] to good behaviour. There is also some chit-chat against Laski, who wrote something rude in some American paper about the trade unions being a brake on the political movement, and against Shinwell. Dukes[1] said, 'If I were to make a speech declaring that Laski was not fit to be Chairman of the National Executive next year, I should hit the headlines all right, but that's not the sort of thing I care to do.'

Thursday 29th June
Lunch with the Iranian Ambassador, a small and rather deprecating man. His wife is taller and much fatter and has bright red hair and was born a German – I am told – and could not, when she married him, speak a word of English. He met her when *en poste* in Berlin. I sit next to Leathers who tells me how conceited Salter is and how he had had to tell him off, though in the kindest way, and that Salter bored and infuriated the P.M. by writing him long letters explaining how eminent he was and telling the P.M. just how everything should be done. The P.M. had said to Leathers, 'I've got another long screed from that damned fellow of yours. He's quite impossible. You must get rid of him at once.' And Leathers said he had told the P.M. that Salter had done very well until recently, though he was now becoming *persona non grata* with everybody, British and American alike, in Washington.
...
   Dine, rather against my will, accompanied by Liesching, with four money-lenders – Colonel Rex Benson,[2] Baring,[3] Rothschild[4] and Lord Rennell – at the Connaught Hotel. I thought they were a poor lot. They used to be merchant bankers. They lent large sums to Germany and lost the greater part – serve them right! Anyhow, in their line of business, they are always getting commissions and rake-offs corresponding to no indispensable service. Now they want, though with more pretension than precision, to muscle in on post-war export

1 Charles Dukes, later 1st Baron Dukeston (1881–1948). General Secretary of the National Union of General and Municipal Workers 1934–46. Labour M.P. 1923–4, 1929–31.
2 Lieutenant-Colonel R. Benson, later Sir Rex (1889–1968). Military attaché in Washington 1941–4. Director of Kleinwort, Benson, Lonsdale Ltd.
3 Probably Sir Evelyn Baring, later 1st Baron (1903–73). Governor of Southern Rhodesia 1942–4; High Commissioner in South Africa 1944–51. Formerly Managing Director of Baring Brothers and Co. Ltd.
4 Probably A. G. de Rothschild (1887–1961). Partner in N. M. Rothschild and Sons, Merchant Bankers.

trade and 'get groups together' in various industries. I was rather glad to leave them having, I hope, made no commitments.

Friday 30th June
Sir Arthur Salter to lunch with me. He is sixty-three, but doesn't look it, and is giving up his professorship at Oxford in the autumn. He hopes to remain a Fellow of All Souls and to contest Oxford University again at the next election.[1] He takes himself in deadly earnest. He says, though I don't quite believe it, that he has no desire for political office. Nor does he want to tie himself up with any of the political parties, believing that University representation can only be justified if this educated citizen's second vote goes not to a member of one of the main parties, as his first vote naturally would, but to an Independent. I say, and he agrees, that we cannot carry too many Independents in Parliament and that I think such as we have should be 'atomistic' and as independent of each other as of the main parties. I should much dislike an organised group of Independents. He reminds me that the French had in their Parliament, among other groups, 'the group of members who belonged to no group'. This would not do here.

He wants, as soon as possible, to be rid of U.N.R.R.A. and then will again speak and write freely. He would like to do some more writing in the next year or so. He is demanding to see the P.M. to ascertain whether the latter really desires that U.N.R.R.A. should be a success. If so, Salter believes that some one minister must be put in charge with full authority to do whatever is necessary. ... We spoke briefly of the 'Camarilla' and I said that Cherwell was much better, though erratic, than the two Bs. Salter said the trouble was that Cherwell was expected to advise the P.M. over an immense range of subjects, most of which he could know little about, thus intervening awkwardly between the P.M. and the responsible minister. Salter also said that he had noticed, when at a Cabinet once, that a number of ministers who, he knew, held sensible views on a particular matter, remained silent or said little when Beaverbrook expressed the contrary view. It was painfully obvious that some of them were anxious not to get into the latter's bad books. Salter thought that our Full Employment White Paper was an excellent document and told me that Beveridge thought the same. Beveridge, he gathered, would like to be in Parliament, and as an Independent. I warned Salter that he also might run for Oxford University.

1 He was re-elected as Independent M.P. for Oxford University in 1945.

Tuesday 4th July

Answering P.Q.s. I get the House entirely on my side and dissolved in laughter by saying in reply to a Supplementary, that 'I understand that a "physiotherapist" is what we used, in old-days, to call a masseuse.' Then follows a discussion whether there is not some equally good simple English word for both. I invite suggestions and there are cries of 'rubbers'.

Thursday 6th July

Another Party Meeting on Town and Country Planning, with a very lengthy self-important speech from Latham, and a rhetorical contribution from Moelwyn Hughes. Attlee makes a few inaudible and ineffective remarks which are ill received. He has no grip in these days on the Party Meeting. Most react eagerly and audibly to the suggestion that they should vote against the Bill on second reading. They have an insatiable longing to be in opposition, to vote against things, to refuse responsibility, to dodge detail, to find easy safety in negatives and impotence. The meeting is adjourned until next Tuesday!

A word afterwards with Bevin who says that his officials and mine are trying to put us both into a strait-jacket on delimitation of Development Areas. He doesn't want to find that the officials have drawn a line and someone wants to start a factory three miles outside, and is told by the officials that he can't. I mention a series of particular cases – South Teesside, Blyth and Ashington, Dundee, Swansea, etc., and in all these he agrees with me that the places in question should be inside. He says he will write me a letter on the question. He is by far my best ally on Development Areas, as on a number of other things. It is indispensable that he and I should play ball together, even if he is sometimes tiresome, long-winded and inattentive! ...

Dine with Gladwyn Jebb who is working very hard on 'The Future of the World'.[1] He is shortly going to Washington with Cadogan and other officials to discuss the possibility of a real 'American Alliance'. He repeats what he has said to me before that the P.M.'s attitude to post-war foreign affairs is quite lamentable, that he doesn't understand a thing about it, and that his approach is wholly romantic. And this is no use at all. His personal telegrams to Roosevelt and Stalin are much too soft-soapy and, with Stalin in particular, this is quite the wrong line. Gusev, he thinks now, is intelligent and powerful, though

1 On 7th July, the Foreign Secretary laid before the War Cabinet a Memorandum on Future World Organisation, which Jebb had played a large part in shaping. This presented plans for the post-war international organisation which were to be discussed at the Dumbarton Oaks Conference (see note before the entry for 9th November 1944, p. 804).

his reactions are slow and stereotyped. Lunching there the other day, Winant, after drinking several glasses of vodka, became quite a new man, self-confident, decisive, incisive and the very opposite of all his ordinary qualities. He began to understand how it came to be said that Winant had been, in his day, the slyest Governor they had ever had in New Hampshire. ...

We discussed what would happen if the P.M., for any reason, passed out. I said that many Tories would prefer Anderson to Eden. Jebb, on the other hand, was quite sure that Eden would get the majority. We spoke also of the future of the Foreign Service and of the need both to give opportunity to the younger people already in it, and to recruit a good, well assorted and well spaced new consignment at the end of the war.

Wednesday 12th July
Streat[1] to see me. ... A good number of 'Doodle Bugs' come over while he is with me and I think he likes them less than most people. I find a certain malicious delight in taking him out on to the balcony so that he shall have a chance of seeing one, as they don't have this kind of fun in Manchester.[2]

Though Roosevelt had already served as President of the United States for three terms, he ran for a fourth in 1944 and defeated his Republican opponent, Governor Thomas E. Dewey, on 7th November.

Thursday 13th July
Long talk with Halifax. He thinks that probably Roosevelt will get back, though he is the most bitterly hated man in the U.S., but that Congress will quite certainly have a large Republican majority. He thinks that Dewey[3] has quite a sporting chance. He has seen him, quietly, several times and, though it would never do for this to get out, he thinks that we might very likely get on much better with

---

1 Sir Raymond Streat (1897–1979). Chairman of the Manchester Cotton Board 1940–57.
2 Marginal insertion: 'As one goes past flaming I say, "You see the Germans have invented a new substance – arsalight." He isn't much amused.'
3 T. E. Dewey (1902–71). Governor of New York 1943–55. Republican Presidential candidate 1944, 1948.

Dewey than with Roosevelt for a fourth term. The deadlock between the President and Congress would be frightful and no policy would ever emerge. Further, Halifax thinks Roosevelt is 'not at all secure', rather like Lloyd George, and may, at any time, play politics to our detriment. Dewey had said to him, 'Make a note in your diary. About 15th October Roosevelt will make a strongly nationalist speech, which you will all hate very much.' He would be at the height of his election campaign then. Meanwhile, before then, we may see him over here. Turning to commercial policy, Halifax said that he quite understood our difficulties resulting from divisions in the Conservative Party. On this I expatiate a little, explaining that the main blame was on the Beaver, Amery and Hudson. Halifax said that he thought the P.M. was a little too sensitive to waves of Parliamentary opinion; also that he thought he looked a good deal older since he last saw him, and that he understood he was often very irascible without much reason. Halifax did not think the P.M.'s war-time methods would go down at all in a peace-time Parliament, and that Anderson and others must find it quite infuriating to have to go over everything again, in meticulous detail, in the War Cabinet, after it had been lengthily debated and settled in very competent Ministerial Committees. The P.M., he said, never reads any of the papers that are put up to the War Cabinet, but enters with great zest into the discussion of all of them, asking that everything be explained again from the beginning. (This is, in fact, a most exhausting and ineffective method of government, of which one is sometimes quite despairingly aware.) Halifax said that Dewey had told him that he wondered whether it would not be best, in the interests of both of us, to go all out for free trade between the U.S. and the British Commonwealth. Winthrop Aldrich, a staunch Republican and head of the Chase National Bank, had said the same to him. 'Let's go for Union Now in the economic field.' This might mean little or nothing, Halifax admitted, but one might keep it at the back of one's mind. He said he would be helped if, when we could not reach decisions here, owing to ministerial disagreements, we would frankly tell him so and he could then discreetly convey this to the Americans. They would quite easily understand. They were constantly in that situation themselves. The trouble was that, when months passed without replies to their suggestions and inquiries, we gave the impression of having all gone to ground, and of being sulky, reserved and non-committal. This irritated the Americans a good deal. He had met McCormick[1] of the *Chicago Tribune* once at lunch, and, following a meal-time of banalities had said, 'Tell me, Colonel, do you really

1 R. R. McCormick (1880–1955). Editor and publisher of the *Chicago Tribune*. Republican.

regard co-operation between your country and mine as quite a repellent idea?' McCormick had replied, 'Not so much repellent, as utterly impossible. How can a free and democratic republic like ours co-operate with a monarchical class-ridden country like yours?' And this description was widely believed by many Americans who were much more friendly to us than McCormick.

We then spoke of the Russians. Halifax said that he was quite sure that we must never let ourselves get into the state of mind of asking whether it was better to co-operate with the Americans or with the Russians. We must do our utmost with both and, in particular, must always treat the Russians with the greatest consideration, and never let them think that we were having secrets with the Americans from which they were excluded. Hull, he said, was very good about this. But he was now a very old man and it was very difficult to get him to focus practical issues or to entertain new ideas. Halifax said he had been told 'by those in the Foreign Office who are working on post-war problems' that, if we were to hold the confidence of the Russians, we must make it quite clear to them that we are as determined as they on a 'tough peace' with Germany. He thought there was much truth in this, but he would himself put it slightly differently. We must never let the Russians think that we, or any important section in this country, or, if we could help it, the Americans, were playing with the idea of building up, or allowing to emerge from defeat, a Germany strong enough to be a partner with us in an Anti-Russian policy. It would also be very tricky to get the right relationship, in the post-war political organisation, between great and small powers. The Russians would be very hard-boiled about this. They would want the big powers to have all the real power. The Americans, and Hull in particular, might go too far the other way. He himself thought it was essential that the three Great Powers should retain the right of initiative and the right of decision in all important post-war security issues. But he didn't think this inconsistent, not only with being polite to the smaller powers, but [with] giving them a real opportunity to express their point of view, to argue on behalf of their own interests and to co-operate usefully within the limits of their capacity. I said I had no quarrel with this, but I thought it most essential that we should not drift into any international constitution in which the small people had a big voice on anything that mattered. Otherwise there would be complete unreality and frustration.

Friday 14th July
Lord President's Committee. In view of the damage to arms production in London through flying bombs, I resuscitate the proposition

for the immediate building of standard factories. I remind them that these were held up because Cherwell said, some months ago, that he didn't think anything would ever come of Crossbow.[1]

The Prof, at this, looked rather sheepish and said nothing. It was agreed that the thing should be looked at again. It is stuck, like many other projects, in a morass of interdepartmental delay and obstruction.

Saturday 15th July
With Davenport[2] to Denham, where we visit Korda's laboratories and see something of the preparation of two films: *Perfect Strangers* which Korda[3] is doing, and *Caesar and Cleopatra* which is one of Rank's new undertakings. Korda is very quick and intelligent, but not, I think, a very good co-operator. None the less, I should like to get him on my new Films Council and shall try to find a way of doing this without giving serious offence in other quarters. Korda says that Rank understands nothing whatever about production and that his father told him that he was not clever enough for the milling business. He, therefore, gave him a large sum of money and told him to run away and play with it. Hence his entry into films.

Thence to Hinton Waldrist where I spend two nights in Davenport's Manor House. He is now married to Olga Edwardes,[4] the actress, who is now also taking up films. Also present Brigadier Harker[5] of M.I.5, who was previously an Indian policeman. Not, I think, very bright, but anxious to tell a good story about his show. He offers to assist me to make sure that there are no large undetected black-market scandals in coupons. He says the Ministry of Food have brought in Sir John Teggart,[6] likewise an old Indian policeman, who, he thinks, is very good at his job. He wonders whether my Mr Yandell[7] is quite of the same calibre. I think that Yandell is better than he thinks. Also

---

1 'Crossbow': Allied measures against V-weapons.
2 Nicholas Davenport, q.v., was acting as personal adviser to Korda on the management of the film industry.
3 Sir Alexander Korda (1893–1956). Film promoter. Chairman and Managing Director of M.G.M. London Films Ltd.
4 Olga Edwardes was also working for Korda. Her first husband, Anthony Baerlein, had been killed in action.
5 Brigadier J. Harker. Second-in-Command of M.I.5. When M.I.5 headquarters at Wormwood Scrubs were bombed, the staff moved to Blenheim Palace, and a billeting order was served on Hinton Manor, sixteen miles away. Harker used to drive to Hinton every weekend.
6 *sic*. Presumably Sir Charles Tegart (1881–1946). Special intelligence bureau of the Ministry of Food 1942–5. Previously in the Indian police.
7 G. Yandell. Board of Trade official.

present Anthony Davenport,[1] his son aged twenty-one, who, after being at Stowe, had one year at Oxford and then joined the Army. Also Peter Leese, now in command of Minesweepers, who has previously been in the North-West Mounted Police and something in California, together with his wife. I sleep a lot, play tennis and make a tour of Davenport's trees, about which he has learnt quite a lot since he first came here. He has some wonderful old cedars and a very fine old ilex.

Tuesday 18th July

The post-war Reconstruction machine seems badly blocked again. I had hoped that, when Woolton had got rid of Employment, Social Security, and Town and Country Planning, the way would be cleared for dealing with a lot of other questions, including many in my field. But we are getting no decisions, and everyone, ministers and officials alike, seems to be dragging back and playing for position. No one ever says, 'Go ahead and God bless you'; everyone says, 'I haven't even been consulted. Therefore nothing should be done.' Bevin, in many ways much the best of all my colleagues, is in a suspicious peasant-minded mood about Location. He has written me several stupid letters and doesn't really deal with the points at issue. I ask Jay whether he doesn't think there is some official 'nigger in the wood-pile' at the Ministry of Labour. But he thinks it is the Minister himself, who seems quite incapable of delegating decisions on Location and wants to settle everything himself.

The Allies made no dramatic territorial gains in the first few weeks after the initial D-Day landings. On the Eastern Front, however, there was soon some rapid progress. On 23rd June the Russian army opened a vast offensive on a 400-mile front in Belorussia with an estimated 160 divisions, 30,000 guns and large mortars, more than 5,000 tanks and 6,000 aircraft. On 18th July Soviet forces crossed the Polish border near Chelm.

Wednesday 19th July

Attlee to dine with me at the Étoile, also to my surprise and satisfaction, practically unscathed by fly bombs, though one filled the place with dust some weeks ago. ...

1 Davenport's son by his first wife, Winifred.

The war is going ahead at a great pace and he thinks it quite possible that the Germans may surrender within two months. If the Turks come in and the Bulgars go out, there will be a landslide in S.E. Europe. He is all for weakening Germany economically after the war and for breaking the power of the Junkers and heavy industry. Wherever there is an economic case for it, industry should be located outside Germany, especially in Poland, Czechoslovakia and Yugoslavia. There should be some plan of International control over the Ruhr, whereby the plant here should be used to supply needed peace products for the whole of Europe. A lot of this is much better sense than I had expected from him. He says, as Chairman of the Cabinet Committee on the Post-War World, he gets a lot of his own way. The Foreign Office, he says, want to re-establish Germany very much as before – I don't think this is true – and the War Office want to deal with Germans who can 'keep order' in the post-surrender chaos.

He has got the P.M. to agree that he (Attlee) should visit France, Italy and Greece during the summer to encourage the development of democratic Left governments. He thinks it might be quite useful if he also went on to Moscow. I strongly support this, particularly in view of the hold-up of our Delegation.

He is all for postponing our Annual Conference and thinks that flying bombs give a very good pretext for this, not only as against the Conference in London, but as against bringing a thousand delegates to any other centre where there is great pressure on space for evacuees.

We agree that it would be much the best if we had no election for, say, six months after the German surrender, and if then we could separate from the Tories without too fierce a quarrel. I say it would be a good thing, both for the country and for the P.M.'s own reputation, if the latter were about then to retire, to write the history of these days, and say that he felt the time had come when those who differed sincerely among themselves should fight it out in the country. He doesn't quite despair of the P.M. accepting this view. For the moment the idea of Eden leaving the Foreign Office is off, but, if Eden wants to be a future P.M., he must learn something about Home Affairs and must stick to the leadership of the House of Commons for the present. But this job is going to become more and more difficult.

Thursday 20th July

Viénot died yesterday. This is a sad end, just when his work was beginning to bear fruit. He handled the negotiations here very well. But he had been a sick man for a long time, first T.B. and at the end a heart attack. He got up, unwisely, to do a broadcast to his countrymen on 14th July, speaking of 'the new France which must be born after the war'. He had sent me, through his secretary, a very nice letter in reply to mine congratulating him on the course of the war and his own part in the negotiations and on the success of de Gaulle's recent visits to London and Washington, and excusing himself for not having been able to dine with me owing to illness.

Lunch at Drapers', for the first time for three months. We elect Pooley to be Master for next year and I meet for the first time Powell, the new Clerk.

From Drapers' Hall to Old Jewry (Bank Buildings) to see the damage done yesterday morning by a bomb which fell at 9.30 a.m. in the wall here, smashing up half of our Export Licensing Department, as well as the National Debt Office and the Office of the Public Works Loans Board. A bomb falling in a well does the maximum damage. Six of our staff were killed and two more on the Danger List. Many of them are very shaken. I say a few words to some fifty who have gone back to work at an office in King William Street nearby. The Board of Trade have had more incidents than any other government department, though several of these have done very little damage. But this particular one was a bad one.

Friday 21st July
A bomb at 8.15 a.m. blows out a lot more windows in my bedroom and along the sixth floor. It fell just behind Lambeth Palace and the Ministry of Works and set light to a petrol store.

Saturday 22nd to Sunday 23rd July
Talk to Llewellyn[1] at Lansdowne Club. They have gone slack again lately, since the flying bombs. He will give up the secretaryship as soon as he can after the German war is finished and will go back with his wife to Nairobi, where they have a house. He hopes that his son, now in Ceylon with Mountbatten's Headquarters, will also come to Kenya and take a leading part in the political life. A nice man. We speak of the time when I was at M.E.W., and he says that I was always 'going a hundred miles an hour then' and he wondered how I managed to keep it up.

Monday 24th July
Carol Johnson[2] to lunch. He has a long run in front of him and will, I think, do well. He struck me as being a bit shy and uncertain of him-

---

1 Lieutenant-Colonel J. M. Llewellyn (d. 1945). Secretary of the Lansdowne Club 1936–45. Former colonial administrator in Kenya.
2 C. A. Johnson (b. 1903). Secretary of the Parliamentary Labour Party 1943–59. Labour M.P. 1959–74.

self and of the directions in which he should concentrate his efforts. He had a vague idea of forming groups of M.P.s to study particular questions and work out policies, e.g. the future of the B.B.C. I told him he must be very careful about this. Policy-making was for the National Executive and great dangers of jealousy were possible here. I told him to keep in close touch with Morgan Phillips, who, like himself, had a long run in front of him. For the next twenty years it would be most important that these two should be good friends and work together. He agreed with me that much of the material in the Parliamentary Party was very poor indeed at present.

In June, a V-2 test rocket landed in Sweden, providing advance warning of the production of this new weapon. The V-2 was a rocket with a warhead containing about a ton of explosive. The first to reach England exploded at Chiswick on 8th September. V-2s killed, in total, 2,754 people.

Wednesday 26th July

Labour Party National Executive all the morning. Some still think we should hold our Annual Conference soon. But this is clearly impossible, since hundreds of thousands of people have already left London and more hundreds of thousands are on the way, so that the provinces are being choked up with evacuees. And London is not suitable because, apart from fly bombs, there is thought by some to be a risk of rocket bombs. Shinwell sees this at once and quite agrees with me that London would *not* be a good place for a Conference. It is left that the office shall make inquiries as to where, possibly, a Conference should be held. It is generally agreed that, if we hold a Conference, it should be a full week and not only one or two days. It is also agreed that there shall be no National Executive in August, but we shall meet early in September just before the projected Conference of Commonwealth Labour Parties.

A Joint Meeting of two of our Sub-Committees recommends that we should turn down any proposal for a Left Unity Conference, but that the Labour Party, when the next election comes, should fight as an independent party, aiming at an independent majority. There is nothing new in this. But, later in the afternoon, someone says that this decision should be published. I say that this seems to me not the right moment, but, the general feeling being in favour of publication, it is agreed that this need not take place for several weeks (i.e. not till after Parliament has got up and we have entered on the Silly Season) and it is left that Ellen Wilkinson, Laski, Greenwood and I should settle the 'terms' of the publication. It is agreed that we should emphasize we do not contemplate leaving the Government or breaking up the Coalition until after the war in Europe, at least, is won. This declaration will take a bit of drafting, but we should be able to put it over in such a way as to encourage and satisfy our own people, without arousing any acute political crisis.

In the afternoon a Joint Meeting between National Executive and Administrative Committee on Standing Orders and Discipline. A little group of second-raters – Ellis Smith, Daggar, Dobbie and Barnes – sit in a bunch and object to everything. They are concerned to maintain the right to indiscipline. I leave before the meeting is over, being fed up with the indecision and perverseness of it all.

War Cabinet from 6.30 till after 8.30. More than two hours meandering about manpower. The Chiefs of Staff have been asked to make an estimate of their requirements for the Japanese war and for the occupation of Europe after the defeat of Germany. We have also put in demands for man and woman power for:

   (i) Direct exports
  (ii) Housing
 (iii) Home Front production.

The net effect of all this is to show a deficit of $1\frac{3}{4}$ millions which must be met either by reducing the demands of the Chiefs of Staff or by starving exports and the Home Front. It is quite clear from the start that the P.M. is not prepared that any decision should be taken tonight. And, indeed, the whole thing is highly hypothetical. The notion that, twelve months after the defeat of Germany, we shall have more than $2\frac{1}{2}$ million making munitions, as against 1,150,000 working for direct exports, and about the same number on housing, is fantastic. The truth is that the Americans don't want us to play too large a part in the Japanese war. But the P.M. and others, including Eden and Lyttelton, are really all playing for position in view of the need for early contacts with the Americans on high levels. Everything must really wait on this and on the progress of the war. When the time comes, I have no doubt that the Services and Supply Departments will have to take less and that the 'deficit' will have to fall on them rather than on the Home Front and exports. Cherwell specifically proposes that we should cut Services plus Supply by $1\frac{1}{2}$ millions and ask them what they could do with this. But, though this is a most sensible suggestion, the P.M. does not react to it tonight. He will issue a new directive shortly. Attlee makes the sensible suggestion that we should use the other United Nations in Europe to provide forces for the occupation of Germany. 'They have earned it,' he says. The P.M., moreover, thinks that the French will wish to rebuild their army and without a strong French army the peace of Europe will be unsustainable; and this army can well garrison the Rhineland and other parts of Germany. The Americans have lately been trying to rearrange the zones of British and American occupation of Germany. But they will want to take back, as soon as possible, all their soldiers, alive and dead, to the U.S. (a great claim on our shipping will be the coffins of all the dead American soldiers, whom the U.S. authorities want to bury in the U.S.A.). The P.M. says that the Germans will want very little 'occupying'. He thinks that when they are beaten they will become totally subservient and any Second Lieutenant will be able to give them orders which they will most obediently execute. They will fight very hard till the end but, once they have given in, they will give in totally. He doesn't think there will be much guerrilla warfare by the S.S. in the German mountains.

Friday 28th July
Lunch with Meynell and Miss Kilroy in order that I shall be finally briefed on Design. But the Ministerial Committee on this, which should have taken place this afternoon, is postponed to next week in order that the Cabinet may consider rockets. These are now thought to be an imminent possibility and various plans for partial evacuation are being considered.

In late July, following the arrival of Soviet troops on Polish soil, the Russian government announced that it had entered into relations with the recently formed Communist-dominated Polish Committee of National Liberation. A few days later Russian forces approached Praga, a suburb of Warsaw on the right bank of the Vistula, and established two bridgeheads across the river further south. On 29th July Moscow broadcast an appeal to the people of Warsaw to rise against the Germans. The Warsaw uprising followed, and lasted sixty days – ending in the massacre of the resistance fighters. The Russians not only failed to help, even by air, but refused to allow British or American aircraft to land in Russia after flying over Warsaw. The London Poles, whose relations with the Russians had long been bad, were able to do nothing except make impotent protests and await news of the unfolding tragedy.

Wednesday 2nd August

Dine with Retinger, whom I find established and well cared for in a private suite at the Dorchester. He has, I suppose, succeeded to Sikorski's heritage here. He has been for several months in and around Warsaw, and I am amazed that the Germans did not pick him up. He was dropped from an aeroplane, and this was the first parachute jump he ever made in his life. He landed quite comfortably, he says. This is very plucky, since he still hates the air in all its forms. He looked pretty ill, having both disabling neuritis in his legs and hands and a most frightful-sounding cough. Stanczyk also there. Both say that, if the Russians insist on setting up their own puppet government of Polish nobodies, the Poles will rise and fight against the Russians. I said this would be a total tragedy and must, at all costs, be avoided. Mikolajczyk should, by now, have arrived in Moscow with Romer [1] and Grabski, [2] and I have great hopes that he may pull off something with Stalin. Arciszewski, [3] a veteran Polish Socialist Leader, who has been imprisoned by the Russians, has now arrived in London, having come out of Poland via the Underground and Cairo. He is very anti-Russian. They asked me to agree to see him. They say, as they have often said before, that I am regarded by the Poles as their best friend in England, and that my name is known and loved throughout their Underground. I agree to see him and he comes next day with Stanczyk. He can only speak Polish. He too says that the Poles will rise and fight if the Russians try to force upon them a government contrary to their choice. Both tell me that the Russians have, in certain cases, shot the leaders of the Polish Underground when the latter, seeking to co-operate with them, made contact. The Polish Underground is today rising in Warsaw against the Germans, and we are sending aircraft to drop arms for them.

Early in May 1944, Wavell, as Viceroy of India, asked the Prime Minister for permission to release Gandhi from internment. (Together with other members of the working committee of Congress, Gandhi had been interned at Poona, following the launching of the 'Quit India' movement.) Wavell's grounds were medical: he had been informed of a sudden deterioration in

---

1 Tadeusz Romer (1894–1978). Foreign Minister in the Polish government-in-exile 1943–4. Ambassador to U.S.S.R. 1942–3.
2 S. Grabski (1871–1949). Chairman of the Polish National Liberation Committee (in London).
3 M. Arciszewski (1892–1963). Polish Under-Secretary of State for Foreign Affairs 1938–42.

Gandhi's condition as a result of a malarial attack. Churchill agreed, reluctantly, to the Viceroy's request. 'We can always arrest him again if he commits new offences,' the Prime Minister minuted to Amery, the Colonial Secretary. 'It is of course understood that there will be no negotiations between him and the Viceroy.' Within a few weeks, however, Gandhi had recovered enough to involve himself again in political activity – proposing a common front with Jinnah on the basis of a conditional and partial concession of Pakistan, and demanding a National Government with full control of the civil administration, made up of ministers chosen by elected members of the Legislative Assembly. A correspondence between Gandhi and the Viceroy followed, and Gandhi now proposed that if a declaration of immediate independence were made and a National Government formed subject to the continuance of existing control over military operations, Congress would give its full co-operation in the war effort. He also called for friendly talks. Wavell wanted to respond in a 'receptive' manner to this communication, and asked Amery to approve a conciliatory reply. But the Prime Minister was displeased, and informed the Viceroy on 4th August, following discussion in Cabinet: 'We are much concerned at the negotiations which you have got into with Gandhi who was released on the medical advice that he would not again be able to take part in active politics.'[1]

Thursday 3rd August

Will Henderson to lunch. He still wants to leave the office soon and get back to Parliament, but is rather dissatisfied that stronger efforts are not being made to get him a good constituency. We discuss how much should be said, and how, in pursuance of the last National Executive decision that, at the next election, we shall fight independently. He is shrewd and sensible on this and is inclined to argue that we should let it all slide and publish nothing. But I point out, on the other hand, that, if we publish something, three or four of us can phrase it to the best advantage, whereas, if we leave it over, an independent next Executive may plunge into some inept and damaging form of words. He will make a draft, following our talk today, and will let me have it next week. ...

5.30–8.30 War Cabinet. I am there only because the first item out of eight on the Agenda is the report of the Cabinet Committee, on which I have been a member, on Indian Finance. This is not reached.

1 N. Mansergh (ed.), *The Transfer of Power*, vol. IV, H.M.S.O., London, 1973, pp. ix–xiii, 951.

We begin with some discussion on the oil talks in Washington, not on the Agenda, but on which a draft telegram is handed round. This is finally sent off, with minor amendments, though some ministers think that we are capitulating to the American oil lobby. But, in fact, the phrasing seems pretty safe. Then an infinitely rambling discussion on what the Viceroy should write to Gandhi, to whom he owes a letter. The P.M. pours forth at great length about the Indians and speaks ill of Wavell. 'He was a bad General. He let us down atrociously at Crete. I have been too kind to him.' Wavell had, in fact, never been authorised to 'open negotiations' with Gandhi. Amery[1] – as many outside would be surprised to find – is always in Cabinet the warmest advocate of a 'sympathetic' and 'constructive' policy in India, but is overborne by the P.M. and others. He says that it has long been a habit for successive Viceroys to have a correspondence with Gandhi. The P.M. said that any honourable man would voluntarily return to jail, from which Gandhi had only been released while the P.M. was away in Cairo, because Wavell assured us that, if not released, he would die, that, even if released, he would almost certainly die and that, quite certainly, he would never be able to take any further part in politics. All this had turned out to be false. He was still sticking to his 'Quit India' policy, and there was no doubt that he had been quite prepared to make an arrangement with the Japs whereby the Japanese claw of the pincers could have stretched unopposed across India to join up with the German claw coming down across the Caucasus. Someone asked Herbert Morrison, 'What would you do, if Mosley, whom *you* let out of jail on much the same grounds as Wavell let out Gandhi, were to start a campaign for "Make Peace with Hitler now"!' Morrison said, 'I should put him inside again at once.' And so they rambled on, for most of the three hours. A dozen of them in turn proposing minor changes in the draft of the telegram. Long debate as to whether one should say 'it is a mistake to say that minority problems are due to the British' or 'it is not true to say that ...... ', or 'minority problems are not due to the British'. Further long debate as to whether our statement, when agreed, should be sent to Wavell as a reply which he should send to Gandhi, or as a statement, to be published by Wavell, of H.M.G.'s position, in which case either Wavell himself, or, some ministers thought, one of his Private Secretaries – and there was a long debate about this – should send [it] to Gandhi, while thanking him for his letter. Long debate as to whether the draft should say that we 'welcomed' the forthcoming meeting between Gandhi and Jinnah or that we 'thought it possible that it might serve

1 Leopold Amery, q.v., Secretary of State for India 1940–45.

a useful purpose', or merely that we 'took note' of their intention to meet.

After this totally wearisome proceeding, to which I had nothing to contribute, the P.M. says that he supposes Parliament is now risen. Eden says, 'I hope so', and the P.M. states that all ministers should now take a fortnight's holiday, though leaving a few of their number always available for current business, and thinks with two or three more Cabinets we can clear off all the remaining urgent business.

This altered my timing a little as I had been hoping to get away tomorrow after lunch, but later this afternoon it seems possible we may finish tomorrow morning. Many ministers are anxious to be away and most are pretty tired.

Hear on the 9 o'clock news tonight that the Americans have taken Rennes. It really looks as though there *is* at last the genuine 'breakthrough' in the West.

Friday 4th August
War Cabinet at 12.30 with further endless talk about India. 'The rottenest show I've ever seen,' says the P.M. to Amery. 'This huge Indian army you talk about is just a gigantic scheme of outdoor relief, as Wingate said to me.' In the Cabinet Amery always stands up for India and the Indians and, as the P.M. said this afternoon, 'You who have become, like Wavell and Linlithgow[1] and all the rest of you, more Indian than the Indians, are attacked in the House of Commons as being a narrow-minded old-fashioned reactionary! It serves you right.' Amery and the P.M. shouted at one another quite a lot. Amery said, 'India has saved the Middle East.' 'Rubbish,' replied the P.M. ...

I go off tonight to West Leaze for six days.

On 15th August three American divisions landed between Hyères and Cannes on the Côte d'Azur, preceded by American and British airborne troops and followed by seven French divisions. This operation ('Dragoon') had been the cause of dissension between the Americans (who favoured it) and the British who did not see the advantage of taking troops from Italy for an attack that could scarcely give immediate help to Eisenhower in the North. In the event, the British were vindicated – 'Dragoon' caused no diversion of forces opposing Eisenhower. Though the operation eventually brought assistance to Eisenhower on his right flank, Churchill always felt that the

1 V. A. J. Hope, 2nd Marquis Linlithgow (1887–1952). Viceroy and Governor-General of India 1936–43.

depletion of the Allied forces in Italy had been an excessive price: without it, the Western Allies might possibly have reached Vienna before the Russians.

Tuesday 15th August

Today at dawn we landed in the South of France, very much where I had for some time been thinking we *should* land. Lots of little beaches that I know – St Raphael, St Tropez, Pardigon, *Aiguebelle*,[1] Cavalaire, Cap Negre etc. There seems, at the start, very little resistance. The withering up of the German forces is going pretty fast, but I am still prepared for a most furious resistance on their own door-step.

Bob Fraser to dine. Betty and Rosalind are still – very rightly – keeping out of London. They have just had a fortnight in Cornwall. He says that, apart from its coast, it is the ugliest county in England, and the coast is being more and more spoiled by bad building. Some day we shall have to pull down a lot of these bungalows.

Wednesday 16th August

Ellen Wilkinson to dine with me, and I afterwards go back and gossip in her flat. She is quite fit again after her various accidents and illnesses. We agree that it would be a mistake, in spite of last month's Executive decision, to make any public statement at present about the next election; or to contemplate a Party Conference in the next few months. We will try and put this over at a small Sub-Committee next week, and then at the National Executive early next month.

Tuesday 22nd August

Meeting of Committee of Labour Party National Executive to consider (i) Conference arrangements and (ii) the publication of the statement agreed on at the last National Executive Meeting about the next general election. Everyone is very sensible including, surprisingly, Laski, who takes the initiative of saying that the Conference must be in London in order to allow ministers and other M.P.s to come and that, therefore, it cannot take place until security permits. All present are against immediate publication of any statement about the next election. It will need careful timing, all are agreed, in order to get any prominence in the rush of the war news and also in order that we shall not seem to be playing politics. Attlee says that he objects to

---

1 Marginal insertion: 'O memory!' Hugh and Ruth spent Christmas and New Year 1927–8 at Aiguebelle, and were so delighted with the area, and with their hotel, that they returned in the spring of 1928.

saying publicly that we shall fight the next election as an independent party as much as he would object to saying that he has not become a Conservative. These things should be taken for granted. We then have a frank discussion as to how this Coalition Government should come to an end. Attlee thinks that after the German surrender we shall all be too busy for a little while to think about this, but that a moment will come when the P.M. will say to him that he hopes, having gone through the war in Europe together, we can go on together through a general election on an agreed programme. Attlee would then reply that he is afraid that this is impossible and that, when the general election comes – and we should do nothing to hasten it – we must offer the country the choice between two alternative programmes. But, Attlee insists and all agree with him, we should aim at closing our association with the Conservatives, and particularly with the P.M., without any bitterness or ill-feeling and with expressions of mutual respect. There might well be an exchange of letters between the P.M. and Attlee, which might be published, in the course of which Attlee would pay a very warm tribute to the P.M. as a war leader and, in that case, he is sure that the P.M. will respond generously towards the Labour Party. I say that I am sure this course is both morally right and politically wise, and this is the general view.

Wednesday 23rd August

Retinger to see me this afternoon to urge me to send for the Polish Socialist leaders and give them a good talking to. He says that some of them are being very difficult about the negotiations with Russia. They won't authorise Mikolajczyk to send his offer to Stalin until this has been submitted to and approved by the Underground in Poland. Also, he says, they are resisting the idea that the new Polish Government should move from London to Warsaw. We try to collect them on the 'phone, but this proves impossible and it is agreed that I shall see them next week. By the time they come, things have moved on and the Underground have approved Mikolajczyk's proposals. Nor is the objection to going to Warsaw being pressed.

Wednesday 30th August

Stanczyk, Grosfeld[1] and Ciolkosz to see me at my request. Things have moved since Retinger tried to arrange this meeting last week. I am afraid that the form of the latest London-Polish proposal to Moscow may make it unacceptable. I speak to them rather frankly and

1 Dr Ludwik Grosfeld (1889–1955). Minister of Finance in the Polish government-in-exile in London 1943–4.

tell them that unless they make friends with the Russians, who are great favourites in this country, there will be nobody left to back the Poles over here except 'a few Roman Catholic priests'. I also tell them that they should not attach too much importance to their own personalities. They may say that they 'represent' this, that or the other pre-war Polish political party, but we cannot take for granted that the Poles in Poland, when liberated, will take quite the same view. On the other hand, it is very hard not to share their bitter views about the Russian failure to co-operate effectively with the brave and, as it now seems, increasingly hopeless rising in Warsaw. This is a frightful affair, on which, without very much fuller knowledge, it is impossible to apportion *all* the blame. But, though I do not say so to the Poles, I am sure that the Russians have behaved very badly over this.

10

Return to Party Politics
September 1944–May 1945

Predictions of a quick German collapse after D-Day proved over-optimistic and the war dragged on through the winter months. In Whitehall, attention shifted to a series of conferences and international meetings – Dumbarton Oaks, Yalta, San Francisco, Potsdam – that would determine the shape of the post-war world. At Westminster, there was mounting speculation about the first general election to be held for a decade. Should this take place in the immediate aftermath of the European war? Should it wait until the autumn of 1945, or even until the defeat of Japan? Could the War Coalition be allowed to survive, or perhaps be re-created after an election? Labour members of the Coalition, including Dalton, were much concerned about these questions, believing that Churchill's great prestige would carry him to certain victory in an early poll.

Dalton's main interest, however, was in his Distribution of Industry Bill, aimed at helping the pre-war Distressed Areas. His one remaining ambition as a Coalition minister was to steer this measure through all its stages and place it on the statute book before the Government broke up.

Friday 1st September
One and a half hours with Bevin, very friendly, very fertile of ideas and a very practical tactician. We discuss, primarily, iron and steel and cotton. I have sent him copies of my drafts on these. He is in favour of an inquiry into iron and steel but advises me to have a word with Anderson before the paper is taken, on personalities. He thinks we should have not less than three nor more than five members and that none should be connected with the industry. He would like a good young-minded employer, a good accountant and, if we could find one,

a good banker. For this last perhaps Beckett[1] of the Westminster. Bankers, he says, are much concerned with our export trade and should have a right bias. And this particular banker is intelligent and might involve Eden (through his wife) and hence the Tory Party. Of industrialists, he mentions Heyworth[2] and Lawrence Cadbury. He doesn't like the latter personally, but he is a good man on efficiency and is on the Bank of England Board. We ought also, I suggest, to have a trade unionist outside iron and steel. Bevin then speaks disparagingly of Citrine and the General Council. Citrine, he says, is always trying to be a super Foreign Secretary and is always flying about, to Washington, Moscow, etc. But he doesn't run his office nearly as well as old Charlie Bowerman[3] and doesn't really get as much out of the Government. The General Council, Bevin thinks, are a hopeless lot. They don't keep their end up against the employers in joint consultation, so that he himself often has to play the part, in such talks, of a trade union leader rather than a minister. The trade unionists come late to such meetings, come in insufficient numbers (a number of those invited simply not turning up with no explanation or excuse), come without having read the papers or studied the questions, and leave early. Meanwhile, the employers all arrive in full force, and up to time, knowing quite a lot about the business, prepared to talk at great length and to sit it out. On the whole, Bevin thinks, George Chester[4] is about the best of the General Council. I mentioned Charlie Dukes but he dismissed him saying that he is bone lazy now and spends all his time breeding dogs and trying to be a country gentleman. ...

He then describes his triumph in the War Cabinet over the Beaver, and his refusal to accept the latter's account of his conversation with Berle 'in a Washington Hotel' as sufficient basis for deciding our policy on Civil Aviation. He finally succeeds in insisting that the P.M. should communicate direct with the President on this. He further says that 'the old boy', i.e. the P.M., wants very much to be 'cock of the walk' after the German war is over and that the Tories are preparing for an early election. Bevin himself thinks that the war in Germany

1 Hon. R. E. Beckett (1870–1955). Chairman of Westminster Bank. An uncle of Eden's wife Beatrice, née Beckett.
2 Geoffrey Heyworth, later 1st Baron (1894–1974). Chairman of Lever Brothers and Unilever Ltd 1942–60. Served on the Company Law Amendment Committee, Board of Trade 1943.
3 C. W. Bowerman (1851–1947). Labour M.P. 1906–31; Secretary of the T.U.C. 1911–23.
4 G. Chester, later Sir George (1886–1949). General Secretary of the National Union of Boot and Shoe Operatives.

will be over 'in a few weeks' and that the Tories will aim at an election next February. This, in my view, would not be too bad and is not what I should mean by 'an early election'. Bevin is tending to think more and more in Party political terms and, I have a faint suspicion, is not excluding the possibility that he might himself one day be P.M. There are plenty of the usual sneers at Herbert Morrison. And no mention at all of Attlee.

Sunday 3rd September

To dine and spend the night with Beaverbrook. He had rung up, and then written and said he wished to discuss something with me specially. But, in fact, he discussed nothing of importance. Also there Margesson, Mrs Randolph Churchill[1] and Henry Luce[2] of *Time* and *Life*, husband of Clare Luce.[3] I didn't like him and I should think he is both insincere and stupid. But visits here are thought to do good to some of these Anglophobes. A good deal of general talk on present events, but surprisingly little of interest.

We hear that Hitler had the German Generals hung so slowly that it took eight minutes for them to die, that this scene was filmed and that the film was distributed to all German military units.[4] These are such curious people that I cannot predict the effect of this. Meanwhile, Franco is very apprehensive of the activities of Spanish Reds who are now crossing his frontier from France, and is trying to get us to take steps to restrain them! Some talk of Poland and Russia. The Beaver is very pro-Russian and anti-London-Poles. It seems clear that the Russians did hope five weeks ago to be able to take Warsaw and that, though it was not co-ordinated, the rising inside Warsaw might reasonably have been expected to succeed. But it has failed, tragically and horribly, because the Russians suffered a genuine and unexpected reverse from three slowly arrived German Armoured Divisions.

The Beaver vehemently maintains that we should have started a Second Front in 1942, and thinks that this issue might, at this time, have brought the Government down. A long tale of his tremendous meeting of 30,000 cheering people at Birmingham on this subject. He

1 Hon. Mrs Randolph Churchill, née Pamela Digby, wife of the Prime Minister's son.
2 H. R. Luce (1898–1967). Founder, editor and publisher of *Time*, *Fortune* and *Life* magazines.
3 Clare Boothe Luce, née Boothe (b. 1903). Republican Congresswoman 1943–7. U.S. Ambassador to Italy 1953–7. Journalist, author and playwright. Former editor of *Vanity Fair*.
4 Following the attempt on Hitler's life. On 20th July, Colonel von Stauffenburg placed a case containing a bomb under the Führer's table at a staff meeting. Several officers present were killed, but Hitler escaped with minor injuries. The conspiracy collapsed, and most of those involved were arrested and executed.

would have risked being pushed out of Europe again because, at that moment, the Russians were stretched to the utmost and in great danger. The Russians were so incensed with us and the Americans making difficulties about their annexation of the Baltic States that Molotov had to be invited to come at once to Washington and London and, when he asked the Americans what would be discussed, they replied 'the Second Front'. We only agreed to the issue of a rather deceiving communiqué, in which we said that we accepted the necessity 'in principle' for a Second Front before the end of that year.

In order to fox the Germans in the last few months, particularly since the fly bombs began, we used every means to persuade them that we intended to make a second landing straight across the Channel to the Pas-de-Calais coast. We maintained a bogus Kent headquarters and let them know the names of the commanders and the troops who were going to invade. There was elaborate signalling and the deliberate loss of documents and the spreading by means familiar to me of 'whispers'. The Germans took all this very seriously and pinned down some ten or twelve Divisions on this coast-line.

Monday 4th September
Bevin this afternoon tells me that some mischief-makers have been trying to put into the P.M.'s head the idea that the Board of Trade is wholly staffed by long-haired professors, who take a sadistic delight in controlling everybody so that, as I think it was the egregious Bracken put it to him, 'You can't' (and here followed a very crude expression) 'even get a permit signed by one of them.' Bevin is always very suspicious of the gang who hang round the P.M., though I am not sure that their influence is always as great as might be supposed.

However, this evening at the War Cabinet, after the Chiefs of Staff now put the finish of the European war not later than the end of December, so that all manpower estimates have now to be revised, and after it has been decided to abolish the black-out as from 17th September, the end of double summer time, I urge that I should have authority to stop the manufacture of black-out material *forthwith* and this is agreed. I send messages to this effect early next morning. The P.M. then asks me whether I am planning, in view of the complete change which has come over the face of the war, an early increase in supplies for the civilians. I say that all plans and programmes are ready and that the only need is a decision to divert materials and labour. Someone suggests there should be a Ministerial Committee on all this but Lyttelton, to my satisfaction, says that he thinks it can best be arranged by consultation between the ministers concerned. I back this up and suggest that it will chiefly be consultations between myself and Lyttelton and Bevin. This is accepted. The P.M. shows no sign of having been unduly got at during the weekend.

'Sooner or later the truth about the handful of power-seeking criminals who launched the Warsaw adventure will out,' Stalin wrote to Roosevelt and Churchill on 22nd August, in reply to a letter from the two Western leaders about the worsening situation in the Polish capital. ' ... From the military point of view the situation, which keeps German attention riveted to Warsaw, is highly unfavourable both to the Red Army and to the Poles.' On 4th September, the British Cabinet responded with a further appeal to the Soviet Government to give whatever help might be in their power, 'and above all to provide facilities for United States aircraft to land on your airfields for this purpose'.[1] On 5th September, President Roosevelt, having received a false report that the rising was over, telegrammed to Churchill that the fighting Poles had departed from Warsaw and the Germans were now in full control. 'The problem of relief for the Poles in Warsaw has therefore unfortunately been solved by delay and by German action, and there now appears to be nothing we can do to assist them.'[2] On 10th September, Soviet artillery began to shell the outskirts of the Polish capital, and Soviet aircraft appeared over Warsaw. On the 15th, the Russians occupied Praga, but went no further. Although a major American shuttle operation was permitted to take place on 18th September, the Soviet authorities refused to allow this to be repeated. On 2nd October Mikolajczyk told Churchill that the Polish forces were about to surrender. The final surrender took place two days later. By then, 200,000 out of a population of a million had died.

Wednesday 6th September
I seem to be seeing Bevin most days now. Today it is about the Poles. Herbert Morrison is also present. The danger seems to be that the Polish Socialists will resign from the Government because not enough help has been sent to Warsaw, in order to show that they have no more confidence in Mikolajczyk and will put in his place Sosnkowski. Bevin wonders whether we Labour ministers might not send a letter to the Polish Socialists telling them how suicidal this would be. Morrison wisely suggests that we should put nothing on paper and it is agreed that I, who Stanczyk has told Bevin am regarded as the

1 See A. Polonsky (ed.), *The Great Powers and the Polish Question 1941–5*, L.S.E., London, 1976, pp. 217–19.
2 W. S. Churchill, *The Second World War, Vol. VI Triumph and Tragedy*, Cassell, London, 1954, p. 126.

Poles' best friend, should see Kwapinski[1] and Arciszewski and dissuade them from such folly. Bevin's view is that the Russians fully intended to take Warsaw five weeks ago but that the Germans, making a desperate effort to prevent them, and bringing up three fresh Panzer Divisions, inflicted on them a severe and unexpected check. Meanwhile, the Poles inside Warsaw had risen and, on the probabilities, it seemed at the time that they were justified in doing so, since the Russian forces were so near and advancing so fast. But the thing went wrong, as it easily might have done in Paris, though the Maquis there were got out of their difficulties by rapid advance of the Americans and, though neither Poles nor Russians were *morally* to blame for the failure of this joint manoeuvre, as usual a most frightful public controversy has sprung up. The Poles have been accusing the Russians of having deliberately let them down and this has made Stalin very bearish, so that he, very wrongfully, made difficulties about British and American planes landing on Soviet airfields after dropping supplies on Warsaw, though pointing out, quite sensibly, that there was no assurance that supplies so dropped would not fall into German hands instead of Polish. But we all agree that to put Sosnkowski in place of Mikolajczyk would be a catastrophe for the Poles in London and for the Polish cause generally. ...

Churchill had visited Italy from 11th–29th August, seeing commanders and troops. He spent 11th–14th August in Naples, where he met Marshal Tito.

See Attlee this afternoon, just back from Italy. He was very pleased with what he saw at the Front. He dined with the P.M. in Naples and they had a frank and friendly discussion about the future. The P.M. quite understands that, when the next election comes, the Labour Party will fight independently. He also thought, Attlee says, that although this is a very old Parliament and badly needs renewal, we ought not to have an election for about six months after the end of the European war, as there would be so much to be done in those first months. Attlee thinks that it should be possible to make the break without any personal crisis or bitterness, but that it would do no good

1 Jan Kwapinski (1885–1964). Leader of the Polish Socialist Party (following the death of Lieberman). Minister of Commerce, Industry and Post-War Reconstruction in the Polish government-in-exile 1942–4. Deputy Premier 1943–4. Minister of Industry, Commerce and Shipping, and Minister of Finance 1944–5.

if it could be said that we 'ran out' before we had really finished our job.

See Morrison for half an hour to check up on the election arrangements. He says that with this new register it would take at least two months from the time when it was decided to dissolve Parliament, and when the register would be frozen, after which it would have to be printed and distributed, until the polling day. Many people would be voting away from their homes, both as evacuees and as 'directed' workers. This would be in addition to the Service vote which, if the men were in this country, could be either by proxy or through absent voters' list, but, if outside this country, must be by proxy, following on the filling up of the necessary form. And this is still being done very slowly in many units.

See Cripps who says that he will have to discharge 500,000 workers by the end of the year and that the Ministry of Labour is being very unhelpful. He and Bevin don't get on well. I find next day that the latter regards Cripps's estimate as quite fantastic and puts it nearer 100,000 a month beginning in November.

SECRET [1]

I saw Kwapinski and Arciszewski tonight. They were both much distressed about Warsaw, and said that they feared all would be over by tomorrow, owing to lack of food and arms for the defenders. All the Socialist members of the Polish government in London, they said, had given in their resignations last night, to take effect in the event of their Prime Minister being unable to obtain today definite assistance for Warsaw. (They spoke at some length of the forms which this assistance might take, including the bombing of bridges, roads and airfields occupied by the Germans, and of the building in Warsaw used by the Gestapo as a torture chamber.) They felt that only by resigning, if help was not now forthcoming, could they justify themselves to their own people in Poland. But they assured me that, although the Government would then have to be reconstructed, there was no possibility that either Sosnkowski or any other soldier would be Prime Minister. They were sure that the President would invite either a member of the Peasant Party or a Socialist to form the next Government. I gathered that they hoped it would be a Socialist and that they also hoped to exclude from the new Government, Kot, Kukiel[2] and Banaczyk.[3] (The first and third of these belong to the

1 This entry, also dated 6th September 1944, is recorded separately.
2 Marjan Kukiel (1885–1973). Minister of War Affairs in the Polish government-in-exile 1942–4. G.O.C. Polish Army Corps, Scotland 1940–42.
3 Wladyslaw Banaczyk (b. 1902). Minister of Home Affairs in the Polish government-in-exile 1943–4.

Peasant Party and the second is a General; they blame these for many intrigues and in particular for the mishandling of the Katyn case which led to the rupture of Soviet-Polish diplomatic relations.) They said a new Government might, they hoped, be better viewed by the Russians and that, in spite of all that the Russians had done and were doing to their people in Poland (of which they gave me many details) it would be not less keen than the present Polish government for a Soviet-Polish settlement.

I had told them, at the outset of our conversation, that in the view of myself and Labour colleagues in the Government it would be a great mistake to upset Mikolajczyk and to put Sosnkowski in his place. Indeed, this last appointment would, I told them, be catastrophic for Polish interests in this country. Having heard their statement, and expressed deep sympathy with those in Warsaw, I strongly urged upon them not to break up the present Government just now. The war was moving very fast both in the West and in the East, and the next few days might bring further great changes. The Russian attack against Warsaw seemed now again to be gathering weight. I, therefore, earnestly pressed them not to insist upon their resignation.

Both Kwapinski and Arciszewski said that they would give most careful consideration to what I had said, but did not definitely commit themselves before leaving me.

Thursday 7th September
John Wilmot, Hugh Gaitskell and I dine with Korda and Nicholas Davenport. Very entertaining for an hour or so, but it lasts too long as that wretched Bracken, trailing Harry Luce with him, comes in just as I was trying to go.

Wednesday 13th September
Citrine and Woodcock to see me. The former is inclined to orate to excess, but I always find him very sensible and good to deal with. Lyttelton, on the other hand, told me the other day that Citrine frequently shouts at him and that he once saw him rise from his seat and shake his fist at the P.M. I have never had such expostulations.

With Hodgson visit the Patent Office, which has been badly bombed, and go round speaking to the staff. A number of these are collected in the Comptroller's room, where I sit in my Uncle's[1] old chair opposite a very good photograph of him which, I am told, always hangs on that wall and was not specially brought in for my benefit today. I say some words of encouragement and thanks to the principal

1 Sir Cornelius Dalton (1842–1920). Comptroller-General of Patents, Designs and Trade Marks 1897–1909.

officials. It must be a deadly dull job in this office and they must need some pluck to keep going. ...

Sir Owen O'Malley then calls, at his own request, to invoke my help in dealing with the Poles. Eden has just flown off to Quebec and has told O'Malley to get the dismissal of Sosnkowski as quickly as possible, saying that, if the Poles won't do it for themselves, the British government will have to ask the President to act.[1] But it would be much better if this were a purely Polish decision. Meanwhile, the Polish Socialists are trying to mix up a reconstruction of the Government with the dismissal of Sosnkowski. O'Malley asks me whether I can bring pressure to bear on them. I promise to do so and let him know, and in particular on Kwapinski and Arciszewski.

It is now 7.30. With some difficulty we collect Kwapinski who comes accompanied by Luba at 9.30. I put the case to them and also tell them what O'Malley had told me earlier, that Russian agreement has now been got to our aircraft, after droppings on Warsaw, landing on Russian airfields; also that the Russian Army advance in this sector is now going better and that the Russian Air Force has been attacking the Germans over Warsaw. I also told them that the British government will stand behind Mikolajczyk, of whom our own P.M. has a very high opinion. But Kwapinski is very determined to get rid of Kot and deploys many arguments for this. I press them emphatically to get rid of Sosnkowski first and reconstruct after, and he says he will tell his colleagues.

It is 10.30 but I get O'Malley along and tell him the result of this conversation. Kwapinski has promised to let me know tomorrow what the Socialists decide (they decide, next day, to demand the dismissal of Sosnkowski, but to require simultaneously a reconstruction of the Government. I so inform O'Malley. I must draw the line somewhere at handling Polish feuds as well!)

Common Wealth was a political party founded in 1942 by J. B. Priestley and Sir Richard Acland to fill the gap created on the Left by the electoral truce. Common Wealth was middle-class and broadly left-wing. For some (including its organising secretary, R. W. G. Mackay) it was just a stand-in for Labour. For others, including Acland, it was an ethical movement calling for personal and economic co-operation that transcended mere

1 On 28th September, under pressure from the British government, President Raczkiewicz replaced Sosnkowski as Polish commander-in-chief with General Bór-Komorowski, Commander of the Polish forces in Warsaw (shortly afterwards captured by the Germans).

government – basing itself on the three principles of Common Ownership, Vital Democracy and Morality in Politics. Proscribed by the Labour Party in 1943, Common Wealth candidates won by-elections against Conservatives at Eddisbury, Skipton and Chelmsford in 1943–5. In the General Election, however, only one of its twenty-three candidates was successful – at Chelmsford, where there was no Labour contestant.

Thursday 14th September
Luba telephones, on behalf of Kwapinski, to tell me that the Polish Socialists are still pressing for reconstruction simultaneously with the dismissal of Sosnkowski. I so inform O'Malley.

Kim Mackay[1] comes, at his own request, to propose the affiliation of Common Wealth to the Labour Party, and to ask whether I thought such a suggestion would be accepted. I said that there would be some opposition, since we are rather against affiliating odds and ends, and it might be felt that it would be more difficult to refuse the Communists if we had already accepted Common Wealth. I said a simpler plan, to which no effective objection could be taken, would be to dissolve Common Wealth and tell all its members to join the Labour Party. (This, I said, was what I had proposed to Maisky once about the British Communists, and he had said it was 'an interesting and novel idea' and he would report it to Moscow. Though nothing more had happened about it.) Mackay said that this would indeed be more logical, but that he was not sure whether all their members, many of whom, he said, were very useful and intelligent middle-class people, and their regional organisers, of whom there were seventeen or eighteen, would follow such a lead. But he was very humble and non-aggressive and obviously felt that he had nothing much to offer. They would not, he said, want to have any separate programme of their own. They would never run a candidate against a Labour candidate (Acland had at once withdrawn from Waterloo when we adopted a Labour candidate, though there had been none in the field when he went there), they had been taking an interest in 180 constituencies, where either there was no Labour candidate or where they felt that they had a better chance of winning than we had. He said that any talk of 'Left unity' was meaningless unless it meant the rallying of smaller forces around the great Labour Party. He thought that they

---

1 R. W. M. ('Kim') Mackay (1902–60). Organising Secretary of Common Wealth. Independent Socialist candidate at the Llandaff by-election 1942. Labour M.P. 1945–51.

could help very much towards getting us a Left victory at the next election. He thought we should get 300 to 350 seats anyhow and that, with their help, we should do much more. (I didn't say so but, unless we can *time* the election well, this seems to me very optimistic.) He said he was in touch with one or two members of our National Executive and George Gibson, who was very friendly to him, had promised to put him in touch with one or two members of the Trade Union section of the National Executive. I said he should be careful not to court a rebuff and therefore not put up the proposal for affiliation formally too soon. Many things were much more easily settled when an election was really imminent, than when it was still some distance away. It is a pity that this man has made two or three serious mistakes – in breaking the truce at Llandaff, in his private affairs and in getting tied up with Bernales – for he has considerable qualities. I should like to get whatever there is in Common Wealth yoked with us. ...

Palmer, Jay and Adams to see me about the threat by the Iron and Steel Control to close Distington. I decide to write a strong letter to Duncan about this and also to stir up Attlee and Bevin. This is a first-class issue, testing all our Development Area policies. I feel tonight almost that I might resign if it went wrong.

Friday 15th to Sunday 17th September
At West Leaze. Wonderful autumn sunshine. I think a good deal about iron and steel, both in general and in relation to the Development Areas, and the threat to close Distington. I remember what Curtin said to me[1] and wonder whether I should ever get so good a case for acting on his advice as this one, on public grounds, on general Labour Party grounds and on constituency grounds. It is always easier to feel adventurous down here than when I have to take for granted the never-ending and very varied rush of duties at the Board of Trade in London where one is in danger of assuming one's own permanence.

Wednesday 20th September
Dine with Duncan, who makes himself very agreeable, though it appears he has been a bit peeved by my putting in a paper proposing an inquiry into iron and steel without consulting him and also sending copies of my letter about Distington to Attlee, Bevin and Lyttelton. He thinks we should discuss these things together first, and that if we did, we could settle them all. He thinks an inquiry into iron and

---

1 See entry for 25th May 1944, pp. 749–50.

steel would be most regrettable and would be very bad for the morale of the industry. He thinks they have done wonderfully well since the beginning of the I.D.A.C. [Import Duties Advisory Committee] regime. He also assures me that there would be no question of any decision being taken to close down any works, especially in Development Areas, without my being fully consulted, and that unless there were very strong reasons to the contrary we should make full use of new and modern plants in preference to old ones. He is having the Distington case specially looked into and proposes that a report should be made jointly to him and me by our officials. He would like a regular high level liaison between him and me on all this. I ask him to transfer one or two high-powered people to me for the switch-over. He says he will think what he can do. (I said that both on my inquiry paper and on Distington I had to act quickly while he was out of reach.)

Thursday 21st September
With John Wilmot and Hugh Gaitskell to dine with Miss Kilroy and Meynell. In every way a very pleasant evening. Meynell has given me his volume of poems.[1] I don't think there are any other poets at the Board of Trade.

Tuesday 26th September
I sit up till 1 this morning with Preston concocting answers to no less than thirty-seven P.Q.s which greet me on the first day of the new session. Few are really troublesome, but they cover a wide field. They go off pretty well, the greatest commotion being about babies' teats, which causes much more concern than Lend-Lease.

Lunch with Levy and Harvie Watt on the former's initiative. Harvie Watt and I discuss next election. He thinks we ought to go on having a Coalition Government and that it might be difficult to re-form it if we break it for the period of the election. I said the Troops should be back to vote in large numbers, or the thing would be indecent and undemocratic; also that it didn't make sense to have an election without a conflict of parties, and that it wouldn't be practical anyhow. If the result of the election was that either of us have a clear working majority, then it should be right that that party should form a government; if we were very close together there would be a case for a new Coalition. He said it would be political damnation for either party to run the Government alone in the post-war years. I must talk to him again.

1 Possibly *Fifteen Poems*, Nonesuch Press, London, 1944.

Dalton was concerned to link investment in the steel industry with his plans for the Development Areas. On 7th October, he told the House of Commons that he was opposed to modernisations in the tinplate industry which would have threatened to take jobs away from South Wales. On 9th October, the Reconstruction Committee discussed a memorandum by him which asked for a comprehensive inquiry 'to enable the iron and steel industry to make its full contribution to the national economy in the post-war years'.[1]

Monday 9th October

Hobble with a stick[2] to Reconstruction Committee in the House of Lords. How damned long these passages seem!

Iron and Steel. I advocate, as in my paper, an independent inquiry into post-war iron and steel. I am careful to say that the wartime control has been a good show, but add that during the war prices haven't mattered much and the Government has sunk more than £45,000,000 in new plant, £41,000,000 being Government owned. Duncan, in reply, is very huffy. He complains that I put the paper in without consulting him – though, if I had consulted him, he certainly would not have agreed – and says that he and not I am the minister responsible for this industry. He is working out a plan for post-war and will put it before us later on. There is no need for any outside inquiry. He is supported by Lyttelton, who says that to suggest an inquiry into a matter being handled by a minister is equivalent to a vote of censure on the latter. I say that, in that case, the Steering Committee – that sober band of officials – passed votes of censure on several ministers, for they suggested inquiries into several industries, and my proposal was merely in support of theirs. I get general support, though not very effective or clear, from the three Labour members of the War Cabinet,[3] but Crookshank says he thinks it is quite wrong to interfere with Duncan. So everything is getting very much on party lines. Woolton [?],[4] beaming at Duncan, asks him whether he doesn't think that iron and steel is so important that it is in the interest of the Government as a whole to look into it. Finally it is left that Duncan, 'in consultation with' me, shall put up proposals to the Committee by the end of the year if possible, or, if not, soon after. This, perhaps, is not a bad outcome.

1 PRO, CAB 87/6 X/PO7917.
2 Dalton had been receiving treatment for a sprained tendon.
3 i.e. Attlee, Bevin and Morrison.
4 Text has: 'W'.

Friday 13th October
This weekend Athens, Belgrade and Riga all fall, and the Hungarians seek an Armistice. Poor Warsaw will be the last capital to be freed!

Monday 16th October
... [W]ith Bevin to his office and have a frank and very useful talk about persons. He says he smells an intrigue in which Lyttelton and Bracken are most prominent, with Duncan supporting. He says that other Labour ministers are inclined to be too passive in face of these intrigues. He is for facing them boldly. He thinks that now I shall get an effective inquiry into iron and steel, as a result of his intervention at a discussion the other day. (This is a very characteristic way of putting it!) He is disposed to be helpful over reinforcements of staff, though he starts with some odd ideas. I press steadily for Bruce-Gardner,[1] with whom I know he is on very good terms. He thinks that I ought to give him the title of Chief Executive for the Switch-Over, rather than a title limited to some particular branch of industry. He suggests that I should think this over and let him know tomorrow what I feel about it.

Wednesday 18th October
12.0 Garro Jones. He tells me that he has formed a small group of Labour M.P.s, including Ivor Thomas, John Dugdale, F. Douglas, and Bellenger[2] – against whom I warn him, but he says that he thinks Bellenger realises he would lose more by blabbing than not.[3] They meet and discuss many things, including the future of the leadership. They consider that, if we leave the Government in the course of next session, the question of the leadership should at once be re-opened, and he thinks there would, in that case, be a majority for Morrison. I say I am not at all sure about this. He says that Bevin is losing ground with the Parliamentary Party, partly because he treats them with such complete disdain – he is widely reported to have said:–

(i) that they were just 'a lot of playboys', and

---

1 Sir Charles Bruce-Gardner, later 1st Bart (1887–1960). Controller of Labour Allocation and Supply at the Ministry of Aircraft Production 1943–4. Chief Executive for Industrial Reconversion at the Board of Trade 1944–5.
2 F. J. Bellenger (1894–1968). Labour M.P. for Bassetlaw 1935–68. Junior minister 1945–6. Secretary of State for War 1946–7.
3 In November 1935, Dalton had held a private meeting in order to canvass a number of new Labour M.P.s on behalf of Herbert Morrison's candidature for the leadership. News of this meeting got into the press, to Morrison's disadvantage. Dalton suspected Bellenger of leaking, and always distrusted him thereafter.

(ii) that they were worse than any Branch Meeting he had ever addressed in the T. & G.W.U. –

and partly because he is, in any case, going in for such egomania, e.g. in talking about founding a new daily paper after the war. Garro thinks this is simply jealousy of the Beaver. We discuss how an election might come and I insist on a point which he had not apparently thought much about, that there would be no appreciable interval between the break-up of the Government and the election. Thus the question of the leadership would have to be settled quickly.

He says that he thinks Lyttelton is very disappointed at not having got on quicker in politics. He had coveted the Treasury and it was the P.M.'s first inclination to appoint him when Kingsley Wood died. But it was thought in certain high quarters that he was not safe in his public statements, and, in particular, in Parliament. And, therefore, Anderson was pressed upon the P.M. in preference. Lyttelton, Garro thinks, would not be at all interested in coming back to the Board of Trade. If he cannot see more prospects arising quite high, he may well prefer to leave politics and go back to business.

The only person Garro ever heard coveting the Board of Trade was Portal. And it would, in any case, be quite impossible to have a peer in that job.

Sunday 22nd October

Dine and spend the night with Beaverbrook. The only other visitors are the American Air General Anderson and Harold Balfour,[1] who goes off after dinner. This is my first trip abroad since this wretched leg trouble. So it is evident that both the Bs think there is a real crisis over the Town and Country Planning Bill, owing to the Tory pressure for increased compensation for various classes of landlords. Balfour says that if he were not a member of the Government he would certainly vote against it. Later in the evening the Beaver, having spoken on the phone to the P.M. who is just back from Moscow, reports that he is in very good spirits but determined to stand fast against the Tory revolt! We go to bed early, after the usual not-very-good film ...

Monday 23rd October

Next morning I drive up with the Beaver and ask him what he thinks of Bruce-Gardner, whose appointment as 'Chief Executive for Industrial

---

1 H. H. Balfour, later 1st Baron (b. 1897). Parliamentary Under-Secretary for Air 1938–44. Minister Resident in West Africa 1944–5. Conservative M.P. for the Isle of Ely 1929–45.

Reconversion' is in the Press this morning. He says he is a first-class man and I have made a very good selection, though perhaps Graham Cunningham[1] from the Ministry of Supply might have been even better. ... The Beaver thinks Portal has made a mess of the prefabricated house and that the P.M. will soon take all housing away from him. He also says, though at this point I doubt his sincerity, that he thinks the Labour ministers of the Government are all doing very well and that there is no doubt that the Labour Party, if it won the next election, would be able to form a first-class Government! He says that Anderson made a complete mess of it when he met the 1922 Committee over compensation to landlords under Town and Country Planning. Anderson, he says, is 'only a civil servant with a swollen head', and Herbert Williams spoke to him very roughly and rudely at the meeting, and asked him who he thought he was and how he had managed to get to where he was. Anderson had made the great mistake of thumping the table at these people and they wouldn't stand it. Anderson, he said, had also committed a most frightful blunder in making a speech on Bretton Woods and on our future Commercial Policy and making no reference to Imperial Preference. This gave very grave offence throughout the Tory Party. I sought to draw the Beaver on the Tory leadership. He ridiculed the idea that Anderson, rather than Eden, might succeed the P.M. Eden, he thought, would have overwhelming support in the Party. Failing him or, as he put it, 'If the P.M. and he crashed in the same plane', the three next possibilities were Oliver Stanley, Hudson and Butler. Of these three he thought that Butler would have the best chance, though he himself would prefer Hudson. Butler has no real grasp of Tory principles as the Beaver understood them; in particular he was not really keen on the Empire. Stanley was clever, but not a strong character. Hudson would be the best, but he was afraid he would not carry the day.

We spoke also of Rank. I said I dared say that he would like a peerage in due course, but that he had never mentioned this to me. The Beaver said, 'Of course not. He'll hope to get that from the Tory Party.' I said I didn't think he ought to get it yet awhile. The Beaver said, 'I quite agree with you. We ought to wait and see how his plans develop. I'll make a note for our Head Office.' He then wrote down on a bit of paper 'Rank must not have a peerage', and put this in his pocket book. This may, of course, all have been play acting. It is noticeable how, in conversation with me, he always talks as though he were deeply embedded in the Tory Party machine, whereas, in fact,

1 Sir Graham Cunningham (1892–1978). Chief Executive and Controller-General of Munitions Production at the Ministry of Supply 1941–6.

he is deeply mistrusted by many of them and occupies a very detached position, exercising influence only through the P.M. on the one hand and his own press on the other. I notice from the Visitors Book that W. J. Brown[1] had been to lunch on the Sunday. The Beaver and I both agreed that he was very intelligent but that he had no political future, particularly since he had incurred the enmity of the trade unions, and particularly of Bevin, by his break-away activities in the past. Of Bevin the Beaver said, 'He is undoubtedly much the most distinguished of the P.M.'s colleagues in the War Cabinet', but, he added, all his relations with Morrison were now so bad that whenever Morrison spoke in the Cabinet, Bevin could be seen and heard sneering. I asked him about Bevin's alleged desire to found a daily newspaper. He said he had no doubt that it was true and that plenty of money would be forthcoming, chiefly from the I.C.I. and other big employers' organisations. This paper would stand for the Corporate State, run by, and for the benefit of, Big Business and the Trade Unions. Also, no doubt, Bevin wanted to get his own back on 'Little Southwood' and Citrine. The latter, he said, was the only man he knew who thought he could walk up, without notice, to No. 10 Downing Street, ring the bell and demand to see the Prime Minister straight away, and if told the P.M. was otherwise engaged, he would be most indignant and affronted.

In September 1944 the Cabinet Committee on Palestine recommended partition – against the advice of the Foreign Office. The Committee reaffirmed this recommendation in a report on 16th October, suggesting that the decision should be announced at the end of the war, without further negotiations with Arabs or Jews. In November, Weizmann made his first wartime visit to Palestine, arriving at the height of a new wave of Jewish terrorism.

Thursday 26th October
Kingsley Martin to see me, at his own request. Very friendly and takes an interest in all I say about the conditions of the next election, and

1 W. J. Brown (1894–1960). Independent M.P. for Rugby 1942–50. Labour M.P. for Wolverhampton West 1929–31. General Secretary, Civil Service Clerical Association 1919–42. Parliamentary General Secretary 1942–9. Brown left the Labour Party to join Sir Oswald Mosley's New Party in 1931, but soon broke away from Mosley and became a pacifist. During the war, he became a keen advocate both of the war effort and of Indian independence.

what I and others are trying to do in the meantime. If he had sat down in my office and written his next leader, I am sure it would have been perfect.

Then Weizmann, who is going out to Palestine very much afraid that Partition is again being discussed and that the P.M. may waver over to it. I say that we should be against it and suggest that he should see Herbert Morrison. Weizmann is going to try really to put a stop to Jewish terrorism in Palestine. I have always liked this man and I think we have always understood each other. He is still very appreciative of the Labour Party Declaration on Palestine and I say that this is now well backed up by the declarations of both Democrats and Republicans in the U.S.A. in favour of unlimited Jewish immigration and rights of Jewish land acquisition in Palestine. ...

Bevin thinks that the appointment of Bruce-Gardner has been a very good stroke and has, for the time being at any rate, silenced many, including another in the Camarilla, who were inclined to criticise the Board of Trade for doing too little to help industry and exports.

Friday 27th October
Lunch with Mrs Phillimore and Comert. The latter is now returning to Paris where he will run *France* as a daily while continuing it under the same title as a 'Journal of Information' in this country as a weekly. He says the new French ministers are all very inexperienced and hardly any speak English, and they are inclined to be shy and backward. He thinks it most important that representative Englishmen should go to France in numbers soon. De Gaulle, against whom he no longer fights, is thought of more and more as being outside the Government rather like a Monarch. F.F.I. [Forces Françaises de l'Intérieur][1] he says are 'very military' and very contemptuous of the old army which broke down in 1940. There will certainly, he says, be a great movement to the Left in France, but the Communists will not acquire great strength. They are widely distrusted and suspected of always 'playing dirty tricks'. I don't know how this man, after four years away, will fit again into the French picture. ...

Gaitskell to dine and we have a discursive talk. Durbin has got Edmonton. A first-class windfall; he should be all right now. So, as I told him the other day, after a long black season of disappointment often in politics the sun breaks out most unexpectedly and quite

1 Forces Françaises de l'Intérieur were set up by General de Gaulle in March 1944. The État-major des Forces Françaises de l'Intérieur eventually took over full responsibility for all aspects of French Resistance.

suddenly. I added that it often goes in again in the same way! Gaitskell thinks very well of Norman Brook.

Saturday 28th October
Irene [Noel-Baker] to lunch. Francis [Noel-Baker][1] is back from the U.S. and frightfully eager, quite naturally, to be in Greece, but Leeper has specially warned the Foreign Office against allowing this dangerous and subversive young man into the country.

Dalton had become concerned that legislation was needed to establish permanent post-war control of location. 'I hope that you will give me your support in pressing on with a Bill for a better-balanced distribution of industry,' he wrote to the Prime Minister on 21st November. ' ... I have long taken a keen interest in this question of Development Areas and have often spoken on it both in Parliament and elsewhere. I know these areas and their people well. Through no fault of their own, they had a very raw deal between the wars.'[2]

Sunday 29th October
Today we hold one of our 'Secret Meetings' of the National Executive and the Labour War Cabinet Ministers at Howard's Hotel. As usual most are quite sensible. Our Declaration that we shall fight the next election as an independent Party has had soothing effects everywhere. Bevin coming in, as usual, very late, says that he can hardly believe his ears. He thought ministers were all supposed to be chained to the Coalition 'and captives of the Tories', but here today everyone is saying we must not hurry the election or the break-up of the Government and everyone, except Shinwell, says that we ought to get the Social Insurance Bill through before the Parliament ends. And this, indeed, is the general mood. I say I also want to get a Location of Industry Bill through. Unless we get Social Insurance through, the Tories will use it as bait for the electors; if we *do* get it through *we* can say that, but for us, nothing nearly so good would have been put forward; and in any case it is *right* to get it through, regardless of party politics.

1 F. E. Noel-Baker, q.v. The Noel-Baker family owned property in Greece.
2 Dalton Papers 7/6 (71), (72).

Monday 30th October
Lunch with Mrs Phillimore, Attlee and Jowitt, to meet Van Kleffens
and a Dutchman, recently come out, one of the leaders of their resistance movement. How brave these men have been, while we have had
so little to endure! Van Kleffens says that a young German officer,
after the occupation of Holland, said one day at The Hague in a mixed
party including both Germans and Dutch, 'Oh dear! I must go, I am
late for an appointment.' When asked, 'What appointment?', he
replied, 'I shall be late for my Welsh lesson' and then seemed suddenly
to realise that he had been indiscreet. 'Your Welsh lesson?' someone
asked, and he replied, rather sheepishly, 'I have got a post on the
staff of the Gauleiter for Wales.'

Van Kleffens also said that he was astonished to read that we had
only caught and executed some fifteen German spies in this country
since the beginning of the war. Jowitt said that some of these German
spies were almost unbelievably incompetent and he could only suppose that they were used as a blind, in the hope that we should think
that there were no really good German spies and so be put off our
guard. The first three German spies he had had to prosecute as Solicitor-General consisted of two men and a woman who had landed on
the Scots coast from an open boat. They had waded ashore and the
men's trousers and the woman's skirt were dripping wet. They walked
into the railway station at Buckie and asked, speaking broken English
with strong German accents, 'what was the name of this station?' When
they were told they asked when the next train left. The porter told
them in an hour and a half. They then asked where that train went to.
He said to Aberdeen and suggested that they should sit and wait in
the Waiting Room. They did so and he went off and rang up the
police. When the police arrived they asked the three visitors to open
their bags. They did so without demur. The bags contained three
wireless sets, a little food, and nothing much else. They offered no
resistance when arrested.

To Westminster Hospital this evening, when I am given gas and
have a minor operation on my finger. It is all very nicely and competently done, though I disliked it a good deal, particularly in prospect. I asked whether I kicked or shouted much when under gas and
they said, 'No.' But I heard myself saying, as I came to, in a tone of
great indignation, 'Just like a bloody Cabinet Committee!' I am to go
back and have the wretched thing dressed each day. But I give them
good marks.

Tuesday 31st October
Following a rather painful first dressing at the Hospital, I go on to a

Distribution of Industry Committee. Here I have a greater success than I had hoped with my paper on the terms of my Location Bill. I have good backing from Bevin in the Chair, and from Johnston, and on most points from W. S. Morrison and Cripps. Anderson is also, on the whole, quite benevolent. The opposition, such as it is, comes from Lyttelton and Duncan, who sit side by side just opposite me, looking like a pair of very sinister capitalists, whispering to one another and suspecting socialism everywhere, both likely to cause more trouble at a later stage.

I am delighted to get agreement for:

(i) Power for the Board of Trade to build factories anywhere, either in the Development Areas or outside, in order to secure diversification,

(ii) Power for the Treasury to grant financial help inside the Development Areas, in the form of grants in aid of interest on capital, or even investment in equities of promising concerns.

...

I feel damned tired tonight.

Wednesday 1st November
Lunch with Retinger to talk to Kot. The plan had been that I should meet Retinger at the Bon Viveur at 1.15, and he should brief me, and that Kot would be invited at 1.30 but, as sometimes, these Polish tactics overreach themselves. I arrive at 1.15 and wait for ten minutes, when Retinger and Kot arrive together! Kot talks at immense length, mostly anti-Russian, and says the Poles are much hurt at the way in which our P.M. is forcing upon them decisions which he took jointly with Stalin, but without consulting them. He demands that they shall agree at once to the Curzon Line and the loss of Lwów and, when Mikolajczyk raised any difficulty, our P.M. gets very indignant and says, 'See what great gains we are offering you in the West in place of all those swamps in eastern Poland!' Kot believes that the Russians won't keep any pledge they give now and that they are determined to destroy the independence of Poland. I tell him that people here are getting very impatient and that if the Poles in London don't accept and sign now they will lose much goodwill both in this country and the U.S.A. Kot has made great play with a number of Polish requirements – that their deportees shall be allowed to return from Russia, that they shall be allowed to bring away from the ceded territories their 'cultural monuments', that they shall be definitely assured that,

if they give up territory in the East, they shall have what is now spoken of in the West, and that some financial provision shall be made for settling Poles from the East in the new territories from which the Germans must be removed. I say that all these are most reasonable propositions, but that the way to handle them at this late stage, after so much fruitless and indecisive discussion, is for Mikolajczyk to say to our P.M. and to the American President that the Poles in London accept the Russian territorial proposals in the East, but that, in so accepting, they take for granted that their requirements, as indicated above, will be met, and Mikolajczyk should urge that a clear promise should be got from Stalin, and that the British and American governments should do everything possible to see that he keeps it, on all these points. Retinger said he thought I had suggested a formula which might do the trick. I told Kot that I was astonished how the Germans had been kept out of our conversation today. The first reference to them had been when Kot had said that German propaganda was active among the Poles in opposition to the Russian suggestions. It was necessary that the Poles, like the Russians and ourselves, should recognise that the Germans had been, were now and, unless we held together, would again become the common enemy of all of us and a formidable threat to all our lives. I also reminded him, not very obscurely, that if he was still a minister in the Polish government in London this was largely due to me, since I had pressed upon my Polish Socialist friends to content themselves with getting rid of Sosnkowski and not to insist on clearing out Kot too!

Thursday 2nd November
I again feel damned tired! This is a great bore.

A day without much incident till the evening, when I sit for two and a half hours in the P.M.'s room at the House at a War Cabinet. Having agreed first to a paper on Building Labour, and then to Bevin's paper on Re-allocation of Civilian Labour, and the continuance, though with modifications, of labour control, we pass to Woolton's paper on the continuance of other economic control. This leads to a first-class squabble. First Attlee and Morrison object to some sentences as committing them to desire a return to *laissez-faire*, and then Beaverbrook and Bracken make a lot of noise the other way and object to the paper as committing them too much to controls. The latter, in his best rude style, tells Woolton that the paper is so badly written that he cannot make sense of it, and then complains that there was no Conservative on the Committee that prepared it. A list of the Committee is then read out. It included: Woolton, Bevin and myself, Anderson, Lyttelton, Duncan and Eden, along with Cripps. Beaverbrook proposes that the matter should be referred back to another Committee on which 'some of us' should sit. After a frightful and most boring wrangle, the P.M. says that he thinks we had better not publish this paper, or anything like it at all, but that Bevin and Duncan should concert a short statement, which could be put along with Bevin's speech on labour control.

After the Cabinet, I said to the P.M. going out that I didn't wish to prolong the discussion, but that there were some controls which I felt it was most indispensable to keep on, especially price control. He said, 'Yes, of course, I quite agree, but are you sure there aren't a lot of controls which you are keeping on now and which could quite well be taken off?' I said I thought not, but that I had set up a Standing Committee, with Waterhouse in the Chair – I thought this might help the P.M. – to keep a constant watch and report to me whenever they thought we could do any de-control. He said, 'You have corrupted Waterhouse. That speech he made at Birmingham has upset a lot of people.' But it was all quite amicable. I asked him whether he knew Bruce-Gardner. He said, 'No.'

Between August and October 1944 a major conference was held at Dumbarton Oaks, near Washington, in order to set up a new international organisation. At this conference the main features of the future United Nations were agreed – including the composition and role of the Security Council and General Assembly, the creation of an Economic and Social Council, the powers of the Secretary General, the role of the Military Staff Committee and various questions concerning human rights and fundamental freedoms. Gladwyn Jebb was the British representative on the conference's 'Formulation Committee', responsible for translating into words decisions of principle made by a small 'Steering Committee'.[1]

Thursday 9th November
Lord Mayor's Luncheon, where they now serve regularly Australian wine! Sit next to Catto who makes no bones about his disagreement with Montagu Norman's policy on many points. We speak again of his projects for new financial institutions and I say that I am in favour of his going ahead with these.

Dine with Gladwyn Jebb whom I had not seen for quite a long

1 See *The Memoirs of Lord Gladwyn*, Weidenfeld & Nicolson, London, 1972, p. 149.

while, not indeed since before he went to Dumbarton Oaks. He is in a rather discouraged mood, and reverts to an old idea of leaving the Civil Service and going into politics. I discourage this, as before. He says that they spend all their time slaving away and then ministers either do nothing about it or do it all wrong. (Gaitskell, to whom I report this, says that all civil servants in *all* departments, and not only in the Foreign Office, must often feel like this!)

Buttering up the Russians, Gladwyn says, is no good. The only result is that they despise you. He liked Stettinius who, he says, doesn't pretend to study detail, but sticks to the large issues and has had an immense personal success in the State Department, where he has smacked all the old boys on the back and made them all call each other by their Christian names – for the first time in their careers. He is said to have 'introduced quite a new atmosphere'. He prefers his Christian names syncopated. He calls himself Ed and, the day after they met for the first time, began to call Gladwyn 'Glad' and in order that everybody should get to know one another better he arranged a party of British, Russian and American delegates to New York where they were entertained and enjoyed themselves for two or three days. The Russians, under this treatment, melted very much, but were paraded before the Russian Consul General in New York, who gave them a pep talk and warned them against being taken in by bourgeois propaganda, or any belief that the U.S. or the U.K. were democracies, or that anything was really better there than in Russia. Gladwyn thinks that, if the Russians were not held in this tight vice, they would be all over the place, completely anarchical and unpredictable. He finds them most intelligent, though still intensely suspicious at the least provocation; it is most difficult to discuss any shop with them not covered by their exact instructions. They say, 'It isn't in the Soviet Memorandum.'

On 3rd November, Dalton wrote to Lord Horder, Physician in Ordinary to the King: 'Just lately I have been feeling a bit weary, and I don't want this to go on. I want all my strength and energy for the last lap of the war, and, not less, for the first post-war years. Could you advise me whom to go to, for some sensible medical guidance?'[1]

---

1 Dalton Papers 8/1 (66).

Friday 10th November
Visit Horder,[1] to whom I had written a few days ago saying that I was
normally so fit that I had no regular doctor but that lately I had been
a bit tired after 4½ years as a Minister of the Crown in this war, with
most of it spent at the Board of Trade. Having gone through all the
obvious tests, and asked me various questions from which it appears
that my condition is not very different from that of a large number of
other people, namely that I am 'a bit stale', and nothing worse, he
says that he will send me some beneficial pills! The rest of our conversation is gossip. He tells me how Beaverbrook pushed him aside
both from being the present P.M.'s Medical Adviser – which he had
been before the latter became P.M. – and also stopped him from
becoming President of the Royal College of Physicians, which he
would normally have been in succession to Dawson of Penn. The
Beaver successfully ran Charlie Wilson, now Lord Moran,[2] for both
these honours. For the latter the Beaver did most vigorous canvassing,
entertaining the electors at dinner and sending emissaries to call upon
them and even sailing, as Horder thought, very close to libel in the
Evening Standard. Here, in the Londoner's Diary, it was stated one
night that the favourite for the post was Sir Charles Wilson. Then
followed a great eulogy, ending up, 'He has absolutely no money
sense.' Then, it was added, 'The runner up is Lord Horder. He has for
years enjoyed a large and lucrative practice.' And nothing more! In
the end Horder was defeated by seven votes. He must be a lot older
than he looks and he told me that he was medical adviser to Bonar
Law, before Ramsay MacDonald. ...

Go to see Attlee and tell him of my concern, already expressed in
a letter, at the omission from the first draft of the King's speech for
next Session of any reference to either Location of Industry or Restrictive Practices. I say that I could not publicly defend the omission
of these two items. He says he has made a covering note on the draft,
in which my views are recorded. I say that I take a very strong view
about this.

Monday 13th November
Since tomorrow there is to be a joint meeting of the International
Policy Sub-Committee of our National Executive to determine and
publish the resolution for the Annual Conference on the International

---

1 T. J. Horder, 1st Baron (1871–1955). Physician in Ordinary to the King; Consulting
   Physician to St Bartholomew's Hospital.
2 Sir Charles Wilson, 1st Baron Moran (1882–1977). Physician to the Prime Minister.
   President of the Royal College of Physicians 1941–50. Dean of St Mary's Hospital
   Medical School 1920–45.

Post-War Settlement, and since I have heard nothing of anyone else drafting anything or of my being expected to draft anything myself, I ring up Transport House at 4.30 to inquire. But neither Gillies nor Morgan Phillips are in their offices! So, in case no one else has done anything, I dictate tonight, near midnight, having just finished all my other jobs, a rough draft of a resolution and have it sent round early next morning to be duplicated and distributed. It is just as well I did.

Tuesday 14th November
At this afternoon's joint meeting I find that no one else has done anything and that my draft holds the field. Moreover, as we go through it, my colleagues swallow it almost whole, with only a few small amendments. Harold Clay, tiresome and persistent on this question, isn't at the meeting. Phil [Noel-] Baker arrives, as usual, very late, and we have settled practically everything, his only suggestions being that we should refer, in relation to Palestine, to the old Mandate, a suggestion which I resisted, and that we should break the resolution up into three parts, the first General, the second on International Political and the third on International Economic Organisation. This had been a suggestion made at our last National Executive by those who didn't really like our original declaration and hoped that on the first part, on German responsibility etc., there might be opposition – and they would have been quite glad to see the Executive beaten on this. But, in practice, it is quite impossible to draft this way and there is no support today for this idea. Little Laski, on the other hand, is most agreeable and co-operative and is very friendly to me, having received my reply to his inquiry as to whether I was engaged in a 'manoeuvre' to limit his Chairmanship of the Party to the few months between next month's Conference and Whitsuntide. I had been able, in a suitable reply, both to deny this and to declare my general view that every Chairman should hold office for at least twelve months and, if the dates of Conference fell awkwardly, always for a longer rather than a shorter period. So he is all for my resolution today!

Thursday 16th November
... [T]o War Cabinet. ... On Distribution of Industry I put in a paper last week embodying amendments suggested during discussion of Distribution of Industry Committee but, since this, Beaverbrook and Bracken have put in a paper disputing some of my proposals, especially the building of factories by the Government outside the Development Areas. There is clearly no time at 8.10 p.m. to go into this in detail and it is clear that hardly any of the twenty-seven persons now sitting round the Cabinet table, exclusive of the officials, has the

faintest idea either of what we have all said in our White Paper on Employment last June or of what is being proposed now, either by me or by the others. The P.M. is apprehensive of promising too much since no one can foresee the length of the war or of the session. Bevin, as I should have expected, is the most helpful of my colleagues and weighs in not quite effectively in favour of some mention of Distribution of Industry, as does Will Whiteley when I say that perhaps the Whips will be able to tell us something of the feeling in the House. Finally, after much to-ing and fro-ing, it is agreed to insert, not a pledge to legislate but a reference to the 'Distribution of Industry' in Development Areas. These last three words are pressed for by the Beaver, and I don't resist them, though they will read oddly in the text of the King's speech. (The only practical result of restricting power to build within the Development Areas will be that the latter will have to be a much longer list, but there is no really serious objection to this, provided administration is sensible.) This is a half success, with which, for the moment, I must content myself. If they had refused to make any mention of either of these topics in the King's speech I should have been inclined to resign.

Tuesday 21st November
I send tonight a letter to the P.M., with a copy to Attlee, on the Development Areas and my great concern at the delays over this ... This is a fairly strong letter and would be a possible foundation for another even stronger if necessary. My paper to the War Cabinet on this was circulated eleven days ago.

Today also Wilmot accepts an invitation from the P.M. to join his Government as Joint Parliamentary Secretary to the Ministry of Supply. When asked to go across to No. 10, he was terrified that he might be asked to be Parliamentary Secretary to the Ministry of Pensions. Even this he had not thought he would really be able to decline in face of scowls from the P.M. The interview was short and he accepted without question. The P.M. said, 'The Minister of Supply will be very glad to have you with him.' I think that a short list of Labour names may have been shown to Duncan, who would, not unnaturally, have chosen Wilmot from such a list. This is all very welcome, and long overdue, though it will make a gap here for me.

On 22nd November there was a minor government reshuffle. Viscount Swinton, who had been appointed Minister of Civil Aviation on 9th October, was replaced as Minister Resident in West Africa by Captain H. Balfour.

Duncan Sandys replaced Lord Portal as Minister of Works, and Sir Edward Grigg took the place of Lord Moyne (who had been assassinated on 6th November by Jewish terrorists) as Minister of State Resident in the Middle East. Dalton invited Tom Fraser, a recently elected Scottish mining M.P., to take the place of Wilmot as his P.P.S.

Wednesday 22nd November
National Executive at 10. Ellen Wilkinson being ill, Laski takes the Chair, and likes it. ...

After the Cabinet I have to go to a meeting with Attlee, Bevin and Morrison at No. 11, when Morrison talks of his idea of putting in a paper on the Government's attitude to industry. Bevin and I are discouraging and Attlee says little. This incident, I can see, helps my relations with Bevin, and the reverse with Morrison; however, that can't be helped for the moment and Bevin is much more use than Morrison on all the things I care most about.

Thursday 23rd November
Privy Council at Buckingham Palace. Attlee, Templewood (ex Sam Hoare), myself and Peake. King's speech impediment is still very bad. There was a long and painful period of at least twenty seconds during which he was struggling to emit the one word 'approved'.

Then to Westminster Hospital, where I am duly discharged by the excellent Dr Hansell, and am now to keep my dry bandage on for a week and then begin very gingerly to wash my finger. They have done a very good job and I pay the Hospital twice what they suggest, even so not much for all their care and labour.

Tuesday 28th November
9.45 a.m. Vast concourse of ministers assembled for this morning on Home Policy Committee to decide what legislation shall be pushed next Session. It is agreed that no more than twelve 'Reconstruction Bills' shall be put 'above the line' and only on these will Parliamentary Counsel be engaged. I get my Location of Industry Bill above the line and with this rest content. ...

Eve of Session Dinner tonight at No. 10, including the Speaker, and all ministers who are Members of the House of Commons, together with Whips, the P.M.'s Private Secretaries, and the Mover and Seconder of the Address ... After the meal, I gave the P.M. the latest telegram from Keynes, Llama Series, suggesting that he might work it into his speech tomorrow. I then sat with Bevin, Herbert Morrison and W. S. Morrison at a table with him and he spoke very freely of the past and the future; of how the Conservative Party in those days had made an organised effort to drive him from public life and how he had no one in the House of Commons to help him 'except Bracken who was always there ready to vote or to do anything' – this dog-like devotion in the past has coloured all the present. Once, he related, on the India Bill he was all but howled down by the Conservative majority when David Kirkwood[1] rose and came to his assistance. He said, 'I can't take as big a part in running the war now as I used to. Now we have got Eisenhower and all these high Generals looking after it. So I have more time to think about houses and post-war plans.' He seemed tonight to be fixed in the idea that, as soon as the German war came to an end, it would be necessary to have a dissolution. I said I thought that if we were in mid-Session and Parliament was engaged on passing good Bills, like the National Insurance Bill and my own Distribution of Industry Bill, all parties would be willing to go on. The P.M. said he did not think that this could be. With the defeat of Germany, it must be inescapably clear where we stood. The least period for this would be two years or until the defeat of Japan, whichever ended first. I am not clear whether he has in mind to try to reopen the whole question with us.

Tuesday 5th December

Meeting at No. 10 of all No. 1 ministers outside the War Cabinet. The P.M. invites us to put questions on anything we like and launches forth into long, discursive and well-phrased replies. We begin with Greece. He doesn't like E.A.M. [Ethnikon Apeteftherotikon Metopon][2] at all and regards them as being under Communist influence. We have armed, fed and liberated Greece. As soon as possible they shall vote freely on their future Government – monarchy or republic etc. – meanwhile we have kept the King over here and our troops must take steps to keep order. If it is true that there were children in the procession of E.A.M., their parents are much to blame for having exposed them to the dangers of rioting and shooting in the streets.

In Belgium it is even clearer than in Greece that we cannot agree to civil war across the lines of communications of our Armies.

In Italy he had seen all the leaders. Bonomi,[3] 'an old boy, quite

---

1 David Kirkwood, later 1st Baron (1872–1955). Labour M.P. for Dumbartonshire Burghs 1922–50; Dumbartonshire East 1950–51.
2 The Greek National Liberation Front, formerly the Popular Front.
3 I. Bonomi (1873–1951). Premier and Foreign Secretary of Italy after the Allies entered Rome June 1944–June 1945. Minister in the Orlando, Nitti and Giolitti Governments 1921. Prime Minister 1921–2.

presentable, though not so good as Badoglio'. The politics there are 'all froth'. Our troops were loudly cheered by the same crowds who loudly cheered the Germans three weeks before. The Communists have some strength, but are biding their time. He met Togliatti[1] – a small man with bright eyes, rather like Reynaud, a very animated manner and rather dissipated appearance. When we liberate Milan etc. we shall find a hungry people in ill-humour both with themselves and everyone else.[2] We shall wish to leave Italy as soon as possible.

Tito is a Soviet Agent. He only appeared on the scene when Russia was attacked. When things got too hot in the mountains he crossed to the Island of Vis (Lissa), where he stayed for four months with British troops, aircraft and ships guarding him. The P.M. met him in Naples. It was hot and the P.M. was in his shirt sleeves, but Tito was wearing a very tight Marshal's uniform made in Russia with heavy epaulettes and gold facings. He was obviously very uncomfortable. 'I did not tell him that anyhow it was only Lend-Lease.' Then suddenly, back at Vis, he left the cave where he was living, under our protection, and went off by air, without telling us anything about it, to Moscow. We did not know where he had gone. But, when the P.M. and Eden arrived in Moscow, Molotov, rather sheepishly, told us that Tito had been there for some time, and hoped that we had no objection. The P.M. said certainly not, but there was no reason why he should not have mentioned it to us. Tito has become very uncivil and has threatened to fire on British Detachments who were trying to help clear the Germans out of Juggery. He wants to get hold of Istria, Trieste, etc., and therefore does not want us to be anywhere near.

Poland, said the P.M., is a very tragic picture. Fortunately the Russians are not now advancing here. Mikolajczyk is a great man and should be head of a Polish Government in Poland. This could have been arranged when they were all in Moscow, but Mikolajczyk thought he had to refer the question back to the Poles in London and that he could get the agreement of his colleagues. But he failed. Now he has resigned, but he is 'lying well' for the next step. The P.M. and Eden saw three representatives of the Lublin Government. They made a very poor impression. Eden said afterwards that they most resembled 'a skunk, a snake and a rat'; they were a most obvious Russian Puppet Government. They said their set pieces. They could not bear to think of having Lwów, etc. Stalin had said that they were a damned nuisance to him. They were always complaining and had no real power in

1 P. Togliatti (1893–1964). Italian Communist leader. Arrived in Italy from Moscow March 1944. Minister without Portfolio 1944; Vice-Premier 1944–5; Minister of Justice 1945.
2 Marginal insertion: 'including us'.

Poland. The Poles shot up their representatives and took to the woods rather than join the Lublin Polish army. Poland, said the P.M., must move westwards. They were entitled to a home in Europe as good as they had before the war. What was the value of Lwów compared to Danzig and 250 miles on the Baltic? Raczkiewicz was a troublesome fellow. More than three years ago we had been told that he couldn't live more than six months.

The battle in the West had been a disappointment. There must now be a pause during the winter. We should not over drive the troops, in order to keep them fighting too long in rain and mud and ruined German towns. The advance on the main Aix to Cologne line had been small and disappointing. The American High Command had made a mistake in trying to attack along too long a front. They should have tried battering ram tactics at some selected point.[1]

In Italy we were holding twenty-eight German Divisions, even though our Army had been much depleted by the Riviera landing.

The P.M. thought that victory in Europe was probable by June 1945. No idea of negotiated peace should be entertained. Any suggestion of this would strengthen rather than weaken the German will to resist, since they would feel that they were wearing us down. Nor would it be wise to let the Germans know the sort of Peace Terms which the Russians wanted. They would be very rough and hard.

Wednesday 6th December
House of Commons Debate on Amendment to Address calling for 'Re-organisation of the Board of Trade', more exports and clearer plans for reconversion. Lyttelton speaks soon after 2 and I wind up soon after 6. ...

Several Labour speakers do quite well, particularly George Benson, who says that if the British industry is in a bad way that is the fault of British industrialists. Lyttelton solemnly reads out a warning by the War Cabinet that there is still a war on and a long way to go before we can think of reconversion on any large scale. This helps me and serves to discount a good deal of criticism. One of the brightest speeches is made by Peter Thorneycroft, who is intelligent, attractive, progressive and an excellent speaker. He is much the best of the Tory Reform Group[2] and should soon be given a post in the Government.

---

1 Marginal insertion: 'as Monty proposed'.
2 'Tory Reform Group': on 17th March 1943, thirty-six Tory M.P.s constituted themselves as the Tory Reform Committee, under the chairmanship of Lord Hinchingbrooke. Members included Peter Thorneycroft, Hugh Molson, Quintin Hogg and Lady Astor. The group sought to identify the Conservative Party with progressive wartime reforms.

I wish I could have him here instead of that damned fool Harcourt Johnstone, who once more makes a complete fool of himself, not being present in the House at the beginning of the Debate. His absence is challenged and I have to get up and say that 'I have taken steps to procure his presence', having arranged with the Chief Whip a moment before to send for him. A little later he appears and stands sheepishly behind the Speaker's Chair, half out of sight. Then he sits at the far end of the Bench and is greeted with ironical cheers. Later he rises and gives an explanation of his absence, which is due to the fact that he was presiding over some Committee of Industrialists in the Department of Trade!! This fool will never get it right with the House. Obviously he should have cancelled all other engagements in order to be here.

When the Germans withdrew from Greece, Churchill ordered the British commander, General Scobie, to resist the threat of a *coup d'état* by Greek Communist guerrillas. 'Do not ... hesitate to act as if you were in a conquered city where a local rebellion is in progress,' the Prime Minister cabled to Scobie on 5th December. ' ... We have to hold and dominate Athens. It would be a great thing for you to succeed in this without bloodshed if possible, but also with bloodshed if necessary.'[1] Details of the instruction got into the American press, raising a political storm, and the Secretary of State, Edward Stettinius, declared that the U.S. expected newly liberated countries to work out their problems of government without outside influence. There was much criticism of Churchill's attitude in Britain as well, especially on the Left. The matter was debated in Parliament on 8th December. Despite a P.L.P. decision to abstain, a total of thirty M.P.s opposed the Prime Minister in the division lobby.

Friday 8th December
Today in the House an excitable Debate, much more like old times, on an unofficial motion of censure on the Government for mishandling Greece etc. Feeling on this runs pretty high, and, as Cripps said to me tonight, it looks as though we have, as so often in our foreign policy, done the right thing in the wrong way. I listened to the tail end of Acland seconding the Amendment and then to the P.M.'s reply; he is in very good debating form but rather trails his coat and gives the

---

1 Churchill, *Triumph and Tragedy*, p. 252. See also entry for 28th December (p. 821 and n.).

impression of enjoying the whole thing rather too much. Many of our M.P.s are unduly sensitive to manner, as against substance, and most abstain in the final division, only thirty, including Independents etc., voting for the Amendment, but the P.M.'s general argument is irresistible. It would be wrong for us to hand over Greece to a clash of private armies. I myself feel baffled by lack of detailed knowledge of E.A.M. etc. Phil [Noel-Baker], of course, is very excited about it and said in the Party Meeting that, if he said some of the things he was saying there outside, he would lose his job in the Government. The Government somehow gets no credit for having kept the King out of Greece. Eden, winding up, makes a much better impression on many than did the P.M. and shows more sympathy and understanding. He offers, if this is the Greek wish, that we, together with our Allies, if they will join us in this, shall ourselves take steps to guarantee a free vote by the Greek people at an early date.

Sunday 10th December
Attlee, Laski, Phil [Noel-Baker] and I have a shot at drafting an Emergency Resolution on Greece for the Conference. We are agreed that the National Executive should take the initiative in proposing such a resolution and should tell the Conference so first thing to-morrow. We also agree that it is essential to keep Greece separate from the general International question, or otherwise delegates' minds will be distracted from the latter and Greece will hit all the headlines.

Because of the D-Day landings and German V-2 attacks on London, the Labour Party Conference had been postponed from Whitsun until the end of the year. It took place on 11th–15th December, at the Central Hall, Westminster. Harold Laski was in the chair.

Monday 11th December
Conference opens and I deliberately neglect the Board of Trade for several days. We had a very easy passage. Discussion on Greece is postponed until Wednesday and it is promised that the National Executive will submit and circulate an Emergency Resolution. This is accepted without challenge.

Our Declaration on Labour and the General Election goes through practically unanimously. There is only negligible support either for the proposal that we should leave the Government before the end of the German war or for the suggestion that we should unite with other 'progressive' elements in a United Front. Both these are overwhelmingly rejected, without card votes, on a show of hands.[1]

Laski in the Chair is a bit too flippant and ironical in some of his

PROGRESS OF LABOUR

observations and George Brown, aged only thirty and about the best of the younger trade union candidates, who, I hope, is going to get Belper in succession to Dallas, tells me to warn Laski that unless he's careful he will find himself moved out of the Chair before the week is over. I pass this on. ...

Arrived at No. 10 at 6.30 and am kept there till 8.45 but my paper is not taken! Other questions, including the release of political agents from the Forces, are put in front of it. This makes me very angry and I decide to send another, rather stronger, letter to the P.M. on the subject, and also to hot up the Labour ministers in the War Cabinet. If this sort of thing goes on much longer, I shall certainly resign.

1 Marginal insertion: 'No mention of electoral truce, nor of a pledge now against a Coalition after the elect[ion]'.

Someone is obviously playing games behind the scenes, but not, I am sure, Bridges, who gives every impression of trying to be helpful.

Hugh Gaitskell says that he is sure that, in addition to the left-wing opposition to the Government policy in Greece, there will be more and more isolationist feeling, equally hostile to the Government, asking why the hell our troops should have to fight in Greece. I think he is right.

In an attempt to steer a course between outright support of the Government over Greece and the hostility felt by many Conference delegates, the N.E.C. submitted a resolution calling for an armistice without delay, and the establishment of a provisional government based on all those who had fought the Nazi invaders.

Wednesday 13th December

Greece this morning. The National Executive Resolution is moved by Greenwood, who is giving an impression at this Conference of having no fire or force left in him, and is finally carried by 2,400,000 to 137,000. This last small vote is purely symbolic. Bevin makes a most powerful and persuasive speech in defence of the Government policy. He has very great power in this Conference. Laski says that last night, in Attlee's room, he took part in a telephone conversation designed to persuade Bevin to come in today; 'it was a fantastic conversation,' he said, 'it was like trying to persuade Tetrazzini to sing.'

First thing this morning, a letter from me to the P.M., which I signed last night, went round to No. 10 and in the lunch interval I sign covering letters to the three Labour members of the War Cabinet and to Thomas Johnston, sending them copies. In this letter to the P.M. I also bring in Restrictive Practices,[1] so that, if there is to be a row, we will have this in as well.

---

1 In addition to his proposed Distribution of Industry Bill, Dalton was pressing 'though less ardently' for a Restrictive Practices Bill. Dalton wanted the Board of Trade to be empowered to refer any firm suspected of a restrictive practice to a Tribunal which could investigate and recommend remedial action – including possible nationalisation. He was not successful. 'On this contentious subject ministers were never in sight of agreement,' he recalled. 'Some wanted something much more complicated, and much less dangerous to monopolists and restrictive trade associations.' (FY, pp. 447–8.)

At the War Cabinet tonight my paper is at the *top* of the Agenda and is taken first (I guess that this is largely due to my letter which he will have got before the Agenda was finally sent out), and finally tonight I get authority to proceed with the drafting of the Bill, which the War Cabinet would like to see again when it's in draft.

Thursday 14th December

Stimulate Low,[1] Sich[2] and Jay, whom I summoned this morning – Overton also coming in – to get on *at once* with making the draft for Parliamentary Counsel for the Distribution of Industry Bill. I tell them this must take precedence over everything else. ...

Lunch with Lady Anderson at 4 Lord North Street, Anderson, Keynes and Monick,[3] Governor of the Bank of France, being present. Monick says that he thinks the French will have to have a capital levy and that it will be quite easy to administer. He has been in France under the German occupation and has not, it seems, been chased as a collaborator. He says that he had great hopes that Weygand would lead a force of 'dissentients' against Pétain, but he thinks the reason why Weygand failed to do this was because 'nobody knows who his parents were' and there were many rumours about his parentage. Some thought he was an illegitimate descendant of the Emperor of Brazil. Anyhow, he was not, by birth, a Frenchman and this has given him a great inferiority complex vis-à-vis Pétain. He was terrified that, if he took a strong line, Pétain would ask publicly, 'Who are this man's parents?'

At the Second Quebec Conference in September 1944 Roosevelt and Churchill reached informal agreement on the amount of aid the United States would supply to Britain during 'Stage II' – the period between the German surrender and the final defeat of Japan. This was followed by two months of detailed negotiations in Washington, led on the British side by Lord Keynes.

---

1 Sir Stephen Low (1883–1955). Solicitor to the Board of Trade 1934–48.
2 R. L. Sich, later Sir Rupert (b. 1908). Board of Trade Solicitor's Department 1932–1948.
3 E. G. M. Monick (b. 1893). French General Secretary of Finance 1944. Financial Attaché at the French Embassy in London 1934–46. Governor of the Banque de France 1945–9.

Keynes says that Helmore[1] did very well at Washington. He thinks we have got much more out of the last talks than we realise and that it is wise publicity to affirm. We have really got all the export freedom we can use and we have *not*, as has been suggested, had our Lend-Lease supplies cut down, but are really getting even more than before. It is generally agreed that the Americans are most anarchic. They all say just what comes into their heads and say it to the Press as well. Stettinius is, in some ways, very simple, and means to be friendly to us, and often has been. But, Keynes said, he is inconceivably press conscious and thinks himself most photogenic. Keynes wanted to have a serious talk with him, they had five minutes together and then Stettinius said, 'I've got the Editor of the *New York Herald Tribune* waiting outside, let's bring him in and see what he thinks.' And, of course, from that moment no serious conversation was possible. When Stettinius came to lunch with the Chancellor and Lady Anderson he arranged that a large number of photographers should come to the Chancellor's house at 2 o'clock, by which time lunch had not been finished, but Stettinius insisted that he should then go upstairs and sit on a sofa beside Lady Anderson, so that the photograph could be taken. It is also quite common, when you meet him in Washington, for a Press photographer to be brought into the office before you are allowed to leave.

Saturday 16th to Monday 18th December
At Diss. Good sleep and very good cooking as usual here.

John Wilmot and I walk as far as the 'Magpie' and have a most interesting and wide ranging conversation in the bar, where the party includes not only a farmer and four or five farm workers, but a little man called Dix who took his B.Sc. as an evening student at L.S.E. in 1922–4 and reminds me of many things I had forgotten, which, he says, I said in my lectures.

...

[Wilmot] told two almost incredible *New Statesman* stories. He went to lunch with them when Gandhi, still in prison, was thought to be in danger of death. Brailsford said, 'If that man dies in captivity, I shall take no further interest in the outcome of the war' and, asked whether he seriously meant this, he stuck to it.

Kingsley Martin rang up Wilmot the day his appointment was announced and said, 'Congratulations, if that's what you think I

1 J. R. C. Helmore, later Sir James (1906–72). Principal Assistant Secretary and Principal Establishment Officer in the Commercial Relations and Treaties Department, Board of Trade 1942–6. Permanent Secretary at the Ministry of Materials 1952; Ministry of Supply 1953–6.

ought to say.' Wilmot said, 'Yes, certainly.' Martin then asked, 'What's the game?' Wilmot said he didn't understand and Martin said, 'Don't you see the game? *THEY* are gunning for the Board of Trade. The first move is to divide you and Dalton and then destroy you both separately. So they've switched you over to a dying Ministry and left him isolated.' Wilmot said, 'I don't understand. I had nothing to do with policy at the Board of Trade.' Martin said, 'Oh nonsense, nobody believes that.' Wilmot said, 'But I was only Dalton's P.P.S.' Martin asked, in great surprise, 'Weren't you the junior minister at the Board of Trade?' Wilmot answered, 'No, of course not. The Parliamentary Secretary is Waterhouse and Harcourt Johnstone [is] at the Department of Trade.' 'Oh!' said Martin obviously quite taken aback. 'That does make it seem a bit different. I could have sworn that you were Parliamentary Secretary and I often said that you and Dalton made a very fine combination.'

As Wilmot said, this was all the more astounding in that it suggested how very little these people really knew about anything to do with politics. He said that Martin had also said, after he had lunch with them one day, and he had told them of a lot of the good work being done at the Board of Trade, 'We mustn't have you to lunch here very often or we shall have nothing left to write about.' This also indicated how they hated to know things were being done well because that was not the sort of thing they wanted to say. Acid and cantankerous criticism based on complete ignorance, modified only by malicious rumour-mongering, is their line.

Monday 18th December
Harvie Watt to lunch. He is very pleased about Wilmot and says that he and Arthur Woodburn have been his selections for some time for the next promotions from the Labour Party to the ranks of junior ministers. Either, he thinks, could have taken on any one of a number of offices. He says that in his reports to the P.M. he has frequently praised Wilmot and also myself, though he has told the P.M. Harcourt Johnstone is a pain in the neck, referring particularly to the incident of his absence at the beginning of the recent debate on Exports. He has urged the P.M. to shift him, but the P.M. doesn't want to make changes in the Government just now because he does not know how much longer it will last. In addition Johnstone is only here as part of Sinclair's quota,[1] though his appointment is commonly regarded as a complete ramp. He also mentions that Johnstone is friendly with Bracken. He knows my views about the latter. I say that I would be most delighted if I could have some lively young Tory instead of

1 i.e. as a Liberal.

Johnstone. My first choice would be Peter Thorneycroft, much the best, I think, of the Tory Reform Group. I invite him to drop this thought into the stream. Harvie Watt himself would like to be Tory Chief Whip. I say that I suppose after the next election the present occupant would have earned a peerage. Harvie Watt says that one of the difficulties is that he is known not to be an admirer of Eden. He would much prefer Anderson to be Prime Minister. He regards Eden as soft and vain and he has no knowledge whatever of domestic questions. He says that if Eden had been even for a short time at the Board of Trade or the Ministry of Supply or even Under-Secretary at the Ministry of Labour, he would have been exhibited as a complete failure.

Tuesday 19th December
Meynell and Pooley to dine. A pleasant evening, full of gossip, ending up at the Savile Club, where I am always astonished at the queer characters hanging around. Story of the King inspecting a file of A.T.S. [Auxiliary Territorial Service] in Italy. Of each girl in turn he asked, with a slight stammer, 'How long have *you* been in Italy?' They had all come out on the same day and this date was monotonously repeated down the file, but it never occurred to the King to ask the next girl a different question.

The story of the Duke of Gloucester[1] inspecting some group of people somewhere else. An important looking man was hanging about in the background and one of the attendants said, 'That's the Judge. I'm sure he would be delighted if you spoke to him.' So the Duke, not quite knowing what to say, asked, 'Do you get much judgin' out here?' Huntin' and fishin' and judgin' – it's all one.

Wednesday 20th December
Overton and Lintott[2] come to break to me the dreadful news that Sir Alexander Maxwell,[3] the Tobacco Controller, wants to be a Parliamentary Candidate – 'in the Conservative interest'. I am rather pleased at this and say that this helps to balance the parties up. Both these two officials support the Treasury view, propounded by Anderson, that no temporary, any more than a permanent, civil servant should be allowed to be adopted as a Candidate. I say I don't agree at all, nor does the P.M., nor the Deputy P.M., and that, provided they show

---

1 Prince Henry, Duke of Gloucester (1901–74). Younger brother of King George VI.
2 H. J. B. Lintott, later Sir Henry (b. 1908). Board of Trade 1935–48. M.E.W. 1939–40. In 1942 Lintott became Principal Assistant Secretary in charge of the Industries Department, Division II, at the Board of Trade.
3 Sir Alexander Hyslop Maxwell (1896–1971). Tobacco Controller at the Board of Trade 1940–45. Tobacco importer. He did not become a candidate.

reasonable discretion in public, I see no reason why a temporary civil servant, particularly in these last stages before the next election, shouldn't be adopted, though I agree that after he fights, whether he wins or loses, he should not return to the public service and that this should be understood beforehand.

Thursday 21st December
War Cabinet on manpower, but a very inconclusive discussion on hypothetical figures. In view of rapid changes on the Western Front the P.M. says the 'time has come to play a strong hand'. We must quickly make a public declaration that we are reinforcing our Armies in France and Belgium by 250,000 fighting men, and this will stimulate our Allies and probably lead to the Americans undertaking to reinforce by a million and redress the balance, now inclined to be seriously tilted towards the Pacific.

Thursday 28th December
Captain Julian Amery to see me. He stays a long time recounting his experience with S.O.E., chiefly in Albania. He thinks that E.A.M. has *now* become completely under Communist influence though it was not so at first. He thinks Stalin is deliberately stirring up trouble for us in Greece. He wonders whether the Labour Party could not have done a bit in Greece and elsewhere in Europe to rally the Socialist as distinct from the Communist elements. I said that in Greece there had never been any to rally. He says that the alleged descents by armed bands of E.L.A.S. [Ellinikos Laikos Apeleftheritokos Stratos][1] on villagers were forays by starving men from the cities. He thinks that Tito is 'simply waiting to intervene' in Greece, via Macedonia, and that the Russians want, in one form or other, to control Salonika. I said that I thought the matter could only be settled by high level

1 The E.L.A.S. (National Popular Liberation Army) and the E.A.M. (National Liberation Front) were the two principal guerrilla forces in Greece. They were both primarily under Communist control. Together they set up a provisional government in the Greek mountains, following the surrender of Italy to the Allies, thus effectively renouncing both the Greek monarch and his government-in-exile. Mutiny in support of the new provisional government broke out among Greek troops outside Greece in April 1944, but this was suppressed, and an uneasy peace was established between the rival factions. Together the two governments formed a coalition under the Liberal, Georgios Papandreou, when the Germans withdrew from Greece in October 1944; but within a short time the Communist members of the coalition had rebelled against orders to disband their guerrilla force, and a civil war broke out in Athens on 3rd December 1944. (See note before entry for 8th December, p. 813.) The Communists eventually disbanded their forces in February 1945, following the Conference of Varkiza.

discussions between us and Stalin. He thinks he may be a Conservative Candidate, in harness with Randolph Churchill, at Preston, but
he doesn't think he agrees with the Conservative Party on most things!
He thinks he is going soon to the Far East with S.O.E.

Dine with Sir Charles Bruce-Gardner at the Café Royal. He is very
delighted having heard that he is to be a Baronet. I say that, naturally,
I had been asked whether I supported this, the initiative coming from
M.A.P. [Ministry of Aircraft Production] and had said certainly yes.
I add that this need not be the end. He is exceedingly good at his
present job. I certainly picked a winner in him.

Friday 29th December
Windle to see me, and we have a good talk about Candidates. We
seem to be laying down quite a large number of good ones.

Wednesday 10th January
National Executive, after which I bring Laski back to lunch. Much
talk this morning on Greece, on which Bevan makes a long speech –
but it is much less easy to be vehement when there are only a small
number of listeners and several of these not very sympathetic. He
claimed to have special knowledge of what the P.M. said to the Greek
King and to the Archbishop of Athens. And, in particular, he *knows*
that the P.M. has offered ten Divisions (what a thought!) for the complete conquest of Greece. He refuses to divulge his source of information. Shinwell moves a Resolution for publication, declaring that we
demand that E.A.M. be brought into the Government and that otherwise we withdraw our troops from Greece at once. He pretends that
this is in line with the Conference Resolution, but fortunately I have
this in my hand and am able to refute him. I move, as an Amendment,
that, as the Chairman had already suggested, we should send a
deputation to the P.M. for general discussion. This Amendment,
rejecting any resolution, is carried by 11 to 6[1] and the deputation is
then unanimously agreed.

Friday 12th January
Leave with Piercy for Shipton and reach Paddington in good time,
but, half an hour before the train is due to leave, an American soldier
in our carriage fidgeting about with the luggage on the rack causes a
large and heavy metal implement to fall on Piercy's bare head. The
window into the corridor is cracked and Piercy is cut and begins to
bleed. I take him along to the First Aid Post where they patch him

---

1 Marginal insertion: 'What luck, considering later evidence, Citrine, Lawson etc!'
  The deputation consisted of Greenwood, Griffiths, Laski and Bevan.

up and tell him that he will probably have a bad headache this evening.

Met at Shipton by Mary Piercy,[1] whom I had not seen for many years, and drive in the dark to Burford, where they live in 'The Great House', but, though the house is a fair size, it is rather a misleading name.

Here I spend, till the morning of 15th January, a very pleasant and peaceful weekend. ...

Piercy is in the running for the Candidature at West Middlesbrough, in succession to Joad. He is one of six or seven. He is going up next week. I like him and I also like Mary, with whom I had a long and interesting conversation about everything under the sun after he had gone. She is still very definitely a Socialist and thinks that he has been slow to come thus far. She looks rather tired with the years and anxieties of war – their son Nicholas[2] is in the Fleet Air Arm, now, for the moment, in South Africa.[3]

Tuesday 16th January
From lunch to International Sub, where Laski, taking the Chair at the opening, proposes that I should be Chairman. No other name is suggested, though Shinwell, who obviously had hopes that he would get the Chair himself, says he objects on principle to a member of the Government being Chairman of any Sub-Committee of the Executive, but no one else supports him. On taking the Chair and thanking my colleagues, I say that, no doubt, the distinction between those who accepted and those who refused invitations to join the Government in May 1940 will soon become much blurred. We then have a report from Laski and Griffiths of their deputation to the P.M. yesterday.[4] It is quite clear, though they don't admit it, that he captivated and, to a considerable extent, persuaded them. Laski then proposes that Gillies should leave the room, and we then discuss whether there should be a re-arrangement in the International Department, to give us a new Secretary. This is unanimously felt to be desirable, and it should be noted that those present included, in addition to those named already, Attlee, Morrison, Phil [Noel-] Baker, Jennie Adamson and Tom Williamson. The latter showed a certain tendency to delay decision but I said we had better first settle the merits, and then go on to procedure. On the merits, or the demerits, of Gillies we were unanimous.

1 Mary Piercy, née Pelham, wife of William Piercy. She and Ruth Dalton had been close friends in the 1920s.
2 Nicholas Piercy, later 2nd Baron (1918–81).
3 Marginal insertion: 'I talk to her about Ruth, to whom she is very grateful for a letter in 1922. This may give an opening one day.'
4 On Greece.

It was then decided that we should recommend to the National Executive that he should be retired – he is just over sixty – but that he should be treated generously, not only as to pension, but by receiving a lump sum of salary paid in advance. It was further decided that I, with Laski, Williamson and Morgan Phillips, should receive him, the others having left, and break this to him. This we did. It was a little difficult since he was obviously so totally unprepared. I began in a deliberately circuitous and muffled fashion, from which he inferred that I thought the strain of war had been bad for his health, and hastened to reassure me that he was really very fit. Whereupon both Laski and Williamson broke in with much greater directness and told him that the Committee had unanimously decided that we should have a new Secretary, and that the best course would be for him to resign. They added that we wished to treat him well financially. He asked that he should have time to think this over, to which we agreed, and I suggested that he might like to make some written communication to Phillips before the next Executive.

Wednesday 17th January

Gladwyn Jebb to dine. I have not seen him for months, and he told me of various formulae he had been making to try to bridge the gap at Dumbarton Oaks between the Russians on the one hand and ourselves and the Americans on the other regarding the rule about Great Powers. The Russians say all these must be unanimous before any action can be taken by the Security Council. We and the U.S. say that a party to a dispute, Great Power or Small, should have no vote. Jebb had suggested that the Anglo-American view should be adopted for the earlier stages of any dispute, i.e. that a Great Power should not have the right to prevent examination of the question by the Council, or by any other method, but that the Russian view should prevail at the last stage, i.e. that after examination no *action* should be recommended by the Council except with the Great Powers unanimous. This had, however, been objected to on high levels, both in the U.S. and here as going too far in the Russian direction and had also been rejected by Stalin as not going far enough! But he still thought that something of this kind might be devised. In fact, if the Great Powers fell out, there would be another war or the whole international organisation would collapse or both. If, however, the Russian view was fully accepted there was a danger that a large number of non-Great Powers, including, perhaps, Canada, would refuse to join the show at all and it would thus become a mere alliance of Great Powers and not an international organisation at all. Shortly after this, and while he was describing a luncheon given by Massigli at which he had been present,[1] he suddenly said that he felt very sick and went out of the restaurant. He then was indeed *very* sick, and fell down, losing consciousness for some moments and groaning most unhappily, also cutting his head behind the ear. The admirable Josef produces various First Aids, including bismuth to be sipped and a rag soaked in vinegar to be rubbed on his face and I then got him, still half unconscious, into the car and took him back to his flat. His wife and family were away and there was no one there except a housekeeper lady in the basement. I got him up in the lift and put him to bed and then started to try to get a doctor. This was a considerable business and took over an hour, involving a telephone call to Horder who gave me three names, but the one I went for proved to have left his residence, as recorded in the telephone book, three years before. I was finally guided to a Maxwell Chance living in 5 Culross Street, and brought him back in my car. He declared that Gladwyn had had a very severe attack of ptomaine poisoning, but having been so violently sick had probably got rid of the poison now, but it had left him rather weak. It is amazing how quickly such a thing can get one right down. I have never seen such a case before. Clearly the damage had been done early in the day, probably at a lunch at the Argentine Embassy – probably they were trying to poison *all* their guests! – for he said he had felt funny in the afternoon. Next day I went to see him in the afternoon and he was out of bed and apparently much better, though he was staying at home and reading Foreign Office papers there. Such an incident makes one feel rather cautious about one's food. I confess this is a new sense of insecurity for me!

Friday 26th January
Captain Raymond Blackburn[2] to dine with me. I had been trying to collect him ever since Chris Mayhew asked me to do so and reported the most astounding conversation at the R.A.C. in the week of the Labour Party Conference. Blackburn is a bit shy. He calls me 'Sir' rather a lot, which is very unnecessary, and is a bit too prone to flatter and too quick to agree. But he is under thirty, quick, able, active and ambitious, though I wouldn't trust him very far. He seems to have done quite well as a solicitor. I don't mention Mayhew.

On 13th December, the War Cabinet authorised the drafting of a Distribution

---

1 Marginal insertion: 'and had seen Ruth – she was looking well, but he thought, rather worried – .'
2 A. R. B. Blackburn (b. 1915). Labour M.P. 1945–50. Independent M.P. 1950–51.

of Industry Bill. Dalton received the first draft of this on 8th January. On 1st February there were discussions on the third draft between the President, Waterhouse, Board of Trade officials and the Parliamentary draftsmen, and Dalton prepared a paper covering the draft Bill for the War Cabinet. This followed a demand from the Legislation Committee for more Bills within the next ten days, and for this Bill in particular on 13th February. 'This unexpected call, for which Attlee is partly, and helpfully, responsible, makes quite a difference in the prospects of getting this Bill passed this session, even though it should not last very long,' Dalton noted. 'It is as though dark clouds had suddenly split open and the sun broken through.'[1]

Friday 2nd February
Lunch alone with Irene [Noel-Baker] who is soon going to Greece. Their house on Euboea was burnt down by the Italians. She thinks Phil ought to resign, but not on any particular issue – not even the Greek issue – but in order to have time to become Chairman of the League of Nations Union and speak freely in the House of Commons and decide about the Peace Settlement. I said I didn't think this would do at all. If you resign from the War Cabinet[2] it can only be on a real issue. The League of Nations Union would make a very unconvincing story. There is not much longer to go before the Government would break up and an election take place, the result of which it would be rash to prophesy. She shrilled a good deal against Attlee, but I said that, in any Labour Government, Phil would certainly have an important office. I also quoted Arthur Henderson's old warning, 'Never fix your mind on one particular office; it only brings disappointment.' It is odd how she – and a lot of other people – don't understand that being in the Cabinet – in *any* office – gives much insight and influence, the amount of which depends much less upon the actual office held than on personal relationships within the Cabinet. Similarly, it is difficult, without revealing to outsiders the composition and procedure of Cabinet Committees (e.g. the A.P.W. [Armistice and Post War Committee] under Attlee), to make clear the extent to which foreign affairs are discussed and foreign policy influenced by ministers other than the P.M. and the Foreign Secretary.

See Attlee later this evening and urge him to get my Distribution of Industry Bill through the War Cabinet next week, so that I can get it, as desired by him, before the Legislation Committee on 13th February.

---

1 Diary, 1st February 1945.
2 Presumably he means 'War Government'. Noel-Baker was Parliamentary Secretary at the Department of War Transport.

He says he will certainly get it through. He adds, 'It would be a good thing to get it through when the old man's away.' Everything seems now at last to be working together for good.

I tell him that A. V. Alexander said yesterday, when I asked his expert opinion, that he couldn't see how the German war could go on more than about two months longer. Attlee said, 'I'm inclined to agree with him, but I don't say so to anybody.' He seemed very cheerful and enjoying this, perhaps, last patch of Deputy Prime Ministership before the kaleidoscope begins to turn. And where will everybody tumble to then?

'The sands are fast running out', Dalton wrote to Attlee on 6th February, 'and I judge that, unless I am able to meet your request and bring the Bill to the Legislation Committee on 13th February, its chances of passing this session will be reduced almost to zero. As you know, I regard the passage of this Bill into law, before this Government breaks up, as one of my most important duties. The day when it becomes clear that I have little or no hope of performing this duty I shall reconsider, most seriously and most coldly, my personal position in the Government.

' ... If after all my efforts this Bill goes down the drain, I think the only right and honest course will be for me to cease to be a member of a Government which will have betrayed, through its procrastination and internal divisions, the populations of the Development Areas ... '[1]

Saturday 3rd February
I send off this morning letters to Bevin, Lyttelton, Woolton and Anderson, each adjusted, to the best of my powers, to the character and outlook of the recipients, seeking to mobilise their support for the Bill. It really begins to look now as though I may just get it through, before the Government breaks up – a Hallelujah Chorus rather than a Resignation Philippic. It would be a terrible bore to fall silently between these two stools!

Tuesday 6th February
Dine with Hugh Gaitskell at the Churchill Club in Westminster, with Mrs Randolph Churchill and others and take the Chair for Van [Vansittart], whom I had not seen for a very long time. He addresses an audience of American, Dominion and British troops on 'The

1 Dalton Papers 7/7 (19).

Problem of Germany'. His plan is to invite questions and answer them at length. On the whole the questions are pretty sensible, but his answers are rather too general and too long. There is, however, I feel, some evidence in this meeting, as elsewhere, of a certain solidifying of sensible opinion about Germany – not hatred nor hysteria, but rational precautions against a third try.

A fresh flurry about my Distribution of Industry Bill. I circulated a draft of this, with a short covering note and particulars of the Development Areas, over the weekend and have been counting on it being taken at the War Cabinet this week, so as to get it to the Legislation Committee next week. Preston had been gently prodding the Cabinet Offices about this and it seemed as though everything was all ready for tomorrow. Then, this morning on the Bench, Attlee says to me that he thinks it would be better to postpone it till the P.M. comes back, in view of the opposition. I say, 'I suppose that damned Bracken has been intriguing again.' He says, 'No, it is the advice of the Secretariat.' I say, 'This is a most serious matter. I must speak to you about it.' I then ask him when he will be free. He is rather evasive and says not much before lunch. I say that I take this most seriously and must insist on having a talk. I then leave the Bench and pick him up later on in the Smoke Room with Jack Lawson who is just back from Greece with shocking stories from our own troops about the atrocities. I then catch Attlee and say that this is a matter on which I feel most strongly and deeply and that, if my Bill is not taken this week, I shall have to consider some very serious decisions. He says, rather feebly, 'Would you go and ask Anderson what he thinks about it?' I do so and catch Anderson just before lunch. He is very friendly and definitely of the opinion that the Bill should be taken this week. He has not heard of any opposition to it and thinks I have met all critics fairly. I then find Attlee in the Dining Room and briefly report this to him. He says, 'All right, I will deal with the matter.'

After lunch – at Drapers' Hall where I attend Queen Mary College Governors – I dictate a very firm letter ... to Attlee in which, more definitely than ever before, I threaten to resign if I don't get my Bill. Already before this letter goes off, the Cabinet Agenda, much delayed, comes round with my Bill No. 1 for tomorrow's meeting. But I think it just as well to send the letter.

Wednesday 7th February

Visit Horder; about three months since my last visit. His dope has obviously been very effective. He says that the tablets contain Vitamin B1 and the pills a little strychnine. He is quite pleased with me and with my health. It appears that I have put on 8 lb. in the last three months! I now weigh just 14 stone. I tell him I am eating, as far as possible, a non-starch diet and he thinks this is quite all right, though there is no sign of sugar in the wrong place.

To see Attlee at his request at 4, the War Cabinet being at 5.30. Following my strong letter of yesterday, he seems a little shy and very conciliatory. I tell him I have just been talking to Lyttelton on the telephone and that he and I have reached complete agreement. Attlee has been well briefed by Gorell Barnes[1] and Piercy on my Bill. He seems anxious to help to get it through. I say that, if I can't get the Bill, it will bring great discredit on *all* Labour ministers. He says he quite agrees.

Entering the War Cabinet room, Lyttelton comes up to me and says he has been working very hard on Max [Beaverbrook] and Brendan [Bracken]. He thinks he has fixed Max but isn't quite sure about Bracken. Max, who looks rather pale and ill, sits absolutely silent throughout a discussion of my Bill lasting for one and three-quarter hours. Bracken only intervenes once or twice and that not too aggressively. Indeed he goes out of his way on one point to accept, quite quietly, a compromise which I suggest. So there is really no opposition. I had told Lyttelton, as we were going away from the Reconversion of Industry Committee, that I should take a very serious view of the failure to get my Bill this week and that relatively speaking, I wasn't much interested in Restrictive Practices. I judge that my intention to resign, unless I get the Bill, has been put round and I think that he will have mentioned it to Max and Bracken and that this largely accounts for their conduct tonight. I think all these three are sharp enough to see that it would do the non-Labour elements in the Government no good if I were to resign on this issue and make a series of speeches about it in Parliament and the country. Anyhow, I get my Bill through the War Cabinet without any serious trouble. Anderson gives steady support and several others butt in helpfully on particular points. But on Section 9,[2] providing for restricted areas, there is the most frightful muddle by Bevin and Woolton[?],[3] both of whom are

1 W. L. Gorell Barnes, later Sir William (b. 1909). Personal Assistant to the Lord President of the Council (Anderson) 1942. Transferred to the War Cabinet Office 1945; Treasury 1946. Personal Assistant to the Prime Minister (Attlee) 1946–8.

2 Clause 9 of the Distribution of Industry Bill would have enabled the Board of Trade to declare any area a Restricted Area, within which permission would be required to construct or extend an industrial building. In fact, this clause was inserted as a 'pious hoax', so that it could be given up at the right moment. The trick worked: after the break-up of the Coalition, the Caretaker Government (which continued to support the Bill) needed a concession to appease Tory back-bench opinion. Clause 9 was dropped, enabling the Bill to pass into law.

3 Text has 'W.': probably Woolton but possibly Waterhouse.

against 'having any areas at all', and in favour of giving some vague power to the Board of Trade to ban any particular factory anywhere. I say that this is absolutely incapable of administration.

So tonight I feel very triumphant. There are still hurdles to be surmounted, but I think that I have got over the worst of them now.

Friday 9th February
Discuss with Attlee, Morrison, Phil [Noel-] Baker and Ellen Wilkinson, the attitude of the Party towards a continuance of conscription. Attlee and Morrison are both inclined to think that we should come out in favour of it, before the election. Phil is against this, mainly on military grounds, holding that our contribution to collective security should be through a powerful Air Force and Navy rather than a large Army. Ellen is against on political grounds. Why should we let the Tories, she asks, manoeuvre us once more into pulling their chestnuts out of the fire? I doubt whether it is necessary to take a decision, beyond what seems the inevitable decision of continuing the call-up for another two or three years so as to allow the demobilisation of large numbers, by age and length of service, in a period when the war against Japan will be continuing and when we shall need a large Army still in Europe.

Wednesday 14th February
[Percy] Cudlipp to lunch. I had not seen him for some time. I never find him very satisfactory. He is always inclined to complain that he is not given a lead, or told things, by the leaders of the Party, but, even when one does talk to him, one doesn't see much result in the paper. We speak of Michael Foot and he says he will arrange for me to have a talk with him soon. It is odd that I have never met this very able, though in some respects mentally perverse, young man. ...

Then Blackburn brings in, as arranged with me earlier, to the same committee room, a party of about a dozen Birmingham shop stewards, who are concerned about the future of the factories there. I explain the procedure for dealing with labour which becomes 'redundant' and with factories which are declared surplus by the Supply Departments. I emphasise that the factories are to be leased not sold, and that I hope a great deal of labour will soon become redundant from arms production, so that I can have more things made for the civilians. I also talk about 'planning' and tried to make them see that you can't just 'make a long-term plan' and then sit back and let the plan take charge, but that, as the Russians have shown us, there must be constant re-adjustment of the plan in the light of ever changing conditions. What will happen in the next few years will depend, I explained, on the results of the next election and then, looking round the table, I ask, 'Do any of you come from King's Norton?' One man says 'Yes', with a broad grin.

This evening I go to dine with Blackburn who was very delighted by this afternoon's performance. He is very quick and eager and has, I can see, considerable aptitude as an intriguer. One of his guests tonight is a young man named Freeman,[1] whom Blackburn is anxious to get adopted as Labour Candidate at Watford where Blackburn has many contacts resulting from his Common Wealth candidature. Freeman, who is a tall, red-haired, rather good-looking, rather serious young man, a Major and a Desert Rat, was at Westminster and Brasenose and then went into an advertising business, makes a very good impression on me. He is still under thirty and became a Socialist at Oxford. He should make a good Candidate and a good M.P.

Friday 16th February
Mary Sutherland[2] to see me at my request. She is inclined to take a grim view about the attitude of a large part of the Party to the International problem and also about the new General Secretary. On the first point I try to get her to take comfort from the terms of our declaration which indeed she thoroughly agrees with, but she is a little over conscious, I think, of our dissidents. On the Gillies case, I encourage her to talk quite frankly and she says that she feels it has been handled the wrong way and that it has created a sense of insecurity in the office, since all of them now think that, if they take a line contrary to that of the National Executive or some of its influential members, they may find themselves slung out. (I thought, though I don't say so, that that might be quite a good thing for them to feel.) She is one of those who still hanker after the idea of a great political leader to be General Secretary of the Party. I don't myself share this view. But she is a nice creature and a great many of her views are very sensible. I arrange with her for an article in the *Labour Woman* on my Distribution of Industry Bill next month.

Then I receive Kingsley Martin, with whom I talk for $1\frac{1}{2}$ hours. I tell him a bit about the Distribution of Industry Bill, but must warn him whether this publicity can be released next week, which is dependent on the day when I can get the Bill printed. He has hardened up quite a lot about the Germans and the Peace Settlement and is now

---

1 John Freeman (b. 1915). Major in the Eighth Army, North Africa. Labour M.P. for Watford 1945–55. Junior minister 1947–51. Editor of the *New Statesman* 1961–5. High Commissioner to India 1965–8. Ambassador to the United States 1969–71. Chairman of London Weekend Television 1971–84.
2 Mary Sutherland (d. 1972). Chief Woman Officer of the Labour Party 1932–60.

engaged in repudiating Brailsford's more extreme view. I tell him that I have tried to make an international policy for the Labour Party which:

(i) will be rational and practical,
(ii) will not lose votes at the next election, and
(iii) will unite all important sections of the party and still the shrill squabbles on side issues, of which we have had too many.

I say I think I have succeeded on all three points. He does not violently disagree.

I get the sense that rather few people run the *New Statesman* now. He is very full of stories of terrible starvation in the Dutch cities behind the German lines and of the spread of typhus. I fear there may be only too much ground for this. But the only remedy is military. The Germans have it in their power to feed these people and simply choose to starve them instead. As to supplies for Belgium and France, I emphasise to him that the chief need is ships, and that the Americans have put too many of these in the Pacific. He should keep hammering on this point.[1]

Monday 19th February
First meeting of Labour Party Campaign Committee this morning. We vote Morrison to the Chair and there is a general discussion. This is a small and useful Committee – Attlee, Morrison and myself, Greenwood, Williamson, Mrs Gould and the Secretary. We want to get a fairly free hand from the Executive to deal with things as they arise.

Tuesday 20th February
9.45 Legislation Committee to consider my Distribution of Industry Bill in draft. The place is packed with ministers, lawyers and other attendants. Attlee in the Chair. The Attorney-General,[2] who is busybodying about the place before the meeting starts, tells me that he doesn't like the Bill at all. I say that all questions of merits have already been settled by the War Cabinet. Then we start and take it clause by clause. Then Greenwood repeats what he said to me, and, rather

---

1 Marginal insertion: '(He went to pieces as usual in his next number, and had a carping article "Retreat from Barlow".)'
2 Sir Donald Somervell, later 1st Baron (1889–1960). Attorney-General 1936–45. Conservative M.P. for Crewe 1931–45. Solicitor-General 1933–6. Home Secretary 1945.

peevishly, what I had said to him. He and the Lord Advocate[1] – a wretched legal pedant – both keep raising points and trying to restrict all powers granted by the Bill. I have the War Cabinet Minutes with me and frequently read out sentences, e.g. 'The War Cabinet decided that Clause 9 should stand as drafted.' These lawyers are most infuriating. Their stuff this morning is all politics rather than law. Then Greenwood, e.g., says once, 'I think it very undesirable to extend the powers of compulsory purchase of land by giving these to fresh Government Departments.' Attlee is very good and steady in the Chair and brushes most of this rubbish aside. Osbert Peake, now Financial Secretary to the Treasury, carefully briefed by Treasury Officials, also raises a lot of difficulties. More than once I have to say to him, 'But I have already cleared this point with the Chancellor. He is quite satisfied with this draft.' Lyttelton, to do him justice, turns up and intervenes several times backing agreements made between himself and me. So *finally* – can it really be *finally*? – I get my Bill ready to be printed. It is to be presented to Parliament tomorrow.

Wednesday 21st February

At 12 noon, at the end of Questions (I present) the Distribution of Industry Bill. That is to say I nod, seated and silent, when the title is called. The Chief Whip then calls 'Second Reading next Tuesday', a formality designed to bring the Bill upon the Order Paper. As we are leaving the Chamber the Chief Whip runs up to me and says the P.M. wants to speak to you. He had been sitting on the Bench. This is his first appearance in the House of Commons after his return yesterday from Yalta and Cairo. He asks me, 'Have you got authority to introduce your Bill?' I say, 'Yes. It has been through the War Cabinet and the Legislation Committee.' He is obviously rather taken aback by this and grumbles something about 'Perhaps we ought to have another look at it.' But things have now gone much too far for this. Some of those damned fellows – Max and Bracken no doubt – have been putting ideas into his head. But all the formalities have now been completed and the Bill will be printed and distributed tomorrow. Today it was only in dummy. (The backers of the Bill are Attlee, Anderson, Lyttelton, Johnston, W. S. Morrison, and Waterhouse. I mentioned to the P.M. today that Lyttelton and I were now quite agreed about it and it was perhaps, following this remark, that the P.M. must have spoken to Lyttelton, for the latter sent, most tentatively and amicably, along the Private Secretary channel, an inquiry

1 J. S. C. Reid, later Baron (1890–1975). Lord Advocate 1941–5. Conservative M.P. for Glasgow Hillhead 1937–48; Stirling and Falkirk Boroughs 1931–5. Solicitor-General for Scotland 1936–41.

as to whether there was anything he could do to help in preparing the way for the Bill. For the moment there is nothing. Later he may be useful with Tory M.P.s. The P.M. has long regarded me as a slightly dangerous character in this field!)

I see Willie Whiteley and ask him to arrange for me to address a special meeting of the P.L.P. next week and also to see the members of the groups affected separately. I also warn him that attempts may be made now to delay the Second Reading. ...

Department of Industry Committee this afternoon. Cripps, who is becoming less and less satisfactory as a departmental minister, is trying to shut down all aircraft production at Short Harlands at Belfast and practically all aluminium stampings at Distington. He seems to be entirely in the hands of his officials and never to give anybody notice of anything.

Dalton's Distribution of Industry Bill, as published on 22nd February, gave the Board of Trade power to build, in the Development Areas, factories, ancillary buildings and houses for key workers; to make loans to non-profit-making trading or industrial estate companies; to acquire derelict land and bring it into use; and to change the definition of Areas subject to an affirmative Parliamentary resolution. It also enabled any minister, with Treasury approval, to make grants or loans to improve basic services on which the development of the Areas depended. It enabled the Treasury to help firms in the Development Areas to raise new capital and it required industrialists to notify the Board of Trade of their intention to build a new factory. Finally, the controversial Clause 9 enabled the Board of Trade, subject to an affirmative Parliamentary resolution, to declare any area a Restricted Area, within which no one might erect or extend any industrial building without permission.

Thursday 22nd February
Today I have been President of the Board of Trade for three years. This is a good deal longer than most of my predecessors. ...

My Distribution of Industry Bill is printed today, a good official Birthday present. I take two press conferences on it, first the Lobby correspondents at the House, and then the Industrial correspondents at the Board of Trade. A lot of them seem rather stupid, but I hope they will get it right in their papers.

At the end of January, British and American Chiefs of Staff met in Malta for discussions before the Yalta Conference. They were joined by Churchill and Roosevelt. The Chiefs of Staff discussions centred around Eisenhower's plans for carrying his forces up to and across the Rhine. It was decided to withdraw three divisions from Greece and three from Italy as soon as possible. It was also agreed that it was 'undesirable that more of Western Europe than necessary should be occupied by the Russians'.[1]

At the Conference at Yalta, in the Crimea, which immediately followed, Churchill, Roosevelt and Stalin discussed plans for future world organisation, settling voting procedures for the proposed United Nations. Zoning policy for post-war Germany was also considered, and it was agreed that France, in addition to Russia, Britain and America, should be assigned a zone. There was a secret agreement concerning the entry of the Soviet Union into the war against Japan after the defeat of Germany. The most vital matter, in the long run, concerned the fate of Poland, now largely occupied by the Russians. Although Stalin accepted that 'free' elections should take place as soon as practicable, he offered no guarantee of international supervision. At the same time, the British and Americans tacitly agreed to a territorial shifting of Poland westward, with the Curzon Line as the Soviet frontier and the Oder–Neisse Line as the western frontier. The outcome of this conference was sharply criticised at home, especially by those who felt that Poland had effectively been sacrificed in the interests of a wider agreement. Following a House of Commons debate on 27th February, twenty-five M.P.s, mainly right-wing Tories, voted against the Government, and one junior minister, H. G. Strauss, resigned.

Friday 23rd February
The P.M. invites all ministers outside the War Cabinet to his room at the House to hear an account of Malta and Yalta. He says it has taken them fourteen months to fix this meeting. Nobody had agreed to any of the places suggested. Finally it is fixed that he shall meet Roosevelt at Malta and the two shall then go on to Yalta, whereat he had sent this message to the President:

> With this final decision let nobody palter,
>   Nor anyone alter,
> From Malta to Yalta let none of us falter.

'I think', he said, 'this may have slightly annoyed the President, who

1 Churchill, *Triumph and Tragedy*, p. 300.

replied rather drily that "he had not heard of any intention to make any change in the arrangements".'

He gave a vivid picture of Yalta. The Russians had made a tremendous effort to prepare for their reception in two of the old palaces of the nobility of Tsarist times. Everywhere all around was destruction. One day a British officer had asked for a lemon and had been given, with great apologies, an orange. Next day there appeared two lemon trees, each covered with ripe fruit, which were rapidly erected in a flower bed outside the palace where the soldiers were staying. The P.M. spoke very warmly of Stalin. He was sure – and Sir Charles Portal had said the same thing to me at the De La Rue dinner last Wednesday – that, as long as Stalin lasted, Anglo-Russian friendship could be maintained.[1] Who would succeed him one didn't know. (Portal had said, 'Perhaps Molotov. He's pretty wooden and he stammers and a stammer in Russian is not a pretty sound.') Several times, when we had pressed our points hard, Stalin had suddenly said, 'Yes. I see the strength of your argument. I will withdraw my proposal.' This had come quite suddenly, when things had not looked favourable to agreement. This was the right way to deal with the Russians. The Americans did not always recognise this. Sometimes they failed to press their points hard enough. All three were agreed that they must meet alone without the French. The Russians, in particular, were very insistent that France had not earned her right to join the Big Three. Stalin measured everything by the number of troops, ships and aircraft each of the Allies put in the field. On this count France was nowhere. The Americans take the same line. We, of the three, were the most favourable to France and we had secured for her considerable gains – a zone of occupation in Germany, a place on the International Allied Control Commission at Berlin, a place among the inviting powers for the San Francisco Conference. On the Dumbarton Oaks difficulty about voting, the P.M. thought that we had reached a pretty good compromise. (This will soon be fully explained, and much discussed by all those interested in international political organisation.) The P.M. had finally persuaded Stalin to accept by illustrating it from our position [over] Hong Kong. If the Chinese clamoured to have it back we should be compelled to allow discussion, and permit the Chinese to state their case and others to express their views upon it. We should have no right to stop any of this, or any recommendations made by any Committee which might be appointed to consider it, but if, after all this, we refused to budge, and the Chinese attacked us and tried to turn us out, they would then

1 Marginal insertion: 'P.M. said, "Poor Neville Chamberlain believed he could trust Hitler. He was wrong. But I don't think I'm wrong about Stalin."'

have become the aggressors. He said that this illustration had made a great impression upon Stalin. There had also been the question of the Russian representation at future conferences of the World Organisation. The Russians had begun by asking for eighteen seats, one for each of their constituent republics. But we had resisted this, though still claiming six seats for the British Empire, which he confessed had struck him, secretly, as rather tall, as against one each for Russia and the U.S.A. Finally we and the Russians agreed that we would keep six and they might have three, including one for the Ukraine and one for White Russia, with a promise never to claim any more. The Americans didn't much like this, but he urged them to try to find some way of having three themselves. Possibly someone from the Senate and someone from the House of Representatives in addition to an official spokesman of the Administration. Roosevelt was going to think this over.

Poland had been much the most difficult question. On this the Big Three had felt more keenly than on anything else which they discussed. After each had stated their opposition, there had been a silence for two or three minutes. Finally an agreement had been arrived at ... Stalin, in the course of the talk on this, had said, 'We are conscious of our great sins against Poland in the past, through occupation and oppression of that country.' The P.M. wasn't sure whether 'sins', the actual word used by the translator, had been quite accurate, but in any case he thought this phrase very significant. No one could tell whether the pledge to make a truly free and independent Poland would be honoured by the Russians or not. We and the Americans would do our best to see that it was. If not, we should be free to continue to recognise the London-Polish government and to refuse approval of the new Polish situation. As regards the taking over of territory previously German, he said that people often spoke of the great difficulties of 'transfer of population', but, in fact, most of the Germans in the territories now taken by the Russians had 'run away already' and this problem would be much easier in practice than had been supposed. He attached great importance to pencilled meetings of the Foreign Secretaries now agreed to and to the undertaking of the Three Great Powers to act together in peace as in war. On the way home he had seen, at Cairo, Ibn Saud[1] who had never before been outside Saudi Arabia and who had made it clear, when invited by Roosevelt to meet him, that he would not come to Cairo unless he was also going to meet the P.M. ...

Sir Montague Barlow to see me at my request. I am anxious to

1 Abdul Aziz II Ibn Saud (1880–1953). Ruler of the newly formed Saudi Arabian Kingdom 1932–53.

mobilise him for my Bill. I think he will play. He is seventy-seven years old and says that he is no longer a Conservative. *The Times* says this morning that my Bill is 'a triumph for the principles of the Barlow Report'. I write this in red ink on a copy of the Bill which I give to him. He is a vain old boy. ...

... [T]o vast reception at Soviet Embassy. I go upstairs to join the Ambassador and some forty or fifty of the elect. Gusev, who looked to me tonight rather like a little pig, was saying to Eden, 'We have been very patient with Mikolajczyk!' I found Citrine with Sidney Hillman [1] and Kuznetsov [2] the Russian trade union leader, who speaks excellent English and seems less mechanical in his responses than most Russians here. Citrine was complaining that, though the Big Six of the Trade Union Conference had today met Eden, Gusev and Winant at a specially arranged lunch to discuss trade union participation at San Francisco, they had got nowhere. Eden had told him that members of our own Government as well had objected 'on principle' to trade union participation. [Citrine] added that, 'Of course it was Bevin' (neither of these two can speak long without an ill word for the other). He then proceeded to say nice things about me, informing Hillman and Kuznetsov that I was the only Labour Party leader who had come out strongly for rearmament in the days before Munich and that in this I had been in complete agreement with him. Some other Labour members of the present Government, he added, probably did not wish to be reminded of the line they used to take then. Kuznetsov, to my regret, is going away tomorrow, otherwise I would have got him to come to our International Conference the weekend after next. I drink a good deal of vodka and not only this, but was also pressed by various of the Russians – who have a most persistent and hospitable trick of forcing food and drink upon one – to taste various Caucasian wines and liqueurs. Remembering an ancient rule of prudence, I continued to eat between the drinks and conducted myself with complete composure while in the Soviet Embassy but arriving back at the Board of Trade I was not able to dictate as much as I had hoped to Miss Wagstaff! [3]

1 Sidney Hillman (1887–1946). U.S. Labour leader. President of the Amalgamated Clothing Workers of America from 1914. Chairman of the C.I.O. Political Action Committee in 1943, which was prominent in the 1944 election campaign. Vice-President of the World Federation of Trade Unions 1945–6.
2 V. V. Kuznetsov (b. 1901). Soviet government official. Chairman of All-Union Central Trade Union Council 1944–54. Deputy Chairman of U.S.S.R. Gosplan 1940–44. Ambassador to China 1953. First Deputy Foreign Minister since 1955.
3 Miss Wagstaff. Diary secretary (in succession to Mrs Dean).
Marginal insertion: 'In fact, I was pretty drunk, and went to sleep on my bed for ¾ hour before seeing my staff!'

Thursday 1st March

After lunch have a further two hours with a large number of Labour M.P.s on my Bill. They are inclined to concentrate on their own constituencies and to ask why these are not in the Development Areas. But, on the whole, the reception is satisfactory, though, as one has so often noticed before, they don't seem to realise how much has been achieved in the face of great difficulties in getting thus far. Silkin[1] strikes the only discordant note saying that he thinks this is quite the wrong way to proceed.

Dine with Herbert Morrison and Ellen Wilkinson at the Howard Hotel, to meet Michael Foot. I find the latter rather disappointing, ideas a bit superficial and too many signs for a man of his age of nervous strain. But he has a gift of phrase and invective which are worth something.

Friday 2nd March

Harcourt Johnstone died last night. He had a stroke in his office in the afternoon and never recovered consciousness. They took him in an ambulance to the Westminster Hospital just round the corner. He was a queer man, and not a satisfactory or loyal colleague. But Mullins,[2] who comes to see me today, tells me that he had for some time been suffering from pains in his head and had been taking a lot of drugs for this. I now understand why he·was so disinclined to go to the House or to show himself in the Smoking Room. He had no really near relatives, the nearest being Listowel's mother.

Lakin,[3] Tory M.P. for Barry, comes to see me. He is most anxious for new developments in his constituency. I tell him he must back my Bill. ...

Molly Hamilton to dine with me. We speak of constituencies and I ask her whether she would be prepared to go back, if invited, to Blackburn. She thinks she would and, in any case, would rather like a Lancashire cotton seat.

Sunday 4th March

Dine this evening with Silkin at his flat at Great Peter Street. His wife,[4] who is a Russian Jewess, is also present, and after dinner the Solicitor-

---

1 Lewis Silkin, later 1st Baron (1889–1972). Labour M.P. for Peckham 1936–50. Minister of Town and Country Planning 1945–50. Father of John and Sam Silkin.
2 A. Mullins (1895–1963). Comptroller-General of the Department of Overseas Trade 1939–46.
3 C. H. A. Lakin (1893–1948). Conservative M.P. for Llandaff and Barry 1942–5.
4 Mrs Rosa Silkin, née Neft (d. 1947).

General[1] and his wife[2] come in. I much prefer the Solicitor-General to the Attorney-General, who is very reactionary and troublesome.

Silkin is an intelligent, though not very prepossessing or attractive, person, and we have quite a useful talk on my Bill, to which the edge of his opposition is now, I hope, somewhat blunted. At the end of the evening, when he and I are alone together, he raises the question of his entering the Government. He says that some time ago he was asked by Whiteley whether he would be willing to accept a Parliamentary Secretaryship. He then said 'No'. He asks my advice as to what line he should take now, saying there are four junior offices vacant. I strongly advise him to accept. It would give him valuable experience, even if he only held office for a few short closing months in the life of this Government. It would also raise his political status and make him more likely to hold important office in a future Labour Government. After discussion he says that he agrees with me and asks me whether I would inform Whiteley that his view is changed. I say that I will do so and promptly do, writing to Whiteley next day (Monday) and confirming this orally with Whiteley on Tuesday. I write to Silkin on Wednesday telling him what I have done, but receive later on the same day a letter from him, which had crossed mine, saying that, after talking it all over with his wife, he has changed his mind and would prefer me to take no action! It is a great mistake to be both changeable and slow.

Monday 5th March

Sir Edward Bridges to see me this evening. This is our first official talk since he succeeded Hopkins.[3] Sandys has asked for Franks[4] to come to the Ministry of Works and to help with housing. I am to be consulted because I have a contingent interest in Franks, who is now running the Raw Materials Control at the Ministry of Supply which will come back in due course to the Board of Trade. I say that housing is so important that, if Duncan will let Franks go, I won't object,

1 Sir David Maxwell-Fyfe, later 1st Earl of Kilmuir (1900–67). Solicitor-General 1942–5. Conservative M.P. for Liverpool West Derby 1935–54. Attorney-General 1945. Home Secretary 1951–4. Lord Chancellor 1954–62.
2 Sylvia Maxwell-Fyfe, née Harrison, later Dame Sylvia, Lady Kilmuir, later Countess de la Warr.
3 Bridges succeeded Sir Richard Hopkins (1880–1955) as Permanent Secretary to the Treasury in 1945.
4 O. Franks, later Sir Oliver, Baron (b. 1905). Permanent Secretary at the Ministry of Supply 1945–6. Temporary civil servant at the Ministry of Supply 1939–46. Professor of Moral Philosophy at Glasgow University 1937–45. Provost of Queen's College, Oxford 1946–8. Ambassador to the U.S. 1948–52. Chairman of Lloyds Bank 1954–62. Provost of Worcester College, Oxford 1962–76.

though I should naturally prefer, on my own behalf or that of my successor, that he should come over with the Controls to the Board of Trade. Bridges is rather against Franks going to Works, thinking he is not quite the man for this job. We then discuss other possibilities relating to the Higher Civil Service, and in particular the top end of the Board of Trade both past and present. No immediate change is likely here, but various future shifts, which might be made with the agreement, and indeed the satisfaction, of those concerned are cursorily canvassed.[1]

Wednesday 7th March
R.I. [Reconstruction of Industry] Committee on:

(i) Light metal industry
(ii) Management.

On the former Bevin is proposing a National Corporation and others, including Duncan, a predominantly private industry but with one or two R.O.F.s [Royal Ordnance Factories].[2] Cripps has put in a paper arguing against both of these. I say that I am much struck by this most impressive presentation of the anti-Socialist case. He doesn't think this at all funny! He says, 'Well you have often done the same thing yourself in the past.' Bevin says, 'Well you have just been taken back into the Labour Party.[3] Do you think you would like to defend this scheme of yours before an Annual Conference?' Finally it is left that Lyttelton, Duncan, Cripps and I should meet and work out a plan in greater detail.

Thursday 8th March
Dine with Blackburn, who produced Stuart Campbell, editor of the *Sunday Pictorial*, who had made a bad impression on me when I had given him lunch long before with Simmonds. He is no better tonight and irritates me a good deal, abusing the Labour Party and its leaders and laying down the law and slithering about from one indefensible proposition to another like an eel. Later, however, he behaves a bit better and says that he intends to urge all readers of the *Sunday*

---

1 Marginal insertion: 'I say that, with a passive President, plus Overton, nothing would ever happen at the Board of Trade! I advise him to look out for a good and honourable berth for Overton somewhere else in the course of the next year or two!'
2 Part of Dalton's plan for keeping industry and employment in the Development Areas after the war involved converting the great wartime Royal Ordnance Factories into industrial estates.
3 Cripps had been expelled from the Labour Party in 1939. For most of the war, he had been an Independent M.P.

Pictorial to vote against the Tories at the next election. I say that this will be all right and that most who follow his advice will vote Labour even if he doesn't directly tell them to. But I really don't want to meet this bounder again.

Friday 9th March
Dine with Phil Noel-Baker. He is a most charming person, though sometimes a little troublesome and over-pressing and subjective in his views.

The labour force in the textile and clothing industries dwindled in the latter part of the war much further than had been intended, with consequent effects on production. Dramatic falls in wholesale clothing stocks in 1944 and early 1945 were not significantly remedied by a 20 per cent switch of manpower from military to civilian clothing authorised by the Prime Minister early in 1945. Only when munitions production in the textile and clothing areas was curtailed was there a lasting improvement.[1]

Monday 12th March
War Cabinet. At long last Lyttelton's paper is taken, recommending that ex-cotton operatives should be withdrawn from munitions and other work 'without prior substitution' and even at the cost of some marginal damage to war production. This is accepted almost without debate; the only query having come from Cripps. The P.M. brushes this aside and says that it is quite clear that we are now so near the end of the war in Europe that some risks can be taken on the aircraft programme. I express thanks, but warn them that I shall have to come back for some more labour soon.

Dine with Gladwyn Jebb, whom I had not seen since his return from Yalta. It was only by a close shave that he and others had escaped death in the air crash which killed Peter Loxley and a number of other Foreign Office and Service people. This party of officials left by two aircraft, Gladwyn being in the first which made its course safely. But the second got far out of its route on the way to Naples and was signalled over Sardinia, then ordered on to Malta and came down in the sea near Lampedusa. Even so the occupants might have been saved,

1 E. L. Hargreaves and M. M. Gowing, *Civil Industry and Trade*, H.M.S.O., London, 1952, p. 475.

but immediately after hitting the surface of the water the aircraft struck a sunken wreck and the passengers, though not the crew, were all killed by the concussion.

At Yalta there was a strange contrast between the unlimited quantities of food and drink provided by the Russians and also the constant service of lady barbers, who smothered all who had a hair cut or a shave in very strong scent (Stalin is always very highly and grossly scented), and the very primitive sleeping conditions, seven or eight high officers and officials being packed together on camp beds in a tiny bedroom so small that all the beds are touching and luggage has to be put underneath them, and bugs in large numbers completed the company until Lord Moran appeared and took violent and effective counter measures. Stalin made a very great impression on all of them. He was exceedingly straightforward and sensible about everything, very good humoured and very patient, with no suggestion anywhere of doctrinaire opinions. He judged everything in terms of contributions to the common pool. He pushed aside the claims of the French to come to Yalta or to be consulted about the war, because, as he pointed out, they had only two or three Divisions on the upper Rhine. When someone suggested that we should pay regard to the views of the Pope – this I think was about Poland – Stalin asked, 'Why should we? How many Army Corps has the Pope got?' Stalin stood out head and shoulders above all the other Russians. Molotov has his points but is very obstinate and slow and, for these reasons, a troublesome person to negotiate with. Vyshinsky[1] is just a tough, though a clever lawyer. Maisky[2] seems to be coming back a bit into his own again, though he looks very unhappy and under-sized in the uniform which he is now always compelled to wear. He was allowed by Stalin to expound the Soviet proposals on reparations. While he was doing this, in English, Stalin was overheard to say, by one of the British party who understood a little Russian, 'I don't understand a word of English, but it sounds to me as though Maisky has got an African accent.' Maisky's thesis was that we should take away from Germany about 80 per cent of all their machines, and a great quantity of their manpower, to work on physical reparation in Russia and thereafter another 80 per cent of their physical production of everything that would be useful to the Allies and particularly to Russia. Gladwyn thought that this was fantastic arithmetic and quite outside the bounds of possibility. The flight of German civilians from East Prussia and Pomerania was on

1 A. Y. Vyshinsky (1883–1954). Soviet Deputy Foreign Minister 1940–49. Foreign Minister 1949–53.
2 Maisky, q.v., was at this time (1943–6) Assistant People's Commissar for Foreign Affairs.

an immense scale. The Russians have literally entered almost empty country. So much for the alleged difficulty of 'transfer of population'. On the other hand, this vast convulsive movement was leading to a crisis, even more severe than might otherwise have been anticipated, within the shrinking borders of the Reich. These Germans had all been fleeing from lands where more food was grown than eaten, to lands where little food was grown. This must lead soon to a catastrophic famine.

Wednesday 14th March

Talks, first with T.U.C. and then with a body of Labour M.P.s, on my Distribution of Industry Bill. The former are quite easy. The latter fortunately contain a majority of Members from the Development Areas, to whom I make a vigorous and slightly demagogic appeal, and get a good response. There are the usual complaints, especially vocal from Burke,[1] of particular areas being left out and Silkin – damned fool! – says that we ought to insist on putting London and Birmingham into the Bill in Clause 9. I say that this is quite the most certain way to wreck it and to deprive the Development Areas of all advantage, for we must, I repeat with tedious reiteration, play football with our heads as well as our feet. This view prevails and I anticipate we shall not only get a solid vote for the Second Reading, but, on the whole, sensible speeches.

Wednesday 21st March

My Bill gets a Second Reading without a division after a long debate, 'the rule being suspended' for an extra hour. I speak for more than an hour and, I hope, expound the thing clearly. I try to avoid giving way to would-be questioners and am surprisingly successful in this attempt, without exciting indignation. Otherwise I should have been going on for a couple of hours and the thread of the argument would have been completely broken up. The habit whereby Members jump up all through a minister's speech in order to put questions, most of which are quite silly, is very bad and I hope I have done something to restore the earlier practice whereby a continuous speech may be made as a basis of a later Debate. Today's Debate is worth reading. Opposition chiefly comes from the Midlands – Wardlaw-Milne, Schuster, W. J. Brown and Higgs.[2] On the other hand, in addition to Labour speakers, support is given by Norman Bower[3] who is sup-

1 W. A. Burke (1890–1968). Labour M.P. for Burnley 1935–59. Junior minister 1945–7.
2 W. F. Higgs (1886–1961). Conservative M.P. for Birmingham West 1937–45.
3 N. A. H. Bower (b. 1907). Conservative M.P. for Harrow West 1944–51.

posed to be speaking for the Tory Reform Group, Trevor Cox[1] and Greenwell,[2] a little bounder who sits for the Hartlepools. Lyttelton is quite good at the end, stressing the strategic argument in favour of control of location. I anticipate a lot of trouble in the Committee upstairs after Easter, but meanwhile we have advanced a definite step forward.

Wednesday 28th March

Labour Party National Executive this morning, in a rather talkative and time-wasting mood. Much discussion about the financial settlement with Gillies who, following Deakin's[3] intervention on his behalf, is to be paid seven-tenths of his present salary for the next $4\frac{1}{2}$ years and then to retire with his full pension. Morrison, Shinwell and Laski oppose this as being too generous, but it is carried by a good majority as a reasonable settlement, likely to prevent any serious row at the Conference. But, we say, it must not be regarded as a precedent in any future case and there is some doubt as to how the rules of our Staff Superannuation Society affect the case of any member proposed to be dispensed with on grounds of inefficiency. Gillies, according to the settlement, is to be 'given leave of absence' on 70 per cent of his salary for $4\frac{1}{2}$ years. It has been argued by the lawyers that, if we said we dismissed him, he could not draw any pension at all from the Fund, but would only be entitled to a refund of his own contribution and this would be a very meagre provision. ...

Dine with Bruce-Gardner at the Café Royal ...

Bruce-Gardner would quite like, I think, to be Chairman of a Public Board to take charge of the iron and steel industry under a Labour Government. He agrees that something of this sort is necessary. He tells how Willie Graham, when President of the Board of Trade in 1930, asked him for a report which, he said, would be of interest to his colleagues, since the Labour Government of the day was thinking of nationalising the industry. Bruce-Gardner repeated this to Montagu Norman and they were then both invited to the Cabinet Room at No. 10 with MacDonald, Snowden and Graham, and no one else. Snowden was 'looking very sardonic'. Bruce-Gardner repeated what Graham had said to him, whereupon the latter blushed

1 H. B. Trevor Cox (b. 1908). Conservative M.P. for Stalybridge and Hyde 1937–45. Later joined the Labour Party. Major A. A. Command H.Q. 1944–6. Served on General Staff, 1940–44.

2 T. G. Greenwell (1894–1967). Conservative M.P. for the Hartlepools 1943–5.

3 Arthur Deakin (1890–1955). National Secretary of the General Workers' group of the Transport and General Workers' Union 1932–46. General Secretary of the Transport and General Workers' Union 1946–55.

and became very confused and denied the story. The meeting then broke up and Montagu Norman said to Bruce-Gardner as they went away, 'I think that's the last we shall hear of that. Of course, you couldn't expect the P.M. in a Labour Government to say that he didn't want to nationalise this industry.' I don't think this story reflects credit on any of the persons concerned.

Thursday 29th March
Leithers [Leith-Ross] to lunch at the Étoile. We talk about the progress of U.N.R.R.A. and his various disappointments. He is finding the Russians difficult. He thinks it partly is because they are excessively bureaucratic at Moscow, though their distrust of foreigners no doubt enters in too. He believes it is inevitable that there will be great starvation in Germany. He does not see how it can be avoided that 10 per cent of them should starve to death. I say that they should be able to live, even though on a very low level, on their present stocks plus their next harvest. But he is doubtful of this. He thinks it very unfortunate that we should have captured in the West, and be feeding very well, a large number of the worst type of Germans from the S.S. etc. ...

Dine alone with Mrs Phillimore. Her prejudice against the Americans is quite an obsession. She can't keep off it.

A conference to set up the United Nations Organisation, along lines agreed at Yalta, opened in San Francisco on 25th April. The British delegation was led by Eden, and included, at senior ministerial level, Attlee and Cranborne.

Wednesday 4th April
Talk with Attlee who is leaving for San Francisco on the 17th. I urge him to have a word with the P.M. before he leaves to make sure that no election will be declared during his absence. He must, in any case, come back for our Party Conference even if he has to return afterwards. He asks what I think of Arthur Jenkins's appointment.[1] I say that I am very pleased with it. He says that he had to fight very hard to get it, since the P.M. first thought of appointing Tories to three of the four vacant Under-Secretaryships, putting in old Jim Rothschild[2] as Sinclair's 'pound of flesh'. Attlee thinks it a very good thing that we

1 Marginal insertion: 'Under-Secretary Town and Country Planning'.
2 J A. de Rothschild (1878–1957). Joint Parliamentary Secretary at the Ministry of Supply 1945. Liberal M.P. for the Isle of Ely 1924–45.

have now promoted two P.P.S.s to be Under-Secretaries. Both are good on merits and in addition it will be good encouragement to the P.P.S.s as a body. I also speak to him about Piercy and advise that he should urge on Shepherd, before leaving, the importance of finding Piercy a seat. I also mention the House of Lords. But he doesn't take much to this, saying, what is quite true, that people who go to the Lords without having had any experience of the Commons aren't much good. If Piercy were in the House of Commons for a year or two he would get on in the other place later. ...

With Bruce-Gardner to see Bevin who tells us, what we knew two days ago, that the provisional date for the end of the war in Europe is now fixed at 31st May. Bevin seems afraid that if we get a lot of labour transferred from munitions to peace production we shan't know what to do with it. I am getting very tired of this. We constantly clamour for more labour, hundreds of thousands more bodies, as distinct from paper plans and programmes, and can absorb [them?] in any area and over a wide range of civilian and export industries. Bruce-Gardner is very persistent and helpful in all this.

Gaitskell is to take two months' rest on doctor's orders. His heart is not quite right.[1] I hope, and think, that this is not really serious, but he has been over working for years and has never seemed physically very strong. He is a bit concerned as to whether the election will come before he has had his rest. I hope, and am inclined to think, it won't, but one can't be sure.

Sunday 8th April
Speak at Alfreton and Belper with, and for, George Brown, who has just been adopted for the Belper Division in succession to George Dallas. A very good type of young trade union candidate. Unless something goes wrong he should win the seat. Both these are good meetings, and at Belper a group of very keen and clear cut young men have taken charge who, till a few weeks ago, were the local Communist Party. They have all come over in a lump and have already, for the first time in history, started to build something real in this town. They give me a sense of great competence and relief, after some of the old buffers who have been muddling along in charge of our local parties for a generation.

Monday 9th April
I walk down Whitehall with Bob [Fraser] and urge him to make up his mind, pretty soon, to cut loose from the Civil Service if he wanted to be a Candidate next time. The political tide was racing, I said, and

---

1 Gaitskell suffered a minor heart attack early in March.

he should by now have made up his mind about the alternative offers which were open to him. He is inclined to be a bit slow.

Tuesday 10th April
Memorial Service to Lloyd George[1] in Westminster Abbey. Rather ironical in view of Lloyd George's hatred and contempt in his younger days for the established Church and his fervent non-conformist radicalism. There is nothing Welsh in today's service. It is one of those impersonal performances, which I have thought before so completely missed out all individuality. Apart from one brief reference to Lloyd George by name, in one of the prayers, it might equally well have been anyone else.

Outside the Abbey door I had a word with Bevin, who had made a heavy attack in a weekend speech upon the Tory Party, and set the press humming with talk of an immediate break-up of the Government and an early election. Bevin, who seems very pleased with himself, grinned and said, 'I wouldn't stand Beaverbrook writing these articles any longer.' There had been many insinuations that Bevin would dissociate himself from other Labour ministers when the time came. I never believed this.

Meet, with one or two of my colleagues, Vernon Bartlett to see whether he would join the Labour Party. He won't – at any rate at present – and will, therefore, I think, be defeated at Bridgwater by the Tory in a three-cornered fight.[2]

Wednesday 11th April
... [M]eeting in Attlee's room with Labour ministers, both large and small, to discuss S. Frisco, whither Attlee and a number of others, including George Tomlinson and Ellen Wilkinson, are going next week. The discussion turns to military commitments for the future and whether we should permanently adopt conscription. The general feeling of the meeting was that we should, but I really don't see why they need keep trying to rush this decision. It will not be raised at S. Frisco in any definite fashion and it is surely enough, for the moment, to say that the present call-up must go on for several years, until we see where we are. Several people made the point that rockets, and extensions of this idea in the future, could only be dealt with by land forces, and not by sea and air alone. Bevin said that if the Russians were on the Oder in the future, they might be able to shoot rockets at

1 David Lloyd George (who had been made 1st Earl of Dwyfor) died on 26th March 1945.
2 In fact, standing as an Independent, Bartlett, q.v., held Bridgwater in a three-cornered fight. He did not stand again in 1950.

this country from that distance. These are not good thoughts.

I speak to Attlee alone after the meeting and urge him to get perfectly clearly from the P.M. an undertaking that while Attlee was away
there could be no question of breaking up the Government or giving
notice of any intention to dissolve Parliament. If this were not clear
I said Attlee ought not to go. He said he was sure that this would be
all right; that he had already spoken to the P.M. who had agreed that
it would be most unfair to do anything of this kind in his absence. I
hope that Attlee and the rest of us are in no danger of being outwitted
as a result of pressure on the P.M. by Max and Bracken.

REMEMBER, GENTLEMEN,
NO QUESTIONS ASKED
ABOUT OUR PRIVATE LIVES
OUTSIDE ..... BUT ALL IS
PEACE AND LOYALTY
WITHIN

JUST A BIG HAPPY FAMILY

Thursday 12th April
War Cabinet on manpower. A shocking show! If an account of this
morning's discussion was published, this Government would perish
in ridicule and contempt. There seems to be complete confusion as
to the meaning and implications of, and the distinctions between, the
following:

(i) V.E. Day. Does this mean that from this day the war with
Germany would be over? If so, will all labour controls cease?

Bevin, supported by Cripps, says 'Yes'. Then there can be no more direction of labour and there is no sense in making any labour 'allocations' for the second half of 1945. What will happen will be that a mass of people will be discharged into an unregulated labour market. This astonishes the P.M. and several others, who say that this is certainly not what was intended. How, in that case, could labour be held in making munitions for the Jap war, or directed toward work of primary importance rather than to inessentials?

(ii) Cease Fire Day. This has already been discussed in connection with workers' holidays. But, if there are still German pockets of resistance to be mopped up, how can we 'cease fire'? Will this, therefore, be before, after or coincident with V.E. Day?

(iii) A 'spontaneous outburst of rejoicing', which might arise here, and in the U.S., when Berlin falls or, even earlier, when the Russians and the Americans meet somewhere near Berlin. Would this not, in effect, be the same as V.E. Day? Beaverbrook has been pressing this argument on the P.M. His game all through is to try to hurry up the election and, therefore, V.E. Day as its preliminary. He is very persistent on all this and it is a bad sign that the P.M., more obviously than ever this morning, is paying heed to him and meeting him off stage.

(iv) The 'end of Hostilities' and

(v) The 'end of the war'. These two last have great legal importance for contracts, etc. How are they related to the others?

Obviously nobody had ever thought all this out. I have no direct Departmental locus, so it is not my responsibility, but it is really a disgraceful omission on the part of some of those concerned. Bevin, as against Beaverbrook, is playing for a postponement of the election and tells me later in the day that the P.M. was very much concerned at what he had said this morning and 'was on to me again about it this afternoon'. It is left that 'the officials' shall go into it and produce a report!

At the close of this morning Herbert Morrison and Eden raised the question of Pollitt being allowed to go to Finland to attend a Communist Conference. It is agreed that he shall be allowed to go, but that no special facilities shall be provided for him. This means that he won't be able to get there. The P.M. winds up a cheerful denunciation of the Communists by declaring that 'They have founded a religion, but they left God out of it. They are Christians without Christ, Jesuits without Jesus!' Morrison says to me, 'I wish he would say that in public.'

Wednesday 18th April
Ness Edwards[1] brings two sleek dark (clothing) Jews to see me. They want a factory at Caerphilly. I am all for their having it.

Lunch with Garro [Jones], who wants to explain to me why he has decided not to stand at the next election. He doesn't like Attlee, who as good as offered him the post of Parliamentary Secretary to Civil Aviation, and then, not being able to bring this off, wasn't frank with him about it. He is not very happy about his constituency, though it should be safe enough at the next election, since there have been moves of a Communist character there. But he admits that his own personal position is quite strong. He has been seeing something of Catto, whom he has known for a long time, and has been talking to him about the possibility of going into business. He finds he doesn't have much time, while in the Government, to see his wife and two young children. He has no difference at all with the Party over policy. He may be able to serve the Party again later in some other capacity. I don't find this, in the total, quite convincing and have never felt that I completely understood him, though he is able, energetic and a good friend of mine. He says he hopes that we shall keep in touch with one another even though he is out of Parliament. It is no good arguing about his decision, since he has both taken it and told his constituents and the press.

Brigadier Taverner to see me. He has just come back after three and a half years as a prisoner-of-war in Germany. His aeroplane came down over the Bay of Biscay when he was flying out from London to take over S.O.E. Middle East for me. Of the fourteen of them, nine were drowned and he was only picked up by a German seaplane after being in a dinghy for three days and nights. He had rather a bad time as a prisoner-of-war, for they threatened to send him to a Concentration Camp as a civilian, because they had ascertained that he had travelled from New York to Lisbon as 'Mr' Taverner. So, they said, he wasn't really a soldier at all but a Secret Agent. In fact, and at that time, before the U.S. were in the war, they all had to travel as civilians. I arranged for Selborne to see him.

International Sub. Only Ellen Wilkinson of the three who are going

1 Ness Edwards (1897–1968). Labour M.P. for Caerphilly 1939–68. Junior minister 1945–50. Postmaster-General 1950–51.

to S. Frisco is there. She gives quite a good account of the discussions with the Dominion representatives. Shinwell is becoming very 'realistic' about Big Powers and upsets Aneurin Bevan who is not really a member of the Sub-Committee but was allowed to come because S. Frisco was to be discussed. When I rebuke Bevan from the Chair for interrupting and tell him that he is only here by courtesy and must listen to other people, he rushes from the room in a temper. They are terribly sensitive to counter-attack, these aggressive people!

Thursday 19th April
See Bevin and give him copies of the P.M.'s Minute to me and my reply on clothing labour. He says that he proposed long ago to the P.M. that we should divert labour from the Services to the civilians but that this was refused then. ...

I say that I am glad to read a statement that he is to act for Attlee during the latter's absence. He grumbles that Attlee only spoke to him about this at the last moment and didn't tell him much of what he was expected to do. Then some desultory talk. He thinks that V. Day has now been considerably postponed. The P.M. got the wind up when he heard all the difficulties about direction of labour after V. Day. Bevin said, 'He's all right as a National Leader, but, when he turns into the Leader of the Tory Party, you can't trust him an inch. He just becomes a crook.' Meanwhile, the row, caused by Bevin's speech followed by Bracken's, has now quite settled down and this weekend Bevin and Alexander are to go to Bristol with the P.M. who will give them both Honorary Degrees in the University. Bevin obviously likes this very much. As regards the possibility of the Government going on until the end of the Jap war he says he told the P.M. that the thing mustn't be discussed in terms of any intrigue. If the P.M. had any suggestion to make, he should make it officially and straightforwardly to the leaders of the other two parties. ...

Dine with Blackburn, who has collected quite an interesting party. Bellenger is one of these and makes a better impression on me than usually. Blackburn wants to accompany me on one of my trips. I say that he can come with me to the North-East the week after next if he is free. Following this there won't be another chance for some time. I take back in my car Fletcher-Cooke,[1] now in the War Cabinet Offices, our Prospective Candidate for East Dorset.[2]

1 Lieutenant-Commander C. F. Fletcher-Cooke (b. 1914). Barrister. Member of Joint Intelligence Staff of the War Cabinet 1942–4. Labour parliamentary candidate 1945. Conservative M.P. for Darwen 1951–83. Junior minister 1961–3.
2 Marginal insertion: '(Freeman, I hear, has been adopted for Watford. One of the very best.)'

Friday 20th April

By train to Swansea, arriving soon after 9 p.m. ... Thence to the Mansion House where I am the guest of the Mayor for three nights. It is a very pleasant house looking out to the south, down a sloping lawn, to some quite magnificent and very well grown trees – which a fool would cut in order to get a better view. In the foreground there are two magnificent ilexes, a superb chestnut, with a well mixed variety at the back, both pines and broad leaved, and some very lovely little flowering trees in the front. The Mayor – Alderman Watkins[1] – is an old collier, a very friendly, simple and typically Welsh personality. The butler is a tall man who looks at me fixedly when I arrive and, following me up to my bedroom, looks at me again and asks whether I remember him. Drawing a bow at a venture I ask, 'Weren't you at the Gnoll?'[2] He is deeply moved at this recognition and says that indeed he was and that he remembers me very well coming there for holidays from school.[3] He is a few months older than I am. He was the boy about the house working under an old tyrant of a butler, whom I well remember, named Veale. He brings to show me a book presented to him by my Grandmother[4] in 1907. He is George Morris and has been in charge of the Mansion House for a number of years.

Tuesday 24th April

Go down to Milland to see Hugh Gaitskell. He has now been in bed for about a fortnight and has another week of the prescribed period to run. After that he is to have two months of pretty complete rest. He is naturally concerned about the election. If he makes reasonable progress and the election is not till the autumn, there should not be much doubt about his being able to fight. But, if it comes this side of August, it might be difficult. And this would be a very bad disappointment for him. We agreed that he should see Horder if any such sudden developments occurred. He has already mentioned this to Hamilton, his G.P., of whom I did not, on his story, think much, and Parkinson, the heart specialist whom he saw. They both said they would welcome Horder's opinion.

---

1 Alderman T. E. Watkins, later Baron (b. 1903). Alderman of Breconshire County Council 1940–74. Labour M.P. for Brecon and Radnor 1945–70. A miner for eight years.
2 The house of Dalton's Welsh grandfather, Charles Evan-Thomas, and Dalton's own birthplace. As a boy, Dalton spent many holidays at the Gnoll, which was later presented to Neath Borough Council by Dalton's uncles.
3 Marginal insertion: 'from Eton'.
4 Cara Evan-Thomas.

He and Dora and his two daughters – of whom I remember Julia[1] very well three years ago at Woburn, she is now just six – are living in a pink washed house which they have just sold, reached through most lovely country. I had forgotten how good the views were from the Portsmouth Road, just before reaching the Devil's Punch Bowl at Haslemere. Gaitskell's mother[2] lives close by and he has an old farmhouse, now broken up and used as two cottages, which he hopes to go into after the war. I hope he will soon get better. I too should be greatly disappointed if he couldn't fight and win at Leeds next time.

Wednesday 25th April
Lunch with Will Henderson. It is on the cards that he will go to the Lords in the Birthday Honours.[3] Ellen Wilkinson spoke to Attlee and so did I. We agreed how few Labour peers were fit to hold office in a Labour Government. We were always 'strengthening the Labour Party' in the Lords but it never seemed to get any better! I said that, of the present lot, only Listowel, Latham and, doubtfully, Winster could, in my view, be considered for office. He again pressed the view that I should go to the Foreign Office if we won. He said that, if I wanted it, 'There are really no competitors.' I said I didn't want to fix my mind too soon, but that, if offered the Foreign Office I didn't think I should have the heart to refuse it! He said, in that case, he would like to be one of my Parliamentary Under-Secretaries, since it would be useful to have one in the Lords as well as the Commons. We agreed that it all turned on keeping the London-Washington-Moscow Triangle in good shape. ...

Dine with Piercy, Wilmot, Jay and Berry at the Reform Club. The old Liberals here are said to be getting very jealous of the Labour Party and horrified to find they have so many members of the Party in the Club! I said that, in that case, we had better be careful in suggesting that I should join it, as I had half thought of doing. There will be a new Club Committee next month and we will wait till then and see who is on it. Beveridge, who is now completely airborne, is a very prominent personage here and it will not make him love the Labour Party any more that we have this very morning endorsed a Labour Candidate against him in Berwick.[4] Probably this will have the result of putting the Conservative in! But Beveridge should have joined the

---

1 Julia Gaitskell, later Mrs McNeal (b. 1939). Gaitskell's second daughter, Cressida, later Mrs Wasserman, was born in 1942.

2 Adelaide Gaitskell, née Jamieson, later Mrs Wodehouse (d. 1956).

3 He did.

4 In the July 1945 General Election, Sir William Beveridge was defeated at Berwick, which he had won for the Liberals the previous year.

Labour Party long ago and it is his own fault if, after lecturing us publicly and boasting of helping to put 500 Liberal Candidates into the field, he finds that we too are not content to be wholly negative!

Thursday 26th April
Talk to George Shepherd about constituencies for a few outstanding people who are not yet fixed. Specially press Bob Fraser, Molly Hamilton and Piercy. Shepherd will send on the first two names to North Aberdeen, now to be vacated by Garro [Jones]. This is a good seat which we have only lost once, in 1931. Both, he says, have Scots names. I say yes, but one talks with a strong Australian accent and the other is a woman. Still it would be very good for either. East Hull is also becoming vacant, through Muff's retirement. He told them, 'If you don't agree with me, you'd better find another Candidate', and to his great astonishment they took him literally. One of the Sunderland seats will probably be vacant through Fred Peart[1] moving across to Workington. But this is less attractive, though the Hull people are said to be both quarrelsome and corrupt. Piercy's name has been sent forward both for the new Coventry Division, which is very good, including part of the mining area in the old Nuneaton Division, and also for Wycombe, which is a new Division and a bit of a speculation. I speak also of Mike Williams-Thompson and understand that it should be possible, even from India, to get him back for the Selection Conference at East Wolverhampton. And, if he is then in the country, we might push him in somewhere else, even if that failed.[2] Tom Williamson should also get fixed up soon, though I don't feel it is my job to push *him*. Shepherd hopes that he will get Silvertown. Apart from a number of the new Divisions in greater London, many of which are pure speculations but some of which ought to come off all right, there is not much left at the moment which looks at all attractive.

Saturday 28th April
Rather a full and tiring day, most of which we spend at Newcastle at the Annual Meeting of the Northern Regional Council. I address the Conference on my Distribution of Industry Bill and get a good reception. Sam Watson makes an excellent Chairman. Then back by car with Will Davies and George Gibson, who always talks one's head

---

1 T. F. Peart, later Baron (b. 1914). Labour M.P. for Workington 1945–76. Minister of Agriculture, Fisheries and Food 1964–8, 1974–6. Lord Privy Seal 1968. Lord President of the Council 1968–70. Leader of the House of Commons 1968–70. Lord Privy Seal and Leader of the House of Lords 1976–9.
  Both Sunderland seats were won for Labour in 1945.
2 Marginal insertion: 'East Wolverhampton'.

off, to a delegate meeting at the Lightfoot,[1] which I address for just over an hour. I tell them that, if the signal for the Election is not hoisted by the middle of June – and it may well be – it is likely to go over till the autumn. They are a wonderfully good loyal lot, but not very talkative. Jack Bell had a tummy ache and George Gibson takes the Chair.

Sunday 29th April

Meet this afternoon at Coundon,[2] about 120 people in the Cinema, but it is all still very dead. And it is very natural that this should be so on a Sunday afternoon, with the war not quite over, and no opposition in the field.

Call, as invited, this afternoon on Dr Cama,[3] whom I had never met before. He has collected quite a party of family and friends and I relate a number of stories, which Will Davies has often heard before, but which interest and, indeed, quite thrill these good people. Dr Cama is, I am told, a Jamaican halfcaste. Dr Cherry,[4] the local doctor who attended me ten years ago when I had lumbago during the Election Campaign, is a Buck Nigger. I think he is probably the better doctor of the two.

Tuesday 1st May

Receive young Tories – Molson,[5] Hinchingbrooke, Hamilton Kerr[6] and Bower – to discuss the Distribution of Industry Bill. They will give me 'steady but not undiscriminating support'. I think they quite like their reception.

Monday 7th May

A great doubt as to whether today would be V.E. Day. Will it be announced tonight? It should have been, but the Americans and the Russians insisted on delaying it till tomorrow so as to get all the surrender business complete.

---

1 In Dalton's constituency.

2 A pit village in Dalton's constituency.

3 Dr L. S. D. Cama. Local doctor; former house surgeon at the Royal Victorian Infirmary, Newcastle.

4 Dr W. J. B. Cherry. G.P. in Barnard Castle.

5 A. H. E. Molson, later Baron (b. 1903). Conservative M.P. for Doncaster 1931–5; High Peak 1939–61. Junior minister 1951–7. Minister of Works 1957–9.

6 H. W. Kerr, later Sir Hamilton, 1st Bart (1903–74). Conservative M.P. for Oldham 1931–45; Cambridge 1950–66. Junior minister 1945.

On 29th April the German commander in Italy, General von Vietinghoff, surrendered unconditionally to the Allies. Next day Hitler committed suicide in Berlin. On 4th May, a delegation from his named successor, Admiral Doenitz, led by Admiral Hans von Friedeburg, surrendered all German forces in Holland, Denmark and North Germany. On 7th May General Jodl surrendered on behalf of the German Supreme Command.

Tuesday 8th May
Today is V.E. Day.

Wednesday 9th May
Meeting of the Three Bodies[1] to consider a statement by Bevin on the future of conscription. He gives many arguments for continuing it and says he thinks the Cabinet should make a statement to this effect before Whitsun. The voluntary army in the past has been largely recruited by unemployment. We can't have this in the future and our full employment policy should, in any case, make it impossible. We shall have for some years to continue the call-up in order to enable the older men and those with longest service to be released, and as a contribution to Collective Security. His idea is that there should be one year's service between the ages of seventeen and twenty-two, this wide choice to allow scope for all sections including apprentices and university students. Thereafter one month a year in the Reserve for five years. Sea and air will be no use against the V. weapons and their development. We must have land plans too.

Bevin relates how Strang, when he saw Stalin in 1939, was asked how many Divisions Britain could put into the field against Germany; Strang said two. Stalin said, 'Soviet Russia will have to put in 500, so that will make 502.' There is a good deal of support for Bevin's view, though some are reluctant to take any responsibility. Dukes says that he can't commit himself without consulting his Executive. We separate into our three sections and after most irritating time-wasting by Shinwell and Bevan, the National Executive agrees to support the continuance, for a term of years, though without prejudice to a long-term policy, of compulsory military service. Bevin says that this is all he wants.

1 The General Council of the T.U.C., the National Executive of the Labour Party, and the Administrative Committee of the P.L.P.

Take Michael Young[1] to lunch at Marsham Restaurant. I don't find him particularly sympathetic, but he is quite capable I think.

Dine with Piercys – William, Mary and Priscilla[2] – at Josef's and afterwards walk about in the crowds on this second Victory night in Trafalgar Square, Whitehall, etc. The flood lighting is again very lovely and everyone, again, as last night, most happy and orderly.

Thursday 10th May

Cecil Malone[3] to see me at Shepherd's suggestion to ask why the National Executive objected to putting him on List 'B'.[4] 'I said they were 'disquieted' by stories of his activities in relation to Finland, the Ukraine and Japan. The first two seemed to be anti-Soviet and the third anti-Chinese. He says that none of this is true and promises to send me a letter. In the first and third cases he was promoting an innocent and non-political Travel Agency, in the second case he had no contacts with the Ukranian Movement organised from Berlin, but only its American and Canadian counterpart. Not a very nice person!

Bevin and Morrison confer with a number of junior ministers. All agree that an October election would be better than one in June. Our stock is steadily climbing and will go on. Where do the two curves cross?

Friday 11th May

Have a word alone with Morrison this afternoon. He and Bevin saw the P.M. earlier today. The latter had his Chief Whip with him. Morrison thinks that the P.M. has not yet made up his mind about the election date. He guesses, however, that the odds are still two or three to one in favour of a June election. The P.M. said that he was under very heavy pressure from the Tory Party to take it quickly. (Bevin had reported that the P.M. had said to him when they were alone,

---

1 Michael Young, later Baron (b. 1915). Secretary to the Labour Party Research Department 1945–51. Sociologist and writer. Director of Political and Economic Planning 1941–5; Institute of Community Studies since 1953. Chairman of the Consumer Association 1956–65; Advisory Centre for Education 1959–76; Social Science Research Council 1965–8; National Consumer Council 1975–7.
2 Priscilla Piercy, later Mrs Taylor (b. 1926). Daughter of William and Mary Piercy.
3 Lieutenant-Colonel C. J. L'Estrange Malone (1890–1966). Coalition Liberal, then British Socialist, then Communist M.P. for East Leyton 1918–22. Labour M.P. for Northampton 1928–31. Worked at the Admiralty Small Vessels Pool 1943–5. Dalton had known Malone since the early 1920s. In 1923 he referred in his diary to Malone's 'record of bloomers' (17th February).
4 'List "B" ': an approved list of potential parliamentary candidates kept by Transport House.

'They know they can't win without me' and also that it was a bitter thought that, having been a national leader for so long, and having been so kindly treated by all, he would soon be attacked and spoken ill of by nearly half the nation!)

Morrison added that he and Bevin had put the case very strongly in favour of an October election, but that he personally had argued against any possibility of further prolonging the life of this Parliament though, he thought, Bevin would like to do this and go on as long as the Jap war. But Morrison thought, and I agreed, that neither the country nor our own Party would swallow any further extension. Morrison said they had used the arguments to the P.M. about the badness of the present Register which would not be renewed until 15th October, and the argument that by October a large number of Servicemen would have returned. The P.M., he thought, was a little afraid of having the Municipal elections on 1st November before the Parliamentary elections, because, if we did very well at the Municipals, this would have a great influence on the Parliamentary. He told the P.M. that, of course, the Labour Party machine was in quite good shape now and we could certainly face a June election. The Tories certainly believe that our machine is less rusty than theirs and this so far as it goes, is an argument for them to wait till October, but the argument on the other side is very much stronger. Attlee and Eden are both returning from S. Frisco and it would obviously be very indecent for the P.M. to make a final decision until he has seen Attlee. But he can't delay the decision very long, if he wants to get the election over before the middle of July, when harvests and holidays begin.

I am inclined, therefore, to bet on a June/July election, though October still remains a possibility.

Bevin said yesterday that we should be in a very strong position if we had definitely offered the P.M. to remain with him until the end of the present Parliament and co-operate in passing good and great measures and taking other necessary action for the transition. If he refused this we should let the facts be known.

Saturday 12th to Monday 14th May
At Birmingham ... An encouraging weekend. We are getting quite a good body of Candidates into the field at the West Midlands, though one cannot have the same confidence in the electorate as in the Candidates.

Listen on Sunday night (13th May 1945) to P.M.'s 9 o'clock broadcast, thinking that he may drop some hint as to whether he was for a quick or a slow election. But there was no hinting. He sounded very tired.

Monday 14th May

Back from Birmingham. Blackburn comes with me and stays to lunch. He has plenty of energy and personality. We speak of Rupert Brooke and I present him with my spare copy of the Memoirs and the Poems.[1]

Thursday 17th May

Lunch with Lyttelton at Drapers' Court. He makes a short amusing speech, then we return together to the Royal Gallery where addresses are presented by the Lord Chancellor and the Speaker to the King, who makes a reply. This is what is called 'An historical occasion'. But it lacked, I thought, any real distinction.

Returning I had a word alone with Attlee, part of which I have noted already. We spoke of the election. He said he thought the P.M. would perhaps make up his mind tonight. He was still quite undecided. He said the Tory pressure on him for a quick election was very strong. On the other hand the 'national points' had been put, especially

(i) that it would be unfair to the civilians because the Register was so bad and so many had moved e.g. evacuees and building trade workers engaged on bomb damage in London,

(ii) that it would be unfair to the Servicemen, none of whom would be home in time to vote now but 500,000 of whom at least would be back before November, and would be reabsorbed in civil life,

(iii) that this was a time when, particularly as there were no difficulties between the parties on International Policy, we should maintain a united front for the next few months and not seem to be absorbed in party conflicts, and

(iv) that there was much useful legislation passing through Parliament which we should complete before the session ended.

I had written all this to Attlee in a letter yesterday and had also told him that Bevin and Morrison had been getting on quite surprisingly well while he had been away! Attlee seemed to think today that the odds were rather in favour of a quick one. On the other hand, Waterhouse, to whom I mention the matter this afternoon, seemed to take – though with some regret – the opposite view.

1 Marginal insertion: '*Tendebantque manus ripae ulterioris amore.*' The reference is to the River Styx (Virgil, *Aeneid*, vi. 314). 'Their hands stretched out in longing for the shore beyond the river' (C. Day Lewis, tr., *The Eclogues, Georgics and Aeneid of Virgil*, Oxford University Press, London, 1966, p. 293).

After the ending of the European war, Churchill was advised by Tory managers to cash in on his prestige and fight an immediate election. Instead, he wrote on 18th May to the leaders of the other Coalition parties offering them one of two alternatives: an immediate election or a continuation of the Coalition until the end of the war against Japan.

Friday 18th May
To Blackpool for Labour Party Conference. I remain here till 23rd May 1945. This is a dramatic Conference, reminding us of that of five years ago at Bournemouth.

Before leaving on Friday (18th) Attlee asked me to come round and see him in the morning. Bevin was also there. Morrison and Ellen Wilkinson had already left for Blackpool. Attlee said that the P.M. had asked him to call just after midnight last night. He had then proposed that we should go on till the end of the Japanese war. Failing this, it seemed that the election would be in July rather than October. Attlee was in favour of going on. Bevin and I were inclined to agree. But we doubted whether the Conference would take it.

The issue of the date of the forthcoming election was discussed at a meeting of the N.E.C. in Blackpool, just before Party Conference.

Saturday 19th May
At Blackpool. Morrison is very definitely against going on till end of Jap war. Wilmot was first in favour, but later changed his mind. So did Bevin and I. Attlee still advised the Executive to agree. But there was a substantial majority the other way. Burrows, Burke and Williamson were inclined to be in favour, all others against. I suggested, but no one backed me up, that we should say we were against a July election; were prepared to go on till November; and, just before November was reached, we would talk again in the light of the state of Jap war. But this was too cunning for the others. Finally we agree that we should not accept end of Jap war and that we would put it to the P.M. that we were still in favour of October election. The letter was to be drafted by three War Cabinet Ministers. But Bevin said he

wasn't interested. Therefore, it was left to Attlee and Morrison and they produced their draft next day and it was read, hurriedly by Attlee on the back of the Platform to N.E.C. We let it go, but it was not too good. In particular, many afterwards thought that reference to Referendum as Nazi or Fascist device was not persuasive. It is clear that the Old Boy has been hustled along by Max and Bracken and by the Tory Head Office.

On the next few days the Conference rises to great heights. We have a finer body of Labour Candidates, including a large number of young Service Candidates, than ever before. It is very moving to see, and hear, these young men. Ellen is an admirable Chairman and always gives the preference to youth on the floor.

The Conference opens on 21st May 1945 and on the next day Morrison begins and I wind up a Debate on 'Let us Face the Future'.[1] We both get a great ovation. I begin by picking up small points about fish, cotton etc., but make an impromptu peroration ten minutes long. The Conference rises at this and I have to rise and bow and make the V. sign.

Next day Attlee and Bevin speak on the International situation and both likewise get an ovation, Bevin the greatest.[2]

Among young Service Candidates I single out Freeman, Desert Rat, who took the surrender of Hamburg and is our Candidate for Watford; Kenneth Younger, just back from Twenty-First Army Group H.Q., Intelligence, Candidate for Grimsby; Raymond Blackburn whom we know; and a bunch of others, including Air Vice-Marshal de Crespigny,[3] whom I introduced to Fred Burrows who said, 'I can't believe it. Either that's not your name or you aren't a Labour Candidate.' The Air Vice-Marshal is, in fact, our Candidate for Newark.

Wednesday 23rd May
Return this afternoon, with Harold Wilson, our Candidate for Ormskirk, and John Pudney,[4] our Candidate for Sevenoaks.

1 'Let Us Face the Future': the title of Labour's 1945 election manifesto.
2 Marginal insertion (at the top of the page): 'Ellen wanted Attlee to retire in favour of Morrison. Couldn't I persuade him? I said it was impossible to change now.'
3 Air Vice-Marshal H. V. Champion de Crespigny (1897–1969). Labour candidate for Newark-on-Trent 1945. A former fighter pilot. Regional Commissioner for Schleswig-Holstein Control Commission in Germany 1946–7.
4 J. S. Pudney (1909–77). Journalist, poet and fiction writer. He became popular in the 1930s with his short stories and first novel, *Jacobson's Ladder*, and won further attention during the war when his lyrics were used in the film *The Way to the Stars*. Literary critic of the *Daily Express* 1947–8. Literary Editor of the *News Review* 1948–50. Contested Sevenoaks for the Labour Party 1945.

On 21st May, the Labour Party decided to leave the Coalition. Two days later, the Prime Minister submitted his resignation to the King, bringing to an end his wartime Government. Churchill now formed a 'Caretaker' administration, composed of Conservatives, National Liberals and a few non-party men, with a Cabinet of sixteen. Former Labour ministers returned to the Opposition benches. For Dalton, whose only London home was at the Board of Trade, this created a problem of accommodation.

Thursday 24th May
Making arrangements for my move. I have a room at 14 Stanhope Gate and arrange with Colonel Llewellyn for an occasional room at the Lansdowne Club. Bob and Betty Fraser are also prepared to put me up at Hampstead. Most of the time between now and 5th July I shall be speaking outside London.

Friday 25th May
Various farewells. I hear that Lyttelton is to come back to the Board of Trade and Waterhouse to remain. This is quite comfortable. I have written to the P.M. both a general letter and one on the Distribution of Industry Bill. I propose to drop Clause 9 and push the rest through. I write on this also to Lyttelton and James Stuart. ...

Horder has seen Hugh Gaitskell and says that he may fight if he doesn't have more than 'two incidents a day'. This is reassuring. At Blackpool I saw the Delegate from South Leeds who was most eager that Gaitskell should go on.

This evening there is a party given by Bruce-Gardner, Warter and Barlow in my honour to which some forty of the principal persons in the Board of Trade are summoned. Speeches are made by Bruce-Gardner, myself, Overton and Waterhouse. It is a pleasant function and I think they are a good lot.

Saturday 26th May
Clearing up papers, personal letters of thanks etc. Oliver Lyttelton is succeeding me. I could not have wished for a more pleasant colleague to whom to hand over. Since he will now combine the Board of Trade and the Ministry of Production, rapid, and I hope, smooth progress should be made in fusing many activities, particularly in the regions. He is also likely to be friendly and accommodating over the Distribution of Industry Bill.

Waterhouse and Summers are also remaining. And the former yesterday, just before our party, was as effusive as such a typically English country gentleman could be expected to be. He and I have liked each other and liked working together. ...

I record for future reference two electoral estimates. Waterhouse said that he did not think the Tories and Liberal Nationals together could lose more than 50 seats net and that he thought they would do better than this, and might lose very few, if any, on balance. A loss of 50 would give a Conservative plus Liberal National majority over all of about 135. Arthur Henderson, on the other hand, son of the best electioneering judge of our times, said that, though he was not as optimistic as some people, he thought we should win at least 80 seats. This would mean a Conservative and Liberal National majority of not more than 75. My own estimate hasn't settled down yet, I am still thinking in terms of a very wide possible variation.

Overton paid me the compliment last night of saying that one of the things that had most impressed him here was my skill in drafting answers to P.Q.s, and Preston said that he thought one of the reasons for this success – I have *never*, in my term of office which had lasted yesterday for three years, three months and three days, been in serious difficulty at Question Time – was that I had always revised these, in consultation with him, without calling anybody else in, though we sometimes got squeaks from along the passage or below ground when my revised answers were shown to them. Many ministers, Preston said, held a serious conference with a crowd of people sitting round when answers to questions were being prepared. He and I agreed that this was not a good plan, though I recall that Henderson at the Foreign Office sometimes used to do this.

Monday 28th May
Move tonight to the Lansdowne Club where I am spending several transitional days.

To the Palace this morning, where a number of ministers are 'taking leave'. I go in between Cripps and Jowitt. Bevin and Morrison, who came earlier, have stayed a bit too long and thrown out the programme. The King has very little to say and doesn't seem to have focused any Board of Trade problem. He says that he thinks it was a pity we 'didn't make an arrangement about coupons for under-clothing'. I am not sure whether he thought that these could be bought without coupons, which was a mistake, or whether he meant that we ought to have arranged to have more underclothes made (though at the cost of what else?) and charged less (or more?) coupons for them. I don't suppose he has ever seen a coupon, either for clothes or food. Anyhow he really had nothing to say, and made no personal impact on me whatever. As nearly inanimate as an animate Monarch could be! Cripps who came out very quickly and didn't even try, as I did, to make some conversation with the poor man, said, 'I said, "Oh well, I suppose your Majesty is very busy this morning so I won't take up your time" ' and came straight out. He said he thought the King was very grateful. ...

At 4.30 an At Home at No. 10. Between 30 and 40 ministers and ex-ministers are present, with a few Private Secretaries and other oddments. Practically all Labour ex-ministers are here, and most of the Tories and Liberals. But Max and Bracken are both absent. The P.M. seemed deeply moved – and I feel the moment a bit too. I have a few minutes alone with him. I ask if he has got my letter. He said, 'Yes, and I shall certainly answer it.'[1] I said that these had been proud and imperishable years, in which we had worked together. I thanked him for all he had done. He said, 'You and all the others have always been exceedingly kind to me, and I should like to thank *you* for all you have done.'

A little later, standing behind the Cabinet table, now draped as a buffet, he addressed us all, with tears visibly running down his cheeks. He said that we had all come together, and had stayed together as a united band of friends, in a very trying time. History would recognise this. 'The light will shine on every helmet.' He was sure that, if ever such another mortal danger threatened, we would all do the same again. (I wondered whether this meant anything. If so, it could only have meant Russia. Probably it was only a phrase.) He went on to say that, when he went to meet Stalin and Truman,[2] he wanted to take with him 'My good friend, Clem Attlee' to show that, whatever happened in the election, we were a United Nation.

Attlee and Sinclair made very brief replies, and then Wolmer[3] suggested that we might all be photographed. This was done in the garden of No. 10. It had begun to rain, the business took some time and the P.M. said, 'We'd better finish this or my political opponents will say that this is a conspiracy on my part to give them all rheumatism!' Then we dispersed.[4]

I had a word with Lyttelton at this party about the Distribution of Industry Bill. I had said that I would myself propose to drop Clause

1 Marginal insertion: 'He never did.'
2 Harry S. Truman (1884–1972). President of the United States 1945–53. Truman succeeded to the Presidency on Roosevelt's death in April 1945.
3 The Earl of Selborne, formerly Lord Wolmer, q.v.
4 Marginal insertion: 'Less than 3 months later, we were photographed again, some of us, as a new Cabinet in that old garden, with its one ilex!'

9. He said he was very grateful. Late that evening Waterhouse rang me up at the Lansdowne and I confirm my proposal on Clause 9.

Tuesday 29th May

At 10.30 we just get a quorum in the Standing Committee on the Distribution of Industry Bill and, as proposed, I got up at the start – this time from the Opposition Bench – and moved to report progress, in order that we might take stock of the changes which have occurred. I then dwell on the great importance of getting the Bill through and propose to drop Clause 9 and finish it this morning. This is generally accepted and, without very much difficulty, the Committee Stage is completed. Fortunately several of those who were threatening to speak at length upon the schedules are absent, and so is silly little Ellis Smith, who has a stupid new Clause giving the President of the Board of Trade power to order any industrialist to go anywhere. This is a great, and, until the last moment, rather an unexpected triumph.

The Bill goes through Report and Third Reading with hardly any difficulty in the following week and passes into law just before Parliament dissolves. This is the best thing I have done at the Board of Trade. If the powers, now conferred upon my successors, are strongly and sensibly used, there will never be any Depressed Areas again. And this means much more than anyone who didn't know these areas in the pre-war years can easily imagine.

Appendix A:
Main Characters

Alexander: Albert Victor Alexander, later 1st Earl (1885–1965). Labour and Co-operative M.P. for Hillsborough 1922–31, 1935–50. Parliamentary Secretary at the Board of Trade 1924; First Lord of the Admiralty 1929–31, 1940–45, 1945–6. Minister of Defence 1947–50; Chancellor of the Duchy of Lancaster 1950–51.

Anderson: Sir John Anderson, later 1st Viscount Waverley (1882–1958). Entered Colonial Office 1905. Secretary to the Minister of Shipping 1917–19. Additional Secretary to the Local Government Board 1919; Second Secretary to the Minister of Health 1919; Chairman of the Board of Inland Revenue 1919–22. Joint Under-Secretary to the Lord Lieutenant of Ireland 1920–22. Permanent Under-Secretary at the Home Office 1922–32; Governor of Bengal 1932–7. National M.P. for Scottish Universities 1938–50. Lord Privy Seal 1938–9; Home Secretary and Minister of Home Security 1939–40; Lord President of the Council 1940–43; Chancellor of the Exchequer 1943–5.

Attlee: Clement Richard Attlee, later 1st Earl (1883–1967). Labour M.P. for Limehouse 1922–50; West Walthamstow 1950–55. Under-Secretary of State for War 1924; Chancellor of the Duchy of Lancaster 1930–31; Postmaster-General 1931; Lord Privy Seal 1940–42; Deputy Prime Minister 1942–5; Secretary of State for Dominion Affairs 1942–5; Prime Minister 1945–51; Minister of Defence 1945–6. Leader of the Labour Party 1935–55.

Beaverbrook: Sir William Maxwell Aitken, 1st Baron Beaverbrook (1879–1964). Canadian newspaper proprietor. Conservative M.P. for Ashton-under-Lyne December 1910–16. Chancellor of

	the Duchy of Lancaster and Minister of Information 1918–1919; Minister of Aircraft Production 1940–41; Minister of State May–June 1941; Minister of Supply 1941–2; Minister of War Production February 1942; Lord Privy Seal 1943–5.
Bevan:	Aneurin Bevan (1897–1960). Labour M.P. for Ebbw Vale 1929–60. Minister of Health 1945–51; Minister of Labour and National Service 1951. Treasurer of the Labour Party 1956–60; Deputy Leader 1959–60.
Bevin:	Ernest Bevin (1881–1951). Labour M.P. for Central Wandsworth 1940–50; East Woolwich 1950–51. Minister of Labour and National Service 1940–45; Secretary of State for Foreign Affairs 1945–51; Lord Privy Seal 1951. Member of the General Council of the T.U.C. 1925–40. National Organiser of the Dockers' Union 1910–21; General Secretary of the Transport and General Workers' Union 1925–40.
Bracken:	Brendan Rendall Bracken, later 1st Viscount (1901–58). Conservative M.P. for Paddington North 1929–45; Bournemouth 1945–50; Bournemouth East 1950–51. Parliamentary Private Secretary to the Prime Minister 1940–41. Minister of Information 1941–5; First Lord of the Admiralty 1945.
Cadogan:	Sir Alexander George Montagu Cadogan (1884–1968). Envoy Extraordinary and Minister Plenipotentiary Peking 1933–5; Ambassador 1935–6. Deputy Under-Secretary 1936–7; Permanent Under-Secretary at the Foreign Office 1938–46. Permanent Representative at the United Nations 1946–50. Chairman of the B.B.C. 1952–7.
Churchill:	Winston Leonard Spencer Churchill, later Sir Winston (1874–1965). Conservative M.P. for Oldham, 1900–4; Liberal M.P. for Oldham 1904–6; North-West Manchester 1906–8; Dundee 1908–22. Conservative M.P. for Epping 1924–45; Woodford 1945–64. Parliamentary Under-Secretary at the Colonial Office 1905–8; President of the Board of Trade 1908–10. Home Secretary 1910–11; First Lord of the Admiralty 1911–15, 1939–40; Chancellor of the Duchy of Lancaster 1915; Minister of Munitions 1917–19; Secretary of State for War and Air 1919–21; Secretary of State for the Colonies 1921–2; Chancellor of the Exchequer 1924–9. Prime Minister 1940–45, 1951–5. Minister of Defence 1940–45.
Cooper:	Alfred Duff Cooper, later 1st Viscount Norwich (1890–1954). Conservative M.P. for Oldham 1924–9; Westminster St George's 1931–45. Financial Secretary at the War Office 1928–9, 1931–4; Treasury 1934–5. Secretary of State for

War 1935–7; First Lord of the Admiralty 1937–8; Minister of Information 1940–41; Chancellor of the Duchy of Lancaster 1941–3. Representative with the French Committee of National Liberation 1943–4. Ambassador to France 1944–7.

Cripps: Sir (Richard) Stafford Cripps (1889–1952). Labour M.P. for East Bristol 1931–50; South-East Bristol 1950. Solicitor-General 1930–31. British Ambassador to the U.S.S.R. 1940–42. Lord Privy Seal and Leader of the House of Commons 1942; Minister of Aircraft Production 1942–5; President of the Board of Trade 1945–7; Minister of Economic Affairs 1947; Chancellor of the Exchequer 1947–50.

Dalton, Hugh: (Edward) Hugh John Neale Dalton, later Baron (1887–1962). Labour M.P. for Peckham 1924–9; Bishop Auckland 1929–31, 1935–59. Under-Secretary of State for Foreign Affairs 1929–31; Minister of Economic Warfare 1940–42; President of the Board of Trade 1942–5; Chancellor of the Exchequer 1945–7; Chancellor of the Duchy of Lancaster 1948–50; Minister of Town and Country Planning 1950–51; Minister of Local Government and Planning 1951.

Dalton, Ruth: ((Florence) Ruth Dalton, née Hamilton Fox (1890–1966). Married Hugh Dalton in 1914. Labour M.P. for Bishop Auckland February–May 1929. Member of the L.C.C. 1925–31; Alderman 1936–42, 1946–52. Assistant Secretary of the Workers' Educational Association 1918–19. Member of the Arts Council 1957–62.

Durbin: Evan Frank Mottram Durbin (1906–48). Economist. Economic Section, War Cabinet Secretariat 1940–42. Temporary Personal Assistant to the Deputy Prime Minister (Attlee) 1942–5; Labour M.P. for Edmonton 1945–8. Parliamentary Private Secretary to Dalton as Chancellor of the Exchequer 1945–7. Parliamentary Secretary at the Ministry of Works 1947–8. His publications included *The Politics of Democratic Socialism* (1940) and *What Have We to Defend?* (1942).

Eden: (Robert) Anthony Eden, later Sir Anthony, 1st Earl of Avon (1897–1977). Conservative M.P. for Warwick and Leamington 1923–57. Parliamentary Private Secretary to Foreign Secretary (Sir Austen Chamberlain) 1926–9. Under-Secretary of State for Foreign Affairs 1931–3; Lord Privy Seal 1933–5; Minister without Portfolio, League of Nations Affairs 1935; Foreign Secretary 1935–8. Dominions Secretary 1939–40; Secretary of State for War 1940; Foreign Secretary 1940–45. Leader of the House of Commons 1942–5.

Deputy Leader of the Opposition 1945–51. Foreign Secretary 1951–5; Prime Minister and Leader of the Conservative Party 1955–7.

Gaitskell: Hugh Todd Naylor Gaitskell (1906–63). Labour M.P. for South Leeds 1945–63. Principal Private Secretary to the Minister of Economic Warfare 1940–42. Principal Assistant Secretary to the President of the Board of Trade 1942–5. Parliamentary Under-Secretary at the Ministry of Fuel and Power 1946–7; Minister of Fuel and Power 1947–50. Minister of State for Economic Affairs 1950; Chancellor of the Exchequer 1950–51. Leader of the Labour Party 1955–63.

Greenwood: Arthur Greenwood (1880–1954). Labour M.P. for Nelson and Colne 1922–31; Wakefield 1932–54. Parliamentary Secretary at the Ministry of Health 1924; Minister of Health 1929–31. Minister without Portfolio 1940–42. Lord Privy Seal 1945–7; Paymaster-General 1946–7. Deputy Leader of the Labour Party 1935–54.

Gubbins: Colin McVean Gubbins, later Sir Colin (1896–1976). Acting Brigadier 1940; Lieutenant-Colonel 1941; Colonel 1942; Temporary Major-General 1943. Director of Operations and Training at S.O.E. 1940–42. Deputy Head of S.O.E. 1942–3. Head of S.O.E. 1943–5.

Halifax: Edward Frederick Lindley Wood, 1st Baron Irwin, 3rd Viscount Halifax (1st Earl 1944) (1881–1959). Conservative M.P. for Ripon 1910–25. Under-Secretary of State for the Colonies 1921–2; President of the Board of Education 1922–4; Minister of Agriculture 1924–5. Viceroy of India 1926–31. President of the Board of Education 1932–5; Secretary of State for War 1935; Lord Privy Seal 1935–7. Leader of the House of Lords 1935–8. Lord President of the Council 1937–8; Foreign Secretary 1938–40. British Ambassador to the U.S.A. 1941–6.

Hoare: Sir Samuel John Gurney Hoare, 2nd Bart (1st Viscount Templewood 1944) (1880–1959). Conservative M.P. for Chelsea 1910–44. Secretary of State for Air 1922–4, 1924–9; Secretary of State for India 1931–5; Foreign Secretary 1935. First Lord of the Admiralty 1936–7; Home Secretary 1937–9; Lord Privy Seal 1939–40; Secretary of State for Air 1940. British Ambassador to Spain 1940–44.

Hore-Belisha: (Isaac) Leslie Hore-Belisha, later 1st Baron (1893–1957). Liberal M.P. for Plymouth Devonport 1923–31; National Liberal M.P. 1931–42; National Independent M.P. 1942–5. Parliamentary Secretary at the Board of Trade 1931–2;

Financial Secretary to the Treasury 1932–4; Minister of Transport 1934–7; Secretary of State for War 1937–40. Minister of National Insurance 1945.

Jay: Douglas Patrick Thomas Jay (b. 1907). Journalist at *The Times* 1929–33; *Economist* 1933–7. City Editor of the *Herald* 1937–41. Assistant Secretary at the Ministry of Supply 1941–3; Principal Assistant Secretary at the Board of Trade 1943–5. Personal Assistant to the Prime Minister 1945–6. Labour M.P. for North Battersea 1946–83. Parliamentary Private Secretary to Dalton as Chancellor of the Exchequer 1947. Economic Secretary to the Treasury 1947–50. Financial Secretary to the Treasury 1950–51. President of the Board of Trade 1964–7. Author of *The Socialist Case* (1937).

Jebb: Hubert Miles Gladwyn Jebb, later Sir Gladwyn, 1st Baron Gladwyn (b. 1900). Private Secretary to the Permanent Under-Secretary of State for Foreign Affairs 1937–40. Chief Executive Officer, Special Operations Executive 1940–2. Head of Reconstruction Department 1942. Counsellor at the Foreign Office 1943–6. Acting Secretary-General of the United Nations 1946. Assistant Under-Secretary and United Nations Adviser 1946–7. U.K. Representative at the United Nations 1950–54. Ambassador to France 1954–60.

Leeper: Reginald Wildig Allen Leeper (Sir Reginald 1945) (1888–1968). Second Secretary in the Foreign Office and Diplomatic Service 1920. First Secretary at the British Legation in Warsaw 1923–4; Riga, 1924; Constantinople 1925; Warsaw 1927–9. Counsellor 1933. Assistant Under-Secretary at the Foreign Office 1940. Head of SO1 1940–43. Ambassador to Greece 1943–6. Ambassador to the Argentine 1946–8.

Leith-Ross: Sir Frederick William Leith-Ross (1887–1968). Private Secretary to the Prime Minister (Asquith) 1911–13. British Representative on the Finance Board of the Reparation Commission 1920–22. Deputy Controller of Finance at the Treasury 1925–32. Chief Economic Adviser to the British Government 1932–46. Member of the Economic Committee of the League of Nations 1932–9. Director-General of Ministry of Economic Warfare 1939–42. Chairman of Inter-Allied Post-War Requirements Committee 1941–3. Deputy Director-General of U.N.R.R.A. 1944–5. Chairman of the European Committee of U.N.R.R.A. Council 1945–6. Governor of the National Bank of Egypt 1946–51.

Lindemann: Frederick Alexander Lindemann (1st Baron Cherwell 1941;
(Cherwell) later 1st Viscount) (1886–1957). Experimental pilot, Director

of Physical Laboratory at R.A.F. Farnborough 1914. Professor of Experimental Philosophy, Oxford 1919–56. Personal Assistant to the Prime Minister 1940–42. Paymaster-General 1942–5, 1951–3.

Lockhart: Robert Hamilton Bruce Lockhart (Sir Robert 1943) (1887–1970). Acting Consul-General in Moscow 1915–17. Head of Special Mission to the Soviet Government 1918. Commercial Secretary to H.M. Legation in Prague 1919–22. Banking in central Europe 1922–8. Journalist with the *Evening Standard* 1929–39. Political Intelligence Department at the Foreign Office 1939–40. British Representative with the Provisional Czech Government in London 1940–41. Deputy Under-Secretary at the Foreign Office and Director-General of the Political Warfare Executive 1941–5. Journalist and author.

Lyttelton: Oliver Lyttelton, later 1st Viscount Chandos (1893–1972). Conservative M.P. for Aldershot 1940–54. President of the Board of Trade 1940–41, 1945; Minister of State 1941–2; Minister of State Resident in the Middle East 1942; Minister of Production 1942–5. Secretary of State for the Colonies 1951–4.

Morrison: Herbert Stanley Morrison, later Baron (1888–1965). Labour M.P. for South Hackney 1923–4, 1929–31, 1935–45; Lewisham 1945–50; South Lewisham 1950–59. Minister of Transport 1929–31. Minister of Supply 1940; Home Secretary and Minister of Home Security 1940–45. Member of War Cabinet 1942–5. Deputy Prime Minister 1945–51. Lord President of the Council and Leader of the House of Commons 1945–51; Foreign Secretary 1951. Deputy Leader of the Opposition 1951–5. Member of L.C.C. 1922–45; Leader 1934–40.

Morton: Major Desmond John Falkiner Morton, later Sir Desmond (1891–1971). Director of Industrial Intelligence Centre 1930. Principal Assistant Secretary at the Ministry of Economic Warfare 1939–40. Personal Assistant to the Prime Minister 1940–46. U.K. delegate to Inter-Allied Reparation Agency. Vice-Chairman of United Nations Economic Survey Mission for the Middle East 1949.

Mountbatten: Sir Louis Francis Albert Victor Nicholas Mountbatten, later 1st Earl (1900–79). Commodore Combined Operations 1941–2. Chief of Combined Operations 1942–3. Supreme Allied Commander S.E. Asia 1943–6. Viceroy of India 1947. Governor-General of India 1947–8. First Sea Lord 1955–9.

Nelson: Sir Frank Nelson (1883–1966). Conservative M.P. for

Stroud 1924–31. Vice-Consul in Basle 1939. Executive director of SO2 1940–42. Wing Commander, Air Intelligence, Washington 1942–5. Air Commodore in Command of Air Intelligence, Control Commission Germany 1945–6. Code name: 'C.D.'

Noel-Baker: Philip John Noel-Baker, later Baron (1889–1982). Labour M.P. for Coventry 1929–31; Derby 1936–50; Derby South 1950–70. Parliamentary Secretary at the Ministry of War Transport 1942–5. Minister of State at the Foreign Office 1945–6. Secretary of State for Air 1946–7; Commonwealth Relations 1947–50. Minister of Fuel and Power 1950–51. Sir Ernest Cassel Professor of International Relations at London University 1924–9. League of Nations Section of British Delegation to the Paris Peace Conference 1919. League of Nations Secretariat until 1922. Principal Assistant to the President of the Disarmament Conference at Geneva 1932–3.

Shinwell: Emanuel Shinwell, later Baron (b. 1884). Labour M.P. for Linlithgow 1922–4, 1928–31; Seaham 1935–50; Easington 1950–70. Financial Secretary at the War Office 1929–30. Parliamentary Secretary at the Department of Mines at the Board of Trade 1924, 1930–31. Minister of Fuel and Power 1945–7; Secretary of State for War 1947–50; Minister of Defence 1950–51. Chairman of the Parliamentary Labour Party 1964–7.

Simon: Sir John Allsebrook Simon (1st Viscount 1940) (1873–1954). Liberal M.P. for Walthamstow 1906–18; Spen Valley 1922–31. National Liberal M.P. for Spen Valley 1931–40. Solicitor-General 1910–13. Attorney-General with a seat in the Cabinet 1913–15; Home Secretary 1915–16. Foreign Secretary 1931–5. Leader of the National Liberal Party 1931–40. Home Secretary and Deputy Leader of the House of Commons 1935–7; Chancellor of the Exchequer 1937–40; Lord Chancellor 1940–45.

Sinclair: Sir Archibald Henry Macdonald Sinclair, 4th Bart, later 1st Viscount Thurso (1890–1970). Liberal M.P. for Caithness and Sutherland 1922–45. Personal Secretary to the Secretary of State for War 1919–21. Private Secretary to the Secretary of State for the Colonies 1921–2. Secretary of State for Scotland 1931–2. Secretary of State for Air 1940–45. Leader of the Liberal Parliamentary Party 1935–45.

Vansittart: Sir Robert Gilbert Vansittart (1st Baron 1941) (1881–1957). Assistant Under-Secretary at the Foreign Office and

873

Waterhouse: Principal Private Secretary to the Prime Minister 1928–30. Permanent Under-Secretary at the Foreign Office 1930–38. Chief Diplomatic Adviser to the Foreign Secretary 1938–41. Charles Waterhouse (1893–1975). Conservative M.P. for Leicester South 1924–45; Leicester South-East 1950–57. Junior Lord of the Treasury 1936. Comptroller of H.M. Household 1937–8; Treasurer 1938–9. Assistant Postmaster-General 1939–41; Parliamentary Secretary at the Board of Trade 1941–5.

Wavell: Sir Archibald Percival Wavell (1st Viscount 1943, later 1st Earl) (1883–1950). Formed Middle East Command 1939. Commander-in-Chief India 1941–3. Supreme Commander South-West Pacific January–March 1942. A.D.C. General to the King 1941–3. Viceroy and Governor-General of India 1943–7.

Wilmot: John Wilmot, later 1st Baron (1895–1964). Labour M.P. for Fulham East 1933–5; Kennington 1939–45; Deptford 1945–50. Parliamentary Private Secretary to Dalton 1940–44. Joint Parliamentary Secretary at the Ministry of Supply 1944–5. Minister of Supply 1945–7. Banker and businessman. Alderman of the L.C.C. 1936–44. Chairman of the London Fire Brigade 1938–42.

Wilson: Sir Horace John Wilson (1882–1972). Principal Assistant Secretary at the Ministry of Labour 1919–21. Permanent Secretary at the Ministry of Labour 1921–30. Chief Industrial Adviser to H.M. Government 1930–39. Seconded from the Treasury for service with the Prime Minister 1935. Permanent Secretary at the Treasury and Head of Civil Service 1939–42.

Wood: Sir (Howard) Kingsley Wood (1881–1943). Conservative M.P. for Woolwich West 1918–43. Parliamentary Secretary at the Ministry of Health 1924–9; Board of Education 1931. Postmaster-General 1931–5; Minister of Health 1935–8; Secretary of State for Air 1938–40; Lord Privy Seal 1940; Chancellor of the Exchequer 1940–43. Member of War Cabinet October 1940–February 1942.

Appendix B:
Coalition Government:
War Cabinet

11th May 1940 to 23rd May 1945

Dates are of War Cabinet membership, and not necessarily of periods of office.

Prime Minister and First Lord of the Treasury Minister of Defence	Winston Churchill (Con.)	11th May 1940– 23rd May 1945
Lord President	Neville Chamberlain (Con.)	11th May 1940– 3rd October 1940
	Sir John Anderson (Nat.)	3rd October 1940– 24th September 1943
	Clement Attlee (Lab.)	24th September 1943– 23rd May 1945
Lord Privy Seal	Clement Attlee (Lab.)	11th May 1940– 19th February 1942
	Sir Stafford Cripps (Ind.)	19th February 1942– 22nd November 1942
Chancellor of the Exchequer	Sir Kingsley Wood (Con.)	3rd October 1940– 19th February 1942
	Sir John Anderson (Nat.)	24th September 1943– 23rd May 1945
Foreign Secretary	Viscount Halifax* (Con.)	11th May 1940– 22nd December 1940
	Anthony Eden (Con.)	22nd December 1940– 23rd May 1945

* Halifax became Ambassador to the United States on 24th January 1941, but remained nominally a member of the War Cabinet until 1945.

Minister of State	Lord Beaverbrook (Con.)	1st May 1941– 29th June 1941
	Oliver Lyttelton (Con.)	29th June 1941– 12th March 1942
Home Secretary and Minister of Home Security	Herbert Morrison (Lab.)	22nd November 1942– 23rd May 1945
Minister of Aircraft Production	Lord Beaverbrook (Con.)	2nd August 1940– 1st May 1941
Dominions Secretary	Clement Attlee (Lab.)	19th February– 24th September 1943
Minister of Labour and National Service	Ernest Bevin (Lab.)	3rd October 1940– 23rd May 1945
Minister Resident in Middle East	Oliver Lyttelton (Con.)	19th February 1942– 12th March 1942
	Richard Casey	19th March 1942– 23rd December 1943
Minister without Portfolio	Arthur Greenwood (Lab.)	11th May 1940– 22nd February 1942
Minister of Reconstruction	Lord Woolton (Con.)	11th November 1943– 23rd May 1945
Minister of Supply	Lord Beaverbrook (Con.)	29th June 1941– 4th February 1942
Minister of (War) Production	Lord Beaverbrook (Con.)	4th February 1942– 19th February 1942
	Oliver Lyttelton (Con.)	12th March 1942– 23rd May 1945

Short Bibliography

Published works cited in footnotes and some others that have been of special value in the preparation of this volume are listed below. A fuller bibliography of published and unpublished sources relating to the whole of Dalton's life may be found in my biography, *Hugh Dalton*, Jonathan Cape, London, 1985, pp. 717–31.

I Biography, Diaries, Letters and Memoirs

J. Amery, *Approach March: A Venture in Autobiography*, Hutchinson, London, 1973.

L. S. Amery, *My Political Life, Vol. III: The Unforgiving Years 1929–1940*, Hutchinson, London, 1955.

J. Astley, *The Inner Circle*, Hutchinson, London, 1971.

Earl of Avon, *Facing the Dictators*, Cassell, London, 1962.

—— *The Reckoning*, Cassell, London, 1965.

Lord Beveridge, *Power and Influence*, Hodder & Stoughton, London, 1953.

Earl of Birkenhead, *The Life of Lord Halifax*, Hamish Hamilton, London, 1965.

A. Boyle, *Poor Dear Brendan: The Quest for Brendan Bracken*, Hutchinson, London, 1974.

V. Brittain, *Pethick-Lawrence: A Portrait*, Allen & Unwin, London, 1964.

R. H. Bruce Lockhart, *Comes the Reckoning*, Putnam, London, 1947.

—— *Giants Cast Long Shadows*, Putnam, London, 1960.

A. Bullock, *The Life and Times of Ernest Bevin. Vol. II: Minister of Labour*, Heinemann, London, 1967.

—— *Ernest Bevin: Foreign Secretary 1945–1951*, Heinemann, London, 1983.

The Memoirs of Lord Chandos, Bodley Head, London, 1962.

W. S. Churchill, *The Second World War*, Collins, London:
I The Gathering Storm, 1948; *II Their Finest Hour*, 1949; *III The Grand*

Alliance, 1950; *IV The Hinge of Fate*, 1951; *V Closing the Ring*, 1952; *VI Triumph and Tragedy*, 1954.

Sir Richard Clarke (ed. Sir Alec Cairncross), *Anglo-American Economic Collaboration in War and Peace 1942–1949*, Oxford University Press, London, 1982.

J. Connell, *Auchinleck*, Cassell, London, 1959.

—— *Wavell*, 2 vols, Collins, London, 1964, 1969.

D. Cooper, *Old Men Forget: The Autobiography of Duff Cooper*, Rupert Hart-Davis, London, 1953.

W. P. Crozier (ed. A. J. P. Taylor), *Off the Record: Political Interviews 1933–1943*, Hutchinson, London, 1973.

H. Dalton, *With British Guns in Italy: a tribute to Italian achievement*, Methuen, London, 1919.

—— *Call Back Yesterday: Memoirs 1887–1931*, Muller, London, 1953.

—— *The Fateful Years: Memoirs 1931–1945*, Muller, London, 1957.

—— *High Tide and After: Memoirs 1945–60*, Muller, London, 1962.

B. Davidson, *Special Operations Europe: Scenes from the Anti-Nazi War*, Gollancz, London, 1980.

S. Delmar, *Black Boomerang*, Secker & Warburg, London, 1962.

Dictionary of National Biography, Oxford University Press, Oxford.

D. Dilks (ed.), *The Diary of Sir Alexander Cadogan 1938–1943*, Cassell, London, 1971.

B. Donoughue and G. W. Jones, *Herbert Morrison: Portrait of a Politician*, Weidenfeld & Nicolson, London, 1973.

P. Einzig, *In the Centre of Things*, Hutchinson, London, 1960.

M. Foot, *Aneurin Bevan: A Biography, Vol. 1 1897–1945*, MacGibbon & Kee, London, 1962.

Gaulle, C. de, *Call to Honour 1940–2*, Collins, London, 1955.

—— *Unity, 1942–4*, Weidenfeld & Nicolson, London, 1959.

The Memoirs of Lord Gladwyn, Weidenfeld & Nicolson, London, 1970.

Sir Arthur Harris, *Bomber Offensive*, Collins, London, 1947.

J. Harris, *William Beveridge: A Biography*, Clarendon Press, Oxford, 1977.

K. Harris, *Attlee*, Weidenfeld & Nicolson, London, 1982.

R. F. Harrod, *The Life of John Maynard Keynes*, Macmillan, London, 1951.

J. Harvey (ed.), *The Diplomatic Diaries of Oliver Harvey 1937–1940*, Collins, London, 1970.

—— (ed.) *The War Diaries of Oliver Harvey*, Collins, London, 1978.

A. Horner, *Incorrigible Rebel*, MacGibbon & Kee, London, 1960.

C. Hull, *The Memoirs of Cordell Hull, Vol. II*, Hodder & Stoughton, London, 1948.

D. Jay, *Change and Fortune: A Political Record*, Hutchinson, London, 1980.

T. Jones, *A Diary with Letters 1931–50*, Oxford University Press, London, 1954.

I. Kirkpatrick, *The Inner Circle*, Macmillan, London, 1959.

Sir Frederick Leith-Ross, *Money Talks: fifty years of international finance*, Hutchinson, London, 1968.

Sir John Lomax, *The Diplomatic Smuggler*, Arthur Barker, London, 1965.

C. Lysaght, *Brendan Bracken*, Allen Lane, London, 1979.

I. MacLeod, *Neville Chamberlain*, Muller, London, 1961.

H. Macmillan, *The Blast of War 1939–45*, Macmillan, London, 1969.

I. Maisky, *Memoirs of a Soviet Ambassador: The War, 1939–43*, Hutchinson, London, 1967.

K. Martin, *Harold Laski 1893–1950: A Biographical Memoir*, Gollancz, London, 1953.

—— *Critic's London Diary: From the New Statesman 1931–1956*, Secker & Warburg, London, 1960.

—— *Editor*, Penguin, Harmondsworth, 1969.

D. E. Moggridge, *Keynes*, Macmillan, London, 1976.

P. Moon (ed.), *Wavell: the Viceroy's Journal*, Oxford University Press, London, 1973.

Lord Moran, *Winston Churchill: The Struggle for Survival 1940–1965*, Constable, London, 1966.

Janet Morgan (ed.), *The Backbench Diaries of Richard Crossman*, Hamish Hamilton and Jonathan Cape, London, 1981.

Sir Oswald Mosley, *My Life*, Nelson, London, 1970.

B. Nanda, *Mahatma Gandhi: A Biography*, Oxford University Press, Oxford, 1981 (first published 1958).

N. Nicolson (ed.), *Harold Nicolson: Diaries and Letters 1939–1945*, Collins, London, 1967.

Obituaries from The Times, Newspaper Archives Developments Ltd, Reading, 1970, 1975.

R. Rhodes James (ed.), *Chips: The Diaries of Sir Henry Channon*, Penguin, Harmondsworth, 1970.

Lord Robbins, *Autobiography of an Economist*, Macmillan, London, 1971.

W. T. Rodgers (ed.), *Hugh Gaitskell*, Thames & Hudson, London, 1964.

E. Spears, *Assignment to Catastrophe. Vol. 1: Prelude to Dunkirk July 1939–May 1940*, Heinemann, London, 1954.

Sir Campbell Stuart, *Opportunity Knocks Once*, Collins, London, 1952.

B. Sweet-Escott, *Baker Street Irregular*, Methuen, London, 1965.

A. J. P. Taylor, *Beaverbrook*, Hamish Hamilton, London, 1972.

Lord Vansittart, *The Mist Procession*, Hutchinson, London, 1958.

Sir Robert Vansittart, *Lessons of My Life*, Hutchinson, London, 1943.

Sir John Wheeler-Bennett (ed.), *Action This Day: Working with Churchill*, Macmillan, London, 1968.

J. W. Wheeler-Bennett, *King George VI: His Life and Reign*, Macmillan, London, 1958.

—— *John Anderson, Viscount Waverley*, Macmillan, London, 1962.

Who Was Who, A. & C. Black, London.

Who Was Who in America, Marquis Who's Who Inc., Chicago.

P. Williams (ed.), *The Diary of Hugh Gaitskell 1945–1956*, Jonathan Cape, London, 1983.

K. Young (ed.), *The Diaries of Sir Robert Bruce Lockhart, Vol. II, 1939–1965*, Macmillan, London, 1980.

II Other Works

P. Addison, *The Road to 1945*, Quartet, London, 1977 (first published Jonathan Cape, 1975).

P. Auty and R. Clogg (eds), *British Policy towards War-time Resistance in Yugoslavia and Greece*, Macmillan, London, 1975.

M. Balfour, *Propaganda in War 1939–1945*, Routledge & Kegan Paul, London, 1981.

E. Barker, *British Policy in South-East Europe in the Second World War*, Macmillan, London, 1976.

F. L. Block, *The Origins of International Economic Disorder: a study of United States international monetary policy from World War II to the present*, University of California Press, Berkeley, 1977.

A. Booth, 'The "Keynesian Revolution" in Economic Policy-Making', *Economic History Review*, vol. xxxvi, 1983.

H. N. Brailsford, *Our Settlement with Germany*, Penguin, London, 1944.

Sir Edward Bridges, *Treasury Control*, Athlone Press, London, 1950.

T. D. Burridge, *British Labour and Hitler's War*, André Deutsch, London, 1976.

D. Butler and A. Sloman, *British Political Facts 1900–1979*, Macmillan, London, 1980.

J. R. M. Butler, *Grand Strategy, Vol. II*, H.M.S.O., London, 1957.

A. Calder, *The People's War*, Jonathan Cape, London, 1965.

D. N. Chester (ed.), *Lessons of the British War Economy*, Cambridge University Press, Cambridge, 1951.

W. H. B. Court, *Coal*, H.M.S.O., London, 1951.

G. Crowther, *Ways and Means of War*, Clarendon Press, Oxford, 1940.

C. Cruickshank, *The Fourth Arm: Psychological Warfare 1938–1945*, Davis-Poynter, London, 1977.

J. Curran and J. Seaton, *Power without Responsibility: The Press and Broadcasting in Britain*, Fontana, London, 1981.

H. Dalton, *Some Aspects of the Inequality of Incomes in Modern Communities*, Routledge, London, 1920.

—— *Practical Socialism for Britain*, Routledge, London, 1935.

—— *Hitler's War: Before and After*, Penguin, Harmondsworth, 1940.

Evan Durbin, *What Have We to Defend?*, Routledge, London, 1942.

M. Elliott-Bateman (ed.), *The Fourth Dimension in Warfare*, Manchester University Press, Manchester, 1970.

M. R. D. Foot, *S.O.E. in France*, H.M.S.O., London, 1968.

R. N. Gardner, *Sterling-Dollar Diplomacy: Anglo-American collaboration in the reconstruction of multilateral trade*, McGraw-Hill, New York, 1969 (first published Oxford University Press, London, 1956).

P. Goodhart and V. Branston, *The 1922*, Macmillan, London, 1978.

J. Grantham, 'Hugh Dalton and the International Post-War Settlement', *Journal of Contemporary History* XIV, 1979.

D. R. Grenfell, *Coal*, Gollancz, London, 1947.

W. K. Hancock and M. M. Gowing, *The British War Economy*, H.M.S.O., London, 1949.

Hansard: House of Commons Debates (H.C. Debs), Fifth Series.

E. L. Hargreaves and M. M. Gowing, *Civil Industry and Trade*, H.M.S.O., London, 1952.

F. H. Hinsley, *et al.*, *British Intelligence in the Second World War, Vols I and II*, H.M.S.O., London, 1979, 1981.

R. Jenkins, *The Pursuit of Progress*, Heinemann, London, 1953.

B. Jones, *The Russia Complex: The British Labour Party and the Soviet Union*, Manchester University Press, Manchester, 1978.

Labour Party Annual Conference Reports, 1940–45.

W. Laqueur (ed.), *The Second World War: Essays in military and political history*, Sage, London, 1982.

J. M. Lee, *Reviewing the Machinery of Government 1942–1952: An Essay on the Anderson Committee and its successors* (mimeo, available from author), 1977.

—— *The Churchill Coalition 1940–1945*, Batsford, London, 1980.

D. Maclennan and J. B. Parr (eds), *Regional Policy: Past Experience and New Directions*, Martin Robertson, Oxford, 1971.

N. Mansergh, *Constitutional Relations between Britain and India 1942–7: The Transfer of Power,* vol. IV, H.M.S.O., London, 1973.

A. Marwick, *Britain in the Century of Total War*, Bodley Head, London, 1968.

W. N. Medlicott, *The Economic Blockade, Vols I and II*, H.M.S.O., London, 1952, 1959.

A. S. Milward, *The German Economy at War*, Athlone Press, London, 1965.

K. O. Morgan, *Labour in Power, 1945–1951*, Oxford University Press, 1984.

Official publications:

    Cmd 6153: *Report of the Royal Commission on the Distribution of the Industrial Population* (Barlow Report), H.M.S.O., London, 1940.

    —— Cmd 6404: *Report of the Committee on Social Insurance and Allied Services* (Beveridge Report), H.M.S.O., London, 1942.

    —— Cmd 6527: *Employment Policy*, H.M.S.O., London, 1944.

R. Page Arnot, *The Miners in Crisis and War*, Allen & Unwin, London, 1962.

H. Pelling, *Britain and the Second World War*, Fontana, London, 1970.

A. Polonsky (ed.), *The Great Powers and the Polish Question 1941–5*, L.S.E., London, 1976.

V. Rothwell, *Britain and the Cold War 1941–1947*, Jonathan Cape, London, 1982.

D. Stafford, *Britain and European Resistance 1940–1945: A Survey of the Special Operations Executive, with Documents*, Macmillan, London, 1980.

—— 'S.O.E. and British Involvement in the Belgrade Coup D'État of March 1941', *Slavic Review*, vol. 36, September 1977.

A. J. P. Taylor, *English History 1914–45*, Clarendon Press, Oxford, 1965.

A. P. Thirlwall (ed.), *Keynes and International Monetary Relations*, Macmillan, London, 1976.

The Times House of Commons, London, 1918–1983.

Sir Robert Vansittart, *Black Record: Germans past and present*, Hamish Hamilton, London, 1941.

D. C. Watt, *Personalities and Policies: studies in the formulation of British foreign policy in the twentieth century*, Longman, London, 1965.

Sir Charles Wheeler and N. Frankland, *The Strategic Air Offensive against Germany 1939–1945*, vol. IV, H.M.S.O., London, 1961.

Whitaker's Almanack, London.

H. Wilson, *New Deal for Coal*, Contact, London, 1945.

Sir Llewellyn Woodward, *British Foreign Policy in the Second World War, Vols I and II*, H.M.S.O., London, 1970, 1971.

G. Worswick and P. Ady (eds), *The British Economy 1945–1950*, Oxford University Press, London, 1952.

Brigadier P. Young (ed.), *The Almanac of World War II*, Hamlyn, London, 1981.

Index

The index includes a glossary of nicknames and the most frequently occurring codenames.

885

889

893

INDEX

Nazis, 40, 544; compared with ordinary
Germans, 147, 152–3; *see also*
Germany, Germans
Nečas, J., 641 and n.
Nedić, General M., 303, 545 and n.
Nehru, Jawaharlal, 480
Nelson, Sir Frank, 51, 64 and n., 72,
97–9, 106, 113–15, 139, 142–3, 146,
149, 156–7, 160, 163–4, 168, 72, 181,
186–8, 193–8, 211, 217, 243–4, 259,
266–7, 300, 308, 311, 314, 325, 335,
339, 346, 364, 371, 380, 383–4, 396,
429–30, 524, 530, 760; takes charge of
SO2, 362–3; goes on sick leave, 411;
S.O.E. Middle East Crisis, 253–5;
reports on Cairo visit, 267; offers
resignation, 285–6; and SO2 row,
301–3; under strain, 305; on future of
SO2, 362–3; goes on sick leave, 411;
retirement, 420; career, 874–5
Nelson, Sir George, 665 and n.
Němec, F., 641 and n.
News Chronicle, 352, 591
Newsome, N., 283 and n.
New Statesman, xxix, 445, 624, 633,
644–5, 721, 733, 818–19, 832; HD
lunches with, 644–5; HD characterises,
819
Newton, Sir Basil, 630 and n.
New Zealand, xxix, 163, 742, 749–50
Nicholls, Doris, 703
Nicholls, J. W., 173 and n., 225
Nicholls, Lieutenant-Colonel L. B., 337
and n., 338–9, 357, 430, 703
Nichols, P. B. B., 29 and n., 30, 174, 225,
254, 327, 334
Nicholson, Sir John, 746 and n.
Nicolson, Harold, xxix, 107 and n., 148,
168, 256, 430; HD's description of, 215
Ninčić, M., 436 and n.
1922 Committee, xxviii, 252, 524, 533,
797; and coal, 417–20, 424, 435–6, 439,
445, 449; *see also* coal; Conservative
Party
Noble, J. S. B., 134 and n.
Noble, Michael, 134 and n.
Noel-Baker, Francis, 327 and n., 358,
800
Noel-Baker, Irene, 298 and n., 358, 615,
702, 800, 826
Noel-Baker, Philip, 12 and n., 55, 120,
128, 143, 156, 252, 256, 281, 298, 310,
314, 336, 360, 365, 371, 445, 498, 545,
567, 582, 605–8, 615, 653, 667, 673,
702, 720, 732–3, 807, 814, 823, 826,
830, 842, 875; on Germans, 152–3;
career, 875

Noguès, General Charles, 49 and n.
Norman, Montagu, 12 and n., 54, 61,
267, 271, 630, 648, 804, 845–6
Normandy landings, 596–7, 681, 692,
710, 728–9; attempt to deceive
Germans on, 785; *see also* D-Day
North Bristol by-election (1943), 559
North-East England, xxxv, 700, 718–19,
726–7, 746, 852; need for more
factories in, 701; survey on joblessness
in, 173; *see also* Distressed Areas;
Durham; location of industry
Northern Ireland, HD visits, 695–6
Northumberland, xxix
Norton, Clifford, 131 and n.
Norton, Mrs, 134 and n.
Norway, Norway debate, 191–2
Nott-Bower, W. G., 387 and n., 388–9,
399
Nowak, Jerzy, 721 and n.
Nowell, R. M., 483 and n.
Nuffield, Lord, 24 and n.

Observer, 721
O'Connor, Major-General, 123
Official Committee on Post-War
Employment (Steering Committee),
617 and n., 637, 673–4, 676–8, 700,
742, 794
Official Secrets Act, 576
Ogilvie, F. W., 33 and n.
oil: and Germany, xvii, xxx, 23, 26, 29,
31–2, 37, 186, 213, 236, 248;
discussed, 134–41, 205; Romanian
targets, 248–9; in Caucasus, 266;
Washington oil conference, 709–10,
777; synthetic, 720–1; *see also*
Prevention of Oil Reaching Germany
Committee
old age pensions, debate on, 470–1,
589–90, 596; *see also* Pensions and
Determination of Needs Bill
'Old Corpse Upstairs', 'Old Man', 'Old
Umbrella', *see* Chamberlain, Neville
Old Rectory (at Woburn), 112, 265–6
Olga, Princess, of Greece, 188 and n.
Oliver, George, 528 and n., 601 and n.,
605
'Oliver Twist', *see* Lyttelton, Oliver
O'Malley, O. S., 9 and n., 429, 790–1
O'Neill, Con, 122 and n.
Openshaw, R., 588 and n.
Operation Torch, 483, 514–15
Overlord, *see* Normandy landings
Overton, Sir Arnold, xxvii, 382 and n.,
401, 407–10, 414, 427, 466–70, 474,
477–8, 482, 491–2, 513, 516, 542, 552,